THE GLOBAL PUBLIC RELATIONS HANDBOOK

THEORY, RESEARCH, AND PRACTICE

EXPANDED AND REVISED EDITION

Communication Series

Jennings Bryant / Dolf Zillmann, General Editors

THE GLOBAL PUBLIC RELATIONS HANDBOOK

THEORY, RESEARCH, AND PRACTICE

EXPANDED AND REVISED EDITION

EDITED BY

KRISHNAMURTHY SRIRAMESH

DEJAN VERČIČ

NEW YORK AND LONDON

First edition published 2003
This edition published 2009
by Routledge
711 Third Ave, New York, NY 10017

Simultaneously published in the UK
by Routledge
2 Park Square, Milton Park, Abingdon, Oxon OX14 4RN

Routledge is an imprint of the Taylor and Francis Group, an informa business

© 2009 Taylor and Francis

Typeset in Times by RefineCatch Ltd, Bungay, Suffolk, UK

Library of Congress Cataloging in Publication Data
The global public relations handbook : theory, research, and practice / (edited) by Krishnamurthy Sriramesh and Dejan Verčič. — Rev. and expanded ed.
      p. cm.
   1. Public relations—Cross-cultural studies—Handbooks, manuals, etc.   2. Intercultural communication—Handbooks, manuals, etc.   I. Sriramesh, Krishnamurthy.   II. Verčič, Dejan.
HM1221.G57 2008
659.2—dc22
2008023417

ISBN10: 0–415–99513–2 (hbk)
ISBN10: 0–415–99514–0 (pbk)
ISBN10: 0–203–88937–1 (ebk)

ISBN13: 978–0–415–99513–9 (hbk)
ISBN13: 978–0–415–99514–6 (pbk)
ISBN13: 978–0–203–88937–4 (ebk)

Contents

IV EUROPE

Epilogue

Contributor Biographies

The Editors

Krishnamurthy Sriramesh is Professor of Public Relations at the School of Business, Massey University, Wellington, New Zealand. Prior to moving to Wellington, he had taught at Purdue University, the University of Florida, and Nanyang Technological University and had served as visiting professor at universities in three continents. He has won the Charles W. Redding Award for Teaching Excellence (Purdue University), Teacher of the Year (University of Florida) and the Faculty Award for Research as well as the Golden Gator Award for excellence in research at the University of Florida. In 2004 he was awarded the prestigious Pathfinder Award from the Institute for Public Relations (USA) for "original scholarly research contributing to the public relations body of knowledge." He has published over 55 journal articles and book chapters and has presented over 60 research papers, seminars, and invited talks in over 20 countries in Africa, Asia, Australasia, Europe, and North America. He has received five top paper awards at international conferences. He is co-editor of the first edition of this book (which received the prestigious PRIDE award from the National Communication Association in the United States) and *Public Relations Research: European and International Perspective* and editor of *Public Relations in Asia: An anthology.* He serves as the Associate Editor of the *Journal of Communication Management* and is a member of the editorial board of scholarly publications such as *Journal of Communication, Journal of Public Relations Research, Public Relations Review, Public Relations Journal, Digital Review of the Asia-Pacific,* and the *Journal of Information and Knowledge Management.*

Dejan Verčič is a founding partner in Pristop, a communication management consultancy based in Ljubljana, Slovenia, and Associate Professor of Public Relations at the University of Ljubljana. He holds a PhD from the London School of Economics and Political Science (LSE). He has published over 200 articles, books, chapters, papers, and reports. In 2000 he received a special award from the Public Relations Society of Slovenia, and in 2001 he was awarded the Alan Campbell-Johnson Medal for outstanding service to international public relations by the UK Chartered Institute of Public Relations (of which he is a Fellow). He has lectured at academic, professional and business conferences and workshops in Austria, Bosnia and Herzegovina, Belgium, Bulgaria, Canada, Croatia, Egypt, Estonia, Finland, France, Germany, Italy, Korea, Macedonia, Mexico, the Netherlands, Portugal, Serbia, Singapore, Slovenia, Sweden, Switzerland, the UK, and the US. He is an active consultant serving major Slovenian and international corporations, political and government agencies and international organizations. He served, *inter alia*, as the chairman of the Research Committee of the IABC Research Foundation and as the President of the European Public Relations Education and Research Association (EUPRERA). Since 1994, he has organized an annual International Public Relations Research Symposium—BledCom. He has recently co-edited *Public Relations Metrics: Research and Evaluation*.

The Contributors

Andréia Athaydes earned a bachelor's degree in public relations from the Federal University of Rio Grande do Sul, Puerto Alegre. She graduated as a communication and political economy specialist from the Pontifical Catholic University of Rio Grande do Sul, Puerto Alegre, and has a master's degree in management and strategic marketing from the University of Business and Social Sciences of Buenos Aires. Andréia is a doctoral student of the University of Málaga's program in organizational communication and between 1998 and 2001, acted as general secretary and president of the Regional Council of Public Relations Professionals of Rio Grande do Sul and Santa Catarina. Currently, she coordinates the Commission of Integration with Latin America of the Federal Council of Public Relations Professionals. She is also professor and director of the Lutheran University of Brazil's Social Communication program and a visiting professor of the Facultades Integradas de Taquara's communication program. From 2000 to 2002, Andréia participated in the Ministry of Education's Commission of Teaching Specialists of Social Communication, evaluating public relations programs in various states of Brazil.

Taye Babaleye, a media/corporate communication consultant, is an accomplished agriculture and environmental journalist, public affairs commentator, and member of the Nigerian Institute of Public Relations (NIPR). Until December 2007 he was Public Relations Manager of the International Institute of Tropical Agriculture (IITA), Ibadan, Nigeria, where he worked for 23 years. He currently teaches public relations at the University of Ibadan, where he is a doctoral degree student in agricultural communication. Taye holds a BA (French), Master of Communication Arts (MCA), and Master of Education (MEd). He is an author, book editor, and newspaper columnist and his love for journalism and development communication has taken him to several countries in sub-Saharan Africa.

Badran A. Badran is assistant provost and professor of communication at Zayed University in Dubai, the United Arab Emirates. He served as training director of the Center for Media Training and Research and director of the Department of Public and Cultural Relations at Zayed University. He holds a PhD in communication from the University of Massachusetts, Amherst, an MA in Journalism from Indiana University, Bloomington, and an International Certificate in Travel and Tourism from Oxford University. He has consulted, lectured and published in public relations, journalism, tourism promotion and publicity, population and environmental communication, and communication and media systems in the Middle East.

Günter Bentele is a full professor for public relations at the University of Leipzig, Germany. In 1994 he was invited to serve as the chair for public relations at the University of Leipzig, a first for any German-speaking country. Prior to joining the university, he was associate professor for Communication Science and Journalism at the University of Bamberg and assistant professor at the Free University of Berlin (1974–1989). He has served as a guest professor in Zurich and Lugano (Switzerland), Jyvaeskylae (Finland), Riga (Latvia), Sofia (Bulgaria), and Klagenfurt (Austria) and was a visiting research scholar at Ohio University in Athens, Ohio. In 1995 he served as president of the German Association for Communication and Media Studies and in 2004 he was president of EUPRERA. He still works as a BoD member in this European organization for PR Education and PR Research. He is author and co-author of 16 books, has edited and co-edited 21 others, and has written more than 280 scientific articles in the fields of public relations, communication theory, journalism and semiotics. He is editor of three book series. In 2004 he received the award of "PR personality 2004" from the German Association for Public Relations, and in 2007 he was honored by the German award "professor of the year" from a field of more than 700 nominees.

Seth A. Center BA Cornell University, PhD candidate University of Virgina. The essay for this volume was written while a Visiting Fellow at the Miller Center of Public Affairs at the University of Virginia. Mr. Center has written on public diplomacy and taught courses in American diplomatic history.

Constance Chay-Németh is an assistant professor at the School of Communication and Information, Nanyang Technological University in Singapore. Her areas of specialization include public relations, issues and crisis management, health communication, and critical and postmodern studies. She is currently interested in studying the effects of the knowledge economy on public relations and knowledge management. Among other professional duties such as reviewing articles for the *Journal of Public Relations Research*, Constance has also worked with public relations consultancies in the United States and Singapore.

Ni Chen is associate professor of communication at the City University of Hong Kong. Before joining the faculty at CUHK, she worked for the Hong Kong Baptist University and universities in the United States. She earned her PhD in mass communication-journalism from E. W. Scripps School of Journalism at Ohio University in 1992. She is the author and co-author of refereed journal articles, book chapters, and conference papers. She is also the co-editor of a book entitled *Internal Public Relations: A Comparative Analysis.* She keeps close contacts with colleagues in Mainland China, doing collaborative research and serving as their life-long distinguished guest lecturer.

Simon Cliffe has previously worked as a Marketing Executive for Cavalier Bremworth Ltd, as a Public Relations and Marketing Communications Lecturer at the University of Auckland, New Zealand, and as a Market Research Consultant. Simon is now traveling and planning to work in the UK.

María Antonieta Rebeil Corella is the Director of the Centro de Investigación para la Comunicación Aplicada (Center for Applied Communication Research (CICA)) at Universidad Anahuac Mexico Norte. She is the Research Coordinator for the Consejo Nacional para la Ensefianza y la Investigación de las Ciencias de la Comunicación (CONEICC), has been named National Researcher by the Sistema Nacional de Investigadores since

2004 and Organizational Communication Research Group Co Chair for the Asociación Mexicana de Investigadores de la Comunicación (AMIC) since 2005. She has edited and co-edited several books, among which are: in 2008, *Etica, Violencia y Television*; in 2006 and 2008 (2nd ed.) *Comunicacion estrategica en las Organizaciones*; in 2006, 2007 and 2008 *XIII, XIV and XV Anuarios de Investigacion de la Comunicacion CONEICC*; in 1997 and 2000 (2nd ed.) *El Poder de la Comunicacion en las Organizaciones*; in 1989, 1991 (2nd ed.), 1997 (3rd ed.) and 2005 (4th ed.) *Perfiles del Cuadrante: Experiencias de la Radio.*

Hugh M. Culbertson is Professor Emeritus in the E. W. Scripps School of Journalism, Ohio University, Athens, Ohio. He co-authored a widely used text, *Fundamentals of News Reporting*, in addition to two texts: *Research Methods in Mass Communication* and *Mass Communication Theory and Research*. He is senior author of *Social, Political and Economic Contexts of Public Relations: A Book of Theory and Cases*, along with *Public Relations Ethics: Some Foundations*. Also, he is senior editor of *International Public Relations: A Comparative Analysis*. Culbertson has co-authored more than 58 articles in refereed journals along with 11 published monographs and book chapters dealing with varied topics in public relations and mass communication. In 1976, Hugh Culbertson was named outstanding Graduate Faculty member at Ohio University; in 1985, he received the Pathfinder Award for excellence in research from the PRSA Research and Education Foundation; and in 1990, he was named Educator of the Year by the Public Relations Society of America. He directed the foundations section of the PRSA Body of Knowledge project in the late 1980s and early 1990s and served on the advisory boards of the *Journal of Public Relations Research* (formerly the *Public Relations Research Annual*), *Journalism and Mass Communication Quarterly*, *Newspaper Research Journal*, and *Public Relations Review*.

Vincent Defourny is UNESCO's representative in Brazil. He joined UNESCO Paris headquarters in 1997 and for five years worked as a program and project evaluation specialist trying to use evaluation as an organizational learning tool. After being closely involved in the elaboration of a new communication strategy for UNESCO in February 2002, he was designated web chief editor. Defourny holds a PhD in communication studies from the Catholic University of Louvain, Louvain-la-neuve, Belgium, where he served in the 1980s as assistant lecturer and until 2004 as visiting professor. Along with his academic activities, he has worked in France, Belgium, and Spain as a consultant for private companies as well as for public and non-profit organizations. From 1981 to 1984, he volunteered in Uganda where he worked in the field in education and on community-based development projects. Defourny published his doctorate thesis on strategic management of communication and wrote articles on other public relations issues. He is also co-author of two books on quality management.

Alberto Montoya Martín del Campo is professor, researcher and consultant for development and public policy at the Research Department of the Universidad Iberoamericana, Ciudad de Mexico, and Vice President of the Centro de Estudios Estrategicos Nacionales (CEEN). In past years he has been Director of Informatics Policies for the Federal Government in Mexico; President of the National Institute of Solidarity; consultant to the Chamber of Representatives; advisor in diverse industrial, workers' and peasant organizations in Mexico. He has written several articles among which are: in 2007 (with V. Suarez), "Ley de Soberania y Seguridad Agroalimentaria y Nutricional: un imperativo para la Nación," in *Rumbo Rural*; and in 2004 "¿Cómo puede Mexico ganar la batalla de la competitividad?," in *Cumbre de Negocios en Veracruz*; and a number of books: in 2004,

Mexico hacia el 2025; in 2000, *Mexico 2010: Pensar y decidir la proxima decada*; in 1992, *Mexico ante la Revolucion Tecnologica.*

Sandra C. Duhé, PhD, is assistant professor and coordinator of the public relations program at the University of Louisiana at Lafayette. Prior to joining academia in 2004, she was a public affairs manager for three multinational corporations working in media relations, corporate brand management, crisis response, community relations, and risk communication. She holds Master's degrees in public relations and applied economics and received her PhD in political economy from the University of Texas at Dallas. Her research focuses on corporate public relations with particular interests in political economy, complexity science, and new media perspectives in public relations practice and theory.

Toni Muzi Falconi is Senior Counsel to Methodos, an Italian based management consultancy specializing in transformation management programs. Since 1962, his experience is essentially in public relations: as manager, consultant and entrepreneur. He now also teaches global relations and intercultural communication at NYU's Master of Science in Public Relations and Corporate Communication; public relations at the Vatican's LUMSA University in Rome, and international public relations at Milan IULM University's Master in Corporate Public Relations. Author of *Il Governo delle Relazioni-Gorel* (2002–2004) Il Sole 24 Ore; *Relazioni Pubbliche e Organizzazioni Complesse* (2004) Lupetti Editore; *In che Senso–Cosa Sono le Relazioni Pubbliche* (2008) Luca Sossella Editore. An honorary fellow of CIPR, he was Chairman of Ferpi (2000–2003), Founding Chairman of the Global Alliance (2002–2004), and received the Alan Campbell Johnson Medal in 2003. He is a member of the Commission for Global Public Relations Research of the Institute for Public Relations.

Maria Aparecida Ferrari is the director of the School of Journalism and Public Relations at the Methodist University of São Paulo, Brazil. She is also an associate professor there in the undergraduate and graduate programs at the School of Communications and Arts. She holds a PhD in Public Relations from the University and an MSc in Public Relations from the same institution (1993). From 1982 to 1992 she worked as a public relations practitioner at the National Industrial Apprenticeship and Training Service (SENAI) and as a consultant with national and multinational companies in Brazil. From 1992 to 1997, she taught public relations in three Chilean universities (Pontificia Universidad Católica de Chile, Universidad del Pacifico, and Universidad de Viña del Mar). In 2002, she founded and is currently the editor of the *Journalism and Public Relations Studies Journal* (*Revista de Estudos de Jornalismo e Relações Publicas*). She is a member of the board of ABRAP-CORP (Brazilian Association of Public Relations and Communication Organizational Researchers) and also a member of the editorial board for the *International Journal of Strategic Communication*. Her research interests are PR theories, culture, and the practice of public relations in Latin America.

Bertil Flodin has close to 40 years of experience in public relations. This includes practical experience as public relations executive for corporations, nongovernmental organizations, and governmental offices. He spent 12 years as an associate professor and an associate dean at the Department of Journalism and Mass Communication at the University of Gothenburg, Sweden. Bertil is the proud recipient of the Gothenburg University Pedagogic Prize, which he received in 1995 for his excellence in teaching. For the past five years, he has worked as a full-time public relations consultant. His assignments have involved strategic communications counsel in crisis communication, public affairs, business intelligence and knowledge management, internal communication, civic information, and the education of professional communicators. He was involved in the creation of crisis communications plans for companies, wrote a handbook on crisis communications for public authorities, and published a number of research reports on public relations and crisis communication.

James E. Grunig is a professor emeritus of public relations in the Department of Communication at the University of Maryland, College Park. He is the co-author of *Excellent Public Relations and Effective Organizations: A Study of Communication Management in Three Countries*, *Managing Public Relations*, *Public Relations Techniques*, and *Manager's Guide to Excellence in Public Relations and Communication Management*. He is editor of *Excellence in Public Relations and Communication Management*. *Excellent Public Relations and Effective Organizations* received the 2002 PRIDE award of the Public Relations Division of the National Communication Association as the best book in public relations in the previous two years. In addition to his books, James has written 225 other publications such as book chapters, journal articles, reports, and papers. He has won six major awards in public relations: the Pathfinder Award for excellence in public relations research of the Institute for Public Relations Research and Education; the Outstanding Educator Award of the Public Relations Society of America (PRSA); the Jackson, Jackson and Wagner Award for behavioral science research of the PRSA Foundation; the Alexander Hamilton Medal for Lifetime Contributions to Professional Public Relations of the Institute for Public Relations; the Lloyd Dennis Award for Distinguished Leadership in Public Affairs (with Larissa A. Grunig) from the Public Affairs and Government Section of PRSA; and the Dr. Hamid Notghi Prize for Career Achievement in Public Relations from the Kargozar Public Relations Institute, Tehran, Iran. He also won the most prestigious lifetime award of the Association for Education in Journalism and Mass Communication (AEJMC), the Paul J. Deutschmann Award for Excellence in Research. He was the 45th annual Distinguished Lecturer of the Institute for Public Relations in 2006.

Larissa A. Grunig is professor at the University of Maryland, College Park, where she has worked since 1978. She teaches public relations and communication research. She has received the Pathfinder Award for excellence in research, sponsored by the Institute for Public Relations; the Jackson, Jackson, and Wagner Behavioral Science Prize; and the Outstanding Educator Award of the Public Relations Society of America. She was cofounder and co-editor of the *Journal of Public Relations Research* and has written more than 200 articles, book chapters, monographs, reviews, and conference papers on public relations, activism, science writing, feminist theory, communication theory, and research. She was a member of an international grant team, sponsored by the IABC Research Foundation, investigating excellence in public relations and communication management. The newest *Excellence* book won the 2002 PRIDE award sponsored by the Public Relations Division of the National Communication Association. Dr. Grunig also serves as a consultant in public relations.

Ahmed Ibrahim Hammad is an assistant professor in the Department of Media at Al-Aqsa University in Gaza. He teaches public relations, political communication and mass communication. He served as Head of the Public Relations Department for the Palestinian Ministry of Higher Education for nearly a decade. He received his doctorate from the

Department of Journalism and Mass Communication, Aristotle University of Thessaloniki, Greece in November, 2005.

Vivian Hirsch is a communication management consultant with a specialization in strategic planning and crisis management. Until 2005, she acted as the Brazilian chief executive officer and vice-president for Latin America of Edelman. She has directed public relations agencies since 1994. Previous to Hirsch's consulting and agency work, she had 20 years of experience as director of public relations for government agencies and corporations, such as Monsanto and American Express. Vivian is fluent in Spanish, English, German, and French.

Øyvind Ihlen is a Post Doctoral Research Fellow at the Department of Media and Communication, University of Oslo; and Associate Professor at Hedmark College, both in Norway. His research focuses on the strategic communication of organizations, particularly regarding corporate social responsibility, the environment, and reputation. Ihlen's research has appeared in a range of journals such as *Public Relations Review*, *Journal of Public Relations Research*, *Journal of Communication Management*, *International Journal of Strategic Communication*, *Corporate Communication: An International Journal*, *Business Strategy and the Environment*, and *NORDICOM Review*, as well as in several anthologies and Nordic journals. Øyvind has been a guest editor of a special issue of *Public Relations Review* on social theory and public relations. He has also published a public relations textbook, a reputation textbook, as well as a book on the framing and reputation management techniques of the Norwegian petroleum industry.

Takashi Inoue is chief executive officer of Inoue Public Relations. He graduated from Waseda University, Tokyo in 1968, majoring in marketing and administration. After a stint in marketing at Yamaha Corporation, he founded Inoue Public Relations in 1970. Takashi Inoue was the first public relations professional to be actively involved in the high-technology industry, beginning with Intel and Apple Computer in the late 1970s and early 1980s. He is one of only a few Japanese public relations consultants to have achieved an international reputation as a spokesperson for Japan. Over the past two decades, he has been especially active and involved in United States–Japan trade-related issues, helping to avert possible crisis situations in the telecommunications, semiconductor, and automotive industries. In 1997, his company won the International Public Relations Association's top award, the Golden World Award for Excellence in Public Relations, for work the company carried out in connection with deregulation of the automobile parts aftermarket in Japan. From April 2004, he became a visiting professor of Waseda University, the first professor in Japan to teach public relations as a regular course subject at a major university. This background led to speaking engagements at universities and other organizations, including the Wharton School, University of Pennsylvania. Takashi is the founder and president of the Japan Public Relations Institute (JPRI), a public affairs PR consultancy. He also has edited *An Introduction to Public Relations*, the first comprehensive book on public relations in the Japanese language and a best-selling business book in Japan. *Public Relations*, which he authored, was published two years later in 2006.

Julia Jahansoozi is a lecturer at the University of Stirling, Scotland where she leads the MSc Public Communication Management programme. She has worked in public relations practice in both Canada and the UK in both consultancy and in-house roles within the private and non-profit sectors. Julia received both her PhD and MSc in Public Relations from the University of Stirling and completed her BSc in Psychology and Political Science at the University of Victoria, Canada. Her areas of research interest include international public relations, organization–public relationships.

Kevin L. Keenan is an associate professor and director of Graduate Studies in the Department of Journalism and Mass Communication at the American University in Cairo, Egypt. He earned his PhD in Mass Communication from the University of Georgia, Athens. His teaching and research interests include communication theory and mass media content and effects and his work appears in the *International Journal of Advertising*, *Journal of Advertising Education*, *Journalism and Mass Communication Educator*, *Journalism and Mass Communication Quarterly*, *Public Relations Review*, and elsewhere. He is active in several professional organizations and has presented over 50 scholarly papers at academic conferences. He has worked in the advertising agency and public opinion research business and currently serves as a consultant for a variety of local, national, and international clients.

Jeong-Nam Kim is an assistant professor of public relations in the Department of Communication at Purdue University in West Lafayette, Indiana. His research areas are public relations and the role of communication and cognition in the problem-solving process. He has developed the communicant activeness in problems solving (CAPS) and the situational theory of problem solving (STOPS) with Dr. James E. Grunig. He is working on studies applying CAPS and STOPS in the areas of public opinion, science communication, health communication, and political communication. He studied communication and public relations at the University of Maryland, College Park.

Yungwook Kim (PhD, University of Florida, 1999) is an Associate Professor of Communication at Ewha Womans University, Seoul, where he teaches crisis management and conflict resolution, government public relations, and international public relations. His current research focuses on crisis management, negotiation and conflict resolution, risk communication, nonprofit public relations, and source competition for deliberative democracy. He taught at Illinois State University prior to his current position. He was also a Fulbright Scholar in the Program on Negotiation at Harvard Law School. His research appears in *Journal of Public Relations Research*, *Public Relations Review*, *Corporate Communications: An International Journal*, *Journal of Promotion Management*, *Journalism and Mass Communication Quarterly*, *Journal of Broadcasting and Electronic Media*, *Journal of Asia Pacific Communication*, *Journal of Business Ethics*, and many other Korean scholarly journals. He has written books entitled, *Understanding Crisis Management: Public Relationship and Crisis Communication* and *Public Relations Communication: Systems, Rhetorical and Critical Approaches*.

Eric Koper has 20 years' international experience in academia and practice. He has demonstrated communication, leadership and management skills in multi-disciplinary research environments when he worked for the Obafemi Awolowo University, FAO, University of Central Lancashire and IITA. He enjoys dealing with complex issues and interacting with various stakeholders such as donors, board members, colleagues, research institutions and partners. As a leader, catalyst and energetic change agent he thrives in active and high pressure multi-cultural environments where he can inject energy, innovation and fun whilst being sensitive to the inherent complexities.

Michael Kunczik is a professor at the Institut für Publizistik (Institute of Communications), Johannes Gutenberg University, Mainz, Germany. He researched mass media effects (especially effects of media violence), international communication, public relations, mass media and social change, media economies, and journalism (especially ethics in journalism). Among his many publications are *Images of Nations and International Public Relations*, *Media Giants: Ownership Concentration and Globalization*, and *Concepts of Journalism: North and South* (also in Portuguese and Spanish).

Ryszard Ławniczak, is a professor at the Poznan University of Economics, Poland, and Head of the Department of Economic Journalism and Public Relations. He was visiting professor at the University of Melbourne (1991) and California State University, Fresno (1984 and 1991). His acadenic research interests include international public relations, foreign economic policies and comparative economic systems. He served as the economic advisor to the President of the Republic of Poland (1997–2005) and is the President of the Western Chapter of the Polish Public Relations Association. He coined the concept of "transitional public relations" and presented it in the first Polish PR books published in English: *Public relations contribution to transition in Central and Eastern Europe. Research and practice* and *Introducing market economy institutions and instruments: The role of public relations in transition economies.* He also contributed a chapter to *Spanning borders, spanning cultures: Public relations in a global setting.*

Shirley Leitch is Dean of the Faculty of Commerce at the University of Wollongong, Australia. She came to Wollongong from the University of Waikato in New Zealand where she was Pro Vice Chancellor of Public Affairs and held a personal chair in corporate communication. Professor Leitch has also held posts at the University of Auckland, Massey University and Victoria University of Wellington and is an A-ranked scholar under the New Zealand PBRF research assessment system. She has undertaken a number of senior advisory roles for government and industry, most recently as research leader of the Growth Culture project for the NZ Government's Growth and Innovation Advisory Board. Over the past two decades, her research work has focused on public communication, particularly on effecting change within public discourses. Professor Leitch has numerous publications including articles in the *European Journal of Marketing*, *Organization Studies*, *Public Relations Review*, *Human Relations*, *Discourse Studies*, *Science and Public Policy*, *International Studies of Management and Organization*, and the *Australian Journal of Communication*.

Jacquie L'Etang is Director of the MSc in Public Relations at Stirling Media Research Institute, Stirling. She is author of *Public Relations: Concepts, Practice and Critique* (Sage 2008), *Public Relations in Britain: A History of Professional Practice* (LEA, 2004) and co-editor of, and contributor to *Public Relations: Critical Debates and Contemporary Practice* (LEA, 2006) and *Critical Perspectives in Public Relations* (ITBP, 1996). She has written nearly 40 book chapters and articles on a range of issues including corporate social responsibility, ethics, history, rhetoric, diplomacy, and education. Her current research interests are in sport, tourism, and religion and she is currently writing a book for Sage on *Sports PR: Issues, Contexts and Practice.* In 2007 she was awarded the Intenational Jordi Xifra Prize (University of Girona). She sits on the editorial boards of *Public Relations Review*, *Journal of Communication Management*, *International Journal of Strategic Communication* and has reviewed for AEJMC and ICA.

Fraser Likely is President and Managing Partner of Likely Communication Strategies Ltd., a PR/Communication management-consulting firm incorporated in Canada in 1987. Likely Communication Strategies provides specialized strategic and performance management consulting services to in-house communications departments in the private, public and not-for-profit sectors. Fraser researches, audits, consults, coaches, trains, writes and speaks in four areas of PR/C function management: function leadership; function strategic management; function structure & organization; and function operational performance & performance measurement. Fraser has been an Adjunct Faculty Member of Royal Roads University's MBA Program in Public Relations and Communication Management as well as in the Department of Communication at the University of Ottawa. Fraser has an M.A. from Carleton University, where his graduate work was on the role of interest or stakeholder groups in societal issues management. As an accredited member of the Canadian Public Relations Society, he has been the Ottawa society President, program chair for three national CPRS conferences, chair of five national committees and task forces as well as recipient of three major National Awards for society leadership. He has been a member of the Advisory Board for the Algonquin College's Public Relations Diploma Program since 1995. Since 1997, he has been a member of Melcrum Publishing's Strategic Communication Management magazine Advisory Board. Fraser was elected to the Institute for Public Relations' Commission on Public Relations Measurement and Evaluation in 2001. He is on the Advisory Board of the International Public Relations Research Conference (IPRRC) and co-sponsor of the IPRRC Jackson-Sharpe Award, a $2000 award given each year to the best joint academic-practitioner scholarly paper.

Jane Masri is Director of Public Relations for Zoom Advertising, based in Ramallah, Palestine. She oversees the public relations and media outreach operations for the firm's local and international clientele. Ms. Masri has co-authored commercially published business guides designed to attract international investors to Palestine and has contributed to hundreds of English-language publications and reports for clients, including the Palestine Investment Fund, Birzeit University, and the Peace Technology Fund. She has more than 15 years of public relations experience and holds a bachelors degree in Economics and English Literature from Bucknell University.

Peter Oriare Mbeke is a public relations, communication and research lecturer at the University of Nairobi, Kenya, and is doing his PhD in media and politics at the same university. He has over ten years' experience teaching public relations in universities such as Daystar University and the United States International University. A graduate of the University of Western Ontario, Canada, he is a renowned pollster in Kenya having pioneered polling there since 1996 and, as a founding director of Strategic Public Relations and Research Limited, conducted the first published exit poll in Kenya in 2002 and another in 2005 during the referendum. Apart from his interest in opinion polls and public relations, he is a peace activist having founded the ISAAA, an agricultural biotechnology think-tank, where he offers communication and research related advice. He is the current chairman for the Education Sub-committee and Deputy Treasurer of the Public Relations Society of Kenya and has written numerous conference papers on public relations in Kenya.

David McKie is a professor in the Management Communication Department of Waikato Management School, Hamilton, New Zealand. As CEO of RAM (Results by Action Management) International Consulting, he also works as a change, communication, leadership, and strategy consultant and runs workshops for individuals and organizations in the private and public sectors in Australia, Europe, India, Sri Lanka, and the USA. A Scot by birth, an Australian by naturalization, a resident of New Zealand by choice, and a citizen of the world by inclination, he enjoys balancing a sense of justice with a sense of humor. David co-authored a Sage book on environmental impacts in 1997, and in 2007 won the PRIDE Prize for the co-authored book *Reconfiguring PR: Equity, Ecology, and Enterprise*. He has also published and spoken widely on: action inquiry and research, applications of complexity sciences, branding in universities, change and leadership, communication; creative industries, emotional intelligence, employee engagement, futures, innovation; media and popular culture, public relations, and strategic entrepreneurship. He is currently seeking a publisher for a book on public relations called "Influencing Israel," while researching a second on "Action Research," and a third on "21C Leadership."

Gary Mersham DLitt et Phil, APR, MPRING, MBTI Admin, AFAWB, is currently Programme Leader for the Public Relations and Communication Management Programmes in the Centre for Social Sciences at the Open Polytechnic of New Zealand. He was previously Professor and Chair of the Department of Communication Science at the University of Zululand. He has taught and consulted as a communications specialist in South Africa, throughout the African continent, and in the USA, Australia, and New Zealand. Gary has a Doctorate in Communication Science from the University of South Africa, and is an accredited Public Relations Practitioner with the Public Relations Institute of South Africa and the Public Relations Institute of New Zealand. He has published and researched widely, authoring eight books and numerous scholarly articles. He shares a passion for the development of African communications and Corporate Social Investment in Africa with colleague, friend and long-time collaborator, Chris Skinner. He is co-author with Chris Skinner of the *Handbook of Public Relations* which has been the leading public relations text in Southern Africa for 25 years. Gary provides strategic counseling, research and communication development services to a number of corporate clients and community groups around the world. He has a blend of 27 years' practical and academic experience in the various fields of organizational and business communications.

Juan-Carlos Molleda is an associate professor and graduate coordinator of the Department of Public Relations, College of Journalism and Communications, University of Florida. He received a Bachelor in Social Communication (1990) from Universidad del Zulia in Venezuela, a Master in Corporate and Professional Communications (1997) from Radford University in Virginia, and a Doctor of Philosophy degree in Journalism and Mass Communications with an emphasis on international public relations (2000) from the University of South Carolina. Juan-Carlos acted as 2008 executive board member of the PRSA International Professional Interest Section, was a founding member of the Commission on Global Public Relations of the Institute for Public Relations, and was 2006–2008 Secretary of the International Communication Association's Public Relations Division. He is member of the editorial boards of the *Journal of Public Relations Research*, *International Journal of Strategic Communication*, and the PRSA *Public Relations Journal*.

Michael Morley is Chairman of Echo Research Inc. Earlier, during a 40-year career at Edelman, Michael founded and built the public relations agency's global network, now the leading independent PR firm with 40 offices worldwide. He served at various times as Edelman's President of International Operations, President of Edelman New York and as Deputy Chairman of Edelman Worldwide. He continues to advise the firm and its clients in an "of counsel" capacity. Michael has managed multi-national PR programmes for companies that include United Parcel Service, AMADEUS Global Travel Distribution, NCR, VISA International, British Airways, Ernst and Young, Roche, Philips, Schering Plough, Warner Lambert, Samsung, S.C. Johnson and Hertz Corporation. He has served as Chairman of the Jury of the IPRA Golden World Awards, and is the author of the book *How to Manage Your Global Reputation*, published by Palgrave Macmillan and in the USA by NYU Press. He is the holder of the CIPR's Alan Campbell-Johnson Medal and is in the ICCO Hall of Fame. He was created Knight of the Order of the Lion by the President of Finland for his contributions to international communications on behalf of that country. He is an adjunct professor at NYU's School of Continuing and Professional Studies.

Danny Moss is the Director of the Centre for Corporate and Public Affairs at the Manchester Metropolitan University and is programme leader for the University's Master's degree programmes in public relations. Previously, as Director of public relations programmes at the University of Stirling, he was responsible for developing and leading the first dedicated Master's programme in public relations in the UK. He is also the co-organiser of the annual International Public Relations Research Symposium, BledCom, which is held at Lake Bled, Slovenia. Danny is the author of a number of books, including two edited collections of papers from the Bled symposium—*Public Relations Research: An International Perspective* and *Perspectives on Public Relations Research*. He has published over 40 journal articles and is the co-editor of the *Journal of Public Affairs*. His most recent book is a volume of case studies edited jointly with Barbara Desanto from the University of North Carolina at Charlotte: *Public Relations Cases: International Perspectives*.

Judy Motion is Professor and Research Director of the School of Management and Marketing in the Faculty of Commerce at the University of Wollongong, Australia. Judy is a New Zealander who has held positions at the University of Auckland and University of Waikato and is ranked an A grade scholar in the New Zealand PBRF research assessment system. Her research adopts a discourse perspective to investigate communication, public relations, marketing, and public policy issues. She is the Australasian associate editor of the *Journal of Communication Management* and *Corporate Communications: An International Journal*, and a member of the editorial boards of the *Journal of Public Affairs*, the *Australian Journal of Communication*, *International Journal of Strategic Communication* and *PRism*. Her research has been published in *Public Relations Review*, *Journal of Public Relations Research*, *Discourse Studies*, *Journal of Communication Management*, *Media Culture and Society*, and *Management Communication Quarterly*.

Jurica Pavicic is Associate Professor of marketing, marketing strategy and marketing for non-profit organizations in the School of Economics and Business at the University of Zagreb, Croatia, where he also received his BSc, MPhil, and PhD. He has professional and academic interests in marketing and all aspects of applied non-profit marketing, management, and communication and is currently working with non-governmental organizations, companies, and research associations to study marketing communications in transition economies. He has published over 20 articles in academic and business journals and other scholarly outlets, including the *British Food Journal*, *Nase Gospodarstvo*, and *Ekonomski pregled*. He also participated in more than 20 international conferences.

Cornelius B. Pratt is communication coordinator in the Office of Communication, United States Department of Agriculture (USDA) Forest Service, Washington, DC. Prior to joining the USDA, he was full professor (1994–2002) in the Department of Advertising at Michigan State University in East Lansing, MI. In 1999, he served as a Fulbright Senior Scholar at three southern African institutions: the University of Zambia, Evelyn Hone College of Applied Arts and Commerce, and the Zambia Institute of Mass Communication Educational Trust, all located in Lusaka, Zambia.

Kjell S. Rakkenes has vast experience from public relations and journalism. He is the Nordic Press Officer for Post Norway (Posten Norge AS)—a post and logistics company based in Norway. Past experience includes Partner and CEO for the largest Norwegian PR and public affairs company JKL Group, Partner with the public affairs consultancy Geelmuyden Kiese and being a journalist in the largest Norwegian business daily, *Dagens Naeringsliv*, the financial daily *Finansavisen* and *Computerworld*. He was the first chairman of the national ethics board of the public relations agencies in Norway.

Ronél Rensburg has been Head of the Department of Marketing and Communication Management at the University of Pretoria since 2000. She is Chairperson of the School of Management Sciences in the Faculty of Economic and Management Sciences and is currently also the President of the Southern African Institute for Management Scientists (SAIMS), and board member of the International Federation of Management Scientists (IFSAM). She is also a board member of the Ron Brown Institute (RBI) for the enhancement of business development in Africa, and a board member of the Centre for Microfinance of Southern Africa. She is coordinator of all international exchange activities, research cooperation and collaboration initiatives for the Faculty of Economic and Management Sciences and has advised 33 doctoral students and more than 30 Masters and MBA-dissertations. She has published books and articles (nationally and internationally) on corporate communication, speech communication, political communication, and corporate social investment and public relations. Her current area of research is the role of reputation management and stakeholder engagement in corporate governance. She has a specific interest in serving the SADC-region of Africa in public relations theory, research and practice.

Adela Rogojinaru holds a PhD in Philology, and is Reader in the University of Bucharest, Romania. She is the current Head of the Department of Communication and Public Relations Studies of the Faculty of Letters and Director of the Centre for Interdisciplinary Research in Communication Sciences and Public Relations. Also a member of professional associations in the field of Communications Sciences such as EUPRERA (European Public Relations Education and Research Association), ECREA (European Communication Research and Education Association), IAMCA (International Association for Media and Comminication Research), and IABC (International Association for Business Communication), she is a Board member of EUPRERA and vice-president of ECREA Section for Organisational and Strategic Communication. In addition to her expertise in communication and public relations, she has developed projects about educational reform process, academic and pre-university curriculum, teacher training, basic literacy, standards and qualification, quality assurance.

Waldemar Rydzak, is a lecturer at the University of Economics in Poznán, Poland. One of the leading Polish specialists in the area of crisis management, he is the author of Poland's first dissertation on that subject. He is founding president of the public relations agency PRELITE and is a member of the Polish Public Relations Association.

Chris Skinner is a visiting senior lecturer and researcher at the University of KwaZulu Natal in the Information Systems and Technology department. He is a Fellow and former Chairman of the Accreditation Board of PRISAS, the Institute of Public Relations and Communication Management, South Africa. He has had more than 30 years' experience in both the corporate and consultancy environment in southern Africa and currently acts as a consultant to both the Federation of African Public Relations Associations (FAPRA) and the Eastern and Southern African Management Institute (ESAMI). He has published numerous books and articles including the definitive *Handbook of Public Relations* which has just celebrated 25 years as the leading public relations text in South Africa.

Gyorgy Szondi is a senior lecturer in Public Relations at Leeds Business School, Leeds Metropolitan University, UK where he is also course leader for the MA in European Public Relations. He holds a BA in Economics, an MA in Public Relations from the University of Stirling, and an MSc in Physics. His PhD at the University of Salzburg, Austria involves researching the concepts of public relations and public diplomacy for the European Union. Before joining Leeds Business School, Gyorgy was teaching in Estonia, where he set up and chaired the public relations program at Concordia International University. His interests and publications include international public relations, public diplomacy, nation branding, risk and crises communication, public relations in Eastern Europe and PR evaluation. He is a regular conference speaker and strategic communication trainer in Eastern Europe, including Hungary, Poland, Estonia, and Latvia. He designed and led training courses for the Health and Safety Executive in the UK; the National School of Government, UK; the Government of Estonia; the Estonian Ministry of Social Affairs; and for several private organizations. His articles have appeared in *Place Branding and Public Diplomacy* and *Journal of Public Affairs* and he has contributed chapters to *The Routledge Handbook of Public Diplomacy*, *Exploring Public Relations* and *Global Public Relations: Spanning Borders, Spanning Cultures*. Prior to academia Gyorgy worked for Hill and Knowlton, the international public relations consultancy in Budapest, and in its international headquarters in London. Besides his native Hungarian, he is fluent in English and Italian, and has a good command of German, French, Polish, Russian and Estonian.

Ana Tkalac is Associate Professor of marketing and marketing communications in the Faculty of Economics, Marketing Department, University of Zagreb, Croatia. She holds a MSc in psychology from the university and is currently finishing her PhD in public relations. She recently returned from the University of Maryland, College Park, where she spent two semesters as a visiting Fulbright Scholar. Her major research interests are focused on attitudes and attitude change in public relations. She has published and co-authored more than 15 papers in the area of public relations and marketing communications, and has also participated in leading international conferences.

Margalit Toledano is currently a senior lecturer in public relations in the Management Communication Department of the Waikato Management School in New Zealand and was accepted as a member of the College of Fellows of the Public Relations Society of America (PRSA) in 2007. An MA in Communication from the Hebrew University, she studied public relations at Boston University on a Hubert H. Humphrey Fellowship Program, became an accredited member of the PRSA in 1985 and served as President of the

Israeli Public Relations Association in 1993–1996. As a practitioner in Israel she served both the public and private sectors and ran her own firm. While managing her PR firm she continued to teach public relations in Bar Ilan University, the Hebrew University in Jerusalem, and Tel Aviv University. Her PhD thesis supervised by Paris 8 University, France, is entitled "The evolution of public relations as a profession in the changing socio-political, economic, and cultural environment of Israel." She is a member of the editorial board of *Public Relations Review* in which she has also published a number of articles. She is now in the process of looking for a publisher for a book about Israeli PR co-authored with Professor David McKie.

Jorge Alberto Hidalgo Toledo is researcher and consultant for social communication at the Centro de Investigacion para la Comunicacion Aplicada (Center for Applied Communication Research) at Universidad Anahuac Mexico Norte and the Endowed Chair Professor of the *Catedra FISAC-Anahuac en comunicacion para la responsabilidad ante el consumo y la sana convivencia.* He is also the Director of *Media and Global Contents* and has been radio producer in Grupo Acir, Radio Centro and news analyst for the newspapers *Reforma* and *El Heraldo de Mexico.* He has published several articles and books among which are: in 2008, a chapter "La mirada perdida: Acoso moral, una apuesta por una victimologia mediatica preventiva" in Rebeil, M.A. and Gomez, D., *Etica, Violencia y Television*; in 2007, "Identidad hipermedial: nuevos medios, nuevas audiencias, ¿nuevas identidades?" for the journal *La Comunicacion en la Comunidad Visual de Mercado*; in 2005, co-author of *Comunicacion Masiva in Hispanoamerica: cultura y literatura mediatica.*

Jacek Trębecki is a lecturer at the University of Economics in Poznán, Poland, and founder of the public relations agency PRELITE, of which he is co-owner. He was a journalist with *Marketing Serwis* monthly and is a specialist in the art of rhetoric, development of information messages, and the evolution of social strategies and campaigns. He is a practitioner in the fields of public campaigns and establishing media relations.

Katerina Tsetsura is an assistant professor at the Gaylord College of Journalism and Mass Communication at the University of Oklahoma. Her interests include international and global strategic communication, global media and public relations ethics, and public affairs and issues management in countries with transitional economies. Her research appeared in internationally recognized books, annuals and journals published on three continents. Dr. Tsetsura also presented papers at numerous research and professional communication conferences around the world, including the UK, Germany, UAE, Poland, Ukraine, Russia, USA, and Mexico. As one of the two leading researchers of the landmark Global Media Transparency project, supported by the Institute for Public Relations (USA), the International Public Relations Association, the International Federation of Journalists, and the International Press Institute, she continues to collect data on media practices around the world for a forthcoming book, *Truth and Global Media Transparency* (together with Dr. Kruckeberg). A former public relations professional, Dr. Tsetsura still provides strategic counseling to agencies, companies and organizations in North American and Eastern European countries in the areas of strategic planning, environmental and public scanning, issues monitoring, and crisis management.

Mark A. Van Dyke has been an associate professor in the School of Communication and the Arts at Marist College in Poughkeepsie, New York since 2004. He teaches graduate and undergraduate courses in public relations, organizational communication, media relations, conflict management, and intercultural communication. A recipient of Marist's college-wide teacher of the year award in 2007, Dr. Van Dyke has established a reputation for using his teaching and research to help prepare students for careers in the public relations profession. He holds a PhD in communication (public relations) from the University of Maryland at College Park (2005) and a master's in public relations from Syracuse University in Syracuse, New York (1989). A graduate of the U.S. Naval Academy in Annapolis, Maryland (1975), Dr. Van Dyke served in the U.S. Navy for 29 years, most of that time as a commissioned public affairs officer. Before retiring from the Navy in 2000, he held senior positions as chief of public information for the North Atlantic Treaty Organization's peace implementation mission in Bosnia-Herzegovina from 1995 to 1996 and as the deputy chief of public information for the U.S. Department of the Navy in Washington, D.C. Dr. Van Dyke has also served as a national defense communication consultant and contributor to news reports about global public relations and international relations. He is a member of the Association of Educators in Journalism and Mass Communication, the National Communication Association, the Public Relations Society of America, and the New York State Communication Association. His research interests include strategic public relations management, conflict resolution, and intercultural communication.

Betteke van Ruler is professor of Communication and Organization at the University of Amsterdam and a member of the Amsterdam School of Communications Research (ASCoR). Prior to that she was an associate professor in communication science and communication management at the Free University of Amsterdam. In 2002–2004 she simultaneously held a funded chair at the University of Twente, focused on professionalism of communication management. Her research focuses on the influence of public relations on journalism and the mediatization of organizations, on the practice of communication management, and on the organization of the communication of the organization. She is a member of several editorial boards such as *Public Relations Review* and *Corporate Communications, an International Journal*. Van Ruler is Past President of the European Public Relations Education and Research Association (EUPRERA) and Past Chair of the Public Relations Division of the International Communication Association (ICA). She is published in *Public Relations Review*, *Journal of Communication Management*, *Journal of Public Relations Research*, and in many Dutch scientific and professional journals. A recent publication is *Public Relations and Communication Management in Europe*, edited in conjunction with Dejan Verčič, and published by Mouton DeGruyter in Berlin. Another recent publication is Van Ruler, Verčič and Verčič, *Public Relations Metrics, Research and Evaluation*, published by Routledge.

Judy VanSlyke Turk is Director and professor at the School of Mass Communications at Virginia Commonwealth University (VCU), Richmond, VA. Prior to joining VCU in March 2002, she was founding dean of the College of Communication and Media Sciences at Zayed University in the United Arab Emirates. Previously, she was dean of the College of Journalism and Mass Communications at the University of South Carolina, and director of the journalism and mass communications program at Kent State. VanSlyke Turk is 2008–2009 president of the Association of Schools of Journalism and Mass Communications and is past president of the Association for Education in Journalism and Mass Communications (AEJMC). She is a member of the Arthur W. Page Society, a past chair of the College of Fellows of the Public Relations Society of America, is a member of the Commission on Public Relations Education, and was named Outstanding Public Relations

Educator in 1992 by the Public Relations Society of America (PRSA). She is associate editor of *Journalism Studies*, an international refereed journal, and is a member of the editorial advisory boards for *Journal of Public Relations Research* and *Journalism and Mass Communications Quarterly*. VanSlyke Turk is co-author of *This is PR: The Realities of Public Relations* (Wadsworth Publishing, now in its 9th edition) and co-editor of *The Evolution of Public Relations: Case Studies From Countries in Transition*, a collection of international public relations case studies published by the Institute for Public Relations, now in its third edition.

Timothy N. Walters is Head of Department, Mass Communication, at the American University of Sharjah. He received his PhD in journalism with a minor in field advertising from the University of Texas at Austin, an MA in history from Indiana University, and a BA with honors in history from Dartmouth College. He has been a member of the advisory board for the Editorial Review committee for *Public Relations Review* since 1994 and is the author of several books and articles. Current projects include examining the media life of college students in the UAE, comparing perceptions of employment readiness among and between students and their prospective employers, and probing how Emirati female college students define their role in society.

Stefan Wehmeier is Junior Professor and represents the chair of communication studies at the Ernst-Moritz-Arndt-University (EMAU) of Greifswald, Germany. He is deputy director of the Institute of Politics and Communication. He received his Doctorate (PhD) in 1997 from the University of Münster, Germany. During 1998–1999 he worked as a journalist and as a PR practitioner and between 2000–2006 he was assistant professor at the University of Leipzig, Department of Public Relations. From January 2007 to October 2007 he was Junior Professor for organizational communication at the EMAU. His research interests include the development of mass media, public relations, and the application of sociological and managerial theories to communication studies.

Jon White is a consultant in management and organization development, public affairs, public relations and corporate communications management. He has worked in public and private sector organizations in Europe, the United States, South Africa, Australia, and Canada. Clients have included companies such as Shell, Motorola, British Airways, National Express and AEA Technology, as well as governments in the UK, Canada, Norway and Macedonia. He has recently worked on executive development programs with the European Commission and with the Foreign and Commonwealth Office of the UK Government. A visiting fellow at Henley Management College in the UK, he is also an honorary professor of public affairs in the University of Birmingham's School of Business and a visiting professor at the University of Central Lancashire and the University of Cardiff's School of Journalism, Media and Cultural Studies. A Fellow of the UK's Chartered Institute of Public Relations, he has a doctorate in psychology from the London School of Economics and Political Science, where he has also led seminars in corporate communication.

R.S. Zaharna is an associate professor in the School of Communication at the American University in Washington, DC. She has written extensively on intercultural and international public communication, and specializes in American and Arab cross-cultural communication. She is author of the forthcoming book, *Redefining Strategic U.S. Public*

Diplomacy in a Global Communication Era (Palgrave-Macmillan). Dr. Zaharna served as a Fulbright Senior Scholar in the West Bank (1996–1997) and holds an undergraduate degree in Foreign Service from Georgetown University and graduate degrees in Communication from Columbia University.

Foreword

Never has cross-cultural communication been so important to different types of organizations (such as governments, corporations, and non-governmental organizations) as it is today. Since the end of World War II, the United Nations and its specialized agencies, such as UNESCO, were the main practitioners of transnational communication, which was an integral part of how they fulfilled their respective missions. A few multinational corporations, mainly from the western world, also engaged in cross-cultural communication. However, in the past decade, cross-cultural communication has become an important focus for a larger number and a wider variety of organizations.

Even the most experienced organizations face challenges when they need to engage in cross-cultural communication, not least because the relationship between an organization and its environment is never static. UNESCO was created to be a permanent worldwide forum of intellectual and ethical exchange and a laboratory of ideas. In 2001, the 188 Member States decided to place all the activities of the current Medium-Term Strategy (2002–2007) under a unifying theme, namely: "UNESCO contributing to peace and human development in an era of globalization through education, the sciences, culture and communication." The context of an ever-globalizing world requires UNESCO to keep its practice of cross-cultural communication under constant review, especially with a view to encouraging a spirit of knowledge-sharing, which is vital for building knowledge societies that are open, inclusive, and equitable.

And democratic. Press freedom, free speech, and the free flow of information are essential for democratic debate to take place. UNESCO is strongly committed to defending and promoting these values and principles. We believe that democratic debate needs to be nurtured and that all members of society—individual and institutional, public and private—can contribute to its cultivation. We recognize, moreover, that the new information and communication technologies (ICTs) have great potential to generate exciting opportunities for opening up avenues of exchange, debate, and discussion. At the same time, the exercise of democratic freedom implies certain responsibilities too. As the "voices" of organizations and groups pursuing their specific interests and ideas, professional communicators find themselves at the interface where institutional concerns and public responsibilities meet.

In an age when there is talk of an inevitable "clash of civilizations," when ill-judged remarks can ignite the tinder-box of popular opinion, when the stereotyping and stigmatization of "the other" can suddenly destroy community relations built up over decades, there is a premium on intercultural dialog within and between societies. There is a corresponding need for sensitivity to these matters by organizations and individuals operating in multicultural, multi-faith, and multi-ethnic environments. The ethics and practice of public relations should be attuned to the new demands of the global situation. The code of practice of public relations, of course, must be a matter of professional self-regulation, but it is not difficult to see where particular emphasis might be placed—for example, respect for the views of others, the active cultivation of mutual understanding, developing the capacity to listen, and sensitivity to local cultures and community values. UNESCO would encourage public relations professionals to reflect increasingly on their practices in the perspective of intercultural dialog and communication. This *Handbook*, with contributions from 62 researchers and scholars hailing from 20 countries, is designed to help that process of reflection.

This publication should prove beneficial to public relations and communication professionals who need to operate in diverse regions of the world. Moreover, it should prove very useful to students and research scholars specializing in international public relations. Indeed, the *Handbook* is to be especially commended for its treatment of the international dimension of public relations, a dimension which highlights the vital importance of cultivating intercultural understanding and dialog. By discussing public relations practice not in isolation but as a function of the political, sociocultural, economic, media, and activist environment in which global organizations must operate, this volume points the way toward fresh approaches to public relations in this age of accelerating globalization.

KOÏCHIRO MATSUURA
DIRECTOR-GENERAL,
UNESCO

PREFACE

The twentieth century was undoubtedly the era of democratization in many parts of the world. The century also saw a concomitant development of more scientific and sophisticated forms of public relations, particularly in the United States and a few countries of Western Europe. The final decade of the twentieth century also was the decade of globalization, with the founding of the World Trade Organization and the formation of many regional and trans-region blocs such as NAFTA, the European Union, Asia-Pacific Economic Cooperation (APEC), and Asia-Europe Meeting (ASEM). Economic cooperation was the primary focus that drove the formation of these trading blocs resulting in significant increases in cross-national trading and communication. Consequently, public relations professionals have been given the responsibility of managing the majority of this transnational communication particularly in the past 15 years.

The need for a comprehensive body of knowledge that will help public relations practitioners operate strategically in a rapidly globalizing world prompted the conceptualization of this book. It is an undeniable fact that to keep pace with the changes brought about by globalization, public relations professionals and students (as future professionals) would need to increase their knowledge of global public relations concepts and their application to the profession. Therefore, in addition to describing various public relations practices across all regions of the world, there is a need to contextualize such practice by linking public relations practices with socio-cultural variables. We hope that in taking such an approach, this book lays the foundation for establishing a holistic body of knowledge based on a comprehensive conceptual framework. We believe that the contributors to this book, who are seasoned public relations scholars, consultants, and practitioners, are in a fairly good position to describe the state of public relations in their country or region as well as relate such practice to relevant socio-cultural variables.

During the five years that have elapsed since the first edition of this book was published, the world has grown ever more interdependent, resulting in growth in public relations activities around much of the globe. Public relations practice and scholarship have advanced during this period as is evident from the many chapters of this edition including from countries that have been in political and economic transition. The size of this book itself is an indication of the growing body of knowledge of global public relations! As heartening as this development is, much work lies ahead. We hope this book will be the harbinger of many attempts that will build on, and refine, the framework and contents of this book.

Much thought and debate preceded our decisions on the contents of this edition. We also solicited feedback from reviewers who have adopted the first edition over the years who told us that even after two printings, the contents of the first edition continue to be of interest and relevance to readers. Therefore, we thought it was prudent to reprint chapters of the first edition and intersperse those chapters with 20 new ones making this edition much more comprehensive.

Producing this edition has been a challenge spread over about two years. A volume of this scope could never have been completed without the cooperation of colleagues dispersed throughout the world. At the outset, we would like to thank the 60 contributors hailing from over 35 countries for their diligence in providing comprehensive information about public relations in 29 countries and an overview of the practice in two continents (Africa and Latin America) as well as the chapters contained in Sections I and VI. We appreciate the efforts of country-specific authors in adhering to the framework described in Section I as much as possible. We extend special thanks to His Excellency Koïchiro Matsuura, Director-General of the UNESCO, for graciously agreeing to write the Foreword for the book. We worked with Linda Bathgate and Karin Wittig (first edition) and Linda Bathgate and Kerry Breen (second edition) and thank them for their patience and cooperation in seeing a project of this magnitude to fruition despite many challenges including a transfer of ownership.

Krishnamurthy Sriramesh would like to thank his family and colleagues and students at several universities in many parts of the world for educating him and assisting in his continued development leading up to the conceptualization and production of this edition. Dejan Verčič would like to thank his colleagues at PRISTOP Communications for the pleasure of working with them and for their cooperation during his work on this book.

KRISHNAMURTHY SRIRAMESH
DEJAN VERČIČ

Introduction

Krishnamurthy Sriramesh

It may be hard to overstate the importance of a comprehensive body of knowledge to public relations practice. During its first two decades of existence, public relations scholarship was built on experiences from only a few Western democracies, principally the US and the UK. Efforts to gather empirical evidence about public relations activities from other parts of the world based on theoretical underpinnings using sound methodology only began in the early 1990s. Most of these "international" studies predominantly used one, or both, of two conceptual foundations, J. E. Grunig's models of public relations and Broom and Dozier's public relations roles, to describe the public relations practice in a few countries. In the past decade, elements proposed by the *Excellence Project* have also been used as other rhetorical and contingency theories for studying public relations in a few countries.

However, the body of research categorized as being in the "international" or "global" arena is confined predominantly to a few countries of Asia and Western Europe, a chasm that needs to be bridged. The principal goal of this book is to help integrate wisdom from many other regions of the world, despite many obstacles. For example, as described in the chapters on Brazil and Chile and the overview chapter of public relations in Latin America, much of the published work on public relations in Latin America is not in English, thus limiting its global utility.

The existing body of knowledge of public relations is a strong foundation on which more holistic scholarship should be built by integrating understanding of public relations practices from as many regions of the world as possible. Such enrichment can also come from cross-national comparisons of public relations practices based on multi-national studies that describe public relations practices in different countries. Cross-national theorizing should also explore how contextual variables external to the organization (described in Part I of this book) influence public relations activities in various parts of the world. Advocating such an approach using a common conceptual framework is the primary theme of this book. Although there are many benefits to such an approach, the most significant one would be the enhancement of the predictive capabilities of the body of knowledge. In order for professionals to engage in strategic public relations management in a global setting, it is essential that they have the benefit of such a body of knowledge. A comprehensive body of knowledge helps them predict the outcomes of their strategies and techniques vis-à-vis the organization's environment rather than trying to practice based on anecdotal evidence when they are required to operate in an unfamiliar region. Globalization has undoubtedly contributed to the exponential growth in the demand for cross-national public relations—global public relations.

DEFINITION OF GLOBAL PUBLIC RELATIONS

Since the early days of public relations scholarship, scores of definitions of the term *public relations* have been offered. In one of the earliest such attempts, the Foundation for Public Relations Research and Education in the United States (founded in 1956 and currently known as the Institute for Public Relations) sponsored a study in 1975 that sought the opinions of 65 leaders of public relations in the US and also analyzed 472 different definitions of the term. Based on this analysis, a long definition of public relations was offered that contained 88 words.[1] In 1982, the Public Relations Society of America (PRSA) issued an "Official Statement of Public Relations" attempting to define the term and set the parameters of the practice. Authors of many introductory textbooks from different parts of the world have offered various definitions of the term public relations. However, among other things, most of these definitions do not specifically address the multicultural diversity or global nature of organizational publics but leave it to the reader to make such assumptions. Therefore, it is appropriate to begin this book by offering a definition of the term *public relations* that also explicitly addresses the multi-cultural (defining culture very broadly, as in Part I of this book) and holistic nature of the term and the practice:

> *Public relations* is the strategic communication that different types of organizations use for establishing and maintaining symbiotic relationships with relevant publics many of whom are increasingly becoming culturally diverse.

When we deconstruct this definition, we recognize that at its core, public relations is a **communication** activity. Organizations expect us to help them effectively communicate with relevant publics based on sound **strategy**. John Budd Jr., founding member of the Fellows of the Public Relations Society of America (PRSA), argued that by aligning public relations with communication, one would be bringing down the profession to a technician's level. He wanted to divest communication from public relations in order to make public relations a managerial level function because he believed communication is merely a technical activity whereas public relations is the strategy behind that technique.[2] The definition offered here sees *communication* not merely as a technique but as being strategic as well. The communication specialist arrives at sound public relations strategies by conducting empirical research (environmental scanning) to understand the needs, values, and expectations of the organization's relevant publics. Wise organizations use such data to establish overall strategies that seek to first understand the cultures and values of their publics and address their needs and expectations as well.

The term *strategic* here also implies that communication is a **managerial** function (that includes contributing to organizational strategy and policy) and not merely a technical

---

[1] Harlow, R. F. (1976). Building a public relations definition. *Public Relations Review,* 2(4).
[2] Budd, J. (1995). Communications doesn't define PR, it diminishes it. *Public Relations Review,* 21(3), pp. 177–179.

function. Conducting research such as environmental scanning can hardly be termed technical as it contributes to managerial decision making. At the level of global public relations, setting appropriate strategies for communicating with a global audience is not only vital but is very much a challenge as well. Most global public relations managers still continue to be found wanting in setting appropriate global strategies if they are not educated to the diversity they are bound to encounter when they practice public relations at the global level.

All communication should aim to be symbiotic. That is, communication is intended to establish and maintain **mutually beneficial relationships** between organizations and their relevant publics rather than fostering an imbalanced relationship as in the case of mere publicity. Therefore, the motivation to engage in global public relations is not for the organization to merely manipulate or exploit the public but with the intent of being symbiotic where both sides of the equation stand to benefit from the relationship. Making sure that one knows the expectations of a global audience is the first of many challenges for the global public relations practitioner.

I would like to stress that the term **organization** and not *corporation* is appropriate here although it is a common phenomenon in many parts of the developed world to use the term *corporate communication* as a synonym for public relations. This is also the reason for public relations to be perceived by a majority of the public as communication on behalf of business interests and therefore looking down upon public relations as being self-serving. However, public relations practitioners contribute to the efficacy of government agencies and non-profits. As is evident in many chapters particularly from countries in Asia, Africa, and Latin America, communication from government and NGOs is of a much higher volume than that of corporations. Therefore, a true definition of public relations cannot ignore communication from governments and NGOs. I would contend that public relations is seen in a negative light predominantly because it is seen as communication aimed at achieving selfish goals of corporate interests. Such a world view among the general populace ignores the use of public relations for advocating altruistic causes and social development, thereby hurting the profession. An entire section of this book is dedicated to expanding our understanding of the use of public relations by governments, non-profits, and world bodies such as the United Nations and UNESCO to counter some of these misperceptions.

The term **relevant publics** denotes that the organization's communication specialists understand the needs and values of individual homogeneous groups that are affected by organizational activities and have the ability to also influence organizational activities including its success and very existence. We need to recognize that, increasingly, these relevant publics are becoming more and more **diverse and global** because of rapid globalization. In fact, I wonder whether one should talk any longer about "international public relations" or "global public relations" as being a specialty because even "domestic" publics are becoming multinational and multicultural due to globalization. So understanding the needs, expectations, and values of a diverse set of publics is becoming more important even as it is growing more complex, requiring great skills and thereby becoming more and more strategic and less technical. As a result, an effective global public relations manager should be well educated and sensitized to communicating in a global environment. It is apparent from the chapters in this book that several factors have contributed significantly to increasing the transnational activities of organizations around the world, thereby globalizing public relations practice as well.

DEMOCRATIZATION

The democratization of the world, especially in the latter half of the twentieth century, has forced organizations of all types in many regions of the world to consider giving greater importance to public relations and communications management in order to build relationships with diverse audiences in far away lands. One might be surprised that in 1900 the world did not have a single democratic country that had universal suffrage! However, by the end of the twentieth century there were 119 electoral democracies, home to 58 percent of the global population. Of these, 85 countries (covering 35 percent of the world's population) were classified by Freedom House (2000) as liberal democracies. This process of democratization hit a crescendo in the 1990s when the former Soviet bloc countries embarked on the journey toward pluralism. In its latest report (2007), Freedom House put the number of electoral democracies at 123 and noted that about 3 billion people (46 percent of the world's population) "lived in free states in which a broad array of political rights were protected" (p. 6).[3]

As a result, emerging democracies around the world have witnessed a significant growth in public communication, much of which will have to be managed by public relations professionals. Examples of the relationship between democratization and the development of public relations is evident in several chapters of this book that describe the infusion of "modern" public relations by the U.S. and its allies in countries such as Japan (Chapter 7), South Korea (Chapter 8), and even a Western European nation such as Sweden (Chapter 23) especially after the end of World War II. A similar trend is reported from many other countries covered in this expanded edition whose economies are in transition.

THE ADVENT OF ICTS AND TRADING BLOCS

Globalization has also been spurred by the rapid expansion of Information and Communication Technologies that have revolutionized the dissemination of information about products, services, and life styles around much of the world. When combined with the freedom that accompanies democratization, one sees a significant increase in the global demand for products and services, as well as global suppliers who can meet this demand. As a result, countries such as India (which has thrived primarily because of the boom in ICTs) and China have emerged as major centers of manufacturing as well as consumption spurring global communication.

The formation of multinational trading blocs such as NAFTA, EC, ASEAN, APEC (Asia Pacific Economic Conference) and ASEM (Asia Europe Meeting) has also contributed to shrinking the global market thereby increasing organizational activities among, and between, trading blocs. These trading blocs continue to expand by attracting more countries into their fold as is evident in the expansion of the EU to its current strength of 27 countries with at least three candidates waiting to join.

These factors have contributed to a significant spurt in global communication placing public relations practitioners at the forefront of managing the relationships among peoples of varied nations and cultures on behalf of organizations of all types. Therefore, it is essential for public relations professionals to be prepared to meet the challenges of communicating with publics of various countries and cultures. Not confined to communicating only with domestic audiences any longer, public relations professionals can greatly benefit from a comprehensive body of knowledge that is also multinational and multicultural.

---

[3] http://www.freedomhouse.org/uploads/special_report/62.pdf (retrieved July 1, 2008).

Further, as discussed in Chapter 44, public relations educators, who are saddled with the responsibility of helping educate future professionals, should build, and benefit from, a body of empirical evidence about public relations practices in a global context, which can be provided primarily by having a comprehensive (and holistic) body of knowledge of public relations.

PUBLIC RELATIONS: AN INDUSTRY IN TRANSITION

There is ample evidence in a majority of chapters of this book that the public relations industry around the world is evolving from publicity-oriented practices into varying degrees of professionalization. Even the United States, popularly considered to be the leader in the field, "is well beyond [its] rudimentary beginnings" but "not there yet," according to L. A. Grunig and J.E. Grunig (Chapter 30). Chen and Culbertson characterize the public relations profession in China (Chapter 10) as an "adolescent" that is undergoing "growing pains." A similar description of the profession is evident in Chapter 11 where Badran Badran, Judy Turk, and Tim Walters describe the industry in the UAE as "coming of age." There is little doubt that in most of the countries covered in this book, democratization and economic liberalization have resulted in public relations being accorded a greater role by decision makers of organizations. This is bound to spur more professionalism of the practice over the next decade. Globalization has also resulted in the influx of multinational corporations and public relations agencies into new markets, which has helped push the industry in these countries to greater professionalism as seen in Singapore (Chapter 9), South Korea (Chapter 8), the Republic of South Africa (Chapter 17) and Chile (Chapter 33).

THE FRAMEWORK FOR THE BOOK

Each of the country-specific chapters seeks to provide readers information on two principal aspects. First, these chapters seek to describe the current status of the public relations profession in the specific country or region thereby helping increase our knowledge and understanding of the profession in other regions of the world. In providing these descriptions, authors have sought to describe specific public relations practices, the knowledge level and professionalism of practitioners, the impact of professional associations on social responsibility and ethics of professionals, the status of public relations education in the nation, challenges being faced by the public relations industry, and the extent to which organizations used strategic public relations management including measurement and evaluation. Although each chapter may vary in the extent to which it provides information on each of these factors owing to the nature of the profession in a particular country, it is interesting to note that this task seemed to pose little or no challenge to any of the contributors. This is in keeping with the fledgling body of knowledge of global public relations that consists almost exclusively of descriptive studies. I hope that readers will find that this book has included a wider range of factors that can be used to describe the public relations profession in a country. Given the relative novelty of the field, descriptive accounts are quite useful in helping advance scholarship to the analytical level.

The second major task that each chapter seeks to accomplish is to link the public relations practices in a country or region to its socio-cultural environment using the framework described in Chapter 1 and elaborated upon in the chapters contained in Part I. This task appeared to pose a greater challenge to authors primarily because of the paucity of empirical evidence on the linkage between public relations and socio-cultural variables in most regions of the world. As a result, despite their expertise and earnest efforts, contributors have had varying degrees of success in providing empirical data on the variables in the framework as well as in making informed linkages between these variables and public relations practice. The efforts of contributors in responding to this challenge deserve to be lauded because of the relative novelty of using this approach. I hope the framework provided in Part I will be the conceptual underpinning for future studies, which can also refine and extend the framework. One of the primary purposes of this book will have been served if it encourages more studies that go beyond describing public relations in specific regions and also gather empirical evidence on socio-cultural variables and their linkage to public relations practice. Providing this linkage will not only get easier but also more refined as a greater number of studies follow the leads provided in this book.

ORGANIZATION OF CHAPTERS

Another significant goal of this book is to help globalize public relations pedagogy by including contributions from every continent. Our field is in dire need of a more holistic perspective, which I believe is bound to benefit professionals, scholars, and students in various ways. Predictably, the North American continent, Europe, and Asia have relatively better representation in this book than Africa and Latin America. Despite persistent efforts, we were unable to get a few more contributions from Africa and Latin America for a variety of reasons including language barriers and paucity of empirical evidence. It is clear that many such constraints will have to be overcome in assembling a comprehensive body of knowledge of global public relations over the next years. In order to compensate for the lack of representation from individual countries of Africa and Latin America, this edition includes two chapters that provide readers with an overview of public relations in each of these two regions.

In identifying the format for the country-specific chapters, I wondered whether contributors should describe the socio-cultural environmental variables (culture, political system, economic system, etc.) of a country first and then contextualize the description of the public relations practices of that country in light of those variables. After much thought, I decided that because there is a distinct lack of empirical evidence on *all* the contextual variables from most regions of the world, it was prudent to describe the public relations profession of each country first and then have authors try to relate public relations practices to environmental variables as far as possible. Because we currently lack even descriptive data on the public relations industry from many regions of the world, such knowledge is most helpful. Future accounts of global public relations may very well find it useful to describe the socio-cultural variables first and base their description of the status of public relations in a country on these contextual variables.

Part I gives an overview of the conceptual framework consisting of the socio-cultural variables that influence public relations activities. Whereas in the previous edition Chapter 1 synopsized the relevance of these variables, this edition offers expanded discussion of the framework by including individual chapters on each of these variables: political economy, culture, mass media, and activism. The new chapters provide extensive reviews of relevant literature and offer ways of empirically measuring these variables and linking them to public relations. The extended discussion of these variables, it is hoped, will spur empirical research on the linkages between these variables and public relations.

Part II presents chapters on Australasia and seven countries of Asia. East Asia is represented by China, Japan, South Korea, and Singapore and West Asia and the Middle

East by the UAE, Israel and the Palestinian region. Globalization has thrust Asia into the forefront of economic growth propelling many Asian countries (including those represented in this section) toward economic development. Even developed economies such as Singapore are in transition as they have been forced to reinvent their economic priorities and activities in order to keep pace with global and regional competition. I had received several inquiries from readers of the previous edition on why countries such as India had not been included in that edition. Readers will be interested to note that ten countries of Asia including Saudi Arabia, India, Malaysia, Taiwan and Indonesia have been discussed using the same framework as this book in *Public Relations in Asia: An Anthology*.[4] Between the two books, 15 countries of Asia have been covered using the framework presented in Part I of this book.

Part III presents chapters from Africa. Nigeria and Kenya are new additions as is the chapter providing an overview of the public relations profession in Africa. At least three authors from Africa had agreed to contribute chapters for this book but could not finish their manuscripts for various reasons. Such constraints will continue to hamper our efforts to build a body of knowledge of public relations that is truly global. As a substitute for more chapters from countries of Africa, I invited Chris Skinner and Gary Mersham to provide an overview of public relations in Africa. I am grateful to them for taking on the challenge of writing about this diverse continent and producing such an informative manuscript. I hope their overview chapter serves as a worthy substitute for the lack of more individual country chapters from this continent.

Part IV presents chapters from Europe including five new chapters from the U.K., Norway, Italy, Romania, and Hungary. For over 12 years, Freedom House has been reporting on the extent of democratization in the former communist countries of Central and Eastern Europe and Eurasia, calling them Nations in Transit (NIT). In the 2007 report on 29 countries in the NIT region, Freedom House noted that there was "reform fatigue, increasing polarization of politics and societies, and pressure to reduce political pluralism."[5] Much of the reform fatigue is caused, according to the authors, by the lopsided distribution of the benefits of a market economy in favor of a few political elites and a continued lack of efforts to end or at least reduce corruption.

Part V presents public relations in North and South America. The three countries that comprise North America have been covered in this book. Getting participation from scholars who are familiar with public relations in Latin America continues to be a challenge primarily due to linguistic barriers. Several potential contributors were contacted but none was willing to participate in the project. We should continue to strive to get local scholars to write about public relations in the nations of this region. I thank Maria Aparecida Farrari for taking on the challenge of writing the overview chapter, always a challenge given regional diversities.

Part VI seeks to provide an overview of global public relations going beyond individual countries. More importantly, it seeks to extend pedagogy beyond corporate communication by focusing on the public relations activities of NGOs and governments. As already noted earlier in this introduction, one of the contributions that global public relations can make to the body of knowledge is to help reduce the asymmetry in the focus between the public relations activities of corporations and governments and NGOs in

---

[4] Sriramesh, K. (2004). *Public Relations in Asia: An Anthology.* Singapore: Thomson.
[5] Evenson, K. D., and Goehring, J. (2007). Nations in Transit 2007: Pause and pushback for democratization. In Freedom House *Nations in Transit 2007: Democratization from Central Europe to Eurasia.* Freedom House.

public relations pedagogy. The chapters from UNESCO and the UN are included for this purpose as is the chapter on NGOs. Sadly, the wealth of experience from such actors has not been integrated well into the body of knowledge of public relations that continues to be skewed toward corporate communication even though various UN agencies have been communicating with diverse publics from around the world for over 60 years. The chapter on public diplomacy and strategic communication is included to provide a further broadening of our horizons about the use of public relations at the global level. Finally, the epilogue looks to the future of global public relations stressing the need to make the body of knowledge more holistic. I hope this edition is much more comprehensive than the previous one, displaying that the field has made significant progress in five years.

GLOBAL PUBLIC RELATIONS: CONCEPTUAL FRAMEWORK

1

A THEORETICAL FRAMEWORK FOR GLOBAL PUBLIC RELATIONS RESEARCH AND PRACTICE

KRISHNAMURTHY SRIRAMESH
DEJAN VERČIČ

As described in the Introduction, there is very little empirical evidence on the nature of public relations in many regions of the world. We believe that the body of knowledge of international public relations is so young that it is very important to have descriptive accounts of public relations practice from individual countries. But we also believe that it is equally important for this body of knowledge to be able help predict the best way to practice public relations in a particular country or region. This is best done by identifying relationships between public relations and other relevant variables. Therefore, in planning this book, we asked contributing authors to not only describe public relations practice in their countries but to attempt to make informed linkages between environmental variables and the profession. We believe that identifying the impact of environmental variables on public relations practice helps increase our ability to predict which strategies and techniques are better suited to a particular organizational environment.

We believe that the framework presented in this chapter, which was followed in each of the 17 individual country chapters, can be a good starting point in exploring the relationship between organizational environments and their public relations practices. We also recognize that as we begin to build the body of knowledge on international public relations, other variables may emerge. We note that because there is little empirical evidence on the linkage between environmental variables and public relations practice from most regions of the world, currently, we can only conceptualize the linkage between these variables and public relations or base our analyses on anecdotal evidence. Nevertheless, in our opinion, this is a significant first step toward building a comprehensive knowledge base of international public relations.

BACKGROUND

We relied on the three-nation study commonly known as the *Excellence Project* (J. E. Grunig, 1992b) in proposing a three-factor framework for this book that attempts to link environmental variables with public relations practice. Based on the Excellence Project, Verčič, L. A. Grunig, and J. E. Grunig (1996) identified nine generic principles that, they argued, could be used to set up global public relations practices. The authors also suggested that five environmental variables can be used by public relations practitioners to design public relations strategies specific to a given country. The five variables are: political ideology, economic system (including the level of development of the country's economy), degree of activism (the extent of pressure organizations face from activists), culture, and media system (the nature of the media environment in a country).

Culbertson and Jeffers (1992) highlighted the importance of what they called social, political and economic contexts (SPE) to public relations practice at the same time that the Excellence Study was underway, but they did not explore these contexts internationally. As a follow-up to their initial article, Culbertson, Jeffers, Stone, and Terrell (1993) explained SPE contexts as follows:

> As we write this, our definition of elements in the SPE context is still evolving.... As we studied, the social context occupied us more than the political and economic ones. Perhaps this stemmed in part from the fact that, on the whole, we were trained in communication and social psychology not in political science or economics.... However, as we proceeded, we decided there was a deeper reason. Consideration of the political context focuses on gaining support from officials—on power relationships having to do with clients and the public at large. And economic context has to do largely with the distribution of resources. (p. 5)

We agree with J. E. Grunig (1992b) and Culbertson et al. (1993) that these environmental variables have a significant impact on public relations. We note, however, that despite the significance of these variables, 11 years later, few studies have empirically linked environmental variables with public relations. The only exception is culture, which has been linked to public relations, either conceptually or based on empirical evidence, by a few studies in the past 11 years (e.g., Huang, 2000; Rhee, 1999, 2002; Sriramesh, 1992, 1996; Sriramesh, J. E. Grunig, & Dozier, 1996; Sriramesh, Kim, & Takasaki, 1999; Sriramesh & Takasaki, 1999; Sriramesh & White, 1992). The linkage between other environmental variables and public relations remains to be empirically investigated, providing public relations scholars with a challenge and an opportunity.

In this chapter, we present the logic behind linking these variables with public relations and suggest ways of operationalizing each variable as a prelude to future studies. In doing so, we collapsed these five variables into three factors: a country's infrastructure, media environment, and societal culture. We describe each of these three interrelated factors and conceptually identify their relationship with international public relations.

INFRASTRUCTURE AND INTERNATIONAL PUBLIC RELATIONS

We believe that three infrastructural ingredients are key to international public relations: a nation's political system, its level of economic development, and the level of activism prevalent in that country. Each of these variables influences the nature of public relations practiced in a country and each is very closely interrelated, which is why we have collapsed them into one factor. However, we do recognize that each of these factors influences and is influenced by a country's culture and media environment—the other two environmental factors that will be reviewed later in this chapter.

Political System

A country's political system influences its social structure. There is little doubt that public relations practice thrives on public opinion, which would lead one to conclude that only pluralistic societies offer an environment that is conducive for practicing strategic public relations. Available evidence (some of which is described in the chapters in this book) suggests that in societies whose political systems do not value public opinion, the nature of public relations is not sophisticated and tends to be one-way propagandistic in nature. However, democracy comes in many forms as is evident in the fact that almost each of the 192 current member states of the United Nations claims to be a democracy. These countries are able to make the claim because they have their own definitions of what democracy is or should be. As described in the Introduction to this book, comprehensive reports such as the one from Freedom House Karatnycky, A. (2002) are indicative of the variability in the definition and practice of democracy around the world. Such descriptions are invariably helpful to international public relations scholars and professionals.

As noted in the introduction, since the beginning of the 1990s, the world has been evolving rather rapidly, with many countries undergoing political, economic, and societal changes. In particular, many former Soviet bloc countries have embarked on the road toward democratization and market reforms and now have economies in transition. These countries are currently in various stages of democratization and market reforms, offering varied opportunities and challenges to public relations professionals. For many of these countries, the transition has neither been smooth nor consistent. Because the political environment determines the nature of public relations one can practice there, it is essential to conduct comparative research on the linkage between various political ideologies and public relations, a relationship that is yet to be empirically explored in most countries—including countries in transition.

Political ideology is closely linked to economic development because political conditions affect economic decision making and vice versa in every country. Furthermore, the dynamics between political and economic systems often determine a nation's stability and further economic development. Examples abound of how lack of economic development often leaves a society mired in a web of illiteracy and poverty, preventing strong democratic political institutions from taking roots.

Typically, three types of political systems have been used in the past: Western industrialized democracies (the First World); Communist states (Second World); and the predominantly non-Western, developing countries (Third World). The collapse of the Soviet Union and its impact on the global power structure, among other things, makes this distinction moot. Furthermore, there are many newly industrializing countries that no longer fit the definition of developing countries but are also not democratic in the Western sense and, therefore, cannot be categorized as belonging to the First World, according to the aforementioned definition (Wilson, 1995).

Simon and Gartzke (1996) differentiated between political environments on a bipolar continuum ranging from democratic to authoritarian. However, this categorization is too simplistic to provide details about the many nuances and the various political and economic challenges and experiences that many countries experience. The world has witnessed significant political changes in recent years. Thus, we should have a more accurate way to classify the political systems of nations. In fact, the 20th century has been a period of democratization of the world. According to the Freedom House, at the beginning of the 20th century, there was not a single country that could be labeled a democracy! Even countries such as the United States and Britain were not true democracies because they did not have universal suffrage at the beginning of the 20th century.

One of the most comprehensive classifications of political systems, one that we prefer over the others, was proposed by the Freedom House in a project titled: "Democracy's Century: A Survey of Global Political Change in the 20th Century" (http://www.freedomhouse.org/reports/century.html#project). This project examined the political systems that governed the world in the 20th century at the beginning, middle, and turn of the century. In doing so, the study offered the following seven types of political systems:

1. *Democracies* wherein multiple parties and individuals compete in open elections to earn the right to rule for a predetermined period (unless there is a constitutionally mandated reason for earlier elections). In democracies, opposition parties have a fair chance of winning power or participate in power sharing as members of a coalition government.

2. *Restricted democratic practices* in which a single party controls key constituencies such as political institutions, the media, and the electoral process to maintain the status quo. Included in this list are countries that deny voting rights based on factors such as gender, race, and socioeconomic status.

3. *Monarchies* consisting of *constitutional monarchies* (a constitution specifies the powers of the monarch often devolving some power to elected and other bodies), *traditional monarchies*, and *absolute monarchies* (where the monarch rules as despot).

4. *Authoritarian regimes* that usually are one-party states or military dictatorships noted for significant human rights violations.

5. *Totalitarian regimes* wherein a single political party establishes total control over the society including intrusion into private life (e.g., Marxist–Leninist and national socialist regimes).

6. *Colonial and imperial dependencies*, which are ruled by large imperial systems, mostly seen in the first half of the 20th century.

7. *Protectorates* that, of their own accord, request protection from a more powerful neighbor or are temporarily placed under protection by the international community.

Using this classification system, Freedom House synthesized the shift in political systems from the beginning of the 20th century, in 1950, and in 1999.

Table 1.1 reveals that in 1900 there were no true democracies in a world that was dominated by monarchies and empires. Twenty-five countries came closest to being labeled as countries with restricted democratic practices (e.g., no universal suffrage), accounting for just 12.4% of the world population. By mid-century, the postwar world had seen the fall of Nazi and fascist totalitarianism and a spurt in decolonization in many parts of the world. In 1950, there were 22 democracies (covering 31% of the world population) and an additional 21 states with restricted democratic practices (11.9% of the global population). However, by the end of the century, democracy had spread to much of the former Communist world and many regions of Latin America, Africa, and Asia, with electoral democracies making up 120 (62.5% of the world population) of the 192 countries that existed then. Note, however, that of these 120 electoral democracies, only 85 (38% of the world's population) were categorized by Freedom House as liberal democracies

TABLE 1.1

Tracking Polity in the 20th Century

	Sovereign States and Colonial Units			Population (Millions)		
	2000	1950	1900	2000	1950	1900
DEM	120 (62.5%)	22 (14.3%)	0 (0.0%)	3,439.4 (58.2%)	743.2 (31.0%)	0 (0.0%)
RDP	16 (8.3%)	21 (13.6%)	25 (19.2%)	297.6 (5.0%)	285.9 (11.9%)	206.6 (12.4%)
CM	0 (0.0%)	9 (5.8%)	19 (14.6%)	0 (0.0%)	77.9 (3.2%)	299.3 (17.9%)
TM	10 (5.2%)	4 (2.6%)	6 (4.6%)	58.2 (1.0%)	16.4 (0.7%)	22.5 (1.3%)
AM	0 (0.0%)	2 (1.3%)	5 (3.8%)	0 (0.0%)	12.5 (0.5%)	610.0 (36.6%)
AR	39 (20.3%)	10 (6.5%)	0 (0.0%)	1,967.7 (33.3%)	122.0 (5.1%)	0 (0.0%)
TOT	5 (2.6%)	12 (7.8%)	0 (0.0%)	141.9 (2.4%)	816.7 (34.1%)	0 (0.0%)
C	0 (0.0%)	43 (27.9%)	55 (42.3%)	0 (0.0%)	118.4 (4.9%)	503.1 (30.2%)
P	2 (1.0%)	31 (20.1%)	20 (15.4%)	4.8 (0.1%)	203.3 (8.5%)	26.5 (1.6%)
Total	192 (100.0%)	154 (100.0%)	130 (100.0%)	5,909.6 (100.0%)	2,396.3 (100.0%)	1,668.0 (100.0%)

Note. DEM = democracy; RDP = restricted democratic practice; CM = constitutional monarchy;
TM = traditional monarchy; AM = absolute monarchy; AR = authoritarian regime; TOT = totalitarian regime;
C = colonial dependency; P = protectorate.
(*Source*: Freedom House, 2000)

according to a more stringent benchmark that required countries to also respect basic human rights and uphold the law in addition to holding elections.

Among other factors, Freedom House's study highlights the fact that the 20th century has been the harbinger of pluralism in the world. It may be hard to fathom that there was no truly democratic country in the world just a century ago! In a century, the world has come a long way, although much more needs to be accomplished. The study also highlights the fact that, whereas all societies have political institutions, the means for attaining political power varies among countries. Political power may come as a birthright (as in monarchies or the political dynasties in nepotistic cultures), through association with other power elite (as in totalitarian regimes), or through complex political rituals (e.g., elections), which may have various levels of openness and fairness. Although these distinctions do not specifically state it, a number of nations of the world recently leaned toward a theocratic form of governance.

The significance of these shifts to public relations lies in the fact that the Western definition of public relations assumes a democratic political structure in which competing groups seek legitimacy and power through public opinion and elections, which is not always the norm in many parts of the world. Particularly difficult to discern are emerging democracies where alternative views may be encouraged in theory but not in practice, resulting in various forms of covert and overt forms of self-, social, and government censorship.

The impact that each of these political systems has on public relations is yet to be fully explored. However, it is clear that, in addition to being an era of democratization of much of the world, the 20th century has by all accounts witnessed the growth of modern public relations. With an increase in the level of democratization of a society (e.g., the United States and Britain) has come a concomitant increase in the level of sophistication of the public relations profession. There is little doubt, however, that strategic public relations flourishes in pluralistic societies. As the succeeding chapters of this book will affirm, democratization has spurred the growth of public relations in many regions of the world. Now is the time to analyze empirically how the other types of political systems affect public relations practices and the impact that public relations has in the process of democratization and in maintaining a particular political system.

Level of Economic Development

Closely linked to a country's political system, a country's economic development provides public relations professionals opportunities as well as challenges. There is little doubt that a more pluralistic political philosophy favors greater economic freedom. By extension, developed (market) economies tend to favor strategic public relations more than developing (managed) ones. However, public relations has yet to be widely considered a core organizational function in organizations of even developed economies. Instead, it languishes as a superfluous appendage in organizations around the world, including developed nations. As a result, the predominant mindset is that scarce resources need to be spent on more pressing needs that are central to an organization's activities and bring tangible returns. Despite this lacuna, strategic public relations generally thrives in developed countries because the more developed an economy is, the greater the number of organizational players and the higher the level of competition among organizations. These multiple suppliers of goods and services obviously need to compete for public attention, approval, and support—a prime reason to employ public relations professionals as in-house staff or as consultants.

Furthermore, the political system of a country also determines the extent to which private entrepreneurship is valued and encouraged. Prior to the establishment of the World Trade Organization (WTO), most developing countries, even those claiming to be democracies, had favored managed economies built mostly around public sector enterprises that often operated as monopolies. In countries with vast public sectors, the government becomes the primary, if not the sole, relevant public for a public relations professional. Even after the establishment of the WTO, countries have been slower in switching to market-oriented systems. But the change from public sector to private sector investment has begun in many of the 144 WTO members. This is bound to create fresh opportunities and challenges for the international public relations professional.

As reviewed in the section "The media and public relations," the level of economic development of a country directly affects variables such as poverty and illiteracy. These two potent variables have a direct impact on the strategies and techniques that public relations professionals may use in a country. The lack of an adequate communication infrastructure also severely challenges the international public relations professional who attempts to conduct information campaigns in developing nations, where folk and indigenous methods of communication may be the more effective choice.

Activism

We clubbed activism with political system and level of development because we believe that the three are closely interrelated. A country's political system has a direct influence on the extent of activism in that country because only pluralistic societies tolerate activism of any sort. Furthermore, a country's level of economic development also directly influences the level and nature of activism in that country. In most developing nations, people are busy fighting to earn the next square meal for their family, leaving them little time or inclination for participating in other activities. To the extent that their livelihood is threatened, the populace of these nations may engage in activism—predominantly labor unionism. As stated earlier, the 20th century has been a period of democratization of the world. Many developing nations, particularly Africa and Asia, engaged in massive social movements to gain independence from colonial rule. But, after gaining independence, the level of activism in these countries has declined partly due to a lack of democratic traditions but also due to economic factors.

Activism provides public relations professionals challenges and opportunities. These days, it is not uncommon to find public relations professionals representing both sides of an activist movement. Chapter 24 of this book describes some of the international activities of nongovernmental organizations as activists. The public relations body of knowledge has not paid much attention to the relationship between activism and public relations. Young as it is, the body of knowledge of international public relations has yet to study the linkage between activism and public relations.

L. A. Grunig (1992) stated that activist groups are motivated to "improve the functioning of the organization from outside (p. 504)." Organizations have continued to face increasing pressure from activists groups who often take various names such as pressure groups, special interest groups, or social movements. Whereas activists believe that they force organizations (especially corporations) to be socially responsible by challenging them, organizations seek to gain autonomy from such challenges that usually drain resources from a corporation's bottom line. Mintzberg (1983) contended that almost every type of organization faces pressures from activist groups at one time or the other. In addition to activism against corporations, one encounters activism in other forms.

Social movements have won nations freedom from colonial rule, much of which happened after World War II principally in Africa and Asia. Theocratic activism has also influenced the political and social structures of many nations and continues to be a potent factor today in many regions of the world. The recent spate of terrorism around the world is evidence of theocratic activism. Labor activism has often played a key role in the economic and industrial development of countries. Therefore, it is critical for us to assess the nature of activism prevalent in a society and determine how it influences the public relations activities of that country. The international public relations professional cannot ignore activism on a global level.

Legal System

The legal system of a country is also closely linked to the level of political and economic development and poses many challenges to the international public relations professional. Every culture has its ways of regulating and enforcing behavior among its citizens and organizations. Whereas legal codes tend to be explicit in Western democracies, the legal structure may appear to be more nebulous and embedded in the social or religious codes in many other regions of the world, which means we need to study the impact of theocracies on public relations as well. Table 1.2 depicts ways of operationalizing these infrastructure variables.

CULTURE

Communication influences and is influenced by culture. Most definitions of the term public relations originating in the United States and Europe recognize that communication (both mass and interpersonal) is the foundation of the public relations profession and is a means to the end of building relationships between organizations and their relevant publics (e.g., Cutlip, Center, & Broom, 2000; J. E. Grunig & Hunt, 1984, Verčič, van Ruler, Butschi, & Flodin, 2001). Logically, culture should affect public relations, and public relations helps alter culture.

Despite this logical linkage between the two, it is only in the last decade that public relations scholars have attempted to study the impact of culture on organizational processes (e.g., Huang, 2000; Rhee, 1999, 2002; Sriramesh, 1992; Sriramesh, 1999; Sriramesh &

TABLE 1.2
The Infrastructure and International Public Relations

Political system
  What is the basic political structure? Democratic, authoritarian, or theocratic, totalitarian, other?
  Is there political pluralism in the society?
  Is public opinion valued?
  How strong are the political institutions?
  What role do formal institutions play in political decision making?
  Do organizations have avenues of influencing public policy making?

Economic system and level of development
  What is the level of economic development?
  Is economic decisionmaking centralized in the government?
  To what extent has membership in WTO changed the environment for private investment?
  What is the power of the private sector in determining public policy?
  What is the relationship between the private and the public sector?
  What is the level of technological development that may be relevant to public relations professionals?

Legal
  How strong and independent is the judiciary?
  What is the relationship between the judiciary and the legislative and executive branches?
  Are there specific legal codes dealing with communication activities of organizations?
  Does the country have legal codes to regulate the media?

Activism
  Historically, what role has activism played in a country (e.g., social movements)?
  What is the nature of activism prevalent in a country currently?
  Are labor unions major forces in the society?
  Currently, what tools do corporations use to deal with activism?

Takasaki, 1999). These studies have empirically tested the relationship between this important variable and public relations. But culture is so fundamental to communication that it behooves scholars of international public relations to study how this variable affects the choice of public relations strategies and tactics in different regions of the world. Many more empirical analyses of the linkage between public relations and culture are needed.

Before one can identify the relationship between culture and public relations, one needs to understand the term *culture* and all of its dimensions. Even in the field of anthropology, in which the central focus involves studying culture, there is no universally accepted definition of the term. Kroeber and Kluckhohn (1952) listed 164 definitions of the term and found 300 other variations of these definitions, thus highlighting the malleable nature of this vital concept! Tylor (1871) provided the first comprehensive definition of culture as "that complex whole which includes knowledge, belief, art, morals, custom, and any other capabilities and habits acquired by man as a member of society" (p. 1). For Kroeber and Kluckhohn, the culture concept encompasses a "set of attributes and products of human societies, and therewith of mankind, which are extrasomatic and transmissible by mechanisms other than biological heredity" (p. 145).

Determinants of Culture

Having defined the term culture, one needs to ask how societies adopt one or more cultures. Kaplan and Manners (1972) identified four determinants of societal culture. First, *technoeconomics* refers to the level of economic development of a society, which invariably influences the culture of each society. We already discussed this determinant as the first environmental factor. Technologies such as satellite communication and the Internet continue to play a role in shaping cultures in the modern world and have a direct influence on public relations as well. Second, *social structure* is indicative of the social institutions that define relationships among different members or groups of a society. Feudal, caste, and class stratifications are examples of social structure. Third, *ideology* refers to the values, norms, worldviews, knowledge, philosophies, and religious principles that the members of a society espouse. Historically, humans have fought over religious philosophies, and they continue to do so. Theocracy is increasingly becoming an issue in international relations because of its impact on sociopolitical systems. Fourth, *personality* refers to the traits of individuals of a society based especially on the child-rearing practices of that society as well as acculturation in school and the workplace.

These four determinants continue to play a vital role in determining the formation of culture in modern societies. In turn, societal culture seeps into organizations through employees who have different family and other backgrounds, turning each organization into a unique corporate culture (Sriramesh et al., 1996).

Dimensions of Societal Culture

Having identified the factors that determine the cultures of a society, it is important to understand how culture is manifested in a society before we link these dimensions of culture with public relations variables. Admitting that he had not been able to measure culture completely because of its malleability as well as our shifting conceptual perspectives in understanding it, Hofstede (1980, 2001) identified five dimensions of societal culture.

The first dimension, *power distance*, describes the vertical stratification of a society wherein members of different strata are accorded different levels of importance and status. The class system of feudal Europe and the caste system in India are examples of power distance. *Social mobility*, the ease with which members of lower strata can achieve a higher status in society, is another variable that corresponds to power distance. Typically, societies with lower power distance tend to have relatively higher social mobility and vice versa. Societies with higher power distance also tend to have more authoritarian organizational structures. The second dimension, *collectivism*, refers to the extent to which members of a culture value the individual over the collectivity. The communes of China, for example, clearly place the welfare of the collectivity over that of the individual. In collectivist societies, organizational employees tend to have greater loyalty to the organization and think in terms of group goals rather than individual accomplishments. Individualistic cultures foster more calculative organizational cultures in which individual employees think more in terms of individual benefits rather than the growth of the collectivity.

The third dimension, *masculinity–femininity*, refers to the gender-based assignment of roles in a society. The extent to which gender plays a role in determining one's status in the organization clearly affects all facets of organizational behavior. This is especially true of the public relations profession because of the feminization of the workforce in many countries, as described in some of the chapters in this book and elsewhere (e.g., Grunig, L. A., Toth, E. L., & Hon, L. C., 2000). The fourth dimension, *uncertainty avoidance*, refers to the extent to which members of a culture can tolerate and cope with ambiguity. Humans have used technology (particularly automation), rites and rituals (a facet of corporate culture), and formalization (also an aspect of corporate culture) to cope with ambiguity in organizations. Furthermore, high-context cultures are known to tolerate greater levels of ambiguity than low-context cultures (Hall & Hall, 1990). The fifth cultural dimension, initially labeled *Confucian dynamism* but later renamed *long-term orientation*, refers to the tendency where a collectivity values long-term commitments and tradition. In an organizational context, this orientation results in a strong work ethic among employees who also expect rewards in a more distant future rather than more immediate returns. However, change also occurs more slowly in such cultures as opposed to those with lower levels of long-term orientation where change can occur more rapidly because long-term traditions do not obstruct the process of change.

Scholars have identified other cultural dimensions as well. Tayeb (1988) identified *interpersonal trust*, the propensity among members of a culture to place trust readily in fellow humans, as another cultural dimension. Kakar (1971) found *deference to authority*, where subordinates readily accept a superior, to be particularly evident in many cultures in Asia. Sriramesh and Takasaki (1999) found the Japanese concept of *amae* to be a manifestation of deference to authority. They also identified the concept of *wa* (harmony) as influencing communication among the Japanese.

In public relations literature, J. E. Grunig (1992) used two worldviews, symmetrical and asymmetrical, to explain the logic behind the choice of public relations strategies and processes by organizations. Although he did not use the term *culture* to refer to them, conceptual linkages can be made between these two worldviews and culture because humans are so greatly influenced by their environment (culture), which shapes their worldviews.

Corporate Culture

The review of societal culture leads us to the next important step in identifying the linkage between culture and public relations—identifying the influence that societal culture has on organizational culture or corporate culture. Sriramesh, J. E. Grunig, and Buffington (1992) observed that whereas corporate culture is influenced by societal culture, it is also distinct from it. Organizations in the same societal culture have distinctive corporate personalities, which are often based on factors such as the charismatic leadership of the organization, age of the organization, organizational type, and size. Schein (1985) identified three reasons for studying the culture of organizations. First, corporate culture is highly visible and can be felt by all observers and participants. Next, by understanding corporate culture, one can evaluate organizational performance and gain knowledge of how people behave and perceive it. Finally, corporate culture provides organizational members with a common frame of reference, a key ingredient of cohesiveness in organizations.

Corporate culture has also been referred to as the rules of the game for getting along in an organization and the ropes that members of an organization share. Scholars such as J. Martin and Siehl (1983) also noted that organizations do not always have a single culture. Organizations often have subcultures and countercultures. Certain subcultures may enhance the mainstream culture by advocating loyalty to core organizational values (*enhancing subculture*), be slightly different from the mainstream culture (*orthogonal subculture*), or completely at odds with the mainstream culture of the organization (*countercultures*). If the counterculture of an organization has a charismatic leader, it may threaten the mainstream culture itself and lead to core changes in organizations.

Glaser (1994) stressed cooperative relationships among organizational employees as a key to organizational success. Needless to say, such cooperation can only be found in an organization that also values communication, the concept that is of primary interest to public relations professionals. The author found that after 3 years of enhanced communication, the sample organization that was afflicted with dissention and mistrust was transformed into one where employees had mutual respect for one another and were more open to teamwork. Communication is the underpinning of a strong corporate culture and is the "normative glue" (Tichy, 1982) that holds an organization together.

What impact does corporate culture have on organizational health? DiSanza's (1995) ethnographic study chronicled the problems encountered by organizations with weak cultures. The author studied the employee orientation procedures of a bank and identified serious flaws in communication, which resulted in low employee morale and poor customer service. Weak corporate cultures are more prone to developing the kinds of orthogonal and countercultures that J. Martin and C. Siehl (1983) identified. Holladay and Coombs (1993) conducted an experimental study investigating the role that delivery of a message plays in employees' perceptions of the chief executive officer's charisma. They found that differences in message delivery seriously impacted the credibility of the leader among employees. Therefore, we can conclude that both corporate and societal culture have a significant impact on communication in general and public relations in particular. Studying the impact of culture on public relations processes is of vital importance to the field of public relations.

How can international public relations professionals use this understanding of societal and corporate culture? In other words, what is the linkage between societal and corporate culture and public relations practice? Acculturation, which may take place at home, school, and work, instills in humans the value system that affects their daily lives. The values that managers espouse clearly affect the choices they make in charting organizational strategies including public relations. Similarly, other publics within a society also carry values that in turn influence their receptivity to organizational messages and their perception of and behavior toward the organization and in other public settings. Therefore, we need to operationalize culture as a variable and identify the impact it has on public relations practice in a given society. Note that whereas the contributions of scholars such as Hofstede (2001) are significant and useful, one must also not discount the importance of cultural dimensions that are unique to a particular country. It is important to identify cultural dimensions that are generic across cultures (e.g., the ones Hofstede, 2001 identified) and dimensions that are unique to a particular culture (e.g., the concept of *wa* and *amae* in Japanese culture). Drawing from this review of literature, the factors noted in Table 1.3 provide a good foundation on which to build the linkage between public relations and culture.

THE MEDIA AND PUBLIC RELATIONS

One cannot overstate the critical relationship between the mass media and public relations. There is near unanimity among authors of public relations literature that the media and public relations have a symbiotic, sometimes contentious, relationship. Most public relations practitioners would agree that media relations accounts for a significant portion of their public relations efforts because they wish to use the media for publicity purposes. However, public relations professionals also serve the media by providing them with information subsidies.

Wilcox and Nolte (1997) observed that despite the continued tension between public relations professionals and journalists, the symbiosis in the relationship requires that they maintain "a solid working relationship based on mutual respect for each other's work" (p. 285). Newsom, Turk, and Kruckeberg (2000) stated that for public relations professionals, "good working relationships with media personnel are always important for smooth functioning..." (p. 395). In their book, *On Deadline*, Howard and Mathews (2000) stressed the need to practice strategic media relations as part of an overall program

TABLE 1.3
Culture and International Public Relations

Stratification
    What is the level of social stratification in your society?
    How does such stratification manifest itself in organizational activities and in public relations?
    What is the level of social mobility in your culture?

Uncertainty (low vs. high context)
    How tolerant is your culture to uncertainty and ambiguity?
    In organizational communication, are meanings explicit in messages or are they based largely on the
        context of a situation?

Gender-based role identification
    To what extent does gender play a role in assigning organizational roles in your country?
    How does this affect public relations practice?

Collectivism
    In your culture, are the interests of the collectivity valued over that of the individual?
    How does this affect public relations activities?

Orientation to life
    Is your culture oriented toward short-term goals or long-term ones?
    How does such an orientation to life affect organizational activities in general and public relations in
        particular?

Interpersonal trust
    What level of interpersonal trust does your culture allow within organizational settings?

Deference to authority
    Does your culture encourage (expect) deference to superiors in social settings?
    If so, how does this manifest itself in organizational communication contexts?

Other
    What are the other cultural idiosyncracies that are specific to your country that you believe influence
        public relations practice?

of public relations and proposed several aspects of effective media relations, such as the characteristics of a good spokesperson. Cutlip, Center, and Broom (2000) reiterated that public relations practitioners will find media relations to be an "economical, effective method of communicating with large and widely dispersed publics" (p. 304).

Mass Media and the Images of Nations

Central to the assertions of the aforementioned public relations scholars is their recognition of the power of mass media to influence public opinion and shape public discourse. Mass media have a powerful influence on organizational activities in general and public relations in particular. Larson and Rivenburgh (1991) recognized the potency of mass media by linking media coverage with the international images of nations. The authors studied the television coverage of the opening ceremony of the Seoul Olympics by the British Broadcasting Corporation, the United States' National Broadcasting Corporation, and Australia's TEN network and concluded that a large majority of developing countries received no mention at all during these telecasts, whereas a few developed countries received very positive and extended coverage. The authors concluded that the media do play a powerful role in influencing how individual countries are perceived globally. Typically, developing nations are stereotyped positively by most media, whereas developing countries are generally negatively portrayed. The findings by Larson and Rivenburgh (1991) are of particular relevance to international public relations practitioners who are often called on by developing countries to change the way they are perceived by the public of developed nations.

Kunczik (1993), who discusses at length the use of the media by nations for public relations purposes in chapter 19, studied the news and advertisements of developing countries in German media and remarked: "since most people's scope of experience is naturally very limited, and their knowledge of complex social processes in other countries comes mainly from the mass media, there is always the danger that, due to the process of news selection, there are differences between 'real reality' and 'media reality'" (p. 1).

Kunczik concluded that many developing countries often view fighting negative media stereotyping as a losing battle, one that they often choose not to wage primarily due to a lack of resources. But other developing nations recognize the need to be heard in the developed world as part of their public diplomacy because they desperately need foreign aid from developed countries and loans from world bodies such as the International Monetary Fund (IMF) or the World Bank, which requires support from key developed countries such as the United States. Because of the powerful effects that the media have in shaping public opinion nationally and internationally, public relations professionals have given primacy to media relations. To conduct effective media relations, international public relations practitioners need to understand the nature of media environment in a particular country. Only then can they develop strategies for conducting effective media relations suitable to that environment.

Currently, the only source for understanding different global media environments is the body of literature in the field of mass communication that describes normative theories of global media systems first proposed by Siebert, Peterson, and Schramm (1956) and subsequently revised and enhanced by several authors (e.g., Altschull, 1984; Hachten, 1981; L. J. Martin & Choudhary, 1983; Merrill & Lowenstein, 1971).

The media systems concept is outdated because of significant world changes, especially in the 1990s. For example, the fall of the Soviet bloc obviates the Soviet media theory, and the fall of Communism in all but a few isolated countries makes the Communist media theory of limited use. Therefore, there is a need to reconceptualize the media environment around the world. Sriramesh (1999) proposed a framework of three factors (media control, media diffusion, and media access) that should help public relations professionals design media relations strategies that are appropriate to different media environments. Adhering to this framework may make it easier for international public relations professionals to maintain effective channels of communication between their client organizations and relevant media around the world. Furthermore, the framework should help researchers study the nexus between the media and effective public relations practices in different countries.

Media Control

Maintaining effective media relations requires that public relations professionals understand who controls the media organizations in a country and whether such control extends to editorial content. The latest Freedom House survey of media freedom found that 75 countries had media systems that could be classified as free, 50 had partly free media, and 61 were not free (Sussman & Karlekar, 2002). The study found that the number of countries with free media was the highest it has ever been. However, it is interesting to note that 111 countries still have media systems that are either partly free or not free. In his introduction to the 1999 World Press Survey conducted by Freedom House, Sussman (1999) stated that "Not until the fall of the Berlin Wall in 1989 did those areas of the world under Communist domination begin to experience some freedom of the news media" (p. 1). The author also reported that in many regions of the world press freedom was weakened by inexperienced journalists and partisan control of the media. In Freedom House's 2002 survey, there was clear evidence that press freedom was an outcome of more pluralistic regimes.

Around the world, media ownership is limited to a few principal sources depending on the nature of political system and level of economic development of the country, two variables described earlier in this chapter. In developed democracies, it is the capitalistic entrepreneur who invests in the media, sustaining media operations principally through sale of advertisements and relying, to a relatively smaller extent, on revenue from subscriptions. There is minimal direct or indirect fiduciary relationship between the government and media organizations in capitalistic systems. The need to sell news as a commodity is naturally strong in such an environment, leading to interesting choices in coverage.

On the contrary, in developing countries, one can often discern media ownership in the hands of political interests as well as the elites of the society. Maintaining the status quo is often paramount for these media moghuls as an incentive to influence media content. The few theocracies of the world provide us examples of the impact of religious interests on media organizations and media content. In most developing countries, the government typically owns the electronic media and often permits private entrepreneurs to own print media.

It is important to recognize that media ownership does not necessarily result in media control. In many developing countries, even though the media may be overtly owned by private interests, they are strictly monitored and controlled through overt and covert means by political or government forces. Sussman (1999) reported that the Freedom House survey had found that "the muzzling of journalists was increasingly accomplished by more subtle, legalistic methods than through violence or outright repression" (p. 1). Government advertisements are a principal method for political rulers to maintain control over media content. Because advertising income forms the bulk of revenue (and, therefore, the basic means of survival) for a large section of private media in many developing countries, this subtle method of control is often very effective. Controlling the supply of the means of production such as newsprint (often imported by the government and sold to media organizations at subsidized costs) is another effective way for governments to maintain their control over privately owned mass media. It is also not uncommon for political rulers of developing nations to own their own media outlets (usually print media) and use them for controlling public opinion with the sole purpose of maintaining the status quo.

Editorial freedom is directly proportional to the level of economic development of a country. It is the lack of resources and infrastructure that have limited editorial freedom in developing nations. In their study of the relationship between press freedom and social development in 134 nations, Weaver, Buddenbaum, and Fair (1985) concluded that "the stronger the media are economically, the less likely the government is to control these media" (p. 113). The reality is that, in most developing countries, economic independence is a mirage for most media outlets, which also results in various limitations on editorial freedom. As discussed in chapter 20, the proposal for a New World Information Order from developing countries was derailed primarily on the basic of media economics and concomitant issues pertaining to editorial freedom.

Media Diffusion

Placing a story in the media is often a significant part of the media relations activity for the savvy public relations professional. Merely placing a message in a medium does not offer the "magic bullet" effect of having intended effects on one's audience. Audience exposure to messages is only the first step. Other intervening steps such as message comprehension or changes in level of knowledge and attitude need to be traversed by audiences before changes can occur in their behavior. Recognizing this, international public relations practitioners need to understand the extent of *media diffusion* (media saturation) in the countries where they operate as a gauge of message exposure among their audiences. It is safe to assume that most public relations professionals desire to use the media for disseminating information to as wide an audience as possible. Therefore, in their symbiotic relationship of providing information subsidies to media outlets, public relations professionals seek unpaid publicity for their organizations and clients.

However, it is critical for international public relations professionals to note that, despite the perceived power of the media, these purveyors of information may not provide an effective means for wide dissemination of organizational messages in every country. In fact, in most developing countries, media reach a fairly homogeneous, relatively small segment of the total population because of two principal factors: illiteracy and poverty. A country's high rate of illiteracy seriously inhibits the use of the print media. Consequently, media relations in such environments will be limited in scope to specific groups of urban, educated, fairly affluent, middle-class citizens (the elites of the society). To reach the larger populace effectively, the international public relations consultant will have to think of other media that reach out to these untapped publics. In larger developing nations, the lack of infrastructure constrains timely distribution of print media messages to far-flung places.

When illiteracy hinders the dispersion of information through the print media, the next logical alternative for the international public relations professional would be to use electronic media. However, television sets and radios often prove too expensive for a large section of citizens who have limited resources. Inadequate infrastructure, such as lack of rural electrification, also contributes to limiting access to the electronic media for even wealthier rural residents. Therefore, the efficacy of electronic media for conducting public information or other public relations campaigns is open to question. International public relations professionals must recognize that regardless of the sophistication of the media relations they may practice, the efficacy of these efforts is limited to the segment of the population that the media of a country can reach.

However, there are signs of hope for the international public relations practitioner who has to operate in a developing country that has these impediments. Lee (1994) examined the development of mass media in the People's Republic of China since 1949 and found that the country's spurt in economic growth in the 1980s resulted in a sudden increase in television ownership. The author concluded that there seems to be a symbiotic relationship between economic growth and television ownership. He speculated that whereas economic growth has led to increased television ownership, television may also have helped spur economic growth by having unplanned effects such as the creation of demand for products and services, acceleration of electrification in rural areas, and the creation of a diversion keeping people away from "the delicate problems of government and politics" (p. 34).

When local conditions limit the use of Western-style media such as television, radio, newspapers, and magazines, what options do international public relations practitioners have in their effort to reach a wider audience in developing societies? In India, for example, many public information campaigns have used folk media such as docudramas, dances, skits, and plays in rural areas (Sriramesh, 1992). A few multinational companies such as makers of toothpaste have used Indian folk media to publicize their products in rural regions with some efficacy. Similar strategies could be used for effective communication with various publics in traditional cultures in other parts of the world as well.

Pratt and Manheim (1988) critiqued the urban bias that is so characteristic of public communication in most of Africa and other developing regions of the world and called for new communication strategies that empower large, neglected segments of the populace. The authors presented a framework of six integrated agendas for conducting communication campaigns that include the use of traditional, indigenous media. However, it is critical that these traditional media be used judiciously. West and Fair (1993) studied the use of modern, popular, and traditional media in Africa and highlighted the pitfalls of the improper use of indigenous African media (or traditional media) for developmental activities.

Media Access

The flip side of media diffusion is media access. Whereas media diffusion refers to the extent of media saturation in a society, *media access* denotes the extent to which the various segments of a society can approach the media to disseminate messages they deem important. It is imprudent to assume that public access to the media remains constant across societies. Sriramesh and Takasaki (1998), reporting on the nature of Japanese public relations, identified press clubs as interlocutors between the media and other publics, including corporations that might want to gain access to the media. Japanese press clubs

TABLE 1.4
A Framework for Media Relations

Media control
  Are the media of a given country:
    A part of the private sector?
    A part of the public sector (direct or indirect government ownership)?
    Aligned with political parties?
    Aligned with or controlled by theocracy?
  What is the political philosophy of the country?
  How much control do media owners display over editorial freedom?
  How are controls over editorial freedom exercised?
  Are media messages aimed at selling news and information as a commodity (a capitalistic
    orientation), as a method of national development (nation building), or to further theocratic causes?
  What is the media infrastructure of the country?
  Are there established legal and other structures to protect the media from political pressure?
  What kind of professional standards do media persons have?

Media diffusion
  What is the ability of the media to diffuse messages to a wide audience?
  Which segments of the population do the print media reach?
  Which segments of the population do the electronic media reach?
  How does the existing infrastructure of the country affect media diffusion?
  What is the rate of illiteracy in the country?
  What is the rate of poverty in the country?

Media access
  What is the level of access that organizations have to mass media in a particular country?
  If there are gatekeepers between the media and other organizations, who are they and how are these
    gatekeepers selected?
  Do different elements of the society such as activists and corporations have direct access to the media?
  Do the media of the country value information subsidies from public relations professionals or
    agencies?

act as gate keepers between the media and organizations, limiting access by organizations and others to the media.

A savvy international public relations practitioner will recognize that just as an organization's access to the media is critical, so is the extent to which the media are accessible to the organization's opponents, principally activists. As described earlier in this chapter, activism has a profound impact on public relations. L. A. Grunig (1992) stated that although activism contributes to the dynamism of an organization's environment thereby posing threats to its autonomy, activists also provide public relations opportunities to an organization. Organizations are forced to communicate symmetrically when activists use the media to challenge an organization's image in the court of public opinion.

The result is that when the media of a society are accessible to individuals or groups with different points of view, the resulting publicity will increase the fluidity of the environment for organizations. The organization then will be forced to use two-way communication for conducting its public relations activities with a variety of publics, rather than focusing on one or two publics. But if various groups that do not conform to the mainstream ideology are not accorded a forum for publicly voicing their agenda, then the extent of pressure on an organization is drastically reduced, calling for minimal sophistication in public relations. Therefore, understanding the extent to which the media are accessible to various activist and other groups in a society helps the international public relations practitioner by providing, among other things, a gauge on the amount of opposition that the environment might pose.

Table 1.4 identifies criteria that help one assess the extent of media control, media diffusion, and media access in a given society.

CONCLUSION

This chapter highlights the need for us to not only describe the public relations profession in different parts of the world but also link them to environmental variables to help improve the efficacy of international public relations practices. We presented three broad environmental variables and the conceptual linkages between these variables and public relations. The 17 country-specific chapters of this book have used this framework in presenting the current status of public relations practice in these countries. Much of the information on the linkage between public relations and environmental variables presented here is anecdotal. However, it is no less important given that this is the first time that such a collective effort is being made. What we need are many more studies that will use the framework presented here and additional ones that might be relevant to gather empirical data linking environmental variables with public relations. The outcome of such cross-national efforts would be a robust body of knowledge of international public relations that can prove beneficial not only to students and scholars but also to professionals.

REFERENCES

Altschull, H. J. (1984). *Agents of power.* White Plains, NY: Longman.

Culbertson, H. M., & Jeffers, D. W. (1992). The social, political, and economic contexts: Keys in educating true public relations professionals. *Public Relations Review, (11),* 5–21.

Culbertson, H. M., & Jeffers, D. W., Stone, D. B., & Terrell, M. (1993). *Social, political, and economic contexts in public relations: Theory and cases.* Hillsdale, NJ: Lawrence Erlbaum Associates.

Cutlip, S. M., Center, A. H., Broom, G. M. (2000). *Effective public relations.* Upper Saddle River, NJ: Prentice-Hall.

DiSanza, J. R. (1995). Bank teller organizational assimilation in a system of contradictory practices. *Management Communication Quarterly, 9*, 191–218.

Freedom House. (2000). Democracy's century: A survey of global political change in the 20th century. Available at: *http://www.freedomhouse.org/reports/century.html*, retrieved on January 14, 2003.

Glaser, S. R. (1994). Teamwork and communication: A 3-year case study of change. *Management Communication Quarterly, 7*, 282–296.

Grunig, J. E., and Hunt, T. (1984) 'Managing Public Relations', Holt, Rinehart, & Winston, New York.

Grunig, L. A. (1992). Activism: How it limits the effectiveness of organizations and how excellent public relations departments respond. In J. E. Grunig (Ed.), *Excellence in public relations and communication management* (pp. 503–530). Hillsdale, NJ: Lawrence Erlbaum Associates.

Grunig, J. E. (1992a). The effect of worldviews on public relations theory and practice. In J. E. Grunig (Ed.), *Excellence in public relations and communication management.* Hillsdale, NJ: Lawrence Erlbaum Associates. pp. 31–64.

Grunig, J. E. (1992b). *Excellence in public relations and communication management.* Hillsdale, NJ: Lawrence Erlbaum Associates.

Grunig, L. A., Toth, E. L., & Hon, L. C. (2000). Feminist values in public relations. *Journal of Public Relations Research, 12*(1), pp. 49–68.

Hachten, W. (1981). *The world news prism: Changing media, clashing ideologies.* Ames, IA: Iowa State University Press.

Hall, E. T., & Hall, M. R. (1990). *Understanding cultural differences.* Yarmouth, ME: Intercultural Press.

Hofstede, G. (1980). *Culture's consequences.* Beverly Hills, CA: Sage.

Hofstede, G. (2001). *Culture's consequences: comparing values, behaviors, institutions, and organizations across nations* 2nd ed.) Thousand Oaks, CA: Sage.

Holladay, S. J., & Coombs, W. T. (1993). Communicating visions: An exploration of the role of delivery in the creation of leader charisma. *Management Communication Quarterly, 6*, 405–427.

Howard, C. M., & Mathews, W. K. (2000). *On deadline: Managing media relations* (3rd ed.). Prospect Heights, IL: Waveland Press Inc.

Huang, Y. H. (2000). The personal influence model and *Gao Guanxi* in Taiwan Chinese public relations. *Public Relations Review, 26*, 216–239.

Kakar, S. (1971). The theme of authority in social relations in India. *Journal of Social Psychology, 84*, 93–101.

Kaplan, D., & Manners, R. A. (1972). *Culture theory.* Englewood Cliffs, NJ: Prentice-Hall.

Karatnycky, A. (2002). Nations in transit 2002: A mixed picture of change. Available at: *http://www.freedomhouse.org/research/nitransit/2002/karatnycky essay2002.pdf*, retrieved on January 14, 2003.

Kroeber, A. L., & Kluckhohn, C. (1952). Culture: A critical review of concepts and definitions. *Papers of the Peabody Museum of American Archeology and Ethnology, 47*(1). Cambridge, MA: Harvard University.

Kunczik, M. (1993, November). *Public relations advertisements of foreign countries in Germany with special reference to developing countries: Results of a content analysis.* Paper presented at the international conference of the Association for the Advancement of Policy, Research and Development in the Third World, Cairo, Egypt.

Larson, J., & Rivenburgh, N. (1991). A comparative analysis of Australian, United States, and British telecasts of the Seoul Olympic Opening Ceremony. *Journal of Broadcasting and Electronic Media, 35*(1), 75–94.

Lee, P. (1994). Mass communication and national development in China: Media roles reconsidered. *Journal of Communication, 44*(3), 22–37.

Martin, J., & Siehl, C. (1983). Organizational culture and counterculture: An uneasy symbiosis. *Organizational Dynamics*, 52–63.

Martin, L. J., & Chaudhary, A. G. (1983). *Comparative mass media ystems.* White Plains, NY: Longman.

Merrill, J. C., & Lowenstein, R. L. (1971). *Media, messages, and men.* New York: Longman.

Mintzberg, H. (1983). *Power in and around organizations.* Englewood Cliffs, NJ: Prentice-Hall.

Newsom, D., Turk, J. V., Kruckeberg, D. (2000). *This is PR: The realities of public relations.* Belmont, CA; Wadsorth.

Pratt, C., & Mannheim, J. (1988). Communication research and development policy: Agenda dynamics in an African setting. *Journal of Communication, 38*(3): 75–95.

Rhee, Y. (1999). *Confucian culture and excellent public relations: A study of generic principles and specific applications in South Korean public relations practice.* Unpublished master's thesis, University of Maryland, College Park.

Rhee, Y. (2002). Culture and dimensions of communication in public relations: An exploratory study of South Korean practitioners. Paper presented to the Public Relations Division at the annual conference of the International Communication Association (ICA), Seoul, South Korea, July 16, 2002.

Schein, E. H. (1985). *Organizational culture and leadership.* San Francisco: Jossey-Bass.

Siebert, F. S., Peterson, T., & Schramm, W. (1956). *Four theories of the press.* Urbana, IL: University of Illinois Press.

Simon, M. W., & Gartzke, E. (1996). Political system similarity and the choice of allies. *Journal of Conflict Resolution, 40*(4), pp. 617–635.

Sriramesh, K. (1992). *The impact of societal culture on public relations: An ethnographic study of South Indian organizations.* Unpublished doctoral dissertation, University of Maryland, College Park.

Sriramesh, K. (1999). The models of public relations in India. Top Faculty Paper presented to the PR Division, AEJMC, August 4–7, New Orleans, LA.

Sriramesh, K., Grunig, J. E., & Buffington, J. (1992). Corporate culture and public relations. In J. E. Grunig (Ed.), *Excellence in public relations and communication management.* Hillsdale, NJ: Lawrence Erlbaum Associates. pp. 577–598.

Sriramesh, K. (1996). Power distance and public relations: An ethnographic study of Southern Indian organizations. In H. Culbertson & N. Chen (Eds.), *International public relations: A comparative analysis.* (pp. 171–190). Mahwah, NJ: Lawrence Erlbaum Associates.

Sriramesh, K., Grunig, J. E., & Dozier, D. M. (1996). Observation and measurement of two dimensions of organizational culture and their relationship to public relations. *Journal of Public Relations Research, 8,* 229–261.

Sriramesh, K., Kim, Y., & Takasaki, M. (1999). Public relations in three Asian cultures: An analysis. *Journal of Public Relations Research, 11*(4), 271–292.

Sriramesh, K., & Takasaki, M. (1998, July). *The impact of culture on Japanese public relations.* Paper presented to the Public Relations Division, International Communication Association, Jerusalem, Israel.

Sriramesh, K., & White, J. (1992). Societal culture and public relations. In J. E. Grunig (Ed.), *Excellence in public relations and communication management* (pp. 597–614). Hillsdale, NJ: Lawrence Erlbaum Associates.

Sussman, L. (1999). *The news of the century: Press freedom 1999.* New York: Freedom House.

Sussman, L. R., & Karlekar, K. D. (2002). *The annual survey of press freedom 2002.* Available at: *http://www.freedomhouse.org/pfs2002/pfs2002.pdf* (Retrieved on January 15, 2003).

Sussman, L., & Karlekar, K. D. (2002). *The annual survey of press freedom 2002.* New York: Freedom House.

Tayeb, M. H. (1988). *Organizations and national culture: A comparative analysis.* London: Sage.

Tichy, N. M. (1982). Managing change strategically: The technical, political, and cultural keys. *Organizational Dynamics, 11*(2), 59–80.

Tylor, E. B. (1871). *Primitive culture.* London: Murray.

Verčič, D., Grunig, L. A., & Grunig, J. E. (1996). Global and specific principles of public relations: Evidence from Slovenia. In H. M. Culbertson & N. Chen (Eds.), *International public relations. A comparative analysis* (pp. 31–66). Mahwah, NJ: Lawrence Erlbaum Associates.

Verčič, D., Ruler, B. van, Butschi, G., and Flodin, B. (2001) 'On the Definition of Public Relations: A European view,' *Public Relations Review,* Vol. 27, pp. 373–387.

Weaver, D. H., Buddenbaum, J. M., & Fair, J. E. (1985). Press freedom, media, and development, 1950–1979: A study of 134 nations. *Journal of Communication, 35*(2), 104–117.

West, H. G., & Fair, J. E. (1993). Development communication and popular resistance in Africa: An examination of the struggle over tradition and modernity through media. *African Studies Review, 36*(1), 91–114.

Wilcox, D. L., & Nolte, L. W. (1997). *Public relations writing and media techniques.* New York: Longman.

Wilson, F. L. (1995). Teaching comparative politics in the 1990s. *Political Science & Politics, 28*(1), 79–80.

2

POLITICAL ECONOMY AND PUBLIC RELATIONS

SANDRA C. DUHÉ
KRISHNAMURTHY SRIRAMESH

POLITICAL ECONOMY AND GLOBAL PUBLIC RELATIONS RESEARCH AND PRACTICE

Our goal in this chapter is to refine and expand our understanding of two of the infrastructural variables described in chapter 1—political system and economic development. We do so through the theoretical lens of political economy, which is a domain of scholarship in its own right, further reinforcing the earlier choice of combining these two variables under infrastructure. Political economy is a suitable concept for this analysis because we must not only be able to identify the nature of each of the environmental variables in a country, but also understand the critical relationships among them, before we can understand the complex ways in which they influence public relations. The unique interplay between political system and economic system impacts the public relations process—whether in the corporate, nonprofit, or governmental realm—in profound and identifiable ways.

To the best of our knowledge, our work herein is a first attempt to apply a political economy framework to the public relations body of knowledge. Students and scholars who have honed their expertise in public relations may find political economy theory to be unfamiliar territory or perhaps be skeptical of its relevance to the field. Practitioners who have worked for multinational enterprises will readily recognize the effects of the concepts discussed in this chapter, but they may not yet have the vocabulary to characterize their experiences within various operating environments. It is our hope to provide a working understanding of political economy for each of these audiences by demonstrating the undeniable interdependence among these concepts and their role in advancing the study and practice of public relations especially at the global level.

POLITICS, ECONOMICS, AND POLITICAL ECONOMY

Gilpin (2001) provided a contemporary definition of global political economy as "the interaction of the market and such powerful actors as states, multinational firms, and international organizations" (pp. 17–18). However, his definition only included a tacit reference to the NGOs that today comprise a significant portion of the political economy landscape globally. The term "political economy" dates back to the 18th century. Caporaso and Levine (1992) described a fundamental shift in the understanding of an economy. They stated that want satisfaction, once the exclusive realm of individual households, was becoming increasingly political. As a result, both the nature of wants and the means of production and distribution used to satisfy these wants evolved to the extent that individuals were becoming more dependent on people outside of the family (even extended families) for their livelihoods and economic well-being. Responsibility for the overall functioning of a system of want satisfaction began to fall upon heads of state (as opposed to heads of households), explaining why many of the early writings in classical political economy focused on the role governments should play in satisfying societal wants. This vigorous debate of how little or how much involvement government should have in the economic pursuits of its citizens continues today and has only become more shrill in different parts of the world. NGOs and civil society also continue to play a key role in this debate with the increasing democratization seen in many regions of the world.

Politics and economics have various, and often overlapping, meanings across theories of political economy. We provide a synopsis of these thoughts for our purposes here. The concepts of public life, government, power, and the state are familiar to our understanding of politics, which Caporaso and Levine (1992) summarized as "the activities and institutions that relate to the making of authoritative public decisions for society as a whole" (p. 20). The authors further explained that economics can be defined as economic calculation (i.e., deciphering what actions one must take to satisfy wants), material provisioning (i.e., activities involved in the production of goods), or the economy as a socially specific institution.

In the definitions of economics, we see a distinct difference in perspectives. Whereas the economic calculation view of economics focuses on the motivations and behaviors of an individual, the material provisioning view focuses on societal activities occurring outside of, yet still affecting, the individual. References to "the economy" are most applicable to the study of public relations because this definition of economics concentrates on the nexus of relationships between individuals (or organizations) and societal institutions in the pursuit of private wants. Caporaso and Levine (1992) expanded upon this societal view:

> The notion of an economy understands it as an enduring social reality of its own kind capable of influencing, forming, and even determining motivations and ways of thinking. The economy has its own social purpose irreducible to those we associate with politics and family life. . . . The economy is a sphere of pursuit of self-interest, a place that validates preoccupation with our private concerns. The relations we enter into are normally understood to be instrumental to those private concerns. This makes the economy at least potentially a set of relations between persons distinct from the social relations that connect persons politically or personally. (pp. 29–30)

Gilpin (2001) similarly defined the economy along social parameters that are of particular interest to public relations practitioners and scholars:

[T]he economy [is] a sociopolitical system composed of powerful economic actors or institutions such as giant firms, powerful labor unions, and large agribusinesses that are competing with one another to formulate government policies on taxes, tariffs, and other matters in ways that advance their own interests. ... In this interpretation, there are many social, political, or economic actors whose behavior has a powerful impact on the nature and functioning of markets. (p. 38)

Although Gilpin did not use the term, he is essentially referring to different "publics," a term that is familiar to public relations practitioners. Neoclassical political economy defines private transactions on the part of individuals seeking to satisfy their wants as "economic" and the public role of the state in that process as "political" (Caporaso and Levine, 1992). This private/public distinction is a useful way to think of the inevitable interplay between economics and politics in an individual's life. The degree to which individuals are free to pursue their livelihood, own a home, and conduct their economic affairs is subject to constraints set by state regulations, property rights, rule of law, and systems of justice. The nature of regulation as well as which activities elicit different kinds of regulation are determined by those who hold political power in a society such as autocrats, oligopolists, and citizens in pluralistic democracies or religious leaders in theocracies. These constraints also apply to organizations and vary extensively in their development and application across nations. The boundary-spanning role of public relations (Lauzen, 1995) demands that practitioners have an in-depth understanding of how these political constraints affect their organizations' ability to pursue economic as well as social goals while also maintaining harmonious relationships with various relevant publics.

Economic and political phenomena are explicably intertwined in societal life. The study of political economy examines the inherent tensions, unintended consequences, and inevitable influences economic and political activities concurrently impart to society, as opposed to the study of economics, political science, or sociology, which examines these respective dimensions unilaterally. Kollontai (2002) eloquently captured this idea:

Political economies attempt to understand the functioning of an economy in a broader societal context. This is a task of growing complexity, given the constantly increasing division of labour, interdependencies, changing technologies, regulatory mechanisms, and evolving economic, organisational, management and other structures. As distinct from pure economics—which concentrates on the internal logic of economic systems—political economies in varying degrees acknowledge the impact of economic developments of political and (to a lesser extent) ideological, cultural and other societal factors and make it a part of their analysis. (p. 218)

Gilpin (2001) argued that "a true 'political economy' is prerequisite to an improved comprehension of the implications of new developments for international (and, where relevant, domestic) economic affairs" (p. 12). We propose that a political economy perspective provides an ideal basis for an integrated understanding of multiple variables relevant to public relations in general and global public relations in particular.

In political economy theories, the economic perspective tends to dominate the political. That is, the market tends to be the primary unit of analysis, with political and other social activities examined as emanating from, or at least adjacent to, the market. One could make a parallel claim that marketing (consumer driven) dominates public relations (which is more oriented toward societal factors). An example of this can be found in an analysis of the factors that drive the global diffusion of the top international public relations agencies

(Sriramesh and Vercic 2004), which offered several propositions, two of which were that "[T]he supply of international public relations consultancy services corresponds to the general level of social welfare and economic development of a country," (p. 8) and that "[T]he need for public relations is the highest where it is least likely to be supplied (or is available)" (p. 9). Based on data on the presence of the leading multinational public relations agencies around the world, Sriramesh and Vercic had shown that public relations service has followed the money trail and gone first to lucrative markets in developed economies or emerging markets. Further, Sriramesh (2008) has contended that public relations scholarship has also focused much more on corporate communication often to the exclusion of the public relations activities of NGOs whose experiences have much to offer the body of knowledge. We agree with Gilpin's (2001) assertion that political forces are just as powerful, and often an antecedent to, economic ones:

> The ways in which the world economy functions are determined by both markets and the policies of nation-states, especially those of powerful states; markets and economic forces alone cannot account for the structure and functioning of the global economy. . . . The relationship of economics and politics is interactive. (p. 23)

Gilpin aptly viewed markets as "embedded in larger sociopolitical systems" (p. 41) and recognized the influence of norms, values, and culture in determining the market's legitimate role in a given society.

Firms are embedded within a social system of production, referred to by Hollingsworth and Boyer (1997) as the integration of multiple institutions including the industrial relations system among firms, suppliers, and customers; the internal structure of corporate firms; conceptions of fairness and justice; financial markets; state structure and policies; and a society's unique moral principles into a social configuration:

> All these institutions, organizations, and social values tend to cohere with each other, although they vary in the degree to which they are tightly coupled with each other into a full-fledged system. While each of these components has some autonomy and may have some goals that are contradictory to the goals of other institutions with which it is integrated, an institutional logic in each society leads institutions to coalesce into a complex social configuration. This occurs because the institutions are embedded in a culture in which their logics are symbolically grounded, organizationally structured, technically and materially constrained, and politically defended. (p. 2)

To examine the role and influence of socio-cultural, economic, or political factors individually in global public relations would be a useful but partial and insufficient effort if we are to better grasp the intricacies of how these variables interact and exert change pressures on organizations. That is, a political economy approach to public relations examines the interplay between organizations and publics with particular attention paid to the conflicts, expectations, and constraints imparted upon relevant parties by a powerful *combination* of social, economic, and political forces. Contemporary public relations scholarship written from a political economy perspective has included discussion of how these forces working in tandem have, for example, disenfranchised what Dutta-Bergman (2005) described as subaltern publics, placed Arab countries far behind other nations in their access to Internet communications (Eid, 2007), and prioritized wealth creation over the public's right to know about the negative consequences of genetic engineering in New Zealand (Weaver and Motion, 2002). These forces comprise a substructure that is both widely influential and inherently complex in that its values and priorities are not readily categorized as social, economic, or political but rather overlap these spheres in their historical and cultural origins.

Political economies influence the saliency of issues and how organizations choose to respond (if at all) to change pressures related to those issues. For instance, environmental initiatives have political (public policy), social (quality of life), and economic (cost/benefit) implications. Whereas firms within a political economy that values individual wealth creation (e.g., enhancing returns to shareholders) may actively resist NGO pressures to adopt environmental care standards beyond those mandated by law, firms operating in political economies that place comparatively greater value on the collective good of society (in cultural terms, Hofstede, 2001, referred to this as collectivism) may proactively seek working partnerships with environmental NGOs as a normal course of business. Political economies dictate the proper role of firms, special interests, and governments in powerful and lasting ways. Public relations scholars (Berger, 2005; Dutta-Bergman, 2005; McKie, 2001; Motion and Weaver, 2005; Roper, 2005, Sriramesh and Vercic, 2004) have elucidated how the practice (and, to some extent, the study) of public relations sustains the primacy of elite social, political, and economic interests and helps, through its discourse, to preserve hegemonic power. Activism is often rooted in a passionate resistance against the long-standing tenets of political economies as social values and thoughts about the proper role of institutions change, albeit slowly, over time.

THEORIES OF POLITICAL ECONOMY

Political economies vary across nations, and so, too, do their influences on global public relations practice. Caporaso and Levine (1992) described four major schools of political economy—classical, Marxian, neoclassical, and Keynesian—that have evolved over time in response to the historical events and societal concerns of their day. We summarize them next to explain how economics and politics are viewed in each approach as well as to highlight the points of differentiation between them. Upon closer examination, it will become apparent that the fundamental principles and tradeoffs between these two concepts still play an active role in contemporary debates regarding globalization, sustainable development, and social welfare, among other contested issues affecting individuals and organizations worldwide. We shall also attempt to provide conceptual linkages between each school of thought and public relations.

Classical Political Economy

The classical school of political economy dates back to the 18th and 19th centuries. In his prolific volume, Adam Smith (1776) described political economy as "the nature and causes of the wealth of nations" (p. 679). A key tenet of the classical school is that economic life can, and should, be separated from political and social life (Caporaso and Levine, 1992). The economic sphere is viewed as primary, and it is argued that it need not be political. Civil society, in classical terms, refers to an unregulated system of want satisfaction motivated by self-interest for the greater good of all. That is, individuals, referred to as economic agents, should be allowed to pursue their self-interests with minimal interference from the state.

Smith (1776) was a proponent of this laissez-faire approach, in that he believed society's interests were best served by individuals pursuing their own highest good. An "invisible hand," rather than the state, family, or group of individuals, would guide producers and consumers toward an optimum utilization of resources (i.e., a balance of supply and

demand), thereby facilitating a self-regulating market. The role of government, in his estimation, should be strictly limited to three arenas: national defense, a system of justice,
and public works (e.g., highways, schools). These sectors were appropriately reserved for
government administration because their production rendered no benefit (i.e., profitability)
to private suppliers in the market. Yet their provision was of national interest. In Smith's
view, state officials could be neither as efficient nor as competent as market cues (e.g.,
competition) in regulating economic transactions.

In the classical school, profit-seeking is viewed as a private, not a public, endeavor
(Caporaso and Levine, 1992):

> Given the overall amount of capital and labor available to society, the proportions devoted
> to different industries should depend on profitability because profitability measures the
> contribution each industry can make to the size of the social revenue and to the growth of
> social wealth. The only way to assure that profit directs investment is to place that invest-
> ment into private hands and subject it to decisions based on self-interest. This works because
> self-interest is best served by the pursuit of profit. . . . The unregulated but self-ordering
> market will encourage the growth of society's capital stock and achieve the public good.
> (p. 43)

Classical economist Milton Friedman (1962) supported the primacy of profit-seeking when
making his well-known, though frequently challenged, assertion regarding corporate social
responsibility:

> The view has been gaining widespread acceptance that corporate officials . . . have a "social
> responsibility" that goes beyond serving the interest of their stockholders. . . . This view
> shows a fundamental misconception of the character and nature of a free economy. In such
> an economy, there is one and only one social responsibility of business—to use its resources
> and engage in activities designed to increase its profits so long as it stays within the rules of
> the game, which is to say, engages in open and free competition, without deception or fraud.
> (p. 133)

Caporaso and Levine (1992) described the unregulated market as a passive social
mechanism, a characteristic that raises the ire of critics of the classical approach. Each
individual brings his/her "property" (e.g., labor, goods) to the market seeking a voluntary
exchange for something of value (e.g., wages, prices). Inevitably, hardships will occur when
producers find consumers are no longer interested in their products, or discover the market
will no longer bear their desired price. In the classical view, this natural allocation of
winners and losers is a critical signaling device that should motivate agents to adapt their
skills and means of production to changing market demands. Those subscribing to the
classical view do not begrudge the market for its objective rendering of hardship, as it falls
on individuals (not society as a whole), and it should be temporary as long as the producer
is willing to adapt to new market conditions. Individual failure is patently different from
a market failure, the possibility of which is addressed in subsequent schools of political
economy thought.

The classical view of political economy has had a profound and pervasive effect on
public relations literature. Stakeholder theory (Freeman, 1984) has been used as an explicit
rebuttal to the notion of shareholder primary promoted by Friedman and other classical
thinkers. Management and business ethics scholars (cf. Donaldson and Preston, 1995;
Drucker, 1999; Halal, 1998; Jones, 1999; Leichty, 1985; Wijnberg, 2000) called for profit-
making entities to seek value creation beyond that for shareholders alone, and this idea

of organizations heeding the interests of multiple stakeholders is prevalent among public relations scholarship (Broom, Casey, and Ritchey, 1997; Coombs, 1998; J. E. Grunig, 2000, 2006; Heath, 2000, 2006; Ledingham, 2003). The related notion of a "triple bottom line" (Elkington, 1998) suggests that firms must focus not only on profitability, but also on environmental concerns and social justice. Corporate social responsibility has been thrust into the forefront primarily because of this change in world view as seen in a compendium of essays (May, Cheney, and Roper, 2007).

The practice of public relations has been impacted by a growing expectation for corporations to fulfill social responsibilities, which has led to vocal resistance and activism against classical ideas. Such expectations have resulted in increasing interaction between firms, special interest groups, and NGOs. Pishchikova (2006) referred to NGOs as a subcategory of actors in civil society. In a context applicable to both political economy and public relations, she described civil society as a venue for promoting democratic values and broadening stakeholder input:

> Civil society is said to have a special empowering quality, since it tends to include stakeholders whose voice is often not heard in traditional decision making. The new polity is more democratic because it tends to disrupt hierarchies and to spread the power among more people and groups. (p. 52)

Hall (1998) explained that civil society is not the same as democracy because it has qualities all of its own, namely as "a form of societal self-organization which allows for co-operation with the state whilst enabling individuation" (p. 32). In civil society, individuals voluntarily associate with groups and causes in an effort to discover and define themselves. Given its affiliation with both the political and economic realm, civil society, according to Hyden (1997), cannot be separated from states and markets, and its emergence relies on rule of law. It has the empowering potential, he noted, "to serve as a constructive, oppositional sphere, facilitating the inclusion of interests into the public realm" (p. 5).

Contrary to Smith's (1776) argument, a political economy characterized by a free and unfettered market is not necessarily civil in the conventional sense of the term. NGOs and other special interest groups have utilized activism to voice their concerns about classical principles that render winners and losers in the global marketplace. The continued challenges to the WTO regime are a case in point where laissez-faire economics is being challenged in many regions of the world for widening the gap between the rich and the poor. Public relations scholars have only now begun to document the shortcomings of current theory and the challenges to global public relations practice as they relate to activism from civil society.

Marxian Political Economy

Karl Marx's 19th century writings on political economy were rooted in the classical school in that he, too, saw the capitalist economy as a nexus of exchange relationships that is inherently apolitical (Caporaso and Levine, 1992). What sets Marx apart is his particular focus on how economic interests trigger powerful political struggles. Class, defined as "categories of persons who have similar positions in the production process" (p. 64), is the central tenet of Marxian political economy.

In Marx's view, the capitalist economy is a structure of production characterized by deprivation and collectivization (Simon, 1994). In civil society, a person's post in the division of labor determines his wants and interests. Individuals initially see themselves as isolated agents pursuing their own economic self-interests. Those with capital are considered capitalists (i.e., bourgeois); those without capital are relegated to the working class (i.e., proletariat) with only their labor to sell. This individualistic perspective begins to change once social realities set in. Close physical conditions for laborers, such as in a factory, lead to increased interaction through interpersonal communication and an enhanced awareness of commonalities. Workers then become more aware of their multi-faceted deprivation relative to that of capitalists. Thereby, Marx proposes a causal schema in which material-economic interests become political interests: The market economy leads to social reality, which leads to class interest, and thus leads to class consciousness, upon which collective, political action can be based. The party becomes the agent for workers, and the state, working to preserve this social order, becomes the agent for capitalists.

Marx veers from the classical school in that he sees the market not so much as a mechanism for maximizing private interests but as a venue for accumulating capital (Simon, 1994). The gap between the "haves" and the "have nots" widens over time, with capitalists becoming richer and the barriers to becoming a capitalist all the more insurmountable. Marx also disagreed with the self-organizing capacity of markets proposed in the classical school. In fact, he believed that markets would eventually self-destruct. As capital accumulation increases and becomes more concentrated, workers are drawn closer together and organize against capitalist interests.

Critical public relations scholarship has incorporated Marxist thought. Dutta-Bergman (2005) questioned the egalitarian perception of civil society and argued that Third World participants are still marginalized by hegemonic interests. Drawing upon Marx's critique of capitalism, he suggested that NGOs are driven by a capitalist logic (see also Neocloeus, 1995) and that today's working class is oppressed as a result of marginalized areas of the world being opened to Western corporate interests. The Marxist influence on Dutta-Bergman's work is evident in the language of class and power he employed: "At its heart, civil society serves as the channel through which the core exercises its power on peripheral actors and exercises its imperialist and capitalist goals under the chador of democracy promotion" (p. 280). Although they did not refer to Marx specifically, Bardhan and Patwardhan (2004) used terms aligned with his capitalist suspicions when they alerted public relations practitioners to the anxieties felt by nations opening their economies to multinational corporations (MNCs):

> Reasons for resistance towards MNCs are varied including postcolonial fears of cultural and economic imperialism, neocolonial anxieties and suspicion of capitalism against the backdrop of long-ingrained socialist and protectionist market ideologies. (p. 247)

Additionally, Berger (1999) incorporated the writings of Marx, among others, to describe how public relations tactics of distortion were used to create a world view that benefited the manufacturer of a questionable sleep aid in the 1980s.

Marxist philosophy is reflected in public relations practice that focuses on increasing share of voice for groups that are disenfranchised, disadvantaged, or otherwise oppressed by distributions of power in capitalist economies. Examples include practitioners working on behalf of activist labor unions, women's rights organizations, class-related issues, and the poor. Each of these areas involves struggles against powerful institutions and mainstream ideas, and proponents rely on public relations practitioners to heighten awareness, shift public opinion, and encourage collective action in their favor. An entire chapter is devoted to activism in this volume because of the importance of activism and civil society to the health of a society and also because of the impact they have on public relations.

However, it is also important to note that historically, public relations has aligned itself almost exclusively with corporate interests (Sriramesh, 2008) and therefore itself suffers from a poor reputation while trying to sell itself as a reputation builder. Although corporate reputation still consumes a predominant portion of public relations pedagogy, it is heartening to note changes are on the horizon as the body begins to diversify its focus into such areas as social marketing on behalf of governments and non-profit organizations for example.

Neoclassical Political Economy

Introduced at the end of the 19th century, neoclassical political economy, like its predecessors, treated the economy as an entity separate from politics (Caporaso and Levine, 1992). The concepts of constrained choice and rational choice characterize this school of thought. Economic agents seek to maximize their level of satisfaction (also known as utility) within a limited range of choices, and they are presumed to be rational and knowledgeable enough to rank-order their preferences within these constraints. In turn, economic agents are able to maximize their own welfare.

Like the classical school, proponents of the neoclassical approach (also referred to as neoliberalism) support a free market that provides a broad range of choices and allows welfare-enhancing transactions to take place with minimal government intervention (Stilwell, 2006). By doing so, the concept of Pareto optimality is achieved. In other words, leaving the market to its own devices results in optimal social welfare, whereby no single person could be made better off without making someone else worse off. Free markets are considered efficient markets because land, labor, capital, and commodities are allowed to reshuffle in order to reach their highest and best use.

A key difference between classical and neoclassical political economy is acknowledgement by the neoclassical school that markets can fail (Stilwell, 2006). That is, markets will not produce optimal results in the presence of externalities, monopolies, or public goods. In the pursuit of maximizing one's own welfare—whether it be an individual or an organization—an unintended social consequence, or externality, can result. If this unintended consequence provides a benefit to someone who is not party to an economic transaction, it is considered a positive externality. Alternatively, if the consequence is harmful, a negative externality ensues.

A classic example of a negative externality is industrial pollution. In its attempt to maximize its welfare, a plant emits pollutants into the air, which affects near neighbors (e.g., odor nuisance, health problems) who have no self-interest in the economic pursuits of the plant. Nevertheless, these parties are impacted by another's pursuit of welfare maximization in a negative manner. Neoclassicalists recognize the need for state intervention, whether regulatory or judicial, to correct this inefficient outcome (Stilwell, 2006). Taxes or fines can be imparted to better align private costs and benefits with social costs and benefits.

Monopolies are considered market failures because mass concentrations of economic power impede competition and limit the range of choices, which are the essential elements of free markets (Stilwell, 2006). A "perfectly competitive market" is defined as one with a large number of buyers and sellers that renders individual firms, producers, and consumers with little power to affect aggregate supply, demand, or prices. Monopolies violate this principle by interfering with voluntary exchange, efficient allocation of resources, and the optimality of outcomes.

Markets will fail to produce public goods, such as national defense or public radio, because producers are unable to recover enough benefits to justify their costs. Governments, then, must step in to provide what the market refuses to produce (Stilwell, 2006). Related to this idea is the problem of free riders: Individuals cannot be excluded from using public goods, yet they benefit from their use without having to make any contribution to their development or maintenance (Stiglitz, 2000). Free riders are considered an outcome of inefficient markets.

In the neoclassical view, the state's role is primarily that of an instrument to correct market failures. However, the state also plays a role in property and other rights, along with concerns of justice. These fall within the state sphere "not because they can be performed more efficiently there, but because the state rather than the market can best enforce equal protection and treatment" (Caporaso and Levine, 1992, p. 98).

A revolutionary contribution of the neoclassical school was marginal analysis, which contributes to the predominant use of neoclassical thought in modern economies (Stilwell, 2006). Marginal analysis brought micro-level mathematical calculation to the examination of human and firm behavior, with the intent of placing economics (a term that came to replace political economy) on par with the scientific rigor of physics. Marginalization allows firms to calculate the cost and benefit of each additional unit produced and to determine, with suitable precision, a production quantity that will optimize profits and minimize cost. Herein lies the impetus for cost-benefit analysis and the neoclassical tie to public relations research and practice.

Just as economists strove to quantify contributions of their analyses, so, too, do public relations practitioners seek to demonstrate their value to organizations through measurement and evaluation techniques. In fact, it has been a challenge for practitioners globally to "justify" their presence in organizations in quantifiable terms. A wave of research has been dedicated to measurement of public relations (Broom and Dozier, 1983; Hon and J. Grunig, 1999; Newlin, 1991; Paine, Draper, and Jeffrey, 2008; Sriramesh, J. E. Grunig, and Dozier, 1996), which, in large part, is motivated by practitioners' need to quantify public relations results for bottom-line scripted executives who are accustomed to marginal analysis in other areas of their business. Cost-benefit analysis has been addressed in both public relations research (Ehling, 1992; J. E. Grunig and L. A. Grunig, 2000; J. E. Grunig and Repper, 1992; Rawlins, 2006) and practice, particularly as it relates to selective engagement of publics. In an economic sense, firms, and hence practitioners, are faced with scarce resources and must strategically segment and prioritize publics based on their level of activism in a firm's operating environment.

A neoclassical view is particularly relevant to public relations advocacy on the part of NGOs that take issue with the calculus of costs versus benefits. Using marginal analysis, firms will invest in employee safety, community welfare, and environmental care up to the point at which these costs begin to outweigh the benefits returned. Generally speaking, firms will seek to minimize costs while activists seek to maximize societal benefits. These mutually exclusive goals place public relations practitioners in the midst of firm–stakeholder conflicts and require negotiation, mutual understanding, and compromise to address what can appear to be insurmountable differences.

Keynesian Political Economy

Keynesian thought arose in the early 20th century and vigorously challenged the role assigned to government by classical thinkers. John Maynard Keynes (1936) did not believe that an unregulated market could fully leverage society's productive potential: State intervention, not an invisible hand, was needed to optimize the allocation of resources.

Furthermore, Keynes argued that an individual's inability to find an appropriate outlet for his product in the market was not necessarily the result of a poor investment decision that needed adjustment but rather a failure on the part of the market to ensure adequate purchasing power and aggregate demand. In this idea, Keynes aligned with Marx's position on the inability of the market to maintain a smooth system of employment and production, though not to the revolutionary extremes Marx held. Like Marx, Keynes recognized the instability of capitalist markets in that processes such as employment and prices tend to be cumulative and reinforcing (Caporaso and Levine, 1992). That is, increases/decreases in these processes tend to lead to further increases/decreases, exacerbate resulting difficulties, and further justify government intervention.

Keynes' (1936) notion of "perverse effects" is related to his argument that micro-economic rationality (i.e., seeking to advance one's own interests) can lead to macro-economic (i.e., societal) irrationality. This concept is in clear opposition to the classical premise that pursuing one's own best interests serves the greater interests of society. To illustrate, a perverse effect results when investors prefer short-term gains available in the securities market over long-term capital investments in a productive enterprise. Such a shift in funds causes economic instabilities.

Corporations, according to Keynes (1936), play an important role because they are market agents with a long-term view. In turn, they represent a stabilizing force in the economy. Their shareholders, however, may value shorter-term returns and spread their investments across industries as a result. Although Keynes lauds the role of corporations in the economy, he recognizes that firms may or may not act in the public interest.

Expectations and labor markets are key components of Keynesian political economy (Keynes, 1936). The more individuals expect prices to rise or fall, the more they will act in ways for their predictions to come to fruition. Likewise, expectations of demand, not costs of production, drive investment decisions in this school of thought. Economic success depends upon the market's ability to provide individuals with their livelihoods. If aggregate demand fails, and the government does nothing to intervene, individuals are unjustly deprived of their ability to earn a living.

Keynes (1936) called for a much more active government role to avoid perverse effects at the macroeconomic level (e.g., employment, aggregate demand) than his laissez-faire predecessors. He proposed government spending, government borrowing, and taxes as effective policy remedies for the instabilities generated by capitalist economies—ideas that would have been considered blasphemous by early classical proponents.

This "big government" approach is widely seen around the world today and affects public relations in many ways. In most developing countries of the world, the hand of the government looms very large controlling a large segment of the economy through public sector enterprises. In such instances, the government becomes the "sole public" for public relations practitioners (Sriramesh, 1992). As long as public relations practitioners maintain good relations with the government, they can be effective in public relations as the government controls the means of production and distribution as well as the mass media. Coupled with reduced activism and civil society owing to a lack of political pluralism, such environments become fertile grounds for one-way, manipulative public relations activities. Public relations often gets mixed up with propaganda in such economies, affecting the reputation of the field. In the mid-1970s, organizational sociologists (e.g. Aldrich and Pfeffer, 1976, Aldrich, 1979) tried to link organizational processes with the environments in which they operate. Similarly, since the early days of theory building, public relations scholarship has recognized the impact of a political-regulatory environment and activism on public relations practice. Schneider (1985) linked the four organizational types proposed by Hull and Hage (1982) to the models of public relations and found that whereas organizational structure "provided only a minimal explanation" (L. Grunig, J. Grunig, and Dozier, 1995, p. 485) for the relationship between vertical structure and public relations, the mixed mechanical/organic organizational type was a predictor of the model of public relations practiced by an organization. Issues management and lobbying are two examples of using public relations strategies to counter government regulation of corporations. Proactive organizations may resort to "self-regulation" in order to avoid more stringent government regulations.

Other Perspectives on Political Economy

Two additional perspectives on political economy—social corporatism and communitarianism—are worth mentioning here. Social corporatism is a political and economic form of industrial organization whereby firms, governments, and civil society form coalitions to protect shared interests (Teague, 1995). This form of institutional collusion found in Austria, Sweden, and Germany is highly centralized, interventionist, and collective compared to the individualist nature of classical (and neoclassical) political economy. Teague defined the four economic functions of social corporatism as competitive (e.g., wage agreements are restricted so as not to undermine competitiveness), stabilization (e.g., cooperative response to economic turbulence improves resilience of all participants), employment (e.g., unemployment is kept low by placing restrictions on wage growth), and equity (e.g., measures are taken to reduce income inequalities). Trade union and employee organizations establish collective strategies designed to both spread the burden of adjustment to economic shocks and share the gains acquired from growth. A *quid pro quo* arrangement exists in that industrial actors can expect favorable policymaking on the part of government in exchange for their willingness to tolerate wage restraints.

Martin and Swank (2004) suggested that social corporatism elevates firms' understanding of, and appreciation for, collectivist concerns, a view they would not otherwise be privy to in a more individualist form of industrial organization. The authors further claimed that such a centralized arrangement of private and public interests may improve productivity and market stability. Over time, employers organized in collaborative groups that facilitate close working relationships with government and labor representatives tend to develop political positions that are more collectivist in scope and are more accepting of the tradeoffs associated with social protectionism.

J. E. Grunig (2000) introduced the collaborative element of societal corporatism as having the potential to serve as a core professional value in public relations. He highlighted the collectivist efforts of government agencies to work with their publics for the greater good of society and noted that this interaction takes place through symmetrical communication. In his opinion, U.S. political economy, which is exceedingly individualist in its orientation, is becoming more social corporatist.

Culbertson and Chen (1997) promoted the political philosophy of communitarianism as a foundation for symmetrical communication. They drew upon the work of Etzioni (1993) and other major contributors to outline six basic assumptions of communitarianism and explain how each related to symmetrical communication. These ideas align well with the democratic principles of public relations and include a commitment to quality relationships, balancing of rights and responsibilities, commitment to core values and beliefs, and an understanding that a sense of community requires social cohesion, empowerment, and broadening of social perspectives. Zucker (2001) associated this way of thinking with Japanese political economy. Communitarians support civil society rather than self-regulating markets, and their perspective of community (as a primary structure of society) is typically treated as something outside of the economy (Zucker). Etzioni (1993) ascribed what he referred to as the "supracommunity" to the city or nation, but not the economy. Zucker expanded on this idea:

> Communitarianism concentrates on community within subsystems of the economy, such as the firm; investigates economic preconditions of political community; describes non-economic communities, such as the polity, the tribe, and the religious group; and postulates a noneconomic supracommunity at the national level. (p. 17)

For communitarians, individual identities are communally formed in the public sphere of ideas, beliefs, and values. Sriramesh and Rivera (2006) addressed corporatism and communitarianism linking them to e-government and e-governance noting that true e-governance should involve two-way symmetrical communication. Further, Sriramesh, Ng, Soh, and Luo (2007) addressed these two schools of thought in referring to corporate social responsibility.

A State-Centered Approach to Political Economy

As previously noted, economics dominates thinking in political economy. But which is a more significant driver in international political economy and a more appropriate place for public relations analysis to begin: markets or nation-states? Although each is instrumental in global political economy, we agree with Gilpin (2001) that a state-centric approach is the best starting point for analysis. Gilpin describes state-centric realism as a perspective that "emphasizes the state (city, imperial, or nation-state) as the principal actor in international affairs and the fact that there is no authority superior to these sovereign political units; this position asserts that analysis should focus on the behavior of individual states" (p. 16). Of particular appeal to public relations scholars is the recognition of other, equally relevant, actors in a state-centric approach: "[A]lthough the state is the primary actor in international affairs, realism should acknowledge the importance of such nonstate actors as multinational firms, international institutions, and nongovernmental organizations (NGOs) in the determination of international affairs" (p. 17). Whereas the primary concerns of the state are national interests in security and political independence, a state-centric approach also recognizes the role that morals and values play in determining state behavior. Activism is likewise accounted for: "[T]he interests and policies of states are determined by the governing political elite, the pressures of powerful groups within a national society, and the nature of the 'national system of political economy'" (p. 18). Each of these considerations aligns well with conventional public relations scholarship that has recognized the government, citizens (including NGOs and activist groups), and corporations as key publics.

Taking a state-centric perspective does not mean the market is ignored. Rather, it means that we begin by first examining the interests and constraints of the state to better understand the economic phenomena occurring within it. We believe that in the modern era, the state (political leaders) sets the stage for economic activity by setting public policies. Although both markets and nation-state policies determine the functioning of the world economy, states play a dominant role because political ideology determines the nature of the market and economy. Gilpin (2001) stated:

> States set the rules that individual entrepreneurs and multinational firms must follow. Yet, economic and technological forces shape the policies and interests of individual states and

the political relations among states. The market is indeed a potent force in determination of economic and political affairs. For this reason, both political and economic analyses are required to understand the actual functioning and evolution of the global economy. *A comprehensive analysis necessitates intellectual integration of both states and markets.* (p. 24, emphasis added)

The state enjoys a certain level of autonomy. That is, it has the ability to define and pursue a public agenda independent of private societal interests (Caporaso and Levine, 1992). State-centered approaches to political economy reflect the neoclassical view that all things political are public, or associated with the state, and all things economic are associated with the private, or social, sphere. Thus, the terms "economy," "society," and "private sphere" are used interchangeably, as they denote private relations among private agents, whether they be individuals, firms, classes, or groups.

The relationship between societal and state forces is a highly interdependent one: "The state enters into the constitution of society just as society contributes to the constitution of the state" (Caporaso and Levine, 1992, p. 192). Each state is unique, in that its history, culture, and domestic structure define its interests, values, and goals. Although the course of public relations scholarship has provided a better understanding of the societal forces that impact organizations, our lack of exploration into state (and economic) forces renders our analysis incomplete, particularly as we seek to expand our research on the international front.

A POLITICAL ECONOMY FRAMEWORK

Nations vary widely in their economic priorities, political structures, and societal expectations. Anecdotal evidence, such as that presented in several chapters of this volume, indicates that these factors contribute to differences in how public relations is practiced around the world. But we have yet to delineate, much less predict (predictive ability is the hallmark of good research and scholarship), the specific public relations outcomes that result from these societal differences. We therefore propose a political economy research framework based on Gilpin's (2001) description of the major differences between national systems of political economy: (1) the primary purposes of the economic activity of the nation, (2) the role of the state in the economy, and (3) the structure of the corporate sector and private business practices (p. 149).

The purpose of a nation's economic activity can be profit making or protectionism, among other variants (Gilpin, 2001). The more liberal systems of political economy will minimize the role of the state in the private sector, whereas the state will be more interventional in communal or collective systems. Labor unions and NGOs have varying degrees of influence in the business sector, which may work closely in tandem with governmental agencies or vehemently independent of them. Each of these elements impacts how an organization relates to, interacts with, and is affected by a myriad of publics. To illustrate how this framework can be applied to nations, we draw upon Gilpin's (2001) description of American, Japanese, and German systems of political economy. Thereafter, we address the powerful political and economic shifts taking place in several emerging markets before suggesting directions for future research.

American Political Economy: Market-Oriented Capitalism

The primary purpose of economic activity in the U.S. is to benefit consumers by maximizing wealth creation (Gilpin, 2001). Distribution of that wealth, along with the social welfare impact of economic activities, is of secondary importance relative to other political economy systems that consider the subsequent social costs too high. The American system reflects many neoclassical principles in that the competitive market economy is viewed as predominant and separate. The state must have a compelling interest, such as a market failure, to intervene in the marketplace.

Governance over the American economy is diluted in that regulatory authority is divided between the executive, legislative, and judicial branches of the federal government as well as between the federal government and the 50 states (Gilpin, 2001). This political structure is characterized by tensions between political conservatives, who eschew any strong role for the state in the economy, and political liberals, who are concerned with business interests having excessive encroachment upon social and governmental interests. Because of this philosophical and structural divide, it is comparatively easier for U.S. private interests to challenge government actions at multiple points of entry.

Industrial policy, which Gilpin (2001) defines as the "deliberate efforts by a government to determine the structure of the economy through such devices as financial subsidies, trade protection, or governmental procurement" (p. 154), is designed to benefit particular industries or particular firms. This differs from more generalized policymaking by the federal government to improve education or increase research and development (R&D) funding. In the U.S., firm-specific policies are applied to select industrial sectors, such as manufacturing and national defense, that are believed to be more important to the economy than others. This practice of "picking winners" is generally frowned upon because many government officials and business leaders suspect the government will designate some industries as more valuable out of political, rather than sound economic, reasons.

The structure of American business is likewise fragmented (Gilpin, 2001). Strict competition and antitrust policies align with a strong resistance to mass concentrations of corporate power, collusion, and sharing of information between firms. As a result, federal regulatory agencies heavily scrutinize proposed mergers because of their perceived threat to an open and competitive marketplace. Neoclassical principles underlie this commitment to maintain free markets and offer more choices to consumers (Caporaso and Levine, 1992).

Shareholder primacy sets American political economy apart from its international counterparts that are more likely to be concerned with a broader range of stakeholders (Gilpin, 2001). In the U.S., shareholder interests are, for the most part, preeminent, despite the fact that few publicly held companies receive the entirety of their start-up wealth from investors (Blair, 1995). Today, employees and other stakeholders have just as much claim on ownership, yet shareholder capitalism remains the predominant practice in the U.S. Gilpin explained:

> In the American system of shareholder capitalism, a firm's fundamental purpose is to make profits for its investors or shareholders; in principle, the firm has minimal obligations to employees and/or to the communities in which its production facilities are located. Moreover, in the United States, a business corporation is regarded as a commodity that is bought and sold like any other commodity without regard for the social consequences of such transactions. . . . (p. 156)

Other political economies, such as Japan and Germany, place a higher priority on social welfare and give comparatively less attention to shareholder interests than the U.S.

Shareholder primacy presents challenges to public relations practice in that it can generate skepticism and backlash from activist publics who believe powerful organizations have a duty to serve the broader interests of society and not just their stockholders. Rebérioux (2007) argued that the return-driven pressures of shareholder primacy are directly responsible for accounting-related corporate scandals (e.g., Enron, Worldcom) in recent years. An environment of heightened public scrutiny and growing distrust of large corporations, fueled in large part by such scandals, demands that profit maximization be accompanied by a proactive commitment to social responsibility if corporations expect to earn the confidence of multiple stakeholders (Grossman, 2005). Corporate public relations practitioners can help firms to understand and better respond to societal expectations, but they are expected to demonstrate how socially-driven programs bring value to the company.

Shareholder activism (Marens, 2002) is a growing phenomenon whereby a minimum investment in stock provides activists with access to speaking platforms at annual stockholder meetings and the ability to file shareholder resolutions (to be voted upon) demanding change on a myriad issues. As shareholders with voting privileges, these activist individuals and groups have the opportunity to influence corporate governance and policy. Public relations practitioners working on behalf of these activists, who include NGOs and investment fund managers, frequently use media channels to gain exposure for and influence votes in favor of their proposed changes.

Japanese Political Economy: Collective Capitalism

America's primary interest in the free and open functioning of the economy is in stark contrast to Japan's, where the economy is regarded as subordinate to other social and political objectives (Gilpin, 2001). As a collectivist culture, Japan would be expected to give greater prominence to society over the individual. Since World War II, Japan has pursued the dual agenda of becoming a powerful industrial and technologically advanced nation while maintaining a strong commitment to social harmony among its people. Japan's approach to economic policy is best described as neomercantilism, which involves "state assistance, regulation, and protection of specific industrial sectors in order to increase their international competitiveness and attain the 'commanding heights' of the global economy" (p. 157). Mercantilism is often associated with protectionist trade policies (Buzan, 1984) and was a popular approach to policymaking prior to Adam Smith's (1776) seminal work.

Japan's political economy has been described as developmental capitalism, but Gilpin (2001) lists other terms used to describe its unique characteristics, such as "Shinto capitalism, developmental state capitalism, tribal capitalism, collective capitalism, welfare corporatism, competitive communism, network capitalism, companyism, producer capitalism, stakeholder capitalism, strategic capitalism, and, perhaps most famously or infamously, 'Japan, Inc.'" (p. 158). Unlike the U.S., the state plays a central and publicly supported role in Japan's economy, which is distinguished by a concentrated focus on economic development; the major role of large corporations in both business and society; the importance of the group over the individual and the producer over the consumer; and a close, more trusting, relationship between government, business, and labor that is intended to advance the collective good of Japanese society. The state is an integral part of society, to the extent that "the Japanese state [has] supported, or even created, certain social characteristics, including an industrious and highly educated workforce" (p. 159). Gilpin credits the Japanese state for creating today's highly developed Japanese society (see also Garon, 1997).

For the Japanese, economic efficiency is subordinate to social equity and domestic harmony (Upham, 1987). In keeping with this principle, the state recognizes a compelling interest in what many Westerners would consider excessive regulation to protect the weak and defenseless (Gilpin, 2001). Redundant staffs and lifetime employment, designed to promote social harmony, reflect the Japanese resistance to the downsizing, rightsizing, and outsourcing tactics so frequently utilized in the U.S. The concept of social harmony (*wa*) also affects public relations activity in Japan (Sriramesh and Takasaki, 1999). Sriramesh and Takasaki found that other cultural idiosyncracies such as *amae* (the dependence on another's goodness) played a role in internal communication maintaining good relations between superiors and subordinates. *Tataemae* (public persona of an individual) and *honne* (the private self) also contribute to reticence among the Japanese to disagree publicly lest "face" be lost leading to a loss of harmony leading to the use of the personal influence model (Sriramesh, Kim, and Takasaki, 1999).

The state's overarching power is uniquely coupled with bureaucratic fragmentation within the government (Gilpin, 2001). That is, economic and other bureaucracies act independently, with each working to fulfill the best interest of the particular segment of Japanese society it represents. Conflicts often arise, making the Japanese preference for consensus decision-making difficult.

Gilpin (2001) considered industrial policy as "the most controversial aspect of Japanese political economy" (p. 161) because its outcomes are the still the subject of much debate. The government has used trade protection measures, generous subsidies, cartels, low-cost financing, and bureaucratic guidance to promote favored established and emerging industries, including technology, automobiles, and scientific instruments, with mixed results.

As part of its focus on stakeholders beyond just shareholders, the private business sector in Japan takes on a great amount of responsibility for social welfare, which is more often regarded as a public sector burden in the U.S. (Gilpin, 2001). The *keiretsu*, a cohesive group of major firms, suppliers, distribution networks, and a major bank, is a unique Japanese business structure based on mutual trust, long-term relationships, and a shared interest in serving stakeholder needs. Given the close working relationship between business and government, private business associations are largely responsible for policing and regulating business activities, which can result in special treatment. Economic stability is valued more than profitability; therefore, Japanese firms seek to maximize sales and growth in order to advance the power and independence of the nation.

German Political Economy: Social Market Capitalism

German political economy shares characteristics with both the American and Japanese systems but still remains different in a number of ways (Gilpin, 2001; see also Glouchevitch, 1992). Germany, like Japan, values savings, investment, economic stability, and stakeholders beyond shareholders, compared to U.S. preferences for consumption, profitability, and shareholder primacy. Like the American system, Germany allows the market to function freely but is set apart by its attempt to balance social concerns with market efficiency. Because of a national commitment to domestic harmony and the well-being of its people, the German state and the private sector work closely together to provide a highly advanced system of social welfare. Germany's political economy is thus referred to as social market capitalism, also known as social corporatist or welfare state capitalism found in other parts of Europe. In corporatist capitalism, labor and society play a more active role in the governance of corporate affairs than in shareholder capitalism (Katzenstein, 1984).

The role of the German state in the economy is closer to that of the American system (Gilpin, 2001). Although codified law and the central bank (*Bundesbank*) contribute to stability at the macroeconomic level, the state intervenes only modestly at the microeconomic level. Industrial policy is not a major factor in the German economy, though subsidies and protective measures have been used in the coal and shipbuilding sectors.

Germany's system of corporate governance and industrial structure is similar in many ways to Japan's (Gilpin, 2001). National organizations, such as the *Bundesverband der Deutschen Industrie* and those representing the interests of labor, are much more powerful than their American and Japanese counterparts. Gilpin refers to this influential structure as a "system of codetermination at the level of the firm [that] has made German labor a partner, albeit a junior partner, in corporate governance" (p. 171). Medium-sized, privately held firms, referred to as the *Mittelstand*, play a key role in the economy, as do large, publicly held firms, though not as predominantly as they do in the U.S.

Germany's system of political economy, like Japan's, is much more tolerant of concentrations of economic power and cooperation than the American system (Gilpin, 2001). German corporations with strong banking ties are considered the most important, reflecting a high integration of finance and industry in corporate governance. This integrated approach, which includes cross-membership on supervisory boards and bank ownership of corporate stocks, resembles the Japanese *keiretsu* in that long-term relationships are leveraged to facilitate information sharing, access to affordable capital, and joint economic planning. In Germany, however, participants are more concerned with advancing the interests of their firms rather than those of the entire group. Gilpin notes that these ties between industry and banks are diminishing as the German economy becomes more globalized.

Bentele and Wehmeyer (2003) noted that the market economy that exists in Germany, in combination with the political system since World War II, has "generally enabled and necessitated the use of public relations by all kinds of social organizations such as corporations, associations, unions, churches, and NGOs" (p. 211). The authors clearly identified a relationship between the economic system and status of public relations (both in organizations and at the level of agencies) when they noted that the increase in the number of IPOs (Initial Public Offerings) in 2000 and 2001 "increased the demand for investor relations experts, resulting in a short-term paucity for skilled practitioners" (p. 211).

Emerging Markets

We would be remiss to discuss highly developed markets without mentioning the emerging nations expected to wield significant influence in the world economy in coming years. The term BRIC, an acronym for Brazil, Russia, India, and China, was used in a Goldman Sachs report (Wilson and Purushothaman, 2003) that predicted phenomenal growth in these countries over the next 30 years and the possibility of a subsequent shakeup in the world's top ten economies by 2050. Each of these nations has experienced what is referred to as "shock therapy" in that their economies made monumental shifts away from state-centered policies and toward more liberal market reforms, with varying degrees of success.

Jha (as cited in Reardon, 2004; see also Kollontai, 2002) argued that nations transitioning toward more open markets will face significant difficulties if neoliberal economic policies (e.g., monetary and fiscal reforms, free trade initiatives) are implemented too quickly and without the proper state infrastructure (e.g., regulation, rule of law, property rights) in place. In other words, markets cannot spontaneously arise independent of the state. For example, Jha credited India with having fundamental market institutions (e.g., banking system, commercial law, entrepreneurs) already established during its reforms but pointed to a lack of sufficient financial and other supporting functions as the reason China and Russia had to back away from initial efforts to spark growth and return to more interventionist policies. de Soto (2000) argued that property rights are the fundamental reason why capitalism tends to be successful in Western nations but fails in the Third World and former communist nations that are undercapitalized:

> The poor inhabitants of these nations—five-sixths of humanity—do have things, but they lack the process to represent their property and create capital. They have houses but not titles, crops but not deeds; businesses but not statutes of incorporation. It is the unavailability of these essential representations that explains why people . . . have not been able to produce sufficient capital to make their domestic capitalism work. (pp. 6–7)

Transitional economies attempt to balance a mix of international and domestic interests, which can be conflicting and add to the difficulties of international market integration. In response to pressure from U.S. and British governments, the International Monetary Fund (IMF), and the World Bank to open its markets and deregulate, Brazil implemented neoliberal policies in the late 1980s (Saad-Filho, 2003). These reforms proved sufficient for short-term growth and stability but failed to sustain Brazil's economy and currency when foreign capital flows declined the following decade. Neoliberalism had rippling effects through social and political spheres and proved to be "an inconsistent and socially undesirable development strategy" (p. 20).

In their follow-up BRIC report (see O'Neill, Wilson, Purushothaman, and Stupnytska, 2005), Goldman Sachs researchers introduced the Next Eleven: a list of developed and developing countries that, based on demographic profiles, were forecasted to have a growing, stronger presence in the global economy.[1] The list comprised Bangladesh, Egypt, Indonesia, Iran, Korea, Mexico, Nigeria, Pakistan, Philippines, Turkey, and Vietnam. BRICs as well as these emerging areas of the world should be of parallel interest to public relations practitioners, who will be tasked with assisting business, government, and civil society organizations in reconciling conflicting interests, influencing public opinion, and communicating with a variety of stakeholders affected by globalization in ways that must be tailored to the unique expectations of each country. Kollontai (2002) described the challenges for emerging economies in a way that affirms our assertion that a state-centered approach to understanding political economy and its effects on public relations practice is most suitable:

> In late-comer, peripheral countries of the world economy (developing and ex-socialist countries), which are trying to modernise and catch up, by definition the role of politics (and ideology) in economic development is much greater. Decisions have to be taken as to

---

[1] Of the eleven countries, only South Korea and Mexico were considered to have the potential to be as important as BRICs.

what goals should be set and in what priority, what elements of modern societies could be transplanted, in what sequence and timeframe, and so forth. This inevitably leads to periods of condensed social change with extreme political, ideological and economic shifts and confrontations. Moreover, modernisation presupposes profound societal transformations, which give rise to serious problems of legitimacy [for the changes and parties involved]. (p. 218)

POLITICAL ECONOMY RESEARCH RECOMMENDATIONS

We offer here a template of questions as a starting point for researchers to operationalize and investigate political economy variables at a national level. Our hope is that additional research in this area will lead to a better understanding of how political economies affect global public relations practice and thus expand our body of knowledge in a relevant and timely way. Of particular importance is our need to understand and respond to the unique public relations challenges of emerging markets, as these areas of the world will become increasingly prominent in the global economy (Sriramesh, 2004). We believe the collaborative, democratic, and relationship-building functions of public relations have the potential to serve a beneficial role for organizations not only in highly developed economies, but also in those nations ascending to the global marketplace. By enhancing our knowledge of political economy effects at the domestic level first, we can advance our understanding of the global economy and public relations' role within it.

We return, then, to Gilpin's (2001) description of the major differences between national systems of political economy, that is, (1) the primary purposes of the economic activity of the nation, (2) the role of the state in the economy, and (3) the structure of the corporate sector and private business practices (p. 149), to guide our recommendations. We expand upon Gilpin's work by incorporating the important roles of labor, NGO, and other activist involvement when addressing the structure and practices of a nation's business sector and include some questions posed in the first chapter of this book, as shown in the list of research questions offered below.

Primary Purposes of the Nation's Economic Activity

- Aside from promoting the welfare of its citizens, what objective(s) most predominantly drives the national economy: market autonomy/consumer welfare, national power, wealth distribution, collective/communal interests, or some other objective?

- What roles do liberty, equality, harmony, community, or other core values play in national economic interests?

- To what extent is the economy open to the outside world? To what extent is protectionism practiced?

- To what extent is the economy in transition? To what extent is the nation considered developed, developing, or emerging?

- How have history and culture contributed to the current economic objectives of the nation?

- What societal tensions arise as a result of these economic objectives? For example, to what extent do "winners" and "losers" exist in the national economy?

- How do national economic objectives affect relationship building between organizations and their publics? What level of activism exists to promote, refute, or protect these objectives? What publics are disenfranchised or marginalized as a result of these objectives?

The Role of the State in the Economy

- What are the primary responsibilities of government?

- How is government organized to facilitate the economic objectives of the nation? How can its role in economic activity be described: minimal, moderate, or highly interventionist? What is the rationale for government intervention?

- How best can the nation's political system be described: democratic, authoritarian, totalitarian, or some other system? To what extent does political pluralism exist?

- How can the relationship between the executive, judiciary, and legislative branches of government be described? To what extent is a system of codified law developed?

- To what extent can organizations (for-profit, non-profit, etc.) influence public policy-making? Are any particular types of organizations considered more powerful than others in their ability to influence public policy? To what extent does industrial policy favor particular areas of commerce?

- To what extent is activism prevalent in the public sector? What historical role has it played in the public sector?

- What role does government play in banking, finance, and other relevant sectors?

- What is the extent of the regulatory environment? To what extent do firms "self-regulate" their behavior in the marketplace?

- To what extent is communication as it relates to public relations practitioners regulated?

The Structure of the Corporate Sector and Civil Society

- What could be described as the primary purpose of business: profitability, sales, growth, or some other purpose?

- To what extent is government involved in the ongoing conduct of business? How can the relationship between government and business be described: cooperative, adversarial, or in some other way?

- To what extent is corporate power concentrated? To what extent does cooperation and/or competition characterize the private sector?

- What role are corporations expected to play in social welfare?

- To what extent are labor unions influential in society?

- To what extent are NGOs, or any other special interest groups, influential in society?

- To what extent is activism prevalent in the private sector? What historical role has it played in the private sector?

- How is activism regarded by corporations? How do corporations respond to activism?

- What level of technology, including new media, is available to public relations practitioners?

Conclusion

Building on the work of the IABC project (J. Grunig, 1992) and the propositions by Verčič, L. Grunig, and J. Grunig (1996), we have offered political economy as a relevant body of knowledge to public relations practice and scholarship globally and in individual countries. Although J. Grunig began to link macroeconomic theory with consumer behavior and public relations as far back as 1966, we believe the field has not integrated the diversity of political economy seen around the world into the body of knowledge. Practitioners, being forced to operate in new environments, are left to anecdotal evidence or trial and error (some mistakes being quite expensive financially and in reputation) when they practice public relations in unfamiliar political economic systems. We have tried to present in this chapter an overview of literature from political economy to help advance global public relations practice and scholarship. In introducing the above framework to guide research in political economy and public relations, we do not presume to have captured all of the relevant questions. In fact, we feel certain others can and should be added to complete our analysis. We do, however, believe that this framework can serve as a feasible starting point for expanding our understanding and thus our body of knowledge in global public relations. More importantly, we hope that this framework spawns empirical research that will expand the conceptual linkage between political economy and public relations into a predictive science.

REFERENCES

Aldrich, H. E. (1979). *Organizations and environments.* Englewood Cliffs, NJ: Prentice Hall.

Aldrich, H. E., and Pfeffer, J. (1976). Environments of organizations. *Annual Review of Sociology, 2,* 79–105.

Bardhan, N., and Patwardhan, P. (2004). Multinational corporations and public relations in a historically resistant host culture. *Journal of Communication Management, 8*(3), 246–263.

Bentele, G., and Wehmeyer, S. (2003). From literary bureaus to a modern profession: The development and current structure of public relations in Germany. In K. Sriramesh and D. Vercic (Eds.), *The handbook of global public relations: Theory, research, and practice.* Mahwah, NJ: Lawrence Erlbaum Associates. (pp. 199–221).

Berger, B. K. (1999). The Halcion affair: Public relations and the construction of ideological world view. *Journal of Public Relations Research, 11*(3), 185–203.

Berger, B. K. (2005). Power over, power with, and power to relations: Critical reflections on public relations, the dominant coalition, and activism. *Journal of Public Relations Research, 17*(1), 5–28.

Blair, M. M. (1995). *Ownership and control: Rethinking corporate governance for the twenty-first century.* Washington, D. C.: Brookings Institution Press.

Broom, G. M., Casey, S., and Ritchey, J. (1997). Toward a concept and theory of organization-public relationships. *Journal of Public Relations Research, 9*(2),83–98.

Broom, G. M., and Dozier, D. (1983, fall). An overview: Evaluation research in public relations. *Public Relations Quarterly,28*(3), 5–9.

Buzan, B. (1984, autumn). Economic structure and international security: The limits of the liberal case. *International Organization, 38*(4), 597–624.

Caporaso, J. A., and Levine, D. P. (1992). *Theories of political economy.* New York: Cambridge University Press.

Coombs, W. T. (1998). The Internet as potential equalizer: New leverage for confronting social irresponsibility. *Public Relations Review, 24*(3), 289–303 .

Culbertson, H. M., and Chen, N. (1997, summer). Communitarianism: A foundation for communication symmetry. *Public Relations Quarterly, 42*(2), 36–41.

de Soto, H. (2000). *The mystery of capital: Why capitalism triumphs in the West and fails everywhere else.* New York: Basic Books.

Donaldson, T., and Preston, L. E. (1995). The stakeholder theory of the corporation: Concepts, evidence, and implications. *Academy of Management Review, 20*(1), 65–91.

Drucker, P. F. (1999). *The frontiers of management: Where tomorrow's decisions are being shaped today.* New York: Penguin.

Dutta-Bergman, M. J. (2005). Civil society and public relations: Not so civil after all. *Journal of Public Relations Research, 17*(3), 267–289.

Ehling, W. P. (1992). Estimating the value of public relations and communication to an organization. In J. E. Grunig (Ed.), *Excellence in public relations and communication management* (pp. 617–638). Hillsdale, NJ: Lawrence Erlbaum Associates.

Eid, M. (2007). Engendering the Arabic Internet: Modern challenges in the information society. In S. C. Duhé (Ed.), *New media and public relations* (pp. 247–268). New York: Peter Lang.

Elkington, J. (1998). *Cannibals with forks: The triple bottom line of 21ˢᵗ century business.* Gabriola Island, BC: New Society Publishers.

Etzioni, A. (1993). *The spirit of community: The reinvention of American society.* New York: Simon and Schuster Touchtone Books.

Freeman, R. E. (1984). *Strategic management.* Boston: Pitman.

Friedman, M. (1962). *Capitalism and freedom* [1982 reprinted edition]. Chicago, IL: University of Chicago Press.

Garon, S. (1997). *Molding Japanese minds: The state in everyday life.* Princeton, NJ: Princeton University Press.

Gilpin, R. (2001). *Global political economy: Understanding the international economic order.* Princeton, NJ: Princeton University Press.

Glouchevitch, P. (1992). *Juggernaut: The German way of business: Why it is transforming Europe—and the world.* New York: Simon and Schuster.

Grossman, H. A. (2005). Refining the role of the corporation: The impact of corporate social responsibility on shareholder primacy theory. *Deakin Law Review, 10*(2), 572–596.

Grunig, J. E. (1992). *Excellence in public relations and communication management: Contributions to effective organizations.* Hillsdale, NJ: Lawrence Erlbaum Associates.

Grunig, J. E. (2000). Collectivism, collaboration, and societal corporatism as core professional values in public relations. *Journal of Public Relations Research, 12*(1), 23–48.

Grunig, J. E. (2006). Furnishing the edifice: Ongoing research on public relations as a strategic management function. *Journal of Public Relations Research, 18*(2), 151–176.

Grunig, J. E., and Grunig, L. A. (2000). Public relations in strategic management and strategic management of public relations: Theory and evidence from the IABC Excellence project. *Journalism Studies, 1*(2), 303–321.

Grunig, J. E., and Repper, F. C. (1992). Strategic management, publics, and issues. In J. E. Grunig (Ed.), *Excellence in public relations and communication management* (pp. 117–157). Hillsdale, NJ: Lawrence Erlbaum Associates.

Grunig, L. A., Grunig, J. E., and Dozier, D. (1995). *Excellent organizations and effective organizations.* Mahwah, NJ: Lawrence Erlbaum Publishers, Inc.

Hull, F., and Hage, J. (1982). Organization: Structures, processes and outcomes: Beyond Burns and Stalker's organic type. *Sociology, 16,* 564–577.

Halal, W. E. (1998). *The new management: Bringing democracy and markets inside organizations.* San Francisco: Berrett-Koehler.

Hall, J. A. (1998, May/June). The nature of civil society. *Society, 35*(4), 32–41.

Heath, R. L. (2000). A rhetorical perspective on the values of public relations: Crossroads and pathways toward concurrence. *Journal of Public Relations Research, 12*(1), 69–91.

Heath, R. L. (2006). Onward into more fog: Thoughts on public relations' research directions. *Journal of Public Relations Research, 18*(2), 93–114.

Hofstede, G. (2001). *Culture's consequences: Comparing values, behaviours, institutions and organizations across nations* (2nd ed.). Thousand Oaks, CA: Sage.

Hollingsworth, J. R., and Boyer, R. (1997). Coordination of economics actors and social systems of production. In J. R. Hollingsworth and R. Boyer (Eds.), *Contemporary capitalism: The embeddedness of institutions* (pp. 1–47). New York: Cambridge University Press.

Hon, C. L., and Grunig, J. E. (1999). *Guidelines for measuring relationships in public relations.* Gainesville, FL: The Institute for Public Relations.

Hull, F., and Hage, J. (1982). Organization: Structures, processes and outcomes: Beyond Burns and Stalker's organic type. *Sociology, 16,* 564–577.

Hyden, G. (1997, spring). Civil society, social capital, and development: Dissection of a complex discourse. *Studies in Comparative International Development, 32*(1), 3–30.

Jones, M. T. (1999, June). The institutional determinants of social responsibility. *Journal of Business Ethics, 20*(2), 163–179.

Katzenstein, P. (1984). *Corporatism and change: Austria, Switzerland, and the politics of industry*. Ithaca, NY: Cornell University Press.

Keynes, J. M. (1936). *General theory of employment, interest and money*. New York: Harcourt, Brace and World.

Kollontai, V. (2002, January). The new political economies: A view from Russia. *American Journal of Economics and Sociology, 61*(1), 217–232.

Lauzen, M. M. (1995). Toward a model of environmental scanning. *Journal of Public Relations Research, 7*(3), 187–203.

Ledingham, J. A. (2003). Explicating relationship management as a general theory of public relations. *Journal of Public Relations Research, 15*(2), 181–198.

Liechty, D. (1985). On the social responsibilities of business: Contra Milton Friedman. *Management Decision, 23*(4), 54–62.

Marens, R. (2002, fall). Inventing corporate governance: The mid-century emergence of shareholder activism. *Journal of Business and Management, 8*(4), 365–389.

Martin, C. J., and Swank, D. (2004, November). Does the organization of capital matter? Employers and active labor market policy at the national and firm levels. *American Political Science Review, 98*(4), 593–611.

May, S., Cheney, G., and Roper, J. (2007). *The debate over Corporate Social Responsibility*. New York: Oxford University Press.

McKie, D. (2001). Updating public relations: "New science," research paradigms, and uneven developments. In R. L. Heath (Ed.), *Handbook of public relations* (pp. 75–91). Thousand Oaks, CA: Sage.

Motion, J., and Weaver, C. K. (2005). A discourse perspective for critical public relations research: Life Sciences Network and the battle for truth. *Journal of Public Relations Research, 17*(1), 49–67.

Neocloeus, M. (1995). From civil society to the social. *British Journal of Sociology, 46,* 395–408.

Newlin, P. E. (1991, spring). A public relations measurement and evaluation model that finds the movement of the needle. *Public Relations Quarterly,* 36(1), 40–41.

O'Neill, J., Wilson, D., Purushothaman, R., and Stupnytska, A. (2005, Dec. 1). *How solid are the BRICs?* Retrieved February 24, 2008, from http://www2.goldmansachs.com/hkchina/insight/research/pdf/BRICs_3_12-1-05.pdf

Paine, K. D., Draper, P., and Jeffrey, A. (2008, January). *Using public relations research to drive business results.* Retrieved February 22, 2008, from http://www.instituteforpr.org/files/uploads/UsingResearch_Drive Business.pdf

Pishchikova, K. (2006, March). The promise of transnational NGO dialogue: The argument and the challenges. *Cambridge Review of International Affairs, 19*(1), 49–61.

Rawlins, B. L. (2006). *Prioritizing stakeholders for public relations.* Retrieved February 5, 2008, from http://www.instituteforpr.org/research_single/prioritizing_stakeholders/

Reardon, J. (2004, Sept.). The perilous road to the market: The political economy of reform in Russia, India, and China (book review). *Journal of Economic Issues, 38*(3), 873–875.

Rebérioux, A. (2007, July). Does shareholder primacy lead to a decline in managerial accountability? *Cambridge Journal of Economics, 31*(4), 507–524.

Roper, J. (2005). Symmetrical communication: Excellent public relations or a strategy for hegemony? *Journal of Public Relations Research, 17*(1), 69–86.

Saad-Filho, A. (2003). New dawn or false start in Brazil? The political economy of Lula's election. *Historical Materialism, 11*(1), 3–21.

Schneider, L. A. (1985). Organizational structure, environmental niches, and public relations: The Hage-Hull typology of organizations as predictor of communication behavior. Unpublished doctoral dissertation, University of Maryland, College Park.

Simon, L. H. (Ed.). (1994). *Karl Marx: Selected writings.* Indianapolis, IN: Hackett Publishing Company.

Smith, A. (1776). *An inquiry into the nature and causes of the wealth of nations* [1981 reprinted edition]. Indianapolis, IN: Liberty Fund.

Sriramesh, K. (1992). The impact of societal culture on public relations: Ethnographic evidence from India. *Public Relations Review, 18*(2), pp. 201–211.

Sriramesh, K. (2004). Public relations practice and research in Asia: A conceptual framework. In K. Sriramesh (Ed.), *Public relations in Asia: An anthology* (pp. 1–27). Singapore: Thomson.

Sriramesh, K. (2008). Globalization and public relations. In A. Zerfrass, B. van Ruler, and K. Sriramesh (Eds.), *Public relations research: European and international perspectives and innovations* (pp. 346–362). Wiesbaden, Germany: Verlag für Sozialwissenschaften.

Sriramesh, K., and Rivera, M. (2006). Corporatism and Communitarianism as environments for e-governance: The case of Singapore. *New Media and Society 8*(5), 707–730.

Sriramesh, K., and Takasaki, M. (1999). The impact of culture on Japanese public relations. *Journal of Communication Management 3*(4), pp. 337–352.

Sriramesh, K., and Verčič, D. (2004). The innovativeness-needs paradox and global public relations: Some propositions on the need for international public relations subsidies. *Media Asia, 31*(1), 3–13.

Sriramesh, K., Grunig, J.E., and Dozier, D.M. (1996). Observation and measurement of two dimensions of organizational culture and their relationship to public relations. *Journal of Public Relations Research, 8*(4), 229–261.

Sriramesh, K., Kim, Y., and Takasaki, M. (1999). Public relations in three Asian cultures: An analysis. *Journal of Public Relations Research 11*(4), pp. 271–292.

Sriramesh, K., Ng, C. W., Soh, T. T., and Luo, W. (2007). Corporate social responsibility and public relations: Perceptions and practices in Singapore. In S. K. May, G. Cheney, and J. Roper (Eds.) *The debate over corporate social responsibility*, New York: Oxford University Press.

Stiglitz, J. E. (2000). *Economics of the public sector* (3rd ed.). New York: W. W. Norton and Company.

Stilwell, F. (2006). *Political economy: The contest of economic ideas* (2nd ed.). South Melbourne, Victoria: Oxford University Press.

Teague, P. (1995, June). Pay determination in the Republic of Ireland: Towards social corporatism? *British Journal of Industrial Relations, 33*(2), 253–273.

Upham, F. (1987). *Law and social change in postwar Japan.* Cambridge, MA: Harvard University Press.

Verčič, D., Grunig, L. A., and Grunig, J. E. (1996). Global and specific principles of public relations: Evidence from Slovenina. In H. M. Culbertson and N. Chen (Eds.), *International public relations. A comparative analysis.* Mahwah, N. J.: Lawrence Erlbaum Associates.

Weaver, C. K, and Motion, J. (2002). Sabotage and subterfuge: Public relations, democracy and genetic engineering in New Zealand. *Media, Culture and Society, 24*, 325–343.

Wilson, D., and Purushothaman, R. (2003, Oct. 1). *Dreaming with BRICs: The path to 2050.* Retrieved February 24, 2008, from http://www2.goldmansachs.com/ideas/brics/book/99-dreaming.pdf

Wijnberg, N. M. (2000, June). Normative stakeholder theory and Aristotle: The link between ethics and politics. *Journal of Business Ethics, 25*(4), 329–342.

Zucker, R. (2001). *Democratic distributive justice.* Cambridge: Cambridge University Press.

3

THE RELATIONSHIP BETWEEN CULTURE AND PUBLIC RELATIONS [1]

KRISHNAMURTHY SRIRAMESH

INTRODUCTION

In presenting the literature review on corporate culture and public relations, we (Sriramesh, J. Grunig, Buffington, 1992) had begun our chapter by quoting Smircich's (1983, p. 339) succinct statement: "culture is an idea whose time has come." Organizational management literature had begun to accept the relevance of this concept at the dawn of the 1980s. We had contended that the time had come for the public relations body of literature to also integrate culture into its pedagogy because of the significance of this variable to human communication and relationship building.

Sadly, culture has yet to be integrated into the public relations body of knowledge. It appears that culture's time has not yet come after all for our field. Much of the literature and scholarship in our area continues to be ethnocentric with a predominantly American, and to a lesser extent British and Western European, bias even though studies have begun to explore the status of public relations in different regions of the world—especially in the past five years. In 1992, we had written: "to communicate to [with] their publics in a global marketplace, public relations practitioners will have to sensitize themselves to the cultural heterogeneity of their audiences. . . . The result will be the growth of a culturally richer profession" (Sriramesh and White, 1992, p. 611). Unfortunately, well into the 21st century, our hope has not yet materialized. The reality is that in a rapidly globalizing world, our field will ignore culture at its own peril. This is true of the other "environmental variables" that emanated from the Excellence project such as the political system, media system,

---

[1] Revised from the original in Toth, E. (2006) *Excellence in public relations and communication management: Challenges for the next generation.* Mahwah, NJ: Lawrence Erlbaum Associates Inc. pp. 507–527.

economic system, and level of activism. We know conceptually that these variables do contribute significantly to making organizational environments around the world dynamic and challenging. It is important to recognize that there may be other variables, or local variations of the above variables, that need to be identified and integrated to the body of literature.

This chapter seeks to assess the role of one of the environmental variables, culture, on public relations. As mentioned in Chapter 1, we discuss these highly inter-related socio-political variables in isolation only for the sake of conceptual clarity and convenience of explanation. Each of these environmental variables influences the other. As a result, studying their relationship with public relations has not been, and will not be, an easy challenge. This chapter begins with a review of the research studies that have assessed the nexus between culture (both societal and corporate) and public relations. Next, it will offer suggestions to build on these initial attempts and give the culture concept the primacy it deserves in the public relations body of knowledge. In doing so, this chapter challenges public relations scholars to integrate this important variable into the public relations body of knowledge and pedagogy.

ORIGINS OF THE STUDY OF CULTURE AND PUBLIC RELATIONS

One can state with a great deal of confidence that the IABC's Excellence Project spawned research linking culture with public relations. When the Project began in 1987, culture had not yet been discussed as a determinant of public relations strategies or practice in the then fledgling body of knowledge of public relations. This was evident as there was no mention of this variable in the 1988 Body of Knowledge report commissioned by the Public Relations Society of America (PRSA). When public relations practitioners needed to enter a new market and interact with publics of a different culture, they often depended on anecdotal evidence to design strategies that were sensitive to the local culture. To a great extent, this continues to be the case even today because of the anemic growth of knowledge about culture and public relations.

Sriramesh and White (1992) began the literature review for the excellence project by discussing whether public relations practice is *culture-free* or *culture-specific*—terms we had borrowed from Tayeb (1988). Scholars advocating the former had argued that organizational characteristics (such as organizational structure) and their contextual factors are stable across societies. Hickson, Hinings, McMillan, and Schwitter (1974) articulated the culture-free thesis best: "[W]hether the culture is Asian or European or North American, a large organization with many employees improves efficiency by specializing their activities but also by increasing, controlling and coordinating specialities" (pp. 63–64). Scholars advocating the *culture-specific* approach (Hofstede, 1991, Tayeb, 1988, Pascale and Athos, 1981, Ouchi, 1981) have countered this argument by stating that organizations are made up of individuals who are acculturated differently at home, school, and the workplace, which makes each individual a unique personality offering different sets of opportunities and challenges to managers. Organizations, which are themselves cultures, face the challenge of harnessing these individual personalities to their mutual benefit, which is not an easy task.

There can be little doubt that organizations are culture-bound. The linkage between culture and public relations is logical and very obvious. Culture affects communication, and is affected by it. Because public relations is fundamentally a communication activity, it is logical to conclude that culture affects public relations also. Therefore there is the need to conceptually link culture with public relations. In order to do so effectively, we believed it was important to distinguish between *societal* culture (Sriramesh and White, 1992) and *corporate* culture (Sriramesh, J. Grunig, Buffington, 1992). Drawing the distinction between these two types of culture is important because public relations professionals deal with *external* and *internal* publics who are acculturated differently by society and by organizations respectively. As members of a society, external publics are imbued with cultural idiosyncracies specific to a region. Internal publics, although acculturated to the culture of the larger society, also get acculturated to certain unique characteristics that are specific to the organization within which they operate. These two types of culture influence not only the way people communicate but also how they respond to communication within the organization.

Having made this basic distinction, we began an extensive review of literature from fields such as anthropology, organizational psychology, and sociology that helped identify conceptual linkages between public relations and these two types of culture. The next two sections will offer a review of studies that have empirically analyzed the relationship between these two types of cultures and public relations thus far.

SOCIETAL CULTURE

The review of literature on societal culture conducted for the Excellence study included the four cultural dimensions that Hofstede (1984) had identified at that time: power distance, uncertainty avoidance, masculinity/femininity, and individualism/collectivism. Hofstede (1991) added a fifth dimension that he first termed Confucian dynamism but later labeled long-term orientation. A few other studies that used the conceptual framework proposed by the Excellence study later included the fifth dimension also.

We ended our literature review with two conceptual propositions that linked societal culture with public relations. The first stated: "societal cultures that display lower levels of power distance, authoritarianism, and individualism, but have higher levels of inter-personal trust among workers, are most likely to develop the excellent public relations practices identified in this book" (Sriramesh and White, 1992, p. 611). Because we had no empirical data at that time we had chosen to keep this conceptual proposition very broad. Now that we have over a decade of data, albeit from only a few countries, it is possible to rephrase this proposition or divide it into several propositions. For example, it is possible that societies with higher levels of collectivism also can develop excellent public relations practices as long as the levels of other dimensions (such as power distance) are lower. Subcultures and countercultures also play a key role in public relations. As will be discussed later, these are some of the avenues and challenges for future researchers.

The second proposition had stated: "although such occurrences are rare, organizations that exist in societal cultures that do not display these characteristics that are conducive to the spawning of excellent public relations programs also may have excellent public relations programs if the few power holders of the organization have individual personalities that foster [a more] participative organizational culture even if this culture is atypical to [the] mainstream societal culture" (Sriramesh and White, 1992, p. 612). With this proposition we wanted to highlight the fact that an organization can develop an internal culture that is different from the mainstream culture of the society in which it exists, which happens more often than one might expect.

It is important to note that the Excellence study did not attempt to gather data on the dimensions of societal culture and, therefore, did not try to empirically link these dimensions with public relations. Despite the dire need to do so, we refrained from garnering empirical data on societal culture for several reasons. The scope of data gathering for the project had already expanded—especially with the inclusion of the employee questionnaire to elicit information for determining the organizational culture of the sample that also was a critical issue. Including societal culture as another variable to be studied would have increased the project's scope exponentially and affected the efficacy of data gathering. Further, like scores of anthropologists and Hofstede, we recognized that culture is a malleable concept that is hard to define and harder to measure. Therefore, we thought it would be best to design individual studies that break down societal culture into manageable parts and study its impact on public relations in some depth. A few studies have done this as will be reviewed presently.

Although the Excellence study did not gather empirical evidence on the relationship between societal culture and public relations, the literature review and conceptualization based on the project have spawned several studies that have contributed to the body of knowledge. Although these studies have not been large in number, they have contributed significantly toward extending the body of knowledge beyond Anglo-Saxon cultures. In doing this, they have helped reduce, at least to some extent, the extreme ethnocentricity of the field. These studies have principally used one or more of Hofstede's dimensions of culture and attempted to link them with public relations practice.

An ethnographic analysis of southern Indian organizations was among the first studies to assess the impact of societal culture on public relations (Sriramesh, 1992). That study focused in particular on the impact of *power distance* on public relations practice. Inequality exists in all societies and there are differences in power among people of different strata in every society. Like Mulder (1977), from whom he had borrowed the concept of power distance, Hofstede (1984) viewed power distance mostly as a form of oppression by the more powerful. Whereas this may be true in many societies, there is also an implicit practice of *deference to authority* by the less powerful that is often seen in some societies. In the study in India, for example, even though the CEO of a private bank wanted to bring a more participative culture in his bank, there was more discomfort from the lower ranks because of their deference to authority (Sriramesh, 1996, pp. 188–189). However, the study also found that more than half the public relations managers agreed that employees lose respect for a manager who consults them before making decisions, signifying that managers also exhibited high levels of power distance. Interestingly, high levels of power distance also resulted in lower status accorded public relations by organizations. Societal culture was found to affect corporate culture.

In her study of public relations in South Korea, Rhee (1999) used all the five dimensions of culture that Hofstede (1984, 1991) had identified. Her data suggested that except for the masculinity/femininity dimension, the other four dimensions identified by Hofstede correlated strongly with the public relations variables identified by the Excellence study. She noted that "[A]lthough conceptually affiliated with high power distance, . . . Confucianism may not be detrimental to achieving excellence in public relations" (p. 185). She reasoned that certain key characteristics of Confucianism such as the focus on harmonious living and placing high value on family morals logically linked Confucianism with excellence in public relations.

Kim (2003) used documentary analysis and personal interviews to assess the extent to which Confucian dynamism affected the global as well as domestic public relations practices of a South Korean multinational corporation. Her data revealed the organization changed its public relations strategies by region. It predominantly used the personal influence model, and to a lesser extent the mixed-motive model, in relating to domestic publics whereas it used the two-way models for its international publics. Interestingly, the corporation also reported that it employs different cultural strategies for domestic and global audiences. Its domestic public relations strategies were largely driven by Confucian culture whereas its global public relations strategies were designed to be "as rational as possible" (p. 90). In other words, societal culture had a greater bearing on its domestic public relations strategies whereas its global strategies were driven by what the author called "pragmatism" that one could construe as cultural relativism.

As Hofstede himself admitted, his dimensions of culture do not measure the variable in its entirety and so it is important that researchers go beyond these dimensions when attempting to link culture with public relations. This has been lacking in most of the small number of studies that currently exist on culture and public relations. Conducting country-specific studies focusing only on culture will greatly help unearth these nuances. In our analysis of public relations in Japan (Sriramesh and Takasaki, 2000), we found that the concept of *wa* (harmony) had a significant impact on public relations practice. Superior–subordinate relationships in Japanese organizations were influenced by the concept of *amae* (the desire to depend on another's goodness) where the manager attempts to satisfy the *amae* of subordinates who in turn reciprocate the gesture by remaining loyal. *Amae,* we argued, contributes to a strong corporate culture, which directly influences an organization's internal and external communication. We also found that *tataeme* (the public persona and behavior of an individual) and *honne* (the private self) play a crucial role in the way the Japanese communicate. The Japanese are reluctant to express disagreement publicly (practicing *tataeme*) because of the fear that it may destroy *wa* (social harmony). Instead, they prefer to engage in communication in informal and social settings (such as in a bar or restaurant) to build stable relationships, thus practicing *honne*.

The concept of *guanxi*, a uniquely Chinese cultural characteristic, is among the more widely discussed cultural dimensions (Chen, 1996, Kipnis, 1997, Tan, 2000, Huang, 2001, Aw, Tan, and Tan, 2002, Hung, 2003,). *Guanxi* appears to be the Chinese manifestation of the personal influence model of public relations. Like the personal influence model, *guanxi* involves building interpersonal relationships with strategic individuals such as journalists and government officials often by doing favors for them. Such relationship building helps open the "gates" so that when needed, these individuals can be relied upon to return the favor whether it be by publishing a news story or approving a government license.

In an analysis of public relations in three Asian cultures, we (Sriramesh, Kim and Takasaki, 1999) exhorted scholars to build a global theory of public relations by taking into account the *native's point of view* on how public relations is practiced within different political, economic, and cultural contexts. We had hoped that our three-nation comparison would be "the harbinger of many more such attempts because finding the uniqueness in public relations practices of a country is as important as finding commonalities among different countries" (p. 289). However, as will be dealt with at some length later in this chapter, there have been very few studies that specifically evaluate the relationship between societal culture and public relations. Further, to the best of the knowledge of this author, there appear to be no studies on this topic from Latin America, Central America, Africa, the Caribbean, or Eastern Europe—at least they do not exist in English.

In one of the few non-Asian studies that have linked societal culture with public relations, Vercic, L. Grunig and J. Grunig (1996) used the first four of Hofstede's dimensions and interpersonal trust (Tayeb, 1988), to assess the impact of Slovenian culture on public relations. They gathered data through "lengthy personal interviews" with three executives of Pristop Communications, the leading public relations agency in Slovenia. The authors discovered that the interviewees often disagreed among themselves about basic Slovenian cultural idiosyncrasies. The authors attributed these disagreements to factors such as the difficulty of describing one's own culture, the rapid changes that the Slovenian society had been undergoing after becoming an independent nation in 1990, and the varying changes that each of the interviewees had experienced personally because of these rapid post-independence socio-political changes.

This is further evidence that it is very challenging to measure culture. Verčič et al. summarized one of the key findings of their study: "whereas Sriramesh and White's (1992) propositions suggest that societal culture shapes public relations . . . [the Slovenian data] suggested that a professional public relations culture may loosen the grip of societal culture on practitioners, freeing them to help transform that larger culture" (pp. 55–56). This is a significant finding and one that is of great importance to the field because the impact of public relations in shaping societal culture has yet to be explored although it should be a significant area of research in the era of globalization where public relations professionals may be accused of cultural imperialism when they communicate with foreign markets on behalf of multinational corporations.

Vasquez and Taylor (2000) studied the relationship between Hofstede's four dimensions and the models of public relations by surveying 134 members of a Mid-Western city's PRSA chapter in the United States. They found that the power distance perceived by respondents was low and concluded that "American practitioners in this study were not working under heavily controlled or authoritative management" (p. 443). However, the authors seemed perplexed that their respondents preferred the one-way models which led them to ask: "Do public relations professionals practice one-way models because their organizations force them to?" (p. 443). Relying on their data, the authors affirmed that "the answer would have to be no" (p. 443). What the authors seem to have overlooked in this seeming contradiction is the fact that authoritarian corporate cultures can, and do, exist in egalitarian societal cultures (Sriramesh, J. Grunig, and Buffington, 1992, Sriramesh, J. Grunig, and Dozier, 1996). Therefore, in a relatively egalitarian societal culture such as the United States, it is easy to find many organizations with varying degrees of authoritarian corporate cultures. Many studies have repeatedly stressed that it is often the case that public relations managers do not set communication policies, which is often the primary reason why they have no control over the public relations strategies they employ.

It is clear from the above review that even though it is a small body of literature, much of the literature linking culture with public relations emanates from studies conducted in Asia. A significant gap exists as there are few studies in English that have linked societal culture and public relations in Latin America, the Caribbean, or Africa. These are serious deficiencies that need to be addressed by the global community of scholars if the public relations body of knowledge is to become holistic and comprehensive.

CORPORATE CULTURE AND PUBLIC RELATIONS:

In 1986, Downey remarked that "[A] great deal has been written of late about corporate culture." The author contended that the term had become a buzzword and that this increased attention had created "armies of corporate culture vultures" (p. 7). He posited that corporate culture "is the consequence of corporate identity" (p. 7). One would have to take serious issue with the author that corporate culture had become an "overused" term in 1986! In the 1980s, management scholars had just begun to discuss it as an important variable affecting organizational processes. More than two decades since Downey made that comment, the public relations body of knowledge has yet to fully identify the relationship between public relations and corporate culture!

Notwithstanding Downey's comment, the term corporate culture was very new to the public relations field in 1987. Based on the literature review for the Excellence study, Sriramesh, J. Grunig, and Buffington (1992) had made three propositions that conceptually linked public relations with corporate culture. They had largely relied on the work of scholars such as Ouchi (1981) and Pascale and Athos (1981) to identify two principal dimensions of organizational culture that were termed *authoritarian* and *participative* (Sriramesh, J. Grunig, and Dozier, 1996). The data from the Excellence project attempting to link organizational culture with public relations led to the following conclusion reported by L. Grunig, J. Grunig, and Dozier (2002):

> "[P]articipative culture is neither a necessary nor a sufficient condition for excellent public relations. An authoritarian culture does not make excellent public relations impossible because it does not correlate negatively with the Excellence factor. At the same time, a participative culture provides a more supportive, nurturing environment for excellent public relations than does an authoritarian culture. Nevertheless, a participative culture does not produce an excellent public relations department unless that department possesses the knowledge and skills to practice public relations symmetrically (p. 496).

One of the conclusions of the Excellence study was that public relations practitioners would find it easier to conduct strategic public relations in participatory rather than authoritarian cultures.

Cameron and McCollum (1993) also assessed the linkage between public relations and organizational culture. They used personal interviews and a survey to assess the link between the efficacy of internal communication and shared beliefs among managers and employees. They posited that "consensus between employees and management at the level of constructs, ideals, and beliefs is both a product and facilitator of communication between management and employees" (p. 244). Their data suggested that employees are more receptive to communication initiated by management when they perceive that they and organizational managers share similar beliefs about the organization's mission. The authors extrapolated from these findings that public relations practitioners should facilitate greater two-way communication between management and employees that would ultimately result in a stronger corporate culture.

L. Grunig's (1995) critique of the corporate culture of the U.S. Department of State based on her analysis of a sex discrimination class-action suit by women in the foreign service is a good example of a different genre of research on corporate culture. Instead of measuring indicators of corporate culture as is typical of corporate culture studies, she used "primary and secondary sources to . . . look at the subcultures that may exist within the larger organizational context" (p. 139). She found that organizational leaders, formal written codes, and the court order had all wanted, or required, the State Department to cease all sex discrimination. However, these seemingly powerful forces appeared to have consistently been over-ruled by "a grimly determined counterculture" that sought to "undermine significantly the emancipatory efforts of organizational management and the court" (p. 157).

Save for the above studies, one cannot find published information of empirical research that has specifically linked corporate culture with public relations. Everett's (1990) essay, while reaffirming some of the conceptualization of the Excellence study (both essays seem to have been prepared around the same time even though published at different dates), also offered a deeper understanding of the relationship between ethnoecology and public relations. Everett saw organizations as socio-cultural systems just as we (Sriramesh and White, 1992) had done. The significance of Everett's contribution is in the way he logically linked organizations with ethnoecology. Stating that "the view of organizations as sociocultural systems places such concepts squarely in the domain of organizational ethnography," the author contended that "it is this relationship that is best explored using the theoretical features and methodological tools of ethnoecology" (p. 248). He concluded that "an adequate understanding of organizational adaptation [with its environment] necessarily requires an account of interactions of the organizational culture and the organizational environment" (p. 248). It is pertinent to note here that organizational ethnography, a critical tool, has not been the preferred methodology for even a handful of studies in our field.

A few other studies have made references to the direct or indirect linkage between corporate culture and public relations or communication in organizations. Reber and Cameron (2003) mentioned corporate culture as a determinant of public relations and noted that "organizational characteristics. . .[such as] harmony among staff. . ." contribute to the willingness among organizations to enter into dialogue with their stakeholders. However, these authors did not gather empirical evidence on specific indicators of corporate culture, as it was not the primary focus of their study. Although Negandhi and Robey (1977) were not studying the impact of corporate culture on public relations, their remark—that studies focusing on the importance of multinational corporations to economic development have limited efficacy in increasing our understanding of organizational behavior in multicultural settings—is pertinent to our field. The authors posited that researchers should focus also on specific management practices in individual firms (that often reflect corporate culture), which have a greater impact in increasing our insight into effective management practices globally.

The preceding review of literature on societal and corporate culture educates us primarily about how much we do not know about the link between public relations and these two concepts. In keeping with the continued effort of this volume to push public relations scholarship to study the linkage between public relations and culture (and other environmental variables) more closely, the next section explores avenues for future research in this area. Given that most of the chapters were unable to find empirical evidence linking culture with public relations, this chapter challenges the scholarly community to give culture the attention it deserves or neglect it at our own peril.

THE FUTURE

Robust theories generate intellectual debates and provide avenues for further research thereby advancing the body of knowledge. As arguably the largest and most influential research project in the field of public relations, one can state with a great deal of confidence that the Excellence study has certainly achieved both of these lofty goals vis-à-vis culture and public relations. Among other things, it provided the field the conceptual linkage between public relations and socio-political variables (environmental variables) of which culture is a significant one. In addition, the study provided empirical data on the linkage between public relations and two dimensions of corporate culture—authoritarian and participative. Finally, it also provided the conceptual foundation for many studies that have contributed to the advancing of the field by gathering empirical data from different parts of the world on the relationship between culture and public relations.

However, as the preceding review clearly shows, we are far from making definitive, and predictive, linkages between the each of the environmental variables and public relations based on empirical evidence. Predictive ability is the most significant contribution scholarship can make to practice—if a practitioner is able to predict with some uncertainty which strategies and techniques may work in a given culture based on the body of knowledge, it helps build bridges between the two. However, even though culture is the most researched of these environmental variables, in reality, we have barely touched the surface of the impact of culture on public relations based on data from a variety of nations and cultures from all parts of the globe. The next section provides some avenues for future research pertaining to culture and public relations.

Expanding the Dimensions of Societal Culture

Hofstede (1984) himself admitted that his seminal study had serious limitations because culture, being malleable, was hard to define and even harder to measure. Defining culture as "the collective programming of the mind which distinguishes the members of one group from another" (p. 21), the author admitted that the dimensions of culture that he had identified were not comprehensive but only ones that he was able to measure (in fact it took him almost 15 years to add the fifth dimension to the original four). Scholars who have tried to link societal culture with public relations have almost exclusively relied on Hofstede's dimensions. This is partly because of the lucidity with which he described and operationalized these constructs. But it is also because of the ease of replicating his reliable and valid survey instrument.

As useful as all these studies have been in advancing our body of knowledge, it would not be an exaggeration to state that there is a dire need to explore other cultural dimensions that often may be unique to a society, and then explore their relationship with public relations as we had done in the study in Japan (Sriramesh and Takasaki, 2000). Whereas Hofstede sought to study cultural dimensions that were common across cultures, we should not overlook the importance of cultural characteristics that are often unique to a single culture and determine its linkage with public relations. It is pertinent to note here that although he recognized that the corporation he studied had "a distinct corporate identity— a company subculture. . ." for the most part he presented his data as representing the societal culture of the mangers from the 39 countries he studied. His study has often been the target of valid criticism that it did not recognize the impact of the corporate culture of the organization. It is important to note in this context that quantitative methods have their own limitations in studying culture, which is why many ethnographers have relied almost exclusively on qualitative methods (Mishler, 1986). This is also why Everett's (1990) advocacy of organizational ethnoecology is pertinent and useful to our field.

The concepts of *guanzi* and *mianzi* from Chinese culture are good examples of successful efforts to expand the number of societal cultural dimensions that affect public relations. As mentioned earlier, the concept of *guanzi* has been mentioned by several scholars as affecting public relations in Chinese cultures. However, the depth of this concept as well as the manifestation of the concept vis-à-vis public relations, has not yet been fully explored. For example, Huang (2000) offered *Gao guanxi,* which represents the use of personal relations or human networks for personal gain as a cultural extension of *guanxi* in Chinese societies. But its presence and any variations in manifestation have not yet been widely studied by other scholars. This is the case with *mianzi* (face) also, which has yet to be deeply studied and integrated into public relations pedagogy even though it is very relevant in many Asian cultures. Even some studies conducted in Chinese societies often merely refer to these concepts as influencing communication without empirically testing their presence and manifestation. Many, however, take the easy route and indicate these cultural constructs as areas that should be studied in "future research." For example, Lee (2004) studied corporate image in a *Chinese-based context* (emphasis added) and yet did not assess the link between culture and corporate image. Instead, the author suggested *mianzi* and *guanxi* as avenues for future research!

The concepts of *wa, amae, tatamae,* and *honne* have added to our expanding knowledge of Japanese culture and its impact on public relations (Sriramesh and Takasaki, 2000). However, we have yet to explore the relationship between public relations and concepts such as *onjoshugi* (managerial paternalism) discussed by Raz (2002). The author mentioned *katachi de hairu* or "entering self-fulfilment through the rules" as one of the ways Japanese employees (*kobun*) define their relationship with the organization. Yoshikawa (1993) discussed the intermediated communication pattern that Japanese often have used to bring credibility to interpersonal communication. Sometimes, even an introductory letter from a third person who knows the principals serves the purpose of breaking the ice between two people and gets the communication underway. The business card (*meishi*) also serves a similar, important, role. We have yet to study individual societal cultures deeply enough to bring out the impact of such unique dimensions on public relations.

Interpersonal Trust

Although in the literature review for the Excellence project Sriramesh and White (1992) identified interpersonal trust as a key dimension of societal culture and one that has a great influence on public relations practice, only one study (Verčič, J. Grunig, and L. Grunig, 1996) has so far studied the impact of this dimension on public relations. In fact, the significance of interpersonal communication on public relations activities is one of the most important, yet least studied, linkages in the public relations body of knowledge.

In the early 1990s, the "personal influence model" was introduced as a potential fifth model of public relations extending the original four models proposed by Grunig and Hunt (1984). Although studies in three diverse cultures (Sriramesh, 1988, Huang, 1990, Lyra, 1991) initially confirmed the presence of this model and studies from other countries have done so since then, there is clearly a dearth of research that assesses the different ways in which culture affects the interpersonal relationships that the personal influence model describes—in both public relations strategy and practice. Personal influence has been studied by other allied disciplines such as mass communication since the mid-1950s (Sriramesh, forthcoming). Trust is a key ingredient that gives credibility to a source in any communication. Interpersonal trust, then, should take primacy in the way public relations practitioners practice the personal influence model in building relationships with key stakeholders. There can be little doubt that the strategies of developing and maintaining interpersonal trust are culture-specific. Yet, the body of knowledge of public relations has yet to study the linkage between culture, interpersonal trust, and public relations.

Relationship Patterns

The notion of relationship building is related to interpersonal trust although this linkage has not yet been recognized in the literature. Scholars (Hon and Grunig, 1999, Ledingham and Bruning, 2000, Huang, 2001, Hung, 2003) have proposed relationship management as one of the key activities of public relations practitioners. Hon and Grunig offered six relationship outcomes and suggested ways of measuring them: trust, control mutuality, relationship commitment, relationship satisfaction, communal relationships, and exchange relationships. However, culture, although fundamental to any relationship building effort (including all the six outcomes listed by Hon and Grunig), has yet to be integrated into the discussion of relationship building.

Hung's (2003) is among only two empirical studies that have attempted to integrate culture and relationship building. She found that Chinese cultural characteristics such as family orientation, relational orientation (role formalization, relational interdependence, face, favor, relational harmony, relational fatalism, and relational determination) influenced the relationship cultivation strategies of a sample of multinational companies operating in China. Based on her empirical data from an earlier study (Huang, 1997), Huang (2001) added *face and favor* as a fifth relationship dimension, which is laudable. However, the impact of culture on the other four dimensions has yet to be established empirically even though conceptually it appears very logical that such a relationship should exist.

Further, it is also important to assess the cross-cultural nature of relationship building as we live in an increasingly globalizing world. F. Kluckhohn (1953) identified three relationship patterns. She stated that the *individual* pattern is typical of Western cultures where the existence of nuclear families ensures that an individual's relationship within the family is limited in scope and intensity. The *collateral* pattern represents cultures where the family sphere is wider than that of a nuclear family (to include grandparents, uncles, cousins, etc.) and the intensity of relationship is also greater than the individual pattern. The *linear* pattern is indicative of an even wider circle of family members to include distant relatives that may often include the tribe or clan. Future studies should assess the impact that acculturation into one of these patterns has on the way organizational decision makers and public relations practitioners of different cultures manage their relationships with key publics on behalf of the organization.

High and Low Context Cultures

Hall was among the first to identify the differences between high and low context cultures. Despite its importance to success in communication, the relationship between high and low context in culture remains one of the under-researched concepts in public relations. There is a need to assess how context affects interpersonal communication and relationship building, which is crucial to the success of public relations outreach with external publics. Further, context must affect organizational communication internally (perhaps as an indicator of the corporate culture of an organization) and therefore also needs to be studied. Myths, stories, rights, and rituals, are all discussed as ingredients of corporate culture. These also provide the context for internal communication in organizations and therefore need to be studied and integrated into public relations pedagogy.

Finally, we also need to keep in mind that culture affects, and is affected by, other environmental factors such as political system, economic system and level of development, media system, and activism. This relationship is yet to be empirically established and incorporated into the public relations body of knowledge. For example, the spiral of silence theory, which is influenced by the political system of a society, invariably affects the level of openness and communication patterns of individuals of a culture. These are as yet unexplored and certainly not integrated into the body of knowledge despite their relevance and importance.

CONCLUSION

As noted in Chapter 1, Freedom House called the 20th century *Democracy's Century.* It is no coincidence that modern public relations flourished concomitantly with political pluralism in the 20th century. Yet, we have yet to empirically link political systems with public relations practice based on data from different parts of the world. For example, in a study of organizations in Shanghai we found the impact of political ideology on public relations in the form of the *lun zi pai bei* system (Sriramesh and Enxi, 2004). Because those Chinese who are now in their 50s grew up during the cultural revolution when many did not have access to higher education, the Chinese government has an affirmative program that actively promotes employees based on seniority (measured in the number of years one has worked in an organization) rather than on professional qualifications or suitability for the position. As a result, we found instances where the public relations managers of some government agencies had previously been steel mill workers, school teachers, and even chefs!

If the 20th century was Democracy's Century, the 21st century has exploded as the Century of Globalization. In such an environment, where peoples of various cultures are becoming ever more interdependent, it is sad and alarming that the concept of culture is being treated almost as an afterthought in many disciplines including public relations. For example, the *Journal of Public Relations Research,* arguably the premier journal oriented to empirical research in our field, welcomed the new millennium by publishing a special issue titled "Public Relations **Values** [emphasis added] in the New Millennium." The thoughtful essays in that volume, from the leading scholars of our field, discussed the values of the profession because "professions are based on values and a body of knowledge to teach and enhance values" (Toth and Pavlik, 2000, p. 1). Even though values of every profession are steeped in culture, only one of these essays made a mention of culture, albeit briefly, to argue that "[individualistic] Anglo cultures need symmetrical public relations even more than organizations in collective cultures" (J. Grunig, 2000, p. 39).

The other essays in this special issue very articulately discussed the importance of activist values (Dozier and Lauzen, 2000), feminist values (L. Grunig, Toth, and Hon, 2000), rhetorical values (Heath, 2000), and postmodernist values (Holtzhausen, 2000). It is an indication of how culture's time has not yet come in our field that all these discussions seem to have been presented almost completely devoid of any discussion of the impact of culture even though concepts such as values and ethics are so deeply rooted in culture as are all human beings. All the rhetorical theories currently discussed in public relations literature are based in Western philosophy even though Indian and Chinese culture, for example, have a more ancient history that includes rhetorical principles. Public relations scholars, especially from other parts of the world such as Asia, Africa, Latin America, and the Caribbean, most of which have longer histories of human habitation, should take it up as a challenge to integrate the cultural values of their societies into the public relations body of knowledge and help expand it. This appears to be the only way of reducing the extreme ethnocentricity that exists in the current body of knowledge of public relations. It is hoped that many of the chapters of this volume contribute to increasing our understanding of the cultures from around the world and are harbingers of even greater awareness and research.

Culture (or multiculturalism) is almost an afterthought in most public relations books and textbooks. The challenge before us is to conduct public relations research studies indigenous to other parts and cultures of the world such as Asia, Africa, Latin America, and the Caribbean. This is the only way of reducing the ethnocentricity of the body of knowledge thus making it more culturally diverse and holistic. Students who receive training in such a holistic system would truly be "global citizens," which is what it will take for them to succeed in, and be effective contributors to, a global and culturally integrated world.

REFERENCES

Aw, A., Tan, S.K., and Tan, R. (2002) Guanxi and Public Relations: An Exploratory Qualitative Study of the Public Relations-Guanxi Phenomenon in Singapore Firms, Paper presented to the Public Relations Division of the International Communication Association, Seoul, South Korea, July 15–19.

Cameron, G. T., and McCollum, T. (1993). Competing corporate cultures: A multi-method, cultural analysis of the role of internal communication. *Journal of Public Relations Research, 5*(4), pp. 217–250.

Chen, N. (1996). Public Relations in China: The Introduction and Development of an Occupational Field. In H. Culberton and N. Chen (Eds.). *International public relations: A comparative analysis* (pp. 121–154). Mahwah, NJ: Lawrence Erlbaum Associates.

Collectivism, collaboration, and societal corporatism as core professional values in public relations. *Journal of Public Relations Research, 12*(1), pp. 2–48.

CPRE (1999). Public relations education for the 21st century: A port of entry. http://www.prsa.org/_Resources/resources/pre21.asp?ident=rsrc6 (accessed May 23, 2005).

Downey, S. M. (1986). The relationship between corporate culture and corporate identity. *Public Relations Quarterly, 31*(4), pp 7–12.

Dozier, D. M., and Lauzen, M. M. (2000). Liberating the intellectual domain from the practice: Public relations, activism, and the role of the scholar. *Journal of Public Relations Research, 12*(1), pp. 2–22.

Everett, J. L. (1990). Organizational culture and ethnoecology in public relations theory and practice. *Public Relations Research Annual Vol 2,* pp. 235–252.

Freedom House, (2000). Democracy's century: A survey of global political change in the 20th century. Available at: http://www.freedomhouse.org/reports/century.html, retrieved on June 4, 2005.

Grunig, J. E., and Hunt, T. (1984). *Managing public relations.* New York: Holt, Rinehart, and Winston.

Grunig, L. A. (1995). The consequences of culture for public relations: The case of women in the foreign service. *Journal of Public Relations Research, 7*(2), pp. 139–161.

Grunig, L. A., Grunig, J. E., and Dozier, D. M. (2002). *Excellent public relations and effective organizations: A study of communication management in three countries.* Mahwah, NJ: Lawrence Erlbaum Associates.

Grunig, L. A., Toth, E. L., and Hon, L. C. (2000). Feminist values in public relations. *Journal of Public Relations Research, 12*(1), pp. 49–68.

Heath, R. L. (2000). A rhetorical perspective on the values of public relations: Crossroads and pathways toward concurrence. *Journal of Public Relations Research, 12*(1), pp. 69–92.

Hickson, D. J., Hinings, C. R., McMillan, C. J., and Schwitter, J. P. (1974). The culture-free context of organization structure: A tri-national comparison. *Sociology,* 8, 59–80.

Hofstede, G. (1984). *Culture's consequences.* Beverly Hills: Sage.

Hofstede, G. (1991). *Culture and organization: Software of the mind.* London: McGraw-Hill.

Holtzhausen, D. R. (2000). Postmodern values in public relations. *Journal of Public Relations Research, 12*(1), pp. 93–114.

Hon, L. C., and Grunig, J. E. (1999). *Guidelines for measuring relationships in public relations.* Gainesville, FL: Institute for Public Relations.

Huang, Y. H. (1990). Risk communication, models of public relations and anti-nuclear activities: A case study of a nuclear power plant in Taiwan. Unpublished Master's thesis, University of Maryland, College Park.

Huang, Y. H. (1997). Toward the contemporary Chinese philosophy of public relations: A perspective from the theory of global public relations. Paper presented to the Public Relations Division at the 47th annual conference of the International Communication Association, Quebec, Canada, May.

Huang, Y. H. (2000). The personal influence model and *gao guanxi* in Tainwan Chinese public relations. *Public Relations Review, 26,* 216–239.

Huang, Y. H. (2001). OPRA: A cross-cultural, multiple-item scale for measuring organization-public relationships. *Journal of Public Relations Research, 13*(1), 61–90.

Hung, C. J. F. (2003). Culture, relationship cultivation, and relationship outcomes: A qualitative evaluation on multinational companies' relationship management in China. Paper presented at the Public Relations Division in the 53rd annual conference of International Communication Association, San Diego, May.

Kim, H. S. (2003). Exploring global public relations in a Korean multinational organization in the context of Confucian culture. *Asian Journal of Communication, 13*(2), pp. 65–95.

Kipnis, A. (1997). *Producing Guanxi: Sentiment, self, and subculture in a North China village.* Durham, NC: Duke University Press.

Kluckhohn, F. (1953). Dominant and variant value orientations. In C. Kluckhohn and H. Murray (Eds.), *Personality in nature, society, and culture.* New York: Alfred A. Knopf, pp. 342–357.

Ledingham, J. A., and Bruning, S. D. (2000). A longitudinal study of organization-public relationships: Defining the role of communication in the practice of relationship management. In J. A. Ledingham and S. D. Bruning (Eds.), *Public relations as relationship management: A relational approach in the study and practice of public relations* (pp. 55–69). Mahwah, NJ: Lawrence Erlbaum Associates.

Ledingham, J. A., and Bruning, S. D. (2000). *Public relations as relationship management: A relational approach to the study and practice of public relations.* Hillsdale, NJ: Lawrence Erlbaum Associates.

Lee, B. K. (2004). Corporate image examined in a Chinese-based context: Study of a young educated public in Hong Kong. *Journal of Public Relations Research, 16*(1), pp. 1–34.

Lyra, A. (1991). Public relations in Greece: Models, roles and gender. Unpublished Master's thesis, University of Maryland, College Park, MD.

Mishler, E. G. (1986). *Research interviewing: context and narrative.* Cambridge, MA: Harvard University Press.

Mulder, M. (1977). *The daily power game.* Leyden: Martinus Nijhoff.

Negandhi, A. R., and Robey, D. (1977). Understanding organizational behavior in multinational and multi-cultural settings. *Human Resource Management, 16*(1). pp. 16–24.

Ouchi, W. G. (1981). *Theory Z: How American business can meet the Japanese challenge.* Reading, MA: Addison-Wesley.

Pascale, R. T., and Athos, A. G. (1981). *The art of Japanese management.* New York: Simon & Schuster.

Public Relations Body of Knowledge Task Force Report (1988). *Public Relations Review,* XIV(1), pp. 3–40.

Raz, A. E. (2002). *Emotions at work: Normative control, organizations, and culture in Japan and America.* London: Harvard University Press.

Reber, B. H., and Cameron, G. T. (2003). Measuring contingencies: Using scales to measure public relations practitioner limits to accommodation. *Journalism and Mass Communication Quarterly, 80*(2), pp. 431–446.

Rhee, Y. (1999). Confucian culture and excellent public relations: A study of generic principles and specific applications in South Korean public relations practice. Unpublished Master's thesis submitted to the University of Maryland at College Park, Maryland, U.S.A.

Smircich, L. (1983). Concepts of culture and organizational analysis. *Administrative Science Quarterly,* 28, 339–358.

Sriramesh, K. (1992). The impact of societal culture on public relations: Ethnographic evidence from India. *Public Relations Review, 18*(2), pp. 201–211.

Sriramesh, K. (1996). Power distance and public relations: An ethnographic study of southern Indian organizations. In H. Culbertson and Ni Chen (Eds.), *International public relations: A comparative analysis.* Hillsdale, NJ: Lawrence Erlbaum Associates, pp. 171–190.

Sriramesh, K. (2000). The models of public relations in India. *Journal of Communication Management, 4*(3), pp. 225–239.

Sriramesh, K. (2002). The dire need for multiculturalism in public relations education: An Asian perspective. *Journal of Communication Management, 7*(1), 54–70.

Sriramesh, K., (2003). The missing link: Multiculturalism and public relations education. In K. Sriramesh and D. Verčič (Eds.) *The global public relations handbook: Theory, research, and practice.* Mahwah, NJ: Lawrence Erlbaum Associates, Inc. pp. 505–521.

Sriramesh, K., and Enxi, L. (2004). Public relations practices and socio-economic factors: A case study of different organizational types in Shanghai. *Journal of Communication Studies, 3*(4), pp. 44–77.

Sriramesh, K., and Grunig, J. E. (1988, November). Toward a Cross-Cultural Theory of Public Relations: Preliminary Evidence from India. Paper presented to the panel on New Frontiers in the International

Management Environment, Association for the Advancement of Policy, Research and Development in the Third World, Myrtle Beach, NC.

Sriramesh, K., and Takasaki, M. (2000). The impact of culture on Japanese public relations. *Journal of Communication Management 3*(4), pp. 337–352.

Sriramesh, K., and White, J. (1992). Societal Culture and Public Relations. In J. E. Grunig (Ed.), *Excellence in Public Relations and Communications Management: Contributions to Effective Organizations*. Hillsdale, NJ: Lawrence Erlbaum Associates., pp. 597–616.

Sriramesh, K., Grunig, J. E., and Buffington, J. (1992). Corporate Culture and Public Relations. In J. E. Grunig (Ed.), *Excellence in Public Relations and Communications Management: Contributions to Effective Organizations*. Hillsdale, NJ: Lawrence Erlbaum Associates., pp. 577–596.

Sriramesh, K., Grunig, J. E., and Dozier, D. (1996). Observation and Measurement of Organizational Culture: Development of Indices of Participative and Authoritarian Cultures. *Journal of Public Relations Research, 8*(4), pp. 229–262.

Sriramesh, K., Kim, Y., and Takasaki, M. (1999). Public relations in three Asian cultures: An analysis. *Journal of Public Relations Research 11*(4), pp. 271–292.

Tan, S. L. (2000). Guanxi and Public Relations in Singapore: An Exploratory Study. Master's thesis, Nanyang Technological University, Singapore.

Tayeb, M. H. (1988). *Organizations and national culture: A comparative analysis.* London: Sage.

Toth, E. L., and Pavlik, J. V. (2000). Public relations values in the new millennium. *Journal of Public Relations Research, 12*(1), pp. 1–2.

Vazquez, G. M., and Taylor, M. (2000). What cultural values influence American public relations practitioners? *Public Relations Review, 25*(4), pp. 433–449.

Verčič, D., Grunig, L. A., and Grunig, J. (1996). Global and specific principles of public relations: Evidence from Slovenia, In H. Culbertson and N. Chen (Eds.), *International public relations: A comparative analysis.* Mahwah, NJ: Lawrence Erlbaum Associates. pp. 31–66.

Yoshikawa, M. J. (1993). Japanese and American modes of communication and implications for managerial and organizational behavior. In W. Dissanayake (Ed.), *Communication theory: The Asian perspective,* (pp. 150–182). Singapore: The Asian Media Information and Communication Centre.

4

THE MASS MEDIA AND PUBLIC RELATIONS

KRISHNAMURTHY SRIRAMESH

DEJAN VERČIČ

Almost every basic textbook on public relations talks about the significance of the relationship between the mass media and public relations. Newsom, Turk, and Kruckeberg (2000) advised that every public relations practitioner should establish a positive relationship with the media, which elicits "extra consideration when the institution he or she represents may be under attack" (p. 418). In their book entitled *Media Relations,* Howard and Mathews (2000) stressed the need to practice strategic media relations as part of an overall program of public relations and proposed several aspects of effective media relations such as the characteristics of a good spokesperson. Cutlip, Center, and Broom (2000) reiterated that working with the mass media is "a major part of many practitioners' jobs" (p. 323).

Sallot and Johnson (2006) reviewed the relationship between journalists and public relations practitioners over a 15-year period and concluded that journalists interviewed in 2002–2004 valued public relations sources more than those interviewed between 1991–96. The authors also concluded that on average, journalists reported that about 44 percent of media content in the US came from public relations sources. Cameron, Sallot, and Curtin (1997) noted that since the 1960s, more than 150 studies have examined some aspect of the relationships between journalists and public relations practitioners, and in general found that 25 percent to 80 percent of news content is influenced by the "information subsidies" given by public relations practitioners. The majority of the studies conducted since the 1960s that Cameron et al. (1997) reviewed also found the relationship between journalists and public relations practitioners to be contentious but one that they chose to tolerate because of the obvious benefits to both. Sallot and Johnson (2006) commented that "jealousy may fuel some journalists' negative perceptions [of public relations practitioners] because they resent the higher salaries and better working conditions they perceive [public relations] practitioners to enjoy" (p. 157).

Information and Communication Technologies (popular as "new media") have changed many of the dynamics of the relationship between public relations and traditional mass media (print and broadcast media). This trend is bound to continue over the next decades and has a direct bearing on the work of public relations practitioners. When new media technologies were just taking a foothold in the mid-1990s, Pavlik (1996) stated that "journalists, public relations practitioners, and advertisers all use new technology to . . . increase their work efficiency and speed, as well as reduce cost" (p. 6). This relationship is ever more significant in the current media rich environment of the 21st century. Guinivin (2007) discussed how traditional media relations tactics may yield lower returns when dealing with new media such as blogs. The author suggested that organizations should monitor the discussions in the blogosphere using specialized services such as Technorati, Daypop, BuzzMetrics, and VMI. Traditional asymmetrical worldviews also do not work and organizations must engage bloggers through open communication. Constant monitoring of the blogosphere also helps engage activists "in real time" before the damage is done.

Silverstone (1999) suggested, "we should be thinking about media as a process, as a process of mediation" (p. 13). Livingstone (2008) noted that in the context of the Internet, instead of "audiences,' researchers conceptualize and observe "users,' whereas "audience' research is reframed into studying and critiquing media literacy. Reber and Kim (2006) analyzed the use of web sites by activist groups for media relations activities and found that most activist groups they studied did not use the web sites effectively for building relationships with mass mediapersons. For example, although these web sites had inter- active features for members of the public, their press rooms were not equally well-equipped to render the same, if not a higher, level of interactivity with journalists.

As noted in Chapter 1, mass media often play a key role in shaping the images of organizations and nations. But the media also tend to sterotype and often provide, wittingly or unwittingly, distortions of reality. For example, Servaes (1991) investigated the reporting of the U.S. invasion of Grenada in 1982 by leading newspapers in six European democra- cies: Britain, Holland, Spain, France, Germany, and Switzerland. He found media coverage of this incident in these countries to be subjective and often based on extraneous factors such as the political relationship between the country and the U.S. The author remarked that the coverage by the newspapers of these six West European countries "frames the story as an East–West conflict with the United States concerned foremost with Communist "danger' and less interested in Grenada itself" (p. 36). Addressing a similar theme, Entman (1991) studied how the media can influence international opinion by contrasting the coverage of the Soviet downing of KAL Flt 007 and the downing of an Iran Air flight by the U.S. Navy ship *Vincennes*. The author concluded that media portrayal influenced many in the audience to view the former incident as "a moral outrage" but concluded that the latter was the tragic result of a "technical problem."

This review points to the power that the media have in shaping public opinion nationally and internationally. It is the recognition of this critical linkage between media and public relations that has led public relations professionals to give primacy to media relations. However, public relations practitioners need to understand how the media operate in a variety of countries before developing strategies for conducting effective media relations. The most popular source for understanding different global media environments is the literature in the field of mass communication that describes normative theories of global media systems.

THEORIES OF MEDIA SYSTEMS AND THEIR RELEVANCE TO INTERNATIONAL PUBLIC RELATIONS

Because the mass media have enormous power to influence public opinion, it behooves global public relations professionals to understand how the media operate in different societies if they are to establish a strong working relationship with the media of different regions. This sentiment was echoed by Yoon (2005) who stated that most previous literature on media relations has treated the subject unidimensionally from the perspective of information subsidies that public relations practitioners provide the mass media—"the action dimension." The author suggested that it was equally important for public relations practitioners to focus on how the media operate in a society—the knowledge dimension. The author offered eight criteria to operationalize the "knowledge dimension" of a media environment: media deadlines, the kinds of stories that would appeal to target journalists, key journalists that needed to be contacted and how to reach them, realizing the importance of speedy response to media queries, and maintaining good relationships with journalists. However, the author did not mention knowledge of the media system (the philosophy that guides the media of a country or region). Getting *access* (which will be described at length later in this chapter) to the media to place stories there, is one of the objectives of most media relations activities.

The theories of the press first proposed by Siebert, Peterson, and Schramm (1956), and subsequently expanded by others, have helped us understand media culture around the world. However, the world has changed significantly since many of these theories were proposed, making some of the normative theories proposed then obsolete, but they are a good foundation on which one can build new frameworks for understanding international media systems. Therefore, this section briefly reviews the literature on global media philosophies.

In their seminal work, Siebert et al. (1956) identified four theories that they argued help explain the media cultures prevailing in most countries of the world including Asia. The *authoritarian theory* described the situation where the State views the mass media as its instrument at all times. The *libertarian theory* described societies that provide the media unfettered freedom, particularly from government control, so that they are free to report a variety of views available in a free marketplace of ideas as well as serve the "watchdog" function of keeping the all-powerful government in check. The *social responsibility theory* proposed by Siebert et al. was an extension of the libertarian theory but unlike the libertarian theory, which assumed that anyone who had the means and the inclination could use the media to publish anything, the social responsibility theory required the media to observe certain professional norms and codes of conduct in exercising their editorial freedom. The final media theory that Siebert et al. proposed was the *Soviet Communist theory,* which the authors saw as an extension of the authoritarian theory. Under this theory, the media were considered subservient to the proletariat, represented by the Communist party. A major difference between the Soviet Communist media theory and the authoritarian theory was that whereas the former described the use of the media for bringing about societal changes that the Communist party wanted, the latter described a system where the media were used for maintaining the status quo.

Lowenstein (in Merrill and Lowenstein, 1971) revised Siebert et al.'s theories and suggested that when distinguishing between media systems of different countries, the type of press ownership should be taken into account in addition to media philosophy. These authors identified three types of press ownership: *private* (individual ownership of the media supported primarily by advertising and subscriptions), *multi-party* (mostly ownership by political parties), and *government* (funded by the government and often subsidized by license fees collected by the government). Lowenstein also modified the Siebert et al. typology renaming the *Soviet Communist* as *Social-centralist* and *social responsibility* as *social libertarian.* Lowenstein argued that the new nomenclature removed the connotative baggage of the previous terms by eliminating the word *communist* from the former and by highlighting the libertarian characteristics of the latter. Later, Lowenstein (in Merrill and Lowenstein, 1979) added a fifth theory, *social-authoritarian*, which represented the use of the media by the governments of developing nations principally toward achieving national development goals, often at the expense of editorial freedom.

Merrill (1974) critiqued the models offered by Siebert et al. and Lowenstein as being too linear where the various theories appear on a freedom–control spectrum. The author instead saw the relationship between libertarianism and authoritarianism as being cyclical and represented libertarianism and authoritarianism as being on opposite sides of a closed circle. The author proposed that the path from media freedom to totalitarianism may proceed through socialism or capitalism. Hachten (1981, 1993) proposed a five-concept typology modifying the theories of Siebert et al., Lowenstein, and Merrill. In addition, he proposed a new *revolutionary theory* that described the use of illegal or subversive media especially by activists. A good example of the revolutionary theory would be the underground media that helped generate massive support for the movement for democracy in China in 1989 that led to the massive uprising at Tiananmen Square. Merrill combined the *libertarian* and *social responsibility* theories into the *Western* media theory. He removed the connotation to the Soviet system calling it simply *communist* theory and renamed Lowenstein's *social authoritarian* theory as *developmental* theory.

In their analysis of global media environments, Martin and Chaudhary (1983) divided the world into the First, Second and Third worlds representing the developed West, the communist bloc, and the developing countries respectively based on political ideology and economic and industrial development. Differences between these systems, the authors contended, are reflected in the differences in media content and what is news in one society need not be so in another. In developed countries, news is generally traded as a commodity because viewers and readers affect the bottom line, while in developing countries news reporting revolves around educational and national developmental goals. Those in power, who directly or indirectly control the media in developing nations, often determine which information is in conformity with such goals.

Martin and Chaudhary (1983) further classified mass media as autonomous or ancillary. The former, these authors argued, "make their own rules of operation, set their own goals, and decide on their own content" (p. 10). According to them, the purpose of autonomous media is seen in their efforts to publish or broadcast for "profit, self-aggrandizement, or out of altruism." Ancillary media, the authors stated, are owned or directly controlled by a government, political party, or an organization such as a religious system, with propaganda as the main purpose of communication. Most Third World countries fall into this category. Explaining the extent of persuasiveness of the media in different systems, Martin and Chaudhary further posited that while the Western audience recognizes the rights of its autonomous media to persuade readers, listeners and viewers, it does not accept everything media persons say. Its acceptance of persuasive messages is situational. The authors argued that in the Third World, people "expect and accept" persuasive communication from their media because of factors such as culture, tradition, or simply a lack of competing information. Where such media are ancillary, as is the case in most developing countries where the broadcast media are controlled by the government, they invariably disseminate the official version of facts and events. The media of these countries conform to the role of "nation building," disseminating much of their information mixed with officially sanctioned opinion or diktat. Critics of course argue, and not totally inaccurately, that the boundaries between nation building and perpetuating the continued rule of those in political power is blurred in most Third World countries.

The media systems concept is out-dated because of the sea change that the world has undergone in the 1990s. As Hiebert (1992) stated: "political ideology is no longer an adequate way to divide up the world's communication systems" (p. 125). Instead, we ought to see mass communication as process where communication is determined to have taken place only when the dissemination of *effective* messages takes place irrespective of the source, medium, or the content of the message. Strategic public relations professionals recognize that in order for messages to be effective, they have to meet the needs of the publics, and thus be consonant with the use of two-way communication between source and receiver.

MASS MEDIA RESEARCH AND ITS RELEVANCE TO GLOBAL PUBLIC RELATIONS

Besides understanding media systems, we need to understand how they influence our world. We find the seven traditions of mass media research offered by Rosengren (2000) relevant to studying the relationship between the mass media and public relations. The *uses and gratification research* explores the way individuals use the mass media. While there can be no doubt that media do influence people, it is also obvious that this influence is not linear nor is it straightforward because individuals are not simply passive receivers. Many critics of the contemporary global media structures see hegemony and dominance producing boringly similar media artifacts globally and thereby creating similar cultural patterns. But, there are others such as Thussu (2000, p. 206) who hold a contrarian view: "To give just one example—despite 200 years of British colonial subjugation, a vast majority of Indians practice their own religion, speak their own language and pursue their traditional culture. It is therefore unlikely that a CNN or an MTV will achieve what the British Empire failed to do." The truth, we feel, is somewhere in the middle of these two extremes because, taking the Indian example, a native Indian would see a vast change in the India (especially urban areas) of today in comparison with what it was, say, twenty years ago.

A second research tradition is *effects research* that looks for short- and long-term media effects on the individual. One could contend that nowhere is this more seriously considered than in marketing communication. Schultz and Kitchen (2000) published four case studies (on British Telecom, De Beers diamonds company, Dow Chemical and Orange PLC mobile telecommunications company) demonstrating international marketing communication producing behavioral effects in many countries around the globe.

The stream of research focusing on *diffusion of news* explores the process by which news is collected and disseminated to individual members of the population. Its effects are expected in hours and days, but as discussed by Jefford and Rabinovitz (1994) in their critique of *Operation Desert Storm* in Kuwait/Iraq (1990–1991), the 1990s brought us "total television" (Engelhardt, 1994) with "real time' (Caldarola, 1994) coverage of the war that perhaps accidentally enabled CNN to emerge as an international broadcaster (Cowan Shulman, 1994).

Agenda-setting is another school of thought that describes the process by which the media suggest to people what to think about by suggesting that the issues they cover are to be given primacy. Or, as Dearing and Rogers (1996, p. 2) stated, it is about "a hierarchy of importance at a point in time." The effects of agenda setting are usually expected in weeks and months. Agenda setting theory also helps one explore how the human tragedy in Darfur can be so neglected, for example, while "the war on terrorism" is deemed as being so important.

The spiral of silence theory helps explain which views and opinions are perceived as being "correct" or "proper" and which are deemed "less correct" or "less proper" in a society. Chomsky (1989; Herman and Chomsky 1994) directly accused the public relations industry for actively engaging in anti-democratic activities that "manufacture consent" and maintain "necessary illusions": "Across a broad spectrum of articulate opinion, the fact that the voice of the people is heard in democratic societies is considered a problem to be overcome by ensuring that the public voice speaks the right words." (Chomsky 1989, p. 19) Elites control the media and control what is to be considered "correct" and "proper". Its effects are expected in months and years.

Cultivation research is about a process by which the common culture of society is "cultivated" by the mass media. Thussu (2000) in this context raised a question of globalization of Western culture and globalization of the English language as the *lingua franca* of global commerce and communication. Following Ritzer's (1996) notion of *The McDonaldization of Society*, one could explore McDonaldization of the globe facilitated by the global dominance of the Western, predominantly US, media—both online and offline. The effects of cultivation are usually expected in years and decades and in international relations they are seen as a form of (soft) power (for more details see the chapter of VanDyke and Verčič in this book).

The seventh research tradition is that of *Öffentlichkeit à la Habermas* (translated in English as *public sphere*) as a summative result of all the above effects shaped by the overall institutional structure of society. Its effects are expected in decades or even centuries. The notion of *public sphere* is particularly interesting when viewed from the prism of globalization. Two examples from as far back as 1969 help illustrate this point. McLuhan (1969) suggested that television images of the Vietnam war in American households converted viewers into participants in the conflict and offered the notion of "global village." Brzezinski (1969) proposed that "new" technologies of the time (television and telecommunications) made the United States the first "global society." Yet this was only a modest introduction to technology-enabled globalization.

The Internet provided the platform for the next phase, while convergence of the Internet and mobile telephony combined with the development of mobile satellite communication (Kishan Thussu 2000) will open a completely new opportunity with direct effects to international public relations practice. *The Economist* (2008, p. 5) reported recently that "[A]ccording to the International Telecommunications Union, 3.3 billion people, more than half the world's population, now subscribe to mobile-telephone services," and commented that "the internet at last looks set to change the whole world." See Figure 4.1.

The Economist (2008), in a special report on mobile technology, noted the use of SMS text messages by the masses leading to the overthrow of Philippine president Joseph Estrada in 2001, while in 2006 America's National Democratic Institute (NDI) used the near general availability of mobile telephones to monitor the national elections in Montenegro that "instantly became the standard for monitoring other precarious elections." In 2007, *Forbes* dedicated its 90th anniversary issue to the power of networks enabled by contemporary digital technologies, and 28 experts and leaders presented their views as important for the global corporate elite readership of the magazine.

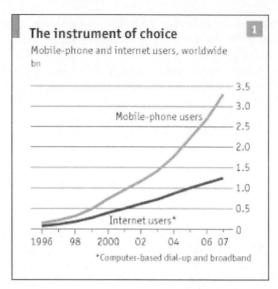

FIG. 4.1   Mobile-phone and internet users, worldwide (reproduced from *The Economist* magazine with permission)

PUBLIC RELATIONS AND THE MASS MEDIA: A REFORMULATION

This chapter proposes that there is a need to reconceptualize ways of understanding media environments around the world especially as far as public relations is concerned. As part of this reformulation, it advocates a framework of three factors (media control, media diffusion, and media access), which should help the international public relations professional in designing an appropriate media relations strategy in most parts of the world. It is hoped that framework will help the global public relations professional understand the media environment in a country and thereby assist in maintaining effective channels of communication between client organizations and relevant media around the world. Further, the framework should help researchers in studying the nexus between the media and effective public relations practices in different countries.

Media Control

In the latest annual survey of freedom of the press in 195 countries and territories, researchers from Freedom House found that "[T]he state of global press freedom declined in 2006, with particularly worrisome trends evident in Asia, the former Soviet Union, and Latin America" (Karlekar, 2007, p. 1). The report also noted that:

> Despite notable improvements in a number of countries, gains were generally overshadowed by a continued, relentless assault on independent news media in a group of geopolitically crucial states, including Russia, Venezuela, Iran, and China, as well as declines in countries with more open press environments, such as Argentina, Brazil, the Philippines, Sri Lanka, and Thailand. Moreover, a growing number of governments moved in 2006 to restrict internet freedom by censoring, harassing, or shutting down sites that provide alternative sources of news and commentary (p. 1).

As part of their media relations activities, public relations professionals constantly seek to use the media to communicate messages to relevant publics. In order to maintain effective media relations, public relations professionals must understand who controls the media, and thereby their content, in a given country. The Freedom House survey found that 58 countries of the world (home to 39 per cent of the world's population) were rated as having media systems that were "partly free" and 63 countries (43 per cent of the world's population) had media that were "not free." By their estimation, then, 82 per cent of the world's population (living in 121 countries) lives in a media system that is not unfettered and mostly under government control. Considering how important it is for public relations practitioners to have effective relationships with the mass media, these numbers offer different types of challenges to practitioners. Quite often, the government becomes the "sole public" in a society because of the control it wields on a wide range of societal matters.

As stated in Chapter 1, in most parts of the world media ownership usually rests with the government or an agency designated by the government or in the hands of capitalistic entrepreneurs depending on the socio-political conditions prevailing in a society. It is important to recognize that media *ownership* does not necessarily result in media *control*. Even though the media may be overtly owned by private interests, they are strictly monitored and controlled through overt and covert means by political or government forces—a trend seen in many developing countries. Freedom House uses three broad criteria that help us understand media freedom or its flip side, media control: "the legal environment in which media operate; political influences on reporting and access to information; and economic pressures on content and the dissemination of news" (Karlekar, 2007, p. 1). The economic, legal, and political systems (three of the four factors that have been termed "infrastructural variables" in Chapter 1) are often under the control of the government in most of the 121 countries where Freedom House reports the media are not fully free. Editorial freedom appears to be directly proportional to the level of economic development of a country. A lack of resources and infrastructure contribute to the limiting of editorial freedom in developing nations. In their study of the relationship between press freedom and social development in 134 nations, Weaver, Buddenbaum, and Fair (1985) concluded that "the stronger the media are economically, the less likely [able] the government is to control these media" (p. 113). Government advertisements, which form a large source of advertising revenue (and a means of survival) for private media in many developing countries, are one method of maintaining control over media content. Controlling the supply of the means of production such as newsprint (often imported and sold at subsidized costs), is another effective way for governments to maintain their control over privately owned mass media. Other forms of censorship including legal harassment abound in many regions of the world. Further, it is also not uncommon for political rulers of developing nations to own their own media outlets (usually print media) and use them for controlling public opinion with the sole purpose of maintaining the status quo—their hold over the reins of power. It is clear that in many developing nations, economic independence is a mirage for most media outlets.

However, it is not uncommon for governments to threaten even financially sound media outlets as evident in an example from Thailand. In March 2002, the government of Thailand banned the editions of two international newspapers and threatened to deport the reporters of these media outlets as retribution for running a story critical of the government. The World Association of Newspapers and the World Editors Forum, which represents more than 18,000 publications in 100 countries, complained to then Prime Minister Thanksin Shinawatra that the proposed expulsion of the two foreign journalists ordered by his government constituted "a breach of the right to freedom of expression." In addition, the Shinawatra government pressured local media to "tone down critical reporting" (Karlekar, 2003, p. 8). Based on these and other factors, the Freedom House report concluded that "as Thaksin consolidates his party's hold over bureaucratic structures and increases the power of the executive, he seems unwilling to allow the press, as well as other independent institutions designed to check corruption, to continue in their role as independent watchdogs of the government" (p. 8). This is a good case study of the influence of the political ideology of a country on media content. Another example from Singapore also highlights the nexus between political ideology and media content. The acting minister for Information and the Arts exhorted the media to play their "social role" as partners (with the government) in nation building despite the "pressures" of globalization:

> Our local media have played an important role in building modern Singapore. By communicating the government's message across to the people, it has [sic] helped to rally support for policies that have brought us progress and prosperity. (*Straits Times*, March 8, 2002.)

Even the young and evolving literature on global public relations has examples of the power of media control in societies with different levels of economic development. Even in the well-developed modern democracy of Japan with a free press, access to the media is controlled through press clubs not due to economic reasons but primarily due to cultural ones (Sriramesh and Takasaki, 1998). Sriramesh and Takasaki concluded that it is critical for public relations professionals operating in Japan to maintain a good working relationship with the secretaries of these press clubs, because these gatekeepers determine whether a press release is even allowed to be disseminated among media members of the club. After studying media relations in another developing country, Sriramesh (1996 in Bardhan and Sriramesh, 2004) reported that many public relations professionals in India agreed that establishing open lines of communication with strategically placed people in the government and industry was a critical part of their activities. These people controlled the media, rather than owned it, and therefore were key stakeholders. The government in India exercises significant control over the privately owned print media through subsidies and advertising. These divergent examples substantiate this chapter's claim that the effective global public relations practitioner must have a good understanding of who *controls* media content in a country regardless of who *owns* the media.

Nevertheless, it is worth noting that media ownership became highly concentrated in the hands of a few corporations particularly in the last quarter of the 20th century. Only five major players (Time Warner, Disney, Viacom, News Corp and Bertelsmann) now control the lion's share of the 37,000 different media outlets in the United States. This number jumps to 54,000 if one counts all weeklies, semiweeklies, and advertising weeklies and all "periodicals," including strictly local ones. The number becomes 178,000 if one counts all "information industries" (Bagdikian 2004, p. 29). That way they effectively control $236 billion spent annually on advertising in the mass media and the approximately $800 billion that Americans spend on media products themselves.

Control extends from traditional to new media on the Internet. As Kalathil and Boas (2001) observe:

> In Singapore, a long-standing semi-authoritarian regime is implementing an ambitious yet carefully planned ICT strategy, using a combination of legal, technical, and social measures to shape the development of Internet use. In military-run regimes such as Myanmar

(Burma), governments can curtail dissident communication by preventing popular access to the Internet and forbidding the use of other ICTs such as fax machines and satellite dishes. In the Middle East, Saudi Arabia and the United Arab Emirates are able to control the political and social impact of the Internet through ambitious censorship schemes.

The authors analyzed strategies used by China and Cuba to control Internet use and found interesting differences:

> The principal difference between China's and Cuba's approaches to the Internet revolved around their reactive measures of control. Cuba's strategy hinges on control of access to the Internet, including a prohibition on individual public access and the careful selection of institutions that are allowed to connect to the Internet. In contrast, China has promoted more widespread access to the Internet and has tried to limit the medium's potential challenges through a combination of content filtering, monitoring, deterrence, and the promotion of self-censorship.

However, one does come across savvy users of these new media who are able to circumvent at least some of the filtering systems used to control access to content.

Online communication is progressively controlled by fewer and fewer companies, mirroring the consolidation seen in offline media as illustrated in Figure 4.2 showing what is owned by the top six online players.

The bottom line is that we live in a world where control of offline and online media is attempted by governments and corporations following the same principles. The media, as a result, increasingly appear similar in many respects around the world.

Media Diffusion

In the previous edition of this book and elsewhere, Sriramesh had used the term "media outreach" to refer to the extent to which the media permeate a given society. The concept of "media outreach" has now been renamed as "media diffusion," for greater clarity. Public relations professionals like to place stories in the media but also know that theory tells us that by merely publishing a message, one cannot claim to have made the desired impact on one's audience. Practicing public relations globally requires that practitioners understand the extent of media *diffusion* in the countries of their choice before they attempt to place information in a particular medium in order to reach a larger section of the populace.

As noted in Chapter 1, high levels of illiteracy and poverty play a critical role in disseminating messages in developing countries. However, it is critical that traditional media be used judiciously. West and Fair (1993) studied the use of what they termed (before the advent of the Internet, of course) "modern," "popular," and "traditional" media in Africa and highlighted the pitfalls of the improper use of indigenous African media (or "traditional" media) for developmental activities. For example, the authors cautioned that it would be inappropriate to use Mozambique's *paiva* genre of song for "transmission of messages originating in an authority external to the very community that maintains them" because historically the songs are "suited to empowerment of the oppressed vis-a-vis authority" (p. 101). It also would be important for the international public relations practitioner to be cautious in using the *Makonde* and *Makua* genre of African sculpture, which is a medium of ridiculing officials (Isaacman and Isaacman, 1983, p. 69, cited in West and Fair) and therefore, may be inappropriate for many information

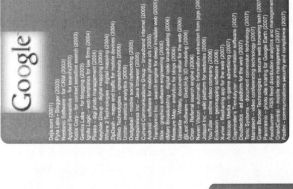

FIG. 4.2 Who owns what on-line (source and copyright 2008: Amy L. Webb, Webbmedia Group, reproduced here with permission)

TABLE 4.1
World Internet Usage and Population Statistics

World Regions	Population (2007 Est.)	Population % of World	Internet Usage, Latest Data	% Population (Penetration)	Usage % of World	Usage Growth 2000–2007
Africa	941,249,130	14.2%	44,361,940	4.7%	3.4%	882.7%
Asia	3,733,783,474	56.5%	510,478,743	13.7%	38.7%	346.6%
Europe	801,821,187	12.1%	348,125,847	43.4%	26.4%	231.2%
Middle East	192,755,045	2.9%	33,510,500	17.4%	2.5%	920.2%
North America	334,659,631	5.1%	238,015,529	71.1%	18.0%	120.2%
Latin America/Caribbean	569,133,474	8.6%	126,203,714	22.2%	9.6%	598.5%
Oceania/Australia	33.569,718	0.5%	19,175,836	57.1%	1.5%	151.6%
WORLD TOTAL	6,606,971,659	100.0%	1,319,872,109	20.0%	100.0%	265.6%

Notes. (1) Internet Usage and World Population Statistics are for December 31, 2007. (2) Demographic (Population) numbers are based on data from the *US Census Bureau*. (3) Internet usage information comes from data published by *Nielsen/NetRatings*, by the *International Telecommunications Union*, by local NIC, and other reliable sources.
Source: http://www.internetworldstats.com/stats.htm (retrieved April 29, 2009)

campaigns. Although we have presented data above showing that particularly mobile telephony offers great potential for nearly-universal diffusion of the Internet, Verčič, Razpet, Dekleva and Šlenc (2000) found that both public relations and Internet use are still unequally distributed around the globe. The authors noted that in the year 2000 both public relations and the Internet were practically absent in Africa, emerging in Asia and in parts of Latin America, globalizing in parts of Europe and Latin America, and were truly globalized only in North America and Western Europe (with Australia and New Zealand). The indicators included in Table 4.1 show that not much has changed since.

However, when dealing with media diffusion, it is necessary to consider in the context of international terrorism, what Dartnell (2005) called "multimedia activism": "Multimedia activism is based in image and text-based representations that transgress identity, space, and the legitimation capacities of states. Multimedia transgresses in a distinct manner by transmitting a dramatic representation of events."

Media Access

The flip side of media diffusion is media *access*. Whereas media diffusion refers to the extent of dispersion of the mass media in a society, media access denotes the extent to which the citizenry of a society can use the mass media as a partner to disseminate messages they deem important. Media access does not remain constant across societies. As noted earlier, Sriramesh and Takasaki (1998), reporting on the nature of Japanese public relations, identified *press clubs* as interlocutors between the media and other publics, including corporations who might want to gain access to the media thereby limiting access to the media in Japan.

A savvy international public relations practitioner will recognize that just as an organization's access to the media is critical, so is the extent to which the media are accessible to those who frequently challenge organization such as activists. Activism has a profound impact on public relations as described in Chapter. While activism contributes to the dynamism of an organization's environment, thereby posing threats to organizational autonomy, activists also provide public relations opportunities to an organization (L. Grunig, 1992). Organizations are forced to communicate symmetrically when activists use the media to challenge their image in the court of public opinion. This also is the kind of two-way communication that Hiebert (1992) proposed in his critique of the normative media theories reviewed earlier in this Chapter. Harold Burson recognized the significance of activists to the public relations profession by stating that it was not until the emergence of intense environmental and consumer advocacy in the 1980s that many CEOs began to appreciate the significance of the public relations practitioner to organizational activities (Parker, 1983). Responding to activists' pressure is at the heart of issue management principles that Jones and Chase (1979) and Crable and Vibbert (1985) proposed. That is precisely why activism has been identified as one of the five environmental variables of critical importance to international public relations practice (Sriramesh and Verčič, 2003).

All these scholars recognize the fact that if the media of a society are accessible to individuals or groups with different points of view, the resulting publicity will increase the fluidity of the environment for organizations. The organization then will be forced to use two-way flow of communication for conducting its public relations activities with a variety of publics, rather than focusing on one or two publics. But if various groups that do not conform to the mainstream ideology are not accorded a forum for publicly voicing their agenda, then the extent of pressure on an organization is drastically reduced, calling for minimal sophistication in public relations. Therefore, understanding the extent to which the media are accessible to various activist and other groups in a society helps the international public relations practitioner by providing, among other things, a gauge on the amount of opposition that the environment might pose.

ICTs—new media—have certainly changed the dynamics as far as access to the mass media are concerned. It is not an exaggeration to say that with the advent of the Internet, many leading print media organizations have felt pressured to alter the way they cover and report the news in order to compete. ICTs have given rise to social media such as Internet forums, message boards, weblogs, wikis, podcasts, pictures and video. Technologies such as blogs, picture-sharing, vlogs, wall-postings, email, instant messaging, music-sharing, crowdsourcing, and Voice Over Internet Protocol (VOIP), are used. These social media have in many ways obviated the need to rely solely on "traditional" media such as newspapers, magazines, radio, and TV.

> Examples of social media applications are Google Groups (reference, social networking), Wikipedia (reference), MySpace (social networking), Facebook (social networking), Last .fm (personal music), YouTube (social networking and video sharing), Second Life (virtual reality), Flickr (photo sharing), Twitter (social networking and microblogging) and other microblogs are Jaiku and Pownce. Many of these social media services can be integrated via Social network aggregation platforms like Mybloglog, a Yahoo property, Blogcatalog, and Plaxo. (Wikipedia 2008)

Because of their pervasiveness and increasing influence by providing a forum for people to disseminate information without going through the traditional gatekeepers such as media reporters and editors, social media are becoming an interesting topic of research in public relations (Wright and Hinson 2008).

CONCLUSION

The mass media are critical to strategic global public relations. One is persuaded by Theus' assertions (1993) that organizations should "develop ways of effectively coorienting with journalists, especially in identifying mutually satisfactory exchanges that benefit each party" (p. 92). The building of such relationships with the media in different countries requires that we move beyond the now dated "theories of the press" and into identifying new frameworks that help us understand media environments and contribute to developing effective methods of conducting international media relations. This chapter has proposed such a framework, one that international public relations practitioners can use to understand the media environment in different countries. By analyzing *who controls* the media in these countries, *how much access* various segments of the population have to the media, and finally the *extent of media outreach*, media relations managers will be better able to strategize their public relations approaches in different countries. They will be able to discern the nature of the challenge they can expect from the media and other sources as well as devise strategies of identifying key mass media (and other) stakeholders who can influence effective media relations. The onset and exponential growth of "new media" is also altering the terrain for global public relations practice. But issues such as the Digital Divide pose interesting avenues for research in how new media contribute to the information sharing dynamics in a society. It is hoped that future research studies will gather empirical evidence on the media environment in different nations based on this framework, thereby exploring the efficacy of this framework to the international public relations professional. Of course such evidence will also help revise and expand this conceptual framework itself.

REFERENCES

Altschull, H. J. (1984). *Agents of power.* White Plains, NY: Longman.

Anderson, T. (1993). Terrorism and censorship: The media in chains. *Journal of International Affairs, 47*(1): 127–136.

Bagdikian, B. H. (2004). *The New Media Monopoly.* Boston: Beacon Press.

Bardhan, N., and Sriramesh, K. (2004). Public relations in India. A profession in transition. In K. Sriramesh (Ed.), *Public relations in Asia: An anthology* (pp. 62–95). Singapore: Thomson.

Brzezinski, Z. (1969). *Between two ages: America's role in the technotronic era.* New York: Viking.

Caldarola, V. J. (1994). Time and the Television War. In S. J. Jeffords and L. Rabinovitz (Eds.), *Seeing through the media: The Persian Gulf War* (pp. 97–105). New Brunswick, NJ: Rutgers University Press.

Cameron, G. T., Sallot, L. M., and Curtin, P. A. (1997). Public relations and the production of news: A critical review and a theoretical framework. In B. R. Burleson (Ed.), *Communication Yearbook 20* (pp. 111–155). Newbury Park, CA: Sage.

Chomsky, N. (1989). *Necessary illusions: Thought control in democratic societies.* London, UK: Pluto Press.

Cowan Shulman, H. (1994). The Gulf War as total television. In S. J. Jeffords and L. Rabinovitz (Eds.). *Seeing through the media: The Persian Gulf War* (pp. 107–120). New Brunswick, NJ: Rutgers University Press.

CPRE. (1999). *Public Relations Education for the 21ˢᵗ Century: A port of entry.* New York: Public Relations Society of America.

Crable, R. E., and Vibbert, S. L. (1985). Managing issues and influencing public policy. *Public Relations Review, 11*: 3–16.

Culbertson, H. M. (1996). Introduction. In H. M. Culbertson and Ni Chen (Eds.), *International public relations: A comparative analysis* (pp. 1–13). Mahwah. NJ: Lawrence Erlbaum Associates.

Cutlip, S. M., Center, A. H., and Broom, G. M. (2000). *Effective public relations,* 8ᵗʰ edn. Englewood Cliffs, NJ: Prentice Hall.

Dartnell, M. (2005). Communicative practice and transgressive global politics: The *d'ua* of Sheikh Muhammed Al–Mohaisany. *First Monday, 10*(7). http://firstmonday.org/issues/issue10_7/dartnell/index.html (retrieved April 29, 2008)

Dearing, J. W. (1996). *Agenda-Setting.* Thousand Oaks, CA: Sage.

The Economist (2008). Nomads at last. A special report on mobile telecoms. *The Economist 387*(8575), April 12th (pp. 1–16).

Engelhardt, T. (1994). The Gulf War as total television. In S. J. Jeffords and L. Rabinovitz (Eds.), *Seeing through the media: The Persian Gulf War* (pp. 81–95). New Brunswick, NJ: Rutgers University Press.

Entman, R. M. (1991). Framing U.S. coverage of international news: Contrasts in narratives of the KAL and Iran Air incidents. *Journal of Communication, 41*(4), 6–27.

Epley, J. (1992). Public relations in the global village: An American perspective. *Public Relations Review, 18*(2), 109–116.

Forbes (2007). The power of networks. *Forbes 179*(10).

Gans, H. (1979). *Deciding what's news*. New York, N Y: Pantheon Books.

Goonasekara, A. (1987). The influence of television on cultural values with special reference to Third World countries. *Media Asia, 14*(1): 7–18.

Grunig, J. E. (1992). Communication, public relations and effective organizations: An overview of the book. In J.E. Grunig (Ed.), *Excellence in public relations and communication management* (pp. 1–28). Hillsdale, NJ: Lawrence Erlbaum Associates.

Grunig, L. (1992). Activism: How it limits the effectiveness of organizations and how excellent public relations departments respond. In J.E. Grunig (Ed.), *Excellence in public relations and communication management* (pp. 503–530). Hillsdale, NJ: Lawrence Erlbaum Associates.

Guiniven, J. (2007). Old media relations models do not work with new media. *Public Relations Tactics, 14*(7): 6–6.

Hachten, W. (1981). *The world news prism: Changing media, clashing ideologies*. Ames, Iowa: Iowa State University Press.

Hachten, W. A. (1993). *The growth of media in the Third World: African failures, Asian successes.* Ames: Iowa State University Press.

Herman, E. S., and Chomsky, N. (1994). *Manufactoring consent: The political economy of the mass media.* London, UK: Vintage.

Hiebert, R. E. (1992). Global public relations in a post-communist world: A new model. *Public Relations Review, 18*(2): 117–126.

Howard, C. M., and Mathews, W. K. (2000). *On deadline: Managing media relations.* Prospect Heights, IL: Waveland.

Jeffords, S. J., and Rabinovitz, L. (1994). *Seeing through the media: The Persian Gulf War.* New Brunswick, NJ: Rutgers University Press.

Jones, B. L., and Chase, W. H. (1979). Managing public policy issues. *Public Relations Review, 5*(2): 3–23.

Kalathil, S. and Boas, T. C. (2001) The Internet and State Control in Authoritarian Regimes: China, Cuba, and the Counterrevolution. First Monday, 6(8). http://firstmonday.org/issues/issue6_8/kalathil/index.html (retrieved April 29, 2008).

Karlekar, K. D. (2007). Press Freedom in 2006: Growing Threats to Media Independence. http://www.freedom house.org/template.cfm?page=131&year=2007&essay=28 (retrieved March 19, 2008).

Kruckeberg, D. (1996). Transnational corporate ethical responsibilities. In H. M. Culbertson and Ni Chen (Eds.), *International Public Relations: A Comparative Analysis* (pp. 81–92). Mahwah, NJ: Lawrence Erlbaum Associates.

Kunczik, M. (1993). Public relations advertisements of foreign countries in Germany with special reference to developing countries: results of a content analysis. Paper presented at the international conference on "The state of education and development: New Directions," Association for the Advancement of Policy, Research and Development in the Third World, November 21–26, Cairo, Egypt.

Larson, J., and Rivenburgh, N. (1991). A comparative analysis of Australian, U.S., and British telecasts of the Seoul Olympic Opening Ceremony. *Journal of Broadcasting and Electronic Media, 35*(1): 75–94.

Lee, P. (1994). Mass communication and national development in China: Media roles reconsidered. *Journal of Communication, 44*(3): 22–37.

Livingstone, S. (2008). Engaging with media—A matter of literacy? *Communication, Culture and Critique, 1*(1): 51–62.

Martin, L. J., and Chaudhary, A. G. (1983). *Comparative mass media systems.* White Plains, NY: Longman.

McLuhan, M., and Fiore, Q. (1969). *War and peace in the global village.* New York: Bantam.

Merrill, J. C. (1974). *The dialectic in journalism: Toward a responsible use of press freedom.* Baton Rouge: Louisiana State University Press.

Merrill, J. C., and Lowenstein, R. L. (1979). *Media, messages, and men.* New York: Longman.

Mintzberg, H. (1983). *Power in and around organizations.* Englewood Cliffs, NJ: Prentice-Hall.

Newsom, D., Turk, J. V., and Kruckeberg, D. (2000). *This is PR: The realities of public relations.* Belmont, CA: Wadsworth.

Parker, R. A. (1983). Potholes lurking on the PR path: An interview with Harold Burson, Burson-Marsteller CEO. *Communication World* (November): 12–13.

Pavlik, J. V. (1996). *New media and the information superhighway.* Boston, MA: Allyn and Bacon.

Pratt, C., and Mannheim, J. (1988). Communication research and development policy: Agenda dynamics in an African setting. *Journal of Communication, 38*(3): 75–95.

Reber, B. H., and Kim, Y. K. (2006). How activist groups use web sites in media relations: Evaluating online press rooms. *Journal of Public Relations Research, 18*(4), 313–333.

Rhee, Y. (1999). Confucian culture and excellent public relations: A study of generic principles and specific applications in South Korean public relations practice. Unpublished Master's thesis submitted to the University of Maryland, College Park, MD.

Ritzer, G. (1996). *The McDonaldization of society: An investigation into the changing character of contemporary social life.* Thousand Oaks, CA: Pine Forge Press.

Rosengren, K. E. (2000). *Communication: An introduction.* Thousand Oaks, CA: Sage.

Sallot, L. M., and Johnson, E. A. (2006). Investigating relationships between journalists and public relations practitioners: Working together to set, frame and build the public agenda, 1991–2004. *Public Relations Review, 32*(2): 151–159.

Schultz, D. E., and Kitchen, P. J. (2000). *Communicating globally: An integrated marketing approach.* Houndmills, UK: Palgrave.

Servaes, J. (1991). European press coverage of the Grenada crisis. *Journal of Communication, 41*(4): 28–41.

Sharpe, M. L. (1992). The impact of social and cultural conditioning on global public relations. *Public Relations Review, 18*, 103–107.

Siebert, F. S., Peterson, T., and Schramm, W. (1956). *Four theories of the press.* Urbana, IL: University of Illinois Press.

Silverstone, R. (1999). *Why study the media?* Thousand Oaks CA: Sage.

Sriramesh, K. (1992). The impact of societal culture on public relations: An ethnographic study of South Indian organizations. Unpublished doctoral dissertation, University of Maryland at College Park, MD.

Sriramesh, K. (1996). Power distance and public relations: An ethnographic study of Southern Indian organizations, in H. Culbertson, and N. Chen (Eds.), *International public relations: A comparative analysis* (pp. 171–190). Mahwah, NJ: Lawrence Erlbaum Associates..

Sriramesh, K. (2002). The dire need for multiculturalism in public relations education: An Asian perspective. *Journal of Communication Management, 7*(1), 54–70.

Sriramesh, K. (2003). Vision statement on Associate Editorship (Asia). *Journal of Communication Management, 7*(3), 193–196.

Sriramesh, K., and Takasaki, M. (1998). The impact of culture on Japanese public relations. Paper presented to the Public Relations Division, International Communication Association, Jerusalem, July 21, 1998.

Sriramesh, K., and Verčič, D. (2003). *The global public relations handbook: Theory, research, and practice.* Mahwah, NJ: Lawrence Erlbaum Associates.

Sriramesh, K., and White, J. (1992). Societal culture and public relations. In J. Grunig (Ed.), *Excellence in public relations and communication management* (pp. 597–614). Hillsdale, NJ: Lawrence Erlbaum Associates.

Sriramesh, K., Grunig, J. E. and Dozier, D. M. (1996). Observation and measurement of two dimensions of organizational culture and their relationship to public relations, *Journal of Public Relations Research, 8*(4): 229–261.

Sussman, L. (1999). *The news of the century: Press freedom 1999.* New York, NY: Freedom House.

Theus, K. (1993). Organizations and the media: Structures of miscommunication. *Management Communication Quarterly, 7*(1): 67–95.

Thussu, D. K. (2000). *International communication: Continuity and change.* London, UK: Arnold.

Verčič, D., Grunig, L. A., and Grunig, J. E. (1996). Global and specific principles of public relations: Evidence from Slovenia. In H. M. Culbertson and Ni Chen (Eds.), *International Public Relations: A Comparative Analysis* (pp. 31–66). Mahwah, NJ: Lawrence Erlbaum Associates.

Verčič, D., Razpet, A., Dekleva, S., and Šlenc, M. (2000). International public relations and the Internet: Diffusion and linkages. *Journal of Communication Management 5*(2): 125–137.

Weaver, D. H., Buddenbaum, J. M., and Fair, J. E. (1985). Press freedom, media, and development, 1950–1979: A study of 134 nations. *Journal of Communication, 35*(2): 104–117.

West, H. G., and Fair, J. E. (1993). Development communication and popular resistance in Africa: An examination of the struggle over tradition and modernity through media. *African Studies Review, 36*(1): 91–114.

Wikipedia (2008). Social media. *Wikipedia, the free encyclopedia.* http://en.wikipedia.org/wiki/Social_media (retreived: April 29, 2008).

Wilcox, D. L., and Nolte, L. W. (1997). *Public relations writing and media techniques.* New York: Longman.

Wright, D. K., and Hinson, M. (2008). Examining the increasing impact of social media on public relations practice. http://www.instituteforpr.org/files/uploads/Wright-Hinson.pdf (retrieved: April 29, 2008).

Yoon, Y. (2005). A scale for measuring media relations efforts. *Public Relations Review 31,* 434–436.

5

ACTIVISM AND PUBLIC RELATIONS

JEONG-NAM KIM

KRISHNAMURTHY SRIRAMESH

INTRODUCTION

When a 23-year-old woman stayed on top of a 180-foot California Redwood tree for 738 days to protest the logging by the Pacific Lumber Company, it was more than news. It was a major challenge by a frail woman of strong convictions to a big company that was founded in 1863. She did not come down the tree until the company had agreed not to cut not only that tree (affectionately named Luna by its savior) but the majestic redwoods in a three-acre buffer zone around it. In another "David vs. Goliath" example, an unemployed former postman and a part-time gardener were dragged to court by McDonald's for libel because the two (and a few of their associates) had distributed leaflets criticizing the multi-billion-dollar corporation for such things as depressing wages, serving unhealthy food and cruelty to animals. The two activists argued their own case against the high-paid libel attorneys that McDonald's could afford, and the trial entered the record books as the longest trial in UK history. In the end, although the judge ruled partially in McDonald's favor and granted a modest 60,000 British pounds, he also agreed with several of the accusations contained in the leaflet and did not offer an injunction against its distribution. The overall effect was that McDonald's lost millions in legal fees and lost hours when corporate executives had to travel to London to testify. The greater damage, however, was in the court of public opinion, and the McLibel case (as it is popularly known) even got its own web site—McSpotlight—that had received some 2.2 million hits by the time the case in the UK had been adjudicated and millions more since then.

These examples highlight not only the potency of activist actions but also the interplay between a pluralistic political system where an individual's freedom of expression is valued, a media system where even the "little voice" or "minority" point of view is liable to be disseminated, and a transparent legal system that ensures that the stronger are not automatically deemed the victors. Of interest to us is that these examples also illustrate the damage to reputation that results from mishandling relationships, and not communicating, with activists. Activists could "improve the functioning" of the organizations through pressure tactics, (re)directing or (re)mobilizing resource for (or against) organizations, and building coalitions as a strategy (Kim, 2002). L. Grunig (1992) and J. Grunig and L. Grunig (1997) recognized activists as a force in our socio-cultural environment with the ability to influence management processes.

Understanding the interplay between activism and public relations is therefore essential to global public relations. As mentioned in Chapter 1, there are strong interconnections among the socio-cultural environmental variables such as culture, political system, economic system and media system as well as the choices of public relations strategies and tactics adopted by the organizations in a society. As a result, these variables increase the frequency and nature of collective actions (i.e., level of activism) seen in a society. This in turn influences public relations practice such as the involvement of public relations in strategic management as well as ethical perceptions of public relations practices in a society. The goal is to be able to use this information to prescribe incremental changes that public relations professionals can make to their strategies and techniques especially as they enter newer socio-cultural environments. With this goal in mind, we propose a model of activism and examine how it can contribute to developing a theory of global public relations practice. We hope this model spawns further empirical research that will enhance the body of knowledge of global public relations.

EXTENT OF ACTIVISM: A CONSEQUENCE OF SOCIO-CULTURAL ENVIRONMENTAL CONDITIONS

Activism is a social phenomenon that can be related to problem-solving actions by individuals or groups who coalesce around problematic situations created by organizational activities (Kim, 2002). This phenomenon is attributable to almost all social changes, turbulence, and emergence of new structure and rules. Major questions for research are: what is activism; why does it arise; and what form does it take based on social contexts and how does it differ across different societies.

One of the most commonly cited definitions of the term *activism* was offered by Diani (1992). He synthesized four different approaches concerning social movements and saw social movements or activism as "a network of informal interactions between a plurality of individuals, groups and/or organizations, engaged in political or cultural conflicts, on the basis of shared collective identities" (p. 1). In his definition, he placed emphasis on *member networks*, *interactions* among those members, *conflicts*, and *shared identities of members* as ingredients of activism. Another sociologist, Tarrow (1994) saw social movements (activism) as:

> collective challenges by people with common purposes and solidarity in sustained interaction with elites, opponents and authorities (p. 4) . . . [The conditions are] a) that movements mount disruptive action against elites, authorities, other groups and cultural codes; b) that they do so in the name of common claims against opponents, authorities, and elites; c) that they are rooted in feelings of solidarity or collective identity; and d) that it is by sustaining their resulting collective action that contention turns into a social movement. (summarized in Klandermans, 1997, p. 2)

Organizational theorist Mintzberg (1983) referred to activists as *special interest groups* and described them as:

> organized groups, outside of government, that seek to represent some kind of special inter-
> est in the External Coalition . . . [special interests groups] may act out of private interests, or
> they may take it upon themselves to represent what they believe to be the public interest,
> especially when they believe that government is too slow or too conservative or not properly
> representative. (pp. 44–45)

Some political scientists have also used the term *interest group* to refer to activists. This term is more common in the U.S. political system and in political science. Browne (1998) specified three conditions for interest groups. First, interest groups are voluntary efforts to bring together members and supporters or joiners. Second, members possess a common characteristic distinguishing themselves from others, and finally, the group's purpose is to serve for the members' common concerns or interests.

Another political scientist, Wright (1996) defined activists or what he called *political interest group* or *organized interest* as:

> [A] collection of individuals or a group of individuals linked together by professional
> circumstance, or by common political, economic, or social interests, that meets the following
> requirements: (1) its name does not appear on an election ballot; (2) it uses some portion of
> its collective resources to try and influence decisions made by the legislative, executive, or
> judicial branches of national, state, or local governments; and (3) it is organized externally
> to the institution of government that it seeks to influence. (pp. 22–23)

Burstein (1998) offered a more inclusive definition of activism and collective behaviors spanning interest groups and SMOs (social movement organization). The key charac-teristics of SMOs and interest groups are that they have some autonomy from government or political parties and make efforts to influence policies. They are trying to elicit govern-mental intervention and influence policy-making process to meet their interests or concerns.

Public relations scholar L. Grunig (1992) defined activism as an effort by "a group of two or more individuals who organize in order to influence another public or publics through action that may include education, compromise, persuasion, pressure tactics, or force" (p. 504). In presenting his situational theory of publics, J. Grunig (1997) borrowed Dewey's definition of the term *public,* which centers around issues (problems generated by adverse organizational consequences on society) and how individuals and groups react to those issues either by being passive or organizing as activists. Activism is also at the heart of issues management where organizations try to influence public policy through such efforts as lobbying.

From the definitions of collective action or activism across disciplines, we have extracted six common cores that help us identify activist collective behavior (including social move-ments) from other social phenomena:

1.   individuals or collections of individuals;
2.   voluntary membership with a specific purpose;
3.   solidarity or collective identity among members;
4.   common interest or cause that binds members as a homogeneous group;

5. marshalling available resources for action such as volunteers and relevant information;
6. efforts targeted at influencing decision-making typically by government agencies and corporations.

Taking the remaining six core components as the basis, we define activism as:

> The coordinated effort of a group that organizes voluntarily in an effort to solve problems that threaten the common interest of members of the group. In the process of problem solving, core members of the group attract other social constituents or publics, create and maintain a shared collective identity among members for the time being, and mobilize resources and power to influence the problem-causing entity's decision or action through communicative action such as education, negotiation, persuasion, pressure tactics, or force.

Two dimensions of the extent of activism for a comparative framework

Having defined the term activism, we turn our attention to another goal of this chapter—to illustrate the relationship between activism as a socioculturual environmental factor and how it affects public relations practice across different societies. We intend to offer a framework that we hope will be useful to studies that seek to link public relations to activism in different global activist environments. Most scholars have concentrated on the causes of activism but there appears to be little attention paid to whether one country's activism is more potent than another's or which factors prompt activism in different countries. Some studies have analyzed the degree of fierceness of confrontational acts such as labor movements or democratization (e.g., della Porta and Diani, 1999; Tarrow, 1998).

We reason that the level of activism consists of at least two dimensions: first, *the degree of intensity of action from an individual or activist group on a given issue* and second, *the number of issues (diversity of issues) in a given society*. The first dimension aims to capture the depth of activism—the general tendency of "fierceness" of confrontation in a given society. From our observation, each society shows different levels of intensity of activist confrontation in relation to common activist issues such as labor movements or democratization. For example, in democratization and labor movement issues, South Korea has shown fiercer confrontation (e.g., frequent suicidal protests in labor movements) and staged organized movement confrontations (e.g., more than one million protestors turned out each day for a month in 1987 and 1991) than other Asian countries (Sanger, 1991).

We thus propose that the differences in political, economic, cultural, media, and organizational conditions will influence the resulting intensity of activist confrontation even in some issues that most countries experience at some point in their history. This notion of activism has been the most commonly taken view of the level of activism that most comparative works adopt.

With regard to the depth of activism, we suggest a few possible operationalization approaches for consideration by future empirical studies. We believe that the intensity of activist confrontation might be observed by using several measures: the frequency of confrontational activity on a given issue and the length and depth of media reporting, the use and frequency of violent action, the extent of publicity generated through non-mass media approaches also (individual campaigning and use of personal influence, for example), and the number of mobilized participants in the confrontational activity. We feel there are more measurement strategies for the proposed conceptual dimensions of the extent of activism.

The second dimension relates to the breadth of activism—the variety of issues available for activists to seize upon in a given society. The extent of fierceness or the confrontational intensity of activists is not the only aspect. Higher levels of activism can also be measured by the variety of issues that are the focus of activist groups. The number of different issues a society experiences varies across countries. Some countries have more diverse issues than others. Again, socio-cultural variables play a role in the spawning of issues for collective action and how these get reported in the media. For example, the activist incidents in the United States are far more diverse and more widely reported than those we find in a country like China. While China has a limited number of issues (at least as evident to the outside world) such as the treatment of AIDS patients or corruption in local governments, the United States experiences numerous kind of issues, such as animal rights, environmental protection, world peace, local issues, individual health issues, political dissents, and economic issues.

In addition to the intensity of confrontation such as the number of mobilized participants in a pressure campaign, the presence of diverse issues publics create and act on becomes critical because those diverse issues are all competing for societal attention and allocation of resources for resolving problems. For example, South Korea is a formerly authoritarian country that had struggled under military dictatorships. As the country democratized in 1987, the intensity of confrontation such as violent pressure tactics or protest through suicides had significantly decreased. However, since then, the breadth of the issues citizens have focused on has expanded rapidly (Kim, 2002). Thus, South Korea still experiences higher levels of activism—perhaps not with the same degree of depth as in the past, but surely of much more breadth.

Generally speaking, the greater the number of issues present in a society, the greater the likelihood that social institutions and entities get involved with collective actions around those issues. Thus, the breadth of issue spectrum reflects the extent or the power of activism in a society. We therefore include the variety or scope of the issues as another key indicator to help us understand the extent of activism in a society. We suggest a measurement strategy where one counts the number of registered interest groups and activist organizations in a society and the number of different issues covered by the mass media in a given period. These two dimensions of determining the extent of activism can vary in degree from high to low (Figure 5.1).

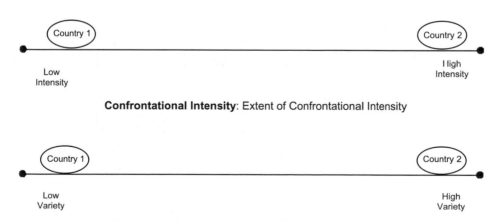

Confrontational Intensity: Extent of Confrontational Intensity

Breadth of Issue Spectrum: Variety or Breadth of Activists' Causes

FIG. 5.1   The depth and breadth continua of the level of activism.

Using these two continua, we propose the model shown in Figure 5.2 for future studies. The diagonal line distinguishes and sorts out high and low activist countries. Our proposed model will be useful for mapping countries in terms of the level of activism.

Next we use a set of comparative variables to explain how and why there is a given level of activism in a country.

THE IMPACT OF ENVIRONMENTAL VARIABLES ON THE LEVEL OF ACTIVISM

As already mentioned, the model we have proposed on the level of activism is influenced by the socio-cultural environmental variables of a society as demonstrated in Figure 5.3.

When the model is currently applied in relation to a country, it is only a conceptual description of how activism is affected by the country's socio-environmental characteristics. Therefore, it helps us understand a part, but not the whole. What is more interesting and important is if one uses the model to conduct empirical studies of a number of countries and assess how these contextual variables influence activism within each country. Such knowledge of activism on a global scale is direly needed and will be of immense help not only to scholars but to practitioners as well.

POLITICAL CONTEXT

As many scholars have agreed, political conditions are most influential in affecting the degree of activism in a society (della Porta and Diani, 1999; McAdam, 1982; McCarthy, 1996). McAdam, McCarthy, and Zald (1988) asserted that social movements are "simply 'politics by other means,' often times the only means open to relatively powerless challenging groups" (p. 699). They believed collective actions of any kind are "insti-

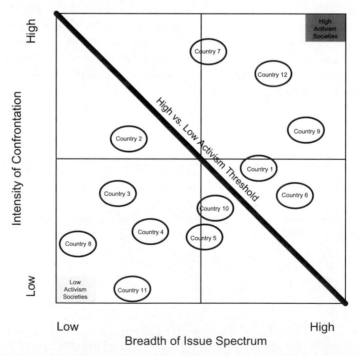

FIG. 5.2   Mapping the level of activism across countries.

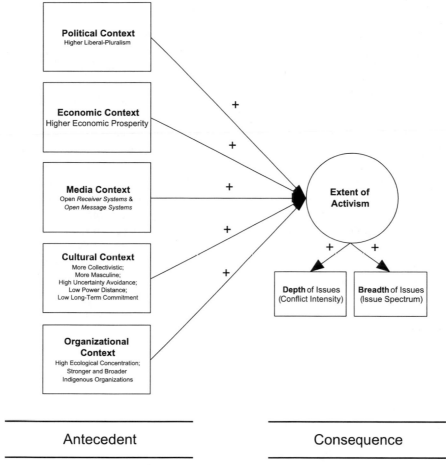

FIG. 5.3 A conceptual model: the effects of socio-cultural environmental variables on the extent of activism.

tutionalized political processes" which are not free from the "political trends and charac-teristics of the regions and countries" (p. 699). The authors stated four major political conditions that result in activism: "structure of political opportunities," "regime crises and contested political arenas," "absence of repression," and "welfare state expansion and the rise of 'new social movements'" (pp. 699–702).

Structure of political opportunities refers to the vulnerability or receptivity of the political system to organized protest from activist publics. *Regime crises and contested political arenas* refers to the period when a society's dominant force has been weakened and is unstable so that those challenging the status quo are in a stronger position relative to other dominant groups or coalitions. *Absence of repression* refers to the absence of, or relatively weaker, counter-activism efforts from dominant social institutions such as government authorities or competing counter movement groups. Finally, *welfare state expansion and the rise of new social movements* refers to the penetration of the state into previously private arenas of life. As a society transitions into a postindustrial capitalist economy, the state or government intervenes in the process of capital accumulation and its use. Thus, the state plays a more active role in complementing the citizens' needs which are not satisfied from an ailing market economy. When such transitions occur, new social movements emerge in response to this unprecedented state penetration into various private spheres of life. Consequently, movements become more diverse in the issues related with women's, environmental, and gay rights. These trends can be seen as efforts to regain control over decisions and areas of life increasingly subject to state control (McAdam, et al. 1988).

These four political conditions are useful variables to characterize the political context of a society. However, these are limited in scope. We believe the characteristics are too particularistic or too general. It is also difficult to operationalize these characteristics in preparation of future data collection. Wilson (1995) offered the First, Second, and Third Worlds and Simon and Gartzke (1996) offered a bipolar continuum spanning between democratic and authoritarian as a way of identifying different political environments in the world. As mentioned in Chapter 1, these two conceptual frameworks for political systems are deficient by being too simplistic and outdated to catch the various nuances observed in diverse countries. Therefore, Sriramesh and Vercic (2003) proposed that one could use the seven categories of political systems relevant to the modern world offered by Freedom House (described in Chapter 1).

We also find Zeigler's (1988) conceptualization of pluralism and corporatism from theories of comparative political systems useful to the present discussion. Zeigler's conceptual framework captured the notion of *relational dynamism* (e.g., competition or cooperation) between state and publics/citizens. The two concepts are also useful in that they can be placed in the opposite extreme of a continuum to make distinctions among different countries (see Chapter 2 for more details).

Corporatism has usually described fascist societies (e.g., Nazi Germany and Italy) (Streeck and Kenworthy, 2005). But, the connotation referred to a society based on a partnership between the state and its component interests, albeit with a dominant partner. Modern notions of corporatism (i.e., neo-corporatism or societal corporatism) have fewer negative meanings. Instead, corporatism hinges on a characteristic of the consensus-oriented democracy, that fits well with "a collectivist view of the role of the state" (Zeigler, 1988, p. 15). Corporatism also involves inclusion of (some would say co-opting) activist groups as members of the government thereby taking away their ability to be counter-cultures (Sriramesh and Rivera, 2006).

In contrast, pluralistic political systems generate a system of multiple competing elites (including interest groups) that determine public policy through bargaining and compromise. This is the assumption on which much of the issues management literature is based that is in the domain of the public relations body of knowledge. The idea of a pluralistic society was rooted in the social contract theory of the seventeenth and eighteenth century philosophers such as Hobbes, Locke, and Madison (Zeigler, 1988). However, in pluralism, the relationship between government and publics tends to be one of "competition" (e.g., competition among interest groups for access to government funds and services as well as for influencing political decision-making); whereas in societal corporatism, the relationship tends to be "collaborative" (J. Grunig and Jaatinen, 1998, p. 15). Therefore, we can reason, as J. Grunig and Jaatinen (1998) did, that pluralistic societies are more likely to tolerate (or even encourage) high levels of activism whereas in corporatistic societies tolerance of activism will be relatively lower.

However, societal corporatism should be understood in a different connotation as compared with pure corporatism (see Chapter 2 for a description of corporatism). In countries that have societal corporatism, government agencies collaborate and even bargain with publics they are supposed to serve or regulate in an effort to balance the interests of those publics with competing interests and motives through symmetrical communication (J. Grunig and Jaatinen, 1998, p 16). Hence, even if the extent of activism such as intensity of confrontation is low in such countries, the influence of activist groups and interest groups (through NGOs) could be of a higher level than in a pluralistic society. Thus, societal corporatism would be in the middle of a continuum with pure pluralism and pure corporatism at either end.

In the model we are proposing, we use a continuum with pure corporatism in one end and pure liberalism at the other. We hypothesize that more corporatistic societies generally tend to have lesser potential for activism or contentious collective actions, whereas in more pluralistic societies there is a far greater potential for higher levels of activism.

ECONOMIC CONTEXT

Most social phenomena require an economic explanation or need to be linked with economic conditions. Not surprisingly, many sociologists have found a strong connection between economic conditions and collective actions (see Chapter 2 for more details on political economy and activism). However, most sociological inquiries on the emergence of activism focused narrowly on the proposition that *a society's low level of prosperity is more conducive to the rise of collective activism.* The two underlying assumptions in this proposition were: 1) the most deprived individuals would be the most likely to participate in activist movements, 2) massive growth in societal wealth would keep people happy and thereby reduce the need for social movements. Yet, researchers began to discard traditional assumptions that low levels of prosperity are more likely to result in higher levels of activism (e.g., Jenkins, 1983; McCarthy and Zald, 1973; Zald and McCarthy, 1977).

McAdam et al. (1988) offered three reasons for the contradictory relationship between prosperity and the frequency of activism. First, a wealthier society's better infrastructure and such things as concomitantly higher levels of new technologies and higher levels of education among the masses gives rise to higher expectations of organizations among the masses and thereby higher levels of grievances among social members. Second, a wealthier society tends to produce a greater number of "entrepreneurs of grievances" (p. 702) who can create new social movements or are more prone to becoming members of movements because they have the expertise, the time, technological aid, and inclination to engage in such movements. Third, a wealthier society tends to have more social resources (infrastructural—such as the media and legal support) that create a conducive environment for collective action. The two examples with which this chapter began are evidence of the confluence of all these factors. In contrast, poverty constrains members of a society making them focus on survival issues such as earning the next meal for the family. Therefore, they have neither the time nor the inclination to engage in activism, save for dire instances that threaten their very survival. Therefore, we postulate that *higher levels of economic prosperity result in concomitantly higher levels of activism.*

MEDIA CONTEXT

The media system and the communication behaviors among members of a society are also important predictors of levels of activism. While scholars from sociology and political science recognized the role of communication and mass media in accounting for collective behaviors, their approaches were limited to the most obvious linkages. Quite often they perceived the mass media only as "manipulative" tools to be used by opposing groups (DeLuca, 1999; DeLuca and Peeples, 2002; McAdam et al., 1988) or by dominant elites of a society (Dow, 2004). Further, scholars whose focus is not primarily mass communication, tended to overestimate the effects and power of the mass media (e.g., McCarthy, McPhail, and Smith, 1996). They also tend to see the mass media as offering opportunities for manipulation. These scholars considered the availability of mass media and communication technology in forming public opinion and maintaining commitment through creating and sharing meaning structures (Kielbowicz and Scherer, 1986; McAdam et al., 1988; Rohlinger, 2006). However, several communication and mass communications scholars have disapproved of such claims of powerful media as a naïve assumption (e.g., Clarke and Kline, 1974, Katz and Blumler, 1974, J. Grunig, 1997). Martin and Chaudhary (1983) synthesized the work of previous scholars and offered a model that attempted to categorize a society's media system according to the extent to which both the *receiver system* and the *message (source) system* are "open" or "closed." The combination of these two variables results in a two-by-two metrics typology: *controlled mass communication*, *open mass communication*, *private communication*, and *directed mass communication*. See Figure 5.4.

Although there are different models for comparing the media across societies, Martin and Chaudhary's model is more useful in this context as it emphasizes the correlations between the media environment and emergence of activism. We propose that a society's activism is dependent on the degree to which the mass media are open or closed both in terms of the audiences (receiver system) and the control of media content (message system).

In Martin and Chaudhary's (1983) model, an "open mass communication system" allows as much audience and message freedom as possible. It is similar to the libertarian, free press, and Western media theories of the press proposed by various scholars (Altschull, 1984; Hachten, 1981; Merrill and Lowenstein, 1971; Siebert, Peterson, and Schramm, 1956). In contrast, the "controlled mass communication system" describes the audience as free to receive messages, but the messages are censored. This system is close to the authoritarian and Communist system. "Private communication" refers to the less developed communication systems that are interpersonal and often the societal communication infrastructures are not well equipped. But these could also occur in very authoritarian systems even if infrastructures are present because individuals cannot voice their dissenting opinions publicly without reprisal. Thus, in most cases, under-civilized primitive societies are placed in this type by Martin and Chaudhary. Finally, "directed mass communication system" refers to a society in which the audience is cut off from

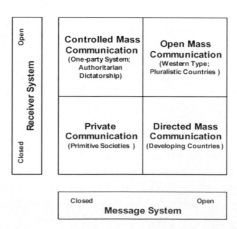

FIG. 5.4   Media typology.

many messages. Such examples are found in Asian and southeast Asian countries where multilingualism prevents portions of the population from receiving the message (Hiebert, Ungurait, and Bohn, 1988).

Using the model, we predict that the presence of more open message and receiver systems in a society will help foster higher levels of activism. Notably, we put more weight on the openness of the message (source) system rather than the receiver system. A society's openness to communication *contents* (the *software* aspects of communication) tends to account for greater variance of emerged collective actions than the format and availability of communication infrastructure (the *hardware infrastructure* of communication). We reason that the tolerance of, or openness to, competing and contentious information among members of a society will increase the shared problem recognitions and collective action potential among them. In summary, we predict that the likelihood of higher levels of activism is greatest in societies with open mass communication systems and is lower in societies that have directed mass communication, controlled mass communication, and private communication in that order.

CULTURAL CONTEXT

The impact of culture on public relations has been discussed for almost two decades. However, there are disappointingly a very small number of studies that have investigated the relationship between culture and activism (see Chapter 3). The difficulty in defining culture and the very malleable nature of the concept, among other things, have contributed to the difficulties in studying how culture affects public relations. Although public relations scholars have advanced the relationship between organizational culture (e.g., participatory culture) and public relations (e.g., Hung, 2003; Rhee, 1999; Sriramesh, 1992; Sriramesh, J. Grunig, and Buffington, 1992; Sriramesh, J. Grunig, and Dozier, D., 1996; Sriramesh and Takasaki, 1999), we do not know of any research that has investigated the impact of culture on activism and linked it to public relations.

Much of the research on the link between culture and public relations has relied on Hofstede's (1984, 2001) dimensions of culture. The most significant benefit of relying on the dimensions of culture he proposed is that we can quickly embark on cross-national comparative studies using a reliable and valid instrument. Although we shall rely on Hofstede's variables for our purposes here, we caution that Hofstede had not been able to identify all dimensions of culture (as he himself admitted) and so there is much scope for further development.

Our model of activism is based on societal culture as defined and explained by Sriramesh and White (1992) and updated in Chapter 3 of this volume. We propose here that societal culture can also influence public relations practice through an intervening variable—the level of activism. We postulate that some characteristics of societal culture are more conducive to the presence of higher levels of activism. This in turn influences the choice of public relations strategies and practices by organizations in those cultures. Our propositions will supplement previous findings about the relationship between culture and public relations at the organizational level.

Hofstede defined culture as "the collective programming of the mind which distinguishes the members of one human group from another" (Hofstede, 1984, p. 21). He saw culture as "systems of values" and values as the building blocks of culture. By adopting Guilford's (1959) definition of culture, Hofstede asserted that culture determines the identity of a human group in the same way as personality determines the identity of an individual.

Consequently, he proposed that culture can be measured the way one measures personality through psychological tests. He identified five dimensions of culture that have been reviewed in Chapter 1.

Existing public relations literature describes the formation of activist groups as originating from the individual. That is, an individual or a small group of people may identify an issue or problem and then organize to do something about it (Crable and Vibbert, 1985; J. Grunig and Hunt, 1984). In the process of organizing a larger group of like-minded persons, we postulate that more collectivistic cultures are likely to foster greater levels of activism because individuals in such cultures tend to share sentiments and are more loyal to the group and show solidarity with the problems of others. Members of a collective culture share an extended self-identity and are more likely to empathize with other members of the group. This increases the potential for collective action more than an individualistic culture where group *loyalty* is often superseded by personal *calculation*. However, it should be noted that collectivistic cultures are generally more tolerant and therefore less likely to engage in activism on a range of issues.

Second, more masculine cultures tend to foster higher levels of activism, because masculine cultures take a more aggressive approach to problems and situations. This leads to greater conflict and higher levels of confrontation against the source of the issue or problem. Third, we predict that societies with higher levels of uncertainty avoidance will experience greater activism because individuals in such societies have lower tolerance for ambiguity. As a consequence, they are more likely to engage in corrective actions to overcome such perceived uncertainties. Fourth, we predict that a society with lower levels of power distance will experience higher levels of activism. Most, if not all, members of such societies consider themselves as being equally powerful to effect societal changes and therefore they will be less shy to challenge perceived problems, injustices, and inequalities. However, we also acknowledge that high power distance has the potential to breed certain types of activism such as social movements (arising from a clash of classes for instance) because of higher levels of oppression over lengthy periods. Finally, societies that are oriented to short-term goals rather than longer term ones will experience higher levels of activism. Members of such societies tend to live more in the present and are less tolerant if the expected rewards (or solution) do not materialize quickly. In contrast, societies that are prone to a long-term orientation to life tend to be more tolerant of problematic situations because they have the patience to wait for anticipated rewards that may come in a more distant future.

ORGANIZATIONAL CONTEXTS

In addition to the political, economic, media, and cultural contexts, factors internal to an organized group also affect the level of activism in a society (Diani and McAdam, 2003; Glenn, 2003; Zhao, 1998). McAdam et al. (1988) stated that "[M]acro-political and economic processes may create the opportunity for successful collective action, but often it is *the internal structure of the population* in question that determines whether this opportunity will be realized" (p. 703; emphasis added). They extracted two specific conditions from previous studies. These were "ecological concentration" and "level of prior organizations" (pp. 703–704). *"Ecological concentration,"* is the degree of geographic concentration in the residential or occupational patterns in the everyday lives of members of a group. Geographic concentration often results in an increase in the frequency of interaction between group members as well as the nature of such interactions, thereby facilitating recruitment of activists. By creating ecologically dense concentrations of relatively homogeneous people, urbanization would tend to increase the structural potential for collective action (Diani and McAdam, 2003; McAdam et al., 1988). The next important condition is when there is a *"high level of prior organization"* in a given population, it is more likely to enhance the prospects for successful collective action (Bernstein, 2004; McAdam et al., 1988, p. 703).

Several studies have supported this hypothesis by examining the civil rights movement, the women's movement, and union membership (Freeman, 1973; Frieman and McAdam, 1992; Morris, 1984; Zald and McCarthy, 1987). Those studies indicated *the strength and breadth of indigenous organization* as the crucial factor in the rapid spread of a movement. For example, union membership was much lower in the United States than in most Western European nations. McAdam et al. (1988) argued this might explain why working class movements have historically played less of a role in politics in the U.S. than in most European countries. Also, the U.S. was especially dense in religiously based social organization compared with Western Europe and Japan, and in this context, many mass movements have been organizationally rooted in churches (McAdam et al., 1988, p. 704).

So, using the two favorable conditions of collective action, we postulate that 1) the higher the ecological concentration one country has, the higher the extent of activism in that country; and 2) the higher the level of prior organizations ("prior organization" is the term McAdams, et al. use to refer to organizations that have been in existence for several years) one country has, the higher the extent of activism it is likely to have.

RELATIONSHIP BETWEEN ACTIVISM AND PUBLIC RELATIONS

To illustrate the relationship between the level of activism and public relations practice, we have offered a conceptual model that also takes into account the other environmental variables discussed in this chapter and presented in Chapter 1. We have offered a definition for the term and discussed the meanings of activism. We have suggested two dimensions that help us understand the extent of activism in a society: the confrontational intensity and the breadth of issue spectrum. To account for the resulting level of activism in a given society, we then reviewed five socioculturual environmental factors. We conceptualized them as the antecedent socioculturual environmental conditions and have offered specific propositions linking each context with the level of activism. We summarize these propositions and the overall model in Figure 5.5.

Based on the conceptual model of activism, we now discuss how the socio-cultural environmental variables affect activism and in turn influence public relations practice in a society. In reviewing their research program on the relationship between activism and public relations, J. Grunig and L. Grunig (1997) linked activism and public relations thus:

> Activism also has assumed great importance as we have attempted to globalize the Excellence theory . . . Activism is particularly important as a specific variable because public relations would lose much of its value to organizations if activists did not exist. Without activists, the environment would be static and placid rather than dynamic and turbulent . . . If environments pose neither a threat nor an opportunity for organizations, as they seemingly do not in an authoritarian culture or political system, organizations could substitute vertically directed, coercive propaganda for horizontal, symmetrical public relations. (1997, p. 7)

We agree that the level of activism in a society has an impact on the way public relations is practiced. Because public relations functions as a boundary spanning function for organizations, public relations practitioners seek information about threats as well as opportunities on behalf of their organizations or clients. The lack of dynamism in the environment leads to a less strategic public relations program as seen in the domination of an asymmetrical and one-way communication approach (including propaganda). This postulation was supported by other studies such as Huang's (1997) analysis of the nuclear power company in Taiwan. She found that with the emergence of a civil rights movement in a previously authoritarian society (that had concomitantly low levels of activism), activism became a key factor that affects public relations practice and helped make it strategic.

In other words, *the higher the frequency and intensity of activism in a society, the greater the need for public relations and the more strategic the nature of the practice.* We extend this proposition further by linking it to socio-cultural environmental variables: *societies that have pluralistic political systems, free or at least partly free media systems, and greater individualism among the populace, are more likely to foster higher levels of activism requiring more symmetrical or strategic approaches to public relations practice.* Organizations that are not sensitive to the dynamism in their socio-cultural environments will pay the price by losing public trust and relationships with key stakeholders. More importantly, they may face threats to their own reputation as identified by the two examples at the beginning of this chapter.

We also rely on the generic principles of public relations to illustrate the impact of activism on public relations by focusing on five of the principles: 1) involvement of public relations in strategic management; 2) two-way model (i.e., mixed-motives model) of public relations, 3) a symmetrical system of internal communication, 4) ethical and social responsibility, and 5) the department has the knowledge needed to practice the managerial

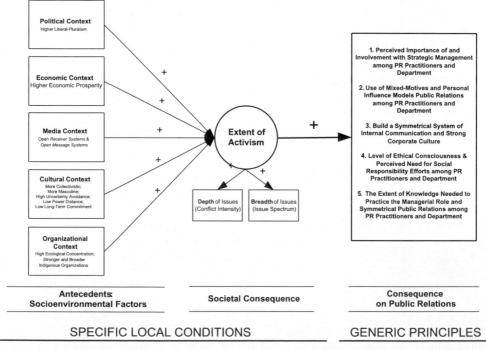

FIG. 5.5 Conceptual model: The effect of socio-cultural environmental variables on the adoption of generic principles of global public relations in a given society.

role and symmetrical public relations. We summarize our propositions linking the level of activism with the characteristics of public relations practices.

SUGGESTED RESEARCH QUESTIONS FOR FUTURE STUDY

In this chapter, we have presented a conceptual model linking activism with public relations as a prelude to discussing the influence of activism on public relations, and by extension, on global public relations. We see the model as being useful for trans-national studies. To facilitate further research using the model, we present some research questions in Table 5.1 that other scholars can use for extending our understanding of the relationship between activism and public relations. With the accumulation of such knowledge, the body of public relations becomes holistic and helps advance global public relations practice as well.

Organizations are going global and among the many challenges they face is having to interact with multinational activist publics. Further, enhanced physical mobility and communication makes it easier for cooperation and collaboration among multinational publics including activists. This has contributed to making the global environment more dynamic requiring the body of knowledge also to keep pace with the demands on the practice. Therefore, empirical knowledge is the need of the hour to complement the body of knowledge of global public relations—much of which, we feel, is conceptual. We hope the research questions will spawn these future studies.

TABLE 5.1
Summary of Research Questions for Future Research using the Descriptive Model of Activism

Research Questions & Propositions	
Socio-cultural Environmental Variables	RQ: Where does the country fall in the corporativistic–pluralistic continuum? If the context is changing, in which direction is the country headed? How have the identified political conditions affected the level of activism in the country?
	RQ: What is the type of economy in the country and its level of economic development? Does the country have the developmental infrastructure to foster activism? If the country is a transitional economy, what is the nature of transition and what are the forecasts for economic growth? How are current economic conditions being received by the populace and what impact have they had on activism in the country?
	RQ: Which media philosophy best describes the nature of the media environment in the country? Who controls the mass media in the country? What is the rate of diffusion of mass media – whom do the mass media reach (focusing on illiteracy and poverty as two limiting factors)? Are activists able to get access to the mass media in order to use them to propagate their cause?
	RQ: Which dimensions of culture best describe the dominant culture of the country? Are there potent subcultures and countercultures in the society? What impact have the dimensions of culture had on activism in the country?
	RQ: What level of ecological concentration and level of prior organization does the country have vis-à-vis activism? What impact have the identified intra-organizational conditions had on the country's activism?
The Extent of Activism in the Country	RQ: What is the history of activism in the country? What is the frequency of activist movements in the country? How intense have the confrontations been? What different tactics have activists used in the past?

(*Continued*)

TABLE 5.1

(Continued)

	Research Questions & Propositions
	RQ: What is the nature of issues that tend to help coalesce activists? How diverse are the various issues that activists seek to address in the given society?
Relationship between the Activism and Public Relations Approach	RQ: Typically, which types of organizations have been targeted by activist groups in this country? How have organizations reacted to activist pressures? Have they preferred to use communication rather than legal or other means to respond to activism?
	RQ: How predictive has the model offered in this chapter been vis-à-vis the level of activism in this country and its impact on the practice of public relations?
	RQ: What recommendations can one make regarding the public relations approach that organizations can make in this country based on the activism environment in the country?
	Proposition: A society whose socio-cultural environmental factors are more conducive to fostering greater levels of activism is more likely to necessitate 1) involvement of public relations in the strategic management process, 2) use of the two-way models (or mixed-motive) approach, 3) presence of a symmetrical internal communication system, 4) higher levels of ethical consciousness and social responsibility, and 5) higher levels of knowledge among practitioners for mixed-motive and strategic approaches in responding to activism.

CONCLUSION AND IMPLICATIONS

This chapter has introduced a conceptual linkage between socio-cultural environmental variables, activism, and public relations practice. What is needed is empirical evidence that can test the conceptual linkages offered here. Therefore, the chapter has offered research questions that could be used by future studies to add empirical evidence and refine the conceptual model presented here. These studies could assess, for example, whether higher levels of activism do contribute to strategic public relations in all societies or whether the socio-cultural environments of different societies deal with activism differently. Studies could also investigate whether being ethical or socially responsible is operationalized in the same way by different societies especially when responding to legitimate demands from activists. When combined with empirical evidence from such studies, we hope the model presented here will provide public relations practitioners with a better understanding of activists in different cultures. The ultimate outcome would also be how best one could adapt to the specific local conditions based on some global principles and strategies— glocalization.

REFERENCES

Altschull, H. J. (1984). *Agents of power*. White Plains, NY: Longman.

Benstein, T. P. (2004). Unrest in rural China: A 2003 assessment. Paper for Conference on "Beyond the Party-State: State, Law, and Society in Contemporary China," Center for East Asian Studies, Institute of Political Studies, Polish Academy of Sciences, Warsaw, June 30-July 1, 2004.

Browne, W. P. (1998). *Groups, interests, and U. S. public policy*. Washington, D.C.: Georgetown University Press.

Burstein, P. (1998). Interest organizations, political parties, and the study of democratic politics. In A. N. Costain and A. S. McFarland (Eds.), *Social movements and American political institutions* (pp. 39–56). Oxford: Rowman & Littlefield Publishers, Inc.

Clarke, P., and Kline, F. G. (1974). Mass media effects reconsidered: Some new strategies for communication research. *Communication Research, 1*, 224–270.

Crable, R. C., and Vibbert, S. L. (1985). Managing issues and influencing public policy. *Public Relations Review,* 11(2), pp. 3–15.

della Porta, D. and Diani, M. (1999). *Social movements: An introduction.* Oxford, UK: Blackwell.

DeLuca, K. M. (1999). *Image politics: The new rhetoric of environmental activism.* New York: The Guilford Press.

DeLuca, K. M., and Peeples, J. (2002). From public sphere to public screen: Democracy, activism, and the "violence" of Seattle. *Critical Studies in Media Communication, 19*, 125–151.

Diani, M. (1992). The concept of social movement. *The Sociological Review, 40*(1), 1–25.

Diani, M. and McAdam, D. (2003). *Social movements and networks: Relational approaches to collective action.* New York: Oxford University Press.

Dow, B. J. (2004). Fixing feminism: Women's liberation and the rhetoric of television documentary. *Quarterly Journal of Speech, 90*, 53–80.

Freeman, J. (1973). The origins of the women's liberation movement. *American Journal of Sociology, 78*, 792–811.

Friedman, D., and McAdam, D. (1992). Collective identity and activism: Networks, choices, and the life of a social movement. In Aldon D. Morris and Carol Mueller (Eds.), *Frontiers of social movement theories* (pp. 156–173). New Haven, CT: Yale University Press.

Glenn, J. K. (2003). Contentious politics and democratization: Comparing the impact of social movements on the fall of communism in Eastern Europe. *Political Studies, 51*, 103–120.

Grunig, J. E. (1997). A situational theory of publics: Conceptual history, recent challenges and new research. In D. Moss, T. MacManus, and D. Verčič (Eds.), *Public relations research: An international perspective* (pp. 3–46). London: International Thompson Business Press.

Grunig, J. E. (2003). Constructing public relations theory and practice. In B. Dervin and S. Chaffee, with L. Foreman-Wernet (Eds.), *Communication, another kind of horse race: Essays honoring Richard F. Carter* (pp. 85–115). Cresskill, NJ: Hampton Press.

Grunig, J. E., and Grunig, L. A. (July 1997). Review of a program of research on activism: Incidence in four countries, activist publics, strategies of activist groups, and organizational responses to activism. Paper presented at the Fourth Public Relations Research Symposium, Managing Environmental Issues, Lake Bled, Slovenia.

Grunig, J. E., and Hunt, T. (1984). *Managing public relations.* New York: Holt, Rinehart and Winston.

Grunig, J. E., and Jaatinen, M. (1998). *Strategic, symmetrical public relations in government: From pluralism to societal corporatism.* Paper presented at the Fifth Annual International Public Relations Research Symposium, Bled, Slovenia, July 10–11, 1998.

Grunig, L. A. (1992). Activism: How it limits the effectiveness of organizations and how excellent public relations departments respond. In J. E. Grunig (Ed.), *Excellence in public relations and communication management: Contributions to effective organizations* (pp. 503–530). Hillsdale, NJ: Lawrence Erlbaum Associates.

Guilford, R. R. (1959). *Personality.* New York: McGraw-Hill.

Hachten, W. (1981). *The world news prism: Changing media, clashing ideologies.* Ames, IA: Iowa State University Press.

Hiebert, R. E., Ungurait, D. F., and Bohn, T. W. (1988). *Mass Media V.* New York: Longman.

Hofstede, G. (1984). *Culture's consequences: International differences in work-related values.* Beverly Hills, CA: Sage.

Hofstede, G. (2001). *Culture's consequences: Comparing values, behaviors, institutions, and organizations across nations.* Beverly Hills, CA: Sage.

Huang, Y. H. (July–August 1997). Impacts of a political system and activism on public relations—A perspective from the theory of global public relations. Paper presented to the Public Relations Division, Association for Education in Journalism and Mass Communication, Chicago, IL.

Hung, C. J. F. (2003). Culture, relationship cultivation, and relationship outcomes: A qualitative evaluation on multinational companies' relationship management in China. Paper presented at the Public Relations Division in the 53rd annual conference of International Communication Association, San Diego, May.

Inkeles, A., and Levinson, D. J. (1969). National character: The study of modal personality and sociocultural systems. In G. Lindzey and E. Aronson (Eds.), *The handbook of social psychology, vol. 4*. Reading, MA: Addison-Wesley.

Jenkins, J. C. (1983). Resource mobilization theory and the study of social movements. *Annual Review of Sociology*, 9, 527–553.

Katz, E. and Blumler, J. G. (1974). *The uses of mass communications*. Beverly Hills, CA: Sage.

Kielbowicz, R. B. and Scherer, C. (1986). The role of the press in the dynamics of social movements. In K. Lang, G. E. Lang, and L. Kriesberg (Eds.), *Research in social movements, conflicts and change* (pp. 71–96). Greenwich CT: JAI Press Inc.

Kim, J.-N. (March 2002). Toward a descriptive model of activism: Applying the working model to Korean activism and the relationship of the extent of activism to the public relations in Korea. Paper presented at the Educators Academy of the Public Relations Society of America, Miami, Florida.

Klandermans, B. (1997). *The social psychology of protest*. Cambridge, MA: Blackwell Publishers Inc.

Kluckhohn, C. (1962). Universal categories of culture. In D. Lerner and H. D. Lasswell (Eds.), *The policy sciences* (pp. 304–320). Stanford, CA: Stanford University Press.

McAdam, D. (1982). *Political process and the development of black insurgency, 1930–1970*. Chicago, IL: University of Chicago Press.

McAdam, D., and Friedman, D. (1992). Collective identity and activism: Networks, choices, and the life of a social movement. In Aldon D. Morris and Carol Mueller (Eds.), *Frontiers of social movement theories* (pp.156–173). New Haven, CT: Yale University Press.

McAdam, D., McCarthy, J., and Zald, M. N. (1988). Social movements. In Neil J. Smelser (Ed.), *Handbook of sociology* (pp. 695–739). Beverly Hills, CA: Sage.

McCarthy, J. D. (1996). Constraints and opportunities in adopting, adapting, and inventing. In D. McAdam, J. McCarthy, and M. N. Zald (Eds.), *Comparative perspectives on social movements* (pp. 141–151). New York: Cambridge University Press.

McCarthy, J. D., and Zald, M. N. (1973). *The trend of social movements in America: Professionalization and resource mobilization*. Moristown, NJ: General Learning Press.

McCarthy, J. D., McPhail, C., and Smith, J. (1996). Images of protest: Dimensions of selection bias in media coverage of Washington demonstrations, 1982 and 1991. *American Sociological Review, 61*, 478–499.

Martin, L. J., and Chaudhary, A. G. (1983). *Comparative mass media systems*. New York: Longman.

Merrill, J. C., and Lowenstein, R. L. (1971). *Media, messages, and men*. New York: Longman.

Mintzberg, H. (1983). *Power in and around organizations*. Englewood Cliffs, NJ: Prentice-Hall.

Morris, A. (1984). *The origins of the civil rights movement*. New York: Free Press.

Parsons, T., and Shils, E. A. (1951). *Toward a general theory of action*. Cambridge, MA: Harvard University Press.

Rhee, Y. (1999). Confucian culture and excellent public relations: A study of generic principles and specific applications in South Korean public relations practice. Unpublished Master's thesis submitted to the University of Maryland at College Park, Maryland, U.S.A.

Rohlinger, D. (August 2006). Mass Media and Discursive Opportunities in the Abortion Debate, 1980–2000. Paper presented at the annual meeting of the American Sociological Association, Montreal Convention Center, Montreal, Quebec, Canada.

Sanger, D. E. (May 17, 1991). Suicides by Korean protesters stir unease and fear of a plot. *New York Times*, Retrieved October 11, 2007, from http://query.nytimes.com.

Siebert, F. S., Peterson, T., and Schramm, W. (1956). *Four theories of the press*. Urbana, IL: University of Illinois Press.

Sriramesh, K., and Rivera, M. (2006). Corporatism and Communitarianism as environments for e-governance: The case of Singapore. *New Media and Society 8*(5), 707–730.

Sriramesh, K., and Takasaki, M. (2000). The impact of culture on Japanese public relations. *Journal of Communication Management 3*(4), pp. 337–352.

Sriramesh, K., and Verčič, D. (2003). *The Global Public Relations Handbook: Theory, Research, and Practice.* Mahwah, NJ: Lawrence Erlbaum.

Sriramesh, K., and White, J. (1992). Societal Culture and Public Relations. In J. E. Grunig (Ed.), *Excellence in*

Public Relations and Communications Management: Contributions to Effective Organizations. Hillsdale, NJ: Lawrence Erlbaum Associates., pp. 597–616.

Sriramesh, K., Grunig, J. E., and Buffington, J. (1992). Corporate Culture and Public Relations. In J. E. Grunig (Ed.), *Excellence in Public Relations and Communications Management: Contributions to Effective Organizations.* Hillsdale, NJ: Lawrence Erlbaum Associates., pp. 577–596.

Sriramesh, K., Grunig, J. E., and Dozier, D. (1996). Observation and Measurement of Organizational Culture: Development of Indices of Participative and Authoritarian Cultures. *Journal of Public Relations Research, 8*(4), pp. 229–262.

Streeck, W. and Kenworthy, L. (2005). Theories and practices of neocorporatism. In T. Janoski, R. R. Alford, A. M. Hicks, and M. A. Schwartz (Eds.), *The handbook of political sociology: States, civil societies, and globalization* (pp. 441–460). New York: Cambridge University Press.

Tarrow, S. (1994). *Power in movement: Social movements, collective action, and mass politics in the modern state.* Cambridge: Cambridge University Press.

Tarrow, S. (1998). *Power in movement: Social movements and contentious politics* (2nd Edn). New York: Cambridge University Press.

Wright, J. R. (1996). *Interest groups and congress: Lobbying, contributions, and influence.* Needham Heights, MA: Allyn and Bacon.

Zald, M. N., and McCarthy, J. D. (1987). Religious groups as crucibles of social movements. In M. N. Zald and J. D. McCarthy (Eds.), *Social movements in an organizational society* (pp. 67–96). New Brunswick, NJ: Transaction Books.

Zeigler, H. (1988). *Pluralism, corporatism, and Confucianism: Political association and conflict regulation in the United States, Europe, and Taiwan.* Philadelphia: Temple University Press.

Zhao, D. (1998). Ecologies of social movements: Student mobilization during the 1989 prodemocracy movement in Beijing. *American Journal of Sociology, 103*, 1493–1529.

ASIA AND AUSTRALASIA

6

PUBLIC RELATIONS IN AUSTRALASIA: FRIENDLY RIVALRY, CULTURAL DIVERSITY, AND GLOBAL FOCUS

JUDY MOTION
SHIRLEY LEITCH
SIMON CLIFFE

INTRODUCTION

As discussed in chapter 1, in recent years, public relations practice has gone global. The strong influence of this globalization is especially evident in New Zealand and Australia. In this chapter we discuss the commonalities as well as the unique features in public relations practice in the two countries. The relationship between the two countries might best be described as a "friendly rivalry" in all spheres. Sporting contests between the two nations, particularly on the rugby field, are fiercely competitive, and victory is highly prized. However, the two nations have always assisted one another during times of crisis and have fought alongside one another in the major conflicts of the 20th century. In public relations, this cooperation can be seen in the joint conferences and the frequent interchanges among practitioners of the two countries. The multinational status of many public relations companies also means that practitioners in New Zealand and Australia find themselves working for the same global companies. Weber Shandwick, Hill and Knowlton, and Burson Marsteller are a few of the many large consultancy chains that operate in both countries. The presence of these consultancies ensures that the standard of public relations in New Zealand and Australia reflects international best practice, whereas competition from local providers ensures that public relations is adapted to fit local circumstances and priorities. This chapter addresses the challenges of distance, bicultural and multicultural policies, activism, technology, and media fragmentation that have influenced the development and practice of public relations in New Zealand and Australia.

History, Geography, and Culture of New Zealand and Australia

The independent nations of New Zealand and Australia, positioned in the southwest Pacific, are often collectively referred to as Australasia. New Zealand lies about 1,000 km to the east of Australia. Australia is situated between the Pacific and Indian Oceans and has Indonesia and Papua New Guinea to the north. Both New Zealand and Australia are relatively sparsely populated, with 3.7 million (statistics New Zealand, 2002) and 19 million (Australian Bureau of Statistics, 2002) inhabitants, respectively, most of whom dwell in urban areas. English is the major language in both countries, although New Zealand also recognizes Maori, the language of the indigenous people, as an official language. Both nations have currencies based on the dollar, but they operate independently. Despite the many similarities between these geographically close neighbors, there also are many differences, especially in politics, economics, and culture.

History has been one point of commonality between the two nations that were once British colonies which, though modern democracies, still recognize the British queen as nominal head of state. The two nations routinely cooperate in a wide variety of areas in the international arena. For example, during World War I, Australia and New Zealand formed a joint army corps—the Australia and New Zealand Army Corps (ANZAC)—to help the allies on the European front. The ANZACs and the hardships they endured constituted an important moment in the formation of each country's distinct national identity (Molony, 1988; Sinclair, 1991). The spirit of cooperation embodied by the ANZACs also defined the notion of mateship, which has been especially predominant within Australian culture ever since.

New Zealand is an archipelago consisting of two main islands: the North Island and the South Island, where the majority of the population resides. It has an indigenous Maori population who have settled in the country since approximately 1000 AD. Discovered by Dutch explorer Abel Tasman in 1642, and circumnavigated by Captain James Cook in 1769, New Zealand was settled predominantly by European traders and whalers, soon to be followed by missionaries who arrived in the early 1800s (Sinclair, 1991). The Treaty of Waitangi, signed in 1840, ceded sovereignty of the land from the Maori to the British empire. This has dominated race relations and continues to do so in the new millennium (Sinclair, 1991). As a British colony, most of the new immigrants after 1840 were of British extraction, which has resulted in the development of close cultural, political, and economic ties with Great Britain. New Zealand once simply adopted British foreign policy as its own and served primarily as a far-flung British farm, producing food and other agricultural products for the British market. These close ties between Britain and New Zealand resulted in New Zealand's almost unquestioning involvement in both world wars. With the adoption of the Statute of Westminster in 1947, New Zealand became a politically independent nation and a member of the British Commonwealth.

In the latter half of the 20th century, New Zealand's biggest challenge had been to combat its declining standard of living relative to other countries (Dalziel, 2002). Like Australia, New Zealand is a member of the Organisation for Economic Co-operation and Development (OECD). OECD's member countries are committed to a market economy and pluralistic government and work to coordinate international and domestic policies in recognition of an increasingly globalized world (Organisation for Economic Co-operation and Development, 2002). In the 1950s, New Zealand was ranked as one of the most prosperous nations in the world (Sinclair, 1991), but its ranking fell to 23rd in the OECD by the beginning of the new millennium. The entry of Britain into the European Economic

Community in the 1970s led to dramatic reductions in the volume of agricultural exports from New Zealand to Britain. The loss of this market caused enormous economic and cultural upheaval in New Zealand and forced the nation to shift its focus from being "Britain's farm" to becoming a distinct nation with its own identity. New Zealand is now a fully participating member of the Asia–Pacific region but has struggled to regain its former economic position.

Australia is the smallest continent but the sixth largest country in the world. The indigenous Aboriginal tribes have inhabited the continent for at least the last 20,000 years. Britain began colonization of Australia in 1788 when Captain Arthur Phillip of the British Royal Navy landed at Botany Bay. Originally, Australia's main role was to serve as a penal colony for Britain's ex-convicts who were the settlers in the early days of the nation (Molony, 1988). Australia did not become a fully integrated colony until 1901 when the various colonies became federated. One of the first actions of the new federal government was to design a "White Australia Policy," which was intended to preserve the Anglo-Celtic heritage of the British settlers (Molony, 1988 p. 294). The policy was made more attractive by the blending of imperial and nationalistic sentiments that proclaimed that Australia's vast empty spaces could support an immense population. World War II revived the old catch-cry, "populate or perish," and a vigorous campaign was launched to encourage immigration from all parts of Europe. Thus, the emphasis shifted from seeking Anglo-Celtic immigrants to seeking immigrants from a variety of European nations. Over the next 4 decades, ethnic diversification gradually intensified with large numbers of Greeks, Italians, and other nationalities, for whom English was not the first language, settling in Australia (Molony, 1988). The 1980s brought heated debates on the relative merits of publicly funded programs for assimilation and for multiculturalism. Between World War II and the late 1980s, approximately 500,000 refugees and displaced persons arrived in Australia. By the 1980s, a quarter of Australians were immigrants, hailing from 120 different countries (Molony, 1988). Today, like New Zealand, Australia has accepted the economic and strategic significance of the Asia-Pacific region given the retrenchment of its traditional European trading partners and has been able to maintain a relatively high standard of living.

Evolution of the Profession

Despite the cultural, economic, and historical differences, public relations has evolved in remarkably similar ways in New Zealand and Australia. The profession began in both countries when journalists, mostly men, began to conduct media relations on behalf of organizations or clients. In New Zealand, the profession's birth can be traced to an historic meeting in the Auckland Star Hotel in 1954 when a group of demobilized military press officers formed what was to become the Public Relations Institute of New Zealand (PRINZ) (Motion & Leitch, 2001). Because of the size of Australia, public relations institutes began at different times in different states and subsequently joined to form the Public Relations Institute of Australia (PRIA). Public relations practitioners in New South Wales became the first to form a professional body in Australia, 5 years earlier than their New Zealand counterparts (Singh & Smyth, 2000). They were followed in 1952 by their colleagues in the state of Victoria. Today, Australia has divisions of PRIA in every state as well as a national body.

In the early years of the profession, almost all public relations practitioners began their professional lives as journalists before entering public relations. There were no opportunities for training public relations professionals in either Australia or New Zealand, an issue recognized by pioneering public relations practitioners. In fact, sharing their knowledge of public relations was the first priority of those who attended the inaugural session of PRINZ in 1954 (Motion & Leitch, 2001). They resolved to circulate whatever books or papers they had among members of the group and actively seek relevant information, particularly from the United States and Europe, which were seen to be leading the development of the field of public relations. In the days before airmail and the Internet, New Zealand and Australia were very isolated from the rest of the world. Newspapers and periodicals took months to arrive by sea and were out of date before they were distributed. There were few opportunities for local practitioners to meet counterparts from other countries. The advent of affordable and regular air services was an important step in exposing the profession in both countries to the ideas of the rest of the world. Air travel made it possible for New Zealanders and Australians to attend conferences and seminars and to learn from a broader range of experiences. However, the significance of the impact of air travel on the development of public relations is probably dwarfed by that of the Internet. For geographically isolated nations, the Internet offers instant access not just to information but also to professional networks.

Status of the Profession

There is no requirement for public relations practitioners to belong to their respective professional associations. Thus, anyone—regardless of education, experience, or understanding of ethics—is able to use the title *public relations consultant* and profit from it. It is difficult to estimate the total number of practitioners who are not members of professional bodies due to the diversity of job titles that are in use. Corporate communications manager, business communications manager, corporate affairs consultant, media relations specialist, press officer, in-house journalist, external relations director, and executive assistant are just a sample of the titles given to or adopted by practitioners. By electing to join either PRINZ or PRIA, practitioners demonstrate their commitment to the development of public relations as a profession with a body of knowledge, accreditation systems, and a code of conduct for ethical practice.

It is estimated that $A250 million is spent annually on public relations in Australia (Tymson & Lazar, 2002, p. 39). Similar figures are not available for New Zealand. In April 2002, PRINZ had a membership of 653, and PRIA's was 2856. The demographics of the members of both associations bear striking similarities. In both countries, approximately 60% of practitioners are women (Peart, 1998; Singh & Smyth, 2000; Tymson & Lazar, 2002). This figure is indicative of the dramatic shift that has occurred since the 1950s when public relations was practiced almost entirely by men. Peart (1998) noted that the older the practitioners were, the more likely it was that they would be male. Singh and Smyth (2000) referred to this gender shift as the "feminization of public relations" (p. 392) and noted some issues associated with feminization, including disparities in salaries based on gender. However, given that men still dominate the senior ranks of public relations in both countries, the full impact of feminization remains to be seen as more experienced female practitioners move into these higher paying positions. Peart's (1998) data suggest that length of experience, rather than gender, is the primary explanation for existing salary disparities. This finding is reinforced by Singh and Smyth (2000) who noted that at least one study in Australia had concluded that women in entry-level positions were earning more than their male counterparts.

Practitioners of both countries face similar professional issues. One of these—technology—has been alluded to already. Technologies, including the Internet, e-mail, databases, mobile telephones, and personal computers, have all had a significant impact on public relations. These technologies were either not invented or were not available in a form or at a price that was accessible when senior practitioners entered the profession. However, technology is only one area of significant change for practitioners. According to Singh and Smyth (2000), Australian public relations is fast becoming a strategic function with ties to the senior levels of management within organizations. This shift from the tactical to the strategic has increased the range of skills and knowledge that practitioners will need to acquire in order to succeed in the profession. A survey by the PRIA showed that major job duties were promotions and publicity (59%), counselling and consulting (52.1%), management (40%), writer/editor/publications (47.2%), internal communications (30.9%), and government relations (27%; Tymson & Lazar, 2002, p. 51).

Professional Education for the Public Relations Industry

The introduction of education and training programs for public relations and the expectation for entry-level practitioners to have relevant training is an important development for the profession, much of which has occurred over the past 2 decades. Nearly 90% of practitioners who took part in a New Zealand study conducted by Peart (1998) had tertiary qualifications. Similar findings resulted from an Australian Committee for Economic Development (CED) study conducted in 1997 (Singh & Smyth, 2000, p. 393). There are no data about the number of practitioners with public relations education, but, given the recent spurt in public relations education, it is likely that a significant proportion of the younger practitioners have some formal public relations education. Thus, the typical public relations practitioner of the future is likely to be a woman with a relevant degree or diploma in public relations.

Formal public relations education began in New Zealand in the late 1960s at Wellington Polytechnic. This part-time course was a joint initiative with PRINZ and was well-supported by the capital city's practitioners, many of whom worked for the government or in the head of offices of New Zealand's largest companies (Motion & Leitch, 2001, p. 661). Now there are degree and diploma courses in public relations at most tertiary institutions in New Zealand. In addition, there are numerous short courses in the area, often offered with the support of the PRINZ. A similar situation exists in Australia with both the tertiary education sector and the PRIA actively offering a range of courses and qualifications for both existing as well as new practitioners (Tymson & Lazar, 2002, p. 38). The major difference between the two nations is that, although PRIA operates an accreditation system for public relations qualifications, PRINZ has a less formal system. Although programs offered in any discipline by New Zealand universities and polytechnics must undergo a stringent approval process, this process is largely overseen by other educationalists, and there are only informal, limited, and piecemeal opportunities for industry input.

Public relations education has been accompanied by a growth in research and scholarship published in local journals such as the *Asia Pacific Public Relations Journal*, the *Australian Journal of Communication*, and *Media International Australia incorporating Culture and Policy*. Reflecting the international trend, public relations theory development in New Zealand and Australia is moving from the predominant systems approach to rhetorical, critical, and poststructuralist approaches.

Practitioner Accreditation

The absence of an accreditation system by PRINZ in New Zealand may be partly explained by the fact that there is a competing organization to which some New Zealand practitioners belong. The strength of this organization in New Zealand—the International Association of Business Communicators—has its roots in the split that occurred within PRINZ following the introduction of accreditation examinations for practitioners (Motion & Leitch, 2001). The accreditation examinations were intended to distinguish full members from associate members of PRINZ. They were not compulsory, and practitioners could continue to belong to and take part in PRINZ activities irrespective of their accreditation status. However, some senior practitioners were unhappy with the suggestion that they needed an examination system administered by their peers to determine their membership status and, therefore, resigned from PRINZ. An accreditation system exists in Australia under the aegis of the PRIA but does not appear to have led to a similar split. There are no data on the number of practitioners who have gained accreditation in the two countries. However, a study by CED in Australia found that about 20% of respondents had gained PRIA accreditation by 1997 (Singh & Smyth, 2000, p. 393). The majority of those surveyed— over 70%—were members of PRIA, suggesting that the majority of PRIA members are not accredited. Peart's (1998) study of senior New Zealand public relations practitioners found that the majority—56%—were accredited members of PRINZ. However, Peart's sample was skewed toward more experienced professionals who are more likely to be accredited.

Codes of Ethics

Accreditation, either of individuals or programs, has the potential to generate controversy. It is only surpassed in this regard by professional codes of ethics or professional practice. Both PRINZ and PRIA operate under such codes, and their content and application have always been the source of lively debate within the profession. In Australia, two separate codes are in operation. The first is the Consultancy Code of Practice, which delineates the general standards to which a consultancy should adhere, a framework within which client relations should be conducted, and a set of guidelines for fees and income. The "General Standards" section of the code begins with the instruction that a registered consultancy: "Accepts a positive duty to observe the highest standards in its business practice and in the practice of public relations; promote the benefits of public relations practice in all dealings; and improve the general understanding of professional public relations practice" (Public Relations Institute of Australia, 2001). This section of the code also states that a registered consultancy: "Adheres to the highest standards of accuracy and truth, avoiding extravagant claims and unfair comparisons and gives credit to ideas and words borrowed from others." There is no legal requirement for any Australian consultancy to either affiliate with PRIA or apply the Code of Practice. However, PRIA operates a register of consultancies in each Australian state, and only those consultancies that adhere to the code are able to list their services. PRINZ operates a similar register for New Zealand consultancies. However, there is no Code of Practice determining which consultancies may or may not list their services. Thus, the PRINZ register serves solely as a reference guide for those seeking to employ a consultancy, a function that could potentially lead to embarrassment for PRINZ in the event of poor or unethical practice by a listed consultant.

The PRINZ Code of Ethics was developed in response to concern over an ethical issue that focused media attention on the profession. Codes of ethics or of public relations practice evolve differently in different countries partly in response to the cases that the ethics committees of the relevant professional bodies confront. In New Zealand, the profession faced a major problem following disclosures in the book entitled *Secrets and Lies: The Anatomy of an Anti-Environmental PR Campaign*. The book, written by two environmental activists, Nicky Hagar and Bob Burton (1998), mapped the role that a prominent New Zealand public relations consultancy had played in assisting the continuation of logging of native forests. The book accused the consultancy of a range of activities including spying, lying, media manipulation, and undermining the democratic process. Such accusations often bring the entire profession of public relations into disrepute and create problems for all practitioners. Given that membership of PRINZ and PRIA is not compulsory, it is difficult for these associations to censure practitioners who choose not to operate within the boundaries of the relevant ethical code. Such practitioners can elect not to join the bodies or can simply resign when controversy erupts to put themselves and their work outside of the jurisdiction of ethics committees.

A new PRINZ code was developed to highlight that public relations practice is a form of advocacy and stress the importance of making the right judgment in balancing corporate and societal obligations: "We must balance our role as advocates for the individuals or groups with the public interest. We must also balance a commitment to promote open communication with the privacy rights of individuals and organisations." (Public Relations Institute of New Zealand, 2002). The code was modeled on that of the Public Relations Society of America and outlined a set of values and beliefs that guide behavior and decision-making processes. These values are advocacy, honesty, expertise, independence, loyalty, and fairness. The code then defines the principles and standards for the practice of public relations in New Zealand. Members are required to balance advocacy and honesty as well as openness and privacy, disclose conflicts of interest, abide by the law, and act in a professional manner. The differences between the codes reflect the lessons learned by the two organizations based on the different situations they have encountered.

Overall, the PRIA code is the more extensive of the two, containing 15 sections compared with the 5 in the PRINZ code. The additional concerns of PRIA primarily relate to the activities of consultancies, with a prohibition on linking fees with results and on seeking payment for unspecified work. The practices of consultancies have clearly been a more prominent issue in Australia than they have been in New Zealand. The PRIA code also requires its members to share information and experiences with one another to assist in the improvement of the general body of knowledge in public relations. Members are barred from misrepresenting their accreditation status in relation to the institute and are also required to act in accordance with the aims, regulations, and policies of the institute. Thus, PRIA is more overt in requiring that members comply with PRIA's standards. PRINZ is, therefore, more prescriptive in its requirements for members in relation to society, whereas PRIA is more concerned with relationships among members and between members and their clients. Both PRIA and PRINZ are members of the Global Alliance for Public Relations and Communications Management (GA) among countries practicing public relations throughout the world. The GA collaborates with a mission to enhance the public relations profession throughout the world. It will, for example, provide opportunities to network, examine ethical practices, and develop a universal accreditation system. A comparison study of codes of ethics was undertaken in February 2002, and the GA is now exploring opportunities to create a global code of ethics.

INFRASTRUCTURE OF NEW ZEALAND AND AUSTRALIA

As mentioned in the overview of this chapter, although both countries are parliamentary democracies with close historical connections to Britain, New Zealand and Australia have developed quite different political and economic systems. However, like other members of the Commonwealth, the two countries have derived their legal systems from British law, and much legislation is still tied to the original British statutes.

An Overview of the New Zealand and Australian Political Systems

New Zealand's parliamentary democracy is based on the British parliamentary model, with legislative power vested in a single house of representatives whose members are elected via universal suffrage every 3 years. The party, or coalition of parties, that holds a majority in the house form the government, with the leader of the dominant party becoming prime minister. The prime minister selects ministers of parliament to form a cabinet, which is the central organ of executive power. The New Zealand Constitution is a combination of both statute and convention, with convention generally taking precedence when there is a conflict between the two.

The Australian system, however, can be described as an amalgam of the British and American political systems. Like New Zealand, it is a parliamentary democracy with the Queen of England as the formal Head of State. However, like the American system, Australia is also a federation of states, and the division of power between the federal government and the state governments is explicitly laid down in a written constitution. The Australian Federation has a three-tier system of government—federal, state, and local. At the federal level, it is based on a two-party system in which the party or coalition of parties with the majority in the House of Representatives forms the government.

The British monarchy is represented in both countries by a governor–general appointed by the monarch at the recommendation of the respective New Zealand and Australian governments. The governor–general has limited powers, but he or she does have the responsibility to protect the constitution and to act in case of a constitutional crisis. Both countries have a tradition of egalitarianism, with New Zealand being one of the first countries to award women's suffrage in 1893 followed closely by Australia in 1894. At present both countries maintain universal suffrage for those age 18 and older.

The New Zealand Political System

In 1993, New Zealand voted to replace its First Past the Post (FPP) system with a Mixed Member Proportional Representation electoral system (MMP) system. Essentially, the MMP system is a proportional voting system in which each voter has two votes: one to elect their representative and one for their preferred party. Parliament currently consists of 67 electorate seats, and 53 party list seats; thus, voters are able to vote for their preferred electorate representative as well as their preferred party. There is a stipulation that for a party to win any list seats it must garner at least 5% of the party list vote or win at least one electoral seat. Elections are held every 3 years.

Historically, under the FPP system, New Zealand politics had been dominated by two major parties, the New Zealand Labour Party (center left) and the New Zealand National Party (center right). Other minority parties include The Association of Consumers and Taxpayers (ACT), the Green Party, the New Zealand First Party, and the United Future Party of New Zealand. Since the inception of the MMP electoral system in 1996, the two major political parties have dominated New Zealand politics, but the MMP system has required them to share power with minority coalition partners. In the current government, the Labour Party was forced to enter into coalition with the left-wing Alliance Party to gain a governing majority in Parliament. The change to the MMP system was based on the rationale of broadening the base of representation in Parliament, thus making Parliament more representative of the wider views of the electorate. In real terms, it has broadened the power base from the executive to the wider members of Parliament, which has made lobbying and power brokering a lot more important and influential in the machinations of government. Lobbying government on behalf of organizations has, therefore, become an important role for public relations consultancies (Aggett, 1996). Weaver and Motion (in press) argued that in New Zealand public relations practices are associated with the neo-liberal political economy where public interest has been subsumed by corporate and market interests. However, a change in government can signal a change in the role of public relations. The current labor-alliance government is more cautious in its use of public relations and has internalized the role, whereas the opposition (National Party) overtly uses public relations consultants.

There has been a high level of political activism in New Zealand. In recent times, the visit by nuclear-powered or armed ships to New Zealand ports, land claims by the Maori, and environmental issues such as genetic engineering have been the major sources of controversy. In the mid-1980s, the government responded to the majority viewpoint that opposed visits by nuclear ships, declaring New Zealand a nuclear-free zone. This effective ban on the warships of allied countries has been a continuing source of strained international relations, particularly between New Zealand and the United States. It has also caused difficulties between New Zealand and Australia and reduced the level of military cooperation between the two countries. More recently, in 2001 the Government held a Royal Commission of Enquiry into genetic engineering. The outcome of the enquiry was to tighten the rules that governed genetic-engineering experiments and trials but not to ban such activity. This issue continues to be a source of controversy in the country as well as a source of votes for the Green Party.

Political activism over a range of issues is, therefore, a continuing concern not only for the government but also other organizations in New Zealand. They must negotiate in an attempt to broker acceptable compromises with a range of stakeholders who often hold strong, often conflicting views. Public relations practitioners are frequently deployed to manage stakeholder relations particularly when political issues are involved. However, public relations practitioners in New Zealand have not always dealt with sensitive political issues in a way that has brought credit on the profession. For example, the tactics used by one consultancy to discredit environmental activists opposing the logging of native forests (Hagar & Burton, 1998) and by another to prevent publicity about mutations occurring in genetically modified salmon (Weaver & Motion, in press) seriously damaged the reputation of public relations as a profession. As already discussed, these incidents have led PRINZ to rewrite its code of ethics and have made professional ethics an important topic for debate in national forums.

The Australian Political System

The Australian electoral system is based on the principles of one person, one vote, and one value. Under the Commonwealth Electoral Act, (Commonwealth of Australia, 2002) Federal elections for the House of Representatives and the Senate are conducted using a preferential voting system, which ensures that a majority of voters have some say in the election of the government, even if their party of choice is not elected. Voters must indicate their preference for every candidate by essentially rank ordering their choices; failure to do so means their vote is not counted. Voters may use ticket voting in the Senate, for which only a mark is required against the name of a political party or an independent, and preferences are then distributed according to that party's official list.

Australian federal politics shares one major commonality with New Zealand in that it has largely been dominated by two major political parties: the Australian Liberal Party and the Australian Labour Party. However, the preferential voting system does encourage minority representation in Parliament, which has made coalitions important in governance. Australian minority political parties include the Australian Democratic Party, the Green Party, the National Party, and the One Nation Party. The multilayered nature of the Australian system, with dual houses in both the states and in the national parliament, presents both challenges and opportunities for public relations practitioners. The complexity of the system ensures that there are multiple points at which public relations practitioners engaged in lobbying activities can attempt to influence the political process. However, this same complexity makes it possible for influence at one level to be countered at a higher level or thwarted at a lower level by opposing lobbyists.

Many of the same issues that divide New Zealanders have also been a source of political activism in Australia, becoming a source of work for Australian public relations consultants. Australia has witnessed a strong environmental movement in areas such as protesting the logging of native forests, the destruction of the environment caused by widespread mining in central Australia, and genetic engineering—particularly of foods. Race relations has also been a contentious issue in Australia. The Aboriginals of Australia do not have the equivalent of the New Zealand Treaty of Waitangi, as a result of which the issue of indigenous land rights has become more complex for both the government and the judiciary system. There are also strong vestiges of traditional beliefs on the White Australia Policy on immigration, and the One Nation Party has emerged as the political voice of this viewpoint. More recently, the current Government regained power in 2001, partly because of its strong stance against refugees from Afghanistan and Asia, who arrive by boat on Australia's northern coastline, by denying them entry.

An Overview of Australasia's Economic Systems

Over the last half century, despite the close economic ties between New Zealand and Australia, Australia has maintained greater economic growth and a higher standard of living than New Zealand in the OECD rankings. The two countries entered into the Closer Economic Relations Agreement in 1983, which has seen the transformation of Australasia into a free-trade zone. Australia benefits from approximately $A7 billion worth of exports to New Zealand, whereas New Zealand exports only over $A5 billion worth of goods to Australia. Much of Australia's trade is dependent on mineral resources and agriculture combined with a growing manufacturing base, whereas New Zealand is very rich in fisheries and agriculture, which contribute to approximately 60% of its export earnings. There is an ongoing discussion about the possible integration of the two economies in the future.

Both countries have highly educated populations, largely because primary and secondary school education is both free and compulsory. Tertiary education is subsidised by the state, and the majority of students study in state-funded tertiary institutions. Both countries possess modern telecommunications systems. The Internet and mobile phone penetration rates in Australia and New Zealand rank among the highest in the world. The availability of broadband is currently an issue confronting the governments of both nations.

The New Zealand Economy

Historically, there has been a large degree of government intervention in the economic of New Zealand. However, there has been a systematic liberalization of the economy and deregulation since 1984. Dalziel (2002) explained these reforms:

> Within a year of change of government in July 1984, interest rates were deregulated, international capital restrictions were removed, the currency was floating freely in foreign exchange markets, and most agricultural subsidies and tax incentives were being phased out. Over the next decade and a half, domestic market regulations were comprehensively reformed in favour of contestability and competition, all import quotas were eliminated and a timetable was set for reducing tariffs to zero by 2006. In 1989, price stability was designated the sole statutory objective of monetary policy. In 1991 labour legislation was radically transformed from a corporatist, union based framework to a decentralised individual based contracts system. Since 1994, the Fiscal Responsibility Act has prohibited budget deficits "on average" over a reasonable period of time. Approximately US $10 billion worth of state assets were privatised between 1988 and 1999, and all remaining central government trading departments have been restructured along the lines of private sector corporations. Social welfare income support entitlements were significantly cut back in 1991, while income tax rates were reduced in 1996 and again in 1998. (pp. 31–32)

Since Dalziel (2002) wrote this piece, the 1991 Employment Contracts Act has been replaced by a more moderate Employment Relations Act, which has attempted to bring the corporate–union relationship back to a more comfortable equilibrium (Rudman, 2002). The top tax rate has also been raised, and some of the cuts to social welfare payments have been reinstated. However, the bulk of the economic reforms remain in place, and they have transformed New Zealand from being one of the most controlled to one of the most deregulated economies in the world. These reforms have resulted in significant economic and social change and upheaval within New Zealand, with a lot of the economic power now focused on the private sector and a much greater emphasis being put on individual responsibility. Deregulation has resulted in numerous public relations opportunities in strategy-oriented work, such as stakeholder relations and corporate identity programs.

The gap between the rich and poor in New Zealand continues to widen. But, compared with the high unemployment figures over the last decade, the current unemployment rate is low at 5.4%. The gross domestic product (GDP) for 2001 was approximately $65 billion (in United States dollars), with the annual growth rate at a modest 2.4%. New Zealand's relatively small population ensures that the country is very dependent on its export earnings. Currently, the economy is in a buoyant state, registering the highest levels of business confidence and consumer spending since the mid 1990s. This buoyancy is largely based on high international prices for agricultural commodities, which are not sustainable over the long term. The government is attempting to reduce New Zealand's reliance on commodities by building what has been called the *knowledge economy*. The longer term economic outlook for New Zealand may well depend on the success or otherwise of this policy, and public relations has played an important role in the policy's implementation. For example, a series of high-profile conferences—most notably the Catching the Knowledge Wave Conference in Auckland and the Innovate Conference in Christchurch—have been staged in an attempt to focus the attention of business and government leaders on the creation of the knowledge economy. Significant media and publicity work was undertaken around these conferences, including live coverage on Sky television, to ensure that the events were available to a wide audience and could provoke national debate around the key economic issues.

The Australian Economy

Although following the reforms of other OECD countries, Australia chose not to move so sharply away from the Keynesian economic model as New Zealand had done. Perhaps the more complex political system to be found in Australia functioned as a source of resistance against such rapid and radical change. Whatever the reasons for moving so slowly, the Australian economy has consistently outperformed the New Zealand economy over the last $1\frac{1}{2}$ decades. Over the past 5 years, Australia's government has played a more interventionist role in the economy, and it has made structural reforms, albeit more gradually than occurred in New Zealand. A key area of the Australian government's structural reform program since 1996 has been the promotion of a more flexible labor market. Significant reforms to workplace relations have included a move from centralized wage fixing to enterprise bargaining. Strong economic growth and moderate wage and price pressures have ensured sustained employment growth. In the last 2 years, however, employment has grown by more than 2% per annum. In March 2001, the unemployment rate was 6.5%, a 4.2% drop from the previous decade's peak unemployment level of 10.7%. GDP is approximately $450 billion (in United States currency according to 2000 estimates). (Australia bureau of statistics, 2002) One of the reasons for Australia's continuing economic strength is the enormous mineral wealth found on the continent. This natural resource has provided the backbone of the Australian economy.

In both Australia and New Zealand, there is a need for investor relations. Tymson and Lazar (2002) outlined the importance of financial public relations in Australia and New Zealand, highlighting the need for merger and acquisition strategies, investor relations, lobbying, and promoting financial products aimed at the consumer market.

An Overview of Australasia's Legal Systems

The legal systems of New Zealand and Australia are based on English common law. In both countries, the judicial branch is separate from the legislative branch to maintain the independence of the judiciary from political interference. However, due to their constitutional differences, the way in which the New Zealand and Australian legal systems manifest themselves is different.

The New Zealand Legal System

In New Zealand, the separation of the judicial and legislative branches has made the judiciary the only source for interpreting and applying the laws enacted by Parliament. The courts in New Zealand are increasingly taking a more independent stance and have begun to play a more significant constitutional and political role with respect to public and administrative law. In addition, some members of the legal community have begun to challenge the traditional doctrine that Parliament may pass any law not binding future Parliaments, contending that certain common-law rights might override the will of Parliament.

New Zealand law is administered by the Department of Justice through its courts. The hierarchy of courts in New Zealand in ascending order (from lowest to highest recognized level) is the District court (which includes disputes tribunals, family courts, and youth courts), the High Court, the Court of Appeal, and the British Privy Council, which can review Court of Appeal cases. Recently, there has been some debate in New Zealand regarding the relevance of having a foreign court involved in the New Zealand legal system. Of particular note, special legislation and land courts—in the form of the

Waitangi Tribunal—have been provided for Maori people, particularly for land claims derived from the Treaty of Waitangi. Over the past 2 decades, hundreds of millions of dollars have been paid out to Maori tribes, known as *iwi*, in recognition of past injustices in relation to the seizure of Maori land by the Crown. Law enforcement is the responsibility of the New Zealand Police Department, a cabinet-level department largely independent (with respect to law enforcement) of executive authority.

A good working knowledge of New Zealand law ensures that public relations professionals can avoid liability and accurately advise clients. Legislation that directly impacts on the practice of public relations includes the Treaty of Waitangi Act of 1975, the Fair Trading Act of 1986, the Broadcasting Standards Act of 1989, the Resource Management Act of 1991, the Defamation Act of 1992, the Human Rights Act of 1993, the Privacy Act of 1993, and the Employment Relations Act of 2000. (Mulholland, 2001).

The Australian Legal System

The Australian Constitution confers the legislative, executive, and judicial powers of the Commonwealth on three different bodies, which are established by the Constitution: Parliament, the Commonwealth Executive, and the Federal Judicature. The demarcation of the branches of government is vague in that there is no strict demarcation between the legislative and executive powers of the Commonwealth. Only the Parliament can pass laws, but these laws often confer on the Commonwealth Executive the power to make regulations, rules, and bylaws in relation to matters relevant to a particular parliamentary act. However, the separation between the judicature on the one hand and the Parliament and the Executive on the other is strict. Only a court may exercise the judicial power of the Commonwealth. In contrast to New Zealand, in Australia, the administration of the law is largely in the hands of the states, each of which has a series of courts culminating in a supreme court. Between them, these courts have comprehensive responsibilities extending to all matters of state and most matters of federal jurisdiction. The states also manage the police, although there is a federal Commonwealth police force that performs general police duties in the Australian Capital Territory and is the principal agency for the enforcement of federal laws. However, for the following matters, the federal judicature take precedence:

- Matters arising directly under any treaty.
- Suits between states, between persons suing or being sued on behalf of different states, or between a state and a person suing or being sued on behalf of another state.
- Matters in which the Commonwealth of Australia or a person suing or being sued on behalf of the Commonwealth of Australia is a party.
- Matters between states, between residents of different states, or between a state and a resident of another state.
- Matters in which a writ of mandamus or prohibition—which concern judicial review of administrative action—is sought against an officer of the federal government or of a federal court. The High Court shares some of its jurisdiction under this section with the Federal Court of Australia. (Attorney-General's Department, n.d.)

Furthermore, in contrast to New Zealand, Australia abolished the ability to appeal to the Privy Council in 1986. In recent years, Australia has also held a referendum on whether or not the British Queen should continue to be head of state. The referendum decided that the connection should remain, but the issue continues to be debated within Australia. In

Australian public relations practice, it is essential to be familiar with relevant legislation because of the potential for liability or negligence. Relevant legislation covers areas such as contracts law, the Design Act of 1906, the Copyright Act of 1968, the Trade Practices Act of 1974, the Australian Broadcasting Act of 1983, the Trademarks Act of 1995, and the Electronic Transactions Act of 1999. Laws relating to business practices, defamation, and lotteries and competitions vary from state to state. The challenge of understanding the law and identifying potential legal problems is, therefore, more complex for Australian public relations practitioners because of the dual systems.

CULTURE AND PUBLIC RELATIONS

Sociocultural Aspects of New Zealand and Australia's Cultural Identities

According to Hall (1996), identities are never unified and, in modern times, are increasingly fragmented and fractured. They are never singular but multiply constructed across different, often intersecting and antagonistic, discourses, practices, and positions (p. 4). Our aim in this section is not to present a unified, essentialized version of cultural identity, but rather to highlight some of the ways that commonalities and shared characteristics are represented in cultural discourses. These commonalities and characteristics serve as points of identification (Hall, 1996) that may be articulated and sutured to form cultural discourses. We now deal with elements of each culture in turn, focusing on cultural elements that are pertinent to understanding the cultures and the public relations practices in both countries.

Although both New Zealand and Australia were originally settled by indigenous people and later became British colonies, significant differences in cultural identity are evident. Both nations emerged as a result of the colonization of indigenous people, but whereas New Zealand has attempted to make financial reparations to these natives, Australia has not (Power, 2000). Maori culture has had a strong influence on the culture of New Zealand. Pacific Island and Asian cultures are also increasingly influencing the New Zealand way of life; so, although New Zealand has a bicultural policy, it has a multicultural focus. Australia, in contrast, is officially multicultural, but the role of the Aboriginal people in the Australian economy and cultural identity is marginal. Cultural identity is thus a political, strategic, positional concept, and bicultural or multicultural policies enable governments to adopt a rhetoric of being considerate to all people or of focusing on indigenous people.

Maori culture is characterized as cooperative, and the *whanau* (extended family) structure of Maori society has influenced an acceptance of cooperation and consensus, as well as a capitalist individualistic approach, in New Zealand society. The Maori have endeavored to save their language and culture by setting up preschool *kohanga reo* (language units) that serve as the starting point of instilling cultural pride and knowledge among their children. The fostering and acceptance of Maori values and knowledge may, however, be contrasted with the disproportionate number of Maori who are poor, face ill health, and appear frequently in crime statistics. As a consequence, the Maori are discursively constructed as either entrepreneurial or welfare dependent.

The national *Pakeha* (New Zealander of European descent) identity has been based on a number of myths: egalitarian society, a heroic settler society, and good old rural values surviving in the suburbs (Bell, 1996). Although traditionally a male-dominated society, a unique recent feature of New Zealand society is that women have succeeded to move to the highest levels. New Zealand was one of the first countries to grant women the right to vote, and currently women hold the four top positions in New Zealand: Prime Minister, Governor General, Attorney General, and Chief Justice. New Zealanders are colloquially referred to as *kiwis*, the name of a flightless native bird. Generally, New Zealanders are characterized as resourceful, self-reliant, outdoors people. Sports play an important part in the New Zealand psyche; for many years, rugby was the predominant sport, with the elite rugby team, All Blacks, attaining iconic status. Rugby is perceived as a sport for the "average bloke." New Zealanders love the water, and from the days of Kupe, the first explorer to reach New Zealand over 1,000 years ago, New Zealanders have had a passion for sailing. Innovation and technology adoption are considered important features of New Zealand culture. For example, competing for and winning the prestigious America's Cup resulted in a number of technological innovations. In addition, New Zealanders are some of the highest mobile phone and Internet users per capita in the world (Tourism New Zealand, 2002). Sensitivity to Maori cultural values, gender equity issues, and environmental management are requisite features of New Zealand public relations practice.

Australian Aborigines were nomadic people who were able to survive in the harsh desert conditions of Australia. The arrival of European settlers led to a dramatic decline in the indigenous population because of conditions of genocide, repression, social and cultural disruption, and dispossession. Australia has not offered Aboriginal people economic settlement for the suffering caused by their colonization. The Prime Minister of Australia, John Howard, refused to apologize on behalf of the Australian government for past injustices done to the Aboriginal people. Power (2000) claimed that an apology would "make people feel more secure that Australia is not now a racist country, it would expunge a sense of guilt and shame that many Australians feel ... the policy of separating children from their Aboriginal parents on racist grounds has been judged by an appropriate body to involve 'gross violations of human rights'" (p. 202). A number of Aboriginal people are beginning to succeed based on Western criteria. However, overall, these people suffer from ill health and welfare dependency. Increasingly, White Australians are questioning the treatment of Aboriginal people and advocating reconciliation and reparation.

The White Australian identity has been based on myths of convict colony, the bronzed lifeguard, and outback hardships. The multicultural nature of Australia and the contrast between urban and outback life make it difficult to categorize Australian culture. Australians are widely regarded as friendly, open people with a dry sense of humor. Generally, New Zealanders are considered more reserved and introverted whereas Australians are considered more extroverted.

Tourism discourses market Australia as a land of contrasts, which also applies to the people: Aborigines, farmers, successful business people, beautiful models, actors, immigrants, and surfers. Australians are recognized for their musical, sporting, and artistic achievements. From opera to rock, Aussie rules to netball, Aboriginal art to Australian film, Australians have succeeded in a global market. Sports are considered the national religion, and both men and women excel in a vast number of sports including Australian rules football, rugby, cricket, hockey, netball, and swimming.

It is difficult to generalize about the impact of culture on public relations practice in the two countries as there is no empirical data on this relationship. But, in general, mostly Western global business practices prevail. However, public relations practice within New Zealand and Australia reflects the multicultural nature of the two countries. Within both countries, conferences address issues of multiculturalism, and there are public relations consultancies that specialize in intercultural communication from Maori, Pacific Island, or a variety of ethnic perspectives.

Hofstede's Dimensions in New Zealand and Australia

The Hofstede's work (1983, 1985) is a useful starting point for a discussion of organizational–cultural dimensions and their implications for the practice of public relations in New Zealand and Australia. The four value dimensions identified by Hofstede and discussed in Chapter 1 do generally apply to both New Zealand and Australia. But the model does tend to act as an essentializing discourse, neglecting the nuances of bicultural and multicultural policies. New Zealand and Australia were both classified similarly by Hofstede. He identified both countries as having a low power distance and weak uncertainty avoidance. Hofstede considered that small power distance plus weak uncertainty avoidance leads to viewing the organization "as a 'village market,' that is an ad-hocracy ..." (p. 353). The author did qualify his view with the observation that the purpose of an organization may also impact on the value system. Obviously, with bicultural and multicultural nations, a variety of organizational models will be present. Hofstede also classified the two countries similarly as being individualistic and masculine, with achievement, self-interest, self-actualization, and assertiveness as some of the norms present in the two countries. The difficulty with this generalization is that conducting business with Maori organizations would require a different approach based on collectivism and relationship-oriented values. The corporate cultures of New Zealand and Australian organizations may also be mediated by the impact of globalization and the origin of multinational organizations.

THE MEDIA ENVIRONMENT

Media Control

The media in both New Zealand and Australia are partly state owned and partly owned by the private sector. The state's involvement is in the area of broadcasting, with the state owning radio and television channels in both countries. The majority of radio and television channels are, however, in the hands of the private sector. The private sector also owns and controls all Australian and New Zealand newspapers. Control of public sector broadcasting is vested with independent boards so as to avoid charges of political interference in or the censorship of program content. The notion of a free press is a recognized and protected part of the democratic political culture of both countries. Thus, public relations practitioners have unfettered access to journalists when they are attempting to communicate the views of their clients or employers.

The democratic ideal of the free press centers on the notion that the media are public watchdogs who monitor political processes and societal activities. It might be argued that this ideal lies at the core of the ongoing commitment to public sector broadcasting because profitability, rather than public service, provides the *raison d'etre* for the private sector. Moreover, as the media become increasingly multinational, their ability to function as a key component of a national—as opposed to global—culture is increasingly brought into question. Major global media companies have significant holdings in New Zealand and Australia. One company–Independent Newspapers Limited, in which Rupert Murdoch's News Limited has a 50% stake–owns all but two of New Zealand's major daily newspapers. In Australia, two companies—News Limited and Fairfax—control all but 3 of the 33 metropolitan newspapers. Such large holdings are more efficient than multiple smaller companies as they are able to share production facilities and journalistic resources through the syndication of stories across multiple media outlets in different Australian states or regions of New Zealand, among other things. However, these efficiencies have come at the price of a reduction in journalistic pluralism with fewer and fewer journalists employed in both countries to cover the news.

In Australia, the government is currently in the process of relaxing the rules governing cross-media ownership in the same market. In the past, these rules have functioned to prevent one company from owning significant portions of the print and broadcast media that serve the same market. The proposed changes would, for example, enable Kerry Packer's company, which owns the Nine Television network and a large stable of magazine titles in both New Zealand and Australia, to also control a major metropolitan newspaper. A relaxation of the rules would enable media companies to offer attractive packages to advertisers that would cover multiple media. Such packages are likely to make it even more difficult for media that are independent of the major companies to compete for advertising dollars, the media's primary source of revenue. However, note that, in both New Zealand and Australia, the domination of traditional media markets by the major companies is already almost complete. At the same time, the Internet is providing a significant threat to traditional media by offering a forum that is characterized by its diversity, its interactivity, and by a low cost structure that makes it widely accessible. Although the traditional media still function as the major source of news and are themselves moving to offer more online offerings, the Internet offers an alternative source of public information for those who choose to seek it out. Perhaps ironically, it is this development of alternative electronic media that has served as a justification in Australia for the cross-ownership law change (Cunningham & Romano, 2000).

In New Zealand, the major recent legal change in relation to the media has gone in a direction contrary to that in Australia. Rather than seeking to strengthen the private sector media, the New Zealand government has sought to strengthen the role of public sector broadcasting through, for example, introducing a 23-point charter that will require state television to offer quality programming that caters to minority interests, including those of the indigenous Maori population. The charter will also require state television to make greater use of local programming. Currently, the two state-owned free-to-air channels are run primarily as profit-making enterprises that compete directly with private sector channels. Under the new charter, they will still be required to run profitably, but profit will no longer be the main or sole objective. Thus, although there are no moves in New Zealand to hinder the growth of the private sector media, the government has decided to ensure that local content that addresses issues of concern to New Zealanders remains freely available.

One significant difference between New Zealand and Australia is that in the latter newspapers have been more likely to display or be accused of displaying a clear bias towards one of the major political parties. Such bias is commonplace in countries such as the United Kingdom in which the public are able to demonstrate their political commitment by, for example, purchasing the *Guardian* newspaper if they support the Labour Party. If a diversity of viewpoints is represented in a freely available range of media products, then it might be argued that such bias in individual newspapers is not necessarily injurious to the goals of a democratic society. One reason for the absence of such demonstrable bias against one or the other of the two major political parties in New Zealand newspapers is arguably that it would run counter to the profit motive. That is, in New Zealand, only one newspaper dominates in each of the major metropolitan areas. The exception—the capital city of Wellington—boasts both a morning and evening daily newspaper owned by the same company. Given the small size of the market, New Zealand newspapers appear to have settled for the mainstream in that they favor neither of the major parties. However, there is also evidence that they put few resources into representing viewpoints from outside of the mainstream of the political center left or center right (Leitch, 1990). Thus, according to Leitch, public relations practitioners working for mainstream organizations or clients have a far easier job in terms of ensuring that their employer's views are represented in the media than do those working for more radical organizations.

Media Outreach

New Zealand and Australia can both be characterized as media saturated countries. Indeed, Australian media scholar Henry Mayer wrote in 1980 that: "You cannot escape from pollution by holding your nose. There is no refuge from the mass media and their effects. Even if you never touch a paper or switch on TV or radio, most people do all three so frequently that the media affect you through them. (cited in Tiffen, 1994, p. 3)

All but a small minority of homes in both countries possess television sets and are, therefore, able to access the multiple free-to-air television channels as well as the satellite pay-TV channels offered by Rupert Murdoch's global network. In New Zealand, for example, some 14% of the population subscribe to the Sky television network, which brings in international programming including CNN. Newspaper readership is declining throughout the Western world, and New Zealand and Australia are no exception in this respect. In the face of growing competition from other media for advertising revenue, the number of newspapers has been reducing in both countries. The implication of this fragmentation of the news audience across multiple media to public relations practice is that it is becoming increasingly difficult and costly to communicate with the masses. However, the increasing specialization of media products means that it is becoming easier to target messages to particular publics who, for example, subscribe to niche publications or Internet newsgroups. Given the focused nature of most public relations work, the ubiquitous, yet fragmented character of the media in New Zealand and Australia is generally a boon to public relations activity.

Media Access

As is the case in most democratic, capitalist countries, access to media is easily available to those who can afford to pay for it. Organizations with resources are able to purchase both advertising and advertorial space or airtime to ensure that their views are heard. However, there are media outlets in both New Zealand and Australia that provide access for organizations with limited resources and minority points of view. For example, the digital television station, BIGTV, run in conjunction with the University of Waikato in Hamilton, New Zealand, provides a forum for local groups to address their community. However, such access shows on radio and television have limited audiences, and few resources are available to assist groups in producing good quality productions.

The media in both Australia and New Zealand are highly dependent on public relations practitioners for many of the news stories they publish. This dependence has been created in part by the declining number of journalists employed by news organizations as they seek to increase profits or reduce costs. Public relations practitioners clearly provide a subsidy to the media by providing free copy that often requires little editing. The reliance of the media on public relations practitioners has also been partly a result of the increasing number of practitioners employed by organizations to handle their media relations. In 2002, for example, the New Zealand government spent more than $N2 13 million on public relations. A spokesperson for one government ministry—Debbie Chin, the Director-General of Health—defended the expenditure, stating that the use of public relations staff reflected the public's right to know what officials and politicians were doing: "This interest reflects the public's right to know. Our approach is to be open and helpful to the media and to recognise they are an important conduit to the general public" (Scanlon, 2002, p. 1). Thus, public relations practitioners have become an established and accepted component of the news-gathering process.

CASE STUDY: 0800 SMOKEY—A PARTNERSHIP APPROACH TO AIR POLLUTION

The following case study is an example of the use of public relations by a major city to help deal with air pollution in New Zealand.

Background

With a population of 1.2 million, Auckland is the fastest growing region in New Zealand. Rapid growth has exacerbated transport problems in Auckland, which has poor systems of public transport and a motorway network that approaches gridlock during peak hours. Although the air is still clean in comparison with that of other major cities, the recent decline in air quality has been of concern to both residents and the local government. Responsibility for monitoring the region's air quality lies with the Auckland Regional Council (ARC), a government environmental agency. Since monitoring of air quality began in 1991, air quality has deteriorated, and levels of pollutants that exceed World Health Organization safety guidelines have been recorded. ARC research showed that over 80% of the air pollution problem in the region was the result of motor vehicle emissions. Moreover, car ownership has been growing at twice the rate of the population, and there is almost one car for every two people in the region.

ARC scientific research attributed the air pollution from vehicles in the region to poor vehicle maintenance, low fuel specifications relative to other developed countries, and the lack of appropriate legislation on the quality of cars being imported from overseas. Market research conducted by the ARC indicated that, although people did attribute pollution to smoky vehicles, they also incorrectly thought that industry was to blame. The challenge for the ARC was to design a campaign that informed Aucklanders of the issues and educated them on the actions they could take.

Campaign Objectives

The objectives of the 0800 Smokey campaign were to:

1. Raise awareness that motor vehicle emissions caused over 80% of the air pollution and that vehicle owners should tune and regularly service their vehicles.

2. Promote the 0800 SMOKEY hotline and web site where people could report smoky vehicles.

3. Give the air quality issue a public context so that the ARC could influence government fuel quality and vehicle import legislation.

The Campaign: Stakeholder Partnerships and Education

The 0800 Smokey campaign was predominantly a public education advertising campaign aimed at raising the awareness of the air pollution problems. A partnership approach was adopted by the ARC to involve key stakeholders and to keep the campaign within the limited resources and budget. Colenso BBDO, an international advertising agency, agreed to provide the creative material on a pro bono basis. The ARC formed a partnership with the Motor Trade Association, a group of automotive repair garages, so that vehicle owners could get a free inspection of their exhaust emissions. Transit New Zealand, a crown entity that directs transport policy and funding, permitted the ARC to use its electronic motorway road signage to promote the campaign. Local businesses were approached and asked to initiate a regular servicing and tuning of their fleet vehicles; replace older fleet vehicles; provide teleworking opportunities; and provide incentives for staff to tune their vehicles, use public transport, or car pool. As a result of its stakeholder partnerships, the ARC was able to run a mass advertising campaign that had local business support and offered free vehicle inspections.

The advertising campaign asked Aucklanders to tune their vehicles and *dob in* (report) those who had a smoky exhaust by calling an 0800 hotline telephone number. A number of key messages were designed:

- "If you see a smoky vehicle, dob it in."
- "Auckland's air pollution exceeds world health standards. Tune your vehicle."
- "If your exhaust smokes for more than 10 seconds, you're poisoning Auckland."

The campaign was launched on Queen Street, the main street of Auckland's business district, with a special event and a number of publicity exercises. Actors had a mock protest wearing gas masks, fire alarms were placed on poles, and stickers placed on shop window mannequins and parking meters that stated, "You're breathing Auckland's filthy air for another . . ." [time indicated on meter].

The launch was widely covered on prime time news programs. The launch message was reinforced by a television commercial that opened with a close-up shot of a billboard that stated, "Our carbon monoxide levels are nearly as high as Auckland's. Tune your vehicle." A wide-angle shot was then used to show that the billboard was on New Zealand House in London with red double-decker buses in the foreground. That shot was replaced by another billboard stating, "Auckland's air pollution exceeds World Health Standards. Tune your vehicle." The comparison of Auckland and London's pollution served to highlight the seriousness of the problem and create controversy and debate through the contradiction of the clean green image that New Zealand has promoted for many years. Controversy was also generated through the use of the word *dob*. A social welfare campaign that encouraged people to report welfare infringements had been termed *dob in a beneficiary* and been very unpopular. Ironically, although this campaign aimed to make people take personal responsibility for air pollution, one of the primary ways in which they were encouraged to do so was by reporting other defaulters.

Evaluation

More than 57,000 calls were made to the 0800 SMOKEY hotline during the campaign. One year later, 2002, 500 calls per week were still being received on the hotline. More than 27,000 vehicles were dobbed in, and 3,000 vehicles were dobbed in 3 times or more. The worst offender—a used diesel-powered car recently imported from Japan—was dobbed in 73 times. Fifty eight per cent of the dobbed in vehicles were diesel powered, but diesel vehicles make up only 14% of the New Zealand vehicle fleet.

A recent telephone survey found that 85% of respondents expressed concern about the impact of exhaust fumes on the environment, an indication that public recognition of the issue remains high. In March 2001, the 10-s smoke law was introduced that allowed police to fine motorists with visible vehicle smoke emissions. This focus on emission levels, rather than on targeting of the mode of transport Aucklanders used, is one explanation of the positive response to the campaign. The long-term solution—a shift to less-polluting public transport—remains to be addressed and is likely to be far more controversial. Given the love affair that New Zealanders have with their cars, convincing them to turn to trains and buses will be a significant challenge for a future public relations campaign.

REFERENCES

http://www.oecd.org/EN/document/0, EN-document-0-nodirectorate-no-13-26640-0,00.html, 30 April, 2002

http://www.stats.govt.nz/, April 29, 2002

http://www.abs.gov.au/ausstats/abs%40.nsf/94713ad445ff1425ca25682000192af2/1647509ef7e25faaca2568 a900154b63!OpenDocument, April 29, 2002

Aggett, M.-J. (1996). Health lobbyists eye up corridors of power. *New Zealand Doctor, 16*, 1–4.

Ansley, G. (2002, April 15). Australia targets New Zealand weaknesses. *The New Zealand Herald*, p. C1.

Bell, C. (1996). *Inventing New Zealand: Everyday myths of pakeha identity.* Auckland, New Zealand: Penguin.

Cunningham, S., & Romano, A. (2000, May). W(h)ither media influence? *Media International Australia, 95*, 19–28.

Dalziel, P. (2002). New Zealand's Economic Reforms: An Assessment. *Review of Political Economy, 14*(1), 31–46.

Hagar, N., & Burton, B. (1998). *Secrets and lies: The anatomy of an anti-environmental PR campaign.* Wellington, New Zealand: Craig Potton Publishing.

Hall, S. (1996). Introduction: Who needs an identity? In S. Hall & P. du Gay (Eds.), *Questions of cultural identity.* (pp. 1–17) London: Sage.

Hofstede, G. (1983). National cultures in four dimensions: A research-based theory of cultural differences among nations. *International Studies of Management and Organization, 13*(1/2), 46–75.

Hofstede, G. (1985). The interaction between National and organizational value systems. *Journal of Management Studies, 22*(4), 347–357.

Leitch, S. (1990). *News talk.* Palmerston North, New Zealand: Dunmore Press.

Molony, J. (1988). *The Penguin history of Australia* (2nd ed.). Ringwood: Penguin.

Motion, J., & Leitch, S. (2001). New Zealand perspectives on public relations. In R. Heath & G. Vasquez (Eds.), *Handbook of public relations* (pp. 659–663), Thousand Oaks, CA: Sage.

Peart, J. (1998, May). The state of public relations. *Marketing Magazine*, 32.

Power, M. R. (2000). Reconciliation, restoration and guilt: The politics of apologies. *Media International Australia Incorporating Culture and Policy, 93*, 191–205.

Scanlon, G. (2002, January 24). PR costs civil service $13 million. The Dominion, p. 19.

Sinclair, K. (1991). *A history of New Zealand* (5th ed.). Auckland, New Zealand: Penguin.

Singh, R., & Smyth, R. (2000). Australian public relations: Status at the turn of the 21st century. *Public Relations Review, 26*(4), 387–401.

Titten, R. (Ed.). (1990). *Mayer on the media: Issues and arguments.* Sydney, Australia: Allen & Unwin.

Tymson, C., & Lazar, P. (2002). *The new Australian and New Zealand public relations manual.* Chotswood, Australia: Tymson Communications.

Weaver, C. K., & Motion, J. (2002 in press). Sabotage and subterfuge: Public relations, democracy and genetic engineering in New Zealand. *Media, Culture and Society. 24*(3), 325–343.

7

AN OVERVIEW OF PUBLIC RELATIONS IN JAPAN AND THE SELF-CORRECTION CONCEPT

TAKASHI INOUE

INTRODUCTION

The modern history of Japan and the country's progress on the path toward Westernization has not been a monotonous journey. The rapid pace of change has resulted in the country repeating many errors at times, causing immeasurable pain not only to the Japanese but also to neighboring countries. The old national slogan was "strong army, strong country." After World War II, democracy replaced militarism and a cooperative system was established between the political, bureaucratic, and business worlds under the single party leadership of the Liberal Democratic Party (LDP). This system was aided by the diligence of the Japanese, and swift economic activity was shown to the world based on Japan's social system. As a result, in the early 1980s, Japan stood at the forefront of modern industrialized societies and was recognized for the high quality of its products and its mass production ability (Sakaiya, 2002).

However, the economic bubble burst in the 1990s due to the appreciation of the yen and the progression of information technology that propelled the globalization of Japanese companies. This created a need to shift management methods from the seniority system, lifetime employment, and group decision-making process that had been established in Japanese culture and institutions to a method that recognized openness, fairness, and speed—characteristics that traditionally did not exist in Japanese firms (Tsurumi, 1997). Since it was founded as a country, Japan has possessed a unique communications format due to the impact of its homogeneity and the influence of Confucianism. Therefore, its forms of communication have differed from that of the West (Inoue, (Ed.) 2001).

A review of the introduction and development of public relations in Japan tells us that the profession did not evolve ideally. In fact, public relations may not have been sought by the Japanese because of the sociological and economic system of the country. Public relations may only exist in a democracy that also has a free, unregulated economy. Ideally, the practice would be a two-way communications (Grunig, J. E., & Hunt. T., 1984) activity in line with the demands of the current worldwide shift toward globalization. This is also an area in which Japan is extremely weak.

A SOCIOCULTURAL PERSPECTIVE OF THE NATION

Japan, located in Northeast Asia, is a nation of thousands of islands, the four major ones being Hokkaido, Shikoku, Kyushu, and Honshu (where Tokyo is located). The land area is slightly smaller than that of the state of California, with a population of 127 million. Since its birth, the economy had been based on agriculture and fishing. Ancient Chinese culture and politics have also influenced Japan. The Tokugawa (Edo) Era that began in the early 17th century established a closed country policy that built a unique culture and societal system. In the latter half of the 19th century, Japan opened itself to external influence with the arrival of Commodore Perry's black ships (Shiba, 1996). The Meiji Restoration, which opened Japan's doors to the West, introduced European science, technology, and political systems with earnest efforts to build a modern state. Initially, Japan modeled itself after the German brand of constitutional monarchy and established an imperial parliament. It also actively promoted rapid industrialization that enriched the nation and helped build the nation's military.

The end of World War II saw the Japanese economy developing swiftly, becoming the second largest in the world next only to the United States in terms of gross domestic product (GDP). In 1990, Japan boasted the highest per capita income in the world (Masamura & Yamada, 2002). There are nationwide television networks, newspapers, magazines, and other forms of media; most of the major media companies are located in Tokyo. Thus, the efficiency of information dissemination and media access is very high. It covers national and international news extensively.

With an increase in the decline of the birth rate, Japan is facing an aging society like many other advanced countries. The average life expectancy in Japan is the highest in the world for both men and women. During much of its history, religion in Japan has centered on Shintoism and Buddhism. The philosophy of Confucianism was introduced in the 6th century, which deeply penetrated Japanese society up to World War II. As a result, Japanese culture differs from the Christian civilization of the West in many aspects. The Confucian philosophy that respects humility and requires strict hierarchical relationships is in direct opposition with the activities entailed in public relations.

THE EVOLUTION OF PUBLIC RELATIONS IN JAPAN

The history of modern public relations in Japan is rather brief. It starts with the occupation of Japan by the United States in 1945 following Japan's defeat in World War II. Public relations was introduced to Japan without the concomitant growth of democracy and free speech seen in the West. There are no materials that enable confirmation of a systematic introduction of public relations by any external source before World War II. However, Shibasaki (1984) wrote that the South Manchurian Railroad had established an independent Public Relations Section under the direct control of the President's Office that was differentiated from propaganda. Kisaku Ikeda, a representative of the Public Relations Institute, commented that the first in-house newsletter in Japan was published in 1903 by Kanebo for its female factory workers. Due to its popularity, this was then followed by the publication of the first official issue of the newsletter for all employees of the company in 1904 (Ikeda, 1997).

According to Ikari, (Ed.) (1998), as for the first public relations magazines, there are many versions of the origin, but Maruzen is said to have issued a magazine beginning in 1897 and Mitsui Gofukuten (presently Mitsukoshi Department Store) in 1899. The Mitsui public relations magazine was 350-pages long! It contained business information, new textile patterns, trends, and even novels by famous authors of the times, such as Koyo Ozaki (Yamaguchi, 1995). The executives of both companies were individuals who had visited America, and it is clear that they created their public relations magazines in Japan after models from corporate public relations magazines that existed in America in the late 1880s.

The Japanese Government and military authorities first recognized the importance of propaganda for their country following World War I. It was the use of the Manchurian Incident as a pretext for occupying Manchuria (the present Northeastern China) by the Imperial Japanese Army in 1931, a precursor of further aggression on the mainland of China, that changed communication attitudes concerning wartime propaganda. As mentioned in a book on the Tokyo Metropolitan Government's PR activities during WW II, published in 1995, Japan's government and military personnel considered the criticism of Japanese military actions by international society as a total defeat in the propaganda campaign, and top priority was given for the creation of a system to manipulate international public opinion.

Based on this, the Ministry of Foreign Affairs established an Information Committee in 1932, and an organization was formed for planning domestic and overseas propaganda in line with national policy. Following a number of transformations, the Information Bureau was established in 1940. This bureau centralized the information and propaganda operations that had been conducted at the respective ministries and agencies (Tokyo Metropolitan Government, 1995). This is similar to reinforcing public relations functions conducted in the United States during World War I and World War II. However, the one distinct difference is that Japan was not a democracy at that time, and the use of public relations was strictly for manipulating public opinion; it led the Japanese into war.

General Douglas MacArthur and the General Headquarters (GHQ) of the Supreme Commander for the Allied Powers introduced to Japan the form of public relations that had appeared in the United States in the early 20th century as a part of the democratization measures after World War II. Before the Occupation, however, some reference to Public Relations was made by Japanese author Tetsuhiko Tozawa, in 1942 in his book entitled *Theory of Propaganda*, as noted by Ikari, (Ed.) (1998). Tozawa's above mentioned book refers to two books by Edward Bernays (1923), *Crystallizing Public Opinion* and *Propaganda*. On May 3, 1947, with the proclamation of the Japanese Constitution based on democracy, GHQ suggested the establishment of Public Relations Offices to central and local governmental offices through the military government offices placed in each region. This resulted in the establishment of independent public relations departments in governmental bodies throughout Japan. One of the first problems faced was in naming the departments because a Japanese word that fit the term *public relations* could not be found. The responsible parties first gathered information and worked earnestly to understand what constituted public relations. As a result, the most commonly used term became *ko(u)-ho(u)*, which literally means public information (which is widely recognized as a rather primitive stage of public relations today). However, many other words such as *ho(u)-do(u)* (news) and *ko(u)-cho(u)* (public hearing) were also used (Ikari, (Ed.) 1998).

By 1949, most of the government bodies nationwide had established public relations departments, and the Civil Information and Education Section of the GHQ held public relations seminars for the staff of the central government. Although these seminar attendees talked about public relations, they primarily focused on the *ko-ho* (public information) of "how a government should convey measures to the people to nurture healthy public opinion (Hikami, 1951, 1952)." But, at the time, it was difficult to differentiate between the public information officer and public relations officer stationed at every military government office by any means other than their titles. Therefore, because the conditions of the conceptually introduced democracy had not taken roots, the terms *public information* and *public relations* became entwined as if they were synonyms (Inoue, (Ed.) 2001).

Thus, the public relations introduced in Japan began with the governmental offices (public centers) and then continued to the private sector's advertising and securities industries. Initially, private companies used the original Japanese translation of the English term *public relations* as is, but in almost all cases the term *ko-ho* is now used. Unlike propaganda that was used before the war as a means of controlling public perception, the modern form of public relations has sprouted on a foundation of democracy based on the awareness of respecting public opinion and social responsibility.

Soon public relations seminars were also being conducted for the private sector. In July 1949, Japan Advertising Limited and Telegraphic Service Company (known today as Dentsu Inc.) held a summer advertising seminar called "About Public Relations," the first seminar of its kind. In his book titled, *PR (w)o Kangaeru* (Thinking About PR), Shigeo Ogura (1990) referred to the seminar and stated that public relations was positioned as a function of management, a policy issue of management, and as a management philosophy.

Note that although the misunderstandings about the role of public relations continued among government public relations departments, the private sector was striving to expand the correct concept of public relations.

In 1951, the Japan Federation of Employers' Associations (JFEA) sent the first postwar business tour to the United States to study human relations and public relations. Based on this tour, a Public Relations Study Group (unofficial English translated name) was formed within JFEA in May 1953. Furthermore, in 1951, the spread of public relations also peaked with the publication of nine educational books on public relations such as *Public Relations Talk* by Shinjiro Kitazawa (1951), *Ko-ho Theory and Practice* by the Japan *Ko-ho* Association (1951), and *Basic Knowledge of PR* by Yoshiro Sasaki (1951). Interestingly, the rapid rise of modern public relations that had continued since its introduction by the GHQ began to stagnate toward the end of 1952 (Koyama, 1975). As the *Thirty Year History of Governmental Ko-ho* by Cabinet Secretary Cabinet Public Relations Office (1990), a complimentary commemorative booklet, noted: "As GHQ left Japan with the conclusion and implementation of the 1952 San Francisco Peace Treaty, a simplification of public bodies related to public relations and the shrinking of budgeting for public relations was sought as this was perceived to be a good chance to re-study the policies under the Occupation, and also because of the tight financial situation."

However, the *Dentsu Advertising Annual* (1956) described public relations in the following manner: "There were many companies who thought that their public relations were a success just by using a lot of money to make a fancy business report or by running a so-called public relations advertisement (advertorial) in the newspaper." Thus, one can infer that conditions did not allow for proper public relations to be conducted.

Riding the wave of democratization, government-related public relations activities even penetrated local government offices. Presently, there is no government office without a public relations department or a section related to it. However, despite the spread, the content of the activities stagnated until the early 1990s. In contrast, public relations activities conducted by corporations were being nurtured, although its theories and technology were not appropriately adopted. The creation of public relations materials was certainly enhanced by the explosion of newspapers, magazines, and broadcast media.

The trend toward the public issue of stocks began in Japan in the 1950s, causing securities companies to use public relations and advertisements in newspapers to solicit shareholders. This solidified several methods used in corporate public relations. Upon entering the country in the 1950s, the Shell Oil Company joined other Japanese firms, such as Japan Airlines, Matsushita Electric, Tokyo Gas, and Mitsubishi Electric, in establishing public relations departments. Many major corporations followed thereafter in the 1960s and through the 1970s (Ikari, (Ed.) 2001).

Advertorials initiated by advertising agencies became the mainstream form of corporate communications in the 1950s. Matsushita Electric and Sony proactively ran advertorials in newspapers and weekly magazines. At that time the advertorials clearly showed an understanding of the importance of nurturing a corporate image while advancing development and research of marketing technologies. However, they did not put into practice the public relations theories that covered a broader range of areas such as government relations, community relations, investor relations, and media relations. Within the increasing commonality of public relations activities by these companies, although superficial in nature, a strong awareness of a company's social responsibility grew centering on the business world.

The outbreak of the Korean War in 1950 brought special war demands to Japan and led the Japanese economy into a fast recovery. This unfortunate event stimulated the rapid growth of the Japanese economy. In addition, the lengthy period under the Liberal Democratic Party (Ozawa, 1993) created the golden triangle of the political, bureaucratic, and business worlds, which in turn helped transform Japan into a country with rapid economic growth. It also was a period that demanded that products be supplied in large volumes, and marketing methods, such as advertorials, sales promotion, and publicity were instrumental in introducing these new products to the public. Marketing is distinct from public relations. Although marketing plays a role in public relations, a misunderstanding concerning these concepts led people to confuse publicity as being public relations; public relations was equated with marketing.

From the mid-1950s through the early 1970s, the Japanese economy experienced a rapid actual growth rate that exceeded 10% per year (Masamura & Yamada, 2002). This marked the arrival of the era of publicity that was used for providing news materials to the media. Unlike advertisements, the key decision of whether to run publicity as news was to be made by the media. Therefore, various ideas began to emerge as effective strategies linked to marketing became more refined in their application to public relations. However, just as a specific prescription must be made available to introduce new scientific technologies, there was also a need at that time to introduce specific public relations technologies. The impact of not doing so led to further misunderstanding of what public relations should be. Advertising for public relations and publicity activities dramatically developed in line with the advanced economic growth and the expansion of various types of media.

However, in the late 1960s, environmental pollution emerged as a major societal issue, which resulted in penalties for companies pursuing profits under the mass production–mass consumption paradigm. The activities of the government became pronounced in this area with the establishment of the Basic Law for Environmental Pollution Control Law (1967) and the formation of the Environment Agency in 1971. In the business world, the New Year's Address of the Japan Association for Corporate Executives in 1969 emphasized the "formation of a society that respects humanity" as its perspective. The Japanese vernacular daily Asahi Shimbun, morning edition, June I, 1969 reported as top news in their social affairs section that a New York Times article criticized Japanese automakers for doing secret recalls of their defective cars. During that period, Asahi Shimbun, in particular, made a negative campaign against Japanese automakers and their faulty cars of that time. A consensus on the recovery of humanity, meaning less emphasis on corporate interests only, was established (Ikari, Ed., 1998). This transformation of society was appreciated by Japan's middle management, especially in the company PR departments, but it did not extend to the executive level.

ECONOMIC FRICTION AND OVERSEAS PUBLIC RELATIONS

One of the pillars of the economic recovery following Japan's defeat in World War II was the establishment of Japan as a trading country, which resulted in the infusion of overseas public relations activities. In 1958, the Japan External Trade Organization was established. The European Economic Community was also established the same year, which signaled increasing intensity in the competition on the international stage. Consequently, strong interest was paid in Japan to overseas public relations activities along with marketing, including establishing overseas sales networks to promote exports and branding Japanese products among overseas consumers. The total volume of Japanese exports grew rapidly from the latter half of the 1960s through the 1970s. The growth was critically described as a "squall," but the trade balance surplus took root at that time. This also led to international criticism that Japan was not working hard to increase imports, resulting in the beginning of trade friction.

Beginning in the 1970s, in many Western countries including the United States, a movement arose to regulate imports of Japanese products. This was evident in the textile negotiations between Japan and the United States during the 1970s; high-technology friction evident in the communications and semiconductor negotiations of the 1980s; and automobile, automobile parts, insurance, finance, and global environmental issues in the 1990s.

The Keidanren (Japan Federation of Economic Organizations), a business organization for Japanese large enterprises, started its activities in 1948. In 1978, it established the Keizai-Koho Center (Japan Institute for Social and Economic Affairs, which handled the public relations function for Keidanren) to address a number of these issues. They made big efforts to disseminate a strong message that represented the Japanese business community (Ikari, Ed. 1998).

The public relations activities of overseas companies in Japan and the overseas public relations activities of Japanese companies took cultural, traditional, and other differences into consideration and proceeded proactively by disclosing large amounts of statistical data and tactics. In addition to using the mass media to publicize their positions to the public, companies also hired specialists such as lobbyists.

THE BIRTH OF PUBLIC RELATIONS FIRMS

During the latter half of the 1950s through the 1970s, which was a period of rapid economic growth in Japan, many public relations firms were established in anticipation of the coming public relations era. These firms included the Chisei Idea Center, International Public Relations, and Cosmo Public Relations established in the later 1950s and Dentsu PR Center, Sun Creative Publicity, Ozma Inc. Kyodo Public Relations, Prap Japan, and Inoue Public Relations established in the 1960s. However, with the exception of a few public relations firms, the services of most companies through the 1980s consisted of marketing to a large extent. Any public relations activity was centered mostly on publicity targeting the media. Interestingly, these public relations firms could be divided into two types. One type focuses mostly on Japanese clients and provides services mainly in the realm of publicity and event management (90%), and the other type includes international clients and provides a wide array of public relations as well as consulting services with a bilingual staff (10%).

With the intensifying international competition of the second half of the 1970s, foreign enterprises seeking to open the Japanese market strengthened their offensive by employing overseas public relations firms such as Burson-Marsteller, Hill & Knowlton, Ketchum, and Edelman. These consultancies either set up local offices or entered into alliances with Japanese public relations firms to develop their business proactively in the world's second largest market. Their method of approaching public relations conveyed a lot of theory and skill to Japanese public relations firms and greatly contributed to raising the level of public relations in Japan.

In 1980, the existing Japan Public Relations Industry Association and Japan Public Relations Association merged to form the Public Relations Society of Japan. It has conducted various educational training sessions and international conferences, and it has worked to spread public relations in Japan. However, because the annual membership fees are higher than that of similar organizations in other countries, the association has been able to attract only a limited number of members (approx. 430 in 2002).

The future of the public relations industry in Japan is very bright due to deregulation and changes into Japanese accounting standards. It is safe to assume that there will be a rapid increase in the need for risk communications, investor relations, and brand management— areas to which Japanese companies had previously paid little attention.

INCREASED INTEREST IN PUBLIC RELATIONS AMONG ORGANIZATION LEADERS

From the 1980s into the 1990s, burgeoning Japanese economic power made the United States-Japan relationship heat up regarding telecommunications, semi-conductors, automobiles and auto parts (Prestowitz, 1985). The difficulty of conducting public relations activities in such an environment of trade friction is that political negotiations are conducted in a realm that differs from the corporate one. Matters also tend to become emotional, with reports in each country becoming vituperative in content as a consequence of poor and inacurrate communication. Even when trying to spread facts, the side receiving the information reacts sensationally and public relations activities often lose their effectiveness. With this in mind, in some cases public relations specialists have been hired and have facilitated calm negotiations even in a charged atmosphere (see the case study at the end of this chapter).

The collapse of the economy in 1991 has exposed the harmful effects of the close ties between the political world, the bureaucracy, and the business world. The Japanese economy has lost its confidence as it faces the need for structural reforms. During its prolonged economic recession, the Japan Society for Corporate Communication Studies, a scholarly society of public relations, was established in 1995. It focuses on corporate communications and the further research and development of public relations involving scholars and business people, as well as practitioners (with 475 individual and 54 corporate members in 2002). The Society conducted a fact-finding study on corporate communications in June 2002 called the *Survey of Corporate Communication Today*. Interestingly, 90% of the 107 Japanese executives who responded to the survey indicated an interest in public relations, and two thirds of those who are company presidents stated that they directed the public relations activities of their organizations. In addition, 80% of the corporate executives indicated that they seek the opinions of individuals responsible for public relations when setting organizational policies, although the extent to which this is done varies. The report, however, doubts the competency of the executives due to their lack of practical experience in the area of public relations. Apart from this issue, these figures indicate that companies have begun to place more importance on public relations activities. This can particularly be said of major companies with 1,000 or more employees that were the primary sample for the study. The results of this survey on the awareness of Japanese top management about public relations are similar to the results of the following study.

This study was entitled the International Public Relations Association's (IPRA's) Gold paper No. 12 (1997), the Evolution of Public Relations Education and the Influence of Globalization (Survey of eight countries), (Wright and Ikari, 1997). I initiated Gold Paper No. 12 as the chairman of the steering committee. There was assistance from top executives from Japanese large enterprises such as Toyota, Sony, NEC, YAMAHA, and Kikkoman, as well as from many foreign enterprise top executives, PR managers from domestic and foreign companies and independent PR consultants.

UNDERLYING PROBLEMS IN JAPANESE ORGANIZATIONS

Japanese organizations face obstacles when conducting two-way communication in a flat and horizontal communication environment. These problems encompass government as well as corporate scandals. Presently, most Japanese realize that they are not particularly skilled in communications, and corporate executives realize the need to strengthen themselves in this area. Currently, Japanese corporations proactively use public relations functions by consulting with outside public relations consultants when crises occur and entrust day-to-day public relations activities to their in-house public relations departments. The problem in Japan is that although executives realize the need for public relations and act as spokespersons for their organizations, they still do not understand its essence.

Furthermore, not only do corporate leaders fail to understand public relations, but there are few experienced practitioners with specialized public relations education in the organization. One must understand that this lack of understanding and education lies deep in the very structure of Japanese companies where personnel are routinely transferred between divisions every 2 to 4 years due to the rotation system. This creates a situation in which leaders cannot obtain professional advice. Nevertheless, as far as ethical issues are concerned, the organizational leaders' failure to confront this matter makes it difficult for awareness of it to penetrate to the far reaches of the organization. In regard to this important issue, in September 2002, Hiroshi Okuda, chairman of Nihon Keidanren (the Japan Business Federation) noted that corporate ethics are vital and necessary to the management of enterprises.

It is apparent to observers that there are very few qualified public relations practitioners in Japan. Today most of the companies listed on the Tokyo Stock Exchange have their own public relations departments, but in many cases these departments are staffed by people who lack sufficient experience. According to a study of 451 companies (most of them publicly listed) by Toray Corporate Business Research, Inc., in 1999, an average of eight members worked in each of the public relations departments of these companies. There is no statistical data on the total number of the public relations departments in Japanese companies, although it may be safe to assume that there may be around 10,000 full-time practitioners, most with few credentials in the companies.

There are about 150 public relations consulting firms in Japan, which are staffed by about 2,000 full-time practitioners, only 3% of whom are proficient in English. Three Japanese universities have public relations faculties. The recent increase in awareness of public relations has led to the offering of 40 specialized public relations courses in Japanese universities. These numbers are expected to increase in the future. Table 7.1 shows the development of public relations in Japan and its problems.

THE LEVEL OF ACTIVISM IN JAPAN

In the late 19th century, labor disputes frequently occurred in Japan as a result of various movements, such as the people's right to freedom and the poor treatment of overworked female laborers in coal mines and textile plants. This led to the repeated formation of labor unions; around 1920, the full-scale unions of Nihon Rodo Sodoumei, Nihon Nomin Kumiai, and Zenkoku Suiheisha (the movement to free the discriminated community called

TABLE 7.1
Evolution and Problems of Public Relations in Japan

	Characteristics	*Objectives*	*Problems*
1925–1945 Early Showa era End of World War II Dawn of public relations	Propaganda to build up national wealth and military strength	Manipulate the masses	Suppressed free speech and manipulated public opinion
1947–1952 Introduction period of public relations in government by the GHQ	Public information (one-way communication)	To assist GHQ in the implementation of occupation policies	Misunderstanding of the concept and functions of actual public relations. In addition, public relations was mixed up with public information
1950–1963 Educational period on American-style public relations	Advertorial and publicity type (one-way communication)	To assist companies in obtaining social approval	Advertising and public relations became indistinguishable. Focus on advertorials
Latter half of the 1950s–1990 Public relations during the high-growth period	Publicity type (one-way communication at the international level)	Sales promotion for creating a mass production and mass consumption cycle	Excessive focus on marketing public relations and lack of introduction of skills for practicing public relations. Worldwide negative image of Japan developed in the 1970s.
1991–Present Public relations after collapse of the bubble economy	Corporate communication (two-way communication)	Developing a sense of social accountability within the corporate world	Multiple scandals and immature two-way communication

Buraku) were formed. These unions were at the very least influenced by the 1917 Russian Revolution. But labor unions formed much more readily after World War II because of the democratization policies of General MacArthur. The labor union movement during the Cold War period often involved idealistic claims, and national strikes sometimes occurred. In particular, intense fights over wage raises happened every spring especially during the high-growth period of the 1960s and 1970s. However, because Japanese per capita wages became the highest in the world in 1990, negotiations between labor and management have become more cooperative (Masamura & Yamada, 2002). The long recession and restructuring of the economy after the collapse of the economic bubble has also contributed to this amity. Especially in the postwar period, these unions had supported certain political parties and thereby gained vast influence on politics. However, their ability to compel union members to vote in certain ways has weakened in recent times.

The consumerism that occurred in the United States in the 1950s spilled over into Japan and has led to greater rebellion against existing authority. The problems of environmental pollution, toxic chemicals, defective automobiles, and other product deficiencies that began occurring in Japan from the latter half of the 1950s served to heighten various consumer advocacy movements. With the increase in citizens' movements, nonprofit organizations and nongovernmental organizations began to emerge to counter environmental pollution, support developing countries, make international contributions, and establish countermeasures for an aging society. In 1998, the Law to Promote Specified Nonprofit Activities (1998) was passed in the Diet. Currently, 5,000 organizations are registered under the law. Some of these organizations do enter into alliances with various international organizations to conduct their activities.

JAPANESE CULTURE AND PUBLIC RELATIONS

According to the concept of United States anthropologist Edward Hall (1976) on high and low context cultures, he characterized Japan as being a high context one. This implies that the level of cultural codes that is implicitly held among communicators in Japan is high, resulting in a proportional limit on the volume of tangible information that is exchanged. In particular, over the past 2,000 years, Japan has treasured the concept of *wa* (harmony) in which people of a single race live together in an island country. In such a society, objectives are not achieved by individuals competing against each other, but rather people are skilled at achieving objectives through group cooperation. Furthermore, the entry of Confucianism into Japan in the 7th century created a society in which people did not make excuses when they did something wrong. This led to an inability to take responsibility and an inability to explain one's actions or express oneself to others clearly. As a result, misunderstandings and friction often occur when the Japanese interact with people from other countries and cultures.

The Japanese have traditionally placed priority on corporate and organizational profit rather than personal profit, and the image of the Japanese has been that of an "economic animal" with an unseen face. The information technology boom of the 1990s brought about a true globalization of many aspects of the culture, and there was a demand for individual strength and creativity in which the individual role was greater than that of the group. Many people believed that for Japan to obtain the know-how for creating high value-added properties (intellectual property) ahead of China and other Asian countries, it must develop a doctrine that respects an individual's free thoughts and actions. Educational reforms are currently underway to achieve this, stressing the inculcation of sound values (morality) at the high school level, creativity rather than rote learning, and a renewed emphasis on English as an international language to help young people live in the global village.

Although this may be a characteristic of an island nation's culture, when two individuals first meet each other in Japanese society, whether through work or on a more personal level, a lot of time is spent getting to know that person. The relationship rests only on a surface level until one party develops sufficient knowledge about the other; in time, an *amae* (overdependency) structure is developed in which each party tries to depend on the other. Drinking with friends and colleagues after work is one ritual that promulgates this structure. The building of mutual trust with an individual within an organization sometimes leads that relationship to take precedence over the organization (Hampden–Turner, 1997). There is also the influence of Confucian thought, which causes this tendency to be even stronger when there is a hierarchical relationship built around deference to authority.

For example, the surprise attack on Pearl Harbor created a negative image of the Japanese. For a long time after World War II, the country was referred to derogatively as "sneaky Japan." In fact, it was due to a delay caused by Japanese incompetence: The declaration of war was transmitted after the actual start of hostilities in Pearl Harbor. Such a fact has been published in some recent books on the war in the Pacific. The fact that this mistake was covered up by the Japanese and never explained to the international community reflected the prevailing value system of the nation. This value system encouraged a tendency for the intraorganizational hierarchy to submit to authority and a cultural sense of value in which domestic interests or the interests of one's organization (to protect one's own comrades) is placed over international interests. This is based on the Japanese cultural concepts of *haji* (or embarrassment—when one refrains from notifying outsiders of facts when a mistake is made), *amae* (over-dependency), and *wa* (harmony) (Sriramesh & Takasaki, 1999). Consequently, these Japanese cultural traits militate against the openness and speediness that is part of the preferred environment of the public relations world.

The essence of the scandal that led to the Pearl Harbor surprise attack is an absolute value judgment within an organizational setting that led to priority being given to individual personal relationships and the organization. This is almost identical to the frequently reported scandals of recent days. However, in the case of the recent scandals, many have become public through internal indictments, indicating that intraorganizational morals and communications based on a new sense of values have begun to function (Inoue, 2002a, 2002b, 2002c, 2002d). The Pearl Harbor anecdote was mentioned by myself in my Melbourne IPRA World Congress speech in 1988, and the Asahi newspaper reported the same story 6 years after that.

THE MEDIA AND PUBLIC RELATIONS

It is difficult to overstate the importance of the relationship between the mass media and public relations. Many believe that media relations activities are at the core of public relations, which makes the need for a robust relationship with the media vital for organizations and public relations practitioners. Japan, which boasts a large gross domestic product, enjoys diverse media coverage nationwide with a high density population and PR's impact on Japanese society is getting stronger. Developing a good relationship with and a deep understanding of the media is crucial in Japan. Moreover, media analysis using information technologies such as the computer and the Internet such as CARMA® (a company which provides Computer Aided Research & Media Analysis), which enables self-correction of two-way communication, is a vital public relations solution in the increasingly complex 21st century.

JAPANESE MEDIA

Broadcasting in Japan began in 1925 when NHK, the Japanese public broadcasting network, began radio broadcasts. In 1951, the first privately owned radio station was opened. In 1953, NHK started the first television broadcasts, and other private television stations began operating the same year. Presently, NHK covers the entire nation with 49 television and radio stations. In addition, Japan has 139 private television stations (including 5 in Tokyo) and 99 private radio stations. Moreover, Japan has satellite-broadcasting stations that began operation in 1987, digital satellite-broadcasting stations that began in 1996, and small FM stations that cover towns and communities.

As mentioned earlier, the first newspaper was issued in Japan in 1871. Presently, there are five national papers—*Asahi Shimbun, Yomiuri Shimbun, Mainichi Shimbun, Nihon Keizai Shimbun*, and *Sankei Shimbun*—with a combined daily circulation exceeding 71 million copies (including morning and evening editions). The national papers enjoy an enormous circulation: The morning circulation for the *Yomiuri Shimbun* exceeds 10 million copies and that of the *Asahi Shimbun* exceeds 8.3 million copies. The annual circulation for newspapers and magazines is the greatest in the world and totals about 4.62 billion issues. Furthermore, a total of 133 million books are published every year. The network of print and electronic media cover 48 million households throughout the nation.

In addition, the Japanese Constitution rejects suppression of free speech and prohibits political intervention in religion, which frequently occurred prior to the war. The media, with the exception of some industries and specialized papers that depend on advertising revenues, are extremely free in expressing their opinions concerning corporations, political parties, or religious groups. There are also newspapers, magazines, and books that are run by political parties and religious groups, such as the *Akahata* newspaper of the Japan Communist Party, *Komei Shimbun* of the Komeito Party, and the *Seikyo Shimbun* of the Soka Gakkai—a Buddhist group.

As for communication activities, there are almost no government regulations outside of some guidelines on ethics. The Japanese Constitution guarantees freedom of speech, expression, and publication. At the same time, the media have also established ethical guidelines for themselves to protect the interests of the public. Thus, journalism enjoys a high level of freedom and credibility in Japan. The mass media, which emerged from the latter half of the 1950s preaching postwar democratic philosophy, became the fourth most powerful entity in Japan following the political, bureaucratic, and business entities in the 1990s. One perspective on the present social reformation being implemented is that it is driven by the mass media supported by public opinion.

Media Outreach

As already mentioned, the various media sources easily encompass all areas of Japan. Furthermore, 47.08 million people use the Internet, and the usage ratio in Japan for mobile telephones is more than half or up to 54.7%. According to the Ministry of Public Management, Home Affairs, Posts and Telecommunications, (2001), (2002). A highly dense telecommunications infrastructure provides a fast and dependable transmission of information by the media. The media network that covers every square inch of Japan broadcasts information to the Japanese people who have a right to know, and an environment has been established in which people can freely select the information they want.

Media Access

Many companies have their own *ko-ho* (public relations) departments, that contact the media when needed. Public relations agencies build relationships with the media in an effort to use the media on behalf of their clients. Although many companies are beginning to adopt two-way communications as part of their media relations, many continue to use one-way communication when disseminating information that is useful to them. Historically, the Japanese media have sought access to organizational leaders to obtain comments directly from them. There are some cases in which organizational leaders have become personally close to journalists and contacted the media directly, thus ignoring the public relations department. However, this sometimes makes the relationship with the media difficult, especially during times of crises. Nonetheless, public relations departments of Japanese corporations are being strengthened because of the heightened necessity to handle corporate public relations due to globalization, environmental activism, and the introduction of new corporate accounting standards. However, there continues to be a lack of very experienced public relations specialists as mentioned earlier. Consequently, when a scandal occurs, it is magnified because the existing staff is unable to initiate appropriate and fast measures.

Furthermore, as previously explained, Japanese media correspondents usually change their departments every 2 to 3 years, which brings up the constant need to establish new relationships. This is mitigated somewhat due to the press club system that originated in 1890 when the Imperial Parliament was inaugurated. Currently, there are about 800 press clubs nationwide that have borrowed space and facilities in the offices of the central government, major political parties, local governments, industry bodies, and major economic organizations.

The Press Club Organization is very exclusive, and fewer than 60 media organizations, including major newspapers, locally strong media, television stations, and wire agencies, are members of a single press club. This system is extremely convenient for the organizations that have a press club on their premises because they can easily disseminate information and messages to their targeted audiences through the media members of their press club. This system worked especially well during the high-economic growth period when organizations that had press clubs were able to achieve their purposes through controlled management of the news, a one-way flow of information. The management of these clubs is done by the club members themselves. As a result, members enjoy autonomy, but the information flow itself is easily controlled by the organizations where each club is located. Press club members mostly have a monopoly on information originating from the organizations where they are stationed.

In the press club system, there are few opportunities for scoops as all the media members of a club are provided with the same releases and briefings by the organizations where the clubs are located. The exclusivity of press clubs and their tradition of keeping non-Japanese out led to intense demonstrations by foreign journalists in the early 1990s, and the clubs started becoming more open. For example, in the press club of the Ministry of Economy, Trade and Industry, there are currently 61 media members including two foreign media (Reuters and Bloomberg). Of these 61 members, 23 media organizations, including Reuters and Bloomberg, have work space for their representatives in the club. The press club of the Ministry of Foreign Affairs has about 10 foreign media members such as the Associated Press, Reuters, CNN, AFP and Bloomberg, in addition to Japanese press members. There are other signs of reform among the press clubs. For example, after the renowned author Yasuo Tanaka assumed the post of governor of Nagano Prefecture, he abolished the press club that had existed in the prefectural offices and changed the rules to allow anyone to attend a media briefing. Increasingly, access to the media has become easier for organizations and persons such as activists.

CONCLUSION

Japan opened up to external influence in the latter half of the 19th century through foreign pressure when Commodore Perry's black ships arrived. Japan's economic growth has been guided by central authorities in a one-way direction and with a top to bottom fiat style of management. This has taken place despite the influence of foreign cultures, science, and technology; the various policies led by the *zaibatsu* (major corporate groupings with an old, industrialist, famous-name founder, such as Iwasaki of the Mitsubishi group and Mitsui of the Mitsui group); the former military plan to catch up with the advanced countries of the West; and the building of a modern democracy under the leadership of the GHQ after Japan's defeat during World War II. However, with emerging societal issues, such as slumping stock prices, the recession, organizational scandals, the collapse of the family, and the increase in violent crimes, the mature Japanese society is still unable to find ways of building a new social system through a structural reform of the present system.

Nonetheless, Japan is now in an era of major transformation on a global scale, as the capitalist doctrine that Japan and the advanced countries of the West pursued during the last century has come to a dead end. The country must shift from an economic development model based on material wealth and build a new model that seeks coexistence with nature and emphasizes a high sense of ethics and wisdom for resolving diverse global problems, such as a lack of food in many nations, population issues, environmental problems, tribal disputes, conflicts between different cultures, and the digital divide. There is a demand for escape from a system that only pursues efficiency and material goods to a system formed from the creation and sharing of a new sense of values that takes into account changes in organizational environments that are horizontal and a two-way process, that accepts failures, respects people, and honors unique cultures and spiritual values.

Presently, information is shared more broadly on a daily basis, and greater speed is sought in handling situations. Within the rapidly changing society and flood of information, the ability to communicate with the targeted public is a critical issue that can mean life or death for a country or corporate body. However, the public may have difficulties in distinguishing the accuracy of the news with the great volume of information constantly being thrown at them. There is a chaotic appearance in the relationship between the information source and recipient. It seems that we are entering an era of unpredictability where humankind experiences rapid changes as never before.

Public relations is the ultimate real-time "software" in which specialists can provide solutions based on a situational judgment within this fast-changing society. The roles and duties of practitioners intermediating between information transmitters, information receivers, and the media are very critical. The key to the future as the problem solver of an increasingly changing and complex society lies in the implementation of a new model of public relations. Its goal should include global peace that strives toward harmonious and prosperous societies in which people are respected. This model consists of two-way communication but also possesses a self-correction function that is one step advanced from the traditional coordination and adjustment function for optimal results.

A final word is appropriate on what I mean by the newly proposed self-correction function. It refers to the ability to reflect on one's past mistake or misjudgment and it also means to make whatever correction is needed as soon as possible to prevent a recurrence of the error or misjudgment and to make a remedy for it when possible. It is not just a passive or superficial understanding of a past mistake or misjudgment, which reflects the old way of thinking. This model that includes the self-correction function envisages a society comprised of newly built values and takes a direction suitable for the 21st century (Inoue, 2002e).

Case Study: Tenneco—Deregulation of the Japanese Auto Parts Aftermarket, by Inoue Public Relations, Tokyo, Japan[1]

Statement of Problem/Opportunity. Tenneco Automotive, a major American auto parts manufacturer, had made little progress in selling its shock absorbers (including its top-selling Monroe ® brand) in Japan despite its efforts over a 20-year period. Of the 1.5 million after-market shock absorbers sold during 1994 in Japan by automobile owners, Tenneco's share was a mere 3.5%. The company and many industry experts agreed that the closed nature of the Japanese aftermarket was the source of the problem. Tenneco hired Inoue Public Relations (Inoue PR) in early 1994 to find a way to open the Japanese market to their various products, including the Monroe shock absorbers. The campaign was a 3-year program concluding at the end of 1996.

Research. Inoue PR, working closely with Tenneco's local subsidiary, Tenneco Automotive Japan, conducted extensive research into legislation and regulations affecting the import of automotive products into Japan. It also interviewed 50 industry experts, auto trade journalists, and representatives of auto repair shops, retailers, auto and auto parts industry groups, and government car inspection and registration centers to gather more data on the environment for automotive products. The research disclosed that a web of government legislation spun over a 40-year period establishing standards for car safety and maintenance and the inspection system itself protected the domestic auto-parts aftermarket from imported products. In the process, domestically manufactured auto parts were labeled "genuine original equipment (OE) parts," whereas imported parts were handicapped from the start with the label "non-OE parts." Furthermore, most of the certified auto repair shops were controlled by top Japanese automakers who also had relationships with domestic parts manufacturers. In addition, the operators of the nation's repair shops were culturally conservative, resisting change of any kind. Finally, imported parts were made more expensive by the complexity of Japan's distribution system. Inoue PR compiled these findings into the Tenneco Report.

Planning. In consultation with Tenneco, Inoue PR set three objectives for the campaign:

1. Secure the deregulation of the Japanese auto parts aftermarket.
2. Once deregulation was under way, find new business partners for the distribution of Tenneco products in Japan.

---

[1]The program was submitted in 1977 to the IPRA Golden World Awards, Category 4: Public Affairs, and it was awarded IPRA's Excellence in Public Relations Grand Prize, which is the top award and the first one awarded in Asia and the Pacific.

3. Because deregulation alone would not ensure expansion in a market that had been heavily influenced by government regulation for more than 40 years, create new demand by re-educating Japanese car owners regarding the purchase of shock absorbers.

To achieve these objectives, Inoue PR developed two key messages. The first, targeted at the government, advocated the idea that deregulation creates new business opportunities in the Japanese aftermarket. The second, targeted at consumers, exhorted them to replace shock absorbers every 30,000 km to enhance driving safety and comfort. The specific audiences among these two broad publics were the key ministries in the Japanese Government, industry groups such as Japan Auto Parts Industry Association, car shops, prospective new distribution channels such as gas stations, and industry experts. Among the media, Inoue PR concentrated on general newspapers, news agencies, business and trade publications, television stations, and the foreign press.

Execution.   In the United States, Tenneco delivered the Tenneco Report to both the United States Department of Commerce and the Office of the United States Trade Representative. It was then presented to the White House. In Japan, Tenneco Japan and Inoue PR submitted the report to high-ranking officials at Japan's Ministry of Trade and Industry (MITI) and Ministry of Transport (MOT), as well as the American Embassy in Japan. Unofficial briefings were also provided to MITI and MOT. Meanwhile, on October 1, 1994, President Clinton declared the United States' intentions to apply Section 301 Trade Sanctions to Japan's auto parts aftermarket. Typically, Inoue PR and the Tenneco Japan office were responsible for lobbying done in Japan, and the Tenneco head office was responsible for the lobbying done in Washington, DC.

Inoue PR had originally planned to release the Tenneco Report at a press conference. However, because the behind-the-scenes efforts with both the Japanese and American governments were proving effective, Inoue PR decided this would not be appropriate. Instead, Inoue PR gave individual off-the-record briefings to Japan's five major newspapers and two major television stations. These media had been dependent on the Japanese government for their information on the auto parts aftermarket, and the briefings opened their eyes to the unfairness of this market to Japanese consumers.

Meanwhile, negotiations between the United States Trade Representative and the Japanese government stalled just before the June 28, 1995, deadline. The United States threatened to enforce sanctions, which had the potential to set off rounds of tit-for-tat retaliation. Under these circumstances, the Tenneco Report proved to be a critical source for both governments in arriving at a settlement. Using information provided during our briefings, the major media wrote articles about the negotiations, which had a tremendous impact on public opinion, putting pressure on the Japanese government to settle.

Once deregulation was under way, Tenneco and Inoue PR, through their connections, approached and proposed distribution partnerships with Toyota Motors, Autobacs, an auto parts chain with 380 outlets nationwide, and Japan Energy—one of Japan's major oil companies with 6,400 JOMO (Joy of Motoring) gas stations nationwide.

To launch the sale of Tenneco shock absorbers at JOMO gas stations, the first press conference in Japan ever held at a gas station was conducted. It featured officials from Tenneco, MITI, and the American Embassy in Japan. It attracted more than 100 Japanese and foreign journalists. Inoue PR also provided a crucial update on the situation in Japan to Dana Mead, chairman & chief executive officer of Tenneco Inc. Mead met with high-ranking Japanese officials to obtain their support for further opening the auto parts aftermarket. Throughout the campaign, Inoue PR arranged more than 20 one-on-one interviews with major Japanese and foreign media and distributed eight press releases gaining extensive quality coverage.

Evaluation. The campaign made great progress toward achieving the objectives. First, on October 20, 1995, Japan's Ministry of Transport, taking unusually quick action, officially decided to exclude four items—shock absorbers among them—from the list of auto parts requiring inspection. This made possible the sale of shock absorbers at locations not certified as inspection stations. Second, prior to the conclusion of the American–Japan negotiations, MITI sent a notice to distributors instructing them not to discriminate against foreign-made products. Third, the Ministry of Transport instructed auto repair shops not to discriminate and to give consumers the opportunity to select the shock absorbers they wanted. Fourth, Tenneco was able to form business partnerships with Toyota, Autobacs, and Japan Energy to distribute Tenneco shock absorbers nationwide.

As a result, the sale of Tenneco's shock absorbers in Japan increased by more than 40% between 1995 and 1996. President Clinton honored the achievements of Tenneco in Japan in an April 1996 White House press conference, marking the successful end of American–Japanese auto negotiations. The Japanese financial newspaper *Nihon Keizai Shimbun* (equivalent to the United Kingdom's *Financial Times* or the United States' *Wall Street Journal*) wrote a special report after the settlement was reached in Geneva between the two countries. The story revealed the existence of the Tenneco Report and its influence on the talks. On January 14, 1997, Japan's authoritative newspaper *Asahi Shimbun* reported on an evaluation of 45 major American–Japanese trade agreements that were made between 1980 and 1996. The study, conducted by the American Chamber of Commerce in Japan, revealed that 13 of these agreements proved to be successful, 18 partially successful, and 10 were failures. The auto parts negotiations were highlighted as a success by the study.

REFERENCES

Bernays, E. L. (1923). *Crystallizing public opinion.* (reprinted in 1961). New York: Liveright Publishing Company.

Cabinet Secretary, Cabinet Public Relations Office, (1990). *Seifu ko-ho 30nenshi no hakkan ni atatte* [The thirty years history of Japanese Government *ko-ho*] Tokyo: Author

Dentsu Advertising Co., Ltd. (Ed.) (1956). *Dentsu kokoku nenkan* [Dentsu AD annual 1956.], Tokyo: Author. p. 450.

Discovered document: Inefficiency was the cause of the delayed Declaration of War announcement to the U.S. by the U.S. Japanese Embassy (1994, November 21). The Asahi Shimbun, front page, morning edition.

Grunig, J. E., & Hunt, T. (1984). *Managing public relations.* New York: Holt, Rinehart & Winston.

Hall, E. T. (1976). *Beyond culture.* New York: Doubleday.

Hampden-Turner, C., & Trompenaars, A. (1997). *The seven cultures of capitalism* (K. Uehara & M. Wakatabe, Trans.). Tokyo: Nihon Keizai Shimbun Sha.

Higuchi, Y., & Ishiwatari, S. (2002). *Globalization.* Tokyo: St. Paul.

Hikami, R. (1951). *PR no kangaekata to arikata* [The concept and practice of PR]. Tokyo: Sekaishoin.

Hikami, R. (1952). *Jichitai ko-ho no riron to gijutsu* [Theory and techniques of public relations in local governments]. Tokyo: Sekaishoin.

Ikeda, K. (1997). *Shanaiho-hyakunenshi* [100 years of in-house publications], April issue, Tokyo: Gendai-keiei Kenkyukai

Ikari, S. (Ed.). (1998). *Kigyo no hatten to ko-ho sen-ryaku-50nen no ayumi to tenbo* [Corporate development and the strategy of public relations—a 50 year history and perspective]. Tokyo: Nikkei BP-Kikaku.

Inoue, T. (2002a, March). Kyogyubyo ni taisho suru kikikanri ho [How to do crisis management to counter the BSE problem]. Opinion leaders' *Seiron Magazine, 3,* 342–349.

Inoue, T. (2002b). *Mad cows, bad system in Japan. IPRA Frontline, 24*(2) p. 8, 13.

Inoue, T. (2002c). *The need for two-way communications and self-correction. IPRA Frontline, 24*(4) p. 17–18. and the erratum, 2003 March, 25(1) p. 5.

Inoue, T. (2002d). Deficiency of Japanese diplomacy. *Japan Today.* Retrieved May 29, 2002, from http://www.japantoday.com/e/?content=comment&id=191

Inoue, T. (2002e). United States public relations in transition: Analysis of evolution and proposal for a new model. In the Proceedings of the Japan Information-Cultural Society. Vol. 9 No. 1, pp. 61–75.

The Japan Society for Corporate Communication Studies. (2002). *Senryo-ki no ko- ho/shanai-ho* [Public relations/house organ during GHQ occupation]. Tokyo: Author.

The Japan Society for Corporate Communication Studies. (2002). *Survey of corporate communication today.* Tokyo: Author.

The Law to Promote Specified Nonprofit Activities, Ordinance No. 7 of 1998, March 25, Cabinet Office

Kitazawa, S. (1951). *Public relations kowa* [Public relations talk]. Tokyo: Diamond-sha.

Koyama, E. (1975). *Gyosei ko-ho nyumon* [An introduction to government public relations]. Tokyo: Gyosei.

Masamura, K., & Yamada, S. (2002). *Nihon keizairon* [The Japanese economy]. Tokyo: Toyo Keizai Shinpo-sha.

Ministry of Public Management, Home Affairs, Post and Telecommunications, (2001), *Tsushin-riyou-doko-chosa* [2001 Communication usage trend survey]. Tokyo: Author.

Ministry of Public Management, Home Affairs, Post and Telecommunications, (2002), *Joho-tsushin hakusho* [*2002 WHITE PAPER Information and Communications in Japan*]. Tokyo: Gyosei.

Nihon-Koho-Kyokai (1951). *Koho no genri to jissai* [Ko-ho theory and practice], Tokyo: Nihon Dempo-Tsushin-Sha

Ogura, S. (1990). *PR wo kangaeru* [All about PR]. Tokyo: Dentsu.

Ozawa, I. (1993). *Nihon kaizo keikaku* [Plans for Japanese structural reforms]. Tokyo: Kodansha.

Public Relations Association of Japan, (2002). PR techo (*Public relations hand book*). Tokyo: Author.

Prestowitz, C. (1985). Nichibei gyakuten [*Trading places: how we allowed Japan to take the lead*]. (M. Kunihiro, Trans.). Tokyo: Diamond-sya.

Sakaiya, T. (2002a). *Jidaiga kawatta* [The Era has changed] Tokyo: Kodansha.

Sasaki, Y. (1951). *Pr no kiso-chishini* [PR basic knowledge], Tokyo: Toyoshokan.

Shiba, R. (1996). *Kono kuni no katachi* [The shape of Japan, Vol. 6]. Tokyo: Bungei-Syun-Jyu.

Shibasaki, K. (1984). *Kigyo-joho-sanbogaku* [Corporate policy maker], Tokyo: Diamond-sha

Sriramesh, K., & Takasaki, M. (1999). The impact of culture on Japanese public relations. *Journal of Communication Management, 3*, 337–351.

The Basic Law for the Environmental Pollution Control Law No. 132 of 1967. August 3, Ministry of Health and Welfare.

Tokyo Metropolitan Government. (1995). *Senjika tocho no ko-ho katsudo* [Public relations activities of the Tokyo Metropolitan Office during World War II]. Tokyo: Tokyo Metropolitan Archives, Tokyo Metropolitan Government Archives.

Tsurumi, Y. (1997). *High speed senryaku* [World class strategy] Tokyo: Sogo-Horei

Wright, D., & Ikari, S. (1997). *The evolution of public relations education and the influence of globalization— survey of eight countries' IPRA gold paper, No. 12, November 1997.* London: International Public Relations Association.

Yamaguchi, M. (1995). *Haisha-no seishinshi* [Psychological history of the defected], Tokyo: Iwanami-shoten.

8

PROFESSIONALISM AND DIVERSIFICATION: THE EVOLUTION OF PUBLIC RELATIONS IN SOUTH KOREA

YUNGWOOK KIM

South Korean public relations scholars, with help from American colleagues, are in the process of describing public relations in South Korea using various theoretical constructs. By all accounts, it is evident that public relations in South Korea is still early in its development and continues to be under the strong influence of the publicity-ridden *hong-bo*. The term *hong-bo*, often used in South Korea as a substitute for the term *public relations*, can be described as disseminating information in a wide coverage using mass media or to make organizations or persons known to the public broadly (J. Park, 2001). *Hong-bo* often refers to publicity activities aimed at evading negative media coverage of organizations. Further, *hong-bo* is deeply rooted in the collaboration between the authoritarian government and the powerful *chaebol* system during the 1970s. Y. Park and M. Kim (1997) defined *chaebol* as "a business group consisting of many companies that are owned and managed by family members in diversified business areas" (p. 97).

Theorizing about public relations in South Korea should logically begin by drawing distinctions between public relations and *hong-bo* because traditional *hong-bo* tactics conflict with the current desire among many professionals for professional practice. Although publicity dominates much of the public relations activities in South Korea, some practitioners do practice more diversified public relations activities such as community relations, crisis management, and investor relations (Y. Kim & Hon, 1998). Although traditional Korean culture represents closed and personalized approaches to communication, the younger generation is more inclined to practice more open communication, seeking long-term relationships between the organization and publics. This, and the entry of multinational enterprises due to rapid globalization, is forcing public relations practitioners in

South Korea to practice more sophisticated forms of public relations (Y. Kim & Hon, 2001). One can conclude that tradition and change are two forces that have influenced current public relations in South Korea. In this chapter I describe the history of public relations in the country and explain the linkage between environmental variables and public relations practice, thus delineating the dialogical interaction between two forces that may lead to more professional and diversified public relations in South Korea.

DEVELOPMENT OF THE FIELD

History

The emergence of public relations in South Korea is deeply rooted in the public information function by the government (often referred to as *gong-bo*). The arrival of American military forces at the end of World War II, after decades of Japanese domination (from 1910 to 1945), helped introduce South Korea to the public information activity by the government (Oh, 1991). The government used the Public Information Department to control public opinion and establish the new policies proposed by the American military government. After the American military government gave way to the newly established South Korean dictatorship in 1948, *gong-bo* was continued to be used to manipulate public opinion until the civil revolution of 1960. Even though what the American military and the South Korean government did was far from professional public relations, the introduction of the public information function (*gong-bo*) to government public relations was a key juncture in the development of public relations. The democratic government initiated by the 1960 civil revolution did not last long. After the 1961 military coup led by General Chung-Hee Park, the nation saw a highly authoritarian rule that eliminated press freedoms (Choe, 1992). The cold-war confrontation between South and North Korea also contributed to such a political climate.

However, a strong governmental drive for industrialization provided immense financial and political support for big companies, which in turn created what became known as the *chaebol* system, a network of conglomerate business groups. The government provided preferential financing to these groups in exchange for illegal political funds (Y. Kim & Hon, 1998). Amidst this collusion, the development of ethical and professional public relations was virtually impossible.

The public relations profession changed significantly in 1988 during and after the Seoul Olympics because of the participation of multinational public relations companies such as Burson–Marsteller and Hill and Knowlton in big government projects (Choe, 1992). The demise of dictatorship and the advent of social democracy during the 1989 civil upheaval provided a fertile ground for the development of professional public relations. Authoritarian processes are no longer effective in the current democratic society in South Korea. Organizations are being forced to take a new perception of public relations in this new environment. These forces of change are typified by increasing globalization, higher degrees of press freedom, the demand for diversified public relations activities, and the growing participation of grassroots citizens in organizational decision making.

In the 1990s, public relations received a boost from scholars who had studied in the United States and returned home to apply their knowledge to study South Korean public relations. The profession also gained significantly with the entry of several multinational public relations companies. Various crisis situations also gave the public relations departments of corporations the motivation to insist on better relationships with diverse publics.

The Current Status of the Profession

It is estimated that almost 200 public relations companies are striving for survival in South Korea (J. Kim, 2001). This increase in the number of public relations companies has lead to an artificial swelling of the public relations industry. Yet, this growth in numbers does not imply a concomitant advancement in the sophistication of public relations services and relationships with client organizations.

Most public relations agencies have actively affiliated themselves with well-known firms such as Hill and Knowlton and Fleishman-Hillard to exchange information and broaden organizational knowledge related to communication and promotion overseas (J. Kim, 2001). Another reason for these affiliations is the increasing challenges resulting from the diversified needs of clients. Leading international agencies also are eager to penetrate the South Korean market, signaling the potential for growth in this market. However, fierce competition among public relations agencies calls for a new set of business standards and ethical guidelines. Low profits resulting from high competition and the lack of sophisticated public relations practices due to an overdependence on media relations are the major limitations of the public relations industry in South Korea (J. Park, 2001).

This growth in numbers has more positive effects than negative ones. Interviews with 24 practitioners and scholars revealed that South Korean companies increasingly appreciate the value of public relations in the pluralistic and integrated society that South Korea has become (Y. Kim & Hon, 2001). Some public relations firms have begun to carve out niches in areas such as crisis management, new technology communication, cyber communication, marketing public relations, public affairs, and investor relations (Rhee, 1999). Crisis management has become a critical part of public relations in South Korea as several big corporations have experienced crisis situations since 1991. One of the most serious cases was the so-called *phenol crisis.* Doosan Electronics, a *chaebol,* discharged a toxic substance known as phenol to the Nakdong River on March 16, 1991, and was confronted with a major lawsuit by those affected by this pollution. (This case is explained in detail at the end of this chapter.) This crisis also instigated the nationwide boycott of Doosan products resulting in the payment of a huge legal compensation. Since that disaster, South Korean companies have realized that they cannot rely solely on their close ties to the government as a strategy for concealing their misdeeds. Instead, they have begun to focus on building relationships with diverse publics as a critical corporate function in a democratic society. They seem to have learned that public relations could offer effective ways of handling crises and, therefore, have begun viewing public relations as a managerial function.

In 1989, the Korean Public Relations Association was established to advance the interests of the profession in South Korea (Choe, 1992). The Korea Public Relations Consultancy Association (KPRCA) was also established in 2000 to prevent public relations companies from conducting unlawful and illegitimate practices (J. Kim, 2001). In 1998, the Korean Academic Society of Public Relations (KASPR), which is the first association for those involved in public relations education, was established. The KASPR publishes the scholarly quarterly journal, the *Korean Journal of Public Relations Research.*

The Models of Public Relations. The established tradition of media-oriented public relations is hard to change in a short time span. In South Korea, as far as organizational information is concerned, personal relationships with journalists rather than news value still determine which stories get published in the media, representing the personal influence model (Sriramesh, 1992; Sriramesh, Y. Kim, & Takasaki, 1999). The public relations activities of Korean *chaebols* have traditionally been restricted mainly to obtaining positive publicity in an effort to counter public criticism about many irresponsible corporate activities.

Y. Kim (1996) surveyed 167 South Korean practitioners to determine which public relations model (J. E. Grunig & Hunt, 1984) they used and the level of job satisfaction among these practitioners. Results showed that Korean practitioners predominantly used the craft models of press agentry and public information. But results also showed that these practitioners aspired to practice the two-way professional models. The study revealed that practitioners who used the two-way models were more satisfied with their jobs than those practicing the one-way craft models. Conveying factual information, or being a neutral disseminator, is a tough task in South Korea because Korean organizations prefer to withhold information. Some practitioners were also found to consider information manipulation as a major public relations strategy attempting to get favorable publicity into the media while keeping unfavorable publicity out of media focus.

Rhee (1999) replicated the excellence study (J. E. Grunig, 1992) and found that South Korean public relations practitioners are primarily involved with media relations. However, results from her study also showed that these practitioners recognized the importance of mutual understanding as well as persuading the public, which is the essence of the two-way models. Yoon (2001) also found that practitioners working for public relations agencies have more symmetrical worldviews than practitioners of their clients. This implies that agency practitioners can function as powerhouses for making the field more professional.

However, results of another study indicated that existing public relations theories, developed largely in the United States, do not fit the public relations function in South Korea perfectly (Y. Kim & Hon, 2001). Qualitative interviews with 24 chief executive officers (CEOs) and public relations executives in South Korea revealed the pitfalls of applying Western models of public relations to the South Korean situation as explained by a mass communication professor interviewed for the study:

> Public relations in Korea is struggling to get to the stage of the public information model but the progress is very tardy because of other environmental factors surrounding the organization such as the level of democracy, government-business collusion, and the pre-modern press system. The slow development of public relations models has made public relations practitioners skip the developmental stage of the public information model. Even though public relations activities are not based on the belief in disseminating true information, they are trying to conduct research before a public relations program and look at the outcome of attitude surveys about publics. Also many companies describe the purpose of public relations as mutual understanding between an organization and publics. (Y. Kim & Hon, 2001, p. 271)

This indicates that the two-way models are already being used to some extent by South Korean public relations practitioners. But, for the most part, the press agentry/publicity model is the most prevalent. However, if this essay takes into consideration the media's unbalanced reporting habits in South Korea, public relations practitioners do not bear all of the responsibility for the dominance of press agentry. Some practitioners in government and public relations agencies said that they have tried to publicize accurate stories about their organizations or clients, rather than trying to manipulate information. It is evident that they know that, in the long run, disclosing and distributing accurate information is better than concealment.

In addition to J. E. Grunig's four public relations models, other models (J. E. Grunig, L. A. Grunig, Sriramesh, Huang, & Lyra, 1995) were revealed during the interviews. Some comments indicated that the personal influence and cultural translation models reflected some important aspects of public relations in South Korea. Public relations practitioners value personal network in resolving organizational conflicts with publics. For example, practitioners turn to networks such as alumni associations, personal links, family members, and relatives and friends for help when organizational problems arise. In-group solidarity, a characteristic of Korean culture, can be reinforced through give-and-take interactions. One corporate public relations director talked about personal influence:

> A unique business background exists in every country. Personal influence is very important under the Chaebol system. The strategies of the Chaebols' PR departments tend to be defensive to avoid criticism from the press and negative coverage. In this case, if a public relations practitioner has an acquaintance or the closeness of friendship with a reporter or a gatekeeper, he can ask to take an unfavorable article out or minimize the size of the headline or article. For continuing this relationship, practitioners have to prepare regular gifts and provide *Ddukgab* (money for buying Korean cake, sometimes similar to bribery) (Y. Kim & Hon, 2001, pp. 273–274).

Foreign businessmen in South Korea often refer to public relations practitioners as consultants and rely on them for help in understanding the unique business practices of South Korea, an indication of the cultural translator model. The trend toward globalization will only add momentum to the use of the cultural translator model.

INFRASTRUCTURE AND PUBLIC RELATIONS

Social, Political, and Economic Contexts

As already mentioned, the replacement of dictatorship with social democracy has contributed to the development of public relations in South Korea. After General Park's coup in 1961, the military government did not encourage a wholesome relationship between the organization and publics through open and reciprocal communication. The government gave favors to *chaebols* in exchange for political funds. For their part, although the *chaebols* led the economic development, they did so under political policies that benefited them greatly. The South Korean media occasionally exposed the alliance between the government and *chaebols* as government intervention resulted in civil protests under the authoritarian regime. However, the media lacked sufficient freedom, and in exchange for securing information sources and achieving financial stability, they often failed to cover certain sensitive issues. The *chaebols*, backed by the government's industrialization drive, did not care for the other publics except the media. All these circumstances created *hong-bo*, explained earlier (Jo, 2001; Rhee, 1999).

Emphasis on government public relations and crisis management is a key to understanding public relations in South Korea. In the United States, it is against the law for the government to spend appropriated money on public relations efforts to gain support for government projects (Wilcox, Ault, Agee, & Cameron, 2000). However, there are no regulations or laws that block public relations activities by government agencies in South Korea. Instead, the government has invested money in significant public relations projects. Public relations by the government can be characterized as developmental public relations because of its emphasis on national development projects, such as spurring industrial drive, in developing countries.

The development of social democracy, the 1988 Seoul Olympic games, and the effects of globalization are key factors in the development of public relations in South Korea. However, the Asian economic crisis of 1997 has altered the optimistic observations and cast doubts on the development of public relations in South Korea. The South Korean government could not secure enough financial resources to repay its debt and sought assistance from the International Monetary Fund. The government-led economic system, including *chaebols*, came under great pressure in this dynamic international business environment, resulting in the collapse of several *chaebols*. The government began economic reforms including the modification of the *chaebol* system because neither the government nor the *chaebols* could adjust to the openness of a global environment.

Therefore, one can conclude that the introduction of political democracy in 1987 and the economic crisis of 1997 has brought about some maturity to the South Korean business environment. However, South Korean business practices still possess serious weaknesses. Despite its efforts, the government has not succeeded in revamping the *chaebol*-oriented economic system completely. Other factors contributing to the failure include fierce labor disputes and the growing chasm between the haves and have-nots, leading to conflicts between the two.

The South Korean legal system protects the right of free speech fully even though it harbors a conservative orientation, a vestige of previous authoritarian regimes. Youm (1996) noted that the South Korean press has evolved from being a voluntary servant of the regime to a harsh critic since the democratic reforms of the 1987 civil democratic movement. Thus, there are no statutory obstacles to freedom except National Security Laws that prohibit association with North Korea. Most trade associations in the mass communication industry have voluntary regulations prohibiting unethical and illegitimate practices. For instance, the KPRCA and the Korean Advertising Agency Association have voluntary ethical codes of conduct. Related to public relations, social customs and cultural uniqueness may be more important for optimal practices than legal fundamentals.

ACTIVISM AND PUBLIC RELATIONS

The conspicuous characteristic of the current South Korean society is the advent of the civil activism era. Civil activism has been reinforced through the democracy movement that protested the authoritative ruling of the military regime. Also, labor movements for better work conditions have stimulated empowerment of civil movements and led to the birth of diverse nongovernmental organizations (NGOs). NGOs are taking an active role in policy making and often oversee and object to the wrongdoings of the government and *chaebols* (Cha, 2001).

By 1999, there were over 2,000 NGOs in South Korea, with a total membership of 20,000. The typical dues-paying member of an NGO is young and educated. The number of NGOs had been increasing drastically since the 1987 uprising for democracy. Statistics show that 70% of NGOs were established after the 1987 democratic movement. This spurt can be attributed to social democratization, maturation of the grassroots democracy, and active participation in political decision making.

However, NGOs are not financially independent from the government. Their public relations strategies revolve mostly around garnering media publicity for their causes. They often use sensationalism to invoke media interest. They seem to prefer the win–lose strategy, such as illegal protests and premature accusation without prior conversation, over the win–win strategy, such as public hearing and dialogue with the organization. Cha (2001) argued that NGOs and the targets of their attacks could have a win–win relationship through two-way and balanced communication. However, if the two-way symmetrical model is used by NGOs, it may be interpreted as a compromise with the socially unjustified in South Korean society. This may be why they shun such mutually negotiated outcomes, another indication of the impact of culture on public relations activities.

Pressure from NGOs forces organizations to engage in ethical and more transparent public relations practices. Many South Korean organizations that practice unethical public relations feel constrained to establish a wholesome relationship with NGOs. The notion that only the powerful utilize public relations to maintain the status quo has been introduced to scholarly research with the development of NGOs and activist public relations.

Several examples illustrate the power of activist groups in South Korea. In 1998, activist groups opposed to the construction of a dam across the Dong River in the province of Kangwon made the government reevaluate and ultimately cancel its construction plans. In April 2000, an activist movement to oust unfit candidates from politics produced successful results in National Assembly elections. The Citizens' Alliance (an NGO) succeeded in preventing 59 of 86 candidates whom it had opposed from getting elected. In February 2001, mounting pressure from activist groups for media reform led the National Tax Administration and the Fair Trade Commission to investigate the tax evasion case and unfair trading practices by media companies. In April 2002, the Citizens' Coalition for Economic Justice, one of the biggest civic movements in Korea, demanded prosecutors to investigate the scandals involving President Kim Dae-jung's two sons. Increasingly, activist groups have begun to influence all sectors of the Korean society as a third power (political and economic interests are the other two).

CULTURE AND PUBLIC RELATIONS

South Korea is identified as a society with high power distance, high collectivism, less tolerance of uncertainty, high masculinity, and high Confucian dynamism (Hofstede, 1980; Hofstede & Bond, 1987). Confucianism, a main philosophy among South Koreans, has been a widely discussed key to understanding Korean culture (Hofstede & Bond, 1987; K. O. Kim, 1997; Yum, 1987a) and communication styles (Yum, 1987a, 1987b). Harmony based on recognizing individual inequalities is pursued, and individual interest can be sacrificed for the benefit of a society (Kincaid, 1987). This subjugation of personal objectives and loyalty to authority have been the guidelines for maintaining spiritual harmony in Korean society since the adoption of basic Confucian principles during the Lee dynasty in the 14thcentury (Yum, 1987a).

Challenging tradition and breaking established rules by social members have been considered inappropriate communication behaviors. The rule of propriety among social members has priority over ethical judgment (Yum, 1987a). In this context, personal connections or selective treatment through favoritism takes precedence over professionalism (Yum, 1988). Particularly, the lack of professional practices based on vocational conscience has worked toward establishing a bad reputation for the public relations field in South Korea.

Yum (1988) described this characteristic in her study comparing East Asian and North American communication patterns. She categorized five Confucian-based dimensions of interpersonal relationships that she observed in East Asia: particularism (devising particular rules depending on the relationship), reciprocity, the in-group and out-group distinction (different treatment for in-group members and out-group members), the role of intermediaries (the need for persons who can introduce new relationships), and the overlap of personal and public domains (blurred distinction between personal and professional relationship). Yum (1988) also categorized four impacts of Confucianism on South Korean communication patterns: process orientation (as opposed to focusing on communication outcomes), differentiated linguistic codes (different languages used depending on people and situations), indirect communication emphasis (as opposed to explicit communication), and receiver-centered communication (emphasis on listening).

The impact of Confucian culture on public relations remains ambivalent. Huang (2000) insisted that Confucianism blocks ethical public relations practices and develops a unique cultural characteristic, *gao guanxi* (exploiting personal relations or human network not unlike the personal influence model), that implies a negative manifestation of Confucian principles. However, Rhee (1999) argued that collectivism and Confucianism are correlated positively with public relations excellence in South Korea. Confucianism may foster social harmony through individual sacrifices. However, relationships among parties in such a society turn into superficial and disharmonious ones. If public relations excellence is achieved through collectivistic harmony, interpersonal liberation or social reform could be restrained. Such interpersonal and critical aspects of public relations are imperative in this context. The impact of Confucianism on public relations requires more study and also demands more interdisciplinary cooperation.

The South Korean socioeconomic system follows the American capitalism model to a large degree. Yet, marked differences exist in corporate cultural norms and the public relations practices between South Korean and American companies. American companies have more freedom to communicate compared to South Korean companies. Traditional Confucian standards in South Korea value social harmony and indirect communication based on diverse linguistic codes rather than the free flow of communication (Kincaid, 1987). Y. Kim and Hon (2001) identified four Confucian rules based on interviews with 24 South Korean public relations professionals: indirect communication, the family chief orientation, the Confucian worldview, and face saving.

Indirect Communication

Information is best delivered through personal gatekeepers. One related notion is, 'A metaphor is better than a direct exhibition.' South Korean publics tend to mistrust information announced officially by organizations, thereby requiring public relations practitioners to communicate indirectly through interpersonal channels. Indirect communication is one of the four effects of Confucianism on South Korean communication patterns (Yum, 1988). However, South Korean business leaders have realized that keeping a low profile is not always beneficial to their company's operations. They have found this to be especially true after experiencing several crises. Thus, this cultural norm of concealing and remaining silent is fading to some extent.

Family Chief Orientation

Kincaid (1987) explained the Eastern spiritual belief as "the subjugation of individual interest and inclination to a strong hierarchical authority" (p. 6). In South Korean society, communication functions to achieve this spiritual harmony at the expense of individual wants. As is typical of most Asian countries, all social systems are hierarchical in South Korea (Yum, 1988). For example, parents have absolute power over other family members. This hierarchy extends to the social family (considering a social organization as a family) as well. Thus, a top manager, the father figure in a professional setting, can regulate the communication system of the organization without interference and mandate the organization's stance on issues. Public relations practitioners can only afford little input because all communication processes depend on the family chief's decision. One communication director described how this system affects public relations:

> All important decisions are made by the chairmans of *Chaebols*. The educational function of public relations department is very weak because most CEOs do not consider public relations an important function of company management. But this is very interesting. Even though most CEOs underestimate the effectiveness of public relations, the importance of public relations is drastically increasing. This is partly because of crisis situations. No other department can handle the crisis situation better than public relations. However, the main reason for having public relations still is its function of deflecting bad news and the CEO's dependence on the personal information network of public relations practitioners. (Y. Kim & Hon, 2001, pp. 276–277)

Confucian Worldview

As Yum (1988) indicated, Confucianism has defined appropriate behaviors for specific situations without regard to the changing patterns brought on by new social systems. The inflexibility of Confucianism makes values such as personal contacts and loyalty to one's organization to be unquestioned. Confusion over legitimate public relations activities could be attributed to the characteristics of Confucianism itself. Although South Korean public relations practitioners generally have displayed considerable moral standards and loyalty (Y. Kim, 2001), their primary allegiance has been to their organizations. Thus, ethical standards often are determined by in-group agreement. Loyalty to the organization sometimes makes public relations activities more complicated because employees' faithfulness is often related to personal bonds and group memberships. This tension is explained by the in-group/out-group distinction that Confucianism imposes on communication (Yum, 1988).

Face Saving

South Koreans try to save face in interpersonal relationships, which extends to the social level as well. Even though it could be beneficial to their business, South Korean public relations practitioners seldom take advantage of competitors' vulnerabilities. Most of the time, a company that criticizes other companies would be an outcast in that business circle. Yet, organizations have often attacked their competitors by releasing unfavorable information about them to the media (Sriramesh et al., 1999). Saving anothers' face as well as that of oneself should be a prime consideration in public relations practices.

THE MEDIA ENVIRONMENT

Most print and broadcasting companies have been affected by the 1997 financial crisis that sank the South Korean economy into recession. Most press companies depend on advertising income. Thus, the reduction in advertising during the 1997 crisis caused serious managerial difficulties. The financial crisis also created a strong impact on editorial emphasis and reporting patterns of journalists. The business section has been reinforced, and articles on topics such as business reconstruction and induction of overseas capital have been highlighted. Furthermore, the South Korean press has put great emphasis on the issue of economic reform.

Internationalizing and reconstructing the economic system is on the national agenda to revitalize the South Korean economy after South Koreans identified the lack of understanding in international affairs and the *chaebol*-oriented monopoly system as the major causes of the 1997 crisis. Globalization and reconstruction also have become the focus of media coverage among the South Korean press. Such business-oriented media content has become an opportunity for the public relations field.

In 2000, the Ministry of Culture and Tourism reported that South Korea had a total of 112 daily newspapers and 1,999 weekly magazines. However, 10 Korean-language national dailies and 2 English dailies are the major competitors at the national level, whereas many regional newspapers serve regional markets. *The Chosun Ilbo, Dong-A Ilbo*, and *JoongAng Ilbo* are influential national print media. *The Hangeorye Sinmun* is influential among comparatively young and progressive readers. *The Korea Herald* and *Korea Times* are the only two English newspapers in South Korea. There also are several business dailies. *The Yonhap News* is the only news agency that feeds news to dailies and broadcasting companies.

The Ministry of Culture and Tourism also reported that broadcasting services were provided by the Korean Broadcasting System (KBS) with 25 subsidiary stations, the Munwha Broadcasting Corporation (MBC) with 19 subsidiary stations, the Seoul Broadcasting System (SBS), and 8 specialized commercial broadcasters (EBS, CBS, BBS, PBC, FEBC, WBS, TBS, and TBN). Cable television is operated by 29 program providers and 77 stations.

Television has higher approval ratings than newspapers about news credibility, and the Internet is emerging as a new agenda setter, as described by the Korea Press Foundation Report of 2001:

> While television gained more approval in 2000 than in 1998, the comparative rating for newspapers declined. It is particularly noteworthy that newspapers' influence dwindled by more than a half in two years, and in usefulness ratings they lagged behind Internet. What is new is the Internet's rapidly growing role as a tool of mass communication. Its success is significant in that it reflects the growing consumer aspirations to be heard vis-à-vis government and traditional mass media and highlights a potentially crucial role to be played by individual consumers in new system of checks and balances. (http://www.kpf.or.kr, 2001).

Media Control

The print media are privately owned. The government retains a marginal indirect ownership through public funding, but it has minimal influence over the print media, especially after social democratization. Private owners have almost complete control over the employment of reporters, operation of editorial desks, and even editorial content. Private owners control major dailies such as *The Chosun Ilbo, Dong-A Ilbo*, and *JoongAng Ilbo*. Media control by private owners has become a serious dilemma in the democratizing media environment. Powerful media owners have obstructed undistorted communication and influenced editorial content. Conflicts between the print media and the government over tax evasion by media owners in 2001 brought into focus the problem of unprincipled ownership of a section of the print media. Media control by private owners fosters systematic distortion in the development of public agenda and obstructs the development of professional public relations in South Korea.

Although in principle the South Korean press is free from government and other external influences, various political and business interest groups do influence editorial content. *Chaebols* are one of the primary groups that are able to wield such influence. Some *chaebols* own media companies and participate in management decision making. Most media companies depend on advertising revenue provided by *chaebols*. Consumer and civic groups also have their agenda for press reform. One example is the anti-*Chosun Ilbo* movement initiated by civic groups to condemn the paper's cold-war mentality. The 2001 Korean Press Foundation Report analyzed:

> The anti-Chosun movement is remarkable in that it does not merely represent an outburst of grievances against a particular newspaper but bring into focus the deep-rooted structural flaws of the country's newspapers. The anti-Chosun movement, as an exercised form of consumers' legitimate right, has served the worthy purpose of establishing an active watchdog function over media for general consumers. (http://www.kpf.or.kr, 2001).

The South Korean television channels include the government-run KBS 1, KBS 2, and Educational Broadcasting System (public channel); semigovernment sponsored MBC; and private SBS and eight provincial broadcasting companies. The Korea Broadcasting Commission regulates the broadcasting industry legally. The purpose of regulation lies in public interest, not governmental control of the media. Most television programs need postbroadcast appraisal to assess whether their content is in the public interest.

In general, the government does not control journalistic content prior to broadcasting. However, the print and broadcasting media often display a strain in relations with each other, as the print media believes that the government influences the editorial content of broadcast media to attack print media.

Media Outreach and Access

The print and broadcasting media diffuse similar messages to South Korean people repetitively. Therefore, accessing information is not a difficulty. Provincial broadcasting companies and regional newspapers also report on the regional news. With a high rate of literacy and education, South Korean people also utilize the Internet for information gathering. The problem lies in information selection, not information outreach.

South Korean newspaper readers are becoming sophisticated, critical, and have high expectations for the quality of information. There is little argument that reporters need better and greater amounts of information from public relations practitioners if their papers are to remain competitive (*Advertising Yearbook*, 2000). This situation may eventually lead to symmetrical relationships between public relations practitioners and journalists, as stated by a professor of mass communication:

> The newspaper industry has faced fierce competition among itself because the number of papers has increased since 1992. This competition has provided a good opportunity for PR practitioners to cater to reporters' need to attract readers with more interesting and newsworthy stories. This is surely a chance for public relations. (Y. Kim & Hon, 2001, p. 280).

The introduction of cable television and local broadcasting has led to greater competition in the telecommunications industry and enlarged media outreach. The dominance of advertising by a few national network companies has declined in this new environment.

Smaller and newer companies have more marketing opportunities. Similar to what occurred within the newspaper industry, the proliferation of broadcasting channels causes the increased dependence on information from news releases and demands cooperation with public relations practitioners to save production costs. Public relations practitioners have easy access to the media. However, the level of access depends more on personal networks than professional relationships.

It is important to note that South Korea is one of fastest growing countries in the world on Internet use among its population. The number of Internet users has been growing drastically in recent years due to the fast growth in penetration of broadband. The number of Internet users reached 1 million in 1997 and surpassed 10 million in 1999. According to the 2001 Nielsen/Net Ratings Global Index for January, more than half of the population in South Korea has access to the Internet. Furthermore, South Korea leads the world in terms of the number of households with Internet access, and it has the fourth largest Internet-reliant population in the world. A high penetration of broadband Internet access and a sophisticated telecommunication infrastructure make such wide usage of the Internet possible.

Cyber media is emerging as an alternative to newspapers and broadcasting. As the 2001 Korea Press Foundation Report described:

> Consumers' approval rating of the press that had declined in 1998 turned upward in 2000. The good news, however, is attributed to Internet service that has outdone television broadcasting services and newspapers in approval rating. Thus, the Internet has come to stay as a very satisfactory mass media. The most noticeable among the Internet news services was "OhmyNews." Launched in February 2000, OhmyNews has done much to differentiate itself from other forms of mass communication. (http://www.kpf.or.kr, 2001).

Public relations practitioners are increasingly utilizing the Internet as a direct medium to reach target publics. The South Korean government created the cyber spokesperson and distributes information directly to citizens (http://www.allim.go.kr). Many companies also utilize the Internet for direct communication with the public. Newspapers and broadcasting channels also create home pages on the Internet to enhance their interactivity.

CONCLUDING COMMENTS

Social democratization brings with it the development of public relations. The South Korean-style *hong-bo*, which focuses heavily on media relations and personal connections with journalists, is not effective in the rapidly changing democratic South Korean society. The changing economic, political, and legal system provides organizations with more opportunities to practice professional public relations. The traditional communication characteristics of the East are now being combined with the individualistic perspectives of the West as the South Korean public relations industry adapts to new environmental demands.

Although there continues to be a shortage of experienced public relations professionals, and public relations agencies rely heavily on foreign clients, optimism for the public relations industry has been growing among practitioners in South Korea. The demand for public relations services by South Korean companies is increasing along with a concomitant increase in their understanding of the benefits of public relations (J. Kim, 2001). The real potential for growth may lie in the retention of agency services by large-scale South Korean companies. South Korean companies need to build positive long-term relationships with key publics and are beginning to formulate long-term public relations strategies and invest in them. Another encouraging aspect of South Korea's public relations industry is the swelling ranks of enterprising practitioners (*Advertising Yearbook*, 2000).

In the scholarly world, the KASPR spearheads the establishment of Korea-accustomed theories and their applications to the industry (Rhee, 1999). Scholarly journals deal with many topics such as the organization–public relationship, evaluation and measurement, crisis management and image restoration, and ethical issues. With a deep-rooted tradition of activism, public relations studies on NGOs, governmental public relations, and nonprofit organizations have produced prolific discussions. Absolute democracy and free press will contribute more on the development of this trend.

Case Study: Doosan Phenol Crisis Management

In March 16, 1991, an unidentified odor was detected in the tap water in the southeastern area of South Korea. The Environmental Bureau's investigation led to the discovery of the toxic substance, phenol, in the water. A government investigation team discovered that phenol had accidentally leaked to the Nakdong River from Doosan Electronics Company, a member of the Doosan *chaebol* group, that manufactures PCI board for computer chips.

Environmental groups and residents of the southeastern area challenged the Doosan group. Many government officials of the local Environmental Bureau and related workers were charged as a result of the investigation. A large demonstration took place in front of the headquarters of the Doosan group. The National Supermarket Association initiated a campaign to boycott Doosan products. This caused a major reduction in the sales of the Doosan group as a significant portion of its products were sold at supermarkets. Over 10,000 people, including pregnant women, filed a lawsuit against the group. Incredibly, in April 23, 1991, phenol was again found to have leaked from the Doosan Electronics Company, resulting in the forcible resignation of the chairman of Doosan group.

The Doosan group handled this situation very poorly because South Korean *chaebol* conglomerates had traditionally solved such problems by personal networks and collusion with the government. However, this was not possible because of the changed situation due to social democratization. The government could not protect the *chaebol* groups any more and had to accede to the demands by activists for an impartial investigation. Media sensationalism worsened the situation further. Doosan's crisis management strategies were too dated to handle the situation in the changed atmosphere. Doosan did not announce the outbreak of the incident right away but rather tried to conceal the situation. It prevented access to the information rather than providing the media with accurate information. This created many rumors that proved to be detrimental to Doosan. The result was a complete loss to Doosan.

Ironically, this became a monumental incident for the development of public relations in South Korea. *Chaebol* groups have, therefore, started to recognize the need for proactive public relations and reinforced their public relations function. Many *chaebol* groups have experienced major crises, and crisis management became a salient function. This trend is related closely with social and political democratization in South Korea. Publics do not tolerate corporate wrongdoings and unprincipled governmental intervention anymore as they once did under the authoritative regime. One CEO of a public relations firm commented on this new changing pattern:

> After experiencing a big crisis situation, some companies appointed the head of the public relations department as a vice president. This means public relations began to participate in the process of corporate decision-making. Traditionally, public relations practitioners had

been perceived as a speechwriter, publisher for an organization, or a post-journalist job. But, with social democratization, many companies came to the realization that they should prepare for a crisis situation against a reinforced social watchdog system. Crisis management is a very important factor that enhances public relations at the managerial level. (Y. Kim & Hon, 2001, p. 281).

Organizations, including corporations and the government, have learned that communicating with their publics and winning their understanding is a prerequisite for success. Public relations practitioners have also started playing a managerial role due to frequent crises and open communication demanded for ethical practices. Doosan appointed a public relations vice president for the first time in South Korea and began to communicate with publics, including consumers, community members, NGOs, and governmental officials, on various issues. They also exerted much effort in environmental protection with reinforced safety measures. Doosan's new programs include (a) devising proactive and comprehensive risk-management system, (b) training public relations practitioners to deliver the organization's key messages and to coordinate the public's demands, and (c) introducing environmentally friendly products and production systems. Doosan has regained its market share as a result of such new programs.

REFERENCES

Advertising yearbook. (2000). Seoul, Korea: Jeil Communications.

Cha, H. W. (2001). *The win–win strategy of public relations by NGOs (Korean).* Unpublished doctoral dissertation, Ewha Womans University, Seoul, Korea.

Choe, Y. (1992). *Hyundai PR Eeron* [Modern public relations theory]. Seoul, Korea: Nanam.

Grunig, J. E. (1992). *Excellence in public relations and communication management.* Hillsdale, NJ: Lawrence Erlbaum Associates.

Grunig, J. E., Grunig, L. A., Sriramesh, K., Huang, Y., & Lyra, A. (1995). Models of public relations in an international setting. *Journal of Public Relations Research, 7,* 163–186.

Grunig, J. E., & Hunt. T. (1984). *Managing public relations.* New York: Holt, Rinehart, and Winston.

Hofstede, G. (1980). *Cultures consequences: International differences in work-related values.* Beverly Hills, CA: Sage.

Hofstede, G., & Bond, M. H. (1987). The Confucius connection: From cultural roots to economic growth. *Organizational Dynamics, 16*(4), 4–21.

Huang, Y. (2000). The personal influence model and Gao Guanxi in Taiwan Chinese public relations. *Public Relations Review, 26*(2), 219–236.

Jo, S. (2001, June). *Models of public relations in South Korea: The difference between HongBo and public relations.* Paper presented at the International Communication Association conference, Washington, DC.

Kim, J. (2001, September). The status and future of the Korean public relations industry. *Goanggogye-Donghyang (Korean Adverting Information),* 21–23.

Kim, K. O. (1997). The reproduction of Confucian culture in contemporary Korea: An anthropological study. In T. Wei-Ming (Ed.), *Confucian traditions in East Asian modernity* (pp. 202–227). Cambridge, MA: Harvard University Press.

Kim, Y. (1996). *Positive and normative models of public relations and their relationship to job satisfaction among Korean public relations practitioners.* Unpublished master's thesis, University of Florida, Gainesville.

Kim, Y. (2001, June). *Ethical standards and ideology among Korean public relations practitioners.* Paper presented at the Korea Academic Society of Public Relations conference, Seoul, Korea.

Kim, Y., & Hon, L. (1998). Craft and professional models of public relations and their relation to job satisfaction among Korean public relations practitioners. *Journal of Public Relations Research, 10,* 155–175.

Kim, Y., & Hon, L. (2001). Public relations in Korea: Applying theories and exploring opportunities. *Journal of Asian Pacific Communication, 11*(2), 259–282.

Kincaid, D. L. (1987). *Communication theory: Eastern and Western perspectives.* San Diego, CA: Academic Press.

Nielson/Net Ratings Global Index (2001). New York: A. C. Nielson. http://www.nielson-netratings.com

Oh, D. B. (1991). *PR communication gae-ron* [Introduction to PR]. Seoul, Korea: Nanam.

Park, J. (2001). Images of "Hong Bo (public relations)" and PR in Korean newspapers. *Public Relations Review, 27*, 403–420.

Park, Y., & Kim, M. (1997). *Understanding Korean corporate culture.* Seoul, Korea: Ohrom.

Rhee, Y. (1999). *Confucian culture and excellent public relations: A study of generic principles and specific and applications in South Korean public relations practice.* Unpublished master's thesis, University of Maryland at College Park, College Park.

Sriramesh, K. (1992). Culture and public relations: Ethnographic evidence from India. *Public Relations Review, 18*(2), 201–212.

Sriramesh, K., Kim, Y., & Takasaki, M. (1999). Public relations in three Asian countries. *Journal of Public Relations Research, 11*, 271–292.

The Korea Press Foundation Report (2001). Seoul: The Korea Press Foundation. http://www.kpf.or.kr.

Wilcox, D. L., Ault, P. H., Agee, W. K., Cameron, G. (2000). *Public relations: Strategies and tactics* (6th ed.). New York: Longman.

Yoon, Y. (2001, August). *Public relations worldview and conflict levels in the client–agency relationship.* Paper presented at the meeting of the Association of Educators for Journalism and Mass Communication, Washington, DC.

Youm, K. H. (1996). *Press law in South Korea.* Ames, Iowa: Iowa State University Press.

Yum, J. O. (1987a). Korean philosophy and communication. In D. L. Kindaid (Ed.), *Communications theory: Eastern and Western perspectives* (pp. 71–86). San Diego, CA: Academic Press.

Yum, J. O. (1987b). The practice of *Uye-ri* in interpersonal relationship in Korea. In D. L. Kindaid (Ed.), *Communications theory: Eastern and Western perspectives* (pp. 87–100). San Diego, CA: Academic Press.

Yum, J. O. (1988). The impact of Confucianism on interpersonal relationships and communication pattern in East Asia. *Communication Monograph, 55*, 374–388.

9

BECOMING PROFESSIONALS: A PORTRAIT OF PUBLIC RELATIONS IN SINGAPORE

CONSTANCE CHAY-NÉMETH

PUBLIC RELATIONS AND THE GEOPOLITICS OF SINGAPORE

The practice of public relations in Singapore may be understood by exploring the relationship between the geopolitics of the island republic and the important role of the government in political, economic, and social engineering. This chapter begins with a brief description of the geopolitical conditions of Singapore and continues with an analysis of the government's role in the political and economic life of the state and its effects on the practice of public relations.

The Republic of Singapore is located 137 km north of the equator. The mainland (606.7 sq km) and 63 offshore islands occupy a total land area of 682.7 sq km. Its immediate neighbors are Malaysia to the north and Indonesia and Brunei to the south. Its population of slightly over 4 million constitutes ethnic groups such as the Chinese (76.8%), Malays (13.9%), Indians (7.9%), and others (1.4%). The four official languages are English (the language of administration), Malay (the national language), Mandarin, and Tamil. Mainstream religions include Buddhism, Taoism, Islam, Christianity, and Hinduism.

In 1819, Sir Stamford Raffles, a representative of the British East India Company established Singapore as a trading port under agreement with the Sultan of Johor and the Malay ruler of the island. In 1824, the Sultan ceded the island in perpetuity to the British East India Company, and the island became a British colony until its occupation by the Japanese colonialists from 1942 to 1945. In September 1945, the Japanese surrendered to the British who resumed colonial control of the island until its independence on August 9, 1965.

The period between 1945 and the early 1960s was tumultuous, demonstrating local activism at its zenith. It is commonly known that local nationalists of the time were battling colonialism, communalism, and Communism. With Communalism came clashes and riots among the different ethnic groups as they became pawns in the hands of colonial divide-and-rule tactics. Communism reared its head in the form of insurgency against the establishment. These insurgent acts were conducted through the use of front organizations such as labor and Chinese school unions. To combat the latter, the British implemented the detention of communist suspects without trial, or what is known today as the Internal Security Act (ISA, 1986).

In 1959, Singapore gained autonomy from the British. The People's Action Party (PAP) has been in power since it was first elected in 1959. Through a series of brilliant political, economic, and social management strategies, the PAP has successfully kept a tight reign over communalism and communism. Today, Singapore's economy ranks among the most competitive in the world economy. In 2000, its per capita gross national product was S$42,212 (Singapore Department of Statistics, 2001). Its next economic lap runs in tandem with the global drive toward a knowledge-based economy (KBE).

EVOLUTION OF PUBLIC RELATIONS IN SINGAPORE

The early models of public relations in Singapore evolved from those used by the British colonialists. They were primarily propagandists seeking to promote the credibility of the British especially after their defeat by the Japanese army in World War II. Publicity and public information were issued from the Department of Publicity and Printing under the British Military Administration (Yeap, 1994). Lord Llyod, the Parliamentary Under Secretary of State for the Colonial Office, best summed up the mission of public relations during colonialism: "It was everywhere of first importance both for British interests and for the colonial interests of the people concerned that we put across with all possible power and persuasion the ideas for which we stand" (cited in Nair, 1986, pp. 3–4).

In the 1950s, the multinational companies entered the oil industry in Singapore. This period also marked the emergence of in-house public relations departments both in the private and public sectors. The government continued with the press agentry and public information models (Grunig & Hunt, 1984) used by the British propagandists. However, now the mission of public relations was to promote national development. The Ministry of Culture and Information recruited individuals professionally trained in journalism and mass communication as public relations personnel. They were responsible for organizing the many public education programs that followed such as the antilitter, antispitting, and speak Mandarin campaigns (Yeap, 1994).

Since the 1980s onwards, more multinational companies and international public relations consultancies have entered the Singapore economy. Local in-house public relations departments and consultancies have also mushroomed. In the 1990s and to date, the Singapore economy has been rapidly globalizing and shifting toward a KBE. With the latter and the entry of many more multinational companies, the public relations industry is in transition—shifting from one-way communication models to two-way communication models and the strategic management of public relations. However, the shift has been slow. The local industry still has much to learn in developing skills, expertise, and knowledge that would prepare it for a global and KBE. Whereas practitioners belonging to international public relations consultancies and public relations departments of larger organizations recognize the importance of public relations as strategic management, those belonging to smaller local organizations continue to focus excessively on the tactics of public relations in media relations, event management, and publicity (Chow, Tan, & Chew, 1996; Tan, 2001; Yeap, 1994).

This shift toward two-way communication and the strategic management of publics also manifests itself in the government's relations with local communities. The Singapore 21 vision, an ongoing government project, advocates the cultivation of a more active citizenry (The Singapore 21 vision, 1997). The vision reflects the opinions of some 6,000 Singaporeans solicited via public forums, surveys, and web site feedback channels. This shift toward symmetry in government–community relations is aptly described by George Yeo, the then Minister of Information and the Arts: "In the old days, the issues were stark, black and white, left or right, up or down . . . bread and butter issues for which there were clear, unequivocal answers. But I think we have passed that stage" (cited in Yeap, 1994).

CURRENT STATUS OF PUBLIC RELATIONS IN SINGAPORE

The public relations profession in Singapore may be said to be in transition from a preprofessional to a professional status. Preprofessionalism is typically marked by an excess of focus on one-way communication models such as press agentry (Gruning & Hunt, 1984), publicity, and the subordination of public relations to a marketing tool "to gain awareness of a client, perhaps to keep TV ratings up or turnstiles clicking" (Culbertson & Jeffers, 1992, p. 54). Professional public relations is a holistic practice. Although it acknowledges the importance of the technical and tactical functions of public relations (e.g., writing press releases and organizing events), more important, it recognizes public relations as a strategic management function. Public relations as strategic management seeks to manage the interactions among organizational knowledge, information, publics, and environmental variables (social, political, and economic infrastructure) to create a win–win situation for the organization and its key publics. "In fact, it can be argued this type of activity distinguishes the true public relations professional from the publicist or hack" (Culbertson & Jeffers, 1992, p. 63).

Dominant Coalitions and Public Relations

The professionalism of public relations, or its lack, is related not only to the strategic or tactical practice of public relations but also to the significance accorded it by the dominant coalitions of organizations. In Singapore, dominant coalitions determine the type of public relations that is eventually practiced. The following paragraphs describe the perceptions of dominant coalitions regarding public relations and their effects on preprofessional and professional public relations in Singapore.

A recent study of the state of public relations in Singapore (Tan, 2001, pp. 8–9) showed that the top four public relations practices performed were media relations (88%), corporate communications and branding (86%), community relations (64%), and government relations (51%). As mentioned earlier, preprofessionalism is characterized by an excessive focus on media publicity. The importance that dominant coalitions attach to media relations and publicity is also borne out by recent e-mail interviews I conducted with 20 public relations practitioners in Singapore.

For instance, one practitioner from an international public relations consultancy said: "Bigger multinational firms have a better understanding about the importance and function of public relations while smaller, especially local, companies may not see any need in it, or they judge results solely through press coverage." Hence, when the number of column inches of press publicity does not match the organization's investment in public relations, the latter is seen as ineffective and a waste of money. Preprofessional public relations often attributes more importance to media publicity than it does to building rapport with key publics.

Other dominant coalitions see public relations in purely tactical and mundane terms. One consultant reported:

> Whilst our clients generally believe that public relations is important and of value to the company, they lack a full understanding of its value. One client still resorts to heavy wine and dine, with so much emphasis placed on superficial matters, e.g., the quality of the paper, the outer appearance of the press kit folder etc, to the point of ignoring strategic and sensible thinking.

The failure to recognize public relations as a strategic function and hence its subordination to a support role is observed by a consultant from an international public relations agency: "Public relations is viewed as a service industry, providing arms-and-legs support on various communications. This is opposed to public relations professionals being viewed as strategic consultants in other countries, especially in the West."

Thus, as long as public relations is still perceived by dominant coalitions to be a tactical function—mundane, peripheral, and publicity centered—it should not be surprising that the public relations industry in Singapore still has one foot caught in preprofessionalism.

Preprofessional Public Relations in Singapore

Preprofessionalism as practiced in Singapore bears specific characteristics. First, public relations is a purely technician role. A practitioner from the in-house public relations department of a government organization observed that practitioners as technicians primarily "book advertising spots," act as "event organisers or even troubleshooters who reply to unfavorable reports/letters." The technician and tactical role of preprofessional public relations in Singapore also extends into its fixation with media relations and publicity. Hence, it is not surprising that practitioners here spend many hours on cultivating good working relationships with journalists, getting them to attend events and press conferences, and writing press releases rather than on strategic management of their clients' affairs.

Second, preprofessional public relations in Singapore is rarely, if ever, strategic and proactive. One practitioner said: "Like most parts of Asia, public relations is still equated with events and other arms- and-legs functions. The strategic element is lost to most clients, including the marketing departments of even many MNCs. . . . " Reactive public relations also implies that local organizations place little importance on environmental tracking in relation to issues and crisis management.

Third, preprofessional public relations in Singapore suffers from a lack of definition and clear conceptualization of the nature and functions of public relations. It is a free-for-all industry wherein public relations is mistaken variously for marketing, advertising, sales, human resource management, lounge hostessing, and the like. One practitioner aptly summed up this dilemma: "This image problem maybe related to the lack of definition regarding what constitutes 'public relations' work in Singapore, where public relations functions are incorporated into various types of job descriptions such as corporate communications, marketing communications, agency & advertising accounts, etc." And because "public relations is still viewed as a sales or marketing function, and often secondary in importance," its practitioners are similarly accorded a low status by many local organizations.

Finally, preprofessional public relations in Singapore is marked by a practice of situational ethics. However, this does not mean that codes of professional ethics do not exist. On the contrary, the Institute of Public Relations Singapore (IPRS) and most multinationals possess their own brands of ethics. For instance, the IPRS observes the code of ethics of the International Public Relations Association. Rather, the problem lies in putting ethical codes to practice in day-to-day public relations conduct and situations. One practitioner aptly summed up this dilemma:

> While almost every reputable consulting firm I know of has a code of ethics, I don't think most consultants pay much attention to ethics on a day-to-day basis. I suppose the only time there are concerns about ethics is when we are pitching for a new client whose business poses conflicts of interest with existing clients. I think, in Singapore we have not yet reached the level of professionalism as in the states or UK. I feel that many of the practitioners here are themselves not clear on the role of public relations, and do not conduct themselves professionally.

The difficulty in performing ethically is further compounded by the lack of power of practitioners for autonomous action. As such, practitioners are tempted to practice situational ethics rather than abide steadfastly to a code of professional ethics. One practitioner observed: "Management at corporate organisations need to understand the function of public relations in order to leverage public relations in reputation management. And, they pretty much determine the level of professionalism in the industry since they pay the salaries or the bills."

Hence, professional ethical conduct is not primarily determined by the public relations industry and its practitioners but dictated instead by the master who pays their bills. Grunig (2000) aptly summed up this dilemma of preprofessionalism: "Professionals, in other words, have the power to carry out their work based on the knowledge and standards of their profession. Nonprofessionals do not have that power. Instead, clients or superiors in the organization tell them what to do—and often those orders violate professional standards" (p. 26).

Toward Professional Public Relations in Singapore

However, there are signs that public relations is rising to a professional status in Singapore, assisted by changing environmental conditions. The government's push toward globalization and a KBE has stimulated the recruitment of more foreign talent to meet the needs of the new KBE.

Imported talent appears to raise the professionalism of the public relations industry in the following ways. First, dominant coalitions formed by imported talent tend to recognize the importance of public relations as a strategic management function. The practitioner from an international public relations agency reported: "The status of public relations has certainly risen slowly but surely over the years. Obviously, MNCs have been at the forefront in recognising public relations as a strategic business management tool."

These enlightened dominant coalitions perceive the strategic importance of public relations in diverse ways. Some practitioners of multinationals see public relations as a "necessary and strategic senior function which must be networked into the regional organization." Others perceive public relations as strategic communication specialists and gate-keepers of organizational information and knowledge. They asserted that public relations practitioners function as "the gatekeeper of company information and a communication channel," while giving "counsel on their communication strategies." Yet other dominant coalitions are said to perceive practitioners "as strategic partners, not just normal resource for e.g., press conference expertise." Overall, enlightened dominant coalitions perceive public relations as being very important because practitioners offer knowledge and experience to companies that lack public relations expertise and contacts. Public relations is also important to dominant coalitions who see practitioners as the link to their public.

In addition, foreign multinational talent brings to the public relations industry diverse knowledge, skills and expertise, as one practitioner from an international public relations consultancy reported: "Global industry leader companies from the US and UK not forgetting closer home from Australia, . . . has brought positive impact because of the generation of new skills and industry expertise knowledge and industry specialist experiences."

Further, a KBE and technology intensive economy also aids in professionalizing public relations in Singapore. One consultant of an international public relations agency suggested that the accessibility of alternative information via the Internet and the potential of cyberactivism have increased the importance of corporate branding as a form of corporate protection:

> The Internet has widened everyone's perception of the power of communications hence it has raised issue of the liability and damaging impact of global networking that can destroy brands or corporations credibility. Consequently, management and clients willingly invest in a sound communications programme, headed by specialists to protect and promote their corporate and product interests.

Others see the development of public relations into specialist and niche areas with the increase of dot.com businesses: "With the onset of internet technology and the overnight boom of dot.com businesses requiring specialist communications promotion. There is more specialist or niche practice expertise available too."

As organizations become increasing affected by the new knowledge-based economy, public relations is slowly moving away from an excessive focus on media relations and publicity. As one practitioner observed: "Now organisations have realised the importance of specialised public relations skills ranging from investor relations to corporate imaging. Certainly more organisations are calling for more strategic usage of public relations even though they may not entirely understand how it works."

Finally, one cannot underestimate the catalytic effect of a turbulent and volatile environment in increasing the professionalism of public relations in Singapore. A few practitioners have observed that the strategic value and importance of public relations increases during crisis situations. One practitioner reported: "On the whole, I find that the image is slowly improving and that management is beginning to regard public relations as a potential area that can make or break a company, especially after recent events such as the SQ006 crash and OUB takeover bids."[1] Yet others suggested: "As a consequence to the Sep 11 events and the increased voice of NGOs, public relations now goes beyond media relations to help organisations manage issues and crisis as well as NGO communication."

As discussed, the functions of managing organizational knowledge, issues, and crises appear to be gaining in importance in Singapore. In fact, the importance of crisis communication is registered by the recent inauguration of the Public Relations Academy in 2002. The academy is run by the Ministry of Information and the Arts for the purpose of

---

[1] The SQ006 crisis involved the crash of a Singapore Airlines plane in Taiwan, November 2000. The Overseas Union Bank (OUB) crisis emerged when the financial representative of the Development Bank of Singapore (DBS) released statements of a defamatory nature regarding the OUB and United Overseas Bank (UOB) board of directors. As a result of this debacle, the DBS issued a public apology and paid the banks S$2 million. The money was paid to local charities.

training top civil servants in more savvy communication with the media and other publics in the event of crisis situations.

Improving Public Relations Professionalism in Singapore

Although there are clear indications of the public relations industry becoming more professional in the future, it remains that this transition to professionalism is slow, lagging behind professionalism in the Western world. To hasten the transition to professional public relations, the industry would need to address the following areas according to a majority of practitioners interviewed.

First, some practitioners have suggested increasing the visibility and profile of the IPRS: "Public relations in Singapore is still in its infancy in some aspects. We lack a reputable organisation in governing the practices of public relations practitioners. The IPRS aims to do something, but it lacks the buy in of key organizations." In other words, professionals need to support each other through membership with a professional body. A recent study showed that most practitioners are not members of any professional associations (Tan, 2001, p. 15). About 53% of practitioners surveyed in consultancies were members of the IPRS. Only 22% of practitioners in private organizations and 16% of those in government agencies were members of the IPRS.

Others suggested the need to improve public relations training and education for practitioners to prepare them for public relations as strategic management beyond technician duties. One practitioner observed: "Some private schools and local training courses are lacking in depth and only manage to cover a brief scope of public relations and how it can be utilised at a higher level." However, a more crucial need lies in changing the way in which public relations is taught to potential practitioners in the local institutions: "The problem, however, is that Asian universities do not teach their students how to think and the exposure of the practitioners is limited because of a lack of reading and reflection." This is a critical shortcoming for practitioners operating within a KBE, with clients demanding more value-added strategic services.

In short, professionalism includes developing the following: (a) sound training in the technical aspects of the profession, (b) cultivating a wide body of interdisciplinary knowledge refined by critical thinking and creative application to organizational problems, and (c) membership to professional associations that would support the practice of professional values and codes of ethics.

INFRASTRUCTURE AND PUBLIC RELATIONS

Earlier, I mentioned that the practice of public relations in Singapore may be understood by exploring the role of the government in economic, political, and social engineering. One political commentator (Yuen, 1999) observed:

> It is usually agreed that nothing much can be done without government approval, support and coordination to marshall the necessary resources.... Once an idea like this takes hold, it is self-fulfilling: any proposal not backed by the government, or by people known to be in favour with the government, would be given little support by everyone else and are consequently likely to fail. (p. 6)

In this regard, public relations practitioners would do well to include the government as one of their key publics whenever engaged in strategic planning and management.

In the past few years, government leaders have advocated a paradigm shift in the Singapore economy—from the old economy of brick-and-mortar businesses to the new economy of knowledge and technology intensive businesses. This paradigm shift is articulated clearly in the speech of David Lim, the Minister of State for Defence and Information and the Arts, during the Prism Awards ceremony.[2] Here are excerpts of his speech indicating impending changes in communication style, issues management, and the nature of "cyber-publics" that are likely to affect the practices of public relations:

> Already, Internet penetration to the homes in Singapore—at 42%, has exceeded the rate of penetration in the US—at 40%. Media companies, both globally and right here in Singapore, will have to adjust their strategies, add new capability and venture into new services and business alliances if they are to keep up. . . .
> Such structural changes to the media industry will also have a big impact on the Public Relations industry. You will have to watch the trends carefully, to catch new opportunities to get your message through, and to capture new audiences. (Lim, 2000)

In this context, it would be pertinent to ask how an economic paradigm shift to a KBE would affect the status and practices of public relations. It is likely that a KBE may also stimulate an increase in government public relations or public affairs, community relations, activism, issues management, and crisis communication. If this is true, it would appear that the transition to professional public relations is given a boost by changing external conditions such as the economy and its attendant effects on the political and social infrastructures of the system. The following paragraphs describe the effects of the government's new economic initiative on public relations practices in public affairs, activism, and organizational practices.

KBE and Public Affairs

In the past decade or so, the political landscape of Singapore has seen significant changes. Although technically labeled a democratic socialist state governed by a parliamentary system, political observers (Chua, 1995; Ho, 2000; Yuen, 1999) have been quick to label the island's political style variously as authoritarian, fascistic, or a benign dictatorship. For instance, one political observer (Yuen, 1999) said: "Singapore is a place that arouses deeply divided feelings among observers. Economically, it is one of the great success stories of this century, but it is also widely seen as an authoritarian state that limits freedom of speech and political rights" (p. 1).

Hitherto, this political style has also translated into a similar style of public affairs, that is, a top-down and paternalistic approach to communication between the state and its constituencies (Chua, 1995). Within such a political framework, consensus is typically valued over dissent and individual interests are subsumed under group interests in the name of economic necessity, pragmatism, and Asian democracy (Ho, 2000).

In this political framework, the business sector plays a minor role in decision making: "Organized business . . . has little formal role in policy making" (Ho, 2000, p. 203). However, personal networking with key government personnel obviously pays off in terms of influencing policy making: "Its influence is largely derived from personal contacts and informal inroads into policy-making circles in Singapore." (S. P. Tan, 1993–94, p. 77).

---

[2]The Prism Awards is conferred annually to individuals and organizations practicing excellent public relations in Singapore.

This use of personal contacts is akin to the personal influence model reported in some Asian cultures (Sriramesh, Kim, & Takasaki, 1999).

In summary, the style of public communication hitherto adopted by the government with its constituencies may be summed up as follows: (a) It typically practices one-way asymmetrical communication. Decision making is monopolized by the government with little participation from the constituencies. The government defines key issues and sets the agenda for discussing them. The task of government public relations practitioners is primarily to inform and educate the masses about government decisions and policies via the pro-government mass media. (b) It promotes consensus rather than confrontation. Constituencies have been socialized to expect the government to take the lead and intervene in solving community problems. This makes for highly passive publics. Perhaps this also explains the excessive importance of media relations in the public relations industry— that is, the media functions as a vehicle for engineering consent with passive publics. (c) As a corollary, the government and its constituencies have yet to develop productive mechanisms for managing conflict and dissensus. This implies the improbability of a two-way symmetrical style of communication with constituencies in the immediate future. For this to occur, it will require drastic changes in the political philosophy and infrastructures of the system.

In spite of this rather bleak scenario, there are emerging signs that the style of government–community relations is changing for the favorable. Demographic changes such as the emergence of a more affluent and larger middle class population, better educated and well-traveled citizenry, the economic paradigm shift to a KBE and its attendant requirements for the development of niche knowledge areas, and critical and creative applications of knowledge to problems and opportunities all seem to contribute to a slowly but surely emerging communitarian democracy (Chua, 1995).

These changing conditions bode well for a more equitable relationship between the government and its constituencies. The Singapore 21 vision is a clear indicator of a change in the government's style of public communication.[3] It suggests the emergence of a two-way communication process between the latter and community publics. It also encourages the formation of a more active citizenry with increasing interest in social responsibility and public debate. To facilitate the latter, the government has created more channels for feedback from its constituencies (Ho, 2000). These include (a) the mass media as channels through which the constituencies may voice their opinions and concerns on government policies; (b) weekly meet-the-member of Parliament (MP) sessions in which constituencies may voice grievances and complaints to the MP; (c) feedback units set up and sponsored by the government to solicit public opinion on public issues; (d) the government's involvement of selected NGOs in the policy-making process; and (e) the use of parapolitical organizations such as community centers, citizens' consultative committees, and town councils to communicate and explain government policies to the constituencies.

In a nutshell, a communitarian democracy requires the establishment of formal institutions, such as a free press and the right of citizens to be consulted, as it does in liberal democracies (Chua, 1995). The emphasis placed on consensus rather than dissensus in communitarian democracies also implies the need to free up the press so that it may reflect

---

[3]The Singapore 21 vision describes five core values for maintaining the prosperity and survival of the nation in the new century. These values include active citizens, strong families, the fact that every Singaporean matters, the Singapore heartbeat, and opportunities for all.

more honestly grassroots sentiments and popular concerns instead of suppressing them. It also implies the need for a free flow of information if citizens are to make well-informed contributions when consulted by the state. Further, it implies the right of citizens to be consulted in policy making if popular consensus is to be achieved. Finally, the shift to KBE also encourages a pluralistic diversity of ideas and the necessity of dissent if creative solutions are to be found to increase the system's performance and survival.

KBE and Activism

These changes to the political philosophy and politicoeconomic infrastructures have made slow but steady incursions into civic life. In the field of public relations, activism is viewed with mixed reactions by practitioners.

For instance, one practitioner said: "Activism is not prevalent in Singapore. Our regional work has encountered activists on environmental, political and trade issues." Others, however, reported increasing activism on different fronts. One practitioner reported an encounter with environmental activism:

> Yes we have, and surprisingly they were rather loud voices, despite our client being a government statutory board. This proves that the local activist groups are starting to grow in strength and courage, as they often see the importance in putting their views and opinions across, and in seeking a change in course of action.

Another reported an emergence of minority shareholder activism: "Activism in Singapore is not as overt as in other markets. However, there is a growing grassroots movement amongst minority shareholder groups which are increasingly getting their views heard, and companies must acknowledge that and deal with it." The rise of minority shareholder activism is also supported by the local media's (Sreenivasan, 2001) advocacy of protection for the latter.

Consumer activism is also emerging. In a recent case, some 5,000 club members filed a class action suit against their town club for misrepresentation and a breach of contract (Tay, 2001). Club members alleged that the club had falsely advertised itself as an exclusive club when it was, in fact, not so.

Perhaps the event that marks the height of recent civil activism lies with the *tudung* issue ("Singapore: Four Muslim," 2002). Local Muslim activists, supported by Malaysian activists have challenged the state's constitutional right in banning the use of the *tudung* (a headscarf worn by Muslim girls and women) at local public schools. The activist who initiated the issue was the president of Fateha.com., an Internet site hosted by a segment of the local Muslim community. Two outcomes of the *tudung* issue have emerged. The first relates to the withdrawal of four Muslim children by their parents from local public schools when they were asked not to wear the *tudung* to school in conformity with the uniform dress code. The second concerns the decision by these parents to sue the state for banning the *tudung* from public schools, an act considered as unconstitutional by the parents. Currently, the issue is still being negotiated between the parents who withdrew their children from the public schools and the state, with intervention from leaders of the Muslim community.

Although these changes in the level of activism are slowly emerging, practitioners would do well not to underestimate the power of increasingly well-educated and vocal young, active publics. It is likely that practitioners conducting government, community, consumer, and employee relations will have to become more responsive to the interests and demands of this segment of young and active publics in the future.

Responding to Activism

How do public relations practitioners in Singapore respond to activism when it does arise, albeit in limited and rather tame forms? Practitioners interviewed suggest several methods. The most popular of which includes a two-way symmetrical communication approach of engagement and dialogues whenever possible. Another suggested a process of compromise and negotiation:

> We made sure that there was consultation of their views and opinions, and provided avenues of feedback such as hotline, briefing sessions with the activist groups, exhibition explaining the rationale of the client, direct communication channels, e.g., brochures specially printed for the activist groups. There had to be some give and take as well, to show the activist groups that we were also listening to their concerns, and that it was not just a one-way communication process. Of course, the client had already prepared in advance to give some leeway regarding some of the issues.

Yet others suggested more aggressive tactics: "The basic tactic is to aggressively inform all audiences about the facts of the case, and engage activists if, and when, appropriate" and to use "issue and crisis management tactics to manage negativity in media reports on client company, product or service."

With the ongoing shift toward a KBE and the extensive use of electronic communication, practitioners anticipate changes in the style of managing activism. The most obvious difference between offline and online media is the increase in the speed of communication that the latter provides. Practitioners suggested two possible effects that may emerge from the latter: (a) Organizations will need to learn to communicate more quickly and accurately to breaking news in the media. Hence, activist access to the media via new electronic technology means a "higher possibility of the media breaking news and organisations would have to be prepared to react quickly." (b) Organizations will need to improve on their ethical conduct, good corporate governance, and transparency. As one practitioner succinctly put it:

> Instantaneous access translates to more competitive reporting which means every journalist will strive to be the first to file a report. Because of the new environment, it is now even more imperative that corporates take on a more proactive role in communicating their business practices and truths to the media. Corporate governance and transparency will help preempt misundertanding.

Further, practitioners anticipate a major change in the demographics and nature of publics who use the Internet. One potential change is the emergence of a younger and better educated public, perhaps more politically conscious of their rights as consumers and citizens. This compels organizations to become more socially responsible, as one practitioner observed:

> With the Internet, these interest groups have an added media channel that has unlimited reach. Interested publics would also have increased accessibility to the various sources of information. These publics would be in a better position to evaluate claims and challenges

by interest groups. Organisations would also have to increase engagement with these activist publics so understand and address their concerns. The Internet can also be used as a tool to engage these activist publics.

In addition, the Internet also enables activists to target organizational stakeholders more directly than traditional media. One practitioner observed: "Obviously the penetration rate of the Internet into homes and businesses in Singapore provides avenue for direct targetting of stakeholders." This direct activist access to organizational stakeholders allows for rapid national and transnational coalition building to occur. It also suggests the necessity for increased organizational surveillance of the environment and heightened issues-tracking and management systems. One practitioner observed:

> We will definitely have to be more savvy when it comes to issue management; currently the interest groups are still rather passive; they are definitely not as active or strong as the activists in other countries. However, that will change as the local interest groups have easy access to similar groups in other countries—there will be exchange of ideas and strategies in lobbying policy change, etc. We will need to strategise new methods of managing and communicating to the activist groups.

Thus, it is likely that a shift to a KBE will eventually stimulate organizations and practitioners to pay more attention to ethical corporate performance and transparency, speed up their communication transfers with greater accuracy, strengthen environmental surveillance and issues management strategies, and become more socially responsive and symmetrical in their relations with key publics.

Limits to Activism

Although a more vibrant civil society appears to be in the making, political analysts argue that the development of local activism is retarded by the following factors: (a) legal restrictions such as the ISA, which allows the government to detain indefinitely political suspects without trial, and the Societies Act, which bars nonpolitical societies from making political statements against the establishment under the pressure of being deregistered by the government; (b) the institutionalization of out-of-bound (OB) markers that circumscribe what may be said about religious, racial, and political issues;[4] and (c) a culture of self-censorship that stifles dissenting political opinions (Gomez, 2000).

Hence, local activism in its limited forms may be classified into pseudoactivism and real activism. Practitioners described pseudoactivism variously as grassroots activism from environmental councils that are "not a real threat" to the establishment. Pseudoactivism is also associated with NGOs that are "aligned with the government" or have been coopted by the government. Such activist groups would then be tolerated or legitimized by the government. Pseudoactivism may also take the form of front organizations with hidden agendas. One veteran practitioner argued that the latter is activism with a hidden agenda to benefit the activist leaders and not the masses whose interests they represent. Thus, it may be deduced that real activist are those who challenge the established status quo and are less likely to be tolerated by the government.

---

[4]OB markers are implicit rules of censorship. Although they do not clearly define what may not be articulated in the public sphere, they define categories of topics that may not be articulated. These categories include matters pertaining to religion, race, and politics.

In the context of such a sharp demarcation between pseudoactivism and real activism, where do business organizations stand with local activists? One chief executive officer (CEO) from a foreign multinational business operating in Singapore offered his perspective (Faithfull, 2000):

> Currently, there appears to be an assumption in some quarters that business and government stand on one side, and civil society organizations on the other. The latter thus often expresses skepticism about the trustworthiness of business corporations as partners in development, seeing identity of interests between them and the government. According to this view, businesses may be reluctant to enter into cooperation with civil society organizations for fear of objections from the government, that is, if business could overcome and convince the NGOs of its genuine intent in the first instance. Such a skeptical conception of different alliances between the three parties can be a serious obstacle in the way of productive collaboration of all three parties in furthering the interests of the society as a whole. (pp. 87–88)

If this description holds water, it is unrealistic to expect much productive engagement and dialogue to occur between activists and the business sector. This would also mean that two-way symmetrical communication and relations may not occur with real activists who suspect business of being co-opted partners of the government.

KBE and Organizational Practices

Practitioners suggested that a shift to a KBE would affect organizational and public relations practices in various other ways, besides those of public affairs and activism already detailed.

First, a KBE encourages the emergence of active publics. Practitioners suggest that organizations need to engage in more two-way communication practices to productively engage active publics. One practitioner said: "Also, with publics becoming more active, we will need to pursue different communication strategies, and reach out to them more directly."

Second, a KBE creates the need to seek endorsement from regional media organizations as local media lose their monopoly over target audiences. One practitioner noted:

> The publics will be more savvy, and they will have access to different sources of info regarding matters of particular concern to them, especially with the Internet, making it easy to access foreign media. This means that the way we communicate will be all the more crucial—we will need to gain the endorsement of regional media with strong credibility, and not just relying on our local STs [*Straits Times*] and BTs [*Business Times*], as people will tend to be more disbelieving.

Third, a KBE changes the tactics of communication in terms of content, channel, and style. For instance, practitioners observed that already more organizations are using the Internet as an added "push technology" to communicate as it "opens up possibilities for more direct targeting other than traditional media." Others suggested that the Internet when "used properly . . . can also provide greater interaction and tracking capability." Yet others noted: "We are already e-mailing journalists more often than faxing. (Some public relations people I know are even sms-sing!)" Also, practitioners have been "directing them [journalists] to downloadable resources on the Internet."

Fourth, the shift to a KBE also reduces costs for organizations and their clients. Practitioners will need to build expertise in niche areas, specializing in online communication strategies and tactics as clients increasing depend on the Internet to reach out to young and Internet-savvy publics. One practitioner observed:

> Yes, the switch does affect the strategies and tactics used by my organization. The organization that I serve now has an interactive and a technology department whose jobs are to give value added services to clients such as web design, online marketing, database marketing, etc. The way we serve our publics is no longer mainly through offline media but through online media which are more cost effective.

Finally, a KBE critically changes the way in which practitioners will need to conceptualize problems and opportunities. The cutting edge no longer appears to be how much one knows but how creatively one applies that knowledge to create value-added solutions to problems. One practitioner put it succinctly:

> I would define knowledge-based economy (KBE) as an economy where all workers are not only content with just problem solving but they have to be more enterprising, innovative and adding value to the economy. Hence, creative and innovative ideas are very much appreciated as they can be transformed for economic gains.

CULTURE AND PUBLIC RELATIONS

Kiasuism is perhaps the quintessential character of Singaporean culture. It may explain the following organizational features in the republic: political caution on the brink of political paranoia and the general lack of entrepreneurial risk taking with regard to innovative ideas and practices.

The word *kiasu* is derived from the local Hokkien dialect. Literally, it means to be afraid to lose out. As one social critic (Chan, 1994) saw it, *kiasuism* takes the following forms in local culture: (a) a conformist and play-it-safe mentality resulting in "a herd mentality where everyone goes after the same things and avoids the same things. No one wants to be different" (p. 71); (b) a narrow and highly materialistic conceptualization of success reducible to the possession of "a piece of property, a car and security in a well-paying job" (p. 72); (c) an education system that tends not to cultivate independent, critical, and creative thinking; and the moral fiber to accept risk taking and challenges; and an unforgiving attitude to failures (p. 73); and add (d) a culture of political paranoia. This chiefly translates into the institutionalization of OB markers and self-censorship.

Thus, an educational system that breeds young students into conformity and a fixation with passing examinations as a means to material success also churns out working adults with similar cautious and conformist mentalities. One practitioner from an international public relations agency observed:

> The problem, however, is that Asian universities do not teach their students how to think and the exposure of the practitioners is limited because of a lack of reading and reflection. . . . Singaporean employees generally have a high standard of education and command of English. But like many Asian countries there is little of the aggression and extrovertion [*sic*] needed in the profession. Ambition is also curbed by an economically sheltered mindset.

This conformist and play-it-safe mentality does not bode well for organizations shifting rapidly toward a KBE. As one practitioner assessed, the new economy requires practitioners to function more as strategic experts and managers of knowledge than as tacticians. This implies the need for practitioners to engage in critical analysis and creative synthesis. The practitioner stated:

> Increasingly the sharper clients want "value added strategic services". In plain English they need advise and ideas on the big picture of things and creative ideas which are essentially an ability to synthesise disparate, seemingly unconnected ideas into something relevant for them. They also want trends, or the ability to spot them and advise on what to do to tap into them.

Kiasuism, which cultivates a culture of political paranoia, is also manifested at the organizational level. Practitioners practice self-censorship: "Even if there are no hard and fast rules, public relations practitioners self-regulate." Others try hard not to infringe on OB markers of ethnic sensitivities: "I think race and religion are two important values that could affect public relations practices. At this moment, especially, these two issues are highly sensitive and public relations practitioners would have to be careful in conveying their messages so they won't cause social disintegration." Yet others are wary of political OB markers: "We urge our clients not to criticize the government in a way that can be construed as inappropriate."

The concern with cultural and ethnic sensitivities may be traced back to the geopolitical and historical conditions described much earlier. Practitioners here recognize the importance of not treading on the toes of the minority groups. In particular, there are efforts at not offending the sentiments and cultural taboos of local and neighboring Islamic constituencies. Whenever possible, practitioners advocate "sensitivities to race and religion [to] be displayed. This is in terms of food served, in speeches, press releases and articles written. We try to create an atmosphere of pleasantry and harmony in all campaigns due to our multi-racial/religion make-up."

In addition to observing the OB markers of race and religion, practitioners also try not to infringe on OB markers pertaining to establishment politics. Giving face to political leaders is a mark of the local culture's deference to those in political authority. One practitioner remarked: "The concept of "face" plays into public relations in that there are often extra sensitivities to consider." Another advised: "Taking note of Government policy and statement helps guide our thinking and advice to clients wishing . . . us [to do] public relations here in terms of angles and approach, which might gain positive media interest."

However, human cultures are typically never static. Even *kiasuism* is likely to change in the distant future as the shift to a KBE encourages greater pluralism and diversity of lifestyles and reduces the local media's monopoly over information. It is certain that the culture of deference to the political elite is already giving way to a desire for more equitable relations between the government and its constituencies.

Economically, these changes may be translated into an adoption of key American entrepreneurial attributes such as: "emphasis on personal independence and self-reliance, a respect for those starting new businesses, [and] acceptance of failure in entrepreneurial and innovation efforts," as articulated by the ex-Prime Minister, Lee Kuan Yew, in a recent public address (Lee, 2002). In short, this is a willingness to embrace risk taking.

THE MEDIA AND PUBLIC RELATIONS

Currently, media relations is the most important public relations activity in the private and public sectors of Singapore. Media relations is the top revenue earner for most public relations consultancies, followed by strategic planning and counseling and then event management (Tan, 2001, p. 12).

The importance of media relations in Singapore takes precedence from the historical model of public relations practiced by the colonialists—practitioners as propagandists for the colonial government. Then and now, the media continue to be powerful vehicles for the dissemination of information on government policies and important agents in engineering consent for state policies among the masses. The media play this role by their agenda-setting function. They possess the power to construct political and social reality for the masses besides reflecting popular opinion to the political elite (Ho, 2000). The importance of the media in government public affairs is reflected in the way in which it is regulated and controlled by the state via licensing, national security laws, and the 1974 Newspaper and Printing Presses Act (George, 2000).

Media Control

What are the effects of the state's control and regulation of the media in the public relations industry? In general, many practitioners agreed that the local media are sufficient for broad outreach to the masses: "Singapore is a relatively small media market so blanket coverage of most stakeholders can be achieved through a few publications." There is apparently no shortage of publication outlets for reaching out to publics interested in technology, women's issues, entertainment, and lifestyle issues. However, just as many practitioners claimed that media outlets are scarce for niche areas such as vertical sector trade publications, medical and health care media catering to the graying population, among many others.

More important, practitioners observed that the monopoly of the local media and its regulation by the state cripples the ability of practitioners to reach out to critical and active publics. That is, although the local media provide sufficient outreach for most target audiences, they lack the credibility and legitimacy to be used as third-party endorsement for special publics. One practitioner noted that the local media's "quality of thinking, analysis and interpretation is below par, and hence [there is] a lack of credibility among the more critical audiences who matter. The international media and internet provide viable alternatives though." In sum, the local media are sufficient and excellent in catering to broad outreach to the masses but fall short where the special publics are concerned.

Media Access

In light of the importance of media relations, it is heartening to note that practitioners are generally able to access the local media easily. Also, media relations are generally cordial, especially for the bigger and more well-established public relations consultancies: "Being a recognized public relations consultancy helps, as the media is aware of the clientele we are handling, and will tend to take us more seriously." It also improves for practitioners who have spent much time and resources in cultivating friendly media relations: "We place great importance on relationship building sessions with the media, to cultivate our media contacts and resources. It is really useful, and we usually are able to rely on these contacts which we have carefully nurtured when we need to contact them."

KBE and Media Relations

Just as a KBE affects the style of government public affairs, activism, and the culture of *kiasuism*, it also affects media relations. Although some practitioners did not anticipate a significant change in the latter, many others suggested that an increase in the use of electronic communication is likely to affect media relations in the following ways.

First, the access of publics to online alternative foreign media is likely to reduce the monopoly of local media. Also, practitioners are able to access alternative media for the dissemination of press releases, third-party endorsement, and the like: "Media industry would have lesser control on releasing certain press releases because public relations firms would have greater media network to send their press releases to. In fact, media industry would have to compete locally and globally."

Second, the shift to a KBE is likely to increase the relationship of dependency between the media and public relations and increase respect for the public relations profession for the following reasons, according to one practitioner:

> With an emphasis on KBE, both the practitioners and the media are expected to be able to have a wider variety of skills beyond the basic, and to provide value-added services—for public relations practitioners, it also means having more in depth knowledge of the particular industry their client is in, and having diverse knowledge across different yet related industries. With that, the media relations would deepen and change, as the mutual need and dependency for one another reaches new heights. With the public relations practitioner displaying a higher level of expertise and skills, more respect to the role of public relations will be accorded, and the media will start to consult the public relations practitioner more frequently. At the same time, the public relations practitioner will no longer be contented to take a back-seat role to the media and play a beggar's role, as he/she will become an expert in the client's business and industry.

In fact, some practitioners observed that public relations professionalism is likely to increase as practitioners play the roles of gatekeepers to organizational information and educators of the media. One practitioner described this greater media dependency on public relations in the following way:

> I think KBE is when content/information becomes the core business rather than playing a supportive role. That is to say, the management of information rather than technical skills possessed by the employees of an organization becomes more important to the organization.
> If that is the case, public relations has a more significant role to play as organizations will need professional help to streamline and package the information into readily digestible content. By reducing jargon and reorganizing content, public relations can help journalists understand the issues at hand, who will in turn be able to transfer that knowledge to the readers . . . because there will be so much more information, often brimming with jargon, the media needs public relations more to sift out info that is relevant to them.

Third, because a KBE facilitates direct engagement with target audiences at a lower cost than traditional media, it is likely to encourage the practices of audience segmentation, rather than the indiscriminate targeting of mass audiences. This also implies a potential decrease in the reliance on traditional mass media for outreach to audiences. In a nutshell, the media market is likely to become more fragmented, departing from the monopolistic monolith that is was and is. Practitioners and activist groups would need to become more media savvy in recognizing the strengths and limitations of different media and customizing them for specific interests (George & Pillay, 2000).

Fourth, a KBE puts pressure on journalists and public relations practitioners alike to produce information content that reflects greater critical analysis, independent judgment, and creative thought because local media and public relations practitioners would be competing with the best practitioners worldwide for the attention of increasingly critical and active audiences. One practitioner put it this way:

> A knowledge-based economy would be an environment in which a person has access to various sources of information. Presented with this wide variety of information sources, people selectively choose the information they receive and evaluate information independently. A KBE would encourage journalists to develop more independent thinking as readers, who have access to the same information, would look toward more evaluative, independent writing. Public relations practitioners will no longer be able to feed information to journalists and expect a regurgitation of information.

In sum, although current public relations in Singapore continues with an emphasis on media relations and tactical public relations, other public relations activities are also slowly emerging in importance. They include public relations as a function of strategic management, corporate branding, community relations, public affairs, and issues management. The next section features a case study showcasing the importance of a strategic management of media relations in Singapore.

A CASE STUDY OF SUCCESSFUL STRATEGIC MANAGEMENT OF MEDIA RELATIONS

In 1998, the Ogilvy Public Relations Worldwide office in Singapore was retained by Andrew Tjioe, the President and CEO of the Tung Lok Group, an international restaurant chain, for assistance. Although the restaurant chain is well-known in Singapore and the region for its excellent cuisine, it had hitherto received little publicity. The CEO wanted the agency's assistance in launching a new theme restaurant and publicizing its new culinary consultant from Canada. The agency's initial research revealed that the restaurant company and its chain of local restaurants did not possess a systematic public relations structure. Calls from the media were handled ad hoc from individual restaurants, and restaurant promotions were not well-publicized in the media. These problems compounded the already insignificant publicity that the chain had then been receiving.

The agency adopted a two-pronged strategy to address the organizational and publicity problems. One of its first strategies was to set up a systematic public relations structure for the client's company and restaurants. The agency created a two-way communication system for the client in the following ways: (a) New work procedures were instituted for the restaurants to provide feedback to the agency on restaurant promotions; (b) the agency met with restaurant managers for regular brainstorming sessions during which communication issues and new promotions were discussed; (c) the agency also trained media spokespersons to develop and deliver key messages, manage media inquiries, stock press kits, and manage requests for photo shoots; and (d) the agency served as the center for coordinating media inquiries.

Its second strategy was to increase publicity for the restaurant chain and publicize the launch of the new restaurant and the culinary consultant. Media publicity and the cultivation of media relations took the following forms: (a) Quarterly media events were generated to introduce the client and the restaurants to key journalists; (b) a friendly and open communication with key media personnel was established by inviting journalists to sample the restaurants' products; (c) a media luncheon was organized at the new restaurant to introduce the CEO and the culinary consultant to journalists; (d) regular updates on the new restaurant's products and promotions were sent to the media; (e) to promote the new restaurant internationally, the agency established contact with the Singapore Tourism Board (a government statutory board) to promote the use of the new restaurant as an attractive venue for media meetings with foreign media invited to Singapore; and (f) to broaden the outreach of publicity for the new restaurant beyond the food and beverage industry, the agency customized news pitches for other media outlets in the fashion, business, lifestyle, and interior designer industries. For instance, fashion stylists, editors, and interior design companies were encouraged to use the new theme restaurant as a location for photo shoots.

In all, the agency's aims were to increase the publicity profile of the restaurant chain among local and international media and to promote the new restaurant, its CEO, and the culinary consultant. An evaluation of the agency's efforts demonstrated that it had made a significantly positive impact on increasing the revenue of the restaurant chain and increasing positive publicity for the client and the chain. In the weeks after the launch of the new restaurant, sales soared and the new restaurant reached breakeven in the first month, a record first in the 18-year history of the restaurant chain. With international publicity offered from various media outlets such as BBC, CNBC, *Asian Wall Street Journal*, the *Cosmopolitan* in Germany, the National Radio in Denmark, Reuters, and a host of other international media houses, the new theme restaurant even stimulated international inquires about the potential for franchise opportunities. Six months later with profits still up, in spite of the then Asian economic crisis, a second new restaurant was opened in Singapore. The client and his new restaurant continued to be the talk of town. Local media coverage was extensive and positive. The new theme restaurant stimulated more articles written on theme restaurants, debates in the dailies, requests from top fashion publications to use its location for photo shoots, and interior design magazines to feature the thematic designs of the restaurant in their publications.

Overall, the client and the chain received very favorable publicity from local and international media. And, to crown the glory, the agency was engaged on a retainer basis to manage the entire restaurant chain's public relations program. In 2001, Ogilvy entered its fourth consecutive year of partnership with Tung Lok. Andrew Tjioe, who was voted Tourism Entrepreneur of the Year (2001) said: "We are pleased to continue partnering with Ogilvy public relations. They have provided us with valuable counsel and helped propel Tung Lok, the brand, to the forefront of the F&B [food and beverage] industry" (Four in a Row, November 2000).

ACKNOWLEDGMENT

The work for this chapter would not have been possible without the contributions of public relations practitioners in Singapore. They gave of their valuable time, energy, and resources to enrich the knowledge and practice of public relations. I thank Mathew Yap of BP Amoco, Agnes Chang and Sylvia Yu of Weber Shandwick Worldwide, Sharolyn Choy of Edelman Singapore, Huw Hopkin of Impiric, and many more practitioners who have assisted me in the process of writing this chapter. Last but not least, special thanks and appreciation must also go to Ogilvy Public Relations in Singapore and the Tung Lok Group for permission to feature them in the case study.

REFERENCES

Chan, D. (1994). Kiasuism and the withering away of Singaporean creativity. In D. da Cunha (Ed.), *Debating Singapore* (pp.71–75). Singapore: Institute of Southeast Asian Studies.
Chow, H. W., Tan, S. J., & Chew, K. L. (1996). Organizational response to public relations: An empirical study of firms in Singapore. *Public Relations Review, 22,* 259–277.

Chua, B. H. (1995). *Communitarian ideology and democracy in Singapore.* London: Routledge.

Culbertson, H. M., & Jeffers, D. W. (1992). Social, political, and economic contexts: Keys in educating true public relations professionals. *Public Relations Review, 18*, 53–78.

Faithfull, T. W. (2000). Corporate citizenship and civil society. In Gillian Koh & Giok Ling Ooi (Eds.), *State–society relations in Singapore* (pp. 77–91). Singapore: Oxford University Press.

Four in a Row for Tung Lok and Ogilvy PR. (November 1, 2001). *AdVoice, p. 8.*

George, C. (2000). *Singapore: The air-conditioned nation.* Singapore: Landmark Books.

George, C., & Pillay, H. (2000). Media and civil society. In G. Koh & Geok Ling Ooi (Eds.), *State–society relations in Singapore* (pp. 189–202). Singapore: Oxford University Press.

Gomez, J. (2000). *Self censorship Singapore's shame.* Singapore: THINK Centre.

Grunig, J. E. (2000). Collectivism, collaboration, and societal corporatism as core professional values in public relations, *Journal of Public Relations Research, 12*, 23–49.

Grunig, J. E., & Hunt, T. (1984). *Managing public relations.* New York: Holt, Rinehart & Winston.

Ho, K. L. (2000). *The politics of policy-making in Singapore.* Singapore: Oxford University Press.

Internal Security Act (chapter 143). Singapore: Government Printer, 1986.

Lee, K. Y. (5 February, 2002). *An entrepreneurial Culture for Singapore.* Lecture presented at the Singapore Management University. Retrieved from http://Search.yahoo.com Retrieval date: 17 January, 2003.

Lim, D. (2000). *Speech by Mr. David Lim.* Minister of State for Defence and Information and the Arts, at Prism Awards. Retrieved from http://www.iprs.org.sg/pages/prism.html Retrieval date: 9 September, 2001.

Nair, B. (1986). *A primer on public relations practice in Singapore.* Singapore: Institute of Public Relations and Print N Publish Pte. Ltd.

Singapore: Four Muslim Primary One Students forbidden to wear the Tudung. (30 January, 2002) *Singapore Straits Times.* Retrieved from www.ahrchk.net/news Retrieval date: 17 January, 2003.

Singapore Department of Statistics. Retrieved from www.singstat.gov.sg Retrieved date: 20 November, 2001.

Sreenivasan, V. (31 August, 2001). It's time the law protects minority shareholders. *The Business Times Online.* Retrieved from http://business-times.asia1.com Retrieval date: 9 March, 2001.

Sriramesh, K., Kim, Y., & Takasaki, M. (1999). Public relations in three Asian cultures: An analysis. *Journal of Public Relations Research, 11*, 271–292.

Tan, R. (2001). *The state of public relations in Singapore.* Singapore: Singapore Polytechnic.

Tan, S. P. (1993–1994). *Roles of organized business in public policy making in Singapore: changes and continuities.* Academic exercise, Department of Political Science, National University of Singapore (NUS).

Tay, C. K. (15 April, 2001). Membership does not come with privileges. *The Straits Times Interactive.* Retrieved from http://straitstimes.asia1.com.sg Retrieval date: 17 January, 2003.

The Singapore 21 vision. Retrieved from Singapore Government website: http://www.gov.sg/singapore 21 Retrieved date: 7 March 2000.

Yeap, S. B. (1994). The state of public relations in Singapore. *Public Relations Review, 20*, 373–394.

Yuen, C. K. (1999). *Leninism, Asian culture and Singapore.* Retrieved from http://www.sintercom.org and www.comp.nus.edu.sg/~yuenck/new. Retrieved date: 15 March, 2000.

10

Public Relations in Mainland China: An Adolescent With Growing Pains

Ni Chen
Hugh M. Culbertson

INTRODUCTION

The People's Republic of China is the world's most populous nation with about 1.3 billion people (Yan, 2000). Also, it is one of the most enduring countries, having remained intact for about 5,000 years. Survival of a state requires ongoing support or, at the very least, lack of effective opposition from sources such as citizens. Thus, such longevity could be viewed in part as a public relations achievement.

[handwritten margin note: Starbucks was seen as a threat in Hidden City]

The country's history has featured long periods of political stability interspersed with dramatic, sudden, often violent change (Latham, 2000; Schoenhals, 1999). Forces for stability include the teaching of the classic philosopher, Confucius, who advocated that it was functional for societies to have stratification with citizens feeling reverence for their fathers, local and provincial leaders, and ultimately the emperor who was often called the son of God (Ng, 2000, pp. 49–52). The famous sage also focused on the interdependence of people and social roles and the importance of the collective rather than the individual. And, he stressed harmony rather than disruption and order rather than chaos (Lu, 2000, p. 7). Such thinking within the imperial court set the stage for a rather complex, rigid, meritocratic bureaucracy centered around the throne.

Furthermore, China has long been largely a peasant society. Peasants devote much of their life and energy to raising food and simply surviving. Chinese intellectuals and leaders long viewed them as being unable to determine their own fate or contribute meaningfully to social and political processes (Park, 1998). Peasants endured much suffering, which might have induced them to feel a need for change. Only 60 years ago, Chairman Mao

Tse-tung understood the latent power and strength of the vast peasantry (Schramm, Chu, & Yu, 1976, p. 87). Geographic isolation, anger at being exploited and bullied by foreign invaders and traders, and ethnocentric pride have also contributed to resistance to change among the Chinese (Xiao, 2000, p. 169).

In the 20th century, however, change came rapidly, often, and violently. The collapse of the Qing Dynasty in 1911 was followed by a variety of conflicts. The first was among warlords, with Chiang Kai-Shek and the Kuomintang Party eventually getting the upper hand by 1927. The Communist revolt then featured the famous Long March for survival by Chairman Mao and other leaders in 1935. Japanese invasion and partial occupation of the country in the 1930s created great suffering and turmoil as it co-existed with the civil war between Chiang's and Mao's forces. Mao prevailed and established the People's Republic of China (PRC) in 1949.

Mao Tse-tung sought to change Chinese society dramatically with forced farm collectivization and other social and economic experiments. Eventually, he feared that a reactionary bureaucracy was gaining control by the early to mid-1960s under Liu Shaoqi. This fear led Mao to unleash the violent Cultural Revolution which lasted for almost a decade until his death in 1976. By 1979, supreme leader Deng Xiaoping called for "opening to the West" and modernization. He believed China would escape from poverty and exploitation only if it adopted Western technology and economic institutions—and adapted them to Chinese needs and characteristics. At the same time, he sought to ensure political dominance by the Chinese Communist Party (Qiu, 2000).

This two-track approach to governing—including economic change and political stability—has helped create a kind of split personality in the new field of Chinese public relations. The profession first gained a presence in China in the early 1980s (Chen, 1992, p. 7). Mirroring recent change in the country, public relations grew rapidly for a few years only to decline for a time in the early 1990s. Recently, it has grown once more, as noted later in this chapter.

Authoritarian rule, crises, and culture have contributed to closedness in China. Communication has often been one-way—with little careful listening or attention to dissenting viewpoints as emphasized by Western scholars (Dozier, L. A. Grunig, & J. E. Grunig, 1995; J. E. Grunig, 1992). However, recent opening and modernization have contributed to gradual change (Chen & Culbertson, 1992).

In this chapter, we link China's culture to public relations practice in the country. Second, we provide an overview of Chinese public relations. Third, we examine Chinese media—control of them, their reach, and citizen access to them—discussing media relations practice in the process. Fourth, we explore current trends in Chinese society that provide opportunities and challenges for public relations practice.

CHINESE CULTURE AND PUBLIC RELATIONS

According to Kroeber and Kluckhohn (cited in Sriramesh & White, 1992), there is no unanimity about the definition of the term *culture*, with at least 164 definitions of the term in anthropological literature. Culture basically includes a complex, stable pattern of beliefs about what is, what is right, and what is important. These beliefs help shape behavior and thought in many areas. Also, cultural beliefs tend to be viewed as obvious, leading people to take them for granted. Scholars (e.g., Sriramesh & White, 1992; Sriramesh, 1996; Sriramesh, J. E. Grunig, & Dozier, 1996) have argued that culture influences the character of public relations practice within a nation. Research in this area has been framed largely by five dimensions of culture proposed by Geert Hofstede (1984, 2001). These dimensions and their relation to public relations in general are discussed in some detail in chapter 1 of this book. In this chapter, we link these cultural dimensions with public relations in China. Finally, we consider implications of culture, in general, and of certain specific features of Chinese culture, in particular.

Much of Hofstede's early work was completed in the 1960s and 1970s, at a time when mainland China was closed to Western scholars. Fortunately, after China had "opened to the West" in the late 1970s, Michael H. Bond, a professor at the Chinese University of Hong Kong, conducted a parallel project called the Chinese Value Survey. Hofstede and Bond (1984, 1998) found that the first three dimensions (power distance, masculinity–femininity, and individualism–collectivism) were clearly evident in China, in similar though not identical form, much like Hofstede's data from other countries. Long-term orientation appeared to be salient and clearly defined only in China and other Confucian societies, and uncertainty avoidance was evident only in other lands.

Hofstede suggested that uncertainty avoidance is consistent with Westerners' search for truth. In the age of modernity, Westerners have assumed there was truth accessible to reason, empirical observation, and religious faith. In contrast, Asian philosophers doubt that such truth really exists. They focus on virtue—the realm that seems to underlie long-term orientation (Hofstede, 2001, pp. 71, 363; Lu, 2000, p. 10). Hofstede (2001, p. 357) observed that, across nations, the dimensions are quite independent of each other with one exception. Power–distance and individualism correlate negatively ($r = -.77$). In short, collectivist societies tend to be hierarchical—with relatively unquestioning acceptance of strong leadership.

Hofstede (2001) also affirmed that nations tend to be stable on these dimensions. In particular, this holds true in China and India (p. 34). However, Yankelovich (1981, pp. xii–xx) argued that beliefs and values within a culture can change as proponents interact with outsiders and are affected by various social forces. Later, we note some areas of possible change in China over the past 50+ years under the influence of communism and opening to the West.

In general, the dimensions do not seem to converge and correlate increasingly over time. However, increasing wealth does seem to contribute to a nation's individualism (Hofstede, 2001, pp. 432, 454).

Comparing of China with other nations is quite challenging. Hofstede (2001, p. 502) concluded that:

1. China is relatively high in power–distance but low in individualism. As already noted, these two dimensions correlate negatively and strongly across nations in general. And, on these dimensions, China differs dramatically from the United States and other Western democracies.

2. China ranks low in uncertainty avoidance but high in masculinity. On these dimensions, the Middle Kingdom resembles the United States quite closely.

3. China ranks highest, by far, of seven nations compared on long-term orientation. The United States and Great Britain, in contrast, rate low here within a separate batch of 29 countries.

We now examine the dimensions' implications.

The Implications of the Dimensions of Culture

Power–Distance. China's high power–distance doubtless stems largely from its imperial tradition. As noted earlier, emperors were viewed as sons of God until 1911. In contrast, the intelligentsia have regarded the millions of peasants in the country as igno-rant, passive, and resigned to a life of bare survival (Park, 1998). Confucius argued that the stability of society was based on unequal relations in which low-level people owe their superiors respect and obedience in exchange for protection and consideration (Hofstede, 2001, p. 114; Ng, 2000, pp. 51–2).

Communist rule, beginning in 1949, has been very authoritarian. Chairman Mao de-manded unquestioning obedience in his effort to build a utopian state. Conversely, communist ideology points toward an egalitarian, selfless, classless society as an ideal. Such thinking seems likely to moderate power-distance somewhat. Also, ancient Chinese philosophers called on intellectuals to question leaders of the state when they erred dra-matically (Lu, 2000, p. 5; Shi, 2000).

Turning to public relations, Sriramesh (1996) suggested that higher levels of power–distance in societies make it difficult for public relations practitioners, as staff workers, to become part of dominant coalitions that ultimately set organizational policy. Access to the dominant coalition is seen by many scholars as being important to public relations excellence (e.g., Verčič, L. A. Grunig, & J. E. Grunig, 1996, p. 37). These conclusions gain support from two arguments:

1. In societies with high power–distance, power often is based on coercion and referent power, with the latter stemming from leaders' charisma and followers' identifying psychologically with them. Public relations people, as staff employees operating in behind-the-scenes support roles, seldom are in a position to coerce or show charisma.

2. In contrast, leaders in low power–distance cultures often exert influence primarily by demonstrating expertise, something that the bright, studious public relations practitioner can demonstrate through day-to-day performance (Hofstede, 2001, p. 97).

In another realm, Taylor (2000) suggested that high power–distance creates special challenges for practitioners. In such societies, people tend to blame leaders quickly when things go wrong. Even today, Chinese leaders often are perceived as leading under a "mandate from heaven" akin to that which supported emperors prior to 1911. When bad things happen, many doubt that the mandate still holds (Lu, 2000, p. 9). This suggests a particular need to act quickly and decisively in dealing with a crisis and to communicate leaders' decisiveness.

Hofstede (2001, pp. 97–98) noted that, in high-power–distance societies, leaders tend to display their status—presumably through such trappings as cheering crowds, fancy palaces, and luxurious limousines. Such trappings may seem excessive, connoting arro-gance, to people from more egalitarian countries such as the Netherlands where leaders feel at home "slumming" with ordinary folk. In light of this, practitioners from other countries must remember to show Chinese leaders the respect they feel they deserve. Such respect for leaders may not come naturally to die-hard egalitarians (Hofstede, 2001, pp. 430–431).

High power–distance also may call into question one important principle of negotiation emphasized in the United States. Mediators there are called on to ensure that negotiators focus on contestants' substantive interests, rather than their positions within an organi-zation or community. With high power–distance, however, positions never cease to be central. One cannot easily put them aside and achieve meaningful discussion (Hofstede, 2001, p. 436; X. Yu, 2000).

Dobson (2002) noted that third-party endorsement, especially by credible authorities supporting a project or product, is especially important in China. This is due in large part to the respect accorded to authority figures.

Collectivism–Individualism. The deep-seated nature of Chinese collectivism is shown by the fact that the Mandarin language has no word corresponding to the English *personality* which denotes a personal identity distinct from the society and culture. The Chinese word for human being, *ren*, includes the person's intimate societal and cultural environment (Hofstede, 2001, p. 210). Another sign of collectivist sentiment is the Chinese nomenclature protocol in which a person's family name precedes the given (first) name, defining the status of the individual by linking with the family. Chinese who migrate to the United States surely find it rather painful to Americanize their names by writing surnames last, as demanded by the telephone company and the Social Security Administration.

A major aspect of Chinese collectivism is *guangxi*—one's network of connections and friendships that seem necessary to get most anything, such as a train, a theater ticket, medicine, or a job! Yang (1994, p. 147) suggested that *quanxhi* helped avoid complete chaos during times such as the Great Cultural Revolution of 1966–1976. However, *quanxhi* poses certain challenges for public relations practitioners. These include:

- A need to spend much time developing relationships of trust before one can get down to business and close a deal. Efficiency-oriented Westerners sometimes are inclined to fly in, get down to substantive business right away, and then leave.

- Hiring and promotion of friends and relatives, often with little regard for ability or actual performance. In joint-venture firms, this strikes Western partners as nepotism or favoritism, perhaps leading to morale problems. Talcott Parsons (1951, p. 30) noted that Chinese are particularistic, taking specific relationships and circumstances into account. In contrast, Americans idealize universal standards of evaluation.

- Demands for money when one requests a permit, license, or shipment. Such "back-door" payments are widely viewed as respectful gifts in China. However, they often look like bribes to naive Westerners who must decide how and whether to offer or receive them (Culbertson, 1994).

- A tendency to talk—in rather personal ways—about people within one's company, department, or circle of friends and coworkers. At its best, such talk can be a genuine expression of personal concern and willingness to help. At its worst, however, personal discussion degenerates into hurtful gossip surely of special concern to internal relations practitioners.

- A perception that non-Chinese are outsiders—and perhaps just a bit inferior. Such thinking can seem ethnocentric to non-natives who are affected by such behavior. This poses relation problems for Western suppliers, customers, investors, technical experts, tourists, and joint-venture partners (Brady, 2000). We examine this issue further later in this chapter.

- Giving credit to the group, as well as to the individual, is important. In one experiment, Chinese management trainees performed best when told their performance would be measured for groups of 10 and their names would not be marked on the completed group product. In contrast, U.S. trainees did best when told their work would be measured individually and their names listed. Also, Chinese subjects performed poorly when told their group mates were strangers from all over the country (Earley, 1989). X. Yu (2000, pp. 124–130) noted that feelings of indebtedness, loyalty, and interconnectedness motivate people strongly in Chinese organizational contexts. Throughout the nation, one owes special allegiance to one's fellow residents or community, province, or region, unlike in most Western cultures.

Masculinity–Femininity. Historically, China has been a male-dominated, patriarchal society. Confucius once said that there are two kinds of people who are very artful, immature, and thus hard to deal with—women and children. According to Confucian ethics, men are superior and women inferior. The popular belief was that man is to woman as the sun is to the moon. He leads, she follows; thus, harmony reigns. Based on this philosophy, women are to obey fathers when young, husbands when married, and adult sons when widowed. Further, China remains, to a degree, a peasant society. In agrarian societies, women, especially those in the countryside and rural areas, generally have little opportunity for education and career growth apart from that of their fathers and husbands. However, Chairman Mao Tse-tung sought to enhance the status and role of women compared with men. "Women are capable of supporting at least half of the sky," he declared in the 1950s.

Since the public relations profession gained recognition as an occupational field in China during the 1980s, women have played a prominent role. They have served often in guest relations. Some fear this lowers the field's status among patriarchal leaders who largely equate public relations with young ladies of charm and beauty (B. Zhu, personal communication, July 11, 1994). However, this is not an obvious, simple conclusion, as discussed later. A masculine society offers at least two challenges for public relations. First, it suggests that male egos be stroked and strength be respected in negotiations. Second, it entails a kind of masculine stubbornness that resists compromise and may even lead to violence. Practitioners must deal with such tendencies in tactful, sensitive ways (Hofstede, 2001, p. 436).

At least one study supports these ideas. In a simulation, experienced business people from 11 countries, including China, negotiated the prices of three commodities. Players from highly masculine, individualistic cultures made high profits—and enjoyed the game—whereas collectivists did not (Graham, Mintu, & Rogers, 1994). We now discuss two rather culture-specific dimensions.

Uncertainty Avoidance.   This dimension seems very complex. And, as noted earlier, it does not show up very clearly in the Chinese Value Survey, although China does rate low, overall, on it. A key notion of Western thought about civic life is that people with differing views must hunt for compromise. If they are to avoid constant turmoil and disruption, they must recognize that no one participant in dialogue is all right or all wrong (Siebert, Peterson, & Schramm, 1956, pp. 39–71). Each person should feel some uncertainty about her or his position. In contrast, Mao Tse-tung, Chiang Kai-Shek, and other Chinese leaders have viewed contests for leadership as fights to the death—with little possibility for compromise or formation of lasting coalitions (D. A. Jordan, personal communication, June 7, 2001).

Recently, more pragmatic leaders have brooked some dissent, but they have cracked down when protests seemed loud and challenging. Such heralded liberalization efforts as the One-Hundred Flowers campaign of the l950s have led eventually to harsh crackdowns known as Anti-Right Movements (Chu, 1999; He, 2000). Much the same thing occurred with Deng Xiaoping's treatment of student protesters at Tiananmen Square in 1989. Of course, Deng Xiaoping had decreed in 1979 that his country should adopt useful Western ideas and adapt them to China's situation. Surely journalists and public relations practitioners engage in some self-censorship because of uncertainty as to where the boundary between what is and what is not acceptable lies at a given moment. This is discussed further in the section on media control.

Long-Term Orientation.   This dimension really came to the fore in the Chinese Value Survey noted earlier (Hofstede & Bond, 1984). It emphasizes certain features of Confucianism that impact on strategic thinking and tactical planning in public relations. One aspect is its emphasis on patience, hard work, and perseverance. Typical Chinese students in the United States have these attributes. They often study in the library when their American counterparts are visiting bars! Furthermore, they seem inclined to spend an extra term in school—or an extra month working on a thesis—to truly excel. In one study, only 14% of workers in China described leisure time as very important. That compares with 68% in the most leisure-oriented of 23 countries covered, Nigeria (Hofstede, 2001, p. 356).

Clearly, cross-cultural differences in patience can create relational problems. At times, a foreign joint-venture partner expects quick results, whereas a Chinese partner does not. Such differences must be faced, discussed, and worked out early in a business relationship (Hofstede, 2001, p. 446; Mann, 1989).

A related element is a long-standing emphasis on education (X. Yu, 2000, p. 132). Young Chinese prepare with great effort for tests so they can enroll in the best available schools. Education is valued so much in China that students seem shocked when someone questions its importance.

Clearly, public relations people working in China can count on a motivated audience when they communicate within universities and schools. However, a down side to this is that great emphasis is placed by the Chinese on rote memory as opposed to independent thinking. Further, students often fail to ask questions in class because they have been taught that this is disrespectful to the professor or teacher. Orientation in this area seems crucial in educational exchange programs.

Taken together, collectivism and long-term emphasis on virtue contribute to a major idiosyncracy of Confucian societies—preserving face. In China, loss of face is often considered to be worse than loss of a limb (Hofstede, 2001, p. 354)! This surely motivates people to work hard and be virtuous. Unfortunately, however, it may also lead them to conceal problems and withdraw from relationships to avoid embarrassment. At least one commentator claims AIDS education and prevention in China have suffered because local government officials sought to save face by ignoring the disease (Yanhai, 2000–2001). Communication professionals must work hard to help ensure candor and continued participation or their client organizations may suffer.

When working in China, public relations professionals must plan their activities so that they do not create a situation in which a native might encounter loss of face. Praising people for positive aspects of their work while acknowledging the negative may help. So does providing face-saving alternatives when a job is eliminated or an effort falls short (Goffman, 1971, pp. 95–187). Actions that may seem irrational to a nonnative are often carried out in China to save face. For example, when the nation is accused of human-rights violations, it often charges the accuser of similar violations. Lu (2000, p. 12) suggested this may be a tactic of saving face.

Emphasis on personal relationships (*guangxi*), along with the drive to save face, surely contribute to an oft-mentioned feature of Chinese life—a government based on people, not laws. This does appear to be changing. In recent years the Chinese legislature, known as the Congress of People's Deputies, has enacted thousands of formal laws (Burns, 1999; Yan, 2000). However, such laws generally are applied within the context of particular situations and relationships. That, in turn, complicates life for the public relations practitioner.

We now turn to several lessons relating to culture that should inform public relations strategists and tacticians:

- Luo (1999) found that the greater the cultural distance between China and that of a joint-venture partner, the smaller the venture's chances of success. Obviously partners need to understand each other, along with the common interests and factors that separate them. This poses a real communication challenge.

- At the same time, cultural similarity does not guarantee successful relationships. Many civil wars have been fought by ethnic groups with very similar cultural values. Those who have a long history of violence—or find themselves in what they see as win–lose relationships—frequently do battle with deadly results (Hofstede, 2001, p. 432).

- Relational and communication problems often develop with transnational organizations such as the World Trade Organization or United Nations. Theoretically, such organizations work to support shared values of all member states. However, workers and leaders come from different countries. And, as shown in a study of American journalists, a person cannot easily hang her or his values in the cloakroom when she or he goes to work each day (Gans, 1980, pp. 182–213). Focusing on common values becomes especially difficult when one or a few member-states contribute disproportionate resources, leading some to feel they should gain hegemony (Hofstede, 2001, pp. 432–433). A good deal of communication effort and training are needed to overcome such problems.

- Westerners tend to idealize a free marketplace in which all ideas are expressed. However, Asian concern for face makes this difficult, as noted earlier. Such concerns also have an up side. Discussing cultural differences can polarize people and lead to conflict. After all, culture consists of well-established beliefs about which belief holders have high personal involvement. Questioning such ideas can amount to questioning people's basic identity, a painful process (Hall, 1965, p. 165; Hofstede, 2001, p. 453). Practitioners need great skill and patience when working in this area.

- "White lies" such as excessive flattery, criticized by some Western philosophers as hypocritical and counterproductive (Bok, 1979, pp. 61–2), are seen as acceptable tools in enhancing a person's face and boosting relationships in China (Lu, 2000, p. 16). This may lead to perceptions of insincerity and deceitfulness across cultures.

- Chinese people tend to view problems and other objects as a whole, whereas Westerners analyze parts of that whole and relationships among these parts (Guan, 2000, p. 34). These tendencies seem to complement each other. However, unless each party is aware of this difference, misunderstandings and a lack of respect could result.

It is important to note that this analysis raises several questions and hypotheses regarding the management of cross-cultural communication. Further study is needed to answer them. Next, we provide a broad overview of Chinese public relations as it has developed within this cultural setting.

CHINESE PUBLIC RELATIONS: AN OVERVIEW

Defining the status and scope of public relations in China is not easy. The country, its provinces, and its cities have more than 150 public relations associations. But none covers the entire field or collects exhaustive data about job titles, practitioner qualifications, and so on. Furthermore, the field's boundaries are not clearly defined. Guest relations, translation, and guiding of tours—areas often viewed as separate from public relations in the West—occupy center stage in the PRC. And political strategy, an important focus in Western public relations, seems to be viewed by many as a separate realm in China.

To identify current trends and developments, Ni Chen, the senior author, who has conducted several studies previously in China (e.g., Chen, 1992; Chen & Culbertson, 1992, 1996a), interviewed 10 people working in the field in 2002. Included in the current study were four educators, four government officials, one agency executive, and one corporate communication manager. In this section, we rely extensively on their comments and draw on data from earlier studies. In general, all the participants agreed on the key areas of the current status of public relations in China, lending weight to their views. Hereafter, we refer to the 10 respondents simply as "our informants."

When Ni Chen collected data for her dissertation on public relations between 1990 and 1991, the young field was growing rapidly. Dozens of educational institutions were offering related courses. Agencies were multiplying. And employment opportunities seemed bright (Chen, 1992, pp. 45–53). However, the next few years witnessed a sudden decline in the field, according to our informants. Approximately one third of the public relations departments in large business organizations were eliminated. The number of newspapers and journals dedicated to public relations declined from 33 in 1989 to only 2 a few years later. The Ministry of Education refused to accredit public relations as a major for study in universities, allowing only Zhongshan University in Guangzhou to offer a public relations program on a trial basis.

Why the decline? Informants suggest several likely reasons. The Asian economic slow-down in the mid-90s affected China as well, causing a trimming of budgets. Public relations was subordinate to marketing in the thinking and practice of many firms. Tensions with foreign governments and firms following the government crackdown on students at Tiananmen Square in June 1989 may have contributed to questioning of "Western imports," including public relations. Many felt that public relations practitioners contributed to widespread government and business corruption. Some cautioned that the field had grown too rapidly—with no well-developed foundation based on Chinese needs and concepts.

Within a few years, however, public relations began to grow once again. According to a 2000 survey by the Chinese International Public Relations Association (CIPRA), earnings from public relations services grew from 200 million RMB ($24 million) to over 2 billion RMB ($242 million) within about 3 years. PRC-owned PR firms grew by 30% per annum in the last several years of the 20th century, whereas foreign-owned agencies in the PRC had a growth rate of 15%. The CIPRA survey suggested that the number of practitioners in the country had surpassed 100,000 by the end of the century. Also, the vice-president of Zenith Integrated Communication noted substantial growth in high-technology and other specialty areas.

Why the growth at the dawn of the new millennium? Informants cited several factors:

- Pressure for transparency in the wake of growing concern about government and business corruption. Executives realized they would need to make accounting and other procedures public—or risk prosecution and even execution—in light of anticorruption programs. Such publicizing required public relations expertise.

- An increasing number and variety of media outlets (described later).

- Growing talk of public relations as an important element, on a par with advertising, in the marketing process. Integrated marketing communication gained much attention in academic, corporate, and agency circles.

- Growth of adult education in support of China's focus on economic, social, and political development. Public relations courses showed up increasingly in adult-education curricula.

- Growth of varied businesses and joint-venture firms in combination with a society-wide tendency to decentralize government and business institutions (Wu, 2000). Each organization has its own public relations concerns.

Communication appears to have different characteristics within different sectors of the industry, according to our informants. In small corporations, practitioners operate largely as technicians. In particular, they help firms build images through publicity. In medium-sized organizations, public relations often plays a communication-management role. Emphasis is on facilitating communication between managers and employees—and between client organizations and external publics. In large firms, practitioners become involved in strategic planning. Building corporate culture is a major focus. Corporate image and logo design have become responsibilities of public relations units. However, the study and development of corporate culture remain in their infancy in China.

Turning to government communication efforts, the central government in Beijing often uses the press-agentry model (J. E. Grunig & Hunt, 1984, chapter 2), including propaganda. Certainly officials did so in the wake of the famous crackdown on students at Tiananmen Square on June 4, 1989. Specifically, PRC leaders did the following:

- Held trials of dissidents during the Persian Gulf War in 1991. The United States government and Western media paid little attention because their focus was on Kuwait and Iraq.

- Hosted the 11th Asian Games in September 1990. President Jiang Zemin and Premier Li Peng saw this as a chance to show the world that China deserved respect.

- Spruced up their showmanship in dealing with journalists. For example, President Jiang dressed in a Western business suit and answered Barbara Walters' questions with smiles—and a few English words here and there. Old-timers like Mao Tse-tung and Zhou Enlai would hardly have used such tactics to reach a Western audience (Chen & Culbertson, 1992).

In contrast, local government officials moved toward two-way communication. An early leader of this strategy was Li Ruihuan, then mayor of Tianjin and later a prominent figure at the central leadership compound, the Zhongnanhai, in Beijing. As mayor, Li held public meetings to gather input from the people. He encouraged citizens to express their views to the media. He began a series of annual surveys to measure public opinion about city government. Further, he used people in the media to obtain information from citizens who had been hesitant in speaking to the government (Chen & Culbertson, 1992). More recently, such two-way efforts have become common in commercial centers of southern China, especially in Shanghai, Guangzhou, and Shenzhen, according to our informants. These cities have long been major entry points for new Western ideas (Chen, 1992, pp. 164–169).

Women in Public Relations

As noted earlier, female practitioners play a central role in the field, often acting as translators and guest-relations experts. Some observers equate public relations with beautiful, charming ladies, creating what supporters of the field in China call the "Miss PR" problem. This often implies a professional who lacks drive, professional training, and ability to think strategically (B. Zhu, personal communication, July 20, 1994). Our informants agreed that such thinking stems from executive ignorance about what public relations really is—and what it can contribute to organizational effectiveness. As suggested earlier, such stereotyping is inaccurate. In fact, guest relations and translation require a high level of understanding, dedication, and sensitivity. Further, a survey of 43 female practitioners found that many thought like managers but behaved as technicians in highly constrained settings (Chen & Culbertson, 1996a, p. 294). Stereotypes about women contributed to this tendency (Chen & Culbertson, 1996a). Overall, according to one senior United States practitioner who has worked in China recently, young women appear to be very sophisticated and assertive in their professional activity (Capozzi, 2002).

Our informants reported that female practitioners quite often play management roles in government agencies, emerging nongovernmental organizations, hospitals, educational institutions, and associations that represent women, laborers, and youth. In these organizations, women in charge of external communication and public relations play leading roles in setting and implementing communication policy. However, male as well as female practitioners play only limited parts in setting overall organizational policy.

Certainly female practitioners have gained high standing in some Chinese firms, such as the huge Capital City Iron and Steel Corporation. A former vice-president of Shanghai Foreign Studies University, now the vice-commissioner of foreign trade and economy in the Shanghai Municipal Government, confirmed recently to the senior author that her appointment to this important post was largely due to her demonstrated ability to make major decisions and her skill in communicating them to relevant constituencies. In her new position, she is able to bring issues of policy promotion, image building, and campaign execution to the top level of decision making. Overall, young Chinese women entering the field appear to be very aggressive and sophisticated (Dobson, 2002).

Public Relations Societies

About 150 public relations societies exist throughout China at the local and provincial, as well as national, levels. CIPRA, with over, 1,000 members, seems to have come to the fore, according to our informants. The association seeks to enhance professionalism through case-study competitions, conferences, and surveys. It also has lobbied successfully to define public relations as a recognized occupation within the national occupational classification record. In 2001, CIPRA introduced the first-ever nationwide accreditation exam for public relations practitioners. The association's current president is Li Daoyu, previously China's ambassador to the United States. His stature "rubs off" on CIPRA. However, many continue to see the organization as heavily oriented toward government practice. A second organization, the Public Relations Society of China, is said by our informants to be losing ground largely because of political fighting among its leaders.

Public Relations Education

As suggested earlier, Chinese public relations education has gone through many ups and downs. When we studied the field in the early 1990s, growth and innovation were apparent (Chen & Culbertson, 1996b). A decline soon after that was followed by more recent growth, according to our informants. Change has been so rapid that even if we had the time to study public relations education and the space to report on it fully, our report would be out of date before it came off the press! Therefore, we venture only to make a few generalizations.

First, public relations education in China is diverse. It is offered in departments of journalism or mass communication, in units focusing on speech and interpersonal communication, and in interdisciplinary programs. It is also offered in 4-year baccalaureate-degree programs, in 2-year technical colleges, and through television distance learning aimed largely at older, nontraditional students (Chen & Culbertson, 1996b). Second, professors appear to strike a reasonable balance between theory and practice; although they often fail to link the two very effectively. Western perspectives get attention, as do Confucius and other classic Chinese philosophers. The latter seem important because they suggest a need for caution and compromise in searching for win–win solutions. Also, the classics focus on long-term interests and on respect needed to build lasting relationships. Third, educators rely heavily on guest lectures. Also, they work hard to arrange internships and hands-on experience. These steps seem especially important because many professors, although perhaps learned, lack practical experience.

We now focus on an interesting and long-standing feature of PRC communication, mass mobilization campaigns.

Mass Mobilization Campaigns

Throughout their history, the Chinese Communist Party and government have sought to enhance the character and spirit of the people through mass mobilization campaigns focusing largely on officially designated heroes. No doubt this squares with the long-standing tradition of worshipping emperors and scholars mentioned earlier in this chapter. Chairman Mao, in particular, came to be viewed widely as a God-like figure during the Cultural Revolution (Zhang, 2000). Such campaigns usually present ideal role models and encourage people to emulate them. Perhaps the best known was Lei Feng, a poor peasant soldier who died when a tree fell on him. Lei Feng was presented as a selfless, virtuous, heroic person.

In recent years, such campaigns have sought to combat "spiritual pollution" and other bourgeois evils. For example, a 24-year-old medical student named Zhang Hua was presented as a hero after he supposedly attempted to rescue a 69-year-old peasant from drowning in a polluted pit. Both Zhang and the peasant were overcome by methane gas fumes and later died (Rosen, 2000, pp. 163–164). Not surprisingly, given the current cynical atmosphere in China, Zhang's heroism soon took a beating. Letters to the editors of certain newspapers questioned his validity as a role model. Shangai's *Wenhui Daily* ran a letter arguing that his supposedly heroic act damaged the interests of the state. He was a young person with much to contribute to the "Four Modernizations." The state already had invested much in him. Thus, it was foolhardy and contrary to the state's interests for him to risk his life for an old peasant whose potential for serving the state was limited at best. Furthermore, press reports alleged that Zhang was not a totally unselfish servant of the party and nation. In fact, against university rules for a medical student, he had a girlfriend (Rosen, 2000, pp. 163–164)!

As this example suggests, mass mobilization campaigns often face uphill battles. Primarily, this problem stems from a lack of faith in various institutions and people in China. Many feel the Communist Party really is Communist in name only (He, 2000, p. 128). Thus, it is viewed widely as a vehicle for making a good living, gaining status, and being safe—not as a focus of faith or deep-seated belief in ideals. In recent years, formally designated role models have had major problems. Their portrayal of selfless dedication to the party, its ideals, and the people at large has seemed somewhat at odds with Deng Xiaoping's widely quoted statement that "to get rich is glorious" (Zhang, 2000, p. 67). Their role in standing against corruption has often received only lukewarm support from party members, some of whom have been corrupt (p. 77).

As elsewhere, media play an important part in Chinese public relations. We now turn to an overview of the nation's media, discussing ways in which media outreach, control, and access impinge on public relations practice in accordance with the framework of this book.

MEDIA IN CHINA: AN OVERVIEW

Media Outreach

In China, as in most developing countries, radio has played a prominent role partly because of the high rate of illiteracy (P. S. Lee, 1994). However, recent strides in education have lifted the literacy rate in the PRC to an estimated 81.5%. Further, the gross national product per capita was about 31,400 RMB ($3,800) in 2001. Although low by Western standards, this income level greatly exceeds that of many developing countries and allows the vast majority of Chinese to afford television sets and purchase newspapers, books, and magazines (Presbyterian Mission Board, 2001, p. 180).

Chinese media were decimated from 1966 to 1967. Chairman Mao Tse-tung closed possible opposition voices and sent journalists, as well as other writers and professionals, to work in the countryside during the Cultural Revolution. Magazines declined from 790 titles circulating in 1965 to just 21 in 1970. Newspapers shrank from 343 to 42 during that period (P. S. Lee, 1994).

When the nation regained sanity following Mao's death in 1976, the media began to flourish. By 1988, 1,579 newspapers were distributed openly (Yan, 2000). Nationwide circulation and readership data are not available, but the high literacy rate indicates a huge potential audience. By 2002, 8,000 specialized and general-interest magazines operated, many of them with circulations exceeding 2.5 million (Dobson, 2002). Further, by 1997, 2,000 local radio stations formed a highly developed system, beaming programs to 417 million receivers, about one for every three Chinese people. By 1999, the nation had 400 million television receivers, with almost 90% of all households having at least one set (Yan, 2000). Early in the new millennium, China Central Television's 12 channels reached about 650 million viewers (Dobson, 2002).

Of course, media outlets are not distributed evenly throughout the land. In 1997, for example, Guangdong, the province adjacent to Hong Kong which the central government viewed as a haven for quick development and Western ideas, had 62 newspapers. Guizhou, a nearby but less developed large province, had just 27 (Wu, 2000, p. 49). Further, there is unequal distribution in buying power as well. Twelve million Chinese workers lost their jobs in just 1997, as privitization and reform almost eliminated the *iron rice bowl*—the guarantee of a job and living wage for everyone that Chairman Mao had sought to implement (Schoenhals, 1999).

In an effort to enhance readership, listenership, and viewership, Chinese media have become more lively and varied. Writing also became more timely and less drab after 1976. Magazine covers feature many glamorous ladies. Sensational content has become common. Even *People's Daily*, the official organ of the Chinese Communist Party, almost tripled the categories of news it covered and reduced its politicized writing about revolutionary themes that had dominated during the Cultural Revolution (Chu, 1999).

The Internet has grown rapidly among elite, highly educated Chinese. By 2002, the number of web users in China was estimated at 56 million (Dobson, 2002). Although impressive, this figure amounts to only about 4% of the nation's total population of roughly 1.3 billion. No doubt this figure is growing rapidly. Yet, dependence on other technology limits expansion. At the beginning of this century, only 5% of Chinese households had telephones, and only 2% had personal computers (C. C. Lee, 2000, pp. 20–21).

Media Control

All media in China are owned by the government. For almost the first 30 years of the PRC, content consisted largely of preaching the party line. However, Deng Xiaoping and Jiang Zemin have been more pragmatic, viewing the press as a tool to enhance modernization and reform (FlorCruz, 1999; Hong & Cuthbert, 1991; Kissinger, 1997; X. Yu, 1994). Exposing the incompetency and corruption of technocrats and lower level administrators have been widely seen as helpful in achieving reform (Chang, 1989, pp. 47–50). Of course, journalists are not permitted to criticize top leaders or the Communist Party or the basic political system (Latham, 2000). Every now and then, the authorities fire an editor or close a web site when they fear things may spin out of control (Dahun, 2000-2001). For example, publication of a two-volume book purporting to detail the events leading to the June 4, 1989, crackdown on students at Tiananmen Square led to a strong government reaction. Officials suppressed the book's circulation, searched for sources of media leaks, and began a general security crackdown on activists (Nathan, 2001). The Communist Party and government have railed recently against "spiritual pollution" by Western ideas and against notions of "peaceful evolution" toward a capitalist and/or democratic society (Qiu, 2000, p. 257).

In this context, the government has cut subsidies even to party papers. Publications began to depend heavily on advertising revenues, which skyrocketed from 248 million RMB ($30 million) in 1985 to 13.6 billion RMB ($1.65 billion) a decade later (Pan, 2000, p. 72). In China, as elsewhere, the person who pays the piper calls the tune to a degree! Officials sometimes tolerate coverage that irritates them because they have to rely on media outlets to reach their publics (Rosen, 2000). Decentralization also has helped loosen government control over the press. Publications have become more and more diverse. Increasingly, the central government has had to rely on local authorities to implement political control. Freedom to operate without government control is greater in the social than the political realm, and in smaller departments and agencies than in central ministries (Wu, 2000, pp. 61–62).

Although somewhat chaotic, financially driven press restructuring and expansion also have extended to the Communist Party press. Throughout the history of the PRC, the party has often operated a morning newspaper and an evening paper in any given large city. The morning paper has been controlled quite strictly and has emphasized party decrees and pronouncements. The evening paper has provided a great deal of soft news and entertainment. From 1992 to 1993, the party began "weaning" media outlets from press subsidies to save money. All newspapers became increasingly dependent on advertising and circulation revenue. Partly because of their readable style and focus on ordinary people, evening papers gained in both areas, whereas morning papers declined.

In response, morning papers were allowed to establish "city evening papers" as cash cows to support them. These new papers sprung up in at least 20 urban areas between 1994 and 1998. Operating independently of party supervision, these papers have often become quite sensational. They report on small social problems, such as missing children and prostitution, and shy away from major controversies. They provide a valuable outlet for public relations people who need to disseminate useful information like bus schedules and instructions on how to do a variety of things (Hang, 2001).

It is important to note that the national media are more closely censored than local and provincial media (Ma, 2000, p. 22). Furthermore, party journalists now are mostly college-educated people exposed to non-Marxist ideas. Thus, today's cadres tend to be more critical and independent than their predecessors (Chu, 1999, p. 13). The Internet has brought many foreign ideas to China. The government often regards this as subversive, leading it to view the medium without much enthusiasm. Authorities have done a great deal to regulate the Internet and little to promote use of it (Yan, 2000). Some web sites have been shut down because they were deemed dangerous (Dahun, 2000–2001).

We now turn to practitioner and news-source access to the media.

Source Access to News Media

Until fairly recently, press coverage in the PRC stemmed largely from government and party directives. In 1994, we met with practitioners in a public relations agency in Hangzhou that was owned by the Xinhua News Agency. One host quipped that "It is rather nice working with the media when you and they have the same boss!" However, the growth, popularity, and limited critical role of the media have complicated things considerably. Young reporters often take the initiative in contacting news sources (Chang, 1989, p. 123).

Although sometimes criticized in official circles, *quanxhi* still operates in China, as noted earlier. Reporter–source relations involve gift giving and reciprocal favors dependent in part on family and geographic ties. All of this makes media relations more complex than in the West.

Reporters, editors, and media relations practitioners share a common uncertainty. They must report critically with a concern in the back of their minds that too much criticism of the wrong people could bring official wrath. China has no official censors who tell journalists in advance what crosses the line. Training of reporters and editors helps them censor themselves (Chang, 1989, p. 256). Our informants believed that most press relations people work with journalists in defining all-important "lines" between what is acceptable and what is not. Such collaboration may reduce press criticism of some client organizations.

Organizations in China gain press coverage in the following ways:

1. Often a newspaper will seek financial sponsorship from a news source for editing a special section or writing an in-depth story. Sometimes the sponsor covers travel and other expenses. At other times, the sponsor may bring cash in so-called "red packets" (Pan, 2000, p. 85). In fact, "red packet" has become a code phrase for corruption in some journalistic quarters, and government officials have railed against it. However, it continues, according to our informants.

2. Sometimes an editor receives a commission of 10% to 20% from advertising and sponsorship revenue that her or his special section brings to a newspaper or magazine (Pan, 2000, pp. 85–86). This, in turn, motivates aggressive advertising sales and promotion by media. And, it leads to in-depth coverage of organizations that may spend their advertising budgets at a publication or station.

3. It is not uncommon for newspapers to contract an external party to edit and produce a special insert or section. Often the public relations people who work for the sponsoring party end up writing and editing such sections (Pan, 2000, p. 87).

4. On occasion, a reporter working for a particular paper or magazine may place her or his story in another publication when a policy or administrative fiat precludes publication in the publication she or he works for. Westerners might call this moonlighting (Pan, 2000, p. 92).

Our informants feared that such arrangements may compromise the integrity of the press as well as public relations, especially when sponsorship and other arrangements are not acknowledged for all to see. Many informants called on educators and leading practitioners to create ethics classes that deal with these matters more forcefully.

Reliance on advertising and circulation revenue appears to give the news media some independence from government. However, this independence may be more apparent than real for one basic reason. The government itself is heavily involved in business, often maintaining partial ownership (Sparks, 2000, pp. 35–49). Furthermore, much as in the West, mergers and conglomerates worry advocates of watchdog journalism. Media conglomerates in Guangzhou and elsewhere have components that may receive little hard-hitting coverage because it would "kill the goose that lays the golden egg" (He, 2000, p. 113).

Although not independent of government, the press appears to be playing a modern public relations role rather than a propaganda role these days in China. Coverage is less ideological than 20 years ago. As He (2000) put it, the main mission is not to brainwash or impose an ideology. Rather, it is to boost the party's image and justify its existence. Some refer to the government and party information system as "Publicity, Inc." (He, 2000).

Much as in the West, reporters move back and forth between work in politics, business, and public relations. Such ties help set the parameters of news and press coverage (Wu, 2000, p. 104). In the final analysis, press coverage relies heavily on government sources in China, much as it does elsewhere (Chang, 1989, p. 84; Culbertson, 1997; Culbertson & Chen, 2001).

We now turn to several developments and concerns in modern China that create important challenges and opportunities for public relations.

SOME CHALLENGES AND OPPORTUNITIES

Social and Economic Development

Chinese leaders have tried, at least since the end of the Qing Dynasty in 1911, to lift out of poverty the mass of peasants who accounted for more than one-half of the population. Chairman Mao Tse-tung's Great Leap Forward, featuring the collective operation of huge farms, and his infamous project of the late 1950s to build backyard steel mills were among the drastic steps taken toward this end. During the first 20 to 25 years of the PRC, radio was viewed as a key vehicle for development instruction. Peasants, many of whom were illiterate, would gather in village squares to hear radio programs. Party cadres would be on hand to answer questions, give instructions, and seek peasant commitment for steps designed to reduce suffering and starvation (F. T. C. Yu, 1963, pp. 277–279).

Recently, as word of urban prosperity spread in the countryside, peasants flocked to cities such as Shanghai, Guangzhou, and Beijing by the millions to search for jobs. Such huge "floating populations" have taxed the infrastructure of these cities beyond limits. The government has reacted by taking the following steps:

1. Instituting a family-responsibility system under which farm families could run their own operations and keep more and more of their own profits.

2. Promoting township and village industries that employ farmers driven off the land by improved technology and other factors. These people, it is hoped, would make a living close to home—rather than migrating to the already overcrowded cities.

3. Supporting certain industries and firms through tax breaks, trade fairs, training programs for workers, infrastructure development, and so on (Belcher & Shue, 2001).

4. Taking land from farmers to build special economic zones, highways, and other development-related infrastructures (Guo, 2001).

Such moves have created an increasingly competitive environment for people who, under Communism, had been taught that competition is basically evil. Competition creates losers as well as winners, and losing is especially painful for folks who have endured centuries of upheaval and near starvation. Sometimes government officials have treated the losers in ways which savvy public relations people would object to.

For example, in the rural Banyan Township of remote Yunnan province, things became so desperate that activists went to Beijing to protest that the meager payments they received for land taken from them were unfair. Beijing officials explained that this was a local matter—outside their jurisdiction. The activists were sent to their provincial capital, Kunming. There they were treated courteously, given a free meal to soothe their feelings, and sent home (Guo, 2001)!

In the wake of such cases, many Chinese people have come to see the national government as their savior, whereas local authorities are seen as corrupt, arbitrary, and unfair (Guo, 2001). Clearly, as decentralization occurs throughout the country, local governments must have legitimacy to operate effectively. Our informants saw a great need for public relations counsel at the village and township levels.

Development has gotten much attention from PRC leaders. Given the widespread reach of television today, development-related programs have become common on China Central Television (CCTV), the nationwide network. For example, CCTV arranged for production of an educational soap opera on family planning. Produced at great expense, the program finally went on the air in 2001 after being bumped from the program schedule for 1 to 2 years by network executives (L. Ren, personal communication, February 10, 2002). Such delays surely hamper development planners to a great extent.

Development news has been featured extensively in party newspapers such as *China Daily* (Culbertson, 1997), and in Xinhua News Agency dispatches. In a study of the latter from 1957 to 1988, Elliott (1998) found heavy emphasis throughout on clarification of development plans and policies, instruction about what local officials and citizens could do to implement these plans, and context relating to progress in other regions and previous goals or claims. However, critical assessment of relevance, success, and failure was quite rare—doubtless reflecting the government's dominant role among news sources (Culbertson, 1997) and its desire to promote development in a positive way (Elliott, 1998).

Some scholars of development communication see current trends in the field as moving away from long-standing Chinese practice. China's highly centralized political system seems ill-suited to dialogic, two-way models relying on grassroots input and support (Freire, 1997). Further, the nation's history of systematic nationwide planning deviates from current emphasis around the world on the identity of specific social groups. A focus on economic growth in isolation from other realms also seems inconsistent with new social movements focusing on personal and group identities (Huesca, 2001). Public relations people need to address such issues. However, our informants reported little practitioner effort to date on these matters.

Institutional Changes

The recent openness and resulting reform have led to institutional innovation in the PRC. Three areas require a great deal of public relations expertise. These are social organizations, local elections, and ties with foreign interest groups. We briefly review each of these realms.

Social Organizations. In recent years, the government and Communist Party have been unable, due partly to a lack of personnel and financial resources, to meet all Chinese social and welfare needs. Thus, officials have permitted the formation of social organizations numbering almost 190,000 according to one published 1996 estimate (quoted in Saich, 2000). These groups operate with various degrees of government support and control (Saich, 2000). Such organizations have been both a blessing and a dilemma for Chinese authorities. The government realizes they are needed but fears they may spin out of control. Crackdowns sometimes occur. In 1998, several leaders of an emerging political party, the Chinese Democratic Party, were jailed for trying to organize in opposition to the Chinese Communist Party. In 1996, the first home for battered women in Shanghai was closed in light of claims that it was improper for a nongovernmental organization to run such a service. The Falungong religious sect was "de-registered" in 1997 after it surprised leaders by organizing a sit-in with 10,000 supporters at the party headquarters in Zhongnanhai (Saich, 2000).

Clearly such organizations need to spell out clearly what they are about and why. Further, government officials must grant such organizations a more stable and well-defined status, as well as opportunities for dialogue. Public relations expertise can certainly help in this process. However, our informants view this as an underdeveloped area of public relations.

Local Elections. Recent prosperity throughout the country appears to have been accompanied by declining revolutionary zeal and party membership. Beginning in the late 1980s, the national government began addressing this problem by encouraging elections for village leadership so local citizens could choose their own leaders and hold them accountable. The Ministry of Civil Affairs, the agency responsible for local elections, did not collect data on how many of China's 930,000 villages hold elections (Pastor & Tan, 2000). Opinions vary as to how effective such elections have been in the past. Anecdotal evidence does suggest that some of these elections are transparent, contested vigorously, and free in the sense that candidates can speak freely and voters vote in secret (Pastor & Tan, 2000). However, some observers insist that free elections must be built on the foundation of independent branches of government, a free press, and freedom of association. These areas are evolving rather slowly in China. Legislative, judicial, and executive branches do exist. But our informants emphasized that the executive branch tends to dominate the other two branches. Furthermore, the Chinese Communist Party dominates all three branches.

Surveys have been done on the interest among Chinese citizens in politics, their propensity to consume news about it, their interest in affecting it, and their perceptions about the need to reform the nation's political system. Shi (2000) concluded that grassroots attitudes and informal knowledge are as supportive of democracy as those found in some societies widely regarded as democratic. President Jiang Zemin and other national leaders have spoken in favor of local elections, viewing them as a tool in developing Chinese Communist Party leadership. However, some worry that village politicians might spin out of party control (Diamond & Myers, 2000). Therefore, the national government has allocated few resources to supervise and support village-level elections (Pastor & Tan, 2000).

In small villages, candidates usually campaign very informally as they feel they already are well-known in their areas. Perhaps partly for this reason, little planned public relations appears to occur during such campaigns—or for women's groups and labor unions. Our informants see these as areas for future growth.

Ties With Foreign Interest Groups. Deng Xiaoping called for adaptation of foreign ideas to Chinese needs and contexts. His pragmatism, still embraced by his successors, leads to some zigs and zags that surely pose public relations problems for the government and for international relations.

For example, an organization called the International Education Foundation became affiliated with the controversial Unification Church of South Koreaunder Reverend Sun Myung Moon. Both groups supported efforts in schools to advocate sexual abstinence as the only effective way to control AIDS and other sexually transmitted diseases. Also, both condemned homosexuals. PRC leaders apparently saw this initially as a useful approach in combating evil Western influences. However, when the organization began to gather a following, the government opposed it as anti-Communist—and as somewhat cult-like in ways reminiscent of the Falungong movement (Yanhai, 2000–2001). We now focus on a final area of concern to the Chinese government.

Dealing With Foreigners

Welcoming Tourists. During a 1-month-long lecture tour in the Middle Kingdom, Hugh M. Culbertson, the junior author of this chapter, commented often that Chinese people really wrote the book on hospitality, after experiencing the bountiful banquets and servings of Peking Duck, considerate tour guides, bright simultaneous interpreters, and comfortable accommodations in Western-style hotels and "dormitories for foreign experts." Interestingly, the very title of foreign expert gave his ego a boost! While in China, he truly had the experience of a lifetime. However, he eventually came to realize three things about the hospitality shown him.

First, although genuine, the hospitality was quite scripted. Activities were highly planned. Banquets were elaborate, as were tours and introductions. Activities seldom seemed completely spontaneous, and this became just a bit disconcerting to an American used to spontaneity. Second, arranged activities often seemed to say implicitly, in light of their formality, "We welcome you warmly, but you are not Chinese. We don't want to forget that you are outsiders visiting our country." Such an insider–outsider distinction was emphasized in several ways, such as dual pricing at the Forbidden City and in certain stores, providing Westerners accommodation in hotels where Chinese could not stay, and so on. Third, the government and party seemingly try, often in subtle ways, to control their guests. A word, *waishi*, denotes such an effort to control relations with guests while welcoming and serving them thoughtfully and warmly (Brady, 2000).

These factors did not really bother the American junior author and his American wife. Feelings of separateness and a need for control seem understandable in light of history—the exploitation of China by the West through parts of at least two centuries, Chinese isolation, Chairman Mao's insistence on the need for self-sufficiency, and so on. Nonetheless, if the nation is to attract Western tourists, such cultural differences deserve careful thought.

Cultural Exchange Balance. Chinese students and workers flock to the West in huge numbers. At any one time in the past 20 years, an average of 40,000 PRC students have attended classes in the United States. These students appear to learn and contribute a great deal. However, relatively few Westerners study or live in China for very long. No doubt this reflects in part their low proficiency in Chinese language. Because of its complexity and utter lack of similarity to Western languages, Chinese seems very daunting. That is especially true in the United States where language studies are notoriously weak. Overall, the number of Chinese students in Europe outnumber the European students in China by almost 20 to 1 according to one study (Meissner, 2002). Contemporary communication scholars stress the importance of symmetry (J. E. Grunig, 1992). That implies mutual understanding among participants in an exchange. And such inequities in the balance of exchange seem apt to hinder mutuality.

CONCLUSIONS

Clearly public relations, a very new field in China, is changing rapidly as it defines itself. Western practices do not set well with the Chinese people. In fact, development of the field appears to have been opposite to that in the West, over time, as to communication channels emphasized. In the United States, early public relations practice focused largely on mass media. Recently, however, interpersonal approaches have gained importance due in part to the following:

- Growing emphasis on employees, stockholders, and other internal publics.

- Widespread development of niche marketing and audience segmentation in strategic thinking as well as tactical practice.

- Growth of the Internet and other technologies that facilitate interaction among small, specialized groups.

In mainland China, in contrast, the field began just 20 years ago with great emphasis on interpersonal communication. Guest relations and simultaneous translation were popular public relations techniques. This stemmed in part from the subtleties of *guangxi*, culture-based collectivism, and low credibility of government-owned media. Recently, however, the mass media appear to have gained in importance. Contributing factors include the following:

- Growth in the number, credibility, diversity, and appeal of media, along with media receptivity to public relations pitches and contributions.

- Marketing of products to large and diverse audiences, as growing purchasing power has expanded markets.

- Great concern for appealing to foreign investors and consumers, using international media, as China has opened its doors to the outside world.

More research obviously is needed to document and clarify such trends.

REFERENCES

Belcher, M., & Shue, V. (2001). Into leather: State-led development and the private sector in Xinji. *China Quarterly, 166*, 368–393.

Bok, S. (1979). Lying: Moral choice in public and public life. New York: Vintage Books.

Brady, A. (2000). Treat insiders and outsiders differently: The use and control of foreigners in the People's Republic of China. *China Quarterly, 164*, 943–964.

Burns, J. P. (1999). The People's Republic of China at 50: National political reform. *China Quarterly, 159*, 580–594.

Capozzi, L. (2002, August). *Public relations in China and Japan today.* Teleconference presentation sponsored by the International Section of the Public Relations Society of America.

Chang, W. H. (1989). *Mass media in China: The history and the future.* Ames, IA: Iowa State University Press.

Chen, N. (1992). *Public relations in China: The introduction and development of an occupational field.* Unpublished doctoral dissertation, Ohio University, Athens.

Chen, N., & Culbertson, H. M. (1992). Two contrasting approaches of government public relations in mainland China. *Public Relations Quarterly, 37*(3), 36–41.

Chen, N., & Culbertson, H. M. (1996a). Guest relations: A demanding but constrained role for lady public relations practitioners in mainland China. *Public Relations Review, 22,* 279–296.

Chen, N., & Culbertson, H. M. (1996b November). *Public relations education in the People's Republic of China: A tentative look at the process.* Paper presented at the meeting the Association for the Advancement of Policy, Research, and Development in the Third World, Cancun, Mexico.

Chu, L. L. (1999). Continuity and change in China's media reform. *Journal of Communication, 44,* 4–21.

Culbertson, H. M. (1994, August). *Cultural beliefs: A focus of study in cross-cultural public relations.* Paper presented at the meeting of the Association for Education in Journalism and Mass Communication, Atlanta, GA.

Culbertson, H. M. (1997). China Daily coverage of rural development: A broad window or a small peep-hole? *Gazette, 59,* 105–120.

Culbertson, H. M., & Chen, N. (2001). Nationality 1, audience 0: A study of factors shaping news about the 1997 Hong Kong handover. *International Communication Bulletin, 36*(1–2), 4–19.

Dahun, X. (2000–2001, Winter). Our life-long struggle for human rights. *China Right Forum,* pp. 13–21.

Diamond, L., & Myers, R. H. (2000). Introduction: Elections and democracy in greater China. *China Quarterly, 162,* 365–386.

Dobson, B. (2002, August). *Public relations in China and Japan today.* Teleconference presentation sponsored by the International Section of the Public Relations Society of America.

Dozier, D. M., with Grunig, L. A., & Grunig, J. E. (1995). *Manager's guide to excellence in public relations and communication management.* Mahwah, NJ: Lawrence Erlbaum Associates.

Earley, P. C. (1989). Social loafing and collectivism: A comparison of the United States and the People's Republic of China. *Administrative Science Quarterly, 34,* 565–581.

Elliott, C. (1998). Defining development news values: An examination of press releases from the New China News Agency. In B. T. McIntyre (Ed.), *Mass media in the Asian Pacific* (pp. 72–84). Philadelphia: Multi-lingual Matters Ltd.

FlorCruz, J. A. (1999). Chinese media in flux. *Media Studies Journal, 13*(2), 42–46.

Freire, P. (1997). *Pedagogy of the oppressed.* New York: Continuum.

Gans, H. J. (1980). *Deciding what's news.* New York: Vintage Press.

Goffman, E. (1971). *Relations in public.* New York: Harper Torchbooks.

Graham, J. L., Mintu, A. T., & Rodgers, W. (1994). Explorations of negotiation behaviors in 10 foreign cultures, using a model developed in the United States. *Management Science, 40,* 72–95.

Grunig, J. E. (1992). *Excellence in public relations and communication management.* Hillsdale, NJ: Lawrence Erlbaum Associates.

Grunig, J. E., & Hunt, T. (1984). *Managing public relations.* New York: Holt, Rinchart & Winston.

Guan, S. (2000). A comparison of Sino–American thinking patterns and the function of Chinese characters in the difference. In D. R. Heisey (Ed.), *Chinese perspectives in rhetoric and communication* (pp. 25–43). Stamford, CT: Ablex.

Guo, X. (2001, June). Land expropriation and rural conflicts in China. *China Quarterly, 166,* 422–439.

Hall, E. T. (1965). *The silent language.* Greenwich, CT: Fawcett.

Hang, C. (2001). China's state-tabloids: The rise of "city newspapers." *Gazette, 63,* 435–450.

He, Z. (2000). Chinese Communist Party press in a tug of war: A political–economy analysis of the *Shenzhen Special Zone Daily.* In C. C. Lee (Ed.), *Communication patterns and bureaucratic control in cultural China: Power, money and media* (pp. 112–151). Evanston, IL: Northwestern University Press.

Hofstede, G. (1984). *Cultural consequences: International differences in work-related values.* Beverly Hills, CA: Sage.

Hofstede, G. (2001). *Culture's consequences: Comparing values, behaviors, institutions, and organizations across nations.* Thousand Oaks, CA: Sage.

Hofstede, G., & Bond, M. H. (1984). Hofstede's cultural dimensions: An independent valuation using Rokeach's value survey. *Journal of Cross-Cultural Psychology, 15,* 417–433.

Hofstede, G., & Bond, M. H. (1998). *Masculinity and femininity: The taboo dimensions of national cultures.* Thousand Oaks, CA: Sage.

Hong, J., & Cuthbert, M. (1991). Media reform in China since 1978: Background factors, problems and future trends. *Gazette, 47,* 141–158.

Huesca, R. (2001). Conceptual contributions of new social movements to development communication research. *Communication Theory, 11,* 415–433.

Kissinger, H. A. (1997, March 3). The philosopher and pragmatist. *Newsweek,* pp. 42–47.

Latham, K. (2000). Nothing but the truth: News media, power and hegemony in south China. *China Quarterly, 163,* 633–654.

Lee, C. C. (2000). Chinese communication: Prisms, trajectories and modes of understanding. In C. C. Lee (Ed.), *Communication patterns and bureaucratic control in cultural China: Power, money and media.* (pp. 3–44). Evanston, IL: Northwestern University Press.

Lee, P. S. (1994). Mass communication and national development in China: Media roles reconsidered. *Journal of Communication, 44*(3), 22–37.

Lu, X. (2000). The influence of classical Chinese rhetoric on contemporary Chinese political communication and social relations. In D. R. Heisey (Ed.), *Chinese perspectives in rhetoric and communication* (pp. 3–23). Stamford, CT: Ablex.

Luo, Y. (1999). Time-based experience and international expansion: The case of an emerging economy. *Journal of Management Studies, 36,* 505–534.

Ma, E. K. (2000). Rethinking media studies: The case of China. In J. Curran & M. J. Park (Eds.), *De-westernizing media studies* (pp. 21–34). New York: Routledge.

Mann, J. (1989). *Beijing Jeep: The short unhappy romance of American business in China.* New York: Simon & Schuster.

Meissner, W. (2002). Culture relations between China and member states of the European Union. *China Quarterly,* 181–203.

Nathan, A. J. (2001). The Tiananmen papers: An editor's reflections. *China Quarterly, 167,* 724–737.

Ng, R. M. (2000). The influence of Confucianism on Chinese conceptions of power, authority, and the rule of law. In D. R. Heisey (Eds.), *Chinese perspectives in rhetoric and communication* (pp. 45–55). Stamford, CT: Ablex.

Pan, Z. (2000). Improvising reform activities: The changing reality of journalistic practice in China. In C. C. Lee (Ed.), *Communication patterns and bureaucratic control in cultural China: Power, money and media* (pp. 68–111). Evanston, IL: Northwestern University Press.

Park, M. (1998). On Lu Xin's attitude toward the masses. *Chinese Culture, 39*(1), 93–108.

Parsons, T. (1951). *The social system.* London: Routledge & Kegan Paul.

Pastor, R. A., & Tan, Q. (2000). The meaning of China's village elections. *China Quarterly, 162,* 490–512.

Presbyterian Mission Board (2001). China: *Evangelism* and *leadership development,* In the 2002 Mission Yearbook. Louisville, Ky. Presbyterian Church U. S. A.

Qiu, J. L. (2000). Interpreting the Dengist rhetoric of building socialism with Chinese characteristics. In D. R. Heisey (Ed.), *Chinese perspectives in rhetoric and communication* (pp. 249–264). Stamford, CT: Ablex.

Rosen, S. (2000). Seeking appropriate behavior under a socialist market economy. In C. C. Lee (Ed.), *Communication patterns and bureaucratic control in cultural China: Power, money and media* (pp. 152–178). Evanston, IL: Northwestern University Press.

Saich, T. (2000, March). Negotiating the state: The development of social organizations in China. *China Quarterly, 161,* 124–141.

Schoenhals, M. (1999). Political movements, change and stability: The Chinese Communist Party in power. *China Quarterly, 159,* 595–605.

Schramm, W., Chu, G. C., & Yu, F. T. C. (1976). China's experience with development communication: How transferable is it? In G. Chu, F. Hung, W. Schramm, S. Uhalley, Jr., & F. T. C. Yu (Eds.), Communication and development in China (pp. 85–101). *Communication Monographs* (Vol. 1). Honolulu, HI: East–West Center.

Shi, T. (2000). Cultural values and democracy in the People's Republic of China. *China Quarterly, 162,* 540–559.

Siebert, F., Peterson, T., & Schramm, W. (1956). *Four theories of the press.* Urbana, IL: University of Illinois Press.

Sparks, C. (2000). Media theory after the fall of European communism. In J. Curran & M. J. Park (Eds.), *De-westernizing media studies* (pp. 35–49). London: Routledge.

Sriramesh, K. (1996). Power distance and public relations: An ethnographic study of southern Indian organizations. In H. M. Culbertson & N. Chen (Eds.), *International public relations: A comparative analysis* (pp. 171–190). Mahwah, NJ: Lawrence Erlbaum Associates.

Sriramesh, K., Grunig, J. E., & Dozier, D. (1996). Observation and measurement of two dimensions of organizational culture and their relationship to public relations. *Journal of Public Relations Research, 8,* 229–261.

Sriramesh, K., & White, J. (1992). Societal culture and public relations. In J. E. Grunig (Ed.), *Excellence in public relations and communication management* (pp. 597–614). Hillsdale, NJ: Lawrence Erlbaum Associates.

Taylor, M. (2000). Cultural variance as a challenge to global public relations: A case study of the Coca-Cola scare in Europe. *Public Relations Review, 16,* 277–293.

Verčič, D., Grunig, L. A. & Grunig, J. E. (1996). Global and specific principles of public relations: Evidence from Slovenia. In H. Culbertson & N. Chen (Eds.), *International public relations: A comparative analysis* (pp. 31–65). Mawhaw, NJ: Lawrence Erlbaum Associates.

Wu, G. (2000). One head, many mouths: Diversifying press structures in reform China. In C. C. Lee (Ed.), *Communication patterns and bureaucratic control in cultural China: Power, money and media* (pp. 45–67). Evanston, IL: Northwestern University Press.

Xiao, X. (2000). Sun Yat-Sen's rhetoric of cultural nationalism. In D. R. Heisey (Ed.), *Chinese perspectives in rhetoric and communication* (pp. 165–177). Stamford, CT: Ablex.

Yan, L. (2000). China. In S. A. Gunartne (Ed.), *Handbook of the media in Asia* (pp. 497–526). Thousand Oaks, CA: Sage.

Yang, M. M. (1994). *Gifts, favors and banquets: The art of social relationships in China.* Ithaca, NY: Cornell University Press.

Yanhai, W. (2000–2001, Winter). A strange love affair. *China Rights Forum,* pp. 3–9.

Yankelovich, D. (1981). *New rules: Searching for self-fulfillment in a world turned upside down.* New York: Random House.

Yu, F. T. C. (1963). Communications and politics in communist China. In L. W. Pye (Ed.), *Communications and political development* (pp. 259–297). Princeton, NJ: Princeton University Press.

Yu, X. (1994). Professionalization without guarantees. *Gazette, 53,* 23–41.

Yu, X. (2000). Examining the impact of cultural values and cultural assumptions on motivational factors in the Chinese organizational context: A cross-cultural perspective. In D. R. Heisey (Ed.), *Chinese perspectives in rhetoric and communication* (pp. 119–138). Stamford, CT: Ablex.

Zhang, N. (2000). Official role models and unofficial responses: Problems of model emulation in post-Mao China. In D. R. Heisey (Ed.), *Chinese perspectives in rhetoric and communication* (pp. 67–85). Stamford, CT: Ablex.

CHAPTER

11

SHARING THE TRANSFORMATION: PUBLIC RELATIONS AND THE UAE COME OF AGE

BADRAN A. BADRAN
JUDY VANSLYKE TURK
TIMOTHY N. WALTERS

Much like the country itself, the practice of public relations in the United Arab Emirates (UAE) has undergone a profound evolution during its short history of 30 years. As the country has grown, so too has the practice of public relations. Once no agencies existed, but today global multinational public relations firms have established a presence in the UAE, some with an equity relationship with their local partners, some as fully owned branches of global firms based in the United States or Europe, and others through affiliates. Companies like Team: Young and Rubicam, Gulf Hill and Knowlton, and Burston–Marsteller operate alongside local, smaller companies, competing for the same dollars and dirhams.

Fueling the development of these agencies has been the explosive growth of the country. The simple, clear, and deep understanding of national priorities set by President His Highness Sheikh Zayed bin Sultan Al Nahyan, who has led the country since its formation in 1971, has moved the UAE to a diversified economy with one of the world's highest standards of living. Once petrocarbons dominated, but now the UAE has broadened its economic scope. The federal government has invested heavily in tourism, aviation, re-export commerce, and recently telecommunications, and it has made progress in shifting the UAE economy from its sole dependence on oil.

The practice of public relations has experienced a parallel growth and increase in sophistication. What once was viewed as the domain of good-looking people who received visitors, provided hospitality, and arranged protocol, is now looked at as a business function, dedicated to managing the resources of the organization for achieving organizational goals.

198

Helping to make the industry more professional is the Middle East Public Relations Association (MEPRA), which was launched in 2001 with the goal of increasing awareness, raising the level of professionalism, and providing a voice for the public relations industry. One of the association's main goals is to assure that its members adhere to a professional code of conduct.

HISTORY AND DEVELOPMENT OF THE COUNTRY

At about 83,000 km², the UAE occupies territory a little smaller than state of Maine in the United States or about four fifths the size of Tasmania. The UAE, a union of seven emirates, is a land of stark contrasts, combining natural wonders such as mountains, beaches, oases, and desert with gleaming man-made modern cities (Babbili & Hussain, 1994, p. 294; see also *Dubai Explorer*, 2001). Two geographical features—the ocean and the desert—have long dictated the pulse of life in this region (Babbili & Hussain, 1994, p. 294). Offshore islands, coral reefs, and salt marshes fill the Arabian Gulf coast, whereas gravel plain and barren desert span the vast inland. To the east the Hajar Mountains rise from the desert, lumbering northward into the Musandam peninsula at the mouth of the Arabian Gulf and reaching an apex of 1,527 m at Jabal Yibir. The western interior of the federation, most belonging to Abu Dhabi, consists mainly of desert dotted with oases (*UAE Yearbook*, 2000/2001, pp. 29–30).

The UAE lies in an arid belt extending across Asia and North Africa, bisected by the Tropic of Cancer. Noticeable variations in climate exist among the coastal regions, interior deserts, and mountains. From November to March mean daytime temperatures are 26°C; nighttime temperatures drop to an almost crisp 15°C. In the summer, temperatures can top out at a life-threatening 50°C. An average of less than 6.5 cm of annual rainfall occurs mainly between November and March, makeing the country's rising population dependent on expensive desalinization (*UAE Yearbook*, 2000/2001, pp. 29–30; *Dubai Explorer*, 2001; CIA, 2001). Sand storms often occur usually from the shamal, a powerful wind from the north or west, that kicks up sand during the winter, whereas the hot-tongued khamsin blows hot air and sand during the summer.

Archaeological evidence has painted a picture of human inhabitance stretching back several thousand years, perhaps as early as 5000 B.C. Early records show sophisticated societies that successfully exploited the environment, raising herds of sheep, goats, and cattle where possible, traversing the long "sand sea" trade routes when necessary, and using the 1,318 km-long coastline to dive for pearls and engage in seafaring occupations such as fishing and trading across the gulf (*UAE Yearbook*, 2000, 2001, pp. 42–43, 46, 51–52, 56).

Some premodern forces shaping the UAE are similar to those affecting other regions in the Middle East. These include the tribal system, a form of governmental rule and societal organization reaching back thousands of years. Ibn Khaldun (1332–1406) provided insight into this organization, much of which is as pertinent to society today it was 6 centuries ago (Barfield, 1990, pp. 154–163). Ibn Khaldun observed that the tribal system relied on actual descent and blood or marital ties for the lower ranks and on political ties for the higher ranks. Continued rule was based on respect and veneration (the notion of *asabiyya*) rather than coercion. It still is, although the blend of these principles varies from emirate to emirate (Van Der Meulen, 1997, pp. 21, 33).

During the British occupation, tribal forms of government were encouraged for the sake of domestic tranquility. The consequences of the decision to manage through the tribal system was far-reaching, confirming the rulers' autonomy and power (Van Der Meulen, 1997). When the UAE moved to independence in 1971, these power organizations carried forward. That meant that the structure and the history of the estimated 42 to 45 Arab tribes located within the UAE were reflected in the country's political process. So, by both law and custom, the Supreme Council of Rulers, the presidency, the Council of Ministers, and the Federal National Council respect and confirm the power of the ruling families in each emirate and the ruling families' relationships with the prominent tribes (Van Der Meulen, 1997, p. 10).

The paramount role of the tribes and their rulers has continued to date; consequently, the legitimacy of the families is unchallenged (Barfield, 1990, p. 156; Van Der Meulen, 1997, p. 10). That means any discussion of UAE's governmental structure must begin from the standpoint of internal tribal origins, partly because many members of the extended family hold high governmental and nongovernmental positions (Tibi, 1990; Van Der Meulen, 1997). That also means family names such as Al Nahyan, Al Maktoum, Al Qasimi, Al Mu'alla, Al Nuaimi, and Al Sharqi appear on the rosters of those holding vital governmental and key business positions.

EVOLUTION AND DEFINITION OF THE PUBLIC RELATIONS PROFESSION

The Western model of public relations in the UAE is a new phenomenon that emerged in the early 1970s. As Cutlip and Broom (1985) noted, the term *public relations* has greatly varying connotations in the United States. Sriramesh and White (1992) argued that cultural differences among societies must affect how public relations is practiced by people within different societies (p. 597). In the Arab World, the nature, goals, roles, and functions of public relations are often described as "vague" (Al Enad, 1990, p. 24).

The vagueness has more to do with the traditional view of public relations than the modern one. Traditionally, public relations was used to describe those individuals and departments whose duties usually were restricted to procuring visas, arranging transportation, and performing hospitality functions (Ayish & Kruckeberg, 1999, p. 124). Moreover, many so called "public relations offices" secured contracts for domestic maids from Southeast Asian countries to work in the UAE and provided secretarial services, such as typing and copying documents (Badran, 1994, p. 3).

The Department of Mass Communication at the UAE University (UAEU) surveyed public relations perceptions and activities in public and private organizations in four major UAE cities in 1994 (Badran, 1994). The survey indicated that most respondents viewed public relations as embodying visitor reception and hospitality, protocol arrangements, and information documentation. Very few respondents viewed public relations as part of the institutional decision-making mechanism.

As for perceptions of a professional public relations practitioner, many respondents thought of him or her as good-looking, educated, open-minded, and highly sociable. Almost all placed a high value on building positive images for their organizations and on satisfying the needs and tastes of the general public. Among the functions not considered within the domain of public relations practice in the UAE were planning; counseling management; anticipating, analyzing, and interpreting public opinion; and managing the resources of the organization for achieving its goals (Badran, 1994, p. 9).

Although some job descriptions for public relations officers in public and private organizations today still reflect the early press agentry model of public relations practice, by and large the modern definition of public relations as a management function is taking hold in the UAE. This change was caused by the arrival of professional public relations agencies in the 1970s and the introduction of public relations education in the country in the 1990s. Though programs generally are heavily oriented toward courses on new technologies, communications departments at the University of Sharjah, American University of Sharjah, American University of Dubai, UAEU, and Zayed University teach either public relations or advertising courses or both.

In the Arab world, the advertising and public relations business reportedly dates back to the 1930s. It began in the Levant as a simple industry, catering to basic needs (Ghassoub, 2002, p. 64). The Lebanese civil war in the mid-1970s forced many advertising and public relations professionals to flee Lebanon. Some, like Eddie Moutran, Akram Miknas, Talal El Makdessi, and Ramzi Raad, chose to work in the gulf. These professionals and a few others like Burhan Beidas and Tareq Noor are usually referred to as advertising legends in the Middle East. They founded successful agencies like Fortune Promoseven, Memac, Intermarkets, and PubliGraphics in Bahrain, Saudi Arabia, the UAE, and elsewhere ("Talking Heads," 2001).

According to Joseph Ghassoub, vice president of the International Advertising Association and managing partner of Team: Young and Rubicam, the real explosion came with the boom in satellite television after the Gulf War. The free-to-air satellite channels that began beaming into people's homes and a concurrent boom in the print media led to this upsurge. Since then, Ghassoub (2002, p. 64) contended, advertising and public relations budgets have been growing at an average rate of 15% per year throughout the region. Standard practice in the UAE and the rest of the gulf was the establishment of an all-purpose company that would offer all advertising, marketing, public relations, and below-the-line services. Nowadays, full-service agencies have given way to segmented and specialized operations.

To mark the development and growing sophistication of the public relations industry, MEPRA was launched in 2001 and officially licensed by the government the following year. MEPRA's main role is "to increase awareness and gain real understanding for public relations as an important economic activity in the region, raise the level of professionalism in public relations and provide a unified voice for the public relations industry to advise, inform and educate the Middle East market about public relations practice."

MEPRA's Chairman Sadri Barrage said public relations is becoming much more widely understood by business and government organizations in the UAE and is becoming increasingly recognized as a strategic communications tool. "The market here has still a lot to learn, however, and this is one of MEPRA's main objectives." Nevertheless, he acknowledged that the public relations industry is still facing a great deal of ignorance (S. Barrage, personal communication, March, 2002). One of MEPRA's key objectives is to create educational forums in the region for young nationals to consider public relations as an exciting career opportunity (MEPRA, 2002). MEPRA defines public relations as "the discipline that looks after reputation with the aim of earning understanding and support, and influencing opinion and behavior." According to MEPRA, public relations also embodies the planned and sustained effort to establish and maintain goodwill and mutual understanding between an organization and its publics (S. Barrage, personal communication, March 15, 2002).

STATUS OF THE PROFESSION

Despite its short history of about 30 years, the UAE public relations and advertising market today includes both global players and local agencies. Global multinationals have established a presence in the UAE, some with an equity relationship with their local partners, some as fully owned-branches, and some through affiliates. The largest professional agencies have their headquarters in Dubai, the UAE's center for business and commerce. The capital, Abu Dhabi, has one or two large agencies and a number of smaller agencies. The same is true in Sharjah, the third largest emirate.

Until recently, the main practitioners of public relations and buyers of public relations services have been multinational businesses and institutions. This is not just because of their economic size but also because of their appreciation of the importance of public relations. Organizations in the area are becoming increasingly sophisticated in their use of communications, which in turn is resulting in public relations becoming a more common practice in the region.

Promoseven PR is part of the Promoseven Network and is considered the market leader in the UAE. Promoseven is an affiliate of McCann–Erickson World Group. In a recent *Gulf Marketing Review* survey of local and multinational advertisers, this agency ranked first among agencies and was the agency with the highest awareness level among clients ("Shining Stars," 2001). Promoseven PR provides public, press, and government relations to independent clients and the agency's advertising clients. It provides organizational services of press offices for sporting events and international exhibitions, conferences, and seminars. In addition, it has an Arab media monitoring service and a specialized unit for product launches, conferences, and special events in all the Gulf Coast Council (GCC), Levant, and North African countries (*Promoseven*, 2001).

Promoseven PR reports that only 30% of its clients have appointed them on a project basis, with the remainder either on a retainer basis or a mix of retainer and project. What is interesting is that 10% of its customers also have an in-house unit.

Other major players include Asda'a Public Relations (the regional affiliate of Burson-Marsteller), Memac, Ogilvy and Mather, Team: Young and Rubicam, Gulf Hill and Knowlton, RSCG, and Bates Pan Gulf. These and smaller agencies compete for approximately $25 million spent on public relations annually in the UAE.

These firms consider people, time, and knowledge as the key resources for generating revenue for a public relations consultancy. Generally, UAE public sector organizations adopt one of two solutions for their public relations needs. They either have in-house departments of media or public relations or they outsource public relations services with professional agencies. Those who feel the need for a full in-house department staff it with public relations professionals who perform functions such as media relations, event management, exhibitions, media production, and public opinion research. An example of this group is the Dubai Municipality.

For those who choose to hire a professional public relations agency, the available services are comparable in quality and quantity to anywhere else in the world. For example, Emirates Internet and Multimedia (EIM), a unit of the UAE's sole telecommunications and Internet service provider, is a client of Asda'a public relations. EIM can avail itself of the following services from its public relations firm: perception management, issues management, business-to-business communication, consumer awareness and education, internal communications, media relations, government relations, investor relations, technology communications, media training, crisis communications, corporate advertising, event management, publishing (both print and web-based), and media monitoring.

Jock Wilson, regional director of Promoseven PR, noted that there is a tendency among UAE clients to focus too much on media relations. Public relations, he said, should be "the active management of an organization's reputation to this stakeholders' audience." Stakeholders include employees, customers, investors, suppliers, government institutions, and the media (Mirabel, October 2001, p. 41). Chair of MEPRA Sadri Barrage has confirmed that media relations is the most commonly used public relations function in the UAE. "Most consultancies in our region offer a wide range of services that cover the entire spectrum of public relations activities but depending on the client profile, I would say that media relations remains the cornerstone of our practice" (S. Barrage, personal communication, March, 2002).

Asda'a's Managing Director Sunil John shares this view. "A typical client's view," John said, "is that public relations is a media relations service and is all about press conferences and press relations." He added, however, that this attitude is changing as more clients today look to public relations more as a strategic consultancy (Mirabel, 2001, p. 42). Current public relations services offered include media monitoring and evaluation, lobbying, sponsorships, events, promotions, and competitions. Future growth areas include corporate communications, covering employee and investor relations, crisis management, and the release of financial information.

PROFESSIONALISM IN THE PUBLIC RELATIONS INDUSTRY

According to MEPRA, most local and regional consultancies enjoy a high level of professionalism. Generally speaking, private and public sectors vary in the level of professionalism exhibited. Although the majority of public relations agencies maintain high professional standards, the public sector, which has in-house public relations departments, practices a narrower range of functions with varying degrees of professionalism. The quality of public relations services rendered also varies between the main urban centers of Dubai and Abu Dhabi and the rest of the country. Outside of these two cities, practices are less professional due to the scarcity of skilled and trained professionals.

Several issues face the profession in the UAE. One is price-cutting (undercutting the competition). This is the practice of smaller operators who cater to price-conscious clients. Price-cutting, although not practiced by all, affects standards and leads to price wars. Another issue is the practice of managing accounts for two or more competitors simultaneously, which is perhaps more of a problem in the advertising industry but it also occurs in the public relations industry. Lastly, gifts and other contributions that some public relations agencies and organizations offer to media professionals in exchange for positive editorial coverage raise serious ethical questions. Anecdotal evidence exists of offers of expensive items as "gifts" to reporters and editors in the UAE.

The practice of publishing press releases verbatim is also customary in some UAE publications compared with the West where the media closely scrutinize and edit news releases. MEPRA's chair says that the adherence of its members to the association's professional code of conduct ensures adherence to high ethics. For us, Barrage said, this a crucial matter of survival. "PR ethics . . . are high on the list of any professional discussions we may have" (S. Barrage, personal communication, March, 2002).

INFRASTRUCTURE AND INTERNATIONAL PUBLIC RELATIONS

The Nation's Political System

Seven rulers exercise political power over a federation established in 1971. None of the emirates has any democratically elected individuals or institutions, and their rule has been both tradition based and patriarchal (United States Department of State, 2001). Because political parties and elections are prohibited, the citizens of the UAE cannot change their government democratically. Citizens may express concerns directly to their rulers by traditional means including the *majlis*—a public forum (International Press Institute [IPI], 2000; also see United States Department of State, 2001).

The seven emirate rulers constitute the Federal Supreme Council, the highest legislative and executive body. The council selects a president and a vice president from its membership, and the president appoints the prime minister and cabinet. The cabinet manages the federation on a day-to-day basis. A consultative body, the Federal National Council, comprised of advisors appointed by the emirate rulers, has no legislative authority, but it questions government ministers in open sessions and makes policy recommendations to the cabinet (United States Department of State, 2001).

Each emirate retains control over its own oil and mineral wealth, some parts of internal security, and some regulation of internal and external commerce. The federal government has primacy in matters of defense and foreign policy, some aspects of internal security, and, increasingly, in the supply of government services (United States Department of State, 2001).

The judiciary generally is independent, but political leaders can review its decisions. The legal system of the UAE is based on a constitution approved by the Federal National Council in 1996, replacing the provisional documents that had been renewed every 5 years since the country's creation in 1971 (www.infoprod.co.il/uae2a.htm). Based on tradition, the constitution, and legislation, the legal system of the UAE has been influenced by Islamic, Roman, and French law (www.law.emory.edu/IFL /legal/UAE.htm; also see www.uottawa.ca. world-legal-systems/eng-common.htm). Common law principles have become important in commercial contracts, and Federal Law No. 40 modernized intellectual property law in 1992 (Abu Ghazaleh, 2002; Dubaiinc, 2001; IPR, 2001). Local government varies from emirate to emirate and is very much a product of the country's growth and urbanization. Hence, the largest, most prosperous emirate, Abu Dhabi, has the most complex local government (*UAE Yearbook*, 2000/2001).

One notable feature remaining from the honored past is the custom of the *majlis*. Traditionally, the sheikh or ruler of an emirate was the leader of the most powerful tribe, and each individual tribe, and often each of its various subsections, also generally had a chief or sheikh. Such leaders kept their authority only as long as they could retain the loyalty and support of their people. Part of that process was the unwritten (but strong) principle that the people should have free access to their sheikh by means of a frequent *majlis*, or public council, in which his fellow tribesmen could voice their opinions.

Today, the *majlis* has maintained its relevance. In large emirates, the ruler and several senior family members hold open *majlis*es. In smaller emirates, the *majlis* of the ruler himself, or of the crown prince or deputy ruler, remain the main focus. To these come traditional-minded tribesmen who may have waited months for the opportunity to speak with their ruler directly, rather than to pursue their requests or complaints through a modern government structure.

In the *majlis*, often heated discussions between sheikhs and other citizens cover everything from questions about governmental policy to relations with neighboring countries. On matters more directly affecting individuals, debates occur before a consensus approach evolves. Frequently, that consensus is later reflected in changes in government policy (taken from http://www.iornet.org /newiornet/uae2.htm).

Level of Economic Development

The UAE has undergone a profound transformation from an impoverished region of small desert principalities to a modern state with a high standard of living. The simple, clear, and deep understanding by President His Highness Sheikh Zayed bin Sultan Al Nahyan of national priorities has fueled this growth. Growth flowed from one early decision on managing water:

> The first fundamental change, and the most important . . . (was) the availability of drinking water. The bringing of water was . . . important. After (water came) everything started changing. Housing became available when there was none before, then infrastructure and everything else. Our policy was first to concentrate all our efforts to develop this country, and to develop its citizens. (*UAE Yearbook*, 1995, p. 19)

Today, the UAE reflects His Highness President Nahyan's dream. It has an oil-and-gas driven economy with an estimated 2000 gross domestic product (GDP) per capita of approximately $22,800 (in purchasing power parity [PPP]) and Human Development Indicators ranking it in the top portion of the Human Development Index (CIA, 2001; Human Development Indicators, 2001, p. 141; *UAE Yearbook*, 2000/2001). These figures compare favorably to PPP figures of neighboring countries: Bahrain, $15,900; Egypt, $3,600; India, $2,200; Iraq, $2,500; Kuwait, $15,000; Oman, $7,700; Pakistan, $2,000; Qatar, $20,300; Saudi Arabia, $10,500; and Syria, $3,100 (CIA, 2001).

Although overall per capita PPP is high in the UAE, disparity exists between the emirates. Income distribution is skewed toward Abu Dhabi and Dubai, a product of oil and gas production. Abu Dhabi and Dubai have per capita GDPs of $23,929 and $16,094, respectively; Sharjah's is $9,838, Ras Al Khaimah's is $8,076, Ajman's is $6.047, Fujairah's is $7,955, and Umm Al Quwain's is $7,154 (Al Sadik, n.d., p. 203). Thus, economic development in the UAE is much the tale of its two largest cities.

As oil and gas revenues flow from the wellhead, life is lived large with the Emirati equivalent of two cars in every garage because the emirate of Abu Dhabi is generous with its oil revenue. The federal government supports the trappings of an easy life with low-cost education and medicine, high-paying jobs, short working hours, and inexpensive housing loans for nationals. Inspired by the benevolent leadership of President His Highness Sheikh Zayed bin Sultan Al Nahyan who has led the country through its entire existence, the UAE has blossomed in the desert and has taken steps to move away from its oil dependence.

The federal government has invested heavily in tourism, aviation, re-export commerce, and, more recently, telecommunications. It has made progress in shifting the UAE economy from an overdependence on petrocarbons. In 1975, crude oil contributed to about 68% of the total economy. By 1998, that figure had fallen to about 22%. As oil dependence fell, manufacturing grew from less than 1% of the economy in 1975 to 12.4%. Commerce, restaurants, and hotels went from about 9% to about 14% and real estate from 2.5% to 10.5% (Shihab, n.d., p. 253).

In facilitating this shift, the country's leadership has recognized that the UAE must make more of its human resources. Devoid of most natural resources except for petrocarbons, the UAE, particularly the emirate of Dubai, has invested billions of dirhams in high technology. The great dream is that this human capital, with its various skills and abilities, can create income-yielding activities and serve as pillar of the future (G. J. Walters, 2001, p. 82). Technology (and technology-related communication) is a great hope for the future; yet, although it offers promise, it presents significant challenges as well. As information technology science and technology come to propel the economy, that same science and technology will not only provide jobs but gateways to knowledge capable of empowering individuals. This empowerment is sure to challenge traditional notions of society and how that society functions in the UAE.

Level of Activism

In Arab and Islamic societies people serve families and families serve society, with the individual finishing last (Nawar, 2000; Patai, 1983). For most, the rule of the family is the norm. There are no political parties and no freedoms other than those the ruler offers his "family" or those that the head of a household offers his wife and children. Across the UAE, families also share many common characteristics—the first of which is an abiding dedication to Islam. Muslims have experienced no need for the development of secularism, as has the West. Indeed, Islam is not a "matter of religion as Westerners understand it, "said Mary-Jane Deeb, adjunct professor at American University. Islam is perceived by Muslims as a total way of life. "Conservative Muslims see the West imposing an entire system of economic, political and social values that strike at the heart of Islamic way of life. Westerners would consider most of these values secular, but to conservative Muslims almost nothing is secular. The Koran governs everything . . ." (cited in Ringle, 2001 p. C01). Thus, in the UAE Islam is normative, the sustaining force. It permeates the entire society (Lewis, 1994; Patai, 1983).

Besides Islam, other strands of a long, proud history are woven into the tapestry of society. The Arabic language is one strand. It carries with it emotions, feelings, and thoughts, creating an artistic expression of sound and rhythm that Naguib Mahfouz described as "searching for tunes in the air" (Mahfouz, 1986, p. 33). Loyalty and an emphasis on honor, both drawn from a simpler past, are other valued traits (Patai, 1983).

The advent of political Islam has made issues inherent in economic modernization of society a triangulated problem. The government has the power to control and suppress. Some religious fundamentalists fear those who advocate too much change too quickly and are concerned about the destruction of the traditional values they hold dear. Others, anxious for development, advocate enhanced (and Westernized) freedoms (Nawar, 2000). Thus, navigating the shoals of change will require steady hands and a delicate touch as the Emirates comes to grips with the demands of a new economy (see Kristof, 2002).

Legal Infrastructure

Law by itself does not determine how free, pluralistic, or independent the media will be. That is because the interaction between legal and social–cultural institutions define this freedom (Price & Krug, 2000, pp. 8–10). Laws help, of course, but even authoritarian societies have mastered the vocabulary of free expression (and access to that expression) and have written it into their constitutions (see International Constitutional Law, n.d.).

The will of the people and the development of civic society have great impact on the reality of what actually happens (Bryant, 1995; Diamond, 1994; Geremek, 1992; O'Donnell & Schmitter, 1986). Civic society exists above the individual level but below that of the state and is institutionalized and generalized through law, custom, and practice. In civic society, complex networks of economic, social, and cultural practices based on friendship, family, the market, and voluntary association influence daily life (Wapner, 1995). Sometimes, but not always, civic society is a precursor to a democratic state (Bryant, 1995; Diamond, 1994; Geremek, 1992; O'Donnell & Schmitter, 1986).

Such civic forces are in play in the UAE, where kinship and marriage count, and extended family networks wield enormous power in all aspects of life. So anything related to lifestyle becomes inexorably intertwined with family, tradition, religion, and heritage (see, e.g., Essoulami, 2001; Za'Za', 2002).

CULTURE AND PUBLIC RELATIONS

Social Cultural Aspects of the UAE

As explained in chapter 1, culture provides a road map for how an individual should function in society, and the defining markers of that roadway include knowledge, beliefs, art, morals, law, custom, capabilities, habits, and values acquired by individuals in their daily living. We are not born with the knowledge of how to decipher this map. Culture (and its constituent parts) is a learned, shared, compelling, interrelated set of symbols whose meanings provide orientations for members of a society.

A focus on the individual, isolated, and independent is embedded in the values and culture of Western societies such as the United States (Connard, 1996). Traditionally, Arabic and Islamic societies such as the UAE have focused more on the group and on interrelated networks, defined in no small measure by religion and circles of kinship. But the underlying social environments are undergoing change as the UAE moves toward a more urban, diverse, and modern economy. This transition may be producing a transitional society (Connard, 1996).

Women in the UAE, as in other places, have several models of choice for life. One is a three-way model suggesting that those choices are leisure, paid work in the office or unpaid work in the home (Jalilvand, 2000). The UAE government's public policy views women in a dual role. They are both the hand that rocks the cradle and the force that runs the economy. It is the policy of the government to increase the number of women from the current level of about 15% of the workforce to about 50% by the year 2020. As this unfolds, women, and no doubt all of society, will feel the tug of push–pull forces affecting personal and societal values and shaking the traditional model of the household (Jaliivand, 2000, p. 27; also see Iglehart, 1979; Mott & Shapiro, 1983). Some driving forces that are helping to catapult the current pioneering generation of women into the marketplace are the changes in education, the perceived worth of education, the restructuring of the economy, and increasing urbanization. These have a profound effect on the evolving society in the UAE as well.

Perhaps equipoised is the best description of Arabic and Islamic society as it relates to the transitional woman. Much of what has occurred in the UAE since its formation as a nation in 1971 has been the product of the aging President His Highness Sheikh Zayed bin Sultan Al Nahyan whose birth year is listed as somewhere between 1908 and 1915 (Van Der Meulen, 1997 p. 109). Whether the country stays the course after his death is unclear.

Is the UAE undergoing a cultural revitalization? Does the whole culture believe that the old ways do not work best? Or, is there a hard core that will return to traditional mores and ways if the leadership that succeeds His Highness President Zayed is less forward-looking than that of the founding President (Walters, T. & Walters, L., 2002)?

The answers, though unclear, will chart the course for the UAE's future, because of Islam's relationship to all things. Traditional Islamic order asserts that all things spring from the God-given Holy Law of Islam (Lewis, 1994, p. 37). Islamic order does several things: It creates a shorthand for operating in life, impacts a set of values, and establishes order in the family. Moreover, it serves as a reference point so that Muslims can say that something is taboo (*haram*—forbidden) or permitted (*halal*—permissible or allowed).

For conservative Muslims, alteration of core values is nothing less than an attack on their faith. "Brought up in a complex but functioning system of social loyalties and responsibilities, (a conservation male) finds those loyalties, defined by faith and kin, denounced as sectarian and nepotistic, and those responsibilities derided and abandoned in favor of capitalistic acquisitiveness or socialistic expropriations" (Lewis, 1993, p. 39). Many male Muslims will not want to see their supremacy lost in their own homes "to emancipated women and rebellious children" (p. 40). Because children develop within the family and because outside forces are buffeting the family ecosystem, the roles of children and adults could be subject to change.

Qualities of UAE Culture

In many ways, the culture of the UAE has begun to diverge from that of the other countries on the Arabian peninsula. Although they share a common religion, high regard for the family, and similar style of governance, the UAE is at the crossroads of modernization. Higher education is greatly valued because the country's leadership wants to develop the UAE as the high-technology hub of the Middle East. Women have become valued not just as wives and mothers but as potential leaders in the workplace, and as this new generation of educated women evolves, so too must the role of men in the society.

So too will the army of expatriate workers on whom the emirates now depends to fuel the country's growth. Today, Nationals comprise about 20% of the 3 million plus population; natives of India and Pakistan account for more than 60%, and fewer than 2% of the population are European. As the announced policy of emiratization takes hold, these proportions will drastically change. As they do, the nature of the society will change as well.

THE MEDIA ENVIRONMENT

Media Control

With the exception of a few privately owned newspapers and radio stations, the UAE broadcast and print media are owned and operated by government departments or government-controlled organizations. Smaller media working in design, photography, advertising, public relations, and printing, among other areas, are privately owned. There are no media in the UAE that are affiliated with political parties. There are only publications by public and private organizations, licensed professional associations, and other nongovernmental organizations.

Recently, there have been signs of a decline in government subsidy for public media and more dependence on advertising or sponsorship for revenue. In fact, the Ministry of Information and Culture has taken the lead in requiring its own media to play by the rules of the private sector. This is in line with a drive by some emirates, such as Abu Dhabi, to privatize their public institutions in a bid to expand sources of income (www.uaeinteract.com, 2001).

The UAE media scene has seen significant changes in the last decade, led by Abu Dhabi and Dubai's efforts to modernize, expand, and create new media enterprises. Developments include an increase in new media outlets, a reform and modernization of older media, creation of Dubai Media City (DMC), application of intellectual property laws in the country, and a new vision of more freedom and less censorship.

In terms of infrastructure, each of the emirates has its own distinct media set up and runs them based on its particular philosophy regarding public media. Abu Dhabi has transformed its media from local to Pan-Arab, with emphasis on strong news and sports programs. Dubai's focus is on business, entertainment, sports, and promoting Dubai as a tourist destination. Sharjah's public media emphasize Islamic, cultural, historical, and children's programs. The Omran brothers, Abdulla and Taryam, own Dar Al Khaleej for Press, Printing & Publishing Ltd. in Sharjah. It publishes *Al Khaleej*, the best selling Arabic daily in the UAE with a circulation of 96,000 (The Times Group, 2002). *Al Khaleej* is a strong proponent of national issues and Pan-Arab causes.

Ajman TV has positioned itself as a favorite station for quiz and game shows, as well as drama and entertainment for the family. In addition to radio stations broadcasting in Arabic in the northern emirates, there are broadcasts in Hindi, Urdu, Malayalam, and English by stations like Umm Al Quwain, Ras Al Khaimah, Radio Asia, and Asianet (*TV and Radio-Guide*, 2002). These broadcasts are mostly intended for Asian expats from India and Pakistan who live and work in the UAE.

Not unlike many other countries, the UAE guarantees freedom of expression in its written constitution. Article 30 protects "freedom of opinion and expressing it verbally, in writing or by other means of expression shall be guaranteed within the limits of the law" (Human Rights Watch, 1999b). Article 31 guarantees "freedom of communication by post, telegraph, or other means of communication and (that) the secrecy thereof shall be guaranteed in accordance with the law" (Human Rights Watch, 1999b).

However it is Article 7 of the Constitution that gives an idea of what "accordance with the law" really means in the UAE. This article declares Islam the official state religion and Islamic *shari'a* (law) the principal source of legislation (Legal Profiles, Islamic Family Law). *Shari'a* is derived from principles of the Koran, explicated by Ijma, or rules that develop through debate and the resultant consensus of religious leaders (Kabbani, n.d.). So the law in the UAE is religious, not secular.

Although controls exist on the media in the UAE, these media are relatively free, particularly when compared with other gulf states (United States Department of State, 2001). The Minister of Information and Culture, a son of His Highness President Zayed, has been quoted as telling the media to "criticize freely," although there is no evidence that journalists have complied, particularly with respect to Emirati rulers and their extended families (Al Bakry, 2001; Human Rights Watch, 1999b; Owais & Matthew, 2000). Federal Law 15 of 1988 requires that all publications be licensed with the Ministry of Information and Culture and delineates acceptable subjects of reporting.

Reporters have established boundaries themselves, practicing self-censorship akin to prior restraint. Journalists censor themselves on sensitive subjects such as the ruling families, Islam, national security, government policy, religion, and relations with neighboring states. "Freedom without responsibility may invite chaos," Ayesha Ibrahim Sultan, head of the UAE journalists association, said. "Freedom and responsibility have to go hand in hand. If we separate them and allow total freedom, it will lead to chaos . . ." (Rahman, 2001). Freedom, then, is not absolute. It is limited because certain social aspects including the morals and values guiding a society must be considered (Rahman, 2001).

In establishing boundaries for expression, the UAE is no different than other societies. The First Amendment of the United States Constitution does not allow complete freedom, and Article 19 of the United Nation's Universal Declaration of Human Rights has exceptions in which governments can restrict information to protect certain interests such as national security, public order, or health or morals in what amounts to prior restraint (Human Rights Watch, 1999a).

The differences about what constitutes a threat to national security, public order, or health or morals rest in the eyes of the beholder. Stakeholders are considering what the limits should be. In a 1998 editorial, Abu Dhabi-based Al Ittihad urged people to adopt a modern cultural concept of freedom and make responsible decisions in real life. The article called for the formulation of an Arab concept of freedom (UAE Editorials, 1998). Just what that formulation might be remains the subject of vigorous debate. Some social forces have voiced hostility to the very pervasive modern media. The UAE, sensing an economic opportunity, has been more liberal than GCC sister states Saudi Arabia or Kuwait (Dubai Press Club, 2002). On May 10, 2001, His Excellency General Sheikh Mohammed bin Rashid Al Maktoum, Crown Prince of Dubai and UAE Minister of Defense, speaking in rather de Tocquevillean terms at the launch of DMC, said:

> We who live in today's cyber age increasingly understand the importance of information and the media that carries this information. The TV set, the newspaper, the radio and the mobile phone are the tools that allow us to utilize this information. But pause and think. If knowledge is power, then the media that brings it to us is the source of that power.
>
> As we look at the dynamic and fast changing media world around us we are continually reminded of the power of media. Improvements in technology are breathing new life into familiar media like TV, radio and print. New and advanced technologies such as the mobile phone and the computer have expanded the horizons and transfer of knowledge and information, making the world like a small village where people can communicate with each other.
>
> I guarantee freedom of expression to all of you. . . . Let us do so responsibly, objectively and with accountability and in the spirit of the social and cultural context in which we live.
>
> This freedom will allow and encourage the Arab media to return home, to broadcast and publish once again from Arab land, and contribute to this new regional media industry.
>
> Always remember, the human mind, once stretched by a new idea, never returns to its original size. It only grows larger. Media has the power to effect change and evolve. (*Gulf News*, 2001 online 11 May for more information see Wheeler, 2001)

The Federal National Council has echoed this sentiment, offered its support for freedom of expression, and stressed the need to support efforts to guard freedom of opinion and expression as provided by the constitution (Dawood, 2001). Although pursuing knowledge has been (and remains) essential to UAE society and is embodied in the Quran, the UAE walks a tightrope between unfettered information flow and protecting cultural heritage (Babbili & Hussain, 1994).

Media Reach

For generations, oral communication was the preferred form of transferring information and stories, and news was passed down from person to person. This has changed as the UAE has modernized. In the 1970s, only 15% of the population was literate. By 2002, that figure had jumped to about 85%, one of the highest on the Arabian Peninsula. At the same time, education in the UAE evolved too. In the school year 1974–1975, the total number of students enrolled in all levels of education was 60,254, with 520 students enrolled in colleges and universities. By 1994–1995, those figures had jumped enormously. The total number of students enrolled in all levels of education was 480,973, with 20,570 students enrolled in colleges and universities. Today these numbers are even higher (Al Sadik, n.d., p. 203).

As education grew, so too did means of communication. Partly because the UAE had not been a reading society and partly reflecting the development of an economic base for advertising, newspapers were slow to develop in the UAE. Even in the late 1960s, no indigenous newspapers were published, and the few newspapers available were imported. Kawas Motivala began publishing a small bulletin several times a week in 1967, but circulation was low. Two years later, *Al Ittihad* (meaning union) became the first permanent regular newspaper, and by 1971 *Emirates News* began its run (Babbili and Hussain, p. 297).

From these modest beginnings, the print industry has grown to include six Arabic language and three English language daily newspapers and more than 160 magazines and journals. Among these are newspapers such as Abu Dhabi-based *Akhbar Al Arab* (founded in 2000), *Al Ittihad* (founded in 1969), *Al Fajr* (founded in 1975), *Al Wihdah* (founded in 1973), Dubai-based *Al Bayan* (founded in 1980), *Khaleej Times* (founded in 1979), the *Gulf News* (founded in 1979), and Sharjah-based *Al Khaleej* (founded in 1970) and *Gulf Today*. Many of these have online versions.

The broadcast media, much like their print counterparts, have a short history in the UAE. Before independence, the British began the first radio service in Sharjah. Radio Abu Dhabi was the first station to broadcast Arabic programs in 1969. In 1971, installation or commissioning of modern studios in Abu Dhabi and Ras Al Khaimah and commercial stations in Abu Dhabi and Sharjah were completed (Babbili & Hussain, 1994, pp. 299–302). The history of television is much the same. The first black-and-white television pictures were broadcast from Abu Dhabi on August 6, 1969. Two years later, PAL color equipment was instated in Abu Dhabi; Dubai television's first broadcast was in 1972 (p. 304).

In January 1999, His Highness President Zayed issued a decree creating Emirates Media Incorporated (EMI) to replace all existing broadcast services. EMI, which is attached to the Ministry of Information and Culture, controls 6 of the country's 14 radio stations and three of the eight television channels. Based in Abu Dhabi, it is run by a board of nine directors, all of whom are nationals. His Excellency Sheikh Abdullah bin Zayed Al Nahyan, the Minister of Information and Culture, serves as chair (*UAE Yearbook*, 2000/2001, pp. 232–233).

Television is delivered over the air, via satellite, or on cable, offering a surprisingly broad menu of viewing alternatives assembled from across the gulf and around the world. The UAE now has eight satellite-delivered channels plus about 30 free-to-air channels. Because of the country's size and relatively flat topography, over the air radio and television reach most parts of the country, except the Hajar Mountains in the east. Electronic fare also includes Orbit Satellite Television, billed as the world's first fully digital, multi-channel, multilingual, direct-to-home, pay-TV and radio satellite service, with over 30 television and radio channels; Showtime Network Arabia, a satellite pay-TV network for the Middle East offering exciting Western entertainment for the entire family; and ART Network, a Pan-Arab satellite pay-TV network. E-Vision Cable TV, operated by Etisalat, the government-run monopoly telecoms provider, offers a basic service of 63 channel: 28 in Arabic, 16 in Hindi, 16 in English, 2 in English, and 1 in German.

The Emirates News Agency, WAM, is run through the Ministry of Information and Culture. It delivers news and features in Arabic and English to radio, television, and local newspapers and has exchange agreements with more than 20 Arab countries. WAM employs about 180 people inside the UAE in bureaus located throughout the emirates and has offices in cities such as Cairo, Beirut, Damascus, London, Paris, Islamabad, Tehran, Washington, DC, and New York.

The UAE is also working hard to develop new media. Launched in November 2000, multibillion dirham DMC was designed to make Dubai the regional center for media businesses and new technology workers (*UAE Yearbook*, 2000/2001, p. 233). Rising next to it on the 500 carefully manicured and watered hectares are Dubai Internet City (DIC) and Dubai Knowledge Village (DKV) (Quinn, 2002 p. 9).

The DIC was the region's first information technology zone and has been viewed by His Excellency General Sheikh Mohammed bin Rashid Al Maktoum, Dubai Crown Prince and the country's Defense Minister, as a project that would benefit Dubai's economy. In September 2001, an estimated 95% of the DIC area had already been spoken for by leading high-technology firms. According to DMC Chief Executive Ahmed bin Bayat, around 500 companies will be located in DIC by the end of 2002, many of them moving from Europe to Dubai (2000 World Press Freedom Review, 2001).

DKV describes itself as "connected learning community that will develop the region's talent pool and accelerate its move to the knowledge economy" (http://www.kv.ae/about/). DKV hopes to achieve several things:

1. Position the Dubai technology, e-commerce, and media free zone as a center of excellence for learning and innovation.
2. Provide the infrastructure for developing, sharing, and applying knowledge.
3. Lead, promote, and facilitate the use of e-learning in education and training in the region.
4. Develop key initiatives to bridge the talent gap in the region.
5. Work with DIC and DMC companies to develop the skills and know-how of the industry http://www.kv.ae/about/).

The main aim of the multibillion dirham DMC, DIC, and DKV complex is to create a clustered economy comprising educators, incubator companies, logistic companies, multimedia businesses, telecommunication companies, remote service providers, software developers, and venture capitalists in one place. The hope is to create a critical mass for the new economy (Arabiata, 2002).

With excellent countrywide penetration, UAE media have the ability to diffuse messages to a vast audience. Although precise numbers are difficult to obtain, the UAE had 170 daily newspaper copies, 355 radio receivers, 134 television sets, 87 personal computers, and 362 main telephones lines per 1,000 inhabitants in 1997, according to the United Nations Educational Scientific and Cultural Organization. That penetration surely has increased.

If one special communications device accents the Emirati culture and lifestyle best, it is the mobile telephone. One of every two persons in the UAE has a mobile telephone, making it the top cellular phone user in the Arab region and the 11th in the world, according the a study by Dubai-based Al Dhaman Stocks Portfolio. The study showed there are 58.5 mobile phone lines for every 100 people in the UAE, Compared to (estimated) 30.05 in Bahrain, 24.8 in Kuwait, 19.9 in Qatar, 6.4 in Oman, 6.3 in Saudi Arabia, and 2.14 in Egypt (Castillo, 2001; CIA, 2001).

Emirates Internet and Multimedia (EIM), the country's sole Internet service provider, puts the current number of Internet subscribers at more than 210,000 and the number of users at about 775,000. According to an International Telecommunications Union (ITU) report, "The UAE is the most wired nation in the Arab world and one of the top nations of the on-line world. With a customer base of about a quarter million, EIM has around 25 percent of the Internet users in the Arab world." ITU further said: "Thirty percent of the 565,000 households in the UAE have access to the Internet (Emirates Internet & Multimedia, 2002)."

An EIM study showed that 51% of the UAE's Internet subscribers are Asians, followed by expatriate Arabs (19%), Nationals (10%), and Westerners (4%). The study also reveals that 36% of Internet subscribers are women. "Our audience profile ranges from the Generation-Xers to the upper-income audience," observed the study. Up to 40% of the subscribers are in Dubai, followed by Abu Dhabi with 30%; 15% live on the west coast and 10% in the city of Al Ain. This research found that 45% of the subscribers surf the net for 5 to 10 hr per week; another 37% surf for 5 hr a week. Only 18% surfed for an average of 10 hr per week. Officials said the EIM portal generates 7 to 8 million page views a month. "Consumers in the UAE are spending less time on traditional media and more time on the Internet," the EIM report said. On the business front, 45% of businesses have access to the Internet. "At present, there are 55 Internet Surfing Centres (ISC) in the UAE. The number is expected to grow significantly" (Emirates Internet & Multimedia, 2002).

The print media, both local and foreign, reach an estimated 74% of the country's literate population. Print is generally considered to be less influential than television. The more educated, middle- and high-income segments of the population read the print media, and expatriates in particular probably constitute a large segment of the print media's readership.

The electronic media appeal to a larger segment of the UAE population than the print media. Part of the reason is the size of country's younger generation, which constitutes more than one third of the total population and favors television and radio. With the proliferation of satellite receivers, consumers all over the country can view local and international channels, both free and for a fee.

Theaters have proliferated in the UAE in recent years, especially in larger cities. According to the Ministry of Information and Culture, there are more than 40 theater complexes in the UAE, some offering multiscreen venues and state-of-the-art facilities. These offer Arab, Indian, and Western films that are rated by the ministry.

Media Access

Government departments have full access to the UAE media. Officials holding press conferences or issuing press releases usually get media coverage in the country's dailies and broadcast media. Most dailies publish WAM stories describing policies, announcements, or events without editing. Some supplement these stories with their own reporters' accounts as well.

Local businesses are successful in accessing the media in varying degrees. Big companies that hire public relations agencies or who have a professional in-house public relations unit usually get their messages across regularly. Also, specialized media like Dubai TV's Business Channel tries to cover business news generated by such companies every day. For smaller players, the task of gaining access to the media becomes more challenging. Editors will publish press releases sent to them if they think the story is newsworthy. Otherwise, they would rather publish the information as paid advertising. The Letters-to-the-Editor section of newspapers is another outlet for the public and organizations to air their views about local and international issues. UAE readers send e-mails or fax letters containing their views to dailies that edit and publish them regularly. Letters dealing with sensitive internal issues are routinely censored.

Radio listeners and viewers of talk shows on UAE television stations can air their views live on various issues. Many public affairs, religious, health, and variety programs invite audience participation regularly. Some stations also offer gifts to listeners and viewers in a bid to attract more audiences for their programs.

Influences on Public Relations

As in other countries, public relations practitioners are subject to internal and external forces. And, as in all other things in the UAE, the practice of public relations is much the story of Abu Dhabi and Dubai, the twin cities that dominate most things. The major economic and governmental centers are located here and, by extension, pervasive religious and cultural influences emarate. The major media centers are also located here. Thus, Abu

Dhabi and Dubai could, if the ruling families so chose, leave the other emirates further behind because of the vast influence that they have both in the economy and the media.

Besides the possibility of internal threats, public relations practitioners are, as are most others in this smaller nation, subject to the vicissitudes of external forces. If the world economy suddenly crashes or if the khamsin wind brings war, then public relations practitioners, like all others, would suffer greatly. The risk also exists that, faced with the unfamiliarity of a downturn, public relations practitioners might entirely abandon any code of ethics, resorting to the most virulent forms of press agentry.

CASE STUDY: THE BURJ AL ARAB HOTEL

Introduction

Because of the vibrant local economy with an almost constant stream of new business developments, product launches are frequent in the UAE. That means that a product launch, which certainly is representative of the economy at large, is the almost perfect incarnation of public relations in the UAE. Use of the launch of the Burj Al Arab Hotel is an almost perfect representation of what is occurring on the toe of the Arabian Peninsula. First, the hotel launch was one of the first times that a local brand was taken international. Second, the Burj Al Arab Hotel symbolizes the dynamism and the drive of today's UAE. As such, it represents the desire of the rulers of the city to create a symbol that would stand for the "epitome of Arab hospitality" (D. Murphy & D. Ibrahim, personal communication, January 28, 2002).

Agency Background: Fortune Promoseven

Founded in the Middle East in 1968, Fortune Promoseven, which has grown along with the region and its clients, now offers a full range of public relations and advertising services in all major countries of the Middle East and North Africa. With offices in 12 countries and a total of 750 employees, the company had billings of more than $299 million in 2000. Among the services it offers are an independent public relations division that is integrated into the network, a direct marketing division, an independent e-commerce division in three countries, and an independent below-the-line division. The Dubai branch of Fortune Promoseven was founded in 1975.

Although Fortune Promoseven shepherded the Burj Al Arab Hotel through a successful launch, the agency and Jumeriah International, owners and managers of the Burj Al Arab Hotel, later parted company. Fortune Promoseven resigned the account in July 2001.

Client Background: Burj Al Arab Hotel

The Burj Al Arab Hotel was conceived to be not only as a luxury hotel, but a symbol "of the opulence, ingenuity and the Arabian spirit" (Burj Al Arab Hotel p. 7). The product of a government–private partnership directed under the leadership of His Excellency General Sheikh Mohammed bin Rashid Al Maktoum, Dubai Crown Prince and Defense Minister, the Burj Al Arab Hotel (translated from Arabic means Arab Tower) was conceived to be a wonder of the modern world (D. Murphy & D. Ibrahim, personal communication, January 28, 2002). The Maktoum family, who envisioned Dubai as a multifaceted hub of the Middle East, viewed the Burj as a magnificent piece of the overall economic puzzle both as a luxury hotel and as a gleaming symbol of progress.

The builders of this architectural wonder clearly achieved their marketing goals. From its opening on November 2, 1999, the Burj has stood apart from other hotel properties. Clustered with the distinctively wave-shaped Jumeriah Beach Hotel on a man-made island of tranquility and hospitality amid Dubai's economic hustle and bustle, the Burj rises like a sail 321 meters into the sky. From the moment a visitor enters the causeway leading to the hotel, the property's style is self-evident. Guests walk past a flaming fountain at the circular entrance into the soaring 180-m-high lobby with its colorful architectural details, computer-programmed "dancing" fountain, and aquarium.

Two hundred two duplex suites, all of which have floor-to-ceiling windows, each feature a private butler, spectacular views, and the convenience of a reception desk on every floor. Club suites include a private dining room and snooker room, and the Presidential Suites have two bedrooms, a private dining room, lounge, and library. Two themed restaurants are on the property. The Al Muntaba Skyview Restaurant, resting spectacularly 200-m above the Arabian Gulf, offers breathtaking sundown views; the Al Mahara Seafood Restaurant offers dining surrounded by glassed-in multicolored marine life from the gulf (Burj Al Arab Hotel pp. 3–14).

The Public Relations Problem

The public relations problem was an opportunity as well as a marketing problem: An international brand for the Burj Al Arab Hotel had to be established. This marked one of the first times that a local brand had been marketed globally. Usually, it is the other way around: A national or regional brand needs tweaking for introduction into a local market. But the problem was not just taking an established local product global; it was starting from scratch. The Burj was new to the UAE and to the rest of the world, although the operating company, Jumeriah International, was well-known.

The company wanted to create brand awareness and a brand attitude for the property. These twin goals revolved around helping to establish Dubai as a center for Middle Eastern tourism, making the Burj Al Arab Hotel a symbol of modern Arab identity and creating an attitude that the Burj was "dedicated to exceeding the expectations of even the most discerning guests" (D. Murphy & D. Ibrahim, personal communication, January 28, 2002).

Target audiences included the tourism and travel industry trade and consumers. Marketing focused on two consumer groups. The first was business and personal travelers who wanted to be pampered, pleased, spoiled, and comforted at an elite destination. The second was to the average "Joe Soap," not someone who would stay at the hotel, but someone who would come to see it, tour it, have "high tea," and then talk about it afterward.

Research and Fact Finding

Before the planning began in November 1998, Jumeriah International issued a request for proposal (RFP). The primary reason for doing so was the public–private nature of the project. "The politics required an RFP because government money was involved," said Dee Murphy, director of marketing for Fortune Promoseven who in 1999 managed the Burj Al Arab Hotel account. "They really had to open it up" (D. Murphy & D. Ibrahim, personal communication, January 28, 2002). The RFP covered production of a whole range of items, including corporate material for the opening and launch of the Burj Al Arab Hotel (D. Murphy & D. Ibrahim, personal communication, January 28, 2002).

"Developing the public relations plan was all about building relationships," said Murphy (D. Murphy & D. Ibrahim, personal communication, January 28, 2002). Gerald Lawless, chief executive officer and Chief Operating Officer of Jumeriah International, had done a lot of previous business with Fortune Promoseven both at Jumeriah International and for other hotels for which he had worked in the UAE. Fortune Promoseven, part of the worldwide network of McCann–Erickson, had previously done corporate identity work for Jumeriah International.

Once notified that it had won the account, Fortune Promoseven created a dedicated special eight-person project team (although at various times everyone at the agency worked on the launch). Work began 1 year before opening, with countless meetings between hotel and Fortune Promoseven staff. The team spent a full 3 months just researching the Arab culture so that they could capture the spirit of the brand.

The size of the project was monumental. "It was a nightmare of a project," said Murphy. "Strategy sessions drove everyone crazy" (D. Murphy & D. Ibrahim, personal communication, January 28, 2002). Those sessions involved discussion of filling many needs such as publicity for the hotel's launch, all corporate identity materials (from matchbooks to tie pins and menu covers), brochures, photography, advertising, trade show displays, corporate videos, and so on.

Goals and Objectives of the Launch

A major challenge was portraying the Arab world, particularly Dubai, as a modern society with good values, a place tolerant and accepting of diversity, to both the tourism trade and to consumer groups. "Even if their countries are at war, people live and work here with mutual respect," said Mary McLaughlin, media relations manager for Jumeriah International. One of the objectives of the launch was to let people know that "there's positive energy generated by the multiple races and ethnic groups that work so well together" (M. McLaughlin, personal communication, February 18, 2002).

Besides making the trade and consumer groups aware of the brand, another goal was to create a specific brand image. FP7's task was establishing the Burj as a "landmark in luxury and Arabian hospitality" with "grandeur, warmth and personal service" offering an "experience of hospitality without equal" (D. Murphy & D. Ibrahim, personal communication, January 28, 2002).

The Launch

The team assembled in the fall of 1998, and planning and coordination continued until the official opening of the hotel on November 2, 1999. A full range of tactics was used to support the strategy of establishing the brand and creating a brand attitude. A barrage of marketing materials was directed at the targeted consumer and trade audiences. These included publicity for the hotel's launch; all corporate identity materials; and advertising, public relations, trade show appearances, and corporate videos.

But media relations activity was emphasized above all else in response to journalistic clamor for information. Five months before opening, "we began receiving media inquiries," said M. McLaughlin (personal communication, February 18, 2002). And they have not stopped.

Results

For months before the inauguration, Fortune Promoseven fielded media inquiries that created quite a buzz. "Everyone was talking about this amazing wonder," said McLaughlin.

"People were watching and waiting. We had their attention without even seeking it. BBC, Canadian TV, CNN, Discovery Channel and many others in Asia, the Middle East and Europe aired features or documentaries" (M. McLaughlin, personal communication, February 18, 2002). BBC News online waxed prosaic about "the billowing, sailed shaped structure," Architectural Record talked about the people who built the hotel and the products that they used, and Forbes.com described the two royal suites as a "gleeful explosion of all things gold, glittery and marble" while gushing over the hotel. Finally, the 160-page commemorative book became a collector's item published in multiple languages and available for $65. Perhaps more important, the hotel had its application accepted as a member of the Leading Hotels of the World, joining storied company such as The Breakers in Palm Beach; Peninsula hotels in Kowloon, Beverly Hills, and New York; and the Mansion on Turtle Creek in Dallas, TX.

Culturally Distinctive Features of the Case

The marketing program for the Burj Al Arab Hotel shows the relevance of knowing about the culture in building a successful brand around the best aspects of that culture. In Dubai that meant modern, cutting edge, on one hand, but steeped in Arabic tradition and custom, on the other. The campaign also shows that cultural knowledge and successful use of that knowledge derives from using people with local expertise and from establishing a timeframe that allows for research and careful strategic planning.

This case also demonstrates that public relations in the UAE is practiced in a manner adapted to conditions. This was a product launch, an almost classic example of the press agentry approach to public relations. The public information model is also alive and well in the UAE, primarily in the governmental sector—an adaptation that fits the government's goals of educating and informing the public. As yet, these two models are the only incarnations of public relations in the UAE. Whether practitioners and firms in the UAE adopt two-way, asymmetrical or symmetrical models of practice is likely to depend on how the country's business culture evolves and the role and function that public relations occupies in that culture.

REFERENCES

Architectural Record. (n.d.). Burj Al Arab/Jumeriah Beach Resort. http://ArchRecord.construction.com/projects/lighting/Archives/0005Jumeriah.asp.

Abu Ghazaleh. (2002). *Copyright law of the UAE*. Retrieved from http://www.agip.com /laws/uae/c.htm

Al Bakay, A. (2001, October 24). Media told to exercise freedom. *Gulf News*, Section 1, p. 3.

Al Enad, A. H. (1990). Public relations roles in developing countries. *Public Relations Quarterly, 35*(1), 24–26.

Al Sadik, A. T. (n.d.). *Evolution and performance of the UAE economy 1972–1998*. Retrieved from http://www.uaeinteract.com

Arabiata. (2002). *Dubai internet city*. Retrieved from http://www.arabiata.com/Services/cc.htm

Ayish, M., & Kruckeberg, D. (1999). Abu Dhabi National Oil Company (ADNOC). In J. Turk & L. Scanlan (Eds.), *Fifteen case studies in international public relations*. The Institute for Public Relations.

Babbili, A. S., & Hussain, S. (1994). United Arab Emirates. In Y. R. Kamalipour, H. Mowalna, & Y. Kamplipur (Eds.), *Mass media in the Middle East* (pp. 293–308). Westport, CT: Greenwood.

Badran, B. (1994, july). *Public relations in the United Arab Emirates: Public perceptions and academic needs*. Paper presented to the 44th annual conference of the Internal Communication Association, Sydney, Australia.

Barfield, T. J. (1990). Tribe and state relations: The inner Asian perspective. In P. S. Khoury & J. Kostiner (Eds.), *Tribes and state formation in the Middle East* (pp. 153–182). Berkeley, CA: University of California Press.

B.B.C. (1 December, 1999). World's tallest hotel opens its doors. http://news.bbc.co.uk/1/bi/world/middle_east/545949.stm

Bryant, C. (1995). Civic nation, civil society, civil religion. in J. Hall (Ed.), Civil society: Theory, history, comparison (pp. 136–157). Cambridge, MA: Polity Press.

Burj Al Arab. (1999). *Commemorative book.*

Castillo, D. J. (2001, October 6). Staying even more in touch on the move. *Gulf News*, mobile phones advertising supplement, p. 1.

CIA. (2001). *The world factbook 2001.* Retrieved from http://www.cia.gov/cia/publications/factbook

Connard, R. (1996). *The ecology of the family: A background paper.* Portland, OR: Northwest Educational Laboratory.

Creating the right waves. (2002, February 21). *Gulf News Supplement.*

Cutlip, S., Center, A., & Broom, G. (1985). *Effective PR.* Englewood clitts, N J: Prentice-Hall.

Dawood, A. (2001, January 11). FNC declares support for freedom of the media. *Gulf News.*

Diamond, L. (1994). Rethinking civil society: Toward democratic consolidation. *Journal of Democracy, 5*(3), 4–17.

Dubai Explorer 2001. (2001). Dubai, United Arab Emirates: Explorer Publishing.

Dubaiinc. (2001). *Facts and figures.* Retrieved from http://www.dubaiinc.com/

Dubai Media City. (2002, February). *Entrepreneur,* 12–19.

Dubai Press Club. (2002, November 5). *Dubai launches its Media City.* Retrieved from http//www.dpc.org.ae

Essoulami, S. (2001). *The press in the arab world: 100 years of suppressed freedom.* Retrieved from http://www.cmfena.org/magazine/features/100_years.htm

Emirates Internet & Multimedia. (2002). Retrieved from http://www.Emirates.net.ae/

Forbes.com. (n.d.). Burj Al Arab. http://www.forbes.com/2002/03/07/0307font_12.html

Geremek, B. (1992). Civic society then and now. *Journal of Democracy, 3*(2), 3–12.

Ghassoub, J. (2002, April). Risks and rewards. *Arabic Trends,* No. 52, p. 64.

Gulf News online. (2001, May 11). Power of ideas and media.

Human Development Indicators. (2001). New York: United Nations Development Program.

Human Rights Watch. (1999a). *Freedom of expression on the internet.* Retrieved from http://www.hrw.org/wr2k/Issues-04.htm

Human Rights Watch. (1999b, June). *The Internet in the Middle East and North Africa: Free expression and censorship.* Retrieved from http://www.hrw.org/advocacy/internet/mena/

Iglehart, A. P. (1979). *Married women and work.* Lexington, MA: Lexington Books.

International Constitutional Law. (n.d.). Retrieved from http://www.uni-wuerzburg.de/law/info.html

International Press Review. (2000). *2000 world press review: UAE.* Retrieved from www.freemedia.at/wpfr/uae.htm

International Press Institute. (2000). Retrieved from http://www.freemedia.at

IPR. (2001). *United Arab Emirates.* Retrieved from www.infoprod.co.il/country/uae2a.htm

Issa, N. (2001). *Dubai technology, e-commerce and media free zone.* Retrieved from http://www.eworldreports.com/viewarticle.asp?ArticleID=364

Jalilvand, M. (2000, August). *Monthly Labor Review,* 26–31.

Kabbani, S. H. M. (n.d.). *Questions on IJMA' (consensus), Taqlid (following qualified opinion), and Ikhtilaf Al-Fuqaha' (differences of the jurists).* Retrieved from As-Sunna Foundation of America, http://www.sunnah.org/fiqh/ijma.htm

Kristof, N. D. (2002, April 30). Stoning and scripture. *New York Times.* Retrieved from http://www.nytimes.com/2002/04/30/opinion/30KRIS.html

Lewis, B. (1991). *Islam and the west.* New York: Oxford University Press.

Mahfouz, M. (1986). The beggar (K. W. Henry & N. K. H. al-Warraki, Trans.). Cairo, Egypt: The American University in Cairo Press.

Media. (2002). Retrieved from http://www.uae.gov.ae/Government/media.htm

Middle East Public Relations Association. (2002). Retrieved from http://www.dubaimediacity.com/associations.asp

Mirabel, E. (2001, October). Message received? *Gulf Marketing Review,* p. 41.

Mott, F. L., & Shapiro, D. (1983). Complementarity of work and fertility among young American mothers. *Journal of Population Studies,* 239–252.

Nawar, I. (2000, May & June). *Freedom of expression in the Arab world*. Paper presented at the Aspen Institute Conference on Freedom of Statement, Wye River, CO.

O'Donnell, G., and Schmitter, P. (1986). *Transitions from authoritarian rule: Tentative conclusions about uncertain democracies*. Baltimore, MD: Johns Hopkins University Press.

Owais, R., & Matthew, A. P. (2000, November 5). Media City launched as beacon of creativity. *Gulf News*. Retrieved from http://www.gulfnews.com/Articlesv /News.asp?ArticleID=1898

Patai, R. (1983). *The Arab mind*. New York, New York: Charles Scribner's Sons, pp. 307–313.

Price, M., & Krug, P. (2000). *The enabling environment for free and independent media: Programme in Comparative Media Law & Policy*. Oxford, England: Oxford University Press.

Privatization drive to stay, says Khalifa. (2001). Retrieved from http://www.uaeinteract.com

Promoseven Agency Profile. (2001). Dubai, United Arab Emirates: Fortune Promoseven.

Quinn, S. (2002). Teaching Journalism in a Changing Islamic Nation. *AsiaPacific MediaEducation, 11*, 6–21.

Rahman, S. (2001, May 1). Media freedom without responsibility 'may invite chaos.' *Gulf News* online.

Ringle, K. 23 October, 2001. The Crusaders' giant footprints: After a millennium, their mark remains. *Washington Post*, p. C01.

Shining Stars. (2001). *Gulf Marketing Review*,

Shihab, M. (n.d.). *Economic development in the UAE*. Downloadable as a pdf file at http://www.uaeinteract. com/uaeint_misc/pdf/12.pdf

Sriramesh, K., & White, J. (1992). Societal culture and public relations. In J. E. Grunig (Ed)., *Excellence in public relations and communication management* (pp. 597–614). Hillsdale, NJ: Lawrence Erlbaum Associates.

Talking Heads: Advertising Legends in the Middle East. (2001). *Gulf Marketing Review*,

The Times Group. (2002). http://www.indianadsabroad. com/alkhaleej.shtml

Tibi, B. (1990). The simultaneity of the unsimultaneous: Old tribes and imposed nation-states in the modern Middle East. In P. S. Khoury & J. Kostiner (Eds.), *Tribes and state formation in the Middle East*, Berkeley, CA: University of California Press.

TV and Radio-Guide. (2002). Retrieved from http://uaeinteract.com/news/ tv_radio.asp

UAE Editorials: Zayed's talk to FNC stresses freedom of expression. (1998.) Retrieved from http://www.uaeinteract. com/uaeint_main/newsreport/19980106.htm

United Arab Emirates Yearbook 1995. (1995). London: Planet Publishing.

United Arab Emirates Yearbook 2000/2001, (2001). Abu Dhabi, United Arab Emirates: Trident Press and Ministry of Information and Culture.

United Nations. (2001). *Human development report*. Downloadable as a pdf file at http://www.undp.org/hdr2001/

United States Department of State. (2001). Country report on human rights practices 2000–United Arab Emirates. Retrieved from http://www.unher.com/ and www.humanrights-usa.net/repo45w/unitedarab Emirates.html

Van dee Melen, H. (May 1997). The role of tribal and kinship ties in the politics of the United Arab Emirates. The Platenew School of Law and Diplomacy.

Wapner, P. (1995). Politics beyond the state: Environmental activism and world civic politics, *World Politics*, 47:311–340.

Walters, G. J. (2001). Human rights in an information age. Toronto, Ontario, Canada: University of Toronto Press.

Walters, T. N., & Walters, L. (2002). *Transitional woman? A case study of values in the context of an Arabic/Islamic Society*. Unpublished manuscript, Zayed University, Dubai, United Arab Emirates.

Wheeler, J. (2001, January 21). Dubai launches Media City. *BBC News*. Retrieved from http://news.bbc.co.uk/1/bi/world/middle_east/1128899.stm

Women account for 36pc of Internet subscribers. (2001). *The Khaleej Times*. Retrieved August 27, 2001, from http://uaeinteract.com/news/default.asp?cntDisplay= 10&ID=177#685

Za'Za', B. (2002, January 8). Summit debates freedom of speech. *Gulf News*, Section 1, p. 6.

12

PALESTINIAN PUBLIC RELATIONS—INSIDE AND OUT

R.S. ZAHARNA

AHMED IBRAHIM HAMMAD

JANE MASRI

Palestine has yet to find her place on the world's map as an independent, sovereign state. Throughout much of its history, Palestine—also known as the Holy Land because it is sacred to the three main monotheistic faiths—has been conquered, occupied and ruled over by foreign entities. In this regard, Palestine shares the fate of many countries around the globe. However, it is Palestine's recent history that makes it somewhat unique from other country studies contained in this book. For, unlike other countries with established borders, economies, institutions, and even mass media, Palestine is still seeking independence and statehood. The Palestinians' quest for statehood is at the heart of the Israeli–Palestinian conflict that has consumed the Middle East and much of the world.

This ongoing conflict has profoundly shaped Palestinian public relations and communication. As other countries were gaining their independence or developing their economies and mass media, the fuel for public relations, Palestine has struggled with a unique set of public relations challenges. Internally, there was the need to keep the Palestinian people together, despite separation and exile. Externally, the Palestinians sought to present their case to the international community. The Palestinian press, under occupation, was heavily censored. The first Palestinian-controlled radio and television inside Palestine only emerged in 1994. At present, the Palestinians are engaged in nation building. This chapter offers an overview of Palestinian public relations and public communication and links it with the Palestinian socio-political environment.

PALESTINE OVERVIEW

The Land

Palestine has long been a part of the geography and history of the Middle East. It lies at the crossroads of Asia, Europe and Africa, within what is known as the Fertile Crescent. Mandate Palestine, as it was known under British rule, extended from Gaza, bordering Egypt, up the Mediterranean coast to Lebanon, and west to Jordan. Today, Palestine consists of the West Bank and Gaza, two separate, non-contiguous land masses separated by the state of Israel. The West Bank is 5,800 sq km or 2,178 sq miles in area and is divided into 11 governorates (Jenin, Tulkarem, Qalqiliya, Nablus, Ramallah-Al-Bireh, Jerusalem, Jericho, Bethlehem, Hebron, Tubas, and Salfit). Gaza covers 365 sq km or 139 sq miles and is divided into five governorates (North Gaza, Gaza, Deir Al-Balah, Khan Yunis and Rafah). Gaza has one of the highest population densities in the world, approximately 10,279 persons per square mile, compared to the West Bank's population density of 1,130 persons per square mile. Three-quarters of Gaza's population are refugees, according to the United Nations Relief and Work Agency for Palestinian Refugees (UNWRA, 2007). Although the 1993 Oslo Accords between the Israelis and the Palestinians call for freedom of movement of Palestinians between the West Bank and Gaza, to date, "there has been near total separation of economic and social interaction between the West Bank and Gaza" (World Bank, 2007a, p. 12). This geographic separation has social, economic and political repercussions for the Palestinians.

The History

The history of Palestine extends back more than two millennia to a land inhabited by the agrarian Canaanites and the trading and seafaring Philistines (Farsoun, 2004). The Prophet Abraham (Ibrahim), revered by Judaism, Christianity, and Islam, journeyed from Ur to Canaan around 1900 B.C. Around 1200 B.C., the Prophet Moses (Musa) led the Israelite exodus from Egypt into Palestine. Palestine was controlled by the Hebrew Israelite tribes until the Roman conquest in 63 B.C. Palestine became predominantly Christian with the emergence of Christianity in Palestine under the Byzantine rule based in Constantinople. After the emergence of Islam, Palestine was a province under the Islamic Umayyad Dynasty based in Syria (A.D. 661–750) and then a province of the Islamic Abbasid dynasty based in Iraq (A.D. 750–1258) (The Palestine Center, 2007). During this period, Islam became the dominant religion and Arabic the dominant language. The Crusaders invaded Palestine and established a Latin Kingdom in Jerusalem (1099–1187).

The recent history of Palestine has been one of continuous occupation and turmoil. From 1517 to 1917, Palestine was an administrative territory of the Islamic Ottoman Empire based in Turkey. When Great Britain captured Jerusalem during World War I, control passed from the Ottomans to the British. At the time, Palestinian Christians and Muslims composed more than 90 percent of the population and owned 97 percent of the land (United Nations, 1990). The British controlled Palestine, first as an occupying power (1917–1920), then under U.N. Mandate (1920–1947). The British made conflicting promises, assuring the indigenous Palestinian people national independence, while pledging to European Jewish leaders "a homeland"—both in Palestine (United Nations, n.d.). During the Nazi persecution of Jews in World War II, there was large-scale Jewish immigration to Palestine. As a result of the conflict, national ambitions and promises, turmoil ensued in Mandate Palestine. The British turned the fate of Palestine over to the

United Nations, which in November 1947, voted to partition Palestine into Arab and Jewish states. The violence intensified. In 1948, Israel announced its independence, absorbing much of the Palestinian state. The Palestinians in the northern region were under Israeli military control from 1948 to 1966 and were eventually absorbed into Israel as citizens of the new Israeli state. The West Bank was annexed by Jordan, while Egypt took administrative control of Gaza. In the aftermath of the June War of 1967, the West Bank and Gaza came under Israeli occupation (see United Nations, 1990). In the mid-1960s, the Palestine Liberation Organization (PLO) emerged and in 1974, gained international recognition as the national representative of the Palestinian people. In 1993, direct, secret negotiations between Israel and the PLO produced the Oslo Accords. Under the stipulations of the Oslo Accords, the PLO returned to Gaza and the West Bank and established the Palestinian National Authority, interchangeably referred to as the Palestinian Authority (PA). Negotiations between the PA and the Israelis have continued in the search for a resolution to the Palestinian–Israeli conflict.

The People

The state of Palestine, regardless of what its final borders will be, is small and limited in natural assets. Its people are its primary resource. Today there are close to nine million Palestinians around the world who continue to identify with their homeland and their compatriots living on Palestinian soil. Today, more than sixty percent of Palestinians are scattered across the globe. According to the Palestinian Central Bureau of Statistics (2006), the combined population for the Palestinians in the Palestinian territories is estimated at 3.7 million. Another 1.4 million Palestinians live in Israel, and approximately 4.6 million Palestinians live in exile, with 2.2 million in refugee camps in neighboring Jordan, Syria, and Lebanon (PASSIA, 2007).

PALESTINIAN HISTORY and PUBLIC RELATIONS/COMMUNICATION

The historical roots of Palestinian public communication stem from its origins as a traditionally agrarian society and tribal Arab culture. The intimate familiarity within the society and economy based on cottage industries lent itself to word-of-mouth reputation management. In the later period of the Ottoman rule, a vigorous Palestinian press emerged (Khalidi, 1994).

British Rule

Under British rule (1917–1947), Palestinian public communication took on new dimensions. With the influx of foreigners, banners and public signs, including street signs, became more common (Ayalon, 2004).The Palestinian press, which had been dormant during the transition from Ottoman to British rule, re-emerged in the 1920s, albeit under strict British censorship (Khalidi, 1997). During the 1937 uprising of Palestinians against the British, to halt foreign immigration, the press played a limited role as the Palestinians organized primarily through their national committees (Kabha, 2003).

Dispossession and Exile

The period between 1947 and 1949 is known among Palestinians as the Nakbah or "the catastrophe." This is when, instead of national independence, the Palestinians found their homeland torn apart. More than 700,000 Palestinians became refugees as a result (U.N. Report, 1952). The emotional trauma of the experience spawned the intense sense of nationalism that permeates much of Palestinian communication today. Following the Nakbah is the period sometimes referred to as "the Lost Years" (Khalidi, 1994), as the Palestinian people were largely invisible, scattered and leaderless. At the time, the Palestinians faced a two-fold public communication challenge. Internally as a people, the challenge was to maintain a sense of national identity and unity. National symbols took on increased significance along with public anniversaries of historic events; two trends that continue today. The Palestinians also faced the challenge of communicating their plight and gaining support for statehood with external publics. As Christison (2000) notes, "because Palestinians had lived in Palestine for centuries, they felt no need to organize, propagandize or publicize in order to advance their goal of continuing to live and form a nation in Palestine" (p. 22). After the Nakbah, Palestinians became more acutely aware of the need to communicate with foreign publics.

Palestinian Identity and Expression

The 1960s marked a new phase in Palestinian communication, with the establishment of the Palestinian Liberation Organization. The PLO embodied the national aspirations of the Palestinian people. The PLO took on the two public communication challenges. Internally, the PLO itself represented an intense social network comprised of political factions and unions, which cut across the various sectors of Palestinian society. Information was circulated through the members and within society. The PLO also launched radio broadcasts, created a news agency (WAFA), issued press releases, distributed its own newspaper, established a research center, and opened information offices (Hamid, 1975). A historic milestone in Palestinian public communication was international recognition of the PLO as the "sole legitimate representative of the Palestinian people." This recognition accorded a recognized voice for the Palestinians in the international community. In the 1970s, the efforts of Palestinian fighters to bring attention to the Palestinian cause through violence achieved their goal of capturing world attention, but cast the Palestinians as terrorists. This image became the dominant Palestinian image in much of the Western media (Adams, 1981; Ghareeb, 1983; Shaheen, 1984; Zaharna, 1995a).

Military Occupation

For the Palestinians living in Palestine, 1967 began the start of military occupation, which severely affected the political, economic and social life of the people (see, for example, Aruri, 1984). Under occupation, all forms of Palestinian national and cultural expression in the territories of the West Bank and Gaza were suppressed. Books were banned. Possession of publications of the PLO or other illegal materials resulted in arrests and imprisonment. The colors of the Palestinian flag were outlawed; even the word "Palestine" could mean a jail sentence (Said, 1989, p. 24). The Palestinians lost control over much of their public forms of communication. Palestinian universities (students and faculty members) were among the most vocal and hence harshly targeted Palestinian institutions (Aruri, 1984; Fashed, 1984; Johnson, 1986).The Palestinian press was heavily censored by Israeli military authorities. The "Defense Emergency Regulations of 1945, No. 88," left over from the British occupation, were still in effect. "Every article, picture, advertisement, decree and death notice must be submitted to military censors" (Friedman, 1983, p. 99). Local news was the most rigidly controlled, followed by Jewish settlement activity,

PLO statements and activities, and Palestinian resistance to Israeli rule, including school closings, demonstrations, arrests or deportations (Khalili, 1991, pp. 12–13; Friedman, 1983, pp. 99–100). A decade after the beginning of the occupation, organized grassroots nationalist political activity emerged in the occupied territories. This movement brought large sectors of society that had not been active before, including students, workers, and women, into nationalist activities (Hammami and Tamari, 1997, p. 277). This extensive social network laid the groundwork for the Palestinian uprising in 1987.

1987 First Palestinian Intifada

The first Palestinian uprising referred to as the "Intifada" represents another important milestone in Palestinian public relations/communication. The Palestinian Intifada is significant for several reasons (see Zaharna, 2003). First is the level of public participation. Although the Intifada started spontaneously as a result of a traffic accident in Gaza, it was transformed into a massive and sustained socio-political movement that eventually involved every segment of Palestinian society. Second, mobilizing Palestinian public sentiment and securing society-wide participation was achieved without the use of the mass media. Under occupation, the media were not a reliable channel for news or information for the Palestinian society. During the early days of the Intifada, newspapers could publish almost nothing, including photographs, casualty figures, or comments by PLO officials (Jamal, 2000, p. 47). The primary information channels were communiqués or one-page leaflets issued by an anonymous underground leadership composed of political and religious factions. These communiqués dealt with everything from the timing of demonstrations or duration of commercial strikes, to encouraging the public, providing guidance for students on how to study when universities were closed, to how to assist the needy (Mishal and Ahorni, 1994, pp. 25–29). The public waited in anticipation for these communiqués and rapidly circulated them through the social networks. Another prominent communication channel was "graffiti" painted at night by a network of youth activists. Walls, buildings, and almost any flat surface became public bulletin boards containing important announcements and proclamations (Oliver and Steinberg, 1993). While the Intifada was very much an internally directed campaign to mobilize Palestinians within the occupied territories, it evolved to include an external focus to include communication with the international publics, media, and political bodies (Zaharna, 2003). The political outcome, if not the success of the Intifada, is also significant, in that it led to the Middle East peace talks in Washington between 1991 and 1993. The peace talks eventually led to negotiations between the PLO and Israelis and the dramatic images of the signing of the Oslo Accords on the White House lawn in September 1993.

1994 Palestinian National Authority: Public Relations and Nation-building

The Oslo Accords laid the foundation for the current milestone in Palestinian public communication. In mid-1994, under the terms of the Oslo Accords concluded between Israel and the PLO, the exiled Palestinian leadership returned to Palestine and worked with Palestinians in the territories to establish the Palestinian National Authority (PA). The PA immediately faced two public communication challenges. The first was nation-building. The second was the public diplomacy goal of achieving support for the establishment of a Palestinian state.

STATUS OF PUBLIC RELATIONS IN PALESTINE

Despite its rich history of public communication, public relations as a profession, industry and field of study is in its infancy in the West Bank and Gaza. Some of the factors shaping the PA media and public relations are common to other Arab countries. With the exception of a few privately owned newspapers and radio stations, the Palestinian broadcast and print media are owned and operated by government departments or government controlled organizations as well as political forces. Palestinian governmental organizations are primarily involved in information, promotion, publicity and facilitating services (Hammad, 2005). As for as the private sector, they are involved with marketing communication which, at least in the United States, is not considered public relations (Grunig and Hunt 1984, p. 357).

About two-thirds of those considered as public relations practitioners or officers are employed in the public sector (government and semi-governmental organizations). Establishing an exact number of public relations practitioners in Palestine is a challenge because there is no widely accepted or well-defined occupation category for public relations, advertising, and press agencies. Distinctions between marketing communication, advertising, and public relations in the Palestinian territories are blurred. What one calls public relations in the NGOs and private sector is mostly seen as a combination of marketing communications and communication management.

Despite these drawbacks in definition, public relations remains the profession of the future in Palestine, due to the fact that the government, organizations, and society need it very badly. One can look at the status of public relations in Palestine in terms of sectors: public or government, non-governmental organizations (NGOs) and the private, professional public relations industry.

Government Public Relations: The Palestinian Authority

For the Palestinian Authority, public relations has become a critical part of nation building and governance. Governmental organization places the practice of media and public relations squarely at the center of building civil society in Palestine. Government public relations efforts, particularly public information campaigns, seek to create awareness, generate acceptance of public policies and programs, and mobilize public participation in development undertakings. Public relations is also an important element in implementing government policy. Publics are affected by government decisions and vice versa. As relations between the different sectors of the government and the various publics become more complex, it is necessary for the government to maintain an open, constructive communication climate, cultivate relationships with the public, and project a positive image.

The Palestinian Authority has five governmental agencies that deal with media and to some extent public relations: Ministry of Information, The Palestinian News Agency (WAFA), State Information Service (SIS), National Guidance Foundation, and Palestinian Broadcast Corporation. New departments of public relations have been organized in a number of governmental organizations and have now become an integral part of their structures. Most, if not all, public relations practitioners, especially in ministries, are based in Ramallah (West Bank) and are occasionally found in other major cities such as Nablus and Gaza. According to Braid (1990), one of the major problems of any existing government information system was the duplication of mandate, duties, and responsibilities among government information offices. The problem of duplication is particularly acute for the PA and Palestinian society as a whole given the forced separation of the West Bank and Gaza.

Hammad (2005) conducted one of the first studies of public relations of Palestinian governmental organizations. He found that almost all Palestinian government organizations and agencies have public relations departments. The public relations department is the second most important information source when Palestinian audiences are targeted. However, while public relations is now practiced widely in various types of Palestinian governmental/public organizations, there is a misconception of public relations that has led to a wide gap between top management and the department of public relations. Hammad counted seven different formal names for public relations departments, ranging from "public relations," to "public relations and information," or "international cultural and public relations." Within organizations, overlap often occurs between public relations functions and other departments. Additionally, more than one-quarter of public relations departments performed functions generally not considered to be public relations duties. Public relations management may well have a place within organizations, however in practice public relations revolves mainly around editorial and "facilitation" work and is not concerned with conducting research, planning or decision-making.

Hammad (2005) found that while most of the Palestinian governmental organizations were involved in internal and external public relations activities, they focused predominantly on external publics. Information disseminated by the governmental organizations via mass media channels was directed primarily toward educating the public while simultaneously promoting favorable images of the government. (Many corporations in the private sector and NGOs adhere to a similar philosophy of one-way public relations communications.) While the internal public may appear unimportant, a public relations program will be seen as ineffective by employees if the organization provides poor public service to the community.

"Communication technician" was the most common public relations role in Hammad's (2005) study. The most-often performed activities were "storing newspapers and magazines" (71 percent), "facilitators: traveling, visas, hotel reservations, other services" (56 percent), and "producing leaflets, brochures, and print materials for their organization" (49 percent). The high percentage of "hosting" or "facilitating" activities may seem unusual to Western readers. However, it is important to point out that the political and economic conditions of the Palestinian people and continuing interest of the international community in the unresolved political conflict generates an unending stream of international delegations visiting Palestine. More than half of the organizations reported "always" receiving delegates. Having on hand printed material for distributing to visiting delegations is part of the public relations requisites as visitors inevitably request them.

The public relations activities considered effective by most of the organization's respondents were those that helped reach the largest audience. Television and newspapers are used to reach the general public. Announcements are used to quickly and efficiently target either small groups such as individual organization members or large groups such as the entire community. Successful receptions and special events with large attendance or good media coverage are also considered useful. The municipality of Gaza, for example, engaged in sponsorships of cultural events and sports shows, because these brought the municipality into contact with their target audience (Gaza City Directory 2002, p. 73). However, many of the managers indicated those activities required a high amount of staff time and attention. Press conferences were very common for the Palestinian public sector organizations, while the political organizations tended not to hold as many press conferences. Other activities included organizing dinners and receptions for major suppliers, distributors, and audiences.

The lack of financial resources is a perennial problem in government public relations and information offices. Most public relations departments suffer from insufficient and unqualified personnel, lack of budget and logistics support. Public relations is often considered a luxury and is, therefore, neglected. Because of dissatisfaction with their salaries and promotion, many professionally skilled government practitioners seek to work with NGOs and private sector firms that offer better salary scales than government ministries.

Palestinian NGOs and Public Relations

Given the Palestinian historical experience—the absence of a governmental authority and foreign occupation that neglected the socio-economic needs of the Palestinian society— NGOs have been an enduring staple of Palestinian society (Al-Shouli, 2006; Hanafi and Tabar, 2003; Sullivan, 2000). The number of NGOs in Palestine has been estimated between 800 to 1,500 (Hammami, 2000; Sullivan, 1996). This number has been growing rapidly in recent years, according to the Palestinian Ministry of Interior, which registers NGOs. Palestinian professional and grassroots NGOs provide 60 percent of all health-care services, 80 percent of all rehabilitation services and nearly 100 percent of all preschool education (Jarrar, 2005). NGOs are also working in agriculture, housing, small business and credit services.

Public relations is a pivotal component of Palestinian NGOs, given their two central public communication functions and audiences. Because NGOs tend to provide critical services or goods to the Palestinian population, an organization has the immediate task of informing the local population of its mission and activities. In addition to informing the public about their services, NGOs often seek to cultivate public goodwill, support, and involvement in their activities. As result, NGO public relations tend to engage heavily in relationship-building activities. Examples include launching community outreach programs, hosting special public functions, or participating in public events. Such activities help the NGO enhance its social capital and expand its social network within the local Palestinian population, which tends to value interpersonal and social communication. Fundraising is another important public relations function necessary for NGOs.

Palestinian NGOs have also formed their own networks and are actively using the internet in their communications. The Palestinian NGO Network (PNGO.net) and Palestine-NGOs.net are examples of Palestinian NGO network sites where members share experiences, post announcements and publish reports. These websites not only help communication within the Palestinian professional community, but provide a valuable source of information for the international community.

The Public Relations Profession

Public relations in Palestine is a relatively young industry composed of a small but growing group of professionals. It resembles the West in its activities, although there have been recent attempts to localize and to be responsive to both industry needs and national development priorities. It is also largely an urban phenomenon in both orientation and concentration. The number of media and advertising agencies grew rapidly in the Palestinian territories after the establishment of the Palestinian Authority. Few such agencies existed before due to Israeli obstacles and military regulations imposed in the occupied territories. The growth of these agencies was also spurred by the proliferation of communication technology throughout society.

The Palestinian public relations industry is similar to public relations in the Arab countries in that it tends to emphasize certain specialties. Political public relations (public affairs), media relations and corporate relations are the most popular areas in public relations practice (Hussein, Mohmammed and Harron, 1991; Mansour, 1993; Alanazi, 1996). Palestinian public relations practitioners also face professional challenges common to their counterparts in other Arab countries such as lack of resources and recognition by top management (Hussein, Mohammed and Harron, 1991, p. 30).

The first independent firm dedicated exclusively to the practice of public relations was founded in the West Bank in 2000 by a young Palestinian who had received his B.A. in public relations at a U.S. university. Most of the firm's early clients were the local operations of international firms, such as British Gas and the Coca-Cola Company, or donor-funded operations such as the Palestinian Banking Corporation, a development and investment bank managed by foreign nationals. The firm's bilingual staff focused primarily on writing press releases (usually taken on board verbatim by the local Arabic language newspapers), and managing press conferences. They also heavily engaged in corporate social responsibility, investing the majority of their effort in staging giveaway events for school children, launching children's libraries at local hospitals, or organizing photo opportunities for donors with local and international dignitaries at the scores of ribbon-cutting ceremonies, project office openings, and official visits by stakeholders from abroad.

After watching the success of this early public relations firm, other communication operations added a public relations component. For example, Sky Advertising, established in the early 1990s primarily as a billboard design and rental operation, added public relations to its roster of services in 2005. Sky was followed into the PR business by En-Nasher Printing and Publishing, another graphic design and publishing house. What is noteworthy about this seeming expansion of the public relations industry in the West Bank is that none of the practitioners could claim any substantive experience or even formal training in the discipline.

In 2004, Zoom Advertising joined the market as the fourth major industry player. Demand for professionally conducted PR campaigns is on the rise, although to date, only the 4 largest firms have the staff and infrastructure required to be a serious contender for the public relations campaign work regularly outsourced by NGOs, government ministries and other international organizations. Today, Ellam Tam, Sky, En-Nasher and Zoom dominate the public relations industry in Palestine, and compete energetically for market share. Virtually all PR professionals with significant experience or educational training in the field work for one of the four major firms.

Another early phenomenon was the "partnering" of the major local public relations practitioners with large, prestigious public relations firms from the West. Ellam Tam captured the attention of Bates Pan Gulf, the Burston Marsteller affiliate headquartered in Dubai. Similarly, Asda'a Public Relations partnered with Sky in Ramallah, and Promo7 partnered with En-Nasher. The formal affiliations resulted in a small but perceptible rise in the level of professionalism among the major West Bank public relations firms. The local firms were able to create systems that mirrored those of the larger mentor, particularly in the area of systematic media scanning and assessments of the impact of media coverage on the client.

The general public has little to no understanding of the profession, either in theory or in practice and tends to confuse it with advertising and journalism. Small to medium sized enterprises view public relations as the realm of the larger corporate players across the board in most economic sectors. The size of the country and market is such that crisis management is handled behind the scenes whenever possible, and among individuals, although recently several quasi-governmental agencies have sought the assistance of the local industry firms in the area of reputation management.

Public Opinion Research

Poll results are used by a wide variety of individuals and organizations, including political leaders, researchers, local and foreign press, diplomatic community members, and local grassroots institutions. Most public opinion research comes from three sources: academic institutions, governmental organizations, and independent research centers. A few research universities (such as Birzeit University, An-Najah National University, Al-Azhar University and Islamic University-Gaza) have generated public opinion research programs, and more are planning to follow suit. But they seldom receive the necessary research funds to begin and continue long-term research projects. The Palestinian Center for Policy and Survey Research (PSR) is an example of an independent, nonprofit institution founded in 2000. PSR has become known and respected internationally for its polling work and its efforts to further objective survey research methodology in the area.

Public Relations Education and Training

Whereas journalism and mass communication (traditionally housed in political science departments) and marketing (traditionally housed in business departments) have long been on the roster of Palestinian university majors, the study area of public relations is considered to be a new academic subject in communication and media studies. Public relations education began in the Islamic University of Gaza in the 1998, followed by Al-Azhar University. Today, all Palestinian universities teach public relations, either as a program (within Journalism or Mass Communication) or as a separate major. Public relations training is also new, albeit growing. Since the establishment of the Palestinian Authority, organizations have sought and sponsored various types of communication training. The Palestinian Academic Society for the Study of International Affairs (PASSIA), for example, has several seminars on public relations, public speaking, communication skills, advocacy and lobbying, and fundraising as part of its human capacity development program (www.passia.org/seminars).

In spite of the confusion about just exactly what public relations is and the many problems that the contemporary public relations practitioner faces in Palestine, public relations continues to be one of the most exciting and fastest growing professional areas.

INFRASTRUCTURE and PUBLIC RELATIONS IN PALESTINE

Palestinian Political Structure

In 1994, as part of the Declaration of Principles on Interim Self-Government Arrangements in 1993 (also known as the Oslo I agreement), the leadership of the PLO returned to the Palestinian territories and established the Palestine National Authority (PA). The Palestinian Authority, which functions as the Palestinian government or "self-rule authority" in the West Bank and Gaza, has three main branches. The Palestinian Basic Law or constitution, adopted in 2001, delineates the powers of the three branches of government as well as the relationship between them. The legislative branch, the Palestinian Legislative Council (PLC), is comprised of eighty-eight democratically elected representatives chosen in electoral districts. All meetings of the PLC and of its committees are open to the public (Palestine Human Development Report 2002).

The executive branch is the highest executive administrative body in the Palestinian Authority. The Palestinian basic law divided political power in the self-rule authority between the president and the prime minister. The late president Arafat, who was the chairman of the PLO, was elected directly by popular vote as the first president of the Palestinian National Authority in 1996. In 2003, the law was modified to shift powers of the presidency (then President Arafat) and to a newly created position of prime minister. The prime minister would be charged with appointing ministers, the daily running of the government, and negotiating on behalf of the Palestinians.

In January 2006, the Hamas party won the majority vote in the nation-wide parliamentary elections monitored by the International Election Commission. Ismail Haniyeh of the Hamas party became the Prime Minister and was given the mandate for running the Palestinian government. The Presidency was held by Mahmoud Abbas of the Fatah party. Citing Hamas' political philosophy, the U.S. and European countries politically boycotted the elected Palestinian Hamas leadership and suspended its funding, and Israel blocked Palestinian tax receipts and transfer of foreign funds. In his "End of Mission Report," Special U.N. envoy Alvaro de Soto highlighted the repercussions of this external political and financial pressure in fueling internal Palestinian tensions (BBC, 2007, de Soto, 2007). Despite efforts in February 2007 to help the Fatah and Hamas parties forge a unity government, tensions continued to escalate and led to armed confrontation between the two groups in Gaza in May 2007. At the time of writing, Hamas is in control in Gaza. The United States, the EU and Israel have announced political support and new funding for President Abbas and the West Bank. The political situation remains fluid, greatly hampering effective government internal public relations with the Palestinian domestic public as well as Palestinian public diplomacy with international publics.

Economic Factors

The Palestinian economic situation has been greatly impacted by the ongoing conflict (World Bank, 2004, 2006, World Bank–IMF, 2007). During the years of occupation (1967–1993), the Palestinian infrastructure languished (Roy, 1991; Rubenberg, 1989). While the Palestinian Authority assumed responsibility for the civil administration of the territories in 1994, it has no control over its water or electricity supplies, or its borders to this day. According to reports by international financial institutions, "external closures" and "internal restrictions on movement" of Palestinian people and goods continue to have the most detrimental effect on the Palestinian economy (World Bank, 2004, 2007b). There are no Palestinian-controlled borders, ports or airports. Agricultural produce, one of the main exports, is ruined when permits are delayed or denied. Imports, necessary for business development, can also be denied. Internal restrictions of movement also great affect the economy. Since June 1967 until now, the Government of Israel (GOI) has "retained full control of the Palestinian population registry," which "allows the GOI to issue ID cards and determine the place of residence of every Palestinian in the West Bank and Gaza over the age of 16" and via a permit system, "to control nearly all facts of Palestinian movement outside of an individual's immediate village or municipal area" (World Bank, 2007a, p. 3). Without permits, Palestinians in the West Bank cannot enter or visit Gaza, and vice versa. This separation has meant a duplication of personnel, work and materials for government ministries, NGOs and private businesses and "high transaction costs," while "the uncertainty restricts Palestinian entrepreneurs from making investments" (World Bank, 2007c, p. 6). A public relations practitioner interviewed for this chapter told of designing and printing a client's brochure for distribution in the West Bank, then having to send the brochure design via the internet so that it can be reprinted in Gaza.

At present, the Palestinian economy is severely depressed. According to the World Bank (2006), the Palestinian economy has become increasingly dependent on foreign aid. In 2005, 44 percent of Palestinians were living below the poverty line of US$2.3 per person per day and an estimated 15 percent were living in extreme poverty, with incomes insufficient to afford basic subsistence (World Bank, 2007b). In January 2006, following the election of the Hamas party to head the Palestinian Authority, Palestinian finances were blocked, preventing government employees from receiving their salaries. This includes staff in government offices, medical personnel in clinics, and teachers throughout the public school system. While many have remained in their jobs, the economic effect has reverberated throughout Palestinian society. Unemployment rates, along with malnutrition, have grown. Almost one-third of the 15–25 year olds and over half of 25–29 year olds are neither employed nor studying (ILO, 2004). The severity of the Palestinian economy makes public relations expenditures a luxury for most organizations and businesses (Hammad, 2005). While public relations is still considered important, basic operational expenses such as employee salaries, electricity, transportation as well as office maintenance and supply take financial precedence over media and publicity costs.

Another important note is the impact of the economic situation on the availability of independent media outlets, an important vehicle for public relations. Most independent media cover their operating costs through advertising sales. However, given the economic climate in the West Bank and Gaza, Palestinian media are unable to survive on advertising revenues alone and have relied on the patronage of political sponsors (Khatib, 1999). As a result, Palestinian public relations practitioners must be politically aware in their media relations.

Legal Infrastructure

The legal situation of Palestine is complex and unique. The successive occupations of the country have deeply affected Palestinian political and legal structures in that the successive divisions of Palestine resulted in a composite of legal systems in Gaza, the West Bank and Jerusalem (As'ad, 1995). While each area evolved separately, none have completely divorced from its historical heritage. Following the 1948 War, the West Bank, including East Jerusalem, became part of the Hashemite Kingdom of Jordan and was subject to the Jordanian continental legal system. Gaza fell under the administrative rule of Egypt and continued with the common law system established during the British Mandate. After the 1967 war, Israel took over the administration of the Palestinian legal system by imposing military law in the occupied West Bank and Gaza Strip. East Jerusalem fell under the jurisdiction of Israeli domestic law and was annexed in 1980 by Israel. One of the major challenges facing the Palestinian Authority today is unification and harmonization of the various legal systems in the Palestinian territories.

In June 1995, the Palestinian President signed a new Palestinian Press Law. This replaced the Israeli military regulations and orders in the occupied territories and defined the relationship between the newly established Authority and society as a whole. The fact that the Press Law was among the first laws issued by the Palestinian Authority reflects the sensitivity of expression and the attention paid to it by Palestinian officials. The spirit of the law illustrates the importance the Palestinian Authority attaches to freedom of the press (Jamal 2005; Hammad 2005). The law stipulates that freedom of opinion should be permitted to every Palestinian individual who attains the absolute right to express his opinion in a free manner either verbally, in writing, photography, or drawing, as a different means of expression and information (Palestinian Press Law, 1995, p. 3). Censorship is not an officially condoned behavior. However problematic this provision might be in practice, it provides the local media with a legal framework unknown in other Arab countries. Palestinian public relations practitioners are aware of these parameters, and like journalists, seek to expand them.

Activism

Despite the heavy censorship, Najjar (1994) called the Palestinian press "unabashedly political." This description of the Palestinian press applies to most of the Palestinian society. Inside Palestine, there is the continuing struggle against occupation and the restrictions on daily life. However, as Nabil Khatib (1999) noted, "attempts to mobilize people through the media were not always successful because all the material had to go to the Israeli military censor." Outside Palestine, Palestinian activism has focused on education and mobilization (Hijab, 2004). Palestinians in the diaspora have also been particularly active in trying to gain understanding for the plight of the Palestinians. Human rights has been a central issue, along with statehood and the right of return. The battle over media images and accuracy has been a long standing issue for Palestinians (see, for example, Hatem, 1974) and the Israelis (see, for example, Toledano (2005)). During the first Intifada, Palestinian and non-Palestinians established new activist organizations to explain the Palestinian position to the public and media, using primarily media relations and public outreach programs. During the second Intifada, Palestinian organizations took to the internet. As Shadid (2002) noted, among the "best and richest resources of pro-Palestinian activism" are such Palestinian websites as the Palestine Chronicle, the Electronic Intifada, Al Awda, Palestine Media Watch, and Palestine Remembered. Palestinian activists, especially those in the diaspora who are trying to increase awareness and understanding of Palestinian concerns among Western publics and media, have tried to increase their public relations skills and efforts. Groups focused on media monitoring have become more sensitive to the way messages are constructed and propagated in the mainstream Western media. Palestinian activists have created media and action alerts to mobilize the community, urging them to contact media outlets or political representatives. For example, Palestinian activists have tried to enhance their media relations skills by developing training manuals and conducting workshops. Khoury-Machool in a study of Palestinian youth and political activism also noted a sharp increase in internet use in Gaza and the West Bank and observed that it helped "foster new socio-political solidarities" (2007, p. 31). This interaction between Palestinian activists in and outside the Palestinian territories has helped increased the overall level of Palestinian public relations in the political realm.

CULTURE AND SOCIETY

Whereas a nation's political, economic and legal structures may dictate what public relations activities are feasible, cultural attributes suggest what communication approaches may be most effective (Zaharna, 2001). Palestinian culture reflects much of the attributes of the Arab culture (Al-Hourani, 2002). Islam, the dominant religion, also has a strong and important influence on Palestinian life. The Palestinian's collective folk heritage can be traced back to ancient times (Barghouthi, 1994). However, again because of its recent history, traditional Palestinian culture has been shaped by its experience with foreign occupation and suppression of national expression (Farsoun, 2004).

One of the most dominant Palestinian cultural communication features is its tendency toward high-context communication. High-context communication places more of the meaning in the context or setting than in the code or actual speech (Hall, 1976). The meaning or value of a communication may not be obviously apparent, but rather may be buried, blurred or suggested. In the Palestinian experience, because overt expression of national aspirations could risk retaliation by the occupying authority, Palestinian communication is rich with symbolism. Examples of dominant nationalistic symbols include the gold "Dome of the Rock" of Al-Aqsa Mosque (which symbolizes the Palestinian capital Jerusalem), "the olive branch" (which symbolizes peace) or the olive tree (which symbolizes Palestinians' long connection to the land). Such symbols are interwoven in the often elaborately detailed logos of Palestinian organizations. Interestingly, under occupation, the watermelon became a high-context substitute for the colors of the national flag—red, green, black and white. While watermelons are plentiful, displaying the national colors was illegal.

Palestinian culture also tends toward collectivism over individualism (Zaharna 1995b). The tendency to value group over individual goals is reflected in the strong family connections. Communication that highlights group interests tends to be more effective than individual choice. Collectivism is also reflected in the media consumption patterns; television viewing tends to be a group experience (Zaharna 2004), while a newspaper circulates through an average of eight readers. Palestinian communication also tends to exhibit the strong in-group and out-group distinctions found in collectivist cultures. Reference to in-group can enhance a communication's persuasive value. While Palestinian society has a collectivist, group orientation, Palestinians have also been described as having a "deep sense of individualism" (Berger, 1962, pp. 274–275). As one scholar noted, Palestinian individualism is not expressed in the nonconformist behavior of Western individuals, but in "demands for equality and reciprocity" (Quandt, Jabber and Lesch, 1973, p. 80).

Similarly, traditional Palestinian culture is very much a "being" culture that stresses "who one is" and relationships to others as opposed to a "doing" culture that stresses what one does (Zaharna, 1991). Palestinian family status or village/town of origin is often prominently stated. Press releases tend to focus on the "who" as opposed to the "what." Palestinian communication also tends to reflect a past-oriented time perspective, in which references to history and tradition are prominent and even essential components. This time perspective, however, can make future-tense public relations strategizing sometimes difficult (Zaharna, 1996). Communication plans are often confined to "the foreseeable" future of six months, rather than the detailed five-year projection.

Palestinian culture tends to be an oral culture that values the spoken word over the printed text. Public dialogue has long held a special place in the Muslim world (Eickelman and Anderson, 2003, p. 2). As Najjar (1994) noted, every time the PLO radio was shut down, efforts were quickly made to broadcast from another venue. Palestinians, like many in the Arab world, also place a premium on direct, interpersonal communication. As Rugh (2004) observed, information from trusted, familiar friends is viewed as more credible than impersonal mass media channels. For the Palestinians, who lacked control over their own media, the credibility of the mass media is doubly suspect.

A final important cultural note relates to gender. Hammad (2005) described Palestinian public relations as a male dominated field. He attributed the observation to the responsibility that public relations workers have for hosting foreign guests. Most public relations managers feel that it is inappropriate to expect women practitioners to go out at night to receive or bid farewell to a guest of the institution. This conforms to traditional Palestinian Arab culture and customs (Al-Hourani, 2002; El-Enad, 1990). While the male dominance in public relations goes against the trend in the United States and even in other Arab countries (e.g., U.A.E.), female enrollments in public relations programs in Palestinian universities are beginning to match or surpass male enrollments.

The rapid rate of entry of women into the field is being seen in the private sector. At present, many female public relations graduates and senior female professionals apply for and are offered positions by the four largest public relations firms (Ellam Tam, Sky, En-Nasher and Zoom). Within the past two years in the West Bank, women have increasingly assumed highly visible, high profile roles in the management and execution of public relations campaigns and events. Three of the four firms have women holding high-level managerial positions in the operation and one of Zoom Advertising's managing partners is female. In Gaza, which tends to be more conservative than the West Bank, female practitioners still face problems with working the longer hours or at night that public relations often requires.

MEDIA

While the media is a core component of most public relations, Palestinian-run media are a very recent phenomenon. As of 1993, there were no Palestinian-controlled radio or television stations in the occupied West Bank or Gaza (Najjar, 1994, p. 221). The signing of the Oslo Agreement and the establishment of the Palestinian Authority marked a major change in the landscape of the Palestinian media. The PA created the Palestinian Broadcasting Corporation (PBC), and introduced the first official Palestinian-run radio and television in Palestine. Palestine radio (Voice of Palestine) began broadcasting from Jericho on 1 July 1994. Palestine TV began broadcasting in 1996. Gaza's first local radio station began broadcasting in 2001 and Gaza still had no private television as of 2005.

Media Control

Palestinians have eagerly made use of the right to establish private media. Today, there are approximately 13 newspapers, 45 private television and 28 radio stations. All of the stations are local (restricted to the major districts) because of the limited transmission power (MIFTAH 2005). Two Palestinian journalists, exiled during the occupation period, returned and introduced two different newspapers into the Palestinian market. The names of the newspapers symbolize the Palestinian hope for a peaceful solution in the region (Hammad 2005) and focus on nation-building (Jamal 2000). *Al-Hiyat al-Jadida* (The New Life), which appeared in November 1994, is partially subsidized by the PA and distributed free in government offices. *Al-Ayyam* (The Days), which started in December 1995, is private and independent. Al-Quds (Jerusalem), the private daily established in 1951, has the largest readership and ad revenue. However, it is published in Jerusalem and is still subject to military censorship. Print media from the religious political parties include *al-Watan* (The Homeland), *al-Risala* (The Message), and *al-Istiqlal* (Independence). As the names of print media suggest, they represent a political medium rather than a neutral public relations tool.

The four major West Bank public relations firms are rapidly learning to cultivate relationships with newspaper editors, staff reporters and freelance journalists, and helping public relations clients gain an understanding of how print media can be engaged in information and awareness campaigns. The level of professionalism and sophistication in crafting press releases and staging press conferences is on the rise, especially in the West Bank city of Ramallah. The print industry sees the relationship as mutually beneficial, and readily responds to attempts of the local PR practitioners to engage them.

Media Reach and Access

Palestine is becoming a media-rich society. According to the Palestinian Central Bureau of Statistics, approximately 91 percent of households own a television and 97 percent own at least one radio. Palestinians spend approximately 14 hours per week watching television and nearly a third of Palestinians listen to radio daily. In additional to the PA official broadcast channels, West Bank cities can receive Jordanian stations, while Gaza can receive Egyptian stations. Nearly half of Palestinian households possess a satellite dish. Among households with satellite dishes, Al-Jazeera television is the most popular satellite channel followed by Arab Radio and TV Channel (ART) and the Middle East Broadcasting Corporation (MBC). Whereas the print media are strongly political, television and radio are primarily entertainment and spot news information media. Among Palestinian households there was a strong preference for recreational and artistic programs (47 percent), music and song concerts (12 percent), news bulletins (10 percent), and religious programs (10 percent). Prime-time television viewing for most households is 8:00–10:00 p.m. For children (aged 6–17), favorite viewing times are between 2:00 and 6:00 p.m. The print medium is the least accessed among the traditional media.

In terms of new media, according to PCBS 2000 statistics, 44 percent of Palestinian households had one member who possessed a mobile phone (51 percent in the West Bank and 30 percent in Gaza). Internet use has been growing steadily throughout Palestine; cybercafés can be found in town centers and refugee camps. In 2000, approximately 11 percent of Palestinian households possessed computers. Internet access was much lower (2.3 percent for West Bank and 1.1 percent for Gaza) because access require both a fixed phone line and personal computer. Approximately, 5.4 percent of Palestinians over 18 years had access to the internet and access differs significantly for males (7.9 percent) and females (2.8 percent). Most accessed the internet from their place of work or study rather than home. According to the International Telecommunication Union, the number of internet users has grown from 35,000 in 2000 to 160,000 by 2005.

Information and awareness campaigns are often broadcast on local radio stations, and simple, low-cost television spots are created by local firms and broadcast on the local television stations. Generally speaking the high cost of advertising on the popular satellite TV and radio channels, as well as a lack of sophisticated tools for impact assessment, have thus far discouraged Palestinian clients, both government and corporate, from including satellite channel messaging in their public relations campaigns or for product advertising. Internet advertising, such as the use of banner ads on web sites, is slowly attracting attention, but has still not attained a measurable level of significance as a PR tool. Private firms have also been integrating SMS messaging, which is transmitted to mobile phones, as another method of maintaining communication and building relations with customers.

COMBINED IMPACT OF INFRASTRUCTURE AND CULTURE ON PALESTINIAN PR

Public relations—the need for an entity to communicate and forge positive relations with publics—has been ever present in Palestine. Indeed, even in pre-modern times, public relations flourished throughout the Middle East (Hatem, 1975; Kirat, 2005). Kruckeberg (1996) argues that while sophisticated public relations are practiced in the Middle East, the models used are not identical to those in the United State or other Western countries. The Palestinian approach to public relations is somewhat different from that presented in U.S. public relations texts that rely predominantly on messaging strategies and the mass media. The impact of infrastructure, especially political and economic factors, combined with cultural features has produced what appears to be a relationship-building and social networking approach to Palestinian public relations.

First, in terms of infrastructure, the political component has been the dominant force propelling the emergence, evolution and growth of Palestinian public relations as a whole. Rather than being primarily a commercial business function, driven by economic necessity of a competitive market place, Palestinian public relations was a political necessity. Public relations was seen as a necessity for communicating internally among the Palestinians inside the territories and throughout the Palestinian diaspora as well as externally with foreign publics. The public relations of international Palestinian activism is comparatively more sophisticated than commercial public relations within the Palestinian territories.

Second, the Palestinians have lacked a strong or long tradition of an independent media, a key component of public relations. Politically, from 1917 up until 1994, the Palestinian media was under heavy censorship by foreign political powers. Economically, the prolonged distortions of occupation hampered the development of a base capable of enabling the Palestinian media to survive on advertising revenues alone. Instead, Palestinian media have relied on the patronage of the various political sponsors. As a result, rather than becoming a neutral channel of communication, the mass media became a political tool with pronounced biases reflecting those of their sponsors. For all these reasons, the mass media has not been a dominant source of credible news and information for the Palestinian people or a reliable communication vehicle for public relations activities.

In the absence of reliable mass media channels to communicate with a dispersed population, Palestinian public relations tapped into a strong cultural feature: interpersonal communication and social networks. Interpersonal communication via social network remains the most credible channel of information. In Arabic, "truth" and "friend" are derived from the same root stem (s-d-q). Interpersonal communication is also valued for immediacy and emotional quality, features that impersonal mass media sources often seek to duplicate but inevitably lack.

Culturally, social networks have long been a dominant feature of Palestinian society, one which pre-dates the mass media and has endured even into cyberspace. As Hadi (1997) noted, during the Ottoman period in the late 19th century, Palestinians established cultural societies and clubs to advocate public policy issues and mobilize the public. During the British Mandate, Palestinians established a mixture of religious, family-based and political organizations. Under Jordanian/Egyptian rule, Palestinians established a variety of professional and charitable organizations run by a new, educated political elite. As Hamid (1975) noted, the PLO itself was a vast network of political factions and unions (students, women, teachers, etc.), which helped maintain the unity of Palestinians in exile. Among the strongest and most enduring Palestinian social networks have been the women's unions. Not only do these unions have extensive connections throughout the society, providing family services, pre-school education and charitable assistance, they are also engaged in information activities. This tradition of communicating through social networks is present today. Today, one of the most ambitious communication ventures for creating a dialogue among Palestinian in the diaspora, CIVITAS sponsored by Sussex University, is built upon social networks (see CIVITAS, "Communication Channels"). PALESTA (Palestinian Scientists and Technologists Aboard), is another example of a Palestinian community network that has been created using the new media (Hanafi, 2005).

Interpersonal communication using social networks has also proven to be highly efficient, especially given the political restrictions. Until very recently and all during the occupation period, because of the predominance of oral communication, information dissemination was tied to transportation, literally. Taxi drivers transporting passengers and goods between towns would be among the first to deliver news. As the taxi stands were often located in the bustling town marketplaces, the news was then passed to shopkeepers, who passed it to customers, who passed it to family members and neighbors. Because most people shop for food daily and rely on public taxis, which allow for small group personal exchanges, news was readily circulated. Within hours and without any employing mass media channel, a town of 100,000 would learn the news. By the next day, people across the territories were discussing the news. Today, cell phones have replaced taxis, but have not lessened the preference for first-person accounts and reliance on interpersonal relay networks for passing information.

Mosques are another example of the importance of interpersonal communication and social networking in Palestinian society. Because the five daily prayers are spread out from dawn to nighttime, mosques are within walking distance from people's homes and work. The Friday noon prayer, the largest congregation of worshippers, is often when important community announcements are circulated. As one Palestinian media report noted, "some Palestinian political factions use the mosques as their main media outlets" (MIFTAH, 2005, p. 3). Islamic parties also reach out into the community providing social, educational and charitable assistance. This direct and often sustained personal contact allows for strong relationship creation. Not surprisingly, religious parties are able to create a formidable social network for communicating and persuading publics.

Tied to the predominance of social networks as a dominant, enduring and efficient communication channel is the importance of relationship building and maintenance strategies. (There is perhaps a correlation between dominant communication channel and communication function.) Again, this stems from the combined impact of infrastructure and culture.

Palestine is a small geographic territory with a close-knit society built around an inter-connected family system as old as the olive trees. Knowing one's family name is often an indication of what area or even village people are from, their economic standing, social connections, religion and political affiliation. In such a setting, maintaining a strong social image and reputation is extremely important as it represents part of the social capital one uses to operate in the society.

Culturally, the social networking approach plays a valuable role in maintaining public images and reputation. Public relations press agentry publicity models (Grunig and Hunt, 1984) strive to "get the word out" and enhance one's image. In the Palestinian setting, rather than generating publicity, the veracity of the viral communication and inter-connecting social networks makes "managing the word" or reputation management more critical than "spreading the word."

Public relations in U.S. texts tends to focus on message design and delivery relying primarily on mass media channels; students are taught how to craft messages for target audiences, develop media relations skills, and assess public opinion polls. In contrast to this message and media-driven approach, the social network approach among the Palestinians focuses on relationship creation. Skills involved identifying and cultivating relationships and then extending those relationships via a vibrant social network. Instead of relying on the mass media to *disseminate* information, the Palestinian public relations approach tends to rely on the extensive network of social relationship to *circulate* information.

In addition to cultural features, there are also economic features that make relationship-building and social networking more financially sound than using the mass media in public relations activities even today. Economically, Palestine is still dominated primarily by cottage industry. Businesses are predominantly family-owned and operated, and like the families, are long time members of the community. Family reputations often extend to the business's product or services. Palestinian businesses also tend to have a direct personal relationship with their patrons and community members. In such an economic setting, reputation management and relationship marketing practices are important, along with social responsibility activities. Crisis tends to be handled via interpersonal networking rather than through mass media pronouncements. More important than media placement, critical public relations activities include attending social functions (i.e., wedding or funeral service), sponsoring community events, and personally visiting or inviting community leaders for informal gatherings. As mentioned previously, social responsibility activities are among the dominant functions Palestinian public relations firms conduct for their international clients.

In turning from the commercial to the political sector, the 2006 parliamentary victory of the Hamas political party to head the Palestinian Authority is very much illustrative of the social network approach of Palestinian public relations. The political arena still represents Palestinian public relations forte. As part of the U.S. administration's push for democratic reform in the Arab world, the Palestinians were urged to hold legislative elections and Hamas, which had previously boycotted elections, was encouraged to join the political process. The ruling Fatah party, which fielded a wide array of candidates in a high visibility campaign, had a well-known reputation for corruption. The mass media, for reasons cited above, played a minimal role in political advocacy. Western analysts, who closely monitored the Palestinian media and public opinion polls, were stunned by the Hamas election victory. However, if one looked at the party's extensive social network, which was well integrated into Palestinian society and paid attention to relationship creation, reputation management and social responsibility, then perhaps the election outcome may not have been so surprising

That Western observers missed the key components of relationship-building and networking in the Palestinian approach to public relations is understandable. The dominance of the media-based public relations model found in U.S. texts may help explain the confusion about "what is public relations" not only in Palestine, but also in other countries which have a tradition of strong social structures and restricted media access and censorship. The social network approach to public relations among the Palestinians appears to be a natural outgrowth of the intensive and extensive social connections within the Palestinian society and the infrastructure (particularly political and economic) that precluded the development of a Palestinian-controlled independent mass media. Palestinians have a vibrant strain of public relations—it is just different. Rather than being message and media-based, it is relationship- and network-based.

REFERENCES

Adams, W.C. (1981). *Television coverage of the Middle East*. Norwood, NJ: Ablex.
Al-Barzinji, S. J. (1998). *Working principles for an Islamic model in mass communication*. Herndon, VA: International Institute of Islamic Thought.

Al-Hourani A. (2002). The Palestinian family between the past and present time. *Cultural Journal of State Information Service*, *(Rou'ya)*, 15, Gaza (in Arabic).

Al-Shouli, S.A. (2006). NGOs in Palestine: The relationship between the Palestinian National Authority and the Palestinian nongovernmental organizations. Virginia Tech University. Unpublished Master's thesis.

Alanazi,, A. (1996). Public Relations in the Middle East: The Case of Saudi Arabia. In Hugh M. Culbertson and Ni Chen (eds.), *International public relations: A comparative analysis*. Mahwah, NJ: Lawrence Erlbaum Associates, pp. 239–256.

Aruri, N. (1984). Universities under occupation: Another front in the war against Palestine. In N. Aruri (Ed.), *Occupation: Israel over Palestine*. London: Zed Books.

As'ad, M. (1995). Palestinian Press Legislations from the Ottoman era until the Israeli occupation. *Samed*, no. 102, October–November, Samed Organization, Beirut, Al-Karmal Publications, Lebanon (in Arabic).

Aswad, B.C. (1970). The involvement of peasants in social movements and its relation to the Palestinian revolution. In N. Aruri (Ed.), *The Palestinian resistance to Israeli occupation*. Wilmette, Ill: Medina Press, pp. 17–24.

Ayalon, A. (2004). *Reading Palestine: Printing and literacy, 1900–1949*. Austin: University of Texas Press.

Barghouthi, A. (1994). Palestinian folk heritage: Roots and characteristics. In S. Kanaana (Ed.), *Folk heritage of Palestine*. Tayibeh: Research Center for Arab Heritage.

Berger, M. (1962). *The Arab world today*. New York: Doubleday.

Botan, C. and Hazelton, V. (2006). Public relations in a new age. In C. Botan and V. Hazelton, *Public relations theory II*. London: Lawrence Erlbaum.

Botan, C. and Taylor, M. (2004). Public relations state of the field. *Journal of Communication*, 54, 645–661.

Braid, F. R. (1990) *Communication for the common good: Towards a framework for a National Communication Policy*. Manila: Asian Institute of Journalism.

Christison, K. (2000). *Perceptions of Palestine: Their influence on U.S. Middle East policy*. Berkeley: University of California Press.

CIVITAS. (2007), Foundations for participation: Civic structures for the Palestinian refugee camps and exile communities/ Running the debates. Retrieved from: http://www.nuffield.ox.ac.uk/projects/Civitas/running_channelsofcommunication.aspx Retrieval date: March 4, 2007.

De Soto, A. (May 2007) End of Mission Report of Alvaro de Soto, Under-Secretary-General, United Nations Special Coordinator for the Middle East Peace Process and Personal Representative of the Secretary-General to the Palestine Liberation Organization and the Palestinian Authority, Envoy to the Quartet. Retrieved from: http://image.guardian.co.uk/sys-files/Guardian/documents/2007/06/12/DeSotoReport.pdf Retrieval date: July 7, 2007.

El-Enad, A. (Spring, 1990). Public relations roles in developing countries. *Public Relations Quarterly*, 35, 24–26.

El-Haddad, L. (December 11, 2003). Intifada spurs Palestine internet boom. *Al-Jazeera.net* (Qatar), December 11, 2003.

Eickelman, D.F. and Anderson, J.W. (2003). *New media in the Muslim world: The emerging public sphere*. Bloomington: Indiana University Press.

Farsoun, S. (2004). *Culture and customs of the palestinians*. Boulder, CO: Greenwood Press.

Fashed, M. (1984). Impact on education. In N. Aruri (Ed.), *Occupation: Israel over Palestine*. London: Zed Books.

Friedman, R.I. (1983). Israeli censorship of the Palestinian press. *Journal of Palestine Studies* 13, 93–191.

Ghareeb, E. (1983). *Split vision: The portrayal of Arabs in the American media*. Washington: The American-Arab Council.

Grunig, J., and Hunt, T. (1984). *Managing public relations*. New York: Holt, Rinehart and Winston.

Hadi, M.A. (August 1997). Ending 30 years of Occupation—The Role of NGOs: Sharing Experiences, Developing New Strategies. PASSIA Seminar: NGO Action and the Question of Palestine, Challenges and Prospects. Palestinian Academic Society for the Study of International Affairs (PASSIA), Jerusalem. Retrieved from: www.passia.org/about_us/MahdiPapers/12-NGO-UN.doc Retrieval date: March 31, 2007.

Hall, E. T. (1976). *Beyond culture*. New York: Anchor Books.

Hamid, R. (1975). What is the PLO? *Journal of Palestine Studies* 4, 90–109.

Hammad, A.I. (2005). Theory and Practice of Public Relations in the Governmental Organizations of

Palestine: The Fashioning of the National Image in A non-Sovereign State. Department of Journalism and Mass Communication, Aristotle University of Thessaloniki, Greece. (Unpublished dissertation.)

Hammami, R. (2000). Palestinian NGOs since Oslo: From NGO politics to social movements? Middle East Report No. 214, Critiquing NGOs: Assessing the last decade, 16–19, 27, 48.

Hammami, R. and Tamari, S. (1997). Populist paradigms: Palestinian sociology. *Contemporary Sociology*, 26, 275–279.

Hanafi, S. (2005). Reshaping geography: Palestinian community networks in Europe and the new media. *Journal of Ethnic and Migration Studies*, 31, pp. 581–598.

Hanafi, S. and Tabar, L. (2003). The Intifada and the aid industry: The impact of the new liberal agenda on the Palestinian NGOs. *Comparative Studies of South Asia, Africa and the Middle East*, 23, 1 and 2.

Hatem, M. A. (1974). *Information and the Arab cause.* London: Longman.

Hijab, N. (June 19, 2004). Palestinian activism in America today. Al-Jazeerah.Opinions/Editorials. Retrieved from: http://www.aljazeerah.info/ Retrieved on: March 3, 2007.

Hussein, S., Mohammed, K., and Harron, R. (1991). The public relations departments in the governmental organizations in the Kingdom of Saudi Arabia. *Riyadh: Public Administration Institute*, 186–191 (in Arabic).

International Labor Organization. (2004). *The situation of workers of the occupied Arab territories.* ILO, Report of the Director General. Geneva: ILO.

International Monetary Fund–World Bank. (March 2007). *West Bank and Gaza: Economic developments in 2006—a first assessment.* Retrieved from: http://www.imf.org/external/np/wbg/2007/eng/032607ed.pdf Retrieval date: July 9, 2007.

Jamal A. (2005). *Media politics and democracy in Palestine: Political culture, pluralism, and the Palestinian Authority*. Brighton: Sussex Academic Press.

Johnson, P. (1986). Palestinian universities under occupation. *Journal of Palestine Studies,* 15, 127–133.

Kabha, M. (2003). The Palestinian press and the general strike, April–October 1936: Filastin as a case study. *Middle Eastern Studies* 39, 169–189.

Khalidi, R. (1997). *Palestinian identity: The construction of modern national consciousness.* New York: Columbia University Press.

Khatib, N. (1999). Media-Communication Strategies: The Palestinian Experience. PASSIA Seminar, Summary of Civil Society Empowerment, Strategic Planning, Policy Analysis, Media and Communication Skills, Palestinian Academic Society for the Study of International Affairs, Jerusalem. Retrieved from: http://www.passia.org/seminars/99/media_and_communication/khatib2.html. Retrieval date: April 11, 2007.

Khoury-Machool, M. (2007). Palestinian youth and political activism: The emerging internet culture and new modes of resistance. *Policy Futures in Education*, 5 (1), 17–36.

Kirat, M. (2005). Public relations practice in the Arab World: A critical assessment. *Public Relations Review*, 31, 323–332.

MIFTAH Media Monitoring Unit (March 2005). Public Discourse and Perceptions: Palestinian media coverage of the Palestinian–Israeli conflict. Ramallah

Mishal, S. and Aharoni, R. (1994). *Speaking stones: Communiqués from the Intifada underground.* New York: Syracuse University Press.

Najjar, O.A. (1994). Palestine. In Y.A. Kamalipour and H. Mowlana (Eds.), *Mass media in the Middle East: A comprehensive handbook.* London: Greenwood Press.

Oliver, A.M. and Steinberg, P. (1993). Information and revolutionary ritual in Intifada graffiti. In A.A. Cohen and G. Wolfsfeld, *Framing the Intifada: People and media.* Norwood, NJ: Ablex.

Palestine Center. (2007). Timeline of Palestinian History and Politics. Retrieved from: http://www.palestinecenter.org/cpap/timelines/timelinepales.html Retrieval date: June 19, 2007.

Palestinian Academic Society for the Study of International Affairs (PASSIA). (2007). Palestine facts and figures. Retrieved from: http://www.passia.org/palestine_facts/pdf/pdf2006/4-Population.pdf Retrieval date: April 7, 2007.

Palestinian Authority. (1995). *Press and Publication Law.* Ramallah: Ministry of Information.

Palestinian Basic Law. (2002). *Palestinian National Authority*. Ramallah.

Palestinian Central Bureau of Statistics (PCBS). (1999). *Population in the Palestinian Territories, 1997–2025.* Ramallah.

Palestinian Central Bureau of Statistics. (2002). *The Social, Cultural Activities and the Use of Mass Media.* Ramallah.

Palestinian Central Bureau of Statistics. (2005). *Labor Force Survey*: (January–March, 2005) Round, (Q1/2005). Press Conference on the Labor Force Survey Results. Ramallah - Palestine. Retrieved from: http://www.pcbs.org. Retrieval date: April 22, 2007.

Palestinian Central Bureau of Statistics (PCBS) (2004). Population.

Palestinian Non-Governmental Organizations' Network (PNGO) http://www.pngo.net/

Palestinian NGOs Network http://www.palestine-ngos.net/

Parvatiyar, A. and Sheth, J.N. (1999). The Domain and Conceptual Foundations of Relationship Marketing. In J. N. Sheth and A. Parvatiyar (Eds.) *Handbook of relationship marketing.* Thousand Oaks, CA: Sage.

Pfau, M. and Parrott, R. (1993). *Persuasive communication campaigns.* Boston: Allyn and Bacon, pp. 25–43.

Quandt, W.B., Jabber, F. and Lesch, A.M. (1973). *The politics of Palestinian nationalism.* Berkeley: University of California Press.

Roy, S. (1991). The political economy of despair: Changing political and economic realities in the Gaza Strip. *Journal of Palestine Studies* 20, pp. 58–69.

Rubenberg, C. A. (1989). Twenty years of Israeli economic policies in the West Bank and Gaza: Prologue to the Intifada. *Journal of Arab Affairs*, 8, (1), 28–73.

Rugh, W.A. (2004). *Arab mass media: Newspapers, radio, and television in Arab politics.* Westport, CT: Praeger.

Said, E. (1980). *The question of Palestine.* New York: Time Books.

Said, E. (1981). *Covering Islam: How the media and the experts determine how we see the rest of the world.* New York: Random House.

Said, E. (1989). Intitfada and independence. *Social Text*, 22, 23–39.

Sayigh, R. (1979). *Palestinians: From peasants to revolutionaries.* London: Zed.

Shadid, Tariq (September 4, 2002). On improving pro-Palestinian activism. *The Palestine Chronicle.* Retrieved from: http://www.zmag.org/content/showarticle.cfm?ItemID=2297 Retrieval date: March 30, 2006

Shaheen, J.G. (1984). *The TV Arab.* Bowling Green, OH: Bowling Green State University Popular Press.

Sullivan, D. J. (1996). NGOs in Palestine: Agents of development and founders of civil society. *Journal of Palestine Studies*, 25, 93–100.

Sullivan, D.J. (2000). NGOs and development in the Arab world: The critical importance of a strong partnership between government and civil society. *Civil Society and Demoncratisation in the Arab World* (Ibn Khaldun Center, Cairo). Retrieved from: http://www.mideastinfo.com/arabngo.htm Retrieval date: April 7, 2007.

Taylor, M. and Kent, M.L. (2006). Public relations theory and practice in nation building. In C. Botan and V. Hazelton, *Public relations theory II.* London: Lawrence Erlbaum.

Toledano, M. (2005). Challenging accounts: Public relations and a tale of two revolutions. *Public Relations Review*, 31, pp. 463–470.

United Nations (25 November 1952). *United Nations Conciliation Commission for Palestine: Report of the UN Economic Survey Mission for the Middle East,* UN Document A/AC.25/6, p. 18; Annual Report of the Director General of UNRWA, Director's Report, UN Document 5224/5223, 25 November 1952. http://www.un.org/unrwa/publications/index.html

United Nations, United Nations Information System on the Question of Palestine (UNIPAL), Division for Palestinian Rights (30 June 1990). *The origins and evolution of the Palestinian problem, 1917–1988, Pt. 1.* Retrieved from: http://domino.un.org/unispal.nsf/frontpage5!OpenPage Retrieval date: April 22, 2007.

United Nations, United Nations Relief and Work Agency for Palestinian Refugees (UNRWA) (2007), Gaza refugee camp profiles. Retrieved from: http://www.un.org/unrwa/refugees/gaza.html Retrieval date: July 7, 2007.

World Bank (October 2004). *Four years—Intifada, closures and Palestinian economic crisis: an assessment.* Retrieved from: http://siteresources.worldbank.org/INTWESTBANKGAZA/Resources/wbgaza-4yrassessment.pdf. Retrieval date: April 22, 2007.

World Bank (May 7, 2006). The impending Palestinian fiscal crisis, potential remedies. Washington, D.C.

World Bank (2007a) *Movement and access restriction in the West Bank: Uncertainty and inefficiency in the*

Palestinian economy. World Bank Technical Team, May 9, 2007. Retrieved from: http://siteresources.world-bank.org/INTWESTBANKGAZA/Resources/WestBankrestrictions9Mayfinal.pdf. Retrieval date: July 9, 2007.

World Bank (2007b). Country Brief: West Bank and Gaza. Retrieved from: http://web.worldbank.org/WBSITE/External/Countries Retrieval date: March 4, 2007.

World Bank (2007c). *West Bank and Gaza investment climate assessment: Unlocking the potential of the private sector.* Report No. 39109-GZ, March 20, 2007. Retrieved from: http://siteresources.worldbank.org/INTWESTBANKGAZA/Resources/294264–1166008938288/ICA2007.pdf Retrieval date: July 9, 2007.

Zaharna, R.S. (1991). The ontological function of interpersonal communication: A cross-cultural analysis of Americans and Palestinians. *Howard Journal of Communication,* 3, 87–98

Zaharna, R.S. (1995a). The Palestinian Leadership and the American Media: Changing Images, Conflicting Results. In Y.A. Kamalipour (Ed.) *The Middle East and the American media.* Chicago: Greenwood Press.

Zaharna, R.S. (1995b). Understanding Cultural Preferences of Arab Communication Patterns. *Public Relations Review,* 21, 241–255.

Zaharna, R.S. (1996). Managing cross-cultural challenges: A pre-K lesson for training in the Gaza Strip. *Journal of Management Development,* 15, 80–92.

Zaharna, R.S. (2001). Toward an In-Awareness Approach to International Public Relations. *Public Relations Review* 27, 135–148.

Zaharna, R.S. (2003). A Tale of Two Intifadas: A Communication Analysis of the Rise and Fall of the Palestinian Image. In I. Alvarez-Ossorio (Ed.), *Informe sobre el Conflicto de Palestina.* Madrid: Ediciones del Oriente y del Mediterraneo (in Spanish).

Zaharna, R.S. (2005). Al-Jazeera and American Public Diplomacy: A Dance of Intercultural Miscommunication. In M. Zayani (Ed.), *Critical perspectives on Al-Jazeera.* London: Pluto Press.

13

The Israeli PR Experience: Nation Building and Professional Values

Margalit Toledano
David McKie

HISTORY, DEVELOPMENT, AND STATUS OF THE PROFESSION

The development of Israeli public relations is interwoven with the history of the Jewish people. The modern state of Israel, which was established in 1948 as a refuge for the Jewish people, is located in the Middle East, in the ancient land from which the Jewish religion and culture originated. However, this chapter identifies the roots of Israeli public relations in the history of the Jewish Diaspora, and in the pre-State nation-building of the Zionist movement.

Two millennia of Diaspora living as a minority without a territorial concentration, and so depending on the mercy of the host countries, and on the internal solidarity of the community, shaped a Jewish public sphere. Not surprisingly, that sphere valued the commitment of the individual to the survival of a collective Jewish identity. "United we stand" is the message that shaped the consciences of the Jewish people through generations and still features prominently in Israel and in Jewish communities all over the world.

In such a collectivist environment, the media were not expected to fulfil the democratic mission of criticizing the political authorities and of protecting individual human rights. Instead, their role was to support the leadership and to promote political agendas set by: the Rabbis in the Diaspora community; the Zionist leaders in the pre-state period; and the leading parties in the State of Israel. From its incubation stage in the mid-19th century in Europe until the 1970s in Israel, most of the Hebrew press was enlisted to promote Jewish international solidarity campaigns, to unify the Jewish people, and to support nation-building. In effect, most Israeli journalists followed the "social-responsibility theory of the press" model whereby: "Freedom of expression under the social responsibility theory is not an absolute right, as under pure libertarian theory" (Siebert, Peterson, and Schramm, 1956, p. 97). Editors and journalists felt somehow part of the political system and were motivated, not only by their professional roles, but also by their involvement as members of a community that was fulfilling a Zionist dream and building a nation.

The 1948 establishment of the Jewish State of Israel was the result of fifty years of intensive political campaigning that included strategic communication and a settlement movement led by the World Zionist Organization. Nachum Sokolow (1859–1936), a politician and a senior leader in the World Zionist Organization, who is also considered the father of Israeli journalism, illustrates these efforts. He is a major representative of the blurring of the lines between the roles of politicians, journalists, and propagandists in the Israeli public sphere. Following a model of "guided" journalism, Sokolow defined the role of the Hebrew press as responsible for Zionist education and national unification. This he viewed as fair and accurate journalism, in contrast to the Yiddish press, who presented arguments and false democracy. Sokolow's "Guide to the Zionist Propagandist" [madrich lamasbir] (see Kouts, 1998, p. 204) founded the concept of Hasbara, a term that means literary "explanation" but is used to describe soft propaganda. Hasbara assumes the need of the authorities to interpret the news and put it into context for media consumers unable to do it for themselves. Hasbara has continued as a synonym for "public relations" and "public diplomacy" in Israel up to the present.

In the absence of journalistic scrutiny, political leaders, who also controlled the modest market activity, did not need to employ experts to manage their media relations. This collaboration between journalists and leaders actually inhibited the development of professional public relations services in Israel, especially the function of media relations, until the 1970s. Prior to that time, most public relations practitioners worked for national or Zionist institutions such as the Jewish Agency, the Israel National Fund, Hadassah Zionist Organisation, and The Hebrew University. In effect, they disseminated the Zionist movement's narratives in collaboration with journalists and school teachers.

The common goal of Hasbara was to connect the new Jewish immigrants to their old-new homeland, to create a new national identity with new myths and traditions, and to motivate the new Israelites to participate in this collective process. Major campaigns in the pre-state period worked to promote the use of the revived Hebrew language as a unifying tool, to increase the employment of Jewish workers instead of the local Palestinian labor (Avoda Ivrit), and to promote the local Jewish products (Tozeret haAretz). Later on, the national consensus helped the leaders of the State of Israel to mobilize Israelis for challenges such as extensive army service, the absorption of mass immigration, and the sacrifice of quality of life (and sometimes life itself), for the sake of defending and building the state. The enlisted or mobilized nature of Jewish and Israeli society stimulated intensive activities in specific public relations services that may be identified with *The Engineering of Consent* (Bernays, 1955) or as "propaganda" (Ellul, 1965, p. 70).

In concert, the Diaspora experience and Zionist nation-building inhibited the development of the media-relations function. On the other hand they stimulated the functions of fundraising and lobbying. Historically, fundraising was a prominent, legitimate, and valued activity in the Jewish community. From the destruction of the Temple in A.D. 70 until the 19th century, professional emissaries from the small Jewish community, which continued to live in Israel, were sent to Jewish communities all over the world. They raised funds to support the community in Israel. Establishing and maintaining the State of Israel similarly involved extensive fundraising from the Jewish Diaspora. Not surprisingly, therefore, the first professional public relations departments developed in institutions—the Zionist national institutions, universities, hospitals and other social services—that depended on donations from Jews abroad. In this very centralized, isolated and non-competitive market, industry and commerce did not use professional public relations services until the 1960s.

Lobbying was another public relations function rooted in the Jewish Diaspora where Jews were often totally dependent on the authorities to grant them any rights. During the 16th, 17th, and 18th centuries, the role of go-between among the Jewish community in Europe and various authorities in the countries where they lived, developed into a professional institution. A Shtadlan, who performed this role as a lobbyist, a representative of the community interests, and a solicitor, became a paid job and part of the community leadership team (the dominant coalition of those times). The Zionist movement harnessed the expertise it inherited from the traditional Jewish community in its lobbying around the world and in its efforts to persuade international public opinion to support Zionist goals.

A process of change towards decentralization developed in Israel following a key event in the history of Israel—the crisis of the 1973 war, when Israel's very survival was threatened. One important outcome was on journalists' self-perception and the re-definition of their role:

> Israeli journalists have moved along a spectrum that began in a journalistic model subservient to political authority and then to the adversarial journalism model. At one pole of this sequence, the press sees itself as an educational tool at the service of the national leadership, disseminating the messages issuing from the political elite. At the opposite pole, it develops the self-perception of a profession that is supposed to provide checks and balances to the national leadership—the perception of the political media as representative of the citizenry facing up to government. (Peri, 2004, p. 89)

The change in journalistic attitudes, which aided the collapse of consensus in Israeli society, opened a door of opportunity for public relations practitioners. Politicians and managers of institutions became more dependent on public opinion and needed communication experts to deal with media that were no longer cooperative. Accordingly, the 1980s were years of growth in the number of public relations practitioners in all sectors, especially in private consultancies. Israeli democracy's move from a highly centralized to a more pluralistic environment was intensified by media changes, as Israel grew from having a solitary television channel (controlled by the government since its inception in 1968), to a multi-channel system in 1993. This contributed to a more media-centered political process and involved more public relations activities. In the 1990s, further political changes democratized the parties and the election system, and, also opened the market to competition from imported goods, which in turn, similarly stimulated an increase in public relations practitioners specializing in political relations, consumer affairs, and lobbying.

The establishment of Israel as a Jewish state involved 125 years of conflict with the Palestinians. Though the Zionist movement was very effective in communicating with world Jewry, and in influencing international public opinion, it failed to develop a dialogue with the indigenous people who had lived in the Jewish homeland for generations. Following the 1967 Arab attack on Israel, the West Bank (formerly under Jordanian rule) and the Sinai and Gaza (formerly under Egyptian rule) regions were occupied and controlled by Israel. With constant growth, the population in 2007 included 5.4 million Jews and 1.4 million Palestinians living within the internationally recognized borders of Israel (the green line), and more than three million Palestinians and 400,000 Jewish settlers living in the occupied territories, mainly in the West Bank (Sinai was returned to Egypt in 1979 and the Gaza strip in 2005). Forty years of occupation had affected the Israeli public sphere and in times of crisis, such as terrorist attacks and war, the public discourse and the expectations from the media followed the enlisted and mobilized model of "United We Stand." Dor's (2001) research into the Israeli print media coverage of the 2000 Intifada crisis concluded that Israeli newspapers played a major propaganda role that favored the then Prime Minister, Ehud Barak:

> A report based only on the spokespeople of the security system does not invite the readers to check the position of the Prime Minister against facts, but rather limits the range of relevant facts to those said by Barak's people. This is not how a newspaper is supposed to function; this is how a public relations agency works. At the end of the Sharem Al Sheich summit the Prime Minister was interviewed on TV one news program and thanked the journalists for "the positive report". . . . He needed "positive" publicity for his public relations campaign and this is what he had received. (Dor, 2001, p. 25; translated from the Hebrew by M. Toledano, hereinafter, ATH (Author Translation from Hebrew).)

Clearly, the traditional model of the Israeli press had not died and its resurrection in times of crisis marginalizes, or replaces (as Dor notes above), public relations practitioners.

These public discourses and traditions represent a challenge for aspiring public relations practitioners. The dominant coalitions of organizations do not see public relations as a management function or practitioners as essential and equal members of the board. In an international comparative study financed by a grant from the International Association of Business Communicators (IABC) in 2003, Israeli public relations practitioners expressed frustration and disappointment at the way management perceived public relations:

> "We have to compete with other projects and fight for the budget all the time."

> "We also need to fight for time resources of management. There is always something more important and more acute."

> "Clients are hiring public relations services without understanding what it should do for them. They don't understand that they would be expected to invest time and more money for the public relations effort to be successful." (Toledano, 2005, Appendix 3, p. 354)

In this research, Israeli practitioners describe how they have to report to management about tactical issues and, how, while they can come up with public relations initiatives, they are not expected to influence policy.

The research was also concerned with international variations in practitioner self image—in particular whether they saw themselves as the ethical consciences of their organizations. While U.S. and New Zealand practitioners were split almost equally on the ethical conscience idea, nearly all of the Israeli participants in the focus groups said that public relations practitioners should not take that responsibility. They said they were not prepared for that job at all and the closest they came was in their role as representative of the media within the organization. That is to say that they could point out how the organization's actions would be interpreted externally. They did not see themselves as representatives of the organization's stakeholders or as any kind of organizational conscience.

In part, this relates to how the profession evolved in Israel. In illustrating how professions developed out of jurisdictional disputes and competition between occupations about work, Abbott (1988) specifically address the professionalization of journalism, suggesting it developed its own professional identity by divorcing itself from public relations (pp. 225–226). In a mirror reflection, the emergence of public relations can be seen as a consequence of its demarcation from journalism and advertising. In the Israeli case it seems that, as late as the 1960s, journalists were still cooperating with government spokes-people and those practitioners who founded the national public relations association (ISPRA) in 1961 deliberately distanced themselves from the advertising profession.

In 2006, according to Israel's largest information corporation, the Ifat Media Informa-tion Center, there were 376 public relations agencies in Israel (a 30 percent increase com-pared to 2005), and 545 spokespeople, of whom 148 were employed by municipalities and city councils, 137 by associations and NGOs, 50 by national and government institutions, 17 by government enterprises, 31 by army and police bodies, 30 by commercial cor-porations, 10 by banks, 30 by the health sector, 33 by education institutions, 25 by art and culture organizations, 13 by media (print, radio, and TV channels), 11 by political parties, and 10 by transportation. (Agencies serve several clients in all sectors) (Boltanski, 2006, pp. 695–749). Based on this report and a survey by advertising agency BDI (2005), we estimate that at least 3,000 people practised public relations in Israel in 2006 and the Israeli Public Relations Association website (ISPRA, 2006) reported about 250 members. In its 2006 annual conference ISPRA members were still debating the lack of funds to employ an administrative secretary (McKie and Toledano, 2006), a recurrent obstacle that reflects the weakness of the organization.

Nevertheless, since its establishment, ISPRA has provided its members with professional training through seminars and has published a code of ethics from 1987. Since 1992, ISPRA has managed an annual award program to recognize an Israeli public figure who used communication effectively to promote a national cause. In 2004, following the example of the International Public Relations Association's (IPRA) Golden Award categories, ISPRA established an annual competition to recognize the best public relations campaigns. Although it offers no accreditation, and is not involved in any academic training program, ISPRA provides services for practitioners and functions as an advocate for the profession.

In 1964 a small group of practitioners went international and joined IPRA. They even succeeded, in spite of opposition from Arab members, in convincing IPRA to convene its fifth congress in Israel in 1970. The interest of Israeli Public Relations practitioners in IPRA, as a window to the international professional community, grew fast. Twenty-five Israelis were members of IPRA by 1988 and a group always attended IPRA's international conferences. In 1992 the Israeli Public Relations Association hosted an IPRA seminar in Israel, with 200 participants from 32 countries. This Congress marked a milestone in Israeli public relations as it attracted media attention and gave positive publicity to the profession.

Until the 1980s Israel did not offer significant business opportunities for the inter-national community and most international public relations agencies were represented by one Israeli agency, Triwaks. A breakthrough came in the second half of the 1990s. Follow-ing the peace process, international corporations became interested in Israel as a market and as a door to the Middle East. The Arab boycott became insignificant and government promises regarding privatization encouraged international investors. Israeli advertising agencies became targets for international agencies, which started to form all kinds of affiliations and partnerships to compete in the Israeli market. Public relations departments and firms followed the advertising model. Porter Noveli, Shandwick, Hill and Knowlton, GCI, Burston Marsteller, and Golin/Harris were among the global leaders who had an affiliation with an Israeli public relations agency. Working with leading international public relations companies had a dramatic impact on Israeli public relations firms. The exposure to professional standards and expectations meant that Israeli practitioners had to prove their value and measure their results. They had to submit business plans and communicate professionally with colleagues abroad.

The major continuing challenge for public relations practice in Israel is the lack of professional training and academic education. In 2007, over 250,000 students were studying in one of Israel's six universities (75,850 students), eighteen public colleges and nine private colleges (71,850), the Open University (39,500) and teacher training colleges (20,900) (Traubman, 2006, p. 5), but none offered a major in public relations. Universities usually include one elective public relations workshop within communication programs focussing on media and society. Haifa University and Sapir College recently introduced courses related to public relations (but taught by staff without public relations qualifications). Four colleges developed significant communication programs that included public relations workshops taught by practitioners. There is still no public relations textbook in Hebrew, and few institutions use textbooks from the U.S. or elsewhere.

In a similarly limiting way, the ISPRA (2007) website presents a narrow idea of the field:

Israel's senior practitioners define public relations as a strategic management discipline that maintains, promotes, and defends the values, interests, products, and services of an organization. ISPRA members . . . typically have responsibility for an organization's media relations, may write and produce corporate and marketing materials, and employee and customer newsletters, may write and deliver speeches and presentations, and may also create and mange special events.

It is significant that ISPRA makes no mention of such management and leadership functions as strategic planning, building relationships with stakeholders, and serving as the ethical conscience of the organization, which are common elsewhere.

INFRASTRUCTURE AND INTERNATIONAL PUBLIC RELATIONS

The Socio-political System

Israel has been considered as the only parliamentary democracy in the Middle East. Nevertheless, it does not have a constitution to protect civil rights, and the nation's Declaration of Independence, which is the legal substitute for a constitution, does not include the word "democracy." From its very beginning, in the pre-state period of the 1920s, Israel's democracy was based on a multiparty system and free representative elections but "during that time, as well as in the early years of statehood, [it] was a formal rather than a liberal democracy, the kind that emphasizes elections and majority rather than the rights of individuals and minorities" (Shapiro, 1978, cited in Perry, 2004, p. 73).

Israel was declared as a Jewish state following the U.N. resolution of November 1947. Since its establishment, the issue of its simultaneous commitment to its Jewish nature, and to democracy, has been the subject of many political controversies. The democratic principle of separation between state and religion has not been accomplished in Israel. The legal system consists of a mixture of English common law and British Mandate regulations but personal civil matters are dominated by the Jewish, Christian, and Muslim religious legal systems. The dependency of the dominant party on its ability to construct a coalition empowers the Jewish religious parties to control the content of holidays and other lifestyle issues.

The Israeli political system was formed long before the establishment of the state. The settlers who immigrated to Eretz Israel at the beginning of the 20th century were organized in parties founded in Eastern Europe as Zionist clubs. From the beginning, in what Wolff-sohn (1987) called a "Party State": "polity and economy, society and culture—even the question of security—were not only closely connected with, but also determined by, party politics" (p. xvii).

The period following World War I until 1948 formed the infrastructure for the state under the rule of the British Mandate. The Jewish community that lived in Israel in this period was called "the Yishuv" and was represented by the democratically elected Assembly and later by the Jewish Agency of the World Zionist Organization, who managed future state issues. These included communication campaigns managed by the Hasbara departments of national institutions, enabling immigration and settlement, promoting the Hebrew language and culture, purchasing lands, and lobbying the U.N. for the establishment of the state. The organized Yishuv under the British Mandate was a political system seeking autonomy, a kind of state in the making. The Yishuv lived in Mandatory Palestine as a minority, next to the Arab majority—two nations that were claiming national independence in the same territory. The Jewish political leadership used the time to develop and grow so that, by 1948, Jews became the majority.

The transformation from embryonic state to full state in 1948 changed the nature of this socio-political environment. The government took over all the functions performed in the Yishuv period by voluntary institutions. The shift from the realities of millennia of state-lessness was characterized by a wave of nationalization of social services and the preference of the state over the society. The new government nationalized the education system and the employment services, and created a single national defence force in what Elon (1983) described as "a cult of 'the state'" which found "expression in the postulate of mamlachtiut—approximately, 'stateism'" (p. 293) and which called "for the state to be the chief regulator curtailing, even substituting for, the free play of semi-autonomous social and political bodies" (p. 294).

Aspects of the mamlachtiut reflected the determination of Ben Gurion, the first Prime Minister (from the Mapai [Labor] party), and the first Israeli governments, to "design" a new Jewish personality, the Hebrew Israeli with a new culture, built partly on denying the Jewish Diaspora culture. The policy of immigrant integration, shaped by the concept of a "melting pot," tried to erase the many cultures and different Jewish traditions that were brought by the new immigrants. The Hebrew language became the unifying force while the original languages of the immigrants were suppressed.

The Mamlachtiut did not allow pluralism. Ben Gurion and his government had a vision and, for them, the state was the tool to achieve the implementation of the Jewish Zionist values. They did not recognize the concept of a "service state" to guarantee the safety, freedoms, and welfare of its citizens. Another aspect of Ben Gurion's government that affected the status of Israeli public opinion was the concept called "Bithonism" (Securitism), which described the school of mind that related to every issue in term of its contribution to state security. It gained widespread support from Israeli public opinion, which was influenced internally by the government and military messages, as much as by the external rhetoric and threatening activities of the neighboring Arab countries' leaders.

The concepts of Mamlachtiut and Bithonism did not allow for consultation with public opinion. Politicians and military leaders presumed to know better and their efforts to influence public opinion were those "of arrogant power elites who believe more in 'educating' the people than in 'serving'" (Elon, 1983, p. 296). The effects of the state ideology, combined with the survival anxieties of Israelis living with continuous external threats, impacted on the public discourse of a state:

with a missionary sense of purpose: from the creation of an "ideal" society (fashioned on socialist or biblical models, or on an amalgam of both) to the strictures imposed upon individuals by the policy of "ingathering of the exiles," to the demand of victory in a "just war" which is often pictured as a struggle between the children of light and the children of darkness. (Elon, 1983, p. 296)

As a continuation of the Jewish experience in the Diaspora, the missionary state kept preaching "unity" rather than freedoms. Factionalism was, and is, condemned.

The Political Transformation

Political events that followed the Six-Day War of 1967, and the Yom Kippur War of 1973, changed the well established national consensus and the political culture of Israel. Following the military success of 1967, Israel gained control over Arab territories that made it three times bigger than its pre-war size. In communication terms, the major change followed the military failure in the 1973 Yom Kippur War. The Labor party was criticized for this "debacle" (Peri, 2004, p. 85) and lost public trust. In 1977, for the first time since the establishment of the State of Israel, a right wing coalition won the elections and formed a government, ending almost thirty years of Mapai dominance. The new government's ideology supported the idea of Israel's control over the occupied territories, was more accommodating to the demands of religious sectors, and promoted a liberal economy. In spite of its activist agenda, this government signed a peace agreement and returned the occupied Sinai land to Egypt.

Key changes in Israel's socio-political environment followed this shift to the right and the erosion of the political center. Peri (2004) described these as consisting of two processes. The first was a form of *Legitimation Crisis* (Habermas, 1976), in which the government lost its exclusive dominance over the public sphere. The second was a "colonial situation" (Peri, 2004, p. 55), which "increased the size and influence of significant groups in the population who lack deep democratic convictions" (p. 55) and made the "internal division over the future of the occupied territories . . . also a cultural battle over what writers call the soul of Israeli society and sociologists define as its collective identity" (p. 55).

As part of the political revolution, Peri (2004) considers another global phenomenon, the decline of the "party state," so that the defeat of the Labor party signified "the collapse of the old party structure, based on one dominant party and its replacement by a new competitive, bipolar structure, also described as polarized pluralism" (p. 60). For public relations, one very significant change was the introduction of internal primaries for the parties' candidates to the Knesset in 1992–3. Until that time candidates were nominated by internal party committees and did not depend that much on public opinion. The new parties' primaries did not improve the democratic system, and failed to give equal opportunities or produce the best lists of candidates, but the new system did elevate the status of public opinion in Israel. This helped establish the need to communicate with, and consult with, constituents.

Activism

The crisis of 1973 shook Israeli society and its self confidence. It inspired protest movements, which demanded changes in the political system, and it instigated changes in the model of journalism from "mobilized" to more open. Journalists, who before the war promoted the myth of the invincible, error-immune Israeli army, did some serious soul-searching and helped catalyze a dramatic change in public discourse.

During the 1980s and the 1990s, Israel went through a very controversial war in Lebanon, a Palestinian uprising in the occupied territories (Intifada), and a peace process. These events sparked protests and demonstrations by both sides of the political spectrum. Lehman-Wilzig (1992), who researched public protest in Israel between 1948 and 1992, concluded that, although the major reason for protest was social issues, political protest grew during that period. Public protest became part and parcel of Israeli culture. From the 1980s onwards, political demonstrations became routine and an accepted tool for civil expression. The protest became a way for public opinion to pressure public institutions and influence decision-making by the government. Nevertheless, in Lehman-Wilzig's (1992) summation:

> The Israeli public's attitude towards the state's democracy is paradoxical. On the one hand, there is a lot of interest in politics; on the other, there is a level of skepticism about the value of the democratic institutions, and a high level of intolerance towards opposing attitudes and worldviews. In terms of political culture, there is a solid democratic norm regarding participation, but a very shaky democratic norm regarding political tolerance—an ideal prescription for wide public protest. (p. 110) [ATH]

Economic Development

There can be few better places than Israel for demonstrating the close connection between political ideology and economic development and the link between an open and competitive liberal economy and the growth of public relations services. Once a traditional economy, based mainly on agriculture, light industry and labor-intensive production, Israel became a knowledge-based economy, with internationally competitive telecommunications, high-tech, and agro-tech industries.

The shift from deep government involvement, and a protectionist and isolated economy, into an open and competitive market happened only in the last two decades of the 20th century. For many years Israel's economy was shaped according to the political ideology of the founders and collective nation-building. There was an expectation that the individual would subject his or her self-interest to the national challenges and sacrifice economic comfort for the collective mission. The Zionist ideology led the Israeli economy of the first three decades in a controlled and monopolistic style. Once that political system changed, the economy also changed dramatically. The Organization for Economic Co-operation and Development (OECD) described the change in a 2002 report:

> Historically Israel's economy was an agrarian three sector economy—the public sector, the Histadruth (General Federation of Hebrew Workers) and the private sector. During the 1980s a process of macro-economic and structural reforms, including disengagement of the government from the economy and deregulation across all sectors, was begun. This was accelerated in the 1990s while at the same time Israel pursued a foreign policy designed to further integrate the country into the world markets, including a range of bilateral and multilateral economic agreements. Today Israel has a modern, technologically advanced economy, with GDP per capita in 2001 at US$17,900, a 50 per cent increase over 1990 figures. (OECD, 2002)

Only a few years later, in 2006 it was estimated that the GDP per capita would be over US$26,000 with a growth rate of 4.5 percent. (CIA, n.d.). In the course of this process, the expansion of market activities, and the increased competition, spurred the development of a consumer culture, which attracted public relations services. Former journalists and advertising people identified the opportunity and opened public relations agencies to assist companies and importers to educate the consumers and to legitimize individualized lifestyles.

During the 1990s, Israel also experienced other intensive transformations, including the integration of a million immigrants from the former Soviet Union, the 1991 Gulf War, the 1993 peace agreement, the assassination of Prime Minister Yitzhak Rabin in 1995, ongoing political instability, and changes of government. At the same time it also turned into a modern technologically-advanced economy in an increasingly global market. The strategic role played by high-tech industries and the foreign investments, which were insignificant before the 1990s, contributed to the rapid expansion. It also created an appropriate environment for the development of public relations.

An important variable for evaluating economic development is the privatization process. Until the mid-1980s the Government, and the Federation of Labor Unions (the Histadrut), were involved as owners and controllers of most public enterprises and dominated economic activity. The privatization process became a political plank of the right wing parties and gained acceptance as a goal for other parties and for the general public. Yet, the implementation of privatization was slow and sporadic. Politicians, after all, are not highly motivated to give up power for the sake of long term benefits for the economy. Moreover, the welfare state principles of solidarity and care for the deprived have been eradicated as a result of privatization. In the new millennium the gap between the haves and the have-nots has grown dramatically. Unemployment rates are between 8–9 percent. In 2005 more than 22 percent of the population lived below the poverty line.

Another change in Israel's economy and society, which further stimulated public relations, was the integration of the Israeli market into a global economy. The process of deregulation and liberalization enabled Israeli companies to operate internationally. Israeli companies are traded in the U.S. Stock Exchange, use up-to-date communication systems and technology, and do much more business abroad than they could do before. In a presentation to OECD Forum 2006, the Israel Bank's Governor, Stanley Fisher (2006), said that the liberalization that took place in the 1990s was very gradual but "by 2003, all capital controls had been removed . . . . Israel also liberalized capital flows. In 2005 outflows amounted to about 9 percent of GDP, roughly equal to the inflows."

Nevertheless, international accountancy firms involved in capital investments in Israel complained about the high level of regulations imposed by the Israel Bank and about high taxation. In spite of these difficulties, and the deteriorating political situation, the second Intifada, terrorist attacks and a war with Lebanon, foreign investment in Israel has continued to grow. According to the Bank of Israel report "Foreign investment in Israel reached an all-time high of $21.1 billion in 2006, up from $9.9 billion in 2005 and $7.2 billion in 2004, a three-fold increase" (Klein, 2007).

Business culture in Israel is very competitive and innovative yet, in some ways, it is still influenced by past values, especially with regard to information. The 2006 Transparency International (TI) organization's *Index of Corruption Perceptions* ranked Israel as number 34 out of 163 countries with a score of 5.9 out of 10 (TI, 2006, p. 5). The index reflects the way corruption is being perceived in each of the countries surveyed. The democratic value of transparency has not been fully absorbed and the idea that the public has a right to know cannot be taken for granted. Research into the phenomenon of information transparency in Israel's public institutions concludes that almost all the economic entities, private and public, are manifestly not transparent:

> The average Israeli director assumes that the public is an idiot and therefore there is no need to provide the public with information in real time and high quality. They would argue that anyway the public would not understand so why make an effort? (Kamir, cited in Cohen, 2003, p. 176) [ATH]

Kamir's research found that the supervising bodies did not publish essential information and that public and taxpayers did not receive any information about the use of the budgets by major organizations. Kamir also reckoned that the media did not bring the important money stories to the public. His findings suggest that Israeli public relations practitioners have not succeeded in opening the companies and institutions, which are their clients, to an open and sincere dialogue with the public.

Culture

The Jewish State of Israel was built by immigrants from more than a hundred countries who contributed to its rich cultural diversity and artistic creativity. Yet, from its pre-state period, the different cultural groups have been struggling to define the collective cultural identity of Israel in what is called often "the war between cultures." Data from 2004 states that 67.1 percent of the Jewish population living in Israel were born in Israel [most of them would be second and third generation of immigrants], 22.6 percent of the Jewish population was born in Europe or America, 5.9 percent in Africa, 4.2 percent in Asia, and, in terms of Israelis religious affiliation in 2004: 76.4 percent were Jewish, 16 percent Muslim, 1.7 percent Arab Christians, 0.4 percent other Christians, and 1.6 percent Druze (CIA, n.d.). But the cultural struggle relates not only to religion and ethnicity because, since the 1950s:

> Israeli society has been divided along five major cleavages: nationally, between Jews and non-Jews, or Palestinians; ethnically, between Ashkenazim [immigrated from Europe and America] and Mizrahim [immigrated from Africa and Arab countries], between religious and secular Jews; politically, between the Right ("the national camp") and the Left ("the peace camp"); and economically, between the haves and the have-nots. (Peri, 2004, pp. 152–153)

In most cases there was an overlap between the groups so that the Mizrahim, who were also the more religious group, were economically deprived, and voted for the Right. The political shift from Left to Right in 1977 marked a cultural change toward the end of the Ashkenazi elite hegemony and the recognition and inclusion of the Mizrahim culture that Kimmerling (2001) called "the end of the Achusalim hegemony" (translating the American term WASPs into the Hebrew acronym: Ashkenazi, Secular, Veteran, Socialist and Nationalist). The "Achusalim" were the founders of the state and, during the first two decades, they shaped the new Israeli culture. Their goal was to create a new united people connected to its old homeland, not a multicultural or pluralistic society. From the 1970s onward, however, repressed cultural groups were moving forward and asserting their separate identities: "The religious-national group, the orthodox-national group (Jewish but not Zionist), the traditional-Mizrachi group, the Russians and the Ethiopians [two 1990s immigrant groups], the Israeli-Arab group, and the veteran and new middle-class secular group" (Kimmerling, 2001, p, 32) [ATH]. Kimmerling (2001) goes on to view the process of cultural fragmentation not as a threat, but rather as an opportunity to develop in the new millennium a civil society that will guarantee cultural rights.

The few professionals, who practiced public relations during the formative era of the pre-state and the first two decades of the state, managed intensive Hasbara campaigns that involved the education system in constructing a new Israeli culture. Their work in the service of Zionist institutions and, later, in Israeli government agencies, helped create and promote new national traditions and supported the revival of the Hebrew language in a unique campaign where it became "a major vehicle in creating a new and more uniform national culture that propagated Zionist ideology and pioneering values" (Zerubavel, 1995, p. 80).

The collapse of centralized consensus and the changing role of journalism stimulated a process of change. The effort to build a collective identity for the new nation and the emphasis on solidarity and sacrifice of individual interests (and sometimes human rights), for the sake of the state (statehood) was replaced by individualism and a shift towards "a civil society bubbling with action and vitality" (Yishai, 1998, p. 160) where people were "no longer mobilized to endorse a national cause but eagerly demand that their interest be considered and then realized" (p. 160). The diversity of voices struggling to be heard, and the competition between them for supportive public opinion, fueled an increase in the demand for professional public relations services, including new consultancies specializing in lobbying in the 1990s.

Part of the Achusalim culture was the myth of the Sabra [native born Israeli Jews], the sons and daughters of the pioneers. These Israeli Jews, who were able to defend themselves and to assert their culture, were to be the complete opposite of the Diaspora Jew. The Sabra myth linked to major aspects of Israeli culture. The first is the centrality of military service in the Israeli experience and admiration for the Sabra fighting skills as ending two centuries of frustrating helplessness of the persecuted Diaspora Jews. The second is the "dugri" way of speaking, translated by Katriel (1986) as "straight or direct talk" (p. 1). Dugri speaking involves a level of directness in speaking that would be considered rude in many other cultures and emerges from different aspects of the Sabra subculture: the need for cultural assertion; the demand for sincerity and truthful expression (expressed in an attitude of "anti-style" with an ethos of naturalness); and the spirit of communitas (Katriel 1986, pp. 17–33).

The centrality of military service is evident in the establishment of the Israeli Defense Force (IDF). From the outset, the IDF had more than a military role. In particular, it was responsible for educating the new migrants and serving as a "melting pot" to unify all Israelis. Military service is obligatory—36 months for men and 21 months for women—and reservists keep training up to a month a year until the age of 49. This service, and for many, the participation in war, and/or situations of danger, are the most intensive experiences of life as Israelis. Afterwards, mobility to management roles, and subsequent promotion, often depended on IDF rank and the social connections with former army comrades.

Although most women serve in the army, few are involved in combat units. This is one of the reasons why few become high-level managers and directors in leading companies. In addition, the declared commitment of the Israeli legal system to gender equality is not supported by Orthodox religious groups, who have a monopoly over personal issues such as marriage and divorce. Girls from such groups are exempt from army service, and religious families do not allow women to participate in political life. Although, according to a recent report of the New Israel Fund:

> Women make up close to 50 percent of the workforce in Israel, . . . they are paid only 62 percent of men's salaries. Women also constitute 70 percent of those earning minimum wage or less. . . .In 2006, only 15 percent of representatives on local councils and only 17 percent of Knesset members were women. (NIF, n.d.)

The impact of this carries over, with variations, into public relations. Women started joining the Israeli Government service in the role of spokesperson only in the late 1970s, but by 1990 women constituted 50 percent of the Government staff responsible for communication and public relations, with most working under the title of spokesperson (Avisar, 1990, p. 10) [ATH]. Women appeared on the Israeli public relations business stage as independent public relations consultants during the 1980s. The number of women in journalism also grew dramatically from the mid-1970s, and during the 1980s, as part of a feminization process of other professions that were considered masculine (Caspi and Limore, 1992, p. 33). Interestingly, the feminization process of the profession did not include any feminist agenda. Israeli women practitioners saw themselves as competing with men in their field according to male rules.

THE MEDIA AND PUBLIC RELATIONS

The first Hebrew newspapers, which started to appear in the second half of the 19th century, and the media in the first two decades of the State of Israel, occupied similar roles. Both were expected to function as unifying agents, to boost the people's morale, and to support the national cause as defined by the leadership. In its Declaration of Independence Israel made a commitment to freedom of the press. However, as soon as the British moved out in 1948, the new temporary government took control of the radio broadcasts services and the Government Press Office (GPO) of the British Mandate, along with its censorship regulations.

In fact, from June 1949, according to the first Government Annual Report, all the information services of different units were concentrated in the Prime Minister's Office. (GAR, 1949/1950, p. 23) [ATH]. In 1950 *Galei Tzahal*, the military radio station, was set up and became a popular channel for the general civil population. The Israeli government kept its control over the broadcast media, the printed press, and Hasbara through different structures within the Prime Minister's Office. In 1965 the Broadcasting Authority was established following the model of the BBC, as a public service governed by a political board. Israeli television broadcasts started as late as 1968 as part of the monopoly of the Broadcasting Authority. For 25 years Israelis could watch only one TV channel, which was governed by the Broadcasting Authority appointed by the government. No commercial advertising was allowed.

In 1990 the Second Authority for Television and Radio was established by law as a public authority to regulate commercial broadcasts in Israel. In November 1993 the first commercial broadcasts started on Channel 2 with three competing private licenses that were limited to a four- to six-year period. The Second Authority also regulated regional radio stations operated by private licenses through commercial financing and under public supervision. The public council, which heads the Second Authority for Television and Radio (n.d.), "appoints its director general based on the recommendations of the minister in charge and the approval of the government." In 2002 it launched TV Channel 10, thus ending Channel 2's monopoly over the television advertising market and, in 2001, the government announced the creation of Channel 3, a second commercial channel. Cable TV, funded by user fees, operates on a regional basis and provides a wide range of channels, mostly foreign news and entertainment channels. About 70 percent of households subscribe to cable television.

A major challenge for Israeli democracy is the cross ownership by a few media moguls of different print and electronic media (including Internet services). The owners' business interests include banks, communications, energy, the food industry, insurance, investments, and tourism. The ownership of media channels empowers this small number of rich businesspeople to use their media assets to promote other interests and intervene in media content behind the scenes. Given the low level of expectations for transparency in Israel, this situation represents a real risk to any public right to know.

The Print Media

Caspi and Limor (1992) pointed out a number of key changes in the Israeli print media that were significant for public relations practitioners:

- The decline of the party-owned press during the 1960s and 1970s. Fourteen dailies were closed down between 1948 and 1981, reflecting the decline in the centrality of the parties in the Israeli socio-political system.

- The consolidation of the private newspapers, mainly the dailies *Ha'aretz*, *Yediot Aharonot*, *Ma'ariv*, and the financial newspaper *Globes*. The private press developed from small informative newspapers in the pre-state and first decade into entertainment corporations managing many economic projects from the 1980s onwards.

- Private ownership enabled political independence and actually "the private newspapers preferred—as a practical and consistent policy—not to be identified with a specific political line but rather to cultivate and preserve ideological independence, and no less than to promote ideological pluralism in the newspaper" (Caspi and Limore, 1992, p. 68) [ATH].

- The rise of local newspapers. This reached its peak during the 1980s and was part of an international process of communication decentralization. The Israeli process reflects a shift, away from an emphasis on unity and consensus during the nation-building period, toward social pluralism.

- The influence of Western journalistic styles and formats—that became an integral part of the transformation of the Israeli society—as it opened to global markets.

- The Arab language newspapers that serve a fifth of the Israeli population went through a similar process of change but in a much shorter time. The "communication revolution" (Caspi and Limore, 1992. p. 91), which occurred in the Arab press during the 1980s, followed a new pluralistic political structure in the Arab sector.

By 2007 Israel media consumers had a choice between 30 dailies, 286 local newspapers, and 255 magazines. There were 958 radio programs and 254 television programs on the different channels and 3,036 journalists, 2,456 editors, and 569 producers worked for the media sector (Boltanski, 2006, pp. 81–83). Because of the often dramatic daily events, and the relevance of political issues to everyday life, Israelis are heavy consumers of news and political programs as well as escapist entertainment programs and sport.

This is matched by high ICT usage according to Orbicom's comparative international index of development "Infostate," which combines the country's "Infodensity" (ICT capital, ICT labor, Networks of Internet, Cable, and Telecommunication), and the country's "Info-use" (ICT uptake and ICT intensity). In Orbicom's 2003 global comparison of "Infostates," Israel is included in the group of "high infostates," and comes 21st in a list of 23 of the most developed countries in the world (Scaidas, 2005, p. 16).

Israelis are enthusiastic adopters of high technology services and major players in the development of new high-tech innovations. The number of cellular phones owned by Israelis is higher than the number of its population. The Internet penetration is high— over 50 percent of the population is connected and broadband services are provided at a reasonable cost. However, where Internet access is concerned, large differences are apparent in the gulf between the information rich and the information poor.

Media Relations

According to Abbott's (1988) model, the emergence and disappearance of professions result from the competition between them. In his account journalism crystallized its professional identity by divorcing itself from public relations. Thus public relations practitioners are assumed to assert themselves as professionals by defining the differences between their practice and the other occupations from which they evolved.

Public relations in the Israeli context did not divorce itself from journalism. The blur between these two occupations is reflected in the ongoing collaborative, and social, relationships between government agency spokespeople and journalists. Historically, too, from early pre-state days, there were financial deals between Hasbara practitioners and news agencies. Hasbara practice in national institutions involved financial support also to film production companies and press photographers. All these took place without even the pretence of transparency and without any respect for the function of independent journalism in a democratic system (Toledano, 2005, p. 323).

These professional values, which were set in the pre-state period by the national institutions, inspired the media sector professionals to this day. In contemporary Israel, journalists still advertise commercial products and services, take public relations jobs, and are deeply involved socially with politicians and public relations practitioners. In an IABC supported research project conducted in 2004, this can be seen in the following comments by a range of Israeli public relations practitioners in a focus group:

> "In Israel companies that conduct themselves ethically are frustrated when they discover the unethical conduct of the media. When, in an article about themselves, they discover bias in favor of the bank where the editor is keeping his private account and the insurance agency of the proof reader—they are disillusioned. The media is breaking the laws of the game."

> "The media is a threat but it can be bought. Any client would be ready to bribe a journalist. I received a letter from a journalist asking to increase the compensation her father was expecting from my client—an insurance company. I decided not to pay the journalist's father more than was deserved but the client considered doing it."

> "Sometimes I forbid my clients when they come up with ideas such as—disseminating false information about competitors via the internet. In the security industry there is a red line and sensitivity of employees to ethical issues but in general the status of ethics in Israel compared to other countries is "day and night". The bottom line is—don't get caught. We are warning them about the possibility of being caught by the media but we don't know what they would be doing behind closed doors" (Toledano, 2005, Appendix 3, p. 355).

The public relations function is still perceived by many Israeli managers as focused on media relations and mainly for the purpose of covering up organizational faults and for the glorification of organizational achievements. In a 2007 New Year congratulations message on video clip, emailed by the Israeli PR agency Gitam-Porter Novelli to its clients, the Director sends the agency's employees out to cut a negative story from all newspapers. The explicit message to the client is "Wishing You a Year of Good News" and the implicit message is "we will use any method possible to protect your reputation." There is no regard given to the ethical implications of the message.

CASE STUDY: MORMONS ON THE MOUNT

The following case illustrates the unique culture that characterizes Israel. It also presents the challenging socio-political and cultural complexity for public relations practice by international groups when they attempt to introduce new ideas or projects and/or transfer them from one culture to the other.

The case concerned Brigham Young University's (BYU) purchase of land in Jerusalem to build a student study center. Brigham Young had run a small study center in an Israeli Kibbutz for years with no problems, and students came from Utah to Jerusalem to study. Difficulties arose when Brigham Young sought to situate their new center next to the Hebrew University on Mount Scopus. The land purchase involved Brigham Young donating a substantial sum of money to the Jerusalem municipality. Since the University is owned by the Mormon Church, orthodox Jewish organizations became alarmed that it might become a Christian missionary outpost for converting Jews. The fears were compounded because the chosen site on Mount Scopus was prominently situated and faced the holy Jewish sites of the old city. Religious and secular Jewish organizations from Israel and the U.S. launched a violent campaign against the building of the study center and organized demonstrations, petitions, publicity and political pressure to stop the project.

BYU hired Gitam, an Israeli advertising and public relations agency, with the following briefs: to influence public opinion and satisfy Israelis that the center would not engage in proselytizing; to convince decision makers to allow the center to be built and to operate; and to help the center be accepted in Jerusalem over the long term. The audiences involved were the general public; the decision makers (especially the Knesset, the government, and the Jerusalem municipality); Jewish religious organizations opposing the center; and "Liberal" Israeli organizations (e.g., democracy movements, human rights workers, and secular organizations).

Gitam undertook research on the opposition, especially the religious organization Yad Leachim, and their backers. The agency also identified potential supporters such as the Mayor of Jerusalem. They researched the reasons for public opposition, and for public support. The opinion surveys found that 20 percent of Israelis opposed the center, 20 percent of Israelis supported the center, and 60 percent could not have cared less. There were three main reasons offered for opposition: distrust of Mormons, through perceptions of their strange way of life and missionary activity; ignorance of Mormons, seen as associated with sects such as Hari Krishna; and feelings that the Jewish people, having already lost too many through the Holocaust, could not afford to lose Jews to other religions.

The four main reasons that emerged for supporting the building of the center were that: Israel as a state was founded in 1948 on a promise that it would be open to, and respectful of, all religions; stopping the Mormons would damage Israel's international reputation (and, especially, the politically-vital relationship with the U.S.); Israel should not be afraid of missionary activity and Brigham Young was not the church; and, as Mormons were credible and trustworthy, to persecute them would be shameful.

The first part of the public relations strategy involved establishing messages to build trust in, and to lessen distrust of, the Mormons. In essence Gitam humanized their clients by presenting them as modern human beings and not as an arcane cult. Gitam implemented the strategy by circulating photographs of Mormons as ordinary people in ordinary clothes doing ordinary things, such as field trips to familiar sites. In addition the agency obtained press coverage of Brigham Young's dance group participating in a local festival. Gitam also circulated the idea that stopping the Mormons would damage Israel's international reputation and enlisted support from influential groups in the U.S. to pressure Israeli decision makers (e.g., the Mormon Congress group organized a declaration signed by members of Congress testifying in support of Brigham Young). Gitam simultaneously publicized positive testimonials about Mormons and their behavior through information kits— provided to Knesset members and the press—that featured a testimonial from the Rabbi of Salt Lake City that more Mormons there converted to Judaism than Jews to Mormonism. This explicitly countered a Yad Leachim organized press conference, in which three individuals testified to Mormon missionary work in Israel.

Finally, Gitam's strategy consciously constructed perceptions of Mormons as being at risk of persecution in Israel, and as the underdog (Toledano, McKie, and Roper, 2004) opposed by larger and more threatening forces. In a retrospective account, Gitam identified a key campaign moment as the time the agency persuaded radio stations to broadcast a recording taken from Brigham Young's telephone answering machine in Jerusalem. The tape contained curses from Jewish religious extremists threatening to kill Mormons if the building expansion went ahead. In the end, two years after the public relations campaign began, Brigham Young's expansion was approved by a Ministerial Committee formed by the government. The Mormon Center was allowed to operate providing that it did not give publicity to activities, that it did not enrol Jews, and that it did not proselytize. The strategy to position the university as the underdog contributed to the success of this campaign. The Brigham Young University Study Center has been built and has served its American students without involving Jewish Israelis and without any incident of proselytizing for the last twenty years.

CONCLUSION

Israel's democracy in the first two decades of the state retarded the development of public relations. The Israeli society at that time, including the media, were mobilised and dominated by the challenge of nation-building, which demanded high levels of unity and consensus. The political system expected the media to support the process, and the leadership's agenda, without questioning or criticizing. At the same time the limited market activities were centralized and controlled by the Government so that competition and consumerist culture was insignificant. As a result, the socio-political and economic environment did not create any need for public relations services. During the pre-state period and the first two decades of the state, the few practitioners worked mainly in the service of national institutions promoting the Zionist narratives in a practice which could be defined as (and was, sometimes, officially called) propaganda.

Though media relations services did not develop until later, the public relations functions of fundraising and lobbying were well rooted and highly developed in the Israeli context. The dependence of Israeli organizations on Jewish Diaspora funds resulted in professional and sophisticated public relations work in the service of major public institutions.

The political changes and economic developments of the 1980s and 1990s provided a more appropriate environment for the development of the profession. The political revolution, which followed the 1967 and 1973 wars, also changed the public discourse and the nature of Israel's democracy in many ways. Its impact on the media and the party system created a need for new professional communicators and stimulated the development of the profession. Continuing challenges remain. These include the concentration of conventional media in terms of major outlets and restricted ownership and the need for increasing transparency in both public and private sectors along with greater ethical involvement by practitioners in their organizations' values and conduct.

REFERENCES

Avisar, A. (1990). 24 hours in the service of the boss and the media: Women conquer state spokesperson role. *Ma'ariv*, 23 March, 1990, 10.

BDI. (2005). Retrieved from http://www.ynet.co.il, 28 December, 2007.

Bernays, E. L. (Ed.). (1955). *The engineering of consent.* Norman, OK: University of Oklahoma Press.

Boltanski, O. (2006). *Infor2006.* Tel-Aviv: Kodaf

Caspi, D., and Limor Y. (1992). *The mediators: The mass media in Israel, 1948–1990* [in Hebrew]. Tel Aviv, Israel: Am Oved.

CIA (Central Intelligence Agency). (n.d.).Downloaded from https://www.cia.gov/cia/publications, 22 October, 2006.

Cohen, N. (2003). A very sealed state. *The Marker*, 21 July, 2003, 15.

Dor, D. (2001). *Newspapers under the influence.* Tel-Aviv: Babel.

Ellul, J. (1965). *Propaganda: The formation of men's attitudes* (K. Kellen and J. Lerner, Trans.). New York: Vintage Books.

Elon, A. (1983). *The Israelis: Founders and sons.* New York: Viking Penguin. (Original work published 1971)

Fisher, S. (2006). Financial market liberalization. Keynote Speech, OECD Forum, "Balancing Globalization," 22–23 May, 2006, Paris, France. Retrieved from http://www.oecd.org, 23 November, 2006.

Habermas, J. (1976). *Legitimation crisis* (T. McCarthy, Trans.). London: Heinemann.

ISPRA (Israeli Public Relations Association). (2007). Website. Retrieved from http://www.ispra.org.il, 5 January, 2007.

Katriel, T. (1986). *Talking straight: Dugri speech in Israeli Sabra culture.* Cambridge: Cambridge University Press.

Kimmerling, B. (2001). *The end of Ashkenazi hegemony.* Jerusalem: Keter Publishing.

Klein, Z. (2007). Foreign investment in Israel at all time high: Tripled in three years. *Globes Israel Business News.* Retrieved from http://www.globes.co.il, 8 January, 2007.

Kouts, G. (1998). Zionism and the Jewish press: Between propaganda and "Objective Journalism." In J. Wilke (Ed.), *Propaganda in the 20th Century: Contributions to its history* (pp. 99–112), Cresskill, NJ: Hampton Press.

Lehman-Wilzig, S. (1992). *Public protest in Israel.* Ramat-Gan, Israel: Bar-Ilan University.

McKie, D., and Toledano, M. (2006). Personal attendance at ISPRA annual conference, 7 December, 2006, Tiberias, Israel.

NIF (New Israeli Fund). (n.d.). Women's rights. Retrieved from http://www.nif.org/content.cfm?cat_id=1520andcurrbody=1, 16 January, 2007.

OECD (Organization for Economic Co-operation and Development). (2002). *OECD investment policy review: Israel overview.* Retrieved from http://www.oecd.org search: Israel, 15 January, 2005.

Peri, Y. (2004). *Telepopulism: Media and politics in Israel.* Stanford, CA: Stanford University Press.

Scaidas, D. (Ed.). (2005). *From the digital divide to digital opportunities: Measuring infostates for development.* Canada: Claude Yves Charron, Orbicom.

Second Authority for Television and Radio. (n.d.). Retrieved from http://www.rashut2.org, 28 January, 2007.

Shapiro, Y. (1978). *Democracy in Israel* [in Hebrew]. Tel Aviv: Masada.

Siebert, F. S., Peterson, T., and Schramm, W. (1956). *Four theories of the press.* Chicago: University of Illinois Press.

Toledano, M. (2005). *Public relations in Israel: The evolution of public relations as a profession in Israel's changing political, socio-cultural, and economic environment* [in French]. Unpublished Ph.D. thesis submitted to Université Paris 8, France.

Toledano, M., McKie, D., and Roper, J. (2004). Theorising practice: Public relations power, U.S. symmetrical theory, and Israeli asymmetric campaigns. *Australian Journal of Communication*, 31(3), 59–70.

Traubman, T. (2006). The number of students doubled in recent decade. *Ha'aretz*, 22 October, 2006, 5.

TI (Transparency International). (2006). Transparency International Corruption Perception Index. Media release, 6 November, 2006 (Gypsy Guillén Kaiser ggkaiser@transparency.org).

Wolffsohn, M. (1987). *Israel, polity, society and economy 1882–1986* (D. Bokovoy, Trans.). Atlantic Highlands, NJ: Humanities Press International.

Yishai, Y. (1998). Civil society in transition. In G. Ben-Dor (Ed.), *The Annals of the American Academy of Political and Social Science, Vol. 555* (January). Thousand Oaks, CA: Sage.

Zerubavel, Y. (1995). *Recovered roots: Collective memory and the making of Israeli national tradition*. Chicago: The University of Chicago Press.

AFRICA

CHAPTER

14

THE NATURE AND STATUS OF PUBLIC RELATIONS PRACTICE IN AFRICA

CHRIS SKINNER

GARY MERSHAM

OVERVIEW

Research on the continental practice of public relations in Africa is for the most part sparse and fragmented, a large proportion of it carried out on specific aspects of practice in specific countries.

There are unfortunately few studies that try to treat Africa as an entity and from a communication perspective. However, the recent report "The Public Relations Landscape in Africa" (2006), carried out by the UK-based consultancy Gyroscope, is one that claims a measure of success in this challenging task.

As the report points out, the continent we refer to as "Africa" is a patchwork of 53 countries, some sharing common borders, with others separated by thousands of kilometres. They range from large, prosperous and cosmopolitan Egypt, to landlocked, impoverished and troubled Chad; and from the scattered Atlantic island state of Sao Tome and Principe to the thriving economies of South Africa, Nigeria and more recently the Democratic Republic of Congo.

The deliberations around NEPAD—the New Partnership for African Development, a continent-wide initiative for the social, economic and political development of Africa—and the "African Renaissance," actively promoted by South Africa's President Thabo Mbeki, in fact highlight the challenges that will have to be addressed before we can speak of an authentically integrated and united Africa

First, there is a daunting lack of physical infrastructure. Road networks radiate from capital cities to the major provincial hubs and the pattern remains constant: the nearer the capital, the better the road. As the roads spread beyond the provinces toward

FIG. 14.1   Countries in the Gyroscope Africa Communications Index.
(see www.gyroscopeconsultancy.com).

the border with the next country, they degrade, often to little more than tracks. Trade and other contact is characteristically either within national borders or extra-continental, rather than intertrade between countries which share borders.

There are relatively few safe, secure and comfortable international road or rail links. Air links are available between major centres, but this raises the problem of cost. The vast majority of people cannot afford to fly, and hence are unable to travel beyond their own country.

This in turn contributes to the second barrier: a profound, mutual ignorance of different countries and cultures. Compared to many other parts of the world, it is very difficult for someone from any given African country to acquire a real knowledge and understanding of just one or two of the countries which border their own.

The third barrier—language—compounds this further (Hooyberg and Mersham, 2000). South Africa alone has 11 recognised official languages; Nigeria has more than 390 distinct dialects; few if any of these are widely spoken in Nigeria's immediate neighbours, such as Chad or Benin, and none of them are spoken in (for example) Egypt or Ethiopia. Even where either English or French is generally understood, linguistic confusion and isolation are common.

The fourth barrier is differential economics and huge discrepancies in the GDPs of Africa's states. Poverty is grinding and widespread. Nations often have small, wealthy elites along with millions of dirt-poor peasants and workers. Elites tend to run major institutions, with a very small middle class providing few checks and balances. As the Gyroscope report (2006:4) puts it, "South Africa can afford a global advertising campaign to build its national brand, and attract investment and tourism; Ghana, which celebrated its 50th Anniversary in 2007, cannot."

Indeed, so challenging is the social, political, geographical and economic diversity of Africa that for many communications professionals in the commercial sector Africa remains out of bounds. For many organisations—NGOs, charities, healthcare managers, educators—operating in Africa is not a choice but a responsibility or a mission. They work there and manage communications there because of the continent's problems, not despite them.

Yet for commercial organizations, Africa is a potentially vast and untapped market, the world's next great consumer market which will require a massive growth in effective marketing communications. Africa is a continent of 800 million people, with an average GDP per capita of $684. This compares with that of China (1.3 billion people, and $780 per capita in GDP) and India (1.1 billion, $440 per capita in GDP). Certainly, within the average GDP per capita in Africa there is an extreme range of personal income levels, from utter poverty to immense wealth—but this range is not significantly more extreme than that of China's or India's inhabitants.

Whether organisations are exploiting Africa's commercial opportunities—either as a market or as a source of raw materials and resources—the need to act as good global corporate citizens is drawn into sharp relief. Clearly there is a responsibility to the continent's people, their development and their environment. Ultimately, then, there are few major organisations that do not need to know more about Africa and how to manage communications there (Gyroscope 2007:5).

Indeed the final Commission Report for Africa (2006) paints a pragmatic and positive story about the continent. Regional economic integration is indeed proceeding apace with major advances in the streamlining of investment and competition policy frameworks, customs regimes and trade policies, and in many other areas. A new initiative on budget reform and public expenditure management has been launched in South Africa with the enthusiastic participation of treasury officials from across the continent (CABRI).

More democratic states and fewer civil conflicts are also just two signs of progress on the political front. The long-awaited European Union–African Summit in Lisbon in December 2007 heard that when leaders of the two continents last met in Cairo seven years previously, there were no fewer than 14 conflicts ranging on African soil, making up 50 percent of violent deaths in the world. These chilling statistics had more than halved by 2007. Africa has also achieved unprecedented macroeconomic stability, which is contributing to better economic growth rates than have been achieved in decades. According to the IMF, the continent's GDP was less than 1 percent between 1995 and 2000. In the first five years of this century it rose to 4.3 percent. Since then it has increased to 5.5 percent and is estimated to have risen to 6.8 percent in 2007. However, it must be said that deep and grinding poverty remains a daily reality throughout the continent, notwithstanding the focus on macroeconomic policy—which is necessary but remains insufficient.

In these circumstances the Commission concludes, Africa is ready and willing to embrace a new kind of partnership. NEPAD's primary objectives are to:

- eradicate poverty;
- place African countries, both individually and collectively, on a path of sustainable growth and development;

- halt the marginalisation of Africa in the globalisation process and enhance its full and beneficial integration into the global economy; and

- accelerate the empowerment of women.

Visit their website at www.nepad.org for further details.

Fortunately the G8 Summit in Gleneagles in Scotland in 2005 has gone some way in providing a comprehensive package to fast track Africa meeting the Millennium Development Goals (MDG) by 2015. These are:

- provide an extra $50 billion aid worldwide and $25 billion for Africa;

- write off the debts of 18 of the world's poorest countries, most of which are in Africa, including $17 billion of Nigeria's debt;

- commit to end all export and domestic subsidies;

- provide as close to universal access to HIV/Aids treatments as possible by 2010;

- provide funding to fight malaria to save the lives of over 600,000 children every year;

- totally eradicate polio from the world; and

- provide access for good quality, free and compulsory education for all children as well as basic health care by 2015.

Although some of these programmes still need to be kickstarted, there is still a commitment from the developed world and its leaders to address the real problems of Africa. (See Gleneagles Plan of Action on climate change, clean energy and sustainable development www.fco.gov.uk.) Overall a significant amount of resources has been channelled into Africa since the MDG were adopted in 2001. Between 2000 and 2005 an estimated $97 billion has reached the continent through official development assistance. African governments themselves have also set aside various percentages of their budgets for expenditure in priority sectors to effect positive change in the lives of the poor.

CHALLENGES FACING THE CONTINENT

The Environmental Dimensions

Africa is the second largest region in the world, accounting for 20 percent of the world's land mass (2,963,313,000 hectares). It stretches 7,680 km from north to south and 7,200 km from east to west. Sixty-six percent of Africa is classified as arid or semi-arid, and it is estimated that about 200 million hectares (32 percent of the suitable area) is cultivated, 30 percent of the total land area (892 million hectares) is used as permanent pasture, and 20 percent of Africa's vegetated lands are classified as degraded and 66 percent of this is moderately to severely degraded. Patterns of land use in Africa are equally diverse and complex, extending beyond agriculture. Source : FAOSTAT 2001.

Some 40 percent of Africa's population live in urban areas. By 2030 this is expected to grow to approximately 54 percent. Africa's rate of urbanisation of 3.5 percent per year is the highest in the world. Forty cities in Africa have populations of more than one million. By 2015, 70 cities will have populations of one million or more. Lagos, Nigeria, with a population of 13.4 million, is the largest city in Africa and the sixth largest in the world. Cairo, Africa's second largest city, has a population of 10.6 million and ranks 19th in the world. Africa's cities account for 60 percent of the region's GDP and are important centres of education, employment and trade. Source : UNCHS 2001. Against this population growth, the devastating effect of HIV/Aids must be set. Still in 2007, there are 33.2 million people living with HIV in the world. The epicentre in Africa is in Southern Africa, where HIV prevalence ranges from 15 percent to 35 percent, in East Africa 2 percent to 7 percent and in West Africa, which includes some of the most populous countries, the prevalence ranges from 1 percent to 5 percent.

However, Africa is faced with three major issues, namely:

- climate variability;
- climate change;
- air quality.

Africa's average annual rainfall has been decreasing since 1968, and drought is now being experienced regularly in Botswana, Burkina Faso, Chad, Ethiopia, Kenya, Mauritania and Mozambique. At the same time, parts of Africa are experiencing excessive rainfall which is causing extensive flooding with extreme loss of life. Ambient air pollution in urban centres is also emerging as an issue of concern for human health in many African countries. Africa emits 3.5 percent of the world's carbon dioxide and this is expected to increase further in the years ahead. Thus as environmental resources dwindle because of global warming, people will begin fighting over scarce resources, particularly water and agricultural land. According to a recent report, "Climate Change as a Security Risk," Southern Africa is one of the areas in the world that is most at risk.

Africa has rich and varied biological resources forming the region's natural wealth on which its social and economic systems are based. These resources also have global importance for the world's climate and for the development of agriculture or industrial activities such as pharmaceuticals, tourism or construction. Of the so-called 25 international hot spots in the world, six of them are in Africa. Hot spots are areas where species diversity and endemism are particularly high and where there is an extraordinary threat of loss of species or habitat. Source: African Environment Outlook 2002.

Africa's hot spots include:

- the Mediterranean Basin Forests;
- the Western Indian Ocean Islands, particularly the island of Madagascar;
- Cape Floristic region in South Africa, being the smallest and richest of the world's floral kingdoms;
- Karoo, being the richest desert in the world, shared between South Africa and Namibia;
- Guinean Forest, a strip of fragmented forest running parallel to the coast of Western Africa through 11 countries from Guinea to Cameroon; and
- Eastern Arc Mountain Forests of eastern Africa which are 30 million years old and are thought to have existed in isolation for at least 10 million years.

The African coastal zone supports a diversity of habitats and resources encompassing mangroves, rocky shores, sandy beaches, deltas, estuaries and coastal wetlands, coral reefs and lagoons. It provides opportunities for employment, tourism, fishing, medicinal preparations and for harvesting resources. Oil and gas resources and other mineral deposits are additional important economic resources for African coastal countries particularly for a number of countries in West Africa (Nigeria and Equatorial Guinea). Major trade and industrial centres have developed around the ports of Lagos, Accra, the Nile delta, Mombasa, Maputo, Durban, Port Elizabeth and Cape Town.

Africa's total forest cover is estimated at approximately 650 million hectares, equivalent to 17 percent of the global forest cover and approximately 22 percent of Africa's land area. It ranges from open savanna to closed tropical rain forest. Africa lost 39 million hectares of tropical forest during the 1980s and another 10 million by 1995. The destruction of the forests has unfortunately gathered pace in the past decade, with grave consequences both for the environment and the people that lived and worked in them.

Of major significance too is that the majority of African countries report over-exploitation of surface and ground water supplies. As a result of inadequate capital investment in this sector by the year 2025, 25 African countries will experience water scarcity or water stress.

Thus as a result of a number of factors, Africa is the only continent in the world in which poverty is expected to rise this century. Up to 65 percent of urban dwellers in some African countries live in poverty, with little or no access to social and urban services, and the position in rural areas is equally dire with periodic droughts worsening an already precarious existence. This is where the humanitarian agencies play a key role together with world bodies such as the UN, the World Bank and the IMF.

The Political and Economic Dimensions

This review provides a snapshot of some of the leading economies on the continent. It is based on a survey conducted in 2006 by Pratibha Thaker, regional director in Africa of the Economist Intelligence Unit and updated from various newspaper reports published in the Mail and Guardian, Johannesburg, South Africa during 2007. It highlights how some of the environmental factors have impacted on the growth and stability of some of Africa's leading economies.

Sudan
The government is based on an uneasy balance of power between the ruling National Congress party in the north, and the semi-autonomous government of Southern Sudan. Although the 2005 peace agreement should hold, complex power- and wealth-sharing mechanisms create a number of potential flashpoints. International relations will be dominated by the question of Darfur. To date only a fraction of the hybrid 26,000-strong African Union–UN peacekeeping force for Darfur is on the ground. But given heavy Chinese investment in the oil industry, the UN Security Council is unlikely to impose serious sanctions, although the US has taken a stand in this regard. Oil output is likely to rise sharply owing to the Petrodar concession but the crude oil is of poor quality. Nevertheless, economic growth will exceed 11 percent.

Somalia
A change of prime ministers in Somalia has seen Ali Mohamed Gedi replaced by Nur Hassan Hussein, but this unfortunately has brought no semblance of peace to the country, which has been without an effective government since the fall of dictator Siad Barre in 1991. Clashes between the Baidoa-based, weak transitional federal government and the ascendant United Islamic Courts (UIC), which has taken control of most of the south of Somalia, intensified during 2007. The transitional government is virtually powerless, but with the support of Ethiopian forces has driven the UIC out of the south. Mediation under the auspices of the African Union and the regional body, the Intergovernmental Authority on Development, continues.

Ethiopia

The Ethiopian People's Revolutionary Democratic Front (EPRDF) retains firm control in the country. Prime Minister Meles Zenawi repeatedly promises to settle his country's border dispute with Eritrea peacefully. Yet six years after signing the Algiers agreement ending the war, Ethiopia continues to dig its heels in against the independent boundary commission's ruling, awarding the town of Badme to Eritrea. The border remains tense. Both sides appear unable to resolve the dispute. Eritrea considers the continued presence of Ethiopian troops in its territory to be a violation of its sovereignty, with the UN taking sides with Addis Ababa. Ethiopia also poured 60,000 troops into Somalia in 2007 to help the transitional government of Abdullah Ysuf drive out the Islamic Courts that controlled the capital Mogadishu. At the beginning of 2008, 35,000 Ethiopian troops still continue to prop up the state in Mogadishu.

Kenya

Kenyans returned to the polls in December 2007. Unfortunately this resulted in a bitterly contested election between President Mwai Kibaki and opposition leader Raila Odinga, which triggered weeks of violence that killed over a thousand people, severely crippling the economy. Key sectors such as tourism, banking and investment have been particularly badly hit and the region as a whole has also suffered. An alliance between the two rival parties has, however, brought some stability to the country in 2008.

Uganda

Uganda has signed a truce with the Lord's Resistance Army that has waged a 20-year insurrection involving dragooning thousands of young people as child soldiers and sex slaves. Unfortunately the deal has not stopped the fighting and Mozambique's former president, Joachim Chissano, has begun mediation efforts to bring the rebels back to negotiations chaired by the Southern Sudanese government.

Burundi

President Pierre Nkurunziza and his party are expected to maintain a firm grip on political power, but internal divisions could weaken the party. The welcome return to peace after so many years of fighting will boost economic growth, but it is doubtful whether the recent ceasefire between the government and the Palipehutu–FNL will evolve into a conclusive settlement. There has unfortunately been no return by either side to the monitoring commission they quit in July 2007—13 months after signing a truce. Donor-financed capital expenditure will play an important role in the development of the economy and construction, trade and manufacturing grew by 5 percent or more in 2007.

Democratic Republic of Congo

Following years of dictatorship, civil war and economic decline, it remains to be seen whether President Joseph Kabila, the leader of the country's first elected government in 40 years in 2006, is capable of leading an administration that can move towards establishing the rule of law and developing the massive economic potential of his country. The United Nations' peacekeeping force, Monuc, is helping the government to contain the Tutsi rebel leader, Laurent Nkunda, in the Kivus on his country's eastern border with Rwanda and Uganda. He is also taking diplomatic heat to facilitate the return of Jean-Pierre Bemba, his chief political rival, from Portugal. The support of donors will remain crucial to financing the operations of government and the business and mining sectors of one of Africa's richest states.

Angola

Angola's economic growth steams ahead. GDP growth since 1995 has averaged 6.6 percent but, on the strength of increased oil revenues, reached 11 percent in 2004 and is forecast by the IMF to have averaged 18 percent a year from 2005–2007. Presidential and parliamentary elections took place in September 2008 and the ruling MPLA party once again was returned to power. The ruling party is in a strong position to win the elections, while the opposition UNITA will struggle to hold together. Angola's on-off relationship with the IMF will remain but relations with China will continue to deepen. Heavy investment in infrastructure and the oil sector will continue to drive economic growth, but the economy will suffer weak structural constraints, including a flawed judicial system, poor regulatory policy and rampant corruption.

Namibia

The country has signed an interim economic partnership agreement (EPA) with the European Union. Economic growth will continue to be concentrated in the minerals sector, and higher output of diamonds, uranium and copper will drive economic growth. However, this will not do much to tackle poverty and income disparity in one of Africa's most unequal societies, where 60 percent of the population share less than 10 percent of the nation's income.

Botswana

Festus Mogae has stood down as President and has been replaced by Ian Khama. Diversification of the economy away from diamond mining will continue, and growth in services is expected to be robust, driven by the good performance of the financial sector, tourism and diamond marketing and sales activities following the transfer of the De Beers activities.

South Africa

South Africa has continued to expand at over 4–5 percent in its GDP in recent years, but severe power cuts announced by Eskom, the country's electricity authority, at the beginning of 2008, are likely to have a dramatic effect on future prospects, possibly reducing growth to 3 percent for the next few years. Important political changes have occurred in recent months with Jacob Zuma being elected to lead the ruling ANC party and Thabo Mbeki being forced to step down as President of the country. All this uncertainty has unfortunately had a negative impact on morale, just two years away from the country hosting the FIFA World Cup in 2010.

Mozambique

As one of Africa's poorest countries, Mozambique is prone to severe flooding, which regularly displaces tens of thousands of people. This occurred in 2007. The port of Maputo, which is used for exports from South Africa, and some industry, notably alumina smelting, together with tourism, provide job opportunities for a growing population.

Zambia

The fall-out from the controversial re-election of President Levy Mwanawasa and his Movement for Multiparty Democracy (MMD) in 2006 has died down. However, compliance with the economic reforms agreed under the country's poverty reduction and growth facility with the IMF may slip, as the government attempts to win back lost voters with lower taxes and labour reform. This could strain but not break relations with the IMF and other donors. The economy will be boosted by increases in copper production, but investment in the sector is unlikely to be maintained at the high levels of recent years. Extensive flooding affecting over one and a half million people in late 2007 has affected the export of food to neighbouring countries, the DRC, Namibia and Zimbabwe, in particular.

Zimbabwe

Zimbabwe's economic decline has been hastened by continued capital flight. Economic analysts say the continued injection of foreign direct investment (FDI) largely depends on the reversal of the Zimbabwean government's controversial political and economic policies. These policies have already affected the country's economic performance, leaving it with record inflation close to the 10,000 percent mark. Despite the continued economic implosion of the country, a new power sharing agreement has been reached between ZANU-PF and the opposition MDC. It is however, unlikely to bring immediate economic relief to millions of Zimbabweans.

Malawi

The ruling Democratic Progressive Party (DPP) faced a challenging period in 2007. Although new investment in the mining sector has got under way, a tailing-off of agricultural recovery and growth in the agro-industries sector after the drought of 2005 is expected to put a brake on overall economic growth. So too have the floods at the end of 2007, which have effected most of Central Africa.

Nigeria

Important elections took place in 2007 which resulted in a highly competitive tussle between Umaru Musa Yar'Adua, the former governor of Katsina State, and the incumbent Vice President, Atiku Abubakar. The former has now assumed power, but conditions still remain tense. His undertaking to work for transparency, accountability and a society free of corruption has won him friends in the West, particularly his undertaking to partner Africom, the new American military command structure for the African continent. It is predicted that an escalation of conflict in the crucial oil-producing areas of the Niger Delta will remain a concern. Non-oil sector growth will remain robust, but political unrest in the Niger Delta will have a negative effect on oil and gas production, pushing down economic growth.

Ghana

The political atmosphere is described as increasingly divisive ahead of the presidential and parliamentary elections in December 2008 when the ruling Patriotic Party and the opposition National Democratic Party will battle it out. Economically, the government's plans to loosen the purse strings will increase both financing and inflationary pressure, while power shortages are likely to impinge on the broader macroeconomic environment. But Ghana will continue to outperform most of its West African peers, with growth rising by almost 6 percent, thanks to strong commodity prices. It celebrated its 50th Anniversary of independence in 2007.

Cameroon

The ruling party, the Democratic Rally of the People of Cameroon, is expected to push ahead with structural reforms to open up sections of the non-oil economy to the private sector, but the progress on the privatisation of the remaining state owned industries may be erratic. Economic growth will benefit from a rise in oil production, growth in the agro-industry and forestry sectors and expansion in aluminium production.

Senegal

The ruling party, the PPDS, continues in power. The economy will be boosted by strong agricultural output growth, rapid expansion of the telecommunications sector and the preparations for the triennial summit of the Organisation of the Islamic Conference in the first quarter of 2008. But the secondary sector will continue to suffer from the negative impact of high oil prices and the ongoing financial difficulties of the country's largest company, Industries Chimiques du Senegal (ICS).

Côte d'Ivoire

2008 is expected to see long-overdue elections. President Laurent Gbagbo and Prime Minister Guillaune Soro have signed supplementary agreements to the Ouagadougou accord signed in March 2007 between the state and rebels in Burkina Faso under the mediation of President Blaise Campaore. The new agreements cover the merging of the official military with the rebel Forces Nouvelles that have controlled the north of the country since it split five years ago. They also lay the groundwork for free and fair elections.

Mauritania

Mauritania remains a beacon of hope in the Maghreb. The military junta that ended Maaiuiya Ould Taya's 25-year authoritarian rule kept to its word to restore democracy to this vast country. Sidi Ould Sheikh Abdallahi, who won the polls in March 2007, has his term as President prematurely ended in August 2008, when he was deposed by a military junta. Although slavery was officially abolished in 1981 by presidential decree, Mauritania's parliament has unanimously passed legislation making the practice of slavery punishable by up to ten years in prison in 2007; reports indicate that it still persists in many parts of Mauritania.

THE MEDIA IN AFRICA

Media channels exist that cover most or all of the African landmass, such as the BBC World Service, Voice of America and Channel Africa (satellite television originating from the South African Broadcasting Corporation) or which are in theory available throughout Africa (such as the Africa Online web portal). However, as practical paths for PR and corporate communications managers, these have limited value: first, in trying to be broadly "African," they lose much of the localism and relevance on which editorial communications depend; and second, they are essentially limited to particular publics: English-speaking, relatively literate and affluent audiences.

The need to plan and manage communications at a local level or country by country basis can be illustrated by considering media availability and habits in just three countries.

Tanzania, for example, with a population of 34 million, has 15 well-established newspapers—dailies and weeklies, in both English and Swahili—including a specialist business newspaper, *The Business Times*. Daily newspaper circulation is around 4 per thousand people. Tanzania also has a mix of independent and state-owned TV and radio stations.

By contrast, South Africa, with a population of 40 million, is currently experiencing a print media boom with 82 newspapers—nationals and regionals, dailies and weeklies, mainly in English or Afrikaans, with several in indigenous black African languages, and including specialist business titles and sports titles. There is a diversity of commercial, state-run and community radio and TV stations, and daily newspaper circulation is around 34 per thousand people.

Algeria, with a population of 32 million, has 26 newspapers, published mainly in French and Arabic, with two English editions, and a small range of TV and radio stations. The press includes weeklies and dailies, as well as nationals and regionals, though distribution of any newspapers outside the major cities is limited. Though the daily press circulation is high by African standards, at 38 per 1,000 people, all media are tightly controlled by the state.

These three countries alone, though broadly similar in terms of population size, demonstrate just some of Africa's remarkable diversity in the availability of media channels, and the potential for editorial access to them. Equally, they indicate the impracticality of trying to plan PR and corporate communications on a "pan-African" basis

Communications Infrastructure

To operate at all, communications managers need access to communications infrastructure: the means to disseminate information in order to change people's perceptions, attitudes and behaviour. Turning to the "new media," huge variations are found throughout Africa. The number of cellular telephone subscribers per 100 inhabitants, and the level of internet access in schools, are illustrative.

Data from the International Telecommunication Union for 2003 (the latest year for which comparable data are available across the relevant countries) shows cellphone subscriptions per 100 inhabitants ranging from 27 in South Africa and 22 in Morocco, down to seven in Egypt, six in Senegal and five in Kenya, with most other countries having fewer than two or three subscriptions per 100 people.

Nevertheless, Africa's uptake of cellular technology has been developing rapidly in the last few years. According to ITU (2006) statistics, the least developed countries with the highest annual growth rate in terms of cellular subscribers over the period 2000–2005 were Djibouti (186 percent), Democratic Republic of Congo (184 percent), Niger (171 percent), Liberia (155 percent), Mali (142 percent), Sudan (139 percent), and Yemen (129 percent). Prepaid services, accounting for almost 90 per cent of the entire market, have contributed to the explosive expansion of the mobile sector in LDCs. In, Chad, Djibouti, Eritrea, Somalia and Niger, all mobile subscriptions were prepaid.

Despite recent progress, African countries continue to face major challenges. Rapid developments in the telecommunications marketplace require new directions to be taken by policymakers and regulators. Many established policies and regulations have become obsolete, leading to inefficient and increasingly untenable restrictions and barriers to the development and dissemination of the benefits of Internet Protocol (IP) convergence. Regulators need to implement policies to encourage new network development opportunities and attract investor financial flows into the sector.

The scarcity of ICT infrastructure, the high cost of international bandwidth, the dearth of relevant local content along with the lack of cooperation among development partners and political instability also remain daunting challenges.

Internet access in schools, another key indicator of the ability to manage communications to specific audiences, was assessed in 2005 by the World Economic Forum for a number of African states. On the WEF's scale (where "1" denotes "very poor" and "7" denotes "excellent'), Egypt scores 3.9, and South Africa scores 3.6; Morocco and Uganda score 2.5; Zimbabwe, Senegal and Tanzania score just over 2; and the other countries all scored between 1 and 2 (in declining order, Ghana, Kenya, Zambia, Nigeria, Algeria, Cameroon, Mozambique, Madagascar, Ethiopia and Angola).

Education and Training

The need to work locally in each African country, combined with the complexities of local languages, cultures and media structures, brings with it the need for locally trained public relations practitioners. Clearly access to such practitioners and the infrastructure existing for their training and development has an important impact on the relative ease and costs of planning and managing communications activity in each country.

Levels of education vary extremely widely, as indicated by the World Economic Forum's 2005 survey of the quality of each country's educational system. In the survey where "1" denotes "very poor" and "7" denotes "excellent," Ghana, Zimbabwe, Kenya and Uganda led with scores of between 3 and 3.5; followed by Egypt (2.9), South Africa and Morocco (2.8), Cameroon (2.7) and Tanzania (2.6). The other countries measured by the WEF all scored less than 2.5.

At tertiary level, UNESCO figures for 2003 (the latest year for which comparable data are available) show that Egypt had around 40 percent tertiary enrolment; South Africa and Algeria both had around 15 percent, and Morocco around 10 percent. In most other countries, tertiary enrolment in 2003 was below 5 percent.

TERTIARY EDUCATION IN PUBLIC RELATIONS

In our work with African teaching and training institutions throughout the continent, we have found wide variations in professional or vocational education in PR and communications management. In many cases, mass communication and journalism programmes continue to be the flagship offering (as it was some thirty years ago in developed countries) containing some public relations focused components. In Uganda, for example, university courses in mass communication are available, with the option to specialise in public relations in the third year. While many countries have no degree courses in communication management, there is a growing trend towards their introduction.

Although the list is not exhaustive, the following teaching institutions offer communications programmes throughout Africa.

South Africa
South Africa has numerous institutions that offer specific communications management and public relations programmes at various levels in the communication departments and business faculties of universities.

Some of the best-known include:

University of Pretoria
University of Johannesburg
University of Zululand
Durban University of Technology
University of the Free State
University of South Africa
NorthWest University
Rhodes University
University of Stellenbosch
University of the Witwatersrand
Nelson Mandela Metropolitan University
Cape Peninsula University of Technology
Central University of Technology
Mangosuthu Technikon
Tshwane University of Technology
Vaal University of Technology

There are also numerous professional colleges that offer programmes; some of the best-known include:

Damelin
Boston
Regent
Intec

Foreign degrees offered locally include those of:

Bond South Africa
Edinburgh Business School
Henley Management College
University of Luton
Monash South Africa
University of Southern Queensland

Ethiopia
University of Addis Ababa

Uganda
Makerere University
Kampala International University

Kenya
University of Nairobi
African Virtual University (AVU)
Daystar University
Tangaza College—Institute for Social Communication

Namibia
University of Namibia

Tanzania
MS Training Centre for Development Co-operation
St Augustine University of Tanzania
University of Dar es Salaam

Egypt
American University Cairo

Ghana
Africa Institute of Journalism and Communications (AIJC)
University of Ghana
Central University
Ghana Institute of Journalism

Nigeria
ABTI-American University of Nigeria
University of Ibadan

Zambia
University of Zambia

PROFESSIONAL STANDARDS AND ETHICS

Standards of professional practice and ethics in the African countries we have researched and worked in range from excellent to very poor. Africa is no different in this respect from other major developing or developed economies such as China, Russia or India.

Countries such as Angola, Ethiopia and Zimbabwe are most at risk where the legal framework of the state is extremely weak; where the judiciary has little or no independence; where Government intervention in commercial relationships has a strongly distorting effect; and where the press is either state-owned, or independent but much oppressed by the state. These countries also tend to score very low on Transparency International's index of corruption.

At the higher end, we find countries such as Ghana, Botswana, South Africa and Namibia, with reasonable standards found in Tanzania, Uganda and Zambia.

African Public Relations Professional Associations

The African Public Relations Association is the successor organisation to the Federation of African Public Relations Associations (FAPRA) which was inaugurated in Nairobi, Kenya, in 1975, as the umbrella body of all National Public Relations Associations in Africa. It is a non-governmental, non-political and non-profit-making professional association, established to foster unity and interaction amongst public relation practitioners in Africa as a whole. Its track record in reaching these objectives has been somewhat inconsistent, but it has been more successful in recent years. In many respects it has benefited from working closely with the highly professional South African-based Public Relations Institute of Southern Africa (PRISA). PRISA, in turn, has benefited from greater contact with its counterparts in the rest of Africa. The two organisations have successfully collaborated to host a number of important conferences on African public relations themes including a joint conference held in Johannesburg in 2006 on "Managing Africa's Reputation."

The following public relations professional associations have been established in Africa and are members of FAPRA:

Arab Public Relations Society [based in Egypt] (APRS)
Institute of Public Relations in Ghana (IPRG)
Public Relations Society of Kenya (PRSK)
Public Relations Association of Botswana
Public Relations Association of Mauritius (PRAM)
Public Relations Association of Sudan
Public Relations Association of Tanzania
Public Relations Association of Gambia
Nigerian Institute of Public Relations (NIPR)
Swaziland Public Relations Association (SPRA)
Public Relations Association of Uganda
Zimbabwe Institute of Public Relations
Public Relations Institute of Southern Africa (PRISA) (based in South Africa)

However, the majority of these have very low key operations and membership is often very small. The Nigerian Institute is the largest national association, followed by PRISA, the Institute of Public Relations and Communication Management based in South Africa. PRISA celebrated its 50th Anniversary in 2007 (see the PRISA website for full details).

Efforts are also on hand to generate a membership data base for public relations practitioners in Africa. South Africa has currently some 2,000 full and 1,500 student members, Nigeria 7,000 full and 3,000 student members. FAPRA has introduced individual membership as well as country membership, which could contribute immeasurably towards its sustainability.

FAPRA also needs to strengthen its institutional links with such bodies as the African Union (AU), New Partnership for Africa Development (NEPAD), African Peer Review Mechanism (APRM) and other sub-regional organisations.

Standards of professionalism, performance and practice in public relations are significantly higher in countries which have a trade or professional association for the industry. The reasons for this include the fact that they generally provide (voluntary) codes of ethics and provide various fora for the discussion of ethical concerns and professional development programmes (for example the Eastern and Southern Africa Management Institute (ESAMI)). However, the various organisations are poorly linked and cooperation is limited.

Public Relations Agencies

While PR and corporate communications agencies of one sort or another can be found in most African countries, the PR and corporate communications agency sector in Africa is significantly under-developed. The Gyroscope report (2006) describes four important categories of agency: the local offices or affiliates of the global PR groups; Africa specialists, with claimed or actual expertise across several countries; local agencies that are genuine PR specialists; and local agencies that claim PR as part of a service offering. Agencies in the latter group are often the local offices or affiliates of global ad agencies.

Global Agencies
Most of the global agency groups are represented in South Africa, generally through affiliates as opposed to owned subsidiaries. Those with a presence in this market include Weber Shandwick, Burson Marsteller, Hill and Knowlton, Porter Novelli, Ogilvy, Fleishman Hillard, Edelman, Manning Selvage and Lee and Brodeur/Pleon. Weber Shandwick, Hill and Knowlton, Ogilvy, Fleishman Hillard and Manning Selvage and Lee are also represented in Egypt.

As well as South Africa and Egypt, Weber Shandwick is also represented in Algeria, Cote d'Ivoire, Kenya, Morocco, Nigeria, Tunisia and Uganda; while Hill and Knowlton is represented in Kenya, Morocco, Nigeria and Uganda. Burson Marsteller has an affiliate in Zimbabwe, and Ogilvy has an affiliate in Kenya. Some "affiliates" are often affiliated to more than one of the global groups.

Africa Specialists
There are a number of consultancies specialising in Africa, often with a focus on business development or market entry, and which offer communications management across several countries as a larger or smaller part of their portfolio. Some are generalist, some specialise in a particular field such as telecoms or pharmaceuticals, and some focus on public and Government affairs, as opposed to consumer or business-to-business communications.

Local PR specialists
South Africa, Egypt and Nigeria have flourishing local public relations industries, with the agency sector also developing fast in Kenya, Uganda, Ghana and Tanzania.

Nigeria is a good example of the pattern of agency development likely to be seen in other countries. Historically, public relations in Nigeria was managed as an adjunct to the advertising industry. As the needs arose clients became more sophisticated and (especially as more and more multi-national organisations began operating in Nigeria), the opportunity for professional public relations agencies grew. There are now some 19 agencies, some trending towards specialisation in areas such as finance, cross-border trade, healthcare, and information technology.

However, developing a viable African Public Relations Consultancy sector remains a challenge for the future as decision makers in both the public and private sectors continue to use foreign based consultancies for jobs that are invariably done by in-country practitioners. Local knowledge of the people, environment, language, history, culture and philosophy would seem essential for successful execution of PR programmes.

THE AFRICA COMMUNICATION INDEX

On some aspects of communications management in Africa there is little or no information; on others, there is far too much information, much of it conflicting, unreliable or plain confusing. To help communication managers to match their needs and objectives in Africa to what is actually possible, and to help them to prioritise their resources in Africa, the UK-based Gyroscope consultancy have created a useful "Africa Communications Index."

The index is a measure of the extent to which PR and corporate communications can be systematically planned, managed and delivered in any given country, and of the extent to which the disciplines can be effective in delivering specific messages to specific target audiences.

Methodology

To develop the index, Gyroscope focused on the 25 African countries for which the World Economic Forum has published recent, robust and comparable statistical data. These countries are shown in Figure 14.1 on p. 266.

The WEF data cover a broad range of indicators, from GDP and other economic factors through to the development and robustness of the IT and communications infrastructure, judicial independence, tertiary education levels and many others. The WEF combines these in the Growth Competitiveness Index—a weighted index showing not just the overall level of economic and social development in each country, but arguably the ability of each country to develop in the short and medium term future.

To develop the Africa Communications Index, Gyroscope selected and weighted a further set of measures, from various sources, including their own research. These include:

Factor	Rationale
Access to staff	Without access to trained—or at least, trainable—staff, a local PR industry cannot develop, and foreign organisations cannot get a foothold. The ease of access to such staff in any given country is therefore a fundamental indicator of whether PR and corporate communications can be managed and delivered there.

Factor	Rationale
Professional body	In more developed countries, the professional bodies for the PR and corporate communications industries may be regarded by cynics as a little irrelevant. However, in many African countries, the professional bodies are actively, even solely, responsible for the development of the industry as a whole. The state of development of a country's professional body is therefore a key indicator of the development of the industry as a whole in that country.
Major agencies	We consider that if one or more of the major global agency groups is represented in a country—either under its own name or through an affiliate that matches the professional standards of the parent—it will tend to have an improving and stabilising effect on general levels of practice and performance.
Adult literacy	Adult literacy is a key indicator of the ability of the population to receive managed communications—such as that distributed through the press, posters or roadshows and sponsored events.
Daily press circulation/ 1,000 population	The number of daily newspapers sold per 1,000 population is a valuable indication of the ability of the media to reach the population.
Press freedom	The freedom of the press (figures published by the WEF) is a further indication of the potential to deliver messages to the population through the media, without bias or corruption.

The Index

The ACI ranges from 0 to 100. The higher the ACI, the easier it is to plan, manage and deliver PR and corporate communications in that country, and the more effective the disciplines can be in delivering specific messages to specific target audiences. The higher the ACI, the higher the potential "Return on Investment" in communications activity.

Alphabetic order		Ranked by ACI	
Country	ACI Max = 100)	ACI (Max = 100)	Country
Algeria	49.51	21.87	Chad
Angola	26.14	22.51	Ethiopia
Botswana	49.56	25.68	Mozambique
Cameroon	41.46	26.14	Angola
Chad	21.87	26.67	Mali
Egypt	80.92	27.85	Malawi
Ethiopia	22.51	28.84	Madagascar
Gambia	36.41	31.84	Senegal
Ghana	62.48	36.41	Gambia
Kenya	68.77	40.51	Zambia
Madagascar	28.84	41.46	Cameroon
Malawi	27.85	43.46	Namibia

(Continued)

Alphabetic order	
Country	ACI Max = 100)
Mali	26.67
Mauritius	52.07
Morocco	45.90
Mozambique	25.68
Namibia	43.46
Nigeria	74.66
Senegal	31.84
South Africa	89.35
Tanzania	46.17
Tunisia	43.81
Uganda	66.55
Zambia	40.51
Zimbabwe	56.90

Ranked by ACI	
ACI (Max = 100)	Country
43.81	Tunisia
45.90	Morocco
46.17	Tanzania
49.51	Algeria
49.56	Botswana
52.07	Mauritius
56.90	Zimbabwe
62.48	Ghana
66.55	Uganda
68.77	Kenya
74.66	Nigeria
80.92	Egypt
89.35	South Africa

Using the ACI

Gyroscope suggest that the ACI should be considered in conjunction with three other factors: the GDP per capita; the population; and the Growth Competitiveness Index (GCI).

Country	ACI (Max = 100)	GDP/capita (US$ per year)	Population (million)	GCI (Max = 7.0)
Algeria	49.51	1,550	31.5	3.39
Angola	26.14	270	12.9	2.60
Botswana	49.56	3,240	1.6	4.56
Cameroon	41.46	600	15.1	2.98
Chad	21.87	210	7.7	2.31
Egypt	80.92	1,380	68.5	3.84
Ethiopia	22.51	100	62.6	2.92
Gambia	36.41	330	1.3	3.93
Ghana	62.48	400	20.2	3.46
Kenya	68.77	360	30.1	3.21
Madagascar	28.84	250	15.9	2.85
Malawi	27.85	180	10.9	3.36

Country	ACI (Max = 100)	GDP/capita (US$ per year)	Population (million)	GCI (Max = 7.0)
Mali	26.67	240	11.2	2.79
Mauritius	52.07	3,540	1.2	4.12
Morocco	45.90	1,190	28.4	3.77
Mozambique	25.68	220	19.7	2.91
Namibia	43.46	1,890	1.7	3.99
Nigeria	74.66	260	112.0	3.10
Senegal	31.84	500	9.5	3.34
South Africa	89.35	3,170	40.4	4.37
Tanzania	46.17	260	33.5	3.49
Tunisia	43.81	2,090	9.6	4.49
Uganda	66.55	320	21.8	3.25
Zambia	40.51	330	9.2	3.10
Zimbabwe	56.90	530	11.7	2.84

Analysis

This tool provides different "views" of Africa according to communication needs. Charities and NGOs, for example, may be more interested in countries which present the greatest needs—in terms of population pressure and social and economic deprivation—and in how to plan their communications and their budgets according to the potential of communications to meet those needs. Certain industries—such as healthcare and telecommunications—also have the need and the opportunity to work in these countries.

Purely commercial organisations, on the other hand, may want to use the data to identify which countries offer the "biggest bang for their communications buck" where spending money on communications is most likely to give the highest return. Other organisations may want to seek a balance: in which they operate as corporate citizens in order to be able to operate also as commercial citizens in Africa.

Gyroscope have analysed the data in three ways, and have drawn some general conclusions.

ACI vs GDP/capita

First, plotting each country's ACI against its per capita GDP suggests five distinct groups.

South Africa and Egypt are "the Pole Stars" of the African continent, with comparatively high GDP figures and very high ACI figures. These are the countries in which corporate communications and public relations can most easily be managed, and where they can be most effective in reaching specific audiences with specific messages.

At the highest levels of GDP, though with lower ACIs, are "the Jewels"—the tourist havens of Mauritius, and Botswana, with its mix of tourism and diamonds. Superficially attractive targets for commercial communications activity, their position on the chart disguises their tiny size: Botswana's population is only 1.6 million, and Mauritius has just 1.2 million.

With an ACI of between 40 and 50, though well below "the Jewels" on GDP, are "the Destinations": Algeria, Tunisia, Morocco and (perhaps) Namibia. With per capita GDPs in the $1,000–$2,000 range, these are amongst Africa's richer countries, and they offer a reasonable capacity for effective communications activity.

Arguably, Namibia should sit alongside this group, but not actually in it: Namibia owes its position more to its small size (just 1.7 million population), its wealth from mining and adventure tourism, and its close economic links to South Africa.

Scoring much higher on ACI—between 60 and 80—though far lower in terms of per capita GDP, are "the Traditional Traders": the well-established regional hubs of Nigeria, Kenya, Uganda and Ghana. Here, robust political, social and economic structures combine with well-established international trade links. Their comparatively low per capita GDP figures reflect their substantial populations: Kenya, Ghana and Uganda all have more than 20 million inhabitants, while Nigeria is Africa's most populous country with 112 million people.

Then there are "the Strugglers": Angola, Chad, Ethiopia, Madagascar, Malawi, Mali and Mozambique. These are the countries—most of them having recently suffered years of man-made or natural disasters—where very low GDP combines with weak or non-existent social, academic or communications structures. Here, a very low ACI indicates that it will be difficult for PR and corporate communications to contribute to economic and social development—for example, by communicating messages about AIDS and other health issues.

ACI vs Population
Plotting the ACI to population of each country, reveals some important differences to ACI vs GDP. First, the tiny size of Botswana, Gambia, Mauritius and Namibia is clearly highlighted, as is the enormous population of Nigeria, which here falls into the same group as South Africa and Egypt.

Second, the "Traditional Traders" again stand out as a distinct group, offering specific opportunities and problems; the group of "Strugglers" at the lower right of the chart is little changed.

Of particular note, however, is the problem of Ethiopia: with a per capita GDP of around $100 dollars per year, and a population of over 60 million, it is extremely difficult for the country's poorly developed communications structures to do much to help in social, educational or economic development.

ACI vs GCI
A third correlation may be made between each country's ACI against its GCI—the Growth Competitiveness Index devised by the World Economic Forum.

Again, the 25 countries fall into some familiar groups: South Africa and Egypt as the Pole Stars; the Traditional Traders; and the Strugglers. However, the chart does reveal two further points of particular interest.

The first is a subtle but detectable relationship between rising ACI and rising GCI, suggesting that developments which raise the ACI of a country will make it better able to grow and develop.

To some extent, this is to be expected, since both indices include (albeit with different weightings) factors such as the state of the country's educational systems. However, since some of the most heavily weighted factors in the ACI include the status of the country's professional public relations industry and the presence or absence of a professional association for public relations, we might conclude that the development of professional standards and structures for public relations can of themselves make a country more competitive.

Based on this, a group of countries—Gambia, Namibia, Morocco, Tanzania, Cameroon, Zambia and (perhaps) Senegal—with an approximately average GCI and a slightly below average ACI, can benefit most, in terms of their social and economic development, from improvements in their professional PR industries. These are termed "the Contenders."

MANAGING PR AND CORPORATE COMMUNICATIONS IN AFRICA

Obviously the best structure for managing communications in Africa for any given organisation will depend on the organisation itself: its objectives, its country priorities, and so on. However, some general observations can be made.

First, a presence (either in-house or through an agency) in Egypt will give access to that market and a degree of access to the markets of Algeria, Tunisia and Morocco and perhaps the north of Nigeria—if only through the common language of Arabic and elements of the common culture of Islam. However, a presence in Egypt is of little use or relevance anywhere further south.

A presence in South Africa gives direct access to that country, as well as to the two states it surrounds, Lesotho and Swaziland. It also gives a reasonable degree of access to Botswana and Namibia, due to their similar standards, economies, and approaches, and (to a lesser extent) to Zimbabwe. A presence in South Africa is also a sign of commitment to Africa, and offers some "exposure through proximity" to the continent's issues and opportunities.

For organisations with broader interests in Africa, both Kenya and Nigeria can operate as regional hubs; Kenya gives easier access to east African, and Anglophone countries such as Uganda and Tanzania, while Nigeria gives access to a group of West African countries, many of them francophone.

An important finding of the Gyroscope report is that corporate communications cannot be effectively managed centrally. Extreme variations from country to country mean that activity must be delivered by locals from each country. The "central" function is therefore to identify the best practitioners in each country, and then to engage, educate and enable them to work effectively. This makes the roles of FAPRA and PRISA and other institutes vital in this respect.

THE FUTURE FOR PR IN AFRICA

Public relations will continue to develop throughout Africa and will contribute to the wider social and economic development of Africa. It is likely that the South African public relations industry will grow faster than the general economy; some of the additional growth will come from the attention focussed on the country by the 2010 World Cup and from steadily improving perceptions of public relations as a commercially valuable discipline. Growth is likely to be strong too in Nigeria, where consumer markets are growing rapidly.

Improving awareness, understanding and appreciation of PR as a profession in South Africa will spill over into southern Africa—Botswana and Namibia as well as Lesotho and Swaziland. Growth in the public relations industries in Nigeria and Kenya, where development of public relations has been relatively strong, will continue, along with steady development in Ghana, Uganda and Tanzania, and perhaps also in Senegal and Cote d'Ivoire (where there have been recent moves to start a professional PR association). This will be led by the increasing availability of graduates with specific education and training in PR and corporate communications.

In the African Arabian countries such as Algeria and Egypt, the impact of economic growth on the industry may be constrained by the strong control exercised by Government in business and the media.

At the 19th All Africa Public Relations Conference held in Johannesburg, South Africa in 2006, the theme was "Managing Africa's Reputation." The conference was mooted as marking the beginning of a new spirit of co-operation between public relations practitioners and public relations professional associations in Africa. Again, the Feder-ation of African Public Relations Associations (FAPRA, 2006) called on all public relations practitioners on the continent to use their skills and expertise to assist in promoting a positive image of Africa to the world.

Public relations professionals were called upon to "intensify training, change orienta-tion, update knowledge of current issues, engage in peer review mechanisms, self-criticisms and assess their contributions to Afro-optimism" and to "provide better advice to African leaders and organizations to enhance good governance and communication."

The need to create an enabling environment of education and training of public relations professionals at Pan-African level, was also stressed:

> Public Relations academics should seek to become value-added agents to the profession by building their image through developing enriched and relevant curriculum with African realities, conducting research on the peculiarities of the practice on the continent, undertake to work closer together with PR practitioners, develop case studies and inculcate excellence in students. (FAPRA 2006)

Thus we do believe the African public relations practitioner is already at the cutting edge of social change. The practitioner is increasingly charged with communicating development messages and facilitating the development process in a context where traditionalism and western oriented globalism meet.

Throughout the African continent, one of the most powerful influences might be broadly encompassed as the African world-view (Mersham, 1992; 1993; Mersham et al. 1995). This concept encompasses the value community and the recognition of the value of all individuals. The philosophy of "Ubuntu"—the idea of being one's brother's keeper—runs deeply throughout African thought and action.

Sociologists have noted that, as modern society becomes increasingly technological and impersonal, people seem to place a greater value than ever on meaningful relationships in their everyday lives. Many traditional African views of communication are connected by the underlying philosophical principles of humanism (*ubuntu*) and communalism (*ubunye*, ubudlelwane). Commonly, the reprocity and mutuality of human relations is emphasized (*isandla sigezesinye*) and the belief that respect should always be reciprocated (*ukuhlo-nishwana kabile*). Becoming a person through one's relations with others (*umuntu umuntu ngabantu*); creating harmonious world relations with others (*ukulingisa endaweni ubuhlobo babantu*), also form part of the ancient African philosophies that relate to communication.

These aspects of African philosophy may explain why public relations theorists, practi-tioners and teachers increasingly find African public relations intriguing, posing challenges to accepted normative approaches, as they seek a conceptualization of a sustainable new global model of the profession.

Scholars have argued that Africa can provide a unique contribution to the global practice of Public Relations. Steve Biko, a celebrated anti-apartheid activist from South Africa, expressed the basis of this contribution in the following way:

> We believe that in the long run the special contribution to the world by Africa will be in this field of human relationships. The great powers of the world may have done wonders in giving the world an industrial and military look, but the great gift still has to come from Africa—giving the world a more human face. (Biko in Coetzee and Roux, 1998:30)

Triple bottom line reporting, comprising the role of organisations in their social, environmental and economic environment, is challenging the business sector around the globe. This new development focuses on all issues of concern to society, and a call for responsibility and urgency to act.

Finally, we might ask how the African humanist approach will impact on the debate on the widening gap between the increasing political, social and economic relevance of the profession in society and the reputation of the profession worldwide.

The World Congress on Communication for Development (WCCD) announced in 2006 that the Global Alliance for Public Relations and Communication Management (www.globalpr.org) had joined the Advisory Body of the Congress to be held in Rome that year. Organized by the World Bank, the Food and Agriculture Organization and the Communication Initiative Network, it is interesting to note that the conference communiqué stated categorically:

> Communication for Development is a social process based on dialogue using a broad range of tools and methods. It is also about seeking change at different levels including listening, building trust, sharing knowledge and skills, building policies, debating and learning for sustained and meaningful change. *It is not public relations or corporate communications as we understand it* . . .(authors' intepretation) (World Congress on Communication for Development. 2007).

We believe therefore, public relations and communication management as a field has still some way to go before it claims the recognition and legitimacy its practitioners have sought for several decades.

REFERENCES

Africa Environment Outlook: Past, present and future perspectives. 2004 New York:UNEP

Arnoldi-Van Der Walt, S.E. 2000. The evaluation of Ubuntu as an Afrocentric management and communication approach. Ph.D. (Communication Management), University of Pretoria.

Berglund, A. 1976. *Zulu thought patterns and symbolism.* Cape Town: David Phillips.

Church, C. "Which way for public relations in Africa?." 2001. *PR Arena,* Newsletter of the Public Relations Society of Kenya, No 1:11.

Dangogo, K. 2007 *The World of Public Relations: Is it the same everywhere?* Abuja: Timex Communications.

FAPRA. 2006. Communiqué from the 19th All Africa Public Relations Conference held in Johannesburg. "Public relations practitioners called on to counter afro-pessimism."

Federation of African Public Relations Associations. http://www.fapra.org/news. Accessed 5 February 2007.

Global Environmental Outlook 2002. New York: UN.

Gumede, M. V. 1990. *Traditional healers: a medical doctor's perspective.* Cape Town: Scottville.

Holtzhausen, D.R.; Petersen, K.; Tindall, T.J. 2002. Exploding the Myth of the Symmetrical/Asymmetrical Dichotomy: Public Relations Models in the New South Africa. Paper presented at the Public Relations Division of the International Communication Association Seoul, Korea—July 2002.

Holtzhausen, D. 2000. Post modern values in public relations. *Journal of Public Relations Research*, 12(1): 93–114.

Hooyberg, V., and Mersham, GM. 2000. "Mass media in Africa: from distant drums to satellite" in De Beer, A. (Ed) *Mass Media in the Millennium : the South African Handbook of Mass Communication*. Pretoria: Van Schaik.

ITU. 2006. *World Telecommunication/ICT Development Report* 2006: "Measuring ICT for social and economic development," 8th edition.

ITU. 2006. *ICT/Telecommunication development in least developed countries* (LDCs). Geneva: ITU.

Johnson, K. 2006. Social Issues and the Environment–PR and Communication Challenges. Address to the joint PRISA/FAPRA conference. Johannesburg, May.

Johnston, A. 2007 50th Anniversary Review. Johannesburg: PRISA.

Leonard, A. and Ströh, U. 2002. "Transcending diversity: The communication manager as ethical/moral ombudsperson in the postmodern organisational setting." *Communicare* 19(2):34–86.

MailandGuardian online. "The year gone by" Jean-Jacques Cornish. Accessed 26 January 2008.

Mersham, G.M. 1992. "The challenges of teaching public relations practice in Africa in the 90s." *Communicatio*, 18 (1): 54–59.

Mersham, G.M. 1993. "Public Relations, Democracy and Corporate Social Investment." *Equid Novi*, 14 (2): 107–126.

Mersham, G.M. 1993. "Public relations: a vital communication function of our times," in de Beer, A.S (ed). *Mass media for the nineties: the South African handbook of mass communication*. Pretoria: Van Schaik.

Mersham, G.M. 1997. Course Curriculum, Communication IV, Technikon South Africa.

Mersham, G.M.; Rensburg, R., and Skinner, C. 1995. *Public relations, development and social investment : A southern African perspective*. Pretoria: Van Schaik.

Mersham, G.M. and Skinner, C. 1999. *New insights into communication and public relations*. Johannesburg: Heinemann Higher Education.

Mersham, G.M. and Skinner, C. 2001. *New insights into the communications and media*. Johannesburg: Heinemann Higher Education.

Mramba, J.H. 2004. "Does PR add to the bottom line?" *PR Arena*, Newsletter of the Public Relations Society of Kenya, No 1: 1–2.

New Partnership for Africa's Development. 2007. http://www.nepad.org. Accessed 20 March.

Ngubane, H. 1977. *Body and mind in Zulu medicine*. London: Academic Press.

Nyambezi, C.L. 1963. *Zulu proverbs*. Johannesburg: University of Witwatersrand Press.

Okereke, M. 1993. "Challenges of public relations practitioners in Africa and recent development in the practice." Paper presented by chairperson of the Federation of African Public Relations Associations (FAPRA) at IPRA Professional Conference, Cape Town, 5 May.

Opukah, S. 2004. The dynamic nature of PR in the 21st century. *PR Arena*, Newsletter of the Public Relations Society of Kenya, No 1: 1–2.

Pratt, C. Public relations and the third world: the African context. *Public Relations Journal.* Vol 42(2): 10–17.

Public Relations Society of Kenya. http://www.prsk.co.ke/arena.htm Accessed 3 February, 2007.

Skinner, J.C., Von Essen, L.M., Mersham, G.M., and Motau, S.J. 2007. *Handbook of public relations*. Cape Town: OUP.

South African Budget Speech 2007. Minister of Finance, Trevor A. Manuel, 21st February 2007. National Treasury: Pretoria.

Steyn, B. 2002. A meta-theoretical framework for the role of the corporate communication strategist. *Communicare*, 21(2): 42–63.

Steyn, B. 2003. A conceptualisation and empirical verification of the "Strategist," (redefined) "Manager" and "Technician" roles of public relations. Paper presented at the 10th International Public Relations Research Symposium, Bled, Slovenia, July 3–6.

World Congress on Communication for Development. 2007. The Rome Consensus: Communication for Development. http://www.devcomm.org/worldbank/admin/uploads/New percent20documents/Rome percent20Consensus.doc. Accessed 7 February.

15

PUBLIC RELATIONS PRACTICE IN NIGERIA

ERIC KOPER

TAYE BABALEYE

JULIA JAHANSOOZI

INTRODUCTION

> The power of Nigerian oratory is measured by the strength of the speaker's legs. This is not a Nigerian proverb, but it ought to be. (Enahoro, 1996, p.29)[1]

Nigeria gained its independence on October 1, 1960. In 1963 it became a Federal Republic and a member of the Commonwealth of Nations. Nigeria is the most populous country in Africa, with about 140 million people (2006 national census) and the largest concentration of Black people in the world. One in five Africans is a Nigerian. There are about 250 ethnic groups, with three major tribes constituting over 40 percent of the population: the Hausa, Ibo and Yoruba. Other major ethnic/linguistic groups include the Tiv, Ibibio, Ijaw, Kanuri, Nupe, Gwari, Igala, Jukun, Igbira, Idoma, Fulani, Itsekiri, Edo, Urhobo and the Anang, and there are approximately 374 dialects within these ethnic groups. The official language is English, but indigenous languages are also commonly used, and most Nigerians understand and speak the "broken English" (Pidgin English). The most popular religions in Nigeria include Islam, Christianity and the worship of several indigenous deities.

---

[1] Peter Enahoro's book *How to be a Nigerian* is highly recommended to anyone who wants to have deeper insight in an accessible style about Nigerian culture written by a Nigerian.

Geography

Nigeria is situated in sub-Saharan West Africa. It lies between longitudes 3° and 14°E and latitudes 4° and 14°N, and covers an area of 923,768 sq. km. It is bordered to the north by the Republics of Niger and Chad, to the west by the Republic of Benin, and to the east by the Republic of Cameroon. The country has about 800km of Atlantic coastline, and has tropical and equatorial regions. In 1991, centrally located Abuja took over as Nigeria's capital city, whilst Lagos remains the commercial headquarters of the country (Nigerian High Commission, 2007).

NATURE AND STATUS OF PUBLIC RELATIONS PRACTICE

Historical Perspectives

Formal public relations practice in Nigeria can be traced back to January 1, 1944 when the British colonial administrators established the first Public Relations Department.[2] The department was headed by Mr D.C. Fletcher, as the leader of a group of staff, which included a public relations officer, an assistant public relations officer, a process engraver, a press officer, a publicity artist, an antiquities officer, a photographer, a films officer, a radio officer and a confidential secretary. The function of the department was mainly to carry out "public enlightenment" programs relating to government activities. The colonial administrators targeted selected publics, such as Nigerian soldiers who participated in World War II as part of the British Army. After Nigeria gained its independence in 1960, the public relations department was transferred to the newly created Federal Ministry of Information (FMI) where it continued with information activities for its various publics. Typical information and public health campaigns focused on the eradication of communicable diseases such as yaws, yellow fever, and tuberculosis, and were often at the request of the WHO (World Health Organization). The FMI was also used to campaign for the success of government education programs through the cinema and open air film shows which encouraged parents to send their children to school.

The first public relations professional body, the Public Relations Association of Nigeria (PRAN), was founded by Dr Samuel Epelle, Director of PR at FMI. Epelle was influential for the development of public relations practice in Nigeria and in 1967, he published the first authoritative book on PR in Nigeria, *Essentials of Public Relations*. Epelle, as PRAN's founder, became its coordinator and chairman and worked to recruit colleagues from other governmental departments and private industries to join him in enlarging PRAN's membership (Oyekan, 1993). In 1969 PRAN was renamed the Nigerian Institute of Public Relations (NIPR) and several years later, it organized the annual Sam Epelle gold medal in his honour, which in 2008 still continues to be awarded.

Events that Shape Professional Public Relations Practice

The establishment of PRAN in 1963 was the first independent step taken by Nigerians to consolidate public relations practice in the country. However, whilst PRAN was still in its infancy the political instability and subsequent 1966 military coup interfered with the professionalization of public relations. At this point the public relations practice did not

---

[2] PR Nigeria at http://www.prnigeria.net/niprnigeria.htm.

have professional standards, educational qualifications, or a developed practitioner "tool kit." PRAN also had to deal with similar issues relating to public acceptance, nomenclature, and reputation that plagued Western public relations professional associations.

Nigerian public relations practice was shaped by both political events and crises. The Nigerian civil war, which began shortly after the first military coup, followed by approximately 30 years of military dictatorships (from 1966–1979 and then again from 1984–1999), had an impact upon the development of public relations practice. As well as this, the Niger Delta crisis and Nigeria's relatively recent democratic governance have continued to influence the shape of pubic relations practice and its professionalization.

The January 16, 1966 coup was organized by a group of Nigerian army officers who were mostly of Ibo ethnicity. It was a bloody coup and many of the politicians that were killed came from Nigeria's Northern and Western regions, and so it was suspected that the Ibo (who were from the Eastern region) had planned the coup. This suspicion was strengthened when General Aguiyi Ironsi, also of Ibo ethnicity, took control of Nigeria. The Hausa and Fulani ethnic groupings dominated the military, and became angry and dissatisfied with the situation, which they felt inadequately represented their interests. Another coup, led by the Hausa and Fulani, occurred in July 1966. Following this coup, Nigerians of Ibo ethnicity were openly harassed and killed. The trust which previously had been evident between the different socio-cultural ethnic groups was broken. By May 1967 the Eastern Region (the Ibo homeland) announced its independence as the State of Biafra[3] under the leadership of Colonel Emeka Odumegwu Ojukwu. Negotiations were unsuccessful and Nigeria declared war on Biafra on July 6, 1967. The civil war continued for 30 months. The years of military rule (1966–1979 and 1984–1999) were characterized by human rights abuses, corruption, and mismanagement. The newly declared Biafra state targeted the international community with a public relations campaign against the Nigerian government, but it was no match for the Nigerian Federal Government. The war ended on January 20, 1970 in favour of the Nigerian Federal Government after Biafra surrendered. To maintain its stand that the war was not an ethnic cleansing, the Nigerian Federal Government was faced with a serious "image-laundering" programme to convince both internal and external observers that the war was purely a Nigerian family affair. The Federal Government under the then Head of State, General Yakubu Gowon, embarked on a rigorous campaign to redeem the image and improve the reputation of the Federal Government. The first catch phrase "no victor, no vanquished" was coined by the Nigerian Government to "soften" the result of the war for the Ibos. Simultaneously, the Federal Government embarked on what it called a "Rehabilitation, Reconstruction, and Reconciliation" programme to repair the war-affected areas and bring the Ibo ethnic group into the mainstream of the Nigerian polity as it was in the beginning. Public relations professionals were recruited and came together to help the Government improve its image and reputation, which led to the birth of what is now considered modern professional public relations practice in Nigeria. The practice which originally was limited to the FMI suddenly became popular with private public relations consultancies and with specialists hired from Europe and America to embark on campaigns aimed at improving the image of Nigeria both at home and abroad. Public relations campaigns were supplemented with advertising as full page adverts were placed in foreign newspapers and magazines, especially in the USA and Europe, in order to reconcile the Ibo population living abroad and to encourage them to return home. Public relations

---

[3] Information is drawn from ICE case studies at http://www.american.edu/ted/ice/biafra.htm "Biafra War" and articles such as the BBC's "Biafra 30 years on" at http://news.bbc.co.uk/1/hi/world/africa/596712.stm. Numerous references to the Biafra war including strong images can be found through Google and Yahoo.

practice grew outside of the government as private corporations and organizations such as the United African Company (UAC), oil and gas companies including Mobil, BP, and Shell, as well other multinational corporations such as Unilever and Nestlé invested in Nigeria and set up their own public relations departments based there. These organizations needed their public relations efforts to improve external attitudes towards their commercial activities in Nigeria.

The second influential event which shaped public relations practice was the prolonged military rule. Generally under military dictatorships, human rights abuses are rampant. The Nigerian case was no exception. Corruption, advanced fee fraud, nepotism and favouritism in high places was standard, whilst the economy declined. All of these ills affected Nigeria's image and reputation and created a challenge for public relations professionals in public and private practice engaged in projecting a favourable image and repairing the reputational damage for various military regimes with the inherited risk of continuing with propaganda that reduces the credibility of the profession. In the private sector, drastic devaluation of the naira, Nigeria's currency,[4] led to soaring inflation levels. This in turn reduced the population's purchasing power and decreased consumer spending. PR professionals, especially in private practice as consultants, were busy advising commercial organizations on how they could improve their businesses and survive the difficult economic conditions (Babaleye, 2005).

Overall the development of public relations practice in Nigeria was perceived to add value after periods of war in order to stimulate the economy and improve Nigeria's image and reputation. Initially public relations practice formally began in the public sector, under the British colonial administrators during World War II. The practice continued to expand after Nigeria's independence in the 1960s with the Federal Ministry of Information (FMI), and gained more prominence after the Nigerian civil war. During the various military governments the public relations practice continued to grow, particularly in the private sector.

ORGANIZATION AND GROWTH OF PUBLIC RELATIONS PROFESSIONAL PRACTICE

Forty-six years after it was introduced by the colonial administrators, public relations practice became a recognized, chartered profession in June 1990,[5] more than a decade earlier than the UK's CIPR. The Nigerian government gave legal backing to public relations practice as a profession and recognized the NIPR as the regulator and only professional body that could admit practitioners into the profession and set standards for its practice in Nigeria. The purpose behind gaining this status was to raise the profile of public relations practice as a respectable, responsible and viable profession within Nigeria. The legislation assures that discipline, standard, and the professional code of ethics are strictly maintained. The NIPR's motto, "Professionalism and Excellence", boldly written under its logo, emphasizes its commitment to ongoing professionalization and high standards within the practice as witnessed through the organization of many short courses.

---

[4] From January 1986 to January 1989 the percentage devaluation of the naira to the dollar was 750 percent: *The Guardian* [Nigeria], April 16, 1989.

[5] The body attained the status of a Chartered Institute in June 1990 through Decree No. 16 (now an Act of the Federal Republic of Nigeria). By virtue of this law, NIPR derived the power to register members, regulate the practice/development of the PR profession and monitor professional conduct through an established Code of Ethics and Professional Conduct regime (http://www.niprabuja.com/aboutus.htm).

As mentioned previously, the NIPR evolved out of PRAN. The NIPR has its national secretariat in Lagos, while there are chapters in more than 28 of the current 36 states of the federation. Membership registers are maintained at both the state chapters and the national headquarters. Memberships are renewed annually at the national headquarters. However not all is that positive, as the Dangogo writes in his article in the Nigerian newspaper *Daily Trust* (November 30, 2007): ". . .the institute has found it rather difficult to monitor the over 6,000 registered members across the country due to insufficient resources. Though PR is regulated in the country via Act 16 1990, the law has not been effectively enforced . . . We've simply failed to develop our institute over the years . . . ." This is not dissimilar to many of the other PR professional bodies across the globe that fail to attract practitioners to their membership.

A factor that influences the current practice of governmental public relations is the strong link between the NIPR and the Nigerian government. Since the enactment of the NIPR Act in 1990, the professional body has been integrated into the three tiers of government to support government activities and programmes at all levels: local, state and federal. Many senior NIPR members have served at various committees of government and community relations bodies to give professional advice on how to attain peace or resolve conflicts on issues requiring government actions and interventions. For instance, Chief Alex Akinyele, a previous NIPR President, was Nigeria's Minister of Information for a period of time under General Ibrahim Babangida's regime in the late 1980s and early 1990s. Chief Mike Okereke, Alhaji Sabo Mohammed, and Chief Jibade Oyekan were all NIPR past presidents and also served in various capacities on Federal Ministry of Information committees. Also several Fellows of the Institute were appointed to head crucial government departments with a view of shaping government policies on crucial issues. Another milestone for the NIPR was the investiture of the Nigerian President, and Governors as patrons of the NIPR at the national and state chapter levels. Indeed this is all based on the importance of government and is an illustration that the origins of public relations can be originated in Government as described for the UK by Jacquie L'Etang (2004) rather than business as popularly referred to in American literature. This "embedding" of the NIPR within the Nigerian government begs questions of independence, legitimacy, and perhaps concerning the level of government control over public relations practice, which could be viewed negatively and reduce public relations and the NIPR as a government "mouth piece" linked with propaganda.

For a long time, the Niger Delta issue has had implications on government public relations practice in Nigeria. The government has its own "publics" which include political parties (in the last dispensation there were more than 50 political parties in Nigeria), through which government policies are disseminated. Others of course include the civil service workforce, organized private sector, labour unions, students, professional bodies and private citizens. The government is required to relate with all segments of society for social, economic and political development. The Federal Ministry of Information (FMI) and all other government-owned media organs such as the Nigerian Television Authority (NTA) and the Federal Radio Corporation of Nigeria (FRCN), as well the Voice of Nigeria (VON) are always integrated into the mainstream of government decision-making bodies to avoid misrepresentation of the government's intentions, so the publicly owned media outlets are clearly not as independent as the BBC, CBC, etc, which whilst publicly funded are not integrated into the government. In addition, the National Assembly (Senate and House of Representatives) provides effective legislation to give backing to people-oriented government policies in the troubled areas. In all of these areas the practice of public relations is given prominence. As it was in the beginning, the public relations department at the FMI is still charged with the responsibility of explaining government policies and activities to the public. More importantly there is a new unit called the National Orientation Agency (NOA), under the directorate of a public relations specialist. The unit has offices in all the 36 States of the federation and Abuja. Its functions are to enlighten the public about government policies and how they affect the citizens. This becomes necessary because of the large percentage of illiterate people in the country. Where necessary there are campaign leaflets published in major Nigerian languages to further educate the people about government activities. Greater understanding is also promoted with the citizens through periodic conferences, seminars and workshops on key national, regional or international issues.

The implications of having such a high level of integration of publicly owned media outlets such as the NTA, the FRCN, and the VON within the Nigerian government are that the independence of the media coverage is questionable. Also the close link with public relations and these government / public-owned media outlets reinforces that the practice engages in mostly press agency and public information tactics, both one-way asymmetrical communication techniques (Grunig and Hunt, 1994).

Public relations activities linked to the petroleum industry and foreign companies such as Shell, Chevron have also increased, as these companies attempt to repair their reputations both within Nigeria, especially the Niger Delta region, and internationally. The ongoing environmental damage, human rights abuses, and the extensive levels of poverty in the Niger Delta region (where the petroleum companies are active) continue to damage the image and reputations of these companies. There are many text-book case studies (for example Tench, 1997; Klein, 2000; Henderson and Williams, 2002; Cornelissen, 2004; Coombs and Holladay, 2007; Curtin and Gaither, 2007; Livesey and Graham, 2007) from the late 1990s onwards that focus on the bad and negligent practice of companies such as Shell regarding their operational activities in Nigeria and the lessons learned. The global attention Shell received before and following Ken Saro-Wiwa's execution resulted in numerous boycotts and demonstrations in other parts of the world. In September 2000 in the US a legal, although non-corporate, precedent was set with *Wiwa v Royal Dutch Petroleum* which was won against Shell Oil defendants in relation to the deaths of nine environmental activities including Ken Saro-Wiwa. (May, Cheney, and Roper, 2007, p. 40).

Given the Nigerian experience of public relations development there is a case to be made that public relations can also emerge as a response to relational crises such as wars and conflicts, rather than business needs. For example, the crisis in the Niger Delta took a dramatic turn in the last two years when militant youth activists protesting for the environmental protection of the region began hostage-taking as a way of gaining the attention of the Nigerian government. The PR implications of the Niger Delta crisis are many, both on the home front and within international circles. Ideologically the basic philosophy underlying public relations practice in Nigeria is that people matter; and that the support of public opinion is of prime importance in all spheres of human endeavour (Eke, 1993 cited in Babaleye 2005). Indeed press freedom in Nigeria is impressive as demonstrated in openly addressing any issue, whether political, business, societal or individual. This may be rooted in the value of knowledge in Nigeria, the many well educated people and the art of rhetorical debate and story telling. It also shows that open expression of opinion does not necessarily mobilize people and direct action, as often assumed by media communication theory. Virtually all the oil companies operating in the area have public relations, public affairs, or external relations departments. In addition, there are public relations consultancies working directly with the in-house public relations departments in these oil companies. The consultancies handle needs assessments surveys, and provide intelligence reports on the behavioural attitudes of people in the Niger Delta, which assists the corporate organizations in how to handle the issues at stake in the area. Through public relations professional interventions the Nigerian government regularly has discussions with the local communities and representatives of the militant youth groups in the Niger Delta region in order to resolve the conflict. The involvement of the private sector in the development of the Niger Delta area under the current Umaru Musa Yar'Adua and Goodluck Jonathan administration is salutary. It is rumoured that before President Olusegun Obasanjo left the stage as Nigeria's president in May 2007, a blueprint was developed in partnership with both the private sector and international donors for a lasting solution to the Niger Delta crisis. With that in view, there is hope and expectation that the long years of neglect, environmental and human rights abuse, and the damage to people's livelihoods, especially through oil spillage and gas flaring, would be adequately tackled.

As well as the heavy utilization of public relations activities by petroleum companies, and recently mobile phone companies such as Glo and MTN, religious organizations also engage in massive public relations campaigns. Typically tens of thousands of worshippers are attracted to mass conventions across the country through media activity, banner displays and peer influence. Oration and narration are strong cultural attributes that come to bear when public relations is practised to strongly influence people's behaviours, especially related to fear appeals probably stemming from a long tradition of naturalitistic beliefs (e.g. "juju," "witchcraft").

CULTURE

> In the beginning, God created the universe; then He created the moon, the stars and the wild beasts in the forests. On the sixth day, He created the Nigerian and there was peace. But on the seventh day while God rested, the Nigerian invented noise. (Enahoro, 1996, p.21)

In Nigeria, communication is varied and interesting. Mass media channels, print and broadcast are widely used and based largely upon the oral tradition. In this tradition people rely mainly on community leaders to brief them about what is happening around them.

In the rural areas village meetings are conducted at the square or at the market place. Communal decisions are taken on issues of interest to the majority of members of the community. It is interesting to note that this is not always a straightforward process as "no Nigerian arrangement is permanent unless that which has been arrived at by negotiated compromise" (Enahoro, 1996).

Oral tradition in Nigeria depends on special custodians of the tradition and culture to remind the people of what happened in the past to predict what could happen in the future. They tell "point-by-point" the history of the community the same way it was handed down to them. These cultural custodians know all the taboos, the location of the shrines for the gods/goddesses, the types of clothes to wear, and the food to eat during traditional festivals. They exist in all the tribes or ethnic groups in the country and relate past events with the political happenings of today alongside advice on how to deal with issues of political interest. Such custodians of tradition and culture are either descendants of the masque actors or praise singers found often in the palaces of the traditional rulers. The praise singers are known to use all sorts of imagery to convey their messages. Chris Ogbondah et al. (1999) describe these as including the drum language, gong language, masquerade dances, and puppet theatre. Drum language ranges from simple signals to elaborately coded messages and is learned through both formal and informal traditional educational processes.

Oral traditional communication lends credence to the importance of public relations practice at the ward and constituent levels in rural communities. Nigerians have a lot of respect for tradition and culture and for example election campaigning cannot succeed in local communities without the blessing of the traditional rulers and the cultural custodians. The rural population to a very large extent relies heavily on the opinion of the traditional rulers who by virtue of the oral culture have an influence upon them. Public relations practitioners have to be aware of the cultural influence that impacts the communication process and behavioural outcomes. A group of people or a whole community can change their mind overnight through the sending of emissaries under cover from the traditional rulers by the use of oral communication. In some places certain masquerades appear to convey messages either in favour of or against an issue, idea or even a person. A thorough understanding of the local culture and tradition would assist public relations specialists to effectively communicate with their various publics in Nigeria.

EDUCATION

Prior to 1960 the Nigerian education system was influenced by Christian and Muslim missionaries who set up and administered schools. Education developed into three tiers: primary, secondary and tertiary. Nigeria saw a tremendous expansion in the number of universities, from six in 1970 to about 240 higher education institutions, and an enrolment of over 1.5 million in 2006 (Okebukola 2006). While the annual enrolment growth rate was rising, the average public expenditures per student in higher education fell significantly during most of this period with detrimental effects on quality.

Public Relations Education

The NIPR has a training school in Lagos where it organizes professional training and qualifying examinations leading to awards of Certificates, Ordinary and Advanced Diplomas. In addition, some universities and polytechnics have been accredited to undertake courses and research projects in PR practice with curricula being periodically reviewed and up-graded by the NIPR to bring both the training and practice of public relations to international "practice" standards. The danger of a professional body such as the NIPR controlling the training and education is the risk that the practice remains static and tactical because of focus on current needs by the practice without necessarily incorporating external and societal influences. NIPR's influence on education is worrying as it seems to serve only short-term practice needs rather than contributing to the establishment and progress of a more advanced body of knowledge. In addition it seems that there's little "self-belief" and exploration of Nigeria's own rich cultural traditions including storytelling, art, religion and use of talking drums as means of communication and relationship building. The University of Ibadan, the University of Lagos, and the University of Nigeria, Nzukka, offer post-graduate courses in Public Relations in Nigeria. Almost all higher institutions of learning with departments of Mass Communication and/or Journalism now offer public relations at first degree level in Nigeria, still rooting it in Media with an emphasis on media relations rather than management, strategy and organizational behaviour. In essence, the highest percentage of public relations practitioners in Nigeria in 2007 have digital and print media backgrounds, followed by mass communication graduates from the universities and polytechnics. Nigerian public relations as such emphasizes press-agency and public information practice and has not yet incorporated management and social sciences as a basis for the practice. This may actually be a result of the strong influence of the professional bodies and is something that other nations should be aware of when empowering these professional bodies as it's a clear illustration of limited progress of the practice being locked in publicity needs. As in most countries where public relations is practiced it is difficult and probably fruitless to define PR as a profession. Although the national secretariat of NIPR and all other state chapters often organize public lectures, seminars, workshops and conferences as refresher courses to train and re-train their members and get them professionally equipped for modern PR practice, it only influences the short-term needs of that practice. At the national secretariat, the education department works in partnership with corporate organizations, universities, polytechnics and other professional bodies to organize quarterly workshops to acquaint members with new initiatives in the ever dynamic functions of public relations. It is noteworthy also that there are some private schools of PR in Lagos, where the proprietors present candidates for overseas international certificates and diploma exams. They include the Kelad School of Public Relations and Okereke and Associates School of PR. Unfortunately these overseas qualifications are also not at the required academic critical level and as such there's still a large void to fill in understanding and progressing the body of knowledge of public relations in Nigeria.

PUBLIC RELATIONS PUBLICATIONS

As an integral part of the research and education department of the NIPR at the national and state chapter levels, journals, newsletters and books are published regularly. At the state levels there are numerous publications and periodicals. However, these publications also demonstrate the lack of a more academic approach towards the public relations practice which is also reflected in this chapter about public relations in Nigeria. It is interesting to note that Nigeria has a well-established reputation for critical thinkers, social critics, and an enormous body of original literature but this has unfortunately not emerged in the development of public relations and to a certain extent may be the reason for its highly tactical practice in Nigeria and for not necessarily influencing more important societal behaviours, including the aforementioned corruption and political complexities.

ECONOMY

Before Nigeria's independence, agriculture was the main economic driver. Nigeria was a major exporter of cocoa, palm oil products, rubber, groundnuts, cotton and animal hides and skins (Ezeala-Harrison, 1993). When Nigeria's petroleum resources were discovered and subsequently exploited, the economic reliance upon agriculture shifted to a dependence upon petroleum exports. It is estimated that petroleum accounts for 20 percent of Nigeria's GDP, which in 2006 was $813 per head (Economist Intelligence Unit, 2008), and 95 percent of exports (CIA World Factbook, 2008[6]). Nigeria was one of the founding members of OPEC (Organization of Petroleum Exporting Countries) and its proven petroleum reserves are ranked as 10th largest in the world. It is also the 12th largest

---

[6] Sources such as CIA World Factbook at https://www.cia.gov/library/publications/the-world-factbook/print/ni.html, BBC country profiles at http://news.bbc.co.uk/1/hi/world/africa/country_profiles/1064557.stm, and country reports at http://www.countryreports.org/country.aspx?countryid=179 provide good and up-to-date country information and supplement the information presented in this chapter.

producer of crude oil and the 8th largest petroleum exporter in the world (OFID, 2007). As well as the petroleum resources there are large mineral deposits such as coal, bitumen, iron ore, gypsum, kaolin, phosphates, limestone, marble, columbite, baryte and gold. Other mineral resources include niobium, lead, tin ore and zinc.

Despite Nigeria's mineral wealth, it suffers from a disintegrating infrastructure, widespread corruption, and poor wealth distribution. Oil production is often disrupted because of the civil unrest in the Niger Delta region where the oil fields are located. There is a history of environmental damage and human rights violations relating to the peoples living in the Niger Delta region (Cayford, 1996). Shell came under international scrutiny for its poor practice in Nigeria and was linked with the death of Ken Saro-Wiwa and eight other environmental activists who were hanged by the Nigerian government in 1995. To date, very little of the wealth derived from petroleum production and export has made its way back to the peoples of the Niger Delta region. As a result there is deep unhappiness in the region, and the civil unrest translates to oil production often falling short of its targets and export capacities.

Besides its mineral wealth, Nigeria has significant agricultural, marine and forest resources. Prior to the discovery and exploitation of Nigeria's petroleum reserves the majority of foreign exchange was earned from agricultural exports. Nigeria's climate, equatorial and tropical vegetation zones enable a diversification of food and cash crops. The agricultural sector accounts for approximately 60 percent of Nigeria's employment. It is overwhelmingly dominated by small scale farms, which tend to be less than one hectare in size. The main food crops grown include cassava, maize, rice, yams, cowpea, soybeans, sorghum, ginger, onions, tomatoes, melons and vegetables. Cash crops are mostly cocoa, cotton, maize, groundnuts, plantain, bananas, palm oil, rubber, coconuts, citrus fruits, pearl millet, yams, sugar cane, and recently cassava. The agricultural sector has declined due to the exploitation of the petroleum and mineral resources and resulted in Nigeria shifting from being a net exporter of agricultural produce to now having to import many of the same crops. As well as the agricultural sector, Nigeria has a forestry industry which capitalizes on its rain forests, and also a leather and textile industry based in a number of cities such as Kano, Sokoto, Ibadan and Lagos.

Recent reforms have improved Nigeria's economy. In 2003, former President Obasanjo embarked on reforming the financial sector in order to open up the Nigerian economy to foreign investment and also to enable Nigerian business to compete internationally. Nigerian banks were able to open branches in other West African countries as the ECOWAS created a more favourable investment climate with its bilateral trade agreements in the region. The economic reforms also encouraged foreign companies to make partnerships with Nigerian partners within sectors such as telecommunications, agriculture, real estate, aviation, and energy. The Nigerian economic reforms have aided the international public relations practice, and Nigeria's negative image is gradually giving way to a more positive and updated assessment of the situation.

At the national level of the government's plan for economic development, relevant microeconomic policies were introduced. The National Economic Empowerment Development Strategy (NEEDS) was specifically designed for effective poverty eradication, even though concerns are being expressed in its implementation. The consolidation of the banking sector owing to a number of mergers and acquisitions has resulted in the increasing competitiveness of the sector. The fight against corruption launched under President Obasanjo's leadership was perhaps the strongest single step taken by the government to sanitize the Nigerian economy. For the first time, governors are being impeached, arrested and prosecuted for corrupt practices. The activities of the Economic and Financial Crimes

Commission (EFCC) have started to reduce the levels of fee fraud, internet scams, and money laundering and have resulted in the high profile conviction of the former Inspector General of Police (IGP), Alhaji Tafa Balogun, who embezzled over N18 billion from police funds.[7]

By reducing corruption levels Nigeria has experienced an expansion in manufacturing, agriculture, and technology. Also the US$18 billion debt relief given by the Paris Club of Creditors has made a significant difference, as this represented approximately 47 percent of Nigeria's foreign debt. The private sector has also become more visible in Nigeria's national economic development with the advent of democratic rule on May 29, 1999 and its engagement with public–private partnerships as well as with privatization initiatives such as within the telecommunications sector.

HUMAN RIGHTS AND ACTIVISM AND PUBLIC RELATIONS PROFESSIONAL PRACTICE

Human rights abuses including illegal arrests, detention, torture and the outright killing of citizens were a source of major concern during the prolonged military rule. Opposition and criticism of the military dictatorship was unwelcome and dissidents were forced to flee the country. With the "state-sponsored" assassinations of Chief Alfred Rewane, and Mrs Kudirat Abiola, wife of Chief M.K.O. Abiola, who won the annulled June 12, 1993 Presidential election, and hundreds of others, human rights abuses peaked under the military administration of General Sani Abacha. The active participation of several human rights organizations, and individual activists such as Chief Gani Fawehinmi, a Lagos-based legal practitioner, the late Dr Beko Ransome Kuti, Chief Femi Falana, and Professor Wole Shoyinka limited the permanence of the military regime.

Public relations practice was not limited to government as the tools and techniques were adopted by a number of human rights organizations including the Campaign for Democracy (CD), Civil Liberties Organization (CLO), National Democratic Coalition (NADECO), which emerged during the military rule and mounted vigorous campaigns against the excesses of the military rulers. The organized labor unions were also involved in the struggle against human rights abuses. The Nigerian Labor Congress, National Association of Nigerian Students (NANS), and the Association of Senior Staffs of Universities (ASSU), organized as pressure groups to give a voice to the voiceless by calling for a stop to military rule in Nigeria. The positive role of activists such as Prof. Wole Shoyinka, Nobel Laureate in Literature, who together with a group of dedicated democrats founded Radio Kudirat (a private radio based in the UK), was instrumental in the fight for democracy.

Nigeria is still coping with other human rights abuses that are still relatively common such as the continued discrimination against women, genital mutilation, and use of child labor. Human trafficking, especially with regard to prostitution, remains a problem. All of these problems provide examples of campaign strategies which are utilized in Nigerian public relations education, which indicates that most of the Nigerian body of knowledge is based on case studies.

Public relations practitioners have developed communication strategies to create awareness of the HIV/AIDS pandemic in Nigeria. The campaign strategies initially focused on

---

[7] Nigeriaworld (2005) at http://nigeriaworld.com/feature/publication/babsajayi/070805.html, last accessed April 2008.

creating awareness regarding the existence of HIV/AIDS and then on its prevention. The campaign now focuses on the need for individuals to have regular HIV/AIDS testing.

THE MASS MEDIA AND PUBLIC RELATIONS

The freedom to "publish and be damned" is apparently firmly entrenched within the Nigerian press.[8] The "founding fathers" of Nigerian journalism, such as Dr Nnamdi Azikiwe, Ernest Ikoli, Chief Obafemi Awolowo, Chief Lateef Jakande and others, fought for Nigeria's independence in the pages of their newspapers. The independent press has stood on the side of the oppressed in society since the colonial era. Nigeria gained its independence from Britain without a "gun battle", which has been credited to the fearless press that existed in Nigeria at the time. Despite a decline in the national economy since the late 1980s, which reduced earnings, the number of newspapers and magazines has continued to grow steadily (Ojo, 1999) and it is estimated that there are over 100 national, regional, and local newspapers within Nigeria (BBC, 2008). Ironically, until about 20 years ago, the majority of Nigerian newspapers and digital media were government-owned. However, the few that were privately owned such as *The Nigerian Tribune, The Punch, Vanguard* and *The Guardian* kept faith with their readers by exposing political and corporate scandals. Although repressive efforts were made by various military regimes to clamp down on the press, they did not succeed. For more than four years under Gen. Sani Abacha's regime (1993–98), *TELL Magazine*, a weekly news magazine, resorted to publishing underground when its editor-in-chief, Nosa Igiebor, was arrested and detained, and the magazine's office was closed by the military government. Prior to Nigeria's independence, editors of *The Nigerian Tribune* were often arrested and detained for attacking the British government's policies.

The Nigerian press can also be viewed as agents of socio-political change. After the annulment of the June 12, 1993 election, believed to have been won by Chief M.K.O. Abiola, a series of repressive attacks were carried out against several media outfits which had supported Abiola's push for democracy (Agbese, 2007). With the recent de-regulation of digital media, the privately-owned media are further exposing incompetent and corrupt politicians and public officials, and maintain pressure for reform. In comparison with the press the broadcast media outlets have had difficulty in achieving independent news coverage. The African Independent Television (AIT) has had a running battle with both the military regimes and unfortunately even with the democratic government under President Obasanjo. However, there is the expectation that the Nigerian press will continue to "wage war" against societal ills as the fourth estate of the realm.

Media Control, Access and Diffusion

Nigeria's vibrant media landscape includes over 100 newspapers (national, regional, and local), state-run radio and TV stations (national and regional), as well as privately owned stations (BBC, 2008), which exist despite the limited advertising revenue that is available for off-setting the high costs involved. Broadcasters have an additional requirement to meet which also is partly responsible for the high operating costs as 60 percent of all programme content must be locally made. Radio remains the most popular source of information.

---

[8] It was referred to in 1960 thus: "It is no coincidence that peaceful Nigeria possesses the freest and most responsible press in black Africa"; see http://www.time.com/time/magazine/article/0,9171,895029,00.html.

The socio-economic and political debates covered by the media increase the awareness of the average Nigerian towards government programs, actions and inactions. The relationship between public relations and the mass media in Nigeria is complex as perceived interwoven interests and idealism may be ethically compromised. The journalist may no longer be seen as the "watchdog" of society and more equated to in-house PR professionals who are perceived as people paid to "cover up" the truth in corporate and governmental organizations especially during crises. With the development of professional training and education for journalists and public relations practitioners, the relational dynamics between journalists and public relations practitioners has become more blurred with inherited potential for reduced societal transparency and accountability.

TRANSFER OF KNOWLEDGE

Public relations and other communication professionals also play an important role in Nigeria's development activities. Earlier mentioned HIV/Aids campaigns are aimed at influencing people's behaviour and positively impacting developmental needs. However, as DfID (2008)[9] reports in sub-Saharan Africa, the number of people living in poverty today is greater than in 1990, the rate of child death has increased and levels of maternal death have remained unchanged, and the livelihoods of 75 percent of the world's poor will continue to depend on agriculture for the foreseeable future. Nigeria is Africa's most populous country, and the country, once a large net exporter of food, now must import food. About 70 percent of its population is employed in agriculture, most of which is at subsistence farming level. There is thus a large community of practice not necessarily labelled as PR, but more often referred to as extension workers that influence agricultural producers, traders and consumers with an aim to improve economic and social development. The "tools" of this trade are more dependent on interpersonal and intergroup communication and require higher levels of trust. As such they serve as excellent examples of how the general public relations practice could move forward. The case study that follows is an example of such a more development related approach.

CONCLUSION

With Nigeria now a democracy, the public relations practice will continue to develop and professionalize. Opportunities now exist for shifting the practice from press agency and public information asymmetric communication models towards more strategic practice that is concerned with relationship management and organizational positioning (Cropp and Pincus, 2001). Chief Toye Ogunnorin, past president of the Public Relations Consultants Association of Nigeria (PRCAN), acknowledged the demand from clients for sophisticated public relations practice. Nigerian public relations consultants are now experiencing a conducive business environment. Politicians, CEOs, and public figures are now retaining the specialist services of consultants to manage their reputation. In-house public relations practitioners and consultants together provide services in the area of speech writing, public speaking, and media training. In the petroleum, manufacturing and the banking and finance sectors of the economy, professional public relations services are being offered and taken up by various corporate organizations which require help positioning themselves in Nigeria's fast-changing socio-economic environment where corporate social responsibility initiatives are replacing the traditional marketing approaches.

---

[9] DfID Annual Report 2008, available at www.dfid.gov.uk.

The way forward for public relations professional practice and the NIPR is to embark on training and educational programs for registered and professional members in order for them to be able to cope successfully with modern trends in the global demands. University public relations education programs should include management, social psychology, as well as mass communication theory and critical perspectives. Skills elements should also be included ensuring that graduates are familiar with campaign planning, strategic communication, and evaluation methods. The NIPR leadership should invest more in development of its membership in order keep up to date with international best practice.

ADDENDUM: CASE STUDY

IITA's Sustainable Tree Crops Program: Developing Relationships with Cocoa Farmers[10]

Problem Identification
In Africa, the use of the conventional extension system to transfer technologies from research institutes to farmers still remains imperfect. The national government extension systems are financially starved and whilst the improved technologies are developed by research institutes, the extension systems lack the means to convey them to farmers in rural areas. The poor rural road network, lack of effective transport system and high levels of illiteracy of rural farmers all contribute to the lack of technology adoption that would improve agricultural practice and food security. There is therefore an information loss between the researchers who develop new technologies and the farmers who need these technologies to improve their productivity. The failure of African farmers to adopt improved technologies can partially be attributed to the poor treatment of information delivery by most African governments. In Nigeria for instance, in spite of over 20 agricultural research institutes farmers seldom feel the impact of agricultural innovations either because they have no access to such vital information or because it is poorly disseminated (Ozonwa, 1995). The non-provision of relevant and effective agricultural information is a key factor that has greatly limited agricultural development in sub-Saharan Africa. In Nigeria, public perception of agricultural research institutes was for a long time that of elitist organizations whose research findings were either ineffective or irrelevant to resource poor farmers. Such public opinion was justified because of lack of effective communication from the research organizations to their publics, especially since research institutes usually do not provide extension services and therefore rarely have direct contact with farmers.

The Sustainable Tree Crops Program
In 1998 a public-private assessment of small-holder agricultural systems based on tree crops such as cocoa resulted in the launch of the Sustainable Tree Crops Program (STCP) in May 2000. There was significant interest from the worldwide chocolate industry in tackling problems relating to the quality and quantity of cocoa being harvested in West Africa, a region known for premium cocoa. The Institute of Tropical Agriculture was asked to host the STCP and provide strategic leadership for this project.

West African cocoa accounts for over 70 percent of the global cocoa supply, and therefore the health of cocoa farming in this region is of paramount importance to the international chocolate industry and to chocolate consumers. Cocoa also has a significant

---

[10] Special acknowledgement to IITA STCP staff for their collaboration and facilitation, especially Stephan Weise, Regional STCP Manager, Chris Okafor, STCP Nigeria Country Manager, and their teams.

impact upon the West African economies as 50 percent of foreign exchange is derived from cocoa exports. Therefore it is no surprise that there are numerous vested interests involved in ensuring that cocoa remains a sustainable tree crop.

The STCP constitutes a coordinated and innovative partnership effort made by farmers and producer organizations, the worldwide chocolate industry, national governments, research institutes, the public sector, policymakers, donors and development agencies to facilitate the improvement of smallholder agricultural systems based on cocoa in West Africa. This was the first time that all the actors involved with cocoa were brought together in order to work for the common good. Previously cocoa development and commercialization was characterized by selfish and narrow interests, and competitive approaches which were of short-term orientation. However within the STCP partnership members now shared a common interest in promoting the production and marketing of quality cocoa, improving market access and income for small-scale producers, and creating systems that would be environmentally friendly, socially responsible, and economically sustainable.

Cocoa Farming in Nigeria

IITA's Dr Stephan Weise was responsible for managing the STCP partnerships, and for overseeing the implementation of research technologies in West Africa that would benefit cocoa farmers in producing increased quantities of high quality cocoa. One of the critical partnerships was with the cocoa farmers. Each of the West African cocoa producing countries had their own particular challenges. In Nigeria cocoa farming had declined partly because of the impact the petroleum industry had on the national economy, making agriculture a less attractive investment; also, the Nigerian government deregulated cocoa, making the quality less consistent.

Cocoa farming compared with other crops such as cassava and yams does not require the same labour intensity. Farmers typically left the cocoa trees alone and only periodically checked on them until the cocoa pods were ready for harvesting. As farmers were not regularly checking the cocoa trees and inspecting the cocoa pods for disease and pests the quality and quantity of cocoa was being reduced. Cocoa farmers needed to learn about new farming techniques that would decrease the impact of disease such as viruses and damage from moulds.

STCP also needed to address the sustainability of cocoa farming. One issue was related to encouraging rural youth to consider becoming the next generation of cocoa farmers. In Nigeria cocoa farmers were getting older and their children were not as interested in becoming farmers. Educational opportunities had opened up alternative occupations which did not include agriculture. Another issue for cocoa sustainability was that STCP needed to support farmers so that they were able to access markets and get the best price for their high quality cocoa harvest.

In order to train the cocoa farmers regarding the latest research technologies, IITA's staff working on the STCP developed Farmer Field Schools (FFS). The IITA STCP role was to:

1. Train farmers via the FFS. Currently there are 14 states in Nigeria that grow cocoa, and IITA STCP is active in all of them.

2. Backstop the STCP FFS program, which entails training facilitators to train / work with the farmers. STCP then monitors the new facilitators and their training to ensure it is going well.

3. Support farmer organizations by helping to organize farmers into cooperative societies so they can bargain for better cocoa prices, gain loans, etc.

IITA's field work staff assigned to STCP worked with approximately 2,500 farmers. As well as recruiting farmers to participate in the FFS, young people and women were also recruited to participate. Field staff would go and meet with the farmers in villages and try to build on the common goal of producing an increased quantity of high quality cocoa. The FFS taught participants about the use of agro-chemicals as well as beneficial farming practices that result in higher cocoa yields and effectively disseminated research technologies and ensured they were adopted.

FFS also encouraged farmers to organize and set up cooperatives so they are empowered to bargain with cocoa processing factories for better pricing as well as getting wholesale prices for farming supplies. Farmers quickly were able to see the benefits of belonging to local cooperatives as they recognized they previously were being cheated by being sold fake or useless agro-chemicals for high prices.

The FFS have helped to reduce the knowledge gap that previously existed. Farmers are empowered and have increased knowledge relating to improving their cocoa harvest. From IITA's perspective, building the partnership with cocoa farmers was a success when the results of what they are doing to improve cocoa production produced a higher quality of life for the farmers and enabled them to have an increased income. IITA also found that trust levels in the relationship field staff had with the farmers increased over time and as farmers and the field staff worked together.

In 2005 the STCP pilot phase came to an end and was evaluated. The STCP public and private partners asked that IITA continue to build upon the pilot achievements and to develop a new five-year program in consultation with national, regional and global stakeholders (IITA, 2006, p.2).

REFERENCES

African Union (2008). URL: http://www.africa-union.org [Date accessed: 23 March 2008].

Agbese, A.A. (2007). *The Role of the press and communication technology in democratisation: The Nigerian story*. New York: Routledge.

Amnesty International (1998). *Annual Report*. Amnesty International Publications, UK.

Babaleye, T. (2005) *A guide to public relations practice in agricultural research*. Ibadan, Nigeria: Banktab Ltd.

BBC (2008). URL: http://news.bbc.co.uk/1/hi/world/africa/country_profiles/1064557.stm#med [Date accessed: 07 May 2008].

Benson-Eluwa, V. (1986). *The practice of human, industrial and public relations*. Enugu, Nigeria: Virgina Creations.

Black, S. (1989) *Introduction to public relations*. London: Modino Press Ltd.

Cayford, S. (1996). The Ogoni uprising: Oil, human rights and a democratic alternative in Nigeria. *Africa Today*, Vol.43, No.2, p.183.

Coombs, W.T., and Holladay, S.J. (2007). *It's not just PR: Public relations in society.* Oxford: Blackwell Publishing.

Cornelissen, J. (2004). *Corporate communications: Theory and practice.* Thousand Oaks, CA: Sage.

Curtin, P.A., and Gaither, T.K. (2007). *International public relations: Negotiating culture, identity, and power.* Thousand Oaks, CA: Sage.

Dangogo, K. (2007). "Nigeria – Way Forward For NIPR" in *Daily Trust*, 30 November 2007. URL: http://allafrica.com/stories/200711300289.html [Date accessed: 05 January 2008].

ECOWAS (2008). URL: http://www.ecowas.int [Date accessed: 23 March 2008].

Emeagwali.com (2008). URL: http://emeagwali.com/nigeria/literature/nigerian-literature.jan93.html [Date accessed: 22 March 2008].

Enahoro, P. (1996). *How to be a Nigerian*. London: Spectrum Books Limited.

Ezeala-Harrison, F. (1993). Structured re-adjustment in Nigeria: Diagnosis of a severe Dutch disease syndrome. *American Journal of Economics and Sociology*, Vol.52, No.2., 193–208.

Henderson, T., and Williams, J. (2002). Shell: Managing a corporate reputation globally. In Moss, D., and DeSanto, B. (eds.). *Public relations cases: International perspectives*, 10–26. London: Routledge.

IITA (2006). *Sustainable tree crops program: A public–private partnership.* Ibadan, Nigeria: International Institute of Tropical Agriculture.

Klein, N. (2000). *No logo.* Toronto: Knopf Canada.

L'Etang, J.Y. (2004). *Public relations in Britain: A history of professional practice in the twentieth century.* London: Lawrence Erlbaum.

Livesey, S.M., and Graham, J. (2007). Greening corporations? Eco-talk and the emerging social imaginary of sustainable development. In May, S., Cheney, G., and Roper, J. (eds.). *The debate over corporate social responsibility,* 336–350. New York: Oxford University Press.

May, S., Cheney, G., and Roper, J. (2007). *The debate over corporate social responsibility.* New York: Oxford University Press.

Mohammed, S.(1993). *NIPR and Decree 16 of June 1990.* The NIPR anniversary brochure, NIPR Secretariat, Lagos.

Nigeria High Commission London (2007). URL: http://www.nigeriahc.org.uk [Date accessed: 22 March 2008].

OFID Newsletter (2007). Vol. XIII, no. 3, Oct.–Dec, OPEC, Vienna.

Ofonri, H.K. (1985). *Guide to PR practice in Nigeria.* Owerri, Nigeria: New African Publishing Ltd.

Ogbondah, C., and Siddens, P. J. (1999). *Defining traditional forms of communication in Nigerian culture within the context of nonverbal communication.* Education Resources Information Center, St. Louis, MO.

Ojo M.A. (1999). *On the beat: In Lagos, religion's above the fold.* Obafemi Awolowo University, Ile-Ife, Nigeria, and the School of Oriental and African Studies, University of London.

Okebukola, P. (2006). *Quality assurance in higher education: The Nigerian experience.* Paper presented at the Quality Assurance in Tertiary Education Conference, Sevres, France, June 18–20.

Oyekan J. (1993). *NIPR–30 years of growth,* The NIPR anniversary brochure, NIPR Secretariat, Lagos.

Ozowa V. N. (1995), Information Needs of Small Scale Farmers in Africa: The Nigerian Example. *Quarterly Bulletin of the International Association of Agricultural Information Specialists,*, Vol. 40, No. 1.

Salu, A. (1994), *Understanding public relations.* Lagos, Nigeria: Talkback Publshers Ltd.

Tench, R. (1997). Corporate advertising: The generic image. In Kitchen, P.J. (ed.). *Public relations principles and practice*, 118–211. London: Thomson Business Press.

16

STATUS OF PUBLIC RELATIONS IN KENYA

PETER ORIARE MBEKE

INTRODUCTION

The Republic of Kenya is in Eastern Africa. It borders Ethiopia to the north, Somalia to the northeast, Tanzania to the south, Uganda to the west, and Sudan to the northwest, with the Indian Ocean traversing its southeast border. Kenya, whose official language is Kiswahili, was given its independence by the United Kingdom in December 1963, and declared a republic the following year. The country of 42 ethnic communities is the forty-seventh largest country in the world, covering an area of 580,367km^2 with a projected population of 32m and density of 59 per km^2.

Kenya faces a number of socio-economic challenges characterized by a population growth rate of 2.7 percent, death rate of 1.1 percent, infant mortality rates of 57 deaths per 1,000 births and HIV/AIDS prevalence rate of 6.1 percent. Slightly more than half of Kenyans live below the poverty line, with a high unemployment rate of 40 percent and a huge public debt of 51 percent of the GDP. Generally, the quality of life in Kenya is low, with a life expectancy at birth of 47.5 years and a GDP per capita (PPP) of USD1,140 (GoK, 2007). In order to mitigate these challenges, the country has embraced progressive democratic change and the principles of free market economy. Since 2003, the economy has rebounded and the GDP rose by 6.1 percent in 2007. The Narc government's economic recovery program, resumption of donor support and improved investor (local and foreign) confidence contributed to the turnaround in the economy. Public relations practice continues to benefit from a buoyant and improved business climate in Kenya today.

This chapter seeks to answer the questions: what is the nature and status of public relations practice in Kenya and what environmental factors influence this practice? The first part of this chapter will deal with the nature and status of public relations in Kenya while the second part will describe the environmental factors that influence the practice of public relations in the country. While the first part will review the evolution of public relations and appraise the prevailing situation, the second part of the chapter will discuss how the level of public relations activism, development of mass media and political, social, economic and cultural factors have influenced the growth and development of public relations practice in Kenya. A case study at the end illustrates the practice of public relations in Kenya.

THE NATURE AND STATUS OF PUBLIC RELATIONS IN KENYA

Public Relations History and Development

The evolution of public relations is closely tied to the civilization of the 42 ethnic communities in Kenya. The practice of and application of public relations techniques is not new to Kenyan communities such as the Luo, Kikuyu, Luhya, Kamba, Nandi, Kisii, among others. Each of these communities had their own communication systems, structures, styles, and even spokespersons. Concepts such as corporate identity, corporate branding, and reputation management were not unknown to them. Members of various Nilotic communities such as the Luos, Tugen, among others, removed the lower teeth as a rite of passage. The Luos removed six while the Tugen removed one. This enabled easy identification of members of these communities, especially during war or multi-ethnic social interactions. Various methods of branding were used to enhance group membership identification. For instance, Masai and Samburu nomadic communities in Kenya used to brand their bodies with various tatoos and ornaments that made them easily recognizable.

Many of the communities practiced public relations during marital affairs. Family reputation was very important in the selection of a spouse. Among the Luos, kinsmen and women scouted for reliable brides and grooms for their young men and women. Upon identifying a suitable young person, the aunt or uncle would befriend such a youth with a view to understand their character, personality and family background. The mediating relative would easily call the deal off if family reputation did not match expectations. The next stage would be to introduce the topic of marriage and identity of the relative before informal contacts between the two would be allowed. The aunts and uncles would act as mediators between the two families and organize initial contact meetings between the two families before presentation of the bride price and wedding ceremony. The objective of such consultations was to improve understanding between the two families. During such meetings and ceremonies, the in-laws maintained high levels of hospitality and charity, with a view to establishing a good reputation with the in-laws. Participants at these meetings were carefully chosen by the bride or groom's family to present a favorable image.

The evolution of public relations is closely tied to Kenya's history and past based on imperialism. The practice of public relations can be traced far back to the time of the early western explorers' forays in Kenya between 1844 and 1884 (Ogot and Ochieng, 1995). The explorers wanted to find the source of the River Nile as well as champion the abolition of the slave trade. Johan Kraft, a German missionary of the Church Missionary Society, was the first European to enter Kenya and start work in Rabai, near Mombasa in 1844. Rebmann and Ehardt joined him in 1846 and 1849 respectively. Both the explorers and the Kenyans practiced interpersonal communications and social public relations then. The practice of public relations by both the explorers and the Kenyan communities improved relations between them. The explorers had to gain the goodwill of the Kenyan communities at the coast, who provided labor and acted as guides during the explorations. There were negotiations and consultations between the explorers and the leaders of various communities for safe passage.

Kraft and Ehardt's reports about equatorial snow-capped Mt. Kilimanjaro in 1848 and Mt. Kenya in 1849 respectively were a publicity masterpiece and caused a lot of interest in Europe. It put Kenya on the global map in such a way that it has attracted millions of tourists and adventurers. The two drew sketch maps to increase understanding of Mt. Kilimanjaro and Mt. Kenya among Europeans. In their own right, these explorers were the early publicists in Kenya.

Owing to improved relations between himself and the Miji Kenda communities at Rabai, Kraft mastered Swahili, the local language. He translated the Bible into Kiswahili, the national language of Kenya, as well as producing the first Kiswahili grammar and dictionary. These were great public relations tools that improved understanding between the explorers and Kenyans. Kraft's work contributed immensely to the evangelization of Kenya by various Christian missions.

The Royal Geographical Society commissioned Joseph Thompson in 1883 to explore the shortest route to the Kenyan coast from the source of the Nile in Uganda. His journeys took him through Kenya and he established good relations with the Masai of Kenya. His humorous book, *Through Masai Land,* a landmark publicity tool, improved the understanding of the Masai and East Africa in Europe. The Masai and their way of life are a major tourism and cultural attraction for Kenya.

The contribution of business in the development of public relations started as early as the 1870s. H.H. Johnson, an English businessman, signed treaties with chiefs in Taveta, a coastal region of Kenya, where he planted wheat and coffee. Johnson wrote numerous petitions to the British government to declare Kenya a British colony, but failed. These are some early examples of lobbying in the country.

The partition of Africa and the building of the railway from Mombasa in Kenya to Uganda between 1884 and 1902 also played a role in the development of public relations in Kenya. The partition of Africa into "spheres of influence" controlled by various European powers set in motion events that not only publicized, but also put Kenya onto the global geo-political map (History World, 2007). Immediately after the partitioning of Africa, English businessmen such as William Mackinnon confirmed and signed new treaties with various chiefs and leaders in coastal parts of Kenya. At the time they practiced social public relations.

Mackinnon formed the British East Africa Association, a trading firm, in 1887, later called the Imperial East Africa Company (1888) to champion the exploitation of Kenyan and Ugandan resources (Wikipedia, 2007). The business interests led to the building of the Lunatic Express, a railway line and train that would reduce the challenges of transportation between the Kenyan coast and Uganda, in 1894. The businessmen used bulletins to create understanding of their interests. Some of the earliest business bulletins are those belonging to the Uganda Railway, advertising the highlands of British East Africa, "winter homes" and "big game" for aristocrats.

The railway and the Lunatic Express opened the Kenyan hinterland to business as new towns and administrative centers sprang up. The Asian and Indian railway laborers remained behind after the construction of the railway and became major sources of social, political and economic development. At the same time, the railway made it easy for European settlers to migrate into Kenya and pursue their dreams. It is noteworthy that the migrant communities made up of Indians, Asians and whites played a key role in the institutionalization of public relations in Kenya. They were the pioneers of public relations practice in the country.

Early British administrators adopted a policy of attracting settlers and visitors to the Kenya highlands to encourage large-scale farming. This involved undertaking information and communication campaigns by putting out notices and bulletins to attract people to the colony. Lord Delamere was one such settler businessmen who took up the British offer. He introduced various commercial crops such as coffee and tea in Kenya, that still play important roles in the economic development of Kenya today (Huxley, 1935). Lord Delamere was a very diplomatic person and had very good relations with Chief Lenana, a Masai leader, who in 1911 sold to Delamere his land rights (Harneit-Sievers, 2002).

Kenya became a British protectorate in 1895 and became a colonial state in 1920 (Makali (ed), 2004; Ochieng and Odhiambo, 1995). The British used the policy of *indirect rule,* in which traditional rulers were responsible for administrative duties within their areas of influence (Chamberlain, 1999). This policy recognized the importance of nurturing good interpersonal communication, consultations and social relations to manage affairs of the colony. The main object for this policy was to nurture goodwill and acceptance among the Kenyan leaders of colonial rule with a view to perpetuating the extraction of resources from the colony (Chamberlain, 1999). The colonial government put in place a top-down communication structure that utilized the chief's *baraza* (public meetings called by the chief) as the focal point for community participation in decision-making. Politicians, business people, clergy and development workers still use the *baraza* model as a focal point for information dissemination and feedback.

Race and Public Relations

The composition of colonial Kenya occasioned a need for public relations to improve racial relations between indigenous Kenyans, Indians, Pakistanis, Goans, Arabs and the English. Racial tensions between the indigenous people of Kenya and the Asian and Arab communities were real at the time. The strained multi-racial setting, occasioned by restrictive racial laws, laid the foundation for public relations practice.

The struggle surrounding the fate of the colony between white settlers and the British administrators also contributed to the evolution of public relations in Kenya. The white settler communities, represented by rich farmers such as Sir Charles Elliot, E.G. Groan and Lord Delaware, wanted to convert Kenya into a white country molded along the Australian and New Zealand models. The protagonists fought this fight along the corridors of power and in the media. Powerful white settler lobby groups held various campaigns and conferences to influence public opinion on the matter. The 1923 Devonshire White Paper, an outcome of the Devonshire conference, finally settled the issue that "primarily, Kenya is an African county and the interests of the African native must be paramount." These were the precursors of lobbying in public relations in Kenya.

The evolution of public relations is also closely associated with the struggle for independence in Kenya. A combination of factors contributed to the fight for independence. The main one was forced annexation of land by white settlers and British administrators, followed by forced taxation and labor. Kenyan communities, especially those living on the white highlands, hated the forced settlements policy which confined many communities, such as the Kikuyu, Meru, Embu, Kalenjin, and Kisii, into "reserves." Rampant abuse of human rights arising from racial laws that restricted and violated the enjoyment of various freedoms by Kenyans encouraged conflict.

The first and second world wars also played a role in the struggle for Kenyan independence. War exposed Kenyan soldiers to the intrigues of politics and produced the forerunners of African freedom fighters and politicians. By the 1920s, several political lobby and pressure groups such as the East African Association, the Kavirondo Taxpayers Welfare Association, the Kikuyu Association and the Kikuyu Central Association had been established. These political associations were the precursors of lobbying organizations and today's political parties. They were led by revolutionaries such as Harry Thuku, Elium Mathu, Jomo Kenyatta, Argwings Kodhek, Oginda Odinga, Tom Mboya among others. These individuals were also the precursors of today's political lobbyists. They organized mass meetings and campaigns to put pressure on the colonial government to change bad laws and allow self-rule.

The Kenyan soldiers who participated in the Second World War were also instrumental in organizing strikes and riots in the city of Nairobi to demand greater freedoms for Kenyans. Former Second World War soldiers formed the Forty Group, a rebel movement that formed the nucleus of armed freedom fighters in Kenya. Later they became known as the Mau Mau freedom fighters, who fought a bitter war from 1946 to 1960 against the colonial government in Kenya.

The British Governor declared a state of emergency in October 1952 and authorized total war against the Mau Mau in Kenya. The British administration used propaganda tactics against the Mau Mau. This involved distribution of propaganda messages through leaflets, posters and radio to pass messages to the settler and African communities. By 1960, when the state of emergency was repealed, over 13,500 Kenyans were dead and over 100,000 detained (Ogot and Ochieng, 1995). The Mau Mau war left the reputation of the colonial administration in shreds.

The growth of mass media is also closely tied to the evolution of public relations in Kenya. The mass media in Kenya trace their origins to the spread of western civilization in Kenya by the white settlers, Christian missionaries and colonial administrators from 1895. The Reverend Albert Stegal of the Church Missionary Society published the quarterly *The Taveta Chronicle* in 1895 and the *Uganda Mail* between 1899 and 1904 in Mombasa (Makali, 2004). The Church of Scotland Mission of Kikuyu published the *Kikuyu News* from 1908 to 1957. M.A. Jevanjee started publishing *The Standard* in 1902. It changed hands in 1905 and became *The East African Standard*. Newspapers catering for the interest of the Asian community, such as *The Hindi Prakash* and the *East African News*, were published in 1915. The colonial press served the interest of the white settlers and Asian immigrant communities (Makali, 2004).

The early freedom fighters used the media to publicize their interests and demands. The *East African Chronicle* published by A.M. Desai in 1919 gave a voice to the Young Kikuyu Association, which was started in 1922. Jomo Kenyatta, the leader of the Kikuyu Central Association, started *Muiguithania*, a monthly newsletter, in 1925 to champion the interest of the Kikuyu (Makali, 2004).

The colonial government also used the media for propaganda purposes. The Native Affairs Department started *Habari*, a monthly newspaper in 1921, to counter rising nationalism and the influence of the African press. The Department of Information produced a weekly bulletin, *Habari za Vita*, to disseminate information about the First World War to relatives and families of soldiers. The colonial government replaced *Habari za Vita* with *Baraza* in 1939, and *Pamoja* newspapers to provide information to the Kenyan public (Makali, 2004).

The colonial government formed the Kenya Information Services (KIS) in 1940 with the objective of popularizing the war among Kenyans. KIS outlived its usefulness after the war and changed its name to Africa Information Services (AIS). However, it served the interests of the white settlers and the colonial administration. In 1953, it became the Department of Information (DOI) with the appointment of the first press officers. DOI served mainly as a propaganda machine, especially during the state of emergency between 1953 and 1960 (PRSK Arena, 2006).

Although the colonial government banned the publication of seditious indigenous newspapers in 1930 and 1939, Kenyan nationalists remained defiant and continued to use the media as a tool for political and civic education. The Kenya African Union published the *Sauti ya Mwafrika* in 1944. By the 1950s there were over 50 indigenous newspapers critical of the colonial administration in Kenya. Most these newspapers were edited by Kenyan nationalists; for example, Paul Ngei edited *Uhuru za Mwafrika,* while W.W.W. Awori edited *Radio Posta* and *Habari za Dunai*, James Gichuru and Joseph Otiende edited *African Leader*, and Bildad Kaggia edited *Inooro ria Agikuyu* and *Africa Mpya* (Makali, 2004).

Early Publicists

Most of the nationalists who led the independence movement in Kenya were actually publicists. They not only edited newspapers, but were adept in the use of the media as propaganda tools. These leaders included: Jaramogi Ochieng Oneko, Tom Mboya, Argwings Kodhek, Jomo Kenyatta, Bildad Kaggia, James Gichuru among others. These leaders organized Kenyans to write protest letters to the press against the colonial administration. They also organized public meetings and made direct petitions to the colonial government (Abuoga and Mutere, 1988).

A good example of the nationalist publicists was Jomo Kenyatta, later the first president of Kenya. Upon his return to Kenya in 1946, Kenyatta organized mass demonstrations and campaigns to mobilize and educate Kenyans about the independence struggle. He published and edited the famous *Muigwithania*, anti-colonial administration newspapers. Kenyatta printed protest letters in the *Muigwithania* to demonstrate grievances against the colonial administration. For instance in 1934, he published letters by Samuel Muindi, a prominent Kamba politician, to support the Kamba campaign against livestock destocking in Kambaland. While in London, Kenyatta also wrote a series of letters to British newspapers such as the *New Statesman* and the *Manchester Guardian* seeking goodwill to change the political trends in Kenya.

The colonial administration formed the Institute of Public Administration in 1922 to train civil servants in effective public sector management. The colonial administration, in a series of articles in the *Journal of The Royal Institute of Public Administration*, (RIPA), argued that public relations was good for smooth and effective public administration. This is evidence that as early as the 1920s, the colonial administration had recognized the importance of effective public relations to facilitate effective delivery of services to the public (Finer, 1931). The colonial government believed that good public relations assisted in communicating public policy to the citizens (Cowell, 1935). The colonial administration therefore encouraged the growth of public relations activities in the colony (Muruli, 2001).

The colonial government established cable and wireless to relay BBC news in English on its transmitting station at Kabete in 1927 (Abuoga and Mutere, 1988). At the time, radio was the only medium of mass communication in Kenya. The African and Asian services started after the outbreak of the Second World War. Initially, broadcasting continued in English. Strategically, the colonial government used radio to support the war machinery. The colonial administration created the mobile information unit in 1940 mainly for propaganda purposes. It was meant to disseminate war information to the Kenyan population (GoK, Kenya Information Annual Report, 1941).

The position of Principal Information Officer for the Kenya Information Office under the Ministry of Information on East African Command was created in 1942. The key responsibility of the PIO was to keep the public informed of the activities of government and its intentions (Kenya Information Annual Report, 1942). A specialized post of public relations was created within the Kenya Information Office in 1944 to foster favorable public opinion towards the war effort. Subsequently, KIO became the technical department with the responsibility of producing and supplying publicity materials.

International Public Relations

The British government established the British Council in 1934 to enhance international public relations and diplomacy through promotional work and exchange programs. With this mandate, the British Council started operating in Kenya in 1947. The objective was to promote mutual exchange of knowledge and ideas about Britain and Kenya. Essentially, the British Council was a tool for communicating British national identity and perpetuating cultural propaganda (East African Standard, 1947).

The colonial government established the Legislative Council in 1927, consisting of various races including one African Kenyan. The creation of the Legislative Council was a strategic move meant to facilitate effective management of public opinion in a multi-racial and multi-ethnic colony.

From the late 1940s, business organizations became increasingly aware of the public virtue and the role of corporate institutions in society (Muruli, 2001). Generally, the demand for political freedoms went hand in hand with increased agitation for economic rights. Increased consumer consciousness led to increased incidences of conflict and confrontation. Workers formed trade unions to demand better pay and rights. In 1959, the 23,000 African port and railway workers went on strike, followed by the East African Posts and Telecommunication African workers strike in 1960 (Muruli, 2001). Such strikes could partly be blamed on lack of or poor internal communication mechanisms within the organizations concerned.

There is evidence that corporations such as British Airways East Africa command used public relations to build good relationships before 1952 (L'Etang, 2001). The Institute of Public Relations *Journal* discussed the qualities of a public relations officer in the Kenyan colony in 1951 (Johnson, 1951). Unilever adopted a policy of public relations immediately after the Second World War because of fear of a big resurgence of political agitation for independence among workers (L'Etang, 2001). They were right.

Public relations consultancies also took root in pre-independence Kenya. The first such consultancy was Dunford, Hall and Partners, registered in 1955. It was a partnership between Michael Dunford and Andrew Hall. The company operated in East, Central and West Africa producing farming and agricultural magazines such as *Ukulima was Kisasa* and *Kenya Farmer* (Abuoga and Mutere, 1988).

The 1960s were a boon for public relations practice. The introduction of television in October 1962 gave PR impetus. Television provided a unique medium for disseminating information to the public.

Kenya got its independence in 1963 and became a republic in 1964. The new government of independent Kenya recognized the role of communication and information. This could be because most of its ministers were nationalists who had largely relied upon the press to disseminate their political platforms. The Department of Information Services, which at independence was subordinated under the Ministry of Constitutional Affairs and Administration, was upgraded to full Ministry of Information, Broadcasting and Tourism in 1964. The ministry had responsibility for information, communication (including broadcasting) and tourism. According to the government, the ministry was to spearhead publicity for development projects through mass education campaigns.

In 1965, the ministry became the Ministry of Information and Broadcasting, which was indicative of the strategic role of public relations in government. The ministry published and distributed free of charge *Kenya Yetu*, a local newspaper with national reach, to disseminate information to the remote parts of the country.

The government at independence also used public relations to support foreign policy. There was an exodus from Kenya from 1960 and soon after independence by whites and Asians because of fear of insecurity and instability under an African government. The new government put in place a massive propaganda campaign to sell Kenya as a peaceful and stable country. The government started and maintained diplomatic missions abroad and even hired public relations firms in countries without diplomatic missions for this very purpose (Daily Nation, 1968). *Kenya Yetu* newspapers were distributed to diplomatic missions abroad to enhance the image of the country abroad. This was a strong PR statement.

Public Relations Education

The new government started the Kenya Institute of Mass Communications in 1965 to cater for the rising training needs of information officers within the civil service and also to work as press attachés in foreign missions. In 1970, the government, with the help of UNESCO and donors, established the School of Journalism at the University of Nairobi to meet the demand for advanced training in information and communications. The school offered public relations as an option in its training programs.

Government ministries and parastatals embraced public relations functions soon after independence. Kenya Power and Lighting Company and East African Harbors Corporation engaged in sponsorships, financial public relations, events and various forms of corporate social responsibility. By 1969 the number of people practicing PR had gone up to over 15 (*East African Standard*, March, 1969). James K. Mwai was the first indigenous Kenyan to become a member of the Institute of Public Relations of Britain (*East African Standard and Daily Nation*, April 4, 1969).

However, the institutionalization of PR in Kenya came several years after independence, and was mostly introduced by foreign organizations that had realized the value of PR as an effective tool of communication with different publics they wanted to address (Mokaya and Rotich, 1991).

Colin Church, a founder member of the Public Relations Society of Kenya (PRSK) and a leading PR consultant, argued that the formal introduction of PR in Kenya took place during the independence period when PR was beginning to expand all over the world.[1] "This came at a time when the media was becoming freer and with it, the PR industry was required by organizations to have messages that they wanted to get across and correct misinformation about their own organizations."[2]

Public relations was first introduced by the local subsidiaries of transnational companies (*The Standard*, June 5, 1987.) The pressure to Africanize the expatriate staff in most companies saw the employment of first-generation public relations practitioners in Kenya. The companies resisted this policy and employed indigenous Kenyans as public relations officers. *The Standard* writer G.M. Anderson argued that organizations did "window dressing," in an article entitled "How Public Relations is Used and Abused" in *The Standard*,

---

[1] See interview with Colin Church, September, 2007.
[2] Interview with the researcher, August 22, 2007.

June 5, 1987. He argues that the companies filled these posts with people without public relations skills but who were nice. "Nice implied unquestionable loyalty to the top management and ability to carry out the wishes of the expatriate without questions." (*The Standard*, June 5, 1987).

The 1970s marked a great milestone in the evolution of public relations in Kenya. The Public Relations Society of Kenya was formed on June 23, 1971 to improve the standards of public relations practice in the country. At the launch, the society had 20 members. The first officials were: Michael Dunford (Chairman), J.H.E. Smart (Vice-Chairman), Miss Raye Low (Secretary), Patrick Orr (Publicity Officer), and committee members were J.E. Opembe, Colin Church, Mohameed Noor and James Mwai. Other members included John Mramba, Shabanji Opukak, Yolanda Taveres, Eunice Mathu, Muthoni Likimani, Muthoni Muthiga. PRSK was registered and ratified its code of conduct based on the Code of Athens (1965).

Training was a major preoccupation of public relations practice in the 1970s. Several Kenyans went to Britain for short training courses in public relations. For example, Charles Kioko of Gailey Roberts Limited went for a two-month training in London in March 1972 while Andrew Ambani of East Africa Cargo Handling Services went to Britain for a short training in public relations in August 1971 (*Daily Nation,* August 8, 1971 and March 3, 1972). In 1974, Jane Daliel got the diploma in communication, advertising and marketing (CAM) from the UK, followed by James Mwai two years later *(East African Standard*, August 24, 1974).

Another milestone in the evolution of public relations in Kenya was the June 1975 PRSK's hosting of an International Public Relations Conference at Kenyatta International Conference Center. The expulsion of the South African delegates from the conference received huge publicity that put PR practice in Kenya on the global map.

Although government and the private sector recognized public relations, many still did not appreciate its strategic importance in the management of organizations. Jessee Opembe, the former chairman of PRSK, once lamented that "Organizations are making a mockery of public relations officers (PRO) by using them as messengers . . . the PRO has not even met the managing director nor seen the chairman of the company. . . this makes the practice of public relations a mockery" (*The East African Standard,* July 24, 1979).

So although public relations practice was integrated in business organizations, the private sector did not perceive it as crucial to management as to employ qualified staff. The main function of public relations practitioners was to whitewash the image of the various organizations they worked for. The main preoccupation of the practitioners seemed to be placing, or at worst killing, stories in the media (Opukah, 2001).

The tremendous growth of Kenya after independence, with a Gross National Product (GNP) of 7% plus, spurred the development of PR (Church, 2007). Organizations used public relations to build their reputation within the emerging markets.

In the early 1980s the PR profession had no focus (Opuka, 1992). The corporate world still misunderstood the strategic importance of PR, with PR practitioners reduced either to mere personal assistants to CEOs or "gin and tonic" press officers. However, as the decades went on, fundamental shifts in the perception of the role of public relations took root. The end of the Cold War ushered in principles and global movements for privatization, democratization, transparency and accountability that led to increased recognition of the strategic importance of public relations in both public and private organizations.

In Kenya, the poor state of government communication led to the appointment of information officers for various ministries in 1983 (Ombara, 2001). President Daniel arap

Moi also played an important role in popularizing public relations. He coined the Nyayo Philosophy of Peace, Love and Unity, and used public relations to popularize it across the country. However, President Moi's PR changed to spin and propaganda soon after the 1982 attempted coup. The President's spin doctors' lies and unethical behavior gave PR a bad name, to the extent that people dismissed government statements as "just PR."

Public relations grew rapidly towards the end of the 1980s. This era was marked by political agitation for more democratic space in Kenya. Pro-democracy movements, civil society organizations and the donor community used public relations to create awareness about their political agendas (Opukah, 1992). Corresponding growth was realized also within the corporate sector as many adverts seeking public relations officers and managers appeared in the local media during this period (Mwembe, 1989).

By 1989, Kenya had over 142 public relations practitioners in senior positions. PR had taken root in Kenya and it was perceived as a management function (Mwembe, 1989).

Public Relations Since the 1990s

The 1990s was a milestone decade for PR growth in Kenya. PRSK hosted the International Public Relations Association conference on *The Pace of Change–Africa's Public Relations Challenge*. The conference debated the implications of the various changes taking place comprising changes in communication, technology, democratization, globalization and increased consumerism (Opukah, 1993). The conference, which was attended by dignitaries including former OAU Secretary General Dr Salim Salim, increased the prestige of public relation in Kenya.

In 1990 and 1993, Kenyan public relations practitioners won global awards in the IPRA Golden Awards. The awards won proved that public relations in Kenya had attained international standards and recognition. This improved the prestige of the practice in Kenya. In 1994, IPRA appointed Colin Church, a PR pioneer in Kenya, to its Board of Directors. This appointment indicated the confidence the international community of PR practitioners had in Kenya PR practitioners.

In 1997, PRSK celebrated its Silver Jubilee. This was a milestone that showed that public relations practice had matured in Kenya. In September 1998, the Federation of East and Central Africa Public Relations Association was launched in Nairobi. This was indicative of the role PRSK played in nurturing the growth of public relations and improving mechanisms for standardization and networking for public relations practitioners across the continent.

Specialized public relations consultancies were formed in the 1990s. Strategic Public Relations Limited was registered in 1996 to champion opinion polling within the industry. Steadman Media Monitoring Limited, another public relations consultancy, focused on provision of media clips to the industry.

Responding to the global business trends to improve efficiency and increase profits by leveraging market positions, Church Orr and Crawford Ellis, rival public relations consultancy firms, merged in 1999.

During this period, PRSK assisted institutions to set up public relations departments. They also assisted institutions of learning such as Kenyatta University to set up undergraduate and postgraduate courses in public relations.

CURRENT STATUS OF PUBLIC RELATIONS IN KENYA

The PR Profession in Kenya Today

It may be said with the wisdom of hindsight that public relations in Kenya has come of age. Public relations is today widely respected and accepted as a management tool both in the public and private sectors. Dr Isaiah Cherutich, a Lecturer at United States International University, argued that "PR was previously relegated to the backburner in most organisations. Now, PR practitioners are answerable to CEOs in many organisations." (Cherutich, 2007).

John Mramba, a PR pioneer, proprietor in Kenya and chairman of a parastatal there, agreed with Dr Cherutich that over the last 10 years there had been "a measure of recognition of PR in the country and the private sector in particular." In fact, most organizations in both the public and private sectors have departments of PR or hire consultants to assist them to manage their communications and project a favorable corporate image.

Despite these advances, Dr Cherutich argued PR practice has not peaked at the ideal levels yet. According to him, poor strategic positioning of PR in organizational management, public ignorance of PR and low remuneration of PR practitioners in Kenya still undermine the potential of public relations practice in Kenya.

Corporates' View of Public Relations in Kenya

Corporate organizations in Kenya today see PR as an indispensable management tool. Corporate organizations are now aware that they need PR to communicate with their publics more than ever before. Colin Church argued that PR was moving from subordinate position to an executive role in the general management, finance and marketing mix (*Daily Nation*, 2000). Most big corporate organizations have public relations departments headed by public relations managers. In organizations such as Standard Chartered and British American Tobacco, public relations functions are positioned at director level. Studies have found out that public relations, initiated by former Managing Director Gareth George, played an important role in the turnaround of Kenya Commercial Bank (KCB, 2005). Kenya Airways, Barclays Bank, Kenya Commercial Bank, Kenya Breweries, and Safaricom Limited, among other leading corporate bodies in Kenya, have invested heavily in mass media campaigns to project an image of good corporate citizenship (Wahome, 2005). Barclays Bank for instance paid Gina Din Corporate Communications, a PR consultancy in Kenya, a retainer fee of about USD13,000 per month in the early 2000s. This indicated the premium value that corporate organizations in Kenya put on effective public relations.

Government's View of PR Today

The Narc Government is keenly aware of the strategic role of public relations in management of public opinion. Soon after coming to power in 2003, it established the Office of Public Communications and strategically positioned it under the Office of the President at a Permanent Secretary Level. Although the office's mandate was to improve the image of the government, Dr Alfred Mutua, the Government Spokesperson, has tended to use the office more often for propaganda than public relations.

The government has been restructuring the Ministry of Information and Communication to make it more responsive to a changing public service. It has initiated an ambitious capacity-building program for information officers, many of whom have been given scholarships to do a master's degree in communication at public universities. Recently, the government advertised 140 vacancies for information officers with relevant degrees.

Mutahi Kagwe, the Minister for Information and Communications, argued that PR remained the crucial ingredient in the change process in Kenya (PR Arena, 2007). According to the minister the government is leveraging the public relations function to play an important role in the socio-economic development of the country.

The government recognizes PRSK. The Media Act 2007 recognized PRSK as a strategic partner in the media sector, and made it a board member of the Media Council of Kenya.

The NGOs' View of Public Relations

The NGO sector in Kenya has embraced public relations practice very well. The growth of public relations practice in this sector is closely tied to the presence of numerous UN agencies and multilateral donor organizations in the country. Most UN agencies and international NGOs and donors use communication as advocacy tools, thereby promoting the expansion of public relations. The sector employs hundreds of communication and public relations professionals in Kenya. As a result of this, the UN agencies and international NGOs have very robust public relations machineries.

The UNDP Kenya Country Office through its capacity building program for the government hired communication and public relations professionals to help strengthen and streamline government communication in various ministries and departments. Multilateral donors such as DFID have also hired and attached communication and public relations specialists to various government programs to improve public communication.

The World Bank, DFID and GTZ are known to have championed best practices in communication and public relations in Kenya. GTZ and WB initiated and entrenched the development of communication strategies to support public restructuring programs in government in Kenya. GTZ supported the water sector reform communication program while DFID gave support for the Public Finance Reform Management Program. UNDP is supporting the communication component of the public sector reform program, which is part of the Economic Recovery Strategy (2007).

The donor group in Kenya through UNDP is currently supporting the media monitoring, media strategy and training component of the 2007 election assistance program in Kenya. The program has hired media organizations and public relations firms such as Media Council of Kenya, Strategic Public Relations and Research Limited and Media Focus on Africa to champion election related research and communication activities. The donor agencies are not only providing employment but also contributing to the growth of the public relations sector.

Level of Professionalism in PR Practice in Kenya

Public relations practice has undergone a sea change—moving from what Opukah called the "era of political and social climbers" to the "era of partnerships rather than patronage." Essentially, this was a shift from corporate sycophancy where PR practitioners pandered to the whims of the management to a more professional approach to their duties (Opukah, 1993).

This seismic shift in PR practice was brought about by the drastic social, economic and political changes that have taken place in the country starting with the introduction of political pluralism and liberalization of the economy in the early 1990s. These changes resulted in a more open society, a more aggressive consumer culture, a vibrant and dynamic media scene, a huge and fairly influential civil society and a rather litigious populace "that has compelled PR practitioners to be more professional in their approach" (Opukah, 2001).

PRSK has played a significant role in nurturing professionalism in Kenya. It has a constitution (1971) and a code of conduct modeled on the Code of Athens (1965). The society has active membership of about 344 (PRSK Status Report, 2006). The membership grew by 70 percent between 2005 and 2006. PRSK has an executive committee that meets once a month to implement the activities of the association. The society has a secretariat hosted by Corporate Reflections, a PR consultancy firm. Although PRSK meets most of its expenses, it is heavily dependent on pro-rated and pro-bono services from PR firms and members of goodwill (PRSK Status Report, 2006). The society recently changed its image and identity by launching a new logo developed by Ogilvy Public Relations. PRSK has developed a draft PRSK Act, which it proposes to sponsor in Parliament for legislation. The act would strengthen the legal framework for public relations practice in Kenya by giving PRSK a legal mandate to enforce standards in the sub-sector. The society has high visibility in Kenya. PRSK was the second public relations body in Africa to become a member of the Global Alliance for Public Relations and Communication (GA). In 2004, the society participated in the First World Public Relations Festival held in Rome, organized by the Italian Federation of Public Relations (FEPRI). It hosted the Federation of Africa Public Relations Associations (FAPRA) All Africa Public Relations conference in June 2005. The society fully participated in the Institute of Public Relations and Communication Management of South Africa's All Africa Public Conference in Johannesburg in 2006. That year it also celebrated its 35th anniversary. The society also actively participated in 2007 FAPRA and GA conferences in Kampala (Uganda) and Cape Town (South Africa).

The society has been active in meeting its social responsibility to Kenyan society. It has supported road safety and security campaigns as well as training the police force. The society was a key partner in the African Peer Review consultations as well as helping the Ministry of Planning M and E Directorate to develop its IEC strategies (PRSK Status Report, 2006).

The society publishes *PR Arena*, a quarterly professional journal for public relations practitioners. *PR Arena* provides a forum for professionals and academics to discuss issues relating to PR practice and education in Kenya. Apart from the journal, the society also operates a well updated website that provides a very efficient point of interaction with members and non-members.

The society has been very active in raising the standards of public relations education and practice in Kenya. It initiated the PR Focus, a student network and outreach programme with the objective of interfacing the institutions of learning, the students and PR practitioners. In 2005 and 2006, PR Focus took place at the University of Nairobi, United States International University, Daystar University, Maseno University and Moi University. PRSK also assisted in the development of the public relations curriculum at the University of Nairobi in 2004. The society runs a quarterly training program for the industry that focuses on media relations, events management, photography for PR, and strategic planning for PR practitioners among others. PRSK also runs the power lunch talk shows that give an opportunity to various industry leaders to interact with PR practitioners.

Education in Public Relations

Today, most people working as public relations officers have been trained in communications, journalism, mass communication and other related fields. This is because of improvements in education and training in tertiary institutions and universities. Today, communication related courses are taught in all the seven public universities and almost all private universities. There has been a mushrooming of tertiary colleges all over the county offering public relations and communication related courses. The School of Journalism at the University of Nairobi and Daystar University became UNESCO centres of excellence in September 2007. Both universities have undergraduate and postgraduate programs in communication with strong emphasis on public relations. The School of Journalism has a Bachelor's degree with two years of specialization in public relations.

Although these developments definitely will improve the quality of professionalism in public relations, accreditation is still problematic. PRSK does not have an accreditation but has voted to use the PRISA accreditation system from 2008. Legislation through the proposed PRSK Act will further strengthen the accreditation system.

State of Professional Prestige and Intellectual Sophistication in Public Relations

Traditionally in Kenya, some of the professions that have enjoyed prestige include law, medicine, engineering, architecture, accountancy and business administration. PR has not featured among the most lucrative of the professions. However, PR is gradually attaining prestigious status if the academic and professional backgrounds of current practitioners are anything to go by.

Opukah (1993) has distinguished two categories of PR people, that is practitioners and professionals. The practitioners are those who occupy some of the senior positions in PR departments especially in the public sector by virtue of their experience and not by professional education or merit. The professionals, on the other hand, occupy their positions mostly in the private sector and in the PR consultancies courtesy of their professional and academic credentials. The latter are intellectually equipped to cope with the various challenges that organisations face in the business world (Opukah, 1993).

Kenya has no public relations professionals with PhDs. Those with PhDs are those who studied Journalism and related courses. The School of Journalism at the University of Nairobi only has one PhD Lecturer in communications. Only Daystar University has a Professor with a communication training background. The state of research and publication in public relations by academics is almost zero. Of course, there is some research conducted by PR consultancies and corporate organizations in this area. However, such research and publication remains in private custody and rarely influences the direction of the practice in Kenya.

A good number of PR practitioners now have MA degrees. The University of Nairobi has over 60 MA graduates in communication studies per year. A similar number will obtain degrees from the undergraduate programme in the next two years.

Indeed, public relations is growing in esteem and prestige. Two ministers in the government are public relations practitioners and proprietors. Hon. Kagwe, the minister of information and communication, is the owner of Tell Em public relations consultancy, while Hon. Tuju, the minister of foreign affairs and international cooperation, is the proprietor of Ace Communications Limited. Currently, most private sector firms and NGOs insist on hiring university graduates to staff their PR departments. Nowadays, it is not uncommon for a vacancy announcement to demand a Master's degree in PR or Communications as part of the requirements for would-be job seekers in PR.

Despite the positive development in public relations, it still faces many challenges. Colin Church argued that one of the biggest challenges "is that PR tends to be subsumed by the advertising industry. Most of the dominant advertising firms that control the over 3 billion shillings industry, run parallel public relations departments or firms." This continues to subdue the strategic role of PR in Kenya.

The growing appreciation of the role of PR by industry and government has created another challenge. Church argued that PR professionals have to match the expanding status of PR with the appropriate academic capacity to practice at senior levels in management. "The PRO must be the CEO's academic and intellectual equal," he noted.

Mwembe argued that the lack of legislation has denied PRSK the ability to rein in what he terms as "quacks" in PR. PR practice in Kenya acquired a negative connotation over the years. Many people associate PR with advertising, propaganda, spin doctoring and marketing which are manipulative. This is made worse by the fact that most of the firms and individuals who offer PR services are also associated with these professions. Advertising, propaganda and spin doctoring usually involve outright lies, misrepresentation of facts and may even be unethical. Worse still, the culture of cash for news is prevalent. A lot of PR practitioners encourage unethical behavior when they give cash for publicity.

Although PR practitioners are visible in the media in Kenya, serious debate about PR issues is muted. Debate often occurs when PRSK activities get covered by the media.

ENVIRONMENTAL FACTORS AND PR PRACTICE

Political Factors and the Development of PR in Kenya

Kenya was a one-party dictatorship after 1969, when former President Jomo Kenyatta banned the Kenya People's Union (KPU), the only opposition party, following disagreements with the former vice president Jaramogi Odinga Odinga. After Kenyatta's death in 1978, his successor, the former President Moi, followed in his footsteps, restricted freedom of expression, outlawed political dissent and perfected political repression and persecution. However, the repeal of section 2A of the Constitution of Kenya, in 1992, dramatically changed the political situation in Kenya. The amendment of section 2A allowed Kenya to embrace a multi-party political system (Opukah, 2001). The changes were brought about by winds of change that were blowing across the African continent after the collapse of the former communist Soviet bloc in Eastern Europe, starting in 1989. In Kenya, the media, civil society and foreign missions were instrumental in bringing political liberalization to the country.

The changes came as a godsend to PR, because democracy is the most fundamental ingredient in the development and growth of PR. Dialogue, engagement of publics and two-way communication, which are important ingredients of a working democracy, are critical principles of PR. The repeal of section 2A led to political pluralism, liberalization of the media, improved freedom of expression and speech, and the outlawing of political repression. PR benefited immensely from these changes in the political, social and cultural environment.

PR thrived in a competitive multi-party political environment because the various politicians and political parties were forced to use public relations practitioners to assist them to communicate more effectively with the electorate and spruce up their images.

According to Dr Cherotich, political parties for the first time greatly relied upon PR consultants to develop and manage their communication campaigns in the 2002 General Election.

The 2005 Referendum on the proposed new Constitution of Kenya also provided an impetus for public relations in Kenya. Once again PR consultants and consultancies played a critical role in running the political communication campaigns for both the "Yes Side" and the "No Side" in the referendum campaigns.

Cherutich argued that "So it means, the voters are much more enlightened, are much more knowledgeable; they need a lot of convincing. That is why people thought of employing PR consultants to sway the voters. It is about public opinion, about perception, about how you project your image in public. PR consultants can polish it."

PR consultancies such as Scan Ad and others were heavily engaged in the launch of the presidential campaigns for the 2007 general elections. PR professionals such as Raphael Tuju, minister for foreign affairs and international cooperation, Mutahi Kagwe, minister for information and communication, Shabanji Opuka, former BAT PLC corporate affairs manager and PR pioneer, Chacha Mwita, former managing editor for the Standard Group, were heavily engaged in campaign strategy for the various political parties, where they belong.

The passing of the Media Council Act 2007 was also a big boon for PR in Kenya. The Act puts in place a legal and regulatory framework that allows for self-regulation of the media industry. The Act recognized that PR professionals are strategic partners of media and made PRSK part of the Media Council Board. This will give PR professionals an opportunity to influence policy on media and communication matters in the country.

Economic Factors and the Development of PR in Kenya

Kenya, a regional center for trade and finance in Eastern and Central Africa, enjoyed a buoyant economy between independence in 1963 and the global economic recession of the 1980s. The 1970s were years of economic boom owing to increased foreign export earnings from tea, coffee and tourism. The high cost of petroleum, low foreign exchange earnings from primary commodities, and bad governance epitomized by endemic corruption, led to a weakening of the economy between the 1980s and 1990s. The weakening of the economy led to the introduction of structural adjustment programs in the public sector in the late 1980s. This led to restructuring of public institutions to increase their efficiency.

The government in 1993, following prodding from the Bretton Woods Institutions, deregulated the economy, thus creating a free market regime. Hitherto protected companies were thereby exposed to competitive markets forcing them to adopt strategies to survive. The downside of this has been contraction rather than the expansion of businesses. The results included retrenchments, mergers, acquisitions, downsizing and the folding or closure of business firms.

As a result of persistent bad governance, the Bretton Woods Institutions suspended financial support for Kenya in 1997, further worsening the country's economic performance. The situation got worse between 1998 and 2000 when the country suffered from a severe drought that adversely affected the agricultural and energy sectors. As a result of this, the GDP dropped to less than 0.2 percent in 2002, rising slightly to 1.1 percent in 2003.

Economic liberalization is good for public relations. "An increasingly liberalised market economy is making corporate competition fight hard to maintain positions in the market place. Only the best survive. In the past, some companies survived through protectionism and monopolies, but this ended with the market economy." (*Daily Nation*,

November, 1998). Public relations has been instrumental in the restructuring processes and in helping companies stay afloat in the turbulent market.

To cope with these challenges various organizations in both the public and private sectors have retrained public relations staff, taken on new talent, revitalized in-house public relations departments, allocated them more resources or contracted public relations consultants to help them establish and maintain their competitiveness in the market.

Soon after coming to power in 2002, the Narc government put in place the Economic Recovery Strategy for Wealth and Employment Creation (ERS), 2003–2007. The ERS focused on increasing economic growth, equity and poverty reduction, improving governance, financing frameworks and putting in place a national monitoring and evaluation system. The ERS program involved the restructuring and re-engineering of government ministries, parastatals and department including the civil service. Part of this strategy involved public service reforms which recognized the utility of public relations and communications to improve service delivery to the public. The government put in place the Rapid Results Initiative to create and nurture a business culture within the civil service (GoK, 2003).

Today, the economy, which had virtually stagnated up to 2002, grows at 6.1 percent annually. The agriculture sector is growing by 5.4 percent, manufacturing by 5.9 percent, the hotels and restaurants sector by 14.9 percent, construction sector by 6.3 percent and the transport sector by 10.8 percent (GoK, 2007). This was an indication of an economic turnaround (GoK, 2003).

Stock market activity is high, with 54 listed companies. Nairobi Stock Exchange Index increased by 314 percent, with market capitalization increasing from KShs.112 billion in 2002 to KShs.792 billion in 2006. This reflected increased confidence in the economy and business profitability. International reserves held by the government grew from USD1.2 billion to USD2.5 billion in 2006 (GoK, 2007).

The Kenya Government sold over 659 million ordinary shares in March 2006, the largest share offer in Kenyan history, through the NSE. Ogilvy and Mather PR were the public relations consultants for the IPO offer (KENGEN, 2006). For the first time in our history, a local PR and advertising firm, Scangroup Limited, became listed on the NSE. Other successful state corporations that successfully offered shares at NSE were Kenya Re-insurance Company and Mumias Sugar. This was an indication of a thriving business environment in Kenya, which has been good for public relations practitioners.

Social Factors and the Development of PR in Kenya

Kenya has witnessed rapid social changes in the four decades since independence in 1963. These changes include an increase in literacy levels, expansion in public education, a better educated and more sophisticated citizenry, and population mobility, universalization of dietary habits and effects of globalization. The country also faces a number of socio-economic challenges characterized by a population growth rate of 2.7 percent, death rate of 11 deaths per 1,000, infant mortality rates of 57 deaths per 1,000 births and HIV/AIDS prevalence rate of 6.1 percent. Slightly more than half of Kenyans live below the poverty line, with a high unemployment rate of 40 percent and a huge public debt of 51 percent of GDP. Generally, the quality of life in Kenya is low with a life expectancy at birth of 47.5 years and a GDP per capita (PPP) of USD1,140 (GoK, 2006).

In order to deal with the above challenges, the government has invested heavily to improve the social welfare of Kenyans. The government introduced universal free primary education, which increased enrolment of pupils by 50 percent by 2006. The government also increased devolved funds. For example, the Constituency Development Fund increased from KShs.1.2 billion in 2003/2004 to KShs.10 billion in 2007/2008; and the Local Authority Transfer Fund increased from KShs.3 billion in 2002/2003 to KShs. 6.5 billion in 2006/2007 and KShs. 9.2 billion in 2007/2008. The increased government expenditures for grassroots development projects helped to increase the disposable income of parents as well as stimulating socio-economic growth at the local level (GoK, 2006).

PR practitioners in Kenya have been forced to take cognisance of these changes, challenges and existing business opportunities in order to serve their clients and organizations better. Dr Cherutich argued that a more enlightened, more educated people will be able to understand PR messages. The more educated the community is, the better it will be able to understand and appreciate the communication.

The enlightened and more sophisticated publics have predictably forced PR practitioners to upgrade their knowledge and research skills so that they can improve on communication between the organizations and these publics.

Cultural Factors and the Growth of PR in Kenya

Cultural factors have played a critical role in the development of PR due to the ethnic diversity of Kenyan society. Kenya has a total of 42 ethnic groups. This creates a special challenge for PR, which has to communicate across the ethnic boundaries. This is because PR involves trying to build goodwill and understanding between an organization and its publics.

One unique cultural factor in the development of PR in Kenya has been language. The diversity of ethnic groups means that there are as many languages as there are communities. PR practitioners in Kenya have made wide use of English and Kiswahili to communicate with their various publics. Kiswahili is recognized as the national language in Kenya while English is the official language. However, at times messages have to be translated in order to access those who cannot speak either English or Kiswahili.

Dr Cherutich argued that Kenyan PR practitioners have been forced to adopt multiculturalism in order to communicate across cultural barriers. "The nature of their work demands that they need to communicate without favouring any community." Public relations practitioners must then create messages in languages that resonate with each ethnic community.

Kenya has gone through a cultural renaissance since 2003, when the Maboomboom cultural festival took place in March. Maboomboom, a Giriama word meaning pounding drums, celebrated Kenya's 40 years of cultural growth of music, art and dance from time-honored traditions to the modern cutting edge. The festival which was the first and biggest multi-discipline arts festival in Kenya, showcased acrobatics, visual arts, applied arts, comedy, cuisine, dance, fashion, film, literature, music and theater for two weeks. This event provided an exciting opportunity for various PR practitioners and consultancies to work with Kenya's fledgling young artists.

The fashion industry has international designers such as Kiko Romeo and African Heritage. Theater life has been active with dramatic organizations such as Phoenix Theatre group and Mbalamwezi Players. TV comedians such as Mwala and Ojwang are household names in Kenya. Kenyan film makers of international repute include film producers Njeri Karago, Bantu Mwaura, Haron Wandago and Mumbi Waigwa. Acrobatic and poetry performance is also growing led by Kikwetu, Neera Kapur, Simba Zambezi, Salto Jamboree and Black Jambo. Redykulaas pioneered stand-up comedy in Kenya followed by Public Noisemakers among others.

Kenya has also witnessed an explosion in contemporary youth music. The scene is packed with award-winning young musicians such as Gidi Gidi Maji Maji, Nameless, Poxie Presha, Nyota Ndogo, Zannaziki, Eric Wanaina, Achieng Abura, and Mercy Myra. The explosion of cultural life in Kenya has presented business opportunities for PR professionals and consultancies to offer communication counseling to the musicians, artists, comedians and various performers.

Mass Media and PR in Kenya

The mass media sub-sector has undergone tremendous growth and development since 1998 when the government liberalized the communication sector through the enactment of the Kenya Communications Act, 1998. The act led to a proliferation of radio stations, television stations and rapid growth in the telecommunications sector. Kenya has over 294,000 main telephone users, 6.5 million mobile phone users, 2.7 million internet users and 2,120 internet hosts. Kenya has a diverse media scene supported by a large middle class that provides a base for substantial advertising revenue. Media liberalization has nurtured a tradition of a relatively independent press.

Kenya has both public and private media. Ownership of private media is in the hands of investors and religious organizations. Kenya boasts an extensive network of international, national and community media. The media is characterized by cross-media ownership and even monopoly. The Nation Media Group owns the Nation Newspapers, Nation Radio, Nation TV, and a host of magazines like *Drum* and *True Love* among others. On the other hand, the Standard Group runs the *Standard* newspapers and Kenya Television Network; and Royal Media Group operates numerous radio networks, Citizen TV and a newspaper. Kenya Broadcasting Corporation, the public broadcaster, has the largest network of radio stations that reach almost all ethnic communities in Kenya. It runs two television networks with numerous programs.

The faith-based media include: Family TV, Hope Radio, Baraka Radio, Waumini Radio among others. Kenya also boasts a strong community radio network characterized by numerous FM stations that reach specific ethnic group audiences. These include: Ramogi Radio, Mulembe, Egesa, Musyi, Inooro and Coro, among others.

The international media is represented by BBC, VOA, Duechewelle and Radio France International, among others. Radio is the most popular medium, reaching over 90 percent of the population. Newspapers and television follow in that order.

The Press Scene

The Nation, published by the Nation Media Group, claims to have three-quarters of the Kenyan newspaper market. It is widely regarded as being independent and balanced.

Other newspapers include:

- *The Standard*, privately-owned daily, and Kenya's oldest newspaper;
- *The East African*, English-language weekly published by the Nation Media Group;
- *Taifa Leo*, Kenya's only Swahili-language daily, published by the Nation Media Group;
- *The Kenya Times*, Kanu party paper, daily;
- *The People Daily*, owned by veteran politician Kenneth Matiba.

Television Scene

- The Kenya Broadcasting Corporation—state-owned, channels in English and Swahili;
- Metro TV—KBC-operated Nairobi station targeting younger viewers;
- Kenya Television Network—first TV station to break state broadcasting monopoly; available in Nairobi, Mombasa, Nakuru, Eldoret, Kisumu;
- Nation TV—Nairobi-based, operated by Nation Media Group;
- Citizen TV—privately-owned;
- Stella TV (STV)—privately-owned;
- Family TV—Christian.

Radio Scene

- Kenya Broadcasting Cooperation—state-owned, services in English, Swahili and 15 other indigenous languages;
- Metro radio—national music-based station operated by KBC;
- Coro FM—KBC-operated Kikuyu-language station in Nairobi;
- Capital FM—private, music-based;
- East FM—private, targets Nairobi's Asian listeners;
- Easy FM—operated by Nation Media Group, relays in Nairobi, Eldoret, Kisumu, Mombasa, Nakuru, Nyeri;
- Kiss FM—private, music-based;
- Kameme FM—private, targets Kikuyu speakers in Nairobi and central highlands;
- Radio Citizen—private, also operates Kikuyu-language Inooro FM and Luo-language Radio Ramogi;
- Rehema Radio—private, Eldoret-based, programmes in Kalenjin.

News Agency Scene

Kenya News Agency is the only state-owned, English-language, medium. Other non-Kenyan news agencies include Reuters News Agency, Agence France-Presse, Kyoto among others.

The media is self-regulating through the Media Act 2007. PRSK is a member of the Media Council Board, which regulates the media sub-sector in Kenya.

PR practitioners aggressively use media in Kenya. In fact, about 80 percent of media content in Kenya is generated by PR practitioners and consultancies.

Public Relations and Activism

Kenya has a vibrant activism culture born out of the long struggle for social, economic and political change. The Central Organization of Trade Unions (COTU) and Kenya National Association of Teachers have been a bastion of employee activism. The trade union leaders over the years have been good at calling press conferences and holding demonstrations and strikes to publicize their cases and demands. Some of them are known to retain either journalists or publicists to offer media liaison services.

The Kenya National Human Rights Commission, Release the Political Prisoners and the Kenya Human Rights Commission are known for their human rights activism which relies heavily on publicity and participatory models of communication. The Kenya National Human Rights Commission has perfected the public inquiries model as a public dialogue and feedback loop to enhance quality of service delivery to Kenyans. Women's affirmative action groups led by UNIFEM in Kenya, have been very active in championing the rights of the child and woman in Kenya. They have relied heavily on media liaison and public dialogue as means of getting their messages out. Activism has contributed a lot to the development of public relations not only because of using public relations techniques but also for employing public relations professions to realize their goals.

PRSK was one of the associations that condemned the government raid on the Standard Media Group in Nairobi in 2004. It also showed solidarity with the media fraternity to reject the draft Media Bill 2007. The media as well as civil society and Parliament rejected the bill because it would have institutionalized punitive media control measures in Kenya. PRSK lobbied the government to amend the offending sections of the bill as well as for inclusion in the Media Council Board.

CASE STUDY: APPLYING PR STRATEGICALLY

The Nairobi Water Company together with Apex Communication Ltd, a communication firm, received a Golden World Award (GWA) for excellence in public relations campaigns. The International Public Relations Association (IPRA) decorated the companies during the 17th issue of GWAs in November 2006, for the Bill Bila Balaa (Bill without a problem) Campaign. Apex Communications Ltd also received the Frontline Award under the GWA, which recognizes a creative entry from a firm where PR is developing. It was the only entry from Africa to receive an award in 2006. The award was an achievement that demonstrated that Kenya has the skill and capacity to compete with top consulting firms in the world in designing and implementing communication and professional PR campaigns that meet world standards.

Winning the award meant that public relations professionals at Apex had won the confidence of the top leadership, a very important ingredient in successful public relations practice. The team built shared vision with the top leadership of the organization and determined what communication can and cannot do. It involved very close collaboration with the leadership of Nairobi Water to design and implement a campaign with all the key elements of a strategic communication program. The program was based on solid understanding of the problem and was deliberate and planned.

The award is a good case study of how a public relations firm can use effective communications to address multiple problems faced by water customers. It is also a lesson in prioritization of issues. The design team settled on the billing campaign for two reasons: it was the top problem, and the company had identified billing as a quick win.

The lessons learned were that the landscape of PR has completely changed. The winning cases for 2006 (www.ipra.org/GWA) put strong emphasis on outcomes. They were designed to resolve problems facing clients. The outcomes were connected to the bottom line. It was a big lesson to PR practitioners in Kenya and the region. PR must serve organizational needs and desires.

(The original case study was published in *PR Arena*, January–April 2007, p.20, with permission from PRSK.)

REFERENCES

Abuoga, J. B. and Mutere, A. A., 1988, *The History of the Press in Kenya (Africa Media Monograph Series, No. 5)*, Nairobi: African Council for Communication Education.

Chamberlain, M. 1999. *Decolonization*. Oxford: Blackwell.

Church, C., Which Way for PR in Africa? (In *PR Arena*, November 2001, Issue No. 1).

Cowell, F. 1935. The Uses and Dangers of Publicity in the Work of Government. *Public Administration* 13, pp. 290–293.

Daily Nation, April 11, 2007.

Daily Nation, February 26, 2000.

Daily Nation, November 4, 1998.

Dangogo, K., "PRSK Hosts FAPRA Conference," in *PR Arena, Gala Issue—2005*.

East African Standard, June 6, 1975.

Finer, H. 1931. Officials and the Public. *Public Administration*, 9, 30.

Government of Kenya. 2004. *Investment Programme for ERS, 2003–2007*. Nairobi: Noel Creative Media Limited.

Government of Kenya. 2006. *Annual Progress Report 2004–2005: Economic Recovery Strategy*. Nairobi: Ministry of Planning and National Development.

Hodgin, T. 1956. *Nationalism in Colonial Africa*. London: Macmillan.

Huxley, Elspeth. 1935.*The White Man's Country*.

Kagwe, Mutahi, "Public Relations: The Driver during Major Change," Speech addressing PRSK members reproduced in *PR Arena*, January–April 2007.

KENGEN. 2006. Prospectus. Nairobi.

L'Etang, J. 1996. Public Relations as Diplomacy in J.L.E. and M.. Piecka (ed.) 1996. *Critical Perspectives in Public Relations* (pp. 12–34). London: Thompson.

L'Etang, J. 1998. "State Propaganda and Bureaucratic Intelligence: The Creation of Public Relations in Twentieth Century Britian." *Public Relations Review*, 24 (2), pp. 413–441.

L'Etang, J. 2000. The Professionalization of British Public Relations in the Twentieth Century: A History. Unpublished doctoral thesis. University of Stirling, Scotland.

L'Etang, J. and Piecka, M (ed.) 1996. *Critical Perspectives in Public Relations*. London: Thompson.

Magaga, A. 1982. *People and Communication in Kenya*. Nairobi: KLB.

Maina, P., 2000. Department of Information and its Historical Origin, (Unpublished article) Nairobi: Department of Information.

Makali, David (ed.) 2004. *Media Law and Practice: The Kenyan Jurisprudence*. Nairobi: Phoenix Publishers.

Mokaya, J. K. and Rotich, S. K. A., A Study of the Relationship Between Journalists and Public Relations Practitioners in Kenya (Unpublished research project presented to the University of Nairobi, 1991).

Muruli, G. (2001). Public Relations in Kenya: The Missing Link 1939–1971. Unpublished Master's thesis, University of Stirling, Stirling, Scotland.

Ochieng, W. and Atieno-Odhiambo, E. 1995. On Decolonization in Ogot, B. and Ochieng, W. (ed.). *Decolonization and Independence in Kenya 1940–1993* (pp. xi-xviii). London: John Currey.

Ogot, B. and Ochieng, W. (ed.) 1995. *Decolonization and Independence in Kenya 1940–193*. London: James Currey.

Ombara, M. 2001. Public Relations in Government (Unpublished article). Nairobi: Department of Information.

Opukah, S., "Developments and Challenges in Public Relations in Africa—A Call for Professionalism," delivered at the First J. E. Opembe Memorial Lecture in Nairobi on June 16, 1993.

Opukah, S., The Transition of PR in Kenya (in *PR News*, November 2001, Issue No. 1).

PRSK 2006, Annual General Meeting Status Report. Nairobi: Corporate Reflections.

Reiss, J. H., 1956, *Department of Information Annual Report 1955*. Nairobi: Government Printer.

17

PUBLIC RELATIONS IN SOUTH AFRICA: FROM RHETORIC TO REALITY

RONÉL RENSBURG

PREVIEW

In South Africa, the public relations field is still characterized by its search for identity, legitimacy, and professional recognition. Nevertheless, South Africa is a new democracy, and public relations practice is essential to democratic societies. In South Africa, the role of public relations practitioners—in all spheres of business—is shaped by the dynamics of an ever-changing and developing society. In this chapter I describe the practice of public relations in South Africa and examine the cultural, developmental, economic, and sociopolitical complexities that impact on the work and effectiveness of public relations practitioners and consultants. Although the chapter mainly consists of factual information, some of the views, expressions, and interpretations are my individual opinions.

PUBLIC RELATIONS IN SOUTH AFRICA: AN OVERVIEW

History and Development of the Country

The Land

The Republic of South Africa occupies the southernmost part of the African continent, covering a surface area of 1,219,090 square km. It has common boundaries with the republics of Namibia, Botswana, and Zimbabwe; the Republic of Mozambique and the Kingdom of Swaziland lie to the northeast. Completely enclosed by South African territory is the mountain kingdom of Lesotho. To the west, south, and east, South Africa borders on the Atlantic and Indian Oceans. Isolated, 1, 290 km southeast of Cape Town in the Atlantic, lie Prince Edward and Marion Islands, annexed by South Africa in 1947 (Government Communication and Information Systems [GCIS], 2001/2002).

In South Africa one finds the world's strangest and most dramatic landscapes; a unique wealth of animal and plant life; a treasure of gold, diamonds, and other minerals; and a kaleidoscope of fascinating cultures. The country is also the home of big game, and the Kruger National Game Park is known throughout the world.

South Africa is divided into nine provinces, each with its own legislature, premier, and provincial members of executive councils. Each of the provinces features its own distinctive landscapes, vegetation, and climate. The provinces are the Western Cape, the Eastern Cape, the Northern Cape, the Free State, North–West, Gauteng, Mpumalanga, KwaZulu-Natal, and the Limpopo (see Appendix Table A8.1).

The People

According to *Statistics South Africa* (2001), the country's population in 2000 was estimated to be 43,686 million, of which 22.7 million were women. The population was classified as follows: 76.7% African, 10.9% White, 8.9% Black, and 2.6% Indian or Asian. The South African population consists of the following groups: the Nguni people (including the Zulu, Xhosa, and Swazi), who account for two thirds of the population; the Sotho-Tswana people, who include the Southern, Northern and Western Sotho (Tswana); the Tsonga; the Venda; Afrikaners; English; Coloreds; Indians; and people who have immigrated to South Africa from the rest of Africa, Europe, and Asia and who continue to maintain their native cultural identity. A few members of the Khoi and San also live in South Africa. South Africa has 11 official languages: Afrikaans, English, isiNdebele, isiXhosa, isiZulu, Sepedi, Sesotho, Setswana, siSwati, Tshivenda, and Xitsonga. Recognizing the historically diminished use and status of the indigenous languages, the government is taking positive measures to elevate the stature of these languages. The official language used in government and business is English.

Almost 80% of South Africa's population adheres to the Christian faith. Other major religious groups are the Hindus, Muslims, and Jews. Freedom of worship is guaranteed, and official policy is one of noninterference in religious practices. Because the traditional religion of the African people has a strong cultural base, the various groups have different rituals, but there are certain common features. A supreme being is generally recognized, but ancestors are of far greater importance, being the deceased elders of the group. They are regarded as part of the community, indispensable links with the spirit world, and the powers that control everyday affairs. These ancestors are not gods, but because they play a key role in bringing about either good or ill fortune, maintaining good relations with them is pivotal, and they have to be appeased regularly by a variety of ritual offerings.

History

Many believe that humankind had its earliest origins in Africa. South Africa is rich in fossil evidence of the evolutionary history of the human family, going back several million years, from the discovery of the Taung child in 1924 to the latest discoveries of hominid fossils at the Sterkfontein caves (recently declared a World Heritage Site). South Africa has been at the forefront of palaeontological research into the origins of humanity. Modern humans have lived in the region for over 100,000 years. The Khoi and the San (the Hottentots and Bushmen of early European terminology), collectively known as the Khoisan and often thought of as distinct peoples, were the first people to roam the southern part of the African continent. Thereafter, other people arrived in South Africa.

The Early Inhabitants.   About 2,000 years ago, Bantu-speaking agro-pastorals began arriving in southern Africa, bringing with them an Iron Age culture and domesticated crops. These farmers spread out across the interior plateau and adopted a more extensive cattle culture. Chiefdoms arose based on control over cattle, which gave rise to patronage and, hence, hierarchies of authority within communities. At several archaeological sites, there is evidence of sophisticated political and material cultures, based in part on contact with the East African trading economy. These cultures, which were part of a broader African civilization, predate European encroachment by several centuries.

The Early Colonial Period.   European seafarers, who pioneered the sea route to India in the late 15th century, were regular visitors to the South African coast during the 1500s. In 1652, the Dutch East India Company set up a station in Table Bay (Cape Town) to service passing ships. Trading with the Khoi soon turned into raiding and warfare. Beginning in 1657, European settlers (French, Dutch, and Portuguese) were allotted farms by the colonial authorities in the arable regions around Cape Town. These settlers expanded northward from the 1830s on, and they provided a myth of the "empty land" which Whites employed to justify their domination over the subcontinent in the 20th century. They became known as *Afrikaner Boers.*

The British Colonial Era.   In 1795, the British occupied Cape Town as a strategic base, controlling the sea route to the East. The Cape Colony was integrated into the dynamic international trading empire of industrializing Britain. By the 1800s, the British brought in settlers and expanded their colonization across the rest of South Africa. During the Anglo-Boer War (1899–1902), British and Boer forces fought for supremacy of the land. The impact of this war has had a seminal influence in the development of Afrikaner nationalist politics. The Boer leaders played a dominant role in the country's politics for the next half of the century. The Union of South Africa came into existence in 1910.

Segregation and Apartheid.   Government policy in the Union of South Africa did not develop in isolation but against the backdrop of Black political initiatives. Segregation and apartheid assumed their shape, in part, as a response to the African's increasing participation in the country's economic life and their assertion to political rights. The African National Congress (ANC), founded in 1912, became the most important organization drawing together traditional authorities and the educated elite in common causes. In its early years, the ANC was concerned with constitutional protest. Worker militancy emerged in the wake of World War I and continued through the 1920s. In 1948, the National Party (NP), with its ideology of apartheid that brought an even more rigorous and authoritarian approach than the segregationist policies of previous governments, won the general election. In 1961, the NP government under Prime Minister Hendrik Verwoerd declared South Africa a republic, after winning a Whites-only referendum on the issue. It also withdrew from the British Commonwealth and a figurehead president replaced the queen as head of state. Racial categories were assigned to the people of South Africa. Under the architects of apartheid a theory of multinationalism was created. This was indeed a separate development wherein the South African population was divided into artificial ethnic nations, each with its own homeland and the prospect of independence. Forced removals from White areas affected some 3.5 million people, and vast rural slums were created in the homelands. Jobs were reserved for Whites only, and many Black people were denied the opportunity to progress in the work environment. The people of the homelands had to carry passbooks to migrate and travel to their work in the cities.

The End of Apartheid and the Birth of a Democratic South Africa. Mass protests, acts of terrorism, and other forms of internal resistance and the employment of harsh sanctions by the United Nations eventually led to scrapping the pass laws in 1986, lifting the ban on liberation movements, and the release of political prisoners like Nelson Mandela in 1990. South Africa's first (in 1994) and second (in 1999) democratic elections saw the ANC emerge as the leading party. South Africa had a new democratic government and a new president in Nelson Mandela. In 1999, Thabo Mbeki succeeded Mandela. Freedom of movement and social mobility of people were guaranteed by the new government. South Africa indeed has had a very complex, and at times confusing, history.

Evolution and Definition of Public Relations as a Profession

Evolution

The evolution of public relations on the African continent, in general, and South Africa, in particular, goes back decades, if not centuries. The application of certain public relations techniques originated at the dawn of African civilization. In ancient Egypt the Pharaohs proclaimed their achievements through word-pictures on impressive monuments. According to Nartey (1988, p. 25), the concept of public relations was practiced in Africa long before the era of colonialism. He drew a parallel between the task of a public relations practitioner and that of a spokesman at the chief's seat of power in traditional South African villages. According to tradition, no African chief or elder statesman spoke directly to a visitor who called at the chief's seat of power. This, incidentally, is still the case in some remote and traditional rural areas of South Africa. All interactions and communication were channeled through a spokesman, a linguist, or an interpreter—sometimes this was one person. Individuals who were appointed to such offices were known to be well-versed in the customs and traditional practices of the village. Such individuals assumed eminent positions and were highly respected by the people. According to Nartey (1988), the concept of public relations also expressed in the African marital affairs such as arranged marriages and *lobola* (bride price)—the African equivalent of dowry, where the parents of the bridegroom would provide cattle (or other goods of commercial value) to the bride's family. At the initial stages and throughout the negotiations of a marriage contract, the go-between or the middle man plays a crucial role in the success of the union. Public relations is also expressed in the use of traditional music, dancing, and the beating of drums to communicate to the inhabitants of the traditional African village. Thus, the concept of public relations is neither alien nor a practice that arrived with colonialism, commercialization, or Western media imperialism. It has been around for centuries on the African continent—in a different format.

According to Lubbe (cited in Lubbe & Puth, 1994, p. 3), two major approaches can be taken when reviewing the historical development of public relations in South Africa. The first is a *systems approach* that illustrates the increasing scope of the practice of public relations in conjunction with the political, social, and economic development of the country. The second is a *structural approach* that depicts the professionalization of public relations in terms of the establishment of professional bodies in the public relations industry. The history of public relations development is well documented in the United States, Great Britain, and a few European countries, as mentioned in the introductory chapter. However, in South Africa, the development of public relations as part of the social and economic development, as well as its establishment as a fully fledged strategic management function in business and industry, has not yet been comprehensively documented and researched. The development of public relations in South Africa has also not been without international influence in terms of practice, research, education, and training—even terminological nomenclature. The phases of development from its initial phase of fundraising, publicity, and press agentry to its more sophisticated level of information dissemination and providing counsel to management coincide with the profession in the United States in particular.

The development of public relations in terms of its professionalization in South Africa, however, has been well documented since the establishment of the Public Relations Institute of Southern Africa (PRISA). The practice of public relations in South Africa is the most advanced compared with the other 14 countries in the southern African region where the profession is served by only a few practitioners, and the industry is growing in size (Rhodes & Baker, cited in Lubbe & Puth, 1994, p. 287).

Defining Public Relations

The PRISA has adopted the following definition of public relations: *"Public relations is the management, through communication, of perceptions and strategic relationships between an organisation and its internal and external stakeholders."* (Mersham, Rensburg, & Skinner 1995, p. 3) This definition emphasizes the fact that public relations should be a deliberate and intentional part of an organization's policy. It is a conscious effort to provide information and create goodwill. Public relations is designed to influence, gain understanding, propagate information, and ensure feedback from those affected by the organization's activities. Messages are tailored to reach identified target publics in accordance with a definite set of objectives (Mersham, Rensburg, & Skinner, 1995).

The definition offered by PRISA has been widely accepted in South Africa among public relations practitioners and scholars alike. It has merit and helps to explain the nature, role, and intention of public relations. However, Mersham et al. (1995, p. 12) contended that South Africa (as well as Africa) needs to continue to seek more substantial and theoretical insights into the place of public relations in the domain of communication science in a developing region. The authors also believed that insights are needed into how the design of communication models can assist in both the application and execution of effective public relations practice, particularly in the context of South Africa.

Status and Image of the Profession: the Search for Legitimacy Continues

In South Africa, much has been done in recent years to bring luster to a profession and academic field in search of legitimacy. Although public relations has undergone extensive change in terms of its activities and its growing importance in modern South African life, it suffers as a result of its unfortunate and pejorative past reputation. Public relations in South Africa may be described as being in a transitional phase. It tries to reconcile and situate its activities within the form of an ethical science. In doing so, it strives to adopt a broader, more humane social vision in which accountability to its stakeholders is given full importance. In spite of substantial changes in the focus and operation of public relations during the last 2 decades, the term public relations has been both misused and misunderstood since the early 1950s. It continues to be incorrectly associated with propaganda, press agentry, and manipulation, and it is often confused with advertising, marketing, and promotion. Practitioners are still suspected of disseminating incomplete, distorted, and biased information, and being the faceless image brokers and spin doctors for rich and powerful individuals, politicians, causes, and organizations.

During the past 2 decades, but particularly after 1994, strenuous efforts have been made by practitioners, academics, and PRISA to stress the scientific nature of the many activities public relations comprises (Cullingworth, 1990; De Beer, 1993; Mersham, 1993; Mersham et al., 1995; Nel, 1993).

The Professionalism of the Public Relations Industry in South Africa

South Africa is far more advanced than other African countries as far as PRISA is concerned. The overall impression is that in South Africa the practice of public relations is also relatively advanced, if not yet fully understood by clients and organizational leaders. But the industry faces a lot of competition from many disciplines that are infiltrating into areas that were traditionally considered to be the domain of the public relations practitioner. Management consultants, auditing firms, advertising agencies, and market research institutions now include the areas of communication consultation—compiling annual reports, product and service brochures, and entire social marketing campaigns and even conducting communication audits. International consultancies are entering the region, and the public relations industry in South Africa needs introspection and self-evaluation on a regular basis. Table A8.2 (see Appendix) shows the industry's current strengths and weaknesses (Rhodes & Baker, cited in Lubbe & Puth, 1994, p. 288).

PRISA started formally in Johannesburg in 1957, although public relations people had been talking about some kind of association for a number of years. The 23 founder members met at the University of the Witwatersrand (Johannesburg), and a chairman was elected. The progress of PRISA as an association is chronicled in Table A8.3 (see Appendix).

PRISA is the first and only public relations association in the world to obtain the International Standards Organization's 9002 certification. PRISA offers a career path for public relations practitioners and encourages skills development in line with the South African Skills Development Act (Act 97 of 1998, South Africa Yearbook 2001/02: 48). Students and practitioners can use PRISA's registration levels to plan their lifelong learning through a Continuing Professional Development Program. PRISA's registration levels can also be used to identify top-notch communicators who will add value to any organization's bottom line. The globally recognized accredited public relations practitioner (APR) is a well-qualified, widely experienced expert who operates at a strategic senior management level. Table A8.4 (see Appendix) states what PRISA strives for and what it offers its members.

The Public Relations Consultancy Chapter (PRCC) is made up of a voluntary committee with a chairman and office bearers. The PRCC's objectives are as follows:

- To unite consultants countrywide under the PRISA umbrella.
- To provide a forum for networking and professional development.
- To gain credibility for public relations consulting nationally.
- To professionalize the public relations consulting industry.
- To align the industry with the aims of development of the country.
- To foster links with allied industries and international consultants.

The PRCC's activities include the following:

- Organizing networking and professional development functions.
- Facilitating the employment and training of disadvantaged public relations practitioners in established consultancies.

- Lobbying and liaising with government.
- Publishing standard client–consultancy and employment contracts for members.
- Presenting the PRISM Award for outstanding public relations consultancy practice.

The public relations consultancies in South Africa and PRISM Award categories are shown in Tables A8.5 and A8.6 (see Appendix), respectively.

The Role of Universities and Colleges in Furthering the Public Relations Profession

Although communication science is offered in most of the large universities like the University of South Africa, the Rand Afrikaans University, and the universities of the Free State, Natal, Port Elizabeth, Potchefstroom, these universities have public relations as a specialization area in their communication science courses or as part of their marketing courses. However, the University of Pretoria is offering a degree course in communication management with a specific focus on public relations. Most of the colleges and technikons in the country offer diplomas, certificates, and courses in public relations. PRISA also has a student chapter for students studying public relations–the Public Relations Student's Chapter (PRSC). There is ongoing research into the national and global issues of public relations as a science and a profession, and a variety of scholars and students are scrutinizing the existing body of knowledge of public relations in a developing world.

Public Relations as Viewed by the Dominant Coalition in Organizations

The theory of public relations emphasizes that public relations is a management function aligned with all the other major functions of the organization such as marketing and financial management. The public relations or corporate communication department of an organization should ideally have a public relations manager or director with input in the formulation of corporate policy and strategy and decision-making authority. The subordinates and specialists in this department should be the technicians, providing technical and expert support in the implementation of public relations programs. In practice, however, the role and function of public relations is often seen only in terms of technical aspects and is relegated to a low status in the organizational structure (Lubbe, cited in Lubbe & Puth, 1994, p. 27).

In some organizations the status of the public relations practitioner or executive is low—reporting to the marketing director in the marketing department where public relations is still being viewed as part of publicity and promotion. The dominant coalition in organizations, notwithstanding numerous strategic sessions and research efforts by leading practitioners and scholars, still regards public relations practitioners as public relations or public affairs officers who are no more than salespeople, tourist guides, special events organizers, personal assistants, or front counter staff. Organizations in South Africa are mainly looking for technicians, not strategists. This stance should not be criticized too harshly by scholars and practitioners. After 1994 organizations are having to cope with cumbersome strategic plans and scenarios and are now looking for pragmatic implementation for these strategies. The technicians can deliver this implementation and produce tangibles. In research in progress, Steyn (2000) found that there is a significant degree of difference between chief executive officer's perceptions and their expectations of the public relations function and the role of public relations practitioners in organizations.

Public relations departments in South African organizations are called by a variety of names such as Corporate Communications, Public Affairs, Corporate Affairs, Public

Relations and Development, Corporate Communication, Marketing Services, and even lately Relationship Management. This is mainly an attempt to capture the essence of what concerns these departments. Note, however, that the term public relations is still the most acceptable and most often used term in this country; it encompasses all of the communication activities with which organizations are normally involved.

A current trend in many South African organizations, large and small, is to outsource the public relations functions and activities to consultancy firms. These organizations may not feel the necessity of having a fully fledged public relations department or even a full-time public relations practitioner. Consultants are called in when specific communication problems or needs arise.

PRISA, together with Research Surveys (a market research group in South Africa), conducted a survey of all corporate PRISA members in 1992, trying to determine, among other things, what they spent on public relations activities annually. The research showed a close correlation between the size of the organization and the amount it spends on public relations. What was and still is of concern, however, is that there are many large organizations in South Africa with frighteningly small public relations budgets (in comparison to the advertising budgets), a reflection of the lack of clout the industry had with management before 1994. This state of affairs, unfortunately, has not changed substantially since then.

Another part of the 1992 research dealt with where organizations rank public relations disciplines for the past 5 years and for the next 5 years. The results of this part of the research are reflected in Table A8.7 (see Appendix; Rhodes & Baker, cited in Lubbe & Puth, 1994, p. 287). Some of the other areas of importance to the future of South African organization are government communication and relations, political action relations, cause-related public relations, regulatory compliance, and risk management communication.

It becomes clear that the public relations industry in South Africa has its strengths and weaknesses. The strengths, however, are still limited. There are very few specialists and too many generalists in the industry. The industry will have to embark on an environmental scanning exercise to determine and take advantage of new opportunities that emerge from the changing environment. It will take some time to correct the poor image the industry has, and it will also take time to convince fully the dominant coalition in South African organizations of the merits and pivotal importance of public relations as a strategic management function.

INFRASTRUCTURE AND INTERNATIONAL PUBLIC RELATIONS

South Africa's Political System

As mentioned previously in this chapter, South Africa has a democratic political system since 1994 when the first all-inclusive elections took place that brought an end to the apartheid regime. These democratic elections have had wide-ranging effects on all South Africans. One of the most significant is that the extensive coverage of the elections by the world's media has underlined the importance of the global connectivity for ordinary people. This has introduced a wider set of global values, trends, and integrative movements than were possible during the apartheid years of isolation. During the 1994 elections, an estimated 5,000 international observers, representing nearly every country around the globe, were present in the country. Observer status was granted by the Independent Electoral Commission (IEC) to 77 international organizations, including the world's largest intergovernmental organizations—the European Union (EU), the United Nations

(UN), the Organization of African Unity, and the Commonwealth—and many other nongovernmental organizations. More than 1 billion rand (R) was allocated in 1994 to the IEC in support of its logistics to carry out a credible election. Public relations programs and voter education efforts were in abundance. The IEC allotted equal media space and time to all political parties in the elections. It was at this point that South Africa's reentry into a host of new global relationships was signaled for the first time (Mersham et al., 1995, p. 20).

This intense world interest, which elaborated and foregrounded the many components and positions of the global dialogue, was mirrored in the South African media and the daily conversations of all South Africans. The ANC—then under the leadership of Nelson Mandela—had a landslide victory, which was repeated in the follow-up elections of 1999. The ANC as a political institution is extremely strong and has been since its inception among many South Africans; it is backed by foreign countries where it operated when it was banned as a political movement (and labeled a *terrorist organization*) by the previous apartheid regime. There is political pluralism in South Africa and ample opportunities for the free expression of public opinion.

Public relations and democracy are not commonly aligned concepts. However, there are some fundamental links (cf. Hiebert, 1984). First, modern public relations can only function within the fundamental rights of freedom of expression and information. Everyone in a democracy should have the right to be heard. This includes the right to communicate on behalf of a cause, an organization, or an individual. This right is not restricted to the owners of newspapers and controllers of the electronic media or the government. Each individual, pressure or activist group, and institution has the right to seek and use public relations counsel and in most democracies do so. Second, public relations is indispensable in democracies with mass societies and mass communication. The various techniques of public relations were formed organically within the processes of urbanization, industrialization, and mass communication. Today these public relations techniques allow a wide spectrum of interest groups to state their messages in a variety of media in such a way that they have a chance to be heard (Mersham et al., 1995, p. 18). Third, public relations defined as an open communication process can only exist in democratic societies. From 1992 to 1994 and thereafter, the abundance of media conferences and releases by groups and movements previously banned by the state is proof of this. In African governments in which one party or one leader determines public policy, there can be no true role for public relations as we define it. The party or leader may use communication techniques as a form of propaganda or manipulation to keep the people in line, but there would be no room for professional practitioners to practice on behalf of those who wanted to challenge or criticize the status quo or propose different ideas, policies, and procedures. Clearly, these communication practices would be labeled subversive, unlawful, and undemocratic. In the new democratic South Africa this principle might ring true, but since 2000, our neighbor Zimbabwe has had other ideas regarding the right to freedom of expression and the role of open communication. In sharp contrast to South Africa's model and peaceful elections stand the 2002 controversial Zimbabwe elections that, unfortunately, continues to impact very negatively on South Africa and the other counties in the region. While writing this chapter, it became official news that, in spite of international pressure and criticism about the election procedure, Robert Mugabe and his Zimbabwe African National Union Patriotic Front (ZANU-PF) party have—questionably—won the elections. This debate, election, and its outcome are not new concepts in Africa where people are becoming used to the fact that politics is a business.

Fourth, public relations is linked to democracy because everyone has a right to articulate his or her version of the truth. There is no one truth because absolute truth exists only in a one-party, totalitarian state. Public relations as we define it exists in open societies where civil society, business, and government are amenable to freely expressed public opinion and the right to criticize existing and proposed policies. The vision of the Government Communication and Information System (GCIS) in South Africa is to make an indispensable and widely valued contribution to society, working with the government for a better life for all by meeting the government's communication needs and the public's information needs.

The GCIS is facilitating the establishment of Multi-purpose Community Centers (MPCCs) as programs for integrated one-stop government information and service points. This initiative is a partnership between all spheres of government, business, and civil society. By the end of March 2003, 60 of these MPCCs will be operating, at least one in each district or metropolitan council (GCIS, 2001/2002, p. 310). Public relations practitioners will play an increasingly important role in government communication.

South Africa's Level of Economic Development

South Africa has one of the most developed economies in Africa and is definitely the economic leader in the Southern African Development Community (SADC). The member states of SADC are Angola, Botswana, the Democratic Republic of the Congo, Lesotho, Malawi, Mauritius, Mozambique, Namibia, Seychelles, South Africa, Swaziland, Tanzania, Zambia, and Zimbabwe. The eyes of the world have been on South Africa since 1994 not only because of the historic unfolding of the democratic process and the peaceful transition but also because South Africa produces 40% of sub-Saharan Africa's gross domestic product and is viewed by many businesses as the gateway to Africa (Palframan, 1994, p. 1).

Blessed with a wealth of natural resources, the country contains wide disparities of wealth, with obvious implications for broader sociopolitical policy directions. Given its history of inequalities and its location, South Africa is a country whose fate is bound up with that of its neighbors. The recent upheaval caused by the 2002 elections in Zimbabwe and President Mbeki's stance of quiet diplomacy toward President Robert Mugabe have resulted in a drop in South African currency (the rand) to a level lower than it has ever been (nearly 10 rand to the American dollar, 10 rand to the Euro, and 16 rand to the British pound). There is also a resurgence of Afro-pessimism by the international community that South Africa might be taking the same route as Zimbabwe and other impoverished countries in Africa. A further challenge is to translate the positive economic conditions into levels of investment high enough to reduce the country's substantial unemployment level. Unemployment remains South Africa's most formidable challenge. *Statistics South Africa* announced in 2001 that the country's official unemployment rate stood at 26.4%. An increasing number of people are entering the labor market. This situation is exacerbated by a constant inflow of illegal aliens from Zimbabwe, Mozambique, and other poor countries in Africa.

Hundreds of international organizations, especially American companies, left the country during the sanctions era before 1994, but with South Africa's acceptance by the international community, many are returning and new companies are establishing themselves here because of the business potential that the country has to offer. They are still reluctant, however, to commit to tangible physical investment. Nearly everything business does is influenced by the government, which creates and enforces the rules by which business is conducted and determines the climate in which business must function (Sadie, cited in Lubbe & Puth, 1994, p. 250). The need for close relations with government is, therefore, evident. The business sector in South Africa is confronted with great future challenges.

There is currently an international campaign to market the New Partnership for Africa's Development (NEPAD). NEPAD's aim to confirm that African countries take responsibility for democracy, human rights, and rules of law and governance. The program was drafted by President Mbeki, Nigerian President Olusegan Obasanjo, and Algerian President Abdelaziz Bouteflika. The program entails moving away from the continent's broad reliance on loans and aid to self-sustaining development and advancement. Developed countries must respond with debt relief, market access to African imports, private investment flows, and increased development assistance.

However, President Mbeki's and Nigerian President Olusegun Obasanjo's recent backing of Robert Mugabe and their description of the elections in Zimbabwe as "free and fair" has tarnished relationships with the international community. South Africa was severely criticized for its stance in local and international media. Trying to save the situation, Mbeki and Obasanjo attempted to convince President Mugabe to avoid suspension from the commonwealth and to opt for a government of national unity, combining efforts with the opposition of Morgan Tsvangarai and his Movement for Democratic Change. This effort was to no avail, and the commonwealth, via its secretariat (a troika including Australian Prime Minister John Howard, President Mbeki, and President Obasanjo), decided to suspend Zimbabwe from the councils of the commonwealth for a period of 1 year effective immediately. The debate on whether sanctions against Zimbabwe will also be imposed continues.

On the macroeconomics side South Africa is a "model citizen" of the international community, which obviously serves the national interest of the country, and the Mbeki administration has delivered on this front. But South Africa fails to attract sufficient foreign direct investment, and the markets massively oversell its currency. Markets are anticipatory by their nature and are moved by perceptions. And it cannot serve the national interest when Mbeki accuses commonwealth countries of racism because they did not agree with him on Zimbabwe (Mulholland, cited in *Business Times*, 2002). This stance could damage his reputation and that of South Africa, put his plans for Africa's rejuvenation in jeopardy, and threaten the NEPAD dream. It reinforces the underlying fear that South Africa will follow the way of Zimbabwe, and international business is weary to directly invest.

South Africa's Legal Infrastructure

The Constitution of the Republic of South Africa (1996; Act 108 of 1996) is the supreme law of the country, and it binds all legislative, executive, and judicial organs of the state at all levels of government. In terms of the constitution, the judicial authority of South Africa is vested in the courts, which are independent and subject only to the constitution and the law. No person or organ of state may interfere with the functioning of the courts, and an order or decision of a court binds all organs of state and people to whom it applies. The Department of Justice and Constitutional Development is responsible for the administration of the courts and constitutional development (GCIS, 2001/2002, p. 365).

South Africa's constitution is one of the most progressive in the world, and it enjoys high acclaim internationally. The preamble of the constitution states that its aims are as follows:

- Heal the divisions of the past and establish a society based on democratic values, social justice, and fundamental human rights.

- Improve the quality of life of all citizens and free the potential of each person.

- Lay the foundations for a democratic and open society in which government is based on the will of the people and every citizen is equally protected by law.

- Build a united and democratic South Africa able to take its rightful place as a sovereign state in the family of nations.

The only apprehension one might have of the constitution is that it is extremely sophisticated, representing values of a developed society and in cases may run the risk of being in conflict with the traditional belief and value system of the majority of South Africans.

The independence of the judicial system in South Africa has been illustrated on many occasions, and it often rules against government at times. The government, and specifically President Mbeki, is backing the now well-publicized dissident's view (in conjunction with AIDS dissident David Rasnick) that there is no proof that HIV causes AIDS. This stance on HIV/AIDS has caused amazement and anger internationally and confusion locally. The government has also faced numerous court battles with multinational pharmaceutical companies. Supporting Mbeki's dissident AIDS theory, the Department of Health refused to make antiretrovirals available to pregnant mothers with HIV/AIDS. The High Court recently ruled in favor of South Africa's Treatment Action Campaign (TAC) and ordered that the drug nevirapine (viramune) be made available immediately and free of charge for the next 5 years to patients at those health facilities with the support structures to dispense the drug. The government has since appealed to the Constitutional Court, and this debate continuous.

The Promotion of Access to Information Act that came into operation in 2001 gives the right of access to information referred to in the constitution (GCIS, 2001/2002, p. 372). The act generally promotes transparency, accountability, and effective governance of all public and private bodies by, among other things, empowering and educating everyone to do the following:

- Understand their rights in terms of the act and exercise them in relation to private and public bodies.

- Understand the functions and operation of public bodies.

- Scrutinize and participate in decision-making by public bodies that affect their rights.

Although there are policies available for telecommunications, marketing, advertising, and government communication, there are no specific legal codes dealing with communication activities. There are, however, codes of conduct that all of these disciplines have to honor.

The Level of Activism in South Africa

For many years South Africa has been notorious for its apartheid regime. Until the 1940s, South Africa's race policies had not been entirely out of step with those in the colonial world. But by the 1950s, which saw decolonization and a global backlash against racism gathering pace, the state was dramatically opposed to world opinion on the question of human rights. The introduction of apartheid policies coincided with the adoption by the ANC in 1949 of the Program of Action, expressing overt militancy. The program rejected White domination and called for action in the form of protests, strikes, and demonstrations.

A decade of turbulent mass action and resistance to the imposition of still more harsh forms of segregation and oppression followed. South Africa was still the last bastion of White supremacy in Africa.

The Defiance Campaign of the early 1950s carried mass mobilization to new heights under the banner of nonviolent resistance to the pass laws. A critical step in the emergence of activism and antiracism was the formation of the Congress Alliance, including the Indian Congress, the Colored People's Congress, a small White congress (called the Congress of Democrats), and the South African Congress of Trade Unions. The Alliance gave formal expression to an emerging unity across racial and class lines that was manifested in the Defiance Campaign and other mass protests of this period—which also saw women's resistance take a more organized character with the formation of the Federation of South African Women.

The state's initial response was to prosecute more than 150 antiapartheid leaders for treason in a trial that began in 1956, but it ended in acquittals in 1961. Matters came to a head at Sharpeville in 1960 when 69 antipass demonstrators were killed. A state of emergency was imposed, and detention without trial was introduced. Black political organizations were banned, and their leaders went into exile or were arrested. Top leaders still inside the country, including members of the newly formed military wing *Umkhonto we Sizwe* (Spear of the Nation), were arrested in 1963 and tried in the Rivonia Trial. Nelson Mandela and other Black leaders were sentenced to life imprisonment.

The resurgence of resistance politics in the 1970s was dramatic. Armed action from beyond the borders abounded but was effectively contained by the state. A wave of strikes by Black labor unions reflected a new militancy that involved better organization and was drawing other sectors, particularly intellectuals and students, into the mass struggle against the state. The involvement of workers in the resistance took on a new dimension with the formation of the Congress of South African Trade Unions. In 1976 a sustained antiapartheid revolt arose by pupils in Soweto against the use of Afrikaans as the language of instruction in their schools.

From the mid-1980s, regional and national states of emergency were enforced. The Inkatha movement—stressing Zulu ethnicity and traditionalism—came into existence with a large following in the rural KwaZulu-Natal area. Battles for turf between the ANC and Inkatha became a very destructive accompaniment to South Africa's transition to democracy. The state embarked on a series of reforms, like scrapping the pass laws in 1986.

In the late 1980s and early 1990s, acts of terrorism occurred while the international community strengthened its support for the antiapartheid cause. A range of sanctions and boycotts was instituted, both unilaterally and through the United Nations. Faced with an untenable situation, the then-President FW de Klerk had no alternative but to release Nelson Mandela and others in 1990 and to unban the liberation movements—creating the environment for open political negotiations. These acts eventually led to the conception of the South Africa's new constitution (Constitution of the Republic of South Africa Act 108 of 1996, in South Africa yearbook, 2001/02, p. 299).

In 1994 the new democratic South Africa was born and many of the liberation and social movements—like the ANC—became political parties. The history of activism in South Africa before 1994 was mainly politically driven and had a moral high ground because of protests against unfair laws that warranted the causes.

There are a number of activist groups currently operating in the country—ranging from environmentalists, anticrime groups, antirape groups, antiabuse of women and children groups, to AIDS activists. In most cases, these activists have valid causes, and they usually address them through recognized channels, at times without valid response and action taken by government. These activist groups demonstrate in public, but they have to apply for permission to do so via procedural regulations. If their nonviolent resistance approaches are not met, these groups usually turn to legal action and the constitution. The AIDS activist group, TAC, recently had a victory in the High Court where they won the battle against the government's refusal to make antiretroviral drugs available to HIV/AIDS pregnant mothers. The activist groups in South Africa have strong and effective communication networks and make continuous efforts to get their story out—locally and internationally. People Against Gangsterism and Drugs (PAG) is a mainly Muslim activist group that argues that government is not doing enough formally to curb crime, violence, and drug abuse, and in the late 1990s this group turned to violent resistance themselves when they embarked on orchestrated acts of terrorism and vigilantism.

As shown in Table A8.8 (see Appendix), there are formalized and registered labor unions, members, employers' organizations, and bargaining councils in South Africa (Statistics South Africa, 2001).

Labor activism also manifests itself in the workplace. South Africa lost an estimated 1.4 million human days to strikes and stay-aways in 2000. According to labor research consultants Andrew Levy and Associates, 500,000 were lost to shop-floor strikes and 900,000 to stay-aways. The major strike trigger was wages. In 2000, the most active unions were the National Union of Mineworkers, the South African Transport and Allied Workers' Union, and the National Union of Metalworkers of South Africa (cited in GCIS, 2001/2002, p. 173).

Organizations have a variety of tools to handle activists, labor unions, and labor problems in general. Human Resources, Industrial Relations, and Corporate Communication Departments usually have mechanisms in place to deal with dispute resolution.

South Africa and the International Environment

Mersham et al. (1995, p. 10) suggested that South Africa and Africa stand poised to enter a positive new era if the people of the African continent are able to accept the value of learning from mistakes and successes of other countries in adapting to the emerging economic and political challenges of the global village while preserving its own unique identity. As trade barriers between nations are reduced, organizations and institutions have to compete in world markets and international arenas. Government too, is now competing on the world stage of international relations. Globally, we are experiencing a growing trend toward a common culture of agreement on a global civil society. South Africa's transition to democracy not only coincides with these major international developments but also stands as a symbol of global integration and reconciliation, the quest for the demise of Afro-pessimism, and the hope for Black renewal and economic realism on a continent marked by political and economic failure.

CULTURE AND PUBLIC RELATIONS IN SOUTH AFRICA

If there is one feature that characterizes South African society in the new millennium it is that of social change. Therefore, the trends and directions of the change process must be taken into consideration when examining public relations in South Africa. At the same time, there is one factor that underlies all social change—communication.

South Africa is extremely heterogeneous with an abundance of cultures and subcultures in the country. The melting pot concept that works well in countries like the United States, Canada, and Australia, however, cannot be transplanted into South Africa. Given the complexity of cultures and levels of development in South Africa, it also becomes evident that intercultural communication, an area with which the present generation of South African public relations practitioners is still largely unfamiliar, will increasingly require more attention as we move into the new millennium.

The complexity of the South African culture has never been fully understood by Western scholars. Culture and the debate about development, underdevelopment, and globalization walk hand-in-hand in South Africa. One can claim that every area of human and societal activity in its community, national, and international context is part of development. As Mowlana (1987, p. 4) put it: *"In short, development is everything and everything is development."*

Optimists view the recent changes in South Africa as the beginning of a new era of development for both South Africa and the countries of the African continent. One of the keys to this optimism lies in unlocking an effective synthesis of Western development policies with indigenous cultures and environments. South Africa is the perfect laboratory for development. It has survived political transition and is a good mixture of Third and First World, in terms of culture and infrastructure. A question arises: How far should South African cultures adapt to Western conceptions of economic and culturally determined ways of doing things? Conversely, how far can Western development models be adapted to South African cultures? Or can African culture afford to become a substitute for Western culture and ignore First World principles—thus entering into a cultural fight for superiority? Answers to such questions vary. Unfortunately, theoretical research on culture does not frequently investigate economic and political development practices. It is not uncommon to hear that a particular developmental project failed in the African context because it did not take the local culture into account (Mersham et al., 1995).

One of the best-known commentators on African culture, Kenyan political scientist Ali Mazrui, argued that both ideology and technology are rooted in culture and that differences in skills are "profoundly affected by culture" (1990, p. 2). He described traditional African society as "impressive when judged by standards of charity and solidarity (p. 3)" but slow in speed. Africa has "cultures of nostalgia rather than anticipation. (p. 5)" African cultures value prestige instead of achievement where "productivity and effectiveness are less than optimal" (p. 202). More critically, Mazrui stated that African rural culture is a "culture of poverty and indigence" (p. 203). Mersham et al. (1995) argued that Mazrui has perhaps misjudged the mood of African people. Africa has an exploding young population, increasingly exposed to the global worldview and hungrily demanding a second wave of change in political and development spheres (p. 25).

Daniel Etounga-Manguelle (1990, p. 72) spoke of the *principle lacunae* of African culture that *"explains our counter-performance in a world based on other values, including a lack of a critical culture, that is, as system of digestion and assimilation of new cultural events that permit popular culture to progress."* He proposed an African solution that is achieved through a "program of cultural adjustment" (p. 72) carried out by Africans, which would transform their worldview to one more consistent with the values of the developed world.

This idea is not far removed from conception of the African Renaissance. The term *African Renaissance* has been around in African political discourse since the colonial period. The Senegalese intellectual Chaik anta Diop first used the term in the context of the struggle against colonial rule, and it was meant to capture the dreams and aspirations of the people of Africa in their quest for self-determination (Cheru, 2001, p. 2). With the end of apartheid in 1994 and the resurgence of democratic ideals throughout Africa, President Mbeki resurrected the term as South Africa aspired to take a leading role in the economic and political transformation of the African continent. But in Africa many of these plans remain merely as rhetoric. The unfortunate result is that rhetoric (communication) and realities no longer coincide, and Africans fail to face up to the need to become something new while remaining authentically African. For the Africa of the 21st century to succeed, Kabou (1991) stated that it must become rational and pragmatic. Underdevelopment is not a matter only of capital or resources, but it originates "inside the heads of Africans." (p. 61) Boon (1998, p. 61) wrote extensively about tribalism and ethnicity and stated that tribalism exists in the present not only in distant rural areas but also in peoples hearts. Boon suggested that people retreat into ethnicity when they are most threatened. Communities then form communication so that they could get the tribe's perspective on the threat posed by massive change. It becomes difficult to adapt and acculturate.

In South Africa, there remains a deep discord between cultural preservationists and developmentalists on cultural preservation. Those in favor of cultural preservation argue that such a transition should not undermine the fundamental value systems of Black society. In Afrikaner circles the same arguments are heard with regard to the preservation of White Afrikaner culture and the Afrikaans language.

Since 1994, there has been greater social mobility in South Africa and South African organizations, but organizational communication continues to be affected by continuing uncertainty and intolerance in the workplace. Although South Africa is largely a paternalistic society, much has been done to preserve rights of women—particularly in the workplace. South Africa is a country with a strong collectivistic approach. This often leads to conflicts when individual performance is at stake. There is also a lack of interpersonal trust within organizational settings. White workers find the issue of affirmative action difficult to overcome. Nowadays, most organizations in South Africa encourage input by individual workers, and dissent is tolerated when it is not detrimental to the health of the organization. A bottom-up approach instead of a top-down network organization is encouraged—but with mixed results.

Turnbull (1994, p. 12) stated that "the job of the public relations practitioner is to shape the perception, that is, to the world, the reality. And it is that which makes public relations not only the first post-modernist profession but an activity of enormous significance in our culture." Questions concerning global culture, acculturation, media imperialism, the resurgence of cultural and religious conflict, and intercultural communication will increasingly occupy the minds of public relations scholars and practitioners in South Africa in the future. Given the centrality of the public relations practice to development concerns and its pivotal role in organizations in South Africa, it will be essential for the practitioner to grasp the issues involved, irrespective of his or her own cultural orientation or worldview.

A most pressing challenge that public relations practitioners will encounter is to find ways of balancing the traditional cultures of South Africa with Western, colonial influences that have influenced the lifestyle of South Africans but have also had an impact in the workplace. There is an inherent distrust in the broad traditional South African community toward organizations fed by a colonial past and the multinationals. This is a very difficult issue for practitioners to contend with, but the heterogeneous make-up of South Africa will have to be managed in the future.

THE MEDIA AND PUBLIC RELATIONS

Media Control

According to the Bill of Rights of South Africa's Constitution (Act 108 of 1996, South African yearbook, 2001/02, p. 299), everyone has the right to freedom of expression, which includes the following:

- Freedom of the press and other media.
- Freedom to receive or impart information or ideas.
- Freedom of artistic creativity.
- Academic freedom and freedom of scientific research.

Several laws, policies, and organizations act to protect and promote the freedom of the media in South Africa. Press Freedom Day is celebrated on October 19. South Africa now has one of the most effective media systems in the world vis-à-vis freedom of expression. Technical and editorial handling of the print media in South Africa rate among the best in the world, as is advanced broadcasting technology. The Broadcasting Act of 1999 (Act 4 of 1999, in South Africa yearbook 2001/02, p. 121–122) is aimed at developing a broadcasting policy to regulate and control broadcasting to, among other things:

- Contribute to democracy, nation building, the provision of education, and the moral fiber of society.
- Encourage ownership and control of broadcasting services by people from historically disadvantaged communities.
- Ensure fair competition in the sector.
- Provide for a three-tier system of public, commercial, and community broadcasting systems.
- Establish a strong and committed public broadcaster to service the needs of all South Africans.

Several organizations and associations play an important role in maintaining the strength of media. The South African National Editors' Forum (SANEF) was conceived at a meeting of the Black Editors Forum, the Conference of Editors, and senior journalism educators and trainers in 1996. SANEF has facilitated the mobilization of the media in the Partnership Against AIDS campaign and in campaigns to end violence against women and children. At a workshop held at the end of 2001, SANEF members and the government agreed that thorough discussion and analysis were needed to improve relations and reach mutual understanding about the roles and functions of the media and the government in a changing society.

Media diversity in any country is a sign of the level of its democracy. South Africa is on its way to achieving as much diversity as possible. The airwaves were deregulated in 2001, but the print media need to catch up as the monopolistic trend in the ownership of publications in the industry continues.

Media Outreach

Because of the very high level of extreme poverty and illiteracy in South Africa, important messages cannot be diffused to all target publics. Radio is still the medium that reaches publics in the rural areas of South Africa, and print media are available to all in the urban areas. In squatter areas, where electricity is available, people can be reached by electronic media. However, media outreach and access are still closely linked to the levels of development in South Africa.

Van Zyl and Tomaselli (1977), Marchant (1988), Tomaselli (1989), Louw (1989), Kaplan (1990), Morris and Stavrou (1991), Mersham (1992, 1993), and Hooyberg and Mersham (1993), among others, argued for the use of the best satellite technology for development purposes in Africa. Satellite communication can provide the foundation for a cost-effective and more beneficial communication infrastructure for southern Africa. Cellular telephony has the potential to become the great connecter of the people of South Africa—provided that with the eradication of poverty and the culture of non-payment for essential services can be addressed.

After 2 years of intense research, negotiations, and tests, the taxi advertising agency ComutaNet announced in 2002 that, under the auspices of Rank TV, it will present big screen television programs at 10 of the busiest taxi ranks (Cab's parking zones) of South Africa (Sake-Beeld, Thursday, 14 March, 2002). ComutaNet will reach approximately 1.2 million economically active South Africans on a daily basis. With taxis being the favorite form of transportation for about 78% of commuters in South Africa, this new communication medium could become an excellent advertising and public relations vehicle.

Media Access

All South Africans, rich and poor, have access to mass media, notwithstanding their location. At the workplace, it is almost impossible for employees not to be reached by controlled and uncontrolled media of all kinds. In 1997, the office of the Ombudsman was opened in Johannesburg. Members of the public who have complaints about reports in the media can submit their grievances to the Ombudsman. The National Community Media Forum is a network that coordinates and represents the interests of community media initiatives from marginalized communities. The Freedom of Expression Institute was formed in 1994 and had as objective the campaigning for freedom of expression during the apartheid years (GCIS, 2001/2002, p. 130).

Activist groups have direct access to the media, and their causes are often taken up and supported by the mass media in the country. For example, no single day passes without media coverage on the crime levels, the farm murders, the rape of women and children, and the issue of AIDS. The control of the news media by news editors in their gatekeeping role is sometimes criticized but also necessary because of the perceived value of a story and the limitations of time and space. A major influence on the choices made by gatekeepers is the policy and ideology of the particular media organization. Factual information can become distorted. Legal legislation and ethics also influence the choices made by media organizations (Mersham & Skinner, 1999, p. 174). But various editorial columns as well as letters to editors are published to keep controversial debates going—like the HIV/AIDS debate. The openness of debates, particularly in the newspapers, is extraordinary.

There are ways of reaching and communicating specifically to rural publics, which consist of local tribes of mixed ethnic groups with different languages and dialects. Some of these publics might live in remote places and may be beyond the reach of the mainstream mass communication media, and they may pay little attention to radio beyond listening to music. They may also be uninterested in the affairs of the world or the cities and show little interest in news bulletins. There have been numerous arguments for or against the utilization of *oramedia, unconventional*, or *folk media* (media based on the indigenous culture produced and consumed by members of a group). The fact is that utilizing folk media still might be useful in the African environment. Unlike mass media, which reach many people at a time but only have cognitive influence (knowledge, awareness, and interest), unconventional media may only reach a few people at a time but can be an effective relay chain to the mass communication media. These media have visible cultural features by which social relationships and a worldview are maintained and defined. They take many forms and are rich in symbolism. These media must be seen as interpersonal or group media speaking to common people in their own language, in their own idiom, and dealing with problems of direct relevance to the situation (Jefkins & Ugboajah, 1986, p. 33). In South Africa, this device has been used adequately lately to promote all kinds of public relations messages and programs, from family planning to efficient farming, primary health care, adult literacy, and the continuous fight against AIDS. There is a wide variety of these media, but some include puppet shows, village gossip, development, improvisation and industrial theater, oratory, poetry and music, praise singing, weddings, funerals, and political rallies.

Although it is widely assumed that remarkable developments in communication technologies automatically improve communication, unfortunately this is not necessarily true for South Africa. We need to monitor continuously what we are communicating and why. In South Africa education about the interpretation of media content will be just as important as the format in which the publics receive communication messages.

Where would these arguments about media access leave South African public relations practitioners? The product and service scope of public relations in South Africa is broad and expanding fast. The time of the traditional professional who believed that maintaining personal influence with the media and the ability to turn out a readable press release would suffice is over. Today, the profession, like other management disciplines, has to have both specialists and generalists, and it should be able to advise on internal and external communication challenges (Rhodes & Baker, cited in Puth & Lubbe, 1994, p. 287). Lobbying, community networking, industrial theater, the innovative use of the visual medium, and social marketing are all realities with which South African public relations practitioners have to come to terms and use effectively in their changing environment. However, mass media remain important channels and important target publics relations practitioners.

ETHICS AND PUBLIC RELATIONS IN SOUTH AFRICA

Worldviews are powerful, and many public relations practitioners are not always aware of the power that they hold over their behavior and outlook. Grunig (1992, p. 38) contended that public relations should be based on a worldview that incorporates ethics into the process, rather than debating the ethics of its outcomes. Pearson (1989) developed an extensive theory of public relations ethics based largely on the theories of the philosopher Habermas (1984). Pearson (1989, p. 315) argued that the profession needed an approach to ethics that combines "moral conviction and tolerance." When people disagree about what is moral, they debate and attempt to persuade one another.

Ethical public relations practitioners must be totally committed to communicating truthfully. However, in attempting to serve clients or management practitioners, avoid taking extreme positions. They will not mount a communication effort to promote the position of a client or organization that—even if, in some sense, literally truthful—will seriously and wrongly compromise or otherwise be injurious to the legitimate concerns and rights of significant third parties (Martinsan, 2000). This is an excellent ideal but difficult to practice in Africa where hired guns are frequently at work. A recent example is President's Robert Mugabe's efforts to fight against the imposition of possible sanctions against Zimbabwe by the international community. He lobbied the international community against the sanctions by involving his ambassadors to the UN, Washington, DC, and the EU. They talked to American congressmen and the Congressional Black Caucus to try to reject the Zimbabwe Bill. Zimbabwe's representatives in the US lobbied African diplomats based in Washington, DC to oppose the bill, while former American ambassador to the UN Andrew Young and the public relations firm Cohen & Woods International were enlisted by the government to fight impending sanctions. However critical we may be of this situation, Andrew Young and the public relations firm merely provided a specialist service to a client and cannot be associated with the ethical implications of the situation. As proposed in this book, public relations ethics in developing countries is one of the many areas of the field that needs more research.

PRISA has a code of conduct to which all practitioners and consultants should adhere. Table A8.9 (see Appendix) describes the code in detail.

SOUTH AFRICAN PUBLIC RELATIONS CASE STUDY

Park Station Partnership Against HIV/AIDS

This campaign won the PRISM Award for the best campaign of 1999. It was submitted by Ad-Uppe Public Relations on behalf of Intersite and the South African Rail Commuter Corporation (SARCC).

Background

The campaign was a full day AIDS-awareness event held at Park Station, Johannesburg, on World AIDS Day, December 1, 1999. It was based on the success of a similar event at Pretoria Station 1 year before, which was also under the management of Ad-Uppe Public Relations and spearheaded by two of the consultancy's major clients, Intersite Property Management Services and its holding company, SARCC. Both companies are agencies of the Department of Transport, functioning as the owners and managers of metropolitan stations in South Africa.

To achieve maximum impact with limited budgets, Intersite, SARCC, and Ad-Uppe Public Relations invited participation from other parties in a joint venture partnership. The ultimate outcome was the Park Station Partnership Against HIV/AIDS, which was made up of the following:

- Intersite (head office, Northern and Southern Gauteng Regions) (participant and sponsor).
- Gauteng Provincial Government (participant and sponsor).
- Spoornet (participant and sponsor).
- Industrial Development Corporation (sponsorship only).
- Metrorail (participant and minor sponsor).
- LoveLife program (participant only).

Following the previous Minister of Transport's support of the fight against HIV/AIDS and considering that the country's roads and railways are fast spreading the pandemic, the project had the full support of the Department of Transport and Minister Dullah Omar hosted the event.

Objectives and Target Publics

The main objective of the event was to make as many people as possible HIV/AIDS aware. The intended message was twofold: (a) to prevent the spread of HIV/AIDS and to (b) care for those with HIV/AIDS. The target publics of the message were commuters, with specific emphasis on the youth. Hence, Park Station was used because 300,000 people pass through the station each day.

Challenges and Obstacles Overcome

As with any state-driven project, there were budget limitations, and the proposed budget had to be tailored from over R 500,000 to R 330,000. When a final decision to go ahead was made 2 weeks prior to the event, only two thirds of the required budget was guaranteed. However, additional sponsorships were obtained, and costs were tailored accordingly. Ad-Uppe Public Relations donated around R 10,000 worth of time.

On the day of the event there were the usual problems as ministers changed their plans, artists arrived late, and so on. All problems were handled smoothly without the crowd's awareness. The biggest challenge of the project was streamlining the needs, wants, and aspirations of the various organizations and individuals involved. Planning meetings often became heated and, as always, a number of members did not deliver as promised. In all cases, Ad-Uppe Public Relations managed to find solutions to these problems and appease almost everyone.

Strategy

The strategy on the day of the event was to make use of the cross-cultural medium of popular music and celebrities to draw a large crowd and deliver the HIV/AIDS message. People living with HIV gave testimonials to make hard-hitting statements of how real the disease is and how people with AIDS are still people that have to live their lives.

Program Execution and Activities Deployed

Prepublicity.   A theme was designed and branded posters, banners, and flyers were displayed and distributed at all major Gauteng stations. A prepublicity media release was issued 2 weeks prior to the event, and invitations were delivered to preferred guests identified by the members of the partnership. These included the entire cabinet as well as provincial and local dignitaries and various industry leaders (potential sponsors for future events).

The Event on Stage.   A stage and sound system were set up on the main concourse of Park Station and a full day (from 6:00 a.m. to 6:00 p.m.) program of guests appeared. The day was divided into four sessions:

- Session 1 (from 6:00 a.m. to 10:00 p.m.) featured community disk jockey's (DJ's) young singer Letoya Makhene as master of ceremony (MC) and popular, yet relatively low-key bands.

- Session 2 (from 10:00 a.m. to 1:00 p.m.) was hosted by radio DJ Grant Shakoane. Popular bands attracted a large crowd before Minister Dullah Omar and other guest speakers

addressed them. A commemorative candle was lit and 1,600 red balloons were released—
one for every new case of HIV reported daily in South Africa.

- Session 3 (from 1:00 p.m. to 4:00 p.m.) included MC Bob Mabena and established music stars performing and addressing the crowd while the preferred guests enjoyed lunch.

- Session 4 (from 4:00 p.m. to 6:00 p.m.) had a very upbeat vibe with popular artists and television stars driving home the message and taking care of the homeward bound commuter traffic.

The Event on the Station.   A team of 200 volunteers, under the guidance of the Gauteng Department of Health, distributed condoms, stickers, and information flyers to commuters on the main concourse thruout the entire day. From 6:00 a.m. til 8:00 a.m., local MECs circulated among the commuter rush, speaking to the people and handing out material. A preferred guest area was set up on the mezzanine level above the concourse, and drinks and a light lunch were served to invited guests. Guests began arriving at 11:00 a.m.

LoveLife used the event to launch their Love Train, which they had parked on one of the station platforms. Preferred guests and others signed their pledges to the fight against HIV/AIDS on the train.

Budget

As already discussed, the budget for the project was extremely limited, and costs had to be kept to a minimum. Sound and stage equipment cost approximately R 80,000; artists' fees were R 65,000; catering for VIPs and workers cost R 38,000; the venue cost R 80,000 (mostly donated by Intersite); visual material were R 31,000, and event management cost R 30,000 (additional time was paid for by Intersite and donated by Ad-Uppe Public Relations). The total budget for the event was R 316,000.

Outcome

The event was a resounding success. All sponsors were satisfied, and the day went off with very few problems. During the lunch hour, an estimated 30,000 people were gathered around the stage. Although a *City Press* article damned the use of music on World AIDS Day, Ad-Uppe Public Relations found it an effective means of reaching a large number of people. The venue was perfect; although there were a lot of hidden logistics behind securing cabinet ministers and controlling large crowds, everything ran smoothly. There was substantial media coverage, both electronic and print (including eTV and SABC1 and SABC 2 news) despite the large number of other initiatives on the same day.

Hundreds of thousands of people heard the message and received background information and condoms to take home with them—which also reached an unquantifiable number of other people. In addition, valuable lessons were learned and contacts made for an even better campaign for 2000. Add-Uppe Public Relations is sure that the Park Station Partnership Against HIV/AIDS made a valuable contribution to the raising of awareness about HIV/AIDS among the people of Gauteng.

CONCLUSION

In this chapter I provided a synopsis of the state of affairs with regard to the evolution of public relations as a profession in South Africa. I also attempted to emphasize the heterogeneous cultural ingredients of South Africa as a country and indicated the level of complexity that public relations practitioners have to confront when operating in a developing world.

APPENDIX

TABLE A.17.1
The Provinces (Statistics South Africa 2001)

Province	Capital	Languages	Population	Area (Square km)	% of Total Area	GGP (1994)	% of Total GDP
Western Cape	Cape Town	Afrikaans English isiXhosa	4.2 million	129,386	10.6%	R81,800 m	14.21%
Eastern Cape	Bisho	isiXhosa Afrikaans English	6.8 million	169,580	13.9%	R29,049 m	7.59%
KwaZulu-Natal	Pietermaritzburg Ulundi (joint)	isiZulu English Afrikaans	9 million	92,100	7.6%	R57,007 m	14.90%
Northern Cape	Kimberley	Afrikaans Setswana isiXhosa	0.873 million	361,830	29.7%	R8,000 m	2.09%
Free State	Bloemfontein	Sesotho Afrikaans isiXhosa	2.790 million	129,480	10.6%	R23,688 m	6.19%
North-West	Mafikeng	Setswana Afrikaans isiXhosa	3.567 million	116,320	9.5%	R21,252 m	5.56%
Gauteng	Pretoria	isiZulu Afrikaans English	7.87 million	17,010	1.4%	R144,359 m	37.73%
Mpumalanga	Nelspruit	isiSwati isiZulu isiNdebele	3 million	79,490	6.5%	R31,175 m	8.15%
(Limpopo)	Polokwane	Sepedi Xitsonga Tshivenda	5.5 million	123,910	10.2%	R14,158 m	3.7%

Note. From Statistics South Africa (2001).

TABLE A.17.2
Industry Strength and Weaknesses

Strengths	Weaknesses
Some in-depth skills	Poor standards
Diversity of skills	Lack of accountability
Flexibility	Low expectations
Can take pressure	Instability
Recognition is growing	Negative image

Note. (Rhodes & Baker, cited in Lubbe & Puth, 1994, p. 288).

TABLE A.17.3

Milestones in the Evolution of Public Relations as a Profession in South Africa

Time	Milestone
1957	Birth of PRISA with 23 founder members. First meeting in Johannesburg and PRISA recognized by IPRA (International Public Relation Association).
1958	First PRISA training course for 49 public relations people. First member newsletter.
1959	First PRISA training committee formed. KwaZulu-Natal region formed.
1960	First PRISA library established.
1962	First public relations booklet printed: *Does Your Bark Bite Your Business?* (Members stand at 71.)
1964	The launch of PRISA's comprehensive education and training program in Johannesburg for 50 students. Immediate examination written in Durban and Cape Town. Pretoria region formed. PRISA registered with the Department of Heraldry. Johannesburg region to be called Southern Transvaal.
1965	Fifty students take the PRISA Intermediate Course and 18 pass. First South African public relations handbook written by Malan and L'Estrange. First South African Public Relations Convention in Johannesburg with 100 delegates. Northern Transvaal region established. (Members stand at 150.)
1966	Eighty students started the Intermediate Public Relations Course, 32 wrote the examination, and 18 passed. Western Cape region formed with seven members.
1967	Decision to establish university Communication courses. An Education and Training Committee appointed. Eastern Cape region established.
1968	Committee on Communication formed with Education subcommittee. Communication courses are instituted at universities. First career pamphlet, *Public Relations as a Career*, Johannesburg PRISA is developed. First seven students write the PRISA's Final Certificate examination. First public relations course offered by the Witwatersrand Technical College. First PRISA Gold Medal awarded to Professor Chris Barnard (first heart transplant surgeon). Advisory committee on public relations research established.
1970	First trophy for house journals awarded. Launch of *Communika* (PRISA's official newsletter). Survey undertaken on the status of the public relations profession. (Members stand on 250.)
1971	The University of South Africa starts the first distance education communication courses and enrolls 300 students for the first year. Southern African Association of Industrial Editors (SAAIE) formed. PRISA Code of Conduct published.
1972	The Constitution is revived. Membership tops 300. Inaugural meeting of the Central region.
1973	The University of the Orange Free State starts the Communication degree courses in the new Department of Communication. PRISA's first Communicator of the Year Award.
1974	PRISA opens its first permanent office. Association of Municipal Public Relations Officers started. Presidential chain of office donated.
1975	SAAIE breaks away from the PRISA. First all-Africa public relations conference with Public Relations Society of Kenya and IPRA. Theme: *Communicating With the Third World.* (members stand at 450.)
1976	PRISA Code of Conduct accepted by members. PRISA welcomes its first Black members. Television documentary, *The Image Makers*, on public relations as a career.
1977	PRISA celebrates the first 20 years. The Consultant's Association formed.

(Continued)

TABLE A.17.3
(*Continued*)

Time	Milestone
1978	PRISA introduces student membership. The National Council produces the first written development plan for PRISA that now has 339 members.
1979	New PRISA logo and membership certificate designed. PRISA survey held on members' needs—100 responses. New Code of Conduct accepted.
1980	Membership increases to 543.
1981	PRISA publishes the *Body of Knowledge* document and all tertiary institutions decide that PRISA should be the examining body for public relations courses.
1982	*Handbook of Public Relations* written by Skinner and von Essen appears. Vaal region established. (Skinner, C & Van Essen (1982))
1985	Public Relations Council of South Africa (PRCSA) is inaugurated.
1986	Launch of Public Relations Council logo. First public relations practitioners accredited. *Communika* wins first prize in the SAAIE house journal competition. In December PRISA signs up its 1,000 member. Management Committee appointed to help run the PRISA.
1987	Official course in the Principles of Public Relations rewritten to meet the needs of the changing market. National Education Committee is reestablished. PRISA is 30 and aims to increase membership and improve services to members. (It now has 1200 members.)
1988	First national education officer appointed. Name returns to the 1957 original. Eighth region—Bophuthatswana formed. PRISA regional assistance program introduced—centralizing mailing and newsletters. PRISA Advanced Principles of Public Relations course designed and presented at main centers. PRISA Basic Principles course packaged and licensed to colleges. (PRISA now has 1,400 members.)
1989	First Head of Education appointed. First strategic planning conference and Education Indaba held. PRISA Professional Development Program was one result. PRISA's Mission Statement published. (It now has 2,000 members.) (Margaret Moscardi)
1991	Academic Conference established at the Pretoria Congress. PRISA is represented at the World Congress in Canada. Transkei region formed. New corporate identity launched for PRISA. Public Relations Consultants' Association closed.
1992	The PRISA Council becomes the accreditation and Ethics Council. First PRISA Management Course implemented.
1993	First academic receives the Educator of the Year Award. The Public Relations Council becomes part of the PRISA. PRISA hosts the first International Public Relations Association (IPRA) congress in South Africa, Cape Town.
1994	The Examination Board (now committee) established. PRISA boasts its first woman president. PRISA embarks on its image campaign. Forty five candidates pass the APR examinations. A new textbook, *Public Relations in South Africa: A Management Reader* (edited by Puth & Lubbe) appears on the shelves. (Isando SA: Heinemann 1994)
1995	Three new courses implemented. PRISA introduces corporate membership. PRISA Consultants' Chapter formed. Another public relations textbook, *Public Relations, Development and Social Investment: A Southern African Perspective* (Mersham et al., 1995) appears.

(Continued)

TABLE A.17.3

(*Continued*)

Time	Milestone
1996	PRISA Education Directorate becomes PRISA Education Center with its own constitution. Community Relations and Development Course implemented. Namibia region formally inaugurated.
1997	The 3-year diploma in Public Relations is implemented. The infrastructure in the PRISA offices is expanded. PRISA is 40 years old.
1998–2002	PRISA grows in stature with now more than 4,000 members (by January 2002, PRISA had 3,430 student members and 1,300 practitioners). The association moves even closer to the academic institutions when, in 1999, for the first time an academic delivers the keynote address at the annual PRISA Conference on Strategic Scenario Planning for the New Millennium. New and revised relations handbooks by Skinner, Von Essen and Mersham appear. The PRISA Education and Training Center is involved in education and training standards generating bodies and the Skills Development Act structures. The Registration of PRISA Education and Training Center as a Higher Education Institution is formed in 2001. PRISA becomes a founder member of the Global Alliance of Public Relations and Communication Management Associations in 2000. PRISA hosts the Global Alliance annual meeting in South Africa in March 2002.

Note: From *PRISA milestones*, by M. Moscardi, 2002, Johannesburg, South Africa: Director of PRISA. Reprinted with permission by Margaret Moscardi (Executive Director: PRISA).

TABLE A.17.4

Vision and Objectives of PRISA

PRISA's vision: Recognition of the public relations profession, PRISA and its members as key role players in Southern Africa and beyond.
PRISA's mission:
- To establish PRISA as the authority for the public relations profession.
- To foster the professionalization of public relations and communication management in Southern Africa.
- To set and maintain professional ethics and standards among members of the institute.
- To provide dynamic value-added services to members of the institute and thereby to its stakeholders.
- To establish public relations as a strategic management function.
- To continually transform the institute to stay ahead of the dynamic changes in the social, political, and economic environment.
PRISA's objectives:
- To promote a general understanding of public relations and communication management and of the value of its practice and to establish and maintain professional status and dignity for public relations practice among registered members of PRISA, employers and the general public.
- To encourage the observance of the highest standards of professional conduct by registered members of PRISA through adherence to the PRISA Code of Professional Standards for the Practice of Public Relations.
- To protect the interests of all concerned in the event of any complaint of malpractice or nonadherence to the PRISA Code of Professional Standards for the Practice of Public Relations being brought against a registered member through the application of a set of disciplinary procedures.

(*Continued*)

TABLE A.17.4
(Continued)

PRISA's values: PRISA is continually transformed to meet the needs and challenges of the next millennium by undertaking tasks that are measurable, monitored, performed to time and quality standards, and add value to all stakeholders.

PRISA will implement leadership that is representative of South Africa, accountable and responsible, professional and informed, and visionary.

These (tasks and leadership) will encourage a culture that is professional, adaptable, liberating, open/transparent, empowering, consultative/decisive, value centered, and dynamic.

PRISA's services: The primary role is to represent the profession of public relations and communication management and enhance the status of practitioners. The benefits of this work are enjoyed by all those who practice public relations. But there is also a wide range of services that are provided specifically as a benefit to individual members:

PR hotline

Professional advice is available to registered practitioners–either from the national office or through the national executive.

Consultancy referral system

PRISA operates a referral system to help members of its Consultancy Chapter. Prospective clients are given a selection of names to approach according to their areas of specialization.

PR job grapevine

This informal job grapevine operates as a contact point between prospective employers and members.

International contacts

Contact with overseas associations and practitioners is maintained at PRISA and benefits all members.

Networking

The single most important reason for belonging to a professional body is networking, keeping in touch, business opportunities and professional development.

CPD information

PRISA is the best source of professional development opportunities through its expanded and varied program of seminars and workshops—on a national and regional level.

Accreditation

PRISA offers members the opportunity of obtaining the globally recognized APR certification

Regional activities

Regional networking and professional development programs are offered for members' benefit.

Discounts

Members and students receive substantial discounts.

PRISA's Membership: Research has shown that one of the most important reasons for joining is networking with peers, sharing and gaining knowledge, and benchmarking practitioners against best practice. Registration with PRISA provides the added advantage of gaining a professional status, as well as the globally recognized APR registration, and gives access to all services at substantial discounts. PRISA will assist members in gaining certification from the Services Seta when this process is in place. There are different categories of registration:

- Individual registration—from affiliate to APR.
- Corporate support—organizations or departments with more than five employees.
- Chapters: Student Chapter for individuals studying public relations and a Consultancy Chapter (PRCC).

(Continued)

TABLE A.17.4

(*Continued*)

PRISA's continuing professional development (CPD): CPD is a global trend and professions around the world have been developing and implementing methods for lifelong learning—at the same time giving senior professionals a formal method of gaining CPD points by contributing their expertise. In essence CPD is a way in which seniors give to and develop the young professional and the young professionals take from seniors and develop themselves. Thus, the profession grows globally, and the status of both the practitioner and the profession is enhanced and its value is firmly established. CPD points will be earned through any or all of these activities:

- Formal further education, completion of formal qualifications.
- Attendance at identified seminars, workshops, and conferences.
- Courses such as time management, and negotiation, and so on.
- Mentoring and coaching.
- Participation in industry and professional bodies.
- Contribution to the body of knowledge, through presentations, the publication of articles, and so on.

PRISA's CPD point system is being finalized now and will become the benchmark for the profession in Southern Africa. It is based on the experience of the IPR in the UK, Public Relations Institute of Australia (PRIA) in Australia, and the Public Relations Society of America (PRSA) in the USA. It follows the guidelines given by the South African Services Seta.

PRISA's awards:

- Vision award: This is an award for developing Black public relations practitioners. It is sponsored by Baird's and Edelmans Worldwide and administered by PRISA.
- President's award: This award is made at the sole discretion of the President of PRISA and is in recognition of outstanding service to PRISA.
- PRISM award for outstanding public relations practice: The Financial Mail PRISM Award is presented to public relations professionals who have successfully blended flair, creativity, and professionalism into public relations programs and strategies that showcase a successful public relations campaign. Presented by the PRCC and supported by the *Financial Mail* newspaper.
- PRISA gold medal award: Awarded in recognition of outstanding public relations service to Southern Africa. Previous winners were Dr. Christian Barnard, Gary Player, President F. W. de Klerk, and President Nelson Mandela.

The purpose of all these awards is to boost standards of professionalism by recognizing and rewarding a clearly defined strategic approach, innovation and creativity.

TABLE A.17.5

Public Relations Consultancies in South Africa

Ad-uppe public relations	Concept communications
Arcay corporate communications	Coralynne & associates
Anthea Johnston & associates	Candid communications
Baird's communications	Corporate communications
Barbara Cousens & associates CC (BC&A)	Debra Anne communications CC
Bay public relations & associates	Fasedemi Newman-Leo Burnett
BSA public relations & event management	Fleishman-Hillard Vallun Wilkins
Bill Paterson (Pty) Ltd	Gillian Gamsy International PR and promotions
Butterfly communications	Gilmark communications
Communications consultants	Grant-Marshall communications CC (GMC)
Cathrall & associates	Grant Thornton Kessel Feinstein
Church Raitt Orr Limited	Harbor public relations & marketing

(*Continued*)

TABLE A.17.5

(Continued)

Image communications	Primary focus
Infokom	Pamela Mgulwa and associates
Integrated communications	Pro-image CC
Joy Cameron-Dow communications CC	Rose Francis communications
Lange public relations	Rosemary Hare public relations
Liz Kneale communications	Sefin marketing communications consultants
Lola Lazarus public relations and promotions (LLPR)	Simeka TWS communications
	Strategic communication consultants
Marcus Brewster publicity	Specialised solutions international
Mandisa communications	Strategic concepts (PTY) limited
Matrix PR & communications consultants	Trish Stewart PR associates (TSPR)
Milkwood communications	

TABLE A.17.6

PRISM Award Categories

Category 1—Overall Institutional
Promoting general relations with all or some publics.

Category 2—Public Service
Promoting societal good with philanthropic motivation (if the principal motivation is a benefit to the sponsor use Category 1 instead).

Category 3—Public Affairs
Specific short-term effort to influence governmental legislation or regulation or to elect a political candidate.

Category 4—Issue Management
Long-term effort dealing with public policy or policies.

Category 5—Emergency
Dealing with a disaster or other unpredicted emergency.

Category 6—Community Relations
Aimed at publics in one or more particular communities in which the company or institution has a special presence or interest.

Category 7—Employee Relations
Designed to increase efficiency or improve morale within the company or institution.

Category 8—Investor Relations
Intended to influence present and prospective investors and the financial community.

Category 9—Product/Service Communication
New product/service or established product/service.

Category 10—Special Event
Concentrated opening, celebration, commemoration, or created event.

Category 11—Environmental
Concerning a real or alleged threat to the environment.

Category 12—Arts
Promoting or fostering the arts by an arts organization or a sponsoring company/institution.

(Continued)

TABLE A.17.6

(*Continued*)

Category 13—Other

Aimed at distributors, members, educators, youth, or other special publics.

2001 Financial Mail PRISM Awards has identified a need for the inclusion of communication pieces that highlight technical skills and expertise, such as editing, writing, design, and photography. They recognize the importance of a communication project's goals and measured results and emphasize the creative process of project execution. It has been decided to include the following as additional category:

Category 14—Publications: Employee publications

Production of external or internal publications in all formats except electronic.

    One- to three-color magazines.

    Four-color (or more) magazines.

    Newspapers.

    Newsletters.

    Special publications.

    Posters.

    Calendars.

Judging will be on writing, editing, design (including photography and graphics), and production.

Note. Gold (Campaign of the Year), silver (outstanding public relations practice), and bronze (runner up to silver) are awarded in the PRISM categories.

TABLE A.17.7

Perceived Importance of Current and Future Public Relations Disciplines

Past 5 Years: What is Currently Important?	*Next 5 Years: What Will be Important?*
General corporate pubic relations	Employee relations
Marketing public relations	Community relations
Community relations	Corporate public relations
Employee relations	Marketing public relations
Investor relations	Investor relations
Special events	Issues management
Public affairs	Public affairs
Issues management	International relations
International public relations	Environmental public relations
Crisis communication	Crisis communication
Environmental public relations	Special events

TABLE A.17.8

Registered Unions, Members, Employers' Organizations, and Bargaining Councils, 1999–2000

Year	*Registered Unions*	*Members*	*Employers' Organizations*	*Private Sector Bargaining Councils*
1999	499	3,359,497	260	78
2000	464	3,552,113	252	73

TABLE A.17.9
PRISA's Code of Conduct

Declaration of Principles

We base our professional principles on the fundamental value and dignity of the individual. We believe in and support the free exercise of human rights, especially freedom of speech, freedom of assembly, and freedom of the media, which are essential to the practice of good public relations. In serving the interests of clients and employers, we dedicate ourselves to the goals of better communication, understanding, and cooperation among diverse individuals, groups, and institutions of society. We also subscribe to and support equal opportunity of employment in the public relations profession.

We pledge:

- To conduct ourselves professionally, with truth, accuracy, fairness, and responsibility to the public and toward our colleagues.
- To improve our individual competence and advance the knowledge and proficiency of the profession through continuing education and research.
- To adhere to the articles of the Code of Professional Standards for the practice of public relations.

Code of Professional Conduct

1. Definition

   Public relations is the management, through communication, of perceptions and strategic relationships between an organization and its internal and external stakeholders.

2. Professional Conduct

   2.1 In the conduct of our professional activities, we shall respect the public interest and the dignity of the individual. It is our responsibility at all times to deal fairly and honestly with our clients or employers, past or present, with our colleagues, media communication, and with the public.

   2.2 We shall conduct our professional lives in accordance with the public interest. We shall not conduct ourselves in any manner detrimental to the profession of public relations.

   2.3 We have a positive duty to maintain integrity and accuracy, as well as generally accepted standards of good taste.

   2.4 We shall not knowingly, intentionally, or recklessly communicate false or misleading information. It is our obligation to use proper care to avoid doing so inadvertently.

   2.5 We shall not guarantee the achievement of specified results beyond our direct control. We shall not negotiate or agree terms with a prospective employer or client on the basis of payment only contingent on specific future public relations achievements.

   2.6 We shall, when acting for a client or employer who belongs to a profession, respect the code of ethics of that of other professions and shall not knowingly be party to any breach of such a code.

3. Toward Clients/Employers Conduct

   3.1 We shall safeguard the confidences of both present and former clients and employers. We shall not disclose or make use of information given or obtained in confidence from an employer or client, past or present, for personal gain or otherwise or to the disadvantage or prejudice of such client or employer.

   3.2 We shall not represent conflicting or competing interests without the express consent of those involved, given after full disclosure of the facts. We shall not place ourselves in a position where our interests are or may be in conflict with a duty to a client without full disclosure of such interests to all involved.

   3.3 We shall not be party to any activity that seeks to dissemble or mislead by promoting one disguised or undisclosed interest while appearing to further another. It is our duty to ensure that the actual interest of any organization with which we may be professionally concerned is adequately declared.

(Continued)

TABLE A.17.9
(Continued)

3.4 In the course of our professional services to the employer or client we shall not accept payment either in cash or in kind in connection with these services from another source without the express consent of our employer or client.

4. Conduct Toward Colleagues

4.1 We shall not maliciously injure the professional reputation or practice of another individual engaged in the public relations profession.

4.2 We shall at all times uphold this code, cooperate with colleagues in doing so, and enforce decisions on any matter arising from this application.

4.3 Registered individuals who knowingly cause or permit another person or organization to act in a manner inconsistent with this code or are party to such an action shall be deemed to be in breach of it.

4.4 If we have reason to believe that another colleague has engaged in practices that may be in breach of this code, or practices that may be unethical, unfair, or illegal, it is our duty to advise the institute promptly.

4.5 We shall not invite any employee of a client to consider alternative employment.

5. Conduct Toward the Business Environment

5.1 We shall not recommend the use of any organization in which we have a financial interest or make use of its services on behalf of our clients or employers without declaring our interest.

5.2 In performing professional services for a client or employer we shall not accept fees, commissions, or any other consideration from anyone other than the client or employer in connection with those services, without the express consent of the client/employer, given after disclosure of the facts.

5.3 We shall sever relations as soon as possible with any organization or individual if such a relationship requires conduct contrary to this code.

6. Conduct Toward the Channels of Communication

6.1 We shall not engage in any practice, that tends to corrupt the integrity of channels or media of communication.

6.2 We shall identify publicly the name of the client or employer on whose behalf any public communication is made.

7. Conduct Toward the State

7.1 We respect the principles contained in the Constitution of the country in which we are resident.

7.2 We shall not offer or give any reward to any person holding public office with intent to further our interests or those of our employer.

8. Conduct Toward PRISA

8.1 We shall at all times respect the dignity and decisions of PRISA.

8.2 We are bound to uphold the annual registration fee levied by PRISA, which fee is payable as determined by registered practitioners at the Annual General Meeting of PRISA.

9. Disciplinary Rules

A registered member who, in the opinion of the Disciplinary Committee of PRISA, infringes the Code of Professional Standards shall be informed in writing. The member deemed responsible for such an infringement shall be given reasonable opportunity to state their defense either in writing or by personal attendance at a meeting of a Disciplinary Committee appointed by the PRISA Board and specially convened for this purpose. Sanctions will take the form of a warning or the practitioner's name will be removed from the register of members. This action will be made public.

REFERENCES

Boon, M. (1998). *The African way: The power of interactive leadership.* (2nd ed.). Sandton, Johannesburg, SA: Zebra.

Cheru, F. (2001). *The African Renaissance and the challenge of globalization* (Working Paper). Geneva, Switzerland: Economic and Social Council of the United Nations.

Constitution of the Republic of South Africa. (1996). (in South Africa yearbook, 2001/2002).

Cullingworth, B. (1990, November). PR comes of age in South Africa. *Review,* 59–61.

De Beer, A. (1993). Journalists could take a leaf from public relations education. *Monitor,* 76–78. Durban, South Africa: The Department of Public Relations and Journalism student publication, ML Sultan Technikon.

Etounga-Manguelle, D. (1990). *L'Afrique: d'un programme d'adjustment culturel?* (Africa: a program for cultural adjustment)? Ivry-sur-Seine: Editions Nouvelle du Sud.

Government Communication and Information System. (Eds.). (2001/2002). *South African yearbook.* Durban, South Africa: Universal Printers.

Grunig, JE. (1992). *Excellence in public relations and communication management.* Hillsdale: New Jersey: Lawrence Erlbaum Associates.

Habermas, J. (1984). *The theory of communicative action* (Vol. 1, T. McCarthy, Trans.). Boston: Beacon.

Hiebert, R. E. (1984). *Introduction.* In B. Cantor (Ed.), *Inside public relations* (pp. xvii–xx). New York: Longman.

Hoogberg, U. & Mersham, G. M. (1993). Mass media in Africa: From distant drums to satellite, in As deBeer (ed.). *Mass media for the nineties:* the *South African handbook of mass communication.* Pretoria: Van Schaik.

Jefkins, F. & Ugboajah, F. (1986). *Communication in industrialising countries* Hong Kong: Macmillan.

Kaplan, D. (1990). *The crossed line: The South African telecommunications industry in transition.* Johannesburg, SA: Witwaters rand University Press.

Kabou, A. (1991). *Et si L'Afrique refusant le devellopement?* Paris: L'Harmatten.

Louw, P. C. (1989). *Communication and Counter Hegemony in Contemperary South Africa. Consideration of a leftist media theory and practice.* Doctoral thesis is, University of Natal, S.A.

Lubbe, B. A., & Puth, G. (Eds.). (1994). *Public relations in South Africa: A management reader.* Isando, Johannesburg, SA: Heinemann.

Malan, J. P., & L' Estrange, J. A. (1965). *Public Relations Practice in South Africa,* Cape Town:Juta.

Mazrui, A. A. (1990). *Cultural forces in world politics.* London: James Curry.

Marchant, H. (1988). *Communication, Media and development.* Durban SA: Butterworths/Does Africa refuse development.

Mersham, G. M. & Skinner, C. (1999). *New insights into Communication & Public Relations.* Sandton, SA: Heinemann.

Mersham, G. M. (1992). *Communication Science in South Africa–The view from Ngoye.* Inaugural Address Kwadlangezwa: University of Zululand Press.

Mersham, G. M. (1993). Public relations: A vital communication function of our times. In A. S. De Beer (Ed.), *Mass media for the nineties: the South African handbook of mass communication.* Pretoria, South Africa: Van Schaik.

Mersham, G. M., Rensburg, R. S., & Skinner, J. C. (1995). *Public relations, development and social investment: A Southern African perspective.* Pretoria, South Africa: Van Schaik.

Moscardi, M. (2002). *PRISA milestones.* Johannesburg, South Africa: Director of PRISA The Institute of Public Relations and Communication management.

Mowlana, H. (1987). *Development: A field in search of itself.* Budapest: International Association for Mass Communication Research.

Nartey, V. (1988). Public relations education and research in Africa. *International Public Relations Review,* 24–28.

Nel, J. J. (1993). From teen to adult. *Communika,* 1.

Palframan, B. (1994). South Africa: Creative alliances work best, *Communication World, 11*(6), 35–36.

Pearson, R. (1989). *A theory of public relations ethics.* Unpublished doctoral thesis, Ohio State University, Athens.

Sakebeeld, Thursday, 14 March, 2002.

Statistics South Africa. (2001).

Steyn, B. (2000). CEO expectations in terms of PR roles. *Communicare, 19*(1), 20–43.

Tomaselli: R. E. (1989). Public Service broadcasting in the age of information capitalism. *Communicate*, 8(2): 27–37

Turnbull, N. S. (1994). Is public relations the first post-modernist profession? *Communika.*

Van Zyl, J. & Tomaselli, K. G. (1997). *Media and change.* Johannesburg, SA: McCraw-Hill.

18

PUBLIC RELATIONS IN EGYPT: PRACTICES, OBSTACLES, AND POTENTIALS

KEVIN L. KEENAN

The Arab Republic of Egypt is located in the northeastern corner of Africa, bordered by Libya to the west, Sudan to the south, and the Mediterranean Sea to the north. The Red Sea borders mainland Egypt to the east, and Israel borders the eastern edge of Egypt's Sinai Peninsula. With a population of 70 million, Egypt is the largest country in the Arab world. The capital city of Cairo, with over 16 million inhabitants, is the center of business, culture, diplomacy, and media in the Middle East.

More than 90% of Egypt's 1 million km^2 area is uninhabited desert, and most of the population resides along the Nile River, which runs the length of the country from south to north. Natural resources include petroleum, natural gas, iron ore, manganese, limestone, and zinc. Agriculture and industry each account for roughly one quarter of Egypt's gross domestic product (GDP) and the services sector makes up the rest, with tourism being an especially important part of the Egyptian economy. Egypt has a trade deficit ratio of 2:1. The country receives substantial foreign aid from the United States, especially after it signed the 1977 Camp David accord with Israel, as well as from the European Union. Through the final years of the 20th century and the beginning of the 21st century, unemployment in the country has hovered between 11% and 12% of the adult population.

Arabic is the official language of Egypt, with English and French understood by many of the upper classes. Approximately 95% of the population is Muslim, and most of the rest are Coptic Christians. Just over half of the population is literate, with the literacy rate for women being lower than that for men. Generally thought of as a developing country, Egypt has been identified as one of several "semiperipheral" nations in the trichotomous approach of world-system theory (McPhail, 2002, p. 17). In world-system terminology, the semiperipheral designation is given to countries that fall between the most highly developed core nations of the United States, Canada, Japan, Australia, New Zealand,

Israel, and the countries of the European Union and peripheral nations, which are the least developed parts of the world, including most of Africa and Latin America and several countries in Asia and the former Soviet Union.

HISTORY AND DEVELOPMENT OF THE COUNTRY AND THE PROFESSION

Although Egypt has a fascinating and documented past extending back 6,000 years, there is little in the history of ancient Egypt that is relevant to modern public relations. Examples of what might be considered the very first forms of agricultural communication can be traced to Egyptian pharaohs (Al-Tohami & Al-Dakoki, 1980) and Alanazi (1996) claimed that something similar to the press-agentry model was practiced as early as 2000 BC in the region that is now Egypt. But clearly, the link between activities in those times and contemporary public relations is not direct. Instead, events and conditions of the last 2 centuries are more important to understanding the practices encompassing, and challenges to the further growth of, the public relations profession in Egypt and will receive the most attention in this chapter.

Beginning in 1798 when the armies of Napoleon invaded Egypt and continuing until the Revolution of 1952, Egypt was intermittently under French control and later under English control. Although this period also included the rule of Mohammed Ali and an era of royal importance under King Fouad and King Farouk early in the 20th century, certain Western influences on Egyptian culture, commerce, and thinking took root during European rule (Botman, 1998; Dykstra, 1998).

By the start of World War I and through World War II, Egypt was essentially a part of the British Empire, with economic and political reliance on Great Britain and British interests having priority in much of what took place in the country. As the role of Britain in Egyptian affairs increased during this period, so did local resentment of such colonialism (Jankowski, 2000). These feelings resulted in a nationalist movement, calls for the expulsion of the British presence, a series of anti-British riots, and a military revolution in 1952 under the command of Gamal Abdel Nasser. Nasser ruled as the president of Egypt until his death in 1970 (Vatikiotis, 1991).

In the half century since the revolution and declaration of independence, Egypt has grown into a position of leadership in the Arab world. During these years, the country has had three presidents, Nasser (1956–1970), Anwar Sadat (1970–1981), and Hosni Mubarak (1981–present), each facing different challenges and concerns, each endorsing different directions and policies, and each in turn having different impacts on the development of public relations in Egypt. Note that all three of Egypt's presidents in the modern era have military backgrounds.

Under Nasser, Egypt adopted a socialist but repressive system of government. Foreign businesses were either expelled or their assets seized, and major industries were nationalized. Political opposition was not tolerated, and numerous cases have been recorded of journalists and opponents being tortured, jailed, or even executed. Political parties, including the Muslim Brotherhood, which had supported Nasser's original coup, were outlawed and thousands of dissidents were imprisoned. During most of the Nasser administration, Egypt was aligned with the Soviet Union. Nasser was a strong proponent of pan-Arabism, and for a brief period from 1958 to 1961, the country was joined with Syria to form the United Arab Republic.

Major accomplishments and activities during Gamal Abdel Nasser's reign as president included taking control of the Suez Canal shortly after the Revolution, the building of the Aswan Dam on the Nile and the resulting changes in electrification and agricultural practices; the United Nations supported military victory over Israel, France, and Britain in 1956; and the rather humiliating defeat by Israel in the Six Day War of 1967. On the whole, however, Nasser's rule was a dictatorship that did little to establish an environment where open expression and the democratic principles necessary for two-way flow of information might flourish. As far as the public relations profession is concerned, his legacy is one that stifled the growth of an open communication system thus limiting the profession principally to propaganda efforts by the government.

When Nasser died in 1970, he was succeeded by his Vice President, Anwar Sadat, who had joined Nasser during the revolution. Under Sadat, Egypt began to liberalize both politically and economically, at least initially. In the early years of Sadat's presidency, many of those imprisoned for political reasons during Nasser's rule were released and restrictions on the formation of political parties were eased. Censorship was reduced for a short span of time, and some amount of press freedom was restored. As will be discussed, in 1977, there was a clampdown on this openness.

On the economic front, Sadat was more open to foreign investment and private sector development than nationalist Nasser. Many in Egypt's upper classes thrived during this period, but conditions for much of Egypt's population did not improve. In fact, ordinary Egyptians suffered due to inflation and other factors related to this openness. In 1977, when government food subsidies were reduced, riots occurred throughout the country prompting the government to quickly reinstate them (Jankowski, 2000).

As a diplomat, Anwar Sadat is certainly best known for the Camp David peace agreement he signed with Israel in 1977. Although international reaction to this move was largely favorable, opinion at home and in the rest of the Arab world was less enthusiastic and hostile among a section of the Egyptian populace. In fact, the backlash among those who disagreed with this move was so great that many of the domestic reforms and moves toward pluralism that Sadat had put in place were reversed. New regulations were reinstated to restrict government criticism and reduced openness and the free flow of information that had characterized the early Sadat years. The combination of dissatisfaction with the poor economic conditions and with the peace accord with arch enemy Israel led to increased unrest in Egypt. This resulted in the rise of a strong Islamist movement and further government crackdowns on open expression and activities deemed threatening to the regime. In 1981, Anwar Sadat was assassinated by a member of the Islamic Jihad, one of the groups targeted by the restrictions put in place during Sadat's final years as president.

In terms of providing an environment conducive to the growth of the public relations profession, the Sadat era can be summarized as a time that offered much promise at the beginning but concluded with repression and limits on expression and activism only slightly less severe than under Nasser. Efforts to establish a private sector economy, encourage open expression, and shifting alliance with the Soviet Union toward the United States and the democratic West would seem like a good start toward a system of democracy, respect of public opinion, and media freedom conducive for modern public relations. But in the end, the Sadat administration reverted to methods of repression and restrictions familiar to Egyptians since their first days of independence.

For the 20 plus years since Sadat's assassination, Mohamed Hosni Mubarak has led Egypt as the country's president. Having served as vice president under Sadat, Mubarak continued the policies of that administration in the early years of his administration. Over time, however, he has put his own mark on Egypt, both domestically and in the global community.

The Mubarak era has seen Egypt's reemergence as a force within the Arab world. After losing favor among much of the region as a result of Sadat's peace with Israel, including the severing of diplomatic relations with most Arab countries and expulsion from the League of Arab States (LAS), Egypt under Mubarak was readmitted to the LAS in 1989, and Cairo currently serves as the headquarters of the LAS. Egypt also took a leadership role among countries of the Middle East in siding with the West during the Gulf War and has led recent regional efforts against terrorism.

Internally, Egypt has faced a variety of issues and opportunities during Mubarak's rule. There has been much discussion and some effort toward further privatizing the economy and introducing competition into industries handled exclusively by the public sector since Egypt's independence. The government has faced varying pressures and threats from Islamist groups and has reacted in ways that have succeeded at times and have brought problems during others. Because it is the Mubarak administration that is leading Egypt into the 21st century, and under whose rule the public relations industry must operate, the following sections concentrate on Egypt under Mubarak. In addition, this chapter focuses on the status of the profession and implications on the profession by environmental factors such as infrastructure, culture, and media systems.

THE EGYPTIAN PUBLIC RELATIONS INDUSTRY

The term *public relations* is familiar to most Egyptians, and jobs bearing that title have existed since privatization became a priority during the last years of the 20th century. However, by Western definitions, the field is rather misunderstood in Egypt and is far less developed than it is in the West or in more progressive parts of the Middle East, such as Lebanon and the United Arab Emirates (Lussier, 2002). In Egypt, public relations is often synonymous with hospitality or customer relations. The industry that is probably most associated with public relations jobs is the service industry. Hotels employ public relations directors responsible for guest services such as arranging airport transportation, hosting dignitaries, and generally putting on a "smiling and friendly face" on behalf of the organization.

There is also a lack of understanding of the parameters of the public relations profession, and confusion exists among Egyptian organizations with regard to the distinctions between public relations, advertising, and marketing (Zaklama, 2001). Most organizations consider sales to be the primary goal of public relations, and there is little interest in or patience for programs or tactics that do not directly contribute to sales. By one estimate, of those individuals who consider themselves part of the public relations business in Egypt, only about 10% are skilled professionals who have a full understanding of the profession in a Western sense (Spiers, 1991). The rest are essentially sales agents of one form or another.

The Egyptian mass media reflect and reinforce the blending of public relations with marketing by linking publicity and news coverage with advertising expenditures. For example, it is accepted practice in Egypt for media use of information contained in news releases and other publicity materials to be contingent on the purchase of advertising space or time. Thus, completely contrary to Western concepts and expectations, publicity truly is paid for in Egypt. An organization either agrees to buy a certain amount of advertising from the publication involved or pays outright for publishing a press release because of the credibility that comes from the information being covered as a news item. Spiers (1991) cited several examples in which media organizations published news stories referring generically to "a pharmaceutical firm" or "a soft drink company" because the organizations involved refused to pay for the privilege of having their company mentioned by name.

The media relations function of public relations professionals in Egypt has traditionally been rather weak and ineffective as well. In part, this is because of the insistence by media gatekeepers that they be compensated for granting access to their audience. It is also an indication of the lack of respect for the profession and the low power public relations practitioners have in deciding their strategies and tactics in most organizations. In addition, it also is probably linked to the fact that most Egyptian public relations practitioners are not considered to be good sources of information by those in the media. As described by one journalist (quoted in Lussier, 2002), "PR departments in Egypt have no power to answer questions on their own. They always have to go back to their superior. They can take your question, and they'll get back to you, but it usually takes days or weeks. It's just not useful for a journalist" (p. 41). Spiers (1991) suggested that problems with media relations are further compounded by the fact that many Egyptian journalists do not work from a permanent office and, therefore, it is difficult to contact them.

Other public relations specialties such as investor relations, sponsorship arrangements, event management, crisis management, and government relations are occasionally found among Egyptian organizations. Lobbying is an underdeveloped tool (Lussier, 2002); as stated earlier, few Egyptian organizations make distinctions between the roles and objectives of public relations and marketing.

Taking these points into account, it is not surprising that the dominant coalitions in most organizations have traditionally not included public relations specialists and, therefore, do not have a very high regard for the contributions that public relations can make to organizational effectiveness. Industry analysts cite many reasons for the underdevelopment of the public relations profession in Egypt and the failure to grasp its purpose and potential. Khorasanizadeh (2001) pointed to the fact that because media and market systems have traditionally involved little or no competition, there has never really been a need for public relations. Stones (1994) proposed that there is a history of government policies and business philosophy in Egypt that actually discourages the sharing of information.

A further factor that likely contributes to the current low status of public relations in Egypt is the lack of formal training in modern theory and practice. Those national universities that include public relations in their curricula generally limit it to a single course in either business or communications departments. At the American University in Cairo, public relations courses are included in an Integrated Marketing Communication specialization. Not surprising, given several of the points already raised, most Egyptian public relations professionals have backgrounds in marketing rather than journalism or any communication area of expertise.

There are some signs, however, of advances in the understanding and sophistication of public relations in Egypt. Zaklama (2001) claimed that a new "mindset" has emerged among leading Egyptian organizations since the last years of the 20th century. The author gave examples of cases in which more sophisticated public relations strategies and techniques have been tried in recent years. These include the use of two-way communication principles by the Egyptian government and the tourism industry in developing public relations approaches in the wake of terrorism incidents in the late 90s and the launching of a successful telecommunications industry during that same period. Recognition that most organizations are likely to have multiple publics each requiring individual attention is also becoming more common, and there is evidence that public relations may finally be emerging as a function distinct from marketing.

As private enterprise continues to increase in Egypt, and as multinational corporations continue to enter the market, there is reason to expect that the worldview that has led to recent advances in the field will continue to spread. International public relations firms, including Brodeur Worldwide, Hill and Knowlton, and Weber Shandwick, have entered into affiliation agreements with local agencies in Cairo. Newly privatized Egyptian businesses in a range of sectors have set up in-house operations intended to treat public relations as something more than just a marketing tool. In their study of the global diffusion of the top 10 international public relations firms, Sriramesh and Verčič (2002) classified Egypt as an emerging nation in terms of factors related to the development of global public relations.

The founding of the Arab Public Relations Society as a modern trade organization has added to the credibility of the profession in Egypt. In October 2002, Egypt hosted the annual conference of the International Public Relations Association, further establishing public relations among Egyptian businesses and decision makers. However, there are numerous obstacles and problems to be dealt with before public relations is fully accepted as an effective and integral organizational function in Egypt. But there seems to be reason for optimism as the country's economic and social systems evolve in the coming years.

INFRASTRUCTURE OF EGYPT

Certain characteristics of Egyptian society and the Egyptian system of government should be recognized as restraints and obstructions to international public relations activities. An understanding of the backgrounds involved and factors related to circumstances faced in dealing with bureaucracies, courts, regulators, and institutions can do much to lessen the barriers faced and to facilitate effective planning of public relations efforts in Egypt. As a country with a developing economy and an important role in regional and global politics, there are opportunities for scholars and practitioners familiar with Egyptian idiosyncrasies to utilize this knowledge to help build a theory of international public relations in addition to considering strategies for conducting effective public relations within Egypt.

Political Structure

Under the constitution passed in 1971, Egypt has a Republican form of government and, in theory, a limited democratic system. The constitution calls for the division of authority among the executive, legislative, and judicial branches. In reality, however, it is the president who wields the most power and who appoints key officials to serve in all areas of government. Islam is the official state religion, and at least indirectly, it guides the direction of most decisions and policies.

For administrative purposes, Egypt is divided into 26 governorates, each with a governor who is appointed by the president. But the system is actually quite centralized, with control ultimately resting with the national government in Cairo. In a public relations sense, the little bit of lobbying that goes on in Egypt is usually concentrated in Cairo.

The legislative branch of Egypt's government consists of two bodies, the People's Assembly of at least 350 members and the smaller Shura Advisory Council. Both the People's Assembly and the Shura Advisory Council are made up of some elected individuals and some appointed by the president.

The concept of political parties and the notions of compromise and exchange, crucial to most democracies and assumed in Western public relations models, are quite limited in Egypt. All political parties must be approved by the government. Although ballots usually include candidates from multiple parties, a single ruling party, the National Democratic Party (NDP), has control of the presidency as well as of both legislative chambers in contemporary Egypt. Since its establishment by Sadat in 1978, the NDP has held anywhere from 70% to 90% of the People's Assembly and Shura Advisory Council, and it is common for those elected as Independents to join the NDP upon taking office. Charges of electoral fraud, corruption, and intimidation are fairly common in Egyptian politics (*Run-Up to Shura*, 2001).

At the executive level, the process of selecting a president involves nomination and approval within the People's Assembly, followed by election in the form of a popular referendum. The term of office is 6 years, with no term limits. In 1999, Hosni Mubarak was elected to his fourth consecutive term, winning 94% support as the only candidate named on the ballot.

The dominant party system that results from this process, with the president designating a portion of the legislature and the legislature in turn nominating the president, is characteristic of many former third-world countries. These emerging democracies commonly end up with power weighted toward the presidency and a government that combines elements of authoritarianism with those of genuine democratic rule. Although there is a place for some limited form of public relations in such a setting, true democracy, with participation and attention to public opinion, has yet to be fully developed in Egypt.

A further indication of the central role of the president in Egyptian government is his executive authority to select (and to dismiss) the country's prime minister, vice-president(s), and the Council of Ministers in charge of overseeing various government responsibilities, industries, and areas of concern. Of these cabinet-level positions, the Ministry of Information is particularly relevant for public relations interests, overseeing the country's media system and serving as the public relations arm of the Egyptian government in a public information sense.

Economic Development

Egypt has the second largest economy in the Arab world, behind only Saudi Arabia. It is a relatively diversified economic system, with oil, tourism, and revenue from the Suez Canal accounting for significant portions of the country's GDP. Agricultural exports and remittances from expatriate Egyptians working abroad also contribute a sizable amount to the economy, as does the $3 billion in foreign aid that Egypt receives annually, most coming from the United States. There is also a substantial hidden economy in Egypt (Roy, 1992), consisting of traditionally undocumented and quasi-illegal activities in several different sectors.

The structure of Egypt's economy has undergone important changes since the days of total nationalism under Gamal Abdel Nasser. It has evolved from the centralized state economy of those times to a system that has much more of a place for private enterprise and, at least in theory, represents a much more fertile setting for the growth of modern public relations practices. Changing from a socialist to a market economy is by no means an easy process, and the country has faced many problems during this period, some of which continue today.

The concept of privatization of large chunks of the economy began receiving lip service in Egypt as part of the open door policy of Anwar Sadat in the 1970s (Gomaa, 1996). It has been expanded as a priority of the Mubarak administration and continues as probably the single most major issue in Egypt's economy in the 2000s. The approach to privatization in Egypt has varied from industry to industry and has evolved over time. In some cases, full ownership of public companies has been sold to private investors, both Egyptian and foreign. In others, only a percentage, often a low percentage, has been sold to private ownership. The range of privatized industries includes banking, construction, hotels, retailing, shipping, and tourism. The government plans to sell additional government-owned businesses working toward the goal of an economy that is 80% privately held by the first years of the 21st century (B. Smith, 1999). This has encouraged a stronger stock market in Egypt.

The public sector in Egypt has a reputation for not being very efficient, and in certain industries, efforts to privatize have been met with low levels of interest among profit-seeking investors. However, privatized industries have seen dramatic improvements in management and marketing (P. Smith, 1999). This appears to bode well for the public relations industry whose value is more likely to be recognized by new organizational leaders.

As might be expected of any economy undergoing radical change from state to market control, there are certain issues and problems that need to be worked out in Egypt. One of these is the increasingly important issue of labor practices and unemployment. Even with the movement toward privatization, over one quarter of Egypt's workforce remains on government payroll, and there are concerns about shifting this large portion of the working population. There are also worries that even a healthy private economy may have trouble supporting Egypt's ever-increasing supply of labor, which looks to increase at a rate of one-half million people per year at least through the first decade of the new century.

Another economic factor of note is the position of small businesses in Egypt. Over 99% of the country's private enterprises have fewer than 50 employees, and the majority have fewer than 10 ("Credit Where," 1999). In addition, most entrepreneurs do not own their own property. This has resulted in a system in which business owners are not able to take advantage of economies of scale and lack collateral for expanding and improving their operations. In facing what amounts to a near daily struggle to remain solvent, these small businesses may consider public relations something of an unaffordable luxury. If the profession is to further establish itself in Egypt, this issue needs to be addressed.

Egyptian businesses of all sizes operate in an economic environment that remains overly bureaucratic and somewhat protectionist in its outlook. Tariffs on imported products average 15%, among the highest in the world. Licenses, permits, taxes, and regulatory rituals can be extremely frustrating, and these laws often make little sense to the outsider. What results is a situation that does little to encourage outside investment in the Egyptian economy.

Legal System

Whereas the Egyptian government and economic systems have changed in ways that are seemingly favorable to the growth of modern public relations, the judicial system has been less progressive. Relying on a combination of Islamic, Ottoman, French, British, and Soviet laws, along with presidential decrees and special "emergency laws" that are passed with some regularity, the Egyptian legal system is often contradictory and inefficient. As a result, it is not uncommon for the simplest of legal contentions to become entangled in the courts for 10 years or more. Judges commonly consider as many as 1,000 cases a day, and postponements are the rule rather than the exception.

The Supreme Constitutional Court is the highest body of the Egyptian legal system, and it oversees issues related to the constitution and resolves cases that have been passed up from lower courts. Beyond that, the Egyptian judiciary consists of two principal branches, the Courts of General Jurisdiction and the Administrative Courts System, each with a rather complex, if not always logical, group of subcourts. One writer characterized the Egyptian system of laws and regulations as "enmeshed in their ancient cobwebs" and described a legal bureaucracy in which it can take 77 separate procedures in 31 different government offices just to register property (B. Smith, 1999, p. 4)!

Although calls for reform are fairly common and blame for the state of Egypt's legal system is often directed at the dominance of the executive branch over the legislature and the judiciary, the current structure is entrenched and is not likely to be overhauled anytime soon. Practitioners and scholars of public relations must recognize that the system they will encounter in Egypt is unlike that of most Western countries. Planners should take into account the delays and inefficiencies characteristic of Egyptian courts and should be aware of the thick bureaucracy involved.

Level of Activism

The subject of activism is a sensitive one in Egypt. Although the country's constitution allows certain rights and protections for all citizens, there is also a history of intolerance and severity in controlling and punishing dissidents. Many of the activities that would be considered legitimate activism in Western democracies are not allowed in Egypt. These prohibitions and their enforcement tend to vary depending on the area or issue at hand. For public relations purposes, it is important to understand the types of issues over which activism is likely to be tolerated as well as the varying enforcement of curbs against activism.

Although restrictions on social and activist movements may seem to be advantageous to businesses fearing activist reaction to their policies or practices, such restrictions also contribute to an environment that stifles expression and promotes repression of the environment as a whole. The result is a situation in which an organization may not have to worry much about activists but may worry about the limited options for involvement with issues of interest to it (issues management).

Among the realms of activism particularly constrained in Egypt are what some would consider basic civil rights of expression, assembly, and association. Reports from Amnesty International (Egypt: Amnesty International, 2002), Human Rights Watch (Human Rights Watch, 2002), and the United States State Department ("Country Reports," 2002) all are critical of the Egyptian government for its heavy-handed methods of dealing with activism. These include closing down newspapers, banning books, outlawing public demonstrations, taking measures to silence trade union representatives and other activists, and placing severe limits on Islamist political activity. Recent examples of government infringement that have attracted international attention include the jailing of a noted sociologist for research work deemed to be "undermining the dignity of the state" (Del Castillo, 2001, p. 53), alleged discrimination against Coptic Christians (Gauch, 1995) and homosexuals (Hammer, 2002), a respected writer being ordered to divorce her husband for making statements considered anti-Islamic (Gauch, 2001), and the passing of a law that places nongovernmental organizations under state control (Mekay, 2000).

However, there are also areas in which activism has been tolerated and is successful in accomplishing various objectives. Feminist groups have used activist methods in campaigns to stem the practice of female circumcision in Egypt (El-Gibaly, Ibrahim, Mensch, & Clark, 2002). Consumer boycotts have become an accepted and widely employed tool for expressing disapproval of an organization's actions (Howeidy, 2001) or the policies of foreign governments (Hanafi, 2002). Thus, although the potential for activism exists in Egypt, public relations planners would do well to recognize that it depends very much on the particular situation, topic, and publics involved.

EGYPTIAN CULTURE

The people of Egypt come from a variety of ethnic and historic subcultures including the more African Nubians of the south, the nomadic Bedouins, and Berber descendents in the western desert. Despite this diversity in background, Egypt has a rich and deep national culture, which most subgroups are proud to share. Egyptian culture is conservative and among the most diverse in the Arab world.

Probably the two characteristics that best distinguish Egyptian culture are the impor-tance of family and the central role of religion. Nearly all aspects of life in Egypt revolve around the immediate and extended family, with marriage, children, and kinship hav-ing particular priorities in all social, educational, recreational, and work-related matters. Women are generally responsible for child care and maintaining the family household, whereas men are expected to provide full financial support, even if that entails working multiple jobs or temporarily separating from the family and moving outside of Egypt to earn a sufficient income (Haikal, 1993).

The place of religion, primarily Islam but also Christianity for the Coptic minority, is so important that it is hard to separate it from basic Egyptian culture. Both Muslims and Christians are very religious people in Egypt. Daily life involves a routine of prayer and devotion to the tenets of one's beliefs; even in the noisy city of Cairo, the broadcast sermons and praying from neighborhood mosques and the ringing of church bells are heard as a constant part of the background. Religious holidays are major celebrations in Egypt, with special importance given to the 1-month-long holy period of Ramadan, a time in which Muslims fast every day during daylight hours and indulge in a daily *iftar* meal at sunset. Ramadan is also a time for charity, with mosques, community groups, and even Christian churches often sponsoring *iftars* for the poor, neighbors or employees, and others. Some more astute organizations have begun to recognize the spirit and meaning of such activities in Egypt and include *iftars* and Ramadan festivities as part of their strategies for dealing with various publics. Ramadan is also the prime season for advertising campaigns in Egypt, as television audiences during this season are more than twice as large as during the rest of the year (Keenan & Yeni, 2002).

In terms of Egypt's dimensions of culture suggested by Hofstede (1980, 1998), little formal study has been done. It appears to a keen observer that the country is stratified socially, it tends toward masculinity and collectivism, it uses high-context communication in most settings, and deference to authority is expected in both social and business contexts.

To elaborate briefly on these points, the stratification of Egyptian society is distinct in terms of education, income, and general standard of living. Gaps between the haves and the have-nots are great and, interestingly, are mostly accepted by both groups. This may be due in part to religious beliefs and the Arabic phrase, "en shah Allah," meaning basically that things are as God meant (willed) them to be.

There is an increasingly large middle class in Egypt, but social mobility is not a defining quality of the culture. Public relations programs based on individual or group mobility motives that might work in the West will not necessarily succeed in Egypt, and it is probably more important for planners to consider the social class of their target publics in Egypt than it is in most other parts of the world.

On the dimension of individualism–collectivism, Egyptian culture values the society and the family over the individual. This collectivism is evident in the rabid patriotism of most Egyptians, the level of charity to help others (again influenced by Islam's teachings), and even in common Cairo street scenes and village settings where citizens cooperate toward a common group goal.

Egypt fits the profile of a masculine culture as laid out by Hofstede (1998)—men are generally assertive, and women are expected to be modest—and there are clear distinc-tions between the roles and expectations of genders. The masculine nature of the culture runs deep, with male children being a special source of pride in most families. Certain oc-cupations, including most of the professions, senior-level management, and high-ranking government and church positions, continue to be almost exclusively the domain of men. In addition, Egyptian laws include elements that discriminate between women and men.

As with most collectivist societies, in Egypt, communication tends to be high in context; people share a wider range of cultural understandings and symbols than in individualistic societies and take more meaning from certain settings and communicators. Combined with the high power distance or deference for authority found in Egypt, the culture is one in which people sort of know their place in a way that might seem inappropriate and unfair to outsiders, especially those from cultures on the other end of the context–power distance continuum.

Both within an organization and for dealing with external publics, it is crucial that public relations practitioners consider these and other cultural factors. It is also important for those whose interest is more scholarly to recognize the characteristics and structure of Egyptian culture in carrying out research on public relations in the country. Unless one is sensitive to the particular nature of the culture and to the interaction of factors such as those discussed here, professional and academic ventures are not likely to have much success. With such sensitivity, the Egyptian culture is one in which there are rich opportunities for public relations work and study.

MEDIA IN EGYPT

The beginnings of modern mass media in Egypt date from 1798, when Napoleon Bonaparte established the first mass circulation newspaper in Alexandria (Dabbous, 1994). Today, the Egyptian press includes national daily and weekly papers and regional publications centered in the larger cities. Magazines have evolved from simple tabloids to a range of full-color, glossy publications to be found on the nation's newsstands in the early years of the 21st century. A limited selection of foreign newspapers and magazines is also available in the country though they tend to be a little outdated by the time they reach Egyptian audiences, especially in the case of foreign dailies.

Radio was introduced in Egypt in 1926 and passed through a stage under Nasser as an important propaganda tool for nationalization and for pan-Arab causes. In contemporary Egypt, AM and FM radio stations offer a full array of programming formats. In 1960, the Radio Corporation of America assisted the Egyptian government in setting up a television system (Gher & Amin, 1999). As of 2002, there are two national broadcast television stations and seven stations with local or regional transmission. There is also one cable television system operating in Cairo, and over 1 million Egyptian households have access to satellite television (Elghawaby, 2000).

As expected, most Egyptian media are in Arabic. There is a daily newspaper and a weekly newspaper in English, and daily newspaper in French. There are also a number of weekly and monthly magazines in English. One of Egypt's television stations, Nile TV, broadcasts both in English and French, and there are several radio stations that have foreign language programming at least part of the day.

Media Control

Since the time of Nasser, Egyptian media have been state-owned or state controlled. The privatization of Egypt's economy has not really included the mass media industry, although some have suggested that the process will just be slower as far as the media are concerned (Napoli, Amin, & Napoli, 1995). With new media such as the Internet and satellite television making inroads, the government is less able to maintain control over what Egyptians view. The result has been a limited loosening of controls, with some private, advertising revenue-supported, publications being permitted. This is true especially among the relatively small circulation English language magazines. Private investment has also been permitted in the operation of Egyptian cable television (Boyd, 1999), and licenses have been granted to private television channels on the government-owned satellite, NileSat (Wahby, 2002).

Despite such developments, Egyptian media remain under government control for the most part. Rugh (1987) described the Egyptian media system as an example of what he called the "mobilization" (p. 31) model of government control, in which the state oversees all media, dictates policy and content, hires and fires media personnel, and exercises strict censorship standards.

The three largest, and most influential, newspapers in Egypt, *Al-Ahram, Al-Akhbar*, and *Al-Gomuhuria*, all remain government owned, as do the English and French language dailies, the primary regional papers, and the country's radio and television stations. In the print segment, an "opposition press" exists but is heavily regulated through laws, taxes, and licensing procedures. Publications that go too far in opposing the government or run content deemed inappropriate to religious and cultural norms are summarily shut down.

In cases when Egyptian media are not owned outright by the government, control is maintained by indirect means such as the supply of newsprint and the distribution of publications, which are under government control. Advertising is also a means of government power in that at least for the print media, the largest advertising spenders are traditionally public sector enterprises (under government control), and the largest advertising agencies in the country are government owned.

The government agency that oversees the ownership, control, and regulation of all media in Egypt is the Ministry of Information. The Egyptian Television and Radio Union, within the Ministry of Information, is responsible for planning, decisions, and implementation of policies related to the broadcast media.

Media Outreach

There are certain factors that should be taken into account in targeting different segments of the Egyptian population, but with proper planning and familiarity with the country, all can be reached through one medium or another. The characteristics and advantages inherent in different media are of course important in public relations work, but in some cases they must be sacrificed in Egypt due to circumstances and obstacles that limit media options for reaching particular groups.

The major national newspapers in Egypt are distributed throughout the country. The largest of these, *Al-Ahram*, has a circulation of over 1 million, and the combined circulation of all Egyptian papers is around 3 million (Gher & Amin, 1999). It is important to recognize, however, that illiteracy remains a problem in Egypt, especially in areas outside the population centers of Cairo and Alexandria. The fact is, that with nearly half of the country's population unable to read, newspaper readership is naturally low, as stressed in chapter 1 of this book. Currently, the low rate of literacy is a priority of the Egyptian government and various nongovernmental organizations. As a result, there is reason to hope that as the portion of the population with reading skills increases, so will the reach of the country's newspapers.

Magazines face the same literacy dilemma as newspapers, and with their typically higher cover price, they also have an audience size that is limited by basic economic affordability in some cases. Although no single Egyptian magazine has a very large circulation, magazines do a good job of reaching narrow audience niches. Magazines specializing in sports, entertainment, religion, women's topics, and other specialized areas are popular among different segments. Distributed through the same *Al-Ahram* newsstand system as Egyptian newspapers, major magazine titles are available throughout the country.

The electronic media offer the greatest opportunity for reaching large audiences and all segments of Egyptian society. Especially with the national radio and television stations, broadcast disseminated messages can be expected to cross boundaries of literacy and socioeconomic status. At the dawn of the 21st century, nearly all Egyptian households have both radio and television receivers, and in areas where television penetration to individual households is low, there is a tradition of communal viewing in neighborhood cafes or village coffee shops. The growth of satellite television among the upper and middle classes has diverted some of the audience that was recently held by domestic channels (Hafez, 2001), but the popularity of certain Egyptian programs and serials and the reputation of special Ramadan programming continues to attract substantial viewership among all classes of society and is even exported and popular throughout the Middle East.

A somewhat unique aspect of Egyptian media outreach involves a category that Dabbous (1994) referred to as "external media services" (p. 70). These include a variety of government-produced radio programs aired outside of the country, the Nile TV channel aimed at foreign audiences, and international distribution of *Al-Ahram* newspaper. Public relations implications of such media include the potential ability to reach expatriate Egyptian publics and the fact that certain messages and media content may "bleed" beyond national borders.

Media Access

The predominant government control over Egyptian media has some obvious impact on the access afforded to those media. One of these is that government organizations and causes have a special advantage in gaining access. By extension, organizations who toe the government line are also much more likely to be permitted access than those with no shared interests or those who oppose the government in some way. Considering this point, government relations practices can be especially important in Egypt; at some level, an overlap of government and media relations should probably be taken into account.

An additional point concerning access to Egyptian media is the confusion between publicity and advertising described earlier in this chapter. As long as it is accepted practice to require either the purchase of advertising or direct payment to the media for media access via releases and other methods, Western conceptions of public relations' role in acquiring media space or time will bear no relation to reality in Egypt. Decisions ought to be made early in public relations planning as to whether an organization is willing to pay for access or will seek other ways through media gatekeepers in Egypt.

Less direct means of gaining media access include letters to the editor, talk shows, audience call-in shows on radio or television, and program-length television infomercials, although the scale and acceptability of such methods are restricted and those involving controversial topics are likely to be heavily censored. For addressing upscale publics composed of Internet users, satellite subscribers, or those exposed to foreign media, there may also be occasions when media strategies might choose to circumvent Egyptian media entirely if access is overly problematic.

In conclusion, the areas of media outreach and media access are closely tied to media control in Egypt. Although the future may see changes in the structure and flexibility of Egyptian media systems, the reality of things now is that the government is all powerful in allowing access and determining who and what will be included in the country's media. Public relations professionals would do well see this as a starting point for planning work to achieve media access.

Considering the current state of factors covered here and the ongoing changes in Egyptian society and business practices, there is reason to think the public relations profession will continue to grow in Egypt. Some obstructions will remain that may constrain this growth, and it is not likely that Egyptian public relations will ever mirror the Western model completely. But as the economy continues to move in the direction of privatization and as the government, Egyptian culture, and the media become more welcoming of the conditions that accompany the privatization, public relations will find an environment where it is increasingly welcome and necessary. In the years ahead, Egypt will offer regular opportunities for public relations consultants to help develop the public relations industry in Egypt and for scholars to study the profession and its development and train future professionals.

CASE STUDY: COCA-COLA EGYPT

Understandably, soft drinks are quite popular in Egypt. The country's dry, hot climate is certainly responsible for their basic appeal. But Egyptians are also notorious for having a sweet tooth. In addition, Islam's prohibition of alcoholic drinks makes soft drinks the beverage type of choice for social gatherings and celebrations.

There are several local soft drink brands on the market, but, like almost everywhere else in the world, the leading sellers are Coca-Cola ® and Pepsi Cola. However, unlike most other countries, in Egypt, Pepsi has always had a larger market share than Coke. In fact Egyptians refer to any soft drink generically as a *Pepsi* (or with colloquial Egyptian pronunciation, as a *Bebsi*) in the same way the term *Coke* is sometimes used to include any and all soft drinks in the United States.

Coca-Cola has been available in Egypt since 1945, but it was nationalized under Nasser and was produced by government-owned bottling plants until 1994 when the Coca-Cola Bottling Companies of Egypt was formed as part of the country's privatization policy. Since then, the company has faced a number of obstacles, including the already established Pepsi Cola as a privatized soft drink bottler in Egypt, occasional consumer boycotts with the identification of the product as a symbol of American imperialism, and a general perception in the Arab world that "Coke is for Jews; Pepsi is for Arabs" (Mikkelson, 1999). But with updated production plants, improved distribution and marketing, and a modern approach to public relations, Coke has made substantial inroads to the point where the brand's current market share is nearly equal to that of Pepsi.

Since its privatization, Coca-Cola Egypt's public relations activities have focused on community service and what most would consider a two-way symmetrical philosophy of emphasizing feedback through research of relevant publics and a recognition that the company must make certain adjustments in its Egyptian operations. Specific efforts have included an employee literacy program that has produced a 100% literacy rate among its 8,000 workers; campaigns in which a portion of all money earned from product sales goes to select charities in Egypt; and sponsorships and participation with nonprofit projects in the areas of education, health, youth sports, and the environment.

In 2000, the company was faced with a potentially devastating situation when a rumor spread through Egypt that Coca-Cola was anti-Islam. A charge was made that if the Coca-Cola script logo was viewed upside down and in a mirror, it read as "No Mohamed. No Mecca." Given the deep importance of religion in all areas of Egyptian life, the supposed message degrading Islam's prophet and the religion's holiest place caused outrage and an instant drop in sales of Coke products nearing almost 20%. Literature decrying the company and calls for its ouster from the country circulated in mosques, schools, and on the streets of cities and villages throughout Egypt. In certain jurisdictions, authorities ordered that all Coca-Cola signage and advertising be removed.

Coca-Cola Egypt's response to this rumor, whose original source was never determined, was immediate, culturally sensitive, and reasoned. The company requested to meet with Egypt's Grand Mufti Sheik Nasser Farid Wassel, the highest religious figure in the country, and also arranged for an official panel of Islamic scholars to consider the matter. Note that in meeting with the Grand Mufti, Coca-Cola's approach was less to plead their case than to seek the input and opinions of the respected religious leader. The convening of the scholarly panel was also done in conformity with tradition and established procedures of Islam.

The outcome of Coca-Cola Egypt's decision to involve local religious experts was that both the Grand Mufti and the group of scholars ruled there was no substance to the rumor of the Coke logo being anti-Islam. The Grand Mufti announced this opinion publicly and went on to scold those who were disseminating the rumor for behavior not befitting their religion and for risking the jobs and welfare of thousands of Egyptian Muslims employed by Coca-Cola.

In the aftermath of this crisis, Coca-Cola took the step of providing its sales force and delivery truck drivers with copies of the Grand Mufti's statement to display and distribute among businesses and customers. The company also followed up with an advertising campaign in which verses from the Holy Koran were included as part of their message, running alongside the recently controversial Coca-Cola logo. Within just a few weeks, Coke regained its prerumor sales level and was once again challenging Pepsi for leadership in the Egyptian soft drink market.

This case shows just how crucial it is for international public relations practitioners to understand what underlies the culture and structure of individual countries. Through no recognizable fault of their own, Coca-Cola had to face perhaps the most serious accusation any company can endure in an Islamic nation. By realizing the severity of the situation and by working with the country's religious leaders in a respectful and cooperative manner, Coca-Cola Egypt managed to avert serious damage and proclaim their innocence and contribution to Egypt's economy.

REFERENCES

Alanazi, A. (1996). Public relations in the Middle East: The case of Saudi Arabia. In H. M. Culbertson & N. Chen, (Eds.), *International public relations: A comparative analysis* (pp. 239–256). Mahwah, NJ: Lawrence Erlbaum Associates.

Al-Tohami, M., & Al-Dakoki, I. (1980). *Principles of public relations in the developing nations.* Beruit, Lebanon: Da Alama'arefa.

Botman, S. (1998). The liberal age, 1923–1952. In M. W. Daly (Ed.), *The Cambridge history of Egypt, 1798–1801* (pp. 285–308). Cambridge, England: Cambridge University Press.

Boyd, D. A. (1999). *Broadcasting in the Arab world: A survey of the electronic media in the Middle East.* Ames, IA: Iowa State University Press.

Country reports on human rights practices: Egypt. (2002, March 4). U.S. Department of State. www.usis.usemb.se/human/2001/neareast/egypt.html

Credit where credit is due. (1999, March 20). *The Economist,* pp. 9–10.

Dabbous, S. (1994). Egypt. In Y. R. Kamalipour & H. Mowlana (Eds.), *Mass media in the Middle East: A comprehensive handbook* (pp. 60–73). Westport, CT: Greenwood Press.

Del Castillo, D. (2001, April 13). Egypt puts a scholar, and academic freedom, on trial. *Chronicle of Higher Education*, pp. A53–A55.

Dykstra, D. (1998). The French occupation of Egypt, 1798–1801. In M. W. Daly (Ed.), *The Cambridge history of Egypt* (pp. 113–138). Cambridge, England: Cambridge University Press.

Elghawaby, A. (2000, March). Egypt: Satellite dishes abound. *World Press Review*, p. 11.

El-Gibaly, O., Ibrahim, B., Mensch, B. S., & Clark, W. H. (2002). The decline of female circumcision in Egypt: Evidence and interpretation. *Social Science and Medicine, 54*(2), 205–221.

Egypt: Amnesty International Report 2002. Retrieved August 12, 2002, from web.amnesty.org/web/ar2002. nsf/mde/egypt

Gauch, S. (1995, February 24). Egypt's Coptic Christians endure harassment by Muslims. *Christian Science Monitor*, p. 10.

Gauch, S. (2001, June 18). Egyptian feminist faces stiff penalty for statements deemed anti-Islamic. *Christian Science Monitor*, p. 9.

Gher, L. H., & Amin, H. Y. (1999). New and old access and ownership in the Arab world. *Gazette, 61*(1), 59–88.

Gomaa, S. S. (1996). The civil debate over privatization in Egypt: Conflicting interpretations and goals. In W. Badran & A. Wahby (Eds.), *Privatization in Egypt: The debate in the People's Assembly* (pp. 179–209). Cairo, Egypt: Center for Political Research and Studies.

Hafez, K. (2001). Mass media in the Middle East: Patterns of political and social change. In K. Hafez (Ed.), *Mass media, politics, and society in the Middle East* (pp. 1–20). Cresskill, NJ: Hampton Press.

Haikal, F. (1993). Family life in modern Egypt. In J. Malek (Ed.), *Egypt: Ancient culture, modern land* (pp. 172–181). Norman, OK: University of Oklahoma Press.

Hammer, J. (2002, February 16). *One man's tale*. Retrieved August 1, 2002 from www.msnbc.com/news/708876

Hanafi, K. (2002, July 22). Egypt: Protest groups boycott United States products. *Islam Online*. Retrieved August 1, 2002 from, www.corpwatch.org/news/PND.jsp?articleid=3148

Hofstede, G. H. (1980). *Culture's consequences: International differences in work-related values*. Beverly Hills, CA: Sage.

Hofstede, G. H. (1998). *Masculinity and femininity: The taboo dimension of national cultures*. Thousand Oaks, CA: Sage.

Human rights watch world report 2002: Egypt. Retrieved August 15, 2002, from www.hrw.org/wr2k2/ menaz.html

Howeidy, A. (2001, April 26–May 2). Secure a victory and move on. *Al-Ahram Weekly On-line*. Retrieved September, 2002 from, www.ahram.org.eg/weekly/2001/531/eg7.htm

Jankowski, J. P. (2000). *Egypt: A short history*. Oxford, England: Oneworld.

Keenan, K. L., & Yeni, S. (2002, August). *Ramadan advertising in Egypt: A content analysis with elaboration on select items*. Paper presented to the Association for Education in Journalism and Mass Communication Conference, Miami, FL.

Khorasanizadeh, F. (2001, April). Sector survey: Marketing and PR. *Business Today Egypt*, pp. 51–58.

Lussier, A. M. (2002, August). The wages of spin. *Business Monthly: The Journal the American Chamber of Commerce in Egypt*, (Vol. 18) 38–45.

McPhail, T. L. (2002). *Global communication: Theories, stakeholders, and trends*. Boston: Allyn & Bacon.

Mekay, E. (2000, September 11). Denial. *New Republic*, pp. 16–17.

Mikkelson, B. (1999). *Red, white, and Jew*. Retrieved January 26, 2003 from www.snopes.com/cokelore/ israel.asp

Napoli, J. J., Amin, H. Y., & Napoli, L. R. (1995). Privatization of the Egyptian media. *Journal of South Asian and Middle Eastern Studies, 18*(4), 39–57.

Roy, D. A. (1992). The hidden economy of Egypt. *Middle East Studies, 28*(4), 689–711.

Rugh, W. A. (1987). *The Arab press: News media and political process in the Arab world*. Syracuse, NY: Syracuse University Press.

Run-Up to Shura Council election marred by a wave of arrests. (2001, December 11). News release from Amnesty International. Retrieved August 1, 2002 from www.amnestyusa.org/news/2001/egypt 05152001.html

Smith, B. (1999, March 20). New and old. *The Economist*, pp. 1–4.

Smith, P. (1999, July/August). Egypt sells off. *Middle East*, pp. 33–36.

Spiers, P. (1991, September). It's not advertising: What is it? *Business Monthly: The Journal of the American Chamber of Commerce in Egypt*, (Vol. 7) 32–33.

Sriramesh, K., & Verčič, D. (2002). *The innovativeness–needs paradox and global public relations: Propositions on the need for international PR subsidies.* Paper presented to the International Communication Association Conference, Seoul, Korea.

Stones, L. (1994, June). The art of image building. *Business Monthly: The Journal of the American Chamber of Commerce in Egypt*, (Vol. 10) 27–30 .

Vatikiotis, P. J. (1991). *The history of Modern Egypt: From Mohamed Ali to Mubarak.* London: Weidenfeld and Nicolson.

Wahby, E. (2002, July). Satellite stations cross red lines. *Business Monthly: The Journal of the American Chamber of Commerce in Egypt*, (Vol. 18) 32.

Zaklama, L. (2001). Public relations Egyptian style. In M. Terterov (Ed.), *Doing business with Egypt*, (pp. 98–103) London: Kogan Page.

IV

EUROPE

19

The United Kingdom: Advances in Practice in a Restless Kingdom

Jon White

Jacquie L'Etang

Danny Moss

INTRODUCTION

The United Kingdom of Great Britain and Northern Ireland is made up of a number of islands off the northwest coast of mainland Europe, its almost 61 million people ruled by a constitutional monarch. The country, as a former imperial power, retains worldwide interests and influence, not least through its links with former dominions and colonies through the Commonwealth. Now, with the years of empire fading into the past, the country is in the process of restless change—re-establishing a role for itself in a world that is changing dramatically as a result of globalisation, and adapting to social and political developments within the country.

Public relations practice in the United Kingdom has made rapid progress in recent years:

- In 2005, the practice was given government recognition through the granting of a charter to the national Institute of Public Relations. The significance of this for the development of the practice will be discussed in more detail later in the chapter.

- Public relations in the UK is marked by debate—in the media, specialist publications and in meetings of practitioners—about the nature and value of the practice (White and Hobsbawm 2007). The debate shows a seriousness of approach to the issues raised by public relations practice, and to the requirements of best practice. In addition, the practice in the UK has been extensively studied in recent years, to assess its contribution to national economic development, and to the effective functioning of business and other organisations.

• Education for the practice is now well developed, setting standards for and raising questions about the practice.

In the UK, it would be true to say—as the late Sam Black, one of the UK's commentators on the development of public relations in the UK and worldwide, suggested—that while public relations practitioners can behave in a professional manner, public relations is not a profession, for reasons we return to later in the chapter. It is probably best described as a practice, but the now Chartered Institute of Public Relations refers to it as an industry and leaders of the "industry" regularly refer to it as a profession. Professional status remains, as we suggest later in the chapter, an aspiration.

    In common with other chapters in the handbook, this chapter examines the nature and status of public relations practice in the UK, and sets it in context, showing how the practice has developed, and how it is influenced by factors such as the country's infrastructure (social, political, economic, and developmental) and the culture within which the practice is carried on, mass media and activism.

    Historical sections in the chapter are based on extensive research in the archives of the Chartered Institute of Public Relations, located at Beccles, Norfolk, East Anglia, England, and oral history, both carried out by L'Etang (2004, 2006). Although an overall history of public relations in the UK context is presented, specialised histories of practice in the constituent parts of the United Kingdom—Scotland, England, Northern Ireland and Wales—remain to be written. However, at least one history of public relations in the Republic of Ireland (where Irish Gaelic and English are spoken) has been written (Colley, 1993).

    Public relations in the UK has evolved as a "London-centric" occupation and this pattern appears to have been established in the 1960s with the fast growth of consultancy practice. In this chapter, the key moments of occupational development are recorded, alongside some indication of the occupation's self-identity, culture and ideology of public relations—aspects that have received somewhat scant treatment in the public relations literature.

THE NATURE AND STATUS OF PUBLIC RELATIONS PRACTICE

History and Development

The United Kingdom is the term that has been used since 1922, when the southern part of Ireland became the Irish Free State (now known as the Republic of Ireland), to refer to the islands of Great Britain and the province of Northern Ireland. "Great Britain" includes England, Scotland, Wales as well as collections of outlying islands such as the Inner and Outer Hebrides and Orkney and Shetland Islands (all off Scotland). The terms "British" and "English" are *not* interchangeable; neither are the terms "UK" and "Great Britain" synonymous. The seat of the UK government is based in Westminster, London.

    Devolution was voted for by Scotland and Wales in 1997 and a Scottish parliament and Welsh assembly came into being in 1999, following centuries of hostility and campaigning by nationalists from these stateless nations. Such campaigns necessarily entail public relations/propaganda. Their national identities were partially eroded by the diminishing use as national languages of Scottish Gaelic and Welsh, although there has been some resurgence of these through new initiatives in media and education.

    The new national legislatures control their countries' destinies in all areas except those areas of "reserved powers," in crucial areas such as defence. These political changes have required adaptation by those in the public affairs and lobbying areas of public relations practice. Public relations in the UK reflects the history of a nation-state that was a major world power in the nineteenth and early twentieth centuries. State communications were needed to support international relations and diplomacy; to engage support from colonised nations and their elite class; to oppose any anti-colonial activities; to promote anti-terrorism. Global warfare, post-war reconstruction, post-war national debt and slow economic recovery all played their parts in the shape of Britain's public relations industry.

Internally, public relations emerged to support the processes of democratisation that had begun in the nineteenth century with the passing of social legislation that required that "subjects" (inhabitants of the UK are not technically "citizens," but subjects of the Royal Highness, the Queen, or King) understood their rights and obligations. Technological developments and increased levels of literacy facilitated mass communications.

This chapter sketches some of the global context that impacted developments in the UK, and then proceeds to explore the specifics of the emergent new occupation of public relations from the 1930s. It should be noted that the term "profession" is limited here to the sociologically derived necessary conditions for the term's employment: that an occupation controls its own boundaries; that it performs a public service, is constrained and regulated by codes of ethics and/or practice; is granted social legitimacy; that it has clear jurisdiction over specified tasks and a body of knowledge (Pieczka and L'Etang, 2001). Quite clearly, public relations in the UK has not achieved this status, even though professional status remains a clear and loudly articulated goal of a relatively small proportion of public relations practitioners active in "professional" bodies.

HISTORICAL CRUXES AND CATALYSTS FOR PR: THE BRITISH NATIONAL CONTEXT

Processes of global flux and transformation have had consequences for national communication policies and processes. Communication that accompanied politics and diplomacy influenced international relations and the development and control of new technology, such as the telegraph, in colonial territories (L'Etang, 2004: 39). The emergence of public relations can be linked to the exercise of power, international conflict and developments in communication technology. The emergence of public relations was due largely to the state at national and local levels. However, transport and utilities were important sectors. For example, Edward Kingsley worked for the Port of London Authority from 1911 to 1948 and developed public relations work from the early 1920s; Sir John Elliot was appointed to support Southern Railways electrification in 1924; Frank Pick worked to improve the image of the Underground; and there were PR departments by the 1930s at the Gas, Light and Coke Company, British Overseas Airways Corporation, Rootes Motors and Brooklands Racing Track (L'Etang, 2004).

Consultancies were set up by Sydney Walton in 1920, Basil Clarke in 1926, as was Watney and Powell's Parliamentary lobbyist company, and Theo Lovell ran a financial PR consultancy in the 1930s. Elsewhere, Harrods, the Dunlop Rubber Company and Vickers all used film for employee communications in the 1920s (L'Etang, 2004).

GLOBAL WARFARE AND PROPAGANDA

The UK was involved in two long world wars (1914–18 and 1939–45) and, following the fall of France in 1940, faced Nazi Germany alone, until the entry of the US into the war following the attack on Pearl Harbor in December 1941 which forced the US into war with

Japan and its ally, Germany. British propaganda in both world wars was the responsibility of the Ministry of Information. Efforts entailed domestic propaganda, intra-colonial propaganda, propaganda aimed at enemy domestic publics, international propaganda tailored for active allies, sympathetic non-participant nations, and hostile nations.

Considerable effort was put into gaining the active involvement of the United States in both world wars, which paid off in 1917, and in the support received from the US in the Second World War prior to and following US entry into the war. A range of staple strategies and tactics was employed. For example, dropping leaflets on enemy territories; publicising false stories about atrocities; censorship; and use of secret agents. A number of those involved in wartime information had later careers in public relations, suggesting a link between the skill sets of propaganda and public relations. Thus, the genesis of public relations was influenced by national and international politics.

Since then, the specialist field of political communication on behalf of politicians and political parties has continued to grow, and the politicisation of the officially neutral non-party political British civil servants of the Government Information Service has been an on-going process since the early 1960s. Government propaganda was also required to support colonial relationships, to counter resistance, and to smooth international, national and regional relations during often-traumatic processes of de-colonisation. Public relations emerged partially in response to, and as part of, globalisation, economic relations, international trade and political conquest. The nature of propaganda in relation to public relations was a matter for debate in government circles from the 1920s onwards.

Peacetime Propaganda

Peacetime propaganda at a national level related to colonial communications with Colonies, Dominions and Commonwealth. It also related to the international status and image of the UK. The formation of the Empire Marketing Board in 1926, and of the British Council in 1934, were important examples of efforts to improve the UK's international status. The British Council exists today as an organization which receives part of its grant from the Foreign and Commonwealth Office and promotes Britain abroad as well as fostering mutually beneficial relations with successor generations in many developed and developing countries overseas. Other examples of peacetime activity include public communication to improve health and fitness levels of the nation, especially after perceived under-performance of national athletes at the Berlin Olympics. Public relations, publicity and propaganda were topics discussed among the governing classes in relation to issues of national and cultural identity and the promotion of British values from the early twentieth century.

DEMOCRATIC EDUCATION, MASS COMMUNICATIONS AND TECHNOLOGY

Democratisation was feared by the elite class, since it gave voice to opinions of those previously excluded: women, the working class, the unemployed, and non-property owners. Opinion management and citizen education thus became an important part of the remit of the political class. New mass media such as films and radio were utilised as part of the democratic education project. The influence of the British Film Documentary Movement led by the Scot John Grierson was important (L'Etang, 2004: 32–35).

At local government level officers had to explain new legislation and welfare rights to the public. Among local government officials there were extensive discussions of the role and scope of public relations in relation to complementary functions of internal and external intelligence gathering, publicity, salesmanship and propaganda, many of which appeared in published form (L'Etang, 2004: 25). The sophisticated understanding of public relations in local government contexts was apparent as early as 1905 when the National Association for Local Government Officers (NALGO) developed a campaign of lobbying, media relations, publicity and promotion (L'Etang, 2004: 23).

In the 1930s developments in statistical research showed that mass opinion could be assessed much more effectively through the use of statistical sampling than the 1934 Peace Ballot, in which the League of Nations sought national opinion by polling eleven and a half million Britons (L'Etang, 2004: 30). The interest in mass opinion, and the ability to research it, provided the conditions for the growth of marketing and public relations. Crucially, in terms of the historical relation between public relations and marketing, it was marketing that took control of market research capability as part of its body of knowledge and jurisdiction. Essentially this meant that marketing, not public relations, developed the intellectual capacity to evaluate (L'Etang, 2004: 30–32).

ECONOMICS AND POLITICAL IDEOLOGY

Britain ended the Second World War as the world's largest debtor nation. The role of the state in economic planning was much debated at a time of economic stringency. For the next half-century governments of various persuasions experimented with various degrees of economic intervention, and the consequent debates over nationalisation and de-nationalisation (otherwise known as "privatisation") created opportunities for public relations practitioners to become advocates on behalf of business (free market ideology) or state (public sector). Private enterprise recruited public relations practitioners to lobby against nationalisation through various activist groups such as the Economic League, Aims of Industry, the Institute of Directors, the Federation of British Industry (now the Confederation of British Industry).

Britain has traditionally had less state ownership than other European countries and it was largely the Labour Party, together with the Trades Union Congress (TUC) that put forward the concept of public ownership in the 1930s and made it a central part of its party manifesto in 1945 (L'Etang, 2004: 84). The ideological underpinnings of nationalisation and anti-nationalisation could be linked rhetorically to international politics and the Cold War. Subsequent state intervention saw periods of de-nationalisation (Conservative Party administration from 1951), re-nationalisation (both Labour and Conservatives from 1964 and 1970, respectively) followed by extensive privatisation during Mrs Thatcher's Conservative administration. Orchestrating the sale of these industries required a major public communication by the Government Information Service and new specialised PR companies established identities, promoted services and worked to maintain customer, shareholder and employee loyalty (L'Etang, 2004: 90).

Post-war economic recovery in the 1960s and the uptake of wartime technology into consumer markets fuelled the growth of consultancies and a public relations practice that was closer to marketing and advertising. By the early 1970s the number of women entering the practice increased rapidly, partly because it was thought they were better suited to consumer PR than men (L'Etang, 2006: 162).

THE "PROFESSIONAL PROJECT"

Definitions, Regulation, Education and the Public Relations of Public Relations

The establishment of the Institute of Public Relations (IPR) in 1948 was driven by local government public relations officers. They had experience of their own professional body (NALGO) and knowledge of what we would term today "strategic public relations" from the local government context. Early concerns included definition of the field, education, and regulation.

Practitioners were concerned to establish status for the occupation and its aspirant professional body. They wished to exclude publicists even though they had a hard time distinguishing publicity from public relations. They had concerns about standards of practice, especially in media relations where there were concerns about the "taste" of stunts and standards of writing; fears about hidden political influence, hospitality and the potential for bribery, fuelled by some quite vicious media criticism that, in the 1960s, extended to hostile television programmes and the establishment of the Society for the Discouragement of Public Relations (L'Etang, 2004: 124–141). Media challenges inhibited chances of social legitimacy and have remained a serious block to the respectability of the occupation both in practice and in academia.

Although the first British code of ethics was written in the 1920s by Basil Clarke, it was not until 1963 that the IPR formulated a code that attempted to protect both the public interest and the interests of employers and clients, rather later than some other European nations (L'Etang, 2004: 156–185). In practice, the Code was often invoked by members against fellow members on grounds of unfair competition, and since membership of the IPR was not required to practice PR, the Code had limited impact. Discussions of PR ethics gradually became subsumed into more general discussions of PR in relation to corporate social responsibility by the 1980s.

The IPR early recognised the importance of education for professional status and in 1949 Norman Rogers argued for qualifications that would be used as an entry requirement to the Institute. For the next half-century IPR members and fellows debated curricula and educational levels in relation to membership criteria, constantly struggling to apply entrance criteria that did not deter new members (and thus threaten the financial viability of the IPR). The Intermediate Diploma was set up in 1957, taught by practitioners, but housed at a central London vocational institution. The Institute edited a textbook the following year. Already practitioners were expressing doubts about the quality of teaching and the need to "teach the teachers," a theme which re-emerged in a European context in the 1990s. In the 1960s public relations qualifications were delegated to the Communication, Advertising and Marketing Education Foundation (CAM). British practitioners who wrote books and became involved in professionalisation processes through education included Sam Black (1962) and Frank Jefkins (1971), whose work achieved international recognition (L'Etang, 2007: 245–247).

University-level education arrived in the late 1980s at post- and under-graduate levels but is still not given full credit by the industry as demonstrated by the fact that student applicants appear not to be given advanced status against graduates of other disciplines to credit them for their PR qualifications. The IPR achieved Chartered Status in 2005 and has continued to develop its own portfolio of training courses and its own educational Diploma course taught on a part-time and on-line basis through various institutions of further and higher education.

In 1960 the IPR recognised the necessity for a separate form of membership to represent the interests of consultancies. Later the same year Prince Yuri Galitzine drove forward a competitor organization, the Society of Independent Public Relations Consultants (known irreverently as "Shipwreck") that excluded advertising-owned firms. Incorporation of the IPR in 1963 required that members were individuals only, not collectivities, which led inevitably to the formation of a separate consultancy body. The rump of SIPREC and limited PR companies that were owned by advertising agencies merged to become the Public Relations Consultants' Association that exists today (L'Etang, 2004: 120–122).

Public relations practitioners have struggled with a conflict in identity that encompasses a vocational idealism with regard to public information and public service on the one hand and advocacy, propaganda and political brokering on the other. "Activists" who carry out issue public relations for pressure groups may be seen as "twisted, frightening reflections of themselves" (Pieczka, 2006a: 288). Occupational mythology includes the glamorous World War II spies, secret agents and propagandists; national promotion; well-connected upper class practitioners positioned at senior levels of organizations with access to high-level politicians helping to form public policy. PR cultures continue to be based strongly on social networks and dining clubs that may be important in producing some occupational norms and discourse (L'Etang, 2006: 157–159, 165; Pieczka, 2006a, 2006b). However, perhaps the most unifying theme is the shared historical concern for the public relations of public relations, which professional status is supposed to resolve. The difficulty for the professional body in terms of regulation, control and credibility is that, by the end of 2007, only around 9,500 of an estimated 48–55,000 practitioners in the UK are members.

Implications

Public relations' historical path in a UK context is unique to its cultural context. Practitioners' understanding of the practice have included societal, organisational, technical and consumer orientations at various times, but there has not been a clear progression, as has been argued for practice in the United States. Rather, British experience suggests that public relations practice has reflected national political and economic responses to developments on the world stage, thus challenging the view that US historical models are relevant to other cultures (L'Etang, 2004: 9–10; L'Etang, 2006: 144).

VIEWS OF CURRENT PRACTICE

Status of the Profession in the UK and the Role and Work of Practitioners

Professional status is an aspiration for the practice of public relations in the UK. A significant step towards this was taken in 2005, when the Institute of Public Relations gained chartered status, which in the UK involves recognition by the government, through the Privy Council, a group of senior advisors to the Queen. Royal Charters awarded by the Council are only granted to professional bodies or organisations that have a solid record of achievement; that represent a field of activity that is unique and not covered by other professional bodies; that work in the public interest and can demonstrate pre-eminence, stability and permanence in their particular field. At the time the charter was awarded it was felt that members of the Institute would benefit as a result of:

- Government acknowledgement that public relations work is valuable to business and society.

- Formal recognition that practitioners are professionals, with specialist knowledge and skills.

- Recognition that, as members, practitioners are obliged to work in the public interest and prepared to be accountable for their actions by signing up to an ethical code of conduct.

- A stronger Institute that can further grow and support members in their career and business.

The Institute sets out a number of key messages about the practice that follow from chartered status. It is committed to raising individual standards in practice and to the accountability of members. The Institute sees itself as leading the profession. Public relations it now defines as being about managing reputation, and it sees public relations as a key to organisational success, and good for business and society. Chartered status is seen as one of the pillars for future professional development for members of the Institute, but an obstacle to fast progress remains the fact that the large majority of practitioners in the UK are not members of the Institute. The lack of control of boundaries to the practice—we saw earlier that the Institute only has 9,500 members out of a practitioner group estimated at 48–55,000—and failure to maintain jurisdictional control over specialist knowledge and skills (much of public relations overlaps with marketing in practice) mitigates against the occupation achieving the status and social recognition it desires.

Outside the Institute and professional groups, the image of public relations has been damaged over recent years by associations with government "spin" raised in many media allusions to the practice. Although senior managers recognise the value of the practice, their preference is to refer to "communication" rather than "public relations" (Murray and White, 2004). Another pillar of professional development has been put in place in recent years, through the emergence of educational programmes at university level designed specifically to prepare entrants for the practice, which is a popular career choice among young people. The Chartered Institute of Public Relations accredits university programmes according to their coverage of a required body of knowledge, and their standards of programme delivery. Educators have raised questions about standards in practice, particularly about ethics in practice (White and Hobsbawm, 2007). They have also been involved in helping set policy for the CIPR on approaches to measurement and evaluation (CIPR Measurement and Evaluation Resource, 2005).

THE SIZE AND STRUCTURE OF THE PUBLIC RELATIONS INDUSTRY IN THE UK

The growing capability of the practice to study itself in the United Kingdom—through increased capacity in national public relations associations such as the CIPR and the Public Relations Consultants Association, and through the academic community now involved in research into practice—has resulted in a number of recent reports into the state of the practice (*The Economic Significance of Public Relations*, Centre for Economics and Business Research, London, 2005; *Unlocking the Potential of Public Relations: Developing Good Practice*, DTI and IPR, 2003; Murray and White, 2004, 2006; Moss, Desanto and Newman, 2005).

In the introduction to the study carried out for the Chartered Institute of Public Relations by the Centre for Economics and Business Research (*The Economic Significance of Public Relations*, 2005), the then president of the CIPR, Chris Genasi, said the report provided hard data to prove the importance and contribution of public relations. He also said:

The picture it paints is of a maturing, confident, growing profession that has become a vital part of so many organizations. Public relations is now firmly entrenched in business, government and the charitable sector, represented increasingly at Board-level. Just as importantly, it shows that PR has developed well beyond traditional media work. PR is now at the heart of strategic reputation management—and organizations are all the better for this development.

The report's key findings showed that:

- A conservatively estimated 47,800 people work in public relations. Of these, most (82 percent) are in-house specialists employed directly by companies, government or not-for-profits.

- Using their estimates of the number of public relations practitioners, a survey of Chartered Institute of Public Relations members and official statistics, CEBR has demonstrated the value of public relations in terms of its financial contribution to the United Kingdom, estimating the turnover of the practice as a whole to be £6.5 billion.

- The practice contributes £3.4 billion to United Kingdom economic activity as well as generating £1.1 billion in corporate profits if the contribution of in-house public relations workers is valued at the same rate as public relations consultants.

- Consultancies and agencies are expected to grow to an average of around 54 employees per company in the next five years.

- Increased spend on public relations activity is expected to come mainly from corporate areas of public relations.

- In-house public relations functions were expected to continue growing as they had in the previous five years.

- At present public relations consultancies whose clients are primarily in the public, health and charities sector account for over a third (36 percent) of turnover of all public relations consultancies.

- In addition, over half (51 percent) of all public relations employees who work in-house are currently employed by organisations in the public, health and charities sector.

- A significant proportion of employees in the practice work in the South East, with a quarter working in London alone.

- The majority of PR employees are graduates, and the range of qualifications held is wide. Over half of practitioners can speak a foreign language.

- The average annual basic salary of a public relations professional is £46,200 but almost half of all employees receive a bonus (on average 8 percent of basic salary) in addition. (Sources: CEBR estimates; CEBR/CIPR survey, August 2005; Office for National Statistics.)

Although there is no single comprehensive source of data on the size, structure and characteristics of the public relations industry in the UK, reports such as the CEBR's 2005 report and a number of industry studies conducted in recent years have helped to generate something of a broad census about the size and profile of the public relations industry in the UK. In addition to the findings above, the 2005 study also found that just over 60 percent of the workforce are female, but only around 6 percent of the workforce come from ethnic minority backgrounds.

Looking at employment trends within the UK public relations industry, employment can be quite cyclical, particularly within the private sector and especially within consultancies.

However, over the past decade or so there has been a trend towards the downsizing of in-house communication and public relations departments. This reflects a wider industry trend towards greater cost consciousness, tighter resource constraints and demands for greater efficiency from all functional departments. Indeed, recent studies both in the UK and US (DeSanto and Moss, 2004) revealed a median in-house department size of just seven people. Part of the explanation suggested for the relatively small size of communication/public relations departments is that organisations have moved towards the use of a mix of in-house and external agency staff to service the fluctuating demands for communication and public relations support.

Any estimate of the numbers employed in public relations within the UK has to be viewed cautiously as there are no official statistics for employment specifically in public relations, as public relations has been treated as part of the professional services sector in official government censuses of employment in UK. Moreover, any attempt to arrive at an accurate estimate of employment within public relations runs into the inevitable problem that many people carrying out public relations type work roles may not be employed in a formal public relations job. Here the problem is not simply about nomenclature, difficult as this may be with many different titles existing for public relations type roles, but people working in other functions such as marketing and human resources may perform a significant public relations role, but this role may not be recognised as such. The problem of nomenclature is a particularly tricky one as fewer and fewer practitioners, particularly at more senior levels, use the term " public relations" in their job title, preferring alternatives such as "corporate communications," "public or external affairs" or simply "communications."

A further problem faced in trying to gauge the size and shape of the industry in the UK stems from the fact that the public relations "industry" comprises a number of different sectors, notably consultancy, in-house corporate departments, in-house local and central government departments as well as the diverse category of practitioners working in not-for-profit/voluntary/charitable organisations. Any attempt to pin down the distribution of employment across these different sectors is made all the more difficult by relatively high levels of employment mobility both within sectors and to a degree between sectors.

PROFILE OF SENIOR PRACTITIONERS AND PUBLIC RELATIONS DIRECTORS

Dolphin (2002) studied the background and work of senior practitioners operating at the PR director level in the UK. He found that the term "PR director" has largely vanished, replaced by a range of alternative titles such as those mentioned above, such as "corporate communications director," or "public affairs director." Although dealing with a relatively small sample, Dolphin found that over 60 percent of senior practitioners had completed a university degree—although not specifically in a communications-related subject.

Only 35 percent of PR directors had what has been viewed as the traditional journalistic background. Indeed, around 25 percent appeared to have had a very generalist working background. What emerges from Dolphin's study is that there is not a clear career pathway to senior status within public relations, rather what matters is the knowledge and skills that the individual possesses and can demonstrate. Yet progression is based solely on these criteria, as contacts, internal "politics" and personality all appear to play a significant part in determining career progression.

In terms of reporting relationships and status, most studies suggest that the majority of senior practitioners/ PR directors in the UK report directly to either chief executives or chairmen in their respective organizations (Dolphin suggests that around 70 percent of PR directors report directly to their CEO or Chairman). What is more difficult to ascertain is the extent to which practitioners contribute directly to senior management policy decisions, rather than simply reporting in on media coverage and operational matters relating to the functioning of the public relations department. Again there is very limited evidence to draw on to date, but anecdotal data suggests that perhaps less than 25 percent of senior practitioners/directors participate regularly in policy-making decisions at the most senior level within their organisations. Participation in senior management decision-making is almost certainly linked closely to top management's perceptions or "worldviews" of the value of public relations, or more specifically, their perceptions of what senior practitioners are able to contribute to the decision-making process.

There are gender differences to be found in UK public relations practice. Studies of the membership of the CIPR have shown that women have become the majority in member- ship in recent years, but that they are a minority in senior management positions in the practice (White and Myers, 1998). Annual salary surveys published by trade publications such as *PR Week* show that women are paid less than men for comparable work. These findings are not unique to public relations practice in the UK where across occupations women tend to be paid less than men for similar work, or to make less progress than men in their careers. In recent years, attention has also turned, through discussions on diversity held by the CIPR, to the representation of ethnic minorities in UK practice, where practitioners from these groups are felt to be under-represented.

TOP MANAGEMENT'S WORLDVIEW

Again, limited detailed information exists about senior management perceptions and understanding of the public relations function's role within organisations. Anecdotally, the "picture" seems quite varied across industry sectors as well as between organisations within the same sector. Indeed, there is little consensus about how far senior management genuinely understand the role and potential contribution of public relations to organisa- tional success.

This lack of understanding of what public relations is and what practitioners actually do has proved a barrier to public relations gaining equal recognition alongside other functions within organisations and, in particular, a barrier to practitioners having a "seat at the top management table" in the majority of organisations in the UK (Dolphin 2002). Evidence gathered from studies such as that conducted by Desanto and Moss (2004) seems to support this notion of a somewhat patchy understanding of public relations amongst senior management within UK organisations. Here, for example, one theme that emerged repeatedly has been that top management appear to see public relations primarily as a reactive media relations function and fail to appreciate how the public relations/communi- cations functions can add value to an organisation, rather than being a "cost centre."

Murray and White's (2004) study of chief executive officers' views of the value of public relations found that the chief executive officers they interviewed (fourteen CEOs in private, public and not-for-profit sector organisations operating nationally and internationally) had an intuitive understanding of the value of public relations. One described the practice as "mission critical" and the group as a whole felt that public relations is essential to the effective management of the modern organisation.

Public relations was not seen by CEOs interviewed as the sole prerogative of the public relations department or director, but a responsibility shared by all members of the organisation, particularly the board members and senior management. The role of the practitioner they felt is to act as coach and advisor to members of management to help them become more effective in this part of the role.

For the CEO making decisions in face of complexity, there was an appreciated need for skilled advisors in matters of relationship management, but the group interviewed felt that there was inadequate investment in this area of management. In a challenge to the practice, they also felt that there were insufficient numbers of practitioners who have the required skills to make the contribution expected. CEO views were echoed in a later study (Murray and White, 2006) of senior practitioners which found that they also had concerns about the numbers of qualified practitioners available to meet the demands of practice, which included complexity of the environment, aggressive media, changes in communication technology, closer scrutiny and increasing regulation.

THE ROLE OF PRACTITIONERS

What do Public Relations Practitioners Do?

While knowledge of the size, structure and rate of growth of the industry in the UK are useful indicators of the development of public relations, they do not in themselves explain the role that practitioners play and the type of work that they undertake on behalf of their organisations or clients.

Much of the discussion about the role of practitioners, within academic circles, has focused on debates about the extent to which practitioners fulfil a predominantly "manager" or "technician" role (Dozier, 1984; Dozier and Broom, 1995). The use of this dual typology of manager-technician roles to explain the work of practitioners has been criticised on a number of grounds, not least that these role typologies only represent *abstractions* for studying the wide range of activities that practitioners perform in their daily lives. The use of these labels has also been criticised by Creedon, 1991; Toth and Grunig, 1993; and Toth et al., 1998 who have argued the "technician" label devalues the often important contribution of technical work which tends to be performed to a greater degree by female practitioners. It is also generally acknowledged that the division of practitioners' work into manager and technician categories is overly simplistic since most practitioners perform elements of both managerial and technical work. A further caveat when looking at the picture of practitioner work portrayed within the academic literature is that the vast majority of the research that underpins the existing categorisation of practitioner roles has been conducted with samples of practitioners working largely in US-based organisations rather than in an international context. However, more recent research has begun to extend the study of practitioner roles to examine practitioner work patterns in organisations operating outside the US.

Practitioner Work Patterns in the UK

Recent research into the pattern of practitioners' work in UK organisations (Moss, Warnaby and Newman, 2000; Desanto and Moss, 2004; Moss, Newman and Desanto 2005) has begun to give a clearer picture of the principal elements of the work performed particularly by more senior public relations practitioners in the UK. It has also provided insights into the way practitioners allocate their time between different activities. While such research is in its early stages and does not provide a definitive profile of practitioner work patterns, it does offer valuable insights into *how* UK practitioners go about performing their roles, into actual practitioner behaviour. What this research suggests is that the image of the practitioner either as the "thoughtful rational planner of programmes," or as "the creative shaper of messages for the media" does not appear to stand up to scrutiny, at least as far as more established senior practitioners are concerned. Rather what emerges is a picture of practitioner work that is typically frenetic, sometimes quite fragmented and unplanned, with practitioners often having to respond to events as they unfold as well as to the demands of others.

This picture of senior practitioner work matches that found in studies of more general management work in organisations, which suggest that managers generally spend relatively little time on strategic thinking and planning, and are often preoccupied with handling the minutiae of running departments and dealing with organisational "politics" (e.g. Hales, 1986; Mintzberg, 1973; Stewart, 1983). Public relations practitioners in managerial roles are, it seems, managers like others. The typical senior UK practitioner's working day revolves around variety of both internal and external face-to-face meetings, administrative duties and external representation of the organisation at events, with a relatively smaller proportion of time spent on planning activities, trouble-shooting activities and writing or technical activities. This profile of senior practitioner work patterns in terms of broad categories of work activity is summarised in Figure 19.1. Here, of course, categories such as "external or internal meetings" which appear to account for close on 50 percent of the typical working week require further explanation. "Internal meetings" were found to span team-briefings, inter-departmental liaison meetings, senior management board meetings as well as meetings with chairmen and chief executives to brief them on relevant developments. External meetings included everything from formal contact with politicians, MPs and civil servants, or local authority representatives, to meetings with community leaders, pressure group representatives and other interest groups. The purpose behind these external meetings appears to be a mix of networking, external representation—ensuring the organisation is understood and its voice is heard—and intelligence gathering.

INFLUENCES ON PRACTITIONER WORK

Of course, in practice, most practitioners acknowledge that there is no such thing as a "typical" working day. Indeed, it might be argued that public relations work is characterised by its variability. Turning to the question of what factors appear to exert the greatest influence on practitioner work, at least four key sources of influence can be identified: the level of seniority of the practitioner within the department/organisation; the industry sector or organisation type; senior management expectations and the situational context.

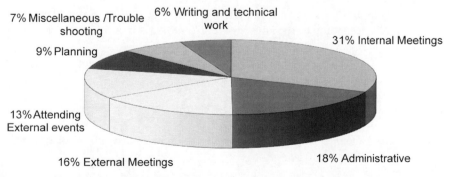

FIG. 19.1   Allocation of UK Senior Practitioner time (%).

The practitioner's level or seniority within their organisational/departmental structure is perhaps the most obvious influence on their individual work patterns. In general, until practitioners have demonstrated their competence and mastery of the more technical and routine administrative tasks, they are unlikely to be allowed to progress to more senior levels where they might have responsibility for supervision of others, leadership and the counselling of senior management. Similarly industry/sector or organisation–type is likely to prove a strong influence on the type of work practitioners typically perform.

Thus, for example, although a generalisation, it appears that practitioners working for fast moving consumer goods (FMCG) companies tend to spend more time engaged in either organising or carrying out technical communications tasks in support of marketing than their counterparts in sectors such as regulated utility companies, transportation or chemical industries. Senior management's expectations of public relations and willingness to sanction particular courses of action inevitably constrain the scope of the work that individual practitioners can perform. Finally, it is perhaps self-evident that the scope of public relations work will almost always depend to a large degree on the particular situation faced. Situations may be relatively short term, determining the type of immediate response options likely to be available, but might also extend into the medium term, setting an on-going agenda for the types of public relations strategies and tactics that may be appropriate.

THE UNITED KINGDOM—THE CONTEXT OF PRACTICE VIS-A-VIS ENVIRONMENTAL VARIABLES

Changes at the National Level

The United Kingdom is changing profoundly. Its past lives on through its involvement in the Commonwealth, an association of nations previously part of the British Empire. It now has a significant—sometimes reluctant—role in European developments, as one of the largest and wealthiest members of the European Union of 27 member countries. The Union itself is in the process of trying to set new rules for its governance through the Treaty of Lisbon, 2007. This treaty—which has been described as a new version of a constitution for the Union (a previous "constitution" was rejected)—sets out the rules by which the European Union is to be governed in the future. It was to be ratified by member states during 2008 and 2009, but an early rejection by the people of Ireland in a referendum in June 2008 has thrown the future of the treaty arrangements into doubt.

The UK is a country marked by social inequality, in which 12.7 million people live in poverty (a figure which is rising year on year, despite government commitments and efforts to raise people out of poverty). At the other end of the income scale, the incomes of the richest fifth of UK households are 16 times greater than those of the poorest fifth—£68,700 compared to £4,200, according to the latest figures from the Economic and Social Research Council (Britain 2008).

The social background to public relations practice in the United Kingdom is provided by:

- complexity in political developments and the uncertainties that this complexity gives rise to;
- social diversity and inequality, which are matched with social dynamism, debates regarding social justice, and creativity;
- demographic change;

- questions of national, economic, social, urban, regional and rural development and impacts of development on the environment.

The challenges faced by the United Kingdom as a country present enormous opportunities for public relations practice, where for example recent political changes associated with devolution have created new requirements for public affairs practice in national capitals in Scotland and Wales, and the issues of increasing social diversity in large cities such as Birmingham demand new and imaginative approaches to community relations and the use of channels of communication to diverse audiences.

Political Structure

We have already discussed the process of devolution, by which central powers have been "devolved" to national assemblies in Wales, Scotland and Northern Ireland. In 2008, nearly ten years after the establishment of a Scottish parliament and Welsh assembly, the implications of devolution for the country as a whole are now becoming apparent, raising questions about national cohesion ("What does it mean to be British?" or "Will the union hold—say, between Scotland and the rest of the country?"), uniformity of provision—in national services, such as the National Health Service, and the governance of England, which lacks a national assembly comparable to the Scottish and Welsh institutions.

Devolution is the latest step in the political development of the United Kingdom. The country is a constitutional monarchy. The monarch, currently Queen Elizabeth II, with parliament, represents the will and aspirations of the people of the country, according to the islands' unwritten constitution. The national parliament is located in London, and made up of two Houses. The first of these, the House of Commons, is elected and, in the end, sovereign, while the second, the House of Lords is made up of appointed members—peers or Lords—with a residual group who are in place on an hereditary basis. Apart from the hereditary peers and a number of bishops, members are appointed by the government of the day, but a balance is maintained of viewpoints and political affiliations.

The government of the day is made up by the party holding a majority of seats in the House of Commons, which has 646 elected members of parliament, elected by constituencies—areas within cities, towns and the country. The major parties are Labour, Conservative and Liberal Democrats. Minor parties represent interests in Wales, Northern Ireland and Scotland, and there are several independent members. In early 2008, the Labour Party, with 352 seats, forms the national government.

In the past ten years, there has been devolution of powers to national assemblies in Scotland and Wales, restoring some rights of self-government to countries that were drawn into union with England in the past—formally in 1536 in the case of Wales and in 1707 in the case of Scotland. Devolved government was restored to Northern Ireland in 2007 after long and sometimes bloody disputes amongst the people who live in the province.

The UK is a former imperial power, with strong links to countries which in one form or another were part of the Empire, such as the US (with which it has a "special relationship", much referred to by national politicians), Canada, Australia, New Zealand, India, Pakistan—and the list can go on, so extensive was the Empire at the end of the 1800s and in the early 1900s. In the twentieth century, the Empire was relinquished, for example when the Raj (British rule) came to an end in India in 1947, or independence was given to African countries, such as Nigeria in 1960. Links are retained through the Commonwealth.

Dean Acheson, a former US Secretary of State, suggested in the 1950s that Britain had lost an empire, but had not yet found a role, and there is uncertainty about the country's future. Is it to be found across the Atlantic, in ever-closer ties to the US, or in an expanding European Union? Or does the UK still have a strong and independent role to play in the world, and if so, does it have the resources to play such a role?

It wields hard power, through its willingness to deploy its limited armed forces abroad, currently in Iraq and Afghanistan, and "soft power," through public and cultural diplomacy, and through institutions such as the British Broadcasting Corporation's World Service and The British Council.

So far, changes to the political structure of the United Kingdom as a consequence of devolution have been piecemeal, and are part of an unfinished political process. There is recognition of a need to set down a constitution for the country, which will clarify the unwritten set of precedents and traditions that serve as the British constitution. These are open to wide interpretation and possible abuse. In concurrent developments, some of the freedoms established under agreements going back to Magna Carta are under threat, as steps are taken to deal with dangers to national security posed by terrorism and religious fundamentalism. Constitutional developments, threats to liberty, privacy and individual rights, and the need for freedom of religious belief are debated vigorously, in the media and other settings.

The political changes accompanying devolution, and the continuing debate about constitutional arrangements have created opportunities in public affairs practice, and raised questions about the part played by political lobbying in the workings of existing and future constitutional arrangements.

Public affairs and political communication in the UK is influenced by a growing number of "think tanks"—politically motivated but theoretically driven organizations—which develop policy options and ideas for debate, for example, the Adam Smith Institute, the Bow Group, the Centre for Policy Studies, Aims of Industry, Demos (L'Etang, 2007: 115). While little research has been done on their PR activities, Magor noted that:

> The think-tank scene has matured in the UK over the last decade and there are now many different types of think tank organizations serving diverse niches . . . Think tanks commonly assert and overplay their impact on policy yet few have measurable performance indicators to determine this . . . the role of some think tank organizations is more akin to that of management consultants (Magor, 2006: 1–2 cited in L'Etang, 2007: 115).

Economic Structure

According to the UK's Economic and Social Research Council, the UK is the world's fifth largest economy behind the US, Japan, Germany and China. London is the world's financial capital (a position that it disputes with New York, with London currently in the ascendancy, according to most financial commentators). It is—on the strength of its history and continuing economic performance, influential in world economic affairs—a member of the G8 group of industrialised economies, a close ally of the US and a substantial member of the European Union.

The country is highly developed economically, with a strong, diverse economy based on freedom of inward investment, trade, financial and professional services, manufacturing and agriculture, and natural resources such as coal, natural gas and oil. Although concerns have been expressed in recent years about the decline in the country's manufacturing base, the country is committed to wealth creation through private enterprise. Business is seen as providing a model for social progress, permeating all sectors of the economy including the public sector. The public sector has adopted the language and practices of the private sector to try to improve performance, with results that are still to be fully assessed. Economic decision-making is decentralised but the inclination of the current, Labour, government is towards centralisation, as recent turbulence in financial markets (which produced "the first run on a British bank in living memory" (*The Scotsman*, December 28, 2007)) has shown.

On questions of economic policy, government in the United Kingdom at all levels is open to discussion and influence as policy is developed. Private and public sector are in close contact, through the activities of individual government departments, companies involved in lobbying and organisations such as the Confederation of British Industry representing their members' interests to government at national and local levels.

UK governments at all levels are committed to e-government, to using the capabilities afforded by technology to improve contact between government, public and interest groups. A number of government services are already accessible and provided through technology, and attempts—not always successful—are being made to offer further government services through use of technology.

Economic policy developments are often initiated in "think tanks"—policy development institutes that are often formed in the first place by political parties to provide ideas for policy that will be adopted in government. A current example of such a policy institute is the Institute for Public Policy Research, which is influential with the Labour government (www.ippr.org).

It has been suggested by a former Downing Street insider—10 Downing Street is the location of the Prime Minister's Office—that ideas for change in government come from outside, from groups such as the policy institutes (Mulgan, 2005). It is vital in public affairs practice, and in approaches to issues management in the United Kingdom, to remain close to developments in the "think tanks."

Government changes and priorities affect the practice of public relations in the UK almost immediately, through public affairs practice, but also the wider practice. In the UK, it has been recognised how much modern government depends on presentation, and on the effective management of key relationships, and almost daily evidence can be found of the importance the government attaches to the practice—although it will hardly ever refer directly to the practice as public relations. As this is written, there is much discussion in the national media of the appointment by the Prime Minister of a new chief of strategy at Downing Street, who was—until his appointment—chief executive of a leading public relations consultancy. It is taken for granted that he will use his skills to guide the government's presentation of itself ("Gordon's new broom needs bold brushwork to fix No 10", *London Evening Standard*, January 9, 2008).

Legal System

The UK's judiciary is independent and strong, able to influence government initiatives on such questions as the length of time suspects can be held without charge. This—a current debate in early 2008—is part of the national approach to dealing with terrorism and threats to national security, where the police, national security agencies and some politicians are arguing for long periods of detention without charge so that evidence can be gathered against potential terrorists.

The relationship between judiciary, legislative and executive branches can be determined partly by the issue under discussion, but as a general rule—and as in other countries—politicians can resent opposition to their plans from the judiciary. Free debate around the issues causing friction between the branches of government is an important means of clarifying the issues, and seeing the roles of the different branches of government clearly. This remains a part of the British political process and is an area where public relations has an important contribution to make. The practice is bound by rules established through self-regulation, by public affairs practitioners, and others regarding the use of influence by and through political advisors and politicians themselves. In the UK, parliamentarians—members of the Houses of Commons or Lords—are able, under certain conditions, to represent interests in the legislature, but they are bound by rules governing standards of behaviour in public life. They are also required to declare their interests in registers of members' interests, and to take specific steps to avoid conflicts of interest.

After some years of delay since it was passed in 2000, the UK government put into effect Freedom of Information legislation in 2005, as part of a stated commitment to open and transparent government. However, already there have been attempts to restrict access to information within the limits set by the legislation, where government departments have argued that responding to requests for information is costly, and costs have to be contained. This is a potential restriction on the amount of information that will be made available.

Another issue in the management of information is data protection, for which rules are laid down in legislation, and their observance monitored by an Information Commissioner. Information relating to individuals and its management are matters of great concern in the UK, which now has a justified reputation as one of the countries most subject to surveillance in the world (Information Commissioner, 2006). Current concern surfaces in debates about government plans for the introduction of identity cards and for a comprehensive data base recording health information for all members of the population. A recent case of data loss by the government, where the UK government's department of revenue and customs managed to mislay discs containing the confidential details of 25 million people, children and adults (including, in the case of adults, bank account details) has fuelled public disquiet about the way personal information is kept by government.

Despite legislation affecting the practice, the practice remains lightly regulated, and mainly expected to manage through self-regulation. This is the opportunity afforded the practice by Chartered status for the Institute of Public Relations, where the Institute has the scope to propose—and gain acceptance for—rules that will govern the practice.

Activism

The UK has a long history of social activism, of groups setting out to define and defend their interests—and in some cases suffering extreme consequences. Recent examples are provided by groups protesting the imposition of local taxation through what was known as the "poll tax," where these protests contributed to the downfall of Prime Minister Margaret Thatcher in the early 1990s, and by groups attempting to block construction projects having significant environmental impact, such as airport runway developments. A protest against a proposed third runway at Heathrow Airport in London is gathering momentum in early 2008.

Less dramatically, the United Kingdom has—like the US—a highly developed voluntary sector, where groups have formed and been active—some for many years—around social issues and their solution, matters of public health, or special interests. Some of the most effective campaigning work in the country is carried on by organisations in this sector, by international organisations such as Friends of the Earth or Greenpeace. Greenpeace, in one much cited example, stopped Shell, the international oil company, from going ahead with plans to dispose of the Brent Spar, an oil rig, in the North Atlantic in the mid-1990s, through aggressive mobilisation of public opinion in the UK and elsewhere in Europe.

Companies in the UK are aware of, and willing to work with, activist groups where this proves possible. They are also aware of their need to anticipate the issues on which their activities may be questioned, and where they will be called upon to meet broader social responsibilities. There is, in the UK, a strong interest on the part of business organisations in corporate social responsibility, and this is channelled through organisations such as Business in the Community—which is an activist group pushing for, and recognising good performance by companies in meeting their social responsibilities. The labour unions have also become skilful in their use of public relations practice in recent years (Davis, 2002).

The right of voluntary sector and other activist groups to make their case in public debate is respected in the United Kingdom, and up to a point social protest is allowed and expected, when issues demand strong action. Limits are reached when individuals, property and social order are threatened, as in the case of protests by animal rights activists. The degree of activism in the United Kingdom means that, for example, large corporate public relations departments have to allocate resources to maintaining close contact with and knowledge of the activities of activist groups. The same is true for government departments and agencies, while some specialist consultancies may build their business on specialist knowledge of activist groups (a good example of this type of consultancy is provided by SIGWatch, www.sigwatch.com).

Culture

Within the country, the population is changing. As in other European countries, the population is an aging population with the 80-plus age group the fastest-growing age group. By 2050, one quarter of the population will be aged 65–79, and ten percent will be 80-plus. These and other figures that follow are drawn from *Britain in 2008*, published in late 2007. The population of the country is nearly 61 million (2006 figures) and growing. Ninety two percent of the population are white. Indians are the biggest single ethnic minority group, followed by Pakistanis. New immigrants—particularly from the countries of Eastern Europe such as Poland, which recently joined the European Union and gained rights of entry for its citizens to the UK—are adding to population growth. Immigration brings with it a number of demands and social problems, such as pressure on social services, but also creates economic benefits for the country

The country is predominantly urban—only 1 in 5 people live in a rural area, while the majority live in urban areas—towns, cities and conurbations around cities like Manchester and Birmingham. London has a population of just over seven million, making it the largest city in Europe and the world's twentieth biggest city (Britain 2008). London occupies a special place in the United Kingdom, as both the national capital and a world financial and cultural centre, described recently by the editor of *The Spectator*, a UK weekly magazine of political commentary, as "almost like a country within a country [with] the reputation of being the financial centre of the world" (Matthew d'Ancona, quoted in *The Independent* newspaper, December 22, 2007).

One consequence of devolution has been a concern about national unity (typified, for example, in an article in *The Guardian*, January 10, 2008, entitled "The Break Up of the Union now seems Inevitable", which talked of "the fabric of the country being torn up and stitched anew.") If Scotland, Wales and Northern Ireland are encouraged to look first to their local assemblies for political leadership, why should the peoples of these parts of the United Kingdom feel an allegiance to the Kingdom as a whole? The concern has emerged in discussions about what it means to be British, and part of these discussions has been a focus on "Britishness"—is there a clearly defined British culture? If so, what are its elements, values, symbols and so on (a useful summary of some elements of Welsh and Scottish culture is to be found in a portrait of the UK prepared for the Global Alliance for Public Relations and Communication Management in 2006, www.globalpr.org)?

The debate about Britishness, carried on in the letters columns of national newspapers, has suggested that the national culture is one that does not have strong defining features and that it is not surprising that people feel closer allegiance to the part of the country that they live in. In any case, the culture is evolving, changing as the impact of immigration, political and technological developments is felt. The impact of immigration has affected tastes in popular music, and reached into social and domestic life, changing the character of several large cities.

If there is a national culture, it is an individualistic, fretful and disputatious culture, reflected most obviously in popular entertainment (television soap operas and television programmes such as EastEnders, Coronation Street or Shameless, which portray the lives of "ordinary" people in the East End of London and Manchester). It can also be seen at work in the political theatre provided by the House of Commons, the conflict in interviews conducted by leading broadcast journalists with public figures on flagship programmes of news and comment such as the national Radio 4 Today programme, and the BBC's Newsnight programme. And, of course, the culture—"the way things are done around here"—can be observed daily on the streets of country villages or major cities, providing one of the attractions of the country to outside visitors.

Paradoxically, the British culture is also to some extent a hidden culture and—in its political expression—a secretive one, which partly explains why it is difficult to draw out in discussions of "Britishness." Characteristics of British social life and conversation are understatement and irony. As in some other cultures, people do not say directly what they mean, but what they say has to be interpreted—which is one reason why argument is seen as a way of bringing issues to the surface for resolution—or at least, clarity in disagreement, "agreeing to disagree." The culture is based on robust argument: relationships are forged through argument, and issues, problems and their solution are clarified. Argument depends on freedom of speech and tolerance for the views of others. (Hall, 1997)

Some coming into contact with the culture may be offended by the freedom of expression that they find, and will on occasions protest against it, as in the example of a Sikh community in Birmingham protesting at the portrayal of aspects of their community in a play staged by the local repertory theatre and forcing the theatre involved to close the production.

The culture described is one in which public relations practice thrives, and has a large role to play in the surfacing and clarification of arguments, and in conflict resolution. The culture is one of high tolerance of differences, but one in which differences are prominent, between classes and between the sexes. There is still differential treatment of men and women in terms of employment opportunities and levels of compensation for similar levels of work. For example, in the early days of 2008, local government employers are having to deal with the economic consequences of "equal pay" settlements where women, for years paid less than men for similar work, are now to be compensated for the years of underpayment.

In the UK, emphasis is placed on individuals over the collective, an emphasis expressed forcefully by Conservative Prime Minister Margaret Thatcher in an interview in September 1987, when she suggested: "there's no such thing as society. There are individual men and women and there are families. And no government can do anything except through people, and people must look after themselves first. It is our duty to look after ourselves and then, also, to look after our neighbours."

A constant theme in national political discussion, taken up again in 2007 by Labour Prime Minister Gordon Brown is one of opportunity, where conditions are to be created to enable people to make best use of their potential. There are difficulties in the UK, in that people start from different positions, and social mobility is influenced by the start that people have in their lives (Britain 2008). Class is still significant in the UK, and determines life chances, and even health and life expectancy. However, deference, where in the past working class would defer to middle class, and middle class to upper class and aristocracy, has long gone.

These class links are apparent in public relations through some of its networking practices, notably dinner clubs, as reported in *PRWeek*, 12 October 2007, pp. 22–27; (Etang, 2006: 157–159).

The UK culture is one conducive to public relations practice, and to practice development. Where it is a hidden or secretive culture, it can be opened out. Where it runs on ambiguity, public relations can help to bring clarity. Where difficult issues are to be debated to resolution, public relations has a clear role in contributing to the quality and content of debate. It is a culture which demands intelligent and sensitive approaches to practice and which, because of this, has the potential to force the development of the practice—if the practice, practitioners and the national public relations associations can respond to the demands made on practice.

THE MASS MEDIA AND PUBLIC RELATIONS

Robust argument in public debate and the practice of public relations in the United Kingdom are set in the context of one of the most demanding media environments to be found anywhere in the world. The United Kingdom is a world media centre—a centre of production which exports its products around the world through the BBC World Service, the BBC itself which has an export arm that sells BBC programmes and other products around the world, and through the work of film and communication production companies.

Within the country, the UK supports a national press, national broadcasting activities, independent television companies, national, regional and local radio broadcasting, operating in both the public and private sectors. Freedom House, which studies freedom and limitations upon it around the world, rates the United Kingdom press at 31 on its ranking of freedom of the press around the world, a ranking headed by the press in the Scandinavian countries (www.freedomhouse.org).

Newspapers emerged in London in the seventeenth century with the publication of the *London Gazette* and developed when allowed to express and promote political and business interests. They have maintained close contact with both since, and can still be categorised according to political leanings and the support they are prepared to give to particular groups, such as the business community or trade unions.

Historically, UK newspapers are generally divided into three groups: mass market tabloids, or "red-tops" (so-called because of their conspicuous mastheads, made prominent to catch attention on newsstands where newspapers are sold) such as *The Sun* and *Daily Mirror*, middle-market tabloids like the *Daily Mail*, judged by many to be the most successful UK newspaper in meeting the interests of its readers, and "quality" newspapers such as *The Times* and *The Guardian* (available in compact format), and *The Daily Telegraph* and *Financial Times*, which still sell as broadsheet, larger format newspapers. Tabloid newspapers can claim they have helped to win elections—*The Sun* newspaper, for example, claimed that it was its influence that resulted in a Conservative victory in a close-run election in the early 1990s.

Their influence and attractiveness to advertisers are based in part on circulation. *The Sun* reaches over three million people a day, while *The Daily Mail* reaches just over two million, and *The Times* has a circulation of around 600,000, according to recent figures from Publicitas. *The Guardian* has a circulation of around 360,000, and is read by 1.9 million people, according to its own figures. Most of the daily newspapers are accompanied by similarly named Sunday newspapers, such as *The Sunday Times* and *The Mail on Sunday*.

The broadcast media are operated in both public and private sectors. The public service British Broadcasting Corporation operates at arm's length from the national government, and is paid for by television license fee revenue, where all owners of television sets are required to pay an annual licence fee. The Corporation negotiates with the government regarding the revenue available to it. The relationship between Corporation and government is a difficult one, and may often involve conflict when government may feel that the Corporation is too critical of government activities, in its news reporting or other programming. The Corporation for its part has to resist what might be felt as excessive government interference, while depending at the same time on continuing government support—which is resented by private sector broadcasting organisations, which feel that the BBC has an unfair advantage over them.

A national regulatory organisation, OFCOM—the Office of Communication—was established in 2002, bringing together a number of existing agencies, to set out rules for broadcasting and other channels and means of communication. It is the independent regulator and competition authority for the UK communications industries, with responsibilities across television, radio, telecommunications and wireless communications services (www.ofcom.org.uk).

The print media are made up of private sector organisations, which are highly competitive in a way which influences their approaches to news gathering, and the ways in which they express their influence and opinions. Some, like *The Sun* and *The Times*, are part of larger international conglomerates such as News International, and because of their reach to large and politically important segments of the UK population as well as the influence of their owners have had significant influence on political decision-making in recent years.

The UK is able to deliver newspapers nationally from centres of production such as London and Manchester in a matter of hours. This has been true since the growth of the railways in the mid-1800s, and now is faciliated by technological developments which allow for even more remote production and distribution. This means that UK newspapers like *The Financial Times* can be produced, in foreign editions, in Europe and North America.

London-centric though many of the national papers may be, they are national papers, which contain similar news on a daily basis, which is delivered throughout the United Kingdom. It will be a preoccupation for any organisation or individual trying to communicate nationally to gain the attention of, and space in these national newspapers. In addition to national—UK—newspapers, there are also newspapers in the countries which make up the UK, such as *The Scotsman* in Scotland, and major regional newspapers in centres like Belfast in Northern Ireland, or Birmingham in the English Midlands. Smaller circulation evening and weekly newspapers are also published across the country, and recent years have seen the emergence of free newspapers, supported by advertising. Editorial approaches taken by these newspapers will reflect local interests, but they may be seen as channels of communication open to those unable to make their point of view heard in the national newspapers.

A point much debated in academic centres where journalistic practices in the country are discussed, such as in Wales, Cardiff University's School of Journalism, in Scotland the University of Stirling's Department of Film, Media and Journalism, or the London School of Economics and Political Science's Media Group, is whether or not owners exert control over content. Realism suggests that owners will control content as they wish, subject to the resistance that can be mobilised against excessive control or the rules that they may establish, by agreement with editorial staff, for the degree of influence that they will seek to have.

Furthermore, the relationship between journalism and public relations has been a focus of critical review by such centres exploring source–media relations and the impact that powerful elites have on media content. The ability of powerful groups such as government and corporates to purchase public relations services is thought to have negative impact on the public sphere (Schlesinger, Miller and Dinan, 2001) Studies at Cardiff University have shown the extensive use made by the media of material derived from public relations sources (Lewis, Williams and Franklin, 2008: Davies 2008).

From the perspective of public relations, it is necessary to know the characteristics and inclinations towards control of owning individuals or groups, so that approaches to the media can be informed by this additional knowledge. In the UK, the media are seen as significant players in the relationship between government and the people of the country. Their part in this relationship has been closely examined in recent years, not least because of the way in which the government has tried to communicate through the media to the national population. This has been extensively studied and reported on with a view to improving relations between government, the media and the public, to rebuild a trust that has been lost (Final Report of the Independent Review of Government Communications, 2004).

The other important development in the UK media has been the move into online delivery of content, where parallel organisations have developed alongside their parent media organisations to use information gathered to feed the demands of online delivery. In this way, newspapers such as *The Guardian* and *The Financial Times* have built up significant web presences, maintained on a moment-by-moment basis, and offering new opportunities to those offering content for consideration by the media.

CEOs and senior practitioners interviewed by Murray and White (2004 and 2006) cited media scrutiny and the demands of increasing numbers of media channels for information as challenging aspects of the business and organisational environments to which they are now bound to respond. The relationship between practitioners and media representatives, such as journalists, has long been and will remain an uneasy one (White and Hobsbawm, 2007; L'Etang 2004), despite recent attempts by presidents of the Chartered Institute of Public Relations to address journalists' perceptions of the practice and to improve the relationship. There are many authoritative guides to the rich UK media environment. One of the most useful available to public relations practitioners is the Hollis Public Relations Annual (www.hollis-pr.com).

Public relations practitioners in the United Kingdom regard the media as a prime audience for practice, according to a series of studies conducted with members of the CIPR over a number of years (for example, White and Myers, 1998), and many public relations consultancies offer media relations as their main service to clients (despite evidence that these services are among the least rewarding that can be offered by public relations consultancies, in terms of their return in fee income to consultancies (White and Myers, 2001)). Because they can deliver large audiences, and help to create awareness and build support, the media are important in UK practice, but can sometimes be given an importance not justified by the immediate demands of the public relations task required. A senior UK practitioner influential in the development of the practice in the UK and internationally, Tim Traverse-Healy, has suggested that public relations practitioners are sometimes too focussed on the media and may overlook the significance of other groups. Media relations work in the UK **is** demanding, because of the aggressive approach taken to newsgathering by the UK media, because of the reach of the UK media, and because of the numbers of media outlets competing for information.

CONCLUDING THOUGHTS

This chapter has created a picture of the United Kingdom, and described significant features of national life that bear on the practice of public relations. The historical sections of the chapter have shown how public relations' development was shaped by the country's experience, as a major power and now as a country on the world stage still influential and economically significant, in close relationships with countries such as the US and members of the European Union and Commonwealth.

The country's experiences in the last century, of two world wars, of loss of empire, and of large-scale immigration are still working through political, economic, social and cultural changes—one consequence of which has been the emergence in the UK of a thriving public relations practice. Practice in the UK is based ultimately on a global outlook, reflected in the confidence of the national Chartered Institute of Public Relations, that "the CIPR is looked to as a source of good practice and a leader of the global profession. This was recognized in [the Institute's] Royal Charter submission" (CIPR Annual Review, 2005). The same review points to the CIPR's role in the work of the Global Alliance for Public Relations and Communication Management (www.globalpr.org) and the European Confederation CERP (www.cerp.org). The Institute sees itself as committed to meeting the education and training needs of an increasingly globalised profession. Within the UK, political, economic and social change, as well as developments in the media and in communication technology, are setting challenges that will force the continuing evolution of the practice and, in the opinion of practitioners inside and outside the country, help to prove—beyond doubt—the value of the practice.

REFERENCES

Biddlecombe, P. (ed) (1971) *Goodwill: the wasted asset*, London, Business Books.

Black, S. (1962) *Practical public relations*, London, Pitman.

Brebner, J. H. (1949) *Public relations and publicity*, London, Institute of Public Administration.

Britain in 2008 (2007): *The State of the Nation*, Swindon, Economic and Social Research Council.

Broom, G.M., and Smith, G.D. (1979). Testing the practitioner's impact on clients. *Public Relations Review 5*, 47–59.

Chartered Institute of Public Relations (2005) Measurement and Evaluation Resource, www.cipr.co.uk/news/research/evaluation_June05.pdf.

Colley, M. (1993) *The communicators: PR–the history of the Public Relations Institute of Ireland 1953–1993*, Public Relations Institute of Ireland.

Creedon, P.J (1991).Public relations and "women's work": Towards a feminist analysis of public relations roles. In L.A. Grunig, and J.E. Grunig (Eds.), *Public Relations Research Annual* (Vol.3, 67–84). Hillsdale, NJ, Lawrence Erlbaum Associates, Inc.

Davies, N (2008) *Flat Earth News*, London, Chatto and Windus.

Davis, A (2002) *Public Relations Democracy: Public Relations, Politics and the Mass Media*, Manchester, Manchester University Press.

Derriman, J. (1965) *Public relations in business management*, London, University of London Press.

Desanto, B. and Moss, D.A. (2004). Rediscovering what PR managers do: Rethinking the measurement of managerial behaviour in the public relations context. *Journal of Communications Management, 9*(2), 179–196.

Dolphin, R.R. (2002) A profile of PR directors in British companies. *Corporate Communications,* Vol 7(1), 17–24.

Hall, E. T. (1997) *Beyond Culture*, New York, Anchor Books.

Information Commissioner (2006) A Report on the Surveillance Society, for the Information Commissioner by the Surveillance Studies Network, London.

Institute of Public Relations (ed) (1958) *A guide to the practice of public relations*, London, Newman Neame.

Jefkins, F. (1977) *Planned press and public relations,* London, Blackie.

L'Etang, J. (2004) *Public Relations in Britain: a history of professional practice*, Mahwah, NJ, Lawrence Erlbaum Associates.

L'Etang, J. (2006), "Public relations as theatre: key players in the evolution of British public relations" In L'Etang, J. and Pieczka, M. (eds) *Public relations: critical debates and contemporary practice*, Mahwah, NJ, Lawrence Erlbaum Associates : 143–166.

L'Etang, J. (2007) *Public relations: concepts, practice and critique,* London, Sage.

L'Etang, J. and Pieczka, M. (eds) (2006) *Public relations: critical debates and contemporary practice*, Mahwah, NJ, Lawrence Erlbaum Associates.

Lewis, J., Williams, A. and Franklin, B. (2008) "A compromised fourth estate? UK news journalism, public relations and news sources" *Journalism Studies* vol. 9 no. 1 (in press).

Lloyd, H. and Lloyd, P. (1963) *Teach yourself public relations*, London, Hodder and Stoughton.

Magor, M. (2006) "Think tanks: some key issues." Unpublished paper.

Mintzberg, H. (1973). *The nature of managerial work*. New York: Harper and Row.

Moss. D.A., Newman, A.J. and Desanto, B. (2005) What do communication managers do? Defining and refining the core elements of management in the public relations/communications context. *Journalism and Mass Communication Quarterly*, 82(4), 73–890.

Moss, D.A., Warnaby, G. and Newman, A. (2000) Public relations practitioner role enactment at the senior management level within UK companies. *Journal of Public Relations Research* 12(4), pp 277–307.

Mulgan, G. (2004) Lessons of Power, *Prospect*, May (cover article).

Murray, K. and White, J. (2004) *CEO Views of Reputation Management: A Study of the Value of Public Relations, as Perceived by Organisation Leaders, A Report by Bell Pottinger*, London, Chime Communications.

Murray, K. and White, J. (2006) *Reputation Management: Leading Practitioners Look to the Future of Public Relations, A Report by Bell Pottinger*, London, Chime Communications.

Pieczka, M. (2006a) "Public relations expertise in practice" in L'Etang, J. and Pieczka, M. (eds) (2006) *Public relations: critical debates and contemporary practice*, Mahwah, NJ, Lawrence Erlbaum Associates: 279–302.

Pieczka, M. (2006b) "'Chemistry' and the public relations industry: an exploration of the concept of jurisdiction and issues arising" in L'Etang, J. and Pieczka, M. (eds) (2006) *Public relations: critical debates and contemporary practice*, Mahwah, NJ, Lawrence Erlbaum Associates: 303–331.

Pieczka, M. and L'Etang, J. (2001) "Public relations and the question of professionalism" in Heath, R. (ed) *Handbook of Public Relations,* London, Sage.

PR Landscapes, The United Kingdom (2006), Global Alliance for Public Relations and Communication Management, London, www.globalpr.org.

Schlesinger, P., Miller, D. and Dinan, W. (2001) *Open Scotland: Journalists, Spin Doctors and Lobbyists*, Edinburgh University Press.

Stewart, R. (1997). *The reality of management* (3rd Ed), Oxford, Butterworth Heinemann.

The Economic Significance of Public Relations (2005), London, Centre for Economics and Business Research.

Toth, E.L. and Grunig, L.A. (1993). The missing story of women in public relations. *Journal of Public Relations Research*, 5, 153–175.

Toth, E.L., Serini, S.A., Wright, D.K. and Emig, A.G. (1998). Trends in public relations roles:1990–1995. *Public Relations Review*, 24 (2), pp. 145–163.

Unlocking the Potential of Public Relations: Developing Good Practice (2003). A report jointly funded by the Department of Trade and Industry and the Institute of Public Relations, London.

White, J. and Hobsbawm, J. (2007) Public Relations and Journalism, *Journalism Practice*, Volume 1, Issue 2, 283–292.

White, J. and Myers, A. (1998) *Survey of Members of the Institute of Public Relations*, London, Institute of Public Relations.

White, J. and Myers, A. (2001) *Fee Setting Practices in Public Relations Consultancies*, A report prepared for the Public Relations Consultants Association, London.

20

FROM LITERARY BUREAUS TO A MODERN PROFESSION: THE DEVELOPMENT AND CURRENT STRUCTURE OF PUBLIC RELATIONS IN GERMANY

GÜNTER BENTELE
STEFAN WEHMEIER

INTRODUCTION

The Federal Republic of Germany with nearly 82 million inhabitants is the country with the highest population in middle Europe. It covers a 356,790 km² area. The North Sea and the Baltic Sea border the national territory to the north, and the Alps border the territory to the south. There are no such natural borders on the east and west. The northern neighbor is Denmark, and Poland and the Czech Republic are the eastern neighbors. The predominantly German-speaking nations Austria and Switzerland border Germany to the south, with France, Belgium, Luxembourg, and the Netherlands bordering on the west. Around 7.3 million foreigners (approx. 9% of the total population) live in Germany. The country ensures freedom of religion. In 2000, the Protestant and Catholic churches had around 27 million members each, with 2.8 million Muslims forming the next largest religious community.

HISTORY OF PUBLIC RELATIONS IN GERMANY

The development of public relations in Germany was shaped by numerous historical conditions. Political, economic, and social influences have had an impact on the evolving public relations profession in Germany. We emphasize the changing political history of Germany since the beginning of the 19th century because the type of state changed several

TABLE 20.1
Periods of German Public Relations

Pre-history:
  Official press politics, functional public relations, development of instruments

Period 1 (mid-19th century–1918) Development of the occupational field	Development of the first press offices in politics and firms, war press releases under the conditions of censorship, first public campaigns
Period 2 (1918–1933) Consolidation and growth	Fast and widespread growth of press offices in different social fields: economy, politics, municipal administration
Period 3 (1933–1945) Media relations and political propaganda and the Nazi Regime	Party-ideological media relations within political propaganda. National and party-related control and direction of journalism, media relations, and inner relations
Period 4 (1945–1958) New beginning and upturn	Postwar development, upturn and orientation to the American model starting in the early 1950s, development of a new professional self-understanding under the conditions of democratic structures (public relations defined as distinct from propaganda and advertisement), fast development of the professional field predominantly in the economic sphere
Period 5 (1958–1985) Consolidation of the professional field in the Federal Republic of Germany and establishment of a socialist public relations in the German Democratic Republic (GDR)	Development of a professional self-consciousness, 1958 foundation of the professional association DPRG, which initiated private training programs. Simultaneous with the developments in West Germany, a type of socialist public relations developed in the GDR from the mid-1960s.
Period 6 (1985–present) Boom of the professional field and professionalization	Strong development of public relations agencies, professionalization of the field, beginning and development of academic public relations education; improvements in the training system, scientific application and enhancement of the instruments; development of public relations as a science

Note. From Bentele 1997: 161

times from the German Alliance during the German Reich to the Weimar Republic, followed by the Nazi Regime, World War II, and the establishment of two German states (one democratic and one socialist), which eventually reunited in 1990. These turning points are also reflected in the periodical structure of German public relations history (see Table 20.1), which is closely related to the general historic periods.

The Press and Freedom of the Press Until 1914

The defeat of France by Napoleon in 1806 officially sealed the end of the Holy Roman Empire. After the Congress of Vienna, this German Empire was succeeded by the German Alliance. It constituted 39 states and existed until 1866. Above all, the claims of sovereignty of some principalities lead to a strong particularism within the alliance (Schieder, 1999, pp. 98–107). A strong and powerful central power was missing, and there was no freedom of the press. For example, on October 18, 1819, the censorship dictate in Prussia since December 1788 was renewed (Koszyk, 1966, p. 59). Only after the failed March Revolution in 1848 was censorship abolished in some states. However, the rulers still kept powerful means of pressure on printing products that they disliked. The most important institute were the granting and cancellation of concessions based on the whims of the rulers (Koszyk, 1966, pp. 120–126).

The German party-related press, such as the social–democratic press, developed under these conditions until the founding of the German Reich in 1871 (Koszyk, 1966, pp. 127–208). Otto von Bismarck, who was prime minister from 1862 and chancellor of the Reich from 1871, tried to either prohibit or exploit the press. Bismarck's treatment of the press was a mix of banning newspapers, legally persecuting journalists and publishers, and manipulating media content (Koszyk, 1966, pp. 229–250).

After the founding of the German Reich, a few more rights and journalistic freedoms were granted by the *Reichspressegesetz* (Reich press law). As a result, the German press experienced an upturn, but it also was an opportunity for advertising gazettes and mass press products of a rather cheap and apolitical character. In 1914, the number of daily and weekly newspapers was around 4,200, and the number of copies printed is estimated to have been 18 million (Pürer & Raabe, 1996, p. 22). This extensive development of the press also caused national organizations and businesses to put more effort into public relations. During this time, public information and public manipulation were often strongly intertwined.

State Press Politics, Municipal Public Relations, and the Evolution of Business-like Public Relations

In 1841, the *Ministerial-Zeitungsbüro* (governmental bureau of newspapers) was established in Prussia as the first political press department. Its function was not only to inform and observe the press but also to avoid negative articles in the media (known as wrong press reports) and the impression of overt censorship (Nöth-Greis, 1997). After the official abolishment of censorship in 1848, the communicative functions of the succeeding institutions such as *Literarisches Cabinet* (Literary Cabinet; 1848–1859), *Centralstelle für Presseangelegenheiten* (Central Office of Press Affairs; 1850–1860), and *Literarisches Büro* (Literary Bureau; 1860–1920) shifted to the observation of the press, the internal information of the Prussian government, and international press relations. However, particularly under Bismarck, this shift included a more subtle influence and control of the press. For example, officious (or government-friendly) newspapers were financially supported (Koszyk, 1966, p. 229ff; Nöth-Greis, 1997). This practice of keeping in leading strings of the press by the government continued after the founding of the German Reich and after the already mentioned liberalization of the press through the Reich press law. Further, the *Pressedezernat des Auswärtigen Amtes* (Press Department at the Office of Foreign Affairs), founded in 1871, had task observation and information of the press and its manipulation. The first corporate press department was established by Alfred Krupp, the founder of the famous steel company, Krupp, in 1870, 4 years after Krupp had seen the necessity to hire a literate. The duty of this literate was to read newspapers from around the world that the organization saw as important as well as to write articles, brochures, and correspondences to publicize the corporation and its products (Wolbring, 2000).

Admiral Alfred von Tirpitz engineered one of the most important public campaigns of the German Reich in his quest to build a strong German Naval fleet. At the end of the 19th century, the German economy developed rapidly, and a section of the political and military elite desired to extend German influence by colonizing new territories. This section of the power elite wanted to counter the dominance of the British Empire by building a strong navy that could not only colonize new lands but also protect German merchant ships. Tirpitz and his supporters had to first convince a majority of the political class, the Kaiser, and the population that this was the right thing for Germany. Tirpitz used different kinds of publicity instruments such as posters, lectures, speeches, and press reports to persuade the relevant target groups. By arguing his case from an economic standpoint, he finally was successful in changing public opinion (Kunczik, 1997, pp. 111–116). Whereas the "fleet campaign" had some manipulative characteristics, the public relations activities at the municipal level mainly were informative. They mostly focused on developing and maintaining relationships with local publics and carrying on the tasks of the cities, thereby actually performing community relations (Liebert, 1997, p. 88).

Besides the political changes of the 19th century, the economic and technical progress also shaped the development of public relations in Germany. Coal mining and the steel industry became pivotal foundations of the German heavy industry and electronics, and chemistry became an innovative growth industry. Alfred Krupp, Emil Rathenau, and Werner von Siemens simultaneously became leading businessmen as well as architects of public relations (Wolbring, 2000; Zipfel, 1997).

In the course of industrialization, friction developed between the powerful trusts and wealthy business families and the evolving working class. Along with industrialization and urbanization, social hardship appeared, which demanded actions from politicians and businesses. Consequently, the late 19th century witnessed the first steps toward social legislation and the first efforts at human relations, such as employee magazines, pensions, sports and singing clubs, and recreation homes for children. The motivation for these moves originated from the ethical pretense of numerous businessmen viewing themselves as fathers of a family of workers on the one hand while fearing strikes and rebellions on the other.

In addition to these internal communication practices, there were early accounts of external communication instruments in companies like Krupp, AEG, and Siemens. Krupp used the First World Exhibition in 1851 in London to present his own efficiency and to show off the biggest steel cube. AEG had already begun systematical analysis of press clippings since the beginning of the 20th century.

Public Relations From World War I Until the Nazi Dictatorship

During the World War I, there was one outstanding national public relations campaign—the loan campaign to raise funds for financing the war. Corporate public relations also was affected by the war, with companies morally supporting their employees on the front with employee magazines (Heise, 2000). At the end of the war and the establishment of the democratic Weimar Republic, public relations made great strides in Germany. A significant number of press offices and news bureaus came into being, and the economic boom of the Twenties convinced the businessmen to carry out active public relations (Kunczik, 1997, pp. 166–182, 290–307).

In contrast, the national socialism (1933–1945) period represented a step backward for the entire field of public communication. Under the Nazi dictatorship, the media were brought in line and exploited to advance the Nazi doctrine. The national socialist state made great propagandistic efforts, and the oppressed media (press, broadcasting, and film) served as loudspeakers of political and ideological content. Although there had existed a relatively diverse and independent media system in the Weimar Republic, public information activities under the Nazis was centralized under the Reich Ministry of Public

Information and Propaganda. The media were cleared of Jewish journalists, and strict penalties were introduced to punish people who did not write stories that pleased the Nazis. Needless to say, the entire system of public communication gained a propagandistic character. Although external media relations and internal information in governmental organizations, associations, communities, cultural institutions, and companies still existed during the Nazi dictatorship, these activities often employed a propagandistic communication style. During this period, German public relations pioneers Carl Hundhausen and Albert Oeckl got their first experience in advertising and public relations. Ivy L. Lee, who at the beginning of the Nazi regime was counselor to a subsidiary of the IG Farben, represented the connection between the development of public relations in Germany and the United States (Kunczik, 1997, pp. 298–301).

From the End of World War II Until Today

After World War II, the public relations field in West Germany was reborn. The American influence on West German society was also widely felt in the development of postwar public relations. Besides German advertising and public relations agencies, branches of American agencies also started to operate in West Germany and bring with them their view of public relations. This, to a certain extent, only meant revitalizing practices that could not be carried out during the Nazi regime. Carl Hundhausen and Albert Oeckl represented both continuity and new beginning for the public relations profession in West Germany. Both of them had already been active in public relations during the Nazi dictatorship, and now they played a crucial role in the development of the profession in the first 2 decades after the war. One of their central achievements was the founding of the professional association of public relations, the Deutsche Public Relations Gesellschaft (DPRG) or the German Public Relations Association. Carl Hundhausen and, later, Albert Oeckl were chairmen of this organization for many years (Binder, 1983).

Until the late 1960s, a rather simple understanding of public relations was dominant in Germany. Public relations was interpreted as advertising for trust. Information and the creation of attention were understood to build trust in organizations and to draw the attention of the media to their products and images. It was only in the early 1970s that an understanding of public relations as the dialogue with different target groups started to develop. The end of the so called economic miracle, resulting in social tensions, and the appearance of environmental activism turned customers into demanding groups with whom dialogue needed to be established. A boom of financial and human resources has been witnessed among public relations agencies since the middle of the 1980s. In addition, public relations was introduced in universities and polytechnics (*Fachhochschulen*), resulting in the intense discussion of ethical standards and the scientific foundation of the field (Bentele & Liebert, 1998, pp. 78–80; Kunczik, 1999).

CHARACTERIZING PRESENT STRUCTURES OF THE PUBLIC RELATIONS FIELD IN GERMANY

The Image of Public Relations

The image of the public relations field varies among different publics. Because public relations is hardly felt directly by the general public, it has a rather diffuse image in contrast to journalists and the media as well as chairmen of companies and other high-ranking persons in organizations who can react directly to public relations activities. Journalists often have an ambivalent image of the public relations field. On one hand, they recognize that public relations is indispensable as a professional information source; on the other hand, they continue to harbor negative expressions such as "PR gags" or "PR pretense" or "typical PR" (these expressions refer to exaggerations or entertaining events with only little content). Especially true of members of the dominant coalition such as the boards of companies, the image of communication experts has significantly improved over the last few decades. In the 1960s expressions like *Sektglashalter* (someone who only holds champagne glasses in his or her hands) or *Frühstücksdirektor* (someone who has a director's position but only dines with guests) were still used to characterize the public relations profession in a negative way. Today, the necessity of communication management and the need to employ well-qualified academics are mainly unquestioned although not yet recognized universally in the country. The bigger an enterprise, the more readily public relations is accepted as an independent function by the organization, preferably combined with other communication functions (Bruhn & Boenigk, 1999, Haedrich, Jenner, Olavarria, & Possekal, 1994). Professional communication experts are treated as partners and as colleagues "on the other side of the desk" by journalists.

Definitions and Different Public Relations Concepts

Just as there are many definitions of terms such as *philosophy, communication,* or *sociology,* there are many definitions of the term *public relations* in Germany. In 1951, Carl Hundhausen (1893–1977) defined public relations as "letting the public or its parts know about yourself in order to advertise for trust" (Hundhausen, 1951, p. 53). Albert Oeckl (1909–2001), who in the 1950s rediscovered the German term *Öffentlichkeitsarbeit* that had been in use in 1917, described public relations as "working *with* the public, working *for* the public, working *in* the public." He continued that "working means the intended, planned, and continuous effort to build mutual understanding and trust and to care about it" (Oeckl, 1964, p. 36). Twelve years later, he defined *Öffentlichkeitsarbeit* as "information + adaptation + integration" (Oeckl, 1976, p. 52). Following a definition by Grunig and Hunt (1984, p. 4), Bentele (1998) described public relations as the "management of information and communication processes between organizations on the one side and their internal and external environments (publics) on the other side. Public Relations serves the functions of information, communication, persuasion, image building, continuous building of trust, management of conflicts, and the generation of social consensus" (p. 33).

To structure the countless definitions in a logical way, different perspectives of public relations should be defined. Bentele (1998, p. 27 ff) distinguished three *starting perspectives* (Who defines public relations?) and three *target perspectives* (How is it defined?). The three starting perspectives are (a) the *everyday life perspective,* (b) the *professional perspective,* and (c) the *scientific perspective.* The target perspectives are the *activity related, organizational,* and *society related* (see table 20.2).

It is not surprising that there are different definitions within the professional perspective. But in the academic perspective, two clearly different perspectives can be distinguished: the *organizational* perspective (subdivided into the communication studies and the business studies perspectives) and the society-related perspective (i. e., public relations is seen and analyzed as a functional element of our modern information and communication society).

Every-day life perceptions of public relations frequently focus not only on neutral fields of activities of public relations practitioners (e.g., providing information) but also on judgments. Those can be positive (e.g., public relations is a cool job and an interesting occupation) or negative (e.g., public relations referred to as embellishments, propaganda, or

TABLE 20.2
Different Starting and Target Perspectives of Public Relations

	Activity related perspective	Organizational perspective	Society related perspective
Every-day life perspective	Interesting profession but also manipulation, extenuation, propaganda, media relations	Activities of public relations agencies, public relations departments in companies etc.	No concept
Professional perspective	Information, talk to the public, care for relationships, keep secrets, and manipulation	Task and function of leadership and management	Basic form of public communication
Scientific perspective	Information, communication, persuasion, acquisition of trust, and soon	Communication studies: communication management. Business studies: instrument of marketing, communication politics	Form of public communication, subsystem of the public communication system

Note. From Bentele 1998: 29

manipulation). Conversely, the conceptions of practitioners mostly are positively connoted but often normatively introduced. Nowadays, professional associations usually label public relations as *dialogue*, but this is more of a normative pretense than an empirical proof. Using a scientifically based viewpoint, public relations can be looked at from an activity-related perspective as well as from an organizational and a macrosocial point of view. The organizational–communication studies perspective poses the question: What does public relations generally contribute to organizations (not only businesses)? Another scientific perspective is the study of marketing which uses public relations as an instrument within communication politics. Communication politics itself is seen as just another part of the general marketing mix (besides product politics, price politics, and placement politics). Thus, public relations in this perspective is in principle subordinate to marketing (for more on this point, see the definitions of public relations, marketing, and advertising in the following chapter). From a society-related (macrosocial) perspective, the question arises: Which social function(s) for the entire society are held by all organizational public relations activities (for more details, refer to Bentele, 1998, p. 32; Ronneberger & Rühl, 1992, p. 249 ff)?

Structures of the Occupational Public Relations Field in Germany

To give an account on the present status of the field in Germany, one can draw on a number of empirical studies that offer important insights from different perspectives. However, a representative study that covers the entire field in Germany does not exist. The total number of full-time public relations practitioners in Germany is estimated to be at least 20,000, of which around 40% work in corporate public relations; 20% in organizations, such as associations, clubs, churches, unions, and so on; 20% in institutions (e.g., political administration on national, regional, and local levels as well as courts); and 20% in public relations agencies (Bentele, 1998). Only an estimated 10% of all public relations professionals are members of one of the professional associations (e.g., the DPRG has approx. 1,800 members: about 4,000 PR practitioners are members of the *Deutscher Journalisten Verband, djv* [the German Journalists Association]. The number of public relations practitioners has increased faster than the number of journalists in Germany. In 1973, the leading public relations agencies founded their own association (Gesellschaft PR-Agenturen—the Association of Public Relations Agencies), which presently accounts for about 30 agencies representing nearly 1,500 professionals.

Professionalization. The degree of professionalization of the public location field, which is strongly interconnected with the training facilities, has been increasing since the beginning of the 1990s. Note that the public relations profession is, in general, academically institutionalized, with 70% to 80% of the practitioners having graduated from an institution of higher education (universities or polytechnic institutions). Some have even earned doctoral degrees (Becher, 1996; Merten, 1997). Nevertheless, the proportion of public relations practitioners who possess a high degree of public relations training (e.g., those who took many public relations courses or majored in public relations) is still under 20% (Röttger, 2000, p. 317). As early as the 1960s and 1970s, the DPRG and some private institutions began offering training courses, with several spread over a few weeks. Yet, it is only since the early 1990s that there has been a boom in public relations training. Many courses, sometimes including government support, were offered by a number of private providers to unemployed academics coming from all disciplines. Some of these courses lasted only 1 day or were spread over a few days, whereas others lasted several weeks or went as long as $1\frac{1}{2}$ years. Universities also began to offer public relations-related subjects, which eventually led to several public relations programs at major universities such as the Free University of Berlin and the Leipzig University. In addition, we currently see some public relations programs at vocational polytechnic institutes (Fachhochschulen) and universities (e.g., Hannover and Osnabrück). Equally important is the fact that several professional associations came together to establish a training academy called Deutsche Akademie für Public Relations—German Academy of Public Relations. There are some 40 other private academies and institutes that offer public relations courses, which are also available in evening schools and as distance learning courses. In the future, the function of public relations training is going to shift to the traditional institutions (polytechnic schools and universities), but private institutions will continue to be important for programs that further education (Bentele & Szyszka, 1995; Brauer, 1996; von Schlippe, Martini, & Schulze-Fürstenow, 1998).

Course Content. The content of academic programs as well as that of private institutions is very diverse and covers the entire spectrum of the profession, including courses such as the basics of communication and public relations, the history of public relations and public relations theories, the methods and instruments of practical public relations and communication management (e.g., media relations, investor relations, event management, internal communication, crisis public relations, and integrated communication), methods of evaluation and empirical communication and social research, and ethics. The training programs also cover economic and legal topics relevant to the profession. At universities, students are expected to take a second major or a minor to develop the required competence in a related discipline, such as political science or business. As far as professional ethics is concerned, the existing ethical codes such as the Code of Athens or Code of Lisbon are not well-known by public relations practitioners (Becher, 1996, p. 187; Röttger, 2000, p. 324). Although ethical attitudes are present among individual practitioners, public discourses on ethics are rare among practitioners. At least the Deutsche Rat für Public Relations (the German Council of Public Relations), a self-regulating organization founded in 1985 by the associations in the field, has been relatively active for some years outlining new guidelines and encouraging discourses about the violation of rules or ethical codes by agencies or practitioners (Avenarius, 1998; Bentele, 2000).

Two other noticeable features of the professional field in Germany are the process of feminization and the openness of the profession, to imports from other professions, such as journalism, law, or engineering. As recently as the late 1980s, not even 15% of public relations professionals in corporations, administration, or associations were women (Böeckelmann, 1988, p. 123; 1991a, p. 155; 1991b, p. 189). A survey by Merten (1997) showed that this proportion rose to 42% by 1996. Further, the present proportion of women among the members of the DPRG (43% in 2001) further confirms this process of feminization of the workforce as does the increase in the number of female public relations students at universities and *Fachhochschulen*, which is more than 60% of the student population.

The fact that the public relations field in Germany is still attracting practitioners from other occupations is proven by a 1989 survey of DPRG members as well as by a more recent study by Becher (1996). Both studies showed that approximately 33% of all people interviewed originally came from journalism, approximately 33% came from business or administration professions, and about 15% had previously worked in advertising and market research. Interestingly, about 20% had no other occupation before entering public relations (Becher, 1996, p. 194; DPRG, 1990).

Concerning the question of self-understanding and role models, Böckelmann's (1991b) surveys indicated that most press speakers (79% in corporations; 56% in organizations such as labor unions, churches, political parties, and business associations; and 53% in institutions such as ministries, parliaments, administration of justice, or municipal administration) identified themselves as being representatives of their respective organization. About 54% to 70% thought of themselves as mediators between the organization and the public, and only 12% (businesses) and 29% (organizations) considered themselves to be journalists (Böckelmann, 1991b, p. 176). This could have resulted from the high number of former journalists among public relations practitioners. Empirical data on the self-assessment and external assessment of public relations technicians and managers do not exist in Germany.

Which activities typically dominate the work of public relations professionals? The lion's share of the daily agenda is used for media relations (press reports, press conferences, organizing talks with journalists, etc.). Internal communication is dominated by analyzing the media as well as by producing and organizing internal media, such as employee magazines and using the intranet.

Are there different standards of quality in the different specialties of the profession? Based on our observations and anecdotal data, the highest qualified public relations practitioners can be found in public relations agencies and in the public relations departments of big companies. These departments are generally fully staffed, and the various specialties are well differentiated. The public relations departments of nonprofit organizations, associations, and public institutions (e.g., museums, theaters, and universities) had employees with the lowest qualifications and worst equipment. The need for public affairs and political communication (not election campaigning) has increased over the last 10 years. As a result, the demand for specialized agencies is high. Particularly during election campaigns, parties do establish large communication departments, which are planned strategically and communicate in a differentiated way. Varying quality standards are more prominent between businesses or agencies and the nonprofit and public field than between different branches (e.g., between the car industry and the financial branch or chemistry).

One of the most ardent desires of public relations associations is the highest possible ranking of public relations practitioners within an organizational hierarchy. According to Merten's (1997), survey, 68% of interviewees held a leading position in the organizational structure. A representative survey among businessmen by Haedrich et al. (1994, p. 4) revealed that 26% of all companies ranked public relations as a line function, whereas 71% ranked it as a management function. The same survey also revealed that 33% of responding companies ranked public relations as being in the top level of the corporate hierarchy, 54% ranked it at the second highest level (i.e., directly under the executive level), 12% ranked it at the third level of hierarchy, and 1% graded it even lower. The same study also found that the bigger a business was, the more independence was granted to the public relations departments; this hierarchy level was similar to that in marketing departments or, in some cases, was even higher than the marketing department. At the same time, the subordination of public relations under marketing or at least the mixing of the two tasks is still apparent especially in small and medium-size firms.

In 1997, the wbpr agency surveyed 3,000 businessmen and found that the ranking of public relations within businesses has improved since the 1990 study. According to those interviewed, 16% ranked public relations as very high, 56% ranked it and as high (wbpr, 1997, p. 9 ff). A recent representative survey among companies confirms these older results and indicates that 80% of the heads of communication departments work on the top hierarchical level with 7% of the public relations department heads even serving as members of the board (Zühlsdorf, 2002, p. 215). These results clearly show that today German companies consider public relations to be relatively important. When public relations practitioners or entire communication departments have a rather low status, this may be due to the fact that public relations practitioners have inferior qualifications at the decision-making level. This situation can be improved not only by continuing the process of professionalization and improving practitioner training but also by academically strengthening the professional standards.

Although it is possible to use existing data to identify the frequency of use of various public relations tools, it does not seem to make sense to rank more complex public relations strategies and methods used in Germany. Presumably, wherever there is public relations, there are at least media relations activities. In addition, one can assume that all of the modern methods of public relations are in use, such as employee relations, investor relations as part of financial relations (this has quickly developed over the last 5 years), crisis communication, issues management (Röttger, 2000a), and event management. Some of the more recent trends, especially at the bigger agencies, focus on change communication (i.e., the management of communication by companies undergoing change), issues management, sustainability communication, brand public relations, corporate governance, and impression management (Bentele, Piwinger, & Schönborn, 2001). These specialties are often organizationally differentiated in bigger companies. Public relations agencies that specialize in event communication, environmental public relations, or change communications are often hired by big corporations. The activities of governmental organizations, municipalities, and associations are dominated by routine public relations, whereas new trends, often imported from the United States, are first applied by the bigger corporations.

THE POLITICAL SYSTEM OF GERMANY

The political experiences of the Weimar Republic and the national–socialist dictatorship have influenced the Constitution of the Federal Republic of Germany. The failure of the Weimar constitution is reflected on in the *Grundgesetz* (Constitution) in four inalterable (nonrepealable) principles. Article 79 (paragraph 3), in combination with Article 1 and 20, defines the principle of human and fundamental rights of democracy, federalism, and the constitutional and welfare state. This constitutional nucleus places the *Grundgesetz* not only on a liberal and democratic structure but also dissociates it from the legal positivism of the Weimar Republic under which everything was legal if decided with the support of a majority of votes (Rudzio, 1997, p. 52). The consequences of the failure of the Weimar Republic are evident in the following four constitutional principles.

1. All political institutions are organized within a parliamentary government system. The parliament can claim exclusive and direct political legitimacy both at the federal (*Bund*) and state (*Länder* or land) levels. All other state institutions derive from the *Bundestag* (lower house of the parliament) or the *Landtag* (state parliament). The chancellor is elected by the parliament and can only be dismissed by a no-confidence majority vote or through the election of a successor. Conversely, the federal president has only representative functions. In Germany, there can be referenda though they are restricted to questions on the new organization of the *Länder* (Rudzio, 1997, p. 60).

2. Germany can be classified as an anthropocentric state. In addition to the traditional features of a constitutional state (i.e., the separation of the powers, the independence of the courts, and the equality before the law), the German *Grundgesetz* also emphasizes the crucial role of inviolable human rights. These human rights are directly effective and can be claimed even at the highest Federal Constitutional Court. In material terms, the fundamental rights belong to the liberal–democratic tradition. Basically, there are two distinct groups of rights (Rudzio, 2000, p. 54): (a) liberal defensive rights against the state (e.g., personal protection and human dignity) and (b) democratic participation rights (e.g., freedom of thought and freedom of association). In particular, the latter refers to just another understanding of democracy. Through Article 9, Germany guarantees the freedom of the citizens to organize themselves, whereas Article 5 and others guarantee the freedom of speech. Freely organized interest groups (e.g., activist groups, citizens' initiatives, demonstrations, and corporations) have the right to stand up actively for their interests and thus to influence the development of political objectives. Due to the possibility of free articulation of interests and their organization in interest groups, Germany can be called a pluralistic democracy where, in principle, all interests can be articulated (Rudzio, 2000, p. 69 ff).

3. Liberal democracies are supported by federalism with the balance of power vertically split between the federal government and individual states. The right to participate in the central decision-making processes is granted to the land governments. The individual states apply federal laws and translate them into action. In this respect, an important feature of the German federalism is the close linkage between the federal (central) government and the states (*Länder*; Rudzio, 1997, p. 53).

4. In contrast to the other constitutional principles, the principle of the welfare state is not elucidated explicitly. It does not contain claim over rights such as the right to work, the right to education, or the right to obtain housing. Still, from the welfare principle, one can draw that it is not legal to leave any individual to his or her fate without a minimum of social care. In addition, the legislator can be obliged to do something about social equalization. How this is done is up to the responsibility of the political majority (Rudzio, 1997, p. 54 ff).

For the purpose of the protection of liberal democratic fundamental rights, the constitution allows a number of legal–administrative procedures (e.g., the prohibition of unconstitutional parties and the right to resist against anyone trying to destroy the fundamental order). For this reason, this democracy is also called a resistant democracy. However, these resistance rights do mainly serve preventive functions to minimize the scope for antidemocratic actions (Rudzio, 2000, p. 46 ff).

On the basis of this constitutional nucleus, a central function of public relations can be derived. The information activities conducted via public relations, that is "making public" (publicizing) information, opinions, attitudes, and demands, corresponds with the concept of a functioning liberal–democratic system (Ronneberger, 1977, p. 12). Pluralistic societies live on public discourses that evoke political objectives and mandatory decisions. Public communication processes make mutual control possible, and the discussion of different interests make mutual corrections possible. The overall aim is to achieve a social consensus of interests (Ronneberger, 1977, p. 13).

The political system of Germany has always had a strong influence on the communication style[1] public relations and its organizational forms. The first German Democracy, the Weimar Republic, enabled rapid development of the public relations profession in all social areas. During the Nazi dictatorship (third period of German public relations history), many issues could not be discussed publicly because of censorship by the state; during, the same time period, the public relations style was propagandistic. During the later periods, public relations developed under the framework of a democratic political system including the growth of organizational forms such as public relations agencies.

THE ECONOMIC SYSTEM IN GERMANY

The concept of a social market economy, which has been present in Germany since 1949, is intertwined with the former federal minister of economy and later Chancellor Ludwig Erhard and his counselor, Alfred Müller-Armack. A social market economy is a special type of economy that pursues the synthesis of legitimized economic freedoms with welfare state ideals of social safety and social justice (Pilz & Ortwein, 1997, p. 250 ff). Considerations to join social and political components evolved at the end of the 19th century when social imbalances started to appear as a result of the development of industrial societies.

The idea of this synthesis grounds on theoretical considerations of the *ordoliberalism*[2], but particular intentions of the Christian social doctrine and liberal socialism were also integrated. Due to this concept, the dissociation from the collectivist socialism and an unbounded capitalism was achievable. The social market economy upholds the liberal economic structures that are constituted by private ownership and private autonomy. Consequently, a *Vergemeinschaftung* (nationalization) of the means of production and a centralized economic control are mostly not feasible. The state confines its own actions

---

[1]Communication styles of public relations can be defined as public communication patterns that consist of combinations of different communication forms (language and textual patters, terminology, or argumentation) and the the selection of publicly discussed topics or themes. At least informative, argumentative, persuasive, and propagandistic public relations styles can be differentiated. They are influenced by social and (especially) political structures.

[2]This word is composed from *liberalism* and the Latin word *ordo* or order. Ordoliberalism is the technical term for the neo-liberal school of thinking (Schmidt, 1995, p. 679).

to setting general frameworks. Social justice, personal freedom, and economic efficiency are interdependent elements of a social market economy (Hennig, 1990, p. 59 ff; Pilz & Ortwein, 1997, p. 251 ff).

The general political framework sets out basic *constitutive* and *regulative* elements for economic politics. Constitutive elements consist of the economic competition (i.e., the free competition of supply and demand), free access to markets, the protection of the freedom to make contracts, and the constancy of economic politics that guarantees a reasonable degree of safety for investments to the businesses (Grosser, 1993, p. 10 ff; Lampert, 1990, p. 36 ff; Pilz & Ortwein, 1997, pp. 252–254). However, economic competition can clash with other state objectives (e.g., the right to equal chances), and competition can also be limited by fusion processes. Therefore, state institutions regulate the conditions of particular processes. Regulating elements are the correction of the market-conditioned income distribution by finance politics, the establishment of a system of social protection that provides minimum social standards (wages, working and time regulations, and regulations on working women and children), and the observation and control of monopolizing processes by cartel institutions (Pilz & Ortwein, 1997, p. 252 ff).

After the end of the economic miracle of the 1960s, the economic–political functions of the state were redefined with the introduction of the *Stabilitätsgesetz* (stability act). This law is also known as the *magic rectangle*, referring to its four objectives. The economic activities of both the federal government and individual states are supposed to contribute to a stable price level, a high employment rate, a balanced international trade, and an appropriate economic growth.

The social and economic structures of Germany have developed and changed significantly. The theoretical conceptualization allowed the building of efficient and liberal structures as well as the integration of a high degree of social market economy achievements (e.g., business constitutions) into the everyday economic activities. However, this structure has been watered down in some fields such as agriculture, pensions, and health insurance. It is now apparent that, due to demographic changes, the quantitative limits of the social sector have been reached. The concept of a social market economy is now facing major challenges.

The system of social market economy, together with a democratic political system, has generally enabled and necessitated the use of public relations by all kinds of social organizations, such as corporations, associations, unions, churches, nongovernmental organizations (NGOs), and so on. Furthermore, different influences of the economic system on public relations could be observed during different phases after World War II. During the 1950s for example, when the acceptance of a social market economy was rather limited, a broad information campaign called *Die Waage* (or pair of scales or the idea to have a socially and economically balanced system in society) was initiated to improve the knowledge and the degree of acceptance of this system. The amount of money in the communication (advertising and public relations) budgets of business enterprises depends directly on the level of ecomomic development. The longevity of public relations agencies also depends on the status of the economy. When corporations slash communication budgets, both in-house public relations and agencies suffer. Advertising budgets were slashed 10% in 2001 after many years of double-digit growth rates. There was a shrinking of the advertising and public relations agency sectors in 2001. This negative trend continues in 2002. Stuctrual changes to the economic system have had positive impacts on some sections of the public relations industry. The great number of IPOs (Initial Public Offering) in 2000 and 2001 has increased the demand for investor relations experts, resulting in a short-term paucity for skilled practitioners.

THE MEDIA SYSTEM IN GERMANY

In pluralistic societies, the mass media serve a key function. Being independent from governmental influence, they generate debate in the public sphere by disseminating information about all important events in politics, economy, society, and culture (Rudzio, 2000, p. 483). The most vital precondition is the freedom of the press which is guaranteed in Article 5 of the German constitution. Paragraph 1 of the constitution guarantees "... freedom of the press and the freedom of broadcast reporting on radio and in film" (*Grundgesetz*, 1994, p. 14) that is free from censorship.

Mass media in Germany are assigned a service function, which includes three main tasks: to encourage the development of public opinion, to control the legislature; the government, and their executing institutions as well as the legal authorities (judicature); and to mediate between the citizens and state institutions (Branahl, 2000, p. 20 ff). At the same time, mass media are economic businesses that have to be regulated. One regulating element is the media diversity, which means that preferential treatment is deliberately granted to the print media because the diversity of the print media market ensures the liberal development of opinions or external pluralism (Papier & Möller, 1999, p. 464). In addition, monopolies can be legally prevented (Pürer & Raabe, 1996, p. 260 ff). The legal regulations for the media can be found in the constitution, verdicts of the Federal Constitutional Court, the media laws of the *Länder*, and cartel and copyright laws (Pürer & Raabe, 1996, p. 261).

The media system of Germany used to be strictly divided into the privately owned print media market and the publicly held broadcasting market until the mid-1980s. The individual types of media can be classified into analytical categories such as publicity, periodicity, topicality, and universality. In Germany, the following basic types of print media can be distinguished: daily newspapers, weekly newspapers, magazines, and advertising journals (Noelle-Neumann, Schulz, & Wilke, 2000, p. 382–412). Due to the technical development of cables and satellites, the argument of a technically limited distribution of television and radio programs became obsolete. Private broadcasting was introduced, and this constituted the dual-broadcasting system in Germany in which public and private commercial broadcasting operate side by side (Stuiber, 1998, pp. 517, 707). Public and private broadcasting are subject to different legal regulations. Public broadcasting has to serve public welfare and ensure the fundamental tasks of providing audiences with information, sports, entertainment, and culture. It has a central integrating function because it articulates the interests of minorities and generates public access among different interest groups (Hesse, 1999, p. 115 ff). For this reason, public broadcasting adopts a strict, internal pluralistic concept (*Binnenpluralismus*) wherein every program has to reflect the actual diversity of the society. Official and independent *Rundfunkräte* (broadcasting boards) control whether these normative demands are fulfilled. In these boards, the representatives of socially relevant groups such as political parties, employers' associations, unions, religions, and science are not allowed to conduct censorship, but they can in retrospect judge the plurality of the programs. Public broadcasting is financed by fees and advertising, which ensures their independence from state budgets (Hesse, 1999, p. 178 ff).

Because private broadcasting depends on incomes from advertising, the constitutional demands are less. As an indirect consequence of economic competition, the concession of private broadcasting activities is expected to result in an increasing diversity of offerings thereby providing more choices for the consumer. This demand is met when at least three stations that cover all general interests are distributed all over Germany by at least three media organizations. Under this condition, the total amount of content provided by private broadcasters has to correspond with the diversity of opinions in the society. To prevent a private broadcasting organization from monopolizing segments of the market, a provider is not given a license to acquire another station if one of the existing stations gathers more that 30% of the audience (Papier & Möller, 1999, p. 465). The media institutions of the *Länder* and the commission for the determination of concentration in the media field (Kommission zur Ermittlung der Konzentration im Medienbereich) are supervising this aspect (Hesse, 1999, p. 243).

Included in the dual-broadcasting system are possibilities for citizens' broadcasting in a local area. Due to the federal structure of the radio and television market, the regulations differ from region to region. In North-Rhine Westfalia, for example, citizens are allowed to produce their own radio and television shows to be broadcast on so-called *open channels*. Open channels distribute their content via private media stations, and these stations are obliged to give technical support for producing the journalistic content (LRG NW, 1995). However, due to the low professional standard of these programs, they are not very popular with audiences.

Media Outreach

An exact measuring system makes precise data about media use by the population possible. The average time of media use is 8.5 hr per day, of which 41% (3.4 hr) is for radio and 37% (approx. 3 hr) is for television. The need for information is mainly met by public stations, whereas private television provides entertainment and relaxation. East Germans watch 30 min more television than West Germans, with the former also watching more entertainment programs. Around 40% of the total population uses the Internet for at least 13 min per day. Each day, 80% of Germans spend 30 min reading the newspaper (Media Perspektiven, 2001, p. 102 ff; 162 ff). In 2001, there were 136 *Publizistische Einheiten* or independent, complete editorial offices with political departments. A total of 386 daily newspapers were produced, with 28.4 million sold copies. Adding local and regional editions, the number of newspapers published rises to nearly 1,600. In addition, there were 23 weeklies (1.9 million sold copies), 845 popular magazines (129.7 million sold copies), and 1,094 professional journals (18 million sold copies; Media Perspektiven, 2001, p. 45). Most daily newspapers are sold through subscriptions. However, seven street-selling newspapers (a total of 43 editions) account for a total circulation of 5.7 million copies. Among these, *BILD* is the biggest street-selling newspaper, with 4.2 million copies per day.

The current media system affects public relations in different ways. First, the growth of a large, private broadcasting market gives public relations more opportunities to be recognized by the media and choose the channels. Second, the increasing number of radio and television stations produces a higher number of journalistic activities and a corresponding increase in public relations activities. Third, on the one hand, it is easier to reach certain publics because of the large number of specialized media; on the other hand, it is more difficult to reach the entire population by performing classical media relations activities because the audience is much more fragmented. Generally, it can be stated that one important reason for the growth of public relations in Germany since the beginning of the 1990s is the growth of the private media market. The public relations boom is coupled—and generated to a great degree—with the marketed media boom. One indicator for the growth of public relations in general is the growth in the number of public relations agencies in the 1990s (see Fig. 20.1).

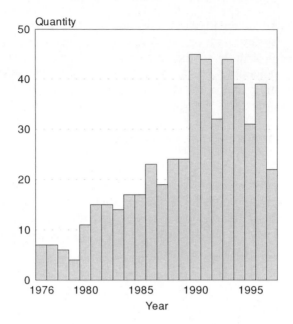

FIG. 20.1. Start up of public relations agencies and free consultants in Germany between 1976 and 1997 (Fuhrberg 1998: 248).

GERMAN CULTURE

Within German history, several social developments that were crucial to the development of cultural values can be named. For example, the enlightenment of the 18th century destroyed the traditionally organized society and emphasized the individual role of any human being on the basis of universal natural rights. Other examples would be the workers' movements and the industrialization processes of the 19th century, World War I and World War II, establishment of the Weimar Republic, and the national socialism movements.

In the rationalized, mechanized, and individualized industrial Germany that is now developing into an information and knowledge society, there is reasonable consensus about the importance of living realms such as family and health as well as work and success. Conversely, there are numerous different life conceptions that can be classified into two dimensions. First, representatives of traditional values establish their priorities on the family's order, work as obligation, and traditional roles of men and women. Second, representatives of more modern values focus on lifestyles that emphasize the possibility of free and independent self-realization and professional success (Lohauß, 1995, p. 215). Since the late 1960s, the importance of obligation and acceptance values has been decreasing in Germany, whereas the importance of self-development values has been increasing (Klages, 1993, p. 32 ff; 1998, pp. 699–703). Examples of obligation and acceptance values are obedience, order, capability, diligence, modesty, and the will to adjust. Self-development values are emancipation, the right to be treated fairly, hedonism, and individualism (e.g., creativity, spontaneity, and self-realization).

The culture in Germany is not only shaped by this change of values but also by the process of individualization, which basically means the liberalization of human beings from traditional norms and collective relations. The decreased standardization of people by social institutions such as churches, schools, and family corresponds with the decreased affiliation to classes. People have greater opportunities to change their social status due to increased social and cultural mobility. This individualization is apparent not only in the enormous increase of single households but also in very flexible party preferences. However, this increase of individual autonomy causes the need to seek more information because this individualized society offers many choices and thus evokes compulsions to make decisions (Beck, 1986; Ebers, 1995).

Due to this individualized and differentiated society and the increasing role of the media, the requirements from communication activities of organizations have significantly expanded. Individualization has an impact on the organizational culture, implying that employees no longer constitute homogenous groups but rather demand heterogeneous communication to communicate extensively and mediate the organization's interests. Furthermore, external dialogue groups have continuously been differentiated, requiring the external communication of organizational interests to analyze and take into consideration the diversity of partial publics and their cultural values. This is essential for the creation and establishment of understanding of and compliance to the activities of an organization in relevant groups.

CONCLUSION

In this chapter we described that, after a long prehistoric period, the public relations industry in Germany has developed into a differentiated field since the middle of the 19th century, influenced largely by the changes in political systems in the country. The public relations industry also has seen obvious influences by the economic and media systems. Looking at the future of public relations in Germany, it can be stated that the ongoing development of the German society into an information and communication society will have an influence on the field. Public relations will gain importance at two levels in this process—organizational and societal. Public relations departments in organizations will gain importance in comparison with other departments, and public relations as a social subsystem will gain relevance within the society as a whole. This will take place in politics, business, culture, sports, and other aspects of society. Techniques and strategies of communication management will be seen as key competences of the 21st century. Especially through online communication, media will develop further—not only mass media but also public relations—to become an established factor of German society.

Projecting to the future, public relations will be more differentiated and specialized within organizations and agencies. That is, complex and institutionalized public relations specialties such as reputation management, issues management, change communication, and so on will become the norm. This change will also be reflected among agencies. In some parts of the professsional field, the integration of different communication disciplines will increase. The process of professionalization will develop further, which also means that more and more programs in university-level education as well as programs of further education will emerge. The existing research is already on the way to becoming an academic discipline, which Germans call *public relations science*. Discussions about appropriate strategies and techniques as well as about ethics will become more important for the entire field. Although public relations cannot reach the status of the classical professions (e.g., law and medicine) for structural reasons, it will grow to a new type of profession with a stronger scientific foundation. The value and equity of organizational communication as well as techniques to measure it will gain much more relevance, and the need for basic and applied research will increase.

Case Study

An important case in German public relations circles was the public conflict between the petrochemical multinational company Shell and the multinational activist group Greenpeace. The two collided in 1995 over Shell's proposal to sink the Brent Spar oil rig in the open sea. The case is remarkable for several, but three primary reasons:

1. The ability of an activist group (Greenpeace) to gain an extraordinary influence on international public opinion.
2. The role and behavior of the media during a clash of two multinationals.
3. The inept communication management by a global corporation such as Shell.

Short Chronology

In September 1991, Shell shut down the Brent Spar oil storage platform. After contemplating various ways of disposing the platform, Shell decided in 1995 to scuttle it in the open sea. On May 10th, 1995, the Scottish Parliament gave Shell the license to dump Brent Spar in its waters. But Greenpeace activists from Great Britain, the Netherlands, and Germany had already occupied the platform 10 days earlier in an effort to prevent it from being scuttled in the open sea. They demanded that the rig be disposed of onshore to prevent hazard to marine life. This conflict resulted in a dramatic media battle.

On May 12th, 1995, Greenpeace protestors were asked to leave the platform, but they refused, emboldened by many European politicians such as the Danish Environment Minister Svend Auken and some representatives of the European Union who by then had declared their resentment about the plan to sink the platform in open sea. By this time, the government of Iceland urged the British government not to dump Brent Spar in the sea. On May 23rd, Shell put an end to the first occupation of Brent Spar.

On May 24th, the youth wing of the leading German Christian Democratic party (CDU) requested the German consumers to boycott Shell-owned gas stations. Six days later, members of the German parliament joined the protest against Shell. Politicians belonging to the Social Democratic Party also urged Germans to avoid Shell-owned gas stations. In a common statement published on May 31st, the German Fishing Association and Greenpeace protested against the sinking as an environmental disaster. The results of a survey published on June 1st showed that the majority of the German population was against the dumping of Brent Spar in the sea. About 75% of those polled were willing to boycott Shell-owned gas stations to display their sentiments.

On June 12th, Shell moved the platform into the North Atlantic Ocean to sink it, but a ship chartered by Greenpeace accompanied the Brent Spar platform to the site. Politicians belonging to both conservative and liberal parties, as well as representatives of churches and business associations, continued to protest Shell's action and called for a boycott of Shell products in Germany. This intense pressure forced the director of Shell in the Netherlands, Jan Slechte, to admit publicly that his company would open a new discussion concerning the disposal of the platform if the British government demanded it. In a meeting with the British prime minister, German Chancellor Helmut Kohl brought up the Brent Spar as the main issue speaking against sinking the platform, whereas other members of the German Government continued to condemn the proposal to sink it in the open sea. On June 16th, two activists of Greenpeace reoccupied the Brent Spar while other members of Greenpeace continued to inform customers about the sinking at Shell gas stations across Germany, Great Britain, the Netherlands, Belgium, Luxembourg, and Switzerland. On the same day, Peter Duncan, chairman of German Shell, hinted at a press conference that the sinking could be postponed. However, this was followed immediately by a declaration by Dutch and British Shell that the sinking would go ahead as planned.

On June 18th, Greenpeace Germany published analyses of samples taken from the Brent Spar that seemed to prove that, in addition to the materials declared by Shell, it contained an unknown quantity of oil that could be hazardous to marine life if the platform was scuttled in open sea. Greenpeace United Kingdom (UK) blamed Shell for leaving close to 5,500 tons of oil in the platform. Other documents published by Greenpeace resulted in the suspicion that the tank also could contain 4,500 l of the chemical Glyoxal that had allegedly been concealed during the authorization procedure. On June 28th, the Brent Spar was only 24 hr away from the North Feni Ridge, the approved location for scuttling the ship. However, that evening it was published that Shell would abandon plans to sink the platform at the ridge and would instead request authorization to anchor the Brent Spar in the Norwegian Erfjord northeast of Stavanger. After extensive consultations, Shell decided to dismantle the platform and recycle some of its parts. Clearly, Greenpeace had come out victorious in this dramatic public conflict and forced Shell, against all odds, to yield to its pressure. However, Greenpeace's victory was not blemishless in retrospect. Later, the activist group admitted to making a misleading statement about there being 5,500 tons of oil left on the condemned rig and apologized to Chris Fay, chief executive officer of Shell UK. Also, the claim that Brent Spar still contained Glyoxal could not be proved by Greenpeace.

Short Analysis

This very well-documented and systematically analyzed case (Klaus, 2001, Krüger and Müller-Henning 2000, and Vowe 2001) shows some mechanisms of the public sphere and the functioning of public communication. With the help of the media, a global activist group was able to mobilize large publics in different countries to participate in its cause with the help of the media. It is pertinent to add here that one of the themes of this case is that the media and activist groups can form a potent adversary to corporations in particular. The result of the intense media and activist pressure was that there was a temporary boycott of Shell gas stations causing economic damage to these independently owned gas stations and, ultimately, to Shell itself.

The communication strategy of Greenpeace has always been to use a "David-against-Goliath-principle" in which it tries to present itself as the weak David fighting against the powerful Goliath (a corporation). In such conflicts, Greenpeace calculates very consciously that a few minor legal transgressions can and ought to be overlooked if the object of its criticism can be shown to contain a greater amount of immorality. Greenpeace was successful in the Brent Spar case in portraying Shell as an unscrupulous and irresponsible big corporation that favors its own economically motivated interests over that of the environment and society itself.

Shell's own organizational structure proved to be a handicap in its battle. Shell UK was responsible for the decision to sink the oil platform, but Shell Germany was a counterpart of Greenpeace protests in Germany. However, Shell was publicly perceived as a single organization! Shell clearly underestimated the sensitivity of the Germany population toward environmental issues. It also did not fore see the influence that media coverage of the Brent Spar event would have on politicians, including leading members of the conservative

CDU party. At the same time, Shell failed to enter into a dialogue with Greenpeace or display open communication with some of its most important publics. Ultimately, Shell had to submit to public pressure generated through contrived events and dramatized media coverage. The company was forced to recognize remarkable losses in reputation and economic damages. After its decision to abandon the sinking of the Brent Spar platform, Shell ordered an "excuse-me" advertisement to minimize loss of reputation. But in doing so, it also had to concede to having made a big mistake.

The media also learned something from this case. Throughout this issue, and in years prior to it, many journalists were very accepting of Greenpeace press releases as shown by an input–output study done by Rossmann (1993). Today many journalists are more careful in adopting press releases by Greenpeace, which lost some of its credibility by misinforming the media and public about the oil and chemicals supposedly left in the platform. Journalists now have a greater distance to this NGO, which continues to be seen as an important information source.

ACKNOWLEDGMENT

We thank Christian Sommer for his helpful input with the following sections: The Political System of Germany, The Economic System in Germany, The Media System in Germany, and German Culture.

REFERENCES

Avenarius, H. (1998). *Die ethischen Normen der Public Relations. Kodizes, Richtlinien, freiwillige Selbstkontrolle* [Ethical norms of public relations: Codices, guidelines, voluntary self-determination]. Neuwied/Kriftel: Luchterhand.

Becher, M. (1996). *Moral in der PR? Eine empirische Studie zu ethischen Problemen im Berufsfeld Öffentlichkeitsarbeit* [Moral in public relations? An empirical study on ethical problems of the professional field of PR] (Vol. 1). Berlin: Vistas.

Beck, U. (1986). *Risikogesellschaft. Auf dem Weg in eine andere Moderne* [Risk society: Approaching a new modernity]. Frankfurt am Main: Suhrkamp.

Bentele, G. (1997). PR-Historiographie und funktional–integrative Schichtung. Ein neuer Ansatz zur PR-Geschichtsschreibung [PR historiography and functional–integral stratification: A new approach on PR historiography]. In P. Szyszka (Ed.), *Auf der Suche nach Identität. PR-Geschichte als Theoriebaustein* (pp. 137–169). Berlin: Vistas.

Bentele, G. (Ed.). (1998). *Berufsfeld PR* [The professional field of PR]. Berlin: PR Kolleg, Loseblattwerk [collection of unbound papers].

Bentele, G. (2000). Ethik der Public Relations—eine schwierige Kombination? [Ethics of public relations—A problematic combination?]. In *PR⁺ plus Fernstudium Public Relations: Vol. 17, Recht und Ethik für PR* (pp. 29–48).

Bentele, G., & Liebert, T. (1998). Geschichte der PR in Deutschland [History of PR in Germany]. In G. Bentele (Ed.), (pp. 71–100).

Bentele, G., Piwinger, M., & Schönborn, G. (Eds.). (2001). *Handbuch Kommunikationsmanagement. Strategien, Wissen, Lösungen* [Handbook of communication management: Strategies, knowledge, solutions]. Neuwied: Luchterhand.

Bentele, G., & Szyszka, P. (Eds.). (1995). *PR-Ausbildung in Deutschland. Entwicklung, Bestandsaufnahme und Perspektiven* [PR training in Germany: Development, current situation and prospects]. Opladen: Westdeutscher Verlag.

Binder, E. (1983). *Die Entstehung unternehmerischer Public Relations in der Bundesrepublik Deutschland* [The development of businesslike public relations in the Federal Republic of Germany] http://kontakt@or-kolleg.com. Münster: Lit.

Böckelmann, F. E. (1988). *Pressestellen in der Wirtschaft* [Press offices in free economy]. Berlin: Spiess.

Böckelmann, F. E. (1991a). *Die Pressearbeit der Organisationen* [PR offices in organizations]. München: Ölschläger.

Böckelmann, F. E. (1991b). Pressestellen als journalistisches Tätigkeitsfeld [PR offices as field of activity for journalists]. In J. Dorer & K. Lojka (Eds.), *Öffentlichkeitsarbeit. Theoretische Ansätze, empirische Befunde und Berufspraxis der Public Relations* (pp. 170–184). Wien: Braumüller.

Branahl, U. (2000). *Medienrecht. Eine Einführung* 3. überarbeitete Auflage [Media law: An introduction] (3rd ed. rev.). Wiesbaden: Westdeutscher Verlag.

Brauer, G. (1996). *Wege in die Öffentlichkeitsarbeit. Einstieg, Einordnung, Einkommen in PR-Berufen* [Paths into public relations: Start, positioning, income in PR professions] (2nd ed.). Konstanz: UVK Medien.

Bruhn, M., & Boenigk, M. (1999). *Integrierte Kommunikation. Entwicklungsstand in Unternehmen* [Integrated communication: On its status quo in businesses]. Wiesbaden: Gabler.

Deutsche Public Relations Gesellschaft (1990). *Auswertung der DPRG-Mitgliederumfrage 1989* [Analysis of the DPRG members survey from 1989]. Bonn: Author.

Ebers, N. (1995). Individualisierung: Georg Simmel—Norbert Elias—Ulrich Beck. *Epistemata: Reihe Philosophie* (Vol. 169) [Individualization: Georg Simmel—Norbert Elias—Ulrich Beck]. Würzburg: Königshausen und Neumann.

Fuhrberg, R. (1998). PR-Dienstleistungsmarkt Deutschland [PR firms in Germany: The German PR service market). In G. Bentele (Ed.), (pp. 241–268).

Grosser, D. (1993). *Soziale Marktwirtschaft—Soziale Sicherheit: Erfahrungen in der Bundesrepublik. Perspektiven im vereinigten Deutschland, Deutschland Report 17* [Social market economy—Social safety: Experiences in Germany. Prospects for the reunited Germany, Germany Report No. 17]. Melle: Ernst Knoth Verlag.

Grundgesetz [The constitution] (32nd ed.) (1994). München: C. H. Beck.

Grunig, J. E., & Hunt, T. (1984). *Managing public relations*. New York: Holt, Rinehart & Winston.

Haedrich, G., & Jenner, T., Olavarria, M., & Possekel, S. (1994). *Aktueller Stand und Entwicklungen der Öffentlichkeitsarbeit in deutschen Unternehmen—Ergebnisse einer empirischen Untersuchung* [Current situation and developments of public relations in German businesses—Results of an empirical study]. Berlin: Institut für Marketing, Lehrstuhl für Konsumgüter-und Dienstleistungs-Marketing.

Heise, J. (2000). *Für Firma, Gott und Vaterland: Kriegserlebnis und Legendenbildung im Spiegel betrieblicher Kriegszeitschriften des 1. Weltkriegs. Das Beispiel Hannover* [For the company, for god and the fatherland: War experiences and the invention of legends in works war magazines of the first world war. Hannover as example]. Hannover: Hahn.

Hennig, B. (1990). Das gesamtwirtschaftliche Zielsystem im Rahmen der Sozialen Marktwirtschaft [The entire economic system of objectives within the framework of social market economy]. In Bundeszentrale für politische Bildung (Ed.), *Wirtschaftspolitik, Schriftenreihe* (Vol. 292, pp. 50–64). Bonn: Bundeszentrale für politische Bildung.

Hesse, A. (1999). *Rundfunkrecht* [Broadcasting law] (2nd ed.). Studienreihe Jura, München: Vahlen.

Hundhausen, C. (1951). *Werbung um öffentliches Vertrauen* [Promoting public trust]. Essen: Girardet.

Klages, H. (1993). *Traditionsbruch als Herausforderung. Perspektiven der Wertewandelsgesellschaft* [The break from traditions as challenge: Perspectives of a value changing society]. Frankfurt am Main New York: Campus.

Klages, H. (1998). Werte und Wertewandel [Values and the change of values]. In B. Schäfers & W. Zapf (Eds.), Handwörterbuch zur Gesellschaft Deutschlands. Bonn: Bundeszentrale für politische Bildung.

Klaus, E. (2001). Die Brent-Spar-Kampagne oder: Wie funktioniert Öffentlichkeit? [The Brent Spar Campaign – Or How the Public Sphere is functioning] In U. Röttger, [ed.] *PR-Kampagnen. Über die Inszenierung von Öffentlichkeit.* (2nd ed., pp. 97–119). Westdeutscher Verlag.

Koszyk, K. (1966). *Deutsche Presse im 19. Jahrhundert* [The German press in the 19th century]. Berlin: Colloquium Verlag.

Krüger, C., & Müller-Hennig, M. (2000): *Greenpeace auf dem Wahrnehmungsmarkt. Studien zur Kommunikationspolitik und Medienresonanz* [Greenpeace on the Reception Market: Studies on Communication Policy and Media Resonance]. Hamburg: Lit.

Kunczik, M. (1997). *Geschichte der Öffentlichkeitsarbeit in Deutschland* [History of public relations in Germany]. Köln et al.: Böhlau.

Kunczik, M. (1999). Öffentlichkeitsarbeit [Public Relations]. In J. Wilke (Ed.), *Mediengeschichte in der Bundesrepublik Deutschland* (pp. 545–569). Bonn: Bundeszentrale für politische Bildung.

Lampert, H. (1990). Die Soziale Marktwirtschaft in der Bundesrepublik Deutschland. Ursprung, Konzeption, Entwicklung und Probleme [Social market economy in the Federal Republic of Germany: Origin, concept, development, and problems]. In Bundeszentrale für politische Bildung (Ed.), *Wirtschaftspolitik, Schriftenreihe* (Vol. 292, pp. 31–49). Bonn: Bundeszentrale für politische Bildung.

Liebert, T. (1997). Über einige inhaltliche und methodische Probleme einer PR-Geschichtsschreibung [On some content-related and methodical problems of PR historiography]. In: P. Szyszka (Ed.), *Auf der Suche nach Identität. PR-Geschichte als Theoriebaustein* (pp. 79–99). Berlin: Vistas.

Lohauß, P. (1995). *Moderne Identität und Gesellschaft. Theorie und Konzepte* [Modern identity and society: Theory and concepts]. Opladen: Leske + Budrich.

LRG NW—Rundfunkgesetz für das Land NordrheinWestfalen in der Fassung der Bekanntmachung der Neufassung vom 24. August 1995 (GV. NW. 1995 S. 994), zuletzt geändert durch Gesetz vom 10. Februar 1998 (GV. NW. 1998 S. 148). Retrieved from http://www.lfr.de/downloads/Lrg-nw.doc

Media Perspektiven. (2001). *Basisdaten. Daten zur Mediensituation in Deutschland 2001* [Basic data: Data on the media situation in Germany 2001]. Frankfurt: Main.

Merten, K. (1997). Das Berufsbild von PR—Anforderungsprofile und Trends. Ergebnisse einer Studie [The professional field of PR—Requirements and trends. Results of a survey]. In G. Schulze-Fürstenow & B.-J. Martini (Eds.), (1994 ff), *Handbuch PR. Öffentlichkeitsarbeit in Wirtschaft, Verbänden, Behörden*, (chap. 3-65, pp. 1–23). Neuwied: Luchterhand.

Noelle-Neumann, E., Schulz, W., & Wilke, J. (2000). *Fischer Lexikon. Publizistik, Massenkommunikation* [Fischer Encyclopedia: Publicity and mass communication] (6th ed.). Frankfurt/Main: Fischer.

Nöth-Greis, G. (1997). Das Literarische Büro als Instrument der Pressepolitik [The Literary Bureau as instrument of press politics]. In J. Wilke (Ed.), *Pressepolitik und Propaganda. Historische Studien vom Vormärz bis zum Kalten Krieg* (pp. 1–78). Köln/Weimar/Wien: Böhlau.

Oeckl, A. (1976). PR-Praxis. Der Schlüssel zur Öffentlichkeitsarbeit [PR practice. The key to public relations]. Düsseldorf; Wien: Ecoh.

Oeckl, A. (1964). *Handbuch der Public Relations. Theorie und Praxis der Öffentlichkeitsarbeit in Deutschland und der Welt* [Handbook of public relations: Theory and practice of public relations in Germany and the world]. München: Süddeutscher Verlag.

Papier, H.-J., & Möller, J. (1999). Presse- und Rundfunkrecht [Press and broadcasting law]. In J. Wilke (Ed.), *Mediengeschichte der Bundesrepublik Deutschland* (Vol. 361, pp. 449–468). Bonn: Bundeszentrale für politische Bildung.

Pilz, F., & Ortwein, H. (1997). *Das politische System Deutschlands. Systemintegrierende Einführung in das Regierungs-, Wirtschafts- und Sozialsystem* [The political system of Germany: A system-integrating introduction into the administrative, economic and social system] (2nd ed.). München/Wien: R. Oldenburg.

Pürer, H., & Raabe, J. (1996). *Medien in Deutschland: Vol. 1, Presse* (korrigierte ed.) [The media in Germany: Vol 1, The press] (rev. ed.). Konstanz: UKV Medien.

Ronneberger, F., & Rühl, M. (1992). *Allgemeine Theorie der Public Relations* [A general theory of public relations]. Wiesbaden: Westdeutscher Verlag.

Ronneberger, F. (1977). Legitimation durch Information [Legitimation by information]. Düsseldorf; Lsien: Ecoh.

Rossmann, T. (1993): Öffentlichkeitsarbeit und ihr Einfluss auf die Medien: Das Beispiel Greenpeace [Public relations and its influence on the mass media: greenpeace as an example]. In *Media Perspektiven* No. 2, 1993 (pp. 85–96).

Röttger, U. (2000). *Public Relations—Organisation und Profession. Öffentlichkeitsarbeit als Organisationfunktion. Eine Berufsfeldstudie* [Public relations—organization and profession. Public relations as organizational function. A study on the professional field]. Wiesbaden: Westdeutscher Verlag.

Röttger, U. (2000a). Issues-Management. Wiesbaden: Westdeutscher Verlag.

Rudzio, W. (1997). Das politische System der Bundesrepublik Deutschland [The political system of the Federal Republic of Germany]. In *Grundwissen Politik Schriftenreihe* (Vol. 345, 3rd ed. rev., pp. 47–89). Bonn: Bundeszentrale für politische Bildung.

Rudzio, W. (2000). *Das politische System der Bundesrepublik Deutschland* (5th ed.) [The political system of the Federal Republic of Germany]. Opladen: Leske + Budrich.

Schieder, T. (1999). *Vom Deutschen Bund zum Deutschen Reich: 1815–1871* (16th ed.) [From the German Alliance to the German Reich: 1815–1871]. München: Deutscher Taschenbuch-Verlag.

Schmidt, M. G. (1995). *Wörterbuch zur Politik* [Political dictionary]. Stuttgart: Kröner.

Stuiber, H. W. (1998). Medien in Deutschland. Vol. 2, Rundfunk, [The media in Germany: Vol. 2, Boardcasting]. Konstanz: UKV Medien.

von Schlippe, B., Martini, B.-J., Schulze-Fürstenow, G. (Eds.). (1998). *Arbeitsplatz PR. Einstieg—Berufsbilder—Perspektiven. Mit einer Dokumentation der aktuellen PR-Bildungsangebote* [Vocation PR: Getting started—professional fields—prospects. Including a documentation of current PR training offers]. Neuwied/Kriftel: Luchterhand.

Vowe, G. (2001). Feldzüge um die öffentliche Meinung. Politische Kommunikation in Kampagnen am Beispiel von Brent Spar und Mururoa [Campaigns for public opinion: Political communication in campaigns, illustrated by the cases of Brent Spar and Mururoa]. In U. Röttger, (Ed.). (2001). *PR-Kamapgnen. Über die Inszenierung von Öffentlichkeit.* (2nd ed., pp. 121–142). Westdeutscher Verlag.

wbpr. (1997). *Wo ist der Schlüssel? Zweite Untersuchung zur unternehmensspezifischen Bedeutung von Public Relations. Eine Untersuchung der wbpr Gesellschaft für Public Relations und Marketing GmbH in Zusammenarbeit mit dem LUMIS-Institut der Universität-GH Siegen und dem Wirtschaftsmagazin Capital* [Where is the key? Second survey on the specific meaning of public relations in businesses. A survey by the PR company wbpr in co-operation with the LUMIS institute at the University Siegen and the business magazine *Capital*]. München/Potsdam.

Wolbring, B. (2000). *Krupp und die Öffentlichkeit im 19. Jahrhundert* [Krupp and the public of the 19th century]. München: C. H. Beck.

Zipfel, A. (1997). *Public Relations in der Elektroindustrie. Die Firmen Siemens und AEG 1847 bis 1939* [Public Relations in the electronic industry: The companies Siemens and AEG from 1847 until 1939]. Köln/Weimar/Wien: Bèohlau.

Zühlsdorf, A. (2002). *Gesellschaftsorientierte Public Relations. Eine strukturationstheoretische Analyse der Interaktion von Unternehmen und kritischer Öffentlichkeit* [Society-oriented public relations: A structural–theoretical analysis of the interaction between businesses and critical publics]. Wiesbaden: Westdeutscher Verlag.

21

PUBLIC RELATIONS IN NORWAY: COMMUNICATION IN A SMALL WELFARE STATE

ØYVIND IHLEN

KJELL S. RAKKENES

INTRODUCTION

Norway is a small kingdom in Northern Europe that has topped the United Nations' list for human development for several years. Unemployment, inequality, and population growth are low among the country's 4.6 million inhabitants. Norwegians enjoy long life expectancy, a high education level, high health expenditure, as well as high income and a high GDP per capita (United Nations Development Programme, 2006). As in the rest of the Scandinavian region to which it belongs, the electoral supremacy of social democracy has been pronounced (Arter, 1999). The Norwegian state has been described as both corporatist and based on an ideology of welfare capitalism, where free market activity is balanced against government intervention. The nation's economy is largely dependent on petroleum; a fourth of Norwegian wealth creation is tied to this industry. Norway is the world's eight largest producer of oil, and only Saudi Arabia and Russia export more oil (Ministry of Petroleum and Energy, 2006). In 2007, the economy is booming and the nation's public relations industry is thriving, as reputation seems to have increased in importance for Norwegian businesses and organizations in general.

Two overarching questions are addressed in the following sections: What is the nature and status of public relations in Norway, and, secondly, how is this practice influenced by environmental factors? The first main section gives a short overview of the history and development of the profession, the status today, the image and standing of the profession, associations, education, and the ethical debate within the field. The second main section highlights the importance of (a) the infrastructure: the political, economic and legislative system, as well as the activism level, (b) the culture, and (c) the media system. These factors are used to discuss the peculiarities of Norwegian public relations, before a short case study illustrates some of these points further. The chapter ends with a conclusion that rounds up the discussion.

THE NATURE AND STATUS OF PUBLIC RELATIONS IN NORWAY

Public Relations History and Development

Going back to the Vikings, Norwegians have a long history of caring for their reputation. The following stanza from *The Poetic Edda* (trans. 1996) is quite telling:

> Cattle die, kinsmen die
> the self must also die;
> I know one thing that never dies:
> the reputation of each dead man.

Although the Vikings made good use of their reputation during two centuries of raids into Europe, public relations in the modern sense is probably more closely linked to the rise of the mass media, industrialization and the introduction of parliamentarism. The first Norwegian weekly newspaper was launched in 1763, and the first daily newspaper in 1819 (Høyer, 1995). It could be hypothesized that the establishment of a market economy during the 19th century also led to increased attempts to get media coverage. At the turn of the 20th century, Norway had become an industrial country, albeit one of the poorer ones in Europe (Hodne and Grytten, 2000). Some years before, in 1884, parliamentarism was introduced, which in turn led to increased lobbying from organized interests representing for instance farming and religious interests (Espeli, 1999).

When Norway gained its independence from Sweden with a referendum in 1905, this was a result of a rising nationalism that probably could not have developed without public relations efforts. Still, little is known about public relations in the late 19th and early 20th century. It can, nonetheless, be mentioned that a newspaper ad from the 1920s invited applicants for a position as "propaganda secretary" in the nonprofit foundation the Norwegian Fire Protection Association. This indicates that at least some organizations did attempt to systematize their public relations activities, although the mentioned job title would go out of fashion some years later, as "propaganda" took on a more sinister meaning.

Some argue that the Norwegian public relations profession really is a phenomenon from the period after the Second World War. The first associations were established in this period, and the first book on public relations was published in 1960. Quite tellingly, the title of the latter was *Public Relations in the U.S.A.* (translated) (Apeland, 1960). The influence from the U.S.A. was important for Norwegian public relations, and the professionalization of the field has largely followed the trends in the U.S.A. (Klasson, 1998).

During the 1950s and 1960s, the personnel department in Norwegian businesses usually handled the internal information, while the marketing department handled the external public relations function. This changed during the 1970s as more businesses set up public relations departments, in part as a product of increased democratization at Norwegian workplaces. When workers' representatives were allowed into the boardrooms, this led to more openness. Another factor that is singled out as important is that a new Public Information Act opened much of the archives of Norwegian government bodies during the same period. This provided new opportunities for Norwegian journalists, which in turn created a need for development of the public relations function in both the public and private sectors (Haug, 1993; Klasson, 1998).

In the 1980s the public relations managers often moved into the boardroom as public relations directors (Haug, 1993). Increasingly, the practitioners have become managers, and started working strategically. Some also claim that public relations has won more professional recognition (Klasson, 1998). However, text production is said to be making up most of the practitioners' work, although the amount of strategic counseling is growing. A study published in 1994 showed that it was more likely for Norwegian practitioners to be technicians, compared with practitioners in Austria and the United States (Coombs and Holladay, 1994).

Status Today

During the first decades after the Second World War, the term "public relations" was in use among practitioners. Later a Norwegian phrase was introduced, literally translated "information and relations with society" ("informasjon and samfunnskontakt") (Haug, 1993). Some authors and journalists argue that this translation was an attempt to get rid of the negative connotations of PR and improve the image of the industry (Allern, 1999). Today, both the media and quite a few practitioners themselves frequently use the short term PR, although "informasjon and samfunnskontakt" is often used in job ads, etc. A host of different job titles are found in such ads, including "communication advisor," "information officer," "information consultant," etc.

As elsewhere in the Western world, the growth of the public relations industry has been immense. Guesses on how many people in total work in public relations in Norway (agencies and in-house) have ranged from under 3,000 at the lowest (Haug, 1993), to 5,000 at the highest (Allern, 1997). The figure 4,000 is the latest found in the literature (Allern, 1999). The numbers are uncertain, as no official statistics exist. In 2007, the Norwegian Communication Association (NCA) has more than 2,600 members. In the latest annual report, however, the association declares that this number is inaccurate and that the potential membership number is much higher (Kommunikasjonsforeningen, 2007).

The first Norwegian public relations agency was probably Apeland Informasjon, established in 1958. In 2007, there are over 30 agencies in Norway. Those associated with NIR—the national agency association (see below)—had a total revenue of NOK 260 million in 2005 (approximately USD 43 million), which is a 25 percent growth compared to 2004 (NIR, 2006a). A reasonable estimate seems to be that the total revenue of the Norwegian public relations industry is close to NOK 400 million (approximately USD 65 million), given the fact that the large NIR outsiders (Geelmuyden.Kiese, JKL, and KREAB) had a combined revenue in 2005 of NOK 95 million (approximately USD 16 million).

The largest agency is the locally owned Geelmuyden.Kiese with 70 employees, and offices in Denmark and Sweden (revenues of NOK 56 million in 2005). Geelmuyden.Kiese is partner for Ketchum in the Nordic region, and has been instrumental in putting the public relations industry on the public agenda as it has kept a rather high profile. Other large agencies include Burson Marsteller (revenues of NOK 43.8 million in 2005), Gambit HillandKnowlton (revenues of NOK 30.7 million in 2005), Apeland Informasjon (revenues of NOK 27.1 million in 2005), and JKL Norway (revenues of NOK 24.5 million in 2005) (*Dagens Næringsliv*, 2006; NIR, 2006b). During the late 1990s and the 2000s, the importance of the agencies increased and several new ones were set up. Anecdotal evidence indicates that in the past few years, the media has more frequently turned to the agencies for expert comments on communication activities of public figures or organizations. A qualified guess is that more or less all the larger companies and public institutions in Norway either use or have used an agency, on a regular or ad-hoc basis. In the 2005 membership survey of NCA, 69 percent said that they had used a public relations agency in the last three years (N = 1148) (Kommunikasjonsforeningen, 2006).

The huge growth has also made it difficult for the agencies to hire qualified personnel, as one of the authors experienced first hand as CEO of one of the larger agencies—JKL. After a period of journalist lay-offs, the media have again started to hire people. Combined with a severe shortage of experienced consultants, the industry has not been able to take full advantage of the increased demand in the market.

In many areas, public relations agencies have replaced advertising agencies in terms of giving strategic communication advice. The fact that many Norwegian public relations practitioners these days have a seat at the decision-making table in their organizations has been used both as an explanation of the growth of the industry and an accompanying dramatic revenue fall in the advertising industry. It is also a sign of a relative recent structural change within the public relations industry itself. Several companies are specializing or diversifying to a much broader extent than before. Agencies like Burson Marsteller and Geelmuyden.Kiese are so-called full service consultancies, offering both strategic advice and operational capacities. Smaller companies are following a different strategy, e.g. the JKL Group which follows a dual brand strategy where it has established a subsidiary (MS&L) to penetrate the product-PR and implementation market. One of the most successful new entrants in the public relations markets recently has been PR Operatørene. This firm is specializing in product PR, and claims that they are all about implementation and creativity. They do not market or sell communication strategies as such. The growth of PR Operatørene has been spectacular, and after just a few years in business the company is among the largest and most profitable in Norway with a revenue of almost NOK 13.6 million in 2005 (NIR, 2006a).

Businesses operating in Norway have traditionally turned to the public relations industry when they have experienced a media crisis or needed an add-on to the marketing campaign launching a new product. This is changing. Demand is increasingly driven by the need for advice when it comes to communication strategy, communication in financial transactions (e.g. M&As, IPOs), investor relations activities or when companies experience regulatory challenges. More and more often blue chip companies or wealthy people turn to the public relations industry when they need access to the networks that the agencies or the individual practitioners have in the media, the Parliament, the Government, or the bureaucracy.

Although the share of strategic counseling is increasing, the demand is still driven by a focus on operational activities. According to an industry survey 23 percent of the revenue in the agencies derives from operational media advice, 20 percent is tied to text production to printed media and 16 percent of the revenue is earned as a result of strategic communication advice. The private sector contributes 65 percent of the total revenue, whereas the public sector demand for public relations services is about 15 percent of the revenue (NIR, n.d.).

The Norwegian agencies are, however, relatively immature as an industry in terms of its body of knowledge. Few companies base their counsel on well-documented processes or methodology. Instead, advice is often rooted in good, common sense situational analysis, the professional experience of the consultants, as well as their gut feeling, and networks in the media, business and government. Among politicians it is apparently a common viewpoint that the agencies often demand good compensation for selling very basic knowledge about the political system (Allern, 2001a). As the clients increasingly regard the advice of the agencies as having strategic value, the agencies are more and more compared to other professional service firms and their processes and methodologies. The industry has therefore identified a need for professionalization.

The need for professionalization also seems to be pressing for in-house consultants. It is, for instance, quite telling that 17 percent of the participants in NCA's latest membership survey said that their organization did not scan their environment in any systematic fashion (N = 1141); 31 percent said that their organization did not have a public relations plan, or that this plan was either outdated or not implemented (N = 1138) (Kommunikasjonsforeningen, 2006).

Image and Standing of the Profession

The Norwegian Prime Minister actually participated at the inaugural meeting of the first Norwegian public relations association. Since then, however, the image and standing of the profession has fluctuated. Media exposés regularly feature practitioners conducting unethical or borderline unethical business. Much of the debate has focused on public relations agencies and their methods in particular. Norwegian agencies have been accused of, for instance, insider trading, constructing front groups, arranging and paying for protest demonstrations, and planting anonymous negative information about their clients' competitors (Ihlen and Robstad, 2004).

In March and April 2007 (as this chapter is written) the largest-ever insider-trading case is before the Norwegian court. A group of investors and one of the most experienced public relations consultants in Norway are accused of insider trading. The public relations advisor, Rune Brynhildsen—a partner at Brynhildsen Woldsdal PR—is accused of distributing inside information on three listed companies to close friends (e.g., Sunnanå, 2007).

The tremendous growth in the industry during the 1990s also led to debate about the very existence of public relations agencies and their influence on democracy. The publication of a book about the industry and the airing of a critical documentary on the main television station set the agenda for this debate (i.e., Allern, 1997; NRK, 1997). The issue was whether the public relations agencies contribute to undue political influence, giving those with the ability and willingness to buy advice ready access to the media and key politicians. The key question was: Would the existence of public relations agencies move the development away from the ideal of "one person, one vote"? Not surprisingly, the agencies themselves defended their existence, arguing that buying public relations advice is just like buying other types of advice. Some practitioners also chose a more aggressive strategy, claiming that public relations in fact improves democracy by offering advice to those who do not have political connections, knowledge about how the media work, or the best ways to present their arguments. While huge corporations often have these resources in-house, selling public relations advice, it was argued, could in fact help counter the privileged influence of these huge corporations by making the knowledge available to others too (Ihlen and Robstad, 2004).

In a corporative society like Norway, there is, however, no doubt that the industry in many cases serves as power brokers for their clients. Most of the large agencies claim that they are able to move political power in favor of their clients, e.g., "Geelmuyden.Kiese moves power and influence in favor of its clients through communication" (translated) (Geelmuyden-Kiese, n.d.). This area needs further study, but anecdotal evidence indicates an increasing trend that senior public relations consultants are influencing political decisions and media coverage on behalf of commercial interests. One of the authors of this chapter argues that political power is for sale, and that companies may exercise real political power if their approach is opportunistic and in consensus with the media and political reality. In an op-ed article he voiced a need for a broad debate on the consequences when democratic and political power is up for grabs for those who have the resources and opportunistic mindsets (Rakkenes, 2006). At the time of writing, NRK, the largest media institution and a public broadcaster, is putting a lot of resources into the production of a documentary series that is to air in 2008, where they try to describe the public relations industry's influence on democracy. The television station is following specific projects involving the weapons industry and the battle to sell new fighter aircraft to Norway, a political party (the Conservative Party), and the race for the winter Olympics 2018.

Another type of criticism of the industry focuses on the relationship with the media, and it points to instances where the media use material from public relations agencies and business without revealing that the coverage was indeed based on such material (Allern, 1997; NRK, 1997). In some journalistic accounts, like the 1997 documentary, public relations is made to look like a type of mysterious source, conducting a type of business that can't stand the light of day. One of the results from the debate that followed was that the media updated their own guidelines for ethical practices and undertook an "ethical cleansing," kicking out 150 public relations practitioners from the Norwegian Press Club (Ottosen, 2004; Raaum, 1999).

Nonetheless, research indicates that the media still make widespread use of material that is provided to them (Valdø, 2005). As pointed out in the 1990s, when the media struggle with downsizing and lack of resources, using public relations material becomes tempting for economic reasons (Allern, 1997). Publicly, though, journalists, and editors in particular, often like to keep a distance from the public relations profession.

Although it seems that journalists and some practitioners thrive on the mystery shrouding the profession, anecdotal evidence indicates that public relations is now an accepted profession. As mentioned, most large organizations, including public institutions, do contract agencies. Still, public relations is an open profession, and the level of professionalism and ethical thinking is unevenly distributed among the practitioners (see later section on ethics). This also contributes to the negative media coverage the profession receives at regular intervals.

Associations

The first public relations association was established in 1949 and named the Norwegian Public Relations Club. Its first president had been head of the Norwegian Information Service in the U.S.A. during the Second World War, and was inspired by the development of the public relations field there. An interesting adaptation to the Norwegian context was that public relations, as acknowledged by the club, should be applied for "the good of society," rather than economic profit. Practitioners from business organizations were not admitted during the first eight years (Mørk, 1994).

In 1969, the club still had only 100 members, and only two were women. In 1972, the club altered its name to the Norwegian Public Relations Association. In 1982, the association merged with an association of editors of internal newsletters, and then in 2000 with the Forum for Public Information. Along the way, the association also changed its name and today is known as the Norwegian Communication Association (NCA).

When NCA merged with the Forum for Public Information, this was the result of a long discussion of the similarities between public relations in the private and public sectors. The latter association had been established in 1975. During the 1960s and the 1970s, the

Government and the state administration became a major actor in the professional development, marking an increasing schism between private and public sector public relations.
The association also enjoyed a close cooperation with the Norwegian Central Information
Service, the central government administration's specialist body. This agency was for many
years a driving force in the professionalization of public relations in the public sector,
publishing reports and arranging conferences. Consequently, the Norwegian Government's
information policy could be seen reflecting thoughts from the public relations body of
knowledge, especially the thoughts on symmetry (Statlig informasjonspolitikk, 1995).

As mentioned, today NCA has over 2,600 members; 61 percent are women, and 55
percent work in the private sector (Kommunikasjonsforeningen, 2007). NCA arranges
seminars, conferences, hands out awards, and publishes its own magazine. Norwegian
public relations agencies are organized in the Norwegian Public Relations Consultants
Association (NIR) which currently (2007) has 23 members. As pointed out, however, some
of the bigger agencies are not members; this includes the largest agency Geelmuyden-Kiese.

Education

Norway has a split structure of public higher education, traditional universities on one
side, and university colleges on the other. The latter have traditionally been vocationally
oriented. In addition, some private institutions do exist and the Norwegian School of
Management business school is first among them. The Norwegian School of Management
also offered the first extensive public relations course in Norway, at the beginning of the
1980s. Starting in the early 1990s the university colleges of Volda and Hedmark followed, at
first offering two-year degrees in Public Information and Communication Management
respectively.

Today these three institutions all offer BA degrees in public relations, but they have a
slightly different profile. Whereas the education at the School of Management is geared
more towards business and the private sector, Volda and Hedmark prepare students
for work in both the private and public sectors. Volda has an emphasis on technical
and managerial courses, also making use of its strong tradition in journalism education.
Hedmark has offered a closer focus on organizational communication, and the public
Norwegian Agency for Quality Assurance in Education has approved the establishment of
an MA in public relations here.

The Norwegian School of Management offers a one-year part-time Master of Management program with a focus on public relations. Several students in media and communication at the University of Oslo and the University of Bergen have also written theses on
public relations. The Department of Media and Communication at the University of Oslo
also offers single BA and MA courses in public relations. Public relations is also taught in
some other institutions, for instance Lillehammer University College that offers a part-time
one-year program in "communication counseling."

Currently there are no full-time full professors in public relations in Norway. Only a few
of the teaching staff holds doctorates and when they do, it is seldom in public relations.
This has led some commentators to argue that Norway is a laggard in Europe in this sense
(Horsle, 2003).

Looking at the top practitioners in the field, few of them have an education in public
relations and many public relations managers are still recruited from the journalist ranks.
One survey of 251 practitioners indicated that more than one out of three had been
journalists (Gabrielsen, 2004). A membership survey from NCA in 2005 indicated that
73 percent of the members had more than three years university education; 44 percent had

1–3 years of education in the field of "information, media or PR," while 17 percent declared they had more than three years education within this field (N = 1148) (Kommunikasjonsforeningen, 2006).

Ethics

Until 2007, NCA had its own deontological (duty) based ethical guidelines, stating, for instance, that the members should strive for transparency, be loyal to their organization, but also protect their integrity, and work to be trustworthy. These ethical guidelines were to be replaced with ethical *principles* in 2007, and it was argued that this could help keep the ethical debate within the field alive (Kommunikasjonsforeningen, 2007). The 2005 membership survey of NCA indicated that 43 percent felt the ethical level in the profession was high, but 45 percent chose the option "neither high, nor low" (N = 1145) (Kommunikasjonsforeningen, 2006). Still, in a survey of 251 Norwegian practitioners, it was shown that the "client syndrome" was widespread, that is, the practitioners were closely attached to their employers. These ties were felt more strongly in the private sector than in the public sector. A clear majority felt that the profession often faces ethical problems (Gabrielsen, 2004).

The association of the agencies, NIR, has a set of ethical norms that currently are under revision. In 2005, the ethics committee of NIR resigned (both the authors were members here), protesting how NIR treated the committee's statements concerning two members, one of them the NIR chair, who had been working for an organization built on a pyramid scheme. Some agencies pulled out in protest afterwards (including JKL), also protesting how the NIR management had asked them not to debate the issue publicly. In an op-ed article in the main business paper, the main author together with the committee's business ethics professor argued for transparency and that professional ethics should be a goal in itself and not a means to improve reputation (Ihlen and Brinkmann, 2006).

The ethics debate is still raised every now and then, and at the time of writing the launch of a new book on "how to succeed with public relations" was accompanied with an attack on the industry. The author of the book argued that the agencies were charging too much for their services, hiding conflicts of interest, and disappointing their customers (Mejlænder, 2007a, 2007b). The practitioners' associations denied the allegations, and accused the author of slander and poor research. Still, it was admitted that the industry did not meet all ideal standards (Jensen, 2007; Lund, 2007).

ENVIRONMENTAL FACTORS AND PUBLIC RELATIONS PRACTICE IN NORWAY

In this section we will first give an overview of the context that affects public relations in Norway regarding the infrastructure (the political, economic, and legal system, and the level of conflict and activism). Then the Norwegian culture and the mass media system are discussed.

Infrastructure

Political and Economic System

Norway is a kingdom in which the King's council—the Council of State—holds the executive power, and the members of the council make up the government. The King has little real political power, but has a symbolic function. The Storting—the Norwegian Parliament—is the legislative and budgetary power, and the government depends on the confidence of the Storting. The Storting currently consists of seven main political parties. The Labour Party (www.dna.no) is a social democratic party that has been the largest party in every Norwegian election since 1945. The Socialist Left Party (www.sv.no), which tellingly positions itself further to the left, has never significantly threatened the position of Labour. At the time of writing, the government is a coalition, made up of Labour, the Socialist Left, and the Centre Party (www.senterpartiet.no).

Although the Conservative Party (www.hoyre.no) has been the second largest party for most of this period, it has had competition from the Christian Democratic Party (www.krf.no), the Centre Party (www.senterpartiet.no), and the Liberal Party (www.venstre.no). The Conservatives and the three other non-socialist parties have all formed governments together. The Conservatives have held office alone on only one occasion, between 1981 and 1983. An additional competitor on the right wing of Norwegian politics has been the Progressive Party (www.frp.no), which from 1989 has become a force to reckon with, although it has never been part of the government. Today, it is the second largest party. Closer analysis and overviews of the Norwegian political system are found in several different books (e.g., Arter, 1999; Christensen, Egeberg, Larsen, Lægreid, and Roness, 2002; Lijphart, 1999; Rønning, 2001; Skare, 1987; Strøm and Svåsand, 1997).

Apparently, Norway seems to violate many of the requirements that are necessary to prosperity, according to mainstream theory of economics. The differences are small, the taxes are high, the public sector is huge, the unions are strong, and the welfare state is generous. Nonetheless, as pointed out in the introduction, Norway has had sustained high growth, low unemployment, and low inequality. In 2006, the research centre ESOP was formed at the University of Oslo to study this paradox (ESOP, 2006).

The Norwegian State plays an active role in Norwegian economy and society, and has a long-held tradition in this regard. From 1945 until approximately 1980, a social democratic program for governance and development of the welfare state prevailed. The Labour Party had a key role in this. During its governance, a range of state-run enterprises were set up and led by people with close ties to the party. Furthermore, during this period the market was largely set aside in favor of a peculiar form of "bargaining economy" between the state on the one side and business and industry on the other. Organizations and corporations were interwoven in the administrative system; political and economic arrangements and decisions were made in negotiation between public and private actors. The Norwegian State during this period has been described as being corporatist and technocratic, as well as permeated by a goal-driven rationale adopted from economic science (Hernes, 1978; Olsen, 1983; Østerud, Engelstad, and Selle, 2003).

Starting in the 1980s, however, reforms were introduced into the Norwegian political system, and market models were increasingly adopted for use in the public sector. It has been argued that the macro-economic policy instruments of the Labour government seemed to fail in the new economic situation of the 1970s. What is certain is that the hegemony of the Labour Party and its social democratic program evaporated. During the 1980s, public companies and property were privatized; public bodies were made independent or turned into companies (Christensen et al., 2002; Østerud et al., 2003).

During this new phase, the day-to-day detailed governance gave way to a governance system which put more emphasis on the ministries' formulation of general guidelines. These guidelines advocated that public companies should have more freedom and pursue commercial interests. These reforms took place, in part, due to increasing public expenditure and pressure on public budgets, but were, by and large, politically driven. The income from the petroleum sector had to some degree shielded the old system. Now, however, "change" and "market orientation" had become overriding values. The official political rationale was that the citizens, in their new capacity as consumers and clients, would be better off with a more effective and responsive system. The effect of the changes has been that the corporatist governance system has been weakened in comparison to professionalized lobbying and mass-mediated influence (Christensen et al., 2002; Østerud et al., 2003). The weakening of the strong corporatist traits, and the new emphasis on the importance of the market, have also meant that public institutions are more concerned for their reputation, and see the value of investing in public relations. Public figures can also be held accountable by the media, and savvy operators in politics or business are increasingly using public relations techniques. The 2005 NCA membership survey showed that 65 percent of the members conducted media training in their organizations (N = 1140), and that 72 percent of these (N = 740) had hired public relations agencies for this task (Kommunikasjonsforeningen, 2006).

As mentioned, Norway is a large producer and exporter of oil, but the nation also has vast reserves of natural gas, and Norway is the third largest exporter and the seventh largest producer of natural gas (Ministry of Petroleum and Energy, 2006). Only a small percentage of Norway's land area is suitable for productive agriculture or forestry, but the country is endowed with natural resources other than oil, among them minerals, fish and timber. Shipping has also been a large industry for 150 years, and today it is claimed that Norwegian companies control 5 percent of the world's merchant fleet (Norwegian Shipowners' Association, n.d.).

However, it was "white coal" that helped the nation to transform itself from being a poor agrarian society to an industrial society in the first place. Few countries in the world have benefited as much from the development of hydroelectric power as Norway. Hydroelectric power provided a cheap energy source that could be harnessed throughout large parts of the country. Between 1905 and 1916, the gross national product was increased by 55 percent, and industry was established as the largest sector in the country (Haagensen, 1984; Nerbøvik, 1999). Energy-intensive production like aluminum has helped several Norwegian communities to thrive.

A 2002 benchmark survey of Norwegian public relations agencies indicated that the biggest customer sector was the category telecom/media/technology, followed by trade and commerce, and public administration (NIR, 2002). In 2006, the agencies reported that IT/telecom/media had increased even more, but also that special interest organizations now made up a considerable portion of the customer base. Although a smaller category, trade and commerce was also mentioned as a growth sector (NIR, 2006c).

Legal system

As stated, the Storting—the Norwegian Parliament—is the legislative power, while the King's council, the government, is the executive power. The third branch of government then, is the Judiciary. The most important courts of law in Norway include the Supreme Court of Justice (Høyesterett), the Interlocutory Appeals Committee of the Supreme Court (Høyesteretts kjæremålsutvalg), the Courts of Appeal (lagmannsrettene), the District Courts (tingrett), and the Conciliation Courts (forliksrådet). The Judiciary is supposed to comprise a relatively independent branch of government. Its role is to implement the legislation adopted by the Storting, but also to monitor the legislative and executive powers to ensure that they comply with the acts of legislation. In principle, the Judiciary has the right to set aside a statute passed by the Storting if it is in contravention of the Constitution, but has been reluctant to invoke this right (Norway: The official site in the United States, 2003).

Freedom of speech is protected by the Constitution that was established in 1814, but excluding protection for racist and blasphemous statements. The latter provision has been largely dormant, although in 1980 the Norwegian Film Authority banned the Monty Python film, *The Life of Brian*. When a Norwegian newspaper printed caricatures of the prophet Mohammed in 2006, complaints were filed but no charges were pressed.

Discussions about libel are more common, and some lawyers specialize in such cases. The Norwegian Press Association, which also comprises the Norwegian Union of Journalists and the Association of Norwegian Editors, runs the Norwegian Press Complaints Commission. Norwegian journalists and media outlets are supposed to follow the Code of Ethics of the Norwegian Press (Norwegian Union of Journalists, 2003). The Complaints Commission frequently issues statements, and if members are found to have acted in breach of the Code of Ethics, they are supposed to print or air a brief statement.

Activism

The Norwegian political system has been relatively open and inclusive. One good example is how Norwegian environmental organizations have been admitted into the decision-making arenas. Whereas, for instance, Friends of the Earth has remained a campaigning group in the U.S.A. and the U.K., the organization has enjoyed close ties to the authorities in Norway. In general, the Norwegian political structure has often integrated organizations and their political goals quickly, and Norway has frequently been described as a state-friendly society. It is normal procedure for Norwegian ministries and their directorates to circulate proposals to solicit comments from affected public or private organizations. The environmental organizations are often included in this regard, and also participate in public committees. Furthermore, the organizations are often partially funded by the public, which also gives them legitimacy. Hence, most of the organizations have reasoned that the benefits of the proximity to the state outweigh the dilemma of being made responsible for the politics. The co-optation process has also run fairly smoothly, since most of the Norwegian environmental movement is pragmatic, moderate, non-fundamentalist, and integrated into mainstream political culture (Bortne, Grendstad, Selle, and Strømsnes, 2001; Bortne, Selle, and Strømsnes, 2002; Christensen et al., 2002; Strømsnes, 2001).

In short, a political culture and tradition have been fostered where it is possible for non-governmental organizations to criticize the state and its politics *and* receive public support at the same time. The possible and preferred perspective of the Norwegian opposition in general is that it does not have to be an alternative on the outside, but might be part of an expanded "normality" (Eriksen, Hompland, and Tjønneland, 2003). Activist organizations have also become increasingly adept at using public relations themselves (Ihlen, 2004, 2006). This holds particularly true for the environmental organizations, but other non-governmental organizations have also been able to exert considerable influence by means of formal and informal contacts with the elected politicians and bureaucrats alike. Other organized interests from the industrial, the agricultural and the educational sectors have also enjoyed such access.

Culture

On Hofstede's scale, Norway scores between 20 and 30 on the power distance measure, a little above 60 on individualism, very low (less than 5) on masculinity, and between 30 and 40 on uncertainty avoidance (Hofstede, 2001, n.d.). Some of these indications can be substantiated with reference to other literature. As for power distance, it is clear that Norway is a rather egalitarian society. These roots are traced to the lack of an upper class in Norway, and the fact that most farming and fishing units have been quite small. Historically, this is also a factor that contributed to tremendous economic growth in the 19th century. The society was egalitarian, many farmers owned their own land and wielded huge political influence, acting together with the bourgeois class of the cities (Hodne and Grytten, 2000).

The experience of a relatively low power distance might also be a result of the fact that Norway is a small country. In 1970, the population was 3.9 million, in 1980 4 million, and presently there are 4.6 million inhabitants (Statistisk sentralbyrå, n.d.). This means that the elites of politics, administration, business, and industry tend to be rather small, and that the actors often know each other. Studies have, for instance, identified that the large companies in Norway (400+ employees) are run by a circle of approximately 500 persons in total, including chief executive officers and chairmen of the boards (Christensen et al., 2002).

A commonly referred to, and legendary phrase in Norwegian political life is "some of us have talked together," indicating oligarchical tendencies (Hjellum, 1992). The real power might reside in small informal networks that make decisions ahead of formal meetings. Such contacts and networks obviously might have explanatory power, but are also difficult to research.

That Norway traditionally has been an egalitarian society with an open political culture has also contributed to a low level of conflict. The immediate period after the Second World War also deserves a mention in this connection. It is often posited that a special cooperative atmosphere dominated the post-war rebuilding process. In addition to the development of the social democratic tradition described above, this contributed to close relations between business interests and the government. A good illustration was mentioned above, when the then Prime Minister took part in the inaugural meeting of the Norwegian Public Relations Club, and "spoke in confidence on hot Norwegian issues for two hours" (Mørk, 1994, p. 10). Since many of today's public relations agencies recruit former politicians (and some even continue as politicians while consulting), this type of social capital is readily available for those who can pay.

Since the country is so small, most practitioners have quite extensive networks, both in politics and in the media. When Shell experienced its Brent Spar crisis, the then public relations director of Shell Norway phoned the Norwegian prime minister to get the go-ahead to tow and dismantle the Brent Spar rig on shore in Norway. Apparently, Shell colleagues in the UK were flabbergasted and used the incident internally as an example of the importance of having a good dialogue with important stakeholders (Rui, 2004).

As for the masculinity scale, it can be mentioned that Norway got its first female Prime Minister in 1981, Gro Harlem Brundtland, and that her cabinet became internationally known for having eight female ministers (out of 18). Norway is ranked as number one on the United Nations list for gender-related development index and gender empowerment measure. Thirty-eight percent of the seats in the parliament are occupied by women, 29 percent of legislators, senior officials, and managers are women, 50 percent of professionals and technicians are female. And while the ratio of estimated female to male earned income is 0.75, this is still among the highest scores in the world (United Nations Development Programme, 2006). Sixty-one percent of the members of NCA are women, and the 2005 membership survey showed that 83 percent of the members agreed that women and men have equal opportunities to succeed as practitioners (N = 1135) (Kommunikasjonsforeningen, 2006).

The Mass Media

The Norwegian media market is described in several English language publications (see Carlsson and Harrie, 2001; Harrie, 2003), and national statistics can also be found on the website MediaNorway (MediaNorway, n.d.). Here we will concentrate on the landscape of newspapers, television/radio, and ownership structures, before discussing the news values of Norwegian media and the standing of the business press.

Newspapers

Norwegian newspapers have had high circulation numbers during the whole post-war period, and the average Norwegian household buys 1.5 newspapers each day (Høst, 1998). During most of the 1990s, the total daily circulation was approximately 3.1 million (Høst 2000, as cited in Østbye, 2001). Given that Norway only has a population of 4.6 million, this is quite a large number. The Norwegian press structure has been rather unique, with local papers, strong regional papers and a nationally distributed press. In total about 220 titles are published (Østbye, 2001). Historically, political parties have owned the Norwegian papers, but this system crumbled during the 1960s (Høyer, 1995). Today, three large owners dominate the market: Schibsted, A-pressen, and Orkla Media.

Television and Radio

Until 1981, the publicly owned Norwegian Broadcasting System (NRK) had a monopoly in television and radio services. In the early 1990s, the commercial television station TV2 and the radio station P4 were granted concessions. Later the television stations TV Norge and TV3 started broadcasting. The Swedish company MTG is principal owner of the latter, which for the last few years has had to fight for its national concession with Kanal24. NRK still held the upper hand with three of four nationwide stations (Harrie, 2003). Seven out of ten Norwegians watch television each day (TNSGallup, n.d.).

Ownership and Regulation

As mentioned, the NRK monopoly was lifted in 1981. Since then, however, the tendency to ownership concentration is noted, which has worried Norwegian politicians. This has given rise to new regulatory bodies (the Media Ownership Authority) and new legislation (the Media Ownership Act) with the aim of ensuring freedom of expression and continued media access. A dual leadership has been the tradition in Norwegian newspapers, with a general manager handling finances, administration, and technology, while the editor-in-chief has been solely responsible for the content. The owners could influence the overall editorial policy, but were expected to refrain from intervening in the day-to-day editorial leadership. During the 2000s, this structure was changed in some newspapers, giving way to a unified management system. The pros and cons of this are also hotly debated (Østbye, 2001). In 2006, another debate was caused when Orkla Media was sold to the British investment company Mecom.

News Values

Starting in the 1960s, the party press structure fell apart, and in the 1990s, new commercial television stations were established. While the largest newspapers previously had an out-spoken party affiliation with corresponding news values, they now tended to rely on a more similar journalistic news ideology. What all the news media have in common is also that they are now owned by investors and publishing companies and more often than not are run on business terms. The news media are turned into profit-making institutions. The conditions for the publicly owned broadcasting stations have changed, and an outspoken policy is that they want to compete with the rankings of the commercial stations in order to preserve their legitimacy as publicly funded (Allern, 2001b).

A striking feature of Norwegian tabloid newspapers is that they serve a mixture of hard-hitting news, political journalism, and celebrity gossip, that sets them apart from, for instance, their German counterpart *Bild-Zeitung* or the British *Sun*. A content analysis of ten Norwegian newspapers showed that the typical Norwegian newspaper was an informative, regional or local paper that carried a wide mixture of content in each issue. The analysis concluded that the Norwegian press by and large was serious and focused on issues of social importance. At the same time, however, it pointed out that few non-powerful sources were used; a preference for elites and patriarchical values could be found (Allern, 2001b). The same elite orientation is documented in studies of business news as well (Slaatta, 2003).

An analysis of the television news of NRK and TV2 indicated that the former covered political news in an idealized citizen perspective, while the latter adopted a consumer perspective. TV2 also put more emphasis on crime, but on the whole it was suggested that the two stations had developed their own news perspectives, representing existing traits found in the Northern European news culture (Waldahl, Bruun Andersen, and Rønning, 2002).

The Business Press

Compared to other countries, the Norwegian business press did not play an important role in the media landscape until the early 1990s. After the turnaround and rebranding of *Norges Handels- og Sjøfartstidende*, Norway finally got its own powerful business and financial daily branded *Dagens Næringsliv* (translated *Today's Business*). The newspaper is printed on pink paper, and has since the beginning of the 1990s enjoyed high credibility both in the business and political community. *Finansavisen*, a competing financial and business daily, was established at the beginning of the 1990s. Although not studied, it is a striking fact that the booming of the business dailies correlates with the rise of the public relations industry in Norway. That Norwegian businesses and organizations increasingly value having a good reputation is illustrated in Table 21.1, and for many of them this is equated with getting good media coverage.

TABLE 21.1

Frequency of the Word 'Reputation' ('Omdømme')
in Norwegian News Media 1996–2006
(search in the database A-tekst:
http://www.retriever-info.com/services/archive.html)

Year	Frequency
1996	229
1997	229
1998	255
1999	245
2000	354
2001	393
2002	396
2003	504
2004	578
2005	760
2006	1044

A peculiar development is that business news has expanded into mainstream dailies. In the popular press, this has been accompanied by a person-oriented type of journalism that "puts a face on" the economic players. Some business sources have expressed frustration over what they feel are unpredictable journalists with viewpoints that differ from case to case, story to story, and that sometimes take on a role as an actor in the economic arena themselves (Slaatta, 2003). For the public relations industry, however, this has also meant that the business of media training is an expanding field (NIR, 2006c).

CASE STUDY: CLOSING DOWN INDUSTRY IN NORWAY

What follows is a case study of the public relations work conducted when a high tech company wanted to move out of Norway, citing high production costs. The identities of the parties involved are hidden.

Background and Problem

In 2003 Norway held local elections and the economy was leveling out on the bottom of a recession. Unemployment was, by Norwegian standards, high and on the rise (expected to climb to 4.7 percent in 2004). The big theme in corporate Norway was the sharp decline in employment related to industrial production. Norwegian industry was moving out of the country; blaming high wages, a strong currency and an unstable regulatory framework. In the parliament all the opposition parties called for the Government to intervene.

The world-leading high tech company "Techno Inc" was also planning to move out of Norway. Low-cost producers from Asia were about to kill the company's competitiveness as sales declined sharply. The board of directors saw only one solution—downscaling. The only activity they would maintain in Norway was 50 jobs tied to R&D due to a good market for engineers with a relevant education.

In many countries, outsourcing and scaling down production is a relatively straight-forward business decision. In Norway, it means that your reputation is at stake. You risk high-level political involvement, huge public debate, and in some cases politicians who put heavy pressure on companies to reverse their plans. In the case of Techno Inc, the effect on the local community would be dramatic. In a two-year perspective a small town would be stripped of its cornerstone industry and 400 people would lose their jobs. Top management feared that their decision would make headline news and become a national theme in the coming campaigning. How could the company implement the decision, without losing credibility in the local community and on the national stage, risking its attractiveness in the labor market for engineers? If a row was caused over bad handling in Norway, the risk of a negative spillover to other markets was huge. The company needed to convince politicians that their decision was right for Norway before the election campaign started.

The Solution

The key to solving such problems in a Norwegian context is to find a way to win over politicians and to avoid them intervening or fueling a political debate over Norwegian industry—using the particular company as an example. Here are the main aspects of the strategy.

Techno Inc expected that the reactions to the downscaling would be based on both emotional factors (*family economies in ruin, crown jewel of Norwegian tech industry is flagging out,* etc.) and on rational facts (*difficult market, high labor cost in Norway, relation-*

ship to the EU, etc.). Employees losing jobs and being forced to sell their homes can be good media stories. Techno Inc understood this, but also that they potentially could win the rational argument by pointing to the tough market conditions and that it would be in the common interest if the company stayed in business and kept at least some jobs in the region. The strategy started with telling a story about Asian low-cost producers entering the market and how the increasing costs caused problems at Techno Inc. The story was told to the media, directly to employees and the local community. The goal was to create a rational understanding that production is expensive in Norway and might threaten the overall survivability of the company.

The second pillar was to find a win–win situation involving key politicians expected to intervene in a possible public debate. Politicians were identified, and meetings were held with the major figures, as well as all the parties in the local election, mayors in the nearby municipalities, relevant politicians at the parliament and two ministers that were expected to engage in the debate. The goal for these meetings was both to inform the politicians about the difficult situation but also to sell the up-side to the decision: that Techno Inc would increase its investments in R&D in Norway and expand its activities in this area. The "bone" that was thrown to the politicians was that if they agreed, they would receive credit for being a part of a solution that gave interesting prospects for the future.

Several local community initiatives were also started. The company, for instance, established a regional high-tech cluster, inviting the local college, politicians, media and other high-tech companies into a network that should work to develop the high-tech industry in the area. When the company had assured the stakeholders, in particular the politicians, they were ready to communicate the decision. Knowing that no politician would heavily criticize the decision, the company felt safe that the media would not be able to get a good spin on this story. No-one would criticize a company that was ready to invest in the region. The company achieved what was aimed for: Little media coverage of the decision and the calm needed to plan the downsizing.

CONCLUSION

The Norwegian public relations industry is thriving, and both agencies and in-house practitioners seem to be experiencing increased demand and influence. Some important driving factors include an increased market orientation in the public sector and an expansion of business news. Still today, the corporatist character of the political and economic system influences the practice as illustrated by the case study. The political culture is inclusive, there are low levels of conflict and the power distance is short. This also means that personal networks are valuable commodities, and the NCA members ranked personal characteristics above strategic knowledge when asked what was the single most important factor to succeed in the profession (Kommunikasjonsforeningen, 2006).

We feel that the latter finding speaks volumes about the current level of professionalism in the field, and argue that the profession still has a way to go in terms of developing methodologies and raising the ethical bar. There seems to be a huge potential for practitioners willing to tap into the international body of knowledge on public relations, and adjust, develop, and implement it in a Norwegian setting. As for now, however, Norwegian practitioners are doing brisk business trading on their networks, common sense analysis, and operational experience.

REFERENCES

Allern, S. (1997). *Når kildene byr opp til dans [When the sources ask for a dance]*. Oslo, Norway: Pax Forlag.

Allern, S. (1999). Nyhetsmediene og PR–bransjen [The news media and the PR–industry]. In B. von der Lippe and O. Nordhaug (Eds.), *Medier, påvirkning og samfunn [Media, influence, and society]* (pp. 267–298). Oslo, Norway: Cappelen Akademisk Forlag.

Allern, S. (2001a). *Flokkdyr på Løvebakken: Søkelys på Stortingets presselosje og politikkens medierammer [Herd journalism at (the Storting): Spotlight at the press box at the Storting and the media frames of politics]*. Oslo, Norway: Pax Forlag.

Allern, S. (2001b). *Nyhetsverdier: Om markedsorientering og journalistikk i ti norske aviser [News values: On the market orientation and journalism in ten Norwegian newspapers]*. Kristiansand, Norway: IJ–forlaget.

Apeland, N. M. (1960). *Public relations i USA [Public relations in the U.S.A.]*. Oslo, Norway: Gyldendal.

Arter, D. (1999). *Scandinavian politics today*. Manchester, UK: Manchester University Press.

Bortne, Ø., Grendstad, G., Selle, P., and Strømsnes, K. (2001). *Norsk miljøvernorganisering mellom stat og lokalsamfunn [Norwegian environmental organization between state and local community]*. Oslo, Norway: Samlaget.

Bortne, Ø., Selle, P., and Strømsnes, K. (2002). *Miljøvern uten grenser? [Environmental conservation without boundaries?]*. Oslo, Norway: Gyldendal.

Carlsson, U., and Harrie, E. (Eds.). (2001). *Media trends 2001 in Denmark, Finland, Iceland, Norway and Sweden: Nordic media trends 6*. Göteborg, Sweden: NORDICOM.

Christensen, T., Egeberg, M., Larsen, H. O., Lægreid, P., and Roness, P. G. (2002). *Forvaltning og politikk [Administration and politics]*. Bergen, Norway: Fagbokforlaget.

Coombs, W. T., and Holladay, S. J. (1994). A comparative analysis of international public relations: Identification and interpretation of similarities and differences between professionalization in Austria, Norway, and the United States. *Journal of Public Relations Research, 6*(1), 23–39.

Dagens Næringsliv. (2006, September 17). Mindre enn GK [Smaller than GK]. *Dagens Næringsliv*, p. 33.

Eriksen, T. B., Hompland, A., and Tjønneland, E. (2003). *Et lite land i verden 1950–2000: Norsk idéhistorie bind VI [A small country in the world 1950–2000: Norwegian history of ideas volume VI]*. Oslo, Norway: Aschehoug.

ESOP. (2006). Equality, Social Organization, and Performance (ESOP): Confronting theory with Nordic lessons. Retrieved March 27, 2007, from http://www.esop.uio.no/

Espeli, H. (1999). *Lobbyvirksomhet på Stortinget [Lobbying at the Storting]*. Oslo, Norway: Tano Aschehoug.

Gabrielsen, K. (2004). Loyalty versus conflict in Norwegian practitioners. *Public Relations Review, 30*, 303–311.

Geelmuyden-Kiese. (n.d.). Hjemmeside [Home page]. Retrieved March 26, 2007, from http://www.geelmuyden-kiese.no/

Haagensen, K. (1984). Kraftutbygging og konflikt: Et tilbakeblikk [Dam building and conflict: A retrospective view]. In K. Haagensen and A. Midttun (Eds.), *Kraftutbygging, konflikt og aksjoner [Power plants, conflicts and direct action]* (pp. 17–37). Oslo, Norway: Universitetsforlaget.

Harrie, E. (2003). *The Nordic media market: Nordic media trends 7*. Göteborg, Sweden: NORDICOM.

Haug, M. (1993). *Informasjon eller påvirkning? Utviklingstrekk ved informasjon og samfunnskontakt som fag [Information or persuasion? The development of public relations as a discipline]* (2 ed.). Oslo, Norway: Bedriftsøkonomens forlag.

Hernes, G. (Ed.). (1978). *Forhandlingsøkonomi og blandingsadministrasjon [Bargaining economy and mixed administration]*. Oslo, Norway: Universitetsforlaget.

Hjellum, T. (1992). *"Noen av oss har snakket sammen" : om fåmannsveldet i Arbeiderpartiet 1945–1973 ["Some of us have talked together": About the oligarchy in the Labour Party 1945–1973]*. Bergen, Norway: Alma Mater.

Hodne, F., and Grytten, O. H. (2000). *Norsk økonomi i det nittende århundre [Norwegian economy in the 19th Century]*. Bergen, Norway: Fagbokforlaget.

Hofstede, G. (2001). *Culture's consequences: Comparing values, behaviors, institutions, and organizations across nations* (2 ed.). Thousand Oaks, CA: Sage.

Hofstede, G. (n.d.). Geert Hofstede Cultural Dimensions: Norway. Retrieved March 27, 2007, from http://www.geert-hofstede.com/hofstede_norway.shtml

Horsle, P. (2003). Norge – en sinke i Europa [Norway: A Laggand in Europe]. *Kommunikasjon, nr. 6.*

Høst, S. (1998). *Daglig mediebruk [Daily media use].* Oslo, Norway: Pax Forlag.

Høyer, S. (1995). *Pressen mellom teknologi og samfunn: Norske og internasjonale perspektiver på pressehistorien fra Gutenberg til vår tid [The press between technology and society: Norwegian and international perspectives on the press history from Gutenberg to our time].* Oslo, Norway: Universitetsforlaget.

Ihlen, Ø. (2004). *Rhetoric and resources in public relations strategies: A rhetorical and sociological analysis of two conflicts over energy and the environment.* Oslo, Norway: Unipub forlag.

Ihlen, Ø. (2006). Substitution or pollution? Competing views of environmental benefit in a gas-fired power plant dispute. *Environmental Communication Yearbook, 3,* 137–155.

Ihlen, Ø., and Brinkmann, J. (2006, February 21). Etikken og målet [Ethics and the goal]. *Dagens Næringsliv,* p. 55.

Ihlen, Ø., and Robstad, P. (2004). *Informasjon and samfunnskontakt – perspektiver og praksis* [Public relations: perspectives and practice]. Bergen: Fagbokforlaget.

Jensen, F. V. (2007). Hemmelig PR-priskveld [Secret PR award ceremony] [Electronic Version]. Retrieved March 27 from http://www.kommunikasjonsforeningen.no/.

Klasson, P. (1998). *Public Relations som profesjonaliseringsprosjekt: Utviklingstrekk ved den norske informasjonsbransjen 1960–1998 [Public relations as a project of professionalization: The development of the Norwegian public relations sector 1960–1998].* Unpublished master's thesis, University of Bergen, Bergen, Norway.

Kommunikasjonsforeningen. (2006). *Medlemsundersøkelse 2005* [Membership Survey 2005]. Oslo, Norway: Kommunikasjonsforeningen.

Kommunikasjonsforeningen. (2007). *Årsberetning – aktivitetsrapport: Landsmøteperioden 2005–2007 [Annual report – activity report: National meeting period 2005–2007].* Oslo, Norway: Kommunikasjonsforeningen.

Lijphart, A. (1999). *Patterns of democracy: Government forms and performance in thirty–six countries.* London: Yale University Press.

Lund, H. (2007). Synsing om PR-bransjen [Unqualified opinions about the PR industry] [Electronic Version]. Retrieved March 27 from http://www.nir.no/vis_arkiv.php?article_id=1530andid2=RTTXhQyhmlMfOnTNWcpQnc8wj.

MediaNorway. (n.d.). Facts about Norwegian media. Retrieved March 27, 2007, from http://medienorge.uib.no/english/

Mejlænder, U.-A. (2007a, February 19). PR-bransjens hemmlighold [The secrecy of the PR-industry]. *Dagbladet.*

Mejlænder, U.-A. (2007b). *Slik gjør du suksess med PR [How to succeed with public relations].* Oslo, Norway: Hegnar Media.

Ministry of Petroleum and Energy. (2006). *Facts: The Norwegian Petroleum Sector 2006.* Oslo, Norway.

Mørk, E. (1994). *Et slag med halen: Informasjonsforeningens historie 1949–1994 [Wagging the tail: The Information Association's history 1949–1994].* Oslo, Norway: Informasjonsforeningen.

Nerbøvik, J. (1999). *Norsk historie 1860–1914: Eit bondesamfunn i oppbrot [Norwegian history 1860–1914: A rural society in change].* Oslo, Norway: Det Norske Samlaget.

NIR. (2002). Benchmarkundersøkelse norske informasjonsrådgivere [Benchmark survey Norwegian public relations consultants]. Retrieved March 26, 2007, from http://www.nir.no/vis_bransjen_statistikk.php?article_id=283andid2=KxTu8YUkrWDdEvvqwT4dIKyRF

NIR. (2006a). Byråstatistikk 2005 [Membership statistics 2005]. Retrieved March 26, 2007, from http://www.nir.no/vis_bransjen_statistikk.php?article_id=1429andid2=NJ4X66mQ04beVz2TpAUoetdUy

NIR. (2006b). Byråstatistikk [Membership statistics]. Retrieved March 26, 2007, from http://www.nir.no/vis_bransjen_statistikk.php

NIR. (2006c). Fortsatt vekst for PR-byråene [Continued growth for the PR agencies]. Retrieved March 26, 2007, from http://www.nir.no/vis_bransjen_benchmark.php

NIR. (n.d.). Produkter i PR-bransjen [Products in the public relations industry]. Retrieved March 26, 2007, from http://www.nir.no/vis_bransjen_statistikk.php?article_id=287andid2=JlsmCo8vgEs8aBxy2iR1P2Yj3

Norway: The official site in the United States. (2003). Facts and Figures: The Judiciary. Retrieved March 27, 2007, from http://www.norway.org/facts/political/judiciary/judiciary.htm

Norwegian Shipowners' Association. (n.d.). Norwegian shipping. Retrieved March 27, 2007, from http://www.rederi.no/default.asp?V_ITEM_ID=914

Norwegian Union of Journalists. (2003). Code of Ethics of the Norwegian Press. Retrieved March 27, 2007, from http://www.nj.no/English/?module=Articles;action=Article.publicShow;ID=1708

NRK. (1997, January 7). Brennpunkt: Bak nyhetene [Brennpunkt: Behind the news].

Olsen, J. P. (1983). *Organized democracy: Political institutions in a welfare state – the case of Norway*. Oslo, Norway: Universitetsforlaget.

Østbye, H. (2001). The Norwegian media landscape: Structure, economy and consumption. In U. Carlsson and E. Harrie (Eds.), *Media trends 2001 in Denmark, Finland, Iceland, Norway and Sweden: Nordic media trends 6* (pp. 239–247). Göteborg, Sweden: NORDICOM.

Østerud, Ø., Engelstad, F., and Selle, P. (2003). *Makten og demokratiet: En sluttbok fra Makt- og demokratiutredningen [The power and the democracy: A concluding book from the Power and Democracy project]*. Oslo, Norway: Gyldendal Akademisk.

Ottosen, R. (2004). *I journalistikkens grenseland: Journalistrollen mellom marked og idealer [In the borderland of journalism: The journalist role between market and ideals]*. Kristiansand, Norway: IJ–forlaget.

Raaum, O. (1999). *Pressen er løs! Fronter i journalistenes faglige frigjøring [The press is free! Frontlines in the fight for professional liberty]*. Oslo, Norway: Pax.

Rakkenes, K. (2006, December 29). Makt i et cocktailglass [Power in a cocktail glass]. *VG*, p. 39.

Rønning, R. (2001). *Vårt politisk Norge: En innføring i stats- og kommunalkunnskap [Our political Norway: An introduction to public policy at the national and local level]* (2 ed.). Bergen, Norway: Fagbokforlaget.

Rui, A. (2004). *Omdømmebygging i Norske Shell A/S [Reputation management in Norwegian Shell A/S]* (Master's thesis). Oslo: University of Oslo.

Skare, L. H. (Ed.). (1987). *Forvaltningen i samfunnet [The administration in society]* (3 ed.). Oslo, Norway: Tano.

Slaatta, T. (2003). *Den norske medieorden: Posisjoner og privilegier [The Norwegian media order: Positions and privileges]*. Oslo, Norway: Gyldendal Akademisk.

Statistisk sentralbyrå. (n.d.). Befolkning [Population]. Retrieved March 26, 2007, from http://www.ssb.no/emner/02/befolkning/

Statlig informasjonspolitikk. (1995). Statlig informasjonspolitikk [The information policy of the Norwegian State]. Retrieved March 26, 2007, from http://www.regjeringen.no/nb/dokumentarkiv/Ryddemappe/423827/423828/423872/423873/423886/Statlig-informasjonspolitikk—-hovedprinsipper.html?id=424477

Strøm, K., and Svåsand, L. (Eds.). (1997). *Challenges to political parties : The case of Norway*. Ann Arbor, MI: University of Michigan Press.

Strømsnes, K. (2001). *Demokrati i bevegelse [Changing democracy]* (Report No. 0111). Bergen, Norway: LOS–senteret.

Sunnanå, L. M. (2007, March 22). Fikk konvolutt med tusenlapper [Received wads of cash in envelope] *Aftenposten*, p. 2.

The Poetic Edda. (trans. 1996). (C. Larrington, Trans.). Oxford and New York: Oxford University Press.

TNSGallup. (n.d.). Seertall [Viewing rates]. Retrieved July 19, 2006, from www.tns-gallup.no/medier

United Nations Development Programme. (2006). *Human development report 2006: Beyond scarcity: Power, poverty, and the global water crisis*. New York: Palgrave Macmillian.

Valdø, H. (2005). *Hvis saken er god, er allting godt? En kvalitativ studie av hva som kjennetegner forholdet mellom journalister og PR-bransjen [If the story is good, is everything ok? A qualitative study of the characteristics of the relation between journalists and the PR industry]*. Norges Teknisk Naturvitenskapelige Universitet [Norwegian University of Science and Technology], Trondheim, Norway.

Waldahl, R., Bruun Andersen, M., and Rønning, H. (2002). *Nyheter først og fremst: Norske tv-nyheter: Myter og realiteter [News first and foremost: Norwegian television news: Myths and realities]*. Oslo, Norway: Universitetsforlaget.

CHAPTER

22

PUBLIC RELATIONS IN THE POLDER: THE CASE OF THE NETHERLANDS

BETTEKE VAN RULER

PREVIEW

In this chapter I draw a picture of the Netherlands and its public relations. The Netherlands is "A fine place to be," (*The Economist*, p. 8, 2002) because "Dutch business is outward-looking and open to new ideas and the rule is common sense." Given such a business atmosphere, one would presume that public relations must have been very successful in the Netherlands. Although Dutch behavior regarding public relations is obviously close to normative, the Dutch public relations industry is not at the level that normative thinking would cast. The question is, why?

I use as many sources as possible to give a broad and deliberate picture of this country and the state of the art and background of public relations as a phenomenon and as an industry. This picture is, however, necessarily subjective, because it is my interpretation of facts and figures as well as my realities and thoughts.

HISTORY AND DEVELOPMENT OF THE COUNTRY

With nearly 16 million inhabitants, the Netherlands is one of the smaller countries of Europe, comparable in population size to Denmark, Greece, and Hungary (about 11 million people), although much smaller in size. The population density is a little over 450 km², which is exceeded only by Bangladesh, Taiwan, and South Korea. The Gross Domestic Product (GDP) for the Netherlands in 1998 was 110, whereas the United States' was 145 and Poland's was 38. The Dutch economy rose sharply to an all-time high during the 1990s thanks to an explosive services sector that accounted for almost 70% of the GDP. Employment is high, with less than 5% unemployed in 2001 and just 13% employed by the government. Nevertheless, 800,000 people of the potential labor force of 7 million are not able to work because of long-standing physical or mental illness. All of these people get an income by the state until their 65th birthday, which is based on their latest earned income level. Everyone above the age of 65 gets a state pension in addition to their private pensions. In 2001, 13.5% of the population was over 65. In a few years, this is expected to be about 20% or even higher, which has the potential to challenge the state pension system.

The Netherlands can be seen as a country of reasonable diversity. One third of the population identify themselves as Catholic (passive or active), almost one third as Protestant of some kind, and the remainder as something else or with no religious affiliation (almost one million is muslim). Most people are Dutch for generations, whereas 1.7 million are first- or second-generation immigrants. Although Dutch women are not as emancipated as women in Scandinavian countries, the Index of Gender Development is almost .7, which is rather high (Gallagher, Laver, & Mair, 2001). This Index measures the degree of women's representation in key areas of political and economic life, taking account of the number of women in national parliaments, women's share of earned income, and their levels of occupancy in a range of professions.

Since the 17th century, the Netherlands has been known for its high level of economic and cultural wealth. The country is famous for painters like Rembrandt and van Gogh, and many continents have had contact with the Dutch because of their entrepreneurial nature and business sense. Many argue that the Dutch became successful because they had to overcome the lack of their own natural resources, inducing them to develop an earthy nature, strict work ethics, and a very strong propensity to negotiate and build consensus. At the same time, the Dutch have built the questionable reputation of pretending to know how people in other societies in the world should behave. *The Oxford Dictionary* defines talking to someone as a *Dutch uncle* as "lecturing him paternally"(Hofstede, 1987, p. 5). The expression *Dutch party* shows a certain ungenerous behavior with money. The country is also famous (or notorious) for its liberal behavior on drugs, which is seen—at least by the Dutch themselves—as the best way to cope with this problem: Drugs are illegal, but the use of them is allowed.

Pillarization, Corporatism, and Consensus

The Dutch have always had a strong outside orientation while maintaining a very tight societal concept. This concept is often characterized by pillarization, corporatism, and consensus (Kickert, 1996). Until the 1970s, Dutch society was segmented by four so-called *pillars*: Protestants, Catholics, Socialists, and Liberal-Neutralists. According to Kickert (1996), this ideological stratification started with the successful 16th-century struggle of the Protestant–Calvinist Dutch for separation from the Catholic Habsburg–Burgundy Empire. In the following centuries, Protestantism was the dominant and preferred religion, and Catholics were seen as second-rate citizens. But almost half of the inhabitants were Catholic. The subsequent necessity for Catholics was to establish a countervailing social and political power. At the end of the 19th century, two other groups in the Netherlands— the socialists and liberals—also started their own social structure, and the ideologically based stratification of Dutch society was a fact. Since then, the social organization of the Dutch state (including political parties, trade unions, employer organizations, schools and universities, the media, health, and welfare) has been performed by many organizations, all based on their (legal) status as private foundations or associations belonging to one of the four pillars and headed by a council of amateurs, as delegated by the pillars. As recently as 40 years ago, a Protestant would not shop in a Catholic grocery or listen to the socialist radio. That is why class stratification was never strong. The secularization of the 1960s has "depillared" society to a large extent. Nevertheless, radio and television as well as primary and secondary schools and other public-oriented and voluntary organizations are still partly organized according to pillarization, and societal culture is still based on this reasonably silent segmentation of society.

According to Kickert (1996), the Netherlands can be seen as an almost perfect example of the modern nonstatist concept of what he called *neocorporatism* (see also Hemerijck, 1993). This (European) model emphasizes the interests represented by a small, fixed number of internally coherent and well-organized interest groups that are recognized by the state and have privileged or even monopolized access to the state. The most important groups in a corporatist society are employers, employees, and the state. However, in the Netherlands all kinds of single-issue pressure groups also are involved in the system.

Another characteristic of the Netherlands is its focus on consensus. Many authors stated (see for an overview: Gallagher, Laver & Mair, 2001) that due to this consensus-building focus of the Dutch, pillarization and corporatism never resulted in a strong polarization of society, even in the turbulent 1960s.

EVOLUTION AND DEFINITION OF THE PROFESSION

Evolution

Another characteristic of the Netherlands is its strong roots in Enlightenment, as developed in the 18th century in France and Germany. Enlightenment has strongly influenced the evolution and practice of public relations in the Netherlands. In the 18th century, science and knowledge were no longer seen as the attributes only of the elite but as things that had to be diffused among all members of the society. The means for this diffusion was *voorlichting*, which means enlightening. The idea of *voorlichting* is based on Kant's expression *sapere aude* (which literally means dare to know): "all people must be willing to be informed on what is going on and made enlightened, so that they can take part in the ongoing debate about and development of society." Besides education, *voorlichting* was seen as the main way to help people to be informed. In the 19th century, *voorlichting* was defined as "giving full information to all people to mature and emancipate." (van Gent, 1995, p. 11) However, many people were afraid of enlightening ordinary people, which is why *voorlichting* is also used to show people how to behave as good citizens and to control them. The history of *voorlichting* can, therefore, be seen as a history of the battle between information and emancipation, on the one hand, and education and persuasion, on the other, but always under the ("Dutch uncle") dogma of knowing what is good. In all theories of *voorlichting*, the rather pedantic premise is that it is given for the benefit of the person or group to be enlightened, even when the people involved do not want to be enlightened at all or at least not in this way. This *voorlichting* influenced public relations to a great extent.

Many like to state that public relations was invented in the United States and crossed the ocean together with Marshall Aid after World War II. This is certainly true for the term *public relations* but not for the practice. When industrialization became a fact, industries started to give information about their well-being to the press as well as to the people at large. The government followed soon after and installed departments to inform journalists. However, Dutch journalists wanted direct access to administrators and politicians. Thanks to the strong pillarization of society in which every pillar had its own media and, therefore, its own political contacts, their lobby was successful for a long time, and the departments had to focus only on foreign journalists.

The characteristics of *voorlichting* can still be found in the practice of the public relations departments of business and government today. The evolution of public relations in the Netherlands cannot, therefore, be captured in terms of publicity or press agentry but more so in terms of public information and well-mentioned but patronizing education.

Definition of Public Relations

After World War II, Dutch society had to be rebuilt. It became important to promote business and societal goods, but society had an even stronger aversion to propaganda than before (Katus, 2001). Therefore, there was a strong debate about the ethics of this kind of promotional activity. Thanks to the propensity among the Dutch toward negotiation and consensus, these problems were solved by creating associations. In 1945, the first professional association was established, initiated by a journalist but open to public relations professionals as well as journalists. The goal of this association was to facilitate the exchange of knowledge between journalists and public relations officers (representing various government agencies and businesses) and to take away the fear for political information, which was strongly associated with Nazi's propaganda.

In 1946, the first professional association was followed by the first public relations association called the Association for Public Contact. A forum for press officers of corporations and the government, it was later renamed as the Association for Public Relations in the Netherlands (now called the Dutch Association for Communication). The primary aims of this association were to help knowledge development among practitioners, provide networking opportunities, and help develop an identity for the profession. Since the founding of this association, there has been a strong debate about the definition of the profession influenced by new knowledge of the profession from the United States and the already existing knowledge of *voorlichting*.

To the definition of public relations borrowed from the United States—"the development of good relationships between an organization and its publics" (Groenendijk, 1987, p. 54)—was added a small but, for the Dutch, very essential clause—"most of all by 'voorlichting.'" It was not until 1966 that this sentence was further discussed. In the beginning of the debate in the 1960s, the official definition remained unchanged except that it did not include the clause, "most of all by voorlichting." By that time, however, the relationships between the government and society and between business and society were very much under pressure. The concept of "good relationships" was seen as "too much aimed at harmony" (Lagerwey, Hemels, & van Ruler, p. 137, 1997) and was soon altered into the more neutral expression of "mutual understanding." This definition remained official (at least for the members of the association) until 1996. During this time, government public relations officers were debating whether they were allowed to persuade "and use the techniques of public relations" (Lagerwey et al., 1997, p. 147). The conclusion was that public relations could not be allowed in governmental communication not because of the concept of mutual understanding, but because of its persuasive character, which was imported from the United States. This debate shows that in reality public relations was seen primarily as propaganda and imagery.

In 1998, the Association of Public Relations in the Netherlands merged with two other smaller associations (the Association of Communication in the Netherlands and the Dutch Association of Corporate Journalists) to become the Dutch Association of Communication.

The board concluded that it served no purpose to try to define the field, and the discussion was over.

The term public relations is hardly used anymore. On the one hand, this is because of the negative connotations of the term itself and, on the other, this is because of the one-way and nonscientific orientation of the practice. Nowadays, the term is used only in a negative way to define what can be seen as bad for one's image and by some consultancies that work for American enterprises and use (aggressive) publicity. The most common current names for the field are corporate communication, communication management, or communication. Defining the public relations field, however, is also not seen as useful because of the mindset that communication management is what communication managers do. Such management is, however, still mainly aimed at *voorlichting* (van Ruler, 1998).

STATUS OF THE PROFESSION

The profession of public relations, with its new nomenclature of communication management or corporate communication, is widely accepted. All organizations have communication employees or at least structural contacts with communication consultancy bureaus. Managers see communication as an important or even as a critical factor for success. Recently, an official state commission advised the prime minister on how to cope with communication in the new information age and was very positive about the necessity of good communication management in the public sector (Commissie Toekomst Overheids-communicatie, 2001). Nevertheless, it is hard to fathom what is meant by *good* in this respect. Even practitioners themselves still call it a diffuse field. But there is no debate on what it is or what it should or could be. Even journalists do not consider it important to debate the practices of communication managers and consultants anymore. There is hardly any debate among professionals about their specific professional ethics. In 1998, the association organized a meeting on ethics and codes. A meager 12 (of over 1,000 members) participated in this meeting. The general conclusion was that a professional code is an old fashioned instrument of no practical significance and that ethics is a situational concept that cannot be debated in general. The discussion has been closed ever since. There is a current debate in the Netherlands about the social responsibility of business as well as on business and societal ethics. The profession is, however, almost totally absent in this debate.

The Visibility of the Profession Within Organizations

A large, representative survey (van Ruler & de Lange, 2000) on the structural representation of communication within organizations with over 50 staff members showed that almost all of these organizations have communication employees and that the responsibility for communication activities is placed at a high level. However, the internal visibility of the profession is very low. Of those responsible for communication activities, less than half (42%) reported to have a job title that relates to communication in one way or another (including external communications, *voorlichting*, public relations, and even advertising). It is no surprise that bearing a communication-related job title corresponds with the presence of a single department coordinating different communication activities, although this correspondence is not complete. Of the over 60% of organizations that reported having a special department to coordinate communication activities, only 55% were headed by a person with some explicit reference to *communication* in his or her job title. The conclusion is that many respondents indicate that there is one special department in which communication activities are coordinated but that these departments are not always led by a real communication manager, a department head, who is named as such. In such cases, the management of communication activities is obviously encroached by another department. Remarkably, if a job title has the word *communication* in it, its hierarchical position is different compared to titles that refer to *marketing*, for example. Staff functions and positions at the middle-management or operational level coincide more often with the use of *communication* in the title, whereas among members of the management team, marketing-related titles prevail. This indicates that communication under the marketing denomination often can be found in a management position. Single communication departments, however, participate less in the board of directors meetings. Obviously, communication management is seen as important, but it is not part of a specialized department at the managerial level.

Another indication of internal visibility is budget. Almost half of the respondents in the study (van Ruler & de Lange, 2000) indicated that either there was no structural budget for communication activities (40%) or that they did not know what this budget was (9%). Communication management is apparently a position at a high level of responsibility, but a structural communication budget is not always available. All in all, communication management may not yet be regarded as being visible within organizations, at least not at a managerial and strategic level, because only 3 of 10 of the organizations in this research comprised a communication department that was visible in the hierarchy as such and had its own structural budget.

PROFESSIONALISM IN THE PUBLIC RELATIONS INDUSTRY

Public relations can be seen as a stable industry in the Netherlands. Of a labor force of about 6 million, public relations accounts for some 30,000 employees with communication duties in organizations, about 50% of whom also have other tasks in personnel, marketing, office management, and other departments. About 25,000 public relations professionals work in public relations consultancies (van Ruler & de Lange, 2000). About 20% of communication professionals are employed in the public sector (government and semigovernmental organizations), as well as at the governmental, provincial, and local levels. The average communication unit employs six people. Marketing communication is included in these figures because it is impossible to make a distinction between marketing communication, advertising, and public relations in the Netherlands. What one calls public relations is mostly seen as (part of) marketing communications, whereas others talk about communication management but actually mean advertising or use marketing communication in such a broad sense that others would call it corporate communication or communication management.

If one were to base their decision on the size of the communication branch alone, one could conclude that public relations has been professionalized. It is questionable, however, whether the profession really meets the traditional criteria of professionalization. Some indicators of professionalism are the educational (knowledge reproduction) system, the knowledge development system, and professional culture. The educational system in public relations is very well-developed at different levels but is focused on the vocational side. There is a well-developed system of education in technical communication activities at a pre-bachelor's as well as at the bachelor's level. At bachelor's level almost all (about 30) professional and scientific universities offer full programs in organizational communication or communication management (with 180 or 240 European credits). Education at the master's level is less developed. There is one university-based master's program in applied communication science (aimed at organizational communication problems); one in corporate communication; one or two in what used to be called *voorlichting*; and one in policy, communication, and organization. There are no doctoral programs in organizational communication or communication management. Researchers of the Netherlands School of Communication Science are much more oriented to mass media and advertising than to organizational communication and communication management. Moreover, there is only one full professor specializing in corporate communication and none specializing in communication management or organizational communication, let alone in public relations. Knowledge production is not at a high level in the Netherlands.

But knowledge reproduction is also not obvious. Of those responsible for communication, 90% have no educational background that has anything to do with communication. This could, of course, be partly caused by the fact that most educational programs have been founded only recently. One could say that lengthy experience could be equalized with higher education. However, 90% of those responsible for communication are in the branch for less than 3 years. It is, therefore, also obvious that it is not a sector for which a special background is needed to get the job. It is also not common to be a member of one of the professional associations. There is a special association for the professionals of the public sector, but only 15% of those eligible actually are members. The Association of Communication has only about 1,000 members from a potential pool of 55,000. There is only one association of consultancies with 40 of 11,500 potential members. These facts lead us to conclude definitively that public relations in the Netherlands is not professionalized.

SUPPLY OF SERVICES IN THE CONSULTANCY SECTOR

The consultancy sector is a booming branch, with approximately 11,500 consultancies. At least three quarters of these are one-person operations. Of the remaining, 90% have fewer than 10 employees. So, it is a large industry with many small businesses. At conferences and in trade publications, the Dutch consultancy sector often claims that it is far ahead in bringing communication management to a strategic level. Van Ruler and de Lange (1999) assessed this claim in their study of the service supply in the consultancy sector. Asked how they typify their own work, professionals working in consulting firms responded that offering communication advice is by far their most common activity, followed by advertising, creative work, and public relations (as in publicity seeking).

Most of the consultancies assessed in the study (van Ruler & de Lange, 1999) had existed for only a short time. One quarter had existed for 2 years or less, and almost half (48%) were less than 5 years old, indicating that this is a young sector. The age of the consultancies correlated positively with their size ($r = .33; p < .01$)—the longer they have been in existence, the larger they are. Does this mean that a consultancy cannot survive if it does not grow? This would imply a correspondence with profitability. One of the outcomes of this study was that the consultancy sector as a whole generates net turnover of more than EUR 4 billion per year. However, profitability per consultancy is low. If the minimal gross income limit is set at EUR 68,000 per employee, then 46% of the larger consultancies and 65% of the one-person consultancies cannot survive, because their turnover lies below this level. If the minimum limit of EUR 110, 000 set by the Vereniging van Erkende Adviesbureaus (VEA) (an association of advertising) is adopted, then fewer than 18% of all consultancies can be expected to survive. There is an almost linear relationship between size and profitability. At the lower limit of EUR 68,000 per employee, a consultancy can survive with seven employees or more; at the VEA standard, a consultancy can survive with 9 employees or more. Thus, the consultancy sector is a young sector with many very small (often one- or two-person) consultancies and their long-term viability is very much at risk. This, of course, has an impact on investments in professionalization.

The Specializations of Consultancies

When asked what their specialization was, although respondents chose the broad denomination of communication most often, advertising, creative work, and public relations were also mentioned (van Ruler & de Lange, 1999). The question is, what are the specializations that the consultancies offer within these denominations? A list of 20 segments of the communication profession was prepared based on a literature review and interviews with directors of consultancies. This list was included in the questionnaire, and respondents were asked to designate the segments they offered. On average the consultancies offered 5 segments, but the individual differences were large: Some consultancies offered only one segment (18%), whereas others offered more than 10 (almost 10%). Predictably, the text consultancies and the creative consultancies had a very limited range of specializations, whereas other consultancies offered a much more diverse range of services. There is, however, hardly any correlation between typification of the supply and the chosen segments.

Aggregate all consultancies, text production scored highest followed by creation and concept development. In the larger consultancies, marketing communication and creation and concept development came first. In the one-person consultancies, text production scores the highest. More strategic issues such as positioning, profiling, and strategic policy advice were mentioned much less frequently. Research was hardly mentioned as a service. Also ethical issues were not apparently regarded as a segment of communication advice. There are not many consultancies that offer advice on strategic issues, but those that do are also more likely to offer research services as well. This applies particularly to the few larger communication and public relations consultancies, not to the consultancies that typify themselves as advertising consultancies. Apparently, providing communicative coaching services is being left to the consultancies that offer organizational advice. It is hardly mentioned in the list of service consultancies delivered in the survey, although it is in demand by communication managers. The supply of communication consultancy, therefore, is limited mainly to tactical and creative (artistic) spheres. The study concluded that the consultancy branch is a sector with a large number of small, relatively young, consultancies. They typically offer services similar to public relations and advertising consultancies and is, above all, tactical and artistic in nature.

INFRASTRUCTURE AND PUBLIC RELATIONS

The Political System

The Netherlands is a constitutional monarchy. The queen opens the parliament every year, but her speech is written by the government. She must sign all legislation, but she has no direct influence on its contents. The queen also has no opinions, at least not in public, and a slip of her tongue to the press is not meant to be made public, although they take the liberty of making these comments public from time to time. The prime minister is politically responsible for everything the queen and her family do or say.

Multiparty System. Similar to Sweden, Dutch politics is highly fragmented. Many parties compete for electoral and parliamentary support, and none of these is in a position to win a working majority on its own. That is why every government is a system of coalitions and alliances. The major parties still represent the ideological pillars of the last century—socialist, liberal, and religious (Catholics and Protestants now work together in one party)—but apart from them, all kinds of interest groups can form their own parties and contest for control of the parliament.

The Polder Model. According to one of the leading political journalists (Kranenburg, 2001), Dutch politics is an oasis of calm where conflict is seen as counterproductive. Like many others, Kranenburg claimed that this is because no single party has ever come close to approaching a majority in parliament. Therefore, a coalition government is inevitable, and today's enemy can become tomorrow's ally. Ever since World War II, the Christian parties (who merged to form the Christian Democratic Union [CDA]) played a pivotal role in these coalitions, aligning themselves with the Social Democrats at times and with the Liberals at other times. This practice ended in 1994 when the "red" of the socialists and the "blue" of the liberals joined to form a coalition known as *purple*. They got along so well that the coalition continued after the 1998 elections as well. Kranenburg described this coalition between labor and capital as "the Third Way *avant la lettre*" (p. 71) (before the term third way was invented) and a most successful one at that. The former trade union boss Wim Kok became prime minister in 1994 and was worshipped by the business community until he retired in 2002. In 2002, the CDA again became a part of the coalition.

This kind of coalition is said to be a natural exponent of Dutch culture, which for centuries has relied on the practice of consultation and the involvement of as many people as possible in decision making. Every issue bearing even the remotest risk of disagreement has a forum of its own in which all interested parties are represented, whether it be traffic issues, defense matters, or education affairs. Kranenburg (2001) showed that this culture has many repercussions in politics: "The more the relevant bodies agree, the less freedom of movement remains for the politicians". It was under these conditions that the now well-known polder model was born in the early 1980s. (*Polder* is a Dutch word for reclaimed land that is made out of water or swamp) (p. 38). At that time, politicians planned to intervene in the country's wage levels and tackle the high rate of unemployment by sharply reducing labor costs. Facing the loss of their freedom of negotiation, labor unions and employers agreed to a voluntary wage restraint in return for a reduction in work hours. The political establishment had no choice but to acquiesce to this "voluntary" agreement between employers and labor unions.

The Dutch Parliament consists of two chambers—the Lower House and the Upper House. The Lower House has existed for more than 500 years and consists of 150 members elected every 4 years by the voters, under a system of proportional representation. The Upper House was installed in 1815, during a short union with Belgium. Its 75 members, part-time politicians, are elected every 4 years by the members of the provincial executives. In the days of the pillarization voting behavior was very clear. As Gallagher, Laver & Mair (2001) stated, "to speak of the majority of voters at a given election as choosing a party is nearly as misleading as speaking of a worshipper on a Sunday 'choosing' to go to an Anglican rather than a Baptist or a Catholic church" (p. 252). Nowadays, there is a massive decline in party identification, with only 28% of voters identifying themselves with a political party. However, this lack of identification could also be partly caused by the fact that voters have several parties to choose from, within the left as well as at the right wings, with about 20 political parties participating in elections at the national or local levels (Gallagher, 2001, p. 258). However, parties do have to campaign, and many observers comment about the "Americanization of politics" when personalities seem to become more important than party programs.

Dutch politics is boring, European Commissioner Frits Bolkestein, once said in a television interview in the 1990s. During the 2002 elections, politics was no longer boring because of a newcomer, the Late Pim Fortuyn, who started the debate about boring politics and politicians. He was murdered 9 days before the elections, throwing the country in shock. His party did well enough to come second behind the Christian Democrats.

However, all parties are arguing for a revised polder model. In government as well as in business, the usual reaction to important and controversial problems is to form a kind of forum to discuss the issue at hand and look for harmonious solutions. This way of solving problems takes a lot of talking, both inside and outside parliament. Long discussions have always been a part of Dutch culture, but they are only allowed when aimed at compromise and consensus. Moreover, the Dutch hate what they call "fried air," or pompous talk and rhetoric (Vossestein, 2001, p. 80). These factors contribute to making politics dull and seldom really innovative. But, as the Dutch say, "Slowly, slowly, then the line will never break . . . "

Level of Economic Development

The Netherlands is a very prosperous country. Despite its small size, the Netherlands is the world's eighth largest trading nation (Vossestein, 2001). It has experienced an even higher employment growth than the United States in recent years. Along with Ireland, Spain, and Finland, the Netherlands is currently one of the more successful countries in Western Europe (Bomhoff, 2001). The exploitation of its large reserves of natural gas has given the Dutch economy a boost since the early 1960s and made the (former) guilder a very strong and stable currency.

Although the Netherlands has a strong agricultural image abroad, just over 2% of all working people are employed in agriculture (Vossestein, 2001). The Dutch economy is predominantly industrial and most of all service-oriented, with a strong international orientation based on the country's long trading tradition and colonial past. Vossestein (2001) contended that this is reflected in the disproportionately high number of Dutch multinational companies, such as Ahold, Akzo-Nobel, DSM, Heineken, KLM, Philips, Shell, Stork, Unilever, Wolters/Kluwer/Reed/Elsevier, ABN/AMRO, Aegon, ING, KPN, Rabobank, which have its roots (and most of the time also their headquarters) in the Netherlands.

Vossestein (2001) described the Netherlands as a mixture of free market economy and fairly strong government control, although the latter is decreasing. Still, there are many rules and regulations on safety, hygiene, salary levels, workers' rights, protection of the environment, limitations on building, and so on, made by consultation with all kinds of groups and coalitions, even more than in many other nations. Strangely, employers do not seem to treat this as restrictive. "A deeply felt need to have everyone share a decent standard of living has led to a system in which, more than in most countries, the national wealth is distributed to all" (Vossestein, 2001, p. 182).

Taxes are high, with a maximum rate of 52%. Rate of taxation is directly proportional to income levels to moderate the income gap between the rich and poor. There is a largely subsidized public transport system, good-quality housing (even for those who cannot afford it; the local government subsidizes high rents if necessary), comprehensive insurance coverage against medical calamities, social security benefits that are higher than in the Anglo Saxon countries, and a significant contribution to overseas development aid (Bomhoff, 2001, p. 60). Of course, this makes the Netherlands an expensive country in which to live. Bomhoff stated that if the Dutch do not want to be cheap, they will have to be smart, implying that if the Dutch cannot comply with international standards they have to be smart to be able to afford it economically. International research clearly demonstrates, he claimed, that the average quality of education strongly influences the level of economic development that a country can attain. Although education is already at a high level, he believed that a change in thinking at the Ministry of Education is needed to increase competition in education. Teachers' unions continue to remain opposed to variable pay for teachers (all teachers at all levels of education are paid by the government and have the same level-based salary scales). The unions also are opposed to any scheme that aims to reward individual schools that do a good job educating their students. Public opinion, he said, is keenly interested in better primary and secondary education, but methods that have been successful abroad always involve more freedom for school managers, a taboo for the Dutch. Other economists believe that the Dutch advantage in Europe will be challenged because of bad innovative power in this field and that competition in the educational system (and selection) has to be introduced for the Dutch to continue to stay wealthy. This could have its influence on the demand for corporate profiling and image making of the educational system, which is at the moment almost nonexistent.

Legal Infrastructure

All legislation is first introduced in the Lower House of parliament where it is debated and can be amended. If it has been introduced by a minister, a bill may be withdrawn up until the final vote is taken. After passage, it is sent to the Upper House where it is adopted or rejected with no provision for making any amendments.

Gallagher et al. (2001, p. 33) made a distinction between two general types of legal systems: the common law tradition and the civil law tradition. Britain and the United States have a common law tradition. Most European countries, including the Netherlands, have a civil law tradition. The difference is that common law systems rely less on law as act of parliaments and more on the accumulated weight of precedents set by the decisions, definitions, and interpretations made by judges. Many key legal principles and rules are thus established not in statutes made by the legislature but in judgments made by the judiciary. The essential feature of a civil law system is that the ultimate foundation of the law is a comprehensive and authoritative legal code. Upon this foundation is built a superstructure of statutes enacted by the legislature. In civil law systems, judges do not make laws, they merely apply the law. Laws are made by parliament and established as legal code. One of the most cited codes in this respect is the Code Napoléon, which emerged as part of the new order after the French Revolution. This code has greatly influenced the Dutch legal system. In practice, Gallagher et al. (2001) explained, the two systems are becoming blurred: "In the Netherlands, the courts have increasingly become interpreters of the law rather than mere appliers of it, partly because the parliament has been inclined to include in statutes 'vague norms' that leave considerable discretion to the judges. In areas such as euthanasia and abortion, the Supreme Court has in effect produced case laws where parliament was unable to pass detailed legislation" (p. 35).

There is a constitutional right to freedom of speech, but this right does not include advertising. That is why it is forbidden to publish certain kinds of advertisements, for example, for cigarettes or liquor. At the same time, public relations and communication managers in these sectors try to avoid this by looking for what they call *brand communication*; they become sponsors for events to attract people to buy their products. This practice is often criticized, and politicians have frequently tried to find ways to end such sponsorships.

In 1970, an official state committee introduced a draft for a Public Access to Government Information Act, which was meant for all individuals. According to Katus (2001), a Dutch scientist on *voorlichting*, "although the Netherlands is a democratic country, it took ten years before this act came into force, legally recognizing the citizens' rights to government information" (p. 28). This has to do with the already-mentioned fear about keeping all people informed at all times and about all subjects. Still, individuals, mostly journalists, have to threaten now and then to get the information they want, and *voorlichters* (communication officers) continue to clash with politicians and bureaucrats who are less inclined toward openness. However, openness is the norm.

Organizations in the Netherlands are not obligated to give any information to individuals. However, they have to file their annual statement of accounts at the Chamber of Commerce, which is obliged to open its files to any interested party as a matter of public record. Most enterprises make these figures public themselves in annual or biannual statements. Although corporations are required to release financial information to stock holders annually, they tend to do so at least twice a year. The law is, however, not as detailed as in the United States. Currently, a public debate on whether to require all organizations to make annual statements regarding financial matters, their record on environmentalism, and their social affairs is taking place. However, many organizations already publish these kinds of data annually.

Level of Activism

Part of Dutch culture is its socio-ideological pluralism. One consequence of pluralism is that there is rarely a majority opinion on any issue, and even if there is one, there will always be factions or individuals with minds of their own and they want to be heard as well (Vossestein, 2001, p. 66). As a result, activism is rather high in the Netherlands but has a unique character because interest or pressure groups are part of the social and political system instead of being outsiders. On all important aspects of social life such as employment, social security, education, health care, energy, environment, and so on, interest groups are trying to get involved in politics and are very successful at it. According to Deth and Vis (2000) it is obvious that pressure groups play an enduring and important role in the political process in the Netherlands and are "part of the system" (p. 229). The constitutional freedom of association is the legal basis for their existence. The number of activists, their expertise on the issue of concern, and their ability to participate in the public debate is the social basis for their success. Almost all Dutch people belong to one or more pressure groups, and they all donate money for the right causes. Activism is, one can say, institutionalized in the Netherlands.

Pressure groups can target public and private interests. Some are small and active because of one local problem, such as building a new chemical plant in a particular area, whereas others are large and internationally oriented. An important example of a pressure group is labor unions. Although only 25% of employees are organized in unions, unions still negotiate with employers thus helping about 83% of the workforce who work under a collective agreement (Deth & Vis, 2000, p. 213). However, 70% to 80% of all employers are united in employers' associations. This could, of course, lead to much polarization, but this is not the case in the Netherlands. Work stoppage strikes are rarely used as weapons, unlike in Germany, Great Britain, or the United States. The obligation to have a well-functioning work council in which the unions are represented helps to establish good relations.

Other pressure groups (also called *social movements*) are aimed at the public interest. Important examples of this kind of pressure groups are the World Wildlife Fund and Greenpeace, which are both very active in the Netherlands, with over 2 million Dutch donors. These groups have pressured governments on public policy issues for years and have now begun to pressure entrepreneurial decision making on a larger scale, with enterprise struggling to cope with this new phenomenon.

All over the world, pressure groups have become professionalized. They have developed in quantity as well as quality. This leaves the Dutch with a fundamental dilemma of according all groups equal rights to be heard. Challenges for politicians today include how to give all pressure groups equal attention and how to keep fair autonomy in decision making. Challenges for entrepreneurs these days in the Netherlands and around the world is to decide which pressure groups they should give attention to and which pressure groups they can afford to ignore. The Dutch society has accepted that pressure groups have become a fact of life and that, in general, they have a right to be heard.

Pressure groups used to be seen from a collective behavior approach, which observes that pressure disturbs social order. But due to the Dutch culture, activism has never reached a violent state. A prominent anti-institutional action group in the 1960s worked under the striking name of the *Gnomes*. They wanted to change the political as well as the economic system and declared a "Gnome state." They started a political party and won several seats in the local parliament of the city of Amsterdam. Most people liked them, and much of the democratization of the region is based on the disturbance they created during the 1970s. Nowadays, most people in the Netherlands see pressure groups from a resource mobilization view, which recognizes collective action as a normal phenomenon of the political system (van Noort, Huberts, & Rademaker, 1992). Moreover, pressure groups have been allowed greater involvement in decision making in the political field as well as in the corporate arena, as long as they are not too violent in their approach. That is why cooperation is an important strategy of Dutch pressure groups. Van Luijk, a professor on business ethics in the Netherlands, called it "democratization of moral authority" and saw it as a trend (van Luijk & Schilder, 1997, p. 16).

Government and private enterprise are developing an interactive approach to policy development, which has proven to be an interesting strategy to deal with activism. It is seen as the best solution for coping with all kinds of pressure in society, and the recent State Commission on Governmental Communication sees it as the key to public policy making.

CULTURE AND PUBLIC RELATIONS

Social Cultural Aspects of the Netherlands

Because of the interactive nature of many of these environmental variables, the previous sections of this chapter have covered many aspects of Dutch social cultural life. Discussing Dutch culture, some authors spoke of a fragmentation of the society due to increasing individualism. Some even spoke of a *tweedeling* (or segregation or apartheid) of society, denoting a split between the beneficiaries of the booming economy and those left out in the cold (Vossestein, 2001). Although no one is financially destitute in the Netherlands, some are left behind due to exploiting economic opportunities. Examples are single mothers, people with mental problems, old people without children living solely on old-age benefits given by the state, and the homeless. Still, Americans who live in the Netherlands mention the ongoing strong family orientation in much of Dutch society (Vossestein, 2001), and most mention the widely felt right to be subsidized by the state. Still, all kinds of signs of individualism can be found in the Netherlands. Fewer and fewer younger people are volunteering these days. This may be a result not only of individualism but also a sign of an increase in workload and other entertaining avenues to spend free time. Some foreign journalists describe the Netherlands as a (far too) liberal society where people do whatever they like such as indulging in drugs and pornography. This is a nation that finds it perfectly normal for gay couples to be married in the town hall and obtain children by artificial insemination or adoption or for doctors to practice euthanasia legally. Luckily for the Netherlands, investors soon discover that much of this image is half true at best and that there is a lot more to Dutch society than this, argued Vossestein (2001).

According to Vossestein (2001), the basic values of the Dutch are egalitarianism and a high work ethic. The Dutch have difficulty in dealing with hierarchy, always trying to maintain a balance between being aware of the hierarchical aspects of a relationship and not wanting to make that awareness too obvious, he argued. In the Netherlands, common people are the norm, so the elite can be mocked. The elite also do not like to be presented as such. They prefer to be pictured riding their bikes or bringing their children to school not for imagery but for practicing the norm. Although working in the Netherlands is highly competitive, competition is not greatly appreciated. One is certainly not expected to compete at the expense of weaker players or colleagues. "Act normal; that is strange enough" and "Never put your head above the surface level" are widely known expressions. Moreover, those with talent should deploy it for the benefit of all, not just for themselves, according to Vossestein (2001). The Dutch like to see themselves as hard-working people with strong work ethics. Hanging around is not seen as fruitful unless it is seen as being deserved after some hard work. In earlier days, girls were not allowed to sit still but had to do needlework when their normal work was done. This is not normal anymore, but sitting still or watching television for example, is still not seen as constructive behavior. However, the Dutch are known for their short work week of 36 hr and their long vacations, ranging from 3 to 5 weeks each year depending on, among other things, their age. However, some Dutch researchers argued that these achievements are no longer sustainable because of globalization (mostly described as Americanization) of the world (see a. o. Bomhoff, 2001).

Hofstede's Dimensions in the Netherlands

In Hofstede's (2001) terms, the Netherlands can be characterized as a nation with a slightly different culture from its neighbors Germany and Belgium and a very different culture from that of the United States, Asia, and Africa. Hofstede treated culture as "the collective programming of the mind, which distinguishes the members of one human group from another" (p. 25). He found five dimensions—power distance, collectivism, masculinity–femininity, uncertainty avoidance, and Confucian dynamism or long-term orientation—as described in some detail in chapter 1. He stated that the Dutch culture is highly feminine and individualistic wherein low levels of power distance is normal, the people act to avoid or minimize uncertainty, and the members of society have a relatively long-term worldview (Hofstede, 1995, 2001). In feminine cultures like the Netherlands, people prefer to solve conflicts by negotiation and compromise. De Swaan (1989), a Dutch sociologist, stated that Dutch society has evolved from a relative command economy (structured by the pillars) into a full negotiation economy in which all people negotiate about everything. This affinity to negotiate makes itself felt in private as well as in public and organizational life. The Law on Works Councils prescribes deliberations on all organizational policy matters. Labor unions have the right to submit their own candidates for these councils and care for the education of council members. Labor unions have less than 30% membership but negotiate with employers on collective agreements that benefit all employees. The general feeling of employers is that labor unions cause trouble but are natural part of life (Hofstede, 1995, p. 121)—a necessary evil.

Hofstede (1987) stated that the Dutch play eight roles in society. The first role is that of the Dutch uncle, explained previously. The second is the role of the housewife (applicable also to men) with a more than normal aim at caring for personal and social environment. The third role is of the nurse (also equally applicable to men). The fourth is that of the innkeeper, always welcoming but never totally altruistic. An interesting aspect of this role according to Hofstede is that the Dutch practice their uncertainty avoidance not as "strangers are dangerous" but as "strangers are strange," which allows room for tolerating unfamiliar behavior. The fifth role is that of the traveller, which is less chauvinistic and rather internationally oriented. The sixth role is the merchant, the seventh is that of the citizen, and the eighth the farmer's wife who denotes a no-nonsense, no-esthetics, hard-working nature. All of these roles are visible in private as well as in social and economic life, and they can be translated into corporate culture. Although the current trend toward globalization tends to export a more Anglo–American culture, many of these roles can still be found in Dutch daily life.

THE MEDIA ENVIRONMENT

Media Control

Freedom of press is a constitutional right in the Netherlands. Diversity of structure and content is a key principle in the Dutch media system ever since the rise of the mass media at the beginning of the 20th century. At that time, the pillarization was a fact and the new mass media were owned or controlled by the pillars and its social institutions from the start. In fact, the Catholic church, several Protestant churches, the Liberal party, and the Socialist party started their own newspapers and nationwide radio stations because they saw these new media as interesting instruments to socialize their people and develop a bond. In view of the very close relations and interaction between people, religion, politics, and the press, it is not surprising that the Dutch press was and remains an opinion press primarily and not an oppression press. Yellow journalism is hardly visible in the Netherlands.

The first daily newspapers were developed in the second half of the 19th century. Hemels (2000) described how the Dutch press was almost entirely run on the basis of corporatist production principles. To boost circulation and reach and hold onto irregular readers, a new generation of managing newspaper publishers offered their readers a very peculiar extra—free accident insurance. At that time, workers had no accident insurance via their employers and were very happy with this extra. According to Hemels, that is why publishers quickly succeeded in penetrating the market of new readers with this rather unique system of subscriptions, which shows the entrepreneurial side of the Dutch. Although this marketing instrument vanished in 1940, until today, most daily newspapers find their ways to their readers mostly via (yearly) subscriptions.

In 1940, on the eve of World War II the daily press had 70 newspapers, with a total circulation of 500,000 copies. Of these, 32 were Catholic, 6 were Liberal, 5 were associated with one of the Protestant parties, 2 were affiliated with the Social Democrats, 1 was Communist, and 1 was National Socialist; the remaining 23 were somehow independent (Hemels, 2000). This segmentation was even stronger with the other new mass medium—radio. Although radio started as a commercial enterprise (by Philips), it was soon taken over by the pillars. The broadcasting system can be typified as external pluriformity in which all pillars had their own broadcasting organization and shared the two available transmitting radio stations. The usual form taken by organizations belonging to a pillar was that of an association governed by its members or by a foundation with a cooperative board. Until the Media Act of 1988 (van Cuilenberg, 1999) commercial radio and television was not allowed.

After the 1960s, the pillared organizations lost their control in society in general and in their own target groups in particular. Some dailies and weeklies that identified with political parties or special-interest groups totally disappeared, whereas others reinvented themselves and broadened their circulation base. The independent popular press increased its market share enormously. *The Telegraph*, for example, reached an all-time high circulation of 1 million copies per day in 1994 (Hemels, 2000).

However, since advertising on television and radio was allowed in 1967, the printed media had to cope with competition for revenues. As compensation, television and radio have been required to pay a portion of their advertising revenue to the press to keep the highest possible plurality in the press system. A special Trade Fund for the Press, paid by radio, television, and government, subsidizes newspapers and magazines for a certain period if they fail to become or stay commercially independent and obviously add to a multiform media system.

Until the 1960s, five (pillar-oriented) broadcasting organizations had a license to broadcast. After years of political struggle and heated public debate about the future of broadcasting, the *open system* was introduced in 1966—new organizations could enter the system as long as they met the principles of noncommercialism, variety, and membership. The Broadcasting Act (see van Cuilenburg, 1999) made it possible for all kinds of ideological or religious schools of thought to engage in broadcasting. However, they were obliged to deliver a comprehensive programming schedule with reasonable proportions of different program categories and to satisfy the population's cultural, religious, or spiritual needs. Since 1988, commercial radio and television has been legalized. In 2002, Dutch television can be said to have a dual system. The first consists of three public television channels programmed by the old (private) pillars and the newer noncommercial broadcasting organizations (including a Muslim broadcaster as well as a very fundamental Protestant broadcaster and other ideologically based organizations), whereas the second other part of the system consists of about 10 commercial channels. Most commercial stations have been owned by or are subsidiaries of the big multinational media corporations such as Bertelsmann and SBS.

Brants and McQuail (1997) described how government policy has been characterized by constant hesitation and decisional hiccups. With the press, there is a growing fear that a diminishing number of publishers will monopolize the market. The adage "government keeping its distance" and hesitation to interfere in press matters has prevented consecutive Cabinets from taking action, they argued. As far as broadcasting was concerned, the government was aware of the financial opportunities offered by selling airtime to commercial parties and the chance that this money would otherwise cross the border and be lost for the development of original Dutch cultural programming. But there was a traditional hesitation about commercialization, and through traditional ties, it tried to preserve both the existing public system and to create a healthy competitive commercial system. The basis of media policy, which used to be "the widest possible dissemination of information from diverse and antagonistic sources" (van Cuilenburg, 1999, p. 10) is still the basis of the media system but becomes blurred with all kinds of commercial and entertaining variables. Regarding pillarization, van Cuilenburg (1999) concluded that there is no longer pluralism among pillars, but a lot of pluralism does exist within each pillar, although they still officially own many of the broadcasting systems and have informal influence on their actions.

Media Outreach

Van Cuilenburg et al. (1999) discussed the overabundance of the Dutch media. In 1940, the Dutch daily newspaper circulation was 500,000 copies. By 1950, it had reached 2.5 million copies per day distributed to 2.5 million households. Currently, the daily press reaches about 80% of the 6 million households who subscribe to one or more periodicals, resulting in a circulation of almost 5 million copies. Van Cuilenburg et al. called the media market a buyers market wherein media consumption is very elastic, which means that the demand for media is directly or even overproportional to media offers and price. A positive consequence of this kind of a media market is a market-oriented diversity by which the public receives the best service; a negative consequence is a middle-of-the-road type of journalism. The commercialization of the media delivers less openness and diversity of meanings, and these are still norms for quality media. Publishers fear a decline of interest in printed information most of all because of the enormous number of television channels and the increase in time spent watching television. They talk about "de-reading." Their answer is a market-oriented one (Lockefeer, 1999), in which they cater to the needs of target groups by delivering niches of information. This means that professional journalism standards are not the only measures of quality of newspapers, but circulation is an important factor as well. Journalism professors, such as Lockefeer, fear for the quality of journalism, because editor-in-chiefs have recently acquired commercial responsibility for newspapers in addition to content.

Radio and television reach almost all households. In almost all households one can find one, two, or more television sets. There is hardly any household without more than one radio. Knulst (1999) did longitudinal research measuring media consumption for the period from 1955 to 1995. He found that, in 1955, respondents listened to the radio for about 15 hr per week, spent 5 hr per week reading newspapers, and watched television for only 25 min per day (very few people owned television sets). The study contrasted this data with data from 1995 when respondents spent 2.5 hr per day watching television; listening to the radio as a single activity was almost not done anymore and newspaper and book readership had also vastly decreased. People with low levels of education and younger people typically watch commercial television, whereas those with higher education and older people watch public television channels. There has also been a steep decline in the reading habits of the Dutch. In 1955, 21% of leisure time was spent on reading, whereas by 1995 it had dropped to only 9%. Reading was restricted to people with higher education and older people. Bronner and Neijens (1995) found that, for most people, television is no longer the intense experience it used to be and has instead become "the water from the tap"—a part of daily life. For the common person, radio is a medium of entertainment nowadays, although experts still think of radio as an information medium. Daily newspapers are used for information, but younger people turn to newspapers only when they have nothing else to do. Reading magazines is still a rather high intense experience. The Internet shows itself as a medium with high usability for all kinds of information.

Since 1995, much time has been spent on new media. In 2001, 59% of all households have a PC (and 97% of all students have one) and about 47% of these households surf the Internet now and then. The average time spent on the Internet and e-mailing currently is 1.8 hr per week (3.4 hr a week for 12- to 19-year-olds; www.scp.nl). Although there are a lot of workshops for older people and the Internet is promoted for all kinds of people, it is still a tool for younger white boys and men. However, trend watchers believe that in a couple of years the Internet will be as normal as the telephone.

Media Access

Although freedom of speech is a constitutional right in the Netherlands, there is a chasm when it comes to pluralism in media access. There are few constraints for anyone to communicate with journalists, but it is extremely hard to get editorial space. This limitation has little to do with any effort to exclude systematically certain organizations or institutions because publicity seeking is part of the communication game of almost all organizations. Two criteria need to be met to get any access to the media. The first is for publicity seekers to be professional. There are numerous books and courses on how to get media attention. Media relations is a key task of communication managers and consultants, and even very small organizations know how to conduct it professionally. As a result, journalists often complain of information overload. The second criterion is the reputation (credibility) of the source of publicity to deliver interesting and well-organized news, as well as being accessible. Some argue that a few pressure groups or social groups get access to media more readily than others. And some of the *allochtonous* (who are not native Dutch citizens) groups in the Netherlands do not have easy access to the media or are only reported in the news in a stereotypical manner. This is partly due to the sociocultural diversity between journalists and these groups and partly due to commercial reasons. Many of these groups do not read Dutch newspapers or watch Dutch television but read their own newspapers and watch their home country stations via satellite dishes. So they often are not considered a part of the Dutch media market.

CONCLUSIONS AND CASE STUDY

Influences on Public Relations

Based on this review, the following conclusions are drawn about public relations in the Netherlands. First, it is obvious that seeking mutual understanding, as prescribed by the normative theory of public relations, is the normal way of doing business in the Netherlands, as the Dutch are culturally inclined to seek consensus. Note that this is not to be seen as something that has been introduced by public relations. Second, concomitantly, relationship building does not have to be introduced as an instrument because it is what we normally do in the Netherlands. Negotiation is our nature. The Dutch multiparty political system, in which today's enemy can be tomorrow's ally, makes it quite normal to cooperate with natural enemies. The economic system shows that reasonably equal division of prosperity and things like empowering people and management of diversity are part of Dutch economic culture. However, the globalizing economy has challenged traditional ways of behaving.

The legal infrastructure is still founded in the civil law tradition (there are no juries). However, the Dutch fear that it will become normal to bring things *sub judice* (the juridization of society) and the introduction of a claiming culture. This will make life harder and could change the nature of public relations in the future into imagery. Still, image building is not seen as the normal way of doing business, but as the American way. The Dutch like image building as long as they can use it, but the norm continues to be "Never make yourself bigger than you are." Image building is seen by many as untrustworthy; hence, this is not a good path for the public relations society in the Netherlands. Working on identities is increasingly seen as more profitable than working on images. Ron van der Jagt, a leading professional, has written a series of articles advocating this school of thought in the journal of the public relations practice, *Communicatie*. Working on identity as a specialty of public relations, however, should not make professionals neglect the basic roots of public relations as proposed in *voorlichting*, whose primary aim is to enlighten people. For centuries, the Dutch have been keeping each other well-informed as a basic societal principle. However, the boundaries of the concept of *voorlichting* are currently being blurred with concepts such as profiling. It is my opinion that the third conclusion drawn, the most important one, is that if there is a need for a normative theory of public relations, it is on *voorlichting*, which produces an informed society where public opinion is the outcome of deliberation and public debate. That is the current focus of many of the Dutch communication scientists.

Case Study

Be Yourself: The Dutch Approach to Repositioning Unilever on the Recruitment Market by Chris Kersbergen[1]

Unilever, one of the world's leading fast-moving consumer goods companies, pursues a multilocal strategy, which pays special attention to local traditions and cultures for successfully marketing consumer brands. One of the foundations of this multilocal strategy is that 90% of Unilever managers are locally recruited and trained. Those responsible for recruitment and management have the freedom to tailor the presentation of Unilever as an employer to suit local conditions.

In 1999, Unilever Netherlands launched a process to reposition itself on the Dutch recruitment market through integrated employer branding. There are two ways in which one can see clear parallels between this strategy and Dutch culture, as explained in this chapter. First, the values and content of the new employer brand are very Dutch. Second, the process by means of which it was developed is in some ways comparable with the so-called 'polder model.'

Authentic Individuals. One of the key characteristics of Unilever is its diversity in all its activities and products and brands but, most importantly, in people. But this was not the image the target group top potential university graduates had. They merely regarded Unilever as a large, formal, and uniform company that was only looking for the "smartest boys in the class." This image did not reflect the richness and diversity that this multinational and its employees represented. Moreover, this image was not very appealing to the recruitment market, where potential recruits rated personal development, low hierarchical levels, informal working culture, interesting colleagues, and quality time (private and at work) as most relevant. Research showed that some of the values that Hofstede (1993, p. 5) termed as "typical of the Dutch culture"—feminine and individualistic with short lines of command—were top-of-the-mind criteria for selecting an employer. Potential recruits look for an environment in which they have the space to learn and grow as individuals. Unilever is that environment, but not everyone who should have known that actually did.

This gap between perception and reality has not yet led to recruitment problems, but one must repair the roof while the sun is shining. That is why Unilever, together with communication consultants at Bikker Euro RSCG, began to develop the new Unilever

---

[1]Chris Kersbergen is a partner at Bikker Euro RSCG, a leading Dutch corporate communications consultancy, and has been responsible for codeveloping the employer brand with Unilever since early 1999.

employer brand. The first step was to match Unilever's company values with those perceived as the most relevant by Dutch recruits. These key brand values were communicated through a remarkable corporate-branding campaign consisting of advertising campaigns and a total redesign of all corporate and recruitment material. By using portraits of credible individuals, using more feminine colors, and focusing on authenticity and personal growth (e.g., using a "be yourself" campaign) Unilever was able to show its Dutch side to local recruits. The employer-branding approach has been very successful in attracting existing and new target groups to apply to Unilever.

A Consensus Model for Brand Development. Apart from the Dutch content and tone of voice of the brand, the process used to develop it was also very Dutch. In the Dutch recruitment market, it is vital to make sure that everything you claim on the outside is a credible reflection of the internal reality. The various networks between students and people working in different companies should never be underestimated. Any graduate thinking of applying to a firm will first contact a friend, family member, or acquaintance who actually works in that company to check "how it really is." After all, you are not just choosing a new toothpaste, you are choosing your working environment and career path for the coming years. So in the recruitment market, and especially in the Dutch network economy, the motto "inside equals outside" rules.

This led Unilever to "involve the involved" in every stage of developing the employer brand, thus making sure that all external claims reflected the internal reality while safeguarding the commitment and support of all Dutch Unilever employees, thus making them ambassadors of the company. Consensus was not a wish but a fundamental necessity to make the campaign credible. Here we can see parallels between the Dutch culture of consensus and coalitions and the so-called polder model.

From the beginning, a group of almost 300 young Unilever managers, all with less than 5 years of experience with the company, were involved in developing the criteria for employer brand fundamentals and the campaign. These young managers became a very cooperative group for the public relations consultants. They witnessed the interviews with students (potential employees) about the image they had of Unilever as an employer and discussed differences between reality and image. When the first visuals of the employer brand were developed, these young managers gave critical feedback. They also contributed in preparing the text for brochures and the web site, and they did the final editing and judging. In many different groups and on many different occasions, this group of young managers actually codeveloped the brand basics and the campaign with the Management Recruitment Department and the agency.

Involvement of senior management was another fundamental factor that contributed to the success of this effort. The Management Recruitment Department showed every proposal to the chief executive officer to get his or her input and consent. Eventually, top management became so involved that they became some of the most enthusiastic ambassadors of the employer brand, conveying that it was not just something from the Management Recruitment Department but part of the corporate story of everyone at Unilever. This not only contributed to making the effort attractive to potential recruits, but it also worked well with current employees. Finally, a lot of attention was paid to informing all other internal and external stakeholders. A special insert in the personnel magazine explained the concepts to all employees before launch. All management recruiters followed special media training focused on explaining the "be yourself" key messages. Finally, all young Unilever managers participated in a pre-introduction day where they were encouraged to translate the campaign messages in their own words.

This consensus model resulted in a very high commitment and an over 90% overall positive evaluation of the "be yourself" campaign among Unilever managers. It helped Unilever become the Number 1 employer of choice in different rankings in 2000 and 2001. But, more important, the "be yourself" philosophy reflects the internal reality and is strongly supported and propagated by Dutch Unilever employees.

REFERENCES

Bomhoff, E. (2001). Not quite smart enough. In *the Netherlands: A practical guide for the foreigner and a mirror for the Dutch*. Amsterdam/Rotterdam: Prometheus/NRC Handelsblad, the Netherlands, pp 58–63.

Brants, J. K., & McQuail, D. (1997). the Netherlands. In B. S. Oestergaard (Ed.), *The media in Western Europe: The Euromedia handbook*. London: Sage. pp. 153–167.

Bronner, F., & Neijens, P. (1999). Hoe beleven mensen hun media? (How do people perceive their media?) In J. van Cuilenburg, P. Neijens, & O. Scholten (Eds.), *Media in overvloed* (Overabundance of media). Amsterdam: Amsterdam University Press, the Netherlands, pp. 118–133.

Commissie Toekomst Overheidscommunicatie. (2001). *In dienst van de democratie. Het rapport van de Commissie Toekomst Overheidscommunicatie* (In the service of democrazy. The report of the Commission on the Future of Government Communication). Den Haag: SDU Uitgevers, the Netherlands.

Cuilenburg, J. van (1999). Het Nederlands mediabestel: Verscheidenheid tussen kartel en concurrentie (The Dutch Media System: a range between cartel and competition). In J. van Cuilenburg, P. Neijens, & O. Scholten (Eds.), *Media in overvloed* (Overabundance of Media). Amsterdam: Amsterdam University Press, the Netherlands, pp. 10–24.

Cuilenburg, J. van, Neijens, P., & Scholten, O. (Eds.), (1999). *Media in overvloed* (Overabundance of Media). *Amsterdam*: Amsterdam University Press, the Netherlands.

Deth, J. W., & Vis, J. C. P. M. (2000). *Regeren in Nederland. Het politieke en bestuurlijke bestel in vergelijkend perspectief* (Government in the Netherlands. The political and administrative system compared). Assen: Van Gorcum, the Netherlands.

Groenendijk, J. N. A. (1987). Public relations in het bedrijfsleven (Public relations in corporations), pp. 49–64. In J. N. A. Groenendijk, G. A. Th. Hazekamp & J. Mastenbroek (Eds.). Public relations & Voorlichting, beleid, organisatie en uitvoering (Public relations and enlightenment, policies, organization and practice). Alphen aan den Rijn, the Netherlands Samson.

Gallagher, M., Laver, M., & Mair, P. (Eds.). (2001). *Representative government in modern Europe*. Boston: McGraw-Hill.

Gent, B. van (1995). Voorlichting in vogelvlucht; bij wijze van inleiding (Overview of enlightenment, an introduction), pp. 9–22. In B. van Gent & J. Katus (Eds.). Voorlichting, theorieën, werkwijzen en terreinen (Enlightenment, theories, methods and fields). Houten, the Netherlands: Bohn Stafleu Van Loghum.

Hemels, J. (2000). Press and broadcasting. In J. Katus & W. T. Volmer (Eds.), *Government communication in the Netherlands*. The Hague: SDU, the Netherlands, pp. 49–69.

Hemerijck, A. (1993). *Historical contingencies of Dutch corporatism*. Unpublished doctoral dissertation, Balliol College, Oxford, England.

Hofstede, G. (1987). *Gevolgen van het Nederlanderschap. Gezondheid, recht en economie* (Consequences of Dutch citizenship. Health, law and economy). Inaugural lecture, University of Maastricht, the Netherlands.

Hofstede, G. (1993). *Images of Europe*. Speech delivered on the occasion of his retirement as a Professor of Organizational Anthropology and International Management, University of Maastricht, the Netherlands.

Hofstede, G. (1995). *Allemaal andersdenkenden. Omgaan met cultuurverschillen* (All dissentient people. How to cope with cultural differences). Amsterdam: Contact, the Netherlands.

Hofstede, G. (2001). *Culture's consequences: International differences in work-related values* (rev. ed.). Newbury Park, CA: Sage.

Katus, J. (2001). Government communication: Development, functions and principles. In J. Katus & W. F. Volmer (Eds.). *Government communication in the Netherlands*. The Hague: SDU, the Netherlands pp. 21–36.

Kickert, W. J. M. (1996). Expansion and diversification of public administration in the postwar welfare state: The case of the Netherlands. *Public Administration Review, 56* (1),

Knulst, W. (1999). Media en tijdbesteding (Time spent on Media) 1955–1995. In J. van Cuilenburg, P. Neijens, & O. Scholten (Eds.), Media *in overvloed* (Overabundance of Media). Amsterdam: Amsterdam University Press, the Netherlands, pp. 101–117.

Kranenburg, M. (2001). The political wing of the "Polder Model." In *the Netherlands: A practical guide for the foreigner and a mirror for the Dutch*. Amsterdam/Rotterdam: Promethuis/NRC Handelsblad, the Netherlands.

Lagerwey, E., Hemels, J., & Ruler, B. van (1997). *Op zoek naar faamwaarde: Vijftig jaar public relations in Nederland* (In search for reputation. Fifty years Public Relations in the Netherlands). Houten: Bohn Stafleu Van Loghum, the Netherlands.

Lockefeer, H. (1999). De krant als baken in een zee van overvloed (The newspaper as beacon in a sea of plenitude)? In J. van Cuilenburg, P. Neijens, & O. Scholten (Eds.), *Media in overvloed* (Overabundance of Media). Amsterdam: Amsterdam University Press, the Netherlands, pp. 54–66.

Luijk, H. van, & Schilder, A. (1997). *Patronen van verantwoordelijkheid: Ethiek en corporate governance* (Patterns of responsibility: Ethics and corporate governance). Schoonhoven: Academic Service, the Netherlands.

Noort, W.J. van, Huberts, L.W., & Rademaker, L. (1992). *Protest en pressie: Een systematische analyse van collectieve actie* (Protest and pressure: A systematic analysis of collective action). Assen: Van Gorcum, the Netherland.

Ruler, B. van (1998). Communication management in the Netherlands. *Public Relations Review, 26*(4), 403–423.

Ruler, B. van, & Lange, R. de (1999). *Trendonderzoek Communicatieberoepspraktijk in Nederland, Monitor Communicatiemanagement en -advies 1999* (Research of the profession of communication managers and consultants in the Netherlands 1999). Beroepsvereniging voor Communicatie (Association of Communication), Den Haag, the Netherlands.

Ruler, B. van, & Lange, R. de (2000). Monitor communicatiemanagement en—advies 1999: De stand van zaken in de Nederlandse beroepspraktijk. *Tijdschrift voor Communicatiewetenschap, 28*(2), 103–124.

Swaan, A. de (1989). Uitgaansbeperking en uitgaansangst: Over de verschuiving van bevelshuishouding naar onderhandelingshuishouding (Restriction of curfew and fear for pleasure seeking: On the move from a rule-governed system to a negotiation-based system). In A. de Swaan. (Ed.), *De mens is de mens een zorg* (A human is a human's concern). Amsterdam: Meulenhoff (inaugural address 28.5.79), the Netherlands, pp. 77–99.

Vossestein, J. (2001). *Dealing with the Dutch: The cultural context of business and work in the Netherlands in the early 21st century.* Amsterdam: KIT. the Netherlaands.

Public Relations in Sweden: A Strong Presence Increasing in Importance

Bertil Flodin

The purpose of this chapter is to introduce readers to the development of public relations in Sweden, discuss the current status of the industry in Sweden, and present some thoughts about the profession's future. At the outset, it is important to recognize that an elaborate history of the public relations profession in Sweden is yet to be written. As such, this chapter provides my personal view of the profession, some of which is based on published information, whereas the rest is based on my 35 years of experience as a public relations practitioner, teacher, and researcher. I begin this chapter with an overview of Sweden as a nation.

CHARACTERISTICS OF SWEDEN

Sweden is a small, highly industrialized country in the northern part of Western Europe. It has less than 9 million inhabitants although it has one of the largest land masses (449,956 km^2) among Western European countries. Sweden is a constitutional monarchy with a parliamentary system of government. As a result, only the king has ceremonial responsibilities as head of state and the parliament sets national policies. The parliament consists of one chamber with 349 members. In the 1998 elections, 149 women were elected to parliament, which is an unusually high proportion compared with the rest of the world. Sweden has a very strong public sector at the national, regional, and local level (Swedish Institute, 1999a).

There are 290 municipalities in Sweden, each with is own popularly elected council. These local councils collect taxes and provide various public services such as schools, child and elder care, housing, and cultural and leisure activities. It is a characteristic feature of the Swedish economy that there is an extensive list of services provided under public auspices. A consequence of this system is that the percentage of taxation is very high.

At the beginning of the 20th century, Sweden was largely an agrarian economy and one of the poorest nations in Europe. However, a rich domestic supply of iron ore, timber, and hydropower enabled the rapid industrialization of the country, transforming it into a modern welfare state (Swedish Institute, 2001). Economic growth was especially strong from the post-World War II period to the middle of the 1970s. During the last 20 years, however, Sweden's gross national product has declined in relation to that of some other European countries. In the early 1990s, Sweden experienced its deepest recession since the 1930s (Swedish Institute, 2001).

After the end of World War II, Swedish politics has been dominated by a power struggle between socialist and nonsocialist groups. Between 1932 and 1976, the Social Democratic Party was in power, either by itself or in coalition with other parties. It regained power in 1994 and remain in power today. Militarily, Sweden is a nonaligned country. One of the implications of this is that it took an extensive period of time and a great many discussions before Sweden was ready to join the European Union (EU) in 1995. As of February 2003, Sweden has not yet made a decision on whether to join the European Monetary Union.

DEVELOPMENT OF SWEDISH PUBLIC RELATIONS

In its modern form, public relations in Sweden began after World War II. In the early days of the profession, media relations was the dominant activity for public relations professionals, which represented corporations and government agencies. In the beginning of the 1950s, several of these practitioners created the Swedish Public Relations Association. In the late 1960s, there was a significant reduction in the number of local governments and an increased interest in active citizenship and democracy. This resulted in a noticeable increase in the number of public relations personnel in the governmental sector as well as the start of a lively debate about what we describe today as asymmetrical and symmetrical communication (Abrahamsson, 1973, 1993). In the beginning of the 1970s, the first courses in communication with reference to public relations were offered at Swedish universities. One of the courses was called *Informationsteknik,* clearly teaching practically oriented techniques as indicated by the title of the course.

After steady progress during the 1980s, the market for public relations exploded during the 1990s, leading up to the new millennium. The tremendous increase in the membership of the Swedish Public Relations Association is an indicator of this development, with a growth in membership from 676 in 1980 to 1,377 in 1990. Today, the association has over 4,400 members. There has been a corresponding increase in the public relations budgets of corporations, organizations, and government agencies as well, particularly in the last decade. It is estimated that public relations spending rose from a total of 4 billion Swedish kronor (SEK) in 1999 to between 5.5 billion and 6 billion SEK in 2001 (Sveriges Informationsförening, 2001a).

Each year, an estimated 4,000 to 5,000 students enroll in communication sciences programs, many of whom have ambitions of entering the public relations profession upon graduation (Högskoleverket, 2001). The public relations profession is becoming more sophisticated to keep pace with rapid globalization, the increase in speed of communication, as well as the expectation that the profession be socially responsible (Flodin, 1999b). The profession is also increasingly perceived as a legitimate and valuable resource by the decision makers in corporations and governmental bodies. As a result, the profession appears to have an interesting future.

CURRENT STATUS OF THE PROFESSION

If we look at the profession from a societal viewpoint, it is evident that the general public does not have an adequate or correct picture of the work performed by committed public relations professionals. In fact, the general perception among the masses is that public relations is merely a publicity activity at best and a concept that encompasses all that is manipulative and propagandistic at worst. To a large extent, this pejorative view of the profession must be considered a reflection of the portrayal of the profession by mass media.

Herein lies the contradiction: The media perceive and describe the profession negatively, whereas public relations professionals produce and deliver a lot of useful information to the media, which the media present to the public daily. Journalists seem to take information subsidies by public relations professionals for granted. One encounters a much more serious and complex understanding of the profession by members of the dominant coalitions of organizations. In a recent study (Sveriges Informationsförening, 2000), the first of its kind in Sweden, 99% of 800 executives in the private and public sector declared that they considered effective public relations a winning concept. The purpose of this study was to obtain a clearer picture of the attitudes among members of dominant coalitions toward public relations and the value these decision makers placed on the profession. The study attempted to ascertain whether members of dominant coalitions had an adequate knowledge of the background, skills, and work assignments of public relations professionals. The sample for the study was diverse, with respondents representing different organizations and industries such as corporations, government agencies, and nongovernmental organizations. Telephone interviews were used to gather data.

The respondents (percentages shown in parantheses after each item) considered the following public relations practices important:

- Creating good relations with stakeholders and publics (88%).
- Advising executives (88%).
- Developing communication strategies (87%).
- Establishing credibility among stakeholders (84%).
- Image creation (83%).
- Crisis management (77%).

This study confirmed that Swedish public relations professionals have established themselves as an important function in the minds of senior managers (57%). Data further revealed that senior managers defined the following competencies relevant to public relations professionals:

- Broad-based competence.
- Sense of design.
- Verbal capacity.
- Good stylistic ability.
- Good social competence.
- Ability to quickly become familiar with situations.
- Good education.
- Keen awareness.
- Excellent communication abilities.

The responses also indicated that senior managers realized the importance of public relations. However, they still do not seem to understand the significant contributions that public relations professionals can have on the overall strategic decision-making process, the business as a whole, and the social intelligence or intellectual capital of the business.

PUBLIC RELATIONS PROFESSIONALS

With 4,400 members from a population of approximately 9 million, Sweden probably has one of the largest, if not the largest, number of public relations professionals per capita in the world. The national association for practitioners—the Swedish Public Relations Association—is strong with a current membership of over 4, 400, making it the second largest in Europe in absolute numbers after the British Institute of Public Relations. The association is very active in a number of areas. It has a highly elaborate professional development program consisting of various communications courses and seminars for members. In addition, it stimulates informal meetings among members working within certain areas (knowledge exchange groups in crisis communication, media relations, etc.). Five years ago, the association started a program exclusively for senior public relations professionals to prepare the professionals to participate in deliberations of dominant coalitions (Sveriges Informationsförening, 2001b).

The Swedish Public Relations Association started in 1996 a research effort on how to measure the impact of public relations (Sveriges Informationsförening, 1996). It also became a partner in a project on how to evaluate the intellectual capital in a company (Nordic Industrial Fund, 2001). A survey of the members of the association (Aldemark, 2001) identified several characteristics of the profession in Sweden. Increasingly, women are dominating the profession. A 1997 survey (Aldemark, 2001) had reported that 70% of public relations professionals were women. However, by 2001, the number had risen to almost 75%. Twenty-five percent of the respondents had the job title of vice president. Most of the respondents (80%) reported that their expertise had been more sought after by their organization in the last 2 years than in the past, a reference to the importance that organizations were placing on the profession. More than 50% of public relations executives were members of the board of management (the dominant coalition) in their respective organizations, another indicator of the significance being accorded to the profession in organizational settings. Of the professionals surveyed, 40% worked in the private sector, 24% in the public sector, 25% in agencies, and 10% in other types of organizations. It was interesting that two thirds of those surveyed worked in the vicinity of Stockholm, the capital. A majority of respondents (85%) had at least a bachelor's degree. When asked about the future, most of the respondents (80%) said that they were convinced that the public relations sector will continue to grow. As far as future growth areas are concerned, respondents believed that strategic planning, profile work, business intelligence, and environmental scanning would be the most important public relations specialities over the next 5 years.

PUBLIC RELATIONS AT UNIVERSITIES

It has been possible to study public relations at Swedish universities since the 1970s although, initially, the number of programs offering it and the number of courses were small. At the beginning of 2001, students were able to take courses in public relations at roughly 12 universities and university colleges (Högskoleverket, 2001). Public relations departments have almost exclusively been situated in programs (schools) of media and communication sciences. In the majority of undergraduate and graduate programs, the number of hours devoted to public relations is rather limited. Ten universities and colleges have specific courses dedicated to public relations. At these institutions, about 15% of the total undergraduate courses (credits) is in public relations, not including credits obtained for doing thesis work (Högskoleverket, 2001). Approximately 40 to 50 exemplary undergraduate (bachelor of arts) theses are produced each year. Postgraduate education in public relations is only represented by two or three universities. There are only three programs (3 years long) at university colleges that focus on professional work in public relations.

The resources available for research in public relations are very limited in Sweden. Presently, there is no full-time professor in public relations and there are no doctoral programs in public relations. Public relations is a growing industry that needs many talented, well-educated young people. There are a large number of students at the undergraduate and graduate levels who want to study public relations. However, the number of qualified public relations teachers is too limited to be able to provide the industry and the students the necessary support and stimulation they need (Dokumentation Information Kultur, 2002). Despite these limitations, about a dozen doctoral students are pursuing research on public relations. Furthermore, about three to five books on the subject are published annually (e.g., Hedquist, 2002; Larsson, 2002; Lidskog, Nohrstedt, & Warg, 2000).

ETHICS AND SOCIAL RESPONSIBILITY

Swedish practitioners have accepted the Code of Athens and the Code of Venice, and they suggested their own ethical codes as well (Sveriges Informationsförening, 2001b). However, these have only existed on paper so far, and very seldom have they been referred to in practice. There also have been no public discussions on the ethics of this industry; so far, almost no public relations practitioner has received sanctions for unethical practices, although it is obvious that practitioners face ethical challenges in their profession regularly (Forsberg, 2001).

At the beginning of the new millennium, some positive signs can be seen in this regard. A number of mentors have accepted to advise younger colleagues on ethical questions, and practitioners have initiated discussions on the subject of social responsibility—an encouraging sign. For example, the Association of Public Relations Consultancies has recently adopted new ethical codes (Föreningen Public Relations Konsultföretag i Sverige, 2002). Even more important is the fact that almost every major Swedish company has adopted communication policies that indicate a strong acceptance of social responsibility and a willingness to use open, transparent, and honest communications. So far there exist no research studies that shed light on whether and to what extent these propositions of high ethical quality are realized in practice.

INFRASTRUCTURE AND SWEDISH PUBLIC RELATIONS

The power of the Swedish parliament has declined during the last decade or so not only because of Sweden's membership in the European Union but also because the Swedish economy is heavily interdependent with the world economy in a globalizing world. Now, in addition to working with the European parliament, Sweden has to work in close cooperation with several other political and economic supranational institutions such as the World Trade Organization and the United Nations (Johnsson, 1999).

An illustrative example is the introduction of commercial television in Sweden. The majority of Swedish politicians did not want commercial television in Sweden. One of their arguments against introducing commercial television was that Sweden already had plenty of commercial messages and advertisements in the print media as well as channels of direct marketing. These opponents also believed that new commercial channels would not match the quality and standard of the public service channels. However, they could not prevent the influx of satellite-broadcast programs from commercial television companies located outside of Sweden. As a result, during the 1990s Sweden saw an influx of terrestrial and satellite television networks, cable television, and commercial radio. For example, 34% of television viewers between 9 and 79 years old watch a Swedish or foreign satellite channel on an average day (Nordicom, 2001). At this point there are few indications that the development of the satellite and cable television networks has had any profound impact on the public relations industry.

Relations between the all levels of the Swedish government and the citizenry can be characterized as being open and transparent. There are numerous opportunities for individuals, groups, and organizations to participate in public debates, and the country has a long tradition of influencing politicians and decision makers. Because of this tradition and the relatively short distance between voters and policy makers (a result of a lack of social stratification), lobbying has only recently expanded in volume and importance as a public relations specialty.

This development escalated even more when Sweden became a member of the EU. One reason for this escalation is that EU bureaucracy is not as transparent as Sweden's is. Furthermore, the complex EU bureaucracy and cultural codes of the EU make it necessary for member countries to have a very specialized knowledge to understand and influence the EU parliament. As a result, it is important to have people who personally know the relevant actors and understand the cultural codes of multiple European decision makers with whom they need to communicate.

Today, the national, regional, and local governments in Sweden use public information as a way of having a dialogue with their stakeholders and publics. These publics can be differentiated along a range of dimensions: citizens, homeowners, shareholders, patients, parents, and environmentalists etcetera. In addition, a great deal of work is being done to communicate with people who have different types of communication problems such as the inability to speak Swedish, not being familiar with the Swedish culture, or being disabled (Landstingsförbundet, 2002).

The political culture in Sweden has affected the public relations profession in a number of ways. The Swedish legislation supports open and free access to information in an attempt to maintain transparency of the government. Examples of this openness can be seen by the way in which the parliament has supported a rich variety of newspapers, public service radio stations, and access to the Internet for everyone for decades. This, in turn, has stimulated the growth and need for a profession in which expertise in media relations is a must. Furthermore, restrictions are not placed on lobbyists, and anybody may call himself or herself a public relations professional and practice the profession.

Swedish political traditions emphasize a strong public sector in which responsibility for schools, health care, and other services are the responsibility of the government. The Swedish public sector is very large; to be able to communicate with the general public and different stakeholders and actors, it is necessary for the public sector to have a large number of public information specialists.

Legal Dimensions

Sweden has a very strong constitutional protection of the rights and freedoms for individuals to express their views without restrictions. The fundamental law of freedom of the press protects the right to publish printed matters without government restrictions and gives citizens the right of access to official documents. The fundamental law of freedom of expression protects this freedom in the media (Swedish Institute, 1999a).

Sweden is believed to have been the first country in the world to establish freedom of the press. In 1776 parliament adopted a Freedom of the Press Act as a part of the Constitution. In 1992 similar legislation was passed for radio, television, film, and other media through the Freedom of Expression Act. The Freedom of the Press Act expressly forbids public censorship of the press as well as other restrictions on publishing and distributing printed matters. This principle is safeguarded with an elaborate combination of measures. First, any periodical appearing four times a year or more must appoint a responsible publisher, who alone is responsible for the content of the publication. Next, the law prohibits the investigation or disclosure of journalists' sources. Finally, the law assures journalists and the public free access to public documents.

Anyone, including aliens, has the right to seek from a state or local government agency any document kept in the agency's files regardless of whether the document is related specifically to the person making the request. Officials are legally required to comply and even to supply copies of the documents requested. This openness is not absolute. Special laws can place restrictions on access as a result of questions concerning personal integrity, the safety of the country, or to prevent criminal acts (Swedish Institute, 1999a).

In practice, this means that journalists check incoming mail daily as a source of accessing different kinds of documents. It also means that public relations practitioners in the public sector always have to base their strategies and tactical work on this principle of openness. The principle of openness in Sweden is unmatched within the bureaucracy of the EU according to Swedish journalists, who have tried to obtain access to EU documents in vain.

This principle of openness also operates within organizations. Sweden has an Employment (Co-Determination in the Workplace) Act (2002), which states that an employer is obliged to inform employees in the organization regularly on matters such as levels of production, the financial health of the organization, and policies regarding personnel. The employer is also required to allow employees the opportunity to examine books, accounts, and other documents. This is governed by the labor union to protect the common interests of its members in relation to the employer (Employment [Co-Determination in the workplace] Act, 2000). This law has been in effect since 1976 and is one of the pillars that make internal communication one of the most important subjects of Swedish public relations practice. By law, this two-way symmetrical communication is forced on every private and public organization.

Presently, the development of information technology (IT) is probably an even stronger force. New media makes available to employees new ways of communicating via the Intranet, the Internet, and e-mail. A recent study of found that 61% of employees interviewed used the Internet daily (Nordicom, 2001). There is general consensus among public relations professionals that different forms of new information technology will be responsible for a significant part of the internal and external communications that they will use in the future. This development is indeed supported by the government, whose ambition is to make Sweden an information society accessible to all (SOU, 2002:20, p. 20).

ACTIVISM

A strong element of Swedish organizational culture during the 20th century has been the understanding between trade unions and employers. This mutual understanding was cemented with a 1930 agreement between trade unions and employers outlining the ways of resolving their differences with a minimum of strikes and lockouts. This consensus model was gradually expanded to encompass the entire political system, which has been characterized by great stability and balance.

Within this system of balance and consensus, activism from different types of social movements and nongovernmental organizations has been witnessed in Sweden. Whether their mission was religious, environmental, or cultural, these activist groups have worked within a democratic system and often have had the support of the parliament and local governments. During the last decades of the last century, new organizations such as Greenpeace and Amnesty International entered the Swedish society and have established themselves as active members of this pluralistic society. For example, Amnesty International has a sponsorship agreement with a Swedish company that produces writing paper.

Until very recently, Sweden had not experienced the use of unconventional or criminal methods by activist groups. Swedish companies had become used to having a dialogue with traditional nongovernmental organizations and supporting them via sponsorships. However, in the last 5 years, activists have been using tactics to grab attention such as climbing on rooftops and chimneys, trying to steal animals from fur farmers, sitting in front of machines that build new roads, sitting in trees to prevent logging, and throwing eggs at ministers. When confronted with this new form of unconventional activist tactics, baffled organizations have often been silent and refused to meet with such activists. Recently, however, corporations and government authorities have been much more open toward inviting activists for constructive dialogues. As one would expect, it is not unusual that these attempts have turned out to be unconstructive and result in dramatic attention-grabbing tactics by activists, who end up being carried away by the police. The most dramatic incident to date took place in Gothenburg when EU held their Summit Meeting in June 2001. Large peaceful demonstrations took place outside the meeting venue, but there were also violent riots resulting in considerable property damage and serious personal injury (Granström, 2002). In the same way that companies track media-exposure and market signals, companies track the activities of activists more closely. This means large companies now have the capability to monitor their environments continuously using new media and forecast potential threats to the company's image by activists. They can now plan communications events with activists based on such environmental monitoring. Most often, organizational relations with activists are framed within crisis management and issues management divisions and not included in the day-to-day activities of the company.

CULTURE AND SWEDISH PUBLIC RELATIONS

The majority of public relations practitioners in Sweden during the 1940s and 1950s were men. Over the years, the proportion of women in the profession has grown to almost 75% by current estimates. Over the 10 years, women have occupied a number of strategic executive positions. There are probably few areas within the Swedish labor market where the proportion of women at senior levels is as high as in public relations.

Another cultural aspect that is very visible is the Anglo-American influence on the Swedish society in general and public relations in particular. English is the first foreign language in the Swedish primary school system and is widely understood in the country. As a result, most public relations textbooks are American from authors such as Cutlip, Center, and Broom. Students are also very familiar with the excellence project (J. E. Grunig, 1992). In addition, students read books on topics such as intercultural communication and strategic communications and scholarly public relations journals published in English. I feel that it is unsatisfactory that the Swedish public relations industry, including research and teaching, is so greatly influenced by British and American experiences and ignores the substantive research that is being done in Germany, Denmark, and Austria.

The research in Europe is more oriented toward questions about the role of public relations in an open society (Gerhard, 2000). Often, this research has a critical reflection and does not take a corporate, profit-oriented perspective (Larsson, 2002). Much research is focused on the role of communication in the dialogue between governmental agencies and citizens. Lately, the relations between individual countries and the EU have started to generate interest among researchers, politicians, and decision makers (Organisation for economic co-operation and development, 2001).

Sweden, by tradition, is very open to the world, particularly during the last decade, Sweden has become quite multicultural. By 1998, approximately 19% of the population resulted from immigration (Johnsson, 1999). By extension, public relations practitioners who have an immigrant background would be expected to be commonplace in Sweden. However, this is not the case, probably because the public relations industry has not yet realized the importance of being able to established multicultural dialogue. As Dozier, L. A. Grunig, and J. E. Grunig (1995) suggested, to be excellent and effective, public relations departments must be much more cultural diversified (see Dozier et al., 1995)—a goal that Sweden must strive to achieve.

Strong laws in support of citizens' rights to access information and the relatively small power distance in Sweden are two strong reasons for the very expanded public information service especially among public sector organizations in Sweden. Currently, thousands of public relations practitioners work for the public sector. They do not use propaganda techniques; they use a combination of the two-way asymmetrical and two-way symmetrical communication models first propounded by J. E. Grunig and Hunt (1992). Examples of these types of communications can be found by visiting the web site www.sverigedirekt.se This site provides access to the entire public sector at all levels. The present trend in Sweden and other countries is to involve citizens as partners in policy-making processes (OECD, 2001).

As public relations has grown in strategic importance, Swedish companies have recognized the importance of knowing and adapting their public relations activities to the different cultural environments of their global markets. They have realized that using different cultural values can create problems. For example, a Swedish company that is used to operating under Swedish regulations and work conditions could encounter public relations problems when they have unjudiciously followed the local practices of a foreign country. For example, the Swedish media have often challenged Swedish companies for hiring child labor abroad. As a result, it is not uncommon today for Swedish companies to have very explicit statements about their policy on such matters. For example, Skanska (2002) declared in its Code of Conduct that "... we provide equal opportunities to people without regard to race, colour, gender, nationality, religion, ethnic affiliation or other distinguishing characteristics" (p. 2).

The awareness among Swedish organizations of the fragility of our environment and the need to preserve it has increased over time. Up until the last decades of the 20th century, the annual reports of Swedish organizations only contained financial information. Then a process was started to incorporate information about the activities performed by organizations to contribute to a sustainable environment. Now Swedish companies like to add information about their relations to society in general and to certain stakeholders in particular in an effort to emphasize their social responsibility.

THE SWEDISH MEDIA

Swedish newspapers have traditionally had a very strong readership as the Swedish are among the most avid newspaper readers in the world (Swedish Institute 1999b). Newspapers have held their position of strength partly because of a very elaborate system of state subsidy introduced in the early 1970s. The aim of the system is to provide each region in Sweden with at least two newspapers. As a result, the less popular newspaper in a region can ask for state support to survive. Besides a very high degree of penetration of the market, Swedish newspapers today are characterized by weak ties to political parties and an almost nonexistent relation to religious movements.

Until the middle of the 1980s, the broadcast media were under monopoly state control. Viewer licensing fees financed the operations, and advertising over this medium was prohibited. As a result of the influx of satellite broadcast channels from commercial companies, the broadcasting situation has totally changed in Sweden. Commercial television broadcasting began in Sweden in 1991, followed by the commercialization of radio stations in 1993.

A recent development is the very rapid introduction and adoption of IT technology in general and the use of the Internet in particular in public relations. A study in 2000 found that at least 64% of the Swedish population between 9 and 79 years old had access to a personal computer in their homes of whom 52% had Internet access (Nordicom, 2001a). The study also reported that the typical Swede uses the Internet 65 min per day, and men use the Internet more frequently than women. The study also found that the Internet is used by middle-aged people more often than by people under the age of 14 or over 65, and the well educated use the Internet more than the less educated.

Table 23.1 provides an overall view of the actual media consumption in Sweden and clearly shows that the Swedish population consumes a variety of media. Furthermore, within each media sector, there are signs of very specialized media consumption. In

TABLE 23.1

Percentage of 9- to 79-Year-Old Swedes Who Use Different Mass Media on an Average Day in 2000

Medium	Percentage
Television	88
Radio	80
Daily newspaper	74
Books	39
Compact disk	37
Weekly magazine	33
Internet	32
Special interest media[a]	32
Text television	31
Evening paper	28
Video	15
Cassette tape	12
Cinema	1

[a] For example, philately and hunting.

Source: Medienotiser 1/2001, Nordicom 2001b, Sweden

addition, the public is exposed to the flow of international news by Swedish and international media such as CNN and BBC. To be competitive, the Swedish media have to be very fast, focus on domestic as well as global issues, provide general as well highly specialized news, and make strategic choices on the degree to which they want to use Internet in their news dissemination. To meet the requirements of the media, Swedish public relations professionals must be able to work with very short deadlines and liaise with national and international media. Furthermore, the field will require highly specialized professionals who can deal with issues such as finance, crisis, legislation, and cultural diversity in a competent way.

The relationship between public relations practitioners and journalists has matured over the years. The earlier unfamiliarity and suspicion between the two has to a large degree been transformed to a professional exchange of information in which both journalists and practitioners are well aware of each other's roles and responsibilities. Of course, this generalization of the industry does not account for many exceptions. In public, however, journalists very often talk about public relations in disparaging terms.

The single most important media development of the last decade both for journalists and public relation practitioners is the rapid introduction and use of the Internet and IT. The amount of information and the speed with which it can be exchanged have created new working conditions for public relations practitioners as well as for journalists (Flodin, 1999a). Today journalists and practitioners exchange information at high speed via the Internet on a daily basis.

The new IT gives professionals the power to create new forms of dialogue with stakeholders and publics and to make all basic information available to the public and to the media. In the long run, this will probably change the working relations between professionals and journalists. Less time will be devoted to the exchange of basic information and more time to proactive and selective efforts.

CASE STUDY: CONSTRUCTION COMPANY SUSPECTED OF CARTEL CONCURRENCE

In March 2001, NCC, one of the leading construction and property-developing companies in the Nordic region, reported seven of its employees to the police for fraud. In the summer of 2001, an anonymous person reported to the Swedish Competition Authority that the NCC was participating in an illegal cartel, an antitrust arrangement with a few of its competitors to lower bids on public tenders. In the morning of October 23, the Swedish Competition Authority suddenly appeared at several of the largest Swedish construction companies to collect data for further investigation. In January 2002, the NCC confirmed at a well-attended press conference that it had participated in this illegal antitrust cartel with some of its key competitors. The press conference resulted in very intensive and negative media coverage. Much of the publicity was of course negative but, as NCC put it, "This is not the time to get good publicity, but to minimize the negative one." The media also began to search for the other members of the cartel.

The press conference was the result of a proactive strategy that the NCC had decided to implement. The key aspects of the strategy were the following: Confirm cartel suspicions, take the initiative, decide when to break the news, be open to internal and external publics, cooperate with the authorities, and supply the media with information. Last but not least was the strategy to take a number of actions to prevent this from happening again, including educating middle management and implementing a compliance program. With this strategy, the NCC wanted to expose the whole affair at one point to prevent a prolonged interest on the subject from the media. The organization also wanted to shift the focus of interest to other actors. The NCC realized that there was an urgent need to rebuild the public's confidence in the board and management of the NCC. In the process, the NCC decided to concentrate on the following key publics: the Swedish Competition Authority, customers, the media, employees, competitors, and the shareholders.

The Swedish Competition Authority was given a full report by the NCC based on an independent investigation by a solicitor's office. The NCC contacted important stakeholders by phone or in person and were given the NCC's version of events. Employees were informed by a combination of Intranet and print media, including a personal letter from the chief executive officer. Just before the press conference, the most important competitors were informed that the NCC intended to break the news about their involvement in the cartel. The first reaction of these organizations was to deny any involvement. Some continue to maintain their innocence. Personal contacts were made with the most important shareholders.

The NCC's own evaluation of public opinion showed that, although a large proportion of the respondents considered the NCC's involvement in the cartel to be serious, a substantial number felt that the NCC had taken care of the situation in a responsible way. Among the employees, the support for the NCC was very strong.

In June 2002, the first phase was over, but the process continues. The NCC awaits court proceedings in 2003, a report from the Swedish Competition Authority, initiatives from other actors, and possible renewed media attention.

The NCC has drawn the following lessons from their crisis:

- It is important to have a powerful crisis management team.
- Organizations have to be prepared for different types of crises.
- Organizations need to solicit second opinions but to keep the initiative.
- Organizations need to scan opinion among important target groups carefully during a crisis.

In conclusion, faced with an embarrassing and dangerous situation, the NCC chose to play by the first rule of the crisis management manual: "Tell it all and tell it fast." So far, this seems to have been a successful strategy, supplemented with the highly demanding ethical standards that NCC has adopted.

REFERENCES

Abrahamsson, K. (1973). *Samhällskommunikation: Om kontakten mellan myndigheter och medborgare* [Public communication: Contacts between authorities and citizens]. Lund: Studentlitteratur, Sweden.

Abrahamsson, K. (1993). *Medborgaren i samhällsdialogen* [The citizen in the public dialogue]. Stockholm: Publica, Sweden.

Aldemark, L. (2001). *INFO 2001 Rapport*. Stockholm: Sveriges Informationsförening, Sweden.

DIK (2002). *Informatörer—ett yrke för framtiden . . . om utbildningarna hänger med* [Public relations officer—a profession for the future . . . if the educations can keep up]. Stockholm: Dik-förbundet, Sweden.

Dozier, D., Grunig, L. A., & Grunig, J. E. (1995). *Managers guide to excellence in public relations and communication management*. Mahwah, NJ: Lawrence Erlbaum Associates, USA.

Employment (Co-Determination in the Workplace) Act. (2000), Sweden.

Flodin, B. (1999a). *Planlagd kriskommunikation* [Planned crisis communications]. Stockholm: Styrelsen för psykologiskt försvar, Sweden.

Flodin, B. (1999b). *Professionell kommunikation* [Professional communication]. Stockholm: Styrelsen för psykologiskt försvar, Sweden.

Föreningen Public Relations Konsultföretag i Sverige. (2002). *Normer för PR-konsultföretagen i PRECIS* [Standards for the Swedish Public Relations Industry]. Retrieved from January 1st, 2003. www.precis. se/standards.

Forsberg, E. (2001). *Sunt-förnuft-konsulter* [Common-sense-consultants]. Örebro: Örebro universitet, Sweden.

Gerhard, J. (2000). Das Öffentlichkeitsdefizit der EU: Theoretische Überlegungen und empirische Befunde. (The public deficit in EU: Theoretical considerations and emperical findings). In B. Baerns (Ed.), *Information und Kommunikation in Europa, Forschung und Praxis*. Berlin: Vistas, Germany.

Granström, K. (Ed). (2002). *Göteborgskravallerna* [The Gothenburg riots]. Report 187. Stockholm: Styrelsen för psykologiskt försvar, Sweden.

Grunig, J. E. (Ed.). (1992). *Excellence in public relations and communication management.* Hillsdale, NJ: Lawrence Erlbaum Associates, USA.

Hedquist, R. (2002). *Trovärdighet—en förutsättning för förtroende* [Credibility A condition for trust]. Stockholm: Styrelsen för psykologiskt försvar, Sweden.

Högskoleverket. (2001). *Utvärdering av medie-och kommunikationsvetenskapliga utbildningar vid svenska universitet och högskolor* [Evaluation of programs in media and communication science at Swedish Universities and University Colleges]. Stockholm: Author, Sweden.

Johnsson, H.-I. (1999). *Spotlight on Sweden.* Stockholm: Swedish Institute, Sweden.

Landstingsförbundet. (2002). *Alla kan vinna* [All may win]. Stockholm: Author, Sweden.

Larsson, L. (Ed.). (2002). *PR på svenska* [PR in Swedish]. Lund: Studentlitteratur, Sweden.

Lidskog, R., Nohrstedt, S. A., Warg, L. E. (Eds.). (2000). *Risker, kommunikation och medier* [Risks, communication and media]. Lund: Studentlitteratur, Sweden.

Nordic Industrial Fund. (2001). *Intellectual capital managing and reporting.* Oslo: Nordic Industrial Fund, Sweden.

Nordicom. (2001a). *Internetbarometer 2000* [Internet barometer 2000]. MedieNotiser 2.2001. Göteborg: Author, Sweden.

Nordicom. (2002). Sveriges 2000 *Mediebarometern 2000,* [Swedish Media barometer 2000]. MedieNotiser 1.2001. Göteborg: Author, Sweden.

OECD. (2001).*Citizens as partners, information, consultation and public participation in policy-making.* Paris: OECD, France.

Skanska. (2002). *Skanska code of conduct.* Stockholm: Author, Sweden.

SOU 2002:20. (2002). *Guide på Internet—ett stöd för medborgarnas möte med det offentliga* [Guide to the Internet—support for the meeting between the citizen and the public sector]. Statens offentliga utredningar. [Swedish Government. official reports] Stockholm: Fritzes. Sweden.

Sveriges Informationsförening. (1996). *Return on communication.* Stockholm: Author, Sweden.

Sveriges Informationsförening. (2000). *Attitydundersökning om informatörer i företag och offentlig sektor* [Survey of attitudes about public relations practitioners in the private and public sector]. Stockholm: Author, Sweden.

Sveriges Informationsförening. (2001a). *INFO 2001 Medlemsundersökning* [Survey among members in the Swedish Public Relations Association]. Stockholm: Author, Sweden.

Sveriges Informationsförening. (2001b). *Nätverk 2001/2002* [Network 2001/2002]. Stockholm: Author, Sweden.

Swedish Institute. (1999a). *General facts on Sweden.* Stockholm: Author, Sweden.

Swedish Institute. (1999b). *Mass media.* Stockholm: Author, Sweden.

Swedish Institute. (2001). *The Swedish economy.* Stockholm: Author, Sweden.

CHAPTER

24

Public Relations in Italy: Master of Ceremonies in a Relational Society*

Toni Muzi Falconi

ITALY TODAY

Despite stereotypes, Italy is a relatively young nation: united only since 1861, and a parliamentary democracy since 1946. Between World War II and the 1989 fall of the Berlin Wall, the Italian people lived in a blocked political democratic system: a system which, on one side, had the largest communist party in the western world—therefore unable to participate in the government because of Italy's membership of NATO—while, on the other side, it accounted for a varied number of small political parties (conservatives, liberals, republicans and socialists) alternating in successive coalitions with the huge, relative majority Catholic party (Democrazia Cristiana)—in an endless dance of musical chairs staged by short-lived cabinets satisfying the power anxiety of a tiny, elitist political clique. At the same time, however, Italy maintained for almost half a century a surprising and stubborn stability in its policies, centered on an indisputable pro-western allegiance, accompanied by a stronger than average active participation of the State in the national economy.

Since 1994—following the collapse of most traditional parties (Catholic, communist and socialist), nurtured by pervasive corrupt practices as well as by the direct political consequences of the fall of the Berlin Wall—the country has moved into a transition. This transition is yet not completed today, seeking as it is, a way towards a bipolar and open political system, with an economy which continues to suffer from insufficiently competitive infrastructures, accompanied by many parallel and apparently consolidated layers of privilege and red tape.

---

* This text was written in the spring of 2007. Although the core contents are fully valid as I sign off in September 2008, clearly some of the more current affairs notions refer to that period (TMF).

484

With almost 60 million inhabitants, Italy is also home of the oldest population in the world, in terms of average age, and its citizens are recognized as—yes!—amongst the prime supporters of the European Union, but also as the last to adopt its directives . . .

Finally, reputed for having the world's greatest cultural heritage, Italy has the lowest percentage of university graduates, as well as book and newspaper readers per inhabitant in western Europe.

PUBLIC RELATIONS IN ITALY

In this context—for a country in which business, financial, cultural, political and media elites amount overall to less than ten thousand connected and related individuals, predominantly male and elderly, whose priorities, rather than to the public interest, rest more on the "preservation of-self + friends-and-family": to the point that sociologists and economists refer to Italy as a "crony society," i.e. a society based on relationships—it should come as no surprise that the evolution of the public relations profession, rooted (as in most other countries) in the easing of relationships amongst elites, has interpreted the role of the "master of ceremonies" to the country's few yet highly segmented leaderships.

Social critics throughout the world are increasingly accusing public relations professionals of advocating mostly on behalf of strong and powerful interest groups, and a similar critique obviously holds true for Italy. On the other hand, the concept of public relations playing the role of "master of ceremonies" to the country's leaderships is coherent with the traditional stereotype that amongst the different roles a professional performs in the organization, that of master of ceremonies (etiquette, cerimonial . . .) is strongly consolidated; as well as with the role which public relators attribute to themselves, as facilitators of smooth relationships between the three traditional segments of a country's leadership (political, economic and media). . . to which, but only in recent years, some scholars also add the social community (thus also, the trend towards corporate social responsibility practices).

When It All Started

Although the first ever public relations function in an Italian organization appeared in the mid-1930s at Linoleum, the floor tile company belonging to the better-known Pirelli Group, it was only after the Allied Forces' occupation of Italy in the mid-1940s that the term began to really circulate. For the first time, specific professionals called themselves public relators and were trained in the Allied Forces headquarters; in the intensely active United States Information Service offices scattered in the various large cities; instead of, as well as inside the international oil companies which had reopened their Italian operations, following the twenty plus years of the fascist period of autarchy. In 1952 the Province of Bologna was the first branch of Italy's public sector to open a public relations office. Also in that same year Roberto Tremelloni, at the time a University Professor of Finance in Milan and soon to become national Finance Minister, opened in Milan the IRP, Istituto per le Relazioni Pubbliche (Institute for Public Relations): a think-tank of professionals and scholars—mostly with a US college background—offering courses to managers, identifying and spreading best practices, attempting to promote the public relations approach to management, inside both private and public sector organizations.

In 1954 the IRP inaugurated the first award of the Oscar del Bilancio, still today's most prominent and reputed annual award (organized by Ferpi, the Italian Public Relations

Federation) for the best financial, social, environmental and governance reporting practices from private, public and social sector organizations.

The First Professional Associations

In 1956 two professional associations were created: the first in Rome, the Sindacato Nazionale Professionisti Relazioni Pubbliche—whose members were for the most part consultants working for the public sector and the political system and, in those years fully separated from Milan, where the business sector mostly resided; the second, the Associazione Italiana Relazioni Pubbliche (AIRP), based in Milan and mostly formed by in-house professionals operating in private sector corporations and related to the business and financial communities.

In the fall of that same year, the two associations promoted together, by the Lake of Stresa, the first ever international conference on public relations in Italy.

Early Best Practices

But it was the Olivetti typewriter company, under the charismatic leadership of owner-intellectual Adriano Olivetti, to mark the foremost maturation of a visionary, local as well as global public relations practice in those years.

Many young architects, writers, designers, poets and philosophers were attracted by Adriano to become public relations operators in the broadest interpretation: including, of course, employee and corporate communication, social responsibility and stakeholder relations, marketing and visual communication, as well as public affairs: all "practices" which today are considered "best" and "fashionable." The Olivetti experience, even after the death of its charismatic leader in 1960, represented Italy's overall best practice well into the 1970s.

Another remarkable public relations experience in those years was that of IRI Group (Istituto Ricostruzione Industriale), a huge conglomerate of State-owned manufacturing companies, where a fairly homogenous group of Catholic CEOs succeeded in dialoguing with hard-line communist trade unionists by deploying effective and creative "inclusive" employee and community two-way relationship programs in order to support and sustain the dramatic economic upturn of the entire country in the 1950s and early 1960s.

Another was ENI (Ente Nazionale Idrocarburi) the national oil company which, under the charismatic leadership of Enrico Mattei, decided to take on the "seven sisters" in the Mediterranean and in Northern Africa, and implemented—by employing as public relators some of the country's most respected journalists and intellectuals—a highly maverick and unconventional public diplomacy program which succeeded in opening effective and operational lines of economic cooperation and trade with many Arab and Soviet countries.

In the 1963 political elections, the leading and central Christian Democratic party decided to use the services of the then famous US public relations consultant Ernst Dichter. Called in late in the campaign he, not unexpectedly, suggested that the party should present a "younger face" and therefore renew its leadership. The party oligarchy interpreted and implemented this reasonable advice by producing a poster with a healthy and smiling young country girl with a strong bosom and a bouquet of flowers in her hand under the headline "DC is twenty years old!" As soon as Palmiro Togliatti, the tough and charismatic leader of the Communist Party, saw the freshly printed poster on the walls outside of his Rome office, he ordered his militants to write by hand on every copy in every corner of the country—as an added pay off—the sentence: "and it's time to screw her!". . . .

It took some thirty years for another famous American political consultant to play an active role in an Italian general election: Francesco Rutelli, now deputy Premier and Minister of Culture, was at the time the electoral candidate for Premiership and hired Stan Greenberg in his losing 2001 campaign against media tycoon Silvio Berlusconi.

Other companies active in public relations in the 1960s, besides Olivetti, IRI and ENI, were Pirelli—with an admirable program of spreading the principles of modern management practice in the private sector through publications, workshops and seminars—and Ferrania, the film manufacturer which had been acquired in 1964 by 3M Company and which ran, until the early 1970s, a very intense public relations program to support young Italian photographers and researchers while developing the major publicly accessible archive on historic and contemporary photography.

Two Associations Merge to Form FERPI and the Profession Develops

On March 17, 1970 in Milan, the two professional associations, IRP and AIRP, united to form the Federazione Italiana Relazioni Pubbliche (FERPI).

Since its inception, FERPI claimed and committed to pursue legal recognition of the profession, an improved relationship with the media, and adopted the IPRA ethics Code of Athens (which, by the way, had been approved in 1961 at an international conference held in Venice organised by Guido De Rossi del Lion Nero, a highly respected Italian public relations professional).

The 1970s were busy years for the association: from 1972 to 1978, four national "provocative" conferences were organized touching on consumerism, public affairs, marketing and journalism. In those years, the association also embarked on an articulated program of professional development for its members, including seminars and workshops on marketing, research, programming as well as evaluation and measurement of public relations effectiveness.

1976 marked the birth of SCR Associati, soon to become Italy's largest and most influential public relations agency. In 1990 SCR was eventually sold to the then UK based Shandwick Group (today Weber Shandwick).

And again in 1976, thanks to the efforts of Giuseppe Roggero (who was then also chairman of SCR) and sociologist Francesco Alberoni, Milan started the first public relations undergraduate course in the IULM Institute, followed a year later by a second evening course organized by Isforp, founded by Aldo Chiappe in Milan, another of Italy's most reputed professionals.

IULM became a full-fledged university in the 1980s and the State therefore recognized the first ever public relations undergraduate course in Italy. Today there are just under 100 under- and post-graduate courses in Communications Sciences, 18 of which are specifically dedicated to either Public Relations, Corporate or Public Communication.

Since the early 1970s, the Italian political system was paralysed, social unrest moved from students to trade unions, while entrepreneurs under considerable political pressure and intense negotiations decided in 1974 to move core employee information and communication activities into the hands of trade unions in a trade-off agreement implying a smaller pay raise than demanded. Also, in the mid-1970s, major corruption scandals exploded involving many private and public sector managers and the country's political leadership. Terrorism struck hard in those years and public relations activities—save for public affairs and political relations—were virtually suspended. It would take more than ten years for major corporations to restore the concept of internal and external public relations as a relevant task of organizational management.

The 1980s

In the 1980s, many companies indulged in cultural sponsorships, image campaigns, logo restyling and other "questionable practices" in media relations and public affairs. As a result, these activities succeeded in creating a nebulous smokescreen which effectively distracted public opinion and covered these companies' increasingly illegal ongoing practices, in full cooperation with the public sector bureaucracy and the political party system.

Also, an integrated and powerful coalition between media tycoon Silvio Berlusconi and powerful Socialist-Party secretary Bettino Craxi forced regulatory boundaries in favor of private/commercial television. This move promptly allowed full broadcast activities to advertizing, private sector and corporate values into what, until then, had been (and partly still is) a lazy pauper communist/Catholic oriented civil society. Mass consumption exploded. Intellectuals call this period the reign of the "culture of image" or of the "culture of visibility," well along the lines of the 1962 work by the American historian David Boorstin, *The Image: what's happened to the American dream?* (Atheneum 1962) or Vance Packard's *The Hidden Persuaders* (David Mckay 1957).

In 1981 six of the country's major public relations firms also formed Assorel, the association of public relations agencies. Not competitive with Ferpi, Assorel recognized the former as the official representative of the profession, and promoted internal (contract, criteria, indicators of an agency vis-à-vis solo or small consultancy) and external activities such as promotion of the public relations agency contribution to potential client organizations.

In 1985, Luca di Montezemolo (today Chairman of Fiat, Ferrari and the National Manufacturers Association)—after having left the position of head of public relations of the Fiat group—created, through his own PR agency, the adventure of Azzurra, the first ever public relations consortium formed by major Italian corporations: a sailboat which raced for the America's Cup. Although Azzurra did not win, it was tremendously popular amongst Italian consumers and sponsors felt very rewarded.

In 1986, for the first time, according to AISM (the Italian association of market research companies) corporations spent more on research into the effects of their communication, rather than into what consumers think and expect of their products.

In the second half of the 1980s, SCR, the agency which was by then one hundred people strong, collectively elaborated and successfully experimented with the public relations methodology GOREL (government of relationships) which, many times updated since, is today adopted by large national and international organizations as a scrapbook reference to public relations governance, evaluation and measurement of effectiveness.

In 1986 Rome also hosted the European Public Relations Congress on "Public Relations in a Changing European Society."

The 1990s

Came 1992, and the *Mani pulite* ("clean hands") corruption scandal erupted, involving a considerable number of public relations professionals accused of intermediating and promoting unlawful operations between businesses, political parties and the media.

A Rome-based association of educators and professionals, *Correnti*, led by Federico Spantigati—a jurist, intellectual and past head of public affairs of Exxon in Italy—theorized that only an organization which communicates factual behavior is credible, and that, following so many years of consociative public policy making between majority and opposition, as well as between those two and the private sector—the identity of an organization was the result of its behaviors and its success in distinguishing itself from others: i.e. positioning came of age.

A much-touted campaign for the privatization of state-owned companies was launched in 1993 by a new transition government headed by Carlo Azeglio Ciampi, the future President of the Republic—with his (at the time and for many years later) public relations assistant, Paolo Peluffo, as well as his then economic advisor and today Governor of the Bank of Italy, Mario Draghi—proposed as a blueprint for the Italian market the UK privatisation schema, where public relations advisors led all communication efforts. This unexpected move relaunched Italy's public relations practice, which had previously received a severe blow from the *Mani pulite* scandal.

Also the "new economy" bubble, with the launch of tens of new entrepreneurial initiatives searching for funds, granted a central role to public relations consultants and agencies. A short-lived phenomenon to be sure, but an unexpected contribution to a significant market rebounce.

In the 1994 political elections, media tycoon Silvio Berlusconi surprised all with a massive "viral" campaign based on thousands of "multipliers" scattered in every corner of the country (many were recruited from his commercial advertising salesforce) and, also with the help of a huge campaign of mega-posters, was elected Prime Minister. Only two years later, in anticipated political elections following the collapse of the shaky Berlusconi coalition, Romano Prodi, supported by his public relations assistant Silvio Sircana, conquered the Premiership, only to be, in turn, replaced two years later by Massimo D'Alema, assisted by professionals Claudio Velardi and Gianni Cuperlo. Three Prime Ministers in six years, who based their success on persuasive communication and . . . their failures on the inability to deliver what they had promised.

A major public relations battle erupted on the stock exchange in 1996 between Olivetti and Telecom Italia over the latter's privatization. Two Italian PR agencies were, for the first time, the real protagonists of this battle: Barabino & Partners on behalf of Olivetti, and Massmedia & Partners (today part of Weber Shandwick) for Telecom Italia.

From 1997, traditional corporations once again became involved in intense communication activities, and the demand side of the market greatly improved in professional competence with the entry of senior professionals inside organizations.

The New Millennium

The election in 1999 of Carlo Azeglio Ciampi to the Presidency of the Republic, accompanied by his public relator Paolo Peluffo, inaugurated seven years (until 2006) of an ongoing and effectively planned public relations program to strengthen the sense of belonging of Italians to the nation, in the wider context of principles of economic behavior from the European Union.

This was a campaign which Paolo Peluffo proudly presented to the world's professional community at the opening in Rome in June 2003 (500 participants from 42 countries) of the first World Festival of Public Relations dedicated to the discussion and subsequent approval of the global ethics protocol proposed by the Global Alliance for Public Relations and Communication Management.

Also in 1999 every Italian organization, similarly to organizations in other countries, was confronted with the threat of the Millennium Bug, a well forecasted and grossly overhyped planetary emergency. The Government, through an ad hoc committee chaired by Franco Bassanini and managed by Ernesto Bettinelli, reunited computer and logistics experts with public relations professionals who, together, planned and executed an intensive communication campaign to reduce the millennium risk. This event possibly marked the most articulated and collaborative public relations campaign ever executed in Italy, involving large, medium and small companies, associations, the public and the social sectors of society throughout the whole country.

Also based on this experience, the year 2000 marked the resounding success of the Vatican's Jubileum where public relations professional Joaquim Navarro Vals excelled in managing the countless religious events and Rome's popular Mayor Francesco Rutelli, effectively supported by communicator Paolo Gentiloni (today Minister of Communication) and assisted, as mentioned, by the US consultant Greenberg, succeeded in earning the dubious privilege of running for and losing, as mentioned, the national 2001 political elections against Silvio Berlusconi's comeback as Premier.

Since the year 2000, corporate communication and public relations practices in Italy took another quantum leap. The 150/2000 national law recognized the strategic role of communication in public sector organizations and made it mandatory for national, regional and local offices of the public administration to establish three distinct functions:

- relationships with publics;
- spokesperson for the political leadership; and
- media relations.

Unfortunately, the latter function was officially reserved for journalists who belonged to that specific professional union ... A government census in 2001 counted some 40,000 public sector communicators. From that same census, Ferpi elaborated that, summing the public, private and social sectors, there were some 70,000 public relations operators in the year 2001. Today the number is close to 100,000.

The non-profit sector is probably the fastest growing segment of the profession, also because it is the smallest. But many of the best practices come from there (see the case history described at the end of the chapter), as well as from the public sector.

In the business and financial sectors the early years of the new millennium registered a period of stagnation in terms of investments, but also showed a significant shift of power from the consultancy and agency sectors to the empowerment of in-house directors of communication in many medium and large organizations. In 1994 only 40 out of the 100 major Italian corporations had a director of communication reporting to top management. In the year 2000 this was 60 and today (2007) it is most probably 100 (according to IULM University Professor Emanuele Invernizzi's ongoing studies), which indicates a strong institutionalization of the function within many organizations.

According to traditional ways of evaluating economic impact as if public relations was a capital intensive profession (i.e. a representative sample of organizations indicate their allocated budgets and these are projected to the universe), the 2006 spend attributed by the annual UPA survey indicates 2.2 billion Euro. According to a different approach, which considers public relations as a labor intensive profession (i.e. the number of professionals multiplied by their gross annual cost to organizations and subsequently multiplied by three to include attributed added value), the 2006 economic impact is approximately valued at 12 billion Euro.

In 2005, Ferpi hosted and organized in the city of Trieste, for the second time running in Italy, the Second World Festival of Public Relations together with the Global Alliance for Public Relations and Communication Management, on the theme communicating for, with and in diversity.

Some 600 professionals and scholars from 48 countries participated.

In general, one can say today that the public relations profession in Italy (also defined as communication, external relations, institutional relations, media relations . . .) is pervasive while most public, private and social sector organizations of a decent size employ at least one professional and/or use external consultants.

There remains, however, much hesitancy in organizations to attribute the term public relations to this function for at least two reasons:

- many—rather than interpreting the term public relations as relationship with publics and therefore "relazioni pubbliche"—prefer to use the term "pubbliche relazioni" (an incorrect translation from English) which is closer in meaning to relationships in public, rather than with publics;

- PR (in the sense of pubbliche relazioni rather than relazioni pubbliche) is also often used to define those young thugs or the young chicks who protect entrances in discotheques and, on occasion, those (mostly) ladies who make a living out of selling their bodies to private clients of the opposite (or even same) sex.

This does not of course help consolidate a positive overall reputation in civil society of the term public relations, also used by the media—which is not less aggressive towards the profession than in other countries—as synonymous with spin and manipulation.

But, having conceded this, it is fair to say that most members of the Italian elite (academics, politicians, business people, financiers, intellectuals) are well aware, recognize (and are also increasingly concerned by . . .) the major role that public relations has today in the formation of public opinion as well as in public, private and social policy decision making processes.

This sentiment has been well understood by the younger generation which increasingly flocks to under- and postgraduate university and professional development courses in public relations. The most recent figures indicate some 60,000 the students currently enrolled, in public relations, corporate or public communication university courses in Italy.

The profession today is still mostly identified with the practices of media relations and public affairs, although there are clear signs that in the more aware segments of the elite, and particularly within organizational dominant coalitions, public relations is being increasingly recognized as essential in the areas of corporate governance, corporate responsibility and the governing of stakeholder relationships. It is also worth mentioning that today the leading candidate for the leadership of the yet to be formed Democratic Party, and potential prime minister should the center left coalition confirm its majority in the next political elections, Walter Veltroni, Mayor of Rome, comes from a long public relations experience on behalf of the now defunct Communist Party.

THE ITALIAN PUBLIC RELATIONS INFRASTRUCTURE

I shall now attempt to describe Italy's overall public relations infrastructure as it appears today (2007)—i.e. the integration of political, economic and legal systems with current trends in social activism, socio-cultural indicators as well as media control, outreach and access.

Political System

From the perspective of its political system, the country's structure is basically democratic, founded on a written Constitution approved in 1947, and subsequently adapted in part to respond, however late, to the many societal changes.

The President of the Republic is elected every seven years by the two chambers: the House of Representatives and the Senate: composed of some 900 individuals elected every five years. The State is supposedly federate, although its 20 Regions have less autonomy than in Switzerland or Germany.

Besides the Presidency, the Government and Parliament, the Public Sector is also composed of some 90 Provinces and 8,000 Municipalities. Its efficiency is rated as 113th out of 117 different countries, yet (or some say, because) there are some 400,000 elected officials in Italy today and some four million public sector employees. Much of the data is derived from articles recently published by the daily newspaper *Il Sole 24 Ore*.

The President (today he is Giorgio Napolitano the first ex-communist to hold this high post) chairs the Superior Council of the Judiciary as well as the Armed Forces. The Premier is formally selected by the President, but in fact indirectly nominated by voters, as the current electoral law obliges coalitions of parties to indicate their joint candidate for the Premiership.

The two chambers (House of Representatives and Senate) have exactly the same roles so, in order to be approved and implemented, any piece of legislation needs to be approved in the same text by both. This feature, originally intended as a guarantee, in fact has severely delayed the pace of legislation and, over the years, has turned into a haven for obstructive lobbying practices: even minor pressure and interest groups were always able to find loopholes in this byzantine process in order to introduce an amendment which would only oblige the bill to go back to the other House. This back and forth procedure would last until the end of a specific legislature, while in the subsequent one the round would begin again.

For example, this practice was successfully adopted by the tobacco industry from 1976 to 1996 to impede the adoption of a bill to prohibit smoking in public places, and the author of this chapter can well cite this case as he was directly and professionally involved in it. Also, this practice has been instrumental in projecting the identity of lobbying as a purely obstructive activity thus contributing to a negative perception of public relations. As a reaction to the pervasiveness of obstructive lobbying, the Executive has over the years succeeded in obtaining from Parliament ample proxies to legislate directly, and more recently accelerated a transition from hard towards soft law practices with the institution of powerful ad hoc Authorities (energy, antitrust, privacy, communication . . .) who today have considerable influence on corporate and other organizational activities.

Compared with the power they once had before 1992, political parties in general have considerably decreased their influence but on the other hand, civil society does not seem to have increased its own. Thus there are many empty power spaces, which are situationally and discretionally filled in—from time to time, objective per objective, item by item—by organized interest groups.

As mentioned, there are a growing number of economists, such as Francesco Giavazzi from Bocconi University and columnist of *Il Corriere della Sera*, Tito Boeri who regularly comments on www.lavoce.info.it and journalists like deputy editor of the *Corriere della Sera*, Massimo Mucchetti or columnist Massimo Riva of *La Repubblica* and many others who continually refer to Italy as a *crony society* when acutely describing the many reasons behind Italy's competitive decline. This has significant consequences on the development of public relations.

The political elite numbers 1400 persons, equal to 26 percent of all national elites, which amount to some 5000 individuals.

There is, however, an overabundance of political pluralism, as the electoral system (due to be once again changed during 2008) has produced something like sixteen different political parties, most of which secure less than 5 percent of the vote.

The two major political parties are Forza Italia (27 percent), founded in 1994 by Silvio Berlusconi and today the focal point of the centre right coalition, and the DS (ex-communist party) with less than 20 percent of the vote and which is the focal point of the centre left coalition. The latter is currently committed to an integration with DL, another central political party of Catholic origin, to form the Democratic Party, expected to become the top party in the country in terms of votes.

Public opinion is valued only inasmuch as the media plays an important role in defining the political agenda. However, few Italians read mainstream print media, while the vast majority form their opinions through the contents of television channels, mostly owned by the duopoly of the State and Mediaset, the Berlusconi owned media group.

There are many studies, but the most recent one is *SPIN* by Giancarlo Bosetti (Marsilio 2007), an excellent pamphlet which describes the recently formed vicious circle by which prime time evening TV news titles dictate the political agenda as well as the front pages of the following day's newspapers.

The positions expressed by the State channels very much adapt to the government agenda—today it is centre left and this guarantees some plurality, because Berlusconi is the leader of the centre right and therefore his channels reflect that position. But when he was premier most TV channels were politically aligned.

All this has significant consequences on the public relations profession, not only, but principally, in its more specific public affairs practice. Given the relatively small number of genuine and powerful public policy makers, public affairs professionals are more committed to develop direct and personal relationships with them, rather than to focus on the contents of their positions and proposals.

And this is yet another reason which explains the poor reputation of public affairs consultants. Organizations tend to use them only tactically to approach those few policy makers and their selection process is mostly dictated by access rather than by competence. This implies that positions and proposals are often developed by other organizational functions within organizations and interest groups, leaving to the public affairs specialists only the role of the advocate, rather than those of the issue manager or of the analyst or of the internal account, thus depriving the public affairs function of three quarters of its internationally recognised role.

Also, media relations have a huge impact on the dynamics of the public policy process as the political elite is highly attentive to its own visibility. This implies that powerful interest groups and organizations make great use of their access to the media in order to ensure visibility for complacent politicians . . . and this has been the very core secret, accompanied by his immense wealth, of Berlusconi's rise to power in that he opened his television studios to candidates which could not afford costly campaigns and set up many credits.

Also, another forceful implication of the strong interrelationships between the political and the business sectors of Italian society, a feature which has been predominant since the inception of professional public relations practices, has led the market to privilege and consolidate public affairs and corporate media relations rather than marketing public relations. Contrary to the UK or USA markets, where marketing public relations is still the prevalent practice, the unintended consequence of this trend by Italian professionals has been to create wide open spaces of public relations support to marketing programs for practitioners in product promotion and advertising, thus contributing not only to increasing pay for play habits with the media, but also to the delay of a serious and long expected debate and confrontation between senior public relations professionals (whose marketing competencies are, in general, minimal) and senior marketing professionals (who consider public relations as a tactical support for their programs either by organising events or handling publicity).

Economic System

Italy's economic system is well entrenched in the European Union and, from this perspective, is similar to that of its many partners.

However, some Italian specificities include:

- a higher than average role of the public sector in the economy;
- a dense framework of small enterprises which supposedly form the backbone of Italy's ailing economic performance;
- a huge practical and operational difference between organizations who operate in a competitive environment and those who operate in protected markets (i.e. so-called liberal professions, public national and local utilities, public sector suppliers);
- a dramatic divide between the north and the south of the country, with the latter representing more than half of the country's 60 million inhabitants;
- a substantial part of the country's economic structure dominated by an intoxicating alliance between legal economic operators and criminality, which strongly influences the recruitment of the elites of the business and political communities, as well as the judiciary. The pervasiveness of organized crime is rated as 103rd out of 117 countries;
- in relative size the country's public debt is the third largest in the world;
- the efficiency of the fiscal system is rated as 114th out of 117 countries.

External constraints imposed by Italy's participation to international economic treaties, as well as those caused by the country's participation in the European Union have succeeded, more or less, in modernizing at least part of the Italian economy—although most of the few large corporations which compete internationally (principally in the energy sector), and with the exception of Fiat (whose extraordinary recent market comeback owes a great deal to its highly innovative internal and employee relations programs) are mostly directly or indirectly controlled, or at least strongly influenced, by the Government.

The country's financial markets are growing but are still considerably immature when compared to the French, German or UK. Quoted companies are mostly family owned who prefer to indulge in opaque practices, and there are no true public companies, in which some sort of control is not exercised by the Government. This leads retail investors to rely on a highly corporative and conservative banking system (which only in recent months has been giving signs of waking up to international competition) while institutional investors negotiate "deals" directly with the owners or even through that same banking system.

The economic dynamics of the country bear a significant impact on the public relations profession not only because investments in this area increase or decrease according to the country's overall economic performance, but also because there is an increasing recognition that public relations has in itself a considerable influence on the elitist financial community, and well as on consumer and political behavior. This awareness enhances—however unfortunately by the adoption of opaque modalities—the profession's role in society.

Finally, both private and public sectors of the economy are engaged in a permanent turf war on who gets the largest share of the national income, and public relations—on both sides—plays a considerable role in advocating the redistribution of that share.

The economic elite is 17.8 percent of the national elite and has considerably decreased in recent years, while the political elite has much increased, and this explains in part the relative deterioration of the economy in recent years compared to that of other European countries.

Legal System

The legal system is considered possibly the weakest element of the country's non-material infrastructure. The judiciary is constitutionally independent, but hardly efficient and effective, plagued by insufficient funds, structures and an archaic procedural system. Today, a state of legality is more of an optional "nice to have" in Italy, while both the executive and the legislative branches of the State appear to be in constant conflict with the judiciary. The time requested for any act of justice to be parsed, let alone implemented, is far longer in Italy than in most other western democratic systems, and this has severe implications on public relations professionals who are often employed to circumvent, delay and create obstacles to the judiciary while searching for other paralegal, when not plainly illegal, procedures to overcome increasing litigation between conflicting interest groups and organizations.

There are myriads of legal requirements and codes affecting communication and public relations practices. Many are aligned and coherent with those of other European Union countries, but just as many are not ... and this creates constant conflicts which entitle organizations to situationally neglect those regulations whose implementation, at that specific moment, appear to be less desirable. To cite just one example related specifically to public relations: there is a legal requirement, stemming from the law 150/2000, for all public sector organizations to maintain a "relationship with publics" office, a "spokes-person" office and a "media relations" office. The latter, so the law states, is operable only by journalists who belong to the State-regulated journalistic union. Seven years have passed since the law was promulgated and formally enacted, but not more than 30 percent of public sector organizations have proceeded to adopt this peculiar regulation. Many municipalities, regions, provinces and central government departments have—yes—one unionized journalist responsible of their media relations, but also employ scores of external consultants, freelancers, services and agencies who, in turn, are (or employ) everything but unionized journalists. This happens because journalists are by law entitled to a separate and more favorable labor contract than that of a public sector employee.

Another impact on public relations of this judiciary freeze is that while organizations do everything possible to avoid turning to the judiciary to obtain justice, they still put a major effort into attempting to create problems for adversaries or competitors (black PR?), with the end result of increasing litigation. This, besides inflating the workload and num-bers of lawyers, has also developed a legal syndrome within public relations departments who carefully double check any statement or tool before releasing it, in fear of legal con-sequences and subsequently devolve discretionary powers to internal legal departments whose opinions are often highly subjective. Today, the relations between organizational public relators and legal counsel are almost as bad as those between public relators and journalists.

Activism

Civil society—in a country with a predominant Catholic and communist mixed cultural background—is less independent, active, lay and open than in many other western democratic countries.

Italian Society Facing New Challenges, a report by Giovanni Moro and Iliana Vannini, Civicus Civil Society Index, May 2006 http://www.civicus.org/new/default.asp?skip2=yes, is of exceptional quality and is a must-read for anyone dealing with Italy today from a public relations practice perspective.

For decades following the Second World War, the non political-party-stimulated voice of social needs was only that of the labor union movement, however closely connected to the major political parties. The first consumerist and environmentalist movements appeared only in the 1980s and still today meet obstacles in being perceived as independent.

Liberal, lay and radical viewpoints do exist, of course, but are mostly represented by some of the smaller political parties rather than by organized civil society. On only a few occasions—for example to avoid the abolition of divorce in 1974 following its introduction in 1971, or to introduce abortion in 1981, or to obtain a first-past-the-post electoral reform in 1993 by a referendum—has civil society succeeded in creating "band wagon" effects.

However, in recent years the non profit and NGO sectors of society have grown considerably grown in number, in popularity and in reputation, to the point that an increasing amount of private and public sector organizations today recognize their associations as active stakeholders and actually make an effort to engage with them.

Consumer, environmental and other social activists have in the meantime also become truly powerful interest groups and effectively lobby Parliament and the public policy process similarly to other private or public sector organizations . . . i.e. by employing public relations professionals who are usually younger and more creative than their peers in the private and public sectors, because there are less financial resources available. Some of the best practices today are realized by this younger generation of professionals.

Socio-cultural System

Italy's socio-cultural system, like that of most other countries, is changing. So much so that it may even seem irrelevant to indulge in describing it, although an effort will be made here to do this critically, describing how things are, but also how they are becoming . . . and mostly, how they impact on the public relations profession.

However it is relevant to state that Italy's peculiar specificity is that its socio-cultural system is far less dynamic in its pace of change than that of most other countries. If it wasn't for the abrupt and recent explosion and discontinuity caused by migrant population, mostly from Africa and Eastern Europe, and the consequences this phenomenon is having on the socio-cultural structure of the country, one could claim that nothing has really happened to accelerate social change in Italy in at least the last two decades. This is mostly due to a much lower than average level of social mobility or, if one prefers, to a much higher than average social rigidity and stratification.

Identified by economists, historians and sociologists mostly as a "relational (or crony) society," the bottom line indicates that in Italy, if one is not somehow related to a member of the elite, it is very difficult to emerge at any significant level of leadership in society. The term "related" may mean different things. It may mean "related" from a family perspective: there are recurring Sir names in diplomacy, the judiciary, politics, journalism, business, finance, academia, culture and . . . public relations. Even a distant cousin is often considered as being "part of friends-and-family."

Another interpretation of the term "related" is the increasing relevance of relational networks and "people one knows" or, at the very least, "may have direct access to." Most forms of career advancement are facilitated when not exclusively determined by relationships, and this is why the head hunting industry is less developed than in other western European countries. As much as this is true for all forms of executive recruitments, it is even more so in the field of public relations where the delicate issue of trust between a professional and his/her boss is highly relevant, and if the boss is normally selected through a relational network, there is no reason why the same process should not apply for his/her public relations manager . . .

Finally, the same term may also be applied to the myriads of clubs, societies, associations to which many "connected" Italians belong (some of which are opaque, secret and some even illegal).

To sum up: belonging is almost always more relevant than competence, while the two together make the best possible combination, but this combination is rare . . . hence, organizations are often hubs of an abundance of incompetence.

Italy has a lower than average tolerance of uncertainty and ambiguity: formally there is a law or a process, a regulation, or a procedure, for just about every possible situation, and if there isn't one . . . someone is likely to be working on it. Very little is implicitly left to an individual's imagination, invention or creativity, if not in finding ways to circumvent formal constraints.

Unfortunately, the consequence is that, whereas coping with ambiguity in many countries may be considered a strength, in Italy it denotes a sign of weakness of the social infrastructure and leaves ample options for interest groups to pursue their own self referred objectives. It is the overriding and pervasive Italian Catholicism, which somehow implies that if you sin you may always confess and be absolved, that drives Italian tolerance of uncertainty and ambiguity.

Specifically in public relations, the concept of ambiguity is often used as a recurrent metaphor of a specific weakness of the discipline, and this also thanks to the fact that Ferpi, since its inception, has always explicitly refused, despite many advances from the political system, to become a union and a state protected profession.

One of the dominating characteristics of Italy is the almost total absence of women in the country's elite. Even in the public relations profession, which as elsewhere is and has been for many years predominantly female, career leadership is mostly assigned to males. In undergraduate public relations courses females count today for 80 percent of the students, and in Ferpi, with its 1,000 members, females are some 65 percent. Take any profession (you name it): politics, academia, business, finance, legal, accounting . . .the women who have succeeded in bypassing the glass ceiling are very few, even compared to other traditional Latin or southern European societies.

This is but one of the dramatic indicators which help analysts understand and explain why, although its economy appears to be improving, the country is in constant decline.

The two fundamental cultural and philosophical backgrounds of Italians—Catholicism and communism—have also profoundly integrated into the country's socio-cultural system and formed what one may define as a structurally collectivist framework.

However, it is fair to say that such oversimplification grossly undervalues some of the more recent dynamics which have stemmed from the already mentioned collapse of traditional, intermediate bodies of society, as both the church and political parties have suffered; the explosion of individual consumptions; the increasing mistrust versus public and private institutions as such. Nevertheless, compared to other European countries, one may claim that Italians are more socially collectivistic and that, at the same time, civil society is becoming more splintered and individually self-serving.

The impact of this structural collectivist culture on public relations is forceful, however, as it obliges the professional to be very much aware of the political and cultural preferences of each interlocutor, much more so than in other countries . . . and this obviously implies indulging more than elsewhere in this relational society which we have often mentioned, in which everyone talks about everyone else, but there are so few people who really count. Or so it has been so far. From this perspective it is probably most relevant for the PR professional to be able to recognize to which stereotype (the traditional or the emerging one) his/her interlocutor belongs.

Interpersonal trust is fundamentally exercised within an organization towards superiors and authorities only in the elder generation, while the younger one takes an opposite stance in that it structurally only trusts its peers, while specifically mistrusting authorities and superiors, save—of course!—for their friends-and-family. Thus public relations, in its more traditional sense (that of Al Pacino's "people I know". . .), is thriving in Italian society.

Basically there is a tradition—also in other cultures which have a Catholic or a communistic culture (Italy has both!)—of deference to authorities and superiors in social as well as organizational settings. Like in French or Spanish, the Italian language uses the plural YOU as a sign of deference. However, it is fair to say that the younger generation tends to stray away from such deference.

Once more, the PR professional needs to be able to recognize in advance which model his/her interlocutor is more comfortable with. But—to draw some conclusion—if this is true for many other countries, it is possibly less true for Italy because, as mentioned at the beginning of this chapter, the pace of change is less dynamic and dramatic.

The Media System

One may guesstimate that media relations account today for at least 60 percent of public relations activities and, only a few years ago, it was much more than that. The implication is that the Italian media system is of particular relevance to the profession.

If we look at the more traditional mainstream printed media and their control, it is fair to say that general and specialized newspapers and magazines are controlled by the private sector, although there are substantial economic and other benefits (such as reduction of postal, printing and distribution expenses) derived from the application of specific laws approved by Parliament and managed by the Government. Also, practically every wire service in the country relies on State contracts for at least 50 percent of its income.

This implies an intense and intimate relationship between owners and managers of mainstream print media and the political system. Of course editors, responsible by law of all editorial content, are formally "independent" from ownership demands. But contracts have expiry dates and the recruitment is done by the owners so that true autonomy, if ever, applies only in the privileged situation in which the editor's opinions coincide with those of the owners, or when the editors' personality and reputation goes well beyond that of the owners.

The number of copies sold by daily newspapers today is exactly the same (approximately 6 million) as it was in 1946, a clear indicator of the non-dynamics of the sector. The advertising industry plays a relevant role and, with only minor exceptions, it is accepted practice that advertising contracts implicitly, and sometimes even explicitly, include or imply trade-offs in favorable editorial coverage of the advertisers' ideas, opinions, products or services.

Only in recent years has newspaper publishing become profitable: but this is due to the combination of an increase in advertising revenue, higher government subsidies and the use of protected newspaper outlets to sell, with newspapers, all sort of books, gadgets and other products/services. Usually, the owner of a newspaper is engaged in other businesses, and publishing is considered a good investment because of the attraction a newspaper has for the political and other elites, and the damage it may cause to competitors. Hence the utmost importance of the assistance and guidance of public relations professionals and their intense and incestuous relationships with journalists. In many cases, and increasingly so in recent years, journalists actually become public relators, working in or on behalf of private, public and social organizations, thus interpreting both roles, alternatively and sometimes even at the same time, with the consequences for published contents which one may imagine.

If one turns to the so called "new media" (i.e. television and radio) Italy's situation in terms of control is frankly rather frightful in terms of pluralism. Two huge conglomerates account for 90 percent of the scene. A Government-controlled entity named RAI owns three TV and radio channels, and a private sector controlled entity called Mediaset (listed on the exchange but controlled by the Berlusconi family) controls another three TV channels. There are also other channels such as La7 owned by Telecom Italia and the whole SKY range of channels which are beginning to dent the duopoly's power. . . but incumbents have joint interests in excluding the growth of others. Of course technology allows today for many other voices to be heard, but these media require substantial resources and so far private capital has been more concerned about gaining political rather than economic benefits from its investments in media.

RAI's chairman is elected by the two Presidents of the House and the Senate, but the rest of the board is elected by the Government, on the principle of a majority of votes to the presently prevailing political majority. When the majority was centre right, the six channels were aligned (although it is fair to say that RAI had at least one channel, the third and least popular, aligned with the opposition). When the majority, as it is now, is centre left, the six channels are clearly not aligned and some political pluralism is available. The impact of this media control scenario on the public relations profession in Italy is and has been powerful.

According to Prof. Carlo Carboni, if you segment Italian elites in three—leaders, concentrated and extended elites—the numbers are respectively 1,924, 5,967 and 17,305.

If you look at the very specific communication components (including senior editors of major newspapers and other media outlets) of these segments the numbers are respectively 148 (7.7 percent), 232 (3.9 percent) and 559 (3.2 percent). And this witnesses a higher concentration in the leader segment of the elite.

The implication is that, if it's true that more than 60 percent of the activities of public relations professionals in Italy are in media relations, a great deal of them are concentrated on supporting the role of the existing leadership rather than in trying to extend both the restricted and enlarged elites in order to introduce more social mobility into society. Once more, the "masters of ceremonies" metaphor appears appropriate.

In terms of media outreach, there is no doubt that mainstream television, as in many other countries, reaches by far the greatest audience and has been doing this for the last 30/40 years. Despite this evidence, it is a fact that public relations culture (including contents delivered by university and professional training programs) is mostly immersed in the stereotype and practice of the written page. Despite the first video news releases in Italy dating back to the late 1970s, and although product placement practices and malpractices in TV programs have become common over recent years, public relators take special pride in a lack of awareness that they are an available tool, and that different media require different approaches and different formats in content presentation. This is especially true in facing up to the new challenges and abrupt, objective change of traditional paradigms posed by the growing pervasiveness of social media, where each individual is a potential medium in itself and where disintermediation is just as intense for journalists as it is for public relators.

This recent phenomenon, clearly not specific to Italy, has a very powerful impact on the media access issue: however restricted it may have been in the past (in proportion to the tiny numbers of both the country's elite and the readers of mainstream printed media), more and more individuals are accessing social media directly, without being harnessed and managed by interest groups or political parties or corporations (as much as this may sound the rhetoric and possibly manipulated, it seems to be fairly true. . . as of today of course), and this obviously poses very relevant consequences for the day-to-day practice of public relators which so far they have failed to appreciate and learn to harness.

CASE STUDY

Involving Media Market's Italian Stakeholders in Supporting Italian NGO Cesvi to Protect South African Women Victims of Gender Violence

Cesvi (www.cesvi.it) is an independent lay non profit association (NGO) founded in 1985 and is today one of the most relevant humanitarian organisations in Italy. With its 30 offices abroad, Cesvi intervenes on every continent to deal with every type of emergency and to promote fair and sustainable development, by helping the poor through participative cooperation.

Current President of Cesvi is Giangi Milesi, an experienced public relations professional with extensive experience in private sector organizations and for many years head of Cesvi's public relations function. Current public relations manager of Cesvi is Myrta Canzonieri.

Media Market is the Italian subsidiary of Media Markt, Europe's largest chain of electronic, telephone, PC, photography, white goods, software, music and multimedia products outlets. Current CEO of Media Market is Pierluigi Bernasconi.

Milesi approached Bernasconi in 2004 and suggested an employee engagement cause related marketing program with the objective of raising funds for a humanitarian cause in parallel with an ongoing cooperation related to a joint humanitarian project in North Korea.

Bernasconi agreed in principle and proposed to hold a two-hour video conference with the then 3,500 Media Market employees scattered around the country's then 52 stores, during which Milesi presented three different project alternatives. A subsequent online referendum witnessed the participation of some 3,000 employees. The three proposed projects were related to the issues of malaria (708 votes), to Aids (1,044 votes) and to gender violence (1,168 votes). The winning project is the most "difficult" and yet the most challenging: building a safe home for abused women and their children in Philippi, one of the most distressed townships in Cape Town. Employees—at all levels—begin to feel moved by and affectionate about the project. The most popular feeling is pride towards a company that not only provides jobs, but cultivates emotions and ideals as well.

The employees wrote:

"The project we discussed and shared during today's video conference is one of the 1,000 reasons why we feel proud of being part of this company . . ." Fabio—Florence

"Thanks for the opportunity to vote and express opinions and sensations. . ." Donatella—Perugia

"It is for me a true joy to realise that the company I work for is not only interested in increasing its turnover, but also in humanitarian deeds. . ." Daria—Milan

"Compliments to my company, for this stunning initiative and thank you for having involved everybody in this difficult and important choice. . ." Luca—Naples

The decision is taken to finance the project by creating, producing and selling over the 2005 Christmas season in all Media Market and Saturn stores a music CD.

The novelty is that the CD is entirely performed by Media Market voluntary employees supported and coordinated, in their free time, by Franco Mussida, the well known historic leader of the Premiata Forneria Marconi (PRF), which was Italy's best contribution to the world rock scene in the 1970s.

All employees are invited to audition. Three hundred volunteer. During two auditions (in Milan and Naples) 68 are shortlisted by Mussida and work begins on the CD, titled Voices from the Heart. Eleven songs are selected (seven new ones and four covers) and a video is shot during the rehearsal and recording phases which take place during weekends.

The final CD is ready for the Christmas season and is sold with particular intensity, passion and energy by employees in all 52 stores. Thirty-two thousand copies are sold, there are 31 articles in the major general and specialized media, and for a week the CD tops the national Best Compilation Hit Parade. A total of 242,000 Euros are collected for the cause.

Other stakeholder groups become involved in the project. Customers are urged by employees to spread the news. Suppliers are invited to financially support the project by using the CD as a corporate Christmas present.

The project receives the 2006 national best cause related marketing project award. The collected money is employed to build the "House of Smile" in the centre of the Philippi Township in partnership with the Province of Cape Town. But more money is needed to employ assistants, psychologists, legal experts. Cesvi and Media Market involve some of the latter's major suppliers like Sony and Legami (a stationery company).

In May 2007, the House is inaugurated in Philippi and the case is officially presented by Ferpi (Italian Federation of Public Relations) at the Fourth World Public Relations Festival dedicated to Communicating for Sustainability held in Cape Town (14–15 May 2007) and organized by the Global Alliance for Public Relations and Communication Management and the Public Relations Institute of Southern Africa. Some 400 senior professionals and scholars from 40 countries participate. During the presentation, Giangi Milesi and Pierluigi Bernasconi announce that the House will be financially supported for a minimum of four years in order to give time to the local managers to find alternative local funds.

REFERENCES

AA.VV. (1956). *Atti del Primo Convegno Internazionale RP*. Franco Angeli.

AA.VV. (1957). *Atti del Secondo Convegno Internazionale RP.* Franco Angeli.

Allern, S. (1997). *Når kildene byr opp til dans [When the sources ask for a dance]*. Oslo, Norway: Pax Forlag.

Bosetti, G. (2007). *Spin.* Marsilio.

Calabrò, A. and Del Giudice L. (2001) *La Finanza Virtuosa e l'Oscar di Bilancio.* Il Sole 24 Ore.

Carboni, C. (2007). *Elite e Classi Dirigenti.* Laterza.

Colarizi, S. (2007). *Storia Politica della Repubblica.* Laterza.

Garbagnati, F. (2007). *Lei e gli Altri (intervista a Toni Muzi Falconi).* Il Sole 24 Ore.

Ginsborg, P. (1990). *A History of Contemporary Italy.* Penguin.

Ginsborg, P. (2001). *Italy and its Discontents.* Penguin.

Hearder, H. and Morris J. (2002). *Italy: A Short History.* Cambridge University Press.

Invernizzi, E. (1976). *RP nelle Organizzazioni Complesse.* Franco Angeli.

Jones, T. (2003). *The Dark Side of Italy.* North Point Press.

Mainini, V. (2002). *Storia delle Relazioni Pubbliche Italiane dal 1946 al 1970.* Graduate thesis IULM University.

Muzi Falconi, T. (2003–2005). *Governare le Relazioni.* Il Sole 24 Ore.

Muzi Falconi, T. (2004). *Relazioni Pubbliche e Organizzazioni Complesse.* Lupetti.

Muzi Falconi, T. (2005). *30 Anni di Comunicazione.* Prima Comunicazione.

Muzi Falconi, T. (2006). *How Big is PR and Why Does It Count.* www.instituteforpr.org.

Roggero, G. (1997). *Relazioni Pubbliche.* Franco Angeli.

Scarpulla, F. (2008). *Storia della Ferpi dal 1970 ad oggi.* Graduate thesis University of Catania (http://www.ferpi.it/navigate.asp?ID=43605).

Van Ruler, B. and Verčič, D. (2004) *Public Relations and Communication Management in Europe*, chapter on Public Relations in Italy by Toni Muzi Falconi and Renata Kodilja. Mouton De Gruyter.

CHAPTER

25

PUBLIC RELATIONS IN AN ECONOMY AND SOCIETY IN TRANSITION: THE CASE OF POLAND

RYSZARD ŁAWNICZAK

WALDEMAR RYDZAK

JACEK TRĘBECKI

INTRODUCTION

Since 1989, the Central European country of Poland has been undergoing a political shift toward democracy and an economic transition from a command economy to a market economy. Several features distinguish Poland from the region's other transition economies. First, only those of Russia and the Ukraine exceed Poland's vast area and population. Second, the process of building democracy in Poland began as early as 1956, a process that was supported by the strong Polish Catholic Church, which operated with varying degrees of intensity throughout the period of Poland's socialist economy. Third, Poland's has had a relatively strong private agricultural sector since World War II, with private farmers holding approximately 85% of the country's total farmland. Fourth, private business ownership in the trade, crafts, and service sectors gained significance after 1956. Finally, Poland has a historic role as a pioneer of transformation including applying *shock therapy*—the process of radical transitioning from a centrally planned economy to one dictated by market forces.

History and Development of the Country

Situated in Central Europe, Poland shares its borders with Germany, the Czech Republic, Slovakia, Ukraine, Belarus, Lithuania, and Russia's Baltic enclave. In the north, Poland borders the Baltic Sea. With an area of 312,683 km² (129,725 square miles) and stretching some 650 km (405 miles) from the east to the west, Poland is the ninth largest country in Europe. At the end of 2001, Poland had a population of 38,632,000, ranking 29th in the world and 8th in Europe. The population consists of 48.6% boys and men and 51.4% girls and women. The average life span is 68.5 years for men and 77.0 years for women. Ethnically, Poland remains fairly homogenous, with ethnic minorities accounting for 2.6% to 3.9% of the population. Poland's prevailing religion is Roman Catholicism.

History.   In early times, western Slavs inhabited the territory that is Poland today. Their adoption of Christianity in 966 AD led directly to the establishment of the Kingdom of Poland in 1025. Poland flourished culturally and economically under the reign of the Jagiellonian Dynasty (1386–1572). By the end Jagiellonian rule, its territory enlarged to several times larger than it is today. For the 2 centuries that followed, the nobility elected kings. Their reign brought about the accelerated growth of towns but also frequent wars that reeked havoc on the economy and led to stagnation in rural areas. Efforts to prevent rapid deterioration came much too late. The neighboring countries of Russia, Prussia, and Austria joined forces to take advantage of Poland's military and economic weakness. As a result, they imposed three consecutive partitions in 1772, 1791, and 1795, effectively wiping Poland off the map of Europe. Significantly, in 1775 Poland remained 2.5 times larger than it is today.

Poland did not regain independence until the end of World War I. Between the World War I and World War II, Poland managed to consolidate itself socially, politically, and administratively. In a time of global depression, the economy proved to be the hardest sector to restore. Following Hitler's invasion of Poland, which marked the outbreak of World War II, the country was occupied by Nazi Germany and the Soviet Union. Approximately 6 million Poles perished during the war. Once it was over, Poland again regained independence. This time, however, its sovereignty was severely compromised by Soviet influence and Communist Party control imposed on the government. After decades of phenomenal growth in the 1960s and 1970s, the inherent flaws of its centrally planned economy led to severe market shortages. The consequence was a lower standard of living, growing dissatisfaction, and social unrest, all of which culminated in the establishment of the Solidarity trade union movement headed by Lech Wałęsa. After a series of strikes and a period of martial law, the Communist government agreed to start roundtable talks with Solidarity representatives. The result was the parliamentary election of June 1989.

These events produced a breakthrough in the postwar political history of Poland. During the roundtable talks, the Communists ensured for themselves a formal majority in the lower chamber of the parliament (the *Sejm*). Solidarity, however, gained an absolute majority in the Senate. By autumn, the first non-Communist government in postwar history was established. In late 1989, the new government and the parliament adopted a package of laws and economic policy measures referred to as shock therapy, thereby abandoning its centrally planned command economy.

Although Poland is a democracy and a market economy today, to this day the legacy of a socialist democracy and central planning is manifested in many areas of social life, including the practice of public relations. The legacy can still be seen in three principal areas, as well as elsewhere. First, there is a common perception that public relations is suspicious propaganda. This view stems from the country's past experience with such things as censorship of the mass media, the subjugation of all such media to a single doctrine, and the resulting stereotypical conviction that the press lies. Second, there is a failure in the society to understand the philosophy behind advertising and promotion of products and businesses or building the images of companies and their executives. This problem stems from the fact that all goods manufactured during the socialist economy were readily sold because of severe shortages and lack of competition. Finally, there is a belief in Polish society that corporations, their owners, and their successes are better left unprompted because such high profiles may bring on additional tax sanctions. This view stems from the fact that, for ideological reasons, all privately owned operations were considered suspicious and were fought with the use of ad hoc taxation.

These characteristics have had a significant impact on the development and current status of public relations in Poland. One might argue that political, social, and economic transformations are responsible for having created a demand for public relations services and for the arrival of public relations experts and agencies, mainly from the West. However, public relations has played the role of an important and useful instrument that has facilitated and accelerated the political and economic transition of the country. One may, therefore, postulate that in Poland, as well as in other transition economies, public relations has a fifth transitional dimension in addition to the other four dimensions characteristic of the developed economies of Europe: managerial, technical, reflective, and educational (van Ruler, 2000).

The Evolution and Definition of Public Relations as a Profession

Evolution.   As can be easily demonstrated, Poland is among the countries for which the concept of public relations has had a long historical and ethnic tradition. Examples of early forms of public relations in the country include attempts by the Polish nobility and kings to gain publicity. The most famous of these were *the Thursday dinners* held by the last Polish King Stanisaw August to promote arts and science, as well as the match-making customs of Polish peasants.

The history of modern public relations in Poland started with a transition from a centrally planned to a market economy and the shift from socialist democracy to a pluralistic political system that began in the early 1990s. With a track record of a little more than 1 decade, Poland's public relations market is relatively young. Yet, as early as the 1970s during Poland's Communist era, information on public relations trickled into Poland from Western Europe and the United States through Polish researchers who maintained scientific links with the West. The year 1973 marked the publication of the article, "Public Relations in the Socialist Economy" (Želisawski, 1973), which most likely was Poland's first published article on public relations. Yet, principally, Polish public relations is a product of the country's systemic transformation and the need to communicate about the environmental variables resulting from the transition to a market economy.

The evolution of public relations in Poland has followed two tracks. The first track is that the systemic transformation has created opportunities for establishing broader foreign contacts, thereby allowing for foreign investment and privatization to enter the country. Numerous Western enterprises that recognized the need for public relations services have moved into the Polish market. Some of this demand was satisfied by foreign agencies that established branch offices in Poland. These included Burston Marsteller, which opened its Warsaw office in 1991. One year earlier, however, the first two domestic public relations agencies—First Public Relations and Alcat Communications—were formed.

The second track is that before establishing certain market instruments, mechanisms, and institutions (e. g., the stock exchange) that were absent in the command economy, the Polish government engaged public relations agencies to carry out public information campaigns. An example is the use of such agencies during the levying of direct and indirect taxes and upon the introduction of the national privatization program in the 1990s. Financing for such campaigns has come from foreign sources, mainly from the PHARE fund (Poland and Hungary Aid for Economic Restructuring). Since the Polish public relations market was virtually nonexistent, the government hired Western companies, which relied on the help of Polish consultants. In this way, even though external funds ultimately ended up in the pockets of external contractors, the transformation provided an impetus for the emergence of the Polish public relations industry.

Between 1990 and 1994, only 11 newly established companies claimed to have made public relations their core business. Still, their actual focus was on advertising. Nevertheless, thanks mainly to big government contracts (for the already-mentioned public information campaigns), the first 5 years of public relations evolution in Poland witnessed rapid development of the market, with an annual growth rate of 12%. In 1997, the annual sales of one of the agencies reached a staggering $3.7 million. By comparison, the market's growth from 2000 to 2001 was less than 5% per annum (Laszyn, 2001).

The years 1995 to 2000 saw further dramatic growth of public relations in Poland. For most of the period, this growth was mainly quantitative. It was not until the late 1990s that actual qualitative improvements were made as the need for crisis communication (in the wake of the Russian crisis of 1998), internal public relations, and investor relations were recognized. Starting in 2000, a growing number of public relations agencies recognized the need for specialization. The formerly fragmented public relations market consolidated through mergers and acquisitions. Many agencies were pushed out of business partly because the first stage of transformations had been completed by then and the government no longer had large contracts to offer to big Western agencies. In addition, many smaller agencies were adversely affected as the economy declined into recession. However, this is when another stage in the development of public relations, one of professionalization and internationalization, began in Poland.

In October 2001 in Berlin, Warsaw-based Business Communications Associates won three Golden World Awards from the International Public Relations Association (IPRA). One of their prize-winning programs was also nominated to receive a United Nations award. In July 2002, in its new strategy for administrative reform drawn up to the European Commission's recommendations given for Polish tax administration, the Ministry of Finance resolved to establish 16 public relations units at local and regional tax offices by January 1, 2004. The ministry's new communications strategy for promoting a good name for tax administration would be developed and implemented in the PHARE 2001 project in close cooperation with French and Swedish experts.

Defining Public Relations. There is no Polish equivalent for the term *public relations*. Although a great number of attempts have been made at translating this term into Polish, no proposal accurately expresses the idea behind it. Therefore, the English term is commonly used. Another term that is gaining popularity in Polish language is *komunikacja społeczna* (social communication), derived from the English word *communication*. The authors of one of two parts of Poland's most popular textbook on public relations (Kadragic & Czarnowski, 1995) have offered the following informative definition of the term: "Public relations is about information. The information is honest and objective, professional and reliable, complete, fast, media- and public opinion-friendly, ethical and responsible."

The approach seemed very appropriate at the time in view of the need to develop public relations as a separate domain in Poland because at that early stage of the profession, the media and public opinion often confused public relations with advertising. Another reason for adopting the above view of public relations was that many public relations practitioners in Poland were former journalists who commonly used language that is similar to that of the media and that is often misunderstood even while practicing public relations. Another factor affecting the perception of public relations in Poland was offered by Goban-Klas (1995):

> The transfer from a command to a fully privatized and highly competitive market economy was not complete. The predominant approach to doing business was to seek a quick profit, which generates considerable distrust, especially since scams and fraud were commonplace. . . . The government is overly apprehensive about working with the media, revealing its plans and submitting itself to public supervision. In effect, Polish PR campaigns could not be modeled after those developed in other countries, including the United States. (p. 8)

In a textbook published in 2001 which to this day remains the most popular public relations textbook, Wójcik (2001) provided a list of key definitions of public relations from world literature and a list of public relations associations from a range of countries. It appears that the definition most quoted in Poland has been taken from one of the most popular American textbooks, which defines public relations as "a management function that deals with evaluating public attitudes, identifying the policies and procedures of an individual or an organization with the public interest, and planning and executing a program of action to earn public understanding and acceptance" (Cutlip, Center, & Broom, 1994, p. 3).

Status and Image of the Profession

By mid-2002 public relations had become one of the most fashionable professions, measured in terms of the number of and demand for public relations programs at state and private institutions of education. Paradoxically, public relations practices have not been officially included in the list of professions pursued in Poland despite the efforts of the Association of Public Relations Firms, established in 2001, which continues to lobby state administration to recognize the profession.

The public relations profession in the country is dominated by women. Most public relations practitioners are young, well-educated women around 30 years old. According to a mid-2002 ranking of the major public relations agencies by the magazine *Impact* (July/August 2002 issue), half of the chief executive officers of such companies are women. Iskra (2001) reported that when asked why they chose public relations as their profession, most practitioners mentioned the opportunity to be creative and performing diverse tasks. The second most quoted reason was the independence and responsibility associated with the profession. A decent remuneration (at an average of approximately 2,500 euros in 2001) was also among the key reasons for respondents to select a career in public relations. The pay factor has clearly contributed to boosting the demand for postgraduate programs in Poland.

Even today, public relations work is often confused with marketing and press agentry and associated with the misused propaganda by the government. According to the founder of Poland's first public relations agency whose opinion may appear to be too critical:

> Polish PR remains far removed from world practices and often stands in complete contrast to them. This, of course, is due largely to market circumstances as Polish media differ widely from those in the rest of the world—rather than serving the mission of informing the public, the media in Poland frequently yield to the paranoia of concealed advertising. Differences can also be found in the way public opinion reacts—the media in Poland are still expected

to provide sensational rather than informative news, customers make their purchases on the basis of price, not quality. Other differences concern the clients of PR agencies—clients in Poland often expect agencies to manipulate the media, corrupt and blackmail journalists rather than disseminating reliable and honest information. (Czarnowski, 1999, p. 1)

The Professionalism of the Public Relations Industry in Poland

As of mid-2001, public relations services were being offered by some 500 agencies and the approximate annual worth of the public relations market was estimated at $100 million (Łaszyn, 2001). Only about 50 of these agencies are fully professional, offer a wide range of services, operate on a long-term basis, and seek to establish lasting relationships with their clients. Other agencies, typically run by one or two individuals, have been set up by journalists and public relations experts who have chosen to leave their jobs in corporate public relations departments or large public relations agencies. Most of these professionals (85%) are natives.

Even today, only a few foreign public relations agencies such as the Rowland Company and Prisma International operate in Poland. Burson Marsteller, which had operated in Poland since 1991, closed its Warsaw office in April 2001. The move appears to be a failure on the part of the company to adapt to the specific requirements of an economy and society in transition. Nearly all of Burson Marsteller's former Polish employees, who gained experience when the agency operated in Poland, currently head Poland's leading public relations agencies. Burson Marsteller's experience in Poland supports that central theme of this book: environmental variables such as nature of the economy, culture, and media are important predictors of success in public relations.

Poland's leading agencies are affiliated with reputable Western multinational consultancies. These include BCA (which won three Golden Awards in Berlin), Edelman PR World Wide, Sigma, Weber Shandwick World Wide, ComPress, Fleishmann Hillard, United Public Relations, Manning, Salvege & Lee, and Hill and Knowlton. Sigma International was ranked as the public relations agency with the largest sales according to a ranking by the monthly *Impact*, with an estimated $4.5 million in revenues and a staff of 60 (*Rzeczpospolita*, 2002).

The Role of Professional Associations. The rapid growth of the public relations market in the 1990s has increased the demand for the establishment of a professional association of practitioners. As a result, the Polish Public Relations Association was established in 1994, and it currently has 184 members. Another public relations association, the Association of Public Relations Firms, was established on January 18, 2001, to represent public relations agencies. Currently, this association has 16 leading agencies as members, with 5 others applying for membership in 2002. The mission of the Association of Public Relations Firms is to protect the rights of its members; represent members in dealings with state authorities, state administration, local governments, and other institutions, as well as with corporate and natural persons; and to strengthen the position of and disseminate knowledge on public relations professions. As this association became more professional, it joined international organizations in the public relations industry. In August 2001, the association was admitted to the International Communications Consultancy Organization. In the same year, it signed a cooperation agreement with the IPRA and joined the Polish Confederation of Private Employers. To date, these are the only public relations associations in Poland. In view of the size of Poland's public relations market and its evolution, it is unlikely that any other associations will be established in the near future.

Ethics: The Hot Issue for Public Relations. Public relations ethics has been debated quite heatedly since the establishment of the Polish Public Relations Association, which adopted a Code of Ethics at its second Congress in 1996. The Association of Public Relations Firms followed suit, drafting its own Statement on Professional Public Relations Practices in 2001. The latter document set out detailed ethical guidelines for its members. The problem with both of the codes is that they are very general and the standards they describe are frequently violated in by public relations professionals. There are three most common violations. The first is the corruption of journalists (Wielowiejska, 2000) and political decision makers. There is a practice of offering material benefits to journalists to influence them, among other things, to include desirable messages in their articles, which is referred to as *nonstandard advertising*. Corruption of political decision makers through unethical lobbying practices is apparent. The second is the unofficial practice by an organization of furnishing the media with anonymous messages aimed at tarnishing the image of the organization's competitors. This practice is referred to as *black PR* in Poland. The third is the use of public relations to acquire funds illegally from state owned- or state-controlled corporations for the purpose of financing the election campaign of a favored political party, for instance.

The Role of Universities and Colleges in Furthering the Public Relations Profession. The origins of public relations education in Poland go as far back as the early 1970s when the country's first course in public relations was offered by the former Main School of Planning and Statistics. At that time, the course was a lecture given on an elective basis by Professor Krystyna Wójcik, who later authored what today is a primary public relations textbook. Since 1989, this course has been a core requirement in the Economic Journalism specialization program offered by Dr. Agenor Gawrzyał at the Poznań University of Economics. Starting in mid-1990s, teaching public relations has gained popularity in both state universities and private business colleges, which have cropped up in great numbers. The first two textbooks on public relations were published in 1992 (Wójcik, 1992; Zemler, 1992).

Today, public relations programs are offered by almost all major state and private institutions of higher education in the country. For the most part, public relations is taught in universities of economics and in some humanities-oriented institutions. Occasionally, it is also taught in institutes of technology. The majority of such institutions offer public relations at the postgraduate, undergraduate, and graduate levels (mainly to holders of other undergraduate degrees). These undergraduate and graduate programs usually focus on a specialization (e.g., public relations, spokesmanship, public relations, media relations, or communication). These specializations are offered as part of programs in economics, sociology, journalism, political science, management, and marketing. The programs are 3 years in duration at the undergraduate level and 4.5 to 5 years in duration at the graduate level (with 2 years focused on the public relations specialization).

Most common, however, are universities with 2-year postgraduate courses, awarding graduates postgraduate diplomas in compliance with the requirements of the Minister of Education. Graduates of undergraduate programs receive bachelor's degrees, whereas persons completing graduate programs are granted master's degrees documented with proper diplomas. Students who complete specializations in specific majors receive master's or bachelor's degrees in their majors (e.g., sociology or journalism) and a document certifying their completion of a public relations specialization.

Public relations as an area of research is relatively new to Poland. Some of the first public relations studies were conducted in the early 1990s. The investigators behind these studies focused on general rather than specific issues. The first two dissertations in the public relations field completed in Poland were defended in 1995. By 2002, 38 dissertations in public relations were submitted, 14 of which were at the final stage of approval. The first higher level dissertation (*habilitacja*) has been defended in 2002. Paradoxically, as of mid-2002, public relations has not been given the status of a scientific discipline (according to the classification of the Scientific Research Committee). Yet, experts claim that the real growth of public relations as a scientific discipline has yet to come.

Public Relations and the Business Community

Systemic transformations and, in particular, the uncertainties of an economy in transition have forced the business community to revisit its position vis-à-vis public relations. State-owned enterprises were forced to reform their communications policies to get their foreign shareholders to support privatization and retrenching (Lawacz, 1995). Public relations was used in this context as an important instrument to support the transition of large enterprises from the former command to the new market economy.

Nevertheless, the majority of demand for public relations services in Poland has not come from state-owned companies but rather from international corporations and companies controlled by foreign enterprises. The second largest group of public relations customers was a new generation of large Polish private businesses and privatized State Treasury companies ranked in the top 10 of Poland's largest business organizations. The group least cognizant of the need for public relations includes small- and medium-size entrepreneurs and large state-held enterprises that have not yet been privatized.

Large, privately owned, foreign and domestic corporations are quite successful in articulating and advocating their interests by using different types of public relations strategies and techniques. In their efforts to maintain relationships with the parliament, other branches of the government, and trade unions, corporations are able to call on a highly professional group of lobbyists such as the Business Center Club and the Confederation of Private Employers. The latter has managed to obtain an equal representation in the Trilateral Commission within whose framework representatives of the government, trade unions, and employers negotiate on all key regulations pertaining to the labor market. Much less effective in dealing with various activist groups are medium-size and large enterprises that are either owned or substantially controlled by the state. In less severe cases, such as when faced with environmental protests, these enterprises respond by using press spokesmen. More serious situations are dealt with by external consultants or crisis management companies (Rydzak, 2001).

A study carried out in 2000 has helped identify where public relations is housed in corporations operating in Poland (euroPR Agency Study, 2000). Of the companies analyzed, 44% were found to place public relations in their marketing departments, 22% in their sales departments, 15% in their management board offices, and 10% in their advertising departments. Only 5% of the organizations maintained a separate public relations unit with a direct reporting relationship with the management board.

Interesting insights were uncovered by the same study that also analyzed the goals that enterprises have formulated for their public relations function. According to the study, creating and maintaining a good corporate image was a public relations priority for 22% of the companies. Another 19% of companies used public relations to inform external publics, whereas 17% concentrated on maintaining good relations with customers and on increasing sales. Shaping public opinion was found to be a priority for a mere 9% of the companies, whereas 4% of the surveyed companies sought to concentrate on the need to maintain ties with the media and organize campaigns. The smallest proportion (1%) indicated a focus on lobbying and internal communications.

One study found that 40% of employees are not familiar with the concept of public relations and that only 12% of the surveyed understand the difference between public relations and advertising (Trębecki, 2001). The level of education of people responsible for public relations functions leaves a lot of room for improvement. Only 6 (or 45%) hold degrees in public relations. The largest proportion of public relations practitioners (53%) are economists, whereas 23% hold degrees in engineering. Other professionals had specialized in human sciences (12%) and law (approx. 4%).

INFRASTRUCTURE AND INTERNATIONAL PUBLIC RELATIONS

Poland's Political System

Today's Poland is a democratic, multiparty, parliamentary republic. Poland's head of state is the president, who is elected in general elections. The national legislature is bicameral and consists of the Sejm (lower house) and the Senate. The prime minister is nominated and appointed by the Parliament. The Senate has a supervisory function and was reinstituted in 1989 for the first time since the end of World War II. Executive powers are entrusted to the prime minister and his or her cabinet, which is referred to as the Council of Ministers.

Poland's current political system has evolved through structural reforms of the state that were originally launched as a result of the roundtable talks of February 1989. Even then, the need to establish a new constitutional order was recognized as one of the most important tasks of systemic transformation. In April 1989, soon after the conclusion of the roundtable talks, the Polish Parliament amended the 1952 Constitution. The Constitution was again redrafted in April 2, 1997. The new version contained changes such as the deletion of articles referring to the leading role of the Communist Party and the alliance with the former Soviet Union. Poland was redefined as a democratic state governed by the rule of law. Another key change was the adoption of the principle of the freedom of association, which in effect allowed for the formation of new political parties. Together with articles on ownership rights and the freedom to engage in economic activities, these constitutional provisions form the basis of the present political and economic system of the Republic of Poland.

Another result of the systemic transformation was the formation of the new administrative system. On January 1, 1999, Poland was reorganized from 49 provinces to 16 *voivodships* (provinces), with three city governments (Warsaw, Kraków and Łódź). The most important part of the system is that the representatives of the three new tiers of local government (communes, counties, and *voivodships*) are now elected. The changes were considerably expanded, and decision-making functions delegated to the lowest levels.

Ever since Poland held its first multiparty presidential, parliamentary, and local elections, a new need arose for ways to communicate with the electorate. There was increasing demand for expertise in political marketing and public relations. Nevertheless, politicians in the early 1990s were relatively slow to trust the knowledge and suggestions of public relations experts. Their distrust was due partly to the failure of the 1993 election campaign carried out for the Liberal Democratic Congress Party (*Kongres Liberalno-Demokratyczny*) by the reputable agency, Saatchi & Saatchi. The agency was proved to be totally unprepared to deal with the realities of the Polish transition environment. The

Liberal Democratic Congress never made it to Parliament and, in fact, was soon dissolved as an independent party. Some of the reasons for its failure were the unrestrained and uncritical use of American models (street parades with Dixieland bands) before the party had a chance to establish its image. The party also was hurt by its poor election slogan: "millions of new jobs."

The first instance in the newly formed democratic Poland when public relations played a pivotal role was the presidential election of 1995. Lech Wałęsa rejected an offer by communication specialists who wanted to hone his communication skills. Wałęsa told specialists of social engineering and public relations that he could teach them how to build images and that he was going to win the election. However, Wałęsa opponent, the left-wing candidate Aleksander Kwaśniewski, took the opposite strategy and entrusted himself to the care of Jaques Sequel, a French public relations and political marketing expert. Kwaśniewski's complete trust in his advisor led to an election victory and a loss for Wałęsa. The color blue, built up as the symbol during the campaign (e.g., eye and shirt color), has since become the favorite color among Polish politicians. The paradox in the second round of the election was that just 5 years after Solidarity's thumping victory, Poles were witnessing a confrontation between Lech Wałęsa, a world renowned symbol of victory over Communism, and a post-Communist candidate who was an atheist and commonly considered a career maker. The breakthrough in the campaign came with Aleksander Kwaśniewski's appreciation of the power of public relations and particularly with the televised debate, which experts believe was the direct blow that led to Lech Wałęsa defeat.

The outcome of the 1995 presidential election was also of great importance for establishing public relations as a force in the Polish political scene of the early 21st century. In the 2000 presidential election, image consultants were engaged by nearly every candidate, as none wanted to repeat Lech Wałęsa mistake from the 1995 campaign. This essential turnaround in politicians' perceptions of public relations can be seen as a manifestation of not only a change in their way of thinking but also a pragmatic way of coping with competition. In 2002, a trend has emerged among politicians as well as business executives of relying on the services of very professional, but sometimes also rather incompetent, image creation experts.

Another link between the new politics of democratization and the public relations profession lies in the educational role given to public institutions that were set up during the transition (Barlik, 2001). The transformation process has had a profound effect on public administration. Some market institutions, such as the stock exchange and the securities and exchange commission, that were absent in centrally planned economies were created. Equally new were hitherto unknown concepts such as the value-added tax. Public administration was placed in charge of educating the public on how to deal with such novel instruments and institutions of the market economy. In particular, public officials' main tasks were to dispel fears of the adverse effects of capitalism and to drum up public support for the ongoing systemic reform.

All of these goals have been pursued by the relevant ministries since the early 1990s. The ministries have outsourced public educational tasks to foreign companies (e.g, Ogilvy Adams & Rinehart) often using foreign aid funds to finance these campaigns. A case in point is the information campaign (which was the second such information campaign after the tax awareness effort of 1992–1993) launched in 1999 to pave the way for social reforms in local administration, health care, the pension system, and education. The campaign was conducted from September 1998 to February 1999. Most of its total cost of about $1.1 million was financed by foreign aid *(Rzeczpospolita*, 1998).

Today, most public relations campaigns carried out by the central administration are performed by full-time, in-house professionals employed in newly formed public relations departments. The responsibilities of such departments are defined by modifying the job descriptions of former spokespeople who operated even in the socialist era. Some of the work is outsourced to specialized public relations agencies.

The majority of public relations tasks handled by Polish public administration institutions involve some sort of media relations. Therefore, public relations officers at all levels of Polish administration are employed in press relations, promotion departments, and information or public relations offices. In addition to media relations, their key responsibilities include promotion of organizational activities and creating and writing publications and web site postings. At lower levels of administration, public relations responsibilities are commonly placed in the hands of spokespeople.

Poland's Level of Economic Development and its Market Economy Model

Measures of Economic Development. Poland is a developed, industrial, middle-income economy and is classified as an emerging Central European market. Its per capita gross domestic product (GDP) in 2000 was $8,763 using purchasing power parity (PPP) and $4,078 using exchange rates (*Concise Statistical Yearbook of Poland*, 2002). Poland is the world's leading manufacturer of a wide range of goods. The country ranks among the world's top 10 producers of hard and brown coal, copper, and sulfur. It ranks among the top 20 producers of sulfuric acid, television sets, cars, trucks, and power-engineering products.

In 2000, per capita GDP PPP amounted to 39.2% of the European Union (EU) average for the same year, up from under 34% in 1995 (European Commission, 2001). What enabled Poland to catch up in real terms was the fact that it was one of the few transition economies that experienced substantial and sustained growth in the 1990s (6% to 7% per annum from 1995 to 1998). Since the end of the 1990s, however, the growth has slowed to 1% (in 2001). As a result, unemployment has increased rapidly from approximately 12.5% in 1999 to 17.4% at the end of 2001, and it continues to rise. However, one silver lining that influences the standard of living is the fall of the rate of inflation to 1.3% as of June 2002 (*Gazeta Wyborcza*, 2002).

One of the best indicators of economic development, one that is more accurate than GDP, is the Human Development Index (HDI). This index is used by the United Nations Development Programme (UNDPs) as a measure of the quality of life in a nation. A nation's HDI is a combination of life expectancy, adult literacy, and per capita GNP. Former communist countries including Poland rate rather well in HDI rankings as these countries have always had high rates of literacy, even if their GNP is generally low. Measured with the HDI, Poland ranks 38th in 2001 with a life expectancy at birth of 73.1 years (1999), a youth literacy rate of 99.8% (for 15- to 24-year-olds), an adult literacy rate of 99.7% (1999), and a per capita GDP PPP of over $8,000 (UNDP, 2002).

UNDP also relies on a number of other economic growth indicators that provide opportunities and pose challenges for public relations professionals in any country. Examples of such indicators, given here for Poland for 1999, include human skills (the average years of schooling completed by age 15 and above is 9.8), electricity consumption (2,458 kilowatt hours per capita), telephone penetration (365 mainline and mobiles per 1000 people), and cellular mobile subscribers (102 per 1000), internet hosts (11.4 computer systems connected to the Internet per 1000). According to statistics for the first half of 2002, 23% of Poles regularly access the Internet (*Gazeta Wyborcza*, 2002), and 18% of the respondents indicated they use the Internet regularly. Thus, approximately 5,600,000 people access the Internet at least once per month in Poland.

Market Economy Model Implemented in Transitional Poland. One of the most difficult tasks faced by Poland and other formerly centrally planned economies was to select the best market economy model. When this issue was debated in the early 1990s, neo-liberal economists such as Szomburg (1993) noted that a number of elements in Poland's sociocultural heritage made the Anglo-Saxon model of capitalism best suited for the Polish economic environment. Specifically, what made the model fit Poland so well were Polish qualities such as readiness to take risks, a strong entrepreneurial spirit, the ability to learn fast (mushroming consultancy firms), a deeply ingrained sense of individualism, reluctance to cooperate with others and operate within larger institutional systems, and the propensity to consume (as demonstrated by a skyrocketing demand for Western products, such as cars, satellite television systems, VCRs, cellular phones, etc.). Alternatives to this brand of capitalism included more institutionally and socially oriented varieties that were prevalent in Germany, Sweden, and Japan. However, a number of economists (Fleck & Ławniczak, 1993) have argued that the legacy of the old socialist system lingering in people's minds and in the economy itself, coupled with the fact that the Polish economy was still relatively undeveloped, suggested that Poland was better off selecting the European social market economy model similar to that adopted by Germany.

Poland's final decision on this debate has been written into Article 20 of the redrafted Constitution of April 2, 1997, which stated that "social market economy . . . lies at the heart of the economic system of the Republic of Poland." Despite this constitutional provision, the model that actually prevails in Poland bears more resemblance to the Anglo-Saxon variety. The first Solidarity government applied a neo-Liberal shock therapy strategy that featured a monetarist program of economic stabilization and a liberal doctrine of systemic transformation based on full-scale marketization.

The adoption by Poland of the radical, neo-Liberal, prescription can be explained by:

- "The receptiveness of the Poles to liberal economics, which is evidently not the case in other parts of the region" (Kiss, 1993 p. 50).

- Strong pro-American sentiments.

- The rather successful public relations activities carried out by a number of specific think tanks. These can be described as forms of activism or as organizations aimed at influencing political outcomes and indeed gaining political power or, in other words that have strictly policy advocacy ambitions.

A number of such think tanks, including the Adam Smith Center, the Stefan Batory Foundation, the Center for Socio-Economic Studies (Centrum Analiz Społeczno-Ekonomicznych), the Independent Center for Economic Studies (Niezależny Ośrodek Badań Ekonomicznych), and the Institute for Market Economy Studies (Instytut Badań nad Gospodarką Rynkową), were established soon after 1989. These organizations received funds and know-how from Western governments, institutions, and multinational corporations. Their objective is to carry out scientific research and provide public relations services that promote a liberal economic doctrine. The institutes generate hundreds of documents and publications every year targeted at political decision makers, entrepreneurs, and journalists, or, generally speaking, the so-called *multipliers* who shape public opinion. In the Polish media and, in particular, on Polish television, these institutions seem to

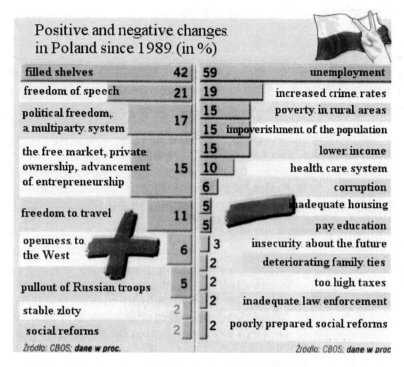

Positive and negative changes in Poland since 1989. (in %)

filled shelves	42		59	unemployment
freedom of speech	21		19	increased crime rates
political freedom, a multiparty system	17		15	poverty in rural areas
			15	impoverishment of the population
the free market, private ownership, advancement of entrepreneurship	15		15	lower income
			10	health care system
			6	corruption
freedom to travel	11		5	inadequate housing
			5	pay education
openness to the West	6		3	insecurity about the future
			2	deteriorating family ties
pullout of Russian troops	5		2	too high taxes
stable zloty	2		2	inadequate law enforcement
social reforms	2		2	poorly prepared social reforms

Źródło: CBOS; *dane w proc.*   Źródło: CBOS; *dane w proc*

FIG. 25.1.   Positive and negative results of the transformation. *Note.* from CBOS study, 1999.

have a monopoly on experts. One of their educational campaigns was conducted in 1992 under the slogan of "Myths about the economy." Materials published in the course of the campaign were published in 18 newspapers, including 13 dailies and 5 weeklies.

The practice of such transitional public relations in today's Poland has helped spread such ideas as the excessive state interference in the economy, the need to replace ideology with economy, privatization as being the key to success, and foreign capital investments always being good for the economy. Such beliefs ran strong practically until 2001 and 2002 which is when unemployment went over the 3 million mark, or approximately 18%. In addition, a growing number of foreign investors (e.g., DAEWOO) filed for bankruptcy and in mid-2002 the world learned of the ENRON and World-Com scandals in the United States. As early as 1999, a Centrum Badania Opinii Społecznej (CBOS) study had explained the balance between the positive and negative results of the Polish transformation, as noted in Fig. 25.1.

These developments have triggered a wave of criticism of the neo-Liberal economic development model. In one critical statement by a journalist, a claim was made that the predominance of neo-Liberal ideas in today's Poland "is not as much an effect of their suitability for the Polish economy but rather of the effectiveness of neo-liberal marketing" (Markowski, 2002, p. 4). Organizations that were promoting neo-Liberal economics launched a public relations campaign of their own to counter such criticism. An example of their response is a large conference entitled, "Foreign Investment—a Driver or Barrier to Poland's Economic Growth," organized in July 2002 by the Polish Confederation of Private Employers (Polska Konfederacja Pracodawców Prywatnych), an organization that had earlier published the "Capitalist Manifesto" (see case study at the end of this chapter).

Legal Infrastructure

The principle sources of law in Poland are the redrafted Polish Constitution of April 4, 1997, legislation passed by the parliament, and subsequent decrees issued by the Council of Ministers or individual ministers. Judicial power is vested in independent courts that answer to the Supreme Court. Civil and criminal cases are tried by juries and by either a professional or a lay judge. The choice of the type of judge to be assigned to a case depends not only on circumstances but also on the kind of court before which the case is brought.

The legal system that has emerged from the systemic transformation in Poland is far from perfect and, as the majority of the Polish population would agree, is in need of extensive modifications and amendments. Public opinion polls regarding the functioning of the justice system carried out in the early 2002 (CBOS, 2002) showed that most of the surveyed believed that Poland suffers from growing crime rates partly because of the inefficient administration of justice. The surveyed attributed inefficiencies of the justice system primarily to poor legislation and corruption and, to a lesser extent, to the fact that judges and prosecutors were intimidated by criminals.

Polish society, however, remains hopeful that one of the positive outcomes of Poland's accession to the EU will be the harmonization of its legislation with that of the community, giving rise to a more effective legal system. (It was announced in October 2002 that Poland and nine other countries may be invited to join the EU in 2004.) Although Poland is not yet a member of the EU, the country concluded the Association Agreement with the Community in December 1991. Poland's obligations under the treaty include bringing foreign trade and investment laws, business regulations, and other legislation into line with European Commission standards. The present legal system and its efficiency problem affect public relations practices in Poland in a two significant ways.

First, the legislature has not yet regulated lobbying. Delays on the issue are constantly reported. The law today allows interest groups to influence the shape of legal regulations. The most powerful of such groups, which represent the interests of foreign armaments, tobacco, pharmaceutical, and alcohol industries, have managed to push through a number of regulations that are not necessarily in the best interest of Polish society at large.

Second, one uniquely Polish example of the impact that legislation has on public relations practice is the ban on concealed advertising that has been written into the new press law. The ban makes it very difficult to provide the public with information, no matter how important and true it may be, if even a reasonable suspicion exists that readers or viewers could be led to discover the name of a company or product involved in the story.

The Level of Activism

Polish activist groups have played a major role in facilitating and accelerating Poland's transition toward democracy and a market economy and continue to do so into the new millennium. At the first stage of the transformation process, these groups contributed mainly by stimulating social initiatives, boosting confidence in the success of revolutionary systemic reforms, fighting for democracy and human rights, and training staff to be assigned to carry out the transition process. Today, NGOs help the society cushion the negative consequences of transformation to a market economy and reinforce and readjust the system of political pluralism and the market economy with a view to building capitalism with a human face.

Historically, activism began with the earliest attempts to liberate Poland from Communist rule. These attempts were made in 1956 when activist groups of rioting workers in

Poznań tried to force the ruling elite to reform the political system using the main slogan, "Yes to socialism, no to corruption." As soon as worker protests in the 1960s induced a certain amount of liberation and democratization in Poland's political system, opportunities opened up for other activist groups. Although such groups were financed to varying degrees and controlled directly by the state and indirectly by the Communist Party, their influence on the systemic transformation in Poland in the 1990s is quite considerable.

A special role in Poland's transition was played by the Association of Polish University Students (ZSP). Its members were given opportunities to learn certain mechanisms of democratic rule, such as direct and secret-ballot voting used in electing officials to the organization's governing body. They were allowed to maintain extensive international contacts with such major-centered student organizations as the Associating Business Administration and Economics Majors and work as interns in developed capitalist countries. In effect, starting from as early as the mid-1960s, Poland's future ruling elite during the transition period began to benefit from the opportunity to engage in international relations and learn about the workings of Western democracies and the market economy. Today, now in their 50s and 60s, these relatively well-educated (many from Western universities as well) former members who also speak several foreign languages have become leaders of political parties, ministers, bank presidents, ambassadors, and other contributors to the success of the Polish transformation.

A special contribution to the Polish systemic transformation, unique in the socialist block, was made by the United Nations Students Association of Poland (SSP ONZ (Studenckie Stowarzyszenie Przyjaciół ONZ)). Its uniqueness stemmed from the fact that, for many years since its establishment in Poland, SSP ONZ was the only youth organization of its kind in the entire socialist block. The advantage of that kind of a monopoly position lies in the very fact that, for many years, acting as sole representatives of socialist countries, representatives of SSP ONZ had been gaining knowledge and experience in international debates and negotiations. This very knowledge is used today to shape the present political and economic system of democratic Poland.

Today's activist and social movements of the Polish transition period can be described as diverse, dependant on available funding, dedicated, and professional. The *Rzeczpospolita* (1999), which is one of the country's two most influential dailies, stated that at the turn of the 20th century: "Non-governmental organizations in Poland are experiencing tough times. Fund raising is not easy, due to sponsor reluctance; earning money is even harder, while state funds are granted not on pragmatic but rather . . . on political considerations. The apparent rule is that governments prefer organizations that are close to them ideologically, a criterion that is far from appropriate."

Because of this ideological slant, organizations that promote liberal ideas of free entrepreneurship (the already-mentioned think tanks and the Confederation of Private Employers) and ideals of a civil society, political pluralism, and integration with the EU (e.g., the Freedom Foundation, Amnesty International, and the Schuman Foundation) are relatively well financed, mostly by foreign sources and the private sector. They can, therefore, afford to maintain in-house experts or engage external consultants to render public relations services in a professional manner.

In the case of other grassroots initiatives and with NGOs engagement in providing social assistance and protecting the environment, public relations efforts are rarely carried out in-house. Instead, the tasks are performed largely by volunteers with little of no training. Nevertheless, some of these organizations in Poland have achieved success unprecedented on the international scene. An example is the Polish public relations achievement of a nonprofit organization conducted by some committed volunteers—the Great Christmas

Aid Orchestra. This unusual project, first launched in 1992, is a special kind of foundation. Journalist Jerzy Owsiak developed the idea of organizing this orchestra in 1991. Each year a concert is held and the event raises funds for a different goal, such as life-saving equipment for newborn babies. The nine events held so far have helped purchase medical equipment worth over $31 million, which was donated to more than 440 hospitals located throughout Poland.

There is little doubt that labor unions have played a central role in the history of the Polish transition. It was the Solidarity trade union (or social movement) that brought down the Socialist and Communist regime. In 2002, in the face of growing unemployment (18% and rising, as already stated), the Solidarity labor union is no longer a major force in society. It was outgrown in terms of importance by OPZZ (Ogólnopolskie Porozumienie Związków Zawdowych), a competing post-Communist trade union. This seemingly paradoxical situation has resulted from a phenomenon referred to by some as the *Solidarity paradox*. This phenomenon describes that, unlike in other post-Communist countries, the Communist system in Poland was abolished by the working class employed in large socialist manufacturing enterprises (e.g., shipyards and mines). It was exactly that section of society that, according to the Communist doctrine, was the mainstay of the system. Meanwhile, however, large and inefficient industrial behemoths were the first to fall victim to the process of market reforms. Governments formed by the Solidarity Party were, therefore, internally torn between their recognition of the need for structural reform and their awareness of the social consequences of such reforms. Both of the competing trade unions now realize the importance of public relations support for their efforts. They use this tool mostly for media relations and, in particular, for dealing with activists and corporations.

CULTURE AND PUBLIC RELATIONS

The value system, standards, and behaviors that distinguish one society from others depend on a country's geographic location and a wide array of natural and historical factors. All of these factors certainly affect the Poles. First, Poland is a predominantly lowland country with no natural borders. Situated between two superpowers, Germany on the West and Russia on the East, Poland has historically served as a corridor for passing foreign armies. This is why, starting in the 17th century, Poland has remained under constant threat of losing its national identity and why so much emphasis has been placed on protecting it. Today Poland has adopted a free market economy and faces tough competition from the West. It also is in danger of losing its cultural values, which is why slogans such as "Polish means good" and "Poland now" that appear on labels against the background of the national flag are increasingly more effective as marketing tools.

The second most important factor shaping Polish culture is the country's history. Several influences from different periods in history have strongly affected the way the Poles perceive the world today:

1. Those tied to the formation of Polish identity have influenced the country since the Polish state first originated. These include the adoption of Christianity in 966, which has made religion a strong influence in both the Polish state and the nation. Poland would wage war against countries representing other religions, such as Islamic Turkey, Orthodox Christian Russia, and predominantly Protestant Germany. Being a real Pole was equated with being Catholic. This association became even stronger during Communism when authorities attempted to secularize the country through force and after Karol Wojtyła assumed the position of the Pope and became Pope John Paul. The Polish brand of Catholicism is

mainly family oriented and underlines the important role of women (e.g., the cult of Virgin Mary of Częstochowa).

2. The influence of the partition is another important factor. During the period when the country was torn between Germany, Russian, and Austria, Poland grew even more devoted to Catholicism and more distrustful of the state and state authorities. Just over 170 years ago, and to some extent during the 5 decades of Communist Poland, the establishment came to be seen as an alien hostile power imposed on the Poles. Civil disobedience and actions aimed at inflicting damage on the state were seen as acts of patriotism and received public support.

3. Another period that strongly affected Poles' collective view of the world was the 5 decades of Socialist Poland. Although sovereign and democratic in theory, Poland remained under Soviet influence during this period, having seen its fate sealed by the Yalta Treaty. Remnants of the old socialist system, based on collectivism, a centrally planned economy, and state regulation of nearly all aspects of the lives of citizens, can be seen to this day. The state has done away with the system of incentives and set up a typically "real Socialism" safety net that has created a special brand of society. Its members, who are in their 50s and 60s, are reluctant to face the challenges of the free market actively, unable to take their lives into their own hands, and incapable of advancing in society. They wait for the state to provide for them. Equally important is their distrust of foreign capital and the capital market. Average workers believe societies are divided into classes that are constantly at war with one another. Rather then recognizing business owners as people whose ideas, effort, and knowledge have helped them succeed, they see them as thieves who built their fortunes by exploiting workers. The cultural legacy of the period is a widespread conviction that everyone is entitled to equal benefits no matter how hard they have worked, what knowledge they possess, and how professional they are. For this very reason, a key task of transitional public relations is to promote entrepreneurship, secure public approval for the concept of private property, and dispel perceptions of entrepreneurs as speculators and exploiters and present them as persons who create jobs and contribute to the economic welfare of the country (see case study). In fact, all major private entrepreneurs in Poland recognize the importance of creating such images and have long maintained teams of public relations experts.

4. The most recent influence comes from the new model of Polish capitalism characterized by growing individualism, Americanization (i.e., the invasion of cheap mass culture imbued with consumerism, violence, and sex), commercialization of life in all of its aspects, and the surge of such new phenomena as gangsterism, unemployment, maximization of profit, and an increasing shallowness in interpersonal relations. The group that best adjusted to these new realities consists of the youth. Paradoxically, however, the beneficiaries of the process of change include Poles in their 50s because many of them have managed to liberate themselves from past political influences.

In analyzing the distinctive features of Polish culture, as fashioned by these factors, one may apply the dimensions of culture proposed by Geert Hofstede (1980). Classified in such a way, Polish society appears to be reluctant to support the government and to trust in its capacity to make a meaningful difference by participating in democratic elections. This is evidenced by voter apathy (the turnout in the presidential elections of 2000 was 61% but dropped to 46.29% in the Sejm elections of 2001) and people's waning interest in politics. Confidence in the transition process also seems to be on the decline. The euphoria of the 1990s, when any change was thought as being for the better, was soon followed by disillusionment and widespread inertia. Economic problems, unemployment, and a growing sense of insecurity provided fertile ground for another wave of populism and collectivism.

History has turned Poles into rugged individualists. Although there is no denying that 5 decades of exposure to a doctrine that advocated collectivism has left a mark especially on the mentality of Poles who are in their 50s and 60s, the tough capitalist competition of the 1990s soon triggered a return to individualism and egoism. However, mainly because of the unusually strong influence of the Polish Catholic Church, the family is cherished in Poland. Poles' devotion to Catholicism was demonstrated during the most recent visit to of the Pope, who drew a record crowd of 2.5 million at an event in Krakow on August 18, 2002. The model of the family promoted by the Church and the political right wing is commonly adopted for practical reasons because in times of insecurity the family remains the only certain source of support. A side effect of such an approach is growing nepotism and a lack of confidence in instruments that promote individuals.

The high esteem in which family values are held in Poland has translated directly into an appreciation of the role of women in Polish society. Respect for mothers and the admiration and adoration of women dates back to the times of nobility and courtly traditions. The period of real Socialism also ensured equal rights and opportunities for women. One of rather famous example of this equalization principle applied in Poland in the 1960s, was the case of appointing women as captains of seagoing vessels. The era of capitalism brought with it a new concept, the businesswoman, who is typically well-educated and very gainfully employed but struggling to reconcile these responsibilities with the traditional role of wife and mother.

Another masculinity–femininity issue can be found in the business environment where the model for solving problems through negotiations is now being abandoned in favor of an aggressive "male" problem-solving mode; an offer to negotiate is often perceived as a sign of weakness. In this context, a special role is played by political parties and trade unions that vie for influence among desperate and disgruntled electorates. This approach creates bidding wars that are won by those parties whose demands are most exaggerated and whose show of strength is most impressive. This system is exploited most effectively by political parties such as the Peasant Self-Defense headed by Andrzej Lepper, a man who rose to his position largely with the help of public relations specialists. This sort of culture puts traditional public relations in a bad light and creates other problems such as the growing distrust of information campaigns, widening income gaps between various levels of society, more extreme attitudes, and, in effect, the perception of traditional public relations tools as governmental propaganda.

THE MEDIA AND PUBLIC RELATIONS

Similar to other Central and Eastern European countries, in the 1990s, Poland saw sweeping changes that affected both the structures of media companies and the rules that governed their operations. Conditions were then created for the media to represent a wide range of views and compete against one another. The state was deprived of its exclusive control over the press, and a number of new private broadcasting companies emerged to compete with public radio and television. Radio and television programming and press offerings became noticeably richer and more diverse. Many of the changes were driven by foreign capital whose presence in Poland proved to be quite fortunate considering how small the budgets of homegrown media companies were at the time. Foreign capital facilitated fast technological and marketing progress. Foreign companies took advantage of the situation and achieved high market penetration, especially in the press sector.

Initially, the emergence of a large number of market-oriented enterprises greatly escalated competition in the media market. Ultimately, however, the market consolidated through mergers and acquisitions, putting both fair competition and diversity at risk. Most recently (in 2002), companies have begun consolidating across media segments (e.g., publishing and radio broadcasting) and emerging into strong multimedia groups. This has given rise to a heated debate over the need to restrict such consolidation. Representatives of foreign publishers have accused the Polish coalition government consisting of Democratic Left Alliance and the Polish Peasants' Party of attempting to constrain the freedom of speech. The government has responded by saying that censorship comes from the market, whose role can be compared to that of a gatekeeper who lets only a select few with sufficient resources have a say in political debates (*Rzeczpospolita*, 2002).

Media Control

The media market has been shaped by a spontaneous and largely unsupervised transition process. Most Polish media have fallen into the hands of and, therefore, under the control of foreign capital. Foreign companies have gained a strong hold over national opinion-forming press controlling Poland's largest dailies, such as *Gazeta Wyborcza* (owned by the American corporation Cox Enterprises, Inc.), *Super Ekspress* (owned by the Swedish group Bonnier), and *Rzeczpospolita* (owned by the Norwegian company Orkla). Magazines catering to women and teenagers are dominated by Gruener + Jahr and Bauer of Germany and Edipresse of Switzerland. The regional and local press also is under the control of Western corporations, especially Passauer Presse of Germany.

Although Western investors have unanimously denied representing the interests of their home countries, parent companies, or other political groups, a strong case can be made to prove that this is exactly what they do. Polish public opinion is increasingly more concerned about the fact that foreign domination of the media results in promoting conservative and neo-Liberal economic views and foreign political and economic interests (*Życie Warszawy*, 1994, *Rzeczpospolita*, 2002). Surprisingly, the most liberal Polish-owned weekly, *Wprost*, known for promoting foreign investments in Poland and other transition economies, published an article criticizing the domination of German investments in the Polish economy, arguing that the government should have a policy enabling the diversification of influence and not allowing the domination of investments from a single country (Nowakowski, 2002). Nowakowski cited banking and mass media as two industries that were predominantly under German ownership. In his opinion, such a situation leads to instances when "in the German bank it will be easier for the German entrepreneur to receive a loan than for his Polish competitor." . . . "On the other hand, in the automobile magazine we can read the 'objective' analysis, from which one can draw a clear conclusion that the cars produced in country of the editor are the best."

Some of the trends seen in the Polish press sector, especially foreign domination of media, have justified governmental efforts to protect the electronic media in Poland. The government has placed stricter controls over the radio and television market by imposing a new system of licensing that includes harsher rules for foreign capital. The Law on Radio and Television Broadcasting provides for the appointment of the National Council for the Supervision of Radio and Television to oversee the radio and television market as well as grant broadcasting licenses. The requirement to disclose any changes in the capital structure of licensed publishers to the council allows the body to monitor market trends on an ongoing basis.

Media Outreach

Thanks to Poland's existing media infrastructure, the virtual nonexistence of illiteracy (.3% in the population segment above 15 years old), and a relatively low poverty rate, the media are capable of disseminating messages practically to the entire population. Daily newspapers reach a relatively unchanging 60% segment of the population; local dailies are the most popular form of press in most provinces. Channel I, which is Poland's most popular radio station, covers the entire country. Channels I, II, and III of Polish radio reach 40% of Poland's population. Public radio in Poland faces strong competition from private stations (most of which are regional and specialize in music and other forms of entertainment) and from private national stations, one of the strongest of which among Polish Catholics is the Catholic radio station Radio Maryja.

Telewizja Polska S.A. (Polish Television), owned exclusively by the state treasury, offers three national channels and one channel abroad via satellite. Channel I of Polish Television is accessible to 98% of the population. Private television, meanwhile, has been steadily gaining market share. In fact, the licensing of private television stations began as early as 1993. In 1997, the ratings of the private station Polsat exceeded those of public television. Many stations in Poland transmit their signals via satellite, which gives them an outreach that transcends Poland's boundary.

Media Access

Throughout the period of Polish transformation, politicians have been warring over access to the media and, particularly, to television. The political victory of the Solidarity faction put an end to the domination of socialist ideology and to state censorship of the mass media. Factors such as excessive public expectations, the deepening stratification of society, and skyrocketing unemployment allowed the leftist coalition of the Democratic Left Alliance and the Polish Peasant Party to rise to power after the 1993 election, which they repeated during the election of 2001. One of the coalition's priorities has been to regain, at least in part, the media access it once enjoyed. Every ruling elite in Poland is well aware of the advantages of controlling the media. Such control can be achieved by acquiring a sufficiently big share in a publishing house or having it managed by people willing to promote their views. Thus, gaining influence over and better access to the media in a market economy requires substantial funds to buy shares and large advertising budgets. Today's market belongs to advertisers for whom the media fight mercilessly.

Public relations professionals and agencies play an important role in providing the media with information subsidies. According to a recent study commissioned by the Association of Public Relations Firms, more than half of public relations practitioners believed that companies are given press coverage in return for placing paid advertisements in a given publication. Over 25% of public relations professionals claimed that press coverage is obtained by bribing a journalist (*Gazeta Wyborcza*, 2002).

All of this shows that direct access to the media in today's transitional Poland differs widely among individual groups of society. Groups such as the government and its institutions (e.g., the Ministry of the Treasury and the Ministry of Finance which publish official announcements in the press), corporations (because of their sizable advertising budgets), and the so-called think tanks among activist groups (which have access to foreign funds and private sponsors) are in a much better position to gain access to the media than the thousands of minor activist groups that deal with issues such as environmental protection, social care, and drug addiction.

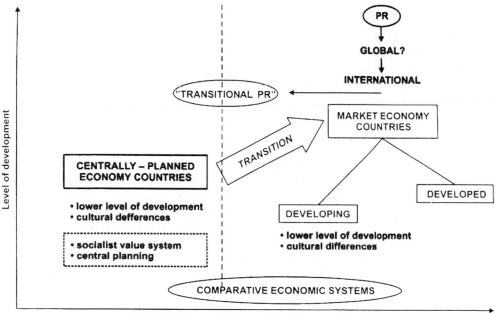

FIG. 25.2. The sources of transitional public relations. *Note.* From *Public Relations Contributions to Transition in Central and Eastern Europe: Research and Practice* (p. 10), by R. Ławniczak (Ed.), 2001, Poznan, Poland: Printer. Copyright 2001 by Ryszard Ławniczak Reprinted with permission.

CONCLUSIONS AND CASE STUDY

Why Transitional Public Relations?

By analyzing Poland as a country in transition, we draw several conclusions. First, Western public relations theory and practice needs to accommodate the unique realities of countries in transition. Second, although one may agree with Verčič's (1996) postulate that there are certain "generic principles of public relations" that may be applicable in every political economic system, we argue that the public relations practitioners in Central an Eastern Europe need to account for the influence of the former and Communist political economic system to a much larger extent. Because of the constraints it previous to efficient use of public relations. Third, the legacy of the former system, as reflected in ways of thinking, the structure of the economy, and the mechanism of resource allocation, has created a unique combination of those constraints on the application of the universal principles of public relations. For this reason, we may speak of *transitional public relations* as a specific brand of international public relations. Fourth, the sources of this concept based on a methodological contribution of the theory of comparative economic systems (Gregory & Stuart, 1985) are presented in Fig. 25.2.

Capitalist Manifesto—A Case Study of Transitional Public Relations

Background. One aspect of systemic transformation in Poland is the state's reorientation from its role as a supervisor protecting the interests of a selected social group to that of a regulator ensuring the proper operation of economic mechanisms. The rationale behind such a reorientation lies in the legacy of the Communist system, which was built on the belief that class struggle is unavoidable, and was committed to ensuring the victory of the working class. Other social groups were thought of as less significant. Private entrepreneurs were described as parasites who lived off the fruit of the toil of workers and peasants. This doctrine was reflected in the official ideology and became the frame of reference for an overgrown administrative apparatus. Restrictions on individual enterprise were written into the law.

Once the systemic transition had taken place, the practice of free enterprise by individual citizens became the cornerstone of the state's economic success. Free enterprise was then manifested by pursuing business through such forms of organization as civil law, joint stock, and limited partnership companies.

State doctrine has also undergone an official change. The state tries to limit its interference in the market and support individual enterprise. High-ranking officials issue statements of commitment to support private business owners. Nevertheless, at its very core, the state apparatus and especially local officials continue to perpetuate old doctrines and portray individual enterprise as a form of exploitation of particular social groups. The approach has led to the imposition of a number of hindrances and administrative barriers for entrepreneurs. The absence of an unambiguous and coherent corporate law has given state officials abundant room to interpret the law at will.

Objectives.   The Confederation of Private Employers (CPE) was established in 1999 to protect the interests of private entrepreneurs. The organization represents private business owners from all industries across Poland. According to its founders, the organization plays a crucial role in securing economic order, as it exercises its statutory right to participate in the formation of law and in public discourse. The CPE's main object is to promote its solutions and integrate them into the body of existing laws. The CPE participates in the work of institutions negotiating Poland's accession to the EU, issues opinions on new legislation, and puts out commentaries on the country's economic situation. Its activities also involve supporting the day-to-day business of its members by, among other things, providing consultations, organizing meetings, and intervening in the ongoing business of employers.

Instrument Used.   One of the most spectacular actions undertaken by the CPE was a campaign to promote the Capitalist Manifesto. The idea came from the Communist Manifesto drawn up in 1847 by Karl Marx and F. Engels for the newly created Communist Association of England; it was to become the party platform and the binding political program. The Communist Manifesto contained the fundamental theses of Marxist political economics, as well as his criticism of the capitalist system and of various currents of socialism of the time. It set out the tasks and goals of the revolutionary labor party and defined the concept of the international proletariat. One of its statements, "Working men of all countries, unite," has become the chief slogan of the Communist Party. In the spring of 2000, over 150 years after the proclamation of the Communist Manifesto, the Capitalist Manifesto of CPE appeared in all Polish press publications. In support of the press campaign, the representatives of the confederations, as well as other promoters of private entrepreneurship, were restating the thesis and the arguments from the Manifesto in their public speeches, presentations in the parliament, meetings with representatives of trade unions, and so on.

Outcome.   Two years after the announcement of the Capitalist Manifesto, the CPE gained the status of one of the most visible and influential lobbying organizations on the Polish political and economic scenes. It has gained equal representation in the Trilateral

Today, private companies in Poland account for:
- 75 percent of Gross Domestic Product
- 70 percent of all employees
- 79 percent of exports

POLSKA KONFEDERACJA PRACODAWCÓW PRYWATNYCH — POLISH CONFEDERATION OF PRIVATE EMPLOYERS

THE CAPITALIST MANIFESTO

Private businesses have become a driving force behind Poland's growth and prosperity. We, Polish employers and employees, can now reap the benefits of their work. Credit for the success of the Polish economy should be given to all the people who, through their hard work and perseverance, developed their businesses, frequently working from scratch. It should also be given to everyone who efficiently works in those companies today.

Free market mechanisms still need to be fully approved by society at large and by politicians. Without a common recognition of the fact that company growth is fueled by profits, even the worthiest of social and public causes will stand no chance of ever being achieved. Even the most heated arguments about how to divide state funds will not generate economic growth. We want to see new jobs created. We also want the right to pursue happiness rather than having poverty shared equally by everyone. Political declarations alone will not force entrepreneurs to want to develop their companies, pay higher taxes, create new jobs, increase exports or investment spending, because those decisions are based on one fundamental measure - acceptable return.

As entrepreneurs and employers, we expect the central and local governments to create favorable conditions for the development of companies. These should be made by ensuring macroeconomic stability, a consistent budgetary regime and making no more promises that cannot be delivered.

It is the duty of both the Parliament and the Government to improve Polish legislation so as to sharpen the competitive edge of Polish companies and products. Let us also seize new opportunities arising with Poland's upcoming accession to the European Union!

WE DEMAND:
- a lower and uniform taxation rate to allow companies to retain funds for future   investment,
- a lower cost of labor, including lower social insurance contributions to allow us to increase employment securely in our companies,
- legislation allowing flexibility in industrial relations,
- mandatory social benefits adjusted to match market requirments,
- stable and coherent legislation that is consistently enforced, unaffected by discretionary powers of officials, and that will effectively help curb corruption,
- public offices and institutions aware of their responsibilities towards entrepreneurs,
- equal rights and obligations for private and state-owned companies,
- equal rights for employer organizations and trade unions.

We hereby proclaim this Manifesto, guided by a sense of responsibility for our companies and our employees, for the economic and social development of Poland and concerned about unique opportunities that we cannot afford to lose.

POLISH CONFEDERATION OF PRIVATE EMPLOYERS

CAPITALISTS OF THE 21st CENTURY, UNITE!

pkpp@prywatni.pl!

FIG. 25.3. The Capitalist Manifesto of Polish Confederation of Private Employers. *Note.* Copyright 2000 by CPE. Reprinted with permission.

Committee, thus breaking the monopoly of the Confederation of Polish Employers, which represents predominantly large state-owned enterprises. Not 1 week goes by without representatives of the Confederation of Polish Employers presenting their position on important economic and political issues, promoting entrepreneurship, and shaping a positive image of the private employer before the media, the parliament, and governmental institutions. See Fig. 25.3.

REFERENCES

Barlik, J. (2001). Public awareness campaigns in Poland and Slovenia: Lessons learned by government agencies and PR practitioners. In R. Ławniczak (Ed.), *Public relations contribution to transition in Central and Eastern Europe: Research and practice*. Poznan: Printer Poland.

Czarnowski, P. (1999, July). *Polskie public relations—jakie jest, każdy widzi*. Paper presented at the meeting of the Polish Association of Public Relations. In Warsaw.

Commission of European Communities. (2002). *Regular Report on Poland's Progress Toward Association*, Brussels.

Concise Statistical Yearbook of Poland, Warsaw. (2002).

Cutlip, S. M., Center, A. H., Broom, G. M. (1994). *Effective public relations*. Upper Saddle River, NJ: Prentice-Hall.

Goban-Klas, T. (1995). *Public relations czyli promocja reputacji. Pojęcia, definicje, uwarunkowania*. Warszawa: BUSINESS PRESS.

Gregory, P. R., & Stuart, R. C. (1985). *Comparative economic systems*. Boston: Houghton Mifflin.

Hofstede, G. (1980). *Culture's consequences. International differences in Work-Related Values*. Newbury Park: Sage (new edition 2001).

Iskra, R. (2001). *Public Relations in zwei Kulturen. PR-Verstaendnisse in Deutschland and Polen und eine empirische Bestandaufnahme des Berufsfeldes PR in Warschau*. Unpublished master thesis. University of Leipzig, Germany.

Kadragic, A., & Czarnowski, P. (1995). *Public relations czyli promocja reputacji. Pojęcia, definicje, uwarunkowania*. Warszawa: BUSINESS PRESS.

Kiss, K. (1993). Western prescriptions for Eastern transition. In H. G. Fleck, & R. Ławniczak (Eds.), *Alternative models of market economy for transition economies*. Warsaw: SORUS Press.

Łaszyn, A. (2001). Poland's pr slowdown. *IPRA FRONTLINE*, October 2001.

Ławniczak, R. (2001). Public relations—an instrument for systemic transformation in Central and Eastern Europe. In R. Ławniczak (Ed.), *Public relations contribution to transition in Central and Eastern Europe: Research and practice*. Poznan: Printer.

Markowski, K. (2002). Ekonomicznie poprawni, *Trybuna*, 31.05.2002

Nowakowski, J. M. (2002). Drang nach Osten, *Wprost*, Nr. 1041.

Ruler, B. van (2000). Future research and practice of public relations, a European approach. In D. Verčič, J. White, & D. Moss, *Public relations, public affairs and corporate communications in the Millenium: The future*. Ljubljana: Pristop Communications.

Rydzak, W. (2001). The application of public relations in crisis situations in enterprises in Poland. In R. Ławniczak, R. (Ed.), *Public relations contribution to transition in Central and Eastern Europe: Research and practice*. Poznan: Printer.

Sriramesh, K., & Verčič, D. (2000). A framework for understanding and conducting international public relations. In D. Verčič, J. White, & D. Moss, (Eds.), *Public relations, public affairs and corporate communications in the Millenium: The future*. Ljubljana: Pristop Communications.

Szomburg, J. (1993). Jaki kapitalizm? *Przegląd Polityczny* (Numer specjalny).

Trębecki, J. (2001). The use of media relations by Polish enterprises. In R. Ławniczak (Ed.), *Public relations contribution to transition in Central and Eastern Europe: Research and practice*. Poznan: Printer.

UNDP. (2002). *Human Development Report.*

Wielowiejska, D. (2000). Korupcja mediów. *Gazeta Wyborcza*, 31.03.2000

Wójcik, K. (1992). *Public relations, czyli jak zjednać otoczenie i tworzyć dobra opinię*. Warszawa: Centrum Szkolenia Liderów.

Wójcik, K. (2001). *Public relations od A do Z* .Warszawa: Placet.

Żelisawski, J. (1973). Public relations w gospodarce socjalistycznej, *Reklama* Nr 6.

Zemler, Z. (1992). *Public relations, kreowanie reputacji firmy*. Warszawa: Poltext.

26

PUBLIC RELATIONS IN A CORPORATIVIST COUNTRY: THE CASE OF SLOVENIA

DEJAN VERČIČ

INTRODUCTION

The public relations profession in Slovenia is very young, having developed only in the 1990s. Its emergence, and early advances, are documented by Ašanin Gole and Verčič (2000); J. E. Grunig, L. Grunig, and Verčič (1996); L. Grunig, J. E. Grunig, and Verčič (1997, 1998); L. Grunig and Verčič (1998); Gruban, Verčič, and Zavrl (1994); Verčič (1993a, 1993b, 2002); Verčič, D., L. Grunig, and J. E. Grunig (1993, 1996); Verčič, Razpet, Dekleva, and Šlenc (2000); and Verčič and van Ruler (2002). This chapter merges these previous reports, updates them, and places them in a broader sociopolitical context, in line with one of the primary purposes of this volume.

L. Grunig and Verčič (1998) described the major attributes that affect the practice of public relations in Slovenia:

> Slovenia has a population of nearly 2 million people, living on 20.296 km^2, and making GDP of US\$ 21 billion. It is slightly larger in size than New Jersey and has about the same population as the Seattle metropolitan area. The contribution of transportation services alone to the United States GDP equals Slovenia's total GDP. The major difference, though, is that Slovenia is an independent country. It is located in the middle of Europe between Austria, Croatia, Hungary, and Italy. From its capital, Ljubljana, it takes two hours by car to get to Venice, Italy, or five to Vienna, Austria. Slovenia gained its independence from Yugoslavia on June 25, 1991, when it also began a transformation from a closed to an open society.

A decade ago, Thurow (1993) predicted that Slovenia would be at the top of the countries that were part of Yugoslavia. The *Economist* (1997a, 1997b) later confirmed Thurow's statement when it noted that "Slovenia has remained the most prosperous country in ex-communist Europe" (p. 45). In 1999, Slovenia's per capita gross domestic product (GDP) surpassed that of Portugal and Greece (both members of the European Union) and entered the new millennium with a per capita GDP that is more than twice that of any of the Central or Eastern European country (Republic of Slovenia, Ministry of Economic Affairs, 2000, p. 11). On October 9, 2002, the European Commission recommended that Slovenia be one of the ten countries that will be invited as full members of the European Union by 2004. It is clear that the first decade of Slovenia's existence as a nation has been good for the country as well as its public relations industry.

History, Development, and Status of the Profession

A History of Slovenia and Its Public Relations-Like Activities

According to the 2002 census, Slovenia has a population of 1,948,250 (943,994 men and 1,004,256 women) of whom 88% are ethnic Slovenians. The population lives in 688,733 households at an average of 2.8 members per household (Statistični urad Republike Slovenije, 2002). The primary official national language is Slovenian, but Italian and Hungarian are also official languages in the regions where Italian and Hungarian minorities reside. The majority of the population is Roman Catholic. In addition, there are 30 other officially registered religious faiths in Slovenia. Life expectancy is 71 years for men and 79 for women. Table 26.1 presents a brief historical overview of the territory and people of Slovenia.

Every nation can claim that it is a product of public relations–like activities. For example, similar claims are made about the use of persuasive communication during the American Revolution in the United States of America (Cutlip, Center, & Broom 2000, pp. 103–104; J. E. Grunig & Hunt, 1984, p. 17; Newsom, VanSlyke Turk, & Kruckeberg, 1996, pp. 35–37). Gruban, Verčič, & Zavrl (1994, pp. 10–13) referred to several key events in Slovenian history starting with the Freising Records, probably dating before 1000 AD as the oldest known record of persuasive speech in Slovenian language. A second communication milestone these authors identified was the publication of the first three Slovenian Alphabetical Primers (in 1550, 1555, and 1556) by Primož Trubar, the first Slovenian author to stress the importance of communication. A third was the publication of the first Slovenian popular science paper intended for farmers, artisans, craftsmen, and intellectuals titled *Kmetijske in rokodelske novice* (Agricultural and Handicraft News) by Kranjska kmetijska družba (the Agricultural Society of Kranj).

The First Trial of Modern Public Relations

The use of contemporary public relations in Slovenia can be traced back to the 1960s, which was a 'liberal' period in communist Yugoslavia. Until 1991, Slovenia was one of the six republics that constituted the former Yugoslavia. During one of his visits to universities in the United States, the founder of communication science at the University of Ljubljana (currently the capital of Slovenia), Prof. France Vreg, met Scott Cutlip and even began translating the second edition of the textbook *Effective Public Relations* (Cutlip & Center, 1960). At the same time, a lecturer at the Department of Communication, Pavle Zrimšek, translated a German book on public relations by Hundhausen (1969). In the early 1970s, final preparations were under way for the introduction of public relations as a separate academic subject to be taught in the Faculty of Sociology, Political Science,

TABLE 26.1

Historical Facts About Slovenia

250,000 BC: The first evidence of human habitation in the territory of the present-day Slovenia

120,000–33,000 BC: Remains from the early Stone Age—the Palaeolithic; among them the oldest musical instrument in the world, found in Slovenia

5,000 BC: Remains found as evidence of a hunting and gathering way of life

3,900 BC: Pile dwellings on the Ljubljana Marshes

1300 BC: Urnfield culture

8th to 7th century BC: Bronze and Iron Age fortifications

4th–3rd century BC: The arrival of Celts; the Noricum kingdom

circa 10 BC: The Roman Empire; the appearance of the first towns

5th–6th century AD: Invasions by Huns and Germanic tribes

After 568: Dominance of Slav people on the territory of Slovenia

7th–11th century: The Duchy of Carantania, the oldest known independent Slavonic state in this area

8th century: The start of conversion to Christianity

9th century: The spread of the Frankish feudal system and the beginning of the formation of the Slovene nation

10th century: The appearance of the Freising Manuscripts, the earliest known text written in Slovene

11th century: The beginning of the development of the Carniola, Styria, Carinthia, and Gorizia regions, and intensive German colonization

11th–14th centuries: The development of medieval towns in Slovenia

14th–15th centuries: Most of the territory of Slovenia including all its hereditary estates is taken over by Habsburgs; in 1456, the Celje counts become extinct—this was the last Slovene feudal dynasty

15th century: Turkish invasion begins

15th–17th centuries: Peasant revolt

1550: Protestantism; first book written in Slovene

18th century: Enlightenment and compulsory universal education

1809–1813: Illyrian provinces

1848: Unified Slovenia, the first Slovene political program

1918: The state of Slovenes, Croats, and Serbs; the kingdom of Serbs, Croats, and Slovenes

1945: The end of the Second World War and the formation of the Federal People's Republic of Yugoslavia

1990: Plebiscite on independence

June 25, 1991: Proclamation of the independent Republic of Slovenia

---

Note. From *Facts About Slovenia* (p. 26), by S. Možina and A. Resman, 2001, Ljubljana: Government of the Republic of Slovenia Public Relations and Media Office.

and Journalism in Ljubljana. Around the same period, some export-oriented companies began experimenting in public relations practice.

However, the 'liberal' period in Yugoslav politics ended in early 1970s and public relations was labeled as 'politically incorrect,' unlike advertising and marketing which were allowed to develop more or less undisturbed both in practice and academia since the mid-1970. As a result, public relations practice with a 'pro-Western leaning' nearly disappeared until 1989. The first academic courses in public relations were offered at the University of Ljubljana only in 1994 (Verčič, 2002).

The First Decade: 1990–2000

The first public relations agency in Slovenia was established in 1989 and 10 practitioners formed the Public Relations Society of Slovenia (PRSS) in 1990. The same year, the first booklet on public relations was published in Slovenian language (Gruban, Maksimovič,

Verčič, & Zavrl, 1990). A year later, the Slovenian chapter of the International Public Relations Association (IPRA) was formed. In 1992, Larissa Grunig and James Grunig, professors of public relations at the University of Maryland, visited Slovenia for the first time and gave a lecture to members of the PRSS. They returned a year later to give the first lecture on public relations at the University of Ljubljana. These visits started an intensive international cooperation between academics and practitioners. Since 1994, when the first international public relations research symposium was organized on Lake Bled, more than 250 top academics and practitioners in public relations from more than 30 countries on five continents have visited Slovenia and exchanged their knowledge and experience. Further, in 1994, the *Excellence in Public Relations and Communication Management* project was replicated in Slovenia and for years its results were used as a benchmark for the development of the profession in Slovenia (Dozier, L. Grunig, and J. E. Grunig 1995, pp. 174–175; Gruban, Verčič, and Zavrl, 1994; J. E. Grunig, L. Grunig, and Verčič 1996; L. Grunig, J. E. Grunig, and Verčič, 1997, 1998; Verčič, 1993a, Verčič, L. Grunig, and J. E. Grunig, 1993; Verčič, L. Grunig, and J. E. Grunig, 1996).

In 1993, the PRSS became a full member of the European confederation of public relations societies—CERP (Confédération Européenne des Relations Publiques—the European Public Relations Confederation) and Slovenia appeared in the *Hollis Europe Book* (a guide to public relations in 35 countries across the European continent) for the first time (Verčič, 1993b). Beginning in 1994, public relations came to be offered regularly as a subject of study at the Faculty of Social Sciences, University of Ljubljana. The following year, the public relations students formed a student section of the PRSS (with members from the two Slovenian universities in Ljubljana and Maribor), with affiliation to the European association of public relations students (CERP Students). In 1996, the PRSS launched its Website (http://www.prss-drustvo.si), and in 1997 organized its first national public relations conference. After the Bled symposia, this became the second regular annual public relations event in Slovenia. In 1998, the Slovenian Code of ethics was adopted leading to a declaration of the ethical unacceptability of hidden advertising. The declaration was initiated by the Slovenian board of IPRA, endorsed by the PRSS, and acknowledged by the Society of Journalists and Marketing Society of Slovenia. In 2000, the PRSS celebrated its 10th anniversary. To mark this milestone, the society began awarding prizes to the best Slovenian cases and the best communicator in management, in cooperation with the Chamber of Commerce and Industry of Slovenia, the Manager's Association of Slovenia, and the Slovenian section of FEACO—the European Association of Management Consulting. By the middle of its first decade in existence, the PRSS had 100 members and by the end of the decade, the number had doubled. It is safe to state that the public relations profession in Slovenia has become an institution (Verčič, 2002).

Definition of Public Relations

The first Slovenian booklet on public relations (Gruban, Maksimovič, Verčič, & Zavrl, 1990) proposed a new translation of the American term "public relations" into Slovenian language: "odnosi z javnostmi." The old term for public relations was *stiki z javnostjo*, which can be literally translated as "contacts with the [general] public." In the 1990s, it was replaced with *odnosi z javnostmi*, whose literal translation is "relations with publics." When the PRSS started a public relations book series in 2002, in cooperation with the major business publishing house GV Založba (with a goal of publishing two books a year, one original and one translation) there was no argument on how the profession is called in Slovenian (Verčič, Zavrl, & Rijavec, 2002). Explanations and defenses of the new term were given in the research report on the Slovenian replication of the *Excellence project* (Gruban, Verčič, & Zavrl, 1994), the first book in the Slovenian language (Gruban, Verčič, & Zavrl, 1997) and the first collection of contributions by practitioners (Gruban, Verčič, & Zavrl, 1998).

The transition from *stiki z javnostjo* to *odnosi z javnostmi* was about the transition from propaganda focused image management to a relational, stakeholder management of public relations. This development was strongly influenced by United States theory and practice (Verčič & J. E. Grunig, 2000). Toward the end of the 1990s, the definition of public relations in Slovenia broadened into "total communication" (Aberg, 1990) between an organization and all its publics (Theaker, 2001) and synchronized with the European approaches (Ruler & Verčič, 2002; Verčič, van Ruler, Bütschi, & Flodin, 2001) that go beyond relational to include discursive and reflective approaches: *celovito komuniciranje* [literally: "holistic communication"] and *komunikacijsko upravljanje* [literally: "communication management"]. Currently, the three terms (*odnosi z javnostmi, celovito komuniciranje,* and *komunikacijsko upravljanje*) coexist in both practice and in academia—their relations and their future are at the moment not decided yet.

A recent study found that typically, Slovenian companies have an average of two public relations professionals (Verčič & Ruler, 2002, p. 7). A linear extrapolation based on this would imply that 7,040 individuals currently work as public relations professionals in the for-profit sector, or approximately 0.05% of the total population. This research also found that 37% of medium and large companies in the representative sample had no specialists in public relations, which means that public relations is practiced by people primarily working in other functional areas (such as general management, human relations, marketing, sales, etc.). In response to questions on the public relations budget, respondents of the study indicated that they spend an average of 16.171 million Slovenian Tolars (SIT) (Euro 74, 675) on public relations annually. With linear extrapolation, the researchers estimated that 57 billion SIT (Euro 263 million) is the total amount of money spent on public relations in Slovenia, amounting to approximately 1.5% of the gross domestic product (GDP) (based 2000 on economic data).

However, one needs to take these numbers with a grain of salt. When asked which department performed the external communication function in their organizations, respondents replied: public relations department (6%), marketing or sales department (31%), no department because the CEO personally attends to this (26%), nowhere and by nobody (25%), and other (12%). When asked which department performed the internal communication function, respondents listed: public relations department (4%), human resources/personnel department (6%), marketing or sales department (19%), the CEO (25%), nobody (26%), and other (20%). When asked which department handles marketing communication (with advertising) respondents replied: marketing and sales department (50%), the CEO (18%), nobody (20%), and other (10%). Respondents also indicated that 60% of the total communication budgets go for marketing communication, 21 for external relations (not primarily marketing), and 19% for internal communication.

Government Practice

In the year 2000, the Government of Slovenia committed itself to implementing the good governance principles defined in the OECD *Citizens as Partners* sourcebook and handbook (see www.oecd.org/puma). The primary principles are accountability (making it possible to identify officials and hold them accountable for their actions), transparency (availability of information about government activities), and openness (seeking and providing appropriate responses). To ensure information society for all and reform of public administration (in line with the aforementioned principles), the government founded a Ministry for Information Society to facilitate the first principle. A position of a Ministerial Counselor in the Office of the Prime Minister was instituted to coordinate work on the second principle. The government as the corporate entity, all the ministries, and many subordinate agencies have Websites (see http://www.gov.si/ and http://www.gov.si/vrs/ang/index-ang.html for general entries, and http://e-gov.gov.si/e-uprava/english/index.jsp for e-Government). To listen to its constituency, the government not only regularly purchases public opinion surveys from the Faculty of Social Science, University of Ljubljana, but also publishes them promptly on the Internet (http://www.uvi.si/slo/aktualno/javnomnenjske-raziskave/pdf/ aktualno.pdf). At the center of the government communication structure is the Public Relations and Media Office with 15 professionals, all members of the civil service, and a Director who is also the spokesperson for the government. The director is nominally a civil servant but has been replaced each time a new government has taken office. This office is divided into three departments, one for managing domestic and one for international communication. The third has been given responsibility for managing the Communication Program for Slovenia's Accession to the European Union. Every ministry employs at least one communication professional, with the Ministry of Interior having the largest department with five communication officers in addition to the eight communication officers the police headquarters and a well-organized structure covering the whole country. The Office of the Prime Minister has three communication officers (see Table 26.2). Although the government has built up its public relations capabilities substantially, it still suffers from inadequate strategic and managerial competence.

Consultancies

As already stated, the public relations industry emerged in the late 1980s and early 1990s in Slovenia. By the end of 1990s, it transformed itself into a "total communication" industry, in line with the development of the definition of public relations given above. Pristop Communications was the first public relations agency in Slovenia. Founded in 1990 with a public relations focus, it entered into other fields of applied communication, including advertising, by the mid-1990s. By the end of the 1990s, Pristop Communications had become not only the largest public relations agency but also the largest advertising agency in Slovenia. All other public relations agencies have followed the same path of providing "total communication" to clients. Therefore, currently there is no public relations agency that exclusively offers public relations services in Slovenia. At the same time, all the advertising agencies also started offering public relations services resulting in a convergence from both professions. There is a Slovenian chapter of the international public relations consultancy organization (ICCO—the International Communications Consultancy Organization, the umbrella association for more than 850 consultancies employing more than 25,000 people through their trade associations in 24 countries) with eight members: Imelda, Informa Echo, NT & RC, Prestige, Pristop, SPEM, Studio 3S, and Studio Kernel, none of whom can be classified as an exclusively public relations consultancy. The largest Slovenian communication consultancies are domestically owned by their founders as limited liability companies, are affiliated with one or more international networks and/or multinationals, and operate in other countries but primarily in South and Eastern Europe. They typically employ up to 40 employees (see Table 26.3).

TABLE 26.2
Republic of Slovenia, Public Relations in Government (plus the President and
the National Assembly), April 2002

Institution	People in Public Relations
Office of the Prime Minister	3
Ministry of Agriculture, Forestry and Food	2
Ministry of Culture	1
Ministry of Defense (with the Slovenian Army)	5
Ministry of Economy	2
Ministry of Education, Science and Sport	2
Ministry of the Environment and Spatial Planning	3
Ministry of Finance	1
Ministry of Foreign Affairs	4
Ministry of Health	1
Ministry of Information Society	1
Ministry of the Interior	5
Police	8
Ministry of Justice	1
Ministry of Labor, Family and Social Affairs	1
Ministry of Transport	2
Public Relations and Media Office	15
Office of European Affairs	2 = 59
Office of the President of the Republic	2
National Assembly (parliament)	5 + 7

Several government agencies and offices have their own public relations staff, including Agency for Agricultural Markets and Rural Development, Agency for Regional Development, Environmental Agency, Government Centre for Informatics, Office for Drugs, Office of Equal Opportunities, Office for Legislation, Office for Metrology, Statistical Office.

Note. From communication between Government and Citizens in Slovenia: A report & recommendations prepared under the auspices of the United Nations Development Programme Regional Bureau for Eastern Europe and the CIS UNDP RBEC sub-regional project RER/01/003/A08/13 "Improving communication from Government to Societies," by D. Verčič and A. Ažman, 2002.

INFRASTRUCTURE AND INTERNATIONAL PUBLIC RELATIONS

Political

The Republic of Slovenia is a constitutional parliamentary democracy, with a president who is directly elected by citizens through a secret ballot. The National Assembly, the highest legislative body, is composed of 90 deputies also directly elected by citizens through a secret ballot following the proportional voting system. As a result of the last parliamentary elections in 2000, the 90 seats in the National Assembly were divided as follows: Liberal Democracy of Slovenia (LDS) 34, Social Democratic Party (SDS) 14, United List of Social Democrats of Slovenia (ZLSD) 11, SLS+SKD Slovene People's Party 9, New Slovenia–Christian People's Party (NSi) 8, Democratic Party of Pensioners of Slovenia (DeSUS) 4, Slovene National Party (SNS) 4, and Youth Party of Slovenia (SMS) 4. The representatives of the Italian and Hungarian minorities have one seat each.

TABLE 26.3

Slovenian Communication Agencies by Turnover in 2002

Agency	Turnover in Million Euro
Pristop	15
S Team Ideas Group	14
Mayer Group	11
Studio Marketing J. W. Thompson	9
Futura DDB	9
Prestige Mythos	9
Luna	9
Formitas BBDO	7
Tovarna vizij	5
Votan Leo Burnett	5

Note. From *Marketing magazine*, "Agencije: promet v letih 2001 in 2000
in napoved za leto 2002," *Marketing magazine*, January 30, 2002.

Slovenia's proportional electoral system seems to produce coalition governments. Even though balloting during elections is not compulsory, Slovenia seems to have a high rate of voter turnout with participation of 83% in 1990, 86% in 1992, 73% in 1996 and 70% in 2000 (Lukšič, 2001, p. 43). Although the general feature of the Slovenian political system is that it is a parliamentary democracy with a proportional electoral system, it is specifically a corporativist system:

> Slovenian political culture contains strong elements of corporatism. A living being that organizes all the main concepts of the body politic and determines political behavior is the best metaphor for corporative political behavior. According to this concept, the state, politics and society are not and cannot be separated. It is because of the tradition of corporatism that the self-management system in its various ideological forms gained so much credence in Slovenia. The fundamental objective of the corporative culture is the survival of the nation because only through the survival of the nation can the lower or sub-communities survive and, indirectly, the individual as well.
>
> In terms of values in the corporative culture, the highest positions are reserved for the stability of the community, equality, unity, justice, solidarity, order and success.
>
> In terms of interest representation, a system of functional representation is being developed which is essentially a complex network of special interests and professional organizations (a better translation of the Slovenian word would be communities) that are incorporated into the political system in one way or another. Political parties are not accepted as an appropriate representative of social interests because of their inevitable politicization and subsequent distortion of authentic interests. During the course of their history, Slovenians have only rarely warmed to the notion of political parties, most recently during the period from 1989 to 1992. A general antipathy to party politics and to parliamentary government is an important ingredient of corporatism. Social alliances leading to consensus among the carriers of vital interests—such as labor unions and employers, physicians, farmers etc.—is one of the most sought-after values. The form of political activity is not as highly valued as its content. For this reason, legal culture does not play a significant role in corporative political culture. Legitimacy is considered far more important than legality. Moral and religious forms of reflection and practice also hold a privileged position in the corporative model while legal and scientific forms and practices are discriminated against on favor of the first two. (Lukšič, 2001, pp. 75–76)

TABLE 26.4

Formal Structure of the National Council

Representatives of employers	4
Representatives of employees	4
Representatives of farmers	2
Representative of craftsmen	1
Representative of free-lance professionals	1
Representative of universities and colleges	1
Representative of educational system	1
Representative of research activities	1
Representative of social security	1
Representative of health care	1
Representative of culture and sports	1
Representatives of local interests	22
Total	40

Note. From *The political system of the Republic of Slovenia: A primer*, 2001, by I. Lukšič (E. J. Debeljak, Trans.), Ljubljana: Znanstveno in publicistično središče.

The most visible feature of this is the second chamber of the parliament, known as the National Council, which is unique to the political systems of Western democracies. It is composed according to the principle of corporative representation (through special interest and professional organizations, like trade unions, employers' and farmers' organizations, universities and colleges, etc.) and its only foreign counterparts were the former Irish senate and the former senate of the Free State of Bavaria (Lukšič, 2001, p. 22). Table 26.4 gives the formal membership in the National Council.

In January 1992, the European Union (EU) officially recognized Slovenia as a sovereign nation and Slovenia became a permanent member of the United Nations in May 1992. In June 1996, the European Association Agreement was signed between the EU and Slovenia, and Slovenia presented its application for full EU membership. Slovenia is a member of Council of Europe, the World Bank, the International Monetary Fund, and the World Trade Organization (WTO). As already stated, on October 9, 2002, the European Commission recommended Slovenia for full membership in the European Union by 2004. A similar recommendation is expected in a few months to give Slovenia NATO membership.

The major influence of the political system to public relations practice is in operation of corporativist structures that favor negotiation and compromise over overt conflict. For example, employers and employees are obliged to talk, negotiate and compromise at micro, mezzo, and macro levels—within large companies employees are represented in supervisory boards and trade unions have special rights, there are general and special industry by industry collective negotiations on wages and terms of employment, and there is a tripartite system of government, employers, and employee negotiations at the national level. Similar formal structures exist in many other areas, including culture, public media, and so on, institutionalizing at least some relationship-building strategies of public relations.

Economic System

The economic strength of Slovenia is indicated in a statement by the BBC during its reporting of the European Commission's recommendation for Slovenia to become a member

TABLE 26.5
Slovenia's Competitiveness: Strengths and Challenges

Strengths
- Stable macroeconomic environment
- Well-educated labor force and fast expansion of higher education
- High female labor force participation rate
- Low corporate income taxation
- Excellent geographic location and connections
- Modern basic information technology infrastructure
- Developed public research capacities and quality of scientific research
- Availability of good health care services and broad coverage of social welfare system
- Biodiversity, forests, and water resources

Challenges for future development
- Structural reforms and reform of public administration
- High unemployment, inflation, and interest rates
- Low foreign direct investments
- Insufficient adult education
- Heavy tax burden on personal income and high social security contributions
- Low volume on Internet-based services
- Insufficient use of energy and low share of renewable energy resources
- Low co-operation between the private business sector and public research institutions
- Underdeveloped entrepreneurial culture
- High health and social welfare costs

Note. From *Benchmarking Slovenia: An evaluation of Slovenia's competitiveness, strengths, and weaknesses* (pp. 7–8), 2000, Ljubljana: Ministry of Economic Affairs, Republic of Slovenia.

of the European Union: "As the wealthiest country in eastern Europe, the former Yugoslav republic of Slovenia is the easiest new member for the Union to digest. As European Commission sources put it, with just 2 million people and living standards almost on a par with Greece or Portugal, it could join in a fortnight" (Vornic, 2002). Table 26.5 gives an overview of strengths and weaknesses of the Slovenian economy.

Slovenia is a small open market economy with a GDP of US $20 billion in 2000. From 1990 to 1999, the average annual growth rate in real GDP was 2.4%. Currently, the per capita GDP is US $10,000 originating from the service industry (58%), industries (38%, of which manufacturing is 28%), and agriculture (4%). The main export destinations are Germany, Italy, Croatia, Austria, and France (which are also the main origins of Slovenian imports). Slovenia spends 7.8% of its GDP on health and 5.7% on education (*Economist*, 2002, pp. 202–203). Table 26.6 gives an overview of the economy.

Legal System

Slovenia is a constitutional democracy with a division of powers between the executive, legislative and judiciary branches. The constitution states that judges are independent within the boundaries of the constitution and the law. Judges are elected by the National Assembly, which acts on the proposal by the 11-member Judicial Council. The country has one supreme court, 4 higher courts, 11 regional courts, and 44 district courts. There are also specialized courts that deal with matters relating to specific legal areas, such as a Court of Audit that controls state accounts, the government budget, and all of public

TABLE 26.6

An Overview of the Slovenian Economy

Population—mid-1999 (1000 persons)	1,985
Surface area (km^2)	20,720
GDP per capita 1998 in PPS (purchasing power standard)[a]	13,700
GDP per capita 1999 in PPS (purchasing power standard)	14,183
GDP per capita as % of EU15 average, 1998	68
GDP at current exchange rate (billion US$), 2000	20
Exports of goods and services as % of GDP, 1998	57
Imports of goods and services as % of GDP, 1998	58
EU share of total exports (%)	66
EU share of total imports (%)	69
Structure of value added by industry (1998), %	
Agriculture	4
Manufacturing	27
Other industries	10
Services	58
Employment by activities (1998), % share	
Agriculture and mining	7
Manufacturing	31
Other industries[b]	9
Market services	36
Non-market services	18
Proportion of employed persons (1999), %	63.3
Unemployment rate, registered (1999 est.), %	13.6
Unemployment rate, ILO (1999 est.), %	7.7
Investment rate, (1998), % of GDP	24
Investment rate, (1998), % of GDP, EU average	20
General government expenditure, (1998), % of GDP	44
Current account balance, (1999 est.), % of GDP	−2.9
External debt, (1998), million US$	4,959
Foreign exchange reserves, (1998), million US$	4,767
Gross public debt, (1998 est.), % of GDP	25

[a]GDP is expressed by Eurostat in an artificial currency called purchasing power standard (PPS) to enable correct comparison of goods and services produced by different countries.
[b]Other industries: electricity, gas, water, and construction.
ILO (International Labour Organization)
Note. From Republic of Slovenia, Ministry of Economic Affairs (p. 12), 2000; *Economist* (pp. 202–203), 2002.

expenditure. The Human Rights ombudsman is responsible for the protection of human rights and fundamental freedoms in relation to state bodies, local administrative bodies and all those with public jurisdiction (Možina & Resman, 2001, pp. 41–44).

The level of corruption in Slovenia is low compared with other Central and Eastern European countries and some member countries of the European Union. The Transparency International Corruption Perception Index in 1999 placed Slovenia at level 6. Slovenia ranked below Denmark, which was listed at level 10 denoting that it had the lowest corruption rate, and Finland (9.8). But Slovenia was above Belgium (5.8), Hungary (5.2),

Greece (4.9), Italy (4.7), the Czech Republic (4.6), and Poland (4.2) (*Republic of Slovenia*, Ministry of Economic Affairs, 2000, p. 17).

The Slovenian constitution protects the freedoms of speech and association, which can be taken as the legal protection of public relations activities. However, the protection of commercial speech is limited and there exist many restrictions related to the promotion of certain services (e.g. legal, medical), products (e.g., alcohol, drugs, tobacco), and targets (e.g., minors). These are changing as Slovenia harmonizes its legislation with that governing the members of the European Union (so-called *acquis communitaire*) in preparation for entry in the EU.

The constitution also contains a clause on the right to information, which is to be operationalized in the newly proposed freedom of information law. Media legislation is extensive and among other things guarantees not only the rights of journalists (guaranteeing them privileged access to information from public bodies), but also of media audiences (a right to correction of wrong information and a right to publish a response). A special law regulates the operation of the public radio and television systems (including its finances based on compulsory subscription fees). There are many other pieces of legislation that affect the practice of public relations in Slovenia: consumer, financial, government, internal, and media relations are all referred to in specific pieces of legislation. Consumer relations are affected with clauses referring to competition, commercial communication regarding specific products (alcohol, drugs, tobacco), informational rights of consumers, and so on. Financial relations are affected by clauses on transparency of financial markets, protection of small shareholders, operation of the stock exchange, and so on. Government relations are affected by clauses on elections and electoral campaigns, organization of civil service, and freedom of information, among others. Employee relations are affected by clauses on informational rights of employees and their representatives, their representation in company supervisory boards, and so on. Although it is impossible to say that any of those pieces of legislation was adopted with public relations profession in mind, they all do affect public relations practice and a professional consulting and execution in the filed of public relations in Slovenia is impossible without a thorough understanding of the regulatory framework.

Activism

Although it has fewer than 2 million inhabitants, Slovenia has more than 14,724 registered nongovernment organizations (NGOs) of which approximately 10,000 are active to varying degrees (Rončević, 2002, p. 62). The majority of these NGO's are founded around specific interests and professions. They form the backbone of Slovenian corporativism:

> A substantial segment of these so-called interest groups had been acknowledged as vital and important to the state and has been elevated to a special status and institutionalized in the National Council. Following an almost identical process, many interest groups are also represented on the board of RTV, Slovenia's national broadcasting company. The specific interests of employers and employees are separately organized or institutionalized within a social partnership system. Only labor unions representatives are allowed to negotiate with employers and the state on behalf of employees. There are 31 such labor unions. (Lukšič, 2001, pp. 54–55)

In addition to having organized labor, Slovenia also has three large associations that bring together employers: the Chamber of Commerce and Industry, the Association of

Employers, and the Trade Chamber. The past decade also has seen special interest groups actively participating in political elections and having a voice in the legislature. For example, the Green Party focused on environmental issues in the previous National Assembly, while the present Assembly has representations from the Youth Party and the Pensioners Party. Besides all of the interest formally represented in the National Council, there are also 31 registered religious organizations.

It is safe to say that corporativism strongly affects the nature of activism in Slovenia. In the 1980s, the implosion of Yugoslavia and its socialism in the country brought to the surface many so-called social movements that championed causes such as the protection of human rights, the environment, and need for pacifism. The majority of these special interests are currently manifested through formal (coorporativist) channels. Yet, there remain some permanent, but not corporativist activist groups such as the anarchist and anti-globalist factions. Activism also often appears at local levels in reaction to en emerging local issue, but it tends to channel itself into regular formal structures of corporativist social organization. This has an important consequence for public relations practice, because it directly links public relations to formal channels of social interaction.

CULTURE

Currently, there exists only one study linking Slovenian culture with public relations (Verčič, L. Grunig, & J. E. Grunig, 1996, pp. 52–56). Although reported in 1996, this study was conducted in 1993, and was based on lengthy personal interviews by North American researchers with three Slovenian practitioners. The authors acknowledged the many limitations of their study, yet remained convinced of its value stating that it was very helpful because "short of a direct cultural encounter with Slovenians or a deep understanding of the cultural roots of that society, scholars from other parts of the world should gain a useful understanding of the way Slovenians as a cultural group view the universe and thus develop a set of rules and behavior" (p. 50).

The theoretical underpinning for Verčič, L. Grunig, and J. E. Grunig's (1996) study was Hofstede's (1980) work on the dimensions of societal culture, which are described in the first chapter of this volume. Verčič, L. Grunig, and J. E. Grunig (1996, p. 56) found that Slovenian culture was high on individualism, power distance, and uncertainty avoidance. They also stated that "the [Slovenian] culture, which had been relatively feminine, is becoming increasingly masculine with the advent of capitalism." So far as societal culture shapes public relations (Sriramesh & White, 1992), the public relations practiced in Slovenia closely resembles that practiced in Austria and other countries in Central Europe.

The central cultural value in Central Europe is "quality of life," which usually refers to a balance between work and family (or leisure). From this balance is derived a clear division between public and private life, which gives a high protection of privacy even to public figures such as politicians and top corporate managers. On the other hand, this same division supports hard work and an authoritarian corporate culture (we are equal and free after work and outside organizations, but not within them), which complements corporativist political structures (favoring negotiations and compromise among equals—but on a collective, not an individual level). The final result of the "quality of life" doctrine is a hierarchy of values often expressed as health, family, and wealth (in that order). All public relations activities need to be adjusted to this fact of *de facto* dualism between public (social, collectivist) and private (individual alone and in family).

THE MEDIA AND PUBLIC RELATIONS

As described in Chapter 1, it is very important to understand the media system in a nation to understand the public relations practiced in that country. Splichal (1999) noted that "whatever the direction of their influence, the mass media represent the most effective influence system in contemporary society" (p. 8). Slovenia has five national TV channels. TV Slovenija 1 and TV Slovenija 2 belong to the public broadcast system RTV Slovenija. POP TV, Kanal A, and TV 3 are private TV channels. Slovenia has 80 radio programs, of which 6 are national (with Radio Slovenija—Program A1, 1. program, Radio Slovenija—Val 202, 2. program, and Radio Slovenija—Program ARS, 3. program, belonging to the public service RTV Slovenija, and the following being the remaining three: Radio Ognjišče, RGL, and Radio SI), 42 regional and 32 local stations.

Currently, 914 newspapers and magazines are regularly published of which 183 belong to companies, associations, societies, and political parties, and 138 to the trade press. A further 91 are local or regional, 53 concentrate on business, finance, and entrepreneurship, 48 have an entertainment focus, and 47 are education oriented. Of the remaining, 38 focus on general interest and current affairs, 35 on issues that interest children, youth or students, and 35 focus on sports and cars. In addition, 32 publications focus on religion and spiritual culture, 30 are oriented toward family issues, 15 are about home, nature, and pets, and 15 are regular supplements to major print editions. A further 11 are oriented toward computers, 9 focus on gastronomy, restaurants, and tourism, 9 deal with health, 7 with music, film, radio, and TV, and 2 focus on border sciences (Mediana, 2002).

The constitution of Slovenia protects freedom of media and expression. In just over a decade, the nation's media system has been significantly affected by the sea changes in policy such as the liberalization of the print media market, privatization of the media, and the introduction law to regulate new media, media monopolization, and commercialization (Hrvatin & Miloslavljević, 2001, p. 7).

Media Control

After studying the issue of media control in Slovenia, Hrvatin & Milosavljević (2001) gave the following overview:

> The Slovene media market is small, so relatively modest financial resources suffice to establish control over it (especially in comparison with the sums involved in the takeovers and acquisitions in other European countries). Before the process of media privatization got underway, the Slovene state expected the invasion of large European and American corporations, similar to what has happened in some other countries in transition. One decade later it is possible to conclude instead that a small number of local owners with stakes in numerous affiliated companies control the major part of the Slovene market. The concentration is still in progress, while cross-ownership ties remain unchanged. It is obvious that the state, or rather its supervising institutions, do not have any mechanism (and no interest) to introduce order into this field. (Hrvatin & Milosavljević, p. 7)

Four big media companies control 90% of the daily newspaper market in the country. Three of them (*Delo, Dnevnik*, and *Večer*), have their roots in the previous socialist system but were privatized through employee (internal) buyouts and internal distribution of shares after the democratization of Slovenia. The fourth daily newspaper, *Slovenske novice,* was established as a partial bypass company of the employees of *Delo* (who established it as a separate and privately owned company using the intangible assets of their primary employer, *Delo,* to form another newspaper and company to which some of them later moved, while others are still employed in *Delo* but participate in profits of *Slovenske novice* as owners).Three other dailies that started after 1990, *Slovenec, Republika,* and *Jutranjik,* closed down because of poor revenue.

This specific form of newspaper privatization was based on several assumptions. The first was that privatization was a safeguard against government intervention into editorial decisions. Next was the notion that employee (internal) buyout was a protection against foreign takeovers. Article 39 of the Mass Media Act of 1994 also prescribed a dispersed ownership of the media to prevent monopolistic practices (Hrvatin & Milosavljević, 2001, pp. 10 and 17). The final result of these practices was that at the end of 1990s, media ownership on the country consisted of a small number of domestic owners except in television where one American and one Scandinavian corporation seized the two largest commercial TV stations and merged into one (Hrvatin & Milosavljević, 2001, p. 97). In Slovenia, media ownership is balanced by a strong Journalist Society that vigorously protects the professional independence of its members and advocates the profession's focus on public service.

The present structure of media ownership is unstable and it will probably change after Slovenia's entry into the EU (2004). Its current consequences for public relations practice are expressing themselves in often conflicting situations between media owners and journalists. While these conflicts have positive consequences in balancing the powers of both sides, they make the life of public relations practitioners working in media relations very complicated.

Media Outreach

Slovenia can legitimately be called a media-rich society because 97.6% of households own a color television set and 98.6% own at least one radio (Mediana, 2001). In 2001, 48.4% of all households owned a computer. In 2001, the average daily media outreach among the Slovenian population aged 12–65 years was: 81% for television, 68% for radio, 44% for daily newspapers, 32% for outdoor media, and 27% for newspapers and magazines (Cati, 2001). Of the 600,000 Internet users in Slovenia (defined as those who have ever used the Internet) 16% can be classified as daily users (RIS, 2002). It is important to recognize that in Slovenia one can simultaneously use the mass media and the corporativist structure of nongovernmental organizations to reinforce messages in an institutionalized two-step model of public communication (impersonal mass media first and personal influence in corporativist institutions later or vice versa). Taken from this perspective, it can be said that media outreach in Slovenia is practically total.

Media Access

Sriramesh and Verčič (2001, p. 115) stated that "the flip side of media outreach is media access." Although Slovenia has reached media saturation in that it is possible to reach everybody through the mass media, it does not mean that every Slovenian has access to use the media for his or her own publicity purposes. Although the media law gives Slovenians a legal basis on which to seek the right to a public voice, such access is not very common. Currently there exist no studies on the issue of media access from the point of view of public relations in Slovenia. For that reason any conclusions on the topic can only be drawn from other fields of interest that were empirically tested. Based both on the data on media control and on the character of the political system, one can conclude that media access belongs to groups and networks that possess other forms of power (economic or political) which they can transform into media access. Such groups typically are different businesses, special interest, and professional, and political organizations acting alone or in coalitions. Public relations in such circumstances becomes 'relationship management' in the literal meaning of the term. Media access in Slovenia can be said to be general, yet mediated by corporativist structures.

From its emergence in 1990 until today, public relations in Slovenia has become an institutionalized practice that attracts many people and resources. Both social culture and the political system have produced a favorable environment for the development of public relations–like activities. Further impetus for the industry is expected when Slovenia becomes a full member of the EU. While professionalization of public relations is still inadequate by theoretical and normative standards, it can be said to be on pair with the best one can find around the world.

CASE STUDY

Several case studies from Slovenia are available in English. Ašanin Gole and Verčič (2000) published 33 cases from the country that have received international awards. Drapal, Verčič, Peterlin, and Ilešič (2002) have presented a case explaining the successful lobbying of institutions of the EU by Slovenia. The case study presented here is a description of the public communication campaign "Raising environmental awareness in Slovenia" that received the United Nations Award given by the International Public Relations Association (IPRA) in cooperation with the UN. Only one such award is given each year to a project that best meets the working guidelines of the United Nations in the domain of environmental protection, and is fully documented by Verčič and Pek-Drapal (2002).

Problem

In an effort to combat air pollution, the Government of Slovenia established the Environmental Development Fund (Eco-Fund) in 1995. One of the objectives of the fund was to provide low-interest loans to households to help them convert their old dirty heating systems to more environmentally friendly modern systems. During the first year of the project (between June 1995 and May 1996), only 117 households applied for loans under this program. Clearly, there was a need to induce greater participation in the program.

In 1996, the European Commission, through its Phare program, issued a public tender for the 'Pilot testing Phase of the World Bank Air Pollution Abatement Programme.' A Slovenian consortium of four consultancies (ITEO, Pristop Communications, Sistemi Shift, and E-Net) was awarded the contract. The total value of the project was ECU 400,000, of which ECU 154,000 were designated for the public communication campaign. The communication campaign began in May 1996. The initial month was designated as the inception phase, the next 11 months as the implementation phase, and the 13th month as the finalization and evaluation phase.

Formative Research

The formative research consisted of individual and group interviews with the management and staff of Eco-Fund and personal interviews with some members of the target audience (including some enabling organizations such as commercial banks that administered the loan scheme). This was followed by a poll of a representative quota sample of 1,163 households from the population of 645,000 households in Slovenia. J. Grunig's (1997) situational analysis of publics was used for identifying the willingness among the population to enter into a dialogue with the project administrators on the key topics of the project. One important finding of this research was that retirees were very interested in the conversion of their heating systems from coal to gas. It was also found that children were prepared to offer financial help to their elderly parents to cover the costs of conversion.

Campaign Goals

The above formative research enabled the project team to set the following five goals for the communication campaign:

- to train and increase communicative capability of the Eco-Fund management and staff;
- to increase awareness about the loan program in the target population;
- to establish consciousness that it is necessary to convert to environmentally friendly heating systems;
- to establish a mutual understanding and strategic partnership between Eco-Fund and their stakeholders;
- to influence the target population and other enabling groups to do the necessary preparatory work, apply for the loans, take the loans, and convert the heating systems.

Stakeholders

Five groups were identified as critical for the success of the program:

- people with old and environmentally unfriendly heating systems needing conversion;
- enabling groups (banks, contractors, natural gas, and district heating distributors);
- media;
- energy consultants and professional associations;
- political entities (Ministry of Environment, pressure groups, etc.).

Messages

Key messages consisted of:

- financial arguments (favorable loans);
- environmental arguments (to convert to environmentally friendly systems);
- convenience arguments (new energy supplies, e.g., natural gas, as reliable, cost efficient, and comfortable);

- enabling arguments (promoting the need for partnership between all organizations that were incorporated into the program).

Tactical Plan

The following were the key elements of the tactical plan:

- a launch "open day";
- training and seminars for Eco-Fund management and staff;
- advertising;
- live radio talk shows;
- media relations;
- a brochure;
- a toll-free telephone number;
- a national round table on air pollution abatement.

Outcome

In the 10 months of the campaign, the number of loans increased from earlier low take-up level of only 117 to 1896. At the end of the program an evaluative research was conducted and the results were fed back to the Eco-Fund.

CONCLUSION

The case we have presented is typical for public relations in Slovenia in that it includes relationship management in its corporativist version (gaining cooperation of many, including political stakeholders without which any project will fail), high managerial sophistication in the field of public relations conceptualization and research (such as the use of Grunig's situational theory in this practical case), straightforward technical execution, and a professional attitude (that is demonstrated in the final feedback to the client at the end of the project that has value only in future use by the client itself). It is worth noting at the end of this discussion that the public relations industry in Slovenia itself must contain elements of corporativism (with a relatively strong association—PRSS being its visible representation). This chapter has only outlined them. A study on the consequences of corporativism on public relations development remains a project for future research.

REFERENCES

Aberg, L. (1990). Theoretical model and praxis of total communications. *International Public Relations Review* *13*(2): 13–17.

Ašanin Gole, P., & Verčič, D. (Eds.). (2000). *Teorija in praksa slovenskih odnosov z javnostmi/Slovenian public relations theory and practice*. Ljubljana: Slovensko društvo za odnose z javnostmi—Public Relations Society of Slovenia.

Cati (2001). *Medijski Monitor*. Ljubljana: Raziskovalna Družba Cati.

Cutlip, S. M., & Center, A. H. (1960). *Effective public relations: Pathways to public favor* (2nd ed.). Englewood Cliffs, NJ: Prentice Hall.

Cutlip, S. M., Center, A. H., & Broom, G. M. (2000). *Effective public relations* (8th ed.). Upper Saddle River, NJ: Prentice Hall.

Dozier, D. D., Grunig, L. A., & Grunig, J. E. (1995). *Manager's guide to excellence in public relations and communication management.* Mahwah, NJ: Lawrence Erlbaum Associates.

Drapal, A., Verčič, D., Peterlin, I., & Ilešič, T. (2002). Slovenia and the EU: An anti-dumping case. In R. Pedler (Ed.), *European Union lobbying: Changes in the arena* (pp. 143–151). Houndmills: Luk Palgrave.

Economist (2002). *Pocket world in Figures, 2002 Edition.* London: Economist.

Economist (1997a, January 3). Slovenia: Canny survivor. *Economist,* pp. 63–65.

Economist (1997b, November 22). A survey of business in Eastern Europe: Eastern Europe recast itself. *Economist,* (Suppl).

Gruban, B., Maksimovič, M., Verčič, D., & Zavrl, F. (1990). *ABC PR: odnosi z javnostmi na prvi pogled.* Ljubljana: Tiskovno središče Ljubljana.

Gruban, B., Verčič, D., & Zavrl F., (1994). *Odnosi z javnostmi v Sloveniji: raziskovalno poročilo 1994/ Public relations in Slovenia: research report 1994.* Ljubljana: Pristop.

Gruban, B., Verčič, D., & Zavrl, F. (1997). *Pristop k odnosom z javnostmi.* Ljubljana: Pristop.

Gruban, B., Verčič, D., & Zavrl, F. (Eds.) (1998). *Preskok v odnose z javnostmi: Zbornik o slovenski praksi v odnosih z javnostmi.* Ljubljana: Pristop.

Grunig, J. E. (1997). A situational theory of publics: Conceptual history, recent challenges and new research. In D. Moss, T. Macmanus, & D. Verčič (Eds.), *Public Relations Research: An international perspective* (pp. 3–48).

Grunig, J. E., Grunig, L. A., & Verčič, D. (1996). The status of public relations in Slovenia: Extending the IABC's Excellence project. Paper presented to the Global Conference on Education for the 21st Century. Association for the Advancement of Policy, Research, and Development in the Third World, Cancun, Mexico. November, 21–23.

Grunig, J. E., & Hunt, T. (1984). *Managing public relations.* New York: Holt, Rinehart & Winston.

Grunig, L. A., Grunig, J. E., & Verčič D. (1997). Are the IABC's excellence principles generic? Comparing Slovenia and the United States, the United Kingdom, and Canada. Paper presented at the IABC Research Foundation at the 1997 International Association of Business Communicators Conference, Los Angeles. June, 9–11.

Grunig, L. A., Grunig, J. E., & Verčič, D. (1998) Are the IABC's excellence principles generic? Comparing Slovenia and the United States, the United Kingdom, and Canada. *Journal of Communication Management,* 2(4), 335–356.

Grunig, L. A., & Verčič, D. (1998). PR in Slovenia: Doing public relations in a small country in transition in Eastern Europe. In J. Felton (Ed.), *Crises in Wired World: How Does PR Handle the Instant Transmission of Problems Globally? Proceedings of International Symposium 2.* Gainesville, FL: Institute of Public Relations, University of Florida.

Hofstede, G. (1980). *Culture's consequences: International differences in work-related values.* Beverly Hills, CA: Sage.

Hrvatin, S. B., & Milosavljević, M. (2001). *Media policy in Slovenia in the 1990s: Regulation, privatization, concentration and commercialization of the media.* (O. Vuković, Trans.). Ljubljana: Peace Institute.

Hundhausen, C. (1969). *Public relations: Theorie und Systematik.* Berlin: de Gruyter.

Lukšič, I. (2001). *The political system of the Republic of Slovenia: A primer* (E. J. Debeljak, Trans.). Ljubljana: Znanstveno in publicistično središče.

Marketing magazine (2002, January 30). Agencije: promet v letih 2001 in 2000 in napoved za leto 2002.

Mediana (2001). *Mediana BGP.* Ljubljana: Inštitut za raziskovanje medijev, Mediana.

Mediana (2002). *Preglednica slovenskih medijev.* Ljubljana: Inštitut za raziskovanje medijev, Mediana.

Možina, S., & Resman, A. (2001). *Facts About Slovenia,* (3rd ed.). Ljubljana: Government of the Republic of Slovenia, Public Relations and Media Office.

Newsom, D., VanSlyke Turk, J., & Kruckeberg, D. (1996). *This is PR: The realities of public relations,* (6th ed.). Belmont, CA: Wadsworth.

Republic of Slovenia, Ministry of Economic Affairs (2000). *Benchmarking Slovenia: An evaluation of Slovenia's competitiveness, strengths and weaknesses.* Ljubljana: Ministry of Economic Affairs, Republic of Slovenia.

Ris (2002). *Research on Internet in Slovenia.* Retrieved on June 15, 2002, from http://www.ris.org

Rončević, B. (2002). Nekaj nastavkov za sociološko obravnavo nevladnih organizacij. In D. Jelovac (Ed.), *Jadranje po nemirnih vodah menedžmenta nevladnih organizacij* (pp. 45–70). Ljubljana and Koper: Radio Študent, Študentska organizacija Univerze v Ljubljani & Visoka šola za management v Kopru.

Ruler, B. van, & Verčič, D. (2002). *The Bled manifesto on public relations*. Ljubljana: Pristop Communications.

Splichal, S. (1999). Ownership, regulation and socialization: Rethinking the principles of democratic media. *The Public* 6(2): 5–24.

Sriramesh, K., & Verčič, D. (2001). International public relations: A framework for future research. *Journal of Communication Management* 6(2), 103–117.

Sriramesh, K., & White, J. (1992). Societal culture and public relations. In J. Grunig (Ed.), *Excellence in public relations and communication management* (pp. 597–614). Hillsdale, NJ: Lawrence Erlbaum Associates.

Statistični urad Republike Slovenije (2002). Popis 2002: Tabelarni pregled—Slovenija. *Retrieved October 10, 2002, from http://www.sigov.si/popis2002/prvi_rezultati_slovenija.html*

Theaker, A. (2001). *Public relations handbook*. London and New York: Routledge.

Thurow, L. (1993). *Head to head: The coming economic battle among Japan, Europe, and America*. London: Nicholas Brealey.

Verčič, D. (1993a, December). Excellence project studied in Slovenia. *Communication World* (pp. 9–10).

Verčič, D. (1993b) Privatisation fuels PR growth. In R. Sarginson (Ed.), *Hollis Europe: the directory of European public relations & PR networks* (pp. 389–390). London: Hollis Directories Ltd.

Verčič, D. (2002). Public relations research and education in Slovenia. In S. Averbeck & S. Wehmeier (Eds.), *Kommunikationswissenschaft und public relations in Osteuropa: Arbeitsberichte* (pp. 157–173). Leizig: Leipziger Universitätsverlag.

Verčič, D., & Ažman, A. (2002). Communication between government and citizens in Slovenia: A report & recommendations prepared under the under the auspices of the United Nations Development Programme Regional Bureau for Eastern Europe and the CIS UNDP RBEC sub-regional project RER/01/003/A08/13, "Improving Communication from Government to Societies." (Unpublished Research Report.)

Verčič, D., & Grunig, J. E. (2000). The origins of public relations theory in economics and strategic management. In D. Moss, D. Verčič, & G. Warnaby (Eds.), *Perspectives on Public Relations Research* (pp. 9–58). London and New York: Routledge.

Verčič, D., Grunig, L. A., & Grunig J. E. (1993). Global and specific principles of public relations: evidence from Slovenia. Paper presented to The International Conference on The State of Education and Development: New Directions. Association for the Advancement of Policy, Research, and Development in the Third World, Cairo, Egypt. November, 22–25.

Verčič, D., Grunig, L. A., & Grunig, J. E. (1996). Global and specific principles of public relations: evidence from Slovenia. In H. M. Culbertson & N. Chen (Eds.), *International public relations: A comparative analysis* (pp. 31–65). Mahwah, NJ: Lawrence Erlbaum Associates.

Verčič, D., & Pek-Drapal, D. (2002). Raising environmental awareness in Slovenia: A public communication campaign. In D. Moss & B. DeSanto (Eds.), *Public relations cases: International perspectives* (pp. 167–179). London & NewYork: Routledge.

Verčič, D., Razpet, A., Dekleva, S., & Šlenc, M. (2000). International public relations and the Internet: Diffusion and linkages. *Journal of communication management* 5(2): 125–137.

Verčič, D., van Ruler, B., Bütschi, G., & Flodin, B. (2001). On the definition of public relations: a European view. *Public Relations Review* 27(4): 373–387.

Verčič, D., & van Ruler, B. (2002). Public relations and communication management in the Netherlands and Slovenia: A comparative analysis. Paper presented to the Public Relations Division, 52nd Annual Conference of the International Communication Association: Reconciliation Through Communication, Seoul, Korea, July 15–19.

Verčič, D., Zavrl, F., & Rijavec, P. (2002). *Odnosi z mediji*. Ljubljana: GV Založba.

Vornic, A. (2002). The EU's uneven new contingent. *BBC News, World edition.* Retrieved January 24, 2003 from http://news.bbc.co.uk/1/hi/world/europe/2314659.stm

CHAPTER

27

CHALLENGES OF REVIVED DEMOCRACIES: THE RISE OF PUBLIC RELATIONS IN ROMANIA

ADELA ROGOJINARU

INTRODUCTION

Public relations stands as a new discipline whose recent past and hybrid nature make it vulnerable against old social sciences. In countries like Romania, the revival of democracy after December 1989 created the context in which all developments in the communication field became embedded in the overall process of social reconstruction. Similar to the evolution of species according to which the ontogeny repeats the phylogeny, local developments repeated global and historical development in the public relations field: one could notice the steady movement from press agency function to information services, a process which will hopefully become completely integrated in the corporate vision and generate symmetrical strategic communication of various organizations (Dozier, Grunig and Grunig, 1995).

In the absence of accurate records, the early moments of public relations in Romania remain one of the post-communist legends. We have been practising it for about fifteen years in both corporate and academic contexts. Attempts to modernise public communication were made spontaneously in the early 1990s, as part of the whole movement towards transparency and public sincerity. "Telling the truth" has been seen as the capital commandment of those times. Concepts of "truth" and "convenience" have been eventually revisited and public communicators learnt to balance prudence and full disclosure in front of their publics.

This chapter looks at the state of public relations in Romania and draws readers' attention to some current tendencies. It presents a reasonable combination of conceptual insights and journalist opinions. The latter views have been taken into account for their anecdotal capacity to capture some of the important public releases on public relations of the last two years. The chapter also tries to link public relations practice in the country to socio-cultural variables.

PROFESSIONALISATION OF PUBLIC RELATIONS: CONTEXT AND HISTORY

Redefinition of Private vs. Public Favours Public Relations

In a few words, we can describe Romania as a country situated in south-eastern Europe, with a population of 21.6 million (UN, 2006), and an area of 238,391 sq km (92,043 sq miles). Romanian (a Romance language) is the official language and Christian Orthodoxy is the major religion. The capital city is Bucharest, also known as "little Paris," for its resemblance in architecture and its urban atmosphere famous in the 1930s. Romania joined the European Union (EU) in January 2007, together with its southern neighbour, Bulgaria, raising the EU membership to 27.

After the fall of communism, in December 1989, Romanian society experienced progressive transitions of at least two kinds: on the one hand, an economic adjustment to free market, and on the other, a complex social, cultural, educational and moral process of democratization. The main challenge in transition countries is that groups at risk are mostly affected by skill mismatch. Patterns of exclusion are linked not only to the labour market, but also to public participation and individual involvement in public life. Social transition basically contributes to changing different social strata and moral order. It thus creates a polarization of goals, needs and expectations. Romanian society faced the occurrence of these phenomena of polarization, which produced the emergence of the so-called transition publics. The power shift created by transition, which led to political polarization, progressively transformed the role of the State versus the private sector. The economic polarization has produced effects of disproportionate mass consumption, including uncritical media exploitation (Zamfir, 2004).

The ambiguous usage and views related to State versus market, and "public" versus "private" accentuated the disruptive process and forced the collective society, ruled by common ideologies, to transform into an individualistic one, ruled by diverted interests. Consequently, private-led viewpoints have emerged in a hectic way in setting up agendas and imposed single, short-term public issues (or "hot issues"). Replicas of mass media favoured private non-regulated issues against public regulated matters, and ended by introducing a certain state of confusion at the level of public opinion. At this point, it might be interesting to note that mass media were not clearly prepared to deal with large complex issues. On the one hand, transition media in Romania adopted a prophetic role and manifested a moralistic simplification of the news, centred on the feeling of guilt and strong accusation addressed to central power (cf. Zamfir, 2004, pp. 152–157). The current accentuation of niche orientation in media should be considered not only a result of specialisation, but also a tendency for news simplification. Different causes may be related to the partisan role of mass media in the transition societies and to their fuzzy idea about raising public issues, based upon which there is no clear distinction between "opinionated" views and "public reasoning" positions. Although party newspapers or media quickly disappeared in Romania during the first years of transition, self-declared "national" or "information" press continues to take sides in open or hidden ways (radio channels are the exception) (Vasilescu, 2001, pp. 165–166). On the other hand, under the global influence of the popular culture, the same media manifest a clear inclination towards show industries, which are considered the sale drivers, especially in TV and tabloid press. Transition mass-media shaped the public sphere by means of hot news and associated "hot-issue publics."

In the given context, it is expected that the role of public relations might increase compared to conventional media as regards the effective treatment of the multifaceted issues, since public relations has always assisted organisations in tailoring public themes and cases for multiple publics. In the post-communist controversy related to private vs. public issues, it seems that public relations (if well practised!) gained some positive features in supporting the second one, while mass media (public channels included!) remain the fervent partisans of the private market and marketing exercise.

Development of Public Relations in Synchrony with Global Practices

Any transition economy implies a deregulation of the social tissue at all levels, especially at the grassroots level. One may wonder if this change is also important for setting up new rules of conduct in public relations or in other communication practices like advertising or direct marketing. We might say that practices like corporate public relations are global and not affected by any other ideological distortions. However, as stated in the previous paragraphs, the nature of practice and the theory of practice in transitional public relations (Ławniczak, 2005) could be better understood by making clearer the characteristics of the *public sphere* (Habermas, 1998) of the society in transition and, subsequently, the specificity of the *communication sphere* (Noelle-Neumann, 2004) of such society. Although phenomena of transition generate various deregulations at social and economic levels, it is difficult to say to what extent such deregulations represent the decisive factor in setting distinct or local models of public communication. General models of public communication, based on persuasion and classic rhetorical structures, do not take into account the implication of "transition" contexts. Actually, the rise of the public relations process (or any "relation building" process) is a response to an emergence of a transitional state of any given structure or society.

We could therefore deduce that the growing avidity for communication of today's publics in Romania was determined by the state of fuzziness that corresponds to any radical change, and, by hypothesis, publicity first, then public relations, have been considered instruments to respond to and convey the fuzzy institutional state into an articulated one. This function corresponding to the approaches of corporate culture and communication sustains a holistic model of public relations (cf. the structuration model and perspective discussed by Witmer, 2006). Although such statement looks hazardous and does not make a real thesis, we could postulate that public relations and publicity have a compensatory function and assist publics in their social recovery within disrupted societies. However, this very statement is challenged by the fact that the media and popular culture produce the same effect in the present post-modern societies. Do public relations and publicity at large introduce deceptively or genuinely communication norms and rules in social structures in which such norms or rules never exist? If so, the state of such social disruption is general and not specific to post-communist states (Fukuyama, 1999) and for that reason the compensatory function of public relations is general. To end this apparent controversy on the role of transition, we conclude that from our viewpoint the transition period served as a good context for the boost in public relations, but it has not created a variant of public relations much different from the international practice.

As far as the national market is concerned, we are indeed confronted in Romania with a communication market dominated by two phenomena: the great expansion of *telecommunications* (mobile phone operations) and the *advertising boom*. Several factors could be considered the main reasons for that, among which are:

- *Increased (disproportionate) consumption* (large divide between consumption and productive investment).

- *Disparities in media consumption, especially electronic media*: in 2007 TV continues to dominate both the news and advertising markets, about 34–25 percent announced increase compared to 2006 (*Media Fact Book*, 2007); disparities are caused mostly by geographic disparities and residence, e.g. urban consumption runs the course for Internet.

- *Fluctuating/disloyal consumption* (traditionalist/past-oriented or experimentalist lifestyles dominate Romanian consumer behaviour (Iliescu and Petre, 2004, pp. 193–199).

- *Orientation towards global and local brands*, which results in amplified visual and anecdotal orientation, based on special events and TV shows.

Based on these four tendencies, we could categorize the publics/media consumers into eight derived opposite styles (Rogojinaru, 2005b). They are either based on consumption orientation: *functional consumers* (value oriented) vs. *ostentatious consumers* (class oriented) or differentiated by media attainment: *visual* vs. *electronic*. Print media audiences tend to be regrouped into the above categories, and television remains the "super- medium" of all media (Drăgan, 2003, pp. 43–49). Publics also show dispersed inclination for loyal/consistent consumption: *long term* (planned) vs. *short term* (short term consumption, based on impulse acquisition caused by sales promotions and advertising), and manifest brand responses and consumption values that are based on *subtle* (global oriented) vs. *acquisitive* (niche oriented).

Within such polarized configuration of publics and opinion formation, the role of public relations is often called back to the very prime functions of public relations such as *public information* or *publicity* (Grunig and Hunt, 1984). As reflected in the service portfolio of public relations agencies, the largest institutional capacity of Romanian public relations is directed toward event management, media planning and publicity (offline as well as online). Strategic counseling or crisis management, once atypical and not evident, has become visible in the agencies' portfolio during the last few years, even though corporate crises tend to be prevented and treated by means of integrated forms of marketing communication rather than by using single public relations techniques: over 80 percent of the areas covered by reported public relations activities are directed to marketing and branding (Daedalus Consulting, 2006). Corporate public relations, which is mostly departmental, is more focused on media tracking, media coordination, reputation management and usually on social and charity work. The Corporate Social Responsibility (CSR) function (see Pratt, 2006) is either included in the social portfolio (together with sponsorship and charity work) or entrusted to corporate foundations to create private-public partnership. Significant steps are made in the area of internal communication and internal social responsibility, due to the high fluctuation of human resources (e.g. the article on safety at work campaign of Petrom, "Siguranţa muncii, mereu în atenţia Petrom," 2007).

Early Forms of Publicity and Political Propaganda Preceded Public Relations

Petcu (2002) points out that although public commercial announcements were made before the industrial period, being notified during the Middle Ages of the Romanian Provinces as part of the commercial regulations by various country rulers ("domnitori"), the modern era of publicity in Romania is to be placed at the beginning of the 19th century. The first modern magazines and newspapers like *Curierul Naţional* and *Albina Românească* included in their pages public announcements and commercial ads. The first media for publicity were newspapers in small format and news-sheets, flyers or leaflets and posters. In this emergent stage, news and publicity presented a blended format and style, the correlated expression of the press in those times being "to publicize for letting know." The first publicity agency was founded at 1880 by the merchant David Anania (Petcu, 2002, p. 57). He had expanded his business into outdoor publicity and encouraged the expansion of the role of the press agents. Commerce and publicity had been allied from the beginning; therefore the motto of the Commercial Almanac (*Almanahul Comercial*) would be "Announcements and advertising are the soul of the commerce." The number of agencies (local and foreign) continued to grow in the first part of the 20th century. The use of testimonials and pseudo-testimonials for endorsement had been included in the promotion of products. From 1928, radio announcements and publicity became important, and electric identification signboards appeared on the facades of stores in Bucharest by 1930 (Petcu, 2002, p. 69). The commercial publicity continued to expand in the Romanian public sphere between 1930 and 1940, a decade which was considered the best years for industrial welfare and commercial publicity of modern Romania before communism (Petcu, 2002, p. 89).

Due to the vicissitudes of Romanian foreign policy during World War II, the end of the war found the Romanian democratic forces and the Romanian monarch King Michael in a complicated diplomatic position of having gained separation from Berlin while sustaining independence from Moscow. Unluckily for Romanian diplomacy, the strategic contribution of the Soviet Union in defeating German and Axis forces resulted eventually in most of Eastern Europe, including Romania, entering the Soviet Union's sphere of influence. Romanian historians outline the biased political attitude of the Allies (USA and Great Britain) in defending the Romanian democratic cause during the negotiations of the Ministries of External Affairs in Moscow 16–26 December 1945 (cf. Constantiniu, 2002, pp. 436–437). The communist era in Romania commenced on 6 March 1945 with the first communist government of Dr. Petru Groza, followed by the abdication of King Michael, the proclamation of the Popular Republic of Romania on 30 December 1947, and the nationalization of industrial properties and collectivization of private rural land in 1948, based on the Soviet model. There followed a period of 45 years of monolithic party and national propaganda. Until its brutal termination in December 1989, the communist regime introduced numerous forms of social, economic and moral spiritual trauma in Romania.

A communist revisionism in the late 1960s and the beginning of the 1970s contributed to an illusory brief relaxation in the public sphere. Small announcements and basic informative publicity for goods of general consumption could be noticed, printed and heard (by radio diffusion). As for the propaganda, from the mid-1970s the political discourses of Ceaușescu became the reference for the whole public expression. Made in a rhetorical way in order to be memorised, invoked and textually repeated in all public and institutional meetings, the discourses were the heart of the public communication (Constantiniu, 2002, p. 486). Press was totally subjugated to the Communist Party and writers were encouraged to propagate the interpretation of the ideology of the "socialist humanism," which constituted a form of heroic illustration of the period. During the 1980s, the regime reached the maximum of its abuse and entered the beginning of its decline. Strengthening relations with China and North Korea confirmed the declared independence from Moscow of Ceaușescu, but condemned Romanian society to extinction. Print media were full of Ceaușescu's discourses and political declarations. Photographic expression was limited to pictorials of the Ceaușescu couple. TV was limited to two hours in the evening, mostly dedicated to news about Ceaușescu. Almost nobody watched, people preferred Bulgarian TV for films and entertainment. Besides Party news, radio did not transmit any other music than Romanian pop music and folklore. In Europe, Romanian dissidents regrouped in Munich around the independent radio station *Europa Liberă* (Free Europe, which had transmitted news from Munich since 1952). For Romanians at home, listening to dissident radio stations like Vocea Americii (Voice of America) in Washington or Europa Liberă was considered a felony and was strictly monitored by Securitate, the secret police.

During the communist period, education and training at tertiary level for political and public communication was offered in the Academia "Ştefan Gheorghiu," an institution subordinated to the Central Committee of the Romanian Communist Party. In its latest form and name, it was active from 1971 to 1989, but its foundation dates back to 1945. This political school (named after a respected leader of the Romanian labour and socialist movements in the first decade of the 20th century, Ştefan Gheorghiu), was defined as "the institution for training and upgrading of all staff ['cadre'] involved in party, state, economic, politic and ideological as well as civic activities" (*Mic Dicţionar Enciclopedic*, 1986, p. 6). The definition makes clear that all forms of management communication, including those applied by civic organisations, were a subject of regulated Communist Party training.

In the 1970s, publicity was however allowed and encouraged in the form of public announcements for commercial goods like home electronics, announcements for industrial services offered by main factories in the country or commercials for promoting healthy food items. The "visible hand" of the centrally planned economy had generated a peculiar practice of state controlled marketing. Unfortunately, even these public announcements gradually disappeared in the mid and late 1980s, being replaced by aggressive party propaganda.

After 1989, post-communist media had an early impact in defining public issues and behaviour. According to political analysts (Mungiu, 1995) political actors using mass media in the early 1990s electoral campaigns were marked by a clear antagonism: on the one hand, the angry anti-communist voice, insisting on full disclosure and denouncement of abuses and propaganda; on the other hand, the versatile position of the residual class, calling for a circumstantial attitude in creating public opinion based upon the assumption that the value of the imposed truth stands in the ability of its intermediation (Mungiu, 1995, p. 27). The entertainment mode gained more and more audience, and over time a "mass-commedia" phenomenon (Vasilescu, 2001) came out. As a result, the opposing cultural journalism continues to criticize the tabloid press for its ridiculousness and call for substantiated news and trustworthy public debates.

Such media heritage did not help in imposing a new communication discipline. It offered a mid point between media influence and political propaganda. It needed some good years to understand the specific nature, object and functions of public and institutional communication. Early practice of public relations developed without clear concerns about theories in use. Imported practical models or experienced practices in public relations and publicity were probably considered enough to respond to an unprofessional market, in which advertising, promotion, publicity and public relations were seen as a melted communication model. Theoretical aspects have became more evident towards the end of the 1990s and beginning of 2000 as soon as Romanian specialists acquired enough knowledge and academic experience to propose titles in the public relations field to editors who up to that time were mostly engaged in translations. Some major publishing houses like Polirom, Comunicare.ro, Tritonic, Institutul European remain the important players in the Romanian editorial market as regards communication, media, and public relations' most circulated titles. This shifting initiative, corroborated with a general growing interest in media and public communication, could be seen as marking the age of maturity in the profession of Romanian public relations.

Development Phases of Public Relations

In spite of the effervescence of commercial publicity in Romania in the first part of the twentieth century and of the timid exercise of publicity in the 1970s, neither the term public relations nor the practice of public relations had been considered before 1990. Due to the unfortunate historical shift to communism, the 1970s and the 1980s, which constituted the development years for most schools of European Public Relations, were a missed opportunity in Romania. Therefore, the practice has to be acknowledged as one of the accomplishments of the post-communist revived democracy.

In a didactic attempt at classification, we would include three distinct phases in the evolution of public relations practice in Romania:

- The pioneer phase of the early 1990s (1991–1995): this phase is mostly based on amalgamated practices of media, publicity and promotional events. Lots of small printing firms started to offer publicity services, larger companies entered the market. The knowledge was imported from abroad, as corporate know-how or background literature. The introduction of the whole specialization and academic degree has been launched by the University of Bucharest (founded as a modern University in 1864, on the premises of the previous academic structure dated 1694), in both the Faculty of Letters (Public relations counts as a single specialization since 1993) and the Faculty of Journalism and Communication Sciences. The first courses in public relations have been also initiated at postuniversity level in the new National School for Political and Administrative Sciences (SNSPA), founded by Government Decision in 1991, courses that have afterwards expanded into full study programs in a separate Faculty of Communication and Public Relations. (Borțun, 2005, pp. 192–195). The first public relations agency was Perfect Ltd. Co, founded in 1992, followed by others like BT Public Relations (1993) and Magnum Communication and Public Affairs (1994).

- The exploratory phase in the second half of the 1990s (1995 till 2000/2001): this phase has served as introductory for public relations studies and transient in the practice. Two major public relations agencies, in Romania, DC Communication and Image Promotion started in 1995, Prais Corporate Communication started in 1998, Ogilvy Public Relations in 1999. Initiative Romania, a media full service agency, starts in 1994 and launches in 1997 the first edition of the *Media Fact Book*. It celebrates 10 years of existence in 2007 (Constantinescu, 2007; Initiative Romania, 2007). The Romanian Association of Public Relations Professionals (ARRP) started in 1995. The academic world benefited to a large extent from this phase seeing that many new sections, departments or faculties have found good grounds to expand. In any case, by multiplication of qualified graduates, Universities produced eventually some pressure on the profesionalisation of the corporate services and corporate and public communication became more aware of their strategic role (see the symptomatic position of Mătieș on "PR or advertising for the image of Romania" in Rogojinaru, 2006, pp. 137–151).

- The consolidation phase from 2001 and ongoing: major events were the formation of the Club of Public Relations Companies (CCRP) in Romania (2003) at the request of whom the first survey on public relations usage and attitudes has been completed at the end of 2006 and publicly reported in the first quarter of 2007 (Păun, 2007). The expansion of both

agencies and academic departments continues as well as the formalization of the qualification for public relations by various accreditation forms. Most recent companies are the
Practice that starts in 2006 and GMP PR in 2007. According to the agencies' reports
published in the special issue of *Campaign Romania* Magazine from June 2007, at present
there are about 28 major public relations agencies and about 15 major BTL agencies with
significant client portfolio in Romania ("Raportul agenţiilor," 2007). But the actual
number of registered agencies certainly exceeds this reported number.

As shown in the above description, public relations has been introduced in Romania after
the fall of communism at the beginning of the 1990s. First public relations activities
emerged in some ambiguity. In the academic community, public relations has been progressively introduced in extension of language, journalism and media studies, being considered
a tool of persuasion in mass communication for influencing large audiences. In institutional practice, it has been placed in the vicinity of protocol and political performance.
The propaganda tools must have been a strong reference practice for developing public
relations practices. At the moment, public information techniques prevail. For the general
public, the interpretation of public relations as interpersonal power-based relations
persists. It is perhaps not far from reality. In any case, current developments and viewpoints
that outlined the strategies of public influence and influence agents magnified this perception (Ellul, 1990, Muchielli, 2002, Wilcox and Cameron, 2006, Pfau and Wan, 2006).
However, major public relations companies insist on the incorporated strategic role of
public relations and make efforts to increase the status of the discipline against other
communication practices.

Professional Status of Public Relations

At present, understanding public relations implies several forms of presence and consequent interpretations:

- **Public relations as practice:** its character and status is internationally defined, as most
  agencies follow the line traced by IPRA or other international and European bodies.
  The facets of public relations practice, especially the ethical ones, form the object of
  debates and actions by practitioners and practitioner bodies like ARRP or CCRP. The
  practice develops at both departmental and agency level. Departments of public relations
  become more specialized nowadays in confrontation with marketing departments. Nevertheless, the study on "PR Communication Usages and Attitudes" (Daedalus Consulting,
  2006; IQAds, 2007) points out that common perception of the public relations role within
  the company counts as 37.4 percent for integration of public relations within the overall
  business strategy while 32.4 percent of the overall perception still considers public relations
  a single part of the marketing plan. The percentages are almost equal; therefore the
  current view of managers considers that public relations should bring solid measurable
  results. The assessment of public relations effectiveness is rather ambiguous: on the one
  hand, there is a total agreement on the fact that public relations should be continuous in
  order to be effective; on the other hand, when exact cost for value measures are asked for,
  about 39.1 percent of the views are not clear if the media value should be accepted as
  lower than the budget invested for media relations (26.9 percent are still inclined to consider it as inefficient public relations, although media relations represents a sole component
  of strategic communication). Agencies define their domain as public relations and/or
  Below-the-Line (BTL). Most agencies cover a large area of interventions, from event

management and communication training to strategic communication (crisis management). Major agencies associated with CCRP point to the fact that their major activity is consultancy. Recent tendencies call for "integrated services" (Păun, 2007b) According to the Daedalus Consulting survey, major outsourced public relations activities are events planning and organization (68.2 percent), media relations (67.1 percent) and media monitoring (62.5 percent); Only 35.2 percent represents outsourced consultancy on communication issues and only 26.1 percent relates to crisis management. The major field of investing in public relations services differentiates amongst companies' interests for either brand PR (13.7 percent) or corporate PR (34.6 percent) or both brand and corporate PR (51.6 percent), which is prevalent among services that companies require constantly.

- **Public relations as profession**: is included in the national classification of occupations in Romania (COR), with four entries, each of them having a specified code and notification on the required level of qualification. Occupations included in COR are approved by the government in consultation with social partners. The occupations are classified based on their necessity defined by employers' associations, employment agencies and professional bodies, whose request used to be submitted to the Ministry of Labour. From 2007, national qualifications and subsequent occupations are subject to approval by the National Qualifications Agency, whose board is tripartite. The occupations listed in the COR for the domain of public relations refer to management positions such as *manager* of public relations and advertising services, for which higher education or equivalent is required, positions of *specialist* in public relations based on a higher education qualification and position of *assistant* in public relations and communication, qualified at secondary and post-secondary level.

- **Public relations as qualification** (starting with level IV EQF): this is an aspect which came recently in the arena of educational and professional debates generated by the restructuring process of European higher education based on the Bologna declaration as well as by the more recent adoption of the certification levels defined by the European Qualification Framework (EQF). At the academic level, the expertise has also resulted from the diversification of domains such as literature, sociology and social sciences in general, philosophy and political sciences, as well as international relations. Open academic levels and certificates are for Bachelor and Master Degrees in Public Relations as well as for Doctoral Degrees in Communication Sciences. Degrees offered used to be accredited by the National Council for Academic Evaluation and Assessment (CNEEA), which has been transformed by law into the Agency of Quality Assurance (ARACIS). All major public universities offer public relations courses at Bachelor and Master degree level: at least four in Bucharest, namely the University of Bucharest, the National School for Political and Administrative Studies (SNSPA), the Academy of Economic Sciences and the National Academy of Information; plus a public one in each of the major cities of Cluj, Timişoara, and Iaşi, and one in small cities like Braşov, Oradea, Sibiu, Suceava, Constanţa, Piteşti, and Târgovişte. Accredited private universities also offer bachelor degree courses and a variable number of masters. Doctoral degrees are normally organized by means of Doctoral Schools in each of the major universities. For the doctoral degrees, titles are conferred for the whole domain of communication sciences, not specifically in public relations. The University of Bucharest has awarded doctoral degrees in communication sciences jointly organized by the Faculty of Sociology and Social Assistance and by the Faculty of Journalism and Communication Sciences.

CURRENT CORPORATE AND POLITICAL PERSPECTIVES ON PUBLIC RELATIONS

The Application of the Principle of Open and Transparent Communication

Besides the appreciation given by various bodies of specialists and professionals, public relations practice is acknowledged and valued, in different ways and degrees, by the managerial level, as previously presented in the results of the survey conducted by Daedalus Consulting in 2006. At the governmental level, general programming documents do not refer to public relations. Yet, official government statements assume general policies related to the development of ITC (Information Technologies and Communication), which are considered necessary for the enhancement of public/civic participation. In the current Program of the Romanian Government for the 2005–2008 period, Chapter 2—Governance principles, the first line under **The principle of communication and transparency** indicates that "The Government will permanently inform the citizens about its activity, both within the stage of public policies assessment, and in the moment of adoption and implementation of decisions, and it will provide at all times complete, objective, and consistent financial information, related to its mission and strategic planning. Within the field of public communication, the Government will use a language accessible to the public." (Guvernul României, 2004).[1]

Access, **quality of services** and **transparency** are the leading terms in the ITC policy declarations. Since the Romanian Government adopts European economic jargon in most of its declarations, the discourse remains more concentrated on market driven trends (e.g. efficiency, competitiveness) than on social or moral aspects of public communication at the national level. This specific governmental statement is subject of monitoring by International Tranparency Romania (www.transparency.org.ro). Although public communication is not explicitly considered a strategic priority, some strategic attributes and powers are transferred to the Agency for Governmental Strategies—ASG (www.publicinfo.ro), a public agency that is entrusted with monitoring the government policies and measures and sustaining the national Romanian identity and image inside the country and abroad. Within its mandate, the Romanian Agency for Governmental Strategies (ASG) produces annual evaluation reports on the application of the Law 544/2001 referring to free access to the information of public interest (ASG, 2007a).

As for setting targets for other partners in civil society, the Romanian Government has refused to tolerate any form of corruption and traffic of influence. One of the political targets is the reevaluation and the implementation of the Corporate Governance Code elaborated in 2000 and updated in 2002, in order to put an emphasis on the financial transparency and also to clarify the role of the transparency centers, whose activities should be extended by means of cooperation between civic and corporate bodies. In addition to the government's targets, each public or private organization has developed at a different speed its own communication strategies, depending on the specific stakeholders.

---

[1] Referring to the *Policy in the field of information technology and communications*, the Romanian government states as follows: "The Romanian Government will promote a set of measures that will allow the improvement of ITandC indicators, will make flexible the structures of central and local administration for the initiation, sustaining and starting ITC projects by the small and medium sized enterprises, as well as open some programs of financing the projects in cooperation with internal and international institutions. There will be promoted at the same time a project for coherent and efficient data processing, in the context of interoperability of local and central public administration." (Guvernul României, 2004)

The private corporate groups and organisations admit public relations practice more and more as an integrated strategy for learning and development. Two dimensions seem to be at issue: programmes of corporate identity, by using blended public relations and advertising techniques or even more integrated programmes of *branding* campaigns, and reputation management, making reference to *crisis public relations and issues management*, concepts which are applied with the same meaning as in the international literature (see Haywood, 2005). From the technical point of view, two public relations domains of applications are favoured: extensive *media relations* and *event public relations*. *Political marketing* is also seen as increasing: image building represents a decisive factor in the political field, hence the increased demand for conducting it professionally (Teodorescu et al., 2007, p. 116). Specialised domains like *Investor public relations* (Investor PR) have spectacularly emerged. Investor PR has been reported rare or even non existent in the Romanian practice of public relations described in July 2005 by the specialized magazine *Săptămâna Financiară* (Financial Week) and retransmitted online by IQAds news briefing (IQAds, 2005b). However, recent description of the agencies' portfolio includes Investor PR in 2007 ("Raportul Agenţiilor," 2007).

At the same time, most of the large companies and holdings like the cement industries and the banking sector manifest the tendency to speak less of public relations and more about corporate responsibility and social investment. Global, European and national pressure related to the competitiveness and stakeholders' approach determined objectives like sustainable development and social/community responsibility, which arose in the last two years as the most chosen corporate topics. Nevertheless, debates of such kind have not yet created a real practice, and most of them remain restricted to intellectual and business elites, as shown by the numerous forums and discussions on corporate responsibility held recently. The best-known events are the seven editions of Forums organized in Bucharest by *Dilema Veche* Magazine together with New Europe College and with the participation of the company EIT Forum Auto Romania (Volvo Importer). These debates have gathered several business executives during 2006 and 2007. It became evident that the corporate social responsibility (CSR) movement was generated mostly by multinationals and a few small companies like EIT Forum Auto that had a strong brand behind it. Various businesses used not to respond to social responsibility or to assimilate it with charity. "CSR in Romania has not yet passed the pre-school level" is the title of a short report on the stage of social responsibility of companies in Romania (Oprea, 2007a, p. 7), in which key aspects of the emergent practice are highlighted, such as the inception stage of CSR in Romania, the vagueness of the terminology used while referring to CSR especially by small and medium size enterprises (SMEs), and the leading role of multinationals in setting the scene. A dedicated issue of *Dilema Veche* Magazine from June 2007 featured even more aspects of CSR, as the Forum itself allowed a friendly debate between the European viewpoints and Romanian interventions of various executives and officials ("Banii în cultură," 2007). On the Romanian side, the speakers have once again referred to the precarious relationship between the State and the private business, considering that CSR should be used as a private tool designed to compensate public deficits in education and culture. The strategic role of CSR has yet to be demonstrated in Romania.

National branding continues to be the issue at governmental level and a challenge for Romanian public relations professionals, but no clear position is taken, although intellectual and professional debates are not rare (cf. Rogojinaru 2007, pp. 5–6, and the whole special issue of the review *Altitudini*, May-June 2007). The latest project proposal for national branding with the theme and slogan *România—Fabulouspirit* has been abandoned by the present minister of external affairs, who claimed that the project did not have national approval ("Explicaţiile Ministerului Afacerilor Externe," 2007).

The Institutionalisation of Public Relations at the Branch Level

The main and the first created professional public relations body is the Romanian Association for Public Relations Professionals (ARRP). It started its business in June 1995, in Bucharest, as a non-profit organization of public relations professionals aiming at promoting the deontological principles of the Code of Athens; elaborating professional standards on which to base the public relations activities in Romania, and consolidating the public trust of various public groups regarding the public relations activity and the body of public relations specialists. ARRP considers itself the main forum for debates around the public relations domain. By its declared mission, ARRP undertakes to actively promote professional exchanges and links to international organizations such as Global Alliance for Public Relations and Communication Management and IPRA (International Public Relations Association).

The presence of the ARRP is large in terms of objectives and ambitious. In terms of impact, there are still efforts to be made in order to influence the real practice. However, despite its ups and downs, the activities of ARRP accumulated in time a certain experience among professionals, and developed various initiatives. Traditional activities are the annual Communication Olympiads, PR days (started in 2005), the National Convention in PR (2005), the Summer PR School (started in 2004). In June 2005, on the occasion of its national Conference, ARRP celebrated a decade of PR, 1995–2005, considering that 1995, its foundation year, was also the starting year for the practice itself.

In 2003, the Club of Public Relations Companies (CCRP) was established as an alternative non-profit professional body of 10 major companies of public relations business in Romania. Its major achievement was the 2006 study entrusted to Daedalus Consultimg on the "PR usages and attitudes." There is no formal link between the ARRP and CCRP, although individual members of ARRP are also part of the CCRP, representing their own managed companies.

In terms of European affiliation of the academic structure, individual professors and later the Department of Communication and Public Relations of the Faculty of Letters of the University of Bucharest joined EUPRERA and IAMCR in 2002, ECREA in 2006 and IABC in 2007. Individual or institutional memberships of various bodies are currently developed by all communication faculties around the country.

Most public relations and BTL agencies are located in Bucharest, following the line of large private capital. In 2005, the number of agencies in Bucharest was reported to be 50 (Borţun, 2005), although 2007 reports give a lower figure (see above, in our previous description, the note on reports of 28 PR agencies and 15 BTL agencies, "Raportul agenţiilor," 2007). There are reports that public relations agencies in the country started to increase their activities, in both profit and client portfolio. However, the most successful are still full service agencies, while the narrowly specialized ones have smaller resources. Moreover, it is noted that the practice of public relations and its benefits are also less understood as a single service outside Bucharest, meaning that agencies in the country combine Advertising, BTL and public relations to satisfy a hybrid market and to respond to cautious or anxious clients. Clients themselves need to be educated for the emergent market of public relations. The level of awareness of the benefits of public relations is not similar among clients. One reason could be the absence of a specific "communication culture" (Borţun, 2005). Yet only big clients are targeted by most public relations agencies, most of them aiming at higher achievements in terms of large investment and sustainable projects ("Raportul agenţiilor," 2007). Only 2.46 percent of the total of small and medium size enterprises (SMEs) made use of consultancy services in public relations in the year 2007, as mentioned by the SMEs Romanian Confederation (CNIPMMRE) and reported during the November conference of ARRP (IQAds, 2007b).

Economic development as well as the education level and mindsets are considered the prerequisites of a steady development in public relations. Most of the agencies consider concentrating on consultancy, although events and media relations remain the core activities. The focus on consultancy responds to strategic positioning of the public relations firms and helps them to capture the competitive advantage. For reasons like credibility, stable profits and professional profile, agencies compete to provide systematic and continuous advice to large corporate clients ("Raportul agenţiilor," 2007).

Following a brief account of the development of public relations in the country (Florescu, 2006), we can say that until 2004 companies outside Bucharest did not consider outsourcing activities in public relations and marketing and made use of "in-house personnel." After 2004, the expansion of the economic business in cities like Cluj, Iaşi, Braşov and Ploieşti encouraged marketing directors to make contracts with specialized public relations companies, assuming the rise in quality. In response, loyalty of the clients has been one of the most appreciated aspects of the quality improvement of communication services in the past two years.

Education and Qualification Programmes for Public Relations

As mentioned earlier, public relations was introduced in 1991, first as single modules of specialization and soon after as a full degree. First intervention was developed by the National School of Political and Administrative Sciences (SNSPA) at post-graduate level. In 1992 the Faculty of Journalism and Communication Sciences from the University of Bucharest presented public relations as a module in last years of studies. For the first time, as a full degree, it has been introduced by the Faculty of Letters in the University of Bucharest, in the academic year 1993–1994. It therefore exists as a subject of study in the university curriculum for almost 15 years. At present, both the Faculty of Letters and the Faculty of Journalism and Communication Sciences of the University of Bucharest include public relations degrees in their curricula. The third large institution offering the degree is the Faculty of Communication and Public Relations "David Ogilvy" of the SNSPA. A Chair of Communication and Public Relations is also organized within the National Academy of Information. All major cities (Cluj, Iaşi, Oradea, Sibiu, Timişoara, Piteşti) have public or private faculties and departments of communication and public relations. The number of students enrolled for public relations increases each year, which is a sign of the growing popularity of the discipline.

The recent legal developments regarding the organization of university studies are providing grounds for the development of a Qualification Framework (QF) in higher education (HE). The legal framework requires learning outcomes described in clear statements of *knowledge*, general and specific *competences*, for each qualification levels. The list of defined sectors to be included in the National Qualification Framework (NQF), as well as the national agreement for adopting NQF, has been formalized through the *Tripartite Agreement on the National Framework of Qualifications*, signed on 23 February 2005 by the Government (Prime Minister), Employers Confederation and Trade Union Confederation in Romania. The sector concerning public relations and publicity is the 15th listed: *Mass-media, publishing and printing*. Public relations represents a qualification provided at both pre-university (upper secondary) and university level. All activities concerning qualifications for young people and adults are subject to coordination and monitoring by the National Adult Training Board (NATB), a body serving as National Qualifications Agency since 2006. For qualifications provided by Higher Education institutions, the regulating agency is ACPART (see below).

In Romania, the Ministry of Education and Research is responsible for deciding on the list of the higher education study domains, whereas universities decide autonomously on the qualifications to be provided within any specific domain, as well as on the certificates of completion for each cycle. The National Agency for Higher Education Qualifications and Partnership with Economic and Social Environment—ACPART (www.acpart.ro) was appointed as national authority for the qualification framework in Higher Education. The methodology for defining QF in higher education has been launched for public consultation by ACPART in October 2007 (ACPART, 2007).

Although existing as an academic specialization for many years, the formal "qualification" for public relations (still called "specialization") has been legally stated in 2006 and listed in the nomenclature of academic qualifications approved by Government Decision. The nomenclature of qualifications formally recognizes the domain of study (equivalent to the qualification domain), which is the "Communication Sciences," and specifies the specialization (degree) as "Communication and Public Relations."

In line with the Bologna Declaration, Romanian universities have already been engaged in the Bachelor–Master–Doctorate (BMD) reform and the NQF will constitute the reference for correlating the BMD system with higher education qualifications levels. The process of consultations initiated by ACPART revealed that Romanian universities are in favour of implementing the respective levels of qualifications corresponding to HE in correlation with the eight reference levels of European Qualification Framework (EQF).

All public and private higher education institutions/universities are subject to accreditation of programmes, and a quality assurance methodology which enables them to produce annual self-assessment reports and improvement plans—subject to external audits—has been introduced. The Romanian Agency for Quality Assurance in Higher Education (ARACIS) was set up by law in order to support the implementation of quality assurance methodology. Quality Assurance in HE follows closely the *Standards and Guidelines for Quality Assurance* in the European Higher Education Area developed by the European Network for Quality Assurance in Higher Education (ENQA).

The Deontology of Public Relations Practice

Ethics in public relations and media has always been a point of discussion and controversy among specialists in Romania. Until recently (2004–2005), practitioners had a tendency to be rather discreet on ethical issues, mostly preaching for "things that work in practice." In recent years, both ARRP and individual companies have been more open towards dealing with ethical issues, especially in connection with the treatment of news and relationship with journalists. However, in practice, mostly at the departmental level, there are practitioners who still consider that paid publicity stands for a kind of effective public relations.

In 2005, ARRP, during the summer school publicly reported that public relations agencies in Romania should actively promote public relations deontology, in order to be a credible partner in Europe and in the international practice (IQAds, 2005). In November 2006, during an interview, the managing partner of DC Communication, Ms. Crenguţa Roşu, insisted upon the fact that clients should understand that public relations is not "the beauty salon" and the public relations advice should not be understood and applied as an institutional make up (IQAds, 2006).

ENVIRONMENTAL FACTORS AND PUBLIC RELATIONS PRACTICE IN ROMANIA

In spite of our point of view about the global perspective on public relations, national and local elements like political, economic and cultural changes shape the practice in forms and meanings specific to each society (Sriramesh and Verčič, 2003). We will attempt to outline those aspects which are considered influential for Romanian public relations.

Political System

Romania is a republic; the political regime of the country is parliamentary democracy sustained by means of a bicameral Parliament formed by Senate and Chamber of Deputies. Various political themes are first dealt with in specialized Commissions, like Education, etc. The political institutions play an important role in the life of Romania. The nation is strongly politically-oriented and political issues are part of the most frequent media and public debates. The State is quite strong, in spite of weak performances in some domains. The State institutions continue to be trusted and looked to for solving public problems. During the year 2007, the political regime has been challenged by different disputes between a liberal Government run by the Prime Minister Călin Popescu-Tăriceanu and a social-democrat President, Traian Băsescu. These disputes show the need of the people for charismatic and populist strong leaders, a phenomenon which might be considered normal in transition times. One of the most important steps in Romanian politics as regards the post-communist presidencies consists of the initiative of current president Traian Băsescu to initiate a presidential commission to elaborate a comprehensive analysis on the communist dictatorship. The Final Report was launched on 18 December 2006 when President Băsescu defended the Report by an official address in the Parliament. It has been recently published by Humanitas Publishing House in Bucharest (Tismăneanu et al., 2007).

Formal institutions play a leading role and formal organizations are more credible than the informal groups. The society is rather vertical and statutory authoritarian; informal grass roots movements are rare and not coordinated. It is not quite clear whether this characteristic is a heritage from the communist past or a structural trait (Barbu, 2004, pp. 71–74; Zamfir, 2004, pp. 149–150). As far as the political pluralism is concerned, there are various political parties, including a large ethnic party, UDMR (The Hungarian Democratic Union). The government used to be formed by a coalition of Liberals, Social Democrats, Conservative Party and UDMR. Given that Social Democrats and Conservatives have withdrawn from power, the current political regime is largely controlled by Liberals in coalition with UDMR.

Freedom of public/political expression is guaranteed by the Constitution. It is valued to the extent that issues are easy to raise; the news market is largely dominated by mass media institutions and opinion leaders valued by media, especially TV. Print becomes extremely specialized, niche oriented, and TV channels are themselves developing into niche channels, the most important being *Acasă* (entertaining) and *Realitatea* TV (news) (Initiative Media, 2007). *Money channel* has been judged the best television channel for market analysis. The public space is largely dominated by hot issues and shows a high level of versatility. The issues keep the front page for only a few days, "important" is less visible than "urgent" and the tendency to tabloid news is increasing. Reactions are often emotional and talk shows are valued only if they try to dig into obscure information (Vasilescu, 2001).

In the relationship between the political environment and the public relations industry, politics do not directly influence the public relations industry, or at least such influence is not obvious. Public relations has been mostly accepted and influential in the private sector, much more than in the public and non-profit sectors, therefore it remains a technical issue and a communication support tool. On the contrary, *political communication* is subject of political education and communication skills are cultivated through the faculties of political sciences or/and administrative studies.

Economic Aspects

Based on the HDI (Human Development Index) for 2004 published by UNDP Human Development Report, Romania is listed as the 60th out of 177 analysed countries, with a value of 0.805. GDP is $8,480 expressed in PPP US$ (purchasing power parity) and gives Romania 63rd place out of 177 countries. Adult literacy rate (over 15 years old) is 97.3 percent and places Romania 26th out of 177 (UNDP, 2006).

The government plays the leading role in setting the economic goals, although decisions may be influenced by private economic groups. The existence of lobbying or any kind of power influence is acknowledged, although no impact analysis has been conducted, any dilemmas being left to public accusations in cases of corruption. Private corporate groups act through various forms of personal and professional lobby, even though their methods of lobbying are neither clear nor declared, but sometimes well managed by Corporate Public Affairs departments.

In terms of the private–public influence relationship, we cannot judge in which way the private sector influences the public policy. The Liberal government contributed more to bringing private views of entrepreneurs into the political debate. The general public tend to consider that the private domain is politically neutral and more involved in generating private capital than influencing the public sphere. This consideration does not include the private owners of media trusts, whose intentions and institutional capacities of manipulating public opinion are evident.

The increasing level of investment in the private business sector claimed more public relations and marketing communication. Major companies invest today in integrated marketing communication (IMC) and CSR, e.g. cement industries, pharmaceuticals and banking and financial operators ("2007. Cei mai mari jucători din economie," 2007). In spite of a hectic relationship between private and public sectors, the two cooperate often in promoting public issues by means of social marketing, cause related advertising, sponsorship and CSR. In the last year, large companies have started to operate with the concept of "partnership," and associate themselves with long-run projects of public institutions like universities or non-profit institutions like NGOs.

As for the technological development relevant to public relations professionals, note that telecommunications in general and the mobile phone industry registered higher rate of growth. Internet connections increased in terms of access and speed, home connections are now provided more easily and faster by cable network companies. Projects for wireless connection have started for major institutions, including universities. The Internet boom, which has been more visible in the last two years, created an emergent important market for online publicity and public relations, counting also a recent but steady development of blogging. The growth rate of internet used as an advertising tool is estimated at 23 percent higher for 2007 than 2006, although far below the TV usage.

Legal Aspects

The public sphere in Romania is overregulated for some issues and insufficient or contradictory in other respects. The legal sector continues to be vulnerable in terms of public credibility. To respond to accusations of traffic of influence and cover-ups, the Executive and mostly the Presidency have launched large anti-corruption measures especially to keep justice in clear separation from political pressures. In spite of various debates, controversies and allegations, the major legal institutions ignore the power of public communication, lack proper communication structures or transmit fragmented and inaccessible information. Juridical institutions continue to be opaque and suspicious in their relations with journalists.

As for specific regulations of the communication sector, the audiovisual media (TV and radio) are subject to scrutiny by the National Council for Audio-Visual (CNA), which is the regulatory institution for monitoring and sanctioning the content of publicity and advertising through audio and visual media. In recent years, ARRP repeatedly approached CNA with a view to introducing further clarification in the laws concerning the nature and function of "public information" and "public issues." There has been an attempt to separate also the domains of advertising and PR in terms of definition and treatment of public issues and newsworthy topics.

Aspects of Social Activism

The unions have been historically active, even in communist times. In the 1970s and 1980s labour unions in the mining and truck industry sectors initiated open revolts against the regime. At present, the unions seem to have lost power, as lots of private employees are not unionized and, on the other hand, human resources departments of companies have changed their career policies from experience-based to individual performance-based systems of evaluation and remuneration. During the 1990s, any form of activism was mostly related to anti-communism. The GDS (Grupul pentru Dialog Social/Group for Social Dialogue) has been continuously the champion of anti-communist and anti-totalitarian debates. At present, student activism seems stronger, with large associations like AIESEC (the Association of Students in Economic Studies) or PRIME, the Association of Students in Communication and PR, or strong student NGOs like Teamwork.

In urban Romania there are few people to take part in civic groups, with the exception of political parties. As for the actual membership of associative structures, it has been stated that 13 percent out of the total population has been or is a member of one association, about 2 percent has been or is present in two associations and about 1 percent is represented in three or more associations (Sandu, 2006, p. 158).

Due to the recent introduction of the practice and to the discreet activities of public relations departments and firms, and probably to the weak or non-existent consumer movement in Romania, no activist group has directly challenged corporate private groups so far. Weak consumer movement might be caused by the wide acceptance of publicity and advertising as key sources of information. In any case, companies carefully prevent any boycott by means of charity and CSR and large branding campaigns addressed to young people, especially students (telecommunications and banks have been more active and clearer in conveying messages to adolescents and young adults). Conventional activism does not seem to be the real threat for public relations departments yet. But blogging or any other electronic network might create a threatening environment for both public and private organizations.

Social Stratification

Far from the times when "the unique working class" was proclaimed by the Communist Party, present Romanian society is highly polarized into business upper class and different layers of working strata, with a significant component of intellectuals who are generally modestly waged, with some exceptions. In a recent study about urban living conditions in 2006 compared to 2005, carried out by Daedalus Consulting and published in January 2007, the results show that 37 percent of Romania's inhabitants living in an urban environment perceive a change for the better in their own life in comparison to the past year. Generally, young persons (18–34 years old) declared that their living standard has improved, and this age group shows, compared to other age groups, a higher level of adjustment to present social conditions. In the case of employers/managers, the presence of other income sources from rents or real estate selling is notable. Employees with a bachelor's degree are more likely to engage in additional activities for increasing their income, besides their main work commitment. Approximately half of Romania's urban population has insufficient revenue, when it comes to the balance between present earnings and needs: 45 percent of Romanians report that their income is sufficient for basic needs at the most (Daedalus Consulting, 2007b).

Social mobility is rather low, the class difference persists and territorial and professional mobility are limited to young ages, under 35. Migration elsewhere in the European Union is the typical solution for young people aged 18 to 30 (Daedalus Consulting, 2007a). Consumer behavior has changed during the years, but not significantly. A book on consumer behavior published in 1996 by Mihaela Miron made clear remarks on the "ostentatious" consumer behavior of Romanians, based on class divisions at the beginning of the 1990s (Miron, 1996). Such stratification does not directly influence public relations, we could see nevertheless the link between the business class and public relations. As public relations is seen and studied as a management-connected discipline, public relations activities are considered an asset for large business—companies, holdings, etc, determined on budget and investment capacity.

The society as a whole shows moderate acceptance of risks, manifests scepticism about radical change, and shows low tolerance to uncertainty and ambiguity; therefore people are inclined to seek details and further guarantees before accepting the consequences of risky actions. Individual responsibility is often transferred collectively or to authorities; individuals are still inclined to blame external bodies or circumstances for their shortcomings. Most meanings are created by opinion leaders, including journalists, since media credibility is quite high. Meanings are rather situational, thus subject to multiple influences and influencers. If not credited by a leader, messages should be explicit and repeated. Public communication uses a high context of construction of meanings, with the exception of multinationals in which communication, both internal and external, is standardized through manuals or codes of conduct.

Gender and Culture

According to the GEM indicator (Gender Empowerment Measure), which reveals how active women are in society (publicly and professionally), Romania ranks 59th out of the 75 analysed countries (UNDP, 2006). Yet, from many points of view, Romanian society can be considered a male culture, in spite of recent steps that have been taken to promote more women in the government and in public life. Although gender is not a formal criterion for assigning organizational roles and although organizational policies value genders equally, corporate practice seems to remain rather masculine. As for the distribution of genders in public relations, most practitioners are women in public relations while advertising is mixed and marketing is rather dominated by male directors. Public relations is considered more social, thus more feminine than the advertising industry. Public relations departments tend to be more feminine, public relations and advertising agencies are more gender-balanced.

In terms of collective/individualistic values, Romanian society manifests traces of a collectivistic society, with great power distance (Hofstede, 2005, p. 83). Networking and personal contacts are important, and there are strong elements of ritualism, which support a cult of celebrities and rich adventurers. This collectivistic value should theoretically sustain public relations activities, for which networking is the key element. Unfortunately, collectivist values do not praise market performance, thus various layers and forms of social resistance maintain a certain level of rigidity. Apart from the strong networking element, interpersonal trust is rather low and most successful organizations create a strong formal environment in order to avoid personal conflicts in the working environment.

Having a high power distance, Romanian culture generally encourages deference to superiors in social settings. The situation is changed in multinational or some smaller firms where the culture is created by specific leadership styles. As expected, private companies act more horizontally whereas public institutions are more hierarchical. Yet, this is not a general rule. As the trust level is low, the organizational openness is also limited and restricted to controlled issues; therefore, many multinationals are rather formal and conventional and often defensive.

Some of the following characteristics may count for Romanian publics: visual inclination (TV is the main important medium for news, ads and entertainment, also outdoor publicity registered in 2006 the highest growth compared to other forms of media advertising), high home and group dependence, large appetite for spectacular details and infotainment, inclination to admire celebrities, strong confidence in multinational brands (in reaction, recent campaigns try to reposition national brands and recreate the golden age of the 1970s). As for multimedia habits, results from a study conducted in April 2007 (Daedalus Consulting, 2007c) show that the best-known ways of electronic communication are SMS and email. Messenger programs and SMS are known by three-quarters of the urban population of Romania and over half of 1021 respondents were aware of chat programs (such as MIRC) and also voice communication programs by Internet (VoiceOverIP). Forums, Chatprograms, blogs or 3G technologies are used by fewer people. More and more teenagers use blogs and chat programs compared to the average.

INFLUENCE OF MASS MEDIA ON THE DEVELOPMENT OF PUBLIC RELATIONS IN ROMANIA

Media Control

Mass-media capacity has expanded in the last 15 years. Factors that augmented media influence were expansion of cable TV at the end of the 1990s as well as increased Internet cable connection at home, in schools, universities and other public places. The influence of the print media has diminished compared to TV and the Internet. Wireless systems and digital TV ("Digi TV") constitute actual alternative offers. In response to the diversification of public tastes and expectations and to answer the global preference for entertainment, TV channels, radio channels and magazines opted for niche specialization. Except for daily newspapers, all mass media are narrowly segmented in order to better serve both direct audiences and advertisers. The outdoor industry occupies a large place, especially in the capital city Bucharest, where the metro allows for generous exposure and repetition ("Publicitatea merge cu metroul," 2006).

Most media channels and media trusts are private property. The Romanian National Channel, TVR, is under the control of Parliament and subject to political monitoring. The fact that TVR is subject to parliamentary control has been understood as the consequence of efforts to increase the public capacity and quality of public services. As for the private groups, their political alignment is not direct, although controlling is exerted through corporate owners. Some of the main national press agencies in Romania are *Rompress* (state owned, general news), *Rador* (state owned, general news), *Mediafax* (private, general news), *AM Press* (private, specialized), *NewsIn* (private, specialized) (Ionescu, 2007, pp. 73–77).

Censorship is no longer the issue, being increasingly replaced by discussions about the degree of manipulation by media. Nevertheless, media news is considered a reliable source of information, especially television, which is the main tool of engaging large publics in campaigns or programs and determining opinion sharing. Emotional inclination and a precarious political education and culture make 36 percent of the urban population acquire necessary information from TV. They read newspapers or listen to the radio to a lesser extent (Sandu, 2006, p. 140).

In terms of political participation and media followers, ever-increasing *civic attitude and participation* remain important public matters. Freedom of speech is a Constitutional guarantee and in recent years, journalists have gained a more important position in public life. Most public institutions opted for nominating a spokesperson, if not an entire Press Bureau. Many public institutions, irrespective of the domain, have chosen to organize a Department for Public Image.[2] News and information represent a service and a commodity. From this point of view, we could say that capitalistic, commercial orientation of news production is prevalent.

Freedom of speech in guaranteed, included media views, but litigation is frequent in consequence of hazardous statements by political persons. In general, litigation between journalists and other persons, especially politicians, tends to be treated publicly. Media play an important role in exposing, disclosing or denouncing and commenting on various tensions and disputes. In this sense, media play an arbiter role (talk shows are the main tool for such arbitrage).

As for media ethics, the Romanian Press Club acts as a professional association, having the responsibility of watching over the press deontology and professional standards. As regards advertising regulation, the National Audio-Visual Council (CNA) is the monitoring body.

The boost in media influence and indirectly the expansion of media relations placed public relations in a privileged position in the communication market and consolidated the professionalization of public relations services in competition with advertising. Public relations events have become one of the most powerful applications due to media involvement. However, ethical issues in media relations persist and often public relations coordinators

---

[2] Data are collected in the current (2006–2008) research project of the Communication and Public Relations department of the Faculty of Letters, University of Bucharest. The interim report is published under the title "Analysis of the communication strategies of public institutions in Romania in the context of European Integration."

make compromises on paid advertising in order to ensure the news diffusion. This is mainly the case in television, the most saturated medium. The correct treatment of "public" information remains the issue for all communication practices and services.

Media Outreach

Due to cable connection and currently to Internet services provided by all telecommunications companies, the media benefit from a wide coverage. Television is the most popular medium, followed by radio, Internet and print media (including online editions of newspapers). Relevant factors for the segmentation of audiences are related to age, education, and the degree of occupational mobility: electronic media are therefore preferred by young people, more educated persons (tertiary level education) and those more flexible in terms of job mobility, while television is largely preferred by a comfortable majority of the lower-middle class. The print media, especially magazines, become niche-specialized according to gender (lifestyle) and occupation (business). Daily newspapers as well as the main TV channels associate audiences geographically and news content is specialized according to national and local coverage. Local TV channels have started to broadcast local news and events and assist the consolidation of local leaders' profiles. Niche segmentation of TV channels, which is considered a trend, implies thematic diversification (specialized news, e.g. business and financial, or entertainment) (Initiative Media, 2007). The capacity of publics to process mediated information of all kinds has improved in the last decade. The literacy level is quite high, which means that adults could easily process functional information. Adult literacy rate has been estimated at 98.7 percent in 1999, according to the UNDP report, and participation in education and professional training has shown a rising trend ever since. The percentage of the adult population, aged 25–64, that graduated at least secondary education was 73.1 percent in 2005 (Guvernul României, 2007). However, the unemployment rate among young people continues to be alarming: 13.1 percent in 2005, higher by 3 percent in urban areas; it appears that the 18–24 age group manifest the highest tendency (23.4 percent) to abandon secondary education without any qualification (Guvernul României, 2007). Current empirical research shows no significant differences in public/political participation in terms of residence, households or TV consumption, but highlights an important increase determined by education level and, to some extent, gender, in favor of more educated, middle class, middle age, higher occupational status males (Sandu, 2006, p. 157).

The large majority of the rural population, with the exception of remote mountain areas, is connected to TV—mostly by cable connection. If connected by cable, rural audiences can reach commercial TV channels. Therefore television remains the main medium for information. TVR 1, the main public TV station (together with TVR2 and TVR Cultural), has passed in 2004 through a rebranding process. Nevertheless, the management failed in getting the required performance. The new director of TVR1 has set the goal of launching a revised formula, in an effort to recapture young audiences (Oprea, 2007b, p. 17).

In spite of the comfortable leadership of television in the media market, an increased role played by business journals and magazines has been considered lately a revolutionary sign as concerns the diversification, specialization and maturity of the print media market (Anton and Oprea, 2007, p. 20).

In relation to effects of social structure upon the public relations industry, we can state that public relations is mostly an urban phenomenon. Municipalities have press and information desks or public relations bureaus. In large communes, local councils have developed internal structures to serve various needs of the public—public information, European affairs, press relations, citizens' assistance, etc. Public relations services serve both public authorities and commercial activities. NGOs that are active in the rural areas occasionally organize campaigns or single issue programmes for public information.

Media Access

The policy of transparency at the Government level is clearly stated. According to the Government Programme—Governing Principle of Participation—the quality and the legitimacy of public policies should be assured through wide consultation of civil society and the business community. This principle is to be correlated to the first governing principle, the one regarding Communication and Transparency, according to which the Government is committed permanently to inform the public by using an accessible level of speech. Constant monitoring has been actively provided by Transparency International Romania. At the same time, ASG promotes actively the governmental policy and fulfils its mandate of monitoring the Law 544/2001 regarding free access to public information (http://www.publicinfo.ro/pagini/accesul-la-informatii-de-interes-public.php), by producing annual reports (ASG, 2007a).

All these statements count for a general political determination in favor of openness and public dialogue, and the effects of this political motivation are visible. As regards corporate and non-profit structures, direct access to the media is fully guaranteed. Needless to say, these corporate strategies differ between organizations: as a general rule, the companies have a higher capacity for media relations and public relations than non-profit bodies, but recently collected information reveals an increasing capacity level in universities and cultural institutions (Rogojinaru, 2006).

The valorization by the media of the information obtained from public relations professionals and agencies has not been researched yet. In principle, journalists respond to public relations bureaus and follow the corporate news via public relations departments. News releases are considered an important source of information, as well as any press event. On the other hand, divergent points of view in terms of treatment of news and agenda setting persist in the real world, in spite of the fact that in most Communication Schools techniques in public relations and media are taught together.

CONCLUSION

From many points of view, both public relations education and industry have emerged from their turbulent childhood and adolescence periods (forced to be faster than others!) and eventually reached their early maturity. There are still aspects to be improved and to consolidate: paradigm shift to be accepted, professional solidarity to be achieved, suspicion manifested by both parts (education and industry) against each other and inside sectors to be passed over, declarations of cooperation to be followed by shared actions, asymmetrical relations to be transformed into symmetrical ones. In any case, the communication market is growing and shows growing acceptance of public relations in all areas of social life and professional activities. The increasing number of people engaged in the communication industry as well as the signs of growing investment in public relations services sustain the optimistic view about the future of the discipline in Romania.

CASE STUDY

EIT-Forum Auto and the Corporate Foundation *Life for Life* Assist the Development of Culture and Education Through Corporate Socially Responsible Initiatives

The description in the following case study presents the activities of the Corporate Foundation "Life for Life," which is associated with the company EIT-Forum Auto, the Volvo importer in Romania. The facts of this case have been provided by Mrs. Raluca Popa, Public Relations Coordinator. The aim of the case study is to outline specific local applications of community public relations in Romania and encourage more local companies to form strategic partnerships in areas like education and culture, as part of their corporate responsibilities towards local communities.

Institutional Context

EIT-Forum Auto, Volvo importer in Romania, sustains and promotes policies of corporate responsibilities. It is part of its corporate value statements that emphasize the humanistic view: "Human values represent the center of Volvo philosophy." Therefore EIT-Forum Auto is one of the companies most involved in cultural and social life, acting in accordance with Volvo values. The year 2006 has been considered the year of consolidating the Volvo Company on the Romanian market as a responsible brand, outlining the honesty, transparency and energetic state of the company. The most important stakeholders are considered the employees, the neighboring communities and local authorities. EIT-Forum Auto contributes to the community by supporting research as well as educational and cultural programmes, in an effort to foster the next generation of employees and strengthen the reputation of Volvo Cars. All CSR programmes have been launched by EIT-Forum Auto and they are currently carried out by the Corporate Foundation "Life for Life."

There are three directions for EIT-Forum to act as a responsible company: 1) sharing the CSR vision, namely creating a corporate platform for debates among major companies in Romania; 2) promoting active and sustainable partnerships with public institutions in promoting excellence in education and culture; 3) providing support through charity programmes for potential talents.

Direction I: Shared Vision of CSR Programmes

Forum Auto has created a platform for major companies in Romania, authorities and non governmental organizations (NGOs) to increase their involvement in the development of cultural and social programmes.

> Generating ideas and producing changes in social mentalities, inducing strong motivations for philanthropic and charity actions in the spirit of social responsibility and human solidarity, conceiving sponsorship as a cultural action, directing the efforts of the community towards supporting self-development aspirations and the creative potential of the individual are, in our vision, the pathways to social progress and a better quality of life. Beyond offering, we are giving people a key to "being" and "becoming" through open-mindedness, knowledge and a professional use of resources, for a better quality of life, now and in the future. (Lavinia Huidan, President/CEO EIT-Forum Auto.)

In order to reach the intended results, the budget for the CSR programme in the year 2006 was 80,000 Euros. The main reported annual achievements noted an increased awareness of company's social responsibility, the active promotion of public–private partnerships, at both national and international level; encouragement of private donations; networking between organizations based in Romania and Romanians worldwide, in promoting humanistic values and maximizing the social impact of the values underlying Volvo's corporate culture.

Direction II: A Partnership for Excellence

The programme aims at supporting the outstanding achievements of young Romanians, encouraging creativity and excellence, and promoting professionalism and competition. The main actions taken in the accomplishment of this goal have addressed gifted young people, those who achieved excellence in mathematics, sciences or arts. A first line of investment, called "Volvo for Intelligence," has aimed at sustaining the national Olympic teams in mathematics and physics. The project supports the Romanian Olympic teams of mathematics and physics, whose remarkable results in international contests have gained worldwide recognition. In 2005, the project has been developed in collaboration with the University of Bucharest, Medicover and Softwin. EIT-Forum Auto has awarded six scholarships for the Olympians who entered the best universities in the world like Harvard, Yale, or Princeton. In addition, some more public support has been offered as yearly prizes to all Olympic students who win gold medals in international contests. Media events have been organized for all these winners, in order to assure the right exposure and media coverage.

A second program referred to supporting young entrepreneurs and very active student associations for developing cultural events. In 2006, Forum Auto has been the partner in the biggest events celebrating the best students in Romania and the company management was part of the jury which selected the best essays on the role of young people in the European Union integration. Forum Auto has supported ORICUM Association and the British Council in the organization of the 2007 Youth Summit in Romania, an event governed by the Presidency of Romania (http://www.youthsummit.ro/en/youth-summit/youth-summit-2007). Forum Auto was the main partner for Bookfest (the Romanian national Book Fair). Forum Auto is also actively involved in supporting academic values and remained a trustworthy private partner of the University of Bucharest, in all debates and projects that encourage young students who can make a difference in the educational system, as well as in participating as official partner in the annual conferences of various faculties and departments.

A third initiative supported direct investment for promoting the national culture and heritage. Forum Auto is the permanent partner of the Romanian Cultural Institute. In 2006, the company launched a structured program of sustaining real values and intelligence in Romania, aiming at raising awareness of Volvo philosophy by concentrating other efforts of major companies in contributing to a better Romanian society. In this context, the company financed the translation of the best Romanian philosophers like Constantin Noica and Mihai Şora into foreign languages. In the same line of duties, Forum Auto was a partner of the European Congress of History of Religion 2006 in order to give the necessary support to establish a special University of the History of Religion.

The fourth and probably the most notable public exercise consisted in the organization of the Forums *Volvo-Dilema Veche*. *Dilema Veche* is a major cultural magazine in Romania, whose founding director is Andrei Pleşu, the Rector of the New Europe College. This platform of debates has been developed since August 2005 and became the well-known place of communication between major companies, authorities, NGOs and other decision makers in order to encourage the dialogue between business and cultural elites. The purpose of all debates is to raise awareness about social and personal accomplishments resulting from professionalism, creativity, intelligence, responsibility, quality and reliability, and to make these values desirable to a larger number of persons. The Forums take place every three months, engaging key representatives of cultural and social life, top management from socially responsible companies, representatives of NGOs, young people involved in educational projects, national and local authorities, editors in chief of the main Romanian newspapers and European invited guests. After each debate, it is *Dilema Veche* that regularly devotes a special issue of its weekly magazine to outline the conclusions of the debate. All meetings have been widely covered in the mass media and obtained TV exposure through live transmissions on Romanian business channels.

Direction III: Corporate Aid

The first part of the charity system developed by Forum Auto aims at assisting young or vulnerable persons to have a good start and to learn how to pursue their projects by themselves. All actions are long term and provide constant follow-up. Within this line of investment, Forum Auto has been a partner of UNICEF in Romania, and also organizes the *Volvo Masters Tournament*, a fundraising special event in aid of the Hospice of Hope in Braşov (Romania). It also organizes the Volvo catamarans championship, during which the Volvo catamarans are used by junior champions for training.

The second part of the charity is addressing people in urgent need. The large social action and financial support provided by Forum Auto in 2005 and continued by Life for Life Foundation has been the *Moldova-Possible Mission* destined to help the people from Bacău County whose homes were flooded: it consisted in a concentrated funding from all partners with the purpose of building twelve new homes for the most badly affected families in the area.

Moral of the Case

EIT-Forum Auto, the Volvo importer is a Romanian company, not a large multinational. The corporate wish seems therefore less imperialistic in its attempts to gain the public trust. Romanian and European vision and values have tried to impose a social balance and a platform for dialogue. What is remarkable in its case is mostly the persistence in accommodating a sound corporate vision to an unstable and fragile social context. The exclusive focus on the "elites" may be questionable, but it is in many ways preferable to "populist" approaches, so visible in private charity nowadays in Romania.

REFERENCES

ACPART (2007). *Metodologia de dezvoltare a Cadrului Naţional al Calificărilor din Învăţământul superior (CNCSIS). Proiect.03.10.2007 [Methodology for the Development of National Qualification Framework in Higher Education.(CNCSIS). Project. 03.10.2007].* Retrieved November 10, 2007, from *ACPART Agency (Agency for Higher Education Qualifications and Partnership with Economic and Social Environment)*, http://www.apart.ro/images/evenimente_noutati/metodologiecncsis.pdf.

Anton, A., and Oprea, R. (2007, April). Revoluţia business [The business revolution]. *Campaign România*, p. 20.

Arghir, V.A.(2007, May–June). România-Fabulospirit [Romania-Fabulospirit], *Altitudini*, 15–16, 19–22.

ASG (2007a). *Raport asupra Implementării Legii Nr. 544/2001 privind liberul acces la informaţiile de interes public în anul 2006 [Report on Implementing the Law 544/2001 regarding the Free Access to the Public Interest Information]. [RAPORT 544_2006 [1]] March.* Retrieved October 10, 2007 from *ASG (Agency for Governmental Strategies)*, http://www.publicinfo.ro/pagini/accesul-la-informatii-de-interes-public.php.

ASG (2007b). Participaţi la programul ROMÂNIA TRANSPARENTĂ [Take part in the programme TRANSPARENT ROMANIA]. Public call for projects. Retrieved October 10, 2007 from ASG (Agency for Governmental Strategies), http://www.publicinfo.ro/pagini/programul-romnia-transparent258.php.

Banii în cultură [Money for culture]. (2007, June 8–14). *Dilema veche*, 174, 9–12.

Barbu, D. (2004). *Republica absentă. Politică și societate în România postcomunistă [The Absent Republic. Politics and society in Postcommunist Romania]*. Bucharest: Nemira.

Borțun, D. (2005). *Relațiile publice și noua societate [Public relations and the new society]*. Bucharest: Tritonic.

Botan, C.H., and Hazleton, V. (2006). *Public Relations Theory II*. New Jersey: Lawrence Erlbaum Associates.

Constantinescu, I. (2007, September–October). Initiative se vrea formatoarea pieței de mass-media. ["Initiative" wants to be the builder in the mass-media market], *Campaign România*, p. 15.

Constantiniu, F. (2002). *O istorie sinceră a poporului Român [A true history of Romanian people]* (3 ed.). Bucharest: Univers Enciclopedic.

Daedalus Consulting (2006). PR Communication Usage and Attitudes. Available in electronic ppt. version PR_Communication_prez_Usage_and_Attitudes. Made available by permission of C. Roșu, managing partner at DC Communication Agency in Romania, personal communication, June 5, 2007.

Daedalus Consulting (2007a). Migrația forței de muncă în România după aderarea la U.E. [Migration of the workforce in Romania after the EU accession]. Available in electronic version migratia_rom.pdf. Retrieved October 10, 2007, from http://www.daedalus.ro/en/index.php?P=380.

Daedalus Consulting (2007b). Living standard of Romania's population. January 2007. Available in electronic version http://www.daedalus.ro/nivelul/nivelul_eng.pdf. Retrieved October 10, 2007, from http://www.daedalus.ro/en/index.php?P=380.

Daedalus Consulting (2007c). Multimedia Habits. April 2007. Available in electronic version http://www.daedalus.ro/multimedia/multimedia_eng.pdf. Retrieved October 10, 2007, from http://www.daedalus.ro/en/index.php?P=389.

Dozier, D. M., Grunig, L.A., and Grunig, J.E. (1995). *Manager's Guide to Excellence in Public Relations and Communication Management*. New Jersey: Lawrence Erlbaum Associates.

Drăgan, I. (2003). Televiziunea—,regină' a comunicării de masă [Televison—"queen" of the mass-communication]. *Romanian Review of Communication and Public Relations*, 6–7, 43–65.

Ellul, J. (1990). *Propagandes*. Paris: Economica.

European Commission (2006). *White Paper on a European Communication Policy*. Brussels, 1.2.2006: COM(2006) 35 final. Brussels: European Commission.

Explicațiile Ministerului Afacerilor Externe [Explanation of the Ministry of Foreign Affairs]. (2007, May–June). *Altitudini*, 15–16, p. 22.

Florescu, L. (2006). Serviciile PR din România [PR Services in Romania]. Retrieved June 30, 2007, from http://www.media ad.ro/article.php?articleId=3916.

Freedom House (2004). *Presa locală. Raportul Freedom House asupra independenței presei locale din România [Local Press. Freedom House Report on the Independence of the Local Press in Romania]*. EU Phare financed project. Bucharest: Freedom House, Romanian Bureau.

Fukuyama, F. (1999). *Marea ruptură. Natura umană și refacerea ordinii sociale [The Great Disruption: Human Nature and the Reconstitution of Social Order]*. Bucharest: Humanitas.

Fundația E.L.I.T.A, Clubul Român de Presă (2006). *Ghidul Mass-media românești 2007 [The Guide of Romanian Mass-Media]*. Bucharest: E.L.I.T.A, House of Guides.

Grunig, J.E. (ed.) (1992). *Excellence in Public Relations and Communication Management*. New Jersey: Lawrence Erlbaum Associates.

Grunig, J.E., and Hunt, T. (1984). *Managing Public Relations*. New York: Holt, Rinehart and Winston.

Guvernul României (2004). *Programul de guvernare 2005–2008 [Governing programme 2005–2008]*, December 2004. Retrieved June 30, 2007, from http://www.gov.ro/obiective/pg2005–2008/program-de-guvernare.

Guvernul României (2007). *Programul Național de Reforme [National Programme of Reforms]*. Available in electronic version pnr_ro_oficial.pdf. Retrieved June 30, 2007, from http://www.gov.ro/obiective/pg2005–2008/program-de-guvernare.

Habermas, J. (1998). *Sfera publică și transformarea ei structurală [Strukturwandel der Öffentlichkeit: Untersuchungen zu einer Kategorie der bürgerlichen Gesellschaft]*. Bucharest: Editura Univers.

Haywood, R. (2005). *Corporate Reputation, the Brand and the Bottom Line. Powerful proven strategies for maximazing value.* (3 ed.). London and Sterling,VA: CIM, Kogan Page.

Hofstede, G. and Hofstede, G.J. (2005). *Cultures and Organisations. Software of the Mind.* (2 ed.). New York: McGraw-Hill.

Iliescu, D., and Petre, D. (2004). *Psihologia reclamei şi a consumatorului. Psihologia consumatoprului [The Psychology of advertising and consumer. Psychology of the consumer].* Bucharest: Comunicare.ro

Ionescu, C. (2007). *Agenţiile de presă din România [The Press Agencies in Romania].* (2 ed.). Bucharest: Tritonic.

Initiative Media Agency (2007). *Media Fact Book.* (10 ed.). Retrieved June 30, 2007, from http://www.initiativemedia.ro/en/download/MFB.pdf

IQAds (2005a). "Relaţiile Publice din România şi practicile internaţionale" [Public Relations in Romania and international practices] Retrieved June 30, 2007, from http://www.iqads.ro/stire_1244/relatiile_publice_din_romania_si_practicile_internationale.html.

IQAds (2005b). IR—o formă de comunicare aproape inexistentă în România [IR- a form which is not existent in Romania]. Retrieved June 30, 2007, from http://www.iqads.ro/revistapresei_1029/ir___o_forma_de_comunicare_aproape_inexistenta_in_romania.html.

IQAds (2006). Crenguţa Roşu: PR-ul nu este "salonul de cosmetică" [Crenguţa Roşu [PR is not the "beauty saloon"]. Retrieved November 10, 2007, from http://www.iqads.ro/interviul_6184/crenguta_rosu__pr_ul_nu_este_salonul_de_cosmetica.html.

IQAds (2007a). CCRP a finalizat primul studiu asupra imaginii si utilizarii relatiilor publice in Romania [CCRP finalised the first study about the image and the usage of Public Relations in Romania]. Retrieved June 30, 2007, from http://www.iqads.ro/stire_6540/ccrp_a_finalizat_primul_studiu_asupra_imaginii_si_utilizarii_relatiilor_publice_in_romania.html.

IQAds (2007b). ARRP organizează conferinţa "Comunicare-Bani-Dezvoltare [ARRP organises the Conference 'Communication-Money-Development']. Retrieved November 22, 2007, from http://www.iqads.ro/stire_7805/arrp_organizeaza_conferinta_comunicare_bani_dezvoltare_html.

Ławniczak, R. (ed.) (2005). *Introducing Market Economy Institutions and Instruments: The Role of Public Relations in Transition Economies.* Poznań: Piar.pl.

Mic Dicţionar Enciclopedic [Concise Encyclopedic Dictionary] (1986). Academia "Ştefan Gheorghiu" [The Academy "Ştefan Gheorghiu"]. Bucharest: Editura Ştiinţifică şi Enciclopedică, p. 6.

Miron, M. (1996). *Comportamentul consumatorului [Consumer Behaviour].* Bucharest: ALL.

Muchielli, A. (2002). *Arta de a influenţa. Analiza tehnicilor de manipulare [L'art d'influencer. Analyse des techniques de manipulation].* Iaşi, Romania: Polirom.

Munglu, A. (1995). *Românll după '89. Istoria unei neînţelegeri [Romanians after '89. History of a misunderstanding]* Bucharest: Humanitas.

Noelle-Neumann, E. (2004). *Spirala tăcerii. Opinia publică–învelişul nostru social [Die Schweigespirale. Öffentliche Meinung–unsere soziale Haut].* Bucharest: comunicare.ro.

Olivesi, S. (dir.) (2006). *Sciences de l'information et de la comunication. Objets, savoirs, discipline.* Grenoble: Presses Universitaires de Grenoble.

Oprea, R.(2007a, February). Responsabilitatea socială [Social Responsibility]. *Campaign România,* p. 7.

Oprea, R. (2007b, February). Mă interesează ca tinerii să revină la TVR1 (Interviu cu Dana Deac, noul director al TVR1) ["I am interested that young audience return to TVR1. (An interview with Dana Deac, the new TVR1 director)]. *Campaign România,* p. 17.

Păun, C. (2007a, March). Primul studiu pentru PR-ul românesc [First study on Romanian PR]. *Campaign România,* p. 43.

Păun, C. (2007b) "Viaţa în agenţiile de relaţii publice" [Living in Public Relations Agencies], *Campaign Romania,* September, 52–55.

Petcu, M. (2002). *O istorie ilustrată a publicităţii româneşti [An Illustrated History of Romanian Publicity].* Bucharest: Tritonic.

Popescu, C.F. (2007). *Dicţionar de jurnalism, relaţii publice şi publicitate [Dictionary of journalism, public relations and publicity].* (2ed.). Bucharest: Niculescu.

Pricopie, R. (2005). *Relaţiile publice. Evoluţie şi perspective [Public Relations. Evolution and perspectives].* Bucharest: Tritonic.

Publicitatea merge cu metroul [Publicity takes the metro]. (2006, December). *Campaign România,* p. 35.

Raportul agenţiilor [The Report of the Agencies]. (2007, June). *Campaign România,* 26–33.

Rogojinaru, A. (2005a). *Relaţiile publice. Fundamente interdisciplinare [Public Relations. Interdisciplinary Fundamentals].* Bucharest: Tritonic.

Rogojinaru, A. (2005b, November 10–13). *Public Relations in transition societies: which publics, which methods, what impact.* Paper submitted at 7th Annual EUPRERA Congress "New Challenges for Public Relations," Lisbon, Portugal.

Rogojinaru, A. (ed.) (2006). *Relaţii publice şi publicitate. Tendinţe şi provocări* [Public Relations and Publicity. Trends and Challenges]. Bucharest: Tritonic.

Rogojinaru, A. (2007, May–June). România–#Imposibilitatea unui brand naţional" [Romania–the impossibility of the national brand]. *Altitudini*, 15–16, 5–6.

Sandu, D. (2006). *Viaţa socială în România urbană [Social life in urban Romania]*. Iaşi, Romania: Polirom.

Siguranţa muncii, mereu în atenţia Petrom [Work safety always in the attention of PETROM]. (2007, September–October). *Campaign România,* p. 59.

Sriramesh, K., and Verčič, D. (2003). *The Handbook of Global Public Relations: Theory, Research, and Practice.* Mahwah, NJ: Lawrence Erlbaum Associates.

Teodorescu, B., Guţu, D., and Enache, R. (2005). *Cea mai bună dintre lumile posibile. Marketingul politic în România—1990–2005 [The best of all possible worlds. Political marketing in Romania—1990–2005].* Bucharest: Comunicare.ro.

Theaker, A. (2001). *The Public Relations Handbook.* London: Routledge.

Tismăneanu, V., Dobrincu, D., Vasile, C. (Eds.) (2007). *Raport final [Final report].* Comisia prezidenţială pentru analiza dictaturii comuniste din România [Presidential Commission for the Analysis of Communist Dictatorship in Romania]. Bucharest: Humanitas.

UNDP (2006). Human Development Report 2006. Human Report Development Indicators, Country Fact Sheet, Romania. Retrieved June 30, 2007, from Human Development Report 2006—Country Fact Sheets—Romania 2006.htm.

Vasilescu, M. (2001). *Mass-comedia. Situaţii şi moravuri ale presei de tranziţie [Mass-Commedia. Situations and habits of the press in transition].* Bucharest: Curtea Veche.

Wilcox, D.L., and Cameron, G.T. (2006). *Public Relations. Strategies and Tactics.* (8 ed.). Boston: Pearson Education.

Zamfir, C. (2004). *O analiză critică a tranziţiei. Ce va fi,după' [A critical analysis of transition.What is next].* Bucharest: Polirom.

Zerfass, A., Van Ruler, B., Rogojinaru, A., Verčič, D., and Hamrefors, S. (2007). *European Communication Monitor 2007. Trends in Communication Management and Public Relations—Results and Implications.* Leipzig: University of Leipzig /Euprera. Retrieved September 30, 2007, from www.communication monitor.eu.

Ziarul Financiar (2007). Cei mai mari jucători din economie [The most important players in economy]. (2007, June). Special issue. *Ziarul Financiar, Anuarul de business al României.*

28

A Hungarian Rhapsody: The Evolution and Current State of Hungarian Public Relations

Gyorgy Szondi

INTRODUCTION

Hungary is located in the heart of Europe with a population of slightly over ten million people, out of which two million live in Budapest, the capital. Four million Hungarians live in neighboring countries, including Slovakia, Romania, Serbia and Ukraine. Hungarians are of Finno-Ugric origin and as a people have been living in the Danube Basin for more than 1,000 years. The Hungarian state was established by King Stephen I, who took up Christianity in the year 1000. In the centuries that followed, Hungary became the leading power in Central Europe until Hungarian lands were subjected to Mongol invasion and later to Turkish occupation in 1526 which lasted 150 years. In the mid-nineteenth century, Hungary established a liberal constitutional monarchy under the Austrian Hapsburgs, which lasted until the Austro-Hungarian monarchy collapsed after the First World War. The Trianon Treaty of 1920 redrew Hungary's borders and took away a third of its territory and 40 percent of the population, resulting in Hungarian minorities in Romania, Slovakia and Serbia. After the Second World War, a communist dictatorship prevented true independence. In 1956, Soviet forces crushed an uprising by Hungarians seeking to liberalize the political and economic system and to break away from Soviet influence. The revolution remains prominent in the country's consciousness.

Hungary played a key role in the collapse of the socialist system, when in May 1989 the country opened its borders with Austria and allowed thousands of East Germans to escape to the West. Despite protests from the East German government, Hungary refused to close the borders. After East Germany sealed its own borders, East Germans took to the streets of Leipzig, Dresden and Berlin, where mass demonstrations led to the fall of the Berlin

Wall in November 1989. In October 1989 the free and independent Republic of Hungary emerged, followed by free elections in 1990. In 1999 Hungary joined NATO and in 2004 became a member of the European Union.

HISTORY, DEVELOPMENT AND STATUS OF THE PROFESSION

Public Relations in the Communist Era

Public relations in Hungary dates back to the 1960s when the country embarked on economic and political liberalization. January 1968 signaled the official launch of a series of economic and social reforms, called the "New Economic Mechanism," which attempted to combine features of central planning and those of the market mechanism. It was a major shift to decentralization in an attempt to overcome the inefficiencies of central planning. The reforms triggered changes in many areas: enterprises won greater autonomy in decisions over production and investment at the expense of central planners; a new pricing system was introduced; there was increased independence from centralized state control in some areas of economy, education and culture, some freedom of travel, and modest social protection and welfare. The reforms were based on a tacit compact between the Communist Party and the people: in exchange for leaving politics to the Communist Party and the government, the people could experience some economic prosperity.

Consumerism emerged during the 1970s, together with a limited private sector in the form of small businesses and business partnerships. Hungary became "the happiest barrack in the bloc." Openness towards the West, which included massive imports of Western goods and know-how, was an important feature of so-called "market socialism" or the "Hungarian model," which seemed to be a feasible system of reforms within the Eastern bloc. To promote and explain the New Economic Mechanism the government engaged in several communication campaigns. One of them was a 24-part TV serial where "Dr. Brain," an animated cartoon figure, explained the basics of market economy to the public.

The publication of the first book on public relations in Hungarian coincided with the start of the reforms, as the book was published in 1968. Its author was József Lipót and the book was entitled *Pubic Relations a gyakorlatban* ("Public Relations in Practice"), including the English term itself. The book was unique in many senses, as it brilliantly adopted and applied public relations as a "capitalist tool" to the socialist economic conditions (one might think of today's China where the term "socialist public relations" better describes the practice).

Mr Lipót's pioneering book was not only the first book devoted to public relations in Hungary but the first public relations book ever published in Eastern Europe. Some 3,800 copies were published, which sold out in a year. It had very positive feedback from business circles, which encouraged Mr Lipót to write a second volume; however, in political circles the book was criticized (one of the critical voices came from as far as East Germany), as the suspicious-sounding "public relations" was considered a capitalist tool. As a result, no publisher was willing to publish another book on public relations, and up to 1990 Mr. Lipót's book remained the only one entirely devoted to public relations.

One of the most noteworthy features of the book was that the author clearly separated public relations from both advertising and propaganda. He provided the following definition:

> Public relations is a more extensive and clearly separate activity from advertising and propaganda. Public relations is a company's or organization's efforts to inform and get informed,

alter its actions and coordinate behavior according to its interests—but at the same time in accordance with facts and truth—through two-way relations established with its publics; ultimately to create and maintain understanding and trust. Public relations work is a continuous, planned, purposeful and complex activity that uses all available means in a complementary way and—under ideal circumstances—starts simultaneously with the establishment of a company or organization until it ceases to exist. (Lipót, 1968: 3).

Mr. Lipót also called for the establishment of public relations departments in organizations. In state-owned companies, advertising and propaganda were combined in one department (Department of Advertising and Propaganda), while press relations were handled by press offices. Only a handful of companies established public relations departments and employed "public relations officers," using the English title towards the end of the 1960s.

Another significant feature of the book was that it was based on personal experience and was therefore very practical. Mr. Lipót started his career at the Hungarian Chamber of Commerce, which was probably the first organization that consciously made use of and promoted public relations in Hungary. The Chamber focused on export promotion and in order to be more effective in foreign markets its attention turned to public relations. The Chamber's aim was to promote exports by creating an international identity and reputation for Hungarian companies abroad and—as an overall goal—to create a strong country image in key foreign markets. Already in the mid-1960s several articles appeared about public relations in Hungary. *Külkereskedelmi Propaganda* (Foreign Trade Propaganda) was the Chamber's bi-monthly trade journal, which devoted a whole issue to public relations in May 1966. The Chamber organized several training courses on public relations during the 1960s and 1970s. In 1966 they invited Sam Black, a leading figure in British public relations, to deliver a seminar on public relations for those who use it or work as public relations officers. As Mr Lipót recalls Sam Black was taken by surprise how much participants had already known about public relations and during the seminar he was asked to go beyond the basics of public relations. All these initiatives and events demonstrate that in Hungary the seeds of public relations were sown in the 1960s when a public relations approach to communication emerged, although confined to certain sectors and companies only. It is important to note that the 1968 reforms marked a new era for advertising and marketing too when two organizations were given monopolistic powers: Hungexpo Advertising focused on external trade and business, while Magyar Hirdető monopolized the Hungarian advertising market. The duty of "socialist advertising" was to inform people about products, their benefits for the consumer and to increase sales in order to make companies and the national economy more profitable.

The other line of development of Hungarian public relations was related to libraries during the 1970s and 1980s, especially to the Széchényi National Library and the National Technical Information Centre and Library which not only published booklets and other materials on public relations but organized several conferences, seminars and clubs about the theoretical and practical aspects of developing and maintaining relations with the public, so contributing to the dissemination of public relations. Some campaigns were also organized to make libraries more popular among the citizens and to promote their use. The "Public Relations Committee" of the Management and Leadership Scientific Society was established in February 1970 and led by Dr. Endre Marinovich, who defended his doctorate about the role of economic and societal relations in the market in 1966. From 1971 until 1987 Dr Marinovich headed the press office of the Ministry of Foreign Trade and often organized public relations training workshops for governmental press officers.

(His wife was the late Dr Márta Németh, who established and chaired the first public relations department in 1994 at the College of Foreign Trade.)

By the 1980s several companies used public relations consciously as a distinct function from advertising and propaganda, including department stores, export companies, trade organizations, libraries and ministries. From 1982 Mr Lipót was the public relations officer of Transelectro, an electrical foreign trade company, where public relations was a planned activity, approved and supported by the director of the company. It was Mr Lipót's initiative to produce annual reports for Transelectro. It was a long and tedious process to collect and compile all the necessary data but his efforts bore fruit when in 1983 the company's first annual report was published in 2,000 copies.

In the 1980s public relations appeared as a chapter in marketing, export marketing and advertising textbooks, following the marketing view of public relations. The first public relations course was taught in 1988 as part of the Marketing Communication degree program although public relations lectures were held at the Carl Marx University of Economics as early as the 1970s. By the mid-1980s public relations was gaining momentum as an emerging profession. In 1988 the International Public Relations Association's (IPRA) annual conference took place in Vienna and the participants were invited to Budapest as well where IPRA's first East–West Public Relations Conference was organized.

Public Relations in Democracy: The First Steps of Professionalization

The Hungarian Public Relations Association (HPRA, *Magyar Public Relations Szövetség*) was established in December 1990 with 40 members. In 1992 public relations became a profession recognized by the Office of Central Statistics as "Business Counseling." In the same year the HPRA developed a standardized public relations terminology. The first public relations degree program at undergraduate level was launched in 1992.

The Foundation for Public Relations Development was established in 1995 at the initiative of HPRA. The Foundation strives for higher standards in and wider recognition for public relations by constantly modernizing and developing the methods and techniques used in public relations. Despite its aim to coordinate research in public relations and further develop public relations education, the Foundation has done very little since the turn of the millennium. The first public relations magazine, *PR Herald* was also launched in 1995 and it was the monthly professional journal until its bankruptcy in 2001. In 2004 the journal was re-launched in an on-line format (http://www.prherald.hu) and serves as the news portal of the communication profession. *Kreatív,* the monthly professional marketing communication journal, devotes a section to public relations too but otherwise no print journal is dedicated to the discipline.

Within the framework of IPRA's annual conference, which was held in Budapest in 1996, the first International Public Relations Film and Video Festival Prince Award was launched. The purpose of the festival, endorsed by IPRA and the European Public Relations Confederation (CERP), is "to maintain the dynamic development of the art and knowledge of public relations as well as to provide opportunity for presenting professional public relations films, videos and different types of multimedia." Budapest hosted the first regional IPRA conference for Central and Eastern Europe in May 2002. The conference concluded with the "Budapest Statement" on the establishment of IPRA's Central and Eastern European Regional Chapter.

HPRA issued four fundamental documents, named after Hungarian cities where the annual meetings took place. The "Gárdony Declaration," adopted in 1993, defines the terminology of public relations, the basic principles and areas of the field. In the

"Székesfehérvár Declaration," HPRA clearly defines the role and functions of public relations in organizations and the different job titles and relevant responsibilities of public relations practitioners. The "Veszprém Declaration," adopted in 1995, is concerned with the relationship between marketing and public relations. The Code of Ethics, adopted in 2000, is based on the professional standards and ethical guidelines of IPRA and CERP. HPRA members have always regarded international relations as particularly important for the development of the practice. Several Hungarian practitioners have been members of international professional organizations from as early as the mid-1980s.

The development of Hungarian public relations was influenced by American, British, German and Austrian public relations practitioners and scholars. When the foundation of Hungarian public relations was emerging during the second half of the 1980s, the founders of the Hungarian PR Association turned to IPRA and the Public Relations Society of America (PRSA) for professional help and support. They participated at IPRA's annual conference in Toronto and went on a study tour in the USA, organized by the PRSA, where they acquired some important know-how and established crucial contacts with leading public relations practitioners. On their return they organized a forum for other Central and Eastern European countries, including Czechoslovakia, Romania and Yugoslavia, with the aim of promoting public relations in the region by passing on their knowledge and experience acquired in North America. During the early 1990s contacts were established with Austrian and German universities whose lecturers provided German textbooks and other publications on public relations.

A factor that negatively influenced the perception of public relations during the 1990s was lobbying due to its unregulated practice. During the past few years, however, the professionalization of lobbying has speeded up. The "First Lobby Association" was established in 2002, the same year when an MA in Lobbying was launched at the University of Economics. So far some 50 people have graduated from the course, many of them CEOs, who often consider lobbying as their own responsibility inside the company. To make lobbying activities more transparent and accountable, the so called "Lobbying Act" was passed in 2006, which defines the duties and obligations of lobbyists. They must be registered and produce quarterly reports, which disclose their lobbying activities, methods, clients and fees. A few books on lobbying and public affairs have also been recently published.

The Status of the Profession

An estimated 5,000 people work in public relations, based on a broad interpretation of the profession. There are around 80 public relations agencies in Hungary, including one or two manned consultancies and depending on how broadly public relations is interpreted. Membership in the Hungarian Public Relations Association is slowly increasing; in 2007 320 practitioners were members. The Association is determined to increase membership and motivate more practitioners to join who are often reluctant to do so or do not see the benefits of joining the organization. HPRA was very passive and nearly invisible around the turn of the millennium. With the 2005 election of Dr Szeles, a pioneering figure of Hungarian public relations who also served as the president between 1991 and 1997, the organization is striving to become an opinion former and more proactive in making the profession's voice heard.

One of the most extensive research projects about the public relations activities of Hungarian companies was done by Annax International Communication Agency. The research was carried out in 2002 and surveyed the top 200 companies (http://www.btl.hu). Fifty-six percent of these companies had a separate public relations department while marketing or human resources departments managed public relations activities in the rest of the cases. Foreign investors owned nearly half of the companies surveyed. Forty-one percent of the respondents referred to the initiatives of these investors as the main reason for engaging in public relations activities, which are often developed and controlled by the foreign headquarters of these multinational companies.

The most frequently quoted purpose of public relations was the need to enhance the reputation of the company. In the light of these attitudes it is not surprising that most companies engage in public relations to "develop a better image" and to "generate trust" towards products, services or the company. In half the companies surveyed, public relations does not contribute to developing business strategies or to the decision-making process. Public relations is brought into play when the decisions have already been made and only need to be communicated to the relevant publics (82 percent). In most cases, public relations comes down to establishing and maintaining effective media relations (93 percent) and to organizing and managing events (86 percent). Other areas, such as internal communication, investor relations and sponsorship, are often managed by other departments, such as the marketing department. Seventy-seven percent of the firms surveyed have already employed a public relations agency and 50 percent were working with at least one agency. Twenty-six percent of respondents reported negative experiences with the services of agencies; only 17 percent were completely satisfied. The rest of the answers included mixed experiences.

In 2005 another survey of the top 200 companies' top executives or managers, to whom the public relations manager or agency report, found that three quarters of those executives considered public relations as an important activity (http://www.marketinginfo.hu). The most common aims of public relations were identified as follows:

1   to enhance the image of the organization (85 percent),

2   to improve the company's market position (59 percent),

3   to support the "fight" against competitors (54 percent),

4   to gain and strengthen the trust of investors (54 percent).

Half of the executives agreed that the company should increase its public relations budget to be more efficient although two thirds of the companies would not change their public relations budget in the following year while a third of the companies would probably decrease their budgets in the following three years. In 2005 the companies surveyed spent 100,000 Euros on average on public relations. When choosing a public relations agency their most important criteria were competency and the professionalism of the consultancy team. Seventy-nine percent of those companies that had employed a public relations agency were satisfied with the agency but this rate dropped to 58 percent as far as value for money was concerned. More than a third of the surveyed managers could not name a single public relations agency which may be interpreted as their lack of direct involvement in public relations decision making or everyday account management.

As far as evaluation is concerned, the only extensive, empirically based research to identify Hungarian practitioners' behavior and attitudes towards evaluation was carried out in 1999 (Szondi, 1999). Seventy-eight percent of the practitioners surveyed valued the role of evaluation in public relations as important or very important, in contrast to 12 percent who did not attribute any importance to it at all. The view that it is possible to measure effectiveness was shared by 47 percent of respondents and a third thought it was impossible. Hungarian practitioners identified effectiveness in public relations with effectiveness at the program level, and only one practitioner mentioned that it should be assessed in relation to organizational goals. A fifth of the respondents considered evaluation as an opportunity to justify their own work to clients or the management, a phenomenon typical of a relatively young profession. Press clippings were the most widely used method to measure output, followed by media content analysis to evaluate public relations efforts in terms of outcome. The former method was mentioned by half of the respondents which suggests that measuring output is more important to practitioners than outcome assessment. A third of Hungarian practitioners rated the intangible and unquantifiable aspect of evaluations as most serious, closely followed by the lack of time and that of budget.

To measure and quantify the results of corporate public relations activities, a public relations and an interactive agency developed "newzeus," a software program which combines stakeholder theory and reporting. The software concentrates on print media coverage and measures the results of media relations by important indicators for the organization. The *Stakeholder Map* presents the stakeholders in terms of their importance/weight within the industry, and the current threat level that they represent (based on their positive/ negative communication activity), using a system of visual coordinates. The *Media Map* displays the various media outlets in terms of their importance/weight and current attitude, using a system of visual coordinates. Finally, the *Newzeus Index* (NI) compares the organization's public relations value with the aggregate average public relations value of the key players (stakeholders) in the industry in which the specific organization operates (http://www.newzeus.hu). The major issue with this software is that it is based on advertising value equivalent (AVE) to enable the organization's communication to be expressed in figures.

Current Issues

By 2000 several consultancies had specialized in sector and industry specific communication, such as health care, IT, energy or financial sector but the relatively small size of the public relations market has prevented agencies from focusing exclusively on one or two public relations specialisms, such as financial public relations or public affairs. After the accession to the European Union, public relations in Central Europe became one of the fastest growing industries. Some local public relations agencies joined international public relations consultancy networks: a strategy to provide global clients with an Eastern European regional approach. In addition, local public relations agencies are creating liaisons across the region, to provide an integrated international service.

Evaluation still remains a key issue in the Hungarian public relations industry. A recent phenomenon is that potential clients are asking for guarantees to secure desired or promised outcomes. In this "payment by results" game some potential clients go as far as wanting the agency to pay a deposit (penalty for non-fulfillment of the contract terms and outcome, which could be as much as 30–40 percent of the total fee) and would guarantee agreed and measurable results. Should the agency not deliver these results or make major mistakes the deposit is lost together with the total or part of the fee. Most public relations agencies are not willing to engage in this process and some might even reduce consultancy fees just to avoid paying deposits or giving guarantees. This can be dangerous as public relations agencies may begin adopting unrealistic evaluation measures and methods to make the impact of their work more tangible. In the light of this, it is not surprising that advertising value equivalents (AVE) remains widely used in Hungary to measure success in media coverage. At the other end of the spectrum, however, a few agencies have managed to get their clients to pay extra, should the agency "over perform" or achieve results which go beyond the goals set in the contract. This is still rare especially since the Hungarian public relations market has become very price sensitive, often at the expense of professionalism. Contracts or tenders are often won by the cheapest offers rather than by the most professional ones, as smaller local agencies are willing to work for less.

Corporate Social Responsibility

Corporate Social Responsibility is gaining ground slowly although it is not an entirely new phenomenon. During state socialism many big state companies used to have their own playground, sports fields, child care system and company holiday schemes to look after their employees and the local communities. After the collapse of communism these units were quickly sold off and about fifteen years later, were "rediscovered" in the form of CSR. Since 2004 the number of forums, conferences and workshops devoted to CSR has been on the increase and the public relations profession has had an important role to play in promoting socially responsible practice. In 2006 the Public Relations Association launched the "CSR Best Practice" initiative to reward the companies with the best CSR programs. A number of issues, however, have hindered the spread of CSR in Hungary. The first one is that in many Eastern European countries CSR is purely associated with sponsorship, which means that many CEOs labor under the illusion that by sponsoring children's hospitals or a good cause, the company has fulfilled its CSR obligations. Second, the Hungarian media have a negative, skeptical and cynical attitude towards CSR which makes CSR communication difficult. The media interpret CSR either as greenwashing or as "hidden advertising" where the companies' sole aim is to increase sales. In 2005 the National Radio and Television Board (NRTB) fined a major media channel when it reported on a CSR event. Under the Hungarian Media Act every time a company's name is mentioned, it is considered to be advertisement and it is banned outside permitted advertisement periods. Instead of reporting on CSR, several print media outlets offer advertising space for companies to communicate their CSR activities. To change the situation and help the Radio and Television Board to be able to separate genuine CSR from hidden advertising, the Hungarian Public Relations Association nominated an independent advisory board to assist NRTB in resolving disputes. To raise awareness of CSR and its importance in society 1 June was declared as the "CSR Day" by eight large corporations and media channels, which grouped together in 2006 to organize a conference on CSR and launch the initiative.

Education

Education in public relations is characterized by numerous vocational courses at postsecondary levels and by academic undergraduate programs. Vocational courses range from some weeks to a complete academic year. At academic level, the first—and so far the only—public relations department was established at the College of Foreign Trade in 1994 (the college is now part of the Budapest Business School); this department was the forerunner of public relations education in Hungary until 2006, when the department was renamed. This is due to the switch to the Bologna system in higher education where only newly accredited programs can be taught. Public relations programs were among the negatively evaluated programs, as the academic community and the accrediting board did not consider it as an academic discipline worthwhile as an independent program of study. Another factor that could have contributed to the assessment of public relations studies is that interdisciplinary studies do not have a long tradition in Hungary.

In order to avoid "public relations" some universities have started to use terms such as "organizational communicator" or "business communicator." Today, eight universities or colleges offer undergraduate public relations courses and/or degrees schemes full-time, part-time or as a distance-learning scheme. Masters level education in public relations does not exist in Hungary. The public relations degree program at Budapest Business School is now hosted by the Department of Media Studies and Social Communication. Students specialize in public relations during their final year of study and prior to that they receive a strong business foundation together with proficiency in two foreign languages. At the rest of the universities, departments of communication or media studies host most public relations courses. Public relations education is evenly distributed across the country, unlike the profession, which has a very strong concentration in the capital.

Each year some 300 students graduate with a public relations degree in Hungary but the demand for public relations graduates is much lower. We could probably conclude that in Hungary there is mass education in public relations at the undergraduate level, which is not necessarily a bad thing. Although it is very difficult to find jobs in public relations as a new graduate, the number of people with basic understanding of the principles of public relations with positive attitudes towards the discipline is increasing in this way.

Practitioners acknowledge the importance of education as a way of improving the status and quality of public relations, but they seem to be critical towards the current level of education. This is partly based on their experiences with new graduates as many public relations agency owners voice their concern about the lack of well-qualified and experienced public relations practitioners. On the other hand, many practitioners teach on public relations courses or are frequent guest speakers which should result in bridging the gap between universities, as producers of knowledge, and the public relations industry as consumers of knowledge.

The most significant forums of professional development are probably the in-house courses and seminars of the public relations agencies. These courses are short in duration but very focused and practice-oriented, and often take place abroad. In 2005 an online knowledge portal—*Practice*—was launched which offers downloadable surveys, articles, studies, video films, educational and other materials in Hungarian and in English. This portal partly fills the knowledge void created by the lack of public relations textbooks in Hungarian, as only a few books have been published and most of them are rather basic. None of the major American or British textbooks have been translated into Hungarian, unlike in other Eastern European countries where these translations dominate the public relations textbook market.

ENVIRONMENTAL FACTORS AND PUBLIC RELATIONS

Political Economy

Hungary is a multiparty democracy. Since the first free elections in 1990, Hungarian democracy has been stable, with all governments serving their full four-year term. Hungary joined the European Union in 2004, prior to which the biggest ever public communication campaigns took place to increase domestic support for EU membership and mobilize citizens to vote in referendum campaigns (Szondi, 2007). The parliament has 386 members: 176 are elected from single-member constituencies, 140 from regional lists and 70 from a national list. The president, whose duties are mainly ceremonial, is elected by the parliament. A proposal to move to pure proportional representation was discussed in 2007 but not yet adopted, as was a proposal to shrink Parliament to fewer than 300 members.

At the last parliamentary elections in 2006, four parties or party alliances passed the minimum threshold of 5 percent: the Hungarian Socialist Party (MSZP), the coalition party Alliance of Free Democrats (SZDSZ), the Hungarian Civic Party (FIDESZ) in alliance with the Christian Democratic People's Party (KDNP), the Hungarian Democratic Forum (MDF) and one independent candidate. The very tight outcome of the elections resulted in the re-election of the previously ruling Socialist–Liberal coalition government, lead by Mr Ferenc Gyurcsány but also in the deepening of the gap between the political "left" and the "right" which has long divided Hungary. Every single issue becomes politicized in Hungary even if it has nothing to do with politics. Public relations practitioners often struggle to keep politics and politicians from interfering in areas in which they are not competent. The division of Hungarian society along political views and strong politicization of anything and everything can be considered as Hungary's cultural black hole.[1]

To create consensus on the EU accession between the political left and right and to link the two sides, a pontoon bridge was built over the river Danube for a few days in March 2003, as a part of the EU referendum campaign. The public relations work for the "Europe Bridge"—which was crossed by almost half a million Hungarians—was done by Hill and Knowlton Hungary.

In September 2006 comments of the Prime Minister, made in a May internal party meeting, were leaked to the press. In the recorded remarks, Gyurcsány, a former communist turned billionaire, admitted that he and his government had repeatedly lied to the electorate about its budgetary and economic performance. A few weeks after his taped comments were revealed, his government survived a no-confidence vote. The ruling coalition parties suffered badly in local elections held later that month, indicating a surviving but much weakened and distrusted government. By 2007 the government's trust index was at an all-time low. The deepening political and economic crises led to the break-up of the coalition between the Socialists and the Liberals, resulting in a minority government from May 2008.

Under communism people learned not to trust the official rhetoric and had to learn how to read between the lines, which still makes many people skeptical towards governmental communication even today. The lack of trust in government, official rhetoric, media and business still prevails and continuous changes during the transition period have not improved the situation. Hungary held the 39th-40th place on the 180-nation global corruption list, based upon the 2007 Corruption Perceptions Index. A government anti-corruption body was created in August 2007 with the remit of tackling sleaze, tax evasion and corruption. However, the ruling Socialist Party's involvement in many scandals and corruption cases further decreased people's trust in the government and its policies.

Politics and political communication have largely contributed to the mixed perceptions of public relations in Hungary. Public relations became widely known between 1998 and 2002, under the conservative government, led by FIDESZ. It was the first government to consciously use public relations. The newspapers close to the government were using the term "public relations" in a positive context, while the journalists not in favor of the government had very negative attitudes towards public relations, associating it with manipulation, propaganda and fake activities (Szondi, 2003). Today, the situation is the same but the Socialists are in government and FIDESZ is in opposition.

After re-election, the Hungarian government embarked on an ambitious four-year consolidation program following another election-year peak in the national budget deficit in

---

[1] Lewis (2007, p.117) defined a cultural black hole as "an undiscussable core belief of such intense gravity that it transcends or distorts any other beliefs, values, or set of principles that enter inside the spherical boundary of its gravitational field and absorbs, indeed swallows up, the precepts held by the 'victim.'

2006 at 9.2 percent of GDP. The origins of the budget deficit date back to the communist era: although Hungary enjoyed one of the most liberal and economically advanced economies of the former Eastern bloc, both agriculture and industry began to suffer from a lack of investment in the 1970s, and Hungary's net foreign debt rose significantly: from $1 billion in 1973 to $15 billion in 1993, due largely to consumer subsidies and unprofitable state enterprises. The budget consolidation program launched in 2006 included slimming state administration by 20 percent, seriously reforming health care, and imposing other cost-cutting measures. Despite Hungary's leading role in its transition during the 1990s and being the most favorably assessed country, in 2007 Hungary was the only country in the EU which did not fulfill any of the so-called convergence criteria to join the Euro zone. The scandal over the prime minister's leaked comments robbed him of the political clout needed to implement the reform program, the necessity of which was very poorly communicated and explained to the public.

The private sector accounts for over 80 percent of GDP (CIA World Factbook). Foreign ownership of and investment in Hungarian firms are widespread, with cumulative foreign direct investment totaling more than $60 billion since 1989. Inflation declined from 14 percent in 1998 to 3.7 percent in 2006. Unemployment has persisted above 6 percent. Hungary's labor force participation rate of 57 percent is one of the lowest in the Organization for Economic Cooperation and Development (OECD). Germany is by far Hungary's largest economic partner.

In 2007 the economy was hit by a temporary inflationary shock: the consumer price index reached 9 percent in March, only to drop slightly again in April. Gross earnings increased 7.1 percent in the first quarter of 2007. Given the 6.2 percentage point difference between gross and net earnings, real earnings declined by 7 percent. Taking into account the strengthening of the forint, the national currency, as well as the anticipated privatization revenues, gross government debt was predicted to remain at 2006 level: approximately 66 percent of GDP. Exports and imports are expanding by 16 percent and 13 percent, respectively. An inflation rate of 7 percent was projected for 2007. The gross domestic product was projected to increase by 3.2 percent in 2007. This rate is lower than those of all other Central European countries, but it is slightly higher than the EU average. Investments were expected to expand by 4 percent (http://www.gki.hu).

TABLE 28.1

Hungary's Key Economic Indicators

GDP (PPP) $172.8 billion
GDP—real growth rate: 3.8 percent
GDP—per capita: purchasing power parity—$17,300
GDP—composition by sector:
agriculture: 3.1 percent
industry: 32.1 percent
services: 64.8 percent
Population below poverty line: 8.6 percent
Household income or consumption by percentage share:
lowest 10 percent: 4.1 percent
highest 10 percent: 21.2 percent
Inflation rate (consumer prices): 3.7 percent
Labor force: 4.2 million
Labor force—by occupation: services 61.2 percent, industry 33.3 percent, agriculture 5.5 percent
Unemployment rate: 7.4 percent
Literacy rate: 99 percent

Source: The CIA World Factbook, 2006

With about $18 billion in foreign direct investment (FDI) since 1989, Hungary has attracted over one-third of all FDI in Central and Eastern Europe, including the former Soviet Union. Of this, about $6 billion came from American companies. Foreign capital is attracted by skilled and relatively inexpensive labor, tax incentives, modern infrastructure, and a good telecommunications system. Public relations played a vital role in attracting investors to Hungary as well as in creating a strong country brand to promote economic, commercial and political interests abroad (Szondi, 2006).

Public relations played a crucial role in turning a centrally planned economic system into a market economy and during the privatizations of state owned companies. The economic conditions have enabled public relations to thrive, but the recent slowdown of GDP growth and the structural reforms have negatively affected the public relations market as well. The polarized and over politicized environment coupled with a lack of trust in politics and politicians have resulted in a very skeptical public, which is not receptive to governmental messages and perceives political and governmental public relations as propagandistic and deceitful. The unprofessional and sometimes unethical use of public relations during election campaigns has also devalued public relations to a certain extent.

Legal System

Hungary has a three-tiered, independent judiciary, in addition to the Supreme Court and a Constitutional Court. The constitution guarantees equality before the law and religious freedom, and provides for the separation of church and state. While adherents of all religions are generally free to worship in their own manner, the state provides financial support and tax breaks to four traditional groups, or "historical churches": the Roman Catholic Church, the Calvinist Church, the Lutheran Church, and the Alliance of Hungarian Jewish Communities. Despite this, Hungary remains one of the most secular countries in Eastern Europe.

Hungarian law is derived from the Roman-Germanic family of law. It bears some similarity to German-Austrian law, in terms of its criminal law and criminal proceedings. Legal guarantees are in place for the freedom of speech, expression, and the press. Declarations of freedom of the press are included in the Constitution, the 1986 Press Law, and the 1996 Media Law. Freedom of the press includes the freedom to launch media outlets, editorial freedom, and the prohibition of censorship. Broadcasting content and ownership in electronic media are regulated by the media law and the main supervisory body overseeing the industry is the National Radio and Television Board. It allocates frequencies and supervises the observation of the media law, including the amount of time taken up by advertising, or the appropriateness of the content of programs. It also has a commission for dealing with complaints from viewers. Freedom of expression is limited by restrictions on the dissemination of harmful content. Hate speech is regulated in the Penal Code, and the Media Law includes passages about it; the National Radio and Television Board can impose sanctions. The Board has often been involved in several disputes where companies and public relations agencies were charged with hidden advertising.

In 2005, parliament passed a law on electronic freedom of information, which obliges government bodies and organizations to make relevant information about their work, including the outcomes of legislative and judicial procedures, publicly accessible on the internet (http://www.ejc.net).

The Law on Business Advertisements absolutely prohibits advertisements of tobacco products in all radio and television broadcasting, and of alcoholic beverages in public service radio and television. Advertisements for alcoholic beverages are allowed in commercial

TV and radio with certain requirements. Tobacco and alcohol producing companies therefore engage in substantial public relations activities and use the services of public relations agencies. Some agencies, however, are not willing to work for tobacco companies.

Social Capital and Activism

During communism governments and governmental organization were discredited and distrusted as many officials and the political elite misused their positions. Communism left a very strong legacy in the political culture of Eastern Europe where an apathetic society, in which people did not trust their new governments and each other, replaced the state instead of a trusting civil society (Badescu and Uslaner, 2003).

As a result of communist legacies Eastern Europe is characterized by weak civil societies. Citizens throughout the region (Howard, 2003, p.148):

1. maintain strong feelings of mistrust of voluntary organizations, resulting from their prior experience with communist organizations

2. continue to make use of private friendship networks, which serve as a disincentive to joining voluntary organizations

3. feel rather disappointed with the new political and economic system, thus discouraging them even more from participating in public activities.

Hungarian citizens' participation in elections remains relatively low, with average turnout at the last two elections 64 percent, and membership in political, professional, and voluntary organizations lower than in the other countries of the EU. In 2005 the number of non-profit organizations reached 57,000 and employed 82,000 people. According to the 1999/2000 European Values Studies, Hungary came last among 25 European countries (including Russia too) regarding spending time in clubs and associations. Concerning active involvement in voluntary organizations Hungarians scored very low (Adam et al., 2005). Only 22 percent of Hungarian respondents believed that "people can generally be trusted," demonstrating a very low level of generalized trust.

After the prime minister's leaked tape in 2006 political activism increased as protesters have regularly demanded his resignation and several anti-government demonstrations were organized. Several political parties, civil groups and other formulations called for the resignation of the prime minister, who did not resign and did not even admit any wrongdoing, prompting many people to label Hungary as a country without consequences. This is an example of the *inefficiency of public communication* when public communicative acts representing some wrongdoing are not followed by the expected consequences (Terestyéni, 2000, p. 45). Inefficiency of public communication is one of the four types of public communicative disorders and failures that contradict democracy and weaken the ethos of building a better world in a post-communist society. Hungarian politics also provides several examples of the other types of defects of public communication identified by Terestyéni: declaring public information official or state secret; communicative intervention into the private sphere of citizens by the authorities and the media; and converting the discussions of public issues into political hostilities without solutions.

Despite Hungarians' low level of involvement in formal organizations, they belong to many different informal groups; social networks and connections are of great importance. People devote time and effort to building and maintaining relationships. Old boys' networks prevail in many areas of political, economic and social life, where informal networks still buy positions, power and success. In terms of how people relate to each other,

Trompenaars and Hampden-Turner's (1997) research also confirmed that Hungarian culture is more particularist than universalist, which means that relationships take precedence over rules. The dominance of connections and informal networks has implications for public relations too, since "knowing the right person" and having the "right connections" are often more important than professionalism. During the 1990s many former journalists set up their public relations agencies relying on their personal connections, while in the 2000s several former government officials and spokespeople who left the public sector set up a public relations agency or work as public relations advisors. Many foreign-owned public relations agencies have faced the challenge of overcoming the lack of informal networks, which often meant that public tenders were won by the smaller, well-connected but less professional public relations firms. Projects and investments funded by the EU require an accompanying communication campaign. The public tenders for these communication campaigns are often won by public relations agencies that have close or good connections with the government.

According to Howard (2003, p.153) these private networks do not serve as the functional equivalent of membership in voluntary organizations: instead of replacing them, private networks serve an important purpose alongside and in addition to public participation. Private networks play an important role in the conception of "social capital," the concept of which is slowly making its way into public relations theory and practice too (e.g. Hazleton and Kennan, 2000). Hungary is characterized—similarly to other post-communist countries—by an insufficient level of social capital. Public relations "from the bottom" can strengthen the civil society but as long as it is used only to strengthen the positions of the elites and the dominance of multinational organizations, its contribution to a more balanced power will remain limited.

Consumer associations have a low profile and Hungarian society is characterized by a low level of consumer awareness. There have been, however, a few national boycotts of products and multinational companies. For example Danone was the subject of consumer boycotts in 2001 when it bought a traditional, well established Hungarian biscuit factory. In spite of its promise not to close the Hungarian factory Danone decided to close it, which resulted in a country-wide boycott of its products and a 10 percent drop in sales. In 2007 activists called for a boycott of Austrian products as a result of pollution of the Raab River, which straddles the border between Austria and Hungary. The river contained over ten times the official limit of phosphate emissions in its water. Hungary blamed the pollution on a leather tannery on the Austrian side of the border and accused the Austrian authorities of "delaying tactics" in dealing with the problem.

A form of consumer activism is consumer nationalism, which is "the invocation of individuals' collective national identities in the process of consumption to favor or reject products" (Wang, 2005, p.225). If their national identity is threatened, Hungarians are united independently of their political orientation. A broken promise, wrongdoings, unjustified lay-offs, unethical treatment or crises may serve as the triggering event that could result in boycotting or pressurizing a multinational company or foreign government. For public relations practitioners, understanding the sensitivity of the Hungarian identity is essential for successful communication.

To counterbalance the dominance of multinational companies, some campaigns have also been organized to encourage Hungarians to buy Hungarian rather than foreign products, which is a response to prevent multinational companies from pushing out local companies from business. In a recent survey on food shopping 64 percent of respondents considered it important to buy Hungarian food products.

Greenpeace and environmental activist groups are present but not very visible: activism is contextual and is not driven by established organizations but evolves around particular issues when ad hoc groups form, making it difficult to identify a group with whom to negotiate. A common public relations mistake is that corporations ignore pressure groups and activists and are not willing to engage in a dialogue, until it is too late. These companies turn to public relations agencies once the issue has escalated into a crisis and they often lack an early warning system. However weak these pressure groups may seem, ignoring them and their demands can result in serious reputational damage. Strategic issues management is either non existent or remains very low profile for the majority of Hungarian organizations.

CULTURE

Hungary's corporate as well as societal culture has been significantly influenced by decades of communism, as have attitudes towards work, power and trust. This section reviews the most important characteristics of the Hungarian national as well as corporate cultures. Hofstede's and other researchers' findings on the different dimensions of the Hungarian culture are often contradictory. This may be attributable to the fact that in transitional countries the different dimensions of culture are not static but may be slowly changing, depending on the economic and social model the transition is aiming for.

Uncertainty avoidance is a critical dimension in transitional countries like Hungary. The transition from central planning to a market economy and from an authoritarian, one-party system into a pluralistic and democratic society has presented great challenges and uncertainty for the whole society and had serious impacts on people's lives. Both Hofstede's (2005) and several Hungarian researchers' findings confirmed that Hungary belongs to the high uncertainty avoidance countries where people prefer stability and predictability, and resist changes. People in these countries are less likely to take risks and tend to avoid decision making. This can have business implications as many managers as well as employees can resist change or hinder the process. The heritage of the socialist past can account for some of these issues as decision making was highly politicized and it was considered safer to avoid making decisions and let someone else "higher up" in the hierarchy do so (Baca, 1999). It has consequences for internal communication insofar as establishing direct communication and cooperation between the different departments can be a difficult issue. Avoiding decision making and responsibility is manifest in Hungarian managers' ability to resolve and handle conflict, which remains poor; consequently they avoid these situations. Another "strategy" of avoiding responsibilities is distorting or withholding information, which is a common feature of internal communication in many Hungarian companies (Borgulya and Barakonyi, 2004, 97). With a new generation of managers, educated in democratic conditions, the situation is slowly improving, however.

According to Hofstede (2005) Hungary is a very individualistic society—he ranked the country on the 4–6th position on his individualism scale. However, several Hungarian researchers found that *collectivism* is more dominant in Hungary than individualism (Heidrich, 2001). The Hungarian culture was influenced by both the Soviet (Russian) "collectivism" for decades and the individualistic Western corporate cultures in the course of the past two decades. Hungarians' high uncertainty avoidance and hesitation in taking risks and making decisions also underpins collectivism, rather than individualism. As Hofstede noted, collectivist societies are characterized by high-context communication where citizens communicate intensively. In a collective society collective interests prevail over individual interests and opinions are predetermined by group membership and social network tends to be the primary source of information. Individualism and collectivism have implications for organizations' and citizens' attitudes and behaviors towards corporate social responsibility and sustainable development. The impact of culture on the evolution, practice and communication of Corporate Social Responsibility (CSR) has been largely under-researched. In a collectivist society an individual's accountability and responsibility are considered limited, and could result in collective "irresponsibility." One of Trompenaars and Hampden-Turner's (1997, 141) cultural dimension is *orientations towards nature*: some societies believe that they can and should control nature by imposing their will upon it while other societies believe that they are part of nature and must go along with its laws. This orientation provides a crucial dimension of CSR context.

The Hungarian culture is affective: people's feelings are often expressed, and they seek for direct emotional response. It is also a diffuse culture where people engage in others in multiple areas and at several levels of personality at the same time. Work and private life are not separate in Hungary: employees discuss their private life with their colleagues openly; social and face-to-face communication at workplaces is of primary importance. Word-of-mouth is therefore an important channel of internal communication while rumor is a challenge.

Hungary belongs to the *high power distance* countries where inequalities among people are expected, privileges, positions and status symbols are important. Centralization and hierarchy are important in the workplace where subordinates expect to be told what to do. Similar to other high power distance countries, Hungary is characterized by large income differentials and by a shrinking middle class. Hofstede also found correlation between power distance and corruption: in large power distance countries corruption tends to be widespread; those in "power" are likely to accept side payments. To avoid fines and court charges the police are well known for accepting payments in Hungary while medical doctors are often given gratitude payments. Low civil service salaries (including doctors and public officials) often force them to accept these payments if they are to make ends meet. Although journalists are not civil servants, there have been cases when they also accepted bribes from public relations agencies or for-profit organizations to publish press releases.

Power distance is important so far as experts are concerned. In high power distance countries experts' opinions are very highly valued and they are among the most trusted people (Hofstede and Hofstede, 2005, 183). Opinions of experts or those in power are rarely questioned and subordinates are not encouraged to voice their own opinions. This has implications for public relations as well, since third party endorsement by opinion leaders and formers remains a very common and effective strategy in public relations. Professional competence rather than managerial skills is expected from superiors. An example of this is that Hungarian hospitals are headed by doctors; schools are "managed" by teachers rather than somebody with a managerial background. Since the opening of Swedish furniture retailer IKEA stores in 1990, the company has been using informal language in its corporate speech and it also addresses customers informally independently of whether they are young or old (using the Hungarian equivalent of the German *Du* or the French *tu*). IKEA was criticized several times for addressing customers informally, which was interpreted as impolite and disrespectful. Another example from public relations is that some clients of public relations consultancies are asking the consultancy to nominate somebody older and more senior to be the account director, as the younger generation are often not taken seriously or need to prove themselves first before being trusted by the client.

Several multinational companies with a low power distance home country which set up businesses or merged with Hungarian companies had to face the challenge of decreasing power distance in corporate culture through internal communication.

Hungary is more a *masculine* society than a feminine one, especially since the free market economy has emerged where challenge, competition, recognition and advancement are important especially in business circles. The implication for the public relations industry is that in masculine societies public relations is associated with females and significantly more public relations practitioners work in public relations while in a feminine society both genders are represented and there is a higher share of working women in professional jobs. According to the worldwide International Standard Classification of Occupations the proportion of women among administrative and managerial workers is the highest in Poland (66 percent), followed by Slovenia (60 percent) and Hungary came fifth (58 percent)

Hungary is a typical *past-oriented culture,* which emphasizes history and tradition, and a lack of vision and positive attitudes towards the future often prevail. In many aspects Hungarian culture is short-term rather than long-term orientated. Hungarians are also well known for their pessimism. Mobility is low, even within the country. People want to find work where they live and are not willing to move. The relatively low number of people who left Hungary for Western Europe after accession to the European Union is another sign of the low level of mobility.

Hungary is a tolerant country although some minority groups are still marginalized and face discrimination, such as the Roma community, which makes up approximately 5 percent of Hungary's population. The first member of the European Parliament of Roma origin was elected in 2004 by Hungarians when the country joined the EU.

Hungary has the biggest Chinese community in Central Europe, and China has recently chosen Hungary as its base for European business. Hill and Knowlton's Hungarian office recognized the importance of the Chinese market as early as 1996 when it started to produce company brochures and promotional materials in Chinese, to attract Chinese clients.

The implications of the above cultural dimensions for public relations activities are:

1   resistance to change which can be overcome by more intense and specific communication;
2   defining clear roles and responsibilities for communication;
3   avoiding dry facts and reasoning in communication and appealing to emotions and affections;
4   identifying and involving opinion leaders and formers;

Language

Hungarian, together with Finnish and Estonian, belongs to the Finno-Ugric language family making it rather isolated among the Slavonic languages that dominate Eastern Europe. Ex-pats and foreign managers moving to Hungary for business purposes usually make very little effort to learn the language and have to rely on interpreters. English has slowly taken over from German as a second language, although in western Hungary German remains widely spoken. In a 2005 Eurobarometer survey of 30 countries, Hungary came last in foreign language competency: 71 percent of Hungarian respondents were unable to converse in a foreign language (http://ec.europa.eu/public_opinion/archives/ebs/ebs_237.en.pdf).

As far as public relations is concerned, Hungarian public relations practitioners did not make much effort to find an adequate translation for the term. They instead had heated discussion whether these two words should be pronounced in English or in Hungarian and whether public relations should be written in lower case or upper case.

MASS MEDIA IN HUNGARY

Hungarian media are politicized, media outlets and journalists having strong political links and views, and therefore impartial, let alone objective, media hardly exist in Hungary. Post-communist media are characterized by a number of problems, which are rooted in the context of transformation in the region (Sükösd and Bajomi-Lázár, 2000). In the early years of the 1990s the dual broadcasting system was established in the region: the commercial channels, which often dominate media markets, and the public service. The crisis of public service broadcasting is manifested in identity and funding problems: commercial media have taken a significant part of advertising revenue from public broadcasters, underfunding makes public media dependent on government funding, thus the media are vulnerable to governments. Each successive Hungarian government has applied financial and political pressure on the media to secure favorable coverage, which, coupled with weak ethical norms among journalists and the low level of journalistic professionalism, has prevented the development of objective, independent news and current affairs programming. Political intervention manifested itself in many ways during the 1990s: newspapers were published by state-owned publishing houses, state-owned banks or other companies associated with the state. Financial support from the government has often had a political price in Hungary, such as removal of critical editors or journalists, or nominating politically loyal chief executives to public TV or radio channels, which often became the loudspeakers of a political party or government. This interlocking of media and politics is so strong in Hungary that politicians are major celebrities and are extensively covered by the press. Media celebrities often become government spokespeople while former government officials become public relations practitioners in contemporary Hungary. These practitioners usually engage in one-way communication since they simply transfer their skills and attitudes in producing unidirectional messages.

Minorities are often under represented in the media and these groups' access to the media is very limited. A unique initiative is Radio-C, a Roma radio station which has been broadcasting for and about Roma people since 2001. Recently talks have started to launch a Roma TV station which would broadcast from Budapest for the Roma minorities in Eastern Europe.

Despite the fact that the Hungarian media market is relatively small, new media products continue to appear. In 2005, 901 daily, weekly and monthly newspapers and magazines were published in Hungary, out of which the daily newspapers number 36. The free newspapers have had an impact on the market, especially *Metro*. Its Budapest edition was launched in 1998 with 160,000 copies and in 2000 the paper went national. Currently *Metro* has 324,000 free copies distributed daily in Hungary. The most frequently read newspapers in Hungary are the local dailies published regionally, while national dailies are read less frequently. Newspaper circulation is falling; in the second quarter of 2007 the circulation dropped by a million compared with the previous quarter. Table 28.2 summarizes the most important national dailies and their circulation in the second quarter of 2007.

Most Hungarian newspapers, weeklies and magazines have online editions. In addition to the content of the print editions, newspaper websites also offer services like discussion forums or newspaper archives, but the content of the sites is not significantly different from the print version. Unlike in many other Central European countries, newspaper websites offer free access to current editions as well as to their archive.

Foreign ownership dominates the Hungarian press. The German Axel Springer, the Swiss Ringier, Sanoma, Westdeutsche Allgemeine Zeitung are among the current owners of newspapers in Hungary where horizontal concentration dominates the newspaper

TABLE 28.2

Major national dailies' circulation numbers. Source: http:www.matesz.hu/data

Dailies	Type	Total circulation
Metro	Free paper	324,000
Blikk	Tabloid	230,000
Népszabadság	Quality (left-wing)	128,500
Nemzeti Sport	Sports	76,400
Színes Bulvar Lap	Tabloid	66,000
Magyar Nemzet	Quality (conservative)	64,500
Népszava	Quality (left-wing)	24,500
Világgazdaság	Economic	13,400

market. While in many EU countries newspaper and magazine publishing is VAT-free, in Hungary the tax is 15 percent, making it one of the highest among European Union countries. Advertisements cover about 50 percent of Hungarian publishers' revenue and the other 50 percent comes from the price of the newspaper. This rate puts the publishers at the mercy of advertisers. Falling circulation numbers mean less revenues for publishers, which results in reducing editorial staff. Journalists made redundant often take up a public relations position. In January 2007 the monopoly of the newspaper distribution company ended and a new company entered the market.

There are three national public service radio stations (Kossuth, Petőfi, Bartók), and two major national commercial stations, Danubius Rádió and Sláger Rádió. There is a significant difference between radio listeners who tune in to commercial or public radio stations. The older generation listens almost exclusively to public radio stations, especially to Kossuth Rádió, which is the most popular public station. According to a representative nation-wide survey, commissioned by NRTC, Sláger Rádió and Danubius Rádió are the most popular commercial stations, 39 percent and 37 percent of respondents listen to them regularly. Sláger Rádió broadcasts hits from the '60s, '70s and '80s and it is the most popular station in the 30–50 age group. Local radio stations—especially commercial ones—are of importance too: 18 percent of the population listen to them regularly. There seems to emerge a clear trend in radio listening habits: for the younger generation radio fulfils an entertainment function and loses its function as a source of information. The second public radio station, Petőfi Rádió, therefore changed its profile in June 2007 to appeal to younger audiences, broadcasting more contemporary music and youth programs and in just four months the number of its listeners quadrupled. Specialized radio stations take up the function of informing and interpreting, such as the Gazdasági Rádió (Economic Radio) or Inforádió, specializing in economics and news/current affairs respectively. A selection of radio stations can also be listened to online.

Until July 2007 Budapest Radio was an important tool of Hungary's public diplomacy efforts, broadcasting English, German, French, Russian and Spanish languages programs abroad about Hungary and her culture. This foreign language service was abolished in July 2007 due to lack of resources. *The Budapest Business Journal*, *Budapest Times* and *The Budapest Sun* are the leading English language newspapers with a circulation of a few thousand.

Until 1997 the state-controlled Hungarian Television (Magyar Televízió, MTV) enjoyed a monopoly. The 1996 Media Law opened the way for creating a dual broadcasting system, modeled on Western European traditions. Currently there are three terrestrial television channels: MTV, the public service channel; TV2, whose majority owner is Scandinavian Broadcasting System (SBS); and RTL Klub, which is owned by a consortium of CLT,

Bertelsmann, Pearson, and the Hungarian national telecom company Magyar Telekom. In June 2007 62 Hungarian language channels were present in the market, competing for the viewers' attention. RTL Klub and TV2 are the most widely watched commercial TV channels followed by M1, the public channel, which is more popular among the 60+ viewers. In the 15–19 year old range RTL Klub dominates, while the 20–29 generation tunes in to TV2 regularly. Television remains the most important news source for 78 percent of the respondents of the NRTC survey, followed by radio (8 percent), the internet (6 percent) and the print press (4 percent). In 2004 people on average spent four and a half hours a day watching television. According to a survey of GfK, a market research institute (http://www.gfk.hu), news programs are the most preferred program type for Hungarian viewers (54 percent), followed by weather forecasts (45 percent), cabaret (34 percent), humor (32 percent) and economics (29 percent). The advertising revenue of RTL Klub and TV2, the two major commercial TV channels' accounts for 90 percent of total TV channels. Both channels have been criticized for their very low standard of programs and news reporting. Ninety-eight percent of Hungarian households have television. Digital television is in an early phase still.

News Sources

According to a 2007 survey of 400 Hungarian journalists (Lenhardt, 2007), every third journalist mentioned the news agencies as the most important news sources, followed by "informators" who are able to provide exclusive stories, while organizations and institutions were ranked as the third most important source. Public relations consultancies were rated very low in terms of news sources. Every second respondent rated news agencies as the most trusted news source, followed by companies and organizations (directly, not via public relations agency) while public relations agencies came last but one as a trusted source of information. The surveyed journalists' most preferred and useful channels of information were the internet, followed by information gained in person or by phone. Professional creative events were as important as news agency reports followed by press conferences and press releases. The least useful—and thus the least used—were newsletters, on-line chats (Skype or Messenger) and on-line press events. 81 percent of journalists surveyed considered personal contacts with CEOs important or very important, 60 percent valued contacts with in-house public relations practitioners as important or very important and only 42 percent thought personal contacts with public relations consultants were important. One of the most interesting findings of the survey was that three quarters of the journalists rely on public relations agencies despite the journalists' less favorable attitudes towards the credibility and competency of these agencies.

Regarding news sources, journalists are often quick to jump on a story without checking the source. In 2007 the Hungarian media widely covered the "discovery" of a Hungarian tribe in Central Africa by Swiss anthropologists. The story turned out to be a hoax, however. It was some media hackers' attempt to demonstrate how the media "work," their hunger for sensationalism and to draw the public's attention to be more alert and skeptical about what they read in the media. It also demonstrated that journalists often do not check the sources of stories. This was not the first hoax in the Hungarian media and probably not the last one either.

In 2005 several newspaper publishers joined efforts to launch a campaign against "unauthorized secondary use" of their articles by media monitoring services. The publishers wanted these services to pay a copyright fee for quoting and using published articles in their reviews. The publishers launched a campaign, "Only from pure sources" to raise awareness of the issue and to fight against "illegal" copying and distribution of their articles. Both the National Association of Hungarian Journalists and the Hungarian Public Relations Association got involved in the debate and mediated between the publishers and the monitoring agencies. Public relations agencies were also affected since they use media monitoring services or do monitoring themselves. The public relations profession argued against fees, given that many articles are fully or partly based on press releases issued by agencies. On the other hand, clients of monitoring firms are big companies who advertise in those newspapers as well. As a result of the negotiations, monitoring (or public relations) agencies—or their clients—now pay between 20 and 50 Eurocent per article to the publisher. The publishers also demanded that the monitoring firms should disclose their clients' names to the publisher, a demand later dropped for public relations agencies thanks to the efforts of the Hungarian Public Relations Association. Another demand was that articles should not be stored for more than two weeks, after which they should be deleted from the monitoring firms' database to prevent competition with the publishers' own archive service.

Magyar Távirati Iroda, the national news agency, was established in 1881 and still dominates the market. It is a state-owned company, managed by a board of trustees which is set up from delegates of the political parties in Parliament.

Social Media

Forty-three percent of households have a personal computer (http://www.nrc.hu). Every third household has internet connection (92 percent of them broadband connection) and 2.5 million Hungarians (20 percent of the total population) use the internet, which is below the EU average (47 percent). Seventy-one percent of the 15–24 age group regularly use the internet, while this ratio drops to 49 percent among the 25–34 age group. The most popular activities on the internet are: job seeking (61 percent), radio listening (55 percent), free online games (52 percent), online phoning (49 percent), and chatting (43 percent). The younger generation does not read print newspapers; online news portals remain their primary source of information.

In 2007 59 percent of Hungarians were digitally illiterate although this number is decreasing year by year. The most visited Hungarian websites and portals are Origo, Startlap, iwiw and Index (news portal). Iwiw, the Hungarian facebook, was launched in 2005 when the number of social media websites was mushrooming. Blogs have not become very popular in Hungary, only 5 percent of regular internet users read them on a regular basis. Forty-nine percent of them use blogs as entertainment, 42 percent as an information source, and 15 percent to gain professional knowledge. Several public relations blogs were launched in recent years, however none of them have become popular.

Seventy-nine percent of Hungarians have at least one mobile phone but the total number of mobile subscribers is 10 million.

Alternative or guerrilla marketing methods that rely on interpersonal communication are slowly penetrating into Hungary, as every fourth Hungarian identifies themselves as an active avoider of advertisements. Viral marketing was first used extensively by political parties and activists during election times in 2002 and 2006 while business organizations have been using it together with buzz marketing and astroturfing since 2005.

CONCLUSION

Although Hungarian economic growth has slowed down and serious reforms are under way to decrease the huge budget deficit, the economic environment provides favorable conditions for public relations to flourish. The political and media environment, in which Hungarian public relations practitioners operate lacks trust and credibility, two major factors in public relations. Given that the Hungarian Public Relations Association defined public relations in the early 1990s as the "art of trust building," the main question for the public relations profession remains: Does public relations contribute to the mistrust or does it have a vital role in creating and building trust? Without doubt the Hungarian Public Relations Association will have a vital role and responsibility in increasing the level of professionalism and showing clear directions for the profession and in making sure that the Hungarian Rhapsody remains in tune.

CASE STUDY

The Saga of the Hungarian SáGa Foods Company and its Bird Flu Crisis

Overview

A bird flu outbreak at one of the largest turkey farms in the UK in February 2007 had a serious impact on British poultry supplier Bernard Matthews, and was potentially damaging to its Hungarian subsidiary SáGa Foods. SáGa asked Weber Shandwick to minimise the effect of the crisis on its operation and avoid negative coverage of SáGa in the media. The agency responded rapidly and managed to keep SáGa's name out of virtually all the coverage of the bird flu outbreak, leaving its reputation and business intact.

Statement of the Problem/Opportunity

On 1 February 2007, vets were called to the UK farm of Bernard Matthews, the biggest turkey producer in Europe, after 2,600 of its birds died. Two days later, European Commission tests confirmed that the turkeys had died from the H5N1 type of bird flu, the strain of the virus most likely to cross from birds to humans, and 159,000 Bernard Matthews turkeys were destroyed.

There was a possibility that the bird flu outbreak in the UK might be associated with the local operations of Bernard Matthews' Hungarian subsidiary, SáGa Foods. UK officials were trying to put the blame on Hungary as a source of the bird flu infection, on the basis that Hungary had reported the occurrence of a similar strain of the virus two weeks earlier. The UK media's speculation was fuelled by only gradually discovering that Bernard Matthews had a Hungarian operation.

In fact, SáGa Foods was not the source of the UK outbreak. Its operations are far away from where avian influenza was found in Hungary, and all official tests proved that the company and its products were safe from the virus.

Nevertheless, the situation was moving fast, and on 5 February, Weber Shandwick in Hungary was charged with the task of ensuring SáGa's name was kept out of the British and Hungarian media's extensive and negative coverage of the latest bird flu outbreaks.

Research

Every local communication had to be in line with Bernard Matthews' communication in the UK, so Weber Shandwick set up direct communications with Bernard Matthews' PR agency in the UK, Hill and Knowlton, to gain first hand information on the UK developments to ensure its actions were aligned with steps taken and messages communicated by SáGa's parent company.

Weber Shandwick swung into action with a thorough—and continuing—monitoring of the UK media to identify the next direction the story might go in and identify the risk to SáGa. After a quick review of the situation, a crisis meeting was held with SáGa's top executives to establish the key messages.

Planning

SáGa already had basic crisis plans in place to handle a bird flu outbreak, but this situation was different: the company was not involved in an outbreak but the media were starting to think it might be.

As the agency had to minimise the amount of communication coming from SáGa at a time when media interest was at its peak, the team needed to clarify the situation without fuelling further coverage or mentions of the company's name.

The overriding objective of the campaign was to fend off even the suspicion in the UK or Hungarian media that SáGa could be affected by bird flu, so protecting the company's name, reputation, and business.

The team and SáGa's management developed a two-pronged communications strategy:

- Limiting SáGa's media communication to critical statements that corrected misinformation and clarified the company's connection with Bernard Matthews.
- Involving third party Hungarian officials who could speak with authority and defend the company at the same time as defending Hungary's preparedness for bird flu.

The key messages were:

- SáGa Foods excludes the possibility that its exported turkey products could be the source of the avian influenza at Bernard Matthews turkey farm in the UK.
- SáGa Foods operates by the strictest EU food safety and biosecurity measures, which would detect any possible infection among its birds.
- There have been no signs of bird flu at SáGa's processing units or any of its supplying farms, and this can be confirmed by the Hungarian authorities.
- Every SáGa product remains safe for consumption by consumers.

Execution

As there was a threat of actually fuelling coverage through multiple interviews and statements, the agency persuaded SáGa's managers to communicate only through a statement that clarified the misinformation carried by the UK press. A statement was drafted by the agency explaining that the Hungarian operation was safe from avian influenza, that it was completely separate from the UK operation, and highlighting the types of goods that travelled between the UK and the Hungarian operations, and how they were moved. The statement was distributed to the Hungarian media and news agencies.

SáGa and Weber Shandwick held a meeting with the Hungarian Agriculture Minister and the Hungarian Chief Veterinary Surgeon and asked them to support SáGa by using their influence to calm the Hungarian media and explain the situation. Both officials agreed to do so.

The issue was made more delicate as the British government and media continued to point the finger at Hungary, and there was mounting anti-British sentiment in the Hungarian media. The team therefore had to balance making the most of local press sympathy with not condemning the British parties involved, and avoiding any political overtones.

The Hungarian chapter of the UK bird flu story came to an end after the Chief Vet held an international press conference in Budapest on 13 February. He was able to show journalists the volumes, locations, trading routes and the types of goods travelling between the UK and the Hungarian companies, fending off charges in the UK media that Hungary was the source of the infection. After this, Weber Shandwick only had to answer a handful of local media enquiries and by February 14 there was no longer a story.

Campaign Outcomes/Monitoring and Evaluation

Weber Shandwick's crisis management campaign for SáGa was a real success. Within eight days the story speculating that SáGa was affected by bird flu was killed, so protecting the company's name, reputation, and business.

What little media coverage there was after 9 February focused on debate about whether the UK bird flu outbreak had originated in Hungary as a country rather than in any particular company, while mentions of SáGa in its local media were sporadic and barely stated more than that it was owned by Bernard Matthews. SáGa's statements enabled the media to clarify how the two companies worked together and reassure Hungarian consumers that they were safe.

The successful management of the crisis probably saved the Hungarian company millions of euro in lost revenue—the result had it been firmly, if wrongly, linked with the UK bird flu outbreak—as well as protecting its image as a quality food manufacturer.

The team responded to the crisis extremely fast, not only fending off negative media coverage, but also managing to mobilise the most credible third party possible, the Chief Vet of Hungary.

Attila Tullner, CEO of SáGa Foods, said:

> The possible connection of SáGa Foods to the avian influenza found in the UK was a serious threat to our business. Fast and effective reaction was needed to avoid possible negative coverage. With the involvement of the Chief Veterinary Surgeon of Hungary, the situation was effectively and quickly closed down, with no long term effect on our brand image.

BIBLIOGRAPHY

Adam, F., Makarovic, M., Rončevič, B., Tomšič, M. (2005). *The Challenges of Sustained Development. The role of socio-cultural factors in East-Central Europe*. Budapest: Central European University Press.

Baca, S. (1999). Cultural Perspectives on Management Issues in Hungary. Foreign-owned production companies in transition. In A. Lorentzen, B. Widmaier and M. Laki (eds) *Institutional Change and Industrial Development in Central and Eastern Europe*. Aldershot: Ashgate.

Badescu, G. and Uslaner, E. (eds.) (2003). *Social Trust and the Transition to Democracy*. London: Routledge.

Borgulya, I. and Barakonyi, K. (2004). *Vállalati kultúra* [Corporate Culture] Budapest: Nemzeti Tankönyvkiadó.

Hazleton, V. and Kennan, W. (2000). Relationships as social capital: econceptualizing the bottom line. *Corporate Communication: An International Journal*, 5, 81–86.

Heidrich, B. (2001). *Szervezeti Kultúra és Interkulturalis Menedzsment* [Corporate Culture and Intercultural Management] Budapest: Human Telex Consulting.

Hofstede, G. and Hofstede, G. J. (2005). *Cultures and Organizations—Software of the Mind.* New York: McGraw-Hill.

Howard, M. (2003). *The Weakness of Civil Society in Post-Communist Europe* New York: Cambridge University Press.

Lenhardt, A. (2007). Újságírók munkamódszerei. [Journalists' working methods] [Online] Available at <http://www.prherald.hu/cikk2.php?idc=20070719-124150>.

Lewis, R. (2007). The *Cultural Imperative: Global Trends in the 21st Century.* London: Nicholas Brealey Publishing.

Lipót, J. (1968). *Public Relations a gyakorlatban* [Public Relations in Practice] Budapest: Közgazdasági és Jogi Kiadó.

Sükösd, M. and Bajomi-Lázár P. (2000). Media Reform in East Central Europe In. M. Sükösd and P. Bajomi-Lázár (eds) *Reinventing Media: Media Policy Reform in East-Central Europe.* Budapest: Central European University Press.

Szondi, G. (1999). *Evaluation in the Hungarian Public Relations Industry,* Unpublished MSc Dissertation, University of Stirling, UK.

Szondi, G. (2003). The image of public relations in the Hungarian print media. *Kommunikáció Menedzsment, 1:* 9–14.

Szondi, G. (2004). Hungary. In Betteke van Ruler and Dejan Verčič (eds.) *Public Relations and Communication Management in Europe: A Nation-by-Nation Introduction to Public Relations Theory and Practice.* Mouton De Gruyter, Berlin/New York.

Szondi, G. (2006). The role and challenges of country branding in transition countries: The Central and Eastern European experience. *Place Branding and Public Diplomacy* Vol.3(1): 8–20.

Szondi, G. (2007). The Eastern European Referendum Campaigns on the Accession to the European Union—a Critical Analysis. *Journal of Public Affairs 7:* 55–69.

Terestyéni, T. (2000). Co-operative and Confrontative Strategies in Public Communication In: N. Schleicher (ed) *Communication Culture in Transition.* Budapest: Akadémiai Kiadó.

Trompenaars, F. and Hampden-Turner, C. (1997). *Riding the Waves of Culture. Understanding Cultural Diversity in Business.* London: Nicholas Brealey Publishing.

Wang, J. (2005). Consumer nationalism and corporate reputation management in the global era. *Corporate Communications: An International Journal 10*(3): 223–239.

29

THE DEVELOPMENT OF PUBLIC RELATIONS IN RUSSIA: A GEOPOLITICAL APPROACH

KATERINA TSETSURA

INTRODUCTION

When one hears about the Russian Federation, or simply Russia, he or she evokes his or her own set of social and cultural images of this country. Some think about an economically struggling post-communist country, while others see quite developed and prosperous cities such as Moscow. Some imagine everlasting winters and miserable countryside roads of peripheral Russia, the poverty and continuous struggle of Russian citizens, while others talk about the successful transformation of the communist regime into a democracy, in which a free market economy develops giving rise to a large middle class.

There is no single answer to how today's Russia and Russian society can be characterized. Opposite viewpoints on a number of issues, analyzed by researches in the social sciences and social studies, have been created not only as a result of different perspectives and approaches to evaluations of the transformation of Russia, but also as a result of examining how certain phenomena perform differently in different parts of the Russian Federation. For example, many public relations scholars discussed theory and practice in Russia by solely constructing their arguments on the evidence from one region or even one city. Clarke (2000) did so based on an analysis of public relations practices in Moscow; Guth (2000) based on a study in St. Petersburg; and McElreath et al. (2001) on the analysis of public relations practice in Moscow and St. Petersburg. Such analyses are incomplete because they do not provide a holistic perspective on all Russian public relations practices.

Contemporary research in the area of international public relations suggests that cultural factors should be examined when one looks at public relations practices in a particular country (Botan, 1993; Culbertson, Chen, 1996; Taylor, 2001). But because the Russian Federation is one of the largest countries in the world and is diverse geographically, politically, economically, and culturally (Chirkova, Lapina, 2001; Lankina, 2001), it is appropriate to assume that Russian public relations can be theorized and practiced differently in different parts of the country. As demonstrated later in this chapter, this assumption is supported by a number of examples.

This chapter seeks to identify the similarities and differences in public relations theory and practice in different metaregions of Russia. Here, metaregions refer to the groups of federal subjects that form the Russian Federation, which are geographically, politically, and economically different and culturally diverse. There are three large types of federal subjects within the Russian Federation: the republics, the territories, and the regions, which are united into metaregions.

This chapter uses a widely accepted categorization of the federal subjects. Five metaregions can be identified: the European metaregion, which includes federal subjects in the Northern, Central, Central Black-Soil, and Southern areas; the Ural metaregion with federal subjects concentrated in the area of Ural mountains; the Central Siberian metaregion with subjects concentrated in the Central Siberian region; the ZaBaikal metaregion, which includes subjects from the Baikal Lake and ZaBaikal (beyond the Baikal Lake) areas; and the Far East metaregion, with federal subjects from the Far East geographic area. In addition, Moscow and St. Petersburg areas all analyzed as a separate metaregion due to a central role these two cities play in the economic, political, and cultural spheres of Russian society. A detailed discussion on why these two cities can be considered as a separate metaregion will be presented later in this chapter.

These metaregions, each having unique geopolitical particularities, should be taken into consideration when one examines the theory and practice of any social field of study, which is new to Russia. This chapter specifically seeks to analyze how public relations practices differ from metaregion to metaregion in Russia and how this fact affects the development of Russian public relations theory. In doing so, the historical particularities of the development of public relations in Russia will first be discussed to provide an evaluation of the status of the profession in today's Russia. The next section will demonstrate how political, economic, and social idiosyncracies of different Russian metaregions create and maintain the field of public relations in Russia. Then, the chapter presents an analysis of some characteristics of Russian culture and will discuss some cultural differences which exist within the Russian Federation in relation to public relations practice and perceptions of the field. Finally, the difference in relationship between the Russian mass media in Moscow and mass media in peripheral Russia and public relations practice in the capital and in other Russian cities is presented. A case study presented in the last section of this chapter will illustrate why it is important to evaluate the differences in public relations practice in different metaregions of Russia when one analyzes contemporary public relations in Russia.

HISTORY, DEVELOPMENT, AND STATUS OF THE PROFESSION

The concept of public relations is relatively new to Russians. Not so long ago, few people had heard of public relations and even fewer knew what public relations entails. The public relations field emerged in Russia less than 20 years ago, and has been developing rapidly since then. Scholars from different fields have turned to this new, unexplored area of promise and have examined the phenomenon in some detail providing their own understanding of what public relations is. This rather eclectic scholarship, based on a number of theories from psychology, social psychology, sociology, political science, philosophy, marketing, and journalism created a diversified perspective of public relations, which later became somewhat of a challenge to a new generation of public relations scholars (Tsetsura, 2000a). The lack of unified understanding of public relations reflects the lack of theoretical development of Russian public relations and the diversity of public relations practices in Russia.

The history of the development of public relations in Russia differs significantly from the development of this profession in the United States. This difference is created not only by the youth of the field in Russia, but also by the lack of Russian scholarly works about the theory of public relations. Perhaps, the primary difference in the origins of public relations education in the United States and Russia is the absence of a communication tradition in Russia. In the United States, communication is a key to understanding the field of public relations. However, in Russia, the communication tradition does not exist. Instead, public relations theory is heavily drawn from journalism, whose impact on Russian public relations has to be addressed.

Traditionally, it was journalism and business scholars who began to define and discuss the conceptual frameworks and worldviews of public relations. They continued to argue about the principles of public relations as well as the methods of teaching public relations. Since then, business scholars have concentrated on the management and marketing functions of public relations (which one can call business-type public relations), whereas journalism scholars have focused on the management-communication function (which one can call journalism-type public relations).

After 10 years of active implementation of public relations courses into programs of higher education in Russia, the significant impact of these two areas became obvious. This impact can be identified not only through the existence of the two schools and the scholarly debates about the business or communication nature of public relations, but also through the contemporary curricula for public relations majors.

The popularity of the field motivated many schools to create their own programs where students could study public relations as a major, minor, or area of emphasis. Faculty members who became interested in the area started to promote public relations courses in their departments. The syllabi they created for classes were based heavily on Western sources and were either marketing or communication based, based on which area they had access to, first. In addition, depending on the scholarly background of these educators, public relations education took either a business or journalism path.

Contemporary public relations education in Russia has a strong orientation to journalism or business depending on its location in the university and the expertise of the faculty teaching at specific programs. As a result, the public relations programs at Moscow, St. Petersburg, Voronezh, and Ural State Universities are journalism-oriented and Moscow State Academy of Management, St. Petersburg Electro-Technical University, and Voronezh State Technical University are business-oriented.

The distribution of public relations programs along these two approaches is fairly even, although the distribution of public relations programs itself is uneven across regions. For instance, the Moscow/St. Petersburg region has a number of programs concentrated in one geographical area, as a result of the active development of public relations practices in the Russian capital. The development of public relations in this region is influenced by incredible free-market opportunities in Moscow, the active relationship building activities among universities in Moscow and St. Petersburg, as well as the linkage between these universities and other European and United States universities.

In April 2000, 56 Russian higher education institutions offered majors or emphases in public relations and more than 65 offered one or more public relations courses (Konovalova, 2000). In September 2001, there were more than 60 public relations programs (*PR News*, 2001). Two years ago, the higher education requirements for public relations majors were formed, and the Federal Russian Committee of Higher Education certified public relations as an official major in universities. This committee, a governmental organ, not only creates the guidelines that universities and colleges should follow but also evaluates these institutions for compliance of federal certification standards (Department of Higher Education of Russian Federation, 2000).

However, only a few programs in Russia actually meet these certification standards (Varustin, 2000). The Moscow and St. Petersburg metaregion has a large number of standardized programs because of an active development of relations with universities in Europe and Northern America. Thanks to the number of federal grants and the volume of financial aid from independent foundations, many universities in Moscow and St. Petersburg such as Moscow State University, Moscow State Institute of International Relations, Moscow Humanitarian Institute, Moscow State Academy of Management, St. Petersburg State University, and St. Petersburg Electro-Technical University, can afford to have American scholars lecture and conduct seminars and workshops on public relations theory and practice quite often (Alyoshina, 1997; Clarke, 2000; Guth, 2000; McElreath, Chen, Azariva, & Shadrova, 2001; Newsom, Turk, & Kruckeberg, 2000).

At the same time, universities in other Russian areas such as the European and Ural metaregions, have fewer programs in public relations and generally offer fewer public relations courses. For example, Voronezh State University, Rostov State University (the European metaregion), and Ural State University (the Ural metaregion) are among the few that offer strong programs in public relations outside of the Moscow/St. Petersburg metaregion. The relationships between Western universities and schools outside of the Moscow/St. Petersburg metaregion are not well developed. For example, between 1995 and 1998, only one educational program brought public relations practitioners to Voronezh State University twice to lecture and conduct seminars, whereas Moscow State University had visiting professors generally once every four months during the same period (S. Martin, personal communication, December 2000). In Voronezh, a city in a Central Black-Soil region with a population of one million, only two universities offer public relations as a major, whereas in Moscow and St. Petersburg there are about twenty programs in public relations. Moreover, in the early days, some regions such as the ZaBaikal metaregion did not have comprehensive programs in public relations. Today, however, all metaregions have standard public relations in higher education institutions.

This analysis suggests that public relations has developed differently in different metaregions as a field of study in higher education. As a result, certain metaregions (such as Moscow/St. Petersburg and European metaregions) have more developed public relations education programs than others, partly because they were created much earlier than in other metaregions (V. V. Tulupov, personal communication, December 2000). These early programs started to offer courses in public relations in 1994–1995. In contrast, Ural State University (the Ural metaregion) offered courses in public relations in 1997, and ZaBaikal State Pedagogical University (the ZaBaikal metaregion) and Dalnevostochnyj State University (Far East State University in Vladivostok, the Far East metaregion) in 1999 (I. Boldonova, personal communication, March 2001). Thus, the development of public relations education has different timelines in different metaregions of Russia. This lag in the development of education has affected the development of the public relations profession in different regions as will be discussed in greater detail in the succeeding pages.

The professional side of public relations in Russia is typified by a greater emphasis on certain specific specialties. Political public relations (public affairs), media relations, and corporate relations are the most popular areas in public relations practice. Several Russian scholars have tried to study public relations in Russia but most of these efforts concentrate on a functional description of practices rather than on theorizing about them (see, e.g., Alyoshina, 1997; Maksimov, 1999; Tulchinsky, 1994).

Governmental and political public relations is a leading specialty in Russian public relations practice. Public relations scholarship is concentrated around this area. Today, the majority of public relations textbooks and case studies published by Russian scholars cover political public relations almost exclusively. For example, Pocheptsov (1998) spent much time on analyzing the nature of political public relations and modern practices in the field. Among the most popular books on public relations are ones that offer practical advice on how to organize political campaigns and use public relations techniques in election campaigns (Pheophanov, 2001). Further, political public relations is often analyzed in conjunction with political advertising, clear evidence that Russian scholars do not make a clear distinction between the two (Egorova-Gantman, & Pleshakov, 1999).

Political public relations practice is constantly criticized by the Russian public partly because, unfortunately, the concept of public relations is not well understood and well communicated in Russian society. Moreover, many unethical practices such as black PR (discussed later in this chapter), have provoked negatively oriented discussions and led to public relations being equated with manipulation. The concept of ethical public relations is often seen as an oxymoron rather than a real phenomenon (V. V. Tulupov, personal communication, December 2000).

Corporate public relations is another specialty that is growing in popularity. This area is becoming more popular as the Russian economy grows and Russia increases its presence in the international market. Unfortunately, many textbooks covering this area as well as many corporate public relations courses cover only basic etiquettes or provide simplistic explanations of the role of modern mass media in society with no information on how to practice strategic corporate communication. Further, such chapters are usually included in books on advertising (Pankratov, Bazhenov, Seregina, & Shakhurin, 2001).

As a profession, public relations has been developing rapidly in Russia. A number of public relations courses are now being taught in Russian universities and colleges. A number of public relations departments are also being created in governmental, corporate, and non-for-profit organizations, signifying a parallel growth in the industry as well. No doubt, Moscow is a leading center for the development of public relations. This concentration is the result of three primary factors. As the capital, Moscow is the center of a high degree of political activity. It is also the center of economic development relative to other cities in Russia. Finally, as mentioned earlier in this chapter, Moscow is the hub of public relations education, having been the pioneer of public relations education in Russia. In contrast, most of the other metaregions, continue to struggle to inculcate strategic public relations practices in business mostly because the phenomenon is neither widely known, nor recognized, by leaders of business and government and by publics. Lately, however, this situation has been changing dramatically.

New departments of public relations have been organized in a number of governmental organizations and have now become an integral part of their structures. For instance, the department of press services in the Yekaterinburg Russian Internal Revenue Service office (in the Ural metaregion) produces publicity and advertising campaigns for the local office. One of its latest efforts featured a series of press-releases aimed at changing the attitudes of taxpayers as well as facilitate communication between these publics and internal revenue service workers, using slogans such as: "have a cup of coffee with your tax service agent" (T. Korchak, personal communication, March 2002).

Most not-for-profit organizations also actively use public relations, mostly for fundraising. For example, Voronezh regional teenage nonprofit organization "New View" (the European metaregion) conducted a number of publicity campaigns to promote its programs. Professional public relations associations in Russia also actively seek to promote public relations as a legitimate profession. Among the biggest and most active are: the Russian Public Relations Society and the Russian Society of Advertising Agencies. It is important to note that many Russian advertising agencies offer public relations services as well, as there are only a few agencies that exclusively practice public relations. These public relations agencies mostly concentrate on political public relations, managing election campaigns with special attention to candidates' image-making (Tsetsura, 2000a). The next section describes one of the most provocative issues in modern public relations in Russia: formulation of the image of the public relations field in relations to "black PR" versus "white PR."

"BLACK" VS. "WHITE" PUBLIC RELATIONS

One of the most interesting and provocative discussions in modern Russian public relations theory centers around two contrasting views on public relations: "white PR" versus "black PR." These two terms were introduced in the early 1990s and soon became very popular among professionals and, later, scholars. Ethics is the main reason behind dividing public relations practices to "black" and "white." "Black PR" is associated with manipulative techniques that are expected to be used mostly in the area of political public relations, particularly, in election campaigns. "White PR," in contrast, presents the Western, ethical view of public relations drawing from the *Excellence Project* (Maksimov, 1999), which is described in the chapter on North America in this volume. In media references, as well as discussions among political relations practitioners, the field is often presented in terms of "black" and "white" PR.

Other scholars, however, reject categorizing public relations practices in these stark terms. Instead of dividing public relations on "black" and "white" terms, they argue, "black" public relations is not a public relations at all, but rather it is propaganda (Tulupov, 1996). Many of them point out that "black vs. white PR" discussions exist mainly because the profession has been slow to adopt ethical standards. Novinskij (2000) argued that in Russia, there is no philosophy and ethics of public relations *per se.* Some scholars from the United States contended that "black" public relations cannot exist because "any misuse or abuse of public relations is a question, not of 'bad' public relations of which only an individual practitioner can be held responsible, but rather such misuse or abuse becomes a question of unethical professional practice which is of collective concern and which must be [the] collective responsibility of all practitioners" (Kruckeberg, 1992, p. 34).

One may conclude that public relations professional ethics is not well understood in Russia. Even though Russian professionals have joined associations such as the International Public Relations Association (IPRA), International Association of Business Communicators (IABC), and the Public Relations Society of America (PRSA) that exhort them to follow codes of ethics, these professionals often consider such codes as idealistic and not practical in the Russian environment (V. V. Tulupov, personal communication,

August 2002). Russian public relations professional organizations often face the same problems as their many counterparts in other countries: the accepted codes of ethics are not enforceable and thus are not practiced (Tsetsura, 2001).

Although the problem of enforcing codes of ethics is not a problem faced only by the Russian public relations industry, the attitudes among some Russian public relations professionals toward this important issue are reason for concern. Many Russian practitioners would readily admit that they do not always practice ethical public relations as presented in the code of ethics of the Russian Public Relations Association. They present what in their view is a plausible excuse for ignoring ethical considerations in their professional practice by citing differences in the mentality of Russian society (cultural differences), which makes it difficult for them to practice specific public relations practices (professional differences). Many of them simply say that it is impossible to practice ethical public relations because nobody would pay for it (Maksimov, 1999).

In addition, Russian society fails to recognize the importance of a wide dissemination of information. Heavily influenced by its Soviet past, senior managers of Russian organizations and governmental agencies do not appreciate the importance and benefits of open communication. Ethical concerns connected to the problem of dissemination of information were clearly evident in the case study of Chernobyl by Jaksa and Pritchard (1996) who described what happened when public relations ethics (government public relations in this case) clashed with the appropriateness (or lack thereof) of particular strategies and practices (such as hiding information from a public who had a right to know what happened at the nuclear station on April 26, 1986).

Jaksa and Pritchard (1996) noted that a group of students from the United States who were on a cultural exchange tour to Kiev, which is about 80 miles away from Chernobyl, were in the vicinity of the disaster on the days immediately following the nuclear accident. Along with this group, hundreds of thousands of area residents were not aware of the accident for almost a week as the group continued its trip in the region. Hiding such critical information, obviously under orders from local and federal government officials, has raised a number of ethical questions about the appropriateness of such actions and the right of publics to have access to information that could present a real or potential threat to health and life. Jaksa and Pritchard concluded that those who have access to important and potentially hazardous information, especially in crisis situations, should be held responsible for disseminating it. This case is an illustration that when government information channels are closed because policy makers intend that to be the best strategy, it is impossible for ethical public relations to be practiced. Unfortunately, even today, government public relations professionals often do not address the ethical aspects of free dissemination of information. Ethics stays on the background as far as the practice of government public relations is concerned.

Thus, the discussion of the practice of ethical public relations leads one to address the impact of environmental variables on the profession and its principles. Therefore, it is helpful to address the political, economic, and activist infrastructure in Russia and the influence of these variables on the development of public relations theory and practice in this country.

INFRASTRUCTURE OF RUSSIAN PUBLIC RELATIONS

Political System

Russia can be characterized as an emerging democracy (Guth, 2000). After the collapse of the Soviet Union, it began to actively seek a national political identity as an established democracy by trying to break its traditional domineering and hierarchical political structure. Aron (2001) contended that Russia had made a significant progress in becoming democratic when he noted that "Russia is by far the freest, most democratic nation of all the post-Soviet states" (p. 79). Others are not so optimistic about Russia's progress as a democratic state. For instance, famous writer and activist Solzhenitsyn (2001) argued that Russia has failed in its quest of becoming a democracy: "There exists no legal framework or financial means for the creation of local self-government; people have no choice but to achieve it through social struggle" (p. 68).

It is worth noting that whereas Solzhenitsyn refers to local governments, Aron talks about the central government. One of the essential features of the Russian political system is that whereas there has been progress toward democracy at the federal level, local governments often remain very conservative and non-democratic. They work under the old scheme of centralized government management. At the same time, when local governments gain additional power that is divested by the central government, they often do not know how to handle it (Lincoln, 2001). For Russia, democracy currently is more of a proclaimed goal than a reality. Many metaregions still do not practice democracy in its true sense, and evidence of that can be found in the contents of the many publications from the central and local Russian media (Brown, 2001).

As mentioned earlier, political public relations is one of the most popular areas of practice in all parts of Russia. Election campaigns are developed and implemented by agencies that engage in political public relations and image-making. Often these are the most popular and well-known public relations agencies. Because of democratization and the resulting ongoing election processes in Russia to elect local, regional, and federal governments, public relations professionals are actively involved in political image-making activities.

Many public relations campaigns such as the All Russian Census Campaign 2001 (which now has been moved to 2002 because of budget cuts) are organized and paid for by the Russian government. Independent public relations firms benefit by winning the contracts to create such campaigns. "Image-Land," a Moscow-based public relations and advertising group, won the account to plan and implement the All Russian Census Campaign 2001.

ECONOMIC SYSTEM AND LEVEL OF DEVELOPMENT

As described the beginning of this book, there is an interrelationship between political philosophy and level of development. This linkage is evident in Russia also where one sees the differences in political systems of various metaregions being closely connected with differences in economic development of the metaregions. The Moscow/St. Petersburg metaregion was central to economic development of the country during the Soviet era, and it continues to maintain that leading position today as well. Most of the investments, Russian and foreign, are concentrated in Moscow and St. Petersburg because of their geopolitical closeness to the federal government. The Ural metaregion is the second most developed metaregion because of its distance from the Moscow area, which also helps it serve as a connecting bridge between the capital and Siberia and Far Eastern regions. The Ural mountains divide Russia into European and Asian parts, and the Ural metaregion (particularly, Yekaterinburg) is considered the single most important connection between the two parts.

Equally important is the Central Siberian metaregion, which has rich natural resources such as gas and oil. Traditionally, this region has had a well-developed heavy industry sector. Most of the largest oil production companies are located in this metaregion. Being important players on the international market for oil and gas products, they practice public relations activities such as lobbying and financial relations. But their primary focus continues to be on positive publicity (press agentry model) rather than strategic public relations.

The economy of the European metaregion has also been growing rapidly in the past decade. Big and small businesses are actively growing in the region, but they do not seem too keen on practicing public relations practices. For the most part, large companies, which work on international markets, try to get involved in some public relations activities albeit at the publicity level.

Although many companies can afford to have public relations practitioners, only a few actually hire more than one professional. This one person is responsible for all aspects of the public relations practices of the organization from technical aspects such as writing press-releases to conceptualizing and implementing strategic campaigns that seek to promote organizational activities. Having one person doing all the public relations work is a common practice in different parts of Russia because very often organizational decision makers (the dominant coalition) do not appreciate the benefits of strategic public relations management. Most senior managers consider public relations to be a technical rather than strategic function one that is not so crucial to the effectiveness of the organization.

Many Russian textbooks and professional workshops organized in different parts of Russia promote the idea that public relations is merely publicity-oriented as is seen in the many publications on public relations that describe the profession as limited to publicity-oriented activities such as organizing exhibitions and thematic presentations, news conferences, and special events (Alyoshina, 1997; Pankratov, Bazhenov, Seregina, & Shakhurin, 2001; Pheophanov, 2001). Seminars and workshops are frequently organized to teach professionals how to create and successfully implement plans for conducting special event luncheons, publicity events, and news conferences. Virtually no information is available in Russia on strategic public relations practices and their connection to overall organizational effectiveness. Some Western textbooks, as well as professional seminars and workshops conducted by Western European and American practitioners and educators, emphasize the strategic nature of public relations. For example, the textbook *This is PR* by Newsom, Turk, and Kruckeberg (2000) is translated to Russian and is widely used by Russian educators.

One of the biggest problems, however, is the lack of economic development among many of Russia's metaregions, which has hampered the growth of public relations in these regions. Organizations and companies not only have a poor understanding of the full value of strategic public relations, but they also do not have the financial resources to invest in public relations departments that can plan, implement, and evaluate strategic campaigns.

Level of Activism

The level of activism in a society demonstrates the extent to which publics are prepared to argue for changes and force the implementation of changes in society. Thus, organizational public relations efforts often reflect the extent to which publics are ready to promote and pursue their goals in the society and thereby posing a challenge to organizations. In Soviet Russia, activism was extremely low because it was a punishable crime. As a result, people learned to stay away from activist groups of any kind. Lincoln (2001), in particular, pointed out that in the Soviet Union, "state propaganda applauded the people's participation in state-controlled civic life, but in reality it was every person for himself [herself]" (p. 87).

As a result of past suppression, post-Soviet Russian publics have been struggling to establish and develop activist groups. Today's Russian activism varies among the different metaregions. Generally, the highest degree of activism is seen in the Moscow/

St. Petersburg, European, and Central Siberia metaregions, generally in the form of labor unions. Most of these activists have focused on economic problems such as salaries and benefits. Because the government still has control over many companies, either directly through government subsidies or indirectly through local and federal legal regulations, efforts of activist groups are directed toward the government as well as toward the management. Most labor unions are not well structured and therefore have poor support even among employees.

For the most part, activism has not spread to other sections of the society. Activist ideas often stay among members of the activist groups and are not known among general publics. Many scholars have examined Russian publics in search of explanations for the reticence among Russians to be active citizens. One explanation is that this is a legacy of the Soviet era and is connected to the poor understanding of activism as a phenomenon. Another is that democracy itself is yet to develop in modern Russia. Lincoln (2001) argued that "Russians today simply lack that sense of civic responsibility that underlines the proper functioning of democratic institutions in the West" (p. 86). He continued that Russians do not understand the concept of a democratic society in which citizens are expected to actively participate in the social life and be responsible for their communities and their neighbors. As a result of underdeveloped activism, corporations in modern Russia do not face pressures from activist groups. For the most part, such groups are rarely seen and those that exist are not powerful (Miroshnichenko, 1998).

Legal Structure

As of today, there is no Russian law regulating public relations practices *per se*. However, there are two federal laws that regulate journalism and advertising, in which some public relations practices are also addressed. The first one is the Media Law of Russian Federation, which specifically addresses a problem of journalistic dignity and states that journalists cannot be paid to publish materials as editorials. Such materials can include positive information about organizations and can be considered "hidden advertising" because their goal is to publicize a product or service by paying for such exposure while not specifying it as such in the media. The Advertising Law of the Russian Federation also addresses this problem, but unfortunately, the statute does not specify the difference between hidden advertising and publicity. As a result of misinterpretation of publicity, materials which are based on press releases are often criticized by the federal organ, Antimonopoly Committee, and its regional departments, which are in charge of implementing the Advertising Law.

The Advertising Law defines hidden advertising as the act of promoting products or services through the media (often published in the editorial pages) without clearly identifying such acts as advertising (with a statement such as "This is advertising"). However, many articles, which are written by journalists but based on organizations' press releases, are often also considered as hidden advertising for which journalists do receive legal warnings from the regional offices of the Antimonopoly Committee (Tsetsura, 2000b). One of the biggest problems is that many of those who work in the offices of this Committee are not familiar with the concept of public relations and do know about the nature of publicity. For instance, the head of Krasnoyarsk Regional Antimonopoly Committee (the Central Siberia metaregion) published a manual for his workers on the ways to uncover hidden advertising in which he stated that any material positively describing an organization or a company can be considered as hidden advertising (Tsetsura, 2000b).

This is not such a big problem in the Moscow/St. Petersburg metaregion because the media there are generally better aware of public relations practices and have more exposure to press releases and publicity events. A different problem, paying journalists and editors for publishing publicity-oriented materials, has now risen in this region and has spread to other Russian metaregions as well.

The slang word *zakazukha* describes the act of publishing material favorable to an organization written by a journalist and printed on editorial pages in return for payment by the organization. Money can go directly to a journalist or an editor. A recent study conducted by Promaco Public Relations, a Moscow-based public relations firm, concluded that 13 of 21 Russian national newspapers and magazines were willing to publish a fake press release (without even checking the facts) for a payment of between $200 to $2000 for the service (Sutherland, 2001). Russian laws define this as hidden advertising but the poor enforcement of the law makes it possible for the practice to continue. As of today, neither journalists nor public relations professionals who engage in this practice have been legally challenged for their activities. Further, codes of ethics of journalism and/or public relations are not enforced either further exacerbating the problem creating a strong negative perception of the field of public relations (Tsetsura, 2000b).

In sum, the preceding pages articulated several major particularities of Russian society that have affected the development of public relations in the country. First, democracy is not well developed in Russia. Next, as a result of the 70-year long Soviet legacy, activism is not well understood or accepted by the Russian public. Third, economic challenges and the ongoing political changes in the country have created barriers to the active development of the public relations profession. Next, because organizational managers and their stakeholders do not have a clear understanding of the nature of public relations, public relations is seen as technical rather than strategic organizational function. Finally, the section has offered certain legal and ethical constraints to the development of public relations. The next section discusses the impact of environmental factors on the public relations profession in Russia.

RUSSIAN CULTURE AND PUBLIC RELATIONS

The editors have discussed the conceptual linkage between public relations and both societal and corporate culture. Culture plays an important role in any field, but it is especially important in the field of public relations which actively relies on communication (Sriramesh, & White, 1992). Russian culture affects public relations practices in two distinct ways. First, Russian culture influences the understanding and conceptualization of Russian public relations as a profession itself. Second, different subcultures within Russia influence the choice of specific public relations practices in different metaregions.

Unfortunately, very little research has been conducted in Russia on cross-cultural communication factors (Ting-Toomey, 1999). Much of the existing research in the area identifies Russia culture as being predominantly individualistic, with higher levels of power distance, but low in context, and with low levels of uncertainly avoidance (Gudykunst, Ting-Toomey, & Chua, 1988). It is important to note, however, that because of the differences in cultures among the metaregions, many cross-cultural indices vary from region to region. For example, the European metaregion generally is considered as a Western-oriented culture with high level of individualism, whereas Central Siberia and ZaBaikal metaregions sometimes are classified as Asian-oriented, collectivist cultures (Richmond, 1996). So far, no formal research has been done to evaluate the cultures of different parts of Russia even though the cultural idiosyncracies of different Russian metaregions require closer examination. Such research would surely be useful in defining the linkage between culture and public relations practices in different metaregions.

Today's Russia is a union of people of almost 100 different nationalities with different subcultural backgrounds. One may safely surmise that these differences might influence the perceptions and general understanding of public relations practices among these peoples. However, it is important to remember that as a profession, public relations developed in the Moscow/St. Petersburg metaregion first and was then transported to other metaregions. The misinterpretations and misunderstandings of the profession, which were developed in the Moscow/St. Petersburg region, thus got transported to these other regions also. In the succeeding pages, the relationship between Russian culture and the public relations profession will be discussed.

The cultural norms of Russian public relations might be explained by:

1. the lack of a well-defined history of public relations as a field;

2. the mixture of Western theories with Russian traditions of communication and relationships;

3. association of public relations with other phenomena (such as propaganda, advertising, promotion, and marketing) in Russia; and

4. the perceptions of public relations by Russian publics.

As would be the case with any new professional occupation, public relations faces a number of problems in modern Russia. Many of these problems have resulted from mis-understandings that have occurred throughout the years that public relations has continued to develop as an area of study in Russia. Because Russia was a part of the Soviet Union for more than 70 years, it has a rich history of negative propaganda practices. This fact has a tremendous effect on the ways in which people perceive public relations in modern Russia. In the next section, a language-related problem is analyzed that affects the philosophy of public relations in modern Russia.

In Russia, the negative meaning of "Soviet propaganda" was broadly used in the middle 1980s, during the early years of *perestrojka*. Negative associations and perceptions of propaganda were very common among Russians who had just gotten freedom of speech and were reevaluating their beliefs and values. At the same time, Russian scholars began working on the neutral nature of propaganda, which still remained shocking for most Russian publics. Western authors Pratkanis and Aronson (1991) were among the first educators to present this "neutral" approach, which was actively extended by other Russian scholars. In their book *Age of Propaganda*, Pratkanis and Aronson supported the idea of a synony-mous meaning of the words "propaganda" and "persuasion." These authors distinguished the two words by defining one as "mindless propaganda" and the other as "thoughtful persuasion." As a result, the word "propaganda" got back its original neutral meaning: it might be positive (open and honest explanations) or negative (lying, manipulative, based on total inspiration, but not on argued evidence).

The concept, although seemingly acceptable, created problems outside of scholarly discussions. Some Russian publics—overwhelmed by the negative perceptions of pro-paganda and remembering old definitions of publicity and public relations, which were wrongly translated as propaganda practices early on (Tsetsura, 2000b)—made inaccurate connections implying that the term "public relations" was a synonym of "propaganda." Thus, the discussion about the differentiation between public relations and propaganda, which Western public relations scholars had been engaged in for many years, has become a matter of urgency to Russian scholars.

The relationship between propaganda and public relations might not be so easy to describe in some of the emerging democracies but an examination of their mutual influence and coexistence could create fascinating discussions. It is especially important to continue to examine these issues because of the need to reevaluating communication phenomena and public relations in the multinational context, as is being done in this volume. At the same time, from the Russian standpoint, it is important to distinguish between public relations and propaganda to establish a clear understanding of which public relations practices are ethical. Misinterpretations in translation and a lack of a clear understanding of the public relations profession has led to the formation of negative perceptions about public relations as a field of practice and an object of study.

MEDIA AND PUBLIC RELATIONS

Media relations is the second most popular area of public relations practices in Russia after political communication involving image building for political figures and political candidates. Most public relations practices are concentrated around the production and dissemination of press releases as well as the creation of special publicity events, as Russia has followed the path of many other countries. Media relations has actively developed in all Russian metaregions, and most public relations and advertising agencies outside of the Moscow/St. Petersburg region almost exclusively offer media relations services.

Media Control

In theory, Russian media can be considered to be private. However, the government (through subsidies) and corporations (investment and advertising) have a significant impact on the media. The financial constraints that the Russian media face on a daily basis have put these media in a disempowered situation of dependency on governments and corporations. Of course, editorial freedom becomes one of the major casualties in this context. This section presents several major factors that have contributed to the creation of a framework for media relations in modern Russia.

Russian media have traditionally been divided into two large categories: national and local. The national media have typically had their headquarters in Moscow, and they traditionally have had the best equipment and personnel. During the Soviet period, national media played an important role in the dissemination of information by the government, which tightly controlled these media. Further, local media always looked up to the national media and never opposed them. Even though the political philosophy of the country has changed, some local media have continued this practices of dependency over national media.

Media Outreach

The outreach of Russian media is tremendous. A massive infrastructure of production and distribution of all types of media, print and broadcasting, was developed during the Soviet era. The high rate of literacy in Russia helped the media establish large readership and viewership during the Soviet period. The public relations implications of these two factors is very clear: this media outreach created an opportunity for fast dissemination of information to the whole country.

The Russian publics, especially in Central Siberia, ZaBaikal, and Far East metaregions, tend to trust the media more than those who live in the European and Ural parts of the country (Kay, 2000; Potcheptsov, 2001). Traditionally, the latter ones have been the more politically and socially active, with better developed, and more diverse, media. The publics in these metaregions do not trust the media as much as residents of other regions and they are especially skeptical about the national media in modern Russia. This fact is important to any/one who wishes to conduct media relations in one of these metaregions.

Editorial pages are often viewed skeptically and critically by these publics. Many problems, or perceived problems, arise when a piece written by a journalist was paid for by a company or an organization or just looks like *zakazukha*. The problem of *zakazukha* exists in all metaregions. At the same time, many publications are the result of the active professional and the legitimate collaboration between journalists and public relations people and should be recognized as such. Public relations practitioners in modern Russia try to find new ways of dealing with public skepticism by demonstrating creativity in organizing publicity events and writing feature press releases (I. Boldonova, personal communication, March 2001; T. Korchak, personal communication, March 2002).

In addition to the many concerns already addressed in this chapter, one must discuss and analyze the self-censorship of the Russian media and its impact on the public relations profession. Self-censorship is practiced by Russian media as a result of financial and legal pressures from government officials and corporations. Self-censorship today is probably the biggest problem of Russian media (GDF, 1999; Tsetsura, & Kruckeberg, in press). The tremendous power of financial groups in Russia coupled with the legal paradoxes of Russian laws on freedom of speech created a situation where the media are trapped between competing forces (Tsetsura, 2002). On the one hand, business conglomerates involve the media often in accusing and attacking one another. On the other, federal, regional, and local government officials try to control the media to keep criticism of their out of the public eye. Even though national media may at times exercise some editorial freedom and resist government and corporate pressures (see Belin, 2001, for the famous NTV scandal case), local media do not have any power to resist such pressures. Belin summed up: "Media in the [other] Russian regions face more restrictions than Moscow-based media. Although no formal monopoly on media ownership exists, there is a dearth of small and medium-sized businesses to support private media through advertising" (p. 340).

The problem of editorial freedom among the regional media in Russia is of vital importance to public relations. In the last decade, the federal government has done practically nothing to protect media freedom in the regions. There is no doubt that the local media are highly dependent on local authorities who often directly dictate media content. Brown (2001) argued that:

> Journalists' dependence on those who were subsidizing their newspapers or television channels curtailed their freedoms, while in the republics and provincial Russia the controls exerted by presidents and governors tended to be much more direct and uncompromising. At best, then, this requirement of a democracy, which has already survived turbulent times, remains a fragile growth. (p. 554)

A study that measured freedom of speech in Russia in 1999 found that none of the 88 studied regions, including Moscow and St. Petersburg, had created satisfactory conditions for genuine press freedom to exist. The new federal government was quick to play the role of godfather of local media when Russian president Vladimir Putin signed a law mandating that subsidies to local print media should be paid directly from the federal budget. According to Belin (2001), this new law "could somewhat reduce the print media's reliance on regional authorities, which previously had control over how federal funds were divided locally" (p. 341). The result, one could argue, is that the print media would now begin depending on the federal government's media ministry! In sum, both the national and local media in Russia still have a long way to go to achieve true freedom of speech.

Public relations practitioners should be aware of these constraints and challenges when dealing with Russian media. Specifically, media relations practices should take into consideration that media often exercise self-censorship. Media access is often curtailed and public relations practitioners may frequently find it difficult to access the media. Further, *zakazukha*, cash for editorial publication, is often an ethical dilemma for public relations practitioners.

CONCLUSION

Public relations in Russia has come a long way. This relatively new profession is developing incredibly. Yet, there are many political, social, educational, and cultural peculiarities that can create not only different perceptions of public relations as a field, but also lead to different practices in various metaregions. Contemporary Russian public relations scholars have begun to study and examine these differences so that they can be used to further develop public relations practice and scholarship. In spite of the many problems that contemporary public relations faces in Russia, it continues to be one of the most exciting and fast growing professional areas. Continuous theoretical and practical contributions certainly will help the field grow, and the future of public relations in Russia looks promising.

REGIONAL PUBLIC RELATIONS PRACTICES: A CASE STUDY

This section illustrates some of the concepts and idiosyncracies of Russian public relations practice which, as already stated, vary from metaregion to metaregion. The case study presented here deals with a public relations campaign "KidSoft," whose aim was to promote an annual festival of computer creativity among children and teenagers. The campaign was conceived and implemented in 1998 by the Voronezh regional youth nonprofit organization called "New View" (the European metaregion). The author of this chapter was the head of the public relations department of the organization at the time. This case study demonstrates which public relations practices this nonprofit organization used and how they were adapted to different metaregions, especially to the Moscow/St. Petersburg metaregion.

The "KidSoft" campaign was the biggest project that "New View" had undertaken. The festival had been conducted twice before, in 1996 and 1997. The main feature of the festival was a contest inviting schoolchildren to send their original computer software to the committee. The finalists were chosen by a panel of judges consisting of professional programmers. On the day of the festival, all the finalists were honored with awards, and the winner won a personal computer. There also were a number of small contests and a computer exhibition at the festival. The 1997 festival had attracted about 60 contest participants and about 500 visitors in a single day. In the third year, 1998, the organizing committee of "KidSoft'98" decided to expand the festival by conducting a two-day final event and promoting it at the national level.

Precampaign research showed that enough information was not available to target publics (schoolchildren, volunteers, sponsors, and journalists) about the festival and contests that were a part of the festival. Also, "KidSoft" was unknown outside of the Voronezh region. Further, the fundraising strategies of the client were not well developed, and enough volunteers were not available to help with the organization of the festival. Finally, the media did not pay attention to earlier festivals or to the organization behind the festival—"New View."

Based on this information, several strategies were developed. First, an intense publicity campaign was implemented. Public relations personnel (one full-time specialist, one part-time specialist, and one part-time volunteer) created and distributed press kits to the national, regional, and local media about the festival and about the organization. Seven national media received press kits by mail and three reacted to the kits seeking from the organizational committee more information about the festival and about possibilities of attending the festival. Campaign personnel responded to these reactions with a series of phone calls as well as special news releases via e-mail to these three national media—two broadcasting and one print. Materials about upcoming events were published and aired, and journalists from all three media covered the festival in 1998. All three national media sent representatives to the festival.

It was well-known that the regional and local media in Voronezh do not follow up on press releases and press kits sent to them. So, practitioners personally visited and talked to editors of each medium in order to get publicity and to find journalists who would agree to cover the event. These personal contacts (typified by the personal influence) were proven to be very helpful as journalists from the local media who personally knew public relations practitioners were more willing to publish information.

Fundraising was another big part of this campaign. Efforts included personal meetings with various potential local sponsors. The concept of fundraising was not well developed in Russia, and generally companies did not engage in sponsorship activities. Special hour-long conversations about benefits of sponsorship were developed for potential sponsors.

Volunteer programs were also new to many schoolchildren who were invited through publicity campaigns to participate in the organization of the festival. Many of them did not even know what it means to be a volunteer. Special information sessions about benefits of being a volunteer and a special project "Help KidSoft'98" were implemented. Volunteers were organized in special teams, and each team competed for a grand prize for the best volunteer team. Weekly meetings with workshops on leadership and social activities "Only for our volunteers" were organized.

As a result of these public relations efforts, the number of participants in "KidSoft" increased to more than 100, with participants from seven different regions and three metaregions of Russia. The total number of visitors during the two-day festival reached 4000. In all, 19 national, regional, and local media covered the event, nine of which covered other projects of the organization in separate stories and five of the media published/aired follow-ups on the festival. The number of sponsors doubled and the contest budget was almost tripled.

This public relations campaign had several ingredients that are common to public relations practices in the European metaregion. First, public relations practitioners were actively involved in the local journalistic environment and personally knew journalists, which helped them to get more publicity. Second, practitioners spent a lot of time explaining to various publics such as journalists, sponsors, and volunteers, not only the goals of the project (the festival in this case), but also, more importantly, the *nature of public relations practices per se*. Many asked practitioners about the field of public relations and various practices that are associated with the field. In 1998, there was still a lack of understanding among the general public of what public relations is.

Further, personal meetings with journalists helped promote publicity efforts because most journalists did not know what to do with press kits and news releases. Even today, many journalists from local media hardly see press releases on their desks. Even though practitioners created releases according to national standards, few local journalists wanted to use them as a starting point, preferring instead to base their stories on face-to-face communication with public relations practitioners.

At the same time, journalists from the national media, who were located in Moscow, and from regional media (St. Petersburg youth magazines) were anxious to see press kits and news releases and even requested information in appropriate formats via mail or e-mail. Thus, it was clear that journalists from the Moscow/St. Petersburg metaregion were familiar with media relations practices and expected to have professional relationships with public relations practitioners.

Therefore, one of the major characteristics of Russian public relations is the need to adapt to different publics from different metaregions. When public relations practitioners want to successfully communicate with publics outside of their metaregion, they should know to what extent public relations is developed and practiced in that metaregion. In addition, perceptions and the backgrounds of various publics should be taken into consideration.

Public relations practitioners who plan to work within the Moscow/St. Petersburg metaregion should be ready to practice a Westernized way of public relations; whereas those who practice public relations in other regions should adapt to the well-known and traditionally successful strategies and tactics used in those metaregions. In particular, personal contacts and face-to-face communication are very popular and successful in media relations practices in European and ZaBaikal metaregions (I. Boldonova, personal communication, March 2001) and less popular in Moscow/St. Petersburg and Ural metaregions (T. Korchak, personal communication, March 2002).

REFERENCES

Alyoshina, I. (1997). *Public relations dlja menedgerov i marketerov* [Public relations for managers and marketers]. Moscow: Gnom-press.

Aron, L. (2001). Russia has made a significant progress in achieving democracy. In W. Dudley (Ed.), *Russia: Opposing viewpoints* (pp. 73–82). San Diego, CA: Greenhaven Press.

Belin, L. (2001). Political bias and self-censorship in the Russian media. In A. Brown (Ed.), *Contemporary Russian politics: A reader* (pp. 323–342). Oxford: Oxford University Press.

Botan, C. (1993). A human nature approach to image and ethics in international public relations. *Journal of Public Relations Research, 5*(2), 71–81.

Brown, A. (2001). Evaluating Russia's democratization. In A. Brown (Ed.), *Contemporary Russian politics: A reader* (pp. 546–568). Oxford: Oxford University Press.

Chirkova, A., & Lapina, N. (2001). Political power and political stability in the Russian regions. In A. Brown (Ed.), *Contemporary Russian politics: A reader* (pp. 384–397). Oxford: Oxford University Press.

Clarke, T. M. (2000). An inside look at Russian public relations. *Public Relations Quarterly, 45*(1), 18–22.

Culbertson, H. M., & Chen, N. (Eds.) (1996). *International PR: A comparative analysis*. Mahwah, NJ: Lawrence Erlbaum Associates.

Department of Higher Education of Russian Federation. (2000). *Novyj gosudarstvennyj obrazovatel'nyj standart po spetsial'nosti "Svjazi s obschestvennostiju" (350400)* [New governmental standard in the major "Public Relations." Official document]. Available: http://www.pr-news.spb.ru/

Egorova-Gantman, E., & Pleshakov, K. (1999). *Politicheskaya reklama*. (Political advertising). Moscow: Nikkolo M.

GDF, Glasnost Defense Foundation (1999). *The silent regions*. Moscow: Sashcko Publishing House.

Gudykunst, W. B., Ting-Toomey, S., & Chua, E. (Eds.) (1988). *Culture and interpersonal communication*. Newbury Park, CA: Sage Publications.

Guth, D. W. (2000). The emergence of public relations in the Russian Federation. *Public Relations Review, 26*(2), 191–207.

Jaksa, J. A., & Pritchard, M. S. (1996). Chernobylk revisited. In J. A. Jaksa, & N. S. Pritchard (Eds.), *Responsible communciation: Ethical issues in business, industry, and the professions* (pp. 215–228). Cresskill, NJ: Hampton Press.

Kay, R. (2000). *Russian women and their organizations: Gender, discrimination and grassroots women's organizations, 1991–96.* London: MacMillan Press, Ltd.

Konovalova E. (2000, April). A za PR otvetish' pered . . . sovest'ju. *Electronic version of magazine Sovetnik* [On-line serial]. Available at http://www.sovetnik.ru/archive/2000/4/article.asp?id=2, September 2, 2000.

Kruckeberg, D. (1992). Ethical decision making in public relations. *International Public Relations Review, 15*(4), 32–37.

Lankina, T. (2001). Local government and ethnic and social activism in Russia. In A. Brown (Ed.), *Contemporary Russian politics: A reader* (pp. 398–411). Oxford: Oxford University Press.

Lincoln, W. B. (2001). Russia's history and culture preclude the creation of a democratic society. In W. Dudley (Ed.), *Russia: Opposing viewpoints* (pp. 83–89). San Diego, CA: Greenhaven Press.

Maksimov, A. A. (1999). "Chistye" i "gryaznye" teknologii vyborov: Rossijskij opyt. Moscow: Delo.

McElreath, M., Chen, N., Azariva, L., & Shadrova, V. (2001). The development of public relations in China, Russia, and the United States. In R. L. Heath (Ed.), *Handbook of public relations* (pp. 665–673). Thousand Oaks, CA: Sage Publications, Inc.

Miroshnichenko, A. A. (1998). Public relations v obschestvenno-politicheskoj sphere. Moscow: Ekspertnoe buro.

Newsom, D., Turk, J. V., & Kruckeberg, D. (2000). *This is PR: The realities of public relations* (7th ed.). Belmont, CA: Wadsworth/Thompson Learning.

Novinskij, B (2000). PR: nauka ili remeslo? *RUPR* [Online]. Available at http://www.rupr.ru/news/173192.html?section=articles, February 3, 2001.

Pankratov, F. G., Bazhenov, Y. K., Seregina, T. M., & Shakhurin, V. G. (2001). *Reklamnaya deyatelnost.* (Advertising activities). Moscow: Informatsionno-vnedrencheskij tsentr "Marketing."

Pheophanov, O. (2001). *Reklama: Novye texnologii v Rossii.* (Advertising: New technologies in Russia). St. Petersburg: Piter.

Pocheptsov, G. (1998). *Public relations, ili kak uspeshno upravljat'* obschestvennym mneniem. (Public relations, or how to manage public opinion successfully) Moskva: Tsentr.

Pocheptsov, G. (2001). Public relations dlya professionalov. (Public relations for professionals). Moscow: REEFL-Book.

PR News (2001). Online Periodical Journal. [Online]. Available at http://www.prnews.ru/news, November 2, 2001.

Pratkanis A., & Aronson, E. (1991) *Age of propaganda.* New York: W. H. Freeman.

Richmond, Y. (1996). *From nyet to da: Understanding the Russians* (2nd ed.). Yarmouth, ME: Intercultural Press.

Solzhenitsyn, A. (2001). Russia has failed to achieve true democracy. In W. Dudley (Ed.), *Russia: Opposing viewpoints* (pp. 66–72). San Diego, CA: Greenhaven Press, Inc.

Sriramesh, K., & White, J. (1992). Societal culture and public relations. In J. E. Grunig (Ed.), *Excellence in public relations and communication management,* (pp. 597–616). Mahwah, NJ: Lawrence Erlbaum.

Sutherland, A. (2001). PR thrives in harder times. *Frontline, IPRA, 23,* p. 52.

Taylor, M. (2001). International public relations: Opportunities and challenges for the 21st century. In R. L. Heath (Ed.), *Handbook of public relations* (pp. 629–637). Thousand Oaks, CA: Sage.

Ting-Toomey, S. (1999). *Communicating across cultures.* New York: Guilford.

Tsetsura, E. Y. (2000a). *Conceptual frameworks in the field of public relations: A comparative study of Russian and United States perspectives.* Unpublished master's thesis, Fort Hays State University, Hays, KS.

Tsetsura, K. (2000b, March). *Understanding the "evil" nature of public relations as perceived by some Russian publics.* Paper presented at the Annual Interdisciplinary International PRSA Educators Academy Conference, Miami, FL.

Tsetsura, K. (2001, March). *Can ethics in public relations finally become international? Dialogic communication as basis for a new universal code of ethics in public relations.* Paper presented at the 4th PRSA Educators Academy international interdisciplinary conference, Miami.

Tsetsura, K. (2002, April). *Use and abuse of freedom of information: Monitoring freedom of speech in Russian media.* Paper presented at the Central States Communication Association convention, Milwaukee, WI.

Tsetsura, K., & Kruckeberg, D. (in press). Contemporary Russian journalism: problems and opportunities. In A. S. de Beer & J. C. Merrill (Ed.), *Global Journalism*, 4th ed. Longman.

Tulchinsky, G. L. (1994). *Public relations: Reputatsija, vlijanie, cvjazi s pressoj I obschestvennostiju, sponsorstvo.* St. Petersburg: St. Petersburg GAK.

Tulupov, V. V. (1996) . Public relations in Russia as a new social institution. *Speeches of conference "Public relations in Russia today and tomorrow"* (pp. 17–21). Voronezh, Russia: Voronezh State University.

Varustin, L. E. (2000, summer). Sistema obrazovanija public relations pered novym vyborom. *Online newspaper PR News* [On-line serial]. Available at http://www.pr-news.spb.ru/, November 5, 2001.

THE AMERICAS

CHAPTER

30

PUBLIC RELATIONS IN THE UNITED STATES: A GENERATION OF MATURATION

LARISSA A. GRUNIG
JAMES E. GRUNIG

Writing a chapter characterizing public relations in the United States is daunting. We accepted this invitation with trepidation. We did not write this chapter in an attempt to galvanize opinion within the academic community of public relations worldwide. Understanding that risk, we did our best to avoid the arrogance that so endears North Americans to the rest of the world. Instead, we tried to stake out a position apart from those whose work legitimately might be characterized as ethnocentric.

Most especially, we do not consider public relations professionals and scholars on other continents imitators rather than innovators. Countries like Germany, for example, have a century-plus history of scholarship and practice in the field. Other countries in which public relations has developed more recently, such as Slovenia, already offer a fecund body of knowledge and sophisticated, highly professional practice. Still others, such as South Africa, are developing democracies that often find themselves in crisis; thus, they are pushed to create solutions that their counterparts around the world will emulate. Finally, giants, such as China and Russia, by their sheer size undoubtedly will produce an exceptional body of theoretical and applied work as soon as public relations educational programs there become a critical mass.

In this chapter, we emphasize the importance of the triad of knowledge, shared expectations between the dominant coalition and public relations, and the organizational context in United States public relations practice. To whom do these considerations relate? They relate to nearly 200,000 practitioners who work in this field in the United States, for sure. Beyond that, we believe that the implications of research we have conducted over the last 17 years are significant for public relations colleagues in other parts of the world.

The Excellence theory (Dozier, L. A. Grunig, & J. E. Grunig, 1995; J. E. Grunig, 1992; L. A. Grunig, J. E. Grunig, & Dozier, 2002) seems to work for North America and at least parts of Europe as well.

We offer the criteria we developed and tested in the Excellence study as a set of generic principles for effective public relations practice. These criteria require knowledge and professionalism by the public relations unit. They also require understanding of and support for public relations by senior management. The characteristics of an excellent public relations function can be placed into five categories that are discussed in the following sections.

EMPOWERMENT OF THE FUNCTION

For public relations to contribute to organizational effectiveness, the organization must empower communication as a critical management function. Empowerment of the public relations function subsumes four characteristics of excellent practice. The first three consider the relationship of communication to the overall management of the organization:

- The senior executive in public relations is involved with the strategic management processes of the organization, and communication programs are developed for strategic publics identified as a part of this strategic management process. Public relations contributes to strategic management by scanning the environment to identify publics affected by the consequences of decisions or who might affect the outcome of decisions. An excellent public relations department communicates with these publics to bring their voices into strategic management, thus making it possible for publics to participate in organizational decisions that affect them.

- Communication programs organized by excellent departments to communicate with strategic publics also are managed strategically. To be managed strategically means that these programs are based on formative research, have concrete and measurable objectives, use varied rather than routine techniques when they are implemented, and are evaluated either formally or informally. In addition, the communication staff can provide evidence to show that these programs achieved their short-term objectives and improved the long-term relationships between the organization and its publics.

- The top communicator is a member of the dominant coalition of the organization or has a direct reporting relationship to senior managers who are part of the dominant coalition. The public relations function seldom will be involved in strategic management and public relations practitioners will not have the power to affect key organizational decisions unless the senior public relations executive is part of or has access to the group of senior managers with the greatest power in the organization.

The fourth characteristic of empowerment defines the extent to which practitioners who are not White men are empowered:

- Diversity is embodied in all public relations roles. The principle of requisite variety (Weick, 1979) suggests that organizations need as much diversity inside as outside if they are to interact successfully with all strategic elements of their environment. Excellent public relations departments empower both men and women in all roles as well as practitioners of diverse racial, ethnic, and cultural backgrounds.

COMMUNICATOR ROLES

Public relations researchers (e.g., Broom, 1982; Dozier & Broom, 1995) have conducted extensive research on two major roles that communicators play in organizations—the manager and the technician. Communication technicians are essential to carry out most of the day-to-day communication activities of public relations departments, and many practitioners—especially women (Toth & L. A. Grunig, 1993)—enact both roles. In less excellent departments, however, all of the communication practitioners—including the senior practitioner—are technicians. If the senior communicator is not a manager, it is not possible for public relations to be empowered as a management function. Three characteristics of excellence in public relations are related to the managerial role:

- A strategic manager rather than a technician or an administrative manager heads the public relations unit. Excellent public relations operations must have at least one senior communication manager who conceptualizes and directs public relations programs, or other members of the dominant coalition who have little knowledge of communication management or of relationship building will supply this direction. In addition, the results of the Excellence study distinguished between two types of senior managers: a strategic manager and an administrative manager. Administrative managers typically manage day-to-day operations of the communication function, personnel, and the budget. They generally are supervisors of technicians rather than strategic managers. If the head of public relations is an administrative manager rather than a strategic manager, the department usually will not be excellent.

- The senior public relations executive or others in the public relations unit must have the knowledge needed for the manager role or the communication function will not have the potential to become a managerial function. Excellent public relations programs are staffed by professionals—practitioners who have gained the knowledge needed to carry out the manager role through university education, continuing education, or self-study.

- Both men and women must have equal opportunity to occupy the managerial role. The majority of public relations professionals in the United States are women. Research (L. A. Grunig, Toth, & Hon, 2000) also has established that female practitioners are the best educated in this field and most likely to take advantage of professional development opportunities. If women are excluded from the managerial role, the communication function may be diminished because the majority of the most knowledgeable practitioners will be excluded from that role. When that is the case, the senior position in the public relations department typically is filled by a technician or by a practitioner from another managerial function who has little knowledge of public relations.

ORGANIZATION OF THE COMMUNICATION FUNCTION AND ITS RELATIONSHIP TO OTHER MANAGEMENT FUNCTIONS

Many organizations have a single department devoted to all communication functions. Others have separate departments for programs aimed at different publics such as journalists, employees, the local community, or the financial community. Still others place communication under another managerial function such as marketing, human resources, legal, or finance. Many organizations also contract or consult with outside firms for all or some of their communication programs or for communication techniques such as annual reports or newsletters. Two characteristics are related to the organization of the function:

- Public relations should be an integrated communication function. An excellent public relations function integrates all public relations programs into a single department or provides a mechanism for coordinating programs managed by different departments. Only in an integrated system is it possible for public relations to develop new communication programs for changing strategic publics and to move resources from outdated programs designed for formerly strategic publics to the new programs.

- Public relations should be a management function separate from other functions. Although the function is integrated in an excellent organization, the function should not be placed in another department whose primary responsibility is a management function other than communication. Many organizations splinter the public relations function by making communication a supporting tool for other departments such as marketing. When the public relations function is sublimated to other functions, it cannot be managed strategically because it cannot move communication resources from one strategic public to another—as an integrated function can.

MODELS OF PUBLIC RELATIONS

Public relations scholars (beginning with J. E. Grunig, 1984) have conducted extensive research on the extent to which organizations practice four models of public relations— four typical ways of conceptualizing and conducting the communication function—and to identify which of these models provides a normative framework for effective and ethical practice. This research suggests that excellent departments design more of their communication programs on the two-way symmetrical model of collaboration and public participation than on three other typical models: press agentry (emphasizing only favorable publicity), public information (disclosing accurate information but engaging in no research or other form of two-way communication), or two-way asymmetrical (emphasizing only the interests of the organization and not the interests of publics).

Two-way symmetrical public relations is based on research and uses communication to enhance public participation and to manage conflict with strategic publics. As a result, two-way symmetrical communication produces better long-term relationships with publics than do the other models. Symmetrical programs generally are conducted more ethically than are other models and, as a result, produce effects that balance the interests of organizations and the publics in society. Four characteristics of excellence are related to these models:

- The public relations department and the dominant coalition share the worldview that the communication department should base its goals and its communication activities on the two-way symmetrical model.

- Communication programs developed for specific publics are based on two-way symmetrical strategies for building and maintaining relationships.

- The senior public relations executive or others in the unit must have the professional knowledge needed to practice the two-way symmetrical model.

- The organization should have a symmetrical system of internal communication. A symmetrical system of internal communication is based on the principles of employee empowerment and participation in decision making. Managers and other employees engage in dialogue and listen to each other. Internal publications disclose relevant information needed by employees to understand their role in the organization and to provide employees with a voice to management. Symmetrical communication within an organization fosters a participative rather than an authoritarian culture as well as improved relationships with employees—greater employee satisfaction, control mutuality, commitment, and trust.[1]

ETHICS

Finally, we determined that incorporating ethics and social responsibility into practice is necessary for public relations to achieve excellence. We (L. A. Grunig et al., 2002, p. 554) acknowledged that elaborating on this final principle requires additional research, but even now we understand that public relations practitioners frequently serve as the ethics officers or consciences of their organizations. Why? Public relations is the function that introduces the values and problems of stakeholders into strategic decisions and that establishes a moral element in those decisions.

It may be early to celebrate the implications of the Excellence theory. The project, begun in 1985, was completed with the publication of the third and final book in the series in 2002 (L. A. Grunig et al., 2002). Already, however, it serves as the organizational framework for this book. Results of that research are woven throughout this chapter.

Clichéd though it may be, we contend that at no time in our country's history has public relations counsel based on solid research and theorizing been more important. In the wake of the attacks of September 11, 2001, and financial mismanagement scandals on the part of major United States corporations, the role of corporate conscience (Edelman, 2002) enacted by educated, professional communicators should be central. Some aspects of this societal context encourage that approach to public relations; others, as detailed next, constrain it.

INFRASTRUCTURE

The United States of America is a land of more than 3.6 million square miles (9.4 million sq km) on the continent of North America. It consists of 50 states, 48 of them contiguous. They are bordered by Canada to the north, Mexico and the Gulf of Mexico to the south, the Atlantic Ocean to the east, and the Pacific Ocean to the west. The state of Hawaii is in the Pacific, southwest of California; Alaska is northwest of Canada. There are several territories and possessions in the Caribbean Sea and the Pacific Ocean, in addition to these states.

Washington, DC, is the capital. Other large cities familiar to people from abroad include New York, Los Angeles, Chicago, Houston, Philadelphia, San Diego, Detroit, Dallas, Phoenix, and San Antonio. The population, according to the 2000 United States Bureau of the Census, is 281,421,906. (About 197,000 of these people are public relations practitioners; United States Department of Labor, 1998.) The population is increasingly heterogeneous—creating an immense challenge for public relations professionals and the U.S. organizations that employ them. The primary language is English; although in some cities (e.g., Los Angeles), more students enter the school system speaking Spanish than English as their native tongue.

---

[1]The generic principles of excellence as presented here are taken largely from J. E. Grunig and L. A. Grunig (2001).

Political System

The United States of America is a democracy. Sovereign power is vested in the citizenry as a whole indirectly through elected representatives. Guiding principles of our 2 centuries plus of constitutional self-government include equality of rights, opportunity, and treatment. Equality relates to everyone, without privileges of rank or heredity. Citizens hold dear the notion of the "common people," in reference to political power. (Of course, as Toth's, 2002, essay on postmodern public relations asserted, no single ideology such as democracy exists.)

After the American Revolution in 1776, the states functioned under the Articles of Confederation for 12 years. By1789, representatives of several states had met in Philadelphia and wrote and adopted the more structured Constitution. The United States Constitution calls for three branches of government: executive, judicial, and legislative. (These branches serve as a system of checks and balances on each other.) Congress is composed of two parts. In the Senate, states enjoy equal representation (two legislators per state). Population determines representation in the House of Representatives.

Here is what historian of public relations Cutlip (1995) had to say about the significance of the approval of the Constitution for public relations in the United States:

> The monumental struggle Alexander Hamilton, James Madison, and John Jay waged to win ratification of the United States Constitution, which governs our lives to this day, demonstrates far better than any other public relations campaign the far-reaching effect of public relations' unseen power. Allan Nevins was not exaggerating when he termed this campaign "the greatest work ever done in the field of public relations." (p. 280)

A mere 2 years after its passage, concerned that the Constitution did not protect certain freedoms, citizens pressed for change. The Bill of Rights resulted. The first of these 10 amendments includes the freedoms of speech, the press, and "the right of the people peaceably to assemble" (cited in Jordan, 2002, p. 45). All three aspects of the First Amendment[2] have important implications for United States practitioners of public relations.

Together with its 10 amendments, the Constitution makes possible our advocacy role in public relations. The freedom of speech,[3] freedom of thought, and freedom of assembly all guarantee, in turn, the right of public relations practitioners to represent all points of view in this democratic marketplace of ideas.

However, according to political communication expert Parry-Giles (quoted in Sherman, 2002), democracy is a "vision premised upon interaction between the voter and the leader" (p. 2). At this point in the republic's history, he said, concerned citizens are searching for alternatives to the standard debates and town hall meetings to understand candidates' stances on issues and to stimulate voters to go to the polls. The interaction between political candidates and constituents has become limited for two main reasons, he explained: Politicians want to control the message, and the media that report on the message are imperfect surrogates for the public voice.

---

[2] A good, current reference to the First Amendment can be found in Farber (2002). It includes discussion of the Internet and other electronic media as well as new federal restrictions on soft money in political campaigns and national security issues after 9/11.

[3] There are constraints on these rights, which are discussed in the portion of this chapter that deals with media. Constraints include "fighting words," defamation, and privacy.

Corporate political expression is controlled in the United States, particularly through the Federal Election Campaign Act of 1970. This act limits what organizations—as well as individuals—can contribute to a candidate's campaign. However, corporations can make partisan statements to their stockholders and can sponsor appearances by candidates. Furthermore, they and their unions may help employees contribute to candidates' campaigns by setting up political action committees. This allows corporations significant say in the outcome of elections.

Also, citizens at large have the right to petition the government; when this is done in the halls of the legislature, it is called *lobbying*. In the past, lobbying meant such unethical practices as bribery; today, it more typically involves providing information to legislative aides—information that may prove influential in future votes. Since 1946, lobbyists must register with Congress and file quarterly statements that reveal their expenses and sources of funding. Since the Foreign Agents Registration Act passed in 1938,[4] lobbyists representing other governments must register with the United States government as well.[5]

Legal System

Individual voices, in fact all manner of individual liberties, are protected by the county's supreme legal document: the United States Constitution. Under the Constitution, every aspect of governmental action is codified. Laws are deduced from the principle of rights—rights of the people, rather than rights of the government. Thus, the government's actions as well as the actions of its citizens are regulated under the rule of law. The rule of law, rather than the rule of people with their whimsies or hereditary privilege, even protects the rights of what the country considers to be the smallest possible minority: that of individuals.

The legal system in the United States protects its citizens' rights through three main entities. The *military* protects the country from outside invaders. *Police forces* protect from domestic criminals. The *court system* settles legal disputes and sentences criminals to punishment according to predefined laws and interpretations thereof. The United States Supreme Court serves as the ultimate arbiter.

Public relations functions in an increasingly legal environment in the United States. Sexual harassment, all forms of discrimination, and abuses of labor are growing concerns. So, too, are issues of the quality and safety of products and of protection of the environment while producing those goods. New communication technology makes organizations increasingly vulnerable to charges that they are violating those norms of safety, quality, and fairness.

Public relations practitioners in publicly traded companies need to understand financial reporting requirements of the Securities and Exchange Commission, established in 1934. Major considerations include the need to prepare and distribute annual reports and to disclose information in a timely way and prohibitions related to issuing prospectuses encouraging investors to buy stock.

One final legal consideration for public relations practitioners in the United States is the copyright statute, originally passed in 1909 and revised in 1976,[6] which protects the

---

[4]The act was amended in 1966 to require disclosure by agents engaged in public relations, politics, financial negotiations, consultancies, or other activities on behalf of other governments (Kennedy, 1966).

[5]Diplomats, officials of other governments, journalists for United States publications, and people involved in charitable or religious activities are exempt from registering.

[6]The revision took into account technological developments such as photocopying, cable television, and videotaping.

original author of a work. Copyright law determines whether others can use not only written materials such as brochures or press releases but music and video clips as well. Fair use of copyrighted work depends on the purpose (nonprofit or commercial), the nature of that work, the amount to be used in relation to the entire work, and the effect of use on the market value of the copyrighted material.

Economic System

The motto of the United States democracy is "In God we trust." A typical sign displayed in small enterprises plays on this motto: "In God we trust; everyone else pays cash." Indeed, capitalism is a dominant feature of the U.S. infrastructure. (As with democracy, Toth, 2002, argued that postmodernists dismiss the possibility of any dominant ideology such as capitalism.)

Most U.S. means of production and distribution are privately owned. Indeed, capitalism is a social as well as economic system based on the principle of individual rights. Contemporary capitalism, in the United States and elsewhere, is characterized by privatization, employee ownership, and industry. Enterprises are operated for profit, under competitive conditions for the most part. In 1997, the U.S. gross domestic product was $7,824,008 million.

Capitalism has been consistent with the U.S. political ideal of achieving the common good (Gianaris, 1996; Greenberg, 1985). Increasingly, however, activists are questioning the moral justification for capitalism (van Parijs, 1997). In particular, they challenge the globalization of capitalism (Maitra, 1996). As we were developing this chapter, for example, protestors were massing in the nation's capital, Washington, DC, to demonstrate against the International Monetary Fund and the World Bank.

Activism

Sam Adams and his daring band of revolutionaries were among the earliest activists in what would become the United States of America. The Sons of Liberty formed an activist group determined to change the government from outside its structure. Since then, grassroots activists have prospered under the country's democracy and its free press. The country's individualistic culture, too, has contributed to the sense here that the work of each individual can help change a system that is not working. However, public relations practitioners have been accused of co-opting environmental activists, in particular, "under the veil of grassroots democracy" (Holtzhausen, 2002, p. 258).

For a very current analysis of the growing social activism in the United States, see Crespo (2002). This photojournalist brought together his own experience as well as essays from organizers of such actions as the Million Mom March and protests against the death penalty, the World Trade Organization, Haitian immigration, and logging of the country's redwood forests.

Lerbinger (2001) explored the relationship between contemporary public relations and these types of activism, concentrating on the period that began in the 1960s when social movements such as civil rights, environmentalism, and feminism became better organized than ever before. As a result of concurrent regulation of big business (and media coverage thereof), corporations relied heavily on public affairs to monitor their socio/political environment. Lerbinger credited this development with leading to increased appreciation for and sophistication of public relations practice.

The Excellence project (L. A. Grunig et al., 2002) found much the same thing: One characteristic of effective public relations is the ability to deal with activist groups. Those external constituencies push the organization to improve, to become more competitive, and—in short—to excellence.

MEDIA ENVIRONMENT

As described in chapter 1, one of the first attempts to link the mass media (radio, television, and newspapers) with society and its political system was Siebert, Peterson, and Schramm's (1963) *Four Theories of the Press*. The United States fell under what they called the *libertarian theory*,[7] also known as the *free press*. The idea is that individuals should be free to publish whatever they want. Thus, attacks on government are common, even encouraged. The media are thought to play a watchdog role over government.

Since then, the work of Siebert and his colleagues (1963) has been widely studied, accepted, and critiqued. For example, Skjerdal (1993) condemned these four normative theories used to illustrate the press' position relative to its political environment as outdated and overly simplistic. Altschull (1984) attempted to improve on the four theories by reducing them to three and adding a development component; in his view, journalism throughout the First World (including, of course, the United States) corresponds to the liberal system.[8]

Hachten (1992) added one kind of media system, identifying a total of five types found throughout the world. They are authoritarian, Communist, revolutionary, developmental, and Western. The latter is the system people in the United States and Western Europe[9] have come to equate with freedom of the press. Ownership of broadcast and print media is private, and the government cannot interfere with reporting. In this system, journalists have the right to "talk politics" (p. 19). In return, they are expected to report responsibly.

However, the press in general has been accused of keeping U.S. citizens in the dark and impotent because of growing concentration and commercialization of our mass media. Pseudoevents like Media Democracy Day have been designed to promote an alternative system, one that informs and empowers all members of society. Media Democracy's web site (http://www.communicationism.org/mediademocracyday.org/home) "prioritizes diversity over monopoly, citizen control over corporate choice, cultural development over company profit, and public discourse over public relations."

Despite these and similar criticisms, the notion of the "free press" of the United States is touted worldwide. We put "free press" in quotation marks because the reality, as Skjerdal (1993) pointed out, is that even the U.S. media system contains elements of authoritarianism. He cited Kamen's (1991) analysis of coverage of the Gulf War as evidence of U.S. reporters being required to run battlefield stories past government censors before being dispatched. Nevertheless, the Constitution guarantees the right to free speech,[10] and the government rarely controls the media directly. At the same time, any number of influences shapes media coverage. Public relations is prominent among them.

Most introductory textbooks in the field point out to student readers that nearly one half of the mainstream media's daily content comes from public relation sources. That

---

[7]The other three theories are *authoritarian*, in which the state controls the media; *Soviet*, closely tied to Communist ideology; and *social responsibility*, which emphasizes the media's obligations to (a diverse) society.

[8]Other prominent media scholars who took on the four theories include Lowenstein and Merrill (1990), Martin and Chaudhary (1983), McLeod and Blumler (1989), and McQuail (1987).

[9]Hachten considered this Western concept rare; it exists in few countries outside the United States and Western Europe.

[10]Exceptions include some cases of speech that interferes with war effort (e.g., troop movements in times of war), false statements of fact, incitement or provoking others to violence (including speech advocating crime), threats, appropriation of speech owned by others, invasion of privacy, child pornography, and obscenity.

content, of course, is not necessarily neutral. Like Skjerdal (1993) before him, Cutlip (1995) provided this instance: "The United States military's control of the news of the Gulf War with Iraq in 1991 was a perfect example [*sic*] how news sources, guided by public relations officials, can control and shape the news with the truth a casualty" (p. 283).

This spin on the news provided by public affairs or public relations sources determined to influence public opinion is played out in all forms of media, print and broadcast. Cutlip (1995) alluded to what he called "talk show democracy" (p. 283) in the U.S. news radio.

What about media access? Daily newspaper circulation at the turn of the recent century was 212 per 1,000 people; there were 806 television receivers per 1,000 inhabitants at that same point. (*World Statistics Pocketbook*, 2001).[11] It is hard to imagine any limits. Nearly 10 years ago, even before the information superhighway had ventured into every hill and vale of the country, Cutlip (1995) wrote the following:

> Today's Washington is wired for quadrophonic [*sic*] sound and wide screen video, swamped by fax, computer messages, 800 numbers, and CNN to every citizen in every village in the nation. Its every act or failure to act to [*sic*] blared to the public thanks to C-Span, open-meeting laws, financial disclosure reports, and campaign spending rules, and its every misstep is logged in a database for use of future opponents. (pp. 283–84)

Like radio, saturation of television has important implications for public relations and, for one recent critic (Sanders, 2002), for democracy itself. In Sanders' view, deregulation and ownership by corporate conglomerates have changed television from an information to an entertainment medium in this country. Hollihan (2001) went so far as to suggest that democracy is facing a crisis in light of television's effects on political campaigning: increased cost, higher level of entertainment, more ethical issues, greater cynicism on the part of the public, and decreased political participation.

Even in this era of specialized and online publications, most people in the United States get their news from the mass media such as television and newspapers. Furthermore, what citizens learn from electronic news sources is questionable. In the context of political communication, for instance, sound bites provide little fodder for deep discussion of critical issues. For this reason, groups such as the University of Maryland's Center for Political Communication and Civic Leadership are experimenting with different approaches to mediated campaign information. The center, for example, recently hosted a "Recovering Democracy Forum," wherein gubernatorial candidates were invited to join a range of citizens (including community activists, students, and political leaders) for facilitated and meaningful dialogue. Even so, one founder of the center explained, traditional broadcast media still attract viewers to political news: "It's like gladiators. You want to see who's going to get bloodied up" (Parry-Giles, quoted in Sherman, 2002).

The United States has been at the forefront of the information revolution. Television and Internet consumption and their concomitant influence on social and cultural habits have been attributed to Americanization. However, sages (Nye, 2002) emphasize that correlation is not causation; the United States simply introduced computers at a faster rate than did many other countries. Given today's worldwide immersion in this information medium, the United States influence on culture is likely to diminish.

---

[11]Compare these numbers from the *World Statistics Pocketbook* (2001) with Slovenia, for just one example, where newspaper circulation in 1999 was 199 per 1,000 people and—strikingly different from U.S. figures—television receivers were 356 per 1,000 people.

SOCIETAL CULTURE

Many U.S. practitioners of public relations work in multinational companies. They must be able to understand and interpret cultures other than their own. As retired French practitioner Jacques Coup de Frejac (1991) said, most important, multinational communicators need:

> A new "intelligence" of other cultures. I consider the building blocks of culture to be all the historical, religious, ideological, social and human elements which constitute the heritage of individuals, tribes and people. There cannot be any good Public Relations without a careful appraisal of others in order to be in harmony with their culture. (p. 23)

Societal culture, what Hofstede (1984) called "the collective programming of the mind which distinguishes the members of one human group from another" (p. 21), is based on what he considered mental programs. Hofstede explained that individuals organize what they know, believe, and expect into these mental programs. When groups of individuals share the programs, he added, we call them a culture.

Organizations as well as societies have cultures; organizational culture can have a strong effect on how public relations is practiced. Adler (2002) pointed out that many managers of multinational organizations believe, therefore, that organizational culture will "moderate or erase the influence of national culture" (p. 67). This would mean that managers could ignore the cultures outside a multinational organization as long as they create and maintain a strong internal culture. Research, Adler said, shows otherwise: "Employees and managers *do* bring their ethnicity to the workplace" (p. 67).

Tixier (1993) found also that culture affects public relations. She studied 40 companies in 11 countries and found that different cultures see the role of communication differently. For less developed countries, she found, communicators often simply copy models of public relations from more developed countries. But cultures, she said, "play an increasingly obvious role as countries reach a greater degree of development" (p. 30).

Language also is an integral part of culture. Anyone who wants to be a global public relations practitioner should learn at least one language other than his or her own, even though English has become essentially the language of international relations. Wouters (1991) expressed the importance of language well:

> Command of other languages for Americans is undeniably increasing in importance as an international mentality spreads . . . willingness to learn other languages shows a sophistication and appreciation of other cultures that is still desperately needed in the United States. Even if the language is not essential to the transaction of business, it has always been an asset. (p. 98)

Although it is important for global public relations practitioners to understand the cultures in which they work, the task would be impossible unless a way is found to identify similarities among cultures that can be classified in some way. It may help to understand the need for such a classification by comparing the numbers of cultures with the numbers of individuals affected by an organization. Practitioners cannot deal with every individual affected by an organization, so they group them into types of publics that respond to organizational consequences in different ways. We must do the same with cultures: Look for types of cultures that require different applications of the generic principles of excellence.

For many years, anthropologists have identified different dimensions of cultures. However, the Dutch organizational researcher Geert Hofstede (1984) developed a set of dimensions of culture that have been used widely by management scholars—including public relations scholars—to study the effect of culture on behavior in organizations. He developed these dimensions by studying theories of anthropologists. Then he tested the concepts by using them to measure cultural differences among employees of a U.S.-based multinational corporation—which he called HERMES—in 39 countries. These dimensions explicate cultural effects on public relations. The dimensions and their implications for public relations are discussed in the following sections.

Individualism or Collectivism

Societies range on a continuum from highly individual to highly collective. This dimension describes how individuals relate to larger groups such as extended families, tribes, or organizations. In individualistic cultures, people define their self-worth by their personal achievements and individual welfare. In collectivist cultures, people define their worth in relationship to larger groups. Individualistic societies value competition; collectivist societies value collaboration and teamwork.

In his study of HERMES employees, Hofstede (1984) found that the United States was the most individualistic of the 39 countries. In his reanalysis of the original data, Hofstede (2001) found that the United States still ranked first out of the 50 countries and 3 regions included in that second calculation. He pointed out that individualism correlates with the extent of economic development.

Given the logic of this dimension, the generic characteristics of excellent public relations—especially symmetrical communication and social responsibility—would seem more likely to be adopted in collectivist cultures. This may explain why asymmetrical models of public relations continue to be popular in the United States, for example, and why the symmetrical model may be valued more in Europe and Asia. Practically, it also may mean that public relations practitioners may have to explain the value of symmetrical communication and social responsibility in individual terms in individualistic countries—that communicating symmetrically and being concerned about others also is good for the self-interest of the organization and the people in it.

Power Distance

This dimension describes how cultures deal with inequality. Some cultures are more likely than others to accept an inequitable distribution of power, prestige, and wealth among different classes or groups. In cultures with high power distance, employees are more likely to accept a centralized work arrangement where superiors make all decisions. When power distance is low, management is decentralized and subordinates make more of their own decisions. Hofstede (1984) found the United States ranked just below the midpoint. That ranking changed little in his (2001) reanalysis; the United States ranked 40th out of the 50 countries and 3 regions in terms of power distance.

The greater the power distance, the more difficult it would be to implement the generic principles of public relations. Senior management, for example, would seem less likely to treat public relations managers as equals—thus relegating public relations to a technical support function and excluding it from strategic management. Symmetrical communication works best when power distance is low—especially a symmetrical system of internal communication. Tayeb (1988), for example, found that employee commitment to the organization and the level of interpersonal trust were lowest when power distance is high. Likewise, organizations would value both diversity and social responsibility less when power distance is high.

The generic principles can be applied when power distance is high, but they must be introduced slowly—as Verčič, L. A. Grunig, and J. E. Grunig (1996) found practitioners were doing in Slovenia. If introduced in small increments, the generic principles then can help gradually to lower the power distance in organizations where societal culture accepts high-power distance.

Uncertainty Avoidance

This dimension of culture refers to the extent to which people in a society can tolerate uncertain, ambiguous situations. When uncertainty avoidance is high, people tend to be dogmatic and authoritarian. They also formulate many rules to reduce uncertainty. They are likely to stay in one job for their lifetime. When uncertainty avoidance is low, people are more open to new ideas, new situations, and diversity. According to Hofstede's (1984) initial study, the United States (along with Canada and the United Kingdom, the countries included in the Excellence study) were ranked in the bottom third of all countries studied on this dimension. As with the first two dimensions, the U.S. ranking changed little with Hofstede's (2001) recalculation: The United States was 43rd out of the 53 countries and regions ranked.

Also like the first two characteristics, high-uncertainty avoidance makes application of the generic principles difficult. Diversity introduces uncertainty. As part of strategic management, public relations introduces requisite variety—uncertainty. Symmetrical public relations brings organizational change—more uncertainty. In these situations, public relations practitioners again must introduce uncertainty in small doses and must research their proposals for change as thoroughly as possible to reduce the uncertainty of what they propose. If they do, practitioners still should be able to introduce gradual change in societies that avoid it.

Masculinity and Femininity

Masculine cultures value assertiveness, making money, and acquiring possessions. Feminine cultures value relationships, concern for others, and quality of life. In addition, women occupy fewer managerial roles in masculine cultures than in feminine cultures. According to Hofstede's (1984) original study, the United States was about one third of the way from the highest level of masculinity. It ranked 15th out of 53 in his (2001) reanalysis.

Obviously, the generic principles such as symmetrical communication, diversity, and social responsibility fit better with feminine than masculine cultures. Again, however, they can be introduced incrementally in masculine cultures to change them gradually.

In the second edition of *Culture's Consequences*, Hofstede (2001) reanalyzed his data for 50 countries (rather than the initial 39) and 3 regions. Thus, the new rankings place each country in relation to 52 other areas. Hofstede also added a fifth dimension of culture— long-term orientation (LTO) versus short-term orientation (STO).

LTO Versus STO

Like the initial four dimensions, LTO versus STO was empirically found and validated (Hofstede, 2001). It reflects a choice of focus for people's efforts: future or present. LTO reflects Confucian values of persistence, thrift, personal stability, and respect for tradition. Not surprising, it was found in answers to questions to the Chinese Value Survey of 1985 (samples came from 23 countries, including the United States). Also not surprising, East Asian countries scored highest; Western countries generally scored on the low side. More specifically, the United States ranked 17th out of the 23 countries (cited in Hofstede, 2001).

Implications for U.S. public relations practice are found primarily in the area of relationships. According to Hofstede (2001), low LTO is associated with the expectation of quick results and the sense that the most important events in life have occurred in the past or occur at present. One key difference between it and high LTO is, in business, short-term results: what Hofstede (2001, p. 366) called "the bottom line" so important to cultures with short-term orientation. By contrast, LTO is associated with the sense that most important events will occur in future and—most significantly—with the building of relationships and market position in business. Thus, public relations practitioners in the United States, with its emphasis on short-term results, may face an uphill battle in convincing top management of the importance of relationship building because cultivating relationships is an inherently long-term process.

We looked at each of Hofstede's (2001) five dimensions individually, but they do interact. Some cultures may have characteristics favorable to the generic concepts on some dimensions but not on others. The United States—with its high individualism; moderately low power distance, uncertainty avoidance, and LTO; and moderately high masculinity— does not have a culture particularly conducive to the generic principles, which may explain why so many U.S. practitioners favor an asymmetrical model and a technical role, do not value diversity, and frequently have lapses in ethics and social responsibility.

Culture shapes public relations, but public relations can help to change culture. To do so, however, the generic principles from the Excellence project must be introduced slowly so that they are perceived as fitting within a range of what is acceptable in a particular culture.

Mass communication and modernization have failed to wipe out the idiosyncrasies of local cultures. Even globalization does not necessarily mean homogenization of culture. Nye (2002) offered historical proof in the example of 17th century Japan, which had deliberately isolated itself from attempts at globalization on the part of European seafarers. By the mid-19th century, when Japan became the first Asian country then to embrace globalization, it borrowed innovations successfully from countries throughout the world yet retained its unique culture.[12] Thus, it makes sense to explore any uniqueness of U.S. culture or cultures even in this era when antiglobalization protestors attack transnational corporations. At the same time, we must keep in mind that culture—including U.S. societal culture—is not static. Its customs, values, rituals, and even language can change as it borrows from other cultures.

U.S. PUBLIC RELATIONS

Harold Burson, co-founder of what remains one of the world's largest and most respected public relations firms, Burson-Marsteller, described the evolution of the field this way: With the boom of post-World II, clients knew what they wanted to do and merely asked

---

[12]Globalization and the information revolution actually may reinforce rather than homogenize culture, according to Nye (2002). He explained that the Internet, for example, allows customers to come together in niche markets and geographically dispersed voters to establish political communities.

their public relations agents, "How do I say it?" With the extensive activism of the 1960s, executives became less sure of themselves and asked, "What do I say?" With more and more public relations professionals coming to the decision table by the 1980s, their bosses then asked, "What do I do?"[13]

There is no question that U.S. public relations has become more strategic over time. However, describing the actual history of public relations in the United States is beyond the scope of this chapter. We say this not because of the time span involved—slightly more than 1 century. Rather, that history is contested[14] and—because we are not historians—we choose not to enter the dispute. We do acknowledge that along with history of the field in this country comes considerable baggage. Our earliest practitioners were press agents or publicists at best. Thus, the field is rooted in less-than-effective and –ethical practice. Instead, then, we date the ensuing description of public relations theory and practice from the mid-1980s—the point at which Burson (quoted in Frank, 2000) credited public relations with gaining a seat at the management decision-making table.

Profile of Contemporary Practitioners

From the 1980s to 2000 (projected), the number of practitioners in the United States grew from 126,000 to 197,000 (U.S. Department of Labor, 1998).[15] This rapid growth is likely to continue, with a 55% increase predicted by 2006, according to the "Best Jobs" issue of *U.S. News & World Report* (1997). Cutlip, Center, and Broom (2000) figured[16] that most of these practitioners work in the corporate sector (40%); followed by agencies (27%); associations, foundations, and educational institutions (14%); health care (8%); government (6%); and nonprofit organizations (5%). More than 90% of all practitioners in the United States have college degrees. Nearly 25% of them have some graduate education, a full 25% have master's degrees, and 2% have doctorates (Cutlip et al., 2000).

The most recent and comprehensive salary survey ("Profile 2000," 2000), conducted jointly in 1999 by the International Association of Business Communicators (IABC) and Public Relations Society of America (PRSA), breaks out some figures by country (United States, Canada, and outside the United States and Canada). Average pay for U.S. communicators was $72,000. Consultants' salaries were significantly higher ($110,000) than those with corporate jobs ($63,000). Geographical location in the country also affected pay. Practitioners in the mid-Atlantic region earned the highest ($113,000 on average) and those in the mountain region earned the least ($56,000 on average).

In 1998, 65.7% of those the government (U.S. Department of Labor, 1998) considered to be in public relations were women. About 14% of U.S. practitioners are minorities— primarily of African and Hispanic origin (U.S. Department of Labor, 1998). Minorities comprise about 25% of the U.S. population. Further evidence of the lack of diverse

---

[13]Many in the U.S. public relations industry have heard versions of this story, either from Burson himself or secondhand. We thank Frank (2000) for writing it down.

[14]In addition to the dispute about where contemporary public relations got its start—The United States or Germany—there is the question of whether the field developed as the four models (J. E. Grunig & Hunt, 1984) suggest (from publicity or press agentry through stages of public information and two-way asymmetrical and, ultimately, to two-way symmetrical) or whether all four models have existed since public relations' inception in the late 1800s.

[15]Cutlip et al., (2000) pointed out that this figure undoubtedly is low, because the U.S. Department of Labor's categories of "public relations specialists" and "managers: marketing, advertising and public relations" excludes many others (e.g., graphic designers, lobbyists, and researchers) who work in the field.

[16]Based primarily on PRSA and IABC membership profiles and descriptions.

representation in public relations is the fact that people of Color make up only about 7% of the membership of U.S. professional societies (Cutlip et al., 2000).

What do these practitioners actually do? The Universal Accreditation Board of the PRSA recently surveyed 1,147 members and learned that, overwhelmingly, 89% of them spend their time in strategic planning and implementing. (Of course, we on the Excellence study team learned that strategic planning and management means different things to different people.) The PRSA study used the term strategic planning to encompass working with members of the dominant coalition "to discuss what kind of image the company wants to project and how to go about it" (Frank, 2000, p. 9). After strategic planning, survey respondents described what they spend "a great deal of" or "some time" doing (in decreasing order) as program planning (88%); project management (86%); media relations (78%); account–client management (67%); special events, conferences, and meetings (66%); internal relations (65%); community relations (60%); issues management (55%); relations with special audiences (54%); and crisis management (45%).

The most recent survey[17] of job satisfaction among U.S. practitioners (cited in "Job insecurity," 2002) established that IABC members,[18] at least, are happy with their work. Respondents cited access to technology, benefits, and flexible hours as the most satisfying aspects of their jobs. Mentoring, working from home, and lack of promotion were least satisfying.

Throughout the last 30 years, public relations practice in the United States has been marked by boom times and busts. For example, downsizing characterized the early 1990s. Then, with the emergence of start-up dot coms, practitioners found lucrative work helping attract investment capital. With the economic recession that followed, many practitioners were out of work once again.[19] The bottom line of the recent IABC study (cited in "Job insecurity," 2002) was that communicators see little job security in their field. However, with rampant charges of managerial malfeasance on the part of some of the country's major companies, industry leaders suggest that expert public relations counselors will once again be in great demand (Edelman, 2002). Already, 82% of the IABC members surveyed said they have unlimited or at least weekly access to senior management.

A Generation of Changes in the Field, Explored Through the Lenses of the Excellence Study and Contemporary Practitioners

By 1983, the premier trade publication in public relations had celebrated its first quarter century. In the 26th anniversary issue of *pr reporter*, Editor Pat Jackson listed the four changes he considered "elemental" since his newsletter's inception in 1958: (a) the field had moved steadily from publicity to policy; (b) practice expanded from applied communication theory to behavioral science; (c) the objective went from influencing opinion to motivating behavior; and (d) research, both qualitative and quantitative, formal and informal, became a major (what Jackson speculated might be "*the*" major) factor.

Articulating these shifts might reflect Jackson's (*pr reporter*, 1983) well-known bias toward behavioral change. However, taken together they suggest what he considered the

---

[17]IABC surveyed 1,349 members in the spring of 2002. For more information on the study, contact IABC at www.iabc.com.

[18]Most IABC members are from the United States, although this association includes a broad geographical base of membership.

[19]In spite of the weak economy, women executives in all fields—including public relations—may be inching up the corporate ladder, according to a recent survey by the women's advocacy group, Catalyst (cited in "Items of interest to professionals," 2002).

"scientifically oriented practitioner" (p. 1) whose work is accountable—linked to the organizational bottom line. At the same time, an increasing number of women were reaching the top in public relations; 20% of the people listed in *O'Dwyer's Directory of Public Relations Executives*, cited in that same issue of *pr reporter*, were women (up from 13.7% just 3 years earlier). This profile of the emerging professional in the 1980s is consistent with results of the Excellence project (Dozier et al., 1995; J. E. Grunig, 1992; L. A. Grunig et al., 2002), which began at that same time.

In 1985, we were part of a team[20] that received a major grant from the Research Foundation of the IABC to study excellence in public relations. The Excellence study, as it came to be called, represented the largest support for research in the field until the turn of this new century. One highly respected professional, former head of the Institute for Public Relations, referred to the Excellence study in a memo to institute board members as "the foundation piece of much of our thinking about corporate PR today" (W. W. White, personal communication, May 8, 2002).

Of course, this research has enjoyed its share of critics from all sides. Conservatives with a strictly business bent regard the Excellence theory, with its emphasis on balancing the concerns of the self-interest of the company with the collective interests of society, as idealistic. Liberals see its authors as pawns of the establishment, working to enhance the effectiveness of a function that empowers capitalists at the expense of unempowered publics. Criticisms notwithstanding, the Excellence study has resulted in an unprecedented development in the scope and substance of what we know (and thus can teach) about public relations from the previous generation of knowledge.

We use *generation* here not in the traditional sense of the interval of time between the birth of parents and that of their children (typically 30 years or three generations per century).[21] We do not use the term as in *spontaneous generation*, because that would deny the years of planning, collecting, and analyzing data and reporting of results and implications from the Excellence study that we undertook. Instead, we use *generation* as a stage of development—as in types of computers. We will conclude this section of the chapter by projecting the next generation of theory and practice in the United States—what we predict but has not been realized to date.

In 1985, the year in which the grant for the Excellence study was awarded, eminent public relations professional for Reynolds Metals, Joseph Awad, identified trends that have only increased in this generation of practice. He also made forecasts that have come about at least in part. For example, Awad predicted that public relations would enjoy a growth surge—largely in reaction to mounting external pressures. This has happened both in terms of numbers of public relations students and practitioners in this country and in the responsibility practitioners have taken on in strategic management.

Like Jackson before him, Awad (1985) also believed that public relations would become more accountable—not only to clients and employers but to society. He cited the trend toward the field's efforts being directed at concrete, measurable objectives rather than toward such vague concepts as public image or goodwill. As a result, he prophesied that public relations would become more effective—largely as a result of the increasing emphasis on emerging issues and the participation of the field in issues management. A concomitant shift would be toward greater reliance on research for both planning purposes and

---

[20]Additional members of the team of principal investigators were David M. Dozier, William P. Ehling, Fred Repper (deceased), and Jon White. We were assisted by a number of graduate students, other colleagues, and IABC members.

[21]Collins and Zoch (2002) used this 30-year span for their generational analysis of public relations educators. Their Delphi study encompassed the period from 1960 to 1990.

benchmarking evaluation of results. Today, we applaud the existence of the Measurement Commission, sponsored by the Institute for Public Relations. Members of the Measurement Commission represent the best in both practice and scholarship, working together to determine both the value of measuring effectiveness and the best methods for doing so. However, we decry the field's continuing emphasis on such poorly defined (and perhaps irrelevant) concepts as image and goodwill.

In what seems somewhat comical in this new century, Awad (1985) also speculated that new communication techniques such as computers would become as commonplace as the typewriter and the telephone. In a still-cogent argument, however, he urged practitioners to avoid the pitfall of mere gadgetry and rely on electronic communication to improve understanding between publics and organizations. Kornegay and L. A. Grunig (1998) described cyberbridging as a process wherein women, especially, could benefit from using the information superhighway to scan the environment and thus make the transition from communication technician to manager. Through this interactive process, of course, organizations would come to understand the legitimate concerns of their stakeholders as well. Indeed, J. E. Grunig and his students (described in Burch, 1997) used the Internet effectively to monitor public opinion of selected organizations—part of the scanning process. Results have established that there is much to be gained from the analysis of groups' responses to particular situations. Implications suggest that by using online discussion groups and establishing their own interactive web sites, organizations can carry out truly two-way and symmetrical public relations programs.

Awad (1985) expressed a further concern that resonates more than 20 years later: The profession's top managers, some of whom are or were pioneers in the field, are retiring or dying. This concern has led a number of U.S.-based associations to initiate professional development programs designed to enhance the capabilities of those who report directly to those senior managers. For example, the Institute for Public Relations and the San Francisco Academy offer several such seminars each year. Both the IABC and the PRSA sponsor extensive professional development sessions at every annual conference. Commercial operations, such as Ragan Communications, conduct similar programs. Distance-learning graduate programs, based in universities such as Syracuse, also help to educate midlevel practitioners for greater responsibility.

To fill the void in top-level leadership of the field, Awad (1985) also suggested that education in public relations would expand (although he predicted the emergence of coursework in the curricula of business management schools, a goal yet to be realized but discussed ad nauseum in professional settings; e.g., Pincus, 2002). He further expected that more practitioners would seek and gain accredited status, which remains as elusive as public relations courses in the business school.

All in all, this concern for senior executives in public relations remains. According to Ogilvy Public Relations Chief Executive Officer (CEO) Bob Seltzer, a shortage of qualified people is the biggest issue facing agencies (cited in Frank, 2000). As a result, the Council of Public Relations Firms[22] has developed methods for recruiting midlevel executives from other fields into ours.

---

[22]The council also studied public relations salaries for their competitiveness. It found that in 2000, top executives were earning an average $250,000 per year and general managers were earning $170,000. Top executives in firms received annual bonuses of 36%, which is in line with other industries. However, baseline salaries are significantly lower than those of, say, business consultants and attorneys. Furthermore, Seltzer (cited in Frank, 2000) predicted that higher salaries in U.S. public relations would help achieve diversity of all kinds in public relations practice.

Awad (1985) went on to predict the coordination of all activities involved in public relations, and he did not mean the integrated marketing communication touted so frequently in the 1990s. Instead, he emphasized the importance of coordinating public relations strategy because its numerous specialties, in his view, are less effective when fragmented. As with Awad's previous projections, the Excellence study also emphasized the need to place public relations functions under an umbrella that would allow for the reallocation of resources within communication as publics became more or less strategic.

Awad (1985) may have been most prescient when describing the trend toward increased responsibility and ethics. Changing value systems—coming to the United States as a result of greater diversity at home and among global competitors, suppliers, and customers—challenge public relations professionals here with supporting the large, complex organization as well as its pluralistic publics. As Awad put it, "Public relations can become the voice & defender of the human, the individual, the personal in a world dominated by quantitative or technocratic thinking" (p. 2).

Over the years of the Excellence study, the research team came to focus more and more on the importance of ethics and integrity; we acknowledged the importance of personal integrity on the part of practitioners and on an ethical norm that combines elements of the deontological and the teleological. That is, we emphasized the value of professional standards or rules—such as disclosure—that would help govern practice; at the same time, we also highlighted the relevance of utilitarian or consequence-based ethics. We reasoned that publics are strategic for the organization because they have consequences on it, or vice versa. As a result, one of us[23] (L. A. Grunig) established what we believe to be at least among the first of its kind: a graduate-level seminar in the philosophy and ethics of public relations. It explores ethical concerns reflected in the professional literature: advocacy, accountability, solicitation of new business, whistle blowing, spin, confidentiality, social and public responsibility, diversity issues, concealment versus disclosure, lying, accuracy, codes of ethics (including global ethics), ethics of research and education, professionalism, logical arguments, dealing with the press, front groups, and divided loyalties between the organization and its publics.

Amplifying the voice of publics in the process of organizational decision making demands more of a communicator than technician's skills. It requires someone at the management level who can function as a peer professional among other members of the organization's dominant coalition. Inclusion in that power elite, or at least a direct reporting relationship to the C-suite (with the other chief executives), is a major premise of the Excellence study. It has been a concern among U.S. practitioners at least since the mid-1980s.

In 1987 ("Public relations pros are counselors, not just tactical communicators"), *pr reporter* highlighted the need for counselors rather than technicians. It pointed out that pioneers such as Edward L. Bernays, Arthur Page, Ivy Lee, and Pendleton Dudley considered themselves policy consultants. However, after World War II and the explosion of the communication industry, more and more of the jobs for practitioners in this country were tactical.

So, where do we stand in 2002? To begin to answer, we quote a handful of pundits in the field. We also cite students, who represent the future of public relations.

---

[23]The other of us, J. E. Grunig, revising the textbook *Managing Public Relations* (J. E. Grunig & Hunt, 1984), is substituting a lengthy chapter on ethics for the scant page or so in the original edition. Most current textbooks in the field include substantial discussion of ethics (Hutchison, 2002).

One good measure comes from the final editorial written by the outgoing editor of *PR Week*, another major trade journal in public relations. Bloom (2002) called this "PR's golden era" (p. 6). He explained that public relations has never been so vital than in this time of helping organizations and society at large cope with massing threats. He added, "Nor has PR ever been so valuable to corporate marketers who seek more cost-sensitive ways of reaching consumers against the backdrop of a fragmented media and increasingly cynical public" (p. 6). Bloom also highlighted problems that continue to plague the field: (a) confusion between public relations and marketing, (b) lack of determination (and the ability) to measure public relations outcomes as well as outputs, (c) mere lip service paid to the importance of a diverse workforce in public relations, and (d) too few professionals who understand how to establish good relationships with journalists.

Another editor of the trade press has a different, less optimistic take on the state of affairs of U.S. public relations. On his *O'Dwyer's PR Daily* website, O'Dwyer (2002) offered advice to students that reflects not a golden age but a time when the term *public relations* has been so discredited in the English language that he urged students to call themselves anything but public relations people or communicators. He cited a 1999 study financed by the PRSA and the Rockefeller Foundation[24] that, he claimed, the PRSA was too embarrassed about to publicize. Why? The research showed "PR specialist" ranking 43rd out of 45 public figures[25] as "believable sources of information."

One student (Pulgar, 2002) who responded to O'Dwyer's (2002) piece questioned the desirability of changing the name of the field—surely a tired argument by now. As Pulgar said, "It's a lot easier to discard an idea rather than rebuild it." His suggestions echo those of many professionals and many textbooks in the field: "Let's work to correct all the mistakes the field's forefathers have made. The reason PR practitioners are expendable is because we are not organized. Put together a board, make an association and license our members so not just anyone can do what we do. Only then will people take us seriously."

Since the 1980s, however, public perception of this field may have changed for the better—at least from students' perspectives. In the mid-1980s, one of us routinely began to ask her undergraduate students in the introductory public relations class what public relations meant. With no formal knowledge of the subject, they said "devious," "lying," "propaganda," "superficial," "snow job," and "covering up." Their most benign labels included "publicity," "image," and "packaging." By 1988, students' comments shifted: They still said "propaganda" and "image" but also added "liaison," "mediator," "representation," "communication," "interaction," and "networking." In 1996, their list included "consulting," "management," "media," "promoting," "communications," "information," "link," "liaison," "writing," and "working with people." In our view, these labels suggest a clear trajectory from the unethical to a more accurate representation of what public relations people most probably do today.

Throughout the history of public relations, practitioners and scholars have attempted to identify and name a single concept that defines the value of public relations. Early in public relations' history, publicity by itself sufficed as the answer—"there is no such thing as bad publicity." When public relations people recognized that publicity had to have some effect on a public before it had value, they adopted one faddish term after another. First, it was "image," then "identity" and "image" together. Now the popular terms are "reputation" and "brand."

---

[24] A political scientist at Columbia University conducted the project.
[25] Only famous entertainers and television or radio talk show hosts ranked lower than public relations people.

With the exception of "identity," most of these terms describe essentially the same phenomenon: what publics think of an organization. "Identity" describes what an organization thinks of itself. Subtle differences can be found in the professional and academic literature among reputation, image, brand, and impressions; but all basically describe cognitions that publics hold about organizations. Jeffries-Fox Associates (2000) conducted a content analysis of 1,149 articles in 94 trade and academic publications to compare the use of the terms "reputation," "brand equity," and "good will" and found that "reputation" and "brand equity" were the most frequently used terms. Jeffries-Fox Associates concluded that "the same component ideas are associated with brand equity and corporate reputation" and that the terms are "used interchangeably" (p. 6). At the same time, they concluded that public relations managers are more likely to use the term "reputation" and marketing managers to use "brand equity." As a result, they recommended adopting the term "reputation" to distinguish public relations from marketing.

In spite of the fact that the term "reputation" means essentially the same thing as older, discredited concepts, the public relations profession in the United States is vigorously attempting to associate reputation management with public relations. The "next challenge," according to an editorial in *PR Week* ("Reputation Name Must Be Pushed," 2000), "is to mobilize support for the phrase 'corporate reputation'" first among "PR agencies and in-house practitioners" so that "there is a better chance that the second audience—clients and journalists—will understand and use the phrase themselves" (p. 10). These public relations professionals promoting the concept of reputation have been joined by business scholars (e.g., Fombrun, 1996) eager to enter the intriguing new research area of reputation, marketing experts promoting the concept of branding, and public opinion research firms eager to capitalize on the popularity of reputational evaluative surveys such as those that produce the annual *Fortune* magazine index of corporate reputations.

J. E. Grunig and Hung (2002) reviewed a substantial portion of the literature on reputation and its reputed role in explaining the value of public relations. They provided evidence that the attempts to show an association between expenditures on public relations and reputation and between reputation and financial performance are methodologically and statistically unsound. They argued that a more logical connection could be shown among public relations activities, relationships, and value to an organization.

The Excellence study (L. A. Grunig et al., 2002) showed that public relations makes an organization more effective when it identifies an organization's most strategic publics as part of strategic management processes and conducts communication programs to develop and maintain effective long-term relationships between organizations and those publics. As a result, public relations professionals can determine the value of public relations by measuring the quality of relationships with strategic publics more accurately than by measuring reputation. In addition, they can evaluate communication programs by measuring the effects of these programs and correlating them with relationship indicators.

J. E. Grunig and Hung's (2002) review of the literature and survey research showed the critical effect of management behaviors on both reputation and the type and quality of relationships. They defined reputation as cognitive representations—what collectivities of people think about organizations. They found that the most important cognitive representations consisted of the recall of either good or bad behaviors of organizations. The recall of behaviors, in turn, had the most significant effect of any type of cognitive representation on the way research participants viewed the type and quality of relationships with an organization.

J. E. Grunig and Hung's (2002) research showed that public relations professionals who are interested in protecting or enhancing the reputations and the relationships of the organizations they serve should do so by participating in the strategic management processes of the organization so that they can have a potential influence on the organizational behaviors chosen by management. The traditional public relations approach of putting out strategic messages after decisions are made would have little effect on either reputation or relationships.

By 2002, the field—as indicated by scholarly research and professional development sessions at conferences of such groups as the PRSA—is moving toward the management of relationships. Skilled technicians will always be in demand, but people with knowledge of strategic management and two-way symmetrical communication must work to identify strategic publics and then establish and maintain good relationships with them (L. A. Grunig et al., 2002). Holtzhausen (2002) called the focus on public relations as a management function "the biggest contribution to establish public relations as a serious field of study" (p. 254).[26]

However, because of the well-documented glass ceiling for professional women and people of Color in the United States (Cline et al., 1986; L. A. Grunig et al., 2000; Toth & Cline, 1989), nontraditional employees in public relations have an especially difficult time transcending the technician's role and ascending to management. This is a problem not only for those practitioners but also for the companies that discriminate against them. Recall that Weick's (1979) principle of requisite variety established that organizations need as much diversity inside as exists in their environment. Excellent public relations, then, requires women and men in all roles as well as practitioners of diverse racioethnic backgrounds (L. A. Grunig et al., 2002). We believe that higher education will help overcome the field's perception of low status and the reality of lingering discrimination (L. A. Grunig, 1992).

Education

The first course in public relations in the United States was taught by Bernays at Cornell University in 1923. He began what has become the noble tradition of using his own textbook (in this case, *Crystallizing Public Opinion*) in the class. Since then, more than 300 extensive courses of study have developed in U.S. universities. The most recent ranking of these programs by *U.S. News & World Report* ("America's best graduate schools," 1996) listed the University of Maryland first, followed by Syracuse University and the University of Florida. In addition, professional bodies have designed continuing education programs and some campuses now offer distance learning. One contentious issue continues to be where the public relations program should be situated: journalism? communication? English? business?

There is no question, however, that the body of knowledge has been growing (even though it remains insufficient for any true profession). One of us recalled that when he began teaching at the University of Maryland in 1969, "It took me about six weeks to tell the students everything I knew and everything that was in the literature" (quoted in Burch, 1997). Five years ago, *Books in Print* listed more than 600 titles on public relations— most of them published in the United States. This literature establishes a firm—if not rock-solid—basis on which to teach.

The most commonly assigned textbooks for courses in public relations principles (Hutchison, 2002) are Baskin, Aronoff, and Lattimore's (1997) *Public Relations: The*

---

[26]To the postmodern scholar Holtzhausen (2002), this is not a plus. She condemned both the management and excellence foci as metanarratives that have "drowned out" (p. 256) other discourses she considered equally valid.

Profession and the Practice (4th ed.); Cutlip et al.'s (2000) *Effective Public Relations* (8th ed.); Newsom, Turk, and Kruckeberg's (2000) *This Is PR: The Realities of Public Relations* (7th ed.); Wilcox, Ault, Agee, and Cameron's (2000) *Public Relations: Strategies and Tactics* (6th ed.); and Seitel's (2001) *The Practice of Public Relations* (8th ed.). Similarly, U.S. educators have considerable choice when assigning texts for classes in public relations writing, techniques, campaigns, and cases.

Since 1956, the PRSA (among other organizations) has been studying public relations education in this country. In 1981, close to the starting point of our analysis in this chapter, it established its Commission on Education, which subsequently published a model curriculum consisting of a minimum of five courses in public relations (Ehling & Plank, 1987).

The most recent Commission on Education report (PRSA, 1999) shows a surprising congruity between what practitioners and what scholars believe is critical to the public relations curriculum at this point. It includes recommendations for both undergraduate and graduate education. Curricular models are based on these assumptions: grounded in the liberal arts, theory based, writing across the curriculum, and emphasis on courses rather than departments where those courses are housed. The report recommended that coursework in the public relations major should comprise 25% to 40% of an undergraduate student's total program. Of those courses, at least half should be identified clearly as public relations courses in these topics: principles, case studies, research, writing and production techniques, planning and management, campaigns, and supervised internship. For the 30- to 36-hr master's degree, the Commission on Education report emphasized public relations management and an advanced understanding of the body of knowledge, culminating in a thesis and exam or capstone project (or both). Since 1989, the PRSA has offered a certification program for institutions of higher education that offer public relations courses and degree programs that meet these standards.

A recent study (Collins & Zoch, 2002) identified the U.S. academics who have made the greatest contributions to the theoretical understanding of public relations from 1960 to 1990 in this country. They are (in alphabetical order) Glen Broom, Scott Cutlip, David Dozier, James E. Grunig, Larissa A. Grunig, Robert Heath, Dean Kruckeberg, and Elizabeth Toth. The top four are, first, J. E. Grunig, followed by Cutlip, and—tied for third place—Broom and Heath. Scholar–participants in the Delphi research credited these men with the following: J. E. Grunig, conceptualizing the first deep theory of public relations (situational theory), contributing the four models of public relations, and bringing a scientific approach to the study of public relations; Cutlip, laying the groundwork for public relations theory, studying the history of the field, and bringing together theory and practice in this textbook; Broom, conceptualizing the four roles of public relations and contributing to the Cutlip and Center books; and Heath, adding to our understanding of issues management and risk communication and applying rhetorical principles to public relations.

These educators both publish in and are informed by the two major scholarly journals in public relations published in the United States: the *Journal of Public Relations Research (JPRR)*[27] and the *Public Relations Review*. Several trade publications exist as well: the PRSA's *The Public Relations Strategist* and *Tactics*, the IABC's *Communication World*, *PR News*, *Ragan Report*, *pr reporter*, *PR Week*, and *O'Dwyer's PR Services Report* among them. Such publications help lay the groundwork for establishing the field as a true profession, one with a published body of knowledge.

---

[27]*Public Relations Research and Education*, begun in 1984 by J. E. Grunig, provided the impetus for the subsequent *Public Relations Research Annual* (1989–1991, edited by J. E. and L. A. Grunig), which begat the *JPRR*.

Professionalism

Several professional groups exist for practitioners in the United States. The PRSA—established in 1948 and headquartered in New York—is the largest, with almost 20,000 members. The IABC has more than 13,000 members; it was founded in 1970 and is headquartered in San Francisco. The PRSA sponsors a student membership organization, the Public Relations Student Society of America. In addition to these major bodies, there are numerous specialized, regional, and local associations. They include the Black Public Relations Society, the Arthur Page Society, Women Executives in Public Relations (WEPR), the National School Public Relations Association, the Council for the Advancement and Support of Education, the Florida Public Relations Association, the Public Relations Seminar, and the Wise Men—to name just a few.

One recent development worthy of attention is the effort of 14 such groups to work together on "PR for PR," as David Drobis (chairman of Ketchum Public Relations) put it in his 2002 Distinguished Lecture to the Institute for Public Relations. Drobis, long-term supporter of research and education in the field, described an effort to provide industry positioning on what he and others in such groups as the Page Society, the PRSA, the IABC, the National Investor Relations Institute, the Public Affairs Council, and WEPR consider three critical issues: disclosure, transparency, and ethics.

All of these professional groups emphasize the importance of ethics. A code of ethics is a norm for any such society. Enforcement of a code of professional standards in public relations, however, has been a major problem. The PRSA revised its code in 2000, removing any enforcement mechanism and reducing its 12 standards to 6 provisions. Despite this ongoing commitment to educate about and to encourage ethical behavior, practitioners in the United States have had to acknowledge the problem of their many colleagues who do not belong to any professional society and, thus, are not governed by any stated norms.

In the absence of state licensing, accreditation of public relations practitioners is a central issue to many of these professional societies. The PRSA's program, Accredited Public Relations (APR), may be the best known. The IABC has its Accredited Business Communicator program. However, the goal of developing a single accreditation program (referred to as universal accreditation or UA) has proven elusive for its proponents within the United States, who contend that a single, strongly supported program would move the practice toward professionalism.

Also, at least the PRSA's accreditation efforts have become increasingly controversial. APR status is required for representation in the National (voting) Assembly, as it is for holding any office at the national level. As a result, the 80% of the PRSA's nonaccredited members have expressed a sense of disenfranchisement recently. However, at the most recent assembly meeting (2002), a proposal to decouple accreditation from the assembly was defeated. In addition, the APR program is frequently criticized for its high cost and low passing rate.

Since the heyday of Bernays, often considered the father of U.S. public relations, some practitioners have called for the licensing of communicators.[28] This restriction into

---

[28]One of the most recent proponents of restricting practice responded to the O'Dwyer (2002) web site piece on advice for students. Rather than licensing, however, JM (2002) recommended requiring new practitioners to take the PRSA's APR exam. Without the added credibility of accreditation, he argued, the field could look forward to being regulated as real estate, law, and accounting are now in the United States.

the field, they believe, would help establish public relations as a profession. Professional status, in turn, would enhance its credibility. However, professionalism has been called the Achilles heel for practitioners in this country (Collins & Zoch, 2002). U.S. practitioners and scholars agree for the most part that public relations is not yet a profession. Collins and Zoch (2002) determined that it was a "quasi-profession" (p. 1), after providing a thorough review of the literature in professionalism and applying criteria such as licensing, status, social responsibility, serving the public interest, codes of ethics and standards, specialized knowledge and skill, a body of knowledge, professional values, and autonomy to public relations practice.

Collins and Zoch's (2002) determination that U.S. public relations fails to qualify as a profession is based largely on the fact that licensing[29] is not required. In addition, they cited Cutlip et al.'s (2000) assertion that research in the field contributes little to building and testing theory and, as a result, that the body of knowledge is inadequate for professional status. The country's largest professional body, the PRSA, began to codify that BOK in 1986—close to the time we begin this look at U.S. practice. The project continues to this time. In addition, professional groups such as the PRSA, the IABC, and the Institute for Public Relations have established foundations to support scholarly and applied research.

The PRSA, beginning at its 2000 conference in Chicago, took the lead in establishing what it called the Global Alliance. This coalition of public relations associations from throughout the world, now headed by Italian professional Toni Muzi Falconi, has begun to meet to tackle global issues that include ethics, education, and accreditation. In the United States, most large firms are concerned about their international practice—especially integrating their operations. Daniel J. Edelman (2002), founder and chairman of Edelman Public Relations Worldwide, explained the difficulty of operating dozens of geographically dispersed companies as a single-service unit. He described twin goals of establishing international standards for practice and assuring clients of equivalent quality of work in every office of the firm. He also cited the need to import programs to the United States from other parts of the world (rather than originating programs solely from this country) and to generate programs for domestic companies within their own countries.

As in many countries, practitioners in the United States grapple with nomenclature—what to call ourselves. Over the last generation, substitute terms for public relations have developed; they include "corporate communication," "corporate relations," "communications," "public affairs," and "corporate affairs" (O'Dwyer, 1981). However, like many of our professional and academic colleagues, we prefer "public relations" rather than some euphemism. It reflects our purpose in building relationships with the publics on which organizations have consequences, or vice versa.

FUTURE CHALLENGES

Future challenges for United States practitioners include what may seem obvious: exploiting the potential of constantly changing technology, especially communication technology; growing the theoretical body of knowledge, so the field may move from its careerist

---

[29]These constitutional issues seem to preclude licensing, or permission granted by the state to practice public relations: freedom of expression and people's right to pursue occupations without undo interference from the state.

status; hiring bright, well-educated practitioners (and educators) who embrace professional norms and can take the place of the aging leadership of this field;[30] encouraging aspiration for the strategic managerial role, without selling the field's skill base short; globalizing practice in light of growing economies and privatization around the world; working to eliminate any remaining discrimination against women or people of Color, whether they be practitioners of public relations, employees, customers, or suppliers; raising the ethical bar; increasing professionalism among all practitioners, regardless of whether they join professional societies; enhancing research skills and, thus, helping make public relations more accountable to the organizational bottom line; and legitimizing the concerns of all publics of the organization—internal and external—by dealing with them with balance and sensitivity. Then, the work of U.S. practitioners will have impact beyond their own bottom line; they may affect other individuals, publics, and other organizations in a positive way.

Are we there yet in the United States? By no means. Press agentry remains the most common approach to public relations, despite the wealth of educational programs available, the research base, and the drive toward professionalism. Are we on the way? Yes, but as Kanter (1998) said, "Everything looks like a failure in the middle" (p. 94). We are at some midpoint in the United States—well beyond our rudimentary beginnings yet well short of our goal of truly global, truly professional, truly strategic, truly empowered, truly responsible, truly ethical, and truly effective public relations practice.

Case Study of Public Relations Excellence in a United States Chemical Corporation

In the Excellence study, Larissa A. Grunig, James E. Grunig, David Dozier, and graduate students at the University of Maryland and San Diego State University conducted qualitative interviews of heads of public relations, members of the dominant coalition, and midlevel public relations personnel at 25 organizations that had scored either at the top or bottom of an index of public relations excellence that was calculated from 20 variables. These case studies focused on why the dominant coalition valued public relations; how the public relations function was structured and its role in strategic management; and how the function became, or failed to become, excellent.

One of these case studies, of a U.S. chemical corporation, provides an excellent example of a near-excellent public relations function and how it became excellent. For ethical reasons, the Excellence researchers guaranteed confidentiality to all organizations studied; so we refer to this organization only as Chemical Corporation. For this case study, interviews were conducted in person with the director of corporate communications; the vice-president for strategic planning, investor relations, and public affairs (a member of the dominant coalition); and a midlevel communication specialist assigned to internal communication.

Chemical Corporation had a score on the Excellence factor higher than three fourths of the organizations included in the quantitative portion of the Excellence study. It reached this level of excellence in large part because of the senior communicator's knowledge of two-way communication and of public relations as a strategic management function. The corporation's public relations function did not reach the highest level of excellence, however, because senior management did not perceive public relations to be part of strategic management. After the quantitative questionnaires were completed, the communication

---

[30]One new wrinkle is the defection of high-level public relations counselors to management consulting firms.

department began to report to a new vice-president of strategic planning, investor relations, and public affairs. His background was in strategic planning. The vice-president recognized and made use of the knowledge of two senior communicators—one in corporate communication and one in marketing communication—and the public relations function became part of strategic management.

As a result, this case study provides a profile of an organization that meets most of the standards of excellence in communication management identified by the Excellence study research team. Public relations was involved in strategic planning, it gradually changed the perception among senior managers of the importance of communication, it worked effectively with counterparts in other departments such as human resources, it practiced a symmetrical model of public relations (including elements of both advocacy and negotiation), it tried to create opportunities for women to move into communication management, and it incorporated diversity into the public relations function.

The Value of Public Relations to the Corporation. One of the two major purposes of the Excellence study was to explain the value of public relations and to estimate that value in monetary terms. The member of the dominant coalition who completed the quantitative questionnaire had assigned a cost–benefit ratio of 200% to public relations and 300% to the communication manager. During the qualitative interviews, however, the vice-president said he "could not begin to 'dollarize' the function. In some respects it's an infinite value. In some respects, it's like throwing money in a hole."

Nevertheless, the vice-president described relationships with two publics—employees and the financial community—for which he said communication had an important role. For employees, he said:

> I could not cite an explicit example for you, but to the extent that we're getting all of our employees, through employee communication, oriented around our strategy, which is, number one, to root out work that we do that wastes money, by definition communication is saving us money. It's saving us money by better enabling the people who should be saving us money to go out there and get the job done. Ultimately, that loops around and helps us make money.

For financial relations, he said:

> All I can tell you is that the director of investor relations walked in the door 10 minutes before you did and said: "You might be interested to know our stock just hit an all-time high today." Now, do I believe we accomplished that without the benefit of communication? No, of course not, communication in every respect . . . in causing the underlying performance, in getting out there and making sure that the investment community knew what we were doing, but for those two things our stock would not be at an all-time high today. Now, do I believe that today somehow we got some leverage from the few million dollars we spend on communication each year? Damn right, I do!

Structure of the Communication Function. In one sense, Chemical Corporation did not meet the criterion of excellence in public relations by having its communication function integrated into a single department. In addition, the director of corporate communications, according to both questionnaires, was not a part of the dominant coalition. Nevertheless, Chemical Corporation achieved integration through its vice-president of strategic planning, investor relations, and public affairs, who was a member of the dominant coalition. The vice-president was responsible for strategic management; the directors of corporate communication, marketing communication, and investor relations reported to him. In addition, a director of government relations and state relations reported to the general counsel and secretary of the company.

At the time the quantitative questionnaires were completed, Chemical Corporation did not have a director of marketing communication. According to both the vice-president and director of communication, marketing communication activities then were dispersed throughout the business units of the corporation. These activities now have been brought together in a single function that reports to the vice-president but not to corporate communication. The director said that the company does not practice integrated marketing communication. In fact, he said the company "does not have a staff function devoted to marketing." Instead, each business unit handled marketing. In the chemical industry, according to the director, marketing typically is not a part of the dominant coalition. Instead, the manufacturing function generally has more power. In consumer product companies such "as an IBM," in contrast, he said "marketing more often is in the dominant coalition. It has to do with the culture of the industry and the specific company."

The corporate communications department, therefore, had responsibility for employee communication, relations with "major media," and "corporate advertising if there is a need for it," according to the director. Corporate communications also communicated with shareholder groups by producing annual reports and earnings announcements and by working with the financial media. The investor relations department, in contrast, "deals directly with analysts and institutional shareholders," the director said.

The director of corporate communications said that it would be better to have all communication functions under one department but that integration in Chemical Corporation was achieved through the vice-president. The communication function was structured as it was, he added, for "political and pragmatic reasons." Nevertheless, he said, there was informal collaboration among the communication functions. The critical factor, the director said, is "not who you report to but rather whether you have access. As a communicator, I have direct access to any of the officers at will. Yesterday, for example, we had a meeting with analysts; and I was there with all of the officers of the company."

The communication function, therefore, achieved integration informally. Importantly, it did so through the strategic management function of the corporation.

Public Relations and Strategic Management. The quantitative questionnaires had shown that the director of corporate communications believed he was heavily involved in strategic management of the company but that the member of the dominant coalition did not. In the qualitative interviews, both the vice-president and the director of communication were asked for an explanation. According to the director: "It may be a semantic thing. From a business perspective, I'm not involved in day-to-day business planning. [The vice-president] is more involved in that. If there are strategic issues that require planning, however, I'm involved." The director provided an example of disclosing and discussing "worst-case scenarios" in communities where chemical plants were located. He said he was involved in planning stages for this issue along with people from health, safety, and the environment; legal; and the businesses. He said, "We're not just waiting for it to hit the fan."

The vice-president also reported that the discrepancy had narrowed since he replaced his predecessor. The current vice-president previously had been vice-president for strategic planning and still is responsible for strategic management. He said: "[The communication director] has been given the opportunity to be more involved. What we discuss over lunch gets him involved in strategic planning . . . more than my predecessor could."

The vice-president emphasized the importance of viewing communication as a strategic function: "Some people scratch their heads and say, 'Why in the world does a strategic planning guy have anything to do with public affairs?'" He answered:

> Most people perceive strategic planning over here at this end of the corporation and if you
> get through R&D [research and development], marketing, and manufacturing and all these
> things somewhere at the other end you have someone worrying about public affairs and public
> relations. My answer is that they have a linear view of a corporation. If you view a corporation
> as being a work process and those work processes are cyclical, then you take that linear view
> of the corporation and bend it around into a circle, then it's funny what comes together in the
> circle—strategic planning and public affairs.
>
> In fact, everything you do strategically in a company has to do with relations with the
> outside world. It has to do with your relationship to the customer, your competitors, your
> suppliers. And, of course, public affairs isn't just a transmitting function; it's a two-way
> function. So, in fact, it's perfectly logical for the public relations function to be directly tied
> to the strategic function. What do people most want to know about a corporation? They want
> to know your strategy. So the things really fit together.

The director of corporate communications used a copyrighted flow chart to explain
how his department "moved from being order takers to strategic planners." Previously,
other departments would give the department a "request to communicate," such as human
resources asking for a videotape or the health, safety, and environment department asking
for an environmental report. After the change in orientation, that request was not honored
until the head of public affairs or his designee did an "alignment check." The alignment
check asked whether the request to communicate fit the company's strategic goals: "Is
the message consistent with key messages? Has the audience been identified? Has desired
behavior been defined? What is the 'requestor's' expected timing? What are resources
expectations? What is the benefit of the message to the intended audience?"

The employee communication specialist explained that the communication department
benefited from reporting to a strategic planner because he imposed a strategic view on
communication. She said, "We now have a methodical, planned way to do work that is tied
into the business side of things." In addition, she said, senior management began to "pay
more attention to communication because [the vice-president] has opened their eyes."
Communication staffers at her middle-management level became involved in strategic
planning through teams formed by the vice-president—including teams devoted to the
media, employee communication, and financial communication.

How Did the Communication Department Become Excellent? The senior communicator described the evolution of the department as "a confluence of forces in which I
know I played a role . . . something I take a lot of personal pride in." The senior communicator's knowledge of strategic management appears to have been the necessary condition
that made it possible for three other factors to have an effect: (a) crises that sensitized
senior management to the importance of public relations, (b) a mediating vice-president
who understood public relations and had valuable connections in senior management, and
(c) business and communication knowledge of the senior communicator.

"Gradually," the vice-president said, "the function evolved to what we have today.
It [excellence in public relations] started with the fact we had some good people. If I
hadn't had a couple of talented communication managers, I couldn't have done anything."
Then, he mentioned the second and third factors: "Without a couple of senior managers,
our chairman and COO [chief operating officer], who wanted to treat communication
strategically, I couldn't have done it. I was a nice linkage between those two things
[competent communicators and strategic management]."

Crises and company performance then played a role, according to the vice-president: "The job of the communication function is to get you the reputation you deserve. Until not too long ago, we probably were getting the reputation we deserved, and everyone wanted to blame the communication function for it. One of things that's helped is that we've had a good message to deliver; the company has been performing better." Since the 1984 tragedy in Bhopal, India, he added, the chemical industry has "been more willing to be open to the public."

After the quantitative questionnaires for the Excellence study had been completed, the communication department held an all-day seminar for senior managers on communication during which a member of the IABC Excellence study research team made a presentation that especially emphasized the importance of public relations in strategic management. Both the communication manager and the vice-president mentioned this presentation as an important factor that helped to change the thinking of senior management about public relations.

The vice-president from strategic planning was a valuable link between the communication function and senior management. His background played a part. Although trained as a chemist, he said he appreciated the importance of communication because a parent and relatives had worked in journalism.

In addition to these factors, the senior communicator pointed out the importance of his own knowledge of the chemical business in addition to his knowledge of communication:

> If the communicator doesn't understand the business of the organization, he or she is never really going to get ahead. That took me a long time to understand. I'm not a chemist by training. I don't have an interest in that, but I have an interest in the chemical industry that I did not have five or 10 years ago. That's important whether you're in the auto industry or the computer industry or in government and whatever industry or business people are in. I think that's a tremendous weakness of professional communicators.

The knowledge base of the communication director and of the communication department about communication itself also explains how the public relations function became excellent at Chemical Corporation and how the director gained access to the dominant coalition. Interviews with both the communication director and employee communication specialist showed that they did not formally study public relations but that both gained their knowledge from the IABC, research journals and professional publications, and experience. The communication director did not have a degree in public relations and he had not taken courses in the subject. The director said he gained his knowledge from professional organizations, especially the IABC. He also said he "learned from the world around him." In addition, the director said he reads communication journals regularly, including *Communication Research* and the *Journal of Communication*.

The Need for International Communication. As is typical in many U.S. corporations, this otherwise excellent public relations function did not conduct its international public relations well. Both the director of communication and the communication specialist identified communication at Chemical Corporation's international sites as a problem to which that the department needed to devote more attention. "For all practical purposes, we have no professional communication opportunities outside headquarters," the director said. He explained that the company had some human resources activities—internal communication—at major sites: "One of the problems we have is trying to ensure that site activities are aligned with what we're doing here." In addition, he said the company did not use public relations firms abroad unless there is a crisis. In that case, he added, it used a network of firms.

The communication specialist reiterated that some international subsidiaries have communication specialists, but "nothing major." She said: "Just last week I met with all the international human resources managers. Part of the vision the employee relations strategic work team has is to have communication strategies and plans in place within five years for all of the major locations, including international locations. In the past, we have not focused on the international communication function."

REFERENCES

Adler, N. J. (2002). *International dimensions of organizational behavior* (4th ed.). Cincinnati, OH: South-Western.

Altschull, J. H. (1984). *Agents of power: The role of the news media in human affairs*. New York: Longman.

America's best graduate schools: 1996 annual guide. (1996, March 18). *U.S. News & World Report*.

Awad, J. (1985). *The power of public relations*. Westport, CT: Praeger.

Baskin, O., Aronoff, C., & Lattimore, D. (1997). *Public relations: The profession and the practice* (4th ed.). Dubuque, IA: Brown.

Bernays, E. L. (1923). *Crystallizing public opinion*. New York: Boni & Liveright.

Best jobs. (1997, October 27). *U.S. News & World Report*, 20–28.

Bloom, J. (2002, September 23). One year, many chats, a few lasting thoughts. *PR Week*, 6.

Books in print. (1996). New Providence, NJ: R. R. Bowker.

Broom, G. M. (1982). A comparison of sex roles in public relations. *Public Relations Review, 8*(3), 17–22.

Burch, D. (1997, Summer). A marriage of ideas: Jim and Lauri Grunig and the give-and-take of effective public relations. *College Park, 8*(3), 20–25.

Cline, C. G., Masel-Walters, L., Toth, E. L., Turk, J. V., Smith, H. T., & Johnson, N. (1986). *The velvet ghetto: The impact of the increasing percentage of women in public relations and business communication*. San Francisco: IABC Foundation.

Collins, E. L., & Zoch, L. M. (2002, August). *PR educators—"The second generation": Measuring and achieving consensus*. Paper presented at the meeting of the Public Relations Division, Association for Education in Journalism and Mass Communication, Miami.

Coup de Frejac, J. (1991). The importance of north–south relations in a multicultural world. *International Public Relations Review, 14*(4), 23–25.

Crespo, A. (2002). *Protest in the land of plenty*. Miami: Center Lane Press.

Cutlip, S. M. (1995). *Public relations history: From the 17th to the 20th century*. Hillsdale, NJ: Lawrence Erlbaum Associates.

Cutlip, S. M., Center, A. H., & Broom, G. M. (2000). *Effective public relations* (8th ed.). Upper Saddle River, NJ: Prentice-Hall.

Dozier, D. M., & Broom, G. M. (1995). Evolution of the manager role in public relations practice. *Journal of Public Relations Research, 7*, 3–26.

Dozier, D. M., with Grunig, L. A., & Grunig, J. E. (1995). *Manager's guide to excellence in public relations and communication management*. Mahwah, NJ: Lawrence Erlbaum Associates.

Drobis, D. (2002, November 7). Distinguished lecture to the Institute for Public Relations. New York.

Edelman, D. J. (2002, Fall). A challenging time, a bright future. *The Public Relations Strategist, 8*(4), 46–48.

Ehling, W. P., & Plank, B. (Eds.). (1987). *The design for undergraduate public relations education: The report of the 1987 Commission on Undergraduate Public Relations Education*. New York: Public Relations Society of America.

Farber, D. A. (2002). *The first amendment* (2nd ed.). New York: Thomson.

Fombrun, C. J. (1996). *Reputation: Realizing value from the corporate image*. Boston: Harvard Business School.

Frank, J. (2000, November 6). The industry booms as PR jobs shift focus. *PR Week*, 9.

Gianaris, N. V. (1996). *Modern capitalism: Privatization, employee ownership, and industrial democracy.* Westport, CT: Praeger.

Greenberg, E. S. (1985). *Capitalism and the American political ideal.* Armonk, NY: M. E. Sharpe.

Grunig, J. E. (1984). Organizations, environments, and models of public relations. *Public Relations Research and Education, 1,* 6–29.

Grunig, J. E. (Ed.). (1992). *Excellence in public relations and communication management.* Hillsdale, NJ: Lawrence Erlbaum Associates.

Grunig, J. E., & Grunig, L. A. (2001, May 21). Auditing a pr function through theoretical benchmarking: Jim & Lauri Grunig's research. *pr reporter* (Suppl.), *12,* 1–4.

Grunig, J. E., & Hung, C. J. (2002, March). *The effect of relationships on reputation and reputation on relationships: A cognitive, behavioral study.* Paper presented at the meeting of the Public Relations Society of America's Educator's Academy 5th Annual International, Interdisciplinary Public Relations Research Conference, Miami.

Grunig, J. E., & Hunt, T. (1984). *Managing public relations.* New York: Holt, Rinehart & Winston.

Grunig, L. A. (1992). Toward the philosophy of public relations. In E. L. Toth & R. L. Heath (Eds.), *Rhetorical and critical approaches to public relations* (pp. 65–91). Hillsdale, NJ: Lawrence Erlbaum Associates.

Grunig, L. A., Grunig, J. E., & Dozier, D. M. (2002). *Excellent public relations and effective organizations: A study of communication management in three countries.* Mahwah, NJ: Lawrence Erlbaum Associates.

Grunig, L. A., Toth, E. L., & Hon, L. C. (2000). *Women in public relations: How gender influences practice.* New York: Guilford.

Hachten, W. A. (1992). *The world news prism: Changing media of international communication* (3rd ed.). Ames: Iowa State University Press.

Hofstede, G. (1984). *Culture's consequences: International differences in work-related values* (abridged ed.). Newbury Park, CA: Sage.

Hofstede, G. (2001). *Culture's consequences: Comparing values, behaviors, institutions, and organizations across nations* (2nd ed.). Thousand Oaks, CA: Sage.

Hollihan, T. A. (2001). *Uncivil wars: Political campaigns in a media age.* New York: Bedord/St. Martin's.

Holtzhausen, D. R. (2002). Towards a postmodern research agenda for public relations. *Public Relations Review, 28,* 251–264.

Hutchison, L. L. (2002). Teaching ethics across the public relations curriculum. *Public Relations Review, 28,* 301–309.

Items of interest to professionals. (2002, December 2). *pr reporter, 45,* 4.

Jeffries-Fox Associates. (2000, March 3). *Toward a shared understanding of corporate reputation and related concepts: Phase I. Content analysis.* Basking Ridge, NJ: Report Prepared for the Council of Public Relations Firms.

JM. (2002, September 23). MuddPR@earthlink.net. *O'Dwyer's PR Daily.* Retrieved from http://www.odwyerpr.com, September 25, 2002.

Job insecurity. (2002, December 2). *pr reporter, 45,* 3.

Jordan, T. L. (2002). *The U.S. Constitution and fascinating facts about it* (7th ed.). Naperville, IL: Oak Hill.

Kamen, J. (1991, March). CNN's breakthrough in Baghdad: Live by satellite (censored). *Washington Journalism Review, 13*(2), pp. 24–27.

Kanter, R. M. (1998). Small business and economic growth. In J. J. Jasinowski (Ed.), *The rising tide* (pp. 87–99). New York: Wiley.

Kennedy, Jr., H., (1966). What you should know about the Foreign Agents Registration Act. *Public Relations Quarterly, 11,* 17–18.

Kornegay, J., & Grunig, L. A. (1998). Cyberbridging: How the communication manager role can link with the dominant coalition. *Journal of Communication Management, 3*(2), 140–156.

Lerbinger, O. (2001). *Corporate power strategies: Getting the upper hand with interest groups.* Newton, MA: Barrington.

Lowenstein, R. L., & Merrill, J. C. (1990). *Macromedia: Mission, message, and morality.* New York: Longman.

Maitra, P. (1996). *The globalization of capitalism in third world countries.* Westport, CT: Praeger.

Martin, L. J., & Chaudhary, A. G. (1983). *Comparative mass media systems.* New York: Longman.

McLeod, J. M., & Blumler, J. G. (1989). The macrosocial level of communication science. In C. R. Berger & S. H. Chaffee (Eds.), *Handbook of communication science* (pp. 271–322). Newbury Park, CA: Sage.

McQuail, D. (1987). *Mass communication theory: An introduction.* London: Sage.

Newsom, D. A., Turk, J. V., & Kruckeberg, D. (2000). *This is PR: The realities of public relations* (7th ed.). Belmont, CA: Wadsworth.

Nye, Jr., J. S. (2002, October 6). In the global age, America's not such a big cheese. *The Washington Post*, p. B3.

O'Dwyer, J. (1981, August). Special report: Fewer major corporations have "public relations" departments. *Jack O'Dwyer's Newsletter*, 1–3.

O'Dwyer, J. (2002, September 17). Students should train as writers. *O'Dwyer's PR Daily.* Retrieved from http://www.odwyerpr.com, September 25, 2002.

Pincus, J. D. (2002, Fall). Expanding the MBA. *The Public Relations Strategist*, p. 4.

Reputation must be pushed. (2000, October 2). *PR Week*, p. 10.

pr reporter. (1983, September 26). [No title] *26*, p. 1.

Profile 2000: A survey of the profession. Part II: Compensation survey. (2000). (International Association of Business Communicators) *Communication World, 13.*

Public relations pros are counselors, not just tactical communicators. (1987, April 20). *pr reporter, 30*, 1–4.

Public Relations Society of America. (1999). *Public relations education for the 21st century: A port of entry: The report of the Commission on Undergraduate Education.* New York: Author.

Pulgar, D. (2002, September 24). Senior, Florida International University. *O'Dwyer's PR Daily.* Retrieved from http://www.odwyerpr.com, September 25, 2002.

Sanders, A. (2002). *Prime-time politics.* Glen Allen, VA: College.

Seitel, F. P. (2001). *The practice of public relations* (8th ed.). Upper Saddle River, NJ: Prentice-Hall.

Sherman, C. (2002, September 24). UM group seeks alternatives to Md. candidates' debates. *Daily Record.* Retrieved from http://www.inform.umd.edu/campusInfo/De. . . s/InstAdv/newsdesk/Clips/200210924.htm, September 24, 2002.

Siebert, F. S., Peterson, T., & Schramm, W. (1963). *Four theories of the press.* Urbana: University of Illinois Press.

Skjerdal, T. S. (1993). *Siebert's four theories of the press: A critique.* Retrieved from http://www.geocities.com/CapitolHill/2152/siebert.html, September 25, 2002.

Tayeb, M. H. (1988). *Organizations and national culture: A comparative analysis.* London: Sage.

Tixier, M. (1993). Approaches to the communication function in France and abroad. *International Public Relations Review, 16*(2), 22–30.

Toth, E. L. (2002). Postmodernism for modernist public relations: The cash value and application of critical research in public relations. *Public Relations Review, 28*, 243–250.

Toth, E. L., & Cline, C. G. (Eds.). (1989). *Beyond the velvet ghetto.* San Francisco: IABC Research Foundation.

Toth, E. L., & Grunig, L. A. (1993). The missing story of women in public relations. *Journal of Public Relations Research, 5*, 153–175.

U.S. Bureau of the Census. (2000). *Statistical abstract of the United States: 2000* (120th ed.). Washington, DC: U.S. Government Printing Office.

U.S. Department of Labor, Bureau of Labor Statistics. (1998, January). *Employment and earnings.* Washington, DC: U.S. Government Printing Office.

van Parijs, P. (1997). *Real freedom for all: What (if anything) can justify capitalism?* Cary, NC: Oxford University Press.

Verčič, D., Grunig, L. A., & Grunig, J. E. (1996). Global and specific principles of public relations: Evidence from Slovenia. In H. M. Culbertson & N. Chen (Eds.), *International public relations: A comparative analysis* (pp. 31–65). Mahwah, NJ: Lawrence Erlbaum Associates.

Weick, K. E. (1979). *The social psychology of organizing* (2nd ed.). Reading, MA: Addison-Wesley.

Wilcox, D. L., Ault, P. H., Agee, W. K., & Cameron, G. T. (2000). *Public relations: Strategies and tactics* (6th ed.). New York: Longman.

World Statistics Pocketbook (22nd ed.). (2001). New York: United Nations Publishing.

Wouters, J. (1991). *International public relations.* New York: Amacom.

CHAPTER

31

A Different Country, A Different Public Relations: Canadian PR in the North American Context

Fraser Likely

Public relations practice in Canada and in the United States evolved in similar ways. There are, though, differences between these two countries. Canadian public relations practice is not a mirror image of that practiced in the United States. This chapter explores the evolution of public relations practice north of the 49th parallel in North America and examines the various factors that have contributed to a distinct Canadian brand of public relations.

CANADA: A BRIEF DESCRIPTION AND HISTORICAL OVERVIEW

Canada, based on landmass, is the second largest country in the world. However, most of its 33 million people live within 100 kilometers of its southern border. This border, much of which is along the 49th parallel, divides North America into Canada in the north and the United States of America in the south.

Canada's free market economy is based on natural resources: fishing; forestry; mining; oil and gas drilling; and farming. The state, at all three levels: federal; provincial; and municipal, plays a large part in the country's economy and has a larger percentage of Canada's Gross Domestic Product (GDP) than is the case in some other countries. Canada has been labeled a socialist or semi-socialist country for the larger role the state—rather than the private sector—plays in such social programs as health care, pensions, education, unemployment insurance and child care.

Canada's vast geography has been a great obstacle in the country's development. This has resulted in Canada being a world leader at various points in its history in the development of rail travel, telegraph wire services, telephones, snowmobiles, air travel, fiber optics and high-speed internet connection. Overcoming distance has been a major preoccupation of nation-building. Canada led the world in telephone usage for years and years, and in 2007 the residents of Toronto have become the greatest users of Facebook of any world city.

Canada is a land of immigrants. The country's native or indigenous peoples are believed to have migrated to North America approximately 10,000 years ago, when a land and ice bridge joined North America to Asia. Today, they number just over a million people. Early Europeans next visited Canada somewhere between 900 and 1100 AD. But, it wasn't until the 15th and 16th centuries that the great European powers attempted to settle what has become Canada. In the late 1750s, Britain finally defeated France in North America, and New France became a British colony, part of British North America. After the American War of Independence, those loyal to the crown—United Empire Loyalists—emigrated to what was left of British North America. Subsequent immigration came from the British Isles and the United States. This was followed by immigration from other countries in Western and Eastern Europe, especially after each World War. In the last thirty years, immigration has come from the Caribbean, Africa, the Indian sub-continent and Asia. Canada now welcomes over 200,000 immigrants per year. Large Canadian cities, notably Toronto, its largest, are said to be the most multicultural in the world.

British direct control lasted until 1867, when Canada began a process of becoming its own country. Today, it is a parliamentary, representative democracy and a constitutional monarchy—with the Queen of the United Kingdom as its monarch and head of state. From its beginnings, Canada searched for a distinct Canadian identity. It was not a colony of France or Britain, nor was it "American." Canada enjoyed a mixture of all worlds. Her constitution and parliamentary system are still largely based on the British model. Her legal system is both French and English. Her social and health care approaches are European, particularly Scandinavian. On the other hand, her mass culture is much more American than European. Dependent initially on its trade ties with the mother country, today the Canadian economy is fully integrated with that of the United States following the North America Free Trade Agreement signed in 1992. By law, Canada is bilingual and bicultural—representing the accommodation of generations of French colonists in Canada following the British takeover and the subsequent development of the country based on the premise of "two founding nations" in legal, political and technological systems. In recent decades, Canada has been increasingly willing to accept multi-culturalism, even to the extent of the state supporting the mosaic of national cultures, rather than the US "melting pot" of one culture. With the world's eighth largest economy, the country has tried to present itself to the rest of the world as an independent "honest broker." As a young country with some history, the identity—the idea—of Canada is still forming.

A BRIEF HISTORY OF PUBLIC RELATIONS IN CANADA

From the limited research that has been conducted so far about public relations in Canada, there appear to be five significant periods in public relations' evolutionary process in Canada: from 1604 to 1900; from 1900 to 1940; from 1940 to 1945 (or the years of the Second World War); from 1945 to 1970; and from 1970 to today. Canada experienced many of the same milestones as did the United States, albeit with a slight lag in time. For example, the first American in-house publicity bureau was established at Westinghouse in 1889 (Newsom et al. 1996) and in Canada at Bell Canada in 1914 (Johansen 2005). James

Cowan opened the first firm in Canada to be called a public relations agency in 1930; in the US, Ivy Lee opened the first agency in 1904 (Basin 2007).

The 1604 to 1900 Period

In this period, what is now Canada changed from being a colony of France, to being a colony of Britain, to being its own country. The available research on the history of public relations in this period demonstrates that typical public relations activities were conducted, first in France, then in Britain, then across Western Europe and then in the United States. These were promotional or publicity activities. For example, in 1613 the French explorer Samuel de Champlain "published a book about his exploits that was designed to lure settlers" (Johansen 2005: 111). By the 1880s, the Government of Canada—in its departments of interior, agriculture and immigation—had developed a comprehensive promotional approach. This included: media tours of Canada for European journalists; sponsored visits to Canada for clergymen and farmers; monitoring of newspapers and subsequent letters to editors in newspapers to correct perceived errors in how Canada was portrayed; exhibits and illustrated lectures at European fairs; pamphlets (in numerous languages); advertisements; and lobbying efforts (to have Canadian geography taught in UK schools) (Emms 1995). Summarizing this period, Johansen concludes that " . . . public relations here (Canada) was first embraced by government" (Johansen 1998: 7).

The 1900 to 1940 Period

The importance of the second period can be illustrated by a number of firsts in the evolution of Canadian public relations. These included: the first in-house publicity unit; the first private sector in-house effort; the first publicity agency; and the first public relations consultancy. Johansen (1998: 7) reports that ". . . by the turn of the century, a handful of private institutions had embarked upon full-time publicity operations." Institutions such as Canadian-owned railroads, banks and telephone companies had hired publicity specialists and were conducting publicity, promotion and public affairs (government relations) campaigns by the beginning of WWI. These new publicity specialists for the most part were former newspaper men (Emms 1995; Johansen 2005). Their units were called publicity bureaus, or in some cases, they were part of a larger, existing advertising department. Through the 1930s, the term public relations took on greater usage. The first public relations consultancy was established in Canada in 1930. Brown (Brown 1984: 8), himself a public relations consultant who started his career with Public and Industrial Relations Limited of Toronto in 1952, commented on the emergent role of public relations advisor in the 1930s: "Most early public relations advisors were former press agents or publicists who had started to specialize in the advice function."

The 1940 to 1945 Period (The Years of the Second World War)

Various authors who have written about the evolution of public relations in Canada cite the years of the Second World War as pivotal, both in the development of public relations in the Canadian government and in its subsequent growth in the private sector (Johansen and Ferguson 2005; Johansen 1998; Emms 1995; Donoghue 1993; Brown 1984). Johansen and Ferguson (2005: 112) state that there was little further development of public relations activities in the Canadian government in the 1930s (other than those portrayed above) and it was because of the war "that public relations activities in the Canadian government became truly large scale." Brown (1984: 9) argued that in the private sector "It [the war] also spawned the Canadian public relations business which, until 1939, had only a handful of practitioners." A large number of people, mostly men, were selected from the ranks of journalism, advertising, publicity and public relations to run Canada's information or "propaganda machine" (Brown 1984: 9) during the war.

The 1945 to 1970 Period

Brown suggests that these "wartime information officers . . ., for the most part, did not return to news work, but joined business, government, labor organizations and other institutions as public relations officers" (Brown 1984: 10). The Canadian economy boomed in the 1950s and 1960s. Canada experienced the highest post-war baby boom of any industrialized country. Businesses grew, as did the size and scope of government, particularly as Canada added government-run universal social programs such as medicare. Social activism, led by interest groups, fueled activist governments. Public relations functions, even those still part of an advertising department at war's end, became separate units. In this period of time, the initial development of various sub-functions such as public affairs/government relations, internal communication and investor relations continued. Gollner (1983) traces the growth of public affairs units between 1950 and 1980. Most were in response to growing citizen activism and government intervention. The Canadian Public Relations Society (CPRS) was incorporated officially in 1956. Johansen (1998) cites efforts in this period to professionalize the society: the first university extension training course at the University of Toronto (1949); tough membership application criteria; PR for PR committees to respond to negative references to PR in the media and to promote the benefits of good PR; a CPRS research foundation (1957); a Code of Conduct; an Accreditation Program (1969) and annual conferences and member society training programs.

The Period since 1970

Very little comprehensive research has been published on the evolution of public relations in Canada in the last 35 or so years. By all anecdotal accounts, public relations continued to grow in this period. Patrick Gossage, Chairman of the public relations firm Media Profile, posted this on the blog of the Canadian Council of Public Relations Firms (CCPRF): "Twenty years ago I launched Media Profile in a corner of my brother's promotion company. We were soon two or three, and twenty years later there are over 50 consultants working on a breathtaking variety of clients" (CCPRF July 4, 2007). The sheer number of public relations firms increased in this period at the same time as the ownership of these agencies changed (Bowles 1988: 1). Few medium (defined here as 10–50 consultants) and large-size (over 50 consultants) public relations firms operating in Canada now are fully Canadian-owned. Only a small number of the current CCPRF membership consists of Canadian-owned firms. At the same time, the number of small, independent, "boutique" one to ten person fully Canadian-owned consultancies multiplied steadily, particularly the one or two member specialist firms.

The most obvious evidence of sustained growth is found in the number of post secondary public relations programs. The first degree program exclusively in public relations was founded in French, at Laval University in the the early 1970s. It was followed by a similar program in English at Mount St. Vincent University in 1977. The real growth in this period occurred at the community college level. In the 1980s and 1990s, two and three year diploma programs were developed at community colleges across Canada. Today, the vast majority of graduates of these programs already have an undergraduate degree in another discipline and are looking for a "technical" diploma to enhance their entry into full-time employment.

In the past 15 years, there has also been the development of post-graduation public relations certificate programs, appealing to public relations professionals already in the work force. Offered at many universities and community colleges across the country, these certificate programs are typically a year or two in length, either full-time or as a series of night courses. Finally, Royal Roads University offers an Executive Master of Business Administration in Public Relations and Communications Management. Created in 1999, this distance education program was recently joined by a distance education Master of Communication Management at McMaster University and two graduate level full-time programs in public relations at Mount St. Vincent University. Recently, many of the diploma programs have sought partnerships with university faculties of communication to offer four year degrees in public relations: for example, Mount Royal College with the University of Calgary, Algonquin College with the University of Ottawa and Humber College with the University of Guelph.

CPRS expanded the number of member societies in this period as membership continued to grow, reaching 1700 full members at its height in the 1980s. IABC officially came to Canada when it merged with the Corporate Communicators of Canada Association in 1974. IABC now has 15 chapters across Canada, CPRS 16. There are other, much smaller, associations for practitioners involved in education, in healthcare or in public affairs. IABC has the most members; in fact its Toronto chapter is IABC's largest at 1,400 members and its Calgary chapter the third largest with 550 members—out of IABC's approximate 100 chapters and membership of 14,700 worldwide. The Toronto and Calgary chapters comprise just under 90 percent of Canada's total IABC membership of approximately 2,200 (IABC Toronto 2007; IABC Calgary 2007). IABC has different and more easily attainable membership criteria than does CPRS, with CPRS's being much more selective, limited to full-time employment in public relations. Johansen (1998: 13–15) recounts the early decisions in CPRS to apply fairly stringent criteria, such as "full-time employment of minimum length," "the signed recommendation of two members in good standing," "membership credentials committees at both the local and national levels also passed judgment on the prospect," and "names were then posted to allow objections from any member."

While IABC membership grew in this period, membership numbers in CPRS have remained flat for the last 20 years. Over these years at the national level, CPRS has maintained such activities as an accreditation program, an awards program, and a yearly national conference. In good financial times, the association can support national-level training programs, promotional programs, educational standards programs with education institutions, an active research foundation, additional member benefits such as insurance programs and tours by the national president and executive committee to member societies across the country. A number of factors have affected CPRS's financial situation and thus its ability to grow over the past decade. These include a number of poorly attended national conferences (annual conferences remain very important revenue generators for both CPRS and IABC), a membership fee decrease in the early 1990s and a move of headquarters in 2000 (CPRS Annual Reports 2007). IABC runs association-wide conference, accreditation and awards programs from its international headquarters in San Francisco. Local chapters, be they IABC or CPRS, concentrate on smaller scale professional development and networking activities as well as acting as ground support for national conference, accreditation and award programs. Being relatively small associations with a limited number of paid staff, both CPRS nationally and especially at the chapter level and IABC chapters in Canada must rely on volunteer effort. Volunteers tend to be practitioners at the beginning or in the middle of their careers. While there are some senior volunteers, and a good number of senior practitioners amongst association membership, the majority of senior practitioners practicing across Canada are not members of CPRS or IABC in Canada.

IABC members benefit from being involved in a larger association, one that numbers more than 14,700 members. On the other hand, members of CPRS benefit from a long-standing relationship with PRSA. This relationship goes back to the 1950s. Almost from its inception, each President and members of their executive committee would attend each other's annual national conference and hold joint meetings while there. CPRS members have for decades been able to attend PRSA events, partake in professional development, buy publications, subscribe to journals and join interest groups at PRSA member rates. CPRS has an agreement with PRSA to use the Accredited in Public Relations (APR) designation.

In summary, this period saw the institutionalization of a public relations unit in most Canadian organizations. The number of consultancies grew. The number of people taking public relations education grew, including the number of graduates entering practice. But, compared to the increasing number of practitioners, the membership associations did not keep pace.

THE CURRENT STATUS OF PUBLIC RELATIONS IN CANADA

Canada had 36,800 employed public relations and communication practitioners in 2004, an increase of 56 percent since the mid-1990s (Canadian Government Job Futures 2007). The Center for Media and Democracy (2007) states the following: "it is estimated, however, that less than 10 percent of public relations practitioners in the US belong to PRSA." Combining IABC's 2007 total of Canadian members with those of CPRS would yield a total of 3,800—putting the Canadian percentage very close to that of the American 10 percent. Certainly, there are many more practitioners than members of either association: for example, there are at least 5,000 practitioners in the Canadian federal government. But only a very small percentage of these practitioners are members of IABC or CPRS.

What's important to note is that without a larger critical mass, neither association on its own has been able to further the professionalism of public relations in Canada. There are no universal standards for public relations education in Canada. CPRS first attempted this in the late 1970s (Root 1984: 247). Since then it has never been able to sustain a comprehensive effort nationally, relying more on local societies to maintain a relationship with education institutions in their area. CPRS's latest national effort is the recent establishment of a new Task Force on Public Relations Education (CPRS 2007). IABC in Canada has not addressed public relations education. Both associations have accreditation programs, but neither has the wherewithal to promote the designation in a way that would give widespread recognition, other than buying yearly advertisements in the trade and mass media to promote their successful applicants. Even after 35 years, only a third of CPRS members are currently accredited. Even so, this is a greater percentage than IABC has in Canada. An even smaller percentage of consulting firms belong to an association that sets business conduct or professional ethics standards. In 1988, "fewer than 25 percent of Canadian consulting firms" were members of the Canadian Public Relations Society's Consultants Institute (Bowles 1988). Today, with the CPRS Consultants Institute long dead, the new CCPRF has thirteen members and as yet sets no standards.

CPRS discussed the need for mandatory licensing for Canadian public relations practitioners at various points in its history (Johansen 1998). In the late 1980s in particular, CPRS devoted considerable energies to a research and outreach program (Johansen 2005). The initiative died in the early 1990s, when faced with a severe recession in Canada. IABC, because of its United States-based membership base hovering around 85 percent or more and because of its less demanding membership requirements, never has addressed the question of licensing or regulation in Canada. It should be noted here that under the Canadian constitution and federal system of government, areas like education, accreditation or licensing fall under the authority of the ten individual provincial governments, not the federal government.

Both CPRS and IABC have codes of professional conduct, to which their members are expected to adhere. Outside of these codes of conduct, there is limited discussion of public relations ethics in Canada amongst practitioners—even though Canadian scholars have been active studying ethics (Pearson 1989a, 1989b; 1990; Edgett 2002; Parsons 2004). Textbooks now in use in public relations courses taught in English are primarily the same as those used in American public relations courses. What's worthy of note is that almost as many books have been produced for French-speaking students, though these students represent only 10–20 percent of the public relations student population. Public relations courses taught in French use some American textbooks, some books produced in France but quite a number of books authored by Canadians and set in a Canadian context. Given that education is a provincial matter and given that member associations like CPRS have been sporadic in trying to influence education standards, it is easy to see why each public relations program in Canada develops its programs, courses and reading lists distinct from any other program. There are no common standards; nor does there appear to be sufficient Canadian content. Over twenty years ago, Gollner (1983: 165) discovered that there was not much in the way of case studies with a distinctive pan-Canadian background. That seems to remain the case today. The choice of public relations textbooks illustrates the remaining linguistic and cultural divide between the founding groups. English Canada studies from American texts: French Canada has the choice of many homegrown publications.

Johansen reports that it wasn't until the 1950s that public relations "began to suffer a broad negative image" (1998: 16). Committees were established in CPRS to diffuse negative imagery and to promote the value of public relations to organizations and to Canadian society (Johansen 1998: 16). These committees still exist today. Considered PR for PR committees, they seem to play a less ambitious and far less active role than their predecessors. For example, the presiding officer of the CPRS national Communications and Marketing Committee stated that "the committee monitored the CBC radio series Spin Cycles and determined there was no need for CPRS to react" (CPRS Annual Report 2004). While there still is the occasional negative reference to public relations or the use of the term in derisive and inflammatory ways in the Canadian media (Scrimger and Richards 2003), these occurrences seem to have waned in recent years.

While CPRS and IABC have various vehicles to communicate with their members, it has proven impossible to sustain a pan-Canadian trade magazine devoted to Canadian public relations. The latest—the on-line subscription publication PR Canada that advertised itself as "Canada's only national newsletter for business communicators" (PR Canada 2006)—is now defunct. A number of Canadian focused print trade publications were started in the past fifty years (most with direct or indirect involvement of CPRS) but none lasted long. Publications covering the marketing and advertising fields do not do justice to public relations. For example, Pat McNamara, Chair of the Canadian Council of Public Relations Firms, recently wrote an open letter to *Marketing* magazine "to state my dissatisfaction with your coverage of our industry" (McNamara 2007). Neither CPRS nor IABC member publications reach the majority of Canadian practitioners. Practitioners rely on publications originating in the US or the UK for both academic and practitioner generated research and information.

Statistics from the Canadian Government (Job Futures 2007) indicate that as an occupation, public relations/communications has grown steadily in the last decade, with:

- less self-employed workers at 11 percent than the national average at 15 percent;
- an unemployment rate lower than the national average (though slightly above other professions);
- a salary package that grew more than the national average;
- an increase in the number of part-time workers (rising steadily since 1997); and
- more job seekers than the number of job openings projected by 2009, even with the large number of baby boom practitioners aged 55 and over ready to retire.

Sixty percent of Canadian public relations and communication workers are female, a percentage that has stayed relatively constant since 1997 (Job Futures 2007) and 1991 (Grunig and Grunig 2002: 183). It was during the 1980s that Canadian women in public relations practice started to outnumber men. In the late 1980s for the first time in CPRS history, more women than men were being accredited and were winning national awards. Scrimger studied the growth of female practitioners and concluded "female practitioners in Canada mirror the same handicaps documented in studies of U.S. practitioners" (1985). One difference, though, was that women in Canada headed more departments of public relations (61 percent) than did their peers in the US (51 percent) or in the United Kingdom (40 percent) (Grunig, L.A., Grunig, J.E. and Dozier, D.M. 2002: 184). Today, in the Canadian Federal Government communications community, women hold the majority of the head positions—at the same and equal senior classification levels as any other executive in any other functional area. That is, heads of communications branches are either Directors General or Assistant Deputy Ministers, dependent on the size of the branch. Each would report to a Deputy Minister, the head of the department, like all other policy, program, operations or corporate services heads. Given that there isn't the uniformity in classification levels in the private sector as there is in government, it is difficult to know if a corporate communications/public relations/public affairs head in the private sector with a vice-president or senior vice-president title is at the same classification level as all other functional and operational heads.

In summary, over the past one hundred or so years, the public relations industry in Canada has evolved into a distinct, though small, occupational category. At present, it appears to be an occupation that is accepted by Canadian society, with an image either neutral or at least far less negative than fifty years ago. It is even valued by employers, though less so than by employers in the US or the UK (Grunig, L.A., Grunig, J.E. and Dozier, D.M. 2002: 80). Interestingly, Canadian practitioners seem to think it has less value to management than do their American and British peers (Grunig, L.A., Grunig, J.E. and Dozier, D.M. 2002: 80). Where former journalists were its first practitioners, today it is graduates of post-secondary public relations educational programs. Public relations membership associations represent approximately 10 percent of practitioners, but less than a third of members are accredited. These associations offer networking and professional development opportunities to their members. They have not being able to professionalize the occupation, by developing market monopoly in its jurisdiction, establishing and maintaining educational standards or achieving self-regulation. Educational institutions have yet to build a solid base of Canadian research in public relations and thus establish a unique body of Canadian public relations knowledge. There are few opportunities available to Canadian public relations practitioners outside of association membership for sharing information and knowledge that is solely Canadian in its nature and context. Like the country itself, the public relations occupation in Canada is still searching for its own identity.

ENVIRONMENTAL FACTORS AND CANADIAN PUBLIC RELATIONS

Political System

The Queen of the United Kingdom is Canada's official head of state; her representative in Canada is the Canadian-born Governor General (appointed by the Queen on the advice of the Prime Minister and Cabinet). The monarch's role (and thus the Governor General's) and therefore their power is limited by Canada's constitution and elected parliament. Canada is a parliamentary democracy, with a clear distinction between head of state and head of government. The Prime Minister is Canada's head of government, with provincial Premiers heading duly elected provincial governments. Political parties choose their leaders. The leader and the party's choice in each riding contest constituency seats in a first-past-the-post electoral system. In federal and provincial elections, the party with the most seats forms the government, with that party's leader becoming Prime Minister or Premier respectively. The Prime Minister or Premier heads the government, led by the executive branch or Cabinet (duly elected members of Parliament chosen usually from the party with the most seats by the Prime Minister). The executive branch, and therefore government, depends on the support of the legislative branch or Parliament, through votes of confidence, for its continuance in power.

Historically, there are three main political positions in Canada, traditionally placed differently across a left–center–right continuum. At times, additional political parties have appeared and contested elections, usually at the far left or far right. It is commonly thought that while a political party may campaign from a left or right of center orientation, all elected governments ultimately govern from the Canadian political center. This applies to both economic policy and social policy. Finding that political center for each policy issue is not an easy task and it has forced political parties before elections, as well as governments once in power, to continuously consult with Canadians through polling and face-to-face consultation techniques.

Canada's political culture is undergoing change. Originally, as conceived in the British North America (BNA) Act of 1867, Canada subordinated the rights of the individual to those of the collective. Whereas the United States of America has celebrated individual rights, as stated in the phrase "life, liberty and the pursuit of happiness", Canada preferred "peace, order and good government." The original BNA Act was explicit in its statement of majority and minority collective rights. As a result, governments played a large role in determining and protecting rights in such areas as political representation, religion, language and education. In doing so, the country developed a tradition of accommodation, compromise and tolerance among and between different groups. As a result, political change in Canada—including full independence from Great Britain—has come slowly and incrementally, not through revolution. With the patriation of the Canadian constitution from Britain to Canada in 1982 and the concurrent adoption of the Canadian Charter of Rights and Freedoms as part of the same package, Canada began a process of recognizing and supporting individual rights—such as those based on sexual orientation, gender and age. The country supports social policies addressed to the collectivity, such as official bilingualism, biculturalism (two founding peoples: French and English), universal health care, gun control and environmental activism as well as those supporting individual rights such as same-sex marriages, the disabled in the workplace and multicultural diversity.

To the tradition of accommodation, compromise and tolerance among and between different groups—particularly between the old English and French immigrant groups (official bilingualism and biculturalism) and later among different immigrant groups (multiculturalism)—has been added a new tradition of accommodation, compromise and tolerance among and between individual differences. Ultimately, the country's political culture will have to balance and likely rebalance traditions of collective rights with those of individual rights.

The public relations industry in Canada has been affected by the country's political structure and culture in a number of ways, such as:

- Governments (at all levels), to a greater or lesser extent, have adopted policies and practices supporting open communication—consulting Canadians and providing information—with governments at all levels employing a considerable percentage of Canadian public relations practitioners.

- Canadians, as individuals and as members of interest groups, have multiple access points to the government in power and to the political system in general, making environmental scanning, consultation and performance measurement important tools for Canadian public relations practitioners.

- The necessity of finding and governing from the political center results in political and government communication that usually is neither extreme nor negative, and not attack-oriented.

- Traditions of accommodation, compromise and tolerance, reflecting the support for collective and individual rights, pervade the communication landscape and they reinforce Canadians' expectations for communication that is inclusive.

- Government lobbying efforts typically have a public relations/communications component and most large government affairs or public affairs or lobbying firms have public relations departments or affiliations with public relations agencies.

- Since education and the regulation of recognized professional bodies are provincial matters, each province is responsible for public relations education and public relations licensing. While there are public relations programs in each province, there is no overarching set of standards for the country. No province has yet recognized public relations as a profession nor granted self-regulating powers to a governing body.

Economic System

Canada's economy is ranked in the world's top ten. The country is a member of the G8. Though its economy is still mostly resource-based, it does have relatively robust manufacturing and high-tech industrial sectors. Three-quarters of Canadian jobs are in the service sector. Canada does not provide much of the secondary or tertiary value-added to the resources it extracts, exporting the vast majority simply as raw material for others to refine and use in manufacturing.

Compared to many countries, Canada is affluent, with a high standard of living. For years, it has ranked in the top five of United Nations Human Development Index.

Economic power has shifted westward over the course of Canadian history. First the Altantic provinces were more prosperous than provincial averages, because of water travel, fisheries and forestry. Then, it was the province of Quebec's turn because of agriculture, forestry, mining, banking and train transportation. Ontario followed as Canada's manufacturing heartland. Recently, oil and gas, mining, forestry and access to the Pacific Rim countries have pushed Alberta and British Columbia to become Canada's economic powerhouses.

Canada is a free market economy, with higher government intervention than that of the United States, but less intervention than most countries in Europe. Being resource-based, resources found mostly in public ownership, has led to greater government regulation of various primary industries. Canada also has fairly robust technology and tourist sectors. The service sector comprises retail, business services such as banking, communication services, education services and health services. These are also highly regulated, particularly the last two which are mostly within the public sector. Canada has taken more of a corporatist than a pluarist approach to business–government relations. There are formal mechanisms such as joint committees, think tanks, bargaining structures and regular consultation processes utilized to aid legislative and regulatory decision-making. Regulation notwithstanding, there has been a hollowing out of the Canadian-owned private sector. That is, Canadian founded and owned corporations increasingly are being sold to foreign buyers, mostly American-owned. To some extent, Canada is becoming a branch plant economy, with American interests controlling a good percentage of the Canadian economy.

The public relations industry in Canada has been affected by the country's economic structure in a number of ways, such as:

- Most medium and large Canadian public relations agencies are a branch of, or owned by, an American-based agency.
- Though there is some movement of personnel across the Canada–United States border, Canadian agency employees service Canadian clients or the branch offices of multi-nationals (where the US based agency is the agency of record).
- Canadian public relations practitioners, not expatriates, are employed by the multi-national's Canadian office.
- The size of Canadian in-house PR departments and PR agencies tends to be smaller than American equivalents and to have less resources in specialized areas such as measurement.
- Canadian-owned agencies tend to be small and independent (though they may be part of a national or an international consortium) and focused on a particular geographical region.
- Canadian public relations practitioners are as advanced in new information technologies and social media as any practtioner in any other highly developed country, thanks to the government's long time encouragement and investment in a high speed, digitized, fiber-optic-based telephony and technological infrastructure.

Legal System

As a federation, laws (statutes, legislation, or acts) in Canada are enacted by the federal government with parliamentary approval and by provincial governments with provincial assembly approval. Municipalities, as creatures of the provinces, are delegated some areas of responsibilities to enact local regulations. The Canadian legal system, based on the rule of law, freedom under the law, democratic principles and respect for others, has provided the country a long heritage of societal justice. Criminal law, based on English common law, is uniform across Canada. Canadian civil law is also based on English common law, except in the province of Quebec where it is based on the civil code of France.

In Canada, a system of federal, provincial and municipal courts administer justice. The federal government has exclusive authority in criminal matters, both in federal and provincial courts. Provinces have jurisdiction over civil matters and the operation of provincial lower courts and municipal courts. The highest court of the Canadian legal system is the Supreme Court of Canada. Judges are appointed to the Supreme Court by the Governor General, on recommendation of the Prime Minister and Cabinet. The federal government appoints judges to lower courts. While appointed by the government, the judiciary is at arm's length from the government.

The public relations industry in Canada has been affected by the country's legal structure and culture in a number of ways, such as:

- Canadian public relations practitioners are subject to the same legal conditions as found in the United Kingdom.

- Various freedoms found in the Canadian Charter of Rights and Freedoms—such as freedom of conscience, freedom of religion, freedom of thought, freedom of belief, freedom of expression, freedom of the press and of other media of communication, freedom of peaceful assembly, and freedom of association—apply directly to the practice of public relations.

- The Canadian Charter of Rights and Freedoms describes Canadian language rights, in particular the right to use either the English or French language in communications with Canada's federal government and certain provincial governments. The effect is that, in most cases, public relations materials would be produced in both official languages in the public sector and in some cases in other sectors as well.

- Section 27 of the Canadian Charter of Rights and Freedoms instructs that the Charter be interpreted in a multicultural context. One effect on public relations is that materials must reflect the diverse nature of Canadian society.

- Section 28, which states that all Charter rights are guaranteed equally to men and women, also has an effect on public relations both in terms of how public relations materials reflect men and women and in the employment of men and women.

Activism

Activism has long been a factor in Canadian political life. Traditionally, activists were outside Canada's ruling elites. From the period of British takeover of Canada to well into the years before the Second World War, elite accommodation was the dominant factor of Canadian political culture. Originally developed to smooth the relationship between British elites (controlling the political system, the military, business and industrial interests, importation and exportation) and French elites (controlling the Roman Catholic Church, the civil law legal system, large land holdings that included agriculture and the production of natural resources), the formula evolved to include all economic elites. From small-scale rebellions in the 1830s (to enlarge access to the political system), to the suffragette movement from the 1900s to the 1930s (to allow women equal rights, such as being able to vote and own property), to the labor movements of the 1910s to 1940s (labor unions are nowhere near as strong today as they were during this period), activists fought the elites over inclusivity, the definition of the public good and the allocation of resources and accumulated wealth.

These were more loose social movements than organized formal groups. The rise of organized, formal, institutionized pressure or interest groups occurred after WWII, with the heyday being the 1970s—as Canada expanded the state's role in the social justice arena. Group survival and success depended on the ability to mimic the Canadian federated political structure (have resources sufficient to engage at both the federal and provincial/ municipal levels), to engage and mobilize the Canadian middle class and to play an active role in the policy communities and issue networks where the new subject matter experts or "technocrats" achieved consensus. From the 1950s on, Canada lessened its focus on elite accommodation and moved to increase the accommodation of the country's quickly increasing middle class, particularly the sectors in which they had interest. Sectoral accommodation—sectors such as environmentalism, sexual orientation, non-smokers' rights, religion, ethnic diversity, health, etc—included the development of new mechanisms for relationship-building and input into political decision-making processes. Think tanks, Royal Commissions, joint committees, formal consultations, funding for research conducted by interest groups and even special programs to fund appeals before the Supreme Court of Canada were some of the institutional mechanisms put in place to accommodate sectoral activism.

While activism has been a feature of Canada's political culture for some time, the accommodation of this activism has also been a necessary part of the political process. The accommodation of activism has long been regarded as an important element in Canadian public relations. Government relations, public affairs and issues management are integral public relations functions. In fact, more has been written in this area of Canadian public relations than any other, by authors such as: Andrew Gollner; Peter Bartha; Pat Delbridge; Jon Johnson; Craig Fleisher; and John Wright. The fact that these authors wrote in the 1980s and early 1990s suggests that activism, issues management and accommodation subsequently have become a fairly institutionalized package in Canada. This accommodation extends beyond the public sector to the private sector as for example the extensive consultation processes run by oil and gas companies in Alberta (Forstner and Bales 1992a; 1992b) and even not-for-profit sectors (inter-faith committees). By the mid-2000s, the practice was not simply based on a tactic of extensive consultation but on a strategy of continuous relationship building (Shaw, J. and Shaw, P. 2005).

The Canadian approach to activism is perhaps best explained by a quote from the abstract of John E. Guiniven's article in the *Journal of Public Relations Research* (Guiniven 2002):

> Public relations practitioners who have worked in the United States and Canada often remark how differently activists and public issues are dealt with in each of the countries. Generally, disputes are seen as much less confrontational, much less zero-sum games in Canada than in the United States . . . the greater acceptance of two-way symmetrical communication in Canada than in the United States results from the tradition of compromise embedded in Canadian culture.

The public relations industry in Canada has been affected by the country's accommodation of activism in a number of ways:

- Issue management is a well established process, with well developed tools, in both public and private sector public relations departments;
- Canada has developed a comprehensive body of literature on business–government relations, on interest group activism and on issues management; and

- the Canadian government has established a quota for the minimum number of employees belonging to minority groups that must work in each department. Therefore, public relations departments in the federal government must hire and train minority group employees. Ultimately, this will increase the multicultural diversity of public relations practitioners in the Canadian government and, eventually, outside of the public sector.

Culture

Canada is seen as a mosaic of cultures, a tradition confirmed by the entrenchment of multiculturalism within the Canadian Charter of Rights and Freedoms. That is not to say that there is not an indentifiable Canadian culture. There is, and it reflects the shared experiences of all Canadians regardless of origin. But when compared to that of its southern neighbor, a singular Canadian culture does not appear as obvious or loud.

The major influences on present day Canadian culture are: the cultures of its aboriginal groups; the culture of early French colonists and the evolution of that culture within a Canadian context; the culture of British settlers—English, Irish and Scottish—and of the home country through Canada's evolution from a British colony to an independent country; the culture of the United States and of US immigration to Canada; and the cultures of waves of immigrant groups from such countries as Norway, Italy, Germany, Portugal, India, China, Yugoslavia, the Philippines, Iran, Chile, South Korea, Ethiopia, Vietnam and Haiti.

These major influences, these pieces of the mosaic, are all identifiable—particularly in a Canadian's vast apparel and culinary choices. They are also visible in artistic, musical and literary endeavors. Likewise, they find expression in the public display of social and religious norms, beliefs and customs. There are newspapers and cable televison shows available in many languages. There are annual festivals and celebrations honoring various ethnic backgrounds. Canadian governments fund everything from heritage language classes to Black History Month to Asian Heritage Month to International Day for the Elimination of Racial Discrimination to Urban Multipurpose Aboriginal Youth Centers.

Canada has developed institutions such as the Canada Council for the Arts, the National Film Board, the Canadian Broadcasting Corporation, the Canadian Radio-Television and Telecommunications Commission and the Status of Women Canada, in part to promote this mosaic. For example, the National Film Board helps fund films that depict the diversity of Canadians and supports film festivals that showcase this diversity, such as the First Peoples Festival, the Toronto Hispanic Film Fest, the *Journées du cinéma africain et créole*, and the Toronto Reel Asian Film Festival.

Over the last decade, Canada has taken in more immigrants on a per capita basis than any other country. Given the sheer diversity of these immigrant backgrounds, easy and early inclusion into Canadian culture—even with Canada's practiced multicultural policies—is still a work in progress. Issues remain, such as the recognition of the professional credentials of immigrants and the acceptance of their ability to work to the standards Canadian professional bodies expect. That said, under the last Liberal Party government in the early 2000s, 40 percent of elected Liberal Members of Parliament or their parents were not born in Canada. In Cabinet, 25 percent of Liberal cabinet members or their parents were not born in Canada. In Canada itself, only 19 percent of Canadians were born outside of Canada (Pettigrew 2007). The 40 percent and the 25 percent represent another means of accommodation and thus the lessening of potential issues to do with inclusivity.

All of the above is not to say that this Canadian approach to a pan-Canadian culture is perfect or that there are no inequalities in the mosaic. For example, even with recent legislation, women still earn less than men, for work of equal value. Visible minorities face discrimination at times when searching for housing or when seeking employment. Many Aboriginals are subject to institutionized poverty and class distinctions. Given the global reach and economic strength of American popular culture, Canada has had to legislate the protection of Canadian culture, such as requiring a minimum of Canadian culture in its mass media in the face of the overwhelming onslaught of American cultural vehicles from television shows, to movies, to magazines, to music on the radio.

There are important distinctions in the social aspects of Canadian culture that are worthy of note. For example, over the past two hundred years, Canada has moved from a country with high levels of social stratification—stratification by wealth, power and prestige—to one with lower levels. Initially, Canada had two basic strata: an elite class and a working class. Elites were made up of church leaders, large landowners or landed gentry, military senior staff and governing appointees. Later, homegrown industry and business successes were added to that mix. Gradually, the influence of religious elites through wealth, power or prestige has vanished as religious adherence has waned. A participatory democracy and an enlargement of the elected political class has decreased the wealth, power and prestige of military senior staff, governing appointees and a landed gentry. Finally, Canada maintains an economic elite, but one that is smaller and less influential in terms of its wealth and prestige than even one or two generations ago.

Add to all this the tremendous increase in the middle managerial and professional class, as well as the rise in the influence of the technocrat, and it can be said that Canada is less hierarchial today. In fact, the country has one of the highest rates of upward social mobility in the developed world. Increasingly, Canada has a social system in which positions of influence are achieved, not ascribed. Whereas, from its founding, Canada had more a caste system, today it is more a meritocracy. Status is gained mainly through achievement, and achievement—wealth, power and prestige—is more closely correlated to education achievement than ever before. Canada's distributive or "welfare state" policies have helped the social mobility of immigrants, making the country less elitist and more egalitarian.

Over the past fifty years, there has been a tremendous increase in upper and lower white collar work (managers; professionals; technicians; administrative staff), while there has been a decrease in upper and lower blue collar work in manufacturing, agriculture, forestry and fisheries. Fewer Canadians belong to trade unions than in previous decades. The country's distributive practices have not benefited native born Canadians in terms of their social mobility. For a developed country, Canada still has a fairly large economic under-class, with high levels of poverty and unemployment.

More than ever, greater prestige is given to upper middle class professional and executive ranks. In fact, Canada's political, legal and bureaucratic elites find their origins there, with their rise based more on merit than ever before. Slowly but surely, this prestigious professional/executive class includes more women. Women have broken the barriers in many professions. This advancement is not as true in the corporate world or in politics, where men still dominate positions of authority. Today, Canadians are slightly less deferential to authority than are Americans—an amazing change considering where each country started. Authority in Canada is now typically an upper middle class authority, rather than an upper class authority. Founded on colonial and counter-revolutionary concepts, Canada was, in its early history, tolerant of ruling elites, deferent to authority and accepting of ascribed status. Today, Canadians are less tolerant of an elite class, less deferential and less accepting. Canadians have high tolerance for ambiguity and uncertainity and support a mosaic of opinion. For example, Canadians recognize political parties from across a broad political spectrum—as well as a political party, at the federal level, which has the goal of separating the Province of Quebec from the rest of the country.

The public relations industry in Canada has been affected by the country's evolving culture in a number of ways, such as:

- Practitioners employ a cross-section of cultural and racial sources for marketing and public good messages, including visible minorities and women, rather than rely on traditional elites or men as message authorities.

- Communication programs and communication product messages are conceptualized, developed and implemented differently for various minority subcultures, not only for French Canadians, as one would expect, but also for smaller but still distinct ethnic groups.

- Both the public and private sectors in Canada produce communication vehicles in a variety of languages.

- Canada has a tradition of comedy based on being non-deferential to authority. From Prime Ministers to rock stars to wealthy businessmen, all "elities" are fair game for satire and ridicule. This tradition implicitly permeates public relations practice since most Canadians do not support celebrity-obsessed culture, by adulating and assigning status to celebrities. Canadians believe more in knocking high-flying "stars" down. Canadians go to the United States to be seen as "famous."

- Few Canadian public relations practitioners have earned entry into the upper middle class professional and executive ranks and garnered the prestige that goes with entry. Most practitioners, and academics for that matter, belong to a middle managerial class both in terms of earnings and in terms of power and prestige.

Mass Media

Canada is served by a comprehensive mass media infrastructure that covers the vast majority of the country. This infrastructure includes local and national daily newspapers, local weekly and monthly newspapers, local and national weekly and monthly magazines, local and national radio, local and national television—with many of these on-line, web-based as well. National radio and television networks reach most of Canada, even to the far reaches of Canada's hinterlands. Canada has an arm's-length, state-owned radio and television network. The Canadian Broadcasting Corporation (CBC) broadcasts in English and Radio-Canada broadcasts in French, both right across the country. Funding for the CBC and Radio-Canada comes from the federal government. Only the two television networks are allowed to sell advertising, in order to increase revenues. A handful of separate private interests own and operate a mixture of for-profit, private radio and/or television broadcast networks and/or individual stations, daily, weekly and/or monthly newspapers and/or magazines. Several provinces operate public community television networks. Over 90 percent of television broadcasts are delivered through cable networks, with most of the balance delivered through satellite service. Canada has recently introduced satellite radio broadcasting.

Freedom of editorial expression regardless of ownership views, editorial objectivity, and the extent of Canadian content are three issues that have been debated and on which Canadian governments have legislated. For example, the Canadian Broadcast Act is based on the premise that broadcast media in Canada should allow the free flow of information and reflect the diversity of various points of view. The Canadian Radio and Television Commission (CRTC) regulates all aspects of the Canadian broadcasting system, including licensing, telecommunications common carriers and service providers. This Commission is at arm's-length from government.

Canadian newspapers, radio stations and television stations are not aligned directly with any particular political party. While an individual paper or station may have a particular editorial slant or bias that leans left or right or may favour the policies of a particular party, reporting is arguably objective and each medium provides other viewpoints through the use of independent columnists and/or op ed guest writers. Owners of media outlets are required to take a hands-off approach to editorial control and content. By and large, media editors enjoy a high degree of editorial freedom. For the most part, editorial control is not subject to the "sensationalization" of news and information—the use of news and information as a marketing tool. While the CBC has a mandate to promote Canadian identity, the news section's role is to cover and reflect Canada to Canadians. The role of the CBC is neither to promote the government of the day nor its policies.

Canada has participated along with the United States and other members of the Organization for Economic Cooperation and Development (OECD) in a series of Adult Literacy and Life Skills surveys. Canadian adult literacy scores rank it in the middle to top end of the survey, behind countries such as Norway, but ahead of the United States. Research in Canada shows that newspaper readership is dropping, television viewing is holding steady and internet use is rapidly increasing.

It is generally recognized that most Canadians, individually or as members of groups, have a high degree of access to Canadian mass media. There are no political or legal or military gatekeepers. Governments, corporations and interest group activists have direct access to the media, both to private and to public media outlets. The media in Canada is not paid by information providers to publish information. There are no "information subsidies" required from journalists, in order to ensure the media outlet publishes information they provide.

The public relations industry in Canada has been affected by the country's mass media environment in a number of ways:

- Public relations practitioners have a smorgasbord of options available to them when they want to have the media cover a story.
- Media journalists have professional standards to uphold and for the most part the relationship between journalists and public relations practitioners is on a professional basis.
- Media relations in Canada is about the practitioner pitching a story idea to the media and about responding to media initiated requests for information and interviews.

Case Study

Political change is typically non-violent in Canada, more incremental than revolutionary. Increasingly, this has involved extensive consultation with and engagement of Canadians. This feature has changed the role of public relations in Canada, both in the public and private sectors.

Background

In the 1980s and 1990s, constitutional change engaged Canadians like no other period in the country's history, including the repatriation of the Canadian consitution from Great Britain and the introduction of a Charter of Rights and Freedoms in the early 1980s, the two referendums held in 1980 and 1995 by the Province of Quebec on whether to separate from the Canadian federation, and the two constitutional change processes on the division of federal and provincial powers called the Meech Lake Accord (1987) and the Charlotte-town Accord (1992). It can be argued that in this period the politics of the country changed from politics of elite accommodation to politics of direct democracy.

Situation

The Charlottetown Accord process in the early 1990s was the most telling. Aligned with the *Yes* forces were the country's political and business elites. The *No* side—those opposed to the proposed constitutional changes—were a collection of interest groups and individual citizens (public opinion polls suggested that the majority of Canadians were initially opposed to the proposals). All four of the Grunig and Hunt (Grunig, J. E. and Grunig, L.A. 1992) models of public relations were practiced during the referendum campaign. If the goals of the first three models were respectively manipulation, education and persuasion, the goal of the last model was dialogue. The efforts of the *Yes* forces were concentrated more on models one through three. The *No* efforts were focused on number four primarily, with some application in model two and an occassional foray into number one, especially near the end. Ultimately, the constitutional proposals were defeated.

Analysis

Post referendum research showed that while knowledge (what was in the accord) was important, full understanding (of the consequences of each proposal; of the various positions) was more important. Full understanding only came through active engagement, particularly through personal participation (phoning in to a radio show; going to a public forum; discussing with peers at a meeting; etc.). That is, non-formal political participation trumped a formal information dump. The majority of Canadians were put off by being told how to vote. More citizens changed their initial support based on discussions with peers, neighbors, co-workers and friends than on information received from any other source. After the Meech Lake and Charlottetown Accord processes, it is doubtful if sub-stantive, large-scale political change will occur in Canada without the direct involvement and participation of Canadian citizens. From a public relations perspective, the longer term effect in Canada has been a greater emphasis on consultation and engagement. This onus has transferred to the private sector, notably in regulated industries such as oil and gas development where there now are formal and comprehensive two-way symmetrical communication and consultation processes.

CONCLUSION

Public relations in Canada is a well-developed occupation. Though not a large occu-pational category, the number of practitioners and consultants has grown substantially. Public relations in Canada is not recognized as a profession. Over the years, public relations member associations have shown strengths in networking and professional development, and weaknesses in accreditation, regulation and advocacy. Public relations practice in Canada has been, and is, greatly influenced by that in the United States—from text books to trade and association magazines to ownership of consulting firms. Standards and quality of practice are similar. Emphasis is different, given Canada's differing political structure and culture—one based on accommodation, collective rights, bilingualism and biculturalism, individual rights and multiculturalism.

REFERENCES

Amyot, D. and Likely, F. "Building on Strength: Recent Changes to the Communications Function in the Federal Government." Canadian Government Executive. August/September. 2004.

Anderson, W. "Creating the National Pastime: The Antecedents of Major League Baseball Public Relations." Media History Monographs. Volume 4(2). Retrieved from http://facstaff.elon.edu/dcopeland/mhm/mhmjour4–2.htm September 15, 2007.

Bartha, P. F. "Key concepts of issues management." Canadian Business Review. Summer. 1984.

Bartha, P. F. "Incorporating Public Affairs in Business Management: Problems and Opportunities." In Murray, V.V. (ed) Theories of Business-Government Relations. Trans Canada Press. Toronto. 1985.

Bartha, P. "Issues Management: Theory and Practice." In Baetz, M. (ed.) Readings and Canadian Cases in Business, Government and Society. Nelson Canada. Toronto. 1993.

Basin, I. "A Century of Spin." CBC Radio (A weekly radio Series about Spin, the Spinners and the Spun). Retrieved from http://www.cbc.ca/news/background/spincycles/ September 15, 2007.

Bernier, M-F., Demers, F., Lavigne, A., Moumouni, C. and Watine, T. Pratiques Novatrices en Communication Publiques: Journalisme, Relations Publiques et Publicité. Les Presses de l'Université Laval. Sainte-Foy. 2005.

Bowles, J. "Consultants at the Crossroads." Marketing Magazine Supplement: Focus on Public Relations. January 25, 1988.

Brown, G. D. "A Brief History and Review of Public Relations in Canada." In Herbert, W. B. and Jenkins, R.G. (eds.) Public Relations in Canada: Some Perspectives. Fitzhenry and Whiteside. Toronto. 1984.

Carney, W. W. In the News: the Practice of Media Relations in Canada. University of Alberta Press. Edmonton. 2002.

Center for Media and Democracy 2007. Retrieved from http://www.sourcewatch.org/index.php?title=Public_Relations_Society_of_America September 15, 2007.

Cooper, J. Crisis Communications in Canada: A Practical Approach. Centennial College Press. Toronto. 2007.

Council of Canadian Public Relations Firms. Retrieved from http://www.ccprf.ca/ September 15 2007.

CPRS. "The Future of Public Relations." Position Paper. National Conference Discussion. June. 1989.

CPRS Introduction. Retrieved from http://www.cprs.ca/Welcome/e_Welcome.htm September 15, 2007.

CPRS Annual Report 2004: Page 11; 2007 annual report Page 11. Retrieved from http://www.cprs.ca/files/e_AnnualReport07.pdf September 15, 2007.

Cutlip, S. The Unseen Power: Public Relations A History. Lawrence Erlbaum Associates. Hillsdale, NJ. 1994.

Cutlip, S. Public Relations History from the 17th to the 20th Century: The Antecedents. Lawrence Erlbaum Associates. Hillsdale, N.J. 1995.

Cutlip, S., Center, A. H. and Broom, G. M. Effective Public Relations. 7th ed. Prentice-Hall. Englewood Cliffs, N.J. 1994.

Czarnecki, A. Crisis Communications: A Primer for Teams. iUniverse. 2007.

Dagenais, B. Le métier de la relationniste. Les Presses de l'Université Laval. Sainte-Foy. 1997.

Dagenais, B. Le Plan de Communication. Les Presses de l'Université Laval. Sainte-Foy. 1998.

Delbridge, P. "Advocacy Groups and the Act of Coalition Building." In Wright, W.J. and DuVernet, C.J. (eds) The Canadian Public Affairs Handbook: Maximizing Markets, Protecting Bottom Lines. Carswell. Toronto. 1988.

Devereaux Ferguson, S. Mastering the Public Opinion Challenge. Irwin. New York. 1994.

Devereaux Ferguson, S., and Johansen, P. "History of Public Relations in Canada." In Robert Heath (ed.) Encyclopedia of Public Relations (pp. 111–116). Sage Publications, Thousand Oaks, CA. 2005.

Donoghue, J. PR: *Fifty Years in the Field*. Dundurn Press. Toronto. 1993.

Edgett, R. "Toward an Ethical Framework for Advocacy in Public Relations." *Journal of Public Relations Research*. Vol. 14(1); 1–26. 2002.

Emms, M. "The Origins of Public Relations as an Occupation in Canada." Unpublished Master Thesis. Department of Communication Studies. Concordia University. Montreal. 1995.

Erb, B. M. "Public Relations in Government." In Herbert, W.B. and Jenkins, R.G. (eds.) *Public Relations in Canada: Some Perspectives*. Fitzhenry and Whiteside. Toronto. 1984.

Ewen, S. *PR! A Social History of Spin*. Basic Books. New York. 1996.

Fleisher, C. S. *Assessing, Managing and Maximizing Public Affairs Performance*. Public Affairs Council. Washington. 1997.

Fleisher, C. S. "Global Development of Public Affairs." In Fleisher, C.S. and Harris, P. Eds. *Handbook of Public Affairs*. Sage Publications. London. 2005.

Flynn, T. "A Delicate Equilibrium: Balancing Theory, Practice, and Outcomes." *Journal of Public Relations Research*. Vol. 18(2); 191–201. 2006.

Forstner, G. and Bales, J. "Building Dialog into the Public Consultation Process, Part One." *Public Relations Quarterly*. 37(3). Fall 1992.

Forstner, G. and Bales, J. "Building Dialog into the Public Consultation Process, Part Two." *Public Relations Quarterly*. 37(4). Winter 1992.

Frappier, G. and Likely, F. "Defining Leadership Roles in the Canadian Government." *Strategic Communication Management*. Melcrum Publishing. Vol 9(1). December/January. 2005.

Gausden, M. B. "Public Relations and Canadian Banking." In Herbert, W.B. and Jenkins, R.G. (eds.) *Public Relations in Canada: Some Perspectives*. Fitzhenry and Whiteside. Toronto. 1984.

Geddes, J. "Meech Lake Ten Years After." *MacLean's Magazine*. June 19, 2000. Retrieved from http://www.thecanadianencyclopedia.com/index.cfm?PgNm=TCEandParams=M1ARTM0012191 September 15, 2007.

Gollner, A. B. *Social Change and Corporate Strategy*. Issue Action Publications. Stamford, Connecticut. 1983.

Gollner, A. B. and Shayon, D. R. *Levering the Impact of Public Affairs*. HRN. Philadelphia. 1984.

Gossage, P. Retrieved from http://www.ccprf.ca/ September 15, 2007.

Government of Canada. "Managing Government Communications in the 1990s." Discussion Paper. Federal Communications Council. November 1992.

Government of Canada. Canadian Government Job Futures. Retrieved from http://www.jobfutures.ca/noc/5124p4.shtml September 15 2007.

Grunig, J. E. and Grunig L. A. "Models of Public Relations and Communication." In Grunig, J.E. (ed). *Excellence in Public Relations and Communication Management*. Lawrence Erlbaum Associates. Mahwah, New Jersey. 1992.

Grunig L. A., Grunig, J. E. and Dozier D. M. *Excellent Public Relations and Effective Organizations: A Study of Communication Management in Three Countries*. Lawrence Erlbaum Associates. Mahwah, New Jersey. 2002.

Guiniven, J. E. "Dealing with Activism in Canada: An Ideal Cultural Fit for the Two-Way Symmetrical Model." *Public Relation Review*. Vol 28(4); 393–402. October 2002.

Hallahan, K. "W.L. Mackenzie King: Rockefeller's other public relations counselor in Colorado." *Journal of Public Relations Research*. 29(4); 410–415. 2003.

Hamilton, S. *A Communications Audit Handbook: Helping Organizations Communicate*. Longman. New York. 1987.

Hammond, R. Retrieved from http://www.cprs.ca/Jack_Yocom/Ruth_Hammond.asp. September 15, 2007.

Harris, R. "Go Big or Stay Small." Report on Market Research. *Marketing Magazine*. September 27, 2004. Retrieved from http://www.marketingmag.ca/magazine/current/market_research_rpt/article.jsp?content=20040927_63740_63740. September 15, 2007.

Herbert, W. B. and Jenkins, R. G. (eds.) *Public Relations in Canada: Some Perspectives*. Fitzhenry and Whiteside. Toronto. 1984.

Hunt, T. and Grunig, J. E. *Managing Public Relations*. Holt, Rinehart and Winston. New York. 1984.

IABC Calgary. Retrieved from http://www.iabccalgary.com/advertising/default.aspx September 15, 2007.

IABC Toronto. Retreived from http://toronto.iabc.com/members/ September 15, 2007.

Institute of Communication Agencies. Retrieved from http://www.ica-ad.com/pro-dev-caap.cfm September 15, 2007.

Johansen, P. "Professionalization and the Birth of the Canadian Public Relations Society." Presentation to the Canadian Communication Association. Ottawa. June. 1998.

Johansen, P. "Professionalization, Building Respectability, and the Birth of the Canadian Public Relations Society." *Journalism Studies*. Vol 2(1); 55–71. 2001

Johansen, P. "International Public Relations: Canadian Perspectives." Presentation for preliminary program. International Communication Association. San Diego, California. May. 2003.

Johnson, J. "Issues Management—What are the Issues?" *Business Quarterly*. University of Western Ontario. Vol. 48; 22–31. Autumn. 1983.

Johnston, R., Blais, A., Gidengil, E. and Nevit, N. *The Challenge of Direct Democracy: The 1992 Canadian Referendum*. McGill-Queen's University Press. Montreal. 1996.

Kanji, M. and Nevitte, N. "Who are the most differential—Canadians or Americans?" In Thomas, D.M. *Canada and the United States: Differences that Count*. Broadview Press. Toronto. 2000.

Knott, L. *Plain Talk About Public Relations*. McClelland and Stewart. Toronto. 1961.

Likely, F. "Winning PR War Requires a Different Dialogue with Public." Op Ed Page article. *The Ottawa Citizen*. October 22, 1992.

Likely, F. "Beyond the Manager and the Technician Roles: Exploring an Executive or Executive Leader Role for the Head of a PR/Communication Function." International Public Relations Research Conference. Miami. Proceedings. 2004.

Likely, F. "The Rise of the Relationship Manager." *Strategic Communication Management*. Melcrum Publishing. Vol 9(4). June/July. 2005.

Lipset, S. M. *Continental Divide: The Values and Institutions of the United States and Canada*. Routledge. NY. 1990.

McNamarra, P. Retrieved from http://www.ccprf.ca/ September 15, 2007.

Maisonneuve, D., Lamarche, J-F and St Amand, Y. *Les Relations Publiques dans une Société en Mouvance*. Les Presses de l'Université du Québec. Sainte-Foy. 2003.

Miller, K. S. "U.S. Public Relations History: Knowledge and Limitations." *Communications Yearbook*. 23; 404. 2000.

Mindszenthy, B., Watson, T. A. G. and Kock, W. *No Surprises: The Crisis Communication Management System*. Bedford House Publishing. Toronto. 1988.

Newsom, D., VanSlyke Turk, J. and Kruckeberg, D. *This is PR: the Realities of Public Relations*. Wadsworth. Belmont, CA. 1996.

Parsons, P. "Framework for Analysis of Conflicting Loyalties." *Public Relations Review*. Vol 19(1); 49–5. 1993.

Parsons, P. A. *Manager's Guide to PR Projects: A Practical Approach*. Lawrence Erlbaum Associates. Hillsdale, NJ. 2003.

Parsons, P. *Ethics in Public Relations: A Guide to Best Practice*. Kogan Page. London. 2004.

Parsons, P. Retrieved from http://www.prcanada.ca/columns.htm (from the now defunct PR Canada web site). September 15, 2007.

Pearson, R. "Reviewing Albert J. Sullivan's Theory of Public Relations Ethics." *Public Relations Review*. Vol 15(2); 52–62. Summer. 1989.

Pearson, R. "Business Ethics as Communication Ethics: Public Relations Practice and the Idea of Dialogue." In Botan, C and Hazleton, V. (eds) *Public Relations Theory*. Lawrence Erlbaum Associates. Hillsdale, NJ. 1989.

Pearson, R. "Ethical Values or Strategic Values? The Two Faces of Systems Theory in Public Relations. In Grunig, L.A. and Grunig, J.E (eds) *Public Relations Research Annual*. Lawrence Erlbaum Associates. Vol 2. 1990.

Pearson, R. "Perspectives on Public Relations History." *Public Relations Review*. Volume 16(3): 27–38. Autumn. 1990.

Pettigrew, P. Remarks. Couchiching Institute of Public Affairs. 76th conference. August 12, 2007.

Piekos, J. M. and Einsiedel, E. F. "Roles and Program Evaluation Techniques Among Canadian Public Relations Practitioners." In Grunig, L.A. and Grunig, J.E (eds) *Public Relations Research Annual*. Lawrence Erlbaum Associates. Vol 2. 1990.

Pross, A. P. (ed). *Pressure Group Behaviour in Canadian Politics*. McGraw-Hill Ryerson. Toronto. 1975.

Pross, A. P. *Group Politics and Public Policy*. Oxford University Press. Toronto. 1986.

PR Canada. Retrieved from http://www.prcanada.ca/ September 15, 2007.

PRSA. Retrieved from http://www.prsa.org/aboutUs/mission.html September 15, 2007.

Redmond, J. and Likely, F. "Rebuilding Communication in the Federal Government of Canada." *Strategic Communication Management*. Melcrum Publishing. Vol 6(6). 2002.

Redmond, J. and Likely, F. "Mission Possible: Renewing the Communications Function in the Federal Government." Canadian Government Executive. Issue 4. 2002.

Reid, A. "Canada at the Crossroads: Public Opinion and the National Unity Debate." In Byers, M. (ed) *The Empire Club of Canada Speeches 1990–1991*. The Empire Club Foundation. Toronto. pp. 316–33. 1992. Retrieved from http://www.empireclubfoundation.com/details.asp?SpeechID=1563andFT=yes

Romanow, W. I. and Soderlund, W. C. *Media Canada: An Introductory Analysis*. 2nd ed. Copp Clark. Toronto. 1996.

Root, M. G. "Canadian Public Relations Educational Standards." In Herbert, W.B. and Jenkins, R.G. (eds.) *Public Relations in Canada: Some Perspectives*. Fitzhenry and Whiteside. Toronto. 1984.

Rose, J. W. *Making "Pictures in our Head": Government Advertising in Canada*. Praeger/Greenwood. 2000.

Saykaly, M. C. *Guide to Public Opinion Research*. Ottawa. Optimum Consultants. 1985.

Scrimger, J. "Women in Canadian Public Relations." *Public Relations Review*. Vol 11(3); 40–46. Autumn. 1985.

Scrimger, J. and Richards, T. "Public relations battles and wars: Journalistic clichés and the potential for resolution (Canada)." *Journal of Public Relations Research*. 29(4); 485–502. 2003.

Seiler, T. M. "Melting Pot and Mosaic: Images and Realities." In Thomas, D.M. (ed) *Canada and the United States: Differences that Count*. Broadview Press. Toronto. 2000.

Shaw, J. and Shaw, P. "Stakeholder Relationships in Canada: In Partnership With Community." In Fleisher, C.S. and Harris, P. (eds) *Handbook of Public Affairs*. Sage Publications. London. 2005.

Shiller, E. (ed). *The Canadian Guide to Managing the Media*. Prentice-Hall Canada. Scarborough. Ontario. 1994.

Stanley, G. "Beyond Communications: Issues Managament in the 1980s—an Introduction." Public Issues Group. Ottawa. 1979.

Taylor, I. *Mediaspeak: The Bold New Guide to Public Relations and Reputation Management*. LB Pub. Services. Toronto. 1999.

Tisdall, C. Retrieved from http://www.cprs.ca/Jack_Yocom/Charles_Tisdall.asp. September 15, 2007.

Wilcox, D. L., Ault, P. H. and Agee, W. K. *Public Relations: Strategies and Tactics*. 5th ed. Longman. New York. 1998.

Wright, W. J. and DuVernet, C. J. (eds). *The Canadian Public Affairs Handbook: Maximizing Markets, Protecting Bottom Lines*. Carswell. Toronto. 1988.

32

The Public Relations Industry in Mexico: From Amateurship to the Construction of a Discipline

María Antonieta Rebeil Corella[1]

Alberto Montoya Martín del Campo

Jorge Alberto Hidalgo Toledo

INTRODUCTION

For many years, the public relations industry in Mexico has struggled to become a discipline and get more professionalized. We begin this chapter with an analysis of the nature of the public relations industry, providing the definition of the concept of public relations itself, following with a history of the evolution of the public relations profession in the country, its agencies and its associations. We contend that growing from amateurship and into a professional discipline, public relations activities in the nation owe their maturity to activities carried out by the existing associations and to the fact that public relations is now being formally taught in universities all over the Mexican territory.

In the second part of the chapter we discuss the relationship between public relations and environmental variables. Public relations activities constantly grapple with a complex panorama prevailing in Mexico. The political, economic, legal and activist situations are described as well as their implications for the public relations industry, are put forth in the

---

[1] The authors acknowledge the contributions of the research team of the Centro de Investigación para la Comunicación Aplicada (Center for Applied Communication Research), Escuela de Comunicación, Universidad Anáhuac Mexico Norte: Cándido Pérez Hernández, Guillermo Lemus Legaspi, Rodrigo A. Reyes Chacha and Diana Vega García.

context of these economic and political issues. National conditions that have an enormous influence on public relations activities are the cultural specificities of the country's people and their ways of life. The third part of the study offers an analysis of the cultural traits of Mexican citizens that are specific to them.

The fourth part of the chapter explores the media panorama in Mexico, describing mass communication as it is controlled mainly by economic power and to some extent by public clout, its extension, its penetration capacity and access by different segments in society.

Some of the conclusions the chapter provides have to do with: 1) how public relations activities become more effective as they develop into a part of a more general communication strategy in organizations integrating all facets of organizational communication: advertising, corporate and internal communications, thus creating a global communication strategy; 2) given the complexity of the Mexican economic, political and cultural environment, public relations agencies and associations must keep a constant watch for change, opportunities and difficulties; 3) among the major problems the public relations industry faces in Mexico are clients' limited view of public relations activities and potential, over usage of mass media applications and limited below the line and one-to-one communication strategies; 4) there are abundant perspectives of growth for the industry if some obstacles are efficiently tackled. We conclude the chapter by providing a case study of *Revive Chapultepec (Come Alive, Chapultepec!)*.

THE NATURE AND STATUS OF PUBLIC RELATIONS PRACTICE IN MÉXICO

The early years of development were not easy for public relations professionals in Mexico. The general public considered public relations, first of all, not as a career in and of itself and secondly, as an occupation where professionals sought to gain the goodwill of the media, organizations and other government institutions through apparently obscure means. However, the public relations profession has gained a shine of its own in more recent years. With the exception of few cases, the public relations industry works on the basis of strategic planning and professionalized policies and methods. Among others, a factor that has influenced the profession positively is its coming together into public relations organizations such as the Association of Mexican Public Relations Professionals (ProRP) and the Mexican Association of Communicators (AMCO). By now the profession is also being taught within universities around the nation. Many experts in the country have through the years put forth a basic proposition: public relations should be considered as a component of the comprising concept of Organizational Communication where marketing/advertising communication, internal communication, corporate communication and public relations are included (Llano, 2007[2], Rebeil, 2000).

Public Relations as a Concept

In Mexico, it is a well known fact that public relations is addressed as a subdiscipline of the organizational communication body of theory (Grunig, 1989). We consider that although organizational communication, specifically corporate communication which is a component of it, provides a basic frame of reference for the definition of public relations, (Rebeil, 2000), public relations activities go a lot further than the strategic information/communication/motivation *modus operandi*, of organizational communication. Few theorists have

---

[2] S. Llano (Personal Interview), Oct. 17, 2007.

worked on public relations as a discipline in and of itself. We contend that public relations has a basic and structural purpose in society and as all disciplines and sub disciplines must be practiced on the rationale of social responsibility. We also put forth the idea that organizational communication, as an arena where internal, market/advertising and cor- porative/public relations communications should synchronize their efforts with the purpose of building and making organizations more efficient (Llano, 2007; Rebeil, 2000, 2007).

History of Public Relations in Mexico

In Mexico, as most other countries around the world, the Public Relations discipline was born as an occupation a long time before it began to be taught within universities. The first public relations agency, Agencia Mexicana de Relaciones Públicas, in the country dates to 1949, founded by Federico Sánchez Fogarty (Bonilla, 2002). After that, the industry began growing slowly, at first acting as a support to different bodies such as the Confederación de Cámaras Industriales (COCAMIN), the Cámara Nacional de la Industria Farmacéutica (CANIFARMA) and other associations, rather than to specific firms. Large groupings require a lot of public relations assistance. Gradually, more local public relations agencies began to appear in Mexican territory. It should be said that promotion agencies frequently appeared, sometimes doing public relations jobs as well as promotional activities for their clients. Such are the cases of Grupo Prom (1971); Advertising and Promotion (1978); Marketing and Promotion (1979) and Cosmic (1980) (Baran and Hidalgo, 2005).

By 1987, there were six public relations agencies in the country. However, by 2002 they amounted to 40 (ProRP, 2002). In summary, out of the 90 agencies participating in the 2006 ProRP Report, 12 percent were founded in the 1980s or before; 42 percent were started during the 1990s; 19 percent during the year 2000 and 27 percent were founded between 2001 and 2007 (ProRP, 2006). However, another event was taking place in the country, which was to change the face of the public relations industry in Mexico. Foreign investment and new international joint strategies had begun to penetrate the industry.

Globalization and NAFTA, Their Impact on the Public Relations Industry

GCI Group, affiliated to Grey Inc., was the first external agency to penetrate the Mexican market. This event took place back in 1980 when the Alonso y Asociados Public Relations Agency, a pioneer in the business since 1963, decided to receive investment and to work jointly with the GCI Group. Burson-Marsteller, affiliated to Young and Rubicam Inc., came in next, at first in association with Omo Delta, and later acquired the agency from its owner, Fernando Mariscal. Maning Selvage & Lee came next into the Mexican market by joining together with Sylvia Pendás, a public relations expert. This company is now represented by Dickins y Asociados. Fleischman-Hillard established in the country on its own. Edelman entered Mexico as a joint business with Comunicaciones Interamericanas. At present, Comunicaciones Interamericanas has been absorbed and its new name is Edelman Mexico. Ketchum Public Relations and Hill & Knowlton introduced themselves into the Mexican arena as a business on their own. Porter-Novelli joined Martec. Golin/ Harris merged with Zimat, the property of Bruno Newman and Associates, the case study found at the end of this chapter. As a result, during this brief time span (1980–2007), ten of the USA's most important firms are doing business in the Mexican market. As a response, Mexican institutions and organizations, as well as political parties and their candidates (even Presidents), have contracted these agencies for economic and political services (Bonilla, 2002).

From a total of 90 public relations agencies that participated in the ProRP study (ProRP, 2006), 64 percent of them have an alliance of some sort with international agencies. This fact is advantageous for the agencies themselves because they can provide services in several countries and not only in Mexico. 56 percent of these agencies offer services to US firms and institutions, 56 percent to other Latin American countries, 28 percent to Europe and 8 percent to Canada (ProRP, 2006).

Public Relations Education

Journalism as a discipline and Communication Sciences have been available within Mexican higher education institutions since 1949 and 1960, respectively. Interestingly, by 1976, the first universities to focus on Public Relations as part of the Communication profession were Universidad Latinoamericana and Universidad del Pacífico. Public relations as a discipline was introduced as part of the contents an expert in communication has to master in order to be fully acknowledged as a professional in the area. However, in many Mexican universities, Public Relations alongside Organizational Communication and Advertising were banned from several academic programs on account of being considered less academic and more pro-capitalism and pro-imperialism, during a period starting in the early 1970s and lasting through the late 1980s. This tendency has now been reversed, leaving only a few cases where the discipline is still rejected.

Today more and more universities include in their Communication BA and MA programs, Advertising, Organizational Communication and Public Relations. These disciplines have become the favorite teaching matter in the context of Masters Degree programs seeking to professionalize students. Furthermore, for specialization purposes within the BA degree programs, public relations is a favorite, together with Journalism and Advertising (Rebeil and Hernández, in press).

Public Relations Associations

Although we can date the first public relations agency back to 1949, alliances and grouping among them can be dated to 1960, when pioneer Sánchez Fogarty was elected president of the recently created Asociación Mexicana de Profesionales en Relaciones Públicas (Mexican Association of Public Relations Professionals (ProRP)), and organized the First Inter American Conference of Public Relations Associations. The Asociación Mexicana de Profesionales en Relaciones Públicas lasted through 1978 when it disappeared after a crisis.

However, the need for association among public relations and similar professions led to the founding of the Mexican Association of Internal Communication (AMCI) as early as 1973. In 1986, it changed its name to the Mexican Association of Organizational Communicators (AMCO), in order to include among its associates, public relations experts. In 1992, the Mexican Association of Marketing Research and Public Opinion Agencies (AMAI) was founded, a major grouping which produces many of the industry's statistics and strategic orientations for professionals in communication and public relations.

In 1996, the Mexican Association of Public Relations Professionals (ProRP) reappeared on the Mexican scene, with eight public relations organized agencies. In 2004, it changed its name to Asociación de Profesionales de Relaciones Públicas, leaving out the adjective, *Mexican*. Actually, it has 20 to 30 members including independent professionals. ProRP is a central association providing guidelines for the development of the industry. Its President is Marco V. Herrera from Grupo Public International Agency (ProRP, 2007).

This Association organized the first International Congress of Public Relations, 2007. More than 200 public relations consultants participated in it and it took place in Mexico City.

The Latin American Association of Public Relations B.A. Degrees was founded in August, 1999 in Peru. Of its 12 members, only one is Mexican: the Autonomous University of Guadalajara.

The country has an additional Public Relations Association. It works locally within the South Baja California region. Its name is Public Relations Association of Los Cabos. It has 30 members (Public Relations professionals) and was founded on September 3, 2003 by Ángeles Miroslava Bautista, its first president. Presently, Daniel Uribe Pedraza is the president of the Association (Asociación de Relaciones Públicas de Los Cabos, 2007).

Market Size of the PR Profession and Reason for its Growth in Mexico

Among the strategies agencies use in Mexico for the construction of a brand is the integration of marketing and public relations activities. The strategic combination of marketing activities and public relations has given the industry a renewed boost and made the services it renders more complete.

Looking back, the industry has grown in the following way: in 1997, the industry's earnings were 140 million Mexican pesos ($12,962,962.96 USD), by 2001 they summed to 546 million Mexican pesos ($50,555,555.55 USD),[3] by 2005, it was 714 million Mexican pesos ($66,111,111.11 USD) and in 2006, 800 million Mexican pesos ($74,074,074.07 USD): a significant growth rate of 12 percent for the period 2005–2006 (Ríos, August, 2007) (Banco de Mexico, 2007). Between 2006 and 2007, the industry's earnings increased 100 million Mexican pesos ($9,259,259.26 USD), a growth rate of 12.5 percent for this period (Ríos, August, 2007).

Public relations in Mexico owes its development to several reasons: 1) the specialization public relations agencies have acquired in relation to specific market segments and the positioning of a label or a product; 2) 360 degrees communication strategies; 3) the preference of Mexican publicists for personal communication with consumers; 4) integrated marketing strategies; 5) smaller public relations firms specialization in segments with little or no attention on the part of the larger agencies; 6) universities' endeavors around the country for providing better and more specialized professionals in the area; 7) special attention paid to businesses and public institutions' credibility and reputation; 8) the need for lobbying and negotiation with authorities and specific sectors of society; 9) the search for new market opportunities; 10) crisis prevention; 11) growing need for social responsibility programs on the part of enterprises and public institutions; 12) firms' and agencies' alliances for the provision of more and better public relations courses, seminars and conferences; 13) evolution of the freedom of expression regulation in the country; 14) the closer attention paid to corporations an the part of government and consumers.

Market value of the public relations industry is 1,753 million Mexican pesos (162,314.81 USD). This figure includes income of public relations agencies, and corporations that include public relations departments within their organization (Ríos, August, 2007) (Banco de Mexico, 2007).

---

[3] Exchange rate at 10.80 Mexican pesos per USD, Banco de Mexico, October 15, 2007.

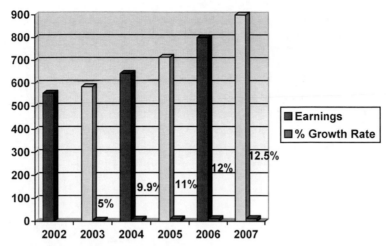

FIG. 32.1 Public Relations Industry Growth in Mexico 2002–2007 (Numbers in millions of Mexican pesos)
Source: Ríos, in *Merca2.0*, August, 2007

The Nature and Status of Public Relations Practice in Mexico

In 2005, public relations agencies were reported to manage a total of 717 different accounts, an amount registering a 28 percent growth rate by 2006. The number of employees in the industry has also increased from 583, for the year 2005, to 689 for 2006. Public relations top 10 agencies earnings vary very little from year to year. The same top 10 have retained their positions for the past five years. Earning differences from the top public relations agency vary significantly from those of the agency in second place. The public relations industry shows a constant growth from 2003 to 2006. The number of accounts varies significantly. For some agencies there is an increase in account numbers. For others, account numbers appear to be lessening. Notwithstanding, earnings continue to increase. Some agencies show a significant growth rate varying from 63 percent to 280 percent (Table 32.1).

The services rendered by public relations agencies in Mexico are: corporate public relations (72 percent of the agencies); integral communication (36 percent); public relations for branding (36 percent); events organization (33 percent); media relations (44 percent); social responsibility (53 percent); crisis communication (44 percent); fashion and lifestyles (25 percent); lobbying (25 percent).

Difficulties for Development

There are several major difficulties affecting the expansion of the public relations industry in the country. Clients in Mexico fall short of understanding and employing the public relations potential to its maximum extent. There is over emphasis on mass media usage. There is limited vision of the potential of organizational organization, marketing and public relations. Next, there is insufficient support provided to public relations activities on the part of CEOs. Although the discipline's professionals are efficient in applying marketing research, promotion and advertising, most marketing agencies in Mexico lack human resources with specialized expertise in public relations. Clients lack sufficient knowledge of the public relations agency's potential to benefit their businesses. There is a generalized

TABLE 32.1

Ranking of PR Agencies in Mexico for 2006, Ríos, in *Merca2.0*, August, 2007

Rank 2005	Rank 2006	Agency	Earnings 2005	Earnings 2006	Growth rate 2005 vs. 2006 (%)	Number of Accounts 2005	Number of Accounts 2006	Accounts Variance 2005 vs. 2006
			Figures in Mexican pesos					
1	1	Zimat Consultores Comunicación Total	118,596,526	138,007,172	16.4	47	48	2.1
3	2	Guerra Castellanos y Asociados Comunicación	32,380,662	43,931,089	35.7	48	63	31.3
2	3	The Jeffrey Group Mexico	34,464,000	39,627,000	15	10	17	70
N/P	4	Edelman Mexico	20,369,580	22,815,640	12	26	16	−38.5
5	5	AB Comunicación	13,170,000	21,895,723	66.3	41	53	29.3
6	6	Infosol	12,500,000	13,500,000	8	20	24	20
8	7	FWD Consultores	10,500,000	13,200,000	25.7	12	31	158.3
N/P	8	Grupo Investiga	6,580,000	12,850,000	95.3	N/D	40	N/D
10	9	PLANECO	10,568,240	12,595,000	19.2	16	11	−31.3
9	10	Arvizu, Comunicación Corporativa	10,124,000	10,254,000	1.3	14	20	42.9
12	11	Organización Internacional	8,680,000	9,850,500	13.5	9	14	55.6
N/P	12	Percepción e Imagen en Medios	6,436,938	9,382,728	45.8	17	12	−29.4
15	13	Alterpraxis	5,460,423	9,070,590	66.1	29	56	93.1
11	14	CB Comunicación	9,000,000	7,000,000	22.2	21	21	0
N/P	15	Par71	1,489,000	5,671,000	280.9	N/D	10	N/D
N/P	16	Mier y Terán & Asociados	3,700,000	5,600,000	51.4	17	19	11.8
7	17	Public International	15,323,000	5,526,000	−63.9	19	6	−68.4
18	18	Contacto, PR & Media Advisors	3,800,000	4,200,000	10.5	8	14	75
N/P	19	Sara Cuéllar Comunicación & Relaciones Publicas	3,960,722	4,156,000	4.9	13	15	15.4
N/P	20	Le Bola de Papel Comunicación	1,200,000	2,000,000	66.7	N/D	10	N/D
N/P	21	IQ PR, Más Que Simple Comunicación	1,600,000	1,800,000	12.5	13	14	7.7
17	22	Consultoría en Relaciones Públicas	1,000,000	1,500,000	50	15	6	−60
19	23	LG Relaciones Públicas	1,601,660	844,933	−47.2	22	9	59.1
N/P	24	Alteizan & Pro	150,000	170,000	13.3	8	7	−12.5

N/D (not available); N/P (non participant).

absence of vision as to the capability of the marketing/public relations mix for boosting an enterprise's credibility and reputation. There is a deficiency of cohesive efforts towards the strengthening of public relations associations in the country. There is a need for promoting the profession at a local level. Competition among agencies has obstructed learning from one another and their successful cases, problems and challenges. Finally, public relations agencies seek more to obtain accounts through competition than through strategic planning policies, hunting for unattended market sectors, the strengthening of their associations' capability to create a better reputation for the industry itself.

Public Relations Industry Challenges in Mexico

Among the most important challenges facing the Mexican public relations industry is the capacity to present itself as an attractive business, one which other firms cannot do without. Corporations and public institutions as well as non government organizations must recognize that the services provided through public relations activities mean added value to the products and services they render to society. This means that the public relations industry should increase its efficiency in selling public relations and providing a clearer idea about how investment in public relations has the potential for increasing sales and a better reputation for any organization.

Introducing the new technologies of information for the support of public relations activities is a vital ingredient in their communication strategies. In Mexico, 22.4 percent of all households own a computer with access to Internet (AMIPCI, 2007). Cellular phones in Mexico have increased from 56 million to 63.2 million between 2006 and 2007 (El Universal, March, 2007). The increase rate is 25.7 percent in 2006 and 13.7 percent in 2007 (AMPCI, 2007) This new technologies increased penetration has given way to more personally directed advertising, promotion and the creation of a reputation that can be carried out more effectively and at a lower cost through the use of Internet and cellular phones. The public relations industry has to make a special effort in packaging its massive communication strategies into the Internet and cellular phones. Other activities, such as generating projects in common with strategic alliances with other groups, organizations and institutions, must be carried out, interpersonally. Thus, interpersonal communication also has an important role but there is a need for training and specialization to be considered seriously by public relations consultants as well as their clients.

Ethics and social responsibility questions are still concentrated within the educational sector in Mexico. However, these ideas and their practice are in the process of becoming more and more popular among firms and institutions of all kinds. The enterprises' image and reputation depend on their ethical behavior. This includes the public relations agencies and individual consultants. A growing interest in the subject is being observed as more conferences are offered on the matter and an increasing amount of books on enterprise ethics and social responsibility are being edited in the country.

ENVIRONMENTAL FACTORS AND THE PUBLIC RELATIONS PRACTICES IN MÉXICO

The Basic Political Structure in Mexico

Mexico is a representative democracy, based on a presidential regime. In the months following the Mexican Revolution of 1910, the *Political Constitution of the United Mexican States* (1917) established a political regime characterized by a focal presidency. This system, which was structured around the strong figure of the President, was reinforced further during the political and economic crisis of 1929–32, given the law that introduced the prohibition of continued reelection of Congress members (Pineda, 2005).

The post-revolutionary regimes that followed this phase consisted of coalitions of regional and class groups, centered around one hegemonic political party, the Partido Revolucionario Institucional (PRI) (Party of the Institutionalized Revolution) which maintained centralized power over a 70-year period, ending in 2000, when the election was won by a different party (Partido de Acción Nacional) (PAN) (National Action Party) (Martínez, 2005).

Revisions and changes within PRI have existed throughout its history. The most remarkable occurred in 1988, the year in which its leftist faction coalesced with several other political forces around Cuauhtémoc Cárdenas, who allegedly was not acknowledged as the winner of the presidential election of that time. The democratic struggle of the left in the following years was repressed through the murder of more than 500 militants and social activists. At that time, several civic groups, social organizations and other political associations emerged. These phenomena promoted and encouraged political change and the evolution of democracy within the country. As a result of these courses of action, the citizens' Instituto Federal Electoral (IFE) (Federal Electoral Institute), a specialized branch of the judiciary power for electoral purposes, was created with the objective of avoiding the executive power's influence in the processes of election of new candidates and the corresponding verification procedures and putting them into the hands of the voters themselves (Martínez, 2005).

Only as recently as 1997, after almost a century of political history, for the first time the hegemonic party (PRI) that held the Presidency for 70 years lost its majority in the House of Representatives. That same year, another event took place: Mexico City's Mayor was elected by the citizens, and not designated directly by the President of the Nation, as had been done from the beginning (Bailleres, 2005).

In the presidential election of 2006, after a bitter and strongly contested campaign, Felipe Calderón was elected President obtaining his triumph by a very slim majority over his opponent, Andrés M. López Obrador, the candidate of the leftist coalition. The vote count difference amounted to no more than 200,000 votes, out of 42 million voters. As a result, the electoral process was considered fraudulent by some parliamentary groups, and the ruling President at that time was not allowed in Congress to deliver his annual address. After the electoral turmoil, it can be said that political institutions in Mexico are still in the process of consolidation (Baqués, 2005).

All of the above has led Congress to discuss even further the election procedures in the country. An additional measure has been introduced in Mexican Legislature through the recent approval (2007) of changes to the Constitution, prohibiting the direct buying of media time by political parties and individuals for the purposes of political advertising in radio and television. This change, still to be ratified by State Legislatures, is the result of the open and uncontrolled political intervention of strong economic groups through the mass media, phenomena made specifically evident in the 2006 presidential election. From now on, media time for political campaigns will be considered as an institutional mechanism for political parties to promote their ideologies and proposals. Political parties, candidates and individuals will not be allowed to buy media time directly and institutional time will be distributed according to the relative vote of political parties in past elections. The media are a contested terrain and these legal changes are aimed at the elimination of paid advertising and information in the media for promoting political preferences, as is now practiced in several European nations (Pineda, 2005).

As of now, formal economic, social and cultural institutions play a limited role in political decisions. There is scant influence on the part of civil society in the political agenda of the country and minimal participation in planning and decisions made within both the legislative and executive powers. These government sections have not provided for fluent and consistent mechanisms for the inclusion of citizens' views in political activities.

There is a lack of development of intermediate institutions within Mexican formal democracy. Rather, the larger business organizations have a much greater capacity to promote their interests and points of view in government. Thus, through the government, large private firms also exercise a big influence in decisions made within workers, peasant and other social organizations (Guerra, 2005).

Political decisions in Mexico are as concentrated as its economic power. It is a natural consequence that social and economic inequalities express themselves in political polarization (Montoya, 2005).

The public's viewpoint is extremely important in this situation because of the fact that public opinion polls and audience research and their changes in perception of public affairs acquire an increased interest for political analysts and for the rest of society. In Mexico also, polls and exit polls following elections are considered progressively more as reference points of citizens' political perceptions and decisions. Electoral results are now constantly compared with previous results in the polls (Alianza Social, 2005).

Public Relations and Political Environment in Mexico

This political environment has a tremendous importance for the public relations industry in an increasingly urban and cosmopolitan society where the scale of the small community has been surpassed by gigantic cities and urban environments, where 75 percent of the Mexican people live. The country needs a public relations industry that is capable of presenting to the public opinion, a pluralistic, diverse, integral and complete view of the country's people and their interests. The different economic sectors, social and ethnic groups that integrate this nation are ever-growing. Public relations' actions have a natural vocation for relating the relevance of particular contributions for the public good, hence an enormous opportunity and responsibility in the Mexican social context where diversity and variety are abundant. Public relations professionals have the responsibility of building bridges among apparently opposing views, clarifying arguments coming from diverse power groups, creating new symbols and images which are inclusive of different opinions and creating an environment of mutual respect and recognition. All of the above, has to do with communicating both form and content, since conflicting social differences must necessarily be resolved if democratic values are to prevail. Public relations activities are relevant in their contribution to a democratic and civic culture, respectful of different groups and supportive of human rights and civil liberties. Furthermore, political candidates seeking public office frequently employ public relations specialists. Public relation agencies have the responsibility of creating the image and reputation of the political candidates, maintaining this image throughout his/her administration period and providing additional support for acquiring either an international public office or locally for the purpose of being hired by national firms as consultant or advisor.

Mexican Economy and Level of Development

Mexico is an emerging medium-sized economy. In 2006, Mexico's GNP was 9,492,312.1 million Mexican pesos (87,899.26 million USD) for a population of 104,860,000, and a

GNP per capita of 8,731.6 pesos (808.48 USD). During a fifty-year period (1932–1982), Mexico had an average 6.5 percent annual growth of GNP, a population growth of 3.5 percent and demonstrated a capacity for increasing its GNP per capita at a rate of 3 percent annually. However, from 1983 to the year 2006, Mexico observed an average 2.4 percent increase in annual growth, and GNP per capita stagnated at an annual rate of 0.3 percent. In short, GNP per capita has languished severely for more than two decades. This structural change left the Mexican government with extremely limited resources for the promotion of wealth in society. In addition to being limited, income distribution skewed even further, Mexico's income and wealth distribution. Today, Mexico is considered among the most unequal societies on the planet, a tendency that has been growing in more recent years. According to the Secretaría de Desarrollo Social (SEDESOL) (Ministry of Social Development) Mexico has 44,700,000 citizens living under poverty conditions, 14,400,000 of which face extreme poverty (SEDESOL quoted in Gómez, 2007). The country, therefore, is having a hard time trying to reduce economic asymmetries and eliminating the still abundant extreme poverty in the nation (Pick and Rebeil, 2005).

The nature of Mexican political economy has changed structurally, emphasizing the role of the private over the public and social sectors; foreign investment over national investment; foreign goods over national production. These tendencies have become particularly strong from the 1988 political regime on, when: a) public policies adopted the strategies of privatizing most public enterprises in the country; b) commercial treaties were established with 42 other nations and specifically NAFTA (North American Foreign Trade Agreement); and c) actions were undertaken, aimed at the reduction of public policies that encouraged the development and growth of the local industrial and agricultural sectors (Corchado, 2000).

Due to the lack of systematic promotion of industrial production from 1998 through 2006, Mexico has accumulated a commercial deficit of 66.4 billion USD. If it were not for the small amount of inbound production and crude oil exports in this period, the commercial deficit would have reached 405 billion USD.

Out of Mexico's total population, 14.7 million are employed formally and almost 3 million employed within the public sector, summing to almost 18 million formal jobs in the country. There is an estimate of 20 million informal jobs out of a total of 42.4 million people within the economically active population. The informal economy has grown exponentially since 1993 (STPS, 2007, Verdusco, 2007).

Public spending for 2006 represents 23 percent of GNP, an extreme reduction compared to the allocation of 44 percent reached in 1982. This curtailment represents an abnormal and limited public spending policy in the country, in comparison to the corresponding levels in the US of 32 percent and an amount for OECD countries of 36 percent, and for European nations an average of 40 percent (Horcacitas, 2005).

Under these conditions it is almost impossible to grow at the rate of 6.5 percent of GNP required for meeting socially demanded employment and for the fiscal resources needed for increasing the nation's competitiveness based on better infrastructure and public services.

In Mexico, economic decisions are highly centralized within the executive power. National planning, fiscal policy, budget programming and operation are public responsibilities concentrated in a single ministry, the Secretaría de Hacienda (Ministry of Finance). Even though the Mexican Congress has increased its independent participation in budget approval, the majority of citizens and their economic and social organizations play only a limited role in the most important and decisive economic resolutions.

Due to the level of economic concentration observed in the Mexican economy, the capacity of larger businesses and organizations in influencing the economic decisions of the executive and legislative powers in government, corresponds to their money-making power. Micro, small and medium-sized businesses play a much more limited role in public economic decision making.

Implications of the Economy for the Public Relations Industry

In general, larger businesses and corporations require important public relations services for their investment initiatives, all through the production process. First of all, it is important to create and maintain enough public awareness of the corporation's prestige in order for it to create favorable conditions for new incoming investments both from foreign and national enterprises. On the other hand, increased global and local competition requires public relations strategies in order to take advantage of market opportunities. Product differentiation and reduced profit margins demand a constant effort for reaching consumers' desires and needs. Thus, public relations, in this context, is strongly related to marketing and advertising.

All of these must be considered as different components of one systematic communication and public relations strategy, and not as isolated efforts. On the other hand, small businesses face more difficult entrepreneurial environments as well as more limited resources to deal with them in an increasingly differentiated business structure with the predominance of few highly concentrated and technologically more advanced businesses. The majority of small businesses in the public relations industry must be capable of providing their services to these smaller economic actors, through innovations in concepts, methodologies and ways of financing public relations services. There lies an enormous challenge but also attractive opportunities, specifically, in the context of an accelerated technological development that opens new perspectives for the businesses in the 21st century.

Mexico has the imperative need to double its annual GNP growth to at least 6 or 7 percent, which would increase job creation to one million jobs annually. Under present conditions, the public relations industry is affected by a semi-stagnant economy that maintains its macroeconomic stability on the basis of oil exports and the reduction of aggregate demand. Therefore, public relations demand is restricted to larger businesses' needs. But this situation can end and must be changed towards the development for increasing national economic competitiveness of all sectors and regions of the country. Public relations can play a vital role in increasing community awareness of economic opportunities and also for improving social cohesion around these objectives. Public relations can be an important bridge that could help bring together the public sector, the economic private institutions and social organizations. It can be thought of, not only as an important means for transforming organizational activities, but also as the mechanism for the development of increased social ties, trust, and consciousness of the general conditions of society, required for transforming and promoting Mexico's economic development.

Mexican Legal Institutions and Their Operations

The evolution of Mexican democracy also changed the strength of its judiciary power. Although the Supreme Court is still strongly influenced by the executive power, there is a clear tendency since the year 2000 towards a stronger and more independent judiciary. Recently, the Supreme Court determined that the executive's point of view prevailed in relation to the demands of unconstitutionality pertaining to budget decisions and energy contracts posed by different legislatures (Macías, 2007).

These cases are hopefully some of the last expressions of a political regime centered on the figure of the president. The role of the Supreme Court is also very relevant in relation to electoral processes in the country. For example, during the 2006 presidential elections, the Supreme Court rejected the demand of citizens to investigate alleged violations of the law. This went through even though, according to Article 27 of the Constitution, the Supreme Court is endowed with the authority to carry out *ex officio* investigations, when according to their own judgment, that presidential election had uncertain results.

The Electoral Court established under Article 99 is the highest authority in electoral matters. Both the Supreme Court and the Electoral Court decided to apply an administrative perspective (instead of a judiciary one) to the alleged violations of electoral law during the 2006 presidential election. This decision left a political climate of uncertainty since such allegations were not investigated thoroughly by the judiciary authority since the decision on the validity of the results was based solely upon the documents, arguments and proofs provided by those making such allegations.

As a result of this experience, reforms to the federal radio and television law and the federal telecommunications law are forthcoming, in order to make changes in accordance with the recent Constitutional reforms, by which no individual or political party is allowed to contract broadcasting time with electoral political purposes (Martell, 2007).

In general, Mexico's judiciary system has had important inefficiencies. First of all, there are heterogeneous legal codes in relation to criminal laws among the different states. Secondly, the institution responsible for receiving and doing the preliminary investigation of crimes is under the jurisdiction of the executive power and not independent of it. Therefore, its research capabilities and police institutions are frequently influenced by the interventions coming from the executive both at federal and state levels. Thirdly, the number of cases presented and the limited technical and human resources within the judiciary result in an enormous delay in decisions. Fourthly, the threat posed by organized crime to police institutions and the judiciary is gigantic on account of the enormous economic resources and extremely violent behavior and capabilities of these organizations. In particular, this national and international problem has escalated into becoming a threat to national security, a fact that has led to a more intense and direct intervention of the Mexican armed forces.

Property rights have formal protection in Mexico and many international treaties have been signed for both intellectual property and investment. However, in Mexico, as in other countries, the effort to clamp down on and eliminate illegal copies and piracy of trademarks requires a continuous and strong effort by different authorities (Casas, 2007).

In the field of telecommunications there are several laws proposed aimed at regulating convergence of modes of communication and providing multimedia services with the objective of increasing the participation of more sectors (González, Soria and Tejado, 2007).

Implications for Public Relations

These strong demands and limited capabilities of the judiciary system require important efforts for public relations since it is often needed to present arguments and proposals which do not have an easy passage under present institutional arrangements. Public relations is very important as a basic support for negotiations and dialogue between firms, executive, legislative and judiciary sectors as well as civic society groups.

Public relations in the context of legal and judiciary issues has several specificities in the country. In the first place, there is a need for thorough revisions of the country's regulation and body of laws related to institutions and norms for investigations and prosecution of crime, which can be enhanced with the participation of experts, academics, and civic groups with the support of public relations strategies.

In the second place, there is a need for the creation of a culture of lawfulness in the Mexican context. The cultural legacy of 300 years as a Hispanic colony, where political and legal decisions were made outside the country and sent as mandates to Nueva España (New Spain) and reinterpreted by local Spaniards, as well as the abysmal inequalities of power and influence existing among *criollos* and *mestizos* and Natives in the American Continent, gave rise to a still prevailing culture of law infringement.

Two centuries of independence have not done away with certain cultural traits in the country. Lawfulness and willingness to abide by regulations need special efforts of social communication and public relations, among the different sectors of Mexican society. For these purposes, it is very important that public relations efforts be carried out in all public and private institutions in order to promote a more thorough knowledge of citizens' rights and responsibilities as a prerequisite for the creation of a lawful culture in the country.

Notwithstanding this, such changes in attitudes and behavior alone are insufficient. Citizens must also have access to full and precise information on the offices, institutions, procedures and mechanisms where they can put through their points of view and demands for justice. This is yet another arena where public relations can do very much to properly inform citizens and provide ample knowledge on the ways and means to gain accurate attention to their demands.

Still another context where public relations is needed in the legal context has to do with information openness and transparency of public institutions. To this day, transparency has been related to providing information on results and public funds allocation. This tendency needs to be reversed so that information is provided to the public all through the processes of decision making and implementation, execution and performance of the governmental projects.

At the present moment, legislative, judiciary and executive powers in Mexico are intensively employing public relations services to pursue their specific interests. The President seeks the support of communication and public relations agencies to achieve efficient agreements and alliances among government and public institutions.

The Supreme Court in Mexico is increasingly aware of the many advantages that the use of mass media can provide public bodies in making civic and communitarian processes more transparent to all citizens. For that purpose, public television networks are being created: the Canal Judicial (Judiciary Channel) and the Canal del Congreso de la Unión (Congress of the Union Channel). Public relations professionals face great responsibility as they are the bridge builders between the government and the mass media. Also, senators, judiciary directors and employees and public office holders in general increasingly demand specialized services from the public relations agencies: media training, crisis communication, construction of a good image and a trustworthy reputation, 360 degree communication solutions, among others.

Public relations professionals face important challenges in the Mexican judiciary and legal arenas. They are being summoned to work on the construction of favorable images for the public organizations and officials. In order to build the public institutions' image and reputation, they have to rely upon the consistency between leaders' discourse and actions. This issue will eventually give way to an increased sensibility on the part of public officials on these matters.

Trade agreements hold important challenges for public relations agencies. At present, peasants and farmers' organizations in the country oppose some of the dispositions in NAFTA where international grain (mainly corn and beans) is being limitlessly introduced into the country, resulting in the deterioration of Mexican food production. Through communication strategies and the promotion of dialogue, public relations professionals can uphold fair commercial agreements that should benefit both national interests and international commerce.

Public relations professionals in the country have for many years overlooked the small businesses arena where most of the economic activity and employment in the country is being provided. A significant percentage (99 percent) of Mexico's production power lies in these medium, small and micro organizations. Public relations and communication strategies that involve offering collective services to these businesses stand in line to be formed and set to work.

A main problem in the Mexican telecommunications industry is the absence of efficient mechanisms where the audiences can provide feedback and actively participate in creating a more democratic mass communication system as well as endorsing quality programming in it. This is another arena where communications and public relations agencies and independent professionals' expertise will be required in the country.

Activism in Mexico

Social movements in Mexico have played an important and active role throughout the history of the nation. In the last three decades, the country has seen many types of social movement rise and settle down again. Activism has involved different social and worker groups and labor unions: railroad workers and medical doctors in the 1960s; students in 1968 and 1971; spontaneous emergency civic initiatives during the earthquakes of 1985; political groups and those in defense of effective voting and democratic elections in 1988; including armed rebellion by the Ejército Zapatista de Liberación Nacional (EZLN) (Zapatist Army for National Liberation), in 1994 (Urreta, 2005).

In the last three years, organized workers, peasants and civil society have addressed the government in requests for more and better jobs, improvement of formal salaries, emergency recovery of salaries, opposition to social security reform measures, renegotiation of the agricultural section of NAFTA, as well as basic nutrition product prices (Díaz, 2005).

As a result of these activist measures and social demands, the government and peasant organizations signed the Acuerdo Nacional para el Campo (Rural National Agreement) in 2003. This Agreement remains the sole pact to be signed between the government and social organizations during the 2000–2006 period political administration. Other civic acts in recent periods that should be referred to are the rejection movements organized against government authorities, during and after the 2006 election processes (Consejo Nacional Agropecuario, 2000; Díaz, 2005).

In 2007, Mexico lived through an especially powerful form of activism, where the country's workers' unions, its farmers' organizations and other civic associations protested jointly in demand for an emergency wage increase in order to compensate for rising food prices. As a result, these forces have established mechanisms for social dialogue, in order to arrange action plans to meet the social demands put forward by these organized groups (Unión Nacional de Trabajadores and FESEBS, 2005).

Labor unions comprise approximately 5 percent of the workers in the country. In other words, the majority of workers are not included within a professional organization. The country's semi-stagnation for the past two decades has resulted in an increased demand for employment on the part of a growing worker population that is increasingly frustrated in its attempts to get a job in the context of lessening opportunities for occupation. As a result, the labor unions' power is being strongly diminished. Furthermore, from 1993 on, the country has seen the multiplication of an informal economy, which has little or no capacity to create its own means of unification and organization (Clavel, 2005).

Notwithstanding the above, there are several independent and efficiently organized and active groups of professionals. These work separately to gain their objectives and up to the present have been unable or unwilling to take a unified stand on issues affecting them as informal workers and small businesses. This is the case of the Comisión Nacional de Electricidad (CFE) (Federal Electricity Commission) workers and telephone companies' employees from Teléfonos de Mexico (TELMEX), the Social Security personnel Instituto Mexicano del Seguro Social (IMSS), public universities' academics and other human resources, many of them brought together under the Unión Nacional de Trabajadores (UNT) (Workers' National Union). Also, elementary and high school teachers organized under the powerful Sindicato Nacional de Trabajadores de la Educación (SNTE) (National Teachers' Union), have gone out to the streets and blocked urban transit and highways, claiming a democratic reform for the Union's internal affairs, their independence from outside forces and the quality of education in the country (Unión Nacional de Trabajadores, 2005).

Generally speaking, social movements in the country pursue both national and economic sectors policies reforms related to salaries and social claims.

Implications for Public Relations

Private enterprises and public institutions in Mexico have initiated a series of policies, strategies and activities related to public services and public relations. They have pushed forward social interest causes through organizing fund raising campaigns in support of nutrition, health and education of the poorer sectors of Mexican society. They have also promoted campaigns aimed at the development of civic culture among the nation's citizens. Naturally, due to the crime and violence prevailing in most large cities, safety has received a lot of attention from the country's private and public sectors. Other important issues undertaken are efforts to persuade private media owners and producers to see the advantages of increasing educational orientations in press communications, radio and television programs as well the Internet, cellular phones and videogames. It should be noted that Mexico is increasingly developing a culture based on philanthropy aimed at helping highly vulnerable persons and groups.

In the context of its historic and imminent activism, Mexico has a large portion of public relations efforts aimed at social welfare, the culture of responsibility, and preventive medicine in relation to cancer, heart failure, and obesity. Considering the need for public policy reform, social movements in Mexico tend to address their demands more to government rather than to the private sector. From the government's perspective, its institutions have set public relations activities into working intensely towards informing citizens on the public institutions services being provided to them, their accessibility and the purposes of improving economic and social conditions they are aimed at.

Quality public information is a must in a country where population has been steadily migrating to its urban areas (75 percent) plus the fact that social structures and culture are becoming more complex. Without effective public information and public relations, institutions cannot function successfully and without efficiency, they can contribute little to the rise of social capital and trust among the people of the country. As a consequence, institutions' and organizations' social legitimacy will grow thinner if specific action isn't undertaken. Recently, Mexican citizens have advanced in formalizing institutions and private enterprises. The current electoral reforms in the country have pointed to the necessary split between institutions' public services and communication for political purposes, which are aimed at electoral objectives. This reform is an important boost for ethical public relations practice in the country.

MÉXICO'S CULTURAL DIVERSITY

Mexico's citizens include significantly diverse cultural manifestations and ethnic groups as it is established in the Nation's Constitution, as a result of more than 3,000 years of history and the coexistence of more than 600 different ethnic groups. The conquest of the country by Spain gave way to the mixing of racial groups (1521–1821), whereby European culture was also included in the country's own version of the melting pot, all through the Spanish Viceroyalty stage lasting 300 years.

Out of the some 108.7 million people (CONAPO, July, 2007) that constitute the country's population, 10 percent speak one of 53 different Indian languages, of which the best known are Náhuatl and Maya. There is, therefore, a multiplicity of coexisting cultures associated with an extraordinarily diverse geographic territory. Also, there is a great religious diversity within the country: 88 percent are Catholic, 4.5 percent are Evangelical; 1.25 percent are Jehovah's Witnesses; 0.71 percent are Protestant, 0.58 are Adventist, 0.25 percent are Mormons; 0.05 percent are Jewish; 3.52 percent are agnostic or atheist (US Embassy in Mexico, 2007).

In the last 30 years, the country has shown growing tendencies towards the mixing of races, increasing urbanization of the population and the acquisition of a more cosmopolitan perspective. At the same time, there is more foreign investment in the country and an increasing globally oriented culture. Due to the fact that the United States is our next-door neighbor, this process has been especially influenced by its North American way of life. These accelerated changes being introduced into a highly asymmetrical social order have produced further educational inequalities and a decidedly heterogeneous society (García, 1990).

Due to the above conditions, there is an increased need for differentiated communication and public relations strategies according to the specific cultural context they face. From the above, it is clear that majority groups in Mexico, including the larger part of the population with its lower socio economic status, rely more specifically on the power of communitarian and labor organizations.

Social Mobility in Mexico

From 1932 to 1982, economic growth allowed a more dynamic process of social mobility than the dominant tendency the country shows now. In the last 20 years, social mobility has been restricted, notwithstanding the fact that income per capita has increased. The lack of job opportunities has led to the emigration of mainly two types of population: the poorer and the most educated. One out of every three Mexicans with a PhD, one out of every five with an MA Degree and three out of every seven with a BA Degree have transferred to the United States or to some other country. In the last five years, Mexico ranks as the country with most population loss. The 2007 estimate by the National Population Council (Consejo Nacional de Población) reports 52 million males and 56 million females in the country (CONAPO, July, 2007).

Uncertainty

The country's recent development and the corresponding deterioration of opportunities and expectations on the part of its citizens, tend to cultivate an attitude of impatience towards the prevailing conditions of uncertainty and ambiguity. On the other hand, both the strong family ties and the predominant Catholic religion provide support and a sense of security, hope and optimism in the face of extremely adverse circumstances.

Masculinity/Femininity: Gender in Roles

Mexico has taken important steps towards recognizing and assigning equal rights to women and men. Both public policies and laws are being endorsed to protect women. Mass media campaigns are constantly launched to prevent and revert violence on women. Some 3.7 million adolescents are attending high school, out of whom 40 percent are female. A growing percentage of women, 4.3 percent from 2005–2006, are now studying high school (Calderón, 2007).

Furthermore, more women are entering higher paid jobs and taking important decisions within the industrial and public sectors. Out of Mexico's economically active population, 36.4 percent are females and 63.6 percent are males (Secretaría de Economía, 2006) (Ministry of Economy). Notwithstanding this, women are still lagging behind in relation to men, with respect to access to public office and to the upper ranking jobs. Gender equality is related basically to three variables: education level, urbanization and the incorporation of women in the labor force. As to the way gender has affected the public relations industry, according to the latest statistics provided by ProRP show that the industry generated 2,252 jobs, out of which 63 percent were taken by females and the remaining 37 percent by males. Public relations is a predominantly female environment in Mexico (ProRP, 2006). This female/male component is probably an expression of the need for feminine qualities in carrying out public relations activities.

Collectivism vs Individualism

In Mexico the interests of the family are placed above the concerns of the collectivity and those of the individual. The family is a pole of attraction for affections, love, and support. Self-esteem in the country depends to a great extent on family ties and pride. A job in Mexico signifies a way to support a family, as well being an opportunity for self-fulfillment and professional satisfaction.

As far as deference to authority is concerned, we can say that it is very important in the Mexican realm. Since pre-Colombian times in the country, all through the Spanish domination, the post-independence regimes, and modern times, government centered around the figure of a strong President, the country has been ruled by authoritarian regimes. This has cultivated through the centuries a vertical and patriarchal culture with a high deference to authority. Parents, teachers, school authorities, job superiors are to be heard and their instructions obeyed. The power that superiors symbolize is a compelling tool.

Public relations professionals coming in from other countries sometimes face inter-cultural communication issues and usually take some time before they understand this facet of Mexican culture. Family ties are very important for opening job opportunities and spaces in the public offices. Friendship and acquaintances are significant assets when seeking business alliances and trust for an organization. Therefore, a period of time and some training is required before a foreigner can start doing a public relations job in the Mexican market.

THE MASS MEDIA AND PUBLIC RELATIONS

Mexico faces extraordinary transformations in the contexts of its mass communication system. Renewed legal processes are changing the means and ways of access and control of the media. New professional clusters, civic society groups and small firms, are slowly entering the mass media scene. In the medium and long turns, more and diverse traditional media will appear in the Mexican sphere as well as more activity being demanded of public relations professionals.

The quantity and quality of media businesses in Mexico is significant and their efficiency is a fact both at the national and the international levels. Some media such as the newspapers *Excelsior*, *El Universal* and *Reforma*, have obtained international awards. The Instituto Politécnico Nacional's Canal Once has gained acknowledgment for its cultural and educational productions. Educational media in the country have been employed as models for similar projects around the World. Radio stations have talented journalists with international recognition, noted for the journalistic professionalism. Mexican film productions has obtained important awards in international movie festivals and is rapidly growing in global commercial circuits.

It is a proven fact that actors, persons, industries, brands, products as well as organizations, that obtain spaces within Mexican media networks, in many cases, acquire presence in the Hispanic world given Mexican media outreach outside the country.

Media Control

The telecommunication sector is one of the fastest growing in the Mexican economy. Its participation in the GNP was 4.9 percent in 2005 and 5.5 percent in 2006. This growth is the result of both private and public investment. In Mexico, in the year 2005, 2,741 million USD and in 2006, 3,506 million USD were invested. On the other hand, this growth is expressed in the industry's earnings: these were amounts superior to those of inflation. In 2006, the annual growth rate reached 16.6 percent compared to that of inflation growth of 4.5 percent. It can be noted that mobile telephone services is a highly dynamic sector, as in 2006 it accounted for 48.5 percent of the total telecommunication sector earnings (COFETEL, 2007).

In Mexico, mass communication media are predominantly privately owned. Private television networks in the country concentrate as much as 80 percent of the audience. Media power is concentrated mainly in two networks: Televisa and TVAzteca. As far as radio networks are concerned, eight private groups concentrate up to 80 percent of radio audiences in the country. Pay TV, is also privately owned by two groups: Grupo Televisa (Cablevision and Sky) and MVS (Mastv). Nowadays, audiences are migrating from open television and into Pay TV. Although, Televisa's audiences prefer Pay TV and are constantly migrating into this type of TV viewing, they continue watching the same channels they do in open television. This is due to fact that Pay TV offers better reception conditions.

Notwithstanding, there are also public media such as Canal 22, pertaining to the National Counsel for Arts and Culture (CONACULTA) (Consejo Nacional para las Artes y la Cultura); Educational Television, the direct ownership of the Secretaría de Educación Pública (SEP) (Ministry of Public Education); TVUNAM, pertaining to Mexico's main university, National Autonomous University of Mexico (Universidad Nacional Autónoma de Mexico); Canal 11, of the National Polytechnic Institute (Instituto Politécnico Nacional); the Mexican Congress TV Channel as well as the Judiciary TV Channel. There are also several radio stations that are publicly owned such as the Mexican Radio Institute (IMER) (Instituto Mexicano de la Radio) and Radio Educación. Locally, there are a total of 17 radio stations with regional outreach and whose main purpose are to provide services, culture and entertainment to different ethnic groups and whose transmissions are carried out in diverse Indian languages.

Mexico is a Republic constituted as a liberal federalist regime. Media owners in Mexico possess a great amount of power in determining editorial policies within their electronic networks as well as newspapers. In many cases this freedom of speech is employed to express the interests and political perspectives of the powerful economic groups, the owners of the media.

The editorial industry in the country has enjoyed a long period of liberty, however, in more recent years it has begun to be threatened through crimes committed against reporters and journalists who investigate the activities of organized crime. After Iraq, Mexico is the country with the greatest number of murders of newsmen and women.

Media news programs are strongly oriented towards providing opinions and editorial contents rather than straight information. Anchormen and ladies provide evaluations and opinions as they read the news in front of the TV cameras and radio stations.

Legal laws are being passed in Congress and evaluated by the Supreme Court to protect the media from political pressure. Recently a piece of legislation was submitted to the Mexican Congress with the purpose of placing new laws and restrictions in the procedures of awarding media concessions to private owners. With the intention of putting off some of the public pressure, media owners are elaborating strong self-regulation projects that include social responsibility campaigns and codes of ethics. The social response to these initiatives on the part of scholars and different associations, have to do with creating media observatories.

The professional standards that media people have are constantly being upgraded in the country. In the last 30 years the country has seen a flourishing of BA degree programs as well as graduate programs offered throughout the Nation's territory by more than 350 universities where more than 72,000 students study. Furthermore, communication research has a long history of endeavors, many of which strive to produce knowledge to make media practices better and provide better contents for programming (Fuentes, 2005; Rebeil, 2006a; Rebeil, 2006b; Rebeil, 2007).

As far as public relations is concerned, the media in Mexico offer a great variety of programming options for the diffusion of advertising, publicity, propaganda, promotion and all other types of messages intended to create favorable circumstances and acceptance for firms, candidates, persons, brands, products, ideas, projects on the part of the different segments of society.

Media Access

Information may reach the media through various means: information agencies, reporters' research work, firms, public relations agencies, and individual persons who report on some of the main events taking place within their realm. Daily, within the different media, a selection of this information is carried out by editors, producers, and reporters. Each one makes observations as to what news seems to be the most relevant. The final decision is always in the hands of the editor. The current events of social relevance are always the main criteria that are taken into account for the inclusion/exclusion of information in the different media.

The main issues that the media pay specific attention to are the owner's ideology and the philosophy of the stakeholders. Also, the specific market segment that each media is trying to access is important. In other words there will always be a threefold tendency: owners' preferences, stakeholders' interests and the target audiences' interests. Media contents are also influenced by the events taking place in the environment: the country's economic, political, social and cultural situation and political climate.

In every case there are specific persons (mostly editors) who influence mass media owners and authorities into publishing or including specific messages. These are usually people who have an extraordinary vision of social dynamics, a great sensibility to see in each information note how successful it can be in print or in programming. They dedicate a large part of their time to writing and to their job. They are selected by the media directors and evaluated upon the results they have had through the years, as well as their life experience.

In general terms, activists and corporations receive an equal amount of attention on the part of the media. It all depends on the issue at hand and who invites the media representatives to a specific press conference or event. When a communication medium receives a direct invitation to publish a piece of information or a news note from a firm, this information is not always taken into consideration by the media. The issue, in order to be included in the programming, has to be a very important social event or the firm has to have a very important presence in the sector it represents. For the purpose of public relations agencies, whenever they send contents referring to branding to the media, this is usually taken into consideration because of the benefits that media may obtain from the firm. Also, the firm that sends the information may be very powerful economically speaking and publishing may represent future alliances and business for a specific media.

Gradually, the tendency for paying for the publication of specific contents is being discontinued. However it still exists and will continue to do so by some media and specifically some individuals who support political interest projects, persons and opinion leaders.

Media Outreach

The capacity of media in Mexico to diffuse messages is practically 100 percent efficient. Media statistics with respect to their outreach are as follows: radio reaches 100 percent of the population, color TV 81 percent, telephone 57 percent, compact disc 53 percent, VCR 47 percent, mobile telephone 45 percent, still camera 44 percent, PC 39 percent, car 35 percent, computer printer 26 percent, pay TV/cable 25 percent, black/white TV 19 percent, videogames 17 percent, video camera 15 percent, answering machine 12 percent, DVD 10 percent, pager 8 percent, fax 6 percent (Consejo de Investigación de Medios, 2006).

Nielsen's population division has three socioeconomic segments (SES): 66.6 percent D+DE, 31.5 percent C+C, 7.9 percent AB (Ríos, August, 2007). The media reach different portions of these segments. Print media reach: 1) magazines: 47.4 percent D+DE, 28.7 percent C, 24 percent ABC+ (Ipsos Bimsa, 2004); 2) newspapers: 61 percent D+DE, 17 percent C, 21 percent ABC+ (Consejo de Investigación de Medios, 2006).

Electronic media audiences are divided into the following socioeconomic levels: 1) TV: 69.9 percent D+DE; 15.96 percent C; 14.35 percent ABC+ (IBOPE AGB, 2005); 2) radio: 64 percent D+DE, 28 percent C+C, 7.5 percent AB. Radio is mostly heard by the AB SES, while driving in their automobile (69.5 percent); the C SES listen to radio at home (50.6

percent) and in the car (49.4 percent); whereas the D SES listen to radio mostly at home (90.6 percent) (INRA, 2005); 3) cinema: 49.2 percent D+DE, 26 percent C, 24.8 percent ABC+ (Data for the year 2004) (Ipsos Bimsa, 2004); 4) internet access: 36 percent at home; 36 percent cyber café; 25 percent office; 11 percent friend's home; and 4 percent at school. As far as SES access to internet, the users are segmented as follows: 38 percent D+DE, 18 percent C, 44 percent ABC+ (AMIPCI, 2007).

With the exception of print media and new information technologies, there is excellent media diffusion and outreach in the country. Until recently, the print media, particularly newspapers, had problems in getting to all corners of the nation, due to the fact that the Newspaper Vendor Union (Unión de Voceadores) avoided working 365 days of the year, alleging that there were special days when work should not be done such as the Annual Presidential Address Day, Labor Day, and others. When the newspaper *Reforma* entered the scene, the situation changed because this important provider of daily news was able to create its own distribution system.

Concerning the Internet, it should be noted that the company Telmex was able to reduce the digital gap significantly by offering PCs at a lower cost to telephone users on the condition that these clients were to buy the Internet connection to this important firm. Interestingly enough, the fastest growing part of the population to access Internet is the lower SES (DE 28 percent growth rate in 2007).

Early years in Mexico's TV history (1950–1985) were hard on reception capacity, particularly in rural areas. However, with Satellite Morelos I and II set in orbit, this situation changed, allowing TV programs to be viewed throughout the country. As of now, Mexican television is moving to HD format. Ahead is a still bigger challenge for Mexican television in the sense that the analog system is going to be converted to digital. The remaining questions are: Will Mexican TV systems be prepared to assume the cost involved in this change in infrastructure? How long will it take Mexican society to attain the outreach capacity it now has with the analog system?

Mexico's rate of illiteracy is 8.6 percent. As far as the media are concerned, the real problems related to literacy are functional illiteracy (people who know how to read and write but have an incapacity to understand explicit and implicit ideas and concepts in the text they read), and media literacy.

The Focus of Organizational Communication in Mexico

Organizational communication in the country attends to several diverse issues and problems influencing the enterprise or institution it serves. At present, many of these efforts tend towards the construction and distribution of messages concerned with threats and opportunities coming in from the outside world. Organizational communication is very busy conceiving effective interpersonal and group strategies that should help the enterprise in the face of an aggressive and globalized environment. A good starting point is the better understanding of what, how and why of globalization and change taking place within Mexican society.

Factors Affecting the Public Relations Industry

The current state of the electronic media outreach in the country facilitates public relations activities. Increasing newspaper outreach is another factor that makes public relations activities more efficient in Mexico. A large percentage of the work in public relations is done through publicity. Magazine penetration to all sectors in society has given an additional impulse to the public relations industry. However, as literacy and education increase in the country, the media consumers tend to reject publicity because they consider it as manipulative. Internet has helped advertising and direct promotion because one-to-one technologies have a more persuasive effect on the user, specifically when the issues are branding and political promotion.

One of the big challenges lying ahead for public relations is the integration of organizational communication efforts of marketing/advertising communication, internal communication, and corporate/public relations communication. For the purpose of providing integral communication solutions and avoiding the media centers' services monopoly, the organizational communication as well as public relations agencies must convince their clients of their capacity to provide total communication solutions. At present public relations agencies are perceived as mere special events organizers or as specific and punctual services providers. All of these misunderstandings can be avoided when organizational communication /public relations agencies work on integrated communications solutions services.

CONCLUSIONS

The Mexican environment in terms of its economic, political, legal and cultural complexity determines the public relations industry's need for being constantly aware of the environment as well as the elements needed for change and adaptation.

In recent years, economic and political situations and change have demanded of the public relations industry the development of different types of services that had never been rendered before by the industry. This has made the industry more efficient and client oriented and a provider of integrated communication services.

To an increasing extent, public relations is considered part of a more global communication strategy that provide organizations, institutions and clients with solutions that are more effective.

Public relations as a discipline is being strengthened by the existence and operations of Public Relations Associations (ProRP amd AMCO) and also through the public relations formal education imparted by the universities in the country as well as the increasing amount of scientific research on the matter.

Media in Mexico show a growing outreach to most sectors in society. This is advantageous for the public relations industry. However, their high concentration in the hands of few owners can be either gainful or detrimental to the public relations agencies given that once they gain entrance to a specific medium, many more doors will automatically open for them. The contrary is also true. If a media network declines to provide its services to a specific agency, many more media will do the same.

The services most often supplied by public relations agencies in Mexico are: corporate public relations; integral communication; public relations for branding; events organization; media training; social responsibility; crisis communication; fashion and life styles and lobbying.

Among the major difficulties for sector expansion are: 1) clients in Mexico fall short of understanding and employing the public relations potential to its maximum extent; 2) over emphasis of mass media usage; 3) limited vision of the potential of organizational marketing and public relations.

CASE STUDY

Revive Chapultepec*: Social Responsibility, Finding the Middle Ground and Public Relations

Clemente Sánchez Uribe, in Collaboration with Guadalupe Albert[4]

Mexico City's Bosque de Chapultepec (Chapultepec Forest) is an icon in the lives of many Mexicans. Considered the oldest urban park in the American Continent, its visitors total 15 million annually and every weekend it receives a massive influx of 200,000 tourists. It covers an area of 686 hectares, space enough to contain a sufficient number of trees to help clean some of the pollution in the largest city of the world.

Notwithstanding its relevance for the people in the City, Bosque de Chapultepec has undergone a series of damages and negative effects due to the excessive number of visitors it receives daily and the growing amounts of vendors who generate an enormous amount of waste in its premises and unfortunately contribute to diminishing the Park's green areas.

Among other factors, in 2004, the above problems led to a public relations and communications initiative to help generate a massive effort directed towards the survival and the improvement of Bosque de Chapultepec. Groups of residents as well as local authorities joined in creating the Fideicomiso Pro-Bosque de Chapultepec (Pro-Bosque de Chapultepec Trusteeship) and the Consejo Rector Ciudadano (Citizens' Governing Council), in establishing the *Plan Maestro de Rehabilitación del Bosque de Chapultepec* (Master Plan for the Rehabilitation of the Forest of Chapultepec), which included and still includes a multiplicity of considerations: environmental, cultural, artistic, recreational, commercial, urban and architectural.

Starting in the Autumn of 2004, a public relations strategy began. Phase 1 of the Plan consisted of sanitary activities. All areas of the park, including trees, creeks and lakes, the Bosque's fauna and recreation areas were sanitized. The activities still continue.

The public relations campaign implemented by both the Trusteeship and the Council has had the responsibility to inform all the City's residents is general and to promote among target audiences, motivations for funding and for doing volunteer work for the rehabilitation purposes. Mass media came on the scene as a tactic for reinforcing the now three-year-old public relations campaign helping to: a) persuade a group of more than 150 firms and entrepreneurs into participating in the initiative; b) implement the one to one money collection activities carried out all over the City's streets; c) create strategic alliances among local and national firms for environmental purposes; d) operate funding initiatives through the rounding up of grocery bills in participating supermarkets; e) organize concerts and cultural events with singers and other movie stars who offer and donate performances for the Bosque's purposes.

Other tactics were the selling of donors' commemorative plaques placed in the *Calzada del Rey* (the King's Avenue), the donation of park benches or ahuehuete[5] trees, and cloth bracelets with the legend: *Revive Chapultepec (Come alive, Chapultepec!)*. These activities were essential for the generation of a sense of belonging in a highly culturally diverse City

---

* *Come Alive, Chapultepec!*

[4]Clemente Sánchez Uribe is a researcher for the Centro de Investigación para la Comunicación Aplicada (Center for Applied Communication Research), Escuela de Comunicación, Universidad Anáhuac Mexico Norte. Guadalupe Albert was Chair of the Pro Bosque de Chapultepec Trusteeship.

[5]Ahuehuete: the City's typical and historic tree species found there since the Prehispanic period.

and the feeling of pride was also enhanced among those who participated and still do, as donors and as volunteer workers in the Master Plan.

All of these activities have been accompanied by the support of public relations communication tools such as press conferences, press news bulletins sent both to national and the international radio and television networks. Public relations activities including lobbying are proof of the extent to which an environmental project can grow and be successful in promoting social responsibility among groups, public institutions, private organizations, and volunteer teamwork. Although the use of mass media is very effective for diffusion and motivation purposes, personal communication, persuasion and other public relations strategies are vital ingredients for philanthropy purposes. *Revive Chapultepec* continues to be dedicated to conscience creating activities as to the Bosque de Chapultepec's importance as a permanent oxygen source for the City. During these years, *Revive Chapultepec* has continuously invited the City's civil society to participate and assume an active role in becoming socially responsible for the Bosque's preservation and survival. It has also become a very important public relations case study for both academic and consulting purposes in the country.

REFERENCES

Alianza Social (2005). Propuesta del foro de la Alianza Social para la transición democrática y el desarrollo con justicia y equidad para la creación del Consejo Económico y Social de Estado. In A. Montoya (Ed.). *Mexico hacia el 2025.* (vol. I). Mexico: Centro de Estudios Estratégicos Nacionales, Instituto Politécnico Nacional, Universidad Iberoamericana, Universidad Autónoma Metropolitana and Noriega Editores.

AMIPCI (2007). *Usuarios de Internet en Mexico: Uso de nuevas tecnologías.* Asociación Mexicana de Internet. Retrieved October 12, 2007 from http://www.amipci.org.mx/temp/Estudio__Amipci_2007_Usuarios_de_ Internet_en_Mexico_y_Uso_de_Nuevas_Tecnologias-0082160001179418241OB.pdf

Asociación Mexicana de Comunicadores Organizacionales (2007). Asociación Mexicana de Comunicadores Organizacionales. Retrieved October 11, 2007 from www.amco.mx.mx

Asociación de Relaciones Públicas de Los Cabos, A.C. (2007), *Asociación Mexicana de Relaciones Públicas de Los Cabos.* Retrieved October 23, 2007, from http://www.rploscabos.com/staticpages/index.php

Bailleres, J. (2005). Gobernabilidad y consolidación democrática en Mexico: elemento para su diagnóstico. In A. Montoya (Ed.). *Mexico hacia el 2025.* (vol. II). Mexico: Centro de Estudios Estratégicos Nacionales, Instituto Politécnico Nacional, Universidad Iberoamericana, Universidad Autónoma Metropolitana and Noriega Editores.

Banco de Mexico (2007). *Convertidor de tipo de cambio.* Retrieved October 15, 2007 from http://www.banxico.gob.mx/PortalesEspecializados/tiposCambio/indicadores.html

Baqués, J. (2005). La perspectiva neoconservadora de la democracia y la participación política de los ciudadanos. In A. Montoya (Ed.). *Mexico hacia el 2025.* (vol. II). Mexico: Centro de Estudios Estratégicos Nacionales, Instituto Politécnico Nacional, Universidad Iberoamericana, Universidad Autónoma Metropolitana and Noriega Editores.

Baran, S. and Hidalgo, J. (2005). *Comunicación masiva en Hispanoamérica: Cultura y literatura mediática.* Mexico: McGraw Hill.

Bonilla, C. (2002). *Relaciones Públicas. Factor de competitividad para empresas e instituciones.* Mexico: Compañía Editorial Continental.

Calderón, F. (2007) *Atención de la Demanda Educativa. Primer Informe de Gobierno del Presidente Calderón.* Retrieved October 25, 2007 from http://www.informe.gob.mx/3.3_TRANSFORMACION_EDUCATIVA/ contenido=243.

Casas, M. (2007). Globalización e identidad nacional mexicana: un análisis desde la comunicación. In M. A. Rebeil (Ed.). *XIV Anuario de Investigación de la Comunicación CONEICC.* Mexico: CONEICC, Universidad Anáhuac, Universidad Autónoma Metropolitana, Universidad del Valle de Mexico, Universidad de Monterrey, Universidad de Sonora and Universidad Simón Bolívar.

Centro de Estudios Estratégicos Nacionales. (2005). In *Mexico 2010: Pensar y decidir la próxima década*. (Vols. I and II). Mexico: Centro de Estudios Estratégicos Nacionales, Instituto Politécnico Nacional, Universidad Autónoma Metropolitana and Noriega Editores.

Clavel, L. (2005). Sociedad y políticas públicas. Las organizaciones sindicales y su incidencia en el espacio de lo público. In A. Montoya (Ed.). *Mexico hacia el 2025*. (vol. II). Mexico: Centro de Estudios Estratégicos Nacionales, Instituto Politécnico Nacional, Universidad Iberoamericana, Universidad Autónoma Metropolitana and Noriega Editores.

COFETEL (2007) *Informe de actividades 2006–2007*. Mexico: COFETEL.

Consejo de Investigación de Medios (2006). *Conexión Media Data*. Consejo de Investigación de Medios: Mexico.

Consejo Nacional Agropecuario: Propuestas de políticas básicas del Sector Agropecuario (2000). In *Mexico 2010: Pensar y decidir la próxima década*. Mexico: Centro de Estudios Estratégicos Nacionales, Instituto Politécnico Nacional, Universidad Autónoma Metropolitana and Noriega Editores.

Consejo Nacional de Población (CONAPO) (2007). *Situación Demográfica 2007*. Retrieved October 29, 2007 from www.comnapo.gob.mx/publicaciones/sdm2007/sdm07_01.pdf.

Corchado, M. C. and Cardoso, M. (2000). La inserción de Mexico en los mercados y regiones dentro de la globalización. In *Mexico 2010: Pensar y decidir la próxima década*. Mexico: Centro de Estudios Estratégicos Nacionales, Instituto Politécnico Nacional, Universidad Autónoma Metropolitana and Noriega Editores.

Del manjar a la dieta. Inversión en Medios. (2008, Edición Especial). *Media Book, 8–1*.

Departament de Periodisme i de Ciencies de la Comunicació (2006). *Analisi. Quaderns de Comunicació i Cultura. Relaciones Públicas*. España: Universitat Autonoma de Barcelona.

Díaz, O. (2005). Modernización del mercadeo de productos agropecuarios: cambio indispensable para erradicar la pobreza en el campo. In A. Montoya (Ed.). *Mexico hacia el 2025*. (vol. II). Mexico: Centro de Estudios Estratégicos Nacionales, Instituto Politécnico Nacional, Universidad Iberoamericana, Universidad Autónoma Metropolitana and Noriega Editores.

Fuentes, R. (2005). La configuración de la oferta nacional de estudios superiores en Comunicación: Reflexiones analíticas y contextuales. In J. Calles (Ed.). *XII Anuario de Investigación de la Comunicación CONEICC*, Mexico: CONEICC, Universidad Anáhuac, Universidad Autónoma Metropolitana, Universidad del Valle de Mexico, Universidad de Monterrey, Universidad de Sonora and Universidad Simón Bolívar.

García, N. (1982). *Las culturas populares en el capitalismo*. Mexico: Nueva Imagen.

García, N. (1988). *Cultura transnacional y culturas populares*. Perú: Ipal.

García, N. (1990). *Culturas híbridas. Estrategias para entrar y salir de la modernidad*. Mexico: Grijalbo.

Gómez, R. (2007, September 19). Viven en Mexico 44 Millones de pobres: SEDESOL. *El Universal on line*. Retrieved on September 27 2007 from http://www.el-universal.com.mx/notas/451590.html

González, F., Soria, G. and Tejado, J. (Eds.). (2007). *La regulación de las telecomunicaciones*. Mexico: Porrúa.

Grunig, J. E. (1984). Organizations, environments and models of public relations. *Public Relations Research and Education, (1)* 6–29.

Grunig, J. E. (1989). Symmetrical presuppositions as a framework for public relations theory. In C. H. Botan and V. Hazleton Jr. (Eds.). *Public relations theory*. Hillsdale: Lawrence Erlbaum.

Guerra, D. (2005). Sistema para la Coordinación Integral de las tareas de gobierno. In A. Montoya (Ed.). *Mexico hacia el 2025*. (vol. II). Mexico: Centro de Estudios Estratégicos Nacionales, Instituto Politécnico Nacional, Universidad Iberoamericana, Universidad Autónoma Metropolitana and Noriega Editores

Horcacitas, E. (2005). Financiamiento e inversión en infraestructura. In A. Montoya (Ed.). *Mexico hacia el 2025*. (vol. II). Mexico: Centro de Estudios Estratégicos Nacionales, Instituto Politécnico Nacional, Universidad Iberoamericana, Universidad Autónoma Metropolitana and Noriega Editores.

IBOPE AGB (2005). *Promedio diario de la composición demográfica del universo nacional IBOPE*. Mexico: IBOPE AGB.

INEGI (2007). *Indicadores seleccionados sobre nivel de escolaridad, promedio de escolaridad, aptitud para leer y escribir y alfabetismo, 1960 a 2005*. Mexico: INEGI.

INRA (2005). *Mediometro y radioautomóviles, Valle de Mexico, 2005*. Mexico: INRA.

Ipsos Bimsa (2004). *Estudio General de Medios (EGM) en 27 ciudades 2002, 2003 y 2004*. Mexico: BIMSA.

Islas, O. (2006). Ventanas de Oportunidades. *Revista Mexicana de Comunicación, (96)*, 27–28.

Macías, H. (2007). Medios de comunicación, percepción de campañas y votantes tijuanenses durante el proceso electoral presidencial 2006. In M. A Rebeil (Ed.). *XIV Anuario de Investigación de la Comunicación CONEICC.* Mexico: CONEICC, Universidad Anáhuac, Universidad Autónoma Metropolitana, Universidad del Valle de Mexico, Universidad de Monterrey, Universidad de Sonora, and Universidad Simón Bolívar.

Martell, L. (2007).La ciudadanía y la sociedad civil del espacio público contemporáneo. In M. A. Rebeil (Ed.). *XIV Anuario de Investigación de la Comunicación CONEICC.* Mexico: CONEICC, Universidad Anáhuac, Universidad Autónoma Metropolitana, Universidad del Valle de Mexico, Universidad de Monterrey, Universidad de Sonora, and Universidad Simón Bolívar.

Martínez, R. (2005). Sistemas de Gobierno de tendencia presidencial. In A. Montoya (Ed.). *Mexico hacia el 2025.* (Vol. II). Mexico: Centro de Estudios Estratégicos Nacionales, Instituto Politécnico Nacional, Universidad Iberoamericana, Universidad Autónoma Metropolitana and Noriega Editores.

Montoya, A. (2005). *Mexico hacia el 2025.* (Vols. I and II). Mexico: Centro de Estudios Estratégicos Nacionales, Instituto Politécnico Nacional, Universidad Iberoamericana, Universidad Autónoma Metropolitana and Noriega Editores.

Pick, J. and Rebeil, M. A. (2005). Los factores de la pobreza en Mexico en la década de los noventa y su comportamiento futuro, 1990–2020. In A. Montoya (Ed.). *Mexico hacia el 2025.* (vol. I). Mexico: Noriega Editores, Instituto Politécnico Nacional, Universidad Iberoamericana and Centro de Estudios Estratégicos Nacionales.

Pineda, J. (2005). Rasgos de la administración pública en transición. In A. Montoya, (Ed.). *Mexico hacia el 2025.* (vol. II). Mexico: Centro de Estudios Estratégicos Nacionales, Instituto Politécnico Nacional, Universidad Iberoamericana, Universidad Autónoma Metropolitana and Noriega Editores.

ProRP (2002). *Directorio de Relaciones Públicas.* Mexico: ProRP.

ProRP (2006). *Reporte de la Industria de las Relaciones Públicas 2005.* Mexico: ProRP.

ProRP (2007). *Reporte de la Industria de las Relaciones Públicas 2006.* Mexico: ProRP.

Rebeil, M. A. (2006a). *Comunicación estratégica en las organizaciones.* Mexico: Editorial Trillas and Universidad Anáhuac.

Rebeil, M. A. (Ed.). (2006b). *XIII Anuario de Investigación de la Comunicación CONEICC,* Mexico: CONEICC, Universidad Anáhuac, Universidad Autónoma Metropolitana, Universidad del Valle de Mexico, Universidad de Monterrey, Universidad de Sonora and Universidad Simón Bolívar.

Rebeil, M. A. and Hernández, J. (in press). *Libro colectivo AMIC.* Mexico: Asociación Mexicana de Investigadores de la Comunicación.

Rebeil, M. A. and Ruiz Sandoval, C. (2000). *El Poder de la Comunicación en las Organizaciones.* Mexico: Plaza y Valdes Editores and Universidad Iberoamericana.

Registra Mexico 56 millones de usuarios de celular. (2007, March 9). *El Universal on line.* Retrieved October 12, from http://www.el-universal.com.mx/notas/411384.html

Ríos, M. A. (2007, August). El avance casi completo. *Merca 2.0.* (64), 58–64.

Ríos, M. A. (2007, September). Respeto por la disciplina. *Merca 2.0* (65), 85.

Salen de Mexico 225 mil jóvenes preparados al año: ONU. (2007, August 10). *El Universal.*

Secretaría de Economía (2006). *El trabajo y las mujeres en Mexico.* Retrieved October 25, 2007 from http://www.economia.gob.mx/pics/p/p1379/documento03.pdf

STPS (2007). *Informe del Empleo al primer trimestre de 2007.* Mexico: STPS.

Unión Nacional de Trabajadores (2005). Por una nueva legislación del trabajo para la reestructuración productiva y la reestructuración democrática. In A. Montoya (Ed.). *Mexico hacia el 2025.* (Vol. II). Mexico: Centro de Estudios Estratégicos Nacionales, Instituto Politécnico Nacional, Universidad Iberoamericana, Universidad Autónoma Metropolitana and Noriega Editores.

Unión Nacional de Trabajadores and FESEBS (2005). Por una reforma laboral y propulsiva para la democracia y la globalización. In A. Montoya (Ed.). *Mexico hacia el 2025.* (Vol. II). Mexico: Centro de Estudios Estratégicos Nacionales, Instituto Politécnico Nacional, Universidad Iberoamericana, Universidad Autónoma Metropolitana and Noriega Editores.

Urreta, A. (2005). La crisis agropecuaria una oportunidad para el cambio. In A. Montoya (Ed.).*Mexico hacia el 2025.* (Vol. II). Mexico: Centro de Estudios Estratégicos Nacionales, Instituto Politécnico Nacional, Universidad Iberoamericana, Universidad Autónoma Metropolitana and Noriega Editores.

U.S. Embassy in Mexico (2007). Informe 2007 sobre Libertad Religiosa Internacional. Sección Mexico. Retrieved October 23, 2007 from http://www.usembassy-mexico.gov/textos/st070914religiosa.html

Verdusco, A. (2007, October 3). Con empleo formal 14.71 millones, reporta el IMSS. *Milenio*.

Xifra, J. (2003). *Teoría y estructura de las relaciones públicas.* España: Mc Graw Hill and Interamericana de España S.A.U.

Zepeda, I. (2007, September). La visión de la industria televisiva. *Merca 2.0 (65),* 44–47.

33

OVERVIEW OF PUBLIC RELATIONS IN SOUTH AMERICA

MARIA APARECIDA FERRARI

The recent history of Latin America is fast, contradictory, and chaotic. The jet plane co-exists with the donkey, the candle with the neon light. . . . Why haven't we been able to resolve our fundamental problem of linking economic growth with social justice, and both these concepts with political democracy? Why haven't we given politics and the economy the continuity that exists in our culture?

Carlos Fuentes, *The Buried Mirror*, 1992.

INTRODUCTION

South American societies have traditionally been afflicted by the whim and designs of specific centers of power and external dominance.

During the twentieth century, continual changes have occurred in differing degrees and circumstances throughout the nations of the continent. The most relevant change was the replacement of dictatorships by (albeit sometimes loosely consolidated) institutional and political democratic systems.

The second important change was to substitute an exhausted model of internal economic development for a model where the economic sector sought a position in the global economy. The third change has taken place in the social structure and has led to an increase of poverty, social inequality, and emergence of precarious labor systems.

This context was to have a decisive effect on the relevance and development of public relations in South America. In the following sections of this chapter, a general contextual analysis, together with a discussion of specific political, cultural and social variables that have affected public relations, will be presented.

A BRIEF OVERVIEW OF THE MODERN HISTORY OF SOUTH AMERICA

The historical and structural focus of European dominance limited the local exercise of power in South America. This focus, based on the strict control of knowledge and production, known as Eurocentrism, permitted the early conquerors and colonizers to exercise unlimited control of the economic resources and products of the region.

Quijano (2005) detailed the workings of this scenario and suggests that a Eurocentric focus continues to persist. Issues such as identity, modernity, unity, development and democracy are the ghosts that still afflict the conscience and imagination of South America. These issues have led to a duality of purpose that needs to be resolved, and requires deciding whether to continue living with these ghosts or finding a means for the renewal of the identity production process.

Identity is an open heterogeneous project and not merely a simple historical issue. The production of a South American identity required the inevitable destruction of the colonial components of power. We cannot forget that the continent was subjected to a vicious and bloody colonization associated with the extinction of the Amerindian nations and the establishment of slavery.

This situation changed, during the early part of the nineteenth century, as result of the wars of independence that were led by Simon Bolívar, Antonio José de Sucre, José de San Martín, Bernardo O'Higgins, and José Artigas, who were able to overthrow the colonizers and to install slave-free republics that, notwithstanding, were to continue in the hands of local oligarchies.

Brazil was the only South American country that continued as a monarchy throughout the greater part of the nineteenth century. The definitive independence from Portugal and the adoption of a republic would only occur in 1889.

The history of South American colonization reveals the cultural and artistic submission of the local population to models imported from England, Portugal, Spain and France. This submission to European hegemony would also be reflected in the communication models found in literary expression, the arts, fashion, and social practices that were, in fact, poorly suited to the new world.

SOUTH AMERICA DURING THE TWENTIETH CENTURY

From the second half of the nineteenth century until approximately 1930, the nations of South America were the focus of a major migratory process which included Europe (Spain, Portugal, Italy, and Germany) and to a lesser degree Asia and the Middle East. There are many reasons behind this phenomenon that include wars, economic crises, epidemics, and unemployment.

The arrival of these immigrants favored the economic transformation of the continent, since the newly arrived dedicated themselves (initially) to colonization and later to the process of industrialization that was to become the major driving force behind the massive urbanization process that affected practically all of South America.

Most Portuguese came to Brazil and Venezuela. The Spaniards came to Argentina, Peru, Colombia, Chile, Paraguay, and Uruguay. The Italians emigrated to Argentina and Brazil. Peru was the focal point of a major influx of Asians that included the Chinese and Japanese. The most expressive concentration of Japanese however is to be found in Brazil (currently more than 1.5 million *nikkey*). Chile and Argentina, in addition to the Spaniards, received a major influx of German, Polish and Palestinian immigrants.

The Europeans readily adapted themselves to the new work regime. Argentina until

1930, for example, was characterized by full employment and in fact offered better working conditions and paid substantially larger wages than those paid in Europe for the same type of labor. It is because of this phenomenon that Argentina came to be known as the capital of South America.

It was during the twentieth century, and after being subjected to centuries of oppression and exploitation, that Latin America as a whole began to affirm its identity. The first decade of the twentieth century was marked in 1907 with a violent miners' rebellion in Iquique (Chile) that would be continued with the Mexican Revolution that began in 1910.

These events were followed by Brazil during the 1920s with the Prestes Column and the Revolution of 1930 that would bring Getúlio Vargas to power. This is one of the major reasons that Brazil was known (during the twentieth century) as the country of revolutions and counter-revolutions.

The emergence of organized labor movements, particularly in Chile and Argentina, occurred at the same time that Communist and Socialist parties were being organized throughout the continent. There were major similarities between the chain of events that led to the emergence of revolutionary leaders such as Augusto César Sandino (Nicaragua), Farabundo Martí (El Salvador), Julio Antonio Mella (Cuba), and José Carlos Mariátegui (Peru).

The reaction of the oligarchies was also equally felt and led to the emergence, for example, of José Vicente Gómez (Venezuela), Fulgencio Batista (Cuba), and Anastácio Somoza (Nicaragua).

This unique combination of events opened the way to major political expressions that led to the Bolivarian Revolution (1952), the Popular Front in Chile (1970), the nationalist movements of Argentina (1946), Brazil (1930) and México with the Institutional Revolutionary Party (PRI) founded during 1929.

The modernization that occurred between 1920 and 1950 required adjusting local economies to the requirements of the worldwide market place. The adjustment needed the substitution of imports, which could only be achieved through the creation of an internal market and, more important, through the implementation of a unique political design. This is precisely what happened during the 1930s with the creation of a national cultural expression where the urban masses became the new social focus.

The 1930s were also characterized by weak and corrupt government, with the emergence of Populist movements and charismatic figures embodying hope, nationhood, and social equality.

The most outstanding expression of these Populist movements was the charismatic president of Argentina, Juan Domingo Perón, who together with his wife Evita was the incarnate voice that vindicated nationalism, anti-imperialism and "trans-classism."

Perón's first government (1946–1955) granted formal guarantees to the less favored social classes known as the "shirtless ones" or "descamisados." With Perón, Argentina achieved one of the most advanced social policies of South America, known as the *star system,* and witnessed the precocious decline of the Left.

In this scenario, the access of the masses to social equality provided the form and the substance to a unique national program that was linked to popular, charismatic leadership. This is exactly what happened with Lázaro Cárdenas in Mexico (1934–1940), with Getúlio Vargas in Brazil (1934–1940 and 1951–1954), and with Juan Domingo Perón in Argentina (1946–1955 and 1973–1974).

It was during the 1950s with the implementation of developmental policies in many nations of South America, where multinational business began to arrive, that public relations became a structured activity that was systematically practiced by these organizations.

The Role of the Military

The idea behind the modernization of South America during the 1960s and 1970s was a model of economic growth that required the transformation of the state and society.

The social and political movements that espoused this idea and that took place after the Cuban Revolution (1959) rattled the status quo of many countries in the continent.

As a result, initiatives that would lead to the consolidation of egalitarian societies were toppled by the dominant oligarchies. Such was the case in Chile, where the government of Salvador Allende (1970–1973) was overthrown by a military dictatorship that would perpetuate itself for seventeen years.

The military dictatorships were the obvious answer to social, political, cultural and labor unrest that had emerged as a by-product of the exploitation, discrimination and oppression of the less able elements of society.

The military dictatorships based their claim to power on the doctrine of National Security, where the militarization of the state gave the armed forces the role of political guardians who governed through the use of repression and censorship. In addition, these regimes entered into strategic alliances with the United States of America in the struggle against Communism.

No South American country escaped from military rule. From the 1950s to the 1970s the military took power in Paraguay (1954), Peru (1962), Brazil (1964), Bolivia (1964), Argentina (1966 and 1976), Chile (1973), and Uruguay (1973).

Not all dictatorships were alike. The military takeover in Brazil occurred during a major expansion of transnational capitalism, which was marked by the strong presence of the state in the economy and through the organization and control of state-owned companies. The presence of the military in Chile was associated with the neo-liberal policies that would become an essential component for modernizing the economy.

The military who took power in Argentina during 1976 witnessed their own stagnation and demise when the entire world was afflicted by a major economic recession. There is widespread consensus that the Argentine military dictatorship was a cruel exercise of misguided power. It is calculated than more than thirty thousand persons were killed or went missing during the dictatorship. One of the more notable manifestations of this tragedy is represented by the mothers of missing political victims, known as the "Mothers of May Square."

Thousands of citizens were jailed, persecuted, maimed and murdered by the military dictatorships that took power in Argentina, Chile, Uruguay, Paraguay and Brazil. These vile repressive acts were often commissioned by the elite and dominant social sectors, which often worked in unison with the Central Intelligence Agency (CIA) or with official military and paramilitary organizations coordinated, for example, through Operation Condor.

This period was marked by the severe censorship of mass communication media. Newspapers and radio were the major vehicles for the diffusion of information. Television arrived in South America during the 1950s and, in practically all nations of the continent, it was introduced by the state. Television was seen from its beginnings as an essential component for the manipulation of mass media by the military and, paradoxically, would come to be regarded as the passport to modernization.

Television arrived in Venezuela in 1952 during the campaign to legitimate the dictatorship of Marcos Perez Jimenez, and was also used in Colombia (1954) as the major vehicle of propaganda for General Gustavo Rojas Pinilla. Chile was a notable exception to this rule. Television arrived during 1959 through the efforts made by the Catholic universities. In Brazil television arrived during 1950 as a result of the political lobbying of an economic group which was closely linked with the state.

Military rule had a devastating effect on civil society in countries such as Argentina, Brazil, Chile, Paraguay and Uruguay. In the majority of these nations, democracy would arrive as a fragile agreement between political classes and economic interests and led to a widespread lack of confidence in the new political players.

The Role of Non Governmental Organizations (NGOs)

During the 1960s a substantial number of European foundations began to assist Non Governmental Organizations (NGOs) in South America.

The 1980s saw a major expansion of NGOs throughout the continent. In Brazil, Peru and Chile this expansion coincided with the re-ordering of political forces into political parties who sought access to power with an effective and generalized discourse of central government with regard to the abdication of state intervention.

These two elements delimited the activities of many NGOs. The first was basically political, and created an institutional space for those political groups seeking access to power.

In Brazil, NGOs such as IBASE would provide important technical and political support to the groups that would later be affiliated with the Brazilian Worker's Party (Partido dos Trabalhadores).

The second element was purely economic and served to provide a structure to these community-based organizations that, in the long term, would achieve effective confidence in the management of their resources and in the efficiency of their interventions with public organizations.

The Return to Freedom

The 1980s and 1990s saw the return of democracy, heavily dependent on external capital. The foreign debt crisis of 1982 was the excuse used to begin the implementation of liberal political policies, which came to signify privatizations, the reduction of customs barriers and the emergence of an extremely flexible labor market.

Privatization brought economic crises, massive outsourcing, bankruptcy and the often criticized handing over of strategic sectors such as gas, water supply and energy to foreign companies.

The industrial deceleration that occurred in many South American nations opened the gates to social discontent. In can be safely concluded that the neo-liberal policies of the 1990s left a negative balance that generally led to the dismantling of the industrial infrastructure implemented between 1930 and 1950. In practical terms, this meant that the economic survival of many nations required the forced adoption of the structural adjustments and recommendations made by the International Monetary Fund (IMF) and the World Bank.

The success of neo-liberal policies required repression and exclusion. Official statistics reveal a sharp drop in the gross income of many South American nations between 1980 and 1990. The analysis of poverty and social inequality indicators during the 1990s reveals that more than 200 million citizens lived in conditions of poverty and extreme poverty. The comparison of this statistic with the statistic for 1970 reveals that there was an absolute increase of 70 million citizens (Sader, 2006, p. 854).

The net result of neo-liberal policies was misery and exploitation for the substantial majority of the population. In Bolivia, for example, 85 percent of the rural population dropped below the poverty line. More than one third of this population has no access to health services. In Brazil, 48 percent of the rural population survives below the poverty line. In Argentina, three million children live in chronic poverty.

On March 23, 1991—and with the explicit intent of articulating commerce, development and the free flow of capital, products and workers—the nations of Argentina, Brazil, Paraguay and Uruguay created the Southern Common Market (MERCOSUR in Spanish and MERCOSUL in Portuguese).

The passing of time revealed that the economic bloc had limited political relevance in many of the member countries. The economic crises that afflicted Brazil and Argentina during the 1990s and the pressure brought by the United States to join ALCA hampered the consolidation of the Southern Common Market.

Despite the participation of nations such as Chile and Colombia, conflicting interests still persist in the Southern Common Market.[1] Chile and Uruguay, who adopted open economic models, have made concerted efforts to join ALCA.

New Governments, New Trends

The twenty-first century arrived with new proposals for government. This was one of the many ways that the citizens of South America replied to the neo-liberal policies of the 1990s. These new proposals moreover have assumed two distinct groupings.

The first group is the group of self-proclaimed Leftist governments that emerged from the ongoing political process, and which did not undertake a radical break with previous political, economic and social policies. This is the case of Brazil, where President Luis Inácio Lula da Silva, who was first elected in October 2002, is currently in his second term of office that will end in 2010.

This first grouping also includes Uruguay, with Tabaré Vasquez (elected in 2005), Alan García of Peru (elected during 2006) and the unique case of Chilean president Michelle Bachelet (elected in 2005) and Álvaro Uribe of Colombia (elected in 2002) who is currently in his second term of office that will end in 2010.

In the second grouping are two governments which emerged from revolutionary processes. Hugo Chavez in Venezuela and Evo Morales in Bolivia (with their own unique traits) are both the products of institutional rupture. The change sought by this group is not merely rhetorical. It is clear that both Chavez and Morales will implement deep changes to the political and economic models of Venezuela and Bolivia.

Chavez is in the process of implementing the "Socialism of the Twenty-First Century" through a unique style of government that is both popular and arbitrary. Morales took office with the promise of establishing a government that would begin with a "productive shock," where the state exercises a decisive role in the nationalization of natural resources and departing from neo-liberal policies. The Morales government seeks to guarantee basic rights such as healthcare, education, and responsible citizenship.

Popular support for both Chavez and Morales is based on the guarantee of a strong, egalitarian State. Hugo Chavez, when beginning his second term of office in December 2006, decided however to control mass communication media. On 28 May 2007, President Chavez decided that he would not renew the concession of RCTV, one of the oldest and most television networks of Venezuela. It is clear that the arbitrary political policies implemented in Venezuela are hampering the continuity of free communication which is free from censorship.

---

[1] Chile joined MERCOSUR during 1996. Bolivia joined during 1997. Peru is a member nation since 2003. Colombia, Venezuela and Ecuador joined during 2004.

Between the two groupings is Argentina. President Nestor Kirchner was brought to power through an open, democratic election. He is the product of the political and economic woes that afflicted Argentina during 2000 and 2001. Although Kirchner is not from the traditional Left (his ties with Peronism are extremely strong), there is no option but to pursue nationalistic policies that will lead to the institutional and economic reconstruction of Argentina.

HISTORY OF PUBLIC RELATIONS IN SOUTH AMERICA

The history and development of public relations in South America has traditionally been dependent on the models and techniques practiced in Europe and in the United States of America. One of the reasons for this dependency was discussed by Ferrari (2003) who pointed out that the practice of public relations in South America was tacitly imposed by multinational business organizations which arrived during the first half of the twentieth century.

Most South American nations experienced an initial phase of industrial growth that occurred between 1930 and 1960. This period was associated with the arrival of many multinational organizations which brought in their hierarchical structures a public relations department, responsible for communicating with internal and external publics.

Table 33.1 shows the formal beginnings of public relations in South America. The first country that implemented public relations was Brazil in 1914, by the Canadian-owned São Paulo Tramway Light and Power Co. Limited. The remaining nations began to timidly adopt the practice of public relations during the 1930s and 1940s.

Public relations arrived in Argentina during the 1930s as a result of initiatives taken by transnational companies such as Lever Brothers (currently Unilever), Shell, Siemens, Swift Armour, Agfa-Gevaert, Price Waterhouse, Goodyear, Citibank, and Kodak. Local companies that adopt the use of PR include Peñaflor, Molinos Río de la Plata, Mastellone Hnos., Loma Negra, Juan Minetti, and Terrabusi. The practice of public relations, during these early years, was informal and often exercised by areas of the company which had no formal expertise in the area of communications.

TABLE 33.1

Decade and Economic Sector where Public Relations Was Instituted in South America

Country	Decade	Sector	Foreign Companies	National Government	Foreign Organization
Argentina	1930	Private	X		
Bolivia	1950	Government		X	
Brazil	1910	Private	X		
Chile	1950	Private	X		
Colombia	1940	Private	X		
Panama	1940	Mixed			X
Peru	1940	Private	X		
Uruguay	1950	Government		X	
Venezuela	1940	Private	X		

Source: Becerra Pajuelo, Nelly Amélia. Perfil das Relações Públicas na América Latina. Masters dissertation, Universidade de São Paulo, 1983, p. 48.

Public relations was introduced to Venezuela by transnational petroleum companies. Shell adopted PR during 1940 with the explicit objective of improving its relations with public opinion.

Public relations formally arrived in Uruguay during the 1950s with the creation of PR departments in the Army, Navy and Air Force. During the 1960s, the state company ANCAP—which is responsible for the administrating the production and distribution of fossil fuels, grain alcohol and Portland cement—established the first PR department.

It was also during the 60s that public relations departments were established in companies such as SUDAMTEX, ILDU, and Canal 4 Montecarlo. Newspapers such as El País and El Día also established their own PR departments. By the end of the decade, there were PR departments in companies such as Angenscheidt (a major retailer), Montevideo Refrescos (Coca Cola), FIAT, ESSO, Agencia Nacional de Informaciones (The National Information Agency) and airlines such as VARIG and PLUNA.

Chile formally established the practice of PR at the Braden Copper Company during 1952. Mario Illanes Peñafiel was the first manager of the Braden PR department. The first PR consultancy was established in 1953 by Ramón Cortez Ponce, formerly director of the School of Journalism at Universidad de Chile.

It is presumed that PR arrived in Bolivia prior to 1952 when the tin barons Patiño, Hoschill and Aramayo needed to improve their public image. The National Revolutionary Movement (MNR) was gaining increasing force and was continually announcing the overthrow of the tin barons. As a result, Rafael Ondorica, a Mexican publicist who was a follower of Ivy Lee instituted the practical application of public relations in Bolivia.

The beginnings of public relations clearly demonstrate the influence of imported PR models in the daily life of many organizations. The imposition of PR practices, brought by transnational organizations to their South American operations, led to local adaptations that were not always satisfactory. Local PR practices did not always meet the needs of specific publics. As a result, there was dissonance between what should have been practiced and that which, in point of fact, was practiced.

Free Communication Moves in an Opposite Direction

The discipline of communications however moved in a radically opposite direction to the pervasive authoritarian regimes that emerged during the 1960s in South America.

Pasquali (quoted in Medina, 2006) notes that "the region was marked by an innovative and progressive renewal of political and social communication theory." In this regard, it is more than likely that the development of communication and free expression in the region was a direct result of the oppression caused by dictatorships and reactionary societies.

One of the more relevant events in the renewal of political and social communication occurred in 1959 when UNESCO created CIESPAL (Interamerican Center for the Study of Latin American Journalism). The theoretical and political influence of CIESPAL would be felt, moreover, only during the 1970s. From that time on, other movements would emerge to foster the creation of communication policies that would challenge the pervading political context.

The Conference on Communication Policies for Latin America and the Caribbean, held during 1976, was the first of a series of regional meetings to be organized throughout the continent. In 1978, UNESCO created an international commission which was mandated to discuss issues and problems unique to the field of communications. This commission, which had among its members Gabriel García Márquez and Juan Somavía, was responsible for the preparation of the "McBride Report."[2]

It was also during 1978 that the Latin American and Caribbean Conference on Cultural Policies was held in Bogotá, Colombia. Immediately thereafter UNESCO created the International Communication Development Program and published in 1980 Resolution 4.19 that established the NOMIC (New World Order of Information and Communication). NOMIC was an international project for reorganizing the global flow of information through the concerted intervention of governments and the third sector. The resolution was unanimously approved in Belgrade during the twenty-first UNESCO conference.

In addition to overcoming a colonialist worldview regarding the creation of instances for the discussion and creation of communication policies, it was also during the 1960s that the pioneering schools of journalism included in their specializations advertising, cinema, radio and television, and public relations.

The creation of the new schools of communication was not always linked, however, to research. Content was focused primarily on professional training, the dissemination of applied research based on the industrial workplace, and heated discussions of theoretical issues.

It was also during the 1960s that these promising initiatives led to the almost simultaneous creation of two organizations dedicated to researching mass communications in Venezuela and Brazil. The Institute for Press Research (Instituto de Investigaciones de la Prensa) was founded by Jesus Marcano Rosas, at the Universidad Central de Venezuela. The Institute for Information Science (Instituto de Ciências da Informação) was founded by Luiz Beltrão, at the Universidade Católica de Pernambuco, Brazil.

Perhaps the most notable event of the decade (which has affected Brazilian PR until the present day) was the publication of the first book on public relations by Cândido Teobaldo de Souza Andrade in 1962. The book, *Understanding Public Relations* (*Para Entender Relações Públicas*) was the practical synthesis of the studies that Professor Andrade had undertaken during the 1950s. A review published by a São Paulo newspaper noted that "Teobaldo de Andrade was the indigenous pioneer of public relations in Brazil."

The military who ruled Brazil since 1964 decided to control the country's communication system through the creation of legislation which had the apparent purpose of protecting the exercise of communication. More than twenty laws and decrees were published between 1967 and 1978, whose chief objective was the imposition of a formal "discipline" on journalism, public relations, advertising, radio, television, the theatre, telecommunications, printed media, and cinema (Teixeira, 2000).

On 11 December 1967, Federal Law 5377 was published as the means to regulate the professional practice of public relations in Brazil. In specific terms, the law defined the profession through a set of controls that established specific parameters and sanctions for the practice of PR in Brazil. Such was not to be the case of neighboring South American nations.

In the final analysis, Brazil was the first nation in the world to adopt specific legislation for regulating the practice of public relations during a military regime.

[2] The MacBride Report, also known as *Many Voices a Single World*, is a document published by UNESCO in 1980. The report was prepared by a commission presided over by the Irish Nobel prize winner Sean MacBride. The objective of the report was to analyze the problems of communication throughout the world and in modern society, and in particular with regard to mass communication and the international press, and to propose a new communications order that would resolve these problems and promote peace and human development.

As a consequence of the law, in 1967 the School of Arts and Communications of the University of São Paulo opened the first four-year professional university-level degree program in public relations. With the exception of Brazil, which instituted a university level PR degree through federal decree, neighboring nations established at first non-degree granting university level programs.

Cavalcanti (1983), in the report prepared to analyze the status of the teaching of public relations, notes that as a result of political motivation, public relations was unjustly persecuted in many nations. The teaching of PR was particularly persecuted and discriminated in a number of state universities.

Humberto López López (1983) noted that the persecution was notoriously effective in Colombia, Mexico, Ecuador, Peru, Chile and Venezuela. In some universities, PR courses and programs were arbitrarily closed. In other universities, PR courses were downgraded to elective status. For example, during 1975, CIESPAL (Interamerican Center for the Study of Latin American Journalism) decided to close the public relations courses taught at the institution since 1959 in its annual seminars.

The influence of the military, as a whole, had a negative effect on the practice of public relations in South America. Public relations became a tool that was used by the totalitarian state to promote its interests and to hamper the free expression of public relations as a democratic activity.

Private organizations curtailed by official censorship focused their attention on protocol and ceremonies, and less on strategic issues. Such was the case of Brazil and Argentina and it was reflected in the content of the materials used to teach and practice public relations.

The Role of Public Relations Associations

The first advances in public relations, which occurred during the first half of the twentieth century, were practically isolated events that were undertaken by highly qualified professionals and executives, from other fields, who had no specific training in PR.

The founding of the associations that convened and prepared public relations professionals occurred, during the 1950s and 1960s, at the same time that the practice of PR was expanding in South America.[3] These associations had an important effect on the development of public relations since they were instrumental in the consolidation and institutionalization of the practice through formal training programs. The associations brought renowned international practitioners such as Harwood I. Childs and Eric Carlson who led specific PR training programs in Brazil and neighboring nations.

Immediately after the creation of the Brazilian Public Relations Association (ABRP) during 1954, a number of international events in the area of PR were organized. ABRP was instrumental in the establishment of the Interamerican Federation of Public Relations Associations (FIARP) on 26 September 1960, during the First Interamerican Public Relations Conference held in Mexico City.

---

[3] Public Relations associations created during the 1950s and 1960s include: the Brazilian Public Relations Association (Associação Brasileira de Relações Públicas—ABRP) in 1954; the Venezuelan College of Public Relations Professionals (Colégio de Relacionistas Públicos de Venezuela—CRPV), in 1956; the Argentine Public Relations Association (Asociación Argentina de Relaciones Públicas—AARP) in 1958; the Uruguayan Public Relations Association (Asociación Uruguaya de Relaciones Públicas—AURP) in 1962; the Paraguayan Public Relations Professionals Association (Asociación Paraguaya de Profesionales de Relaciones Públicas—APPRP) in 1963; The Center for Public Relations (Centro de Relaciones Públicas—CERP) in 1963.

FIARP during the two following decades was focused on the enrichment of university training as a means for improving the professional practice of public relations. Article 5 of the statutes makes it quite clear that FIARP should assure the prestige of the profession and strive to improve and standardize the practice and education of public relations.

The will and foresight of the members of FIARP led to the design of a curriculum that was adopted during the 1970s by the Université de Montreal (Canada), Universidad de Antioquía (Colombia) and Faculdade de Comunicação Social Anhembi (Brazil).

The efforts made by FIARP required that the member nations should promote the adoption of university-level training for public relations based on scientific knowledge and applied research.

The basic universal concept of public relations was approved during the Fourth Annual Meeting of the FIARP Governing Council convened in Rio de Janeiro during October 1963. Public relations was defined "as a socio-technical and administrative discipline which analyzes and evaluates public attitudes and implements a planned, continual and reciprocal communication action plan, based on the interests of the community, that is targeted at achieving an affinity and useful understanding with the public."

FIARP was in existence for twenty-five years. At the annual meeting of the Governing Council held during 1985 in Paraguay, it was decided that FIARP would cease to exist and become CONFIARP (Conferación Interamericana de Relaciones Públicas). Since that date, CONFIARP has become the integrating body for regional or national PR federations.

Arrival of International Public Relations Services

The neo-liberal policies adopted by South American nations during the 1980s and 1990s led to an economic dependency on the IMF and the nations of the First World which also allowed many multinational conglomerates to enjoy unlimited privileges in the region.

Paradoxically, it was also through the multinational companies that many innovative practices and models of communications were transferred to local organizations.

Beginning in the early 1970s, Brazil was to become the port of entry for international public relations companies who were experienced providers of integrated communication services. Many of these organizations chose Brazil as their regional headquarters since it was felt that the geographic extension of the country, population, and market potential provided a more than suitable focus for their operations. Table 33.2 shows when these companies arrived in Brazil.

TABLE 33.2
Arrival Date for International PR Agencies in Brazil

Year	International Agencies	Country	Agreements with National Agencies
1977	Burson Marsteller	USA	—
1980	Hill & Knowlton	USA	—
1995	Edelman	USA	—
1997	Ketchum	USA	In Press
1998	Jeffrey Group		
1999	Fleishman Hillard (*)	USA	Estrategia
2000	Porter Novelli	USA	CDN
2001	Manning, Savage & Lee	USA	Andreoli & Associados
2007	Ogilvy Public Relations	USA	—

(*) Omnicom Group.

The re-democratization of South America during the 1980s and 1990s revealed the need for transparency and symmetry, to both public and private institutions, in their relations with society.

It became apparent that earlier communications models and practices were no longer suitable to the interests of different publics. Consequently, many organizations began to work in a planned and strategic manner designed to achieve their objectives with the different publics.

University Level Education in Public Relations

The 1970s were a decisive period for the education and training of public relations professionals in South America. Table 33.3 shows the beginnings of PR at the formal university level.

TABLE 33.3

Establishment of University Level Degree Granting Programs and Public Relations Associations

Country	Beginning date of university-level PR education	Legal Professional status	Number of university-level PR programs in 2007	Founding date Public Relations Associations
Argentina	1968	NO	13	Consejo de Profesionales de Relaciones Públicas 1958, 1961, 1989.
Bolivia	1999	NO	1	Asociación Boliviana de Relaciones Públicas (ABOREP), 1973. Asociación de Relacionistas Públicos, 1999.
Brazil	1967	1967	106	Associação Brasileira de Relações Públicas (ABRP), 1954 Sistema CONFERP, 1969.
Chile	1992	NO	9	Colegio de Profesionales de RRPP de Chile, 1983.
Colombia	—	NO	—	Centro Colombiano de Relaciones Públicas y Comunicación Organizacional – CECORP, 1963. Academia Colombiana de Relaciones Públicas, 2002.
Ecuador	1990	NO	4 (*)	Asociación de Relacionistas Públicos y Comunicadores Organizacionales Ecuatoriamos (ARPCOE), 2002.
Paraguay	1966	NO	3	Consejo de Graduados en Relaciones Públicas, 1963, 1990, 2004.
Peru	1964	2005	7 (**)	Colégio de Relacionistas Públicos de Peru, 2004. Federación de Relacionistas de Peru, 1989.
Uruguay	—	—	—	Asociación Uruguaya de Relaciones Públicas, 1962.
Venezuela	2005	Ongoing	3 (***)	Colegio de Relacionistas Públicos de Venezuela, 1956. Asociación Venezolana de Técnicos Superiores en RRPP (AVTESURP), 2000.

(*)   There is only one university level degree granting program in Public Relations. The remaining programs offer specializations within a degree program.

(**)   Communication programs that offer master's and doctoral programs in Public Relations.

(***)   Two university level Communications programs offer a specialization in Public Relations.

With the exception of Brazil, which began university level degree granting programs in public relations during 1967, the neighboring nations as a whole began with the implementation of post-secondary technical PR programs.

In 1968, Argentina establishes its first university-level degree granting public relations program at Universidad John F. Kennedy. This initiative was to be followed in 1973 by Universidad Nacional de Lomas de Zamora, and subsequently Universidad de Morón. At present, thirteen university level degree programs are in existence.

Peru established its first post-secondary technical level program in 1964. Presently, a master's level and doctoral public relations programs is offered by Universidad San Martin de Porres.

Post-secondary technical level programs were established in Chile during the 1980s and the first university level program was established in 1992. In 2007, there exist eleven university level degree granting public relations programs and two post-secondary programs.

In Colombia, the practice of public relations in government bodies was formally forbidden in 1974. The net effect of this event was the practical extinction of university level PR education.

Paraguay established its first university level public relations program in 1992. Today, there exist three university level PR programs in the country.

The Uruguayan Public Relations Association (Asociación Uruguaya de Relaciones Públicas—AURP) has promoted public relations education and training since 1962. Nevertheless, there are no university level degree granting public relations programs in Uruguay.

The first university level public relations program was established in Bolivia, during 1982, as a result of the protocol signed by FIARP, the Bolivian Public Relations Association (Asociación Boliviana de Relaciones Públicas) and the Catholic University of Bolivia (Universidad Católica Boliviana). Since there was no student interest, the program was subsequently closed down. Degree granting university level education was re-established during 1999 by Universidad NUR in the city of Santa Cruz de la Sierra.

Public relations began in Ecuador at the post-secondary level, and later on at the university level, when the Faculty of Communication and Social Sciences established the program during 1968. The Universidad Tecnológica Equinoccial (UTE) is the pioneering organization for public relations in Ecuador. Universidad Técnica de Ambato, Universidad de Guayaquil, Universidad del Azuay, and Universidad Particular de Loja offer specific degrees in Communication Science.

Degree granting university level education was instituted in Venezuela during 2005 to substitute existing post-secondary technical programs. Today, there are two universities that offer PR as a major field of specialization.

With the establishment of university level programs, together with the proliferation of post-secondary programs, the teaching of public relations was subjected to a major theoretical influence from the United States of America and, to a lesser degree, from Europe. As a result, the region came to depend on concepts and instruments which, in many cases, were not adequately suited to the diverse contexts found in the continent.

This is the reason that we must comprehend that public relations is still in its developmental phase and that conceptual problems still continue to plague us. One of the major problems lies in the fact that more than 150 multiple definitions have distorted the concept of public relations.

Theoretical underpinnings are deficient, since the rationale for PR is provided by foreign publications that do not fit with the political, social and cultural context of South America. Most of the books authored by local PR practitioners and academics refer exclusively to international practices, and do not present a truly South American theory-based PR perspective.

The textbooks used until the last decade that became the standard reference for the teaching and practice of PR are translations of North American textbooks authored by Cutlip and Center (1952), Carlson (1953), Childs (1964) and Simon (1972). The textbook which became the procedural manual for PR was authored by Beltrand Canfield (1961). Canfield's *Public Relations* was published as a two-volume textbook in both Spanish and Portuguese.

Research undertaken by Ferrari (2004) regarding the publications used for the teaching of public relations in South America, reveals that North American textbooks continue to be used, and that new foreign titles have been incorporated in PR courses.[4]

In Brazil, the scenario has slowly evolved since the publication of the first Brazilian textbook by Cândido Teobaldo de Souza Andrade during 1962. Brazil leads the production of PR publications, and today there are eighty titles written by local authors that are to be found in the principal bibliographic catalogues. Nevertheless, a content analysis of these materials reveals that the majority quote foreign authors and that there was little progress in the discussion and assimilation of national and regional theoretical currents and perspectives.

Ferrari (2004) also pointed out the existence of a number of specific historical studies regarding public relations in South America, which include the studies undertaken in Brazil by Andrade (1962) and Becerra (1983), Délano (1990) in Chile, Escalante (1968) in Argentina, and Merchán Lopéz in Venezuela (1978).

In Uruguay, public relations was portrayed by the Uruguayan Public Relations Association (Asociación Uruguaya de Relaciones Públicas—AURP) and later by the public relations and communications journal *Revista Relaciones Públicas & Comunicación* edited and published by AURP since 1991. Oxilia (1976) described public relations in Paraguay. Sampér (1963) discussed the importance of public relations in Colombia. Flores Bao (1981) analyzed the human interaction of public relations in Peru and Dulfredo Retamozo (1980) defended the practice of public relations in Bolivia.

Graduate Education

The University of São Paulo School of Communications and Arts is a notable exception in the national and international scenario and particularly in South America. The school was the first to teach social communication in Brazil and was also the first to offer an undergraduate public relations degree in 1967 and, beginning in 1971, a graduate degree program in communication science.

It was from this school that the first holders of doctorates and master's degrees in public relations emerged. The success of this graduate program was one of the principal factors behind the prestige gained by PR throughout the region.

---

[4] GRUNIG, James E. (org.) *Excellence in public relations and communication management*. Hillsdale: Erlbaum Associates, 1992. GRUNIG, James E. & HUNT, Todd. *Managing public relations*. Hillsdale: Erlbaum Associates, 1984. CUTLIP, S., CENTER, A. and BROM, G. *Effective public relations*, 9th edition, New Jersey: Prentice Hall, 2005; LESLEY, Philip. *Os fundamentos de relações públicas e da comunicação*. São Paulo: Pioneira, 1995. LERBINGER, Otto. *The crisis manager—facing responsibility*. Hillsdale: Erlbaum Associates, 1997; WILCOX et al. *Relaciones Públicas—Estrategias y Tácticas*. Madrid: Pearson Educación, 2001.

The research studies undertaken at the school during the last four decades became the textbooks that were to be used by other PR schools for the university-level training of new professionals.

Twenty-one graduate level PR/communication science programs are currently operating in Brazil. These programs require the approval of the Federal Ministry of Education which is officially responsible for establishing and controlling graduate education in Brazil.

The largest programs are housed in the School of Communications and Arts (ECA-USP) in the University of São Paulo (USP), the Methodist University of São Paulo (UMESP), and the Social Communication Faculty of the Catholic University of Rio Grande do Sul (FAMECOS-PUC/RS).

In the neighboring nations, post-secondary technical programs became the standard professional training medium.

The fact that these programs did not grant a university level professional degree led to the establishment, during the last two decades of the twentieth century, of complementary programs in public relations and social communication that granted a professional degree or graduate level extension degree. Presently, graduate level public relations programs are found in Peru and Argentina.

Public Relations Loses its Prestige

The boom enjoyed by marketing during the 1980s created tensions with public relations, which was enjoying a period of renewal brought about by the liberalization of politics and the economy.

Marketing emerged with the explicit purpose of increasing market share. Its results were measured in the short term, and were required to bring effective financial gains to the organizations.

At the time, most public relations professionals believed that PR pursued intangible objectives (behavior change or attitude reinforcement, for example) which were not linked to the financial aspects of a company. In other words, PR had nothing to do with the generation of profit.

This point of view allowed marketing to acquire a leading position in the administrative structure of many organizations together with the allocation of massive financial resources for the implementation of its strategies.

Many public relations professionals continued to affirm that their job was to "establish a mutual equilibrium between the organization and its publics." The furnishing of intangible results of their activities to the organization contributed, overall, to a permanent renouncing or abandonment of the space that PR had acquired.

Zapata (1998) explained that this abandonment "was caused by the failure of PR to define itself as an important player for the achievement of financial objectives that were valued by the organization."

The failure to commit itself to the achievement of profit undermined the occupation of a strategic position by public relations in most organizations. The exercise of the profession revealed itself to be distant from the practical mundane objectives of the organization.

To make the scenario complete, academia as a whole did not play an active role in the legitimating of public relations. Referring specifically to Brazil (which always privileged university level PR education), the distorted vision of many universities, which did not privilege research, limited the generation of knowledge regarding the practice of public relations in diverse institutional contexts. The sad truth is that, for all South American countries, the majority of the individuals who are working in PR have no formal training and education in public relations.

A related problem that is common to neighboring nations is the limited application of formal research methods. The use of statistical methods in Brazilian PR research is practically non-existent.

Representative samples and hypothesis testing which can be used to generalize or isolate the effects of practices or expectations is not a relevant characteristic of PR research in Brazil.

The analysis of master's and doctoral theses published between 1980 and 2000 undertaken by Kunsch (2004) revealed that 23 of 126 dissertations used a mix of qualitative and quantitative methods.

This fact reveals that most researchers find it difficult to work with statistics and sophisticated research methods. The analysis also reveals the absence of theory-based PR research and the validation of the contributions made by Brazilian communications theorists. The general trend of the dissertations is to emphasize the use of tools and instrumentation, and to practically ignore organizational communication processes and new theories.

These results reveal that the majority of the research undertaken in Brazil has not addressed the development and testing of a normative theory that can be used to characterize Brazilian behaviors in communication management. Additionally, these studies evidence the theoretical fragility and the pervasive presence of a descriptive model that always shows "how it's done," but never addresses "why it's done."

Until the 1990s CONFIARP continued its mission of integrating national associations and also maintained a strong focus on university level education as the foundation for the practice of public relations.

Despite the efforts made by CONFIARP there was an unprecedented growth of universities throughout the region. Private universities proliferated in all nations of the region. Each institution targeted a specific market and did not ignore external trends. CONFIARP, nevertheless, was unable to monitor the creation and development of university level public relations and communications programs.

The same can be said for national public relations associations. In Brazil, for example, ABRP exercised until the end of the 1980s a predominant role in the training of PR professionals, in addition to promoting national and international scientific events. During the 1990s both ABRP and CONFERP began to lose their influence and prestige because law 5,377 limited the practice of PR only to those who were formally trained. As previously pointed out, the majority of PR practitioners are not from university level PR programs.

With globalization, many organizations sought highly qualified communications professionals independent of the degrees held from higher education institutions. Journalists were generally in the forefront of public relations. The reason for this may be less related to their almost intuitive understanding of the profession than because of the influence that journalism exercises on society as a whole.

Public relations, in point of fact, is a professional activity that is practiced by journalists in many South American nations. Since many nations in the region had no concern with establishing specific university level public relations education, it can be safely assumed that the journalist generally carried out the role of public relations.

Brazil was the most notable exception because of the law published in 1967. A review of the law was undertaken during 1994 in the forum of a National Public Relations Parliament convened by CONFERP. The objective was to rethink the profession and adapt it to modern requirements.

The debates ranged from maintaining the 1967 legislation to outright abolition of the law. In 1997, a document which detailed all suggested modifications was published and presented to the Federal Chamber of Deputies.

Since 1998, a draft for modifying the 1967 law has awaited a final decision by the Federal Chamber of Deputies. The modified law would open the profession to other university level graduates who would have to complete graduate level training in public relations.

It can safely be concluded that Brazilian public relations is undergoing an identity crisis. Many PR professionals are against maintaining the law, since throughout these past 40 years the law hampered instead of leveraging the practice of public relations.

While Brazil is attempting to rid itself of the regulation that hampered the development of the profession, Peru, Puerto Rico and Venezuela are working to create legislation that (in practical terms) creates a "market reserve" for the profession.

Panama in 1990 was the first nation after Brazil to regulate the profession. Peru regulated the profession in 2005, and created the "National College of Public Relations" as the official regulating body.

In 2007 a draft law was awaiting the approval of the Venezuelan National Assembly. The same phenomenon was occurring in Puerto Rico where the College of Public Relations professionals had completed a draft bill for approval by the Senate of the Commonwealth of Puerto Rico.

PUBLIC RELATIONS IN THE THIRD MILLENIUM

The new social order has brought new opportunities for the practice of public relations in areas such as the cultural industry, technology and the third sector. These new dimensions of contemporary society are the focus of communication and consequently public relations. Additionally, non governmental organizations are nurturing the growth of community communication.

Global sustainability and the environment are two concerns for changing the behavior of the new generations, which must be incorporated by organizations and institutions. Bringing this about requires a public relations which is able to communicate the policy and the goals that will enable us to better understand this world in which we live.

Public Relations in Present Day South America

The historical, political and economic panorama lived by South America during the past century helps to explain how public relations was defined and practiced during the last decades of the previous century and until the arrival of the third millennium.

A direct result of this panorama is reflected in the accelerated growth of the communication process in the university and how it was reflected in the consolidation of the region's media industry, and how the pioneering schools of journalism became the breeding place for the new schools of social communication. These institutions were to provide new degrees in advertising, public relations, cinema, radio, television, editorial production, etc.

According to Melo (2006), at the end of twentieth century there were approximately a thousand communications programs in the southern continent. Half of these programs are found in Brazil. In 2001 there was a total of 525 undergraduate communications programs. The content areas of these programs were distributed as follows: advertising (40 percent); journalism (35 percent); radio, TV, cinema and video production (14 percent), public relations (8 percent); editorial production (3 percent).

Recent research completed by Ferrari (2007) shows that the expansion of communications programs in Brazil is due to the direct support of the State which has authorized the opening of new higher education institutions. Year 2007 data reveals the existence of 750 university level communications programs. Of this total, 350 programs are in the field of advertising, 290 in journalism and 106 in public relations.

The contribution of pioneering social communications thinkers that projected South America to the world also needs to be recognized. These pioneers include, for example: José Marques de Melo and Paulo Freire (Brazil); Jesús Martin-Barbero (Colombia); Jorge Fernandez (Ecuador); Néstor García Canclini and Eliseo Verón (Argentina); Antonio Pasquali (Venezuela); Luis Ramiro Beltrán (Bolivia); Juan Diaz Bordenave (Paraguay); Mario Kaplún (Uruguay); Armand Mattelart (Chile).

These researchers were the founders of the Latin American School of Communication. The group emerged with the purpose of thinking through how communication was linked to Latin American culture. According to Melo (quoted in Dias, 2006 page 199), "these studies were a hybrid representation of the school's unique traits." In this mosaic of influences, it can be said that these studies incorporated the thinking of many sources which included European traditions, North American innovations, African values and the Amerindian heritage.

These same researchers were the protagonists in the creation of the many associations that, in one manner or another, were able to gather together public relations researchers. These associations[5] were responsible for research studies, and the production of diverse essential communication products required by the emerging cultural industry which includes public opinion and audience research, mass media, and customer persuasion.

During the past three decades, both the Brazilian Interdisciplinary Society for Communications Studies (INTERCOM—Sociedade Brasileira de Estudos Interdisciplinares da Comunicação) and the Latin American Society of Researchers (ALAIC—Asociación de Investigadores Latinoamericanos de la Comunicación) have worked to promote public relations and have made a concerted effort to disseminate public relations research studies in an effective proactive manner that is uniquely distinct from the efforts made by existing PR organizations. INTERCOM hosts a yearly event that is the meeting place for Brazilian researchers and the researchers of neighboring nations. ALAIC is responsible for the organization of a Latin American congress held every two years. Both ALAIC and INTERCOM have organized Social Communication into twenty research forums, where the most productive forums are public relations and Organizational Communication.

It can be argued that the visibility achieved by public relations in private and public organizations was not occurring in the world of academia. CONFIARP, which is considered to be the "integrator" of the region, was unable to integrate university level public relations education.

The work of CONFIARP became more difficult with the founding of two new competing organizations during the 1990s. ALACAURP, the Latin American Society of Public Relations Programs (Asociación Latinoamericana de las Carreras Universitárias de Relaciones Públicas) was founded in1999. Its membership consists of representatives from eight nations. Its mission is to promote and support university level academic research and graduate education in public relations.

The second new organization is ALARP (Asociación Latinoamericana de Relaciones Públicas). The mission of ALARP is to disseminate public relations throughout the South American continent. Both organizations were founded at practically the same time.

---

[5] CIESPAL (1959); INTERCOM (1977); ALAIC (1987); FELAFACS (1981); ABOIC (1981/1999); ACIC (2000); AMIC (1979).

These initiatives evidence the fragile nature of public relations. The absence of a solid theory-base that rallies its practitioners and the power struggle between the different organizations lead the casual observer to conclude that all these organizations were designed to promote their members, and not to disseminate the theory and practice of public relations.

These organizations, whether supported or not by a university, have been unable to promote neither national nor international research and, on the whole, have become the conveners or organizers of events that have produced little relevant scientific knowledge.

As a part of an effort for legitimating public relations, three journals[6] are being produced in South America. Two of these journals are published in Portuguese. The third journal is published in Peru.

The *Revista de Estudos de Jornalismo e Relações Públicas* was first published in 2003. The second journal *Revista Organicom* began publication during 2004. Both these journals are produced in Brazil. *Revista ALACAURP* is produced by ALACAURP, and began publication during 2004.

Is There a Latin American School of Public Relations?

The Latin-American School of Communication (founded by the researchers discussed in the previous section) was a reaction to functional North American models and to a number of sociological European theories. This reaction also had an impact on the development of public relations in South America.

As the offspring of an imported model, public relations was granted a guaranteed place in the organization and was criticized for being "defenders of capitalism." This precisely was the approach taken by Peruzzo in her book *Public Relations in the Capitalist Mode of Production* (*Relações Públicas no Modo de Produção Capitalista*), published in 1983.

Peruzzo asserted that public relations was used by organizations to create a climate for increasing the cooperation and productivity of the worker and to gain the collaboration of other publics with organizational policy and strategies. From this perspective, public relations was characterized as a set of activities designed to plan and manage the relationship of organizations with their publics and for guaranteeing the reputation of these organizations in society.

At the other extreme were those professionals who adopted "the understanding between parties" focus that was defined in the 1978 Mexico Resolution.[7]

In reality, the only author that addressed public relations as a science and gave it a distinctly unique focus was the Brazilian Roberto Porto Simões who, in 1984 published the book *The Political Role of Public Relations* (*Relações Públicas: Função Política*), where he describes public relations in the context of managing organizational policies. Conflict,

---

[6] *Revista de Estudos de Jornalismo e Relações Públicas*, published by the School of Journalism and Public Relations of the Methodist University of São Paulo is a biannual publication that is distributed through Brazil and South America. *Revista Organicom,* produced by GESTCORP/USP, is a biannual publication with national distribution. *Revista ALACAURP*, produced by ALACAURP, has no fixed distribution dates.

[7] This definition was prepared during the First World Assembly of the Presidents of Public Relations Associations during 9–11 August 1978, in Mexico City: "The professional exercise of public relations requires a planned action, which is supported by systematic communications research and planned participation, designed to elevate the level of understanding, solidarity and collaboration between an organization and the social groups that it interacts with, in the process of fostering legitimate interests that promote their reciprocal development and of the community to which they belong."

according to Porto Simões, is a pervasive social factor where the presence of the public relations professional is required to legitimate the decisions of the organization.

In academic and professional debates, most professionals hold as a universal truth that public relations is a managerial, strategic role and that a technical or tactical focus is not appropriate.

This new focus was disseminated and later adopted in South America by public relations professionals as a result of the assimilation of new European and North American theories for the teaching of public relations developed principally by James E. Grunig and his colleagues from the School of Maryland.

Grunig is considered the leading researcher of contemporary public relations. He has attracted the attention of South American researchers who have applied his models and theories in local research studies. The first of these studies was completed by Ferrari during the year 2000.

Two important international events held during the previous months[8] serve as a factual testimony regarding the importance of work undertaken by James Grunig and his colleagues, which reveals that his systematic approach to public relations is widely accepted and practiced in South America.

A number of important issues and reflections remain at the close of this chapter. Specifically, what is missing in the public relations research of South America? Is it necessary to develop new concepts and theories with roots in the particular experience of the region? Are there sufficient historical and political premises for unique South American thinking for public relations?

The reply to these questions will probably be given by the evolution of each individual nation. South America has gained a critical mass of researchers who can assure the consolidation of public relations. It can also be concluded that the interest in communications research has achieved an important place in both universities and private organizations.

In this scenario, we need to foresee the importance and the need for organizations capable of gathering the thinking of all nations in the continent. Our roads are constantly being renewed. Technology should be used to unite and to delimit a single unique definition of public relations which serves to reinforce the cohesive thinking and action of every professional and academic.

Final Thoughts on the South American Jigsaw Puzzle

A substantial component of the reflections regarding the practice of public relations is the future destiny of democracy in South America. The permanent incompetence shown with rare exception, by many governments in the region, when facing the challenge of eliminating social inequality and economic stagnation reveals an uncertain scenario that is always tainted by a hope which never seems to arrive. Research undertaken by the United Nations Development Program (2002) reveals a generalized dissatisfaction with the performance of democracy throughout the continent.

The analysis of political processes undertaken by Latinobarómetro[9] reveals an important perception, shared by a substantial number of individuals, that the region's leadership is

---

[8] First International Public Relations Seminar, Lima, Peru on 4, 5 and 6 December 2006 where Professor James Grunig was the keynote speaker of the event where he also was awarded the degree of Doctor Honoris Causa. In the First Congress of Communications Researchers held in São Paulo on May 3–5 2007, Dr. Larissa Grunig and Dr. Linda Putnam were the leading speakers of the event.

[9] The project established in 1995 is based on a similar European initiative, carries out yearly opinion surveys in 17 nations, and is an important evaluator for democratic support in the region.

incapable of addressing the expectations that they themselves created. In other words, the political discourse associated with the broad dispersion of power explains why many governments are so poorly rated and why a false link has been created between democracy and economic development.

Socio-economic inequalities have a direct effect on the practice of public relations. The first practical effect of social and economic instability is often the downsizing or outright elimination of public relations in both public and private organizations. Many executives perceive times of crisis as inappropriate for investing in public relations. On the contrary, many executives have expressed the opinion that the elimination of PR, during difficult times, is an important means of preserving scarce economic resources.

The most important threat to the profession, nevertheless, is the generalized lack of knowledge regarding the true role of public relations in organizations and in society as a whole. First and foremost is the generalized belief that any professional can be a successful PR practitioner. Secondly, many executives do not regard public relations as a strategic component of the business. Lastly, there is also the sad fact that many university-level public relations programs have not been capable of preparing truly competent professionals for the job market.

Nevertheless, economic prosperity and the arrival of a large number of transnational organizations have led to an increasing demand for public relations in Chile, Peru, Colombia and Brazil. Many countries have adapted the global practices of the newly arrived organizations to local scenarios, and have created what is being referred to as "glocal practices."

The political and ethical volatility which afflicts many South American nations motivated many public relations professionals to focus their activities on the development and application of strategies for negotiating social conflict.

PR professionals have effectively participated, through direct action with central governments, in the transition to more ethical and participative democracies. As a result, many nations are in the process of institutionalizing public relations through legislation that legitimates the practice of the profession.

It also undeniable that many organizations are slowly becoming more transparent in their practices. Social responsibility is becoming a business philosophy that is also an essential part of social and environmental sustainability. The concerted actions of NGOs and community pressure groups have also induced many organizations to adopt responsible practices with needy communities and the environment.

In this context, public relations emerges as the activity that is responsible for the relations between organizations and their publics. Let us not forget that, despite the fact that we may wish to conceive a single unique definition of public relations in the region, each nation needs to be seen with its own unique characteristics and through its political, economic, social and cultural systems.

Culture has become a crucial issue in the governance of many organizations. The specificities and unique characteristics of our culture have a direct impact on the managerial models of many organizations. Ferrari (2000) noted that "culture is an independent variable that influences the practice of public relations, since organizations and local institutions are integral parts of the national environment. Organizations are culturally conditioned and are subject to the values, principles, and traditions of a specific nation. The products of public relations are, in fact, the result of individual local contexts."

We need to recognize that the lack of true South American integration in the field of public relations is the result of many factors that include: a) the cultural barrier imposed by the use of Spanish and Portuguese; b) the preference for imported principles, concepts, and theories; c) ignoring all that is local and privileging imported foreign models; d) inequalities in the access to technology which have led to the digital exclusion observed in many nations of the region; e) limited financial resources for the funding of university research; f) the disconnected evaluation of undergraduate and graduate programs in public relations offered by different universities; g) insufficient support provided by universities and research centers for the production of local public relations contents.

The growth of public relations will become a reality only when governments, organizations and publics engage in continual dialogue. Communications professionals are ever more aware that the outright adoption of foreign successful models is a useless practice. We need to define the exact meaning and unique characteristics of the public relations that we practice. Everything we do in public relations requires adjusting to local realities that take into consideration the influence of culture, politics, the economy, medias and the idiosyncrasies of each nation. Public relations will be legitimated only when it truly meets the needs of its publics.

BIBLIOGRAPHY

Andrade, Cândido Teobaldo de Souza. *Para entender relações públicas*. 4a. ed. São Paulo: Loyola, 1993.

——. *Curso de relações públicas*: relações com os diferentes públicos. 6a. ed. revista e ampliada. São Paulo: Pioneira Thomson Learning, 2003.

Becerra, Nelly A. Pajuelo. *Perfil das relações públicas na America Latina*. São Paulo, 1983. Dissertação (Mestrado em Ciências da Comunicação)—ECA-USP, 1983.

Cavalcanti, Milton. Situação do Ensino de Relações Públicas na America Latina. *Informe sobre o Centro Interamericano e Estudos Superiores de Relações Públicas*. Punta del Este, 1983, p. 5.

Dias, Eliane P. M. *A voz da comunicação na America latina*. Comunicação & Sociedade. São Bernardo do Campo: PósCom-Metodista, a. 28, n. 46, 2°. Sem. 2006, p.199.

Ferrari, Maria Aparecida. *A influência dos valores organizacionais na determinação da prática e do papel dos profissionais de relações públicas*: estudo comparativo entre organizações do Brasil e do Chile. São Paulo, 2000. Tese (Doutorado em Ciências da Comunicação)—ECA-USP, 2000.

——. Novos aportes das relações públicas para o século XXI. *Comunicação & Sociedade*. São Bernardo do Campo: PósCom-Metodista, a. 24, n. 39,1°. sem. 2003. pp. 53–65.

——. *Perspectivas latino-americanas das Relações Públicas: trajetória da atividade e da profissão*. Paper apresentado no VII Congreso Latinoamericano de Ciencias de la Comunicación de ALAIC. La Plata, 2004.

——. O ensino da Comunicação no Brasil. Paper apresentado no *10°. Congresso de Jornalismo, Relações Públicas e Assessoria de Imprensa*. São Paulo, maio de 2007.

França, Fabio. *Públicos: como identificá-los em uma nova visão estratégica*. São Caetano do Sul (SP): Yendis Editora, 2004.

Fuentes, Carlos. *El espejo enterrado*. México: Fondo de Cultura, 1992, p. 339.

Garretón, Manuel A. La transformación de la acción colectiva en America Latina. *Trampas de la Comunicación y Cultura*. UNLP, Buenos Aires, Año I, no. 10, Fevereiro 2003, pp. 12–27.

Grunig, James E. A função das relações públicas na administração e sua contribuição para a efetividade organizacional e societal. Translated by John Franklin Arce. *Comunicação & Sociedade*. São Bernardo do Campo: Póscom-Umesp, a. 24, n. 39, p. 67–92, 1°. sem. 2003.

——. (org.) *Excellence in public relations and communication management*. Hillsdale: Erlbaum Associates, 1992.

——. and Hunt, Todd. *Managing public relations*. Hillsdale: Erlbaum Associates, 1984.

Kunsch, Margarida M. K. Tendências da produção científica em relações públicas e comunicação organizacional no Brasil. Revista *Comunicação & Sociedade*. São Bernardo do Campo: Póscom-Metodista, a. 24, n. 39, p. 93–125, 1°. sem. 2003.

Medina, Cremilda. Nas trilhas latino-americanas do direito social à informação. Texto apresentado no painel *"America do Sul: Aspectos Políticos, Econômicos e Sociais,"* realizado no IEA/USP em 20 de setembro de 2006.

Melo, José Marques de. O campo acadêmico da Comunicação: história concisa. IN *Pedagogia da Comunicação: matrizes brasileiras* (org.). São Paulo: Angellara, 2006, p. 23—24.

Mineiro, Adhemar S. e DURÃO, Jorge Eduardo. *PNUD*. Seminário "Democracia na America Latina: possibilidades de mudança e limites," 2003.

Peruzzo, Cecilia M. Krohling. *Relações públicas no modo de produção capitalista..* São Paulo: Summus, 1986.

Quijano, Aníbal. Dom Quixote e os moinhos de vento na America Latina. *Revista Estudos Avançados. Instituto de Estudos Avançados da USP.* São Paulo. Vol. 19, no. 55, set/dez, 2005, p. 23.

Sader, Emir (org.). *Latinoamericana: enciclopédia contemporânea da America Latina e do Caribe.* São Paulo: Boitempo, 2006, p. 854

Simões, Roberto Porto. *Relações públicas*: função política. 3a. ed. São Paulo: Summus, 1995.

Teixeira, João Evangelista. *Relações Públicas na Umesp: 30 anos de história.* São Bernardo do Campo: Umesp, 2000, p.28.

Thomazi, Maria Stella. *O ensino e a pesquisa em relações públicas no Brasil e a sua repercussão na profissão.* São Paulo, 1991. Tese (Doutorado em Ciências da Comunicação)—ECA-USP.

Zapata, Julio Henquiquez. *Começando, trinta anos depois do início. O Parlamento Nacional de Relações Públicas como fonte para determinar incertezas e problems da profissão.* Dissertação de Mestrado. São Paulo, Escola de Comunicação e Artes, Universidade de São Paulo, 1998, p. 10.

34

PUBLIC RELATIONS IN BRAZIL: PRACTICE AND EDUCATION IN A SOUTH AMERICAN CONTEXT

JUAN-CARLOS MOLLEDA

ANDRÉIA ATHAYDES

VIVIAN HIRSCH

When public relations arrived in Brazil in the 1910s it had a Canadian influence, but has since acquired the strong flavor of the largest South American country. This unique Brazilian flavor is enhanced by a combination of a nascent scholarship and a young democracy that emphasizes voluntarism and partnerships to overcome great social inequalities. The national iron and steel company (Companhia Siderúrgica Nacional) in Rio de Janeiro founded the first authentic public relations department in 1951 (Kunsch, 1997). The strong influence of Portuguese language and culture have isolated Brazil from its neighbors. This isolation has created a rich and unique rainbow of artistic, culinary, and social expressions. At the same time, that isolation has motivated Brazil to strive to reach out to the international community. The welcoming attitude of Brazilians is rooted in its history. This is a country that had peaceful transitions from Portuguese colonialism to independence and from military dictatorship to democracy.

Even though the country has grown inward, today Brazilians are open and eager to learn from, and share with, the world in every field of knowledge and professional activity, including public relations. As the largest country in Latin America with the eighth largest economy in the world, Brazil is a fertile environment for the growth of public relations. Brazil legalized the public relations profession in 1967 and created the most formal regulatory structure that is known worldwide. Regulating the public relations industry has its supporters and critics. Federal and regional councils seek to control the practice and set ethical and professional standards. This chapter seeks to introduce the reader to the complexity of public relations in this giant South American nation.

HISTORY AND DEFINITIONS OF PUBLIC RELATIONS

According to Dall'Agnol (1998), the evolution of public relations in Brazil can be divided into four periods: the pioneers, the professionals, the academics, and the researchers. The first period started on January 30 of 1914, when a Canadian corporation called The São Paulo Tramway Light and Power Company Limited created a public relations department (Kunsch, 1997; Peruzzo, 1986; Wey, 1986). Eduardo Pinheiro Lobo, considered as the father of the profession in Brazil, headed the first department. From the 1920s to the end of the 1940s, Brazilian public relations developed primarily in the government sector.

The second period of *professionals* began in the 1950s with a series of public relations classes offered at Getulio Vargas Foundation and the University of São Paulo. In both institutions, public relations courses and seminars were closed linked with business administration (Wey, 1986). In 1953, Getulio Vargas Foundation hired American professor Eric Carlson to carry out the first formal public relations program. Carlson worked with Sylla Chaves as translator and a couple of professors and professionals from various parts of Brazil (Chaves, 1963). Large organizations began expecting professionals to possess technical knowledge and skills, a change for a field that until then was considered a job for people with well-known family heritage who could easily develop influential contacts and friendships in cocktail parties (Wey, 1986).

The Brazilian Association of Public Relations (ABRP) was founded in 1954. A group of professionals from the private and public sectors in São Paulo sponsored its creation. According to Sharpe and Simões (1996), many of the founders of the association were related to the Institute for the Rational Organization of Work and the Institute of Administration of the University of São Paulo. The aim was to increase the strategic implementation of public relations in public administration.

The third period, referred to as *academics* by Dall'Agnol (1998), was characterized by the creation of social communication programs in the '60s and '70s expanding the traditional focus on journalism education to other communication disciplines as well. Among the prominent scholars who represent this academic stage are Cândido Teobaldo de Souza Andrade from the University of São Paulo, the first to graduate from a doctoral program in Brazil and author of one of the first books entitled *How to understand public relations* that was published in 1962. Another scholar was Marta D'Azevedo from the Federal University of Rio Grande do Sul (UFRGS), who wrote the book *Public relations theory and process* in 1971. Eugênio Wenhausen, also from UFRGS, coauthored with Roberto Porto Simões the publication entitled *An introduction to public relations* in 1974. Other notable educators were Nemercio Nogueira and Nei Peixoto do Vale (Dall'Agnol, 1998). During this period, public relations programs were created in several institutions of higher education all over the country.

The fourth period is led by Simões who is considered, after Andrade (1986), as one of the first Brazilian scholars to theorize the objectives of public relations. His book *Public relations: Political function* has been considered one of the most influential publications in the field since its publication in 1984. The Superior Council of Communication and Public Relations of Spain published the book in Spanish in 1993. Simões is one of the few, if not the only, Brazilian scholars of public relations who has published academic work in the United States (Sharpe & Simões, 1996; Simões, 1992). Some other scholars and professionals who have contributed to the study of public relations are Margarida K. Kunsch, Cecília Peruzzo, Sidinéia Freitas Gomes, Fábio França, Marcos Fernando Evangelista, Martha Geralda D'Azevedo, Walter Ramos Poyares, Hebe Wey, and Waldyr Gutierrez.

Brazil has one of the largest collections of public relations publications and research papers in Latin America. An impressive number of educators and researchers discuss issues concerning the profession and direct master's and doctoral theses. The Brazilian Society of Interdisciplinary Studies of Communication offers an online database with papers presented in its different congresses (Banco de papers, n.d.). Many universities with public relations programs have their own academic journals to publish studies or commentary papers primarily produced by their professors and graduate students.

The federal and regional councils offer comprehensive lists of publications in the field. The Website of the Regional Council of Public Relations Professionals (Rio Grande do Sul and Santa Catarina) has identified more than 500 publications in Portuguese and Spanish, including more than 100 books with an emphasis on public relations (Livros, n.d.).

DEFINITIONS OF PUBLIC RELATIONS

Official definitions of public relations have been offered by several institutions such as the Inter-American Confederation of Public Relations (CONFIARP), the national Federal Council of Public Relations Professionals (CONFERP), ABRP, as well as a group of scholars. Brazil is a founding member of CONFIARP, created in Mexico in 1960 (Molleda, 2001). Today, Brazilian Antonio-Carlos Lago is the president of the confederation and ABRP. His country is an active participant of the confederation and will host the 25th biannual Inter-American Congress in 2004.

In 1963, at the conclusion of the IV Inter-American Conference of Public Relations in Rio de Janeiro, the first official definition of public relations was approved and adopted by CONFIARP (known at that time as the Inter-American Federation of Public Relations, FIARP) and ABRP. The definition reads:

> Public relations is a socio-technical and administrative discipline with which the opinion and attitude of a public are analyzed and evaluated. Public relations is carried out through a planned, continuous program of reciprocal communication destined to maintain a beneficial affinity with and comprehension of the public. (Pérez-Senac, 2000, p. 22)

This definition emphasizes the influence of social and management sciences for the strategic use of public relations based on two-way symmetrical communication between an organization and its publics. This definition is compatible with those found in the United States body of literature (J. Grunig, 1992; J. Grunig & Hunt, 1984).

At the national level, the 1967 law (details in the legal section below) considers public relations activities as consisting of the following: the diffusion of information of institutional character from an entity to the public through the mass media; the coordination and planning of public opinion research with an institutional purpose; the planning and supervision of the use of audiovisual media for institutional means; the planning and execution of public opinion campaigns; and the teaching of public relations techniques according to norms to be established in the regulation of the law in 1968 (Congresso Nacional do Brasil).

From the legal and professional to the academic sector, public relations has acquired a distinctively Brazilian flavor. Simões (1992) defined public relations as a political function. He stated that an organization needs to convey "that it exists, with permission from a granting power (government) in order to produce something or provide some service to society.... [I]t must act in benefit of all of its partners in society. Its action must be geared toward the common good and never to its own interests. There must be an integration interest" (p. 196). The "integration" theme is present as a key element of the conception of public relations in Latin America (Molleda, 2001).

Additionally, Simões described six common public relations approaches in Brazil and South America:

1. the communication approach includes publicity and internal communication;

2. the marketing approach emphasizes product and organizational promotions;

3. the organizational legitimacy approach focuses on explicit ethical actions;

4. the motivational approach is carried out in conjunction with human resources;

5. the interpersonal approach concentrates on social, technical and political networking; and

6. the event organization approach includes the coordination of social and cultural activities as ends in themselves.

With a distinctive approach, Cicilia Peruzzo (1993) explained the social function of public relations by defining communitarian or popular public relations as "those committed with society transformation toward a stage of higher social equality" (p. 133). Peruzzo (1986, 1993) stated that it implies a new conception of the world and human beings, which includes building a fair and free society; seeking to defend the rights of citizens; seeing civil society as a promoter of change; encouraging the exchange of knowledge between disciplines of study to further political education among citizens, stimulating collective actions, autonomy and the sharing of decision-making power in social movements and other types of organizations.

The study of public relations in undergraduate and graduate programs is producing many master's thesis and doctoral dissertations. The wealth of research is constantly progressing and redefining the scope of the discipline. The next section focuses on public relations education in Brazil.

PUBLIC RELATIONS EDUCATION

In 1965, the International Center of Higher Studies of Communication for Latin America (CIESPAL) conducted four regional seminars to promote the redirection of journalism careers in communication or science institutes of "collective communication" (Meditsch, 1999). At a seminar in Rio de Janeiro, CIESPAL introduced the concept of a "polyvalent communication professional," a professional who could acquire a holistic knowledge of the mass media as well as perform scientific research, public relations and advertising. According to Meditsch, by 1970, a third of the schools in the continent had changed their names from "journalism" to "communication." By 1980, 85% of schools had made this change. The notion of "polyvalent journalists" evolved into the concept of "social communicators." However, it is significant to note that while the name was accepted, the idea of a "polyvalent communicator" was not accepted by educators. Brazil was the pioneer in defending the legitimacy and need for specialized studies in journalism, advertising, political propaganda, and public relations in Latin America. The emphases were offered under the umbrella of social communication.

In 1967, the University of São Paulo's School of Communication and Arts offered the first four-year public relations program. Since then, significant strides have been made in public relations education in the country. According to the Regional Council of São Paulo and Parana, public relations is currently being taught in 78 undergraduate programs and 24 graduate programs across the nation (Cursos de Graduação, 2002; Pós-Graduação, 2002).

In the past decade, under President Fernando Henrique Cardoso, the management and operation of higher education in Brazil has undergone significant changes. The Brazilian education department (Ministério de Educação), under the aegis of its higher education division (Secretaria de Ensino Superior or SESu), has established a rigorous system for evaluating graduate programs nationwide, with the goal of ensuring a minimum level of quality for both new and existing programs. Among the many evaluation instruments established for this purpose are curricular guidelines and quality standards.

To develop these documents, SESu formed committees of education specialists consisting of university professors from across the nation and solicited their input. Although these committees have existed in Brazil since 1985, when José Sarney was president, we have chosen to focus our attention in this chapter on the 1990s because it was during this decade that important changes were made in the teaching of communication, particularly public relations.[1] Based on Regulation Law 146/97 a Committee of Specialists in Communication Education (CEE-COM) was formed. The development of curricular guidelines was the main challenge faced by this committee. Many of the demands of public relations professionals, which were represented in the document developed by the National Parliament of Public Relations, were included in the curricular guidelines for communication.[2] This allowed the narrowing of the gap between educational and professional performance, obviating the need for a judicial-legal solution for the inappropriate practice of public relations by professionals in other areas.

The goal was to ensure that the demands of public relations professionals were addressed through higher education if not by legal means. The document emphasizes the specific abilities, in addition to the ones required for communication in general, that public relations professionals must possess regarding the development of relationships with key stakeholders, establishment of needs assessments and plans, development of strategies for improving relationships; implementation of integration instruments and programs; conduct of activities related to communication strategies; dialog between the typical functions of public relations and the other professional managerial functions that exist in the area of communication or other areas with which it interacts; and, finally, all other activities that common sense or public relations organizations may deem specific to this discipline.

Although the curricular guidelines for communication were not approved by the Higher Education Council until July 4, 2001 (through CES Resolution 16/2002), the final document had already been provided to the division of higher education. Based on this document, members of the newly formed committee developed quality standards for all areas of specialization.

The committees of education specialists completed its term in July 2002. The responsibility to evaluate and recognize graduate education programs in Brazil has been passed on to the National Institute of Statistics and Educational Research, the organization that oversees the national university examinations (known as "Provão"), using the quality

---

[1]The Committees of Education Specialists are made up of professors from different universities to provide assistance to the higher education division in the analysis of different activities within its jurisdiction.

[2]A national discussion regarding the attributes and functions of public relations professionals, which resulted in the development of a document, by CONFERP, aimed at revising the law that regulates the public relations profession in Brazil: Law 5.377/69.

standards developed by the committees.[3] The institute also is responsible for developing the Manual of Evaluation of Education Conditions, with 70% of criteria being common to all disciplines, and only 30% specific to each discipline.

From supranational to national definitions as well as academic and professional initiatives, public relations continues its development in Brazil. In particular, the profession faces a distinctive legal framework that is not found in any other country of Latin America. This regulatory framework has been blamed for excluding the term "public relations" from most private organizations (Kunsch, 1997).

LEGAL STATUS

According to Kunsch (1997), Brazil was the first country in the world to adopt a public relations legislation (Congresso Nacional do Brasil Law 5,377, December 11, 1967). Similarly, Panama has regulated the profession since 1980. Other Latin American countries, such as Costa Rica and Peru, have tried to pass laws to regulate public relations without success.

Federal and regional councils were created to enforce the law and to penalize those who did not comply with it. Professionals must have a public relations degree and be licensed by their states' regional councils to practice public relations legally. Despite the longevity of the law and the work carried out by the regulatory bodies, licensing has been difficult to enforce, especially at times when the scope of public relations has expanded and diversified (Molleda, 2002a).

The government recognized that under the 1967 law, public relations professionals could be licensed if they were practicing public relations since 1965 and they were ABRP members. Professionals must have practiced public relations for more than two years and received their main source of income from this practice. This provisional condition (provisionados) was accepted until 1969 when only professionals with a university degree in communication and an emphasis on public relations from a recognized institution or a foreign degree properly revalidated in Brazil in the Ministry of Education could obtain the professional license. Even though the government itself has gotten involved with law enactments, public relations agencies cannot be hired by government entities unless bids are solicited through advertising agencies. Moreover, public relations firms need to be subcontracted by advertising agencies for work to be directly provided to government. In some cases, public relations can comprise 70% of the marketing mix but will still have to be channeled via an advertising agency for government projects.

The law has lasted without modification for more than three decades and some scholars blame it as being a "serious obstacle for the growth and consolidation of the area" (Kunsch, 1997, p. 22). Public relations associations and councils have repeatedly addressed the nation's political, social and economic advances as a justification for updating the legislation. In 1998, at the conclusion of the four-year National Parliament of Public Relations sponsored by the Federal Council (CONFERP), changes to the law were drafted.

The national debate coordinated by the Federal Council produced a document named "Conclusions of the National Parliament of Public Relations," which was presented at the

[3]A national qualifying examination for 24 university programs. The students are submitted to this exam at the end of their graduating course in order to evaluate and measure knowledge and abilities acquired along the course. In the field of communication, only journalism has been included in this system since 1998. No date has been set for the inclusion of the other communication areas in this evaluation system.

XV ABRP Congress in Salvador, Bahia, in August 1998 (Conselho Federal, 1998). The decisions of the Parliament have not been made legally binding through the modification of the two first paragraphs of Law 5.377/69. As a result, CONFERP, under the direction of Flávio Schmidt, is working toward finalizing the document so it can be put into practice. Federal Council Secretary General Jorge Eduardo Caixeta, in an interoffice memorandum to the regional counsels dated August 20, 2000, noted that:

> In all regulated professions, it is the respective Federal Council that establishes what society should consider in order for concepts, behavior standards, and professional stance to be defined. ... It seems that we suffer from a chronic problem: all of us know what public relations is, what it does, what its specific activities are. And yet, when asked to define these concepts, we stumble, choke, and ... let time go by. Time has gone by and now it is past the time for us to assume the responsibility for doing so.

To achieve this objectives, in early 2002, the federal and regional counsels, in consultation with professionals in their respective states, drafted a resolution proposal that defines public relations professional activities in Brazil. This proposal is based on the original document developed by the Parliament. In August 2002, CONFERP's deliberative group met in Belo Horizonte, in the state of Minas Gerais, to further develop this proposal. The group has had difficulty in achieving consensus on two issues:

1. The definition of the concepts used in the field of public relations such as institutional, corporate, organizational, public, or civic communication. This issue is problematic because existing theories in Brazil regarding these themes include different terminology. Public relations professionals often use these terms interchangeably in their daily work and may also incorporate additional ones.

2. The fact that, because the existing law does not precisely identify the types of activities that are specific to public relations, many of them are currently recognized as appropriate for professionals such as administrators, marketers, journalists, and others. Claiming that these activities and functions belong to public relations will certainly lead to conflicts, perhaps even legal challenges, from these other professions.

Regarding this matter, França (2001) noted:

> It is difficult to determine, thinking ahead to 2000, which directions public relations professional activities will take. The practice of public relations seems fragmented, lacking a strategic positioning and favoring organized, integrative and systemic action. If it were strong enough to elevate the stature of public relations in the market along with those who dedicate themselves to it and the organizations who greatly need it. (p. 3)

Although the situation has improved significantly in the past five years, public relations in Brazil, although guaranteed a legal status, has not yet acquired legitimacy in the eyes of society. To achieve this legitimacy, CONFERP is focusing its efforts on obtaining a clear and objective definition of the functions and activities of public relations professionals, guaranteeing them defense subsidies, even if these are applicable only to legal matters.

The resolution proposal was approved in October of 2002. Highlights include: (1) The definition of the main concepts used in the field; and (2) the definition of varied public relations activities including those related to public relations education, which reflect the curricular guidelines approved in 2002 through State Council of Education Resolution 16/2000.

CONFERP realizes that the existence of the law in and of itself will not guarantee the recognition of public relations professionals by the Brazilian society. This will only occur if public relations graduates demonstrate that they are competent to practice the public relations activities described under the law. In addition to tackling legal aspects, which is its main function, CONFERP has created committees (coordenadorias) that work with higher education institutions to ensure that public relations professionals receive high-quality education.

The recognition of the public relations field by the different segments of Brazilian society is being promoted by the legal redefinition of the profession along with its unification with the national and international education sectors, thus ensuring that it has the theoretical and practical bases required for the full exercise of professional public relations activities.

TRENDS IN THE INDUSTRY

Duarte (2001) stated that despite efforts to regulate the public relations profession, encroachment has persisted over the decades. Journalists frequently perform public relations functions calling themselves "institutional journalists" (jornalismo empresarial). Such journalists see public relations as just the production of corporate publications and the diffusion of information on behalf of the organization. Another trend is the introduction of terms such as endomarketing, institutional marketing, social marketing, relationship marketing, and media training, which incorporate strategies and tactics historically associated with public relations. Professionals of other areas are gaining enormous visibility in the market and now present those approaches as novelties.

Other associations unite those professionals who have a broader view of corporate communication practices, which respond to the trend in integrated or marketing communication in Brazil. For instance, the Brazilian Association of Business Communication (ABERJE) claims to be the major entity representing social communication in Brazil (O que é a Aberje, n.d.). Its objective is to discuss and promote communication as an instrument linked to the strategic management of organizations and strengthening the citizenry. Founded in 1967, ABERJE claims to have a membership of more than 1,000 private and public companies and institutions from five administrative regions (O que é a Aberje, n.d.).

Nevertheless, and despite all these associations and legalities, any journalist in Brazil can open a small firm and call himself/herself a public relations practitioner. Brazilian business executives take these "media relations boutiques" into consideration and solicit bids from these firms also along with large global firms such as Edelman. There is a widespread misunderstanding in Brazil regarding the role of public relations. Most business executives regard public relations as mere media relations and measurement of success is determined by media advertising equivalency. The global messaging strategies and tactics are not yet recognized in Brazil. Instead, business marketing executives and CEOs engage a public relations firm to "put the product or executives in the media" with a positive spin—obviously at 1% or less of the cost of advertising.

According to the most recent association in Brazil inaugurated in 2001—Brazilian Association of Communication Agencies (Associação Brasileira das Agências de Comunicação, ABRACOM)—the size of the public relations market in the country is about US$ 50 million. If true, this would prove once again that the only recognition for public relations is still in its value as a tool of basic media relations activities.

INFRASTRUCTURE AND PUBLIC RELATIONS

This section summarizes the nature of the Brazilian infrastructure as it relates to public relations practices. Relevant aspects of the political and economic spheres as well as the extent of activism embedded in society are addressed.

Political System

Since winning independence from Portugal in 1822, Brazil has been a federal republic, with a new constitution that was promulgated in 1988. The president is popularly elected to no more than two 4-year terms. The 1994 elections marked the second presidential suffrage since the end of military rule. Fernando Henrique Cardoso won that election and won reelection in 1998. Labor Party candidate Luís Inácio "Lula" da Silva was elected president with 61% of the vote on October 27, 2002. This is the first time that a left-wing Workers' Party candidate has been elected President in Brazil's history.

Brazil experienced dramatic changes especially in the '80s and '90s (Ortiz, 1991; Santos & Silveira, 2001). Today, Brazilians enjoy the benefits of a young, vibrant democracy, despite its imperfections. Political rights improved substantially between 1984, when the military was still in power, and the early 1990s. According to Mainwaring, Brinks, and Perez-Linan (2001):

> In 1984, the last of the military presidents was still in office; citizens in state capitals and a number of other cities were not able to elect their own mayor; one-third of the federal senate had been elected indirectly in rules designed to guarantee majorities for the military government; communist parties were outlawed; and the left still faced sporadic repression. (p. 54)

These vestiges of authoritarian rule had been eliminated by 1990. As a result, there are many different political parties in Brazil. "[I]ndividuals are given significant freedom in expressing their beliefs ... this notion dates back to Brazil's founding, where different groups were not forced to assimilate fully to the Portuguese culture" (Gannon, 2001, p. 116).

Government institutions have realized the power of communication in a modern democratic society. In 1997, the Federal Senate created a large-scale communication operation with the purpose of promoting political education among the Brazilian citizens and motivating their participation in the nascent democratic process (Testa, 1999). The mission of the newly founded Secretary of Social Communication was based on the Brazilian Constitution, which emphasizes that citizens actively participate in grassroots democratic traditions. Access to information regarding the Senate, its members and actions, as well as open channels of communication between senators and citizens, were considered fundamental. One of the apparent outcomes of this initiative of the Brazilian Senate, which includes journalists in residence and mass media productions, has been an increase in political coverage by local and national media outlets and an increase in public awareness of the political system. It has motivated more inquiries from citizens about senators and legislation, which has been recorded by the "Voice of the Citizen," a "hotline" of the Department of Public Relations. Such democratic advancements have partly contributed to economic growth and the organization of increasingly active civil societies. A Code of Defense of the Consumer was enacted in 1991. According to Sorj (2000), the advances in consumers' rights have also become a channel of expression for the defense of the rights of citizens.

As democracy advances, Brazilian organizations have endured a hard fight for public recognition. The emerging society is much more oriented toward results. Quality of products and services, environmental protection, and social responsibility have become relevant matters for organizations. Since 1985, the advancement has empowered citizens. The democratic process has also challenged government officials. They are advised and assisted by public relations or social communication professionals who build bridges of participation between ministries and other governmental dependencies, organized groups, and common citizens.

Once a radical leftist, the newly elected president of Brazil portrays a renovated image of moderation and has been building linkages with industrialists, bankers, and stock exchange officials. As a consequence "many business leaders have moved to his side, seizing the opportunity to open an unprecedented dialogue with the leftist candidate [now elected president] and his team" (Lula's historic victory, 2002).

The young but vibrant Brazilian democracy, and the great inequalities the Brazilian population faces are pressuring organizations to increase their community involvement through partnerships with employees, other organizations, community groups, and local and federal government agencies. Nevertheless, Molleda's (2002b) study indicated that Brazilians continue to mistrust their government, which is characterized as being bureaucratic and inefficient. The study focused on the social role of public relations professionals including partnership with the government in developing social and educational programs. The "partnership with government" items created a distinctive dimension of the external social role but those statements were reported to have the lowest mean scores. Molleda (2002b) concluded that despite these results "[i]t is possible that progress toward participative democracy, voluntarism, and a stronger civil society will increase organizations' involvement with government and community initiatives" as a key dimension of the social role of public relations in Brazil (p. 21). This process may be accelerated by Lula's administration despite some skepticism on this issue in some circles.

Economic System

With an estimated 170 million inhabitants in 2000, Brazil has the largest population in Latin America and sixth largest in the world (World Bank, 2002). Eighty percent of Brazil's population lives in the south-central urban area. Whereas this fast growth in urban population has positively influenced economic development, it has also created serious social, environmental, and political problems for large cities.

Possessing large and well-developed agricultural, mining, manufacturing, technology, and services industries, Brazil's economy outweighs that of all other South American countries and is expanding its presence in world markets. In the information technology realm, Brazil is considered one of the 30 leading exporters of high-tech products. It occupies the 27th place in the world, according to United Nations.

However, since the 1960s, Brazil has ridden a roller coaster of high and low economic performance. The late '60s and early '70s were years of double-digit annual growth. In the '80s, however, its performance was poor in relation to its potential (World Bank, 2002). The adoption of a new Constitution in 1988 did not help much to improve the situation. Lack of flexibility was the result of the introduction of major rigidities in budgeting and public expenditure. In the early 1990s the Real Plan motivated economic recovery. The main goal of this plan was to reduce inflation and keep it low, which it did to the appreciation of the masses. The inflation rate before 1994 was four digits but was only a single digit in 1998. Despite the success of the economic program, the country faces the problem of poverty.

The new Brazilian democracy and the social equality challenges are also much more demanding of private organizations. There have been major changes in Brazil's emergent economy as well. During the 1980s, Brazilian companies went trough a process of economic adjustments and improvements that made them less dependent on being favored by the State and more suitable to compete in a world market. Brazilian "[c]onglomerates . . . don't have much more room to expand locally, yet they face increasing international competition at home," Adese says (2002, p. 29). Such is the case of Metalúrgica Gerdau S.A. which is located in the extreme south and is one of the fastest growing steel producers in the world (Rohter, 2001).

Environmental awareness among Brazilians has increased with the noticeable involvement of the private sector and civil society at large in discussions about taking actions to save the environment. While Brazil still has not approved genetically modified organisms (GMOs), the country requires labeling of the few imported products containing genetically modified products so that consumer can choose whether to buy them. Brazil has made significant progress in human development since 1975, which is a comprehensive measure of economic development (United Nations Development Programme, 2001). The state of São Paulo has produced a new index reflecting both human development and social responsibility.

Activism and Social Movements

In general, Latin American citizens, especially the lower strata of the population, are becoming more active and outspoken. The new unionism in rural Brazil, for example, is a consequence of the country's democratic transition during the 1980s. The unionism trend could increase in the administration of Luis Inacio "Lula" da Silva who was a former factory worker and trade union leader. The participation of civil society in the construction of a democratic system entails individual and collective involvement. Herbert de Souza, a.k.a. Betinho, was the principal leader of the Action Movement of Citizenry against Hunger, Misery and for Life (Movimento da Ação da Cidadania contra a Fome, a Miséria e pela Vida). Founded in 1993, this movement responded to the need of motivating citizens to participate in reducing the level of social fragmentation and exclusion (Plasencia, 2001). During its best years of 1993 and 1994, the movement had more than 5000 committees in different regions of the country. Three main campaign themes guided its actions: food for the hungry, work to eradicate the misery of the unemployed, and democratization of land ownership.

According to Plasencia (2001), the movement was inspired by the global promotion of democratic ideals and, paradoxically, the ever-increasing inefficiency of democratic regimes to facilitate ample participation of the people in political activity and public life. Democracy becomes not only the responsibility of political parties and the state, but also of every citizen as well, according to the principles of the Action Movement of Citizenry. It is necessary to discourage indifference and awaken the conscience of people for abandoning the culture of resignation. Even with this enhanced social conscience, Brazilians has yet to follow the steps of more developed nations and it is very difficult to form public interest groups to discuss matters of interest such as medical diseases or to protest against urban violence.

Social movements constitute a space to develop education programs in democracy. State and private organizations have developed partnerships with community groups, philanthropic institutions, and small businesses, creating new forms of solidarity. However, there appears to be more talk than action, especially in the hectic urban centers.

The growth of volunteerism in Brazil is evidence of "the seemingly intractable nature of Brazil's social ills such as the heightened concern over how to solve those problems and the growing impatience with government's ability to address them," according to Buckley (2001, p. A01). "It also is evidence of how the power of democracy . . . can go beyond free elections and fair trials to affect a society in ways that are subtler but no less profound."

The World Social Forum, the counter to the World Economic Forum, took place for the third time in Porto Alegre, capital of Rio Grande do Sul, in January 2003. Bruno (2001) stated that the United Nations has ranked Porto Alegre as Brazil's best metropolis in terms of quality of life: "For 12 years, Porto Alegre's budget has been decided by hundreds of well-organized community and worker groups" (p. 25). The city's mayor and its left-wing coalition from his Worker's Party (PT) have made progress in housing, public transportation, the health system, infrastructure, education, and legal system. This has attracted the attention of urban planners worldwide.

With the assistance of 100,000 activists from 156 nations and more than four thousand journalists, the forum, as one of its best events, had a protest rally against the creation of the Free Trade Area of the Americas (FTAA). Romero (2002) reported the view of Mark Ritchie of the Institute for Agriculture and Trade Policy in Minneapolis: "I was amazed at how the concept of corporate responsibility has grown in Brazil."

The democratization of Brazil and the difficulties of the economy have contributed to the birth of a more active society. A large number of nongovernmental organizations (NGOs) emerged during the 1990s dedicated to the issues of ethics and social responsibility. In this context, a large number of public relations programs have been implemented to support these organizations. The level of development, perhaps, is the aspect that impacts the evolution and practice of public relations in Brazil the most. This largest South American country is rapidly changing because of a vibrant democracy and an emerging economy while struggling to reduce the gap between different socioeconomic classes. This struggle is more pronounced in the large urban centers located primarily in the southeastern zone. The government sector is aware of the struggle and has increased its own internal and external communication activities. The private sector is also in tune with this fact and has contributed to ease the crisis with nonprofit initiatives such as the Ethos Institute of Business and Social Responsibility (Instituto Ethos de Empresas e Responsabilidade Social).

Ethos conducted research in the largest urban areas of Brazil and reported that a more demanding consumer is emerging who stresses the need for socially responsible organizations (Responsabilidade, 2001). Nevertheless, the government is still seen as the most responsible entity for dealing with crime and health problems. Private organizations are seen as a second force capable of contributing to employment and effective social transformation. The active and complex nature of Brazilians was dormant during the military oppression, but those cultural dimensions have always been embedded in the culture.

CULTURAL DIMENSIONS

The most common Brazilian greeting is "tudo bom?" meaning "is everything well?" This optimism is present in social interactions, making Brazilians a very friendly people. Gannon (2001) explained, "Brazilians have tremendous spirit in the face of adversity. . . . The well of this spirit is continually replenished by the Brazilians' passion for life" (p. 113). Brazilian society is very diverse given contrasting European, African, and Asian roots. The Brazilian population is made up of five major ethic groups: the indigenous full-blooded natives who mainly live in the upper Amazon basin and in the northern and western border regions; Portuguese who initiated intermarriages with natives and slaves since colonization in the 1500s; Africans brought as slaves; and, various other Europeans, Middle Eastern, and Asian immigrants who entered the country mainly between 1875 and 1960. Since the mid-nineteenth century, about 5 million Germans, Italians, Spaniards, and Poles have settled in the southern states of Paraná, Rio Grande do Sul, Santa Catarina, and São Paulo. The largest Japanese community outside of Japan is in São Paulo.

Mainly the white elite have cherished the myth of a racially balanced democracy in the country. But, since 1995, when President Cardoso brought the issue to the political arena, discriminatory cases and a different reality has been uncovered (Affirmative action, 2001). Rohter (2002) explained that "[o]fficially, less than half of Brazil's 175 million people are classified as black. But in a nation that likes to consider itself a racial democracy, 70 percent of those living below the poverty line are black, as are 80 percent of those who are illiterate, and some studies indicate that on average, whites live longer than blacks and earn twice as much" (p. A4). Being black seems to be a stigma in Brazil. Forty percent of Brazilians called themselves brown (i.e., mestizo) and only 5% called themselves black. According to the Brazilian Institute of Geography and Statistics, 5.6% of the northeastern population is reported black and 64.5% mixed race (parda) (Distribuição da população, 1999).

In September 2001, Brazilian officials attending the United Nation's antiracism conference in South Africa agreed to support quotas for blacks in universities and the civil service. Already, the State Assembly of Rio de Janeiro has voted to implement the proposal in the two universities it sponsors. Thus, the race issue is complicated. "There is a good amount of income inequality, and much of it is concentrated among those with darker skin pigmentation, even though Brazilians of all types tend to interact more easily in daily life than their American counterparts," wrote Gannon (2001, p. 116).

Brazil is the only Portuguese-speaking nation in the Americas. National identity is strong in spite of the variety of ethnic groups and class distinctions. This multiracial society or "Brazilian rainbow" has been isolated from its Spanish-speaking neighbors on the border regions of the Amazon rainforest and the Parana basin as a consequence of language, geography, and history. "Isolation has bred introversion. That partly reflects Brazil's vast size, self-sufficiency and fairly peaceful history. . . . Its legacies include ugly everyday violence and deep-rooted social inequalities" (Brazil's 500 years of solicitude, 2000, p. 15).

About 80% of the population professes to follow Roman Catholicism, with most others being Protestants or followers of practices derived from African religious cults. "As late as the 1990s, Brazil was recognized as the largest Catholic country in the world," according to Birman and Leite (2000, p. 271). These authors argued that it is not clear whether this is true today: "Doubts abound as we now witness the rapid proliferation of alternative religious movements (led by a burgeoning number of Pentecostal churches and sects), which has led the Catholic Church to adopt measures intended to recapture lost ground." In a strong uncertainty avoidance society such as Brazil, "we find religions which claim absolute truth and which do not tolerate other religions" (Hofstede, 1983, p. 83).

According to Hofstede's (1983) cultural dimensions, Brazil is a culture that strongly avoids uncertainty: "there will be a higher level of anxiety in people, which becomes manifest in greater nervousness, emotionally, and aggressiveness" (pp. 81–83). Nevertheless, Brazilians live in uncertainty because, especially in the political and economic arena, the future is unknown. Therefore, Brazilians seem to find ways to escape their reality with a great passion for life and optimism to overcome the anxiety that unstable scenarios cause.

On two other of Hofstede's dimensions, Brazilians are collectivistic with high power distance embedded in their society. This combination is defined by Triandis (2002) as vertical collectivism. That is, vertical cultures accept hierarchy as a given which is enhanced by the fact that collectivistic cultures are higher in conformity. Societies with high power distance let inequalities such as physical and intellectual capacities "grow over time into inequalities in power and health" (Hofstede, 1983, p. 81). "The latter may become hereditary and no longer related to physical and intellectual capacities at all," according to Hofstede. These aspects seem to be causing struggles within the population that, since 1985, is in the process of overcoming the repression of dictatorships.

According to Hoftede (1983), Brazil is considered a moderately feminine society. The feminine feature could be related to a peaceful transition from colonialism to a federative republic and from dictatorship to democracy. In general, Brazilians put relationships with people before money and appreciate the preservation of the environment (Gannon, 2001). This fact has been emphasized since the World Environmental Summit in 1992, when Brazil became the center of promotion and conservation of biodiversity.

Using Hofstede's (1991) fifth dimension of culture, Confucian work dynamism later described as long-term orientation (Hofstede, 2001), Brazil can be categorized as a short-term orientation society. The fact that the future is always unknown by Brazilians could in part explain this categorization.

Triandis (2002) elaborated on the dimensions of cultures, which could be easily interpreted to explain the complexity of Brazilian society. Subgroups with different interests, beliefs, and attitudes concerning a wide array of issues can be found in Brazil. In the southeast, where the major economic centers are located, the gap between the rich and the poor is great. "Affluence is shifting most rich cultures toward individualism," Triandis wrote (2002, p. 27). "Affluence has the consequence of making people independent of their groups." This reality is overwhelming sociologists.

More specific aspects can be analyzed when focusing on communication behavior and the impact of cultural dimensions. Brazilians as "[c]ollectivists use indirect and face saving communications. . . . This means that e-mail will be less satisfying to collectivists, since they will not have access to the context" (Triandis, 2002, p. 38). Taking into consideration the vertical collectivistic nature of Brazilian society, they limit the information they send to only some "important" people. Dealing with high- or low-status individuals, face-to-face communication will produce higher levels of cooperation among Brazilians. This assumption applies to media relations strategies, in which media owners, editors, and journalists should be approached both personally and through formal channels, with the former being a common and effective practice.

The cultural aspects of Brazil have an impact on public relations practices in the country. People orientation is a must in developing media, community, government and employee relations strategies. Human communication is a primary component of ongoing relationship efforts. Personal contacts, typified by the personal influence model, are essential to develop solid interactions with journalists, editors, and government officials. In public organizations and government agencies, a primary function of public relations is "protocol and ceremonial," which is the consequence of a culture characterized by high power distance.

In their pursuit of high and immediate impact, Brazilian and transnational corporations frequently opt for special events that attract a gathering of the masses. Nationalism and diversity (the Brazilian rainbow) are especially emphasized. This has been enhanced by a campaign promoting voluntarism among common citizens, organized groups, and a variety of institutions. One limitation for public relations planning is the short-term orientation found in Brazilian society whereby most of the strategic public relations programs focus on immediate and reactive actions.

MEDIA INFRASTRUCTURE

Media Control

The emergence of a commercial model of broadcasting in Brazil began in the 1920s. Magazine publishers, press agencies, advertising agencies, and radio and television broadcasters have pressed hard for a commercial media (Herman & McChesney, 1997). The Brazilian government did not establish a public broadcasting system for its propaganda efforts. Instead, it censored the media and tried to exert control over them. The influence of the government on the development of the media infrastructure in Brazil is summarized in the following paragraph:

> The Globo system was rewarded by the generals with huge subsidies in the form of a taxpayer-financed telecommunications network and satellite system, a very large flow of government advertising, discrimination against rival networks, which helped sink several of them. . . . The Globo network absorbs some 80 percent of TV advertising revenue and 60 percent of all Brazilian advertising, and it also controls vast interests in other media sectors (including *O Globo*, the [third] largest newspaper in Brazil, news and advertising agencies, record, printing and publishing companies, and all kinds of radio stations). . . . The ending of the military regime in 1985 did not curb the expansion of the Globo empire; the weak civil liberties that followed did not have the incentive or power to intrude. (Herman & McChesney, 1997, p. 165)

Brazil's largest newspaper is *Folha de São Paulo*, and the second largest is *O Estado de São Paulo*. *O Globo* is the third-largest daily. Nevertheless, the expansion of the Globo conglomerate continues in Brazil, Latin America, and the Spanish-speaking United States. Globo accorded a long-term strategic alliance with News Corporation considered as one of the largest global media oligopolies (Herman & McChesney, 1997). A more recent business partnership has been consolidated between AOL-Time Warner, Banco Itaú, and Globo to create AOL Brasil, which has moved forward the era of media convergence in Brazil.

Like many other Latin American countries, Brazil's media environment is considered to be *partly free* by the *Press Freedom Survey 2002* (Freedom House, 2002). A 1967 press law prescribes prison terms for libel, but this provision is rarely enforced. A 1999 law would penalize prosecutors, judges, and government attorneys for leaking information to the press about ongoing cases. The press is privately owned and newspapers have played a central role in exposing official corruption. There are dozens of daily newspapers and numerous other publications throughout the country. In recent years TV Globo's near monopoly on the broadcast media has been challenged by its rival, Sistema Brasileiro de Televisão (STB). A federal judge ordered the closure of 2000 community radio stations in São Paulo in January 2002 because the stations allegedly interfered with airplane flights! A number of journalists reported incidents of intimidation, including assaults and death threats. In the Ramo Branco electoral zone, media were prohibited from reporting on municipal elections by a local judge.

New information technology is helping to diversify the Brazilian media infrastructure and practices. Brazil has experienced an impressive growth in the number of Internet hosts from 268,000 in 1995 to 1,203,100 in 2000 (United Nations Development Programme, 2001). Between 1998 and 2000, Internet users have increased from 3.8 million to 16.9 million, displaying what a powerful channel of communication this new medium has become.

Brazil has a very sophisticated media infrastructure; some analysts say that the system is more advanced that the level of education of the population. Satellites are used for both the print (e.g., *Gazeta Mercantil*) and the broadcasting industry. Each corner of the vast country can be reached with any combination of media mix.

The sophistication of the media industry makes "media relations" an essential public relations function in Brazil. New information technologies are increasing the use of Internet communication between media and public relations professionals. Public relations professionals are conscious of the power of the media in mobilizing public opinion. Primarily, "information subsidies" or communication activities are oriented toward obtaining a favorable coverage of the organization, hiding unfavorable aspects that could be negative for the organization's reputation and "framing" organizational positions to influence positive responses when perhaps focusing on solving eventual conflicts (Penteado, 2002).

Former and current journalists (converted into public relations practitioners) dominate the media relations function (Penteado 1996, 2002). According to Penteado (1996):

> [P]ublic relations departments are usually divided between the "journalists," who are the press agents, and the mediators in a two way situation that usually deal with external environments; and the "public relations," practitioners who take care of the internal environment and of most events, and also responsible for most of the research. Journalists who, later covert to public relations may be those who tend to use one-way publicity and two-way publicity communication in Brazil. (p. 124)

CONCLUSIONS

To sum up the relationship between the Brazilian environment and public relations in Brazil, it is clear that the country has achieved a significant degree of professionalism and scholarship in public relations. "The profession as an institution is an unquestionable reality by the action of its professionals in several segments of society, in companies, universities" and by professional councils, associations, and labor unions (Dall'Agnol, 1998, p. 9). The legal status of the profession has its supporters and detractors. It is clear that Brazilian professionals can be separated into three camps: members of the regional councils, members of the business communication association, and many others that do not belong to either group.

Public relations is a constantly changing industry but in regions such as Latin America, these changes are much quicker and intense due to a series of socioeconomic factors. For example, one issue is devaluation of national currencies. Because the "recognition" of public relations in Brazil is basically limited to media relations, public relations fees which in the developed world would be of US$ 10,000 per month are only about 10,000 reais in Brazil, which at best be the equivalent of US$ 2800. Moreover, the slowdown of the United States and world economy, recent corporate scandals, and high oil prices are having serious effects on Latin America's economies.

Changes and trends have forced companies to act in a more socially responsible manner. Changes in the public relations industry have clients investing more in other areas of the communication mix that were previously ignored such as promotions and relationship marketing. They are also taking advantage of new technologies such as the mobile internet.

Despite economic difficulties, the public relations industry has grown in Brazil and Latin America over the last five years. The main differences are in the perceptions among executives of large national and multinational corporations regarding the use of communication as tools to pursue business objectives. Although a majority of clients still do not understand the full scope of public relations and insist in believing that media relations is what public relations is all about, some people do understand that public relations can be an effective way to manage organizational communication.

Public relations agencies have felt the effect of these changes such as a growth in the request for proposals, more demanding clients, better acceptance of specialized services and opinions, as well as increased confidence of those who hire their services. But, on the other hand, agencies too have had to strive to consistently provide better services, proactive attitudes and constructive criticism.

That said, agencies still face situations where clients have no idea of what they can do for their company, and still have the expectation of securing results comparable to those of their latest advertising campaign (for 1% of the price). Therefore, the trends we see for the near future are pretty much an evolution of what is already in place. Currently, we observe an explosion of niche publications clearly indicating a segmentation of the market, targeting new or emerging consumer groups. Along with that come the new forms of communicating with these publics. The use of e-publicity (or online media relations) is gradually but consistently replacing the old press-conference/press-kit format. Journalists today go to the Internet not only to find out if anyone has written the story they want to write, but also to analyze and discover new topics to write about.

In summary, an overview of public relations in Brazil and the environmental variables that influence its development allow us to make various assumptions. More democracy and economic complexity in a large nation positively influences the development of public relations as a professional practice and discipline of study. As the Brazilian economy stabilizes and its political system strengthens, public relations will continue to develop in Brazil, positively influencing the rest of the South American nations. A closer relationship between government, the private sector, community groups, media outlets, activists, and social movements may achieve the integration that seems to be the core of the Latin American school of public relations.

CASE STUDY: COCA-COLA AND THE PARINTINS FOLKLORIC FESTIVAL

Founded in 1886, Coca-Cola produces more than 230 brands in nearly 200 countries. Headquartered in Atlanta, Georgia, the corporation's first international bottling plant was opened in Canada in 1906 (Around the world, n.d.). Almost 50 years after it foundation, Coca-Cola arrived in northeastern Brazil in 1942 (A pausa que, n.d.).

The first bottling plants were located in the cities of Recife and Natal. They were called the "Victory Corridor" because this operation was part of the war efforts determined by the then-president of Coca-Cola, Robert Woodruff. During World War II, the corporation promised the United States military servicemen that, wherever they were, they would continue drinking cold Cokes at the same price of 5 cents. The outsourced Brazilian plants supplied the finished product to cargo ships heading toward Europe from the country's northeast coast.

Today, Coca-Cola Brazil is very much engaged in community initiatives. The page named "Example of Citizenship" of the company's Website in Brazil is introduced by these statements:

Citizenship means the consistent exercise of the rights and responsibilities of a citizen with the State. This is the commitment of Coca-Cola since almost 60 years of activities in Brazil, in which it has always tried to play an active role in social development of the communities where it operates in the country. At the end, our success is a fruit of a strong interaction with the public, the partnership between the corporation and the Brazilian society. (Exemplo de cidadania, n.d.)

Among the various social programs Coca-Cola has developed in this giant South American nation are environmental protection and conservation actions, educative programs, sport activities, and cultural programs. The best-known cultural program is the Folkloric Festival of Parintins; an event in which only Parintins residents can parade and participate in the professional choreographies that include themes concerning endangered species and environmental protection.

Legends, music, and complex dances are combined with blue and red colors in a unique jungle carnival. The annual Festival of Parintins, in Parintins, city of the Tupirambarana Island in the Amazon State, has been sponsored by Coca-Cola since 1995. The global beverage corporation partners with local and federal governments as well as community, environmental groups, other corporate sponsors, and the mass media to make this three-day event at the end of June possible. The promotional rights of the arena (bumbodromo) have been licensed to TV A Crítica, a company of the Brazilian System of Television (SBT), which is the main competitor of the largest broadcasting system Globo.

The estimated cost of this folk festival with cattle ranching roots is US$ 3 million (Nogueira, 2002). The Atlanta-based corporation has gradually increased its economic and promotional support from US$ 1 million in 1999, US$ 1.5 million in 2000, to US$ 2 million in 2001 (Coca-Cola, 2001). The festival is based on the rivalry that has divided Parintins in two camps: Garantido Boi (Guaranteed Ox) and Caprichoso Boi (Capricious Ox) supporters. The Garantido Boi supporters built their houses and businesses, which were painted red in one half of the town, while fans of the Caprichoso Boi built their house and business in the other half of the town and painted them blue. According to Darlington (2000), "even Coca-Cola has had to adapt. After Caprichoso supporters refused to buy Coke because of its red cans, the multinational Goliath created huge blue advertising banners, traditionally the trademark color of its rival Pepsi." As a corporate video says, "Coca-Cola wins over a city maintaining impartiality in the use of the red and blue colors" (Coca-Cola Parintins, 1999). The corporation had to invent a new logo for Parintins (Lengsfeld, n.d.).

The legend tells the story of a pregnant wife of a farmer who asked her husband to slaughter a prized ox, which symbolizes love and wealth, so she could eat its tongue. The angry owner searched for the farmer and caught him. The farmer was saved when a shaman (witchcraft doctor) revived the bull. This evolved into a century-old folk rivalry between the Capricious Ox and the Guaranteed Ox. As far as 1913, bands of singers in animal costumes have danced in the streets while improvising lyrics.

The Parintins festival started as an official competition between the Caprichoso and Garantido "bumbás" (groups of dancers) in 1964 (O festival, n.d.). Each group of around 3500 dancers and drummers stage this "Amazon Opera" for three nights, with three hours of spectacle each night. It combines the artistic beauty of the Carnival of Rio de Janeiro and the happy atmosphere of the Street Carnival of Bahia, all captured in the wilderness and density of the rainforest. The unique festival captures and promotes not only local legends but also scenes of daily life in the Amazon homeland.

Coca-Cola brought international attention to Parintins. "The festival has gradually reinvented the poor riverside community, showcasing the beauty and creativity of the far-flung region better known for environmental destruction and lawlessness," Darlington wrote. "But some critics are beginning to wonder if all the attention is helping erode decades-old traditions."

Celso Schvartzer, manager of institutional relations, explains that "Coca-Cola's main goal is to spread the festival in the regions where it still is not known. Here in the Amazon region it is already acclaimed, not just known" (Coca-Cola Parintins, 1999). The Amazon Secretary of State for Culture, Sports and Tourism estimates that approximately 100,000 visitors have attended the event in the last three years (Nogueira, 2002). It is expected that the number of visitors will increase this year because of the promotion of the festival in the Carnival of Rio.

After five years of logistic and financial support, the success of the festival is a concern for the main sponsor. As a consequence, Coca-Cola has limited the number of their national and international guests, which include media personalities, journalists, intellectuals, and opinion makers in general. Darlington (2000) quotes Tim Haas, president of Coca-Cola for Latin America, when he says: "You have to strike a balance between growth and traditional values. You have to be very careful you don't exploit this."

"Today Parintins has a new format, a business format," the Amazon Secretary of Culture, Robério Braga says (Coca-Cola Parintins, 1999). "Both an institutional and business relationship that consolidates the government, Coca-Cola [and] Kuat [aim] to promote the legitimate cultures making the Amazon people proud of their indigenous roots, their natural roots, for Brazil's 500 years we're going to have a green and yellow bull." These are the colors of the national flag.

The public relations efforts of Coca-Cola in Parintins go beyond publicity and media relations. They have nurtured long-term relationships with government officials and community groups as well as celebrities and tourists. The special attention to local political and community leaders is key in a country that is characterized by a vertical collectivistic culture, in which both the hierarchy and integration of society are interlinked.

The sponsoring organization is involved in operative and logistic efforts through its front-runner brand Kuat, called the guaraná of the Amazon. More than 700 workers from Parintins were hired to build and maintain a 200-guest balcony (glass box) inside a 35,000-set arena, or bumbodromo, where the festival takes place, and 50,000 square feet of social and sports club space. All the raw materials needed for the construction of these facilities are from the Amazon region as well as arts and crafts exhibits, furniture, and decorative accessories.

Brazilians enjoy large public gatherings, in which music, colors, and cultural expressions are combined. It seems the global giant has capitalized on that fact as other transnational corporations have done, such as America Online Brazil and its "Rock in Rio" music festival in January 2001. Any corporate engagement that promotes cultural values, concentrates large numbers of participants and spectators and reaches out to communities, celebrities, and government officials is likely to succeed and resonate through time.

REFERENCES

Adese, C. (2002, March). Corporate Brazil goes global: Latin America's largest competitors seek to buy and build international market share. *Latin Trade, 10*(3), 29–35.

Affirmative action in Brazil; I'm Black, be fairer to me; Brazil may adopt quotas, in education and jobs, for the darker-skinned. (2001, October 18). *The Economist*, p. 66.

Andrade, C. T. (1986). *Curso de relações públicas* (3rd ed.). São Paulo: Atlas.

A pausa que refresca 1942/1945. (n.d.). Coca-Cola Brazil Website. Retrieved March 12, 2002 from http://www.cocacolabrasil.com.br/quemsomos/historia/historia.asp

Around the World. (n.d.). Coca-Cola Website. Retrieved March 12, 2002, from http://www2.coca-cola.com/ourcompany/aroundworld.html

Banco de papers. (n.d.). Sociedade Brasileira de Estudos Interdisciplinares da Comunicação. Retrieved September 15, 2002, from http://www.intercom.org.br/papers/indexbp.html

Birman, P., & Leite, M. P. (2000). Whatever happened to what used to be the largest Catholic country in the world? *Daedalus, 129*(2), 271–290.

Brazil's 500 years of solicitude; It's time for South America's giant to shake off its inferiority complex. (2000, April 22). *The Economist,* p. 15.

Bruno, K. (2001). This is what democracy looks like. *Earth Island Journal, 16*(2), p. 25.

Buckley, S. (2001, January 9). Volunteerism is blossoming in Brazil. *The Washington Post*, p. A01.

Chaves, S. M. (1963). *Aspectos de relações públicas.* Rio de Janeiro: DASP.

Coca-Cola Parintins 99; Versão Inglês [English version]. (1999). (Videocassette produced for Coca-Cola in Brazil by AV Produções).

Coca-cola y el festival Parintins bailan nuevamente en el 2001. (2001). Coca-Cola Colombia's Website. Retrieved March 13, 2002, from http://www.cocacola.com.co/cocacolamundo/coca_col_sala_eventos.php#a

Congresso Nacional do Brasil. (1967, December). Law No. 5,377.

Congresso Nacional do Brasil. (1968, September). Decree No. 63,283: Regulation of Law No. 5,377.

CONRERP-SP. (2002). Conselho Regional de Profissionais de Relações Públicas 2ª Região—Retrieved September 15, 2002, São Paulo/Paraná: www.conrerp-sp.org.br

Conselho Federal de Professionais de Relações Públicas. (1998). *Conclusões do parlamento nacional de relações públicas* [Brochure]. Brasilia, Brazil: Comissão Redactora.

Cursos de Graduação. (2002). CONRERP—2ª Região São Paulo/Paraná. Retrieved September 16, 2002, from http://www.abrpsaopaulo.com.br/guiabrasileiro/cursos/gradua_rp.htm

Dall'Agnol, P. (1998). *The historic trajectory of the public relations profession in Brazil.* Paper presented at the First International Interdisciplinary Research Conference of the Public Relations Society of America's Educators Academy. College Park, MD.

Darlington, S. (2000). Brazil parties in the Amazon; festival celebrates Brazil's cattle ranching roots. *Reuters.* Retrieved March 6, 2002, from http://abcnews.go.com/sections/travel/DailyNews/brazilfest000719.html

Distribuição da população por cor ou raça. (1999). Instituto Brasileiro de Geografia e estadística (IBGE). Retrived September 15, 2002, from http://www.ibge.gov.br

Duarte, J. A. (2001). Assesoria de imprensa, o caso brasileiro. In A. T. Barros, J. A. Duarte, & R. E. Martinez (Eds.), *Comunicação: Discursos, Prácticas e tendencias* (pp. 1–14). Rideel: Brazil.

Exemplo de cidadania. (n.d.). Coca-Cola Brazil's Website. Retrieved March 12, 2002, from http://www.cocacolabrasil.com.br/empresa/cidadania/cidadania.asp

França, F. (2001). Relações públicas: visão 2000. In M. M. Kunsch (Ed.), *Obtendo resultados com relações públicas* (pp. 3–17). São Paulo: Pioneira.

Freedom House. (2002). *The annual survey of press freedom 2002.* Retrieved on October 14, 2002 from http://www.freedomhouse.org/pfs2002/pfs2002.pdf

Gannon, M. J. (2001). *Understanding global cultures: Metaphorical journeys through 23 nations* (2nd ed.). Thousand Oaks, CA: Sage.

Grunig, J. E. (Ed.). (1992). *Excellence in public relations and communication management.* Hillsdale, NJ: Lawrence Erlbaum Associates.

Gruning, J. E., & Hunt, T. (1984). *Managing public relations.* New York: Holt, Rinehart and Winston.

Herman, E. S., & McChesney, R. W. (1997). *The global media: The new missionaries of corporate capitalism.* London: Cassell.

Hodess, R., Banfield, J., & Wolfe, T. (Eds.). (2001). *Global corruption report 2001.* Berlin: Transparency International.

Hofstede, G. (1983). The cultural relativity of organizational practices and theories. *Journal of International Business Studies, 14*(2), 75–89.

Hofstede, G. (1991). *Cultures and organizations: software of the mind.* London: McGraw-Hill.

Kunsch, M. M. (1997). *Relações públicas e modernidade: Novos paradigmas na comunicação organizacional.* Brazil: Summus.

Lengsfeld, R. (n.d.). Parintins: A city divided into blue and red. TAM Airline. Retrieved March 6, 2002, from http://www.tamgetaways.com/city.html%BFaction=grt& rtid=15& city_id=9.html

Livros. (n.d.). Conselho Regional de Relações Públicas—4ª Região. Retrieved on September 15, 2002, from http://www.conrerprssc.org.br/

Lula's historic victory. (2002, October 28). Economist Intelligence Unit. Retrieved November 3, 2002, from EIU viewswire database.

Mainwaring, S., Brinks, D., & Perez-Linan, A. (2001). Classifying political regimes in Latin America, 1945–1999. *Studies in Comparative International development, 36*(1), 37–65.

Meditsch, Eduardo. (1999). CIESPAL: progreso y problema del comunicólogo. *Chasqui, 67,* 70–74.

Molleda, J. C. (2001). International paradigms: The Latin American School of public relations. *Journalism Studies, 2*(4), 513–530.

Molleda, J. C. (2002a, March). *The legal status of public relations in Brazil: The views of professionals.* Paper presented at V International, Interdisciplinary Public Relations Research Conference of the Public Relations Society of America Educators Academy. Miami, FL.

Molleda, J. C. (2002b). *International paradigms: The social role of Brazilian public relations professionals.* Paper presented at the 85th Annual Convention of the Association for Education in Journalism and Mass Communication. Miami, FL.

Nogueira, W. (2002, February 26). Bumbás planejan investir R$7,5 milhões no festival. *Investnews-Conteúdo Online Gazeta Mercantil, www.gazetorio.com.br.*

O festival folclórico do parintins. (n.d.). Retrieved March 6, 2002 from http://parintins.com/docs/festival.ph3

O que é a Aberje. (n.d.). Associação Brasileira de Comunicação Empresarial. Retrieved September 15, 2002 from http://www.aberje.com.br/

Ortiz, R. (1991). *A moderna tradição brasileira—Cultural brasileira e indústria cultural.* São Paulo, Brazil: Editora Brasiliense.

Penteado, R. (1996). *Effects of public relations roles and models on quality committed Brazilian organizations.* Unpublished master's thesis, University of Florida, Gainesville.

Penteado, R. (2002). Assessoria de imprensa na era digital. In J. Duarte (Ed.), *Assesoria de imprensa e relacionamento com a mídia; teoria e técnica* (pp. 340–362). Brazil: Editoral Atlas.

Pérez-Senac, R. (2000). Desarrollo y aportes de una corriente Latinoamericana de relaciones públicas. *Alacaurp, 1,* 21–26.

Peruzzo, C. K. (1986). *Relações públicas no modo de produção capitalista.* São Paulo Brazil: Summus.

Peruzzo, C. K. (1993). Relaciones públicas y cambio social. *Chasqui, 46,* 111–114.

Pinheiro, P. S. (1996, September/October). Democracies without citizenship. *Nacla Report of the Americas, 30*(2), 17–23.

Plasencia, J. R. (2001). *Cidadania em ação.* Brazil: DP&A editora.Wey, Hebe. (1983). *O processo de relações públicas.* Riode Janeiro, Brazil: Summus.

Pós-Graduação. (2002). CONRERP-2ª Região São Paulo/Paraná. Retrieved September 16, 2002, from http://www.abrpsaopaulo.com.br/guiabrasileiro/cursos/posgradua.htm

Responsabilidade social das empresas: Percepção do consumidor Brasileiro. (2001). Instituto Ethos. Retrieved March 5, 2002, from http://www.ethos.org.br/pri/open/publicacoes/index.asp

Rohter, L. (2001, August 30). From Brazil, an emerging steel giant. *The New York Times,* p. C1.

Rohter, L. (2002, August 17). The Saturday profile; from maid to Rio governor, and still fighting. *The New York Times,* p. A4.

Romero, S. (2002, February 7). Brazil forum more local than worldly. *The New York Times,* p. A18.

Santos, M., & Silveira, M. L. (2001). *O Brasil: Território e sociedade no início do século XXI.* Riode Janeiro, Brazil: Editora Record.

Simões, R. P. (1992). Public relations as a political function: A Latin American view. *Public Relations Review, 18*(2), 189–200.

Sharpe, M. L., & Simões, R. P. (1996). Public relations performance in South and Central America. In H. M. Culbertson and N. Chen (Eds.), *International public relations: A comparative analysis* (pp. 273–297). Mahwah, NJ: Lawrence Erlbaum Associates.

Sorj, B. (2000). *A nova sociedade brasileira*. Riode Janeiro, Brazil: Jorge Zahar Editor Ltda.

Testa, A. F. (Ed.). (1999). *Marketing politico e comunicação; o Senado e a opinião pública*. Brasilia, Brazil: Senado Federal Secretaria de Comunicação Social.

Triandis, H. C. (2002). Generic individualism and collectivism. In M. J. Gannon and K. L. Newman (Eds.), *The Blackwell handbook of cross-cultural management*. pp. 16–45.

United Nations Development Programme. (2001). *Human development report 2001*. New York: Oxford University Press.

Wey, H. (1986). *O proceso de relações públicas (3a edição)*. São Paulo, Brazil: Summus Editorial.

World Bank. (2002). ICT at a glance: Brazil. Retrieved on October 14, 2002 from http://www.worldbank.org/cgi-bin/sendoff.cgi?page=%2Fdata%2Fcountrydata%2Fict%2Fbra_ict.pdf

35

PUBLIC RELATIONS IN CHILE: SEARCHING FOR IDENTITY AMID IMPORTED MODELS

MARIA APARECIDA FERRARI

Seventeen years of military rule had a severe impact on the culture and behavior of the Chilean people. Under the military regime, few were willing to participate in public issues, because they were afraid of reprisals rather than because of lack of interest or creative ideas. Today's Chilean society is more concerned with daily problems and difficulties and appears indifferent to political and social issues. The legacy of the military has resulted in a striking lack of solidarity among Chileans, who appear to have become more individualistic and self-centered. Paradoxically, the social, economic, and cultural legacy created by the military, which was subsequently adopted by the new democratic regime, attempted to sell Chile as a *jaguar* or as a winner. As a result, the Chilean cultural and communication system has been based on a mystified concept of reality which is a mix of nationalism, leadership, competitiveness, success, and innovation.

Despite the first manifestations of public relations during the 1950s, it wasn't until the 1990s with the reinstatement of democracy and the globalization of the economy, that business expansion made possible the development of public relations in Chile. Notwithstanding the existence of seven university-level public relations programs, the profession is not fully understood and is confused with the activities practiced by journalists. This chapter will examine the impact of historical events on the freedom of expression, the media system, and in the practice of public relations among Chile's private and public organizations.

THE BEGINNING OF PUBLIC RELATIONS IN CHILE

As a profession, public relations formally began in Chile with the founding of the first public relations department at the Braden Copper mining company in 1952, with Mario Illanes Peñafiel as manager. In 1953, Ramón Cortez Ponce, a journalist and professor at the School of Journalism at the University of Chile, founded the first public relations agency in the country. Together with Uruguay, Argentina, and Bolivia, Chile was one of the last countries to integrate public relations to the formal structure of public and business organizations in Latin America (Becerra, 1983). Like the majority of Latin American countries, Public Relations accompanied foreign copper companies into Chile, soon to be followed by companies from the machine sector. Slowly, companies with 100% indigenous ownership such as Cristalerias de Chile, CMPC (Compañía Manufacturera de Papeles y Cartones de Puente Alto), and Compañía de Petróleos de Chile (COPEC) also adopted public relations functions. These companies hired the Ramón Cortez Ponce agency to advise them in designing and implementing their public relations efforts.

EARLY PUBLIC RELATIONS EDUCATION

The history of Public Relations in Chile is closely linked to the evolution of Journalism. The first School of Journalism was founded on May 28, 1953 at the University of Chile. The school also administered short courses on public relations and advertising. Dr. Juan Gómez Millas, Rector of the University of Chile, declared at the time that public relations and advertising courses were "an indispensable complement to Journalism" (Délano, 1990). Ramón Cortés Ponce became the first director of the School of Journalism at the University of Chile. He designed and taught the first course on public relations with the intent of demonstrating how "the similarities and differences between the theoretical and practical training of both professionals augment each other" (Délano, 1990). During the 1960s, several courses and seminars were conducted in other schools of journalism such as the Pontifícia Universidad Católica de Chile (in Santiago), and Universidad de Concepción (in the city of Concepción).

It was also during the 1960s that Carlos Aracena Aguayo wrote the first Chilean document addressing public relations as a formal discipline. The 114-page book, *Las Relaciones Públicas en Acción* (Public Relations in Action), is an unpretentious document presenting the history of public relations in the country together with proprietary course materials and information collected by the author during his participation in seminars and conferences held between 1958 and 1961.

A significant event in the development of public relations in Chile is the official ruling issued by the Controller General of the Republic in 1959. The ruling stated that "Journalists should also be responsible for the discharge of the Public Relations profession." Because they possessed legal recognition, journalists easily became public relations managers in public, state-controlled or municipal organizations. The private sector, however, was not bound by this official ruling. The ruling had great repercussions on the society because at that time, the state owned and controlled 70% of the economy.

El Mercurio, the most influential daily newspaper in Chile, published an article that categorically stated that journalism and public relations were incompatible professions. Despite the fact that each profession is well respected independently, combining the two posed grave risks to the application of ethical standards in public information. The newspaper emphasized that students interested in studying these two disciplines should choose to study only one and be convinced of the fact that both professions are incompatible (Délano, 1990). This early manifestation was the harbinger of the clash in prestige between the two professions where the greater prestige for journalism in Chilean society lowered the standing of public relations in the society in the years to come.

BIRTH OF A PROFESSIONAL ASSOCIATION

The Chilean Institute of Public Relations Professionals (ICREP) was founded on January 25, 1960 with the objective of promoting the professional development and the diffusion of public relations in Chile. ICREP offered a 150-hour, three-level, professional development program to its members. This program was subsequently recognized by The Interamerican Confederation of Public Relations Associations (CONFIARP).

The Chilean Institute for the Rational Administration of the Business Organization (ICARE) was another organization that played an active role in training public relations professionals in the country. ICARE also offered courses in the areas of marketing, finance, and human relations. The first intensive course on public relations was administered by ICARE in 1977. Oddly enough, public relations was the only area that declined in acceptance and did not perpetuate itself.

CLASS ORGANIZATIONS AS A MOBILIZING FORCE FOR PUBLIC RELATIONS

The emergence of national public relations associations in Brazil (1954), Mexico (1955), Venezuela (1956), Argentina and Panama (1958), and Peru and Chile (1960) resulted in the creation of Interamerican Federation of Public Relations Associations (FIARP) in 1960. FIARP was founded with the basic mandate of creating affiliated public relations associations in every Latin American country. The founding members of FIARP were Argentina, Brazil, Chile, Colombia, Cuba, the United States, Mexico, Panama, Peru, Puerto Rico, and Venezuela. The principal objective of FIARP was to defend and consolidate the profession through the organization and promotion of seminars and conferences, and to oversee the ethical practice of the profession. In 1985, FIARP made the transition to become a formally organized confederation currently known as CONFIARP (Interamerican Public Relations Confederation). CONFIARPs principal mandate is to maintain the integrity and identity of public relations in Latin America.

As noted earlier, ICREP (the Chilean Institute of Public Relations Professionals) was created in 1960 with the objective of integrating public relations professionals, and to provide opportunities for professional development through formal courses and training programs. On May 26, 1983, the Council of Public Relations Professionals Chile was founded with the purpose of integrating public relations practitioners and to replace ICREP. The principal motivation for founding this Council was to restate the role of public relations and to legitimize public relations practitioners' roles in society. This was necessitated by the fact that many public relations practitioners did not have formal training in public relations, and, in fact, many did not have formal training in any field of endeavor whatsoever.

However, the strategy of bringing legitimacy to the profession failed to come to fruition. Flanagan (1992) reported based on her research that "62.8% of Chilean executives did not know about the council or any other professional association. This shows that Public Relations does not have the social visibility required for an acceptable professional activity." For the past 19 years, the council has been the only formal representative of Chilean Public Relations professionals. Since there is no legal requirement for affiliation, its members have demonstrated a timid lackluster expression that has not led to an effective diffusion and legitimization of the profession. In September 2002, the council had approximately 500 members and is engaged in the promotion of public relations programs designed for small and medium-size organizations.

THE BIRTH OF PUBLIC RELATIONS EDUCATION IN CHILE

Until the 1970s, the Chilean university system was recognized as one of the best in Latin America. Chilean universities led intellectual developments in the field of modernization, Marxism, and free-market economy and provided the forum for the open discussion of these concepts. The failure of the Chilean socialist experiment and the demise of the Left precipitated the emergence of a right-wing dictatorship and the onset of conservative policies and neoliberal thinking in the economy. With the purpose of achieving structural change, a new higher education system was implemented in 1980. The implementation of the system led to the creation of technical education centers, professional institutes, and private universities. According to Eyzaguirre (1993), "the spirit of the new legislation was to increase the response to the demand for education and to make available resources more in keeping with the geographical and social realities where the new institutions were located." By 1983, Chile had 24 centers of higher education.

As a result of the new university system, professional level public relations programs began in 1980 at the National Public Relations School and at INACAP (National Training Institute). In 1985, public relations courses began to be offered at IPEVE (Professional Teaching Institute). Subsequently, public relations was also offered at the Instituto del Pacífico and DUOC (University Department for Farmers and Workers), which is affiliated with the Catholic University of Chile (Pontifícia Universidad Católica de Chile).

The emergence of professional institutes that offered operational and tactical-level public relations education benefited journalists. The formal requirement of a five-year university-level education allowed journalists to acquire the responsibility (to this day) for the management of communications in public and private organizations. Major political and economic transformations, that began at the end of 1980s, brought about a process of modernization and internationalization of the economy attracting many prestigious and experienced foreign business organizations to Chile.

This process of modernization and internationalization also brought new management styles to the country. The first major achievements became visible during the early 1990s, under the democratically elected government of President Patrício Aylwin. The stable economy was the result of free-market policies implemented during the previous decade. As a result, the potential for the field of communications was indeed extremely positive. Many public and private organizations began to organize their public relations and communications departments with a free-market perspective that needed to be sensitive to the challenges of globalization.

Flanagan (1992) reported in her analysis of 100 Chilean business organizations, that journalists managed 49% of the public relations/communications departments. In the remaining 51%, 12% of professionals were self-taught, 32% had university training in areas such as economics, business administration, law, or engineering, and only 7% had university-level degrees in public relations from foreign universities. Flanagan's findings reveal that public relations has failed to achieve the stature of journalism and other professions. One of the reasons for this lack of acceptance is the delayed recognition of university-level public relations education by the Ministry of Education. It was only in 1992 that the Ministry approved public relations as a field of study, which meant that prior to 1992, most practitioners held public relations positions without the required credentials as well as specific knowledge and skills. Délano (2000) concluded that, "the fact that the managerial and strategic role of Public Relations in Chile was never exercised by a professional specifically trained in Public Relations corroborates Flanagan's conclusions. Exceptions occur when the professional has been trained outside of Chile. In general, professionals in Public Relations positions are either lawyers, sociologists, engineers, or journalists."

The Ministry of Education officially recognized the first university-level public relations program offered by Universidad de Viña del Mar in 1992. In 1993, the programs offered by Universidad Santo Tomás, Universidad de Las Américas, and Universidad de Artes, Ciencias y de Comunicación (UNIACC), all located in the capital of Santiago, were also granted official recognition. In 1995, Universidad del Pacífico began to offer Public Relations education.

The quality of the Public Relations program offered by Universidad de Viña del Mar is noteworthy. The curriculum was reorganized in 1992, with a strategic managerial focus closely aligned to Chilean culture and values, by this author. Students also are required to plan and execute a supervised public relations campaign for the client organization. The education offered by this program, that takes four and one half years to complete, is considered to be the best suited for the requirements of the Chilean market (M. A. Salazar, personal communication, August 2000).

In 1992, the Extension Center of the Catholic University of Chile began to offer short training programs in Public Relations Planning, Corporate Image, Planning of Events, and Protocol. In addition, the concerted efforts of public relations educators made possible the organization of seminars and training programs with the participation of renowned international researchers and academics such as Margarida M. K. Kunsch (Brazil) and Otto Lerbinger (United States) in 1992, Melvin Sharpe (United States) and Roberto Porto Simões (Brazil) in 1993, and James Grunig and Larissa Grunig (United States) in 2000. Today, six private universities offer public relations programs.

In Chile, there is a noticeable difference between the teaching and reputation of public and private universities. Public universities (Universidad de Chile, Universidad de Santiago, and Universidad de Concepción) and the three traditional private universities (Pontifícia Universidad Católica de Chile, Universidad Técnica Frederico Santa Maria, and Universidad Adolfo Ibañez) have been in existence longer and boast of many former students who currently hold important public positions. The private universities, on the other hand, aren't as rigid in the selection of their students and do not have an alumni body comparable to "traditional" universities. The fact that the majority of the faculty has a social sciences or journalism background has given a certain "journalistic" bias to the education of the new public relations professionals. This bias, which is not totally pertinent to the requirements of the public relations market, will cease to exist when university public relations programs have faculty with comprehensive training in public relations, and who are less concerned with "informative" aspects and more with the strategic and managerial aspects of the profession.

Currently, there are no public relations graduate programs in Chile. Graduate-level professional education programs known as "diplomados" are offered in organizational communication by Universidad Diego Portales, Pontifícia Universidad Católica de Chile, and Universidad del Desarrollo (initially in the city of Concepción and currently in Santiago). In general, the curriculum totals 372 hours of class time and requires candidates to present evidence of completion of an undergraduate degree before gaining admission to the program. The programs were not designed to prepare researchers or academics but to train qualified professionals in the area of strategic organizational communication.

BIBLIOGRAPHY AND THEORY BASE

There are four public relations textbooks written by Chilean authors. In 1960, Carlos Aracena Aguayo wrote the first book titled *Las Relaciones Públicas en Acción* (Public Relations in Action). The second book, *Las Relaciones Públicas en Chile: fundamentos prácticos y teóricos* (Public relations in Chile: theory and practice), was written by Bárbara Délano Alfonso in 1990. This book presents the personal biographies and professional history of three early Chilean thinkers in the area of public relations. Délano also details the active principles of public relations and, in the latter chapters of the book, discusses the importance of protocol for the public relations professional. In 1993, Pablo Eyzaguirre Chadwick wrote *Manual de Relaciones Públicas* (Public relations manual) discussing a number of operational definitions and process requirements for public relations, and detailing the importance of protocol and etiquette in the organization of events. Eyzaguirre also wrote a fourth textbook called *Relaciones Públicas* (Public relations) in 1997.

The remaining textbooks used in Public Relations programs are mainly translations of books written by James E. Grunig and Todd Hunt (*Dirección de Relaciones Públicas*, 2000), John Pavlik (*La investigación en Relaciones Públicas*, 1999), Philip Lesly (*Manual de Relaciones Públicas*, 1973), and Scott Cutlip and Alan Center (*Relaciones Públicas*, 1963). The only exception is the book written by Roberto Porto Simões (*Relaciones Públicas: función política*, 1993) which was translated from Portuguese. There are two dissertations that address the practice of public relations in Chile. The first is the doctoral dissertation written in Spain by Catalina Flanagan Simonsen, in 1992. The second is the master's dissertation written by Carmen Gloria Ortega in 1993 at California State University, Hayward. The limited number of Chilean publications on the subject, together with a highly abstract theoretical base from abroad, is one of the principal impediments to the development of research and practice that conforms to local cultural requirements and idiosyncrasies (Ortega, 1993).

The absence of indigenous research and the ensuing lack of dissertations in public relations have made Chile totally dependent on foreign concepts and theory that bear no relationship to Chilean culture and identity. The main question for public relations researchers and academics is whether to follow North American or European models or to develop a unique Latin American identity that is free of foreign influence. This issue is closely linked to the legitimization of university-level public relations programs that have existed for a decade. Similar to what occurred in other Latin American countries, the Council of Public Relations Professionals Chile was unable to achieve a representative stature and to legitimize public relations practice in Chilean society.

There is no available data either on the number of private and public organizations that have a public relations department, or on the number of professionals who have graduated from university-level public relations programs. One of the explanations given to justify this situation is the fact that there is no legislation regulating the practice of public relations (as in Brazil, Panama, and Peru). Further, there exist no additional registration requirements, beyond a university diploma, to monitor the public relations professional.

B. J. A. Délano (personal communication, August 2000) addressed this issue when she emphasized, during her interview with the author, that "universities and professional institutes which provide Public Relations education are not interested in publicizing the true number of graduates. The statistics would reveal that the number of graduates far exceeds available work positions. A number of Public Relations professionals estimate that there are approximately 6000 graduates. Approximately 1000 graduates have achieved placement in the Public Relations job market. Of these placements, about 120 can be found in strategic organizational roles."

CHILE AS A NATION: DEMOGRAPHICS AND A BRIEF HISTORY

From its independence in 1818 until the military coup of 1973, Chile suffered three brief interruptions from civilian democratic rule. During the twentieth century, specifically from 1932 until the fall of Allende in 1973, Chilean constitutional rule had remained intact. Two thirds of the population of (15,050,341) (as of September 2002) live in cities. Since the 1992 census, the population of Chile has increased by 12.8%. After Cuba and Uruguay, Chile has the third lowest population growth in Latin America, with Argentina in fourth place. Due to the accelerated growth of the population aged over 60 years, the base of the demographic pyramid is undergoing a profound change. Chile is one of the more urbanized and industrialized countries in Latin America, and boasts a literacy rate of 95%. The country possesses a sophisticated social security system that is funded by individual capitalization mechanisms. The system has been operated since 1983 by a number of Administrators of Pension Funds (AFP), and requires the participants to deposit part of their monthly income in a savings account that is used to float the pension fund. The ethnic composition of the country is mainly derived from immigrant Europeans with indigenous inhabitants constituting a small percentage of the total population.

CONTEXT OF THE CHILEAN ECONOMIC AND POLITICAL SYSTEM

The main issue for Latin America is the definition of the role of government in promoting development, political stability, and social order. Today, Latin American governments are at the mercy of world markets and the pressure groups, while facing a chronic lack of financial resources. Besides the efforts of the government, Chilean society has met the challenge of addressing the new realities of political power and the pressure to increase public expenditure. Over the past 10 years, new political strategies have led to a political and social consensus that has substantially reduced the social conflict seen in most Latin American nations.

Historical events have had a profound effect on the development of public relations in Chile. The beginning of industrialization of the country occurred during the nineteenth century with the often-dubious support of the British Empire. In 1879, the Chilean bourgeoisie drew the country into a war with Peru and Bolivia over the control of nitrate extraction. The arrival of multinational companies such as Guggenheim converted nitrate mining as the principal source for the economic well-being of the country. After the decline of nitrate, Braden Copper arrived during the 1930s to initiate the massive extraction of copper. International Telephone & Telegraph (ITT) arrived shortly thereafter operating telephone communication services, and later making substantial investments in the hotel sector.

Between 1945 and 1946, the United States and Chile entered into an agreement to strengthen the foundations of a continental defense system. The fragile economic situation experienced by many Latin American countries after World War II was one of the principal motives for establishing such military assistance agreements. In 1950, the Economic Commission for Latin America and Caribbean (CEPAL) was established to assist the region with economic and social development. The history of CEPAL can be divided into five distinct phases. When it was founded, CEPAL provided direct support for the industrialization required to help Chile depend less on imported products. In the 1960s, CEPAL's objective was the facilitation of reforms required for industrialization. During the 1970s, CEPAL provided orientation for the implementation of development strategies and the diversification of exports. In the 1980s, the issue of external debt was tackled through the promotion of structural adjustments coupled with economic growth. The 1990s were devoted to the equitable transformation of production processes.

The great merit of CEPAL was to seek and integrated perspective of development based on an objective interaction with regional governments. The goal was the development of an identity capable of defending regional interests, which would facilitate the implementation of structural change. The main idea was the modernization of the economy based on the adoption of first world technologies that would serve to break economic dependence on the United States that the majority of Latin American nations experienced during the second half of the twentieth century.

The 1960s witnessed the first signs that the Chilean economic system was wavering. The pace of economic growth was unable to induce an equitable distribution of wealth. Unions and left-wing political parties emerged to address the contradictions and injustice of the prevailing economic structure. The Chilean economy exhibited two distinct structural characteristics at this time: the concentration of the means of production in the hands of a reduced number of national and foreign investors, and a substantial foreign debt. Beginning in 1965, there was agrarian reform to diversify ownership that had hitherto been cornered by a minority. By 1970, a substantial number of agricultural estates had been expropriated. In addition, legislation was introduced to allow the Chilean government to acquire a part of foreign capital holdings. This led to the emergence of hybrid, state-controlled organizations that were able to receive foreign investments resulting, for example, in the "Chileanization" of copper mining. As a result, the Chilean government acquired control of 51% of the shares in largest copper mine in the country that was formerly owned by Braden Copper.

During the 1970s, a number of United States, European, and Japanese firms, established themselves in Chile in the areas of food processing, automotive technology, and petro-chemicals. Nevertheless, United States influence continued to play a dominant role in the formulation and implementation of Chilean economic policy. From 1973 to 1990, Chile lived through a military government commanded by General Augusto Pinochet Ugarte. Ideologically, the Pinochet government was a right-wing, anticommunist, conservative dictatorship with a paradoxical vision for progressive economic policies. Nonetheless, the Pinochet government has been singled out as one of the cruelest Latin American dictator-ships, and has earned the dubious reputation of being responsible for the dismantling of state economic intervention implemented during the 1930s.

Despite recent economic crises in different regions of the world (Mexico in 1994, Asia in 1998, and Argentina during 2001), Chile continues to demonstrate the macroeconomic stability that was implemented during the Pinochet government. Chile's financial system has been stable requiring no external economic assistance. Compared to its neighbors, Chile has a privileged economic situation, thereby offering opportunities for investment that are more optimistic than in other Latin America countries.

The Chilean political transition, together with a neoliberal market economy, has af-forded the country a democracy of opportunities ranging from an efficient and respected State through a society with pluralistic perspectives, to organizations which are beginning to be concerned with their publics. Despite the existence of a sound productive structure and a robust economic system, Chilean culture is still attached to the values and behavior of an outdated social model. In this context, business organizations seeking to expand their market share have given special attention to the intangible perceptions of the publics such as their image, reputation, and credibility.

Public relations has been slowly incorporated into organizations, either as an internal department or as an external communication agency. The practice of public relations has not been legitimated by executives, and is still confused with the press agentry practiced by journalists. The combination of economic growth and the consolidation of university level public relations programs could lead to increased participation of public relations in public and private organizations. Societal pressure for a better quality of life will probably force organizations to rethink their mission, objectives, and relationship with their publics. In this context, it will be easier perhaps to demonstrate the importance of public relations practice on business performance.

CULTURE AND POWER IN CHILE: VALUES AND IDIOSYNCRASY

To understand Chilean culture, it is necessary to review the Spanish colonization and its relationship with indigenous inhabitants. From the mixture of these two races, there emerged the mestizo who, because of their desire to be part of the Hispanic world, reneged their native heritage. According to Castellón & Araos (1999), the cultural identity of Chile was the result of three factors: (1) the Spanish language imposed by the conquerors; (2) national boundaries that were determined by distinct geographical features ranging from the desert in the north to the frozen glaciers of the south; (3) interpretation of the world through a hybridization of European Catholicism and the mystic relationship with nature that was native to the land.

Bassa (1996) further developed these concepts by revealing that "from colonial times when the Spaniard longed to return to the homeland, the Creoles wished that they had been born in Europe, the 'mestizos' who did not understand the ambiguities of the past and the Indian who longed for pre-Hispanic times. Even today, each segment of Chilean society hides its true identity and wishes to be the other" (p. 44). The political transition of the past decade and the adoption of a successful economic model reveals that the principal components of the power structure of Chilean society are the state, political parties, businesses, the Catholic Church, the armed forces, emerging ecological and feminist groups, and mass media. The critical boundaries are those that separate civilian society from the state and, within the state, the boundary that separates political power, political parties, and the armed forces.

Traditionally, the Catholic Church had been the leading mouthpiece of Chilean society. During the 1960s, the church was the driving force for social reform. It also played an important role in the area of human rights during the Pinochet regime. Today, the church has withdrawn from the political arena, dedicating itself to issues pertaining to moral order and social values. Nevertheless, the influence of the church is far greater in Chile than in any other Latin American nation.

Three examples serve to illustrate the influence of the Chilean church and its conservative outlook toward world issues. Chile is the only country in Latin America that does not have a law permitting divorce. The implementation of government policies regarding the use of condoms for the prevention of AIDS, proposed by CONASIDA (National AIDS Commission) have been curtailed by the strong negative pressure of the Church. Official discussion of clinical abortion is forbidden in the country. A number of analysts argue that the Catholic Church has "a lobby that is so effective that no one can notice it or be aware of its existence." Because of pressure by the Church, public relations campaigns designed to address these issues have been totally ineffective.

Contemporary Chilean history can be divided into three distinct phases: before, during, and after the military regime of Pinochet. Until 1970, Chile was an extremely conservative and traditional country where interpersonal relationships were closely aligned with family and friends and maintaining group solidarity—similar to the cultural dimension of collectivism that Hofstede (1984) identified. After the military coup in 1973, social relations were severely affected leading to the weakening of personal relationships and a conflict of ideologies. Since the coup, Chile has been divided between those who are "for" or "against" the Pinochet regime. With the return of democracy in 1989, Chile became an active player in the globalization process that led to concomitant cultural changes to which the society had to quickly adapt.

Currently, Chilean culture is in the middle of a transition between a religious paternalistic model characterized by insecurity and improvisation of work tasks, and a new model based upon technology, work rationalization, and the depersonification of social relationships. Researching public relations practice of Chilean organizations, Ferrari (2000) concluded that the public relations model adopted in this country was closely linked to organizational culture, and to the process of political and economic development of recent years. Of the 13 organizations that were studied, 6 could be characterized as having an authoritarian culture. The decision making in these stratified organizations was highly centralized and was made based on traditions. Four organizations studied were undergoing the transition from authoritarian to participative culture. Only three organizations in this study displayed a participative cultural model, where employee participation in organizational decision making was reinforced by the dominant coalition. The predominant organizational values of these organizations were: commitment, honesty, efficiency, and individualism. The stress placed on tangible rewards has intensified individualism and redefined the relationship between employees and the organization.

Another interesting finding of the study (Ferrari, 2000) was with regard to the model of public relations practiced by these organizations. Six Chilean organizations practiced the two-way asymmetric model based on reactive programs operating within an authoritarian cultural framework. Six multinational organizations practiced the symmetrical model, where negotiation and mediation were used to address the highly dynamic environment they faced because they belonged to the vulnerable economic sector that obligated them to a proactive stance with their publics. Only one company practiced the public information model. The study also revealed that 9 of the 13 organizations had former journalists as the public relations manager. Three public relations managers had a university education, but in a different discipline. The public relations manager of only one organization had formal training in public relations. Senior executives of these 13 organizations generally associated public relations practice with organizing events, and arranging parties or cocktails.

These results were confirmed by a study on the "The Best Places to Work" by Levering and Moskowitz (2001). According to this study, of the 10 best companies to work for, 8 were subsidiaries of a multinational corporation with headquarters in the United States, Germany, France, or Australia. The majority of the CEOs interviewed for this study declared that there was a "headquarters culture" that the subsidiaries attempted to reproduce. These CEOs felt that 50% of an organization's success is due to organizational culture. Twenty-five percent of the success of a subsidiary is due to the unique characteristics of the country. The remaining 25% is due to the team spirit that managers are able to achieve. An interesting finding was the paternalistic attitude that Chilean workers expect from their companies. This is different to what normally occurs at headquarters, and closely reflects the existence of a traditional relationship between the superior and a protected loyal subordinate.

PUBLIC RELATIONS AGENCIES

The Chilean communications scene changed during the 1990s as a result of the influx of multinational public relations such as Edelman, Porter Novelli, Ketchum, Burson Marsteller, and Hill & Knowlton. These organizations made a commitment to the development of public relations in Latin America and began work on improving the images of private corporations with the government, the media, and various other publics. Except for Burson Marsteller which operates independently, the remaining agencies have local affiliates. There are approximately 10 Chilean public relations agencies. Both multinational and Chilean agencies have been forced to provide a wide range of services because public relations has not been widely accepted as an independent profession. The majority of these agencies work with journalists who act as public relations professionals. Until the arrival of multinational agencies, Chilean professionals based their activities on a very limited tactical focus. Globalization and the liberalization of the economy have forced many Chilean companies to demonstrate more transparency in their operations. Multinational companies, mainly from the telecommunications, mining, and financial sectors, contract the services of international public relations agencies. Most Chilean public relations agencies, on the other hand, have restricted their activities to managing internal and external communications and press relations. It is quite common for a Chilean company to hire a press agent to transform a company executive into a newsworthy commodity.

PUBLIC OPINION AND THE INFLUENCE OF MASS MEDIA: CENSORSHIP AND FREEDOM OF SPEECH

Despite the new press law of May 2001, limitations to freedom of speech continue to exist in Chile. This is true for a diverse number of mass media vehicles, notwithstanding the efforts made to reimplement and improve the open democratic system that had ceased to exist during the military regime. A change in mentality to end the widespread self-censorship, a vestige of the military regime, which affects freedom of speech and the pluralistic development of mass media, is long overdue. Self-censorship has a great deal to do with the desire to not create problems or trouble for anyone. The journalist practices self-censorship because the effects of causing discomfort to certain interests may be personally disastrous to the journalist (Krohne, 2002).

Public decree no. 3.621 of 1981 transformed all professional councils into associations that had no power to control ethical practices or to require mandatory registration. The return of democracy has been unable to restore to the councils the rights that were withdrawn by this decree instituted during the military regime. This situation affects Chilean society as a whole bacause there are no means to ensure the quality and credibility of the communication professional. Chile is the only Latin American country where censorship of the cinema is enshrined in the Constitution (article no. 19). The long-overdue approval of the motion picture qualification law on December 9, 2002 will require the reexamination of 380 films that were censored during the military regime (1974 to 1990).

From the mass media perspective, the changes of the past had dual consequences. First, there was a demand for greater information on the status of the economy. Second, there was the requirement for improving the technical expertise of journalists and mass media communicators. The ever-increasing demand for high-quality information has forced the media to become a proactive player in the development of a more ethical relationship with society.

Many Chileans regard the press as the fourth power, because of its tremendous influence on public opinion. Others, however, prefer to see the press as an instrument of publicity, which is dominated by market forces. In Chile, television audiences are extremely large. Ninety five percent of Chilean homes possess a television set. Despite the outstanding technical quality achieved by Chilean television, this medium has not become an important element in tailoring public opinion. One of the reasons for the lackluster quality of TV programming includes the fact that public relations and communications professionals are not involved in designing and implementing institutional and issue-focused campaigns.

To summarize the media environment in Chile, one can say that television is primarily an entertainment medium and the press is the principal vehicle for mobilizing public opinion. These facts explain the importance of press agentry in the activities of agencies and communication consultancies. Chileans consider exposure in the printed media as powerful and it is an important means for achieving social prestige. Public relations campaigns focused on strategic public or minority issues have not achieved adequate exposure in the national press. In fact, there is more concern for information which favors the interests of social and economic groups than public issues. The reason for this may well reside in the individualism which permeates all segments of Chilean society, a legacy of the difficult years of military rule, as already stated.

NEWSPAPERS AND MAGAZINES

The open political environment that existed in Chile until 1973 contributed to the emergence of a free press which often resulted in the politicized and controversial behavior of the printed media. With the arrival of the military regime, the situation changed radically and there was severe control of the press for seventeen years. Under the strict control of the military regime, the only exceptions emerged at the end of the seventies with the weekly magazine *Hoy* that was followed by other alternative media. According to Krohne (2002), "these alternative media which included the *Apsi*, *Análisis*, *Cauce*, and *Hoy* magazines and the newspapers *Fortín Mapocho* and *La Epoca* did not survive the end of the military regime" (p. 24).

Some analysts are of the opinion that during the 1980s, the media adapted to the market and its cruelties. The revitalized newspaper conglomerates had a distinct right-wing orientation. For example, the *El Mercurio* group (which in 1973 represented one third of national newspaper circulation) consolidated its market share and during 1988 became the main proprietor of more than 50% of newspapers with national circulation (Krohne, p. 22).

Television took over the market that previously belonged to the print media. Journalism had to modernize to correctly interpret the new national scenario. Today there are few newspapers, magazines, or television channels that are dedicated to politics or that defend a specific ideology, as had been the case in the past. Today, business ideology permeates radio and television because to survive in a neoliberal economy, it is necessary to secure revenue through advertising.

There seems to be public apathy, mainly due to the fear that has persisted since the Pinochet government. In summary, this phenomenon has led to a crisis of values. This crisis, which has been affected by globalization, has led to individualism, the disinterest among the younger generation in politics, and to a disorganized citizenry. Another important effect of the crisis was the weakening of regional printed media that compete with the dominant national press. There are seven national and one state daily newspaper. Six of the dailies have a distinct right-wing orientation. They compete with 42 regional newspapers that have limited technological infrastructure, and practically no access to international news sources.

The *El Mercurio* group, that owns the largest daily in the country, dominates the printed media. The editorial policies of *El Mercurio* are directed to the dominant social coalition with a notable neoliberal orientation to the economy, a conservative stance to moral and ethical issues, and right-wing orientation on politics. The *El Mercurio* group also publishes an afternoon daily, *La Segunda*, which is characterized by a very agile editorial policy that is well in tune with the moral and political agenda of the country.

Copesa is the second print media conglomerate. It is responsible for the publication of *La Tercera* which is directed to the professional sector, and to the emerging groups associated with economic modernization. Third behind these leaders is the state-owned La Nación group that publishes the daily *La Nación*. The newspaper *Ultimas Notícias* targets the middle class. *La Hora* is a free newspaper. *La Cuarta* has a distinct place with the humbler segments of the population with an essentially sensationalist content. *La Época* dedicates itself to economic and political issues. The newspapers *El Diário* and *Estratégia* specialize in financial journalism. Two magazines, *Cosas* and *Caras* cater to women. The *¿Qué Pasa?* is an influential weekly magazine that is characterized by an inquisitive and direct editorial policy.

TELEVISION AND RADIO

Since its creation in 1922, radio has always been managed by businesspeople with clear commercial objectives, unlike the print media. The linking of radios to political parties occurred in the beginning of the 1970s, largely due to the prevailing political conflict. The 1980s saw a structural mutation of Chilean communication media. According to Tironi (1998), until the 1980s there persisted an organizationally primitive and relatively elitist system of print media that was highly dependent on the state, with marked political, cultural, and educational pretensions.

Today, there exist a total of 1264 radio stations (FM and AM) of which 220 are community radio stations. Many radio networks such as Chilena (belonging to the Catholic Church), Cooperativa, and Agricultura have a strong orientation toward news. The rest are dedicated to music and entertainment. In 1973, the formerly subsidized television stations were forced by the government to seek private funding through the procurement of paid advertising and sponsorships. The effects of this policy can be seen today in the quality of the programming aired on Chilean television. Since the 1980s, there has been a massive shift to privatize the ownership of TV stations giving them a strong market orientation and information and entertainment focus. Between 1970 and 1983, the number of television sets increased sixfold. In 1974, there were 53 television sets per 1000 people; in 1980 the figure was 205, and in 1982 there were 302 sets per 1000 people. The massive utilization of satellite technologies also benefited the creation of new FM stations. In contrast, there was a decline in newspaper circulation, partly because of the economic crisis between 1982 and 1984, as well as President Frei Montalva's educational reform on reading habits.

Today, commercial Chilean television is privately owned. There are six stations of which three have national coverage. The Catholic University of Chile owns channel 13. TVN is state-owned. Megavisión belongs to the Televisa/Mexico communications conglomerate. American Media Partners own Chilevisión. La Red belongs to Compañía Chilena de Television S/A. Canal 2 is owned by Compañía Chilena de Comunicaciones. The globalization of communication has induced Chileans to prefer the content of the media of neighboring countries. The lack of domestic cultural television programming has greatly harmed the country.

It is obvious that globalization and new technologies have created an ideal environment for the expansion of communications in Chile. Among the principal characteristics of this expansion are the creation of monopolies and the adoption of North American programming strategies. Radio, because of its closeness to local language and national sentiment, has achieved a stronger cultural bond with its audience. Television, on the other hand, is seen as a privately administrated mass medium which is focused on imported entertainment and news programming.

One of the more noticeable features of the present-day Chilean is the absolute absence of interest in politics, which is made explicit through individualistic behavior. Group participation generally occurs when there is a threat to public safety or to personal and family integrity. As a result, public relations is commonly practiced in the context of internal communication or through press-agentry activities. Public relations is generally not involved in designing and implementing institutional television and radio campaigns for large audiences. Until the present day, over the air television is a mass medium which has not implemented programming oriented to the structuring of issue-conscious publics. In Chile, there is a consensus that the principal mission of television is to entertain whereas the role of the print media is to influence and mobilize public opinion. It is clear that the beginning of the twenty-first century brought market forces to the media.

THE PARTICIPATION OF THE CITIZENRY IN NATIONAL AFFAIRS: NONGOVERNMENTAL ORGANIZATIONS

Like other Latin American nations, Chile does not have a philanthropic culture and a proactive stance on issues of concern to its citizens. As a result, predominantly during the military regime, a number of nongovernmental organizations (NGOs) were founded, with links to left-wing scholarly organizations. Initially, these organizations were funded from abroad and hosted banned political groups that were to ultimately launch the political platform leading to the return of democracy and the first Concertación government. After the return to democracy, these organizations lost external funding, which reduced their political visibility. They engaged in movements for other domestic causes such as defending small businesses, advancing the feminist movement, and advocating environmental issues.

Until 1996, feminist groups received more support than the "green" groups. After 1996, the number of environmental NGOs grew substantially. Some of their initiatives were highly publicized and served to retard the financing of many mega projects that endangered the environment. In summary, these "green groups" will be among the principal social and political forces of the country. To achieve this stature, the "green" NGOs will have to seek alliance with political parties.

The protection of the indigenous Mapuche community reached its heyday during the military regime when activists challenged the illegal occupation of native lands. However, during the political transition (after the end of the military regime), the significance of these activists was substantially reduced. Since the 1990s new activist groups have manifested to protect the rights of indigenous people. Most observers agree that the changes in the behavior of the population were due to the rapid social transformation that was forced by the new economy. Family and work relationships, together with personal friendship, have suffered affecting Chilean culture. The most prominent feature of this change is the individualism caused by fierce personal competition and reduced work opportunities. This individualism is also noticeable in the declining participation of the younger generations in politics, national issues, and in the formation of activist groups. Despite the existence of groups concerned with the defense of natural resources and individual freedoms, it is apparent that many Chileans have lost their cultural identity and their willingness to participate in deciding urgent social and national issues.

With the rapid growth of NGOs in the country, it is believed that there will appear in the near future a solidarity movement capable of implementing structural and social projects. Presently, few NGOs have a permanent communications and public relations department whose principal focus is the design of communication campaigns for disseminating goals and policy objectives. The principal obstacle is the lack of financial resources to invest in planned communication.

Another factor that has hampered the growth of NGOs is the worldview that society expects the state to provide all necessary basic services. The absence of solidarity and citizenship, a legacy of the 1970s and 1980s, are dominating factors in Chilean culture. National and international NGOs that receive foreign financial support are the most visible. Chile—despite the existence of relevant issues such as AIDS, discrimination of women, and the destruction of the environment—has not been able to realize the importance of NGOs.

PUBLIC RELATIONS IN CHILE: THE PAST AND THE FUTURE

From the first public relations department founded by the Braden Copper Company in 1952 until the present day, the evolution of public relations has been hampered by the strong presence of journalism and by the low status the profession enjoys in Chilean society. In addition, at least until the 1980s, multinational companies merely replicated the public relations strategies and tactics dictated from their headquarters. Most often, these practices had no relevance to the organization's environment in Chile, further hampering the growth of the profession. The government sector has established public relations departments to maintain sustained relationships with its diverse publics including the use of mass communication media. Only large Chilean organizations, such as Corpracion Nacional del Cobre (CODELCO) and Empresa Nacional de Electricidad S.A. (ENDESA), have an in-house public relations department, who often rely on the professional services of public relations agencies. Few medium and small organizations currently have a public relations department.

Senior managers often consider themselves to be the public relations professionals of the company regarding public relations purely as a social endeavor, dedicated to maintaining personal contacts with politicians, society and the media (Ferrari, 2000). This is typical of the personal influence model that has been written about in the last decade (Huang, 1990). The difficulty in identifying the principal events in the history of public relations in Chile is due to the absence of a suitable knowledge base. Délano (1990) dedicated her research to an analysis of the importance of three early Chilean thinkers and their personal and professional history. Eyzaguirre (1993) explained the history of public relations education in Chile.

The history of public relations as a professional activity was largely influenced by the political context of Chile during the 1970s and 1980s. This is consonant with the framework used in this book that proposes a country's political system as a key variable in the development and status of the public relations profession. There are two schools of thought on the nexus between the recent political history of Chile and the public relations profession. First, some believe that the military regime (1973–1990) had a positive influence on the public relations profession by legitimizing it, which was a result of the encouraging globalization and privatization of businesses (Délano, 2000). The second point of view argues that the military regime actually hampered the development of the mass media as well as public relations. Public relations, this school of thought holds, was restricted to the organization of parties and cocktails (Ruiz-Velasco, 1995). During the military regime, many public relations posts were in the hands of individuals close to the military. Censorship was also widespread because there was a public office that decided what could and could not be published in the media. This situation lasted until the beginning of the 1990s.

According to many public relations professionals, the current professionalization of public relations is a result of the combination of two unique factors: the return of democratic rule and the implementation of a neoliberal economy. The international exposure of many Chilean companies forced them to become more transparent, not only with their shareholders, but also with their clients, suppliers, the media, and stakeholders. This trend was accelerated largely as a result of privatization, globalization of the companies and the development of mass communication media. Currently, approximately 15 national and international agencies provide integrated communication services including public relations. The more widely known agencies are multinationals. A number of local agencies work in alliance with foreign partners.

There is no reliable record of the number of Chilean organizations that have public relations/communication departments. The Council of Public Relations Professionals, the national body that represents Public Relations professionals, is not considered relevant by businesses. Journalists, who are affiliated to their own professional associations, occupy the vast majority of public relations positions. The number of professionals who have graduated from university public relations programs is still very small given that the first graduates only came to the market in 1995.

According to Veragua (2001), past president of The Council of Public Relations Professionals "the PR professional has an important role in the administration of internal and external communication processes. Without communication there is no organization, and without communication there is no coordination. This is the main reason why PR professionals need to collaborate with the creation of an organizational climate that contributes to the improvement of individuals and the organization."

CASE STUDY MCDONALD'S LETTUCE[1]

In April 1991, following an outbreak of cholera in Latin America, the government of Chile and its Ministry of Public Health prohibited lettuce and other raw vegetables from being served in restaurants. The prohibition presented a significant challenge to McDonald's, whose signature sandwiches such as the Big Mac could not be served with this essential ingredient. Chile was the only country of the 83 in which McDonald's operates where its sandwiches did not include lettuce. Focus group testing demonstrated consumer dissatisfaction with a sandwich without lettuce. But the government was apprehensive about changing the restriction for reasons of public health and politically motivated criticism. Burson-Marsteller Santiago was hired by McDonald's to develop and implement a strategic PR program to address the issue.

---

[1]This case study was furnished by Mr. Ramiro Prudencio, CEO Burson Marsteller Brazil, and Ms. Claudia Adriasola, CEO Burson Marsteller Chile.

Target Audiences and Their Perceptions

There were two primary target audiences. The first was government health officials, who perceived a public health risk to lifting the prohibition. Perceptions dictated that no restaurant had the infrastructure, know-how, or food safety expertise to properly produce and serve lettuce. The sense of risk was compounded by a concern that any outbreak in enteric disease could be used against the ministry for political purposes. Concerns were further heightened by ongoing political conflicts between the Health Ministry and medical worker unions. The second target audience was consumers, who for years had consumed lettuce in restaurants and, after the prohibition, were consistently receiving public health messages concerning the proper handling of raw vegetables and risk of cholera.

Despite the public health messages, consumers felt that a sandwich without lettuce was less satisfying. Moreover, they expressed underlying concerns about the risk that eating improperly handled lettuce might present. Once official approval for serving lettuce was given, the program objective was to reintroduce the consumption of this leafy vegetable in a manner that managed possible consumer concerns and emphasized improved product taste.

Strategy & Implementation

The core concept was to demonstrate McDonald's recognized leadership and expertise in food safety, and to demonstrate that an outright ban on serving lettuce was unnecessary to assure public health. Activities included:

- Development of collateral materials that fully explained McDonald's food safety expertise and its proposed program to control the entire lettuce process from seeding in the field to serving in the restaurant
- Meetings with key public health officials at the ministerial and civil service levels
- Ally development with suppliers, restaurant association, United States Embassy, and others
- Tours of lettuce processing facilities with health officials and media
- Internal communications strategies and activities to prepare staff to address consumer concerns in restaurants or at McDonald's offices
- Media relations activities to underscore McDonald's food safety expertise and lettuce processing and to highlight reintroduction of lettuce on McDonald's sandwiches

Results

On August 18, 1995, McDonald's was the first restaurant to serve lettuce in Chile since April 1991. Sales jumped more than 15% in the days following the announcement, which was carried on every television news program in Chile. McDonald's held this advantage over other competitors, less prepared for the removal of the prohibition, for several weeks.

REFERENCES

Bassa, I. A. D. (1996). *Bases culturales para la formulación de un modelo de gestión estratégica de empresas chilenas* (Cultural bases for a development model of strategic management of Chilean companies). Unpublished master's thesis, Pontifícia Universidad Católica de Chile, Santiago, Chile.

Becerra, N. A. P. (1983). *Perfil das Relações Públicas na América Latina* (Profile of Public Relations in Latin America). Unpublished master's thesis, Universidade de São Paulo, São Paulo, Brazil.

Castellón, L., & Araos, C. (1999). Medios de comunicación e identidad cultural: una reflexión desde la prensa escrita (Levels of cultural identity: A reflection from the printed media). *Anuário Unesco/Umesp de Comunicação Regional*, *II*(2), 91–107.

Cutlip, S. M. & Center, A. H. (1963). *Relaciones Públicas*. Barcelona, España: Ediciones Rialp S.A.

Délano, B. J. A. (1990). *Las Relaciones Públicas en Chile—fundamentos prácticos y teóricos* (Public Relations in Chile: Theory and practice). Santiago, Chile: Universitaria.

Eyzaguirre, P. C. (1993). *Manual de Relaciones Públicas* (Public relations manual). Santiago, Chile: Los Andes.

Eyzaguirre, P. C. (1997). *Relaciones Públicas* (Public relations). Santiago, Chile: Calicanto.

Ferrari, M. A. (2000). *A influência dos valores organizacionais na determinação prática das Relações Públicas em organizações do Brasil e do Chile* (The influence of organizational values in the practice of public relations in Brazilian and Chilean organizations). Unpublished doctoral dissertation, Universidade de São Paulo, São Paulo, Brazil.

Flanagan, C. S. (1992). *Relaciones Públicas: concepto, evolución y practica actual en Chile* (Public Relations: Concept, evolution and current practice in Chile). Unpublished doctoral dissertation, Universidad Complutense de Madrid, Madrid, Spain.

Grunig, J. E. & Hunt, T. (2000) *Dirección de Relaciones Públicas*. Barcelona, España: Ediciones Gestión 2000 S.A.

Hofstede, G. (1984). *Culture's consequences: international differences in work-related values*. London: Sage Publications.

Huang, Y. (1990). *Risk communication, models of public relations and anti-nuclear activism: A case study of a nuclear power plant in Taiwan*. Unpublished master's thesis, University of Maryland, College Park.

Krohne, W. (2002). *La Libertad de Expresión en Chile bajo la Atenta Mirada de La Crítica* (Freedom of expression in Chile as seen by the attentive eye of the media). Santiago, Chile: Fundación Konrad Adenauer.

Lesly, P. (1973). Manual de *Relaciones Públicas*. Barcelona, España: Ediciones Martínez Roca S.A.

Levering, R., & Moskowitz, M. (2001, November 16–29). Los mejores lugares para trabajar (The best places to work). *Revista Capital, Negocios y Mundo*, (73), 120–124.

Ortega, C. G. (1993). Growth and development of public relations in Chile. U.S.A. Unpublished master's thesis, California State University, Hayward.

Pavlik, J. V. (1999). *La Investigación en Relaciones Públicas*. Barcelona, España: Ediciones Gestión 2000 S.A.

Ruiz-Velasco, L. (1995, July). Relaciones peligrosas (Dangerous relationships). *Revista America Economia*, (97), 22–24.

Simões, R. P. (1993). *Relaciones Públicas: función política en la empresa y en la institución pública. 3ª edición*. Barcelona, España: Editorial El Ateneo.

Tironi, E. (1998, April). Los medios y el poder (Power and the media). *Revista Capital, Negocios Y Mundo*, Special Issue: El Poder, 76–79.

Veragua, M. (2001, January). Relaciones Públicas: por un mundo mejor (public relations: for a better world). Retrieved January 21, 2001 from *http://www.dirigible.cl*.

INTERNATIONAL PUBLIC RELATIONS: KEY DIMENSIONS AND ACTORS

36

Transnational Public Relations by Foreign Governments

Michael Kunczik

DEFINITION OF PUBLIC RELATIONS AND STATUS OF RESEARCH

The focus of this chapter will be the field of international public relations with particular reference to the issue of image cultivation by nations. Taking the quantity of publications as an indicator, one has to conclude that the body of research on this topic has large gaps. Even the relationship between news media and images of nations is not well researched and for this very reason the following discussion cannot be treated as complete. The main reason for this gap in research can be seen in the often highly sophisticated methods that states adopt to influence world opinion. Among others, public relations agencies and even the secret service units play a decisive role in these activities, which very often take place far from public view (Kunczik, 1997). Public relations is often perceived as the art of camouflaging and deceiving and it is assumed that for public relations to be successful, target groups (those to be influenced) not notice that they have become the "victims" of public relations efforts.

Because credibility is a decisive variable in the communication process, attempts are constantly being made to influence media reporting by covert means to avoid the impression of manipulation. The aim of such activities is chameleonlike: to adapt to the surroundings while remaining submerged. Attempting to identify the instigators of public relations by nations is often like trying to nail pudding to a wall. Therefore, there is very little literature on this theme. One cannot, after all, do a representative survey of the former KGB (or its successor organization) or the Central Intelligence Agency (CIA), although the United States Information Service (USIA) has been the subject of a published empirical study (Bogart, 1976). The borders between secret services and news agencies are often blurred, as evident from the example of TASS, the former Soviet news agency

(Kruglak, 1962). But besides that, most industrialized as well as developing countries either have created special organizations (e.g., USIA, the British Council, Maison Française, Goethe Institute, and so forth) to improve their country's image abroad or have commissioned public relations agencies to do so on their behalf.

For the nation-state, public relations implies the planned and continuous distribution of interest-bound information by a state aimed (mostly) at improving the country's image abroad. Trying to distinguish between advertising, public relations, and propaganda in foreign image cultivation is merely a semantic game. In Lasswell's (1942) definition of *propaganda* as "the manipulation of symbols as a means of influencing attitudes on controversial matters" (p. 106), one could easily substitute *public relations* for *propaganda.* I treat propaganda and public relations as synonyms following the tradition of one of the founding fathers of modern public relations Edward L. Bernays who stated: "the only difference between 'propaganda' and 'education,' really, is the point of view. The advocacy of what we believe in is education. The advocacy of what we don't believe in is propaganda" (1923, p. 212).

So, public relations for the nation-state comprises persuasive communicative acts directed at a foreign audience. But a famous comment by Walter Lippmann applies also to the changeability of images: "For the most part we do not first see, and then define, we define first and then see" (1922, p. 81). In other words, from the wealth of events and information available, we select those that conform to the already existing image (selective perception) in our minds. Furthermore, can information in which one is not interested in be ignored? For example, in September 1947, a six-month propaganda campaign to promote the United Nations was begun in Cincinnati whose slogan was: "Peace begins with the United Nations—the United Nations begin with you." It was largely unsuccessful because those who paid attention to the message were primarily individuals who already had an interest in, and were informed about, the United Nations. As Star and Hughes (1950) observed, "The conclusion is that the people reached by the campaign were those least in need of it and that the people missed by it were the new audience the plan hoped to gain" (p. 397).

Donsbach (1991) published an extensive study on the selective perception of West German newspaper readers that clearly confirms the phenomenon of *de facto* selectivity. In the precommunicative phase, recipients chose those media that they assumed followed an editorial line as close as possible to their own political persuasions. This implies humans are more likely to select information that confirms their preexisting views than information that challenges preexisting views. Of course, this logic holds water only where there is a choice of free media. Donsbach was able to prove that newspaper readers prefer to read those articles that they expect will confirm their existing opinions. But, and this is very important, the selection rule applies only when positive information is offered. When negative information is offered, both supporters and opponents of a certain position have similar reactions: they heed it. In other words, the protective shield of selective perception works against information that might result in a positive change of opinion, but not against information that might produce a negative change of opinion. Churchill may have been right when he stated: "To build may have to be the slow and laboring task of years. To destroy can be the thoughtless act of a single day" (Howard, 1986/1987).

HISTORICAL OUTLINE OF IMAGE CULTIVATION BY GOVERNMENTS

The following short review of early image cultivation by states makes no claim to completeness but is meant merely to underscore that image cultivation did not begin with the age of the mass media. The Bible contains examples that prove that the character of a nation and its image has concerned humanity from the beginning of its history. As reported in *Genesis* (18:32) if God had found even 10 innocent people in Sodom, he would not have destroyed the city in order to save them. The Apostle Paul, in his letter to Titus (1:12), wrote the following about the Cretans: "It was a Cretan himself, one of their own prophets, who spoke the truth when he said, 'Cretans are always liars, wicked beasts, and lazy gluttons'." Further examples were gathered by Duijker and Frijda (1960, 1):

> Herodotus discusses the characteristic habits of the Scythes, the Phrygians, the Libyans and many others. Vatsayana, in the Kama-Sutra, notices striking differences in the sexual behaviour of the human female, and one of his classifications is based on region of origin. Tacitus presents, in his famous Germania, an elaborate description of the attitudes, customs and morals of the Germans. Juvenal speaks rather sarcastically about the little Greeks in imperial Rome, and makes it quite clear that he considers them a rather contemptible bunch of spineless good-for-nothings.

Alexander the Great (356 BC–323 BC) created what can be described as the first war reporter unit. Reports written to serve his objectives were sent to the Macedonian court, reproduced there, and disseminated with propagandistic intent. Callisthenes of Olynthus (c. 360 BC–328 BC), appointed to accompany Alexander as historian on his Asiatic expedition, spread the claim that the king was the son of Zeus, the supreme god. The sacred oracle of Didyma confirmed the story—surely under the influence of Alexander's "Public Relations department," which probably made skillful use of the oracle's utterance: It is very difficult to fight the son of so powerful a god!

The invention of the printing press by Gutenberg (about 1445) was the point of departure for a new kind of international public relations practice. Emperor Maxmillan I (1493–1519) was the first German leader (and to the best knowledge of this author the first leader of any nation) to manipulate the predecessors of the modern newspaper—then called "new newspapers" (*newe zeytungen*), as an instrument to influence public opinion. With biased war reports, he tried to influence the mood of the public in his empire. Maximilian also tried to communicate with the population of the enemy state, for example, the commoners of the Republic of Venice. In repeated appeals, he tried to incite them to insurrection against the finance aristocracy promising them liberation and a share of the city-state's government and the possessions of the rulers.

In 1576, Rudolf II was elected emperor of the Holy Roman Empire of the German Nation by the Reichstag in Regensburg. The Turks were Rudolf's main opponent as it was their leader Sultan Murad III who had declared war on the German nation. To mobilize support, Rudolf used the instruments of propaganda such as leaflets, coins, medals, festivities, political acts of symbolic value, art, and architecture (e.g., triumphal arches). In 1593, when the Turks attacked, the emperor started his propaganda campaign, including atrocity propaganda. Detailed accounts of Turkish atrocities (e.g., disemboweling a pregnant woman and smashing the foetus against the wall) were published in leaflets and newspapers.

Cardinal Richelieu (1585–1642) the leading minister who asserted absolutism in France, had a press office that used pamphlets to fight France's foreign opponents, especially the Habsburgs. *La réputation* was the political keyword for the cardinal, a master in public relations. Richelieu also established a press department and had a minister for "Information and Propaganda." From the beginning of his career, Richelieu hired writers to produce leaflets that justified his policies and attacked his political opponents. The most important instrument of his press policy was the *Gazette*, a weekly. In 1635 Richelieu established the Académie Française to which leading literati were appointed. Its main task was to standardize French language and influence long-term public opinion. Richelieu also distributed publications, biased appropriately to suit his purpose, in foreign countries. Rome was the center of the world in those days and he who had a good reputation in Rome had a good reputation in the world (i.e., Europe). According to Richelieu, the best way for a sovereign to get a good reputation in Rome was to govern decently. France wanted to become the "Arbitre de la Chrestiente" (Arbiter of Christendom), and in order to achieve this aim, even negative information about other countries was disseminated. Without a doubt, Richelieu was a master of public relations for France's image and can be regarded as a pioneer in public relations for nations.

Public relations for France reached a high point during the reign of Louis XIV. The, "Sun King," who reigned for 54 years (1661–1715), was a master of image construction. His personality, life, and body were put on stage and Louis le Grand was created. To polish the king's image, newspapers were founded, academies were established, castles were built, and birthdays and battle victories were celebrated. Numerous statues of Louis XIV were errected as part of a statue campaign in the 1680s (Burke, 1992). Triumphal arches were built in abundance. The palace at Versailles was imitated all over Europe. Every utterance of the king was recorded by secretaries. Dozens of painters were kept busy. Among those employed to polish the image of the king were the painter Lebrun, the musician Lully, and the poets Corneille, Racine, and Jean-Baptiste Roquelin (Molière). These extravagant activities, however, ruined France. In 1715 when the king died, France, the richest country of Europe, was on its way to ruin.

Louis XIV used publicity to defend France, whose incarnation he believed himself to be ("L'état c'est moi!"), against hostile public opinion in Europe. Burke (1992) examined the parallels between modern publicity agents and the "glory enterprise" of Louis XIV. He analyzed "the selling of Ludwig XIV" (p. 4). According to Burke *gloire* (glory) was a keyword of the time. Louis XIV was a master of impression management. He played the part of the king, living the life of a living image. As Burke pointed out, Louis XIV's image projection was aimed not only at the domestic public: "The foreign public for l'histoire du roi was considered no less important than the domestic one. In 1698, for example, the petite académie was [. . .] to draw up a list of medals suitable for presentation to foreigners" (p. 158). France had practical reasons for image cultivation in, for example, the Ottoman Empire because both had a common enemy in the Holy Roman Empire of the German Nation. But the main target of Louis XIV's image policy were the other courts of Europe: "The ambassadors formed a substantial part of the audience for the court festivals, plays, ballets and operas. They were very often presented with gifts, which would enhance the king's name abroad—medals and tapestries of the events of the reign [. . .] and jewelled portaits of Louis himself" (Burke, 1992, p. 162).

Texts glorifying Louis IV were published in foreign languages. For example, Latin was used to reach the educated people in Europe. Burke (1992) labeled Louis XIV's image policy as "theatre state" and described the life of the king as a grand spectacle. Statecraft became stagecraft. Burke concluded that the main difference between modern image shaping and Louis' image building is technological. Louis was presented by means of print, statues, and medals, whereas twentieth-century rulers have relied on photography, cinema, radio, and television. Burke wrote that "Long before the cinema, the theatre affected perceptions of politics. For his contemporaries the sun-king was a star" (p. 199). Louis used the grandiosity of official architecture and sculpture to dwarf the spectator, to make them conscious of his power.

It is pertinent to mention here that the "founding fathers" of the United States also made use of the media to achieve their foreign policy objectives during times of conflicts or war. James Truslow Adams (1927) who compared World War I propaganda activities with those used by the founding fathers came to the conclusion that the widely held view that propaganda was an invention of thr First World War was inaccurate. He argued that the propaganda activities of the anti-British American revolutionaries were comparable to those mounted between 1914 and 1918. The 1776 revolution had been set in motion by Samuel Adams and a number of other agitators living in Massachussetts. Generally speaking, American public opinion was against the federalists who tried to portray the British as an enemy. Incidents such as the Boston Tea Party were arranged partly for the purpose of attracting public attention through media coverage. Samuel Adams argued: "Put your enemy in the wrong and keep him there" (Baldwin, 1965, p. 8).

PROFESSIONAL INTERNATIONAL IMAGE CULTIVATION

The birth of professional international image cultivation took place during World War I (Kunczik 1998). The first step in this development was the fight for America's neutrality. A commentary in *The New York Times* (September 9, 1914) carried the headline: "The Press Agents' War," whose author argued: "The present European war [. . .] deserves to be distinguished as *first press agents* war" (p. 8). The Germans wanted the Americans to stay neutral and the British wanted to create the impression that there was a fight between the forces of good and evil and that the British cause was America's too. The first British act of war was to cut Germany's overseas cables on August 5, 1914. Germany was cut off from the world's most important neutral country at the very moment when the American public opinion was being formed on the question of responsibility for the outbreak of the war. William Gibbs McAdoo (1931), Secretary of the Treasury and Wilson's son-in-law, reported that because of cable control: "Nearly everything in the newspapers which came from Europe during the war was censored and colored in the Allied interest" (p. 322). Unbiased news simply disappeared out of the American papers about the middle of August, 1914. British intellectuals and the Oxford University took part in the propaganda effort against "Frankenstein Germany" (Kunczik, 1997, p. 179). The authors of the Oxford Pamphlets were able "to give a patriotic bias to the apparent objective presentation of material" (Squires, 1935, p. 17). The British handled journalists perfectly. American correspondents were invited to visit the front and later they were wined and dined in the headquarter chateau. The Neutral Press Committee had the task of influencing foreign journalists. With the Help of *Who's Who* a mailing list of about 170.000 American opinion leaders was compiled. They were bombarded with propaganda material, which was sent by private persons and not by official institutions to increase credibility. Needless to say, these materials received wide press coverage. Even years after the war ended, there lingered the impression that before America entered the war, there had been no British propaganda.

One clever move of British propaganda was to arrange for the translation, printing, and distribution in the United States of works of extreme German nationalists, militarists, and exponents of the "Machtpolitik" (power policy). These nationalistic individuals who had little influence in Germany were created to be the representatives of the terrible character of the German population as worshippers of power and might. According to Millis (1935) "the stupefied Germans discovered themselves convicted before world opinion on the evidence of a few writers whom the vast majority of Germans had never read or never even heard of" (p. 77).

Although the Germans lost the public relations battle in the United States, they weren't really as bad as portrayed. The first step taken to advance the German cause was the establishment of the German Information Bureau. The Germans, like the British, preferred to use interpersonal channels ofcommunication to distribute their point of view. According to Wilke (1998), the German Embassy had a list of 60,000 names (p. 16). The Germans, like the English, made use of the third-party approach and tried to influence public opinion through the publication of books written by Americans. Millis (1935) reported that authors Frank Harris and Edwin J. Clapp were on the German payroll (p. 203). In December 1914, the services of William Bayard Hale, a leading American journalist and former advisor to President Wilson, were secured by Dernburg to wage a publicity campaign (Viereck, 1930).[1] Grattan (1929/1969) elaborated: "He was put in immediate charge of the news sheet, and was detailed to prepare pamphlets and other publicity materials for distribution to the general public. His salary was to be $15,000 a year and he apparently continued in active service for almost precisely a year, although his contract did not expire until the middle of 1918" (p. 87). Among other things, Hale established contacts with the League of American Women for Strict Neutrality, who claimed to have gathered 200,000 signatures for a petition to Congress (Millis, 1935, p. 203). Germany, after having tried in vain to buy *The New York Sun* and *The Washington Post*, bought *The New York Evening Mail* (for $1.5 million) with sole the purpose of reaching a large metropolitan audience (Doerries, 1989).

The Germans had no success in this publicity war, because the British "paper bullets" gradually had already changed public opinion in their favor. On April 6, 1917, President Wilson declared war against Germany. Recognizing public opinion as a major force in the war, on April 14, 1917, President Wilson established the Committee on Public Information (CPI) headed by journalist George Creel to conduct propaganda abroad and in the United States. The task was the "whole business of mobilizing the mind of the world" (Creel, 1920, p. XIII). That is, America should be represented not merely as a strong man fully armed, but as a strong man fully armed and believing in the cause for which he is fighting— for ideas and ideals. According to Creel (1920), the CPI's charter was to carry "to every corner of the civilized globe the full message of America's idealism, unselfishness, and indomitable purpose" (p. 4).

The CPI was able to build on the experience gained in the commercial sector. Creel (1920) described the fight for the minds of men, for the "conquest of their convictions" (p. 4): "In all things, from first to last, without halt or change, it was a plain publicity proposition, a vast enterprise in salesmanship, the world's greatest adventure in advertising" (p. 4). He avoided describing the activity as propaganda because "that word, in German hands, had come to be associated with deceit and corruption" (p. 4). Eric Goldman (1948) characterized America's entry into the war as "brilliant publicity for publicity" (p. 12). Creel (1920) contended that one of his most effective ideas was to bring to the United States, delegations of foreign newspaper men periodically so they might "see with their own eyes, hear with their own ears" (p. 227), and on their return be able to report fully on America's morale and effort. According to Creel, "these trips were of incalculable value in our foreign educational work" (p. 227). Mexico was selected for the initial experiment, the Swiss came next, then Italian journalists, and finally a group from Scandinavia.

---

[1] Hearst was not informed about his correspondent's second job (Doerries, 1989). How close the connections between Wilson and Hale was documented by Josephus Daniels (1944), Secretary of the Navy in Wilson's cabinet. He pointed out that early in the campaign that put Wilson in the White House, the Democratic Party circulated a number of copies of William Bayard Hale's *Woodrow Wilson: The Story of His Life*: "It was the *vade mecum* of all Democratic speakers. It was the best story of Wilson before he became President, that had been written" (p. 76). In 1913 Wilson sent "his personal friend and biographer" (p. 181) Hale to Mexico to make a firsthand study and report on the situation over there; Hale was entrusted with an important and confidential mission in the critical days of Watchful Waiting (Daniels, 1944).

After the end of World War I the character of diplomacy slowly changed. The mediation of foreign policy intensified and today nearly every act in the (open) conduct of foreign policy takes public relations (the effect on the respective image), into account.[2] Immediately after World War I, Carl Byoir and Bernays conducted public relations for Lithuanian groups in the United States. They were agitating for an independent Lithuania, which, like the other Baltic states, had previously belonged to Russia (Bernays 1965, p. 188ff.). From the beginning, the firm Carl Byoir & Associates accepted every client it could get. In 1931, a contract was signed with the Cuban government of General Machado, a ruthless dictator, whose character was very hard to sell positively to the American public. In 1933, this relationship ended when the general was toppled. That same year Byoir opened business relations with the German Tourist Information Office whose links with the Nazis was obvious.

In 1927, in an address on "International Communications," Ivy L. Lee, one of the most influential public relations counsels in the United States, argued that the nations of the world must get matters of importance into print in the newspapers. To accomplish this, Ivy felt nations needed to create an appetite among the reading public by humanizing stories (Hiebert, 1966, 255ff.). Even more important was a lecture Lee gave on July 3, 1934 in London on "The Problem of International Propaganda" in which he developed the idea that international propaganda should be a kind of two-way communication. The motto of Theodore Roosevelt "Speak softly, but carry a big stick" was labeled as old-fashioned. Lee believed that nation states should speak clearly and loudly and without hiding a stick. He argued that complete knowledge of the truth would make people understand each other. Each government should become aware of press relations and understand, that "correspondents of foreign newspapers were there to ascertain facts and facts alone, and to ascertain them promptly and accurately" (Hiebert, 1966, p. 261). According to Lee, the wisest and most enlighted government is the one which effectively assists the press. Lee considered it to be a mistake for governments to rely on the printing presses of other countries to tell their stories for them. Lee proposed to the Soviet Union, which had a bad image due to its refusal to pay Czarist debts, to use paid advertising instead. According to Lee, the Soviet Union had to establish a reputation of good faith, and a desire to comply with every international obligation. Because of his role as counselor to Russia, Lee was attacked as a traitor who worked against American interests. Hiebert (1966, 283) wrote: "Upon notification of American recognition, one of the first things done by Maxim

---

[2]It has become self-evident that foreign policy has to take the media into consideration. Manheim (1994) examined the head-of-state visits of Prime Minister Benazir Bhutto of Pakistan (1989) and of President Roh Tae Woo of Korea (1989) to the United States in the context of public diplomacy. He analyzed how each visit was planned, orchestrated, and conducted with United States and their home country media, elite, and public opinion in mind. Bhutto, for instance, had signed a contract with lobbyist and political consultant Mark Siegel, who waged a campaign with the theme of democratic partnership. Siegel laid emphasis on the political elite and tried to create the impression that Bhutto was the guarantor for democracy. Manheim wrote: "The centerpiece of the visit was Bhutto's address at the Harvard University commencement, where she called for the creation of an association of democratic nations, one in which the richest democracies would aid the poorest and through which economic and political sanctions might be applied against those nations moving away from the democratic ideal" (p. 85). According to Manheim the visit was a complete success. Wooing the mass media, international and domestic, was the primary purpose of the 1994 visits to the beleaguered Bosnian city of Sarajevo by Benazir Bhutto and Turkish Prime Minister Tansu Ciller. The two leaders as "women, mothers and spouses," wanted to show their solidarity with the courageous women of Sarajevo. Before Bhutto went to Sarajevo her main political opponent, former prime minister Nawaz Sharif, had visited Bosnia and made a $3 million personal donation. The press in Pakistan glorified this as a heroic deed, so Bhutto was forced to counter to win the upcoming March 1994 elections.

Litvinov, Soviet Foreign Minister, was to send a cable to Ivy Lee expressing appreciation for the part he had played in paving the way for a closer Russian-American relationship."

Ivy Lee had connections to Nazi Germany also. He worked for the German Dye Trust. Although he had no formal relationship with the Nazi Government he conceded that the advice he offered his client was ultimately intended to guide the German government in its public relations in the United States. Among other things, he made suggestions for German statements on disarmament: "Germany does not want armament in itself. It is willing to destroy every weapon of war if other nations will do the same. If other nations, however, continue to refuse to disarm, the German government is left with no choice except to demand an equality of armament. The German people are unwilling to believe that any people will deny them this right today" (Hiebert, 1966, p. 289). Lee also proposed that Joachim von Ribbentrop, the special commissioner for disarmament, should visit the United States to explain Germany's position to President Roosevelt and also to enlighten the Foreign Policy Association and the Council on Foreign Relations on the issue. Lee testified before a committee of the House of Representatives that he had disseminated no German propaganda in the United States, but that he only acted as adviser. He argued that his advice included the repeated suggestion that "they could never in the world get the American people reconciled to their treatment of the Jews and that Nazi propaganda in the United States was a mistake" (Hiebert, 1966, p. 290).

Regarding Lee's handling of the negative image of Hitler's storm trooperss, Hiebert (1966) reported: "Lee advised that the government issue a frank statement on this subject, including in the information that the storm troops number about 2,500,000 men, were 'between the ages of 18 and 60, physically well-trained and disciplined, but not armed, not prepared for war, and organized only for the purpose of preventing for all time the return of the Communist peril" (p. 289). This was an unimaginable masterpiece of ethical and moral elasticity because simultaneously Lee worked for the recognition of the Soviet Union.

ACTORS IN THE FIELD OF INTERNATIONAL PUBLIC RELATIONS

It is almost impossible to make a clear distinction between the nature of international public relations activities of nation-states, international social/economic organizations (e.g., the World Bank, Greenpeace), international political organizations (e.g., United Nations, NATO, etc.), and multinational corporations (MNCs). Furthermore, the same public relations agency often counsels nation states and MNCs. The following discussion proceeds from the premise that the economy cannot be regarded as a subsystem equal in importance to others. Rather, economics is assumed to be a basic social factor that also decisively influences other subsystems. In particular, this chapter argues that economy and policy are inseparable. All too often, people overlook the fact that MNCs are quite active in moulding foreign policy and interact with states for this purpose. Bernays (1965), working as PR counselor for United Fruit, wrote, "I was struck by the thought that although I was advising a banana company, I was actually fighting in the Cold War" (p. 766).

Nations' worry over their image gives power to such organizations as Amnesty International. Founded in 1961 by British jurist Peter Benenson, Amnesty International seeks to obtain the release of political and religious "prisoners of conscience" through international protest. Benenson was moved to act in 1961 when two Portuguese students were sentenced to 7 years' imprisonment each for uttering a toast to freedom. In January 1989, Amnesty International focused on violations of human rights in Turkey. This may be one reason why in June 1989 the Turkish government hired Saatchi & Saatchi, the well-known advertising agency, to improve the country's image.

A simple classification of those who use international public relations can be developed using two dimensions: for-profit versus nonprofit and public versus private.

	Public	Private
For-profit	State-owned airlines	MNCs
Nonprofit	Governments, international organizations	Foundations

This is only a rough classification. Other actors are also in the field such as individual international influence brokers (e.g., former diplomats and government officials such as Henry Kissinger) and international public relations agencies (e.g., Interpublic, Omnicom Group, Wire & Plastic Products), who often give advice and influence, or at least try to influence, world politics. Walter Isaacson (1992) argued that Kissinger's comments on the crackdown of the democratic movement in China in June 1989 were based on commercial interests, because Kissinger had clients (among them, Atlantic Richfield, ITT, and an investment partnership called China Ventures) with strong business interests in China. After the Tiananmen Square crackdown, Kissinger recommended, in a television interview on ABC, that the United States should maintain good relations with China instead of imposing economic sanctions, as an indication of America's political maturity. Isaacson maintained, that "if the American reaction to the Tiananmen had been mild, as Kissinger urged, China Ventures would have proceeded, and Kissinger would have made a significant amount of money" (p. 749). According to Isaacson, Kissinger's trip to China in November 1989 was staged to show the world that the time to ostracize China had passed. Kissinger met Deng Xiaoping, among others, and later reported on his meetings and the atmosphere within China to President Bush and other top American leaders.

The close interconnections between nations and MNCs are demonstrated by another example involving the Mobil Corporation. In October 1981, an advertisement appeared in *The New York Times*: "Saudi Arabia: Far More Than Oil" (Grunig & Hunt, 1984, p. 521). In 1986 Mobil waged a campaign in the United States for the sale of missiles to Saudi Arabia, which, Mobil argued, would serve America's interests:

> This week, the Senate will attempt to override President Reagan's veto [of the resolution by the Congress to block the sale of missiles to Saudi Arabia], and kill the sale. When the crucial roll call is taken, members should remember a simple fact: They *aren't* voting on just an arms bill for Saudi Arabia. They *are* voting on an arms bill for American interests. Against such a yardstick, we trust the presidential veto will be sustained. (Onkvisit & Shaw, 1989, p. 148)

Mobil also referred to the Red Menace emphasizing Soviet involvement in the Middle East.

The Ford Company also fought against communism. In 1951 Henry Ford took part in the Crusade for Freedom. According to Cutlip (1994), Henry Ford II identified himself with that crusade "making an imaginative, constructive and dramatic effort to fight Communism. Use of Ford-Lincoln-Mercury dealerships throughout the United States as focal points for Crusade collections magnified this identity" (p. 698). In 1953, close to the 50th anniversary of Henry Ford, the film *The American Road* was produced to show that Ford was an American success story. Furthermore, a 50th anniversary book was published with a foreword in the name of Henry Ford II written by the public relations agency of Earl Newsom. The book said, among other things, that "the growth and achievements of Ford Motor Company have been made possible by the kind of world we live in, by American democracy, and the economic opportunity to seek change and progress freely" (Cutlip, 1994, p. 698).

The German DEMAG (Deutsche Maschinenbau AG), which built the steel factories in Rourkela, India, waged a three-year campaign in which the industrialization policies of the Indian government were praised as was the efficiency of German industry. During this period, the Soviet Union built another steel plant in India. The Soviets then waged a campaign against Germany and its industry, alleging that Germans were capitalists who were tyring to colonize India and exploit it by selling German products of poor quality. This fight for Indian public opinion was called "West German-Russian steel battle" (Darrow, Forrestal, & Cookman, 1967, p. 523). DEMAG countered with its own campaign distributing pamphlets to journalists, members of the parliament, and educators. Twenty thousand copies of a picture poster explaining the processes of steel production were donated to schools and universities. Radio Ceylon, popular among the Indian public, aired programs sponsored by DEMAG. Advertisements were published in Indian newspapers and journalists of the most important Indian dailies were visited by the press secretary of DEMAG.

Even rates of exchange can become the target of public relations campaigns of MNCs as was the case with Eastman Kodak (Dilenschneider & Forrestal, 1990). The company knew that its competitive position in the world marketplace was hurt by the then strength of the United States dollar. Kodak's communication division suggested that a public relations program be targeted at this issue. Fact-finding meetings with President Reagan, high-level administration officials, and key national economic and trade groups were arranged. According to Dilenschneider and Forrestal, the company funded a $150,000 study by the American Enterprise Institute, a conservative think tank (18 members of the Institute joined the Reagan Administration in 1981), to research the relationships between the strength of the dollar and the federal budget deficits. The Institute found a relationship between high interest rates required to finance the huge deficits and the dollar's strength. Dilenschneider and Forrestal wrote:

> Kodak believed a public affairs program could play a major role in persuading the government to pass legislation to eliminate federal budget deficit and intervene in currency exchange markets to stabilize the overvalued dollar. Kodak developed a 12-month communications program to reach members of Congress, the administration, and others in a position to influence economic policy. The message was that the overvalued dollar and escalating budget deficits were so damaging to manufacturers that a decisive action was needed (p. 679).

The program, which received a Silver Anvil Award in the 1986 competition sponsored by the Public Relations Society of America (PRSA), included a mailing to Kodak's shareholders, a "Write to Congress" campaign, consultations with leading politicians including Treasury Secretary Baker, and visits by Kodak executives to members of Congress and Cabinet members. According to Dilenschneider and Forrester the campaign played a direct role in changing the government's position and furthermore set the stage for two historic events: the September 1985 Group of Five communiqué pledging dollar stabilization, and the Gramm-Rudman-Hollings Act, aimed at eliminating federal budget deficits by 1991.

MEDIATION OF FOREIGN POLICY

Public relations for states is closely connected to the mediation of foreign policy. Hertz (1982) asserted: It is perhaps no exaggeration to say that today half of power politics consists of image making. With the rising importance of publics in foreign affairs, image making has steadily increased. Today, hardly anything remains in the open conduct of foreign policy that does not have a propaganda or public relations aspect . . . (p. 187).

Kepplinger (1983) concluded that the mass media, originally located outside the political system, have taken over a place within the political system. The media have become a political force which no longer just react, but also act. The functional dependencies of political institutions and the mass media in parliamentary democracies are seen as a matter of both domestic and foreign politics. Through their mediating function, the mass media hold a key position in the political process. The media have the power to put themes on the agenda hitherto ignored by politics and can help establish contacts not possible at the level of diplomacy thereby becoming instruments of foreign policy.

On the significance of the mass media in foreign policy, Karl (1982) wrote: "The media are increasingly a part of the process (if not the entire process) in the communication between governments and publics about international politics" (p. 144). Indeed, governments can come under pressure from what is already on media record. Thus, in the event of a potential or actual conflict, negotiated solutions could become more difficult if it appeared that such a new conciliatory approach might involve a loss of face. Karl wrote: "In an age of media diplomacy, statecraft may have become the hostage—if not the victim—of stagecraft. Only the media have a first-strike capability on both national and international levels" (p. 155).

The mass media of communication have broken into the traditionally exclusive sphere of diplomacy and have themselves become an instrument of international conciliation and mediation as also of conflict. The mass media, by serving in the diplomatic sphere as a source of international information, can contribute to international orientation by establishing a common fund of knowledge that enables or facilitates negotiations, for example. But as to the quality of this common basis of information, many countries (especially developing countries) believe that their positions are not receiving due attention in the world or in a certain region because of the current lop-sided structure of the global information system. Such a situation can be defined as an image crisis when the political elite of a state believe that they do not have a fair and adequate image in a foreign country and believe that they are not given adequate and unbiased media attention.

According to Signitzer and Coombs (1992), the field of diplomacy is shifting from traditional diplomacy toward public diplomacy. They wrote that "the actors in public diplomacy can no longer be confined to the profession of diplomats but include various individuals, groups, and institutions who engage in international and intercultural communication activities which do have a bearing on the political relationship between two or more countries" (p. 139). The authors made a distinction between the tough-minded and the tender-minded schools of public diplomacy:

> The tough-minded hold that the purpose of public diplomacy is to exert an influence on attitudes of foreign audiences using persuasion and propaganda. . . . The tender-minded school argues that information and cultural programs must bypass current foreign policy goals to concentrate on the highest long-range national objectives. The goal is to create a climate of mutal understanding. (p. 140)

The authors argued that neither school is correct, but have to be synthesized. They also made a distinction between political information, usually administered by a section of the foreign ministry or by an embassy, and cultural communication, usually administered by a cultural section of the foreign ministry, cultural institutes abroad, or some semiautonomous body (e.g., the British Council). Two types of cultural communication were identified by the authors. The first, cultural diplomacy, refers to the creation of cultural agreements in a formal sense aimed at presenting a favorable image of one's own culture abroad. The second, cultural relations, does not have unilateral advantages in mind but has the goal of information exchange in order to present "an honest picture of each country rather than a beautified one" (p. 140).

The shifting from traditional diplomacy toward public diplomacy implies that politicians are trying to instrumentalize the mass media. Adaptation of foreign policy to the mass media implies that politicians are accepting public relations counsel. The dominating motive of political action is no longer the substantial quality of policy, but the creation of newsworthy events, and public relations practitioners know how news is selected by journalists. Bernays (1923) argued in his famous *Crystallizing public opinion*: "The counsel on public relations not only knows what news value is, but knowing it, he is in a position to make news happen. He is a creator of events" (p. 197). In his memoirs (1965) Bernays described how he advised the exiled Czech politician, Tomás Garrigue Masaryk, who had been elected president of the Czechoslovak National Council, to issue his country's declaration of independence on a Sunday for public relations reasons because it would get more space in the media, Sunday being a slow news day.[3]

Important to image building are "pseudoevents" (Boorstin, 1961) that are deliberately staged to gain attention or create a certain impression. There are hundreds if not thousands of examples which demonstrate that the staging of pseudoevents has become routine. These make up much of media coverage. Mahatma Gandhi staged pseudoevents in his struggle for India's liberation from British rule. In 1930 he organized the famous march on the salt works of Dharasana (popularly knowns as Dandi March) in violation of government orders against marches, which resulting in the police caning several thousand demonstrators with long sticks with steel nails embedded in the end. More than 2,000 newspapers throughout the world reported this bloodbath. World public opinion condemned the British for this barbaric action and an American senator read a UPI report on the incident in Congress. Physically, the police had been the victors, but morally they had been vanquished.

THE STRUCTURAL NECESSITY OF INTERNATIONAL PUBLIC RELATIONS

Mass media reporting of foreign affairs often governs what kind of image of a country or culture has in another country. International news is selected by criteria similar to those used for national news or local news. Higher ranking (superpower) or geographically and/or culturally close states are most likely to be reported on by the media of a country. Economic alliances and ideological relations also generate more intensive coverage of another country. In the Foreign Images Study for the United Nations Educational Scientific and Cultural Organization (UNESCO), the selection of international news in 29 countries was examined (Sreberny-Mohammadi, 1985). According to this study, selection is done by universally valid criteria, with particular emphasis on the unusual such as disasters, unrest, and coups. Regionalism is particularly pronounced in all media systems. Hence, one cannot speak of a clear predominance of the world centers over the periphery. But negativism (civil war, natural disasters, debt crisis, human rights violations, electoral frauds, etc.)

---

[3]Reading Masaryk's *The Making of a State: Memoirs and Observations, 1914–1918* (New York: Howard Fertig; original work published 1927) is like reading a guide to efficient international public relations.

often remain the only important news factors dominating the coverage of developing countries by the media of developed nations. Aside from this aspect, the media of the Third World do not themselves measure up to the demands made by their representatives at the international level, for they select news according to the same criteria as the Western media. Accordingly, the media of the Third World are noted for using a high proportion of nonpolitical bad news from industrialized nations. The crisis-oriented reporting on the Third World by the Western media corresponds to the bad picture of the Western nations in the press of developing countries. Overall, the cynical journalists' adage, "Bad news is good news," applies to the reporting of international events.

A replication of the Foreign Images Study conducted in 1995 by Robert Stevenson and Annabelle Sreberny-Mohammadi but not yet completely published (Kunczik and Zipfel, 2001, 429ff.) seems to confirm this pattern of news flow. Wu (1998) investigated the determinants of international news flow and concluded that "the everyday representation of the world via news media is far from a reflection of global realities" (p. 507). Recent research on the international flow of television news demonstrates that some countries are in a central position (United States, Great Britain, Russia, France, and Germany) and many countries are in a peripherical position concerning the flow of news (Kim and Barnett, 1996). The flow of television news has a similar structure. The global market of television news is dominated by APTV (Associated Press TV), Reuters Television and WTN (World television News) (Boyd-Barrett 1998).

Given the structural conditions of the international flow of news, countries which need to have a positive image in a certain geographical region for economic or political interests (including those nations that are at a disadvantage from the outset because of the standard processes of gathering and reporting by mass media), must mount active publicity campaigns. Although by definition, public relations for states is always interest-bound communication, it can offset communication deficits resulting from the deficiencies of media structures. This form of public relations activity for states, meant primarily to compensate for structural communication deficits, aims mainly to adapt the image to news values by trying to influence mass media reporting. *Structural* international public relations helps in correcting the "false" images previously created by mass media. *Manipulative public relations*, on the other hand, tries to create a positive image that in most cases does not reflect reality and includes lying and disinformation. The AIDS campaign of the KGB[4]

---

[4]The AIDS disinformation campaign began in 1985 whereby the United States was blamed worldwide for the outbreak of the disease. This report, although dismissed as absurd by all experts, including Soviet medical scientists, met with much positive response, especially in African countries. For example *Afrique Nouvelle*, a weekly newspaper very close to the Catholic church, reported: "According to an authorized scientific source, the AIDS virus was developed in the research center at Fort Detrick, Maryland, where it was grown at the same time as other viruses to be used in biological weapons. It was then tested on drug addicts and homosexuals" (United States Department of State, 1987, p. 71). In August 1986 a study conducted by biophysicist Professor Jakob Segal, his wife Dr. Lilli Segal, and Dr. Ronald Dehmlow of Humboldt University in East Berlin became public. The study claimed that at Fort Detrick in 1977, the United States had synthetically manufactured the AIDS virus by combining two naturally occurring viruses, VISNA and HTLV-I. Experts agree that this hypothesis is untenable, but it circulated nonetheless in the media of Africa, South Asia, and the Soviet Union. Indeed, it was discussed extensively at the eighth conference of the Nonaligned Movement at Harare in September of that year. Both *Pravda* and *Izvestiya* have repeatedly printed articles alleging that AIDS was created in laboratories at Fort Detrick as part of alleged attempts by the United States to create new biological weapons (Walker, 1988). The Soviet media later warned against American soldiers spreading AIDS in other countries. The obvious intention of such reports was to spread mistrust of the American military, but it also affected tourists, businesspeople, and so forth. Indeed, the newspaper *Sovyetskaya Rossiya* reported on January 23, 1987 that in Western Europe AIDS was most prevalent in places where United States troops were based.

and the disinformation campaign of the Reagan administration against Muammar Qaddafi are good examples of this.[5]

IMAGES OF NATIONS AND THE INTERNATIONAL SYSTEM

In literature there is no clear definitive distinction between such concepts as attitude, stereotype, prejudice, or image. We agree with Boulding (1956) that the conception of an image involves not only present image but also aspects of its past as well as future expectations. Therefore, *national image* can be defined as the cognitive representation that a person holds about a given country—a person's beliefs about a nation and its people. Of special importance to political action is the benevolence or malevolence imputed to other nations in images as well as the historical component of the image. Feelings about a country's future are important too.

Boulding (1969) defined *image* as "total cognitive, affective, and evaluative structure of the behavior unit, or its internal view of itself and the universe" (p. 423). Whether our perceptions of the world are real or fictional does not play a large part in our daily lives. One behaves as if one's perception of the world were "true." Boulding (1967) localized an image sphere, which he described as a "world of literary images" (p. 5). In this world the test of reality is the least pronounced. That is, the elimination of errors either does not take place at all, or occurs only at enormous cost. It is in this world that the images of the international system are localized and international decision makers mainly move. Indeed, Boulding regarded the international system as by far the most pathological and costly part of the world system (e.g., costs of military, foreign ministries, diplomatic corps, secret services, and wars).[6] Boulding wrote (1967):

> On the whole the images of the international system in the minds of its decision makers are derived by a process that I have described as "literary"—a melange of narrative history, memories of past events, stories and conversations, etc., plus an enormous amount of usually ill-digested and carelessly collected current information. When we add to this the fact that the system produces strong hates, loves, loyalties, disloyalties, and so on, it would be surprising if any images were formed that even remotely resembled the most loosely defined realities of the case. (p. 9).

Manheim (1991) took the same position, arguing that for top decision makers in the United States, "the likelihod is that most people in our government and others, even at the highest level, received at least as much information about the June 1989 massacre

---

[5]On August 25, 1986, a report appeared in the *Wall Street Journal* claiming that Qadaffi was planning new attacks, that the United States and Libya were again headed for collision, and that the Pentagon was preparing plans for another bombardment of Libya. The report was described as "authoritative," that is, as being reliably sourced, by the spokesman for the White House, Larry Speakes. Other newspapers followed with reports that Libya was sponsoring terrorist activities and that there was the possibility of renewed confrontation with the United States According to Hedrick Smith (1988), George Shultz, the Secretary of State, said: "Frankly, I don't have any problems with a little psychological warfare against Qaddafi" (p. 448), then recalled Churchill's justifying deceptions against Hitler during World War II: "In time of war, truth is so precious, it must be attended by a bodyguard of lies".

[6]In fact, decision makers are usually aware that they are living in a world of images. As the famous French statesman Talleyrand pointed out, in politics what is believed to be true is more important than truth itself. Ronald Reagan knew that "Facts are stupid things" (*Time*, August 29, 1988, p. 52). Kissinger (1969) stated: "Deterrence above all depends on psychological criteria" (p. 61).

in Beijing's Tiananmen Square from media reports as from diplomatic or intelligence sources. They know little more than we know. We are vulnerable" (p. 130). For politicians (foreign ministers, for example), the success of their career has not been dependent on the ability to estimate correctly the images of foreign nations but to meet the demands and stereotypes of their voters. If people believed that the Soviet Union was an "empire of evil" (as Ronald Reagan stated), one can win elections only if one is of the same opinion or at least gives that impression. Although they often refuse to believe it themselves, politicians are as prone to distorted perceptions as anyone else. When such distorted perceptions flow into political decision making, there can be very negative consequences.

ESTABLISHMENT OF TRUST AS THE MAIN AIM OF INTERNATIONAL PUBLIC RELATIONS

The main objective of international public relations is to establish (or maintain existing) positive images of one's own nation or to appear trustworthy to other actors in the world system.[7] Trust is no abstract concept. In the field of international policy, trust is an important factor in mobilizing resources such as receiving political and/or material support from other nations, for example. In other words, if other actors in the world system place their trust in a nation and her future because of her reliability, then trust becomes the equivalent of money. Put simply: trust is money and money is trust. The positive image of a country's currency reflects confidence in that country's future. International business and currency exchange rates are not determined simply by pure economic facts (like currency reserves and gold reserves, deficit or surplus in balance of trade or balance of payment). The image of a nation, the solvency rating of its businesses, the credibility of its politicians and their reliability to tame inflation by tight fiscal and monetary policies are some factors that are of decisive importance. Indeed, a country's reputation for solvency is more important to the stability of her currency than some short-term economic fluctuations.

In 1926 French economist Albert Aftalion published his theory (Théorie psychologique du change) based on the hypothesis that the exchange rate of a country's currency is determined mainly by trust in the future of that country. A deficit of the balance of payments will not cause a devaluation of the currency as long as the belief in the future of the currency attracts foreign capital thus balancing the deficit. There is one main reason for the use of a certain currency as key currency: trust in that currency. Monetary policy is image policy. Money is an illusion, nothing more than the trust people have in their respective currency.

Public relations counselor Ivy Ledbetter Lee certainly was aware of the importance of trust when he argued: "Those who handle a loan must create an atmosphere . . ." (Hiebert, 1966, p. 266). Lee knew that simple statistics were not enough to market a loan. Lee handled loans for Poland, Rumania, France, and other countries, but considered Hungary a difficult case because too many people in America "had a mental picture of the [Hungarian] people

---

[7]Sometimes some countries seem to be interested in having a negative image in certain target groups. In 1991 Austria's Home Secretary, Franz Löschnack, published an advertisement in the Romanian newspaper *Romania Libera*. Romanians wanting to emigrate to Austria were warned against trying to enter Austria. Foreigners were not allowed to work in Austria without official permission and for Romanians no permission would be given. Romanians also had no prospects for asylum in Austria: "There are no more shelters for people asking for asylum." The last sentence of the advertisement was: "You don't have the slightest chance." The compositor of *Romania Libera* protested in a subtle way: Below the Austrian ad was placed an ad for the Bucharest center for disinfection, which fought against rat infestations and rounded up stray dogs.

as a wild, Bohemian lot, instead of the agricultural, sane, and highly cultivated people that they really are" (Hiebert, 1966, p. 267). His advice to Hungary was to create the image that their country was stable and civilized. Argentina had problems attracting investors because of its image of social instability. Lee advised them to send a polo team to the United States to compete with American teams contending that "polo is not played except where there is a very high degree of civilization and a stable society. . . . The galloping gentlemen would tell the story more convincingly than any amount of statistics or mere statements as to the true conditions" (Hiebert 1966, p. 267).

Some examples of attempts by countries to gain trust with the international community:

1. On July 1, 1994 Banco do Brasil advertised in the leading German daily *Frankfurter Allgemeine Zeitung* that Brazil now had a new and stable currency: the *real*. This monetary reform was called the most decisive turning point in the history of Brazil's economy. Brazil now offered investors more opportunities than ever before urging them to have confidence in the new currency, to overcome memories of the old currency that was plagued by inflation. The advertisement closed with the slogan: "BANCO DO BRAZIL. Good for you. Good for Brazil."

2. Estonia published in *Time* (July 4, 1994) a country profile as an advertisement: "ESTONIA: Rebirth of a Nation." The advertisement claimed that after years of quiet opposition to Soviet rule, Estonia had seized the opportunity of the failed coup of August 1991 in Moscow to declare full independence. "Swift and decisive actions underwrote this move: a new constitution was drawn up, free elections held, monetary reform (including a new currency) was initiated, and a fast-track policy of economic renewal was implemented," the advertisement declared. Estonia characterized itself as the champion of free trade and exuded confidence that it could withstand the shock of competition. Information about the economic climate and new opportunities in the Baltics was provided, especially concerning the progress of privatization: "New ownership structures are the single most important aspect of the marketization of economic life."

3. Peru, which had a poor image around the world due to the outbreak of cholera in 1991 and the guerrilla movement Shining Path in 1993, published a special advertising section in the *International Herald Tribune* on November 24, 1993. President Alberto Fujimori emphasized in an interview the "dramatic moves his government has made to improve the country's economic and business climate." One article dealt with the economic comeback of the country. Privatization was described as generating cash and competition. Peru was characterized not only as a country of ancient culture but also as a nation of opportunities.

Many nations have published similar advertisements. Sometimes nations are interested in projecting a negative image strategically, at least to a target group. Mexico became the first country to practically declare itself insolvent by an ad in *The International Herald Tribune* (June 8, 1989). Luis Tellez, the general director of financial planning in the Mexican ministry of finance, signed the text in which the chairman of the Citicorp bank, John Reed, was attacked. The banker was accused of having too restricted a view of things:

> For Mexico, the debt crisis is much more than a discussion of swaps or of the return of flight capital. It is a story of adjustment, of an extraordinary effort to transform an economy and of the hopes of millions of Mexicans for an opportunity to increase their standards of living. All parties involved should begin to look at the situation from both sides. We created the debt

problem together; therefore it is up to both debtors and creditors to find a way out.... We should all realize that there is much to gain by acting together. If banks insist on keeping their eyes closed to economic realities there will be no winners.

THE TACTIC OF WITHDRAWAL

Many countries (especially developiong nations) make considerable efforts and spend vital and often scarce resources to cultivate their images abroad (especially in developed countries) principally to attract foreign aid. No precise linkage between commissioned public relations activities and what appears in the mass media as a result of these activities can be traced. Typically, one can do little more than guess at what suggestions were made, which were accepted, and how they were implemented. The precise nature of the intervention remains a mystery. Manheim and Albritton (1984) studied the influence of the activities of public relations agencies on the images of nations. In particular, they examined the coverage by *The New York Times* of six countries (the Republic of Korea, the Philippines, Yugoslavia, Argentina, Indonesia, and Rhodesia), which had hired public relations agencies in the United States.[8] The major service the public relations firms had offered was to improve their client's access to American journalists. In addition, they wrote press releases, did direct mailings, and sent out newsletters and brochures. In some cases, embassy personnel were trained on how to speak about sensitive issues such as terrorism or human rights. Field trips for the press, visits with editors, and lunches with business groups were organized. One of the main effects of this public relations activity was that with the exception of Indonesia, the media coverage of each country was reduced. This corresponds to research findings on the effects of mass communications where the image of a country that makes negative headlines and also has a negative image in public opinion cannot be changed by the sudden appearance of positive reporting because this would be perceived as incredible. Withdrawal from public attention makes people forget, providing an opportunity to build a positive new image more slowly.

Nevertheless, some of the emphases of the public relations activities can be illustrated (Cutlip, 1994; Kunczik, 1997; Manheim, 1994; Manheim & Albritton, 1984), such as visits by heads of state, the release of political prisoners, press junkets organized by the respective governments or by transnational corporations, establishment of information offices, cosmetic redistribution of power within a country, scheduling of elections, sporting events, and so on. These events have a high likelihood of coverage by the news media. It is useful to adopt some hypotheses that have been developed in mass media research to guide research on public relations conducted on behalf of nations. For example, one hypothesis could be that the more a country depends on trade exports, the more likely and the more intensely it will mount campaigns of image cultivation abroad. Further, a state may be more likely to mount a public relations campaign in another region if the reporting in that region is biased due to the structures of news selection. Another hypothesis could be that the more important (economically and/or politically) an entity (whether country or union such as the European Community), the more likely it is that foreign countries will mount campaigns in that country (e.g., most campaigns are waged in the United States and Western industrialized countries). So far, public relations and/or advertising campaigns for

[8]Coverage of Mexico, which had no contract with any agency, was also monitored. *The New York Times* was chosen because it is the newspaper most widely read by the American elite, is most frequently quoted by political decision makers, and is known from previous research to have a strong agenda-setting effect on public opinion, and provides more foreign coverage than comparable American daily newspapers.

tourism have been the focal point of activities in the area of international public relations (Kunczik & Weber, 1994).

PUBLIC RELATIONS DURING WAR: THE NECESSITY
TO MANIPULATE THE NEWS MEDIA

In times of war, the manipulation of the news media is often considered a necessity. The first military theoretician to recognize this was the Prussian general, Carl von Clausewitz (1780–1831). In his *Vom Kriege* (On War), published posthumously in 1832, von Clause-witz argued that Napoleon's military success was due mainly to the enthusiasm of the French people. According to von Clausewitz, war is an act of violence aimed at forcing the enemy to accept one's will. The central aspect of warfare, he suggested, is not physical force but morale. The goal of war, then, is to break the enemy's morale. The von Clause-witz theory of war takes the following factors into consideration: (1) the government that defines the war's aims, (2) the army that is fighting, and (3) the people.

Important to understanding the theoretical foundation of censorship is the environment in which military actions take place. This environment is characterized by danger, the highest physical strain, and confusion. Von Clausewitz (1832/1873) called this *friktion*, which means all plans developed during practice maneuvers have to be changed during real war. Camouflage and deception are the norm in war. Most intelligence is not secure and very often is wrong. Indeed, von Clausewitz argued, in war most news is false. Secrecy becomes most important because the enemy has to be deceived.

According to von Clausewitz (1832/1873) lying and deceiving are necessities of war. Mastery of deceit and hypocrisy is decisive for successful military actions because the aim has to be to surprise the enemy. The German sociologist Simmel (1920) argued that during war, the basis of social life must be undermined. The enemy must be confronted with unexpected situations. Simmel made the assumption that "all relationships between people are self-evidently based on their knowing something about each other" (p. 256). People have expectations regarding the behavior of others and know that those they are dealing with also have such expectations. Stable social relations are based on the formation of "expectations of expectations," which makes social behavior predictable. During war, one has to deceive the enemy's expectations of one's behavior and undermine the foundations of human coexistence.

In times of war, communication with the enemy requires that we try to pass false intelligence to the enemy even when the enemy is aware that this is our intention. It is a situation of paradoxical communication (Watzlawick, 1976). Decision making in war, then, means making paradox predictions. The higher the probability of a certain action, the lower the chance the enemy will mount it. The lower the probability of an action, the higher the probability the enemy will act that way. The art of disinformation assumes highest importance for survival in times of war. Successful disinformation means the enemy treats false information as credible. The logic of disinformation is as follows: What does the enemy think, about what I think, about what he thinks, and so on (Watzlawick, 1976). Reporting the truth of war might not only give the enemy advantages but also weaken the morale of one's own population and/or troops. Lying and propaganda are important instruments of warfare. If journalists can be instrumentalized and manipulated as tools of propaganda, then they are useful. But reporting the truth in most cases is dangerous for the successful achievement of the aims of war.

Three more reasons for manipulating the media and institutionalizing censorship during war are (1) the morale of the soldiers, (2) the morale of the population, and (3) world public opinion. Any nation waging war has to find stories that justify and ennoble its cause. These are the stories to be disseminated, whereas those that tell of the horrors of war from the soldiers' point of view should be suppressed. The German sociologist Ferdinand Tönnies (1922) argued that when a country is at war, its people believe in the just cause of the war, which was forced upon them by the enemy. To stabilize belligerent public opinion, the government stigmatizes the enemy as aggressor or as a nonhuman monster. President Bush, who characterized Saddam Hussein as another Hitler, argued that "Saddam tried to cast this conflict as a religious war, but it has nothing to do with religion *per se*. It has, on the other hand, everything to do with what religion embodies: good vs. evil, right vs. wrong" (*Time*, March 11, 1991, p. 24).

During war it is of vital interest to the supreme command or the government to control the mass media in order to hinder shifts in public opinion. It can be argued, for instance, that the United States was drawn into the quagmire in Somalia by the influence of television. But television was also probably responsible for America's subsequent withdrawal from Somalia. As Considine (1994) put it:

> The pictures of Michael Duran and other soldiers brutalized in Somalia set off a media and public clamour for American withdrawal. The frenzy prompted Secretary of State Warren Christopher to say that however useful television coverage was to national understanding, edited highlights and pictures taken out of context could not become the driving force for determining American foreign policy. (p. 11)

But Considine maintained that "State Department sources had confirmed that news coverage was driving United States foreign policy" (p. 11). At least the quality of foreign policy has changed under the influence of television; possibly not a turn for the better. There are indications that even warfare is being affected by media coverage. A NATO officer explained why the Allied forces declined to shoot down Serbian helicopters that were violating the no-fly zone: "Even if they were carrying arms, we worried that someone would stick civilian bodies in the wreckage just in time to be filmed by CNN" (*Newsweek*, March 14, 1994). Further, NATO commanders decided not to use napalm or cluster bombs, capable of clearing large swaths of terrain, in Bosnia because: "Bad TV. Napalm leaves it victims shrivelled and charred. Cluster bombs tear them into shreds. The West is worried how they might look on the nightly news" (*Newsweek*, April 25, 1994, p. 13).

The Gulf War (II)

Hill & Knowlton, belonging to Wpp, played a major role in the preparations for the Gulf War.[9] Shortly after the invasion of Kuwait in August 1990, Hill & Knowlton signed a contract with a lobby group called Citizens for a Free Kuwait (CFK). CFK was financed with US $17,861 in contributions from individuals and US $11,852,329 from the Government of Kuwait (MacArthur, 1992; Trento, 1992). Its relationship with CFK brought the agency an estimated US $10 million to 12 million. According to MacArthur, H&K organized a Kuwait Information Day on United States college campuses on September 12. September 23 became a national day of prayer, and September 24 was declared by the governors of

---

[9] Wpp (Wire and Plastic Products) is one of the most important transnational advertising and public relations networks. Besides Hill & Knowlton, Burson Marsteller and Cohn & Wolfe belong to wpp. Ogilvy & Mather; Young & Rubicam and J. Walter Thompsonare advertising agencies owned by Wpp. The gross income of Wpp in 2000 was about $7.97 billion; Kunczik and Zipfel 2001, 450*ff.*)

13 states as a national Free Kuwait Day. Thousands of media kits extolling the virtues of Kuwaiti society were distributed. Media events featuring Kuwaiti "resistance fighters" and businesspeople were organized. Meetings with newspaper editorial boards were arranged. Video news releases from the Middle East were produced. According to Trento (1992), H&K arranged a press conference with a Kuwaiti "freedom fighter" in early September to offset the view that Kuwaitis were fleeing their country and to outline the activities of Kuwaiti resistance. According to Trento, press conferences were arranged to present the image of a strong, gallant Kuwaiti resistance to counter reports of young Kuwaitis partying the war away in the discos of Cairo.

Hill & Knowlton tried to remind members of Congress that Kuwait was a democracy by showing copies of its constitution (Roschwalb, 1994). There is no doubt that Kuwait had certain problems with its image in the United States. H&K also used "atrocity propaganda." MacArthur (1992) emphasized that of all the accusations made against Saddam Hussein, none had more impact on the American public than the one about Iraqi soldiers removing 312 babies from incubators and letting them die on the cold floor in order to steal the incubators. According to Cutlip (1994), Robert Keith Gray, then head of Hill & Knowlton sent a memo to Citizens for a Free Kuwait requesting atrocity stories (p. 771). In October 1990, the Congressional Human Right's Caucus held a public hearing on conditions in Kuwait under Iraqi occupation. Trento (1992) reported that George Hymel of H&K and his staff "provided witnesses, wrote testimony, and coached the witnesses for effectiveness. The PR staff produced videotapes detailing the atrocities and ensured that the room was filled with reporters and television cameras" (p. 381). Nayirah, a 15-year-old Kuwaiti girl, whose last name was kept secret supposedly to protect her family in Kuwait, testified:

> I volunteered at the al-Addan hospital. . . . While I was there, I saw the Iraqi soldiers come into the hospital with guns, and go into the room where 15 babies were in incubators. They took the babies out of the incubators, took the incubators, and left the children on the cold floor to die. (MacArthur, 1992, p. 58)

None of the members of Congress knew that Nayirah in fact was the daughter of the Kuwaiti ambassador to Washington! As Cutlip (1994) commented:

> H&K sent its own camera crew to film this hearing that it had helped cast and direct. It then produced a film that was quickly sent out as a video release used widely by a gullible media. Too late some alert reporter unmasked the story as a hoax and revealed that Nayirah was the Kuwaiti Ambassador's daughter living in Washington. Once more the press served as patsies for the public relations staged event[10] (p. 771).

H&K also ensured that the video was aired by about 700 TV stations. On October 10, 1990, about 53 million Americans watched the tearful testimony on ABC's *Nightline*.

---

[10]Cutlip (1994) was referring to Susan B. Trento's (1992) *The Power House: Robert Keith Gray and the Selling of Access and Influence in Washington* and to John R. McArthur's *Remember Nayirah, Witness for Kuwait?* (in *The New York Times* op-ed page, January 6, 1992), but in the meantime some new evidence has been published and Cutlip's argument has to be modified. (For H&K's version of the Kuwait account, see Pratt, 1994). Roschwalb (1994) pointed out that the story of Iraqi soldiers removing hundreds of babies from incubators "was shown to be almost certainly false by an ABC reporter, John Martin, in March 1991 after the liberation of Kuwait" (p. 271). MacArthur emphasized that Nayirah was the daughter of the Ambassador, had been brought to the Committee by H&K, and that H&K did not respond to the question whether she was in Kuwait in August and September 1990 when the alleged atrocities took place.

According to H&K, the substance of Nayirah's testimony was true and using her as a witness was a stylistic move. The Ambassador verified that Nayirah indeed had been in Kuwait. Kroll Associates, a private investigative company, inquired on behalf of the Kuwaiti government about the alleged atrocities and concluded "that multiple incubator atrocities had taken place and that Nayirah was a witness to one of them" (Pratt, 1994, p. 289). MacArthur (1992) argued that the main result of the investigation was that Nayirah did not work in the hospital, came to the hospital by accident, and did not see babies taken out of incubators.

According to Roschwalb (1994), the atrocity story "seriously distorted the American debate about whether to support military action. Seven senators cited the story in speeches backing the January 12 resolution authorizing war" (p. 271). Decisive in supporting the credibility of the baby incubator story was the fact that on December 19, 1990 Amnesty International published a report on human rights violations in occupied Kuwait. The report included the baby incubator story: "In addition over 300 premature babies were reported to have died after Iraqi soldiers removed them from incubators, which were then looted. Such deaths were reported at al-Razi and al-Addan hospitals, as well as the Maternity Hospital" (MacArthur, 1992, p. 66). President Bush too made frequent use of the atrocity story. On October 15, 1990 he said: "I met with the Emir of Kuwait. And I heard horrible tales: newborn babies thrown out of incubators and the incubators then shipped off to Baghdad" (MacArthur, 1992, p. 65). MacArthur also quoted a speech of Bush to the troops, which he characterized as Bush's best imitation of an H&K press release: "It turns your stomach when you listen to the tales of those that have escaped the brutality of Saddam the invader. Mass hangings. Babies pulled from incubators and scattered like firewood across the floor" (p. 65).

When questioned whether the testimony of Nayirah was decisive in mobilizing support for the war, Frank Mankiewicz, vice-president of H&K, answered that he had been against the war from the beginning and the decision for war was the President's (Der Spiegel, No. 40, 1990). But Mankiewicz also called Kuwait a success for his company. Because the White House, Pentagon, and State Department controlled all information they gave to the media and the public, Trento (1992) argued that it remains a question whether or not H&K's effort on behalf of Kuwait was technically necessary or effective. But it is important to note that it did demonstrate that a public relations firm behaved like a warmonger by distorting facts, distributing atrocity propaganda, and presenting violators of human rights as democrats.

TERRORISM AS INTERNATIONAL PUBLIC RELATIONS

Attracting attention is another aim of international public relations. Certain forms of terrorism, namely, those designed to reach the public through media coverage, are specifically staged for the mass media (Schmid & de Graaf, 1982; Weimann, 1990). Terrorists, normally labeling themselves as freedom fighters, know that journalists tend to regard dramatic and violent events as news. Weimann (1990) quoted a Palestinian terrorist/freedom fighter after the 1972 Munich Olympic Games incident (Palestinian terrorists captured Israeli olympic competitors, resulting in nine Israeli and five Palestinian deaths): "We knew that people in England and America would switch their television sets from any programme about the plight of the Palestinians if there was a sporting event on another channel.... From Munich onwards nobody could ignore the Palestinians or their cause" (p. 16).

The "theatre of terror" (Weimann, 1990) evolved by adjustment to the modes of news selection and international terrorism became a media event and eventually international public relations. Responding to the stigmatization as terrorist, Yasser Arafat argued in a 1988 interview:

> George Washington was called a terrorist by the British. DeGaulle was called a terrorist by the Nazis. What can they say about the P.L.O., except to repeat this slogan? We are freedom fighters, and we are proud of it. According to international law and the United Nations Charter, I have the right to resist Israeli occupation. I don't want to harm anybody. But look how they are treating my people. These savage, barbarian, fascist practices against our children, our women! (*Time*, November 7, 1988)

In the Algerian War, which began in 1954 and lasted 8 years, the Algerian insurgents used the media instrumentally. Abane Ramdane, the FLN liberation movement leader, asked rhetorically: "Is it better for our cause to kill ten of the enemy in the countryside of Telergma, where no one will speak of it, or one in Algiers that will be mentioned the next day in the American press?" (Schmid & de Graaf, 1982, p. 19). In this interplay, symbiotic relationships developed between the freedom fighters and the mass media. Robert Kleinmann of CBS, reporting on the final phase of the Algerian War, said: "If the photographer wanted to be sure to get a picture, it was very useful for him to find out when an assassination was going to take place. Many of the most startling pictures of assassinations in Algeria were obtained in that fashion. . . . There is a very fine line here between reporting and instigating murder. . . . There are competitive pressures on reporters and cameramen in the field" (Schmid & de Graaf, 1982, p. 141).

CONCLUSION

An overarching conclusion that can be drawn from this review of literature on transnational public relations by governments is that there still exist large gaps in research on this topic. Furthermore, there are many aspects of international public relations that have not been discussed here such as the formation of images. Edward W. Said (1978) pointed out that the Orient was almost a European invention since antiquity as a place of romance, exotic beings, haunting memories and landscapes, and remarkable experiences. This contrived Orient helped define Europe (or the West) as its contrasting image. Such images are extremely difficult to change by means of public relations. One finds Japan and India as good examples of this. Suvanto (2002) demonstrated how ancient stereotypes about Japan (geisha, temples, cherry blossom, Mt. Fuji) have survived in Western travel literature. The literature written for Western businessmen has created the image of the Japanese as "sariiman" (e.g., they all look the same in their dark suits, they work in big companies all their lives, they work long days in their offices, their company is a community, etc.). The image of India in the "West" is still influenced by the so-called Alexander-novel (Kunczik, 2000), a work of fiction published about 1.700 years ago. This novel, which was translated into 35 languages, met the demand for entertainment and mysteries. It became a bestseller with the second largest distribution of all books during the Middle Ages with only the Bible having a higher circulation. A content analysis of German schoolbooks found that India still is presented in a way that reflects those very old stereotypes (Kunczik, 2002b). The "Imperatives of Intercultural Education" developed by Gordon W. Allport (1954) in his study about the origin and nature of stereotypes *The Nature of Prejudice* should not be forgotten. Allport calls attention to the decisive role of the school in learning prejudice. Such stereotypes are extremely difficult to change by using public relations.

There is always the danger of the self-fulfilling prophecy. Images can have a dramatic influence on the destiny of whole nations. The famous comment by Thomas and Thomas (1928) is still valid: "If men define situations as real, they are real in their consequences" (p. 572). The image of a country as one in permanent crisis or as economically unreliable, generated perhaps by continuous negative reporting, can influence economic decision-making processes and discourage investments, which in turn can create, or exacerbate, future crises. Barnett et al. (1999) examined monetary and trade networks as part of the process of globalization. Kunczik (2002a) has begun research on the influence of images of nations on the flow of international capital with special reference to the role of the rating agencies (esp. Standard & Poor's and Moody's). Credit rating agencies evaluate financial claims according to their creditworthiness. Sovereign credit ratings are the risk assessments assigned to the obligations of central governments. Sovereign risks consist of three different risks: economic, political, and social. In this context, image policy (public relations) can become quite important, because the rating agencies use "Western" (especially American) criteria to evaluate foreign countries. S. Narenda, "Principal Information Officer of the Government of India" and "Information Advisor to the Indian Prime Minister" emphasized in 2001: "If Standard & Poor say we are poor, we frown." Y. V. Reddy, one of the directors of the Reserve Bank of India, pointed out: "Unquestionably, Indian economy is far stronger now. In view of this unblemished record and current economic strength, it becomes difficult to explain the CRAs' (Credit Agencies') delay in upgrading India's credit rating to investment grade. The ratings of India by these two agencies would appear to convey that India in 1998 is no better off than it was in 1991." Due to globalization one of the main problems for so-called developing countries and/or emerging markets will be their image in the world of international investors. The better the image the easier will be the access to the international capital market. If this assumption is correct, there will be a more intensive image-fight between nations with image polishing becoming a functional equivalent to investor relations.

The Gulf War and the wars in Yugoslavia demonstrated a new trend: the "privatization" of war and atrocity propaganda by public relations firms. Hill & Knowlton's work during the Gulf War is no individual case. Cutlip (1994) pointed out, that "tiny Kosovo, threatened by Serbian aggression after Yugoslavia's break up" asked the American public relations firm Ruder-Finn to wage an intensive public relations campaign in the United States (the firm also worked for Croatia and Bosnia-Herzegovina). The president of Ruder-Finn emphasized: "We helped to formulate the message in a way that Americans could understand." Cutlip (1994) commented like a prophet: "Again the objective is to move public opinion to embroil America in that fratricidal conflict" (p. 771ff.).

As my final remark I emphasize the simple wisdom that image cultivation begins at home, in one's own country, in the way one deals with one's people and one's journalists. The best image cultivation is observance of human rights, establishment of a democratic form of state, and a free press.

REFERENCES

Adams, J. T. (1927). *New England and the Republic 1776–1850*. Boston: Little, Brown.

Aftalion, A. (1926). Théorie psychologique du change, In: Revue d'économic politique (p. 945–986).

Allport, G. W. (1958). *The nature of prejudice*. Garden City, NY: Doubleday. (Original work published 1954)

Baldwin, W. H. (1965). History of persuasion. *Public Relations Quarterly, 10*.

Barnett, G. A., et al. (1999). Globalisation and international communication. An examination of monetary, telecommunications and trade networks. *Journal of International Communication, 6*(2), 7–49.

Bernays, E. L. (1923). *Crystallizing public opinion.* New York: Boni & Liveright.

Bernays, E. L. (1965). *Biography of an idea: Memoirs of public relations counsel Edward L. Bernays.* New York: Simon & Schuster.

Bogart, L. (1976). *Premises for propaganda: The United States Information Agency's operating assumptions in the Cold War.* New York: Free Press.

Boorstin, D. (1961). *The image: A guide to pseudo-events in America.* New York: Harper & Row.

Boulding, K. E. (1956). *The image.* Ann Arbor: University of Michigan Press.

Boulding, K. E. (1967). The learning and reality-testing process in the international system. *Journal of International Affairs, 21.*

Boulding, K. E. (1969). National images and international systems. In J. N. Rosenau (Ed.), *International politics and foreign policy.* New York: Free Press.

Boyd-Barrett, O. (1998). Global news agencies. In O. Boyd-Barrett, and T. Rantanen (Eds.), *The globalization of news* (pp. 19–34), London: Sage.

Burke, P. (1992). *The fabrication of Louis XIV.* New Haven, CT: Yale University Press.

Clausewitz, C. P. G. von (1873). *On war.* (J. J. Graham, Trans., Vols. 1–3). London: N. Trübner. (Original work published 1832)

Considine, D. (1994). Media literacy and media education. *Telemedium: The Journal of Media Literacy, 40.*

Creel, G. (1920). *How we advertised America.* New York: Harper.

Cutlip, S. M. (1994). *The unseen power: Public relations. A history.* Hillsdale, NJ: Lawrence Erlbaum Associates.

Daniels, J. (1944). *The Wilson era: Years of peace, 1910–1917.* Chapel Hill: University of North Carolina Press.

Darrow, R. W., Forrestal, D. J., & Cookman, A. O. (1967). *The Dartnell Public Relations Handbook* (rev. ed.). Chicago: Dartnell.

Dilenschneider, R. L., & Forrestal, D. J. (1990). *The Dartnell public relations handbook* (3rd ed.). Chicago, IL: Dartnell.

Doerries, R. R. (1989). *Imperial challenge: Ambassador Count Bernstorff and German-American relations, 1908–1917* (C. D. Shannon, Trans.). Chapel Hill: University of North Carolina Press.

Donsbach, W. (1991). *Medienwirkung trotz Selektion. Einflußfaktoren auf die Zuwendung zu Zeitungsninhalten.* Cologne, Germany: Böhlau.

Duijker, H. C., J. & Frijda, N. H. (1960). *National character and national stereotypes.* Amsterdam: North-Holland.

Goldman, Eric. F. (1948). *Two-way street: The emergence of the public relations counsel.* Boston: Bellman.

Grattan, C. H. (1969). *Why we fought.* (K. L. Nelson, Ed.). New York: Bobbs-Merrill. (Original work published 1929)

Grunig, J. E., & Hunt, T. (1984). *Managing public relations.* New York: Holt, Rinehart & Winston.

Hertz, J. H. (1982). Political realism revisited. *International Studies Quarterly, 25.*

Hiebert, R. E. (1966). *Courtier to the crowd: The story of Ivy Lee and the development of public relations.* Ames: Iowa State University Press.

Howard, C. M., (1986/87, Spring). How to Say "No" Without alienating reporters. *Public Relations Quarterly.*

Isaacson, W. (1992). *Kissinger: A biography.* London: Faber & Faber.

Karl, P. M. (1982). Media diplomacy. In G. Benjamin (Ed.), *The communications revolution in politics. Proceedings of the Academy of Political Science, 34* (4).

Kepplinger, H. M. (1983). Fuktionswandel der Massenmedien. In M. Rühl & H. W. Stuiber (Eds.), *Kommunikationspolitik in Forschung und Anwendung.* Düsseldorf, Germany: Droste.

Kim, K., & Barnett, G. A. (1996). The determinants of international news flow: A network analysis. *Communications Research, 23,* 323–353.

Kissinger, H. (1969). *American foreign policy: Three essays.* New York: Norton.

Knorr, K. D. (1980). Die Fabrikation von Wissen. In N. Stehr & V. Meja (Eds.), *Wissenssoziologie. Kölner Zeitschrift für Soziologie und Sozialpsychologie, Sonderheft 22.* Opladen, Germany: Westdeutscher Verlag, 226–295.

Kruglak, T. E. (1962). *The two faces of TASS.* Minneapolis: University of Minnesota Press.

Kunczik, M. (1997). *Images of nations and international public relations,* Mahwah, N.J: Lawrence Erlbaum Associates.

Kunczik, M. (1998). *British and German Propaganda in the United States from 1914 to 1917.* In J. Wilke (Ed.), *Propaganda in the 20th century. Contributions to its history.* Cresskill, NJ: Hampton Press, 25–55.

Kunczik, M. (2000). Indian Identity and India's image in historical perspective. Paper presented at the IAMCR Conference, Singapore.

Kunczik, M. (2002a). Globalization: News media, images of nations and the flow of international capital with special reference to the role of rating agencies. *Journal of International Communication, 8* (1), 39–79.

Kunczik, M. (2002b). The image of India in German schoolbooks. An explorative study of textbooks in geography, religion, German lessons and history, Paper presented at the IAMCR conference, Barcelona, Spain.

Kunczik, M., & Weber, U. (1994). Public diplomacy and public relations advertisements of foreign countries in Germany. *The Journal of International Communication, 1,* 18–40.

Kunczik, M., & Zipfel, A. (2001). *Publizistik,* Cologne, Weimar, and Vienna: Böhlau Verlag.

Lasswell, H. D. (1942). Communications research and politics. In D. Waples (Ed.), *Print, radio, and film in a democracy.* Chicago: University of Chicago Press.

Lippmann, W. (1922). *Public opinion.* New York: Harcourt Brace.

MacArthur, J. R. (1992). *Second front: Censorship and propaganda in the Gulf War.* New York: Hill & Wang.

Manheim, J. B. (1991). *All of the people all the time: Strategic communication and American politics.* Armonk, NY: M. E. Sharpe.

Manheim, J. B. (1994). *Strategic public diplomacy and American foreign policy: The evolution of influence.* Oxford, UK: Oxford University Press.

Manheim, J. B., & Albritton, R. B. (1984). Changing national images: International public relations and media agenda setting. *American Political Science Review, 78.* 47, 641–657.

McAdoo, W. G. (1931). *Crowded years: The reminiscences of William G. McAdoo.* Boston: Houghton Mifflin.

Millis, W. (1935). *Road to war: America 1914–1917.* New York: Houghton Mifflin.

Olasky, M. N. (1985, Spring). A reappraisal of 19th-century public relations. *Public Relations Review, 11.*

Onkvisit, S., & Shaw, J. J. (1989). *International marketing. Analysis and strategy.* Columbus, OH: Merrill.

Pratt, C. B. (1994). Hill & Knowlton's two ethical dilemmas. *Public Relations Review, 20.* 3, S.277–294.

Roschwalb, S. A. (1994). The Hill & Knowlton cases: A brief on the controversy. *Public Relations Review, 20* 3, 267–267.

Said, E. (1978). *Orientalism,* New York: Pantheon Books.

Schmid, A. P., & de Graaf, J. (1982). *Violence as communication: Insurgent terrorism and the Western media.* London: Sage.

Signitzer, B., & Coombs, T. (1992). Public relations and public diplomacy: Conceptual convergences. *Public Relations Review, 18,* 137–147.

Simmel, G. (1920). *Soziologie* [Sociology] (2nd ed.). Munich, Germany: Duncker & Humblot.

Smith, H. (1988). *The power game: How Washington works.* New York: Random House.

Squires, J. D. (1935).*British propaganda at Home and in the United States. From 1914 to 1917,* Cambridge, MA.: Harvard University Press.

Sreberny-Mohammadi, A. (1985). *Foreign news in the media. International reporting in 29 countries.* Paris: UNESCO.

Star, S. A., & Hughes, H. M. (1950). Report on an educational campaign: The Cincinnati plan for the United Nations. *American Journal of Sociology, 55,* 389–400.

Suvanto, M. (2002). *Images of Japan and the Japanese. The Representations of the Japanese Culture in the Popular Literature Targeted at the Western Worls in the 1980s–1990s,* Jyväskylä, Finland: University of Jyväskylä.

Thomas, W. I., & Thomas, D. S. (1928). *The Child in America.* New York: Knopf.

Tocqueville, A. de (1946). *Democracy in America,* Vol. II, London 1946: Oxford University Press.

Tönnies, F. (1922). *Kritik der Öffentlichen Meinung.* Berlin: Springer.

Trento, S. B. (1992). *The Power House: Robert Keith Gray and the Selling of Access and Influence in Washington.* New York: St. Martin's Press.

United States Department of State (1987, October). *Soviet Influence Activities: A Report on Active Measures and Propaganda.* Washington, DC: United States Government Printing Office.

Viereck, G. S. (1930). *Spreading Germs of Hate.* New York: H. Liveright.

Walker, F. E. (1988, May). Recent changes in the Soviet propaganda machine. *Journal of Defense & Diplomacy*.

Watzlawick, P. (1976). *How Real is Real? Confusion, Disinformation, Communication*. New York: Random House.

Weimann, G. (1990). "Redefinition of image": The impact of mass-mediated terrorism. *International Journal of Public Opinion Research*, 2, 16–29.

Wilke, J. (Ed.) (1998). *Propaganda in the 20th century. Contributions to Its History*, Cresskill, NJ: Hampton Press.

Wilke, J. (1998). German foreign propaganda in the United States during World War I: The Central Office of Foreign Services.

Wu, H. D. (1998). Investigating the determinants of international news flow. In *Gazette, 60*, 493–512,

37

PUBLIC RELATIONS OF MOVERS AND SHAKERS: TRANSNATIONAL CORPORATIONS

DEJAN VERČIČ

Public relations is a managerial function (Cutlip, Center, & Broom, 2000) and public relations theory originates in economics and strategic management (Verčič & J. Grunig, 2000). Business (Pearson, 1989) and its particular form, the corporation (Olasky, 1987), are the paradigmatic subjects of theorizing in what Verčič & J. Grunig called "the American concept of public relations" (2000, p. 12). Further, this concept was identified by Verčič, L. Grunig, and J. Grunig (1995) as the only global concept of public relations currently available.[1] Yet, while "all public relations is global or international" (L. Grunig, J. Grunig, & Dozier, 2002, p. 541) because all companies affect, or are affected by, the world that lies beyond their borders, it is amazing that we have only a few quality publications on the public relations practices of transnational corporations (TNC).[2] As contemporary companies "should globalize unless they can find very good reasons not to" (Yip, 2001, p. 150), so should research and theorizing in public relations. Public relations is an innovative social

---

[1] Only recently has work been initiated on alternative conceptualizations, primarily in Europe; see van Ruler & Verčič (2002a, 2002b) and Verčič, van Ruler, Bütschi, & Flodin (2001), and reflections from Africa (Rensburg, 2002), Asia (Sriramesh, 2002) and Latin America (Ferrari, 2002); for a North American reflection see L. Grunig & J. Grunig (2002). See also Sriramesh, Kim, & Takasaki (1999).

[2] In this chapter we use the term "transnational corporation" (TNC) as a generic term for business (for-profit) entities operating in more than one country as defined by Dicken (1988, p. 177) and quoted in the chapter. Organizational studies and in international management literature use different names, like "transnational corporation," "multinational corporation," "international corporation," "global corporation," etc., to distinguish between different types of international businesses and one such typology is presented in the chapter. Yet, when it is not explicitly specified differently, we use the term "transnational corporation" to cover all types of international businesses. In the same way we use the term "corporation" as a generic term for a large for-profit organization. "Transnational corporate public relations" in that context is used as a generic name for public relations carried in and on behalf of transnational corporations.

technology (Verčič, Razpet, Dekleva, & Šlenc, 2000) and its global diffusion is controlled primarily by TNCs in their transformation into global institutions (Kruckeberg, 2000).

This chapter intends to provide a presentation of "the beast" by first providing a definition of what constitutes a transnational corporation. Next, it provides a rough estimate of the scope of the diffusion of TNCs, lists the largest among them, and presents how they are classified based on the level of their transformation from a domestic to a global business in organizational studies. Then the chapter focuses on currently available information on transnational corporate public relations. Finally, the chapter provides a plea for a theory of transnational corporate public relations by highlighting the peculiarities of corporate public relations in international arena and concludes with a view toward the future.

THE "MOVERS AND SHAKERS"

Peter Dicken (1998), in his best-selling book on the globalization phenomenon, entitled the translational corporations (TNCs) as "the primary 'movers and shapers' of the global economy" (p. 177) and defined them as follows: "A transnational corporation is a firm which has the power to co-ordinate and control operations in more than one country, even if it does not own them" (p. 177).

Dickens sees TNCs as the primary beneficiaries of the present form of globalization that is characterized by economic deregulation and the privatization of state-owned assets around the world. Yet he doesn't believe that these processes make states obsolete or puts their "economic sovereignty at bay" (Vernon, 1968). Besides TNCs and governments there are also nongovernmental organizations that operate transnationally, giving us three major players we need to consider when analyzing the world beyond one's national borders. TNCs are the primary movers and shakers of the global economy, but they do not act in isolation.

Wallace (1982) warned that multinational businesses are not necessarily organized as firms, as limited liability companies, or as corporations, but rather as groups or networks of entities that have been established under different national regimes with different nationalities and legal forms. Early European multinational business enterprises are generally considered to be the forerunners of modern multinational corporations and they appeared on the world map from 1300 to 1700. Gabel and Bruner (2002) listed several of the early European multinational businesses: the Hanseatic League in Germany, the Merchant Adventurers Company in Britain, the Medici family of Italy, the Muscovy Company in Russia, the Dutch East India Company in the Netherlands, and the British East India Company (known to contemporaries simply as "the Company"). UNCTAD (United Nations Conference on Trade and Development) calculated that by the end of the twentieth century, there were approximately 39,000 parent-company TNCs controlling about 265,000 foreign affiliates (Dicken, 1998, p. 43). The largest among them have revenues of over US $200 billion (Table 37.1), employ over 1 million people (Table 37.2), and have profits of over US $15 billion (Table 37.3).

There are many descriptions of the phenomenon of these large firms that co-ordinate and control operations in more than one country. Based on a review of relevant literature, Stohl (2001) developed a typology of organizations to describe "the transformation and convergence of domestic to global forms of organizing" (p. 328). Her description of the five types "are based on the predominance of a single national/cultural identity, the perceived importance of an international orientation and perspective, the legitimacy of multiple voices and authority, the type of structure, the 'ideal' management model, and the interconnected nature of interactions across a diversity of cultural groups" (p. 328). She labeled the five types of organizations domestic, multicultural, multinational, international, and global.

TABLE 37.1

The World's Largest Companies by Revenues in 2001 US $Million

Rank	Company	Revenues ($million)
1	Wal-Mart Stores	219,812.0
2	Exxon Mobil	191,581.0
3	General Motors	177,260.0
4	BP	174,218.0
5	Ford Motor	162,412.0
6	Enron	138,718.0
7	DaimlerChrysler	136,897.3
8	Royal Dutch/Shell Group	135,211.0
9	General Electric	125,913.0
10	Toyota Motor	120,814.4

Note. Retrieved January 14, 2003 from http://www.fortune.com/fortune/Global500

TABLE 37.2

The World's Largest Companies by Employment

Rank	Company	2001 Number of Employees
1	Wal-Mart Stores	1,383,000
2	China National Petroleum	1,167,129
3	State Power	1,162,645
4	Sinopec	937,300
5	United States Postal Service	891,005
6	China Telecommunications	566,587
7	Agricultural Bank of China	500,000
8	Siemens	484,000
9	Industrial & Commercial Bank of China	429,709
10	McDonald's	395,000

Note. Retrieved November 8, 2002 from http://www.fortune.com/lists/G500/g500_topperf_co_bigemploy.html

Stohl (2001, pp. 329–330) noted that these five types of organizations can be placed on a continuum from being purely domestic to being purely global with distinctions based on six dimensions. The first dimension is a predominantly national orientation as seen in domestic organizations that identify with one country and one dominant culture. Multicultural organizations identify with one country with some recognition by management of the cultural diversity of their workforce. Multinational organizations identify with one nationality while doing business in several countries. International organization identify with two or more countries. Global organization identify with the global system.

The second dimension is the perceived importance of international orientation. Domestic organizations have no international orientation while multicultural organizations give it very little importance. International orientation is important for multinational organizations, extremely important for international organizations, and dominant for global organizations.

The third dimension is the legitimacy of multiple voices and authority. Domestic organizations are parochial, multicultural organizations are ethnocentric, multinational organizations are polycentric, international organizations are regiocentric, and global organizations are geocentric.

TABLE 37.3
The World's Largest Companies by Profits

Rank	Company	2001 Profits ($millions)
1	Exxon Mobil	15,320.0
2	Citigroup	14,126.0
3	General Electric	13,684.0
4	Royal Dutch/Shell Group	10,852.0
5	Philip Morris	8,560.0
6	BP	8,010.0
7	Pfizer	7,788.0
8	Intl. Business Machines	7,723.0
9	AT&T	7,715.0
10	Microsoft	7,346.0

Note. Retrieved November 8, 2002 from http://www.fortune.com/lists/G500/g500_topperf_co_highprofit.html

The fourth dimension is the type of structure. Domestic organizations have hierarchical, traditional bureaucratic, and matrix structures. Multicultural organizations introduce teamwork and flattening of hierarchy. Multinational organizations are hierarchically managed from a central location with national subsidiaries, which are miniature replicas and employ teamwork. International organizations have joint hierarchy and international divisions that integrate global activities with teamwork within subsidiaries but not across. Global organizations have decentralized decision making and share responsibilities.

The fifth dimension is the management model. Domestic organizations are monocultural, multicultural organizations favor cultural dominance, multinational organizations cultural compromise, international organizations cultural synergy, and global organizations cultural integration.

The sixth dimension is the level of international interaction. Domestic organizations may import and export goods and services with a few representatives abroad. Multicultural organizations also import and export with some representatives abroad and also have intercultural communication among workforce. Multinational organizations favor intercultural communication among workforce, management, clients, customers, etc. International organizations are internationally loosely coupled. Global organizations are global networks, integrative and tightly coupled.

It is no wonder that international corporate public relations practices operate along two extremes. The first is when domestic public relations practices are extended to other countries with few, or no, modifications and the other is when international public relations practices are unrelated to domestic public relations programs (Wakefield, 2001, p. 641). To bridge the gap between these two extreme positions, Verčič, L. Grunig, and J. Grunig (1995) and L. Grunig, J. Grunig, and Verčič (1998) proposed a normative theory of generic principles and specific applications (based on five environmental variables) in international public relations.

THE PUBLIC RELATIONS OF TRANSNATIONAL CORPORATIONS: GENERIC PRINCIPLES AND SPECIFIC APPLICATIONS

A normative theory of generic principles in international public relations argues that there are some principles of public relations that can be practiced around the world. Verčič, L. Grunig & J. Grunig (1995) proposed the following generic principles borrowing from the findings of the "excellence study" (reported in Dozier, L. Grunig, & J. Grunig, 1995; J. Grunig 1992; and L. Grunig, J. Grunig & Dozier 2002):

1. Public relations is involved in strategic management.
2. Public relations is empowered by the dominant coalition or by direct reporting relationship to senior management.
3. The public relations function is an integrated one.
4. Public relations is a managerial function separate from other functions.
5. The public relations unit is headed by a manager rather than a technician.
6. The two-way symmetrical model of public relations is used.
7. A symmetrical system of internal communication is used.
8. Knowledge potential for managerial role and symmetrical public relations.
9. Diversity is embodied in all roles.
10. An organizational context exists for excellence.

L. Grunig, J. E. Grunig, and Verčič (1998) tested the application of these principles in Slovenia and confirmed the validity of this general model. Rhee (2002) arrived at similar conclusions based on her study of the principles in South Korea. The impact of specific environmental variables on the international application of the generic principles has been discussed in detail by Sriramesh and Verčič (2001) and in Chapter 1 of this book.

The above conceptualizations have laid out the first frameworks to organize empirical research on public relations practices in transnational corporations. Wakefield (1999, p. 34) conducted a Delphi study on the application of the generic principles proposed by Verčič, L. Grunig, and J. E. Grunig (1995) soliciting responses from 23 public relations veterans in 18 countries. He conducted a follow-up study adding another 31 respondents from 15 countries and developed what he labeled as "factors of effectiveness in multinational public relations" that form the foundation for practicing "world-class" public relations.

He suggested that organizations practicing "world-class" public relations would have a global, but not a "central-mandate" philosophy, and value "outside-in" dialogue over "inside-out" communication. Further, in these organizations, the senior public relations managers in every unit report to the senior executive in a country in which they operate but have dual matrix reporting relationship to headquarters public relations which is located in the country of a TNC's origin. The communication efforts of these organizations are coordinated, both at headquarters and internationally and PR cooperates closely with other departments such as marketing and legal, but is not subordinated to them. The author also suggested that the PR officers in every unit of organizations that practice "world-class" public relations are full-time and have proper training. His other suggestions were that:

- Public relations officers operate as a global team with horizontal reporting relationships.
- Public relations staffing represents the diversity of the firm's transnational publics.
- A central person is a team leader, not a mandate giver.
- Communication between public relations people is "multiway," not just two-way.
- Opportunities for interaction are frequent, and both formal and informal.

Although the studies reviewed above have evaluated corporate public relations in international settings, further studies are needed before we can claim the existence of a theory of transnational corporate public relations.

TOWARD A THEORY OF TRANSNATIONAL CORPORATE PUBLIC RELATIONS

Drucker (1994, p. 96) wrote that "[e]very organization, whether business or not, has a theory of the business." This makes assumptions about the environment (which define what an organization is paid for), about the specific mission (what an organization considers to be meaningful results) and assumptions about the core competencies needed to accomplish the mission (where an organization must excel in order to retain leadership).

A theory of the business has relevance on two levels: it applies to public relations client organizations (organizations employing public relations capacities, internally or/and externally) and to the public relations function in/for these same organizations itself. It is beyond the scope of this chapter to elaborate how theories of business differ between domestic, multicultural, multinational, international, and global firms. Notwithstanding any differences, three commonalities remain:

1. "*All* TNCs have an identifiable home base, which ensures that every TNC is essentially embedded within its domestic environment" (Dicken, 1998, p. 193). No corporation is culture-free or nation-free.

2. "The creation of particular types of demand and the shaping of customer tastes and preferences are an intrinsic part of the TNC system" (Dicken, 1989, p. 249). For that very reason, it is interesting to note a parallel between the dominance of TNCs originating in the United States that are at the top of the list of the largest TNCs in the world and the major United States export industry: "The single largest export industry for the United States is not aircraft or automobiles, it is entertainment—Hollywood films grossed more than $30 billion worldwide in 1997" (UNDP [United Nations Development Programme]), 1999, p. 4).

3. "Global business is not, then, just about business: it has cultural, legal, political and social effects as much as economic ones" (Parker, 1996, p. 485). Three books expressing the intellectual spirit at the dawn of the twenty-first century question practices of TNCs exactly because of these "externalities" (Verčič & J. Grunig, 2000): Frank (2001), Hertz (2001), and Klein (2000). Similarly, Plender (2000) warrants the newest unpopularity of capitalism: "Large corporations are the engines of creative destruction. So they make a large target. For their part, politicians need enemies. In the post-cold war world big business fits the bill."

L. Grunig (1992, pp. 72–73) questioned the purpose of the public relations profession: "Are we in the business of persuasion? of information? of negotiation? of co-optation? of co-operation?" The models of public relations first presented by J. Grunig and Hunt (1984, pp. 21–22) answer the question differently (the press agentry model says that public relations is about presentation, the public information model says that it is about information, the two-way asymmetrical model says that is about persuasion, and the two-way symmetrical model says that it is about negotiation). J. Grunig and L. Grunig (1989) summed up those purposes in two general forms: control of the external environment by the focal organization and adaptation of the focal organization to its environment. So far as transnational corporate public relations is related to markets, it is also involved in control. This explains why Wakefield (2000, pp. 199–200) found that submission of public relations to marketing is more common internationally than in the United States corporate world. While White (1997, p. 159) postulated that "[p]ublic relations is a practical management and business discipline, partly because it is also a moral discipline," this maxim still seems to be in the second tier when firms practice public relations internationally.

TABLE 37.4

The Nine Principles

At the World Economic Forum, Davos, on January 31, 1999, UN Secretary-General Kofi A. Annan challenged world business leaders to "embrace and enact" the Global Compact, both in their individual corporate practices and by supporting appropriate public policies. These principles cover topics in human rights, labor, and environment:

Human Rights

The Secretary-General asked world business to:

Principle 1: Support and respect the protection of international human rights within their sphere of influence; and

Principle 2: Make sure their own corporations are not complicit in human rights abuses.

Labor

The Secretary-General asked world business to uphold:

Principle 3: Freedom of association and the effective recognition of the right to collective bargaining;

Principle 4: The elimination of all forms of forced and compulsory labor;

Principle 5: The effective abolition of child labor; and

Principle 6: The elimination of discrimination in respect of employment and occupation.

Environment

The Secretary-General asked world business to:

Principle 7: Support a precautionary approach to environmental challenges;

Principle 8: Undertake initiatives to promote greater environmental responsibility; and

Principle 9: Encourage the development and diffusion of environmentally friendly technologies.

Note. Retrieved November 8, 2002 from http://65.214.34.30/un/gc/unweb.nsf/content/thenine.htm

Meaningful results in transnational corporate public relations relate above all to the legitimacy of the system (Jensen, 1997) that enables them to operate (Ruler & Verčič, 2002a, 2002b, Verčič, van Ruler, Bütschi & Flodin, 2001). The 1970s saw a more critical attitude toward TNCs starting with the notion of a national "economic sovereignty at bay" (Vernon, 1968) and efforts by many national governments to regulate the activities of TNCs. The 1980s was a decade of deregulation and increased efforts to attract foreign investments, while the 1990s "saw a proliferation of corporate codes of conduct and an increased emphasis on corporate responsibility" (Jenkins, 2001, p. III). Table 37.4 presents an international framework for self-regulating corporate practices around the world.

Kruckeberg (2000) noted that the corporation has traditionally been "a central institution in American culture, with a historical pattern of rights and duties, powers and responsibilities" (p. 150). With an increase in the proportion of the world's population taking part in the global economy from around a quarter to four-fifths in only 25 years (Jefkins, 2001, pp. 6–7), "corporations as global institutions may become far more powerful and pervasively influential" (Kruckeberg, p. 150)—a central institution in global culture!

Public relations competencies in transnational businesses have a special emphasis in dealing with multiple publics with conflicting expectations and interests (Verčič, 1997). The vice president in charge of external affairs of one of the largest TNCs, the Royal Dutch/Shell Group of companies, commented on the results of their research on international publics:

We found that many rational and intelligent people thought that it was a reasonable proposition that companies such as Shell should mediate to reduce tensions between different levels of government, or that they should take positions on social policy matters. At all times we should remember that Shell is a business. Activities as these are not within the normal, legitimate role of a business. Therefore, we cannot meet such expectations. (de Segundo, 1997, pp. 17–18)

The importance of researching factors outside the organization was further emphasized by Drucker (1997): "In fact, approximately 90% or more of the information any organization collects is about inside events. Increasingly, a winning strategy will require information about events and conditions *outside* the institution: noncustomers, technologies other than those currently used by the company and its present competitors, markets not currently served, and so on" (p. 22).

In addition to these general remarks, there is a need to highlight some concrete features of transnational corporate public relations, which is the focus of the next section.

PECULIARITIES OF TNC PUBLIC RELATIONS

There are several features of public relations in and for TNCs that we can only mention here, yet they need further study. In general, we can identify them under the following headings: fewer professionals, more stakeholders, more competitors, and more issue groups.

Fewer Professionals

While normative public relations theory argues for a strategic public relations management function staffed by educated and trained professionals, it is common for the total number of public relations staff in international operations to be well below the total number of business entities they are required to serve and support. In the 1990s, when ABB was among the most admired European TNCs, it comprised of 1000 companies operating in 140 countries with 217,000 employees. These were further fragmented to 5000 profit centers. These 5000 centers in 1000 firms were attended to by a global network of approximately "200 communication specialists (although not all have only communications as their function)" (Robertson, 1997). What is important to understand in this context is that this example is far from extreme—it might well be closer to the norm. It is not uncommon to find some diversified conglomerates that have only a handful of public relations professionals in the HQ being responsible for activities around the world! One may wonder how they succeed and this aspect needs further research.

Downsizing and outsourcing have contributed to the further decrease in the number of public relations professionals working TNCs (Newsom, VanSlyke Turk, & Kruckeberg, 1996, p. 72). Studies that assess collaboration with "global" public relations agencies from a perspective of a "downsized public relations department" are still lacking.

More Stakeholders

There is no doubt that the larger a corporation becomes, the greater the number of stakeholders it needs to contend with. The largest TNCs operating around the globe have more stakeholders than corporations operating within a single country. But that is not all. As Fombrun & Rindova (2000) argued based on the case of Royal Dutch/Shell: "in different settings, the relative importance of stakeholders varies, and the factors that influence reputation are different" (p. 85). In 1995, Royal Dutch/Shell faced two major crises. The first centered on its decision to scuttle its aging offshore drilling platform—the Brent Spar—in the North Sea, which resulted in a vociferous, and successful, opposition from an NGO—Greenpeace (The case study of Brent Spar has been discussed in the chapter on Germany in this book). The other focused on the corporation's human rights record in Nigeria. As a part of its learning experience from these issues, Shell initiated several projects, among which the most interesting from a public relations perspective are the "Assessing Society's Changing Expectations" project and the "Becoming WoMAC (The World's Most Admired Corporation)" project. Fombrun and Rindova noted that "firms that rate well with some evaluators do not always do so well with others" (p. 85). This may open some new questions regarding stakeholder relationship management that is not only complex but qualitatively different in a transnational as opposed to a single-country setting.

TNCs often operate as conglomerates of corporations that have very little in common. They may well have different identities, names and values, and in some cases may be in the process of being bought only to be sold soon after. In recent years, many TNCs have managed "value chains" that have no, or very limited, legal bonds. For example, there may be a link between a Vietnamese textile producer who is outsourced by a branded corporation in the United States who then sells the product via a third legal entity in Europe. The very notions of internal communication and corporate social responsibility need to get completely new meanings under such circumstances. Yet public relations literature is silent on such issues.

More Competitors

Public relations is generally described as being concerned with relations between organizations and their publics. In a single country, it is often the case that corporate public relations opportunities and problems arise out of actions of competitors even if such instances are not so visible. Yet, such instances become much more visible in the international arena. Globalization is about competition, promoting and restricting it, and as such about competitors. Two books that explored the subject of lobbying in the European Union (Pedler, 2002b; Pedler and van Schendelen, 1994) indicated how the lobbying practices TNCs employ in the context of European integration and institutions depend on the practices of their competitors. For example, clean air and the issue of car emissions in Europe pit the interests of car manufacturers and the oil industry, and the interests of the governments of domestic (European, in this case) and foreign countries (e.g., Japan and the United States). Car and oil corporations (with different technologies and interests based on them) play games between themselves and their public relations activities are in that respect both competitive and co-dependent (Pedler, 2002a). Under such circumstances, publics may not be emerging out of issues or problems (J. E. Grunig, 1997), but based on the actions of other corporations.

More Issue Groups

Naomi Klein (2000) introduced counter-corporate activism by stating:

> Dozens of brand-based campaigns have succeeded in rattling their corporate targets, in several cases pushing them to substantially alter their policies. But three campaigns stand out for having reached well beyond activist circles and deep into public consciousness. The tactics they have developed—among them the use of the courts to force transparency on corporations, and the Internet to bypass traditional media—are revolutionizing the future of political engagement. By now it should come as no surprise that the targets of these influential campaigns are three of the most familiar and best-tended logos on the brandscape: the Swoosh,

the Shell and the Arches. (p. 366; the author is referring to Nike, the Royal Dutch/Shell Group of companies, and McDonald's, respectively.)

Not only are there more issue groups around the world than in any single country, but they also perceive themselves as global warriors that are in a global search for causes to oppose. Transnational issues management may well be a different game than one plays domestically.

CONCLUSIONS

Corporate public relations in the world stage is the forerunner of the best in public relations. It demands more work in a more complex environment. Therefore, to study the best in public relations we need to focus on transnational corporate public relations. In the past decade, we have seen the emergence of the first normative theory focusing on corporate public relations at the international level. What we need in this decade are descriptive studies documenting the everyday practice of transnational corporate public relations and analyses of empirical data from individual case studies, cross-sectional and longitudinal surveys, and behavioral data. It is a no-risk strategy to predict that excellent public relations will very soon be only transnational. Global institutionalization of public relations depends on global institutionalization of corporations and their employment of public relations services.

There continues to be little information on the profile of model global corporate public relations practitioner. Are they to be natives in a country in which they are serving or are they to be professional expatriates committed only to their corporations? Are they building lasting relationships with their stakeholders or moving from country to country (as professional diplomats do) so often that this is not possible? Currently, TNCs probably employ the majority of public relations professionals and they will probably employ an even larger share of them in the future. TNCs are public relations' natural environment.

REFERENCES

Cutlip, S. M., Center, A. H., & Broom, G. M. (2000). *Effective public relations*, 8th ed. Upper Saddle River, NJ: Prentice Hall.

Dicken, P. (1998). *Global shift: Transforming the world economy*, 3rd ed. London: Paul Chapman.

Dozier, D. M., Grunig, L. A., & Grunig, J. E. (1995). *Manager's guide to excellence in public relations and communication management*. Mahwah, NJ: Lawrence Erlbaum Associates.

Drucker, P. F. (1994). The theory of business. *Harvard Business Review*, 27(5) September–October, 95–104.

Drucker, P. F. (1997). The future that has already happened. *Harvard Business Review*, 75(5) September–October, 20–24.

Ferrari, M. A. (2002). The Latin American perspective on public relations: The case of Brazil and Chile. In D. Verčič, B. van Ruler, I. Jensen, D. Moss, & J. White (Eds.), *Proceedings of the BledCom 2002: The status of public relations knowledge in Europe and around the world*, (pp. 19–24). Ljubljana: Pristop Communications.

Fombrun, C. J., & Rindova V. P. (2000). The road to transparency: Reputation management of Royal Dutch/ Shell. In M. Schuletz, M. J. Natch, & M. H. Larsen (Eds.), The expressing organization: Linking identity, reputation and the corporate brand (pp. 79–96). Oxford: Oxford University Press.

Frank, T. (2001). *One market under God: Extreme capitalism, market populism, and the end of economic democracy*. London: Secker & Warburg.

Gabel, M., & Bruner, H. (2002).*Global Inc. An atlas of the multinational corporation*. Retreived November 6, 2002, from http://www.globallinksconsulting.com/GIncOnLine.html

Grunig, J. (1992) (Ed.). *Excellence in public relations and communication management*. Hillsdale, NJ: Lawrence Erlabaum Associates.

Grunig, J. E. (1997). A situational theory of publics: Conceptual history, recent challenges and new research. In D. Moss, T. MacManus, & D. Verčič (Eds.), *Public relations research: An international perspective* (pp. 3–48). London: ITP.

Grunig, L. A. (1992). Toward the philosophy of public relations. In E. L. Toth & R. L. Heath (Eds.), *Rhetorical and critical approaches to public relations* (pp. 65–91). Hillsdale, NJ: Lawrence Erlbaum Associates.

Grunig, J. E., & Grunig, L. A. (1989). Toward a theory of the public relations behavior of organizations: Review of a program of research. In J. E. Grunig & L. A. Grunig (Eds.), *Public relations research annual* (Vol. 1, pp. 27–66). Hilsdale, NJ: Lawrence Erlbaum.

Grunig, J. E., & Hunt, T. (1984). *Managing public relations*. New York: Holt, Rinehart and Winston.

Grunig, L. A. (1992). Toward the philosophy of public relations. In E. L. Toth & R. L. Heath (Eds.), *Rhetorical and critical approaches to public relations* (pp. 56–91). Hillsdale, NJ: Lawrence Erlbaum.

Grunig, L. A., & Grunig, J. E. (2002). The Bled manifesto on public relations: One North American Perspective. In D. Verčič, B. van Ruler, I. Jensen, D. Moss & J. White (Eds.), *Proceedings of the BledCom 2002: The status of public relations knowledge in Europe and around the world* (pp. 25–34). Ljubljana: Pristop Communications.

Grunig, L. A., Grunig, J. E., & Dozier, D. M. (2002). *Excellent public relations and effective organizations: A study of communication management in three countries*. Mahwah, NJ: Lawrence Erlbaum Associates.

Grunig, L. A., Grunig, J. E., & Verčič, D. (1998). Are the IABC's excellence principles generic? Comparing Slovenia and the United States, the United Kingdom and Canada. *Journal of Communication Management*, 2(4), 335–356.

Hertz, N. (2001). *The silent takeover: Global capitalism and the death of democracy*. London: William Heinemann.

Jefkins, R. (2001). *Corporate codes of conduct: Self-regulating in a global economy (Technology, Business and Society Programme Paper Number 2)*. Geneva: United Nations Research Institute for Social Development.

Jensen, I. (1997). Legitimacy and strategy of different companies: A perspective of external and internal public relations. In D. Moss, T. MacManus, & D. Verčič (Eds.), *Public relations research: An international perspective* (pp. 225–246). London: ITP.

Klein, N. (2000). *No logo: Taking aim at the brand bullies*. London: Flamingo.

Kruckeberg, D. (2000). Public relations: Toward a global professionalism. In J. A. Ledingham & S. D. Bruning (Eds.), *Public relations as relationship management: A relational approach to the study and practice of public relations* (pp. 145–157). Mahwah, NJ: Lawrence Erlbaum Associates.

Newsom, D., VanSlyke Turk, J., & Kruckeberg, D. (Eds.). (1996). *This is PR: The realities of public relations*, 6th ed. Belmont, CA: Wadsworth.

Olasky, M. N. (1987). *Corporate public relations: A new historical perspective*. Hillsdale, NJ: Lawrence Erlbaum Associates.

Parker, B. (1996). Evolution and revolution: From international business to globalization. In S. R. Clegg, C. Hardy, & W. R. Nord (Eds.), *Handbook of organization studies*, pp. 484–506. London: Sage.

Pearson, R. (1989). Business ethics as communication ethics: Public relations practice and the idea of dialogue. In C. H. Botan & V. Hazleton, Jr. (Eds). *Public relations theory* (pp. 111–131). Hillsdale, NJ: Lawrence Erlbaum Associates.

Pedler, R. (2002a). Clean air and car emissions: What industries and issue groups can and can't achieve. In R. Pedler (Ed.), *European Union lobbying: Changes in the arena* (pp. 104–122). London: Palgrave.

Pedler, R. (Ed.) (2002b). *European Union lobbying: Changes in the arena*. London: Palgrave.

Pedler, R. H. & van Schendelen, M. P. C. M. (Eds.) (1994). *Lobbying the European Union: Companies, trade associations and issue groups*. Aldershot, UK: Dartmouth.

Plender, J. (2000, September 11). Unpopular capitalism. *Financial Times*, p. 18.

Rensburg, R. (2002). The Bled manifesto on public relations: An African perspective and vision. In D. Verčič, B. van Ruler, I. Jensen, D. Moss, & J. White (Eds.), *Proceedings of the BledCom 2002: The status of public relations knowledge in Europe and around the world* (pp. 35–43). Ljubljana: Pristop Communications.

Rhee, Y. (2002). Global public relations: A cross-cultural study of the excellence theory in South Korea. *Journal of public relations research 14*(3), 159–184.

Robertson, M. (1997). How can you possibly think global, act local. In T. R. V. Foster & A. Jolly (Eds), *Corporate communications handbook* (pp. 302–308). London: Kogan Page.

Ruler, B. van & Verčič, D. (2002a). 21st century communication management—the people, the organization. In P. Simcic Brønn & R. Wiig (Eds.), *Corporate communication: A strategic approach to building reputation* (pp. 277–294). Oslo: Gyldendal Norsk Forlag.

Ruler, B., & Verčič, D. (2002b). *The Bled manifesto on public relations.* Ljubljana: Pristop Communications.

Segundo, K. de (1997). Meeting society's changing expectations. *Corporate reputation review, 1*(1–2), 16–19.

Sriramesh, K. (2002). The Bled manifesto on public relations: An Asian perspective. In D. Verčič, B. van Ruler, I. Jensen, D. Moss, & J. White (Eds.), *Proceedings of the BledCom 2002: The status of public relations knowledge in Europe and around the world* (pp. 44–49). Ljubljana: Pristop Communications.

Sriramesh, K., & Verčič, D. (2001). International public relations: A framework for future research. *Journal of communication management, 6*(2): 103–117.

Sriramesh, K., Kim, Y., & Takasi, M. (1999). Public relations in three Asian cultures: An analysis. *Journal of public relations research, 11*(4): 271–292.

Stohl, C. (2001). Globalizing organizational communication. In F. M. Jablin & L. L. Putnam (Eds.), *The new handbook of organizational: Advances in Theory, Research, and Methods* (pp. 323–375). Thousand Oaks, CA: Sage.

United Nations Development Programme (UNPD). (1999). *Human development report 1999.* New York: Oxford University Press.

Verčič, D. (1997). Towards fourth wave public relations: A case study. In D. Moss, T. MacManus, & D. Verčič (Eds.), *Public relations research: An international perspective* (pp. 264–279). London: ITP.

Verčič, D., & Grunig, J. E. (2000). The origins of public relations theory in economics and strategic management. In D. Moss, D. Verčič, & G. Warnaby (Eds.), *Perspectives on public relations research* (pp. 9–58). London: Routledge.

Verčič, D., Grunig, L. A., & Grunig, J. E. (1995). Global and specific principles of public relations: Evidence from Slovenia. In H. M. Culbertson & N. Chen (Eds.), *International public relations: A comparative analysis* (pp. 31–65). Mahwah, NJ: Lawrence Erlbaum Associates.

Verčič, D., Razpet, A., Dekleva, S., & Šlenc, M. (2000). International public relations and the Internet: Diffusion and linkages. *Journal of communication management 5*(2), 125–137.

Verčič, D., van Ruler, B., Bütschi, G., & Flodin, B. (2001). On the definition of public relations: A European view. *Public Relations Review, 27*(4), 373–387.

Vernon, R. (1968). Economic sovereignty at bay. *Foreign Affairs, 47*(1), 110–122.

Wakefield, R. I. (1999). World-class public relations: A model for effective public relations in the multinational. In D. Verčič, J. White, & D. Moss (Eds.), *Proceedings of the 6th international public relations research symposium: Innovation in public relations, public affairs and corporate communication practice* (pp. 30–37). Ljubljana: Pristop Communications.

Wakefield, R. I. (2000). Preliminary Delphi research on international public relations programming: Initial data support application of certain generic/specific concepts. In D. Moss, D. Verčič, & G. Warnaby (Eds.), *Perspectives on public relations research* (pp. 179–208). London: Routledge.

Wakefield, R. I. (2001). Effective public relations in the multinational organization. In R. L. Heath (Ed.), *Handbook of public relations* (pp. 639–647). Thousand Oaks, CA: Sage.

Wallace, C. D. (1982). *Legal control of the multinational enterprise: National regulatory techniques and the prospects for international controls.* The Hague: Martinus Nijhoff.

White, J. (1997). Business and organizational consequences of the moral role of the public relations practitioner. In D. Moss, T. MacManus, & D. Verčič (Eds.), *Public relations research: An international perspective* (pp. 159–169). London: ITP.

Yip, G. S. (2001). Global strategy in the twenty-first century. In S. Crainer & D. Dearlove (Eds.), *Financial Times handbook of management*, 2nd ed. (pp. 150–163). London: Financial Times & Prentice Hall.

38

NONGOVERNMENTAL ORGANIZATIONS AND INTERNATIONAL PUBLIC RELATIONS

ANA TKALAC

JURICA PAVICIC

FABULA DOCET! (STORY TEACHES US)

The nonprofit sector consists of organized individuals or organizations that wish to create a society as a community of responsible individuals oriented toward personal or family interests as well as toward the interests and development of their local community and global society (Pavicic, 2000). For more than 40 years, the social role of the nonprofit sector has been investigated and documented by various authors (Kotler & Zaltman, 1971; Lazer, 1969; Samuelson, 1970). Social analysts have been intensively researching this area since the late 1950s, determining the field through three main elements of modern society—government, community, and the market (Smith & Lipsky, 1993).

Another topic closely related to this field of research includes the concept of social responsibility—taking care of the community, which is for the most part oriented toward resolving social problems and crises. Solving problems such as war, disease, or hunger and promoting international development should primarily be considered part of the standard "business portfolio" of government/governmental institutions.

However, such problems are often resolved by the actions of community actors that are independent, cooperating, and non-governmental (Bellah, 1985; Pavicic, 2000). Why is this so? Many governments and governmental institutions are usually either not able, not prepared, or not willing to be involved in the resolution of specific social problems—especially in "troublesome" cases like human rights, international democracy, democratic elections, or ecology. The only "Robin Hoods" left to help in such situations are nonprofit organizations. Even though nongovernmental organizations (NGOs) have consistently used public relations as a primary tool to mobilize public opinion in their favor, public relations literature on this subject is rather thin.

INTERNATIONAL NGOs AND SOCIETY/THE INTERNATIONAL COMMUNITY— *IN AEDEM ES NAVI!* (THE SAME DESTINY AWAITS US)

Socially engaged activism, especially at the international level, is mostly organized by NGOs.[1] Charnovitz (1997, p. 186) offered the following description of nongovernmental organizations:

> NGOs are groups of individuals organized for the myriad of reasons that engage human imagination and aspiration. They can be set up to advocate a particular cause, such as human rights, or to carry out programs on the ground, such as disaster relief. They can have memberships ranging from local to global.

People and organizations willing and dedicated to work and achieve the above-mentioned goals are derived from one of the key democratic rights—the right of citizens to organize themselves (Pentikainen, 2000). Although there is no general regulation governing NGOs, the basis for obtaining "nongovernmental" status includes three criteria: (1) NGOs should not be constituted as political parties, (2) they should not have profit as a motive, and (3) they should not be criminal in operation—in particular, they should be nonviolent (Willetts, 2002).

These characteristics are formally articulated in documents such as the European Convention on the Recognition of the Legal Personality of International Non-governmental Organizations (Strasbourg, 1986—Council of Europe) and United Nations Economic and Social Council (UN ECOSOC) resolutions.

There is evidence to suggest that the development of nongovernmental organizations (or bodies that are not part of the state or kingdom), as well as the idea of universal *pro bono* activism, can be traced far back in time. Antonides & Van Raaij (1998) emphasized that in the medieval period some theoreticians such as Aquinas, Luther, and Calvin, insisted on the social responsibility of merchants and bankers and suggested that those who ignored the problems of poor people (hunger, disease, poverty), be socially "excommunicated."

Simmons (1998), Paul (2000), and other authors agreed that ideas on the necessity of acting in an organized way for the good of the community have existed since the early 1800s. According to Simmons (1998), the British and Foreign Anti-Slavery Society were the forerunners and even the initiators of government actions against slavery. Those actions resulted in the World Anti-Slavery Convention of 1840. Other forerunners of international nongovernmental organizations such as the World Alliance of YMCA (in 1855) and the International Committee for the Red Cross (in 1863) were founded relatively soon afterward (Paul, 2000).

---

[1]The term "nongovernmental organizations (NGOs)" is sometimes considered a synonym for "nonprofit organizations" or *vice versa*. In many cases there is no significant difference between these two terms that could affect understanding of these words in essence—the difference may only be lexical. However, "nonprofit organizations" should be considered as a superordinate term because it includes a wider range of organizations and institutions. According to Paul (2000), nonprofit organizations also include institutions like museums, universities, and hospitals focused on services with sporadic engagement in advocacy. In contrast, NGOs are significantly dedicated to advocacy.

The development of numerous local, national and international independent societies or organizations led to the formation of the Union of International Organizations (*Union des associations internationals*) in 1910. This union consisted of more than 130 international organizations (Rice & Ritchie, 1995; Willetts, 2002).

Although the international visibility of nongovernmental organizations of that time was quite developed and at times even officially directed through bodies such as the League of Nations, international NGOs were formally recognized only in June 1946 by the United Nations when the Committee on Non-Governmental Organizations was established as a standing committee of the ECOSOC—Economic and Social Council (Economic and Social Council resolution 3 (II), 1946).

NGOs might sometimes consider themselves as the only real representatives and benevolent protectors of the society, often leading to tensions between NGOs and governments. According to Paul (2000), elected government officials and bureaucrats defend themselves against NGO criticism by pointing out that NGO leaders are not democratically elected. However the mission of NGOs is largely directed at helping society's human development by using their "social capital," the potential to cause or hasten positive social changes (Putnam, 1993).

One of the recent concepts very relevant to NGOs is the concept of *civil society.* Although Judge (1994) emphasized the difficulties caused by the fact that civil society is discussed through a variety of terms such as NGOs, voluntary associations, nonprofit and charitable organizations, etc., it is important to grasp the concept's main characteristics. Because the term "civil society" was rarely used prior to 1989, one could argue that "civil society" gained currency as a concept only at the time of the transformation of the U.S.S.R. (Judge, 1996).

However, the main problem with providing a definition for the term "civil society" is in providing a response to the question: Who are its stakeholders? Cohen and Arato (1992) equate civil society with persons, institutions, and organizations that have the goal of expressing or advancing a common purpose through ideas, actions and demands on governments. According to Agenda 21 of the 1992 Rio Earth Summit (Commission on Sustainable Development [CSD] in Gemill & Bamidele-Izu, 2002), civil society might be classified into eight main groups: women, children and young people, indigenous peoples and communities, *nongovernmental organizations*, workers and trade unions, the scientific and technological community, business and industry, and farmers.

Because the problems that NGOs have to deal with are so diverse and encompass the political, economic, and social aspects of human existence, any generalization of the practical methods, goals or actors might be considered an inappropriate simplification. Instead, it might be useful to consider an analysis of the levels of NGO activities offered by Paul (2000). By using the example of the World Court Project, a network of NGOs opposed to nuclear weapons, Paul suggested the following levels:

1. Micro-policy (getting the World Court to accept the case on the illegality of nuclear weapons),
2. Macro-policy (questioning governments' strategic reliance on such weapons), and
3. Norm-setting (persuading the public(s) that nuclear weapons are dangerous and a threat to real security in the world).

Although there are three levels to the action mentioned above, other initiatives might consist only of one or two levels.

TABLE 38.1
Changes in Terminology Related to NGOs

Level of Organization	From 1946 to the Early 1990s	From the Early 1990s Onward
Local	National NGO, at the UN Not discussed elsewhere	Grassroots, community-based or civil society organization, or local NGO
Provincial (United States—state)	National NGO, at the United Nations Not discussed elsewhere	Civil society organization or local NGO
National	National NGO, at the UN NGO, outside the UN	NGO or national NGO or civil society organization
Regional	International NGO	NGO or civil society organization
Global	International NGO	NGO or major group or civil society organization

Note. From *UNESCO Encyclopedia of Life Support Systems*, by P. Willetts, 2000.

The idea of international NGO activism is confirmed by many institutions worldwide. NGOs cooperate with the UN, governments, parliaments, numerous private organizations, and companies. One of the most important symbolic social honors for international NGOs was the 1997 Nobel Peace Prize given to Jody Williams, Head of the International Committee to Ban Landmines. The recognition she received and other widely publicized statements such as the declaration that the main weapon in her campaign was the e-mail, further increased the popularity of international NGO activism (Knickerbocker, 2000).

There is no doubt that NGO activism is a "developing area." Consequently, since 1946, the social, economic, and political environment has brought changes to the widely used terminology covering the international dimension of NGOs (Table 38.1). NGOs are sometimes not taken very seriously and cannot totally avoid the reputation of being utopian, antagonistic to governments, and potentially obstructionist (Dichter, 1999). However, among all other participants in the contemporary globalization process, NGOs might be considered as the person in the famous quotation by Alphonse de Lamartine: "Sometimes, when one person is missing, the whole world seems depopulated." Why is this so? Probably because of the important social role of NGOs in monitoring and forcing local and world leaders to take care of others and championing worthy causes such as democracy, cultural appreciation, universal education, and the preservation of the ecology.

FIGURES— *PLUS ULTRA!* (YET FURTHER)

The problem of inconsistent criteria that makes it difficult to produce any uniform classification, as well as the constant changes in the activities of NGOs, casts doubt on the reliability of various quantifications (e.g., number of employees/volunteers, number of projects, etc.) of the activities of international NGOs. However, since recognition from the United Nations in 1946, there has been considerable development of international NGOs. The largest growth in the number of international NGOs occurred in the period 1990–2000 as indicated in Table 38.2.

TABLE 38.2

Growth of International NGOs Between 1990 and 2000

Purpose	1990	2000	Growth (%)
Culture and recreation	1,169	2,733	26
Education	1,485	1,839	23.8
Research	7,675	8,467	10.3
Health	1,357	2,036	50
Social services	2,361	4,215	78.5
Environment	979	1,170	19.5
Economic development, infrastructure	9,582	9,614	0.3
Law, policy, advocacy	2,712	3,864	42.5
Religion	1,407	1,869	32.8
Defense	244	234	−4.1
Politics	1,275	1,240	−2.7
Total	31,246	37,281	19.3

Note. From *Human Development Report 2002*, by Anheier, Glasius, and Kaldor, 2001.

CURRENT PROBLEMS AND CRITICISMS OF INTERNATIONAL NGOs VERSUS INTERNATIONAL PUBLIC RELATION—*QUAE CULPARE SOLES, EA TU NE FECERIS IPSE!* (DON'T DO YOURSELF, WHAT YOU USUALLY DISAPPROVE OF)

NGOs and all their relevant stakeholders might be negatively influenced by issues that provoke certain public criticisms and, to some extent, go against the idea of modern non-governmental activism and the important international social role it plays. The most notable problems in such a context are:

- *Sometimes the status of international NGO is abused to achieve some latent political, religious or economic benefits—quite different from the formally declared benefits.* There is always one rotten apple in the barrel. The bad apple can rot the others as well as damage the basic idea of eating apples. In the case of NGOs, the "dangerous apples" could be organizations or networks with unacceptable or controversial missions or methods of operation. The most commonly used international example in this context is al Qaeda (Naim, 2002). A different kind of NGO, but still very controversial, is the organization of the Reverend Sun Myung Moon (Paine & Gratzer, 2001). For instance, the Moon organization is working very hard to achieve a leading role in the NGO community at the United Nations declaring:

  > "The organization of the Reverend Sun Myung Moon is seeking a major role in the NGO community at the UN. .... The Moon organization has used the UN for conferences and for publicity events. .... A new Moon-sponsored "umbrella group," known as the World Association of NGOs (WANGO), proposes itself as an authentic voice of the NGO community. ...." (Paine & Gratzer, 2001, pp. 1–24).

  It is also worrying that there are reports on the Moon organization's systematical violation of United States tax, immigration, banking and other laws (Parry, 1997) or information on the Moon organization's criticism of women for acting as men's equals (Paine & Gratzer, 2001).

- *In some countries and regions, international NGOs with large potential and resources could generate misunderstanding and distorted perceptions regarding the concept of being "nonprofit" (which is one of the most important components of their NGO status).* Although NGOs might have an international focus and outreach, they act locally. Local people working for NGOs in some regions might treat them as "cash cows." Some of them might be able to earn several times more by working for NGOs than by working for local businesses or government. Abramson (1999) cited the example of Uzbekistan where although the average state salary was $120 per year in 1998, local drivers, administrative assistants, or receptionists working for international NGOs were earning between $2,400 and $4,800 annually! Some authors emphasized that in many cases such distorted perceptions of nonprofit status and all related disparities could also be caused by so-called "professional do-gooders" or "professional altruists" who, work for international NGOs advocating altruist causes but live in luxurious houses, have expensive cars, and enjoy many such material benefits. These professionals also typically earn ten or twenty times more than the average local wage (Vaknin, 2002)

- *At some stage of their life cycle, some international NGOs become unproductive and bureaucratic.* Such problems affect all types of organizations in both the profit and non-profit sector (Pavicic, 2000). The problem is obvious in organizations that have an increasingly international impact. Through organizational change and growth, these organizations may begin to lose their flexibility, their established values and their effectiveness (Edwards & Hulme [1992] cited in Uvin & Miller, 1994). On the other hand, there are examples from some African countries where local NGOs might consist of only three people (e.g., a director, a secretary, and a driver) and no members (Onishi, 2002). This also reflects negatively on the general perception of NGOs.

- *Some international NGOs may be involved in misuse of financial and other resources* (Paine & Gratzer, 2001). Although only a few NGOs may be guilty of this, they can tarnish the reputation of all NGOs and have a negative effect on NGOs' publics, especially donors.

- *Sometimes international NGOs are seen only through the spectacles of "fashionable case studies"—like the Red Cross (Judge, 1994), Amnesty International, or Greenpeace.* Such case studies can be informative, interesting and educative for practitioners, but such extremely positive examples could generate a certain level of frustration and demotivation among other, less successful, organizations.

- *Some NGOs could have a conflict of interest.* One of the recent cases that might be perceived in this light is the Cafedirect-Oxfam case. According to Vaknin (2002), Cafedirect is a firm committed to the "fair trade" of coffee. The NGO Oxfam owns a 25% stake in Cafedirect. Oxfam started a campaign against Cafedirect's competitors and accused them of exploiting coffee growers by paying them only a tiny fraction of the final retail price. Such involvement in market competing could lead to conflicts of interest and/or unethical behavior among NGOs. A similar type of conflict may be seen in instances where NGOs are partly financed by governments or government agencies (Pharoah, 2002). In such cases, the key questions are "Can I bite the hand that feeds me?" and "Am I really non-governmental?"

- *"Illegality" is illegality!* Although some authors declare that "illegality" is often a matter of interpretation and environment (Judge, 1994), many international NGOs are caught in a "double measures" trap. They insist on a strict social expulsion of NGOs that are obviously illegal, and those that engage in behaviors such as violence, supporting terrorism, or racial segregation. It is also important to observe here that some NGOs do not register themselves with appropriate authorities in countries where they are active, preferring to work illegally (Judge, 1994).

- *NGOs are considered as important social partners in bringing positive social changes.* Therefore, sometimes NGOs are faced with numerous "missions impossible" thrust upon them by other social partners whose expectations are too high and unrealistic (Lewis, 1998; Pavicic, 1997).

- *Large international NGOs from developed countries sometimes develop standards based on "western" traditions and expect these standards to be universally applicable.* The so-called effect of "westernizing" can be seen as a serious image problem (Toulmin, 1994). Moreover, examples of local acceptance of "westernizing" could even culminate in protests or negative consequences for those local organizations that cooperate with international NGOs. For instance, in Jordan, the editor of an independent weekly magazine was expelled from the local union of journalists because he was accused of accepting foreign donations for his projects (Mekki, 2000). According to Vichit-Vadakan (2001), NGOs in Thailand are perceived by many Thais as agents that aim to undermine local society and the Thai way of life. Sometimes this clash can be put in simple stereotypical terms—wealthy countries and their organizations emphasize ecology and democracy, while underdeveloped countries really need jobs and food (Shikwati, 2002).

- *Large international NGOs could attract large donors who perceive them as the only organizations capable of coping with certain social difficulties.* Such donors could also be interested in having a reliable partner institution. Since the number of donors and their funds are limited, smaller national, regional and even international NGOs could be at a handicap in their fund-raising activities.

- *The effects of NGOs' work could be counterproductive (or perceived as such).* There is evidence that the arrival of NGOs might provoke local social polarizations and other clashes, or that NGOs could be perceived as "irritating" (Vaknin, 2002). Vaknin also emphasized the problem of good intentions but bad effects in the case of footballs stitched by children of Pakistan. Because of the actions of NGOs and the fear of worldwide protests against child labor, Nike and Reebok relocated their workshops and took work away from some 7000 children. The NGOs' intentions were good, but the average family income in these extremely poor families fell by 20 percent (Vaknin, 2002). The result was that child labor was eradicated, but, this also meant that the children had fewer clothes and less food! Unfortunately, in this case, both alternatives could be considered as bad, but the affected families probably think that the decrease in income is the worse option.

NGOs AND PUBLIC RELATIONS—*PER ASPERA AD ASTRA!*
(THROUGH A PATH OF THORNS TO THE STARS)

All positive social roles, along with criticism and problems, create space for the implementation of international public relations. Public relations could, in a sense, be considered a catalyst or even generator of positive international NGO practice and an impediment to negative practices. Gemmill & Bambidele-Izu (2002) suggested that civil society, through NGOs, should have one of the most important roles in the following five areas of activities:

- Information collection and dissemination
- Policy development consultation
- Policy implementation

- Assessment and monitoring
- Advocacy for environmental justice

Wilcox, Ault, Agee, and Cameron (2000) stated that traditionally, all nonprofit social agencies were viewed as the "good guys" of society and as high-minded, compassionate organizations whose members were committed to helping people live a better life. This perception has recently been seriously challenged. During the early 1990s different charity organizations came into the center of public attention due, among other things, to extremely high executive salaries and different forms of financial improprieties.

The American Red Cross faced massive public protests over its mismanagement of funds collected after the earthquakes of San Francisco in 1989. The organization collected approximately $52 million and initially distributed only $10 million to those affected by the earthquake. After public pressure, the organization rechanneled the entire amount to the victims (Tate, 2002). After the September 11, 2001 tragedy in New York and Washington, D.C., the Red Cross drew the wrath of the public by announcing that it planned to channel part of the money collected by the Liberty Fund to future projects unrelated to the tragedy. At first, the Red Cross designated only 10% of the fund to the families of victims. After the vociferous public criticism it received, the Red Cross reversed its earlier policy and announced that all the money raised for the Liberty Fund would be distributed to September 11 victims only and not reserved for any future use by the organization (Tate, 2002).

The United Way of America was another NGO that came under public scrutiny for fraud. In one of the most highly publicized scandals, William Aramony resigned in 1992 as president and CEO when he was charged with tax manipulation, misusing huge sums of donor contributions for his own benefit, and filing false income tax returns (Young, 2002). The "United Way of America" story become a topic not only in the news, but also in public relations textbooks (Cutlip, Center, & Broom, 1999; Wilcox, Ault, Agee & Cameron, 2000). Even though the story is now more than 10 years old, the public still remembers it well and this NGO has lost some of its luster.

Such erosion in public confidence has been instrumental in making organizations that depend almost exclusively on the goodwill of people change the way they communicate with the public. Reforms in the way NGOs operate and communicate were aimed at reassuring the public that contributions are being spent for the core charitable mission of these organizations, with minimal spending on administrative costs (Frumkin and Kim, 2001). In the light of these events, public relations has gained new importance assuming responsibility for rebuilding organizational credibility and restoring public confidence.

Modern society is typified by intense media scrutiny in many parts of the world making any attempt to fool the public a fatal proposition. All NGOs are more or less dependent on the support of the public. All are also placed in the middle of various social, political, and economic trends that require high-quality management and good public relations. According to Cutlip, Center, and Broom (1999), the altered climate of the 1990s brought about a significant change in the way that public relations is practiced by NGOs. These authors mentioned five major trends in this area: the introduction of marketing and management concepts in communications strategies; the development of information technology and its implications; the use of advertising in public relations programs; the need for the adaptation of a public relations curriculum; and a constant increase in public relations standards in non-profit organizations.

Marketing concepts and management by objectives are becoming increasingly important to the communication strategies of NGOs. McConkey (1975) claimed that management by objectives was the prominent style of leadership for non-profit organizations. This meant that "association leaders contain their activities in a clearly defined set of organizational goals" (p. 223). Kelly (2000) stated in his article on nonprofit public relations management: "Management by objectives is a central concept in the public relations process, which dictates that activities are planned and implemented in support of functional objectives derived from organizational goals" (p. 90). The challenges that NGOs face in the new competitive and performance-driven world can be met through a better, and more efficient management process. Improving the management of communications, as well as management in general, is seen as a way of raising operational effectiveness.

Technology has widened communication selectivity and reach, but on the other hand, has also raised the question of ethics, privacy and legitimacy. Sanborn (2000) stated: "By using the Web, non-profit groups are beginning to create individual identities and use skills they learned offline to present their message to a new, often global audience" (p. 37). Reis (2000) reported on a recent study from the Mellman Group that showed the vast potential of the Internet in bringing about social change. The study contended that about 50 million Americans over 18 have Internet access and also contribute time and money to charitable or advocacy causes.

On the other hand, the Internet has also proved a crucial tool in organizing activist groups. It has also directly equipped protesters with a powerful weapon. Global Exchange, for example, set up a "virtual activist" tool kit online to protest against Gap's labor conditions. The kit included a standard letter to send to the company, as well as anti-Gap flyers; all documents could be easily downloaded from the Internet site (as quoted by Li, 2001). Another example includes the demonstrations that followed Seattle's 1999 World Trade Organizations meeting that were organized by a coalition of environmental and citizens' groups who had been communicating with each other prior to the demonstrations. About 1500 NGOs signed an anti-WTO protest declaration created online by Public Citizen. The Internet allowed organizers to share ideas and tactics instantly and without much expenditure of scarce resources. Without e-mail, such a massive mobilization would have been impossible (Kettl, 2000).

One of the consequences of the revolution in communication technology is that people are overwhelmed with information overload. The only effective response is a comprehensive and focused strategic communication plan, based on coordinating communication management with the work of public relations professionals (Lauer, 1993).

Paid advertising has become the main communication tactic of NGOs. The American Cancer Society has achieved great success by carefully identifying concerns that people really care about, providing services that connect with major public issues, and communicating its activities effectively through advertising (Gallagher & Vaughan, 2002). Kotler and Andreasen (1996) stated that one of the characteristics of organization-centered nonprofit organizations is that they rely excessively on advertising and promotion to achieve their objectives. The authors added that "this is partly because they have a distorted view of what it takes to change people's behavior" (p. 516).

The need for building coalitions in communities and empowering the people that are being helped requires different skills than those taught in traditional public relations curricula. Ehling (1992) stated that "Although the picture of public relations professionalism has brightened over the years and public relations educational programs have grown and strengthened, all is not well" (p. 456). The principles and specifics of communication in nonprofit organizations have undergone significant transformations in recent years becoming more complex. On the one hand, this increase in complexity needs to be followed by a formalized body of knowledge that is the subject of academic study. On the other, there is a growing need for establishing academic programs that can train professionals to work in this field. Such an education should extend beyond any single traditional discipline encompassing a wide variety of skills instead. Current university public relations programs are not adequately responding to the needs of nonprofit communications specialists or to the requirements of international communicators. To effectively prepare these professionals, specific knowledge and perspectives need to be integrated in educational programs.

NGO Executives have higher expectations for professional public relations providers. Managers of NGOs increasingly recognize how essential public relations is to their success. Cutlip, Center, and Broom (1999) believe that public relations practice in a nonprofit organization includes a wide spectrum of approaches. While a single practitioner may be assisting an NGO by implementing a simple publicity campaign, there may be other instances where NGOs could have a large, professional, public relations department with a strategic plan and an adequate budget.

It is essential to take all these trends into consideration when planning a strategic communication campaign, whether national or international. However, the question that remains is what are the elements of international public relations in the communication strategies of NGOs. Does the development of information technology and the globalization of the media guarantee a place for every "good" cause on the planet?

The process of globalization accentuates the need for the development of international public relations principles. Verčič, L. Grunig, and J. E. Grunig (1996) have identified nine normative generic principles that can be used to describe, and practice, global public relations. These authors also proposed five environmental variables that can be used to construct country specific strategies, which include political ideology, the economic system, the level of activism, culture, and media culture. Sriramesh and Verčič (2001) later reduced these five factors to three: a country's infrastructure, the media environment, and societal culture, which are described in Chapter 1 of this volume. It is easy to see how each of these dimensions influences the public relations strategies of the typical NGO. Taking into consideration the diverse global characteristics and specifics of the different publics around the world, the question is, Are there any universally applicable values?

NGOs AND INTERNATIONAL PUBLIC RELATIONS—*EXTRA MUROS ET INTRA!* (WITHIN AND OUTSIDE THE WALLS)

"Optimistic observers imagine a global meritocracy of suffering in which all deserving causes attract international support" (Bob, 2002, p. 37). Allen L. Hammond of the World Resources Institute recently proposed that the combination of global media, new technologies, and altruistic NGOs may soon empower the "underrepresented" of the world (cited in Bob, 2002). But while there are different groups that have felt the benefits of the globalization of NGOs and the public relations that helps promote their causes, there are many questions in this domain that remain unanswered.

In today's society where the media determine what is "just," NGOs have to struggle to gain public attention among many competing interests while also overcoming indifference of this international audience. They also have to compete with various powerful opponents such as governments, multinational companies, and international financial institutions that are supported by highly organized public relations. In that kind of context the transnational NGO community displays a clear hierarchy of influence and reputation. Large and powerful organizations such as the Human Rights Watch, Amnesty International, Greenpeace, and Friends of the Earth have the resources and expertise to investigate the claims of local groups from distant places and give them legitimacy (Bob, 2002).

"The worldwide reach of media organizations such as CNN [the BBC, and Sky Television] may lead one to think that communication strategies are cross-cultural. They are not. A safe rule of thumb is to simply assume that each time the borders are crossed, the rules of the game change" (Boyer, 1997, p. 485). People live in different countries that often are also culturally distinct. One of the themes of this book (described in Chapter 1) is that every country is a complex system of social relations, religious beliefs, languages, attitudes, and habits, all of which will obviously impact on how communications are received and delivered. It is a basic principle in communications theory that, for any communication to be successful, the sender of the message must understand the frame of reference of the receiver of the message (Schramm, 1954). Obviously, the international NGO must understand the cultural dimensions of its relevant publics in order to be successful, because they may differ substantially from the public of its own home culture.

There are various dimensions of culture such as the degree of traditionalism, the degree of secularism, the degree to which cultures rely on explicit and verbal information (low context cultures) versus implicit and nonverbal information (high context cultures), and the degree to which they are oriented towards the individual rather than being interdependent or relational (Batra, Myers, & Aaker, 1999). For example, many researchers have classified North American and Western European cultures as relatively more secular, low context, and oriented toward the individual, in contrast to Asian cultures, while Hispanic cultures fall somewhere in between (Martenson, 1989). As described in Chapter 1, Hofstede (1980) found that the United States, Great Britain, and Canada represented individualistic cultures, while the United States proved to have low tolerance for ambiguity.

Given these differences across cultures on various environmental variables, it seems logical that the publics in different countries may have different ways of deciding whom to trust, different levels of involvement toward the same cause, and so on. Considering the lack of relevant research in the area of international public relations of NGOs, this question remains unanswered. Despite this lack of empirical evidence, the starting point in formulating the main goals of international public relations for non-governmental organizations should not differ significantly from the objectives NGOs identify for their domestic activities. The objectives that Wilcox et al. (2000) defined for nonprofit organizations (p. 389) can be viewed from an international perspective:

1. *Develop public awareness of the organization's purpose and activities.* All of the trends mentioned earlier, mainly the globalization of media and the fast development of information technology make it possible to communicate globally. Delivering the message to an international public becomes easier in light of those trends, even though the problem of cultural and national differences still remains an issue.

NGOs have become sophisticated communicators and instigators of change in the global marketplace. Wootliff and Deri (2002) reported on a study conducted in the United States, Europe, and Australia which showed that in spite of large differences in size and approach among NGOs, these organizations are "no longer perceived as small brands of activists, but rather as the new 'super brands,' surpassing the stature of major corporations, government bodies and even the media among consumers" (p. 159).

In November 1997, *The New York Times* published a confidential Ernst & Young audit of labor and environmental activists it had conducted for one of Nike's factories in Vietnam. The audit, which was leaked to the newspaper, outlined the bad environmental practices of Nike, generating a series of articles and columns in newspapers across the United States and around the world critical of Nike. The NGO Working Assets Citizen Action followed up on the story and generated 33,000 letters to Nike CEO Phil Knight, urging him to pay workers a living wage and to implement a comprehensive third-party monitoring system.

Pressure was brought upon Nike by NGOs such as Global Exchange and Vietnam Labor Watch who also encouraged universities doing business with Nike to push it into changing its behavior. In 1998 Nike announced its pledge to end child labor, to follow United States occupational health and safety standards, and to allow NGOs to participate in the monitoring of its Asian factories (Wootliff and Deri, 2002).

2. *Induce individuals to use the services the nongovernmental organization provides.* After the public becomes aware of the NGO's purpose, the second and closely related step is connecting with the people at whom the service is aimed. The importance of communication in informing potential users of free medical examinations, clothing, food, counseling, scholarships, and other services is essential. The difficulties in transcending communication barriers are significant even without an international dimension. An example includes health and welfare agencies that need to build a communication bridge between ethnic communities. Traditional programs and communication messages fail to reach various needy publics because of cultural and linguistic differences, limited access to information, and low levels of education (Cutlip, Center, & Broom, 1999).

3. *Create educational materials (especially important for health-oriented agencies).* Again the international factor plays a major role in the formulation of the message but the issue of "speaking the same language" is a problem for NGOs domestically as well as internationally. The main challenge is in understanding the publics with whom the NGO is communicating. For example, in the population control campaigns in many developing countries, a major achievement of public relations campaigns has been to demystify contraception and make it acceptable for public discussion of contraception in general, and specific contraceptive methods in particular (Kotler & Andreasen, 1996).

4. *Recruit and train volunteer workers.* A significant proportion of international nonprofit organizations rely on unpaid volunteers for clerical assistance, fundraising, conducting tours and even volunteer recruitment. This can create two types of problems for the manager of the nonprofit organization. First, the need for a steady inflow of volunteers means that a third public is added to those with whom the manager must communicate. On one hand, programs must be designed to attract paid personnel, while on the other, communicators must be careful about the possible consequences of the proposed programs on existing volunteers, none of which is simplified with the international factor. Second, it is not easy to manage volunteers, because their status allows them to get away with a higher level of unreliability (Kotler & Andreasen, 1996).

Cutlip, Center, and Broom (1999) reported that almost 40 million people volunteer each year in the United States. Because volunteers are an important resource in the life and economy of many NGOs, nongovernmental organizations need to constantly work toward attracting more volunteers. To continue attracting volunteers in the numbers necessary to carry out their programs, organizations need to take innovative approaches in communicating with their publics (Baskin and Aronoff, 1988).

5. *Obtain funds to operate the organization.* The main financial resources of NGOs worldwide consist of large donations from private foundations, large individual public contributions, companies, other NGOs and government/governmental agencies. According to an estimate by Hulme and Edwards (1996), some $5.7–10 billion passes through international NGOs annually. The role of high-quality, transparent international communication strategies in obtaining these funds is crucial.

Finally, one should take into consideration the fact that "communication influences, and is influenced by, culture. Logically, then, culture should affect public relations and, because public relations involves communication, public relations does help alter culture" (Sriramesh & Verčič, 2001, p. 106.). It becomes quite obvious that all the elements of non-governmental operations have significant implications on society as a whole. The changing competitive environments that affect the business world similarly affect NGO which must adapt to the changing social and economic environments. In such a surrounding, "effective communication and public relations strategies will be central to their success" (Boyer, 1997, p. 508).

REFERENCES

Abramson, D. M. (1999). A critical look at NGOs and Civil Society as means to an end in Uzbekistan. *Human Organizations*, Fall, *58*(3), 240–250.

Anheier, H., Glasius, M., & Kaldor, M. (2001). Global Civil Society. Oxford: Oxford University Press. Retrieved October 21, 2002 from http://www.undp.org/hdr2002/ and http://globalpolicy.igc.org/ngos/role/ intro/growth2000.htm

Antonides, G., & Van Raaij, W. F. (1998). *Consumer Behavior*. Chicester: Wiley.

Baskin, O. W., & Aronoff, C. E. (1988). *Public relations: The profession and the practice*. Dubuque, IA: Wm. C. Brown.

Batra, R., Myers, J. G., & Aaker, D. A. (1999). *Advertising management*. New Delhi: Prentice Hall of India.

Bellah, R. N., (ed.) (1985). *Habits of the heart: Individualism and commitment in American Life*. New York: Harper and Row.

Bob, C. (2002). Merchants of morality. *Foreign Policy, 129*, 36–45.

Boyer, R. (1997). Public relations and communications for nonprofit organizations. In C. L. Caywood (Ed.), *The handbook of strategic public relations & integrated communications*. (pp. 481–508). Boston: McGraw Hill.

Charnovitz, S. (1997). Two centuries of participation: NGOs and international governence. *Michigan Journal of International Law, 18*(2), 183–286.

Cohen, J. L., & Arato, A. (1992). *Civil society and political theory* Cambridge, MA. MIT Press.

Council of Europe (1986). European Convention on the Recognition of the Legal Personality of International Non-Governmental Organisations. Strasbourg.

Cutlip, S. M., Center, A. H., & Broom, G. M. (1999). *Effective public relations*, 8th ed. New Jersey: Prentice Hall.

Dichter, T. W. (1999). Globalization ands its effects on NGOs: Efflorescence or a blurring of roles and relevance?. *Nonprofit and Voluntary Sector Quarterly, 28*(4), 38–58.

Edwards & Hulme (1992). In P. Uvin, & D. Miller (Eds.) (1994). *Scalling Up: Thinking Through the Issues*. The World Hunger Program. Retrieved October 23, 2002 from http://www.globalpolicy.org/ngos/role/ intro/imp/2000/1204.htm

Ehling, W. P. (1992). Public relations education and professionalism. In J. Grunig (Ed.), *Excellence in public relations and communications management* (pp. 439–466). Hillsdale, NJ: Lawrence Erlbaum Associates.

Frumkin, P., & Kim, M. T. (2001). Strategic positioning and the financing of nonprofit organizations: Is efficiency rewarded in the contributions marketplace? *Public Administration Review, 61*(3), 266–275.

Gallagher, M., & Vaughan, S. R. (2002). Internal controls in nonprofit organizations: The case of the American Cancer Society, Ohio Division, *Nonprofit Management and Leadership, 12*(3), 313–325.

Gemmill, B. & Bamidele-Izu, A. (2002). *The Role of NGOs and civil society in global environmental governance*. In Esty D. C. & Ivanova, M. H. (eds.) Global Environmental Governance: Options and Opportunities. Yale School of Forestry and Environmental Studies. New Haven CT.

Hofstede, G. (1980). *Culture's consequences*. Beverly Hills, CA: Sage.

Hulme, D., & Edwards, M. (1996). (Eds.). *NGOs, states and donors: Too close to comfort?* New York: St. Martin's Press.

Judge, A. (1994). NGOs and civil society: Some realities and distortions the challenge of "necessary-to-Governance organizations" (NGOs). Adaptation of a paper presented to a Seminar on State and Society at the Russian Public Policy Center, Moscow, December 6–8, 1994. Retrieved October 21, 2002 from http://www.globalpolicy.org/ngos/role/intro/def/2000/civso.htm

Judge, A. (1996). Interacting fruitfully with un-civil Society the dilemma for non-civil society organizations. Presentation to a World Bank Workshop on Civil Society in the FSU and East/Central Europe, Washington, DC, October 16, 1996. Published in *Transnational Associations, 49*(3), 1997, 124–132. Retrieved October 21, 2002 from http://www.globalpolicy.org/ngos/role/intro/def/2000/un-civ.htm

Kelly, K. S. (2000). Managing public relations for nonprofits. *Nonprofit Management and Leadership, 11*(1), 87–95.

Kettl, D. F. (2000). The transformation of governance: Globalization, devolution, and the role of government. *Public Administration Review, 60*(6), 488–497.

Knickerbocker, B. (2000). Nongovernmental organizations are fighting and winning social, political battles. Christian Science Monitor Website/Nando Media, February 6, 2000. Retrieved October 23, 2002 from http://www.globalpolicy.org/ngos/00role.htm

Kotler, P., & Andreasen, A. R. (1996). *Strategic Marketing for NonProfit Organizations*, 5th ed. Upper Saddle River, NJ: Prentice Hall.

Kotler, P., & Zaltman, G. (1971, July). Social marketing: An approach to planned social change, *Journal of Marketing, 35*, 3–12.

Lauer, L. D. (1993). Achieving an admired organization: The essential elements of communicating nonprofits. *Nonprofit World, 11*(5), 36.

Lazer, W. (1969). Marketing's changing social relationships. *Journal of Marketing, 33* (January), 3–9.

Lewis, D. (1998). Interview with Michael Edwards on the future of NGOs. Retrieved October 21, 2002 from http://globalpolicy.igc.org/ngos/issues/edwards.htm

Li, G. (2001). An analysis: The impact of non-governmental organizations on the practice of public relations. *Public Relations Quarterly, 46*(4), 11–14.

Martenson, R. (1989). International advertising in cross cultural environments. *Journal of International Consumer Marketing, 2*(1), 7–18.

McConkey, D. D. (1975). *MBO for Nonprofit Organizations*, New York: American Management Association (AMACOM).

Mekki, H. (2000). Foreign Funding of NGOs fuels anger in Jordan. Agence France Presse, September 11, 2000. Retrieved October 23, 2002 from http://www.globalpolicy.org/nogs/role/globdem/funding/2001/0410jord.htm

Naim, M. (2002). Al Qaeda, the NGO. *Foreign Policy*, March/April, 129, 99–100.

Onishi, N. (2002). Nongovernmental organizations show their growing power. Retrieved October 12, 2002 from http://globalpolicy.igc.org/ngos/0322ngos.htm

Paine, H., & Gratzer, B. (2001). Rev. Moon and the United Nations: A challenge for the NGO community. Retrieved October 21, 2002 from http://www.globalpolicy.org/ngos/analysis/1101moon.htm

Parry, R. (1997). Dark side of Rev. Moon: Generation Next The Consortium, September 8.

Paul, J. A. (2000). NGOs and global policy-making. Retrieved October 23, 2002 from http://globalpolicy.igc.org/ngos/analysis/anal00.htm

Pavicic, J. (1997). *Mogucnosti primjene marketinga i poduzetnickih aktivnosti u humanitarnim organizacijama*: Magistarski rad. Zagreb. Ekonomski fakultet Sveucilista u Zagrebu.

Pavicic, J. (2000). *Upravljanje strateskim marketingom neprofitnih organizacija*. Doctoral dissertation. Zagreb: Ekonomski fakultet Sveucilista u Zagrebu.

Pentikainen, A. (2000). *Creating global governance—The role of non-governmental organizations in the United Nations*. Helsinki: Finnish UN Association.

Pharoah, C. (2002). Who pays the piper? Bond, September 2002. Retrieved October 23, 2002 from http://www.globalpolicy.org/ngos/role/globdem/funding/2002/0902piper.htm

Putnam, R. D. (1993). *Making democracy work*. Princeton, NJ: Princeton University Press.

Reis, G. R. (2000). Fund raising on the Web: Why having a dot—org Website isn't enough. *Fund Raising Management, 30*(11), 22–24.

Rice, A. E., & Ritchie, C. (1995). Relationships between international non-governmental organizations and the United Nations, *Transnational Associations 47*(5), 254–265. Retrieved October 23, 2002 from http://www.uia.org/uiadocs/unngos.htm

Samuelson, P. A. (1970). *Readings in Economics*. New York: McGraw-Hill.

Sanborn, S. (2000). Nonprofits reap the rewards of the Web. *InfoWorld, 22*(25), 37.

Schramm, W. (1954). *The process and effects of mass communication*. Urbana: University of Illinois Press.

Shikwati, J. (2002). Do Not Need White NGOs to Speak for Me Times, September 3.

Simmons, P. J. (1998). Learning to Live with NGOs. Foreign Policy. Fall. Retrieved October 21, 2002 from http://globalpolicy.igc.otg/ngos/issues/simmons.htm

Smith, S. R., & Lipsky, M. (1993). *Nonprofits for hire: The welfare state in the age of contracting*. Cambridge, MA: Harvard University Press.

Sriramesh, K., & Verčič, D. (2001). International public relations: A framework for future research. *Journal of Communication Management, 6*(2), 103–117.

Tate, C. F. (2002). Enron proof oversight. *Association Management, 54*(8), 85–96.

Toulmin, S. (1994). The Role of transnational NGOs in global affairs. Retrieved October 21, 2002 from http://globalpolicy.igc.org/ngos/role/globalact/state/2000/1122.htm

Tse, D. K., Belk, R. W., & Zhou, N. (1989). Becoming a consumer society: A longitudinal and cross cultural content analysis of print ads from Hong Kong, the People's Republic of China and Taiwan. *Journal of Consumer Research, 15*, 457–472.

United Nations (1946). Economic and Social Council Resolution 3 (II) on the 21st of June. Retrieved October 21, 2002 from http://www.un.org/esa/coordination/ngo/committee.htm

Vaknin, S. (2002). The Self-appointed altruists. Business and Economics Desk in United Press International, September 10, 2002. Retrieved October 23, 2002 from http://www.globalpolicy.org.ngos/credib/2002/1009altruist.htm

Verčič, D., Grunig, L. A., & Grunig, J. E. (1996). Global and specific principles of public relations: Evidence from Slovenia. In H. M. Culbertson & N. Chen (Eds.), *International public relations: A comparative analysis*. (pp. 31–65). Mahwah, NJ: Lawrence Erlbaum Associates.

Vichit-Vadakan, J. (2001). Central role in development for Thai NGOs? Retrieved October 23, 2002 from http://www.globalpolicy.org/ngos/intro/general/2002/12thai.htm

Wilcox, D. L., Ault, P. H., Agee, W. K., & Cameron, G. T. (2000). *Public relations: Strategies and tactics*, 6th ed. New York: Longman.

Willetts, P. (2002). What is a non-governmental organization? Article 1.44.3.7. Non-Governmental Organizations. In *UNESCO Encyclopedia of Life Support Systems*. Retrieved October 21, 2002 from http://www.staff.city.ac.uk/p.willetts/CS NTWKS/NGO-ART.htm

Wootliff, J., & Deri, C. (2001). NGO's: The new super brands. *Corporate Reputation Review, 4*(2), 157–164.

Young, D. R. (2002). Organizational identity and the structure of nonprofit umbrella associations. *Nonprofit Management and Leadership, 11*(3), 289–304.

39

PUBLIC RELATIONS, PUBLIC DIPLOMACY,
AND STRATEGIC COMMUNICATION:
AN INTERNATIONAL MODEL OF
CONCEPTUAL CONVERGENCE

MARK A. VAN DYKE

DEJAN VERČIČ

INTRODUCTION

For decades, scholars and practitioners have debated the issue of separation or convergence between public relations and public diplomacy. In the global war against terrorism, these functions have become integral to efforts by nations and international alliances to achieve domestic and foreign policy goals. Recent integration of public relations with public diplomacy and even psychological operations in global, political-military approaches to strategic communication suggest a practical convergence that is moving beyond a theoretical explanation. Without a theoretical framework to guide these programs, the boundaries among communication functions could erode and threaten the integrity of public relations and public diplomacy. This chapter uses a review of historical trends and literature to posit conceptual convergence, promote discussion and research, and propose an international convergence model.

Post-Cold War conflicts—including the war against terrorism—have been punctuated by activists, insurgents, and terrorists who use asymmetrical means to attack alliances, coalitions, or nations that possess much more formidable economic, political, and military power (Nemeth, 2000). To manage these threats and promote support at home and abroad, nations and international alliances are integrating public relations and public diplomacy in global, political-military approaches to *strategic communication*. These strategic communication programs rely on *soft power* (e.g., popular media, cultural programs) to attract others to cooperate and on *hard power* (e.g., political, economic, and military sanctions or force) to persuade or compel others to adopt goals. Public relations and public diplomacy often operate together with other communication functions like psychological operations to support soft and hard power applications. The integration of these disparate communication functions in strategic communication programs and subordinate activities like military *information operations* has led many to question the effect of this convergence on the credibility and efficacy of public relations and public diplomacy.

The dominant perspective views public relations as strategic management of communication and relationships between organizations and publics (e.g., Cutlip, Center, and Broom, 2005; J. Grunig and Hunt, 1984; Sriramesh and Verčič, 2001, 2003a). Public diplomacy is often regarded as a complementary but separate concept characterized by international or intercultural communication between nations and foreign publics (Adelman, 1981; Belay, 1997). However, some scholars and practitioners have drawn parallels between public relations and public diplomacy and even cited convergence between the two concepts (Kunczik, 2003; Signitzer and Coombs, 1992; Signitzer and Wamser, 2006).

Integration of public relations, public diplomacy, and other communication functions in strategic communication, information operations, and other political-military communication programs serves as a catalyst for further study of the public relations–public diplomacy relationship. For instance, the role of public relations in information operations has become the focus of controversy and debate among government and political leaders, public relations professionals, diplomats, and journalists. To some, information operations "can make an important contribution to defusing crises" (U.S. Joint Staff, 1998, p. I-4). To others, information operations as a military strategy conjure images of communication as a weapon (Beelman, 2001; van Dyke, 1997), which raises important ethical questions about the role of public relations in such operations. These perspectives derive from national policies; however, we see these policies as having global implications, since their application extends to public relations and public diplomacy activities that are used to manage *international* conflict.

The integration of public relations and public diplomacy in integrated communication programs that are designed to project hard and soft power raises exigent questions about convergence and credibility that must be addressed in practice and in theory. Unfortunately, public relations scholars have been slow to study this convergence among communication concepts or apply theory in a way that might produce answers to practical problems associated with this trend. Meanwhile, scholars and practitioners in public diplomacy, psychological operations, and other political-military communication disciplines have moved quickly to set and implement policies that determine the role of public relations in integrated communication activities (Robinson, 2006).

Only recently have public relations scholars and practitioners started to complement political-military approaches toward public relations with their interest in strategic communication (Hallahan, Holtzhausen, van Ruler, Verčič, and Sriramesh, 2007). Furthermore, President of the International Public Relations Association Robert W. Grupp has envisioned his organization's mission as promotion of corporate diplomacy, which he defined as complementary to public diplomacy:

> Corporate diplomacy means at least two things. It means a company embeds the value of collaboration deeply into its operations and practices; and it means the company extends the reach of its relationships to include groups, cultures, organizations, even governments, which don't necessarily involve the company or client directly but which ultimately affect the sustainability of the business. (Grupp, 2008, p. 7)

This chapter will review historical trends and review literature from theory and practice to explicate public relations and public diplomacy. This review will document empirical evidence that supports the notion of conceptual convergence between public relations and diplomacy in theory and in practice. Discussion will explore the opportunities, limits, and risks of integrating these concepts in political-military programs like information operations and strategic communication. Finally, we provide a convergence model that explains how public relations and public diplomacy operate together, in theory and in practice, on an international level. We conclude with a call for research to produce contemporary case studies, enlighten scholarship, and narrow the gap between theory and professional practice in public relations and public diplomacy.

In this chapter, we cite literature and examples primarily from the United States and the United Kingdom because our experience is rooted in the study and practice of public relations and public diplomacy in these countries. Furthermore, the products of scholarly study and practice in these countries are more accessible and better documented than in most other countries. However, we know that the subject we cover operates globally. Thus, we look forward to others expanding on our seemingly restricted literature review by adding valuable cases from around the globe to future publications.

LITERATURE REVIEW

Studies of public diplomacy have in recent decades occupied an area of special interest in public relations research. However, the association of public relations and public diplomacy with new, international approaches to strategic communication has attracted scant attention from public relations scholars. This review will explicate relevant concepts in theory and in practice and support subsequent discussion of convergence.

Public Relations and Public Diplomacy

Public relations

Public relations is generally defined as strategic management of communication and relationships between organizations and their publics, or in the public sphere (e.g., Cutlip et al., 2005; J. Grunig and Hunt, 1984; van Ruler and Verčič, 2002, 2005; van Ruler, Verčič, Bütschi, and Flodin, 2004; Seitel, 2007). A global theory of public relations has advanced this view by incorporating political as well as cultural and societal variables (van Ruler and Verčič, 2002; van Ruler et al., 2004; Sriramesh and Verčič, 2001, 2003a, 2003b).

National governments and political-military alliances often refer to the public relations function as *public information* or *public affairs*. This nomenclature grew from the historical model of public information associated with legislation and regulations that restrict public relations activities within the government agencies of some nations (J. Grunig and Hunt, 1984). Figure 39.1, reproduced exactly as it appeared in U.S. Joint Staff (2005), depicts the model of public affairs that operates in support of U.S. joint military operations.

Public diplomacy

The field of *international relations* focuses on relationships among national governments (Signitzer and Wamser, 1996). Within this field, *diplomacy* is conceptualized as the management or negotiation of relationships among these governments through international or intercultural communication (Adelman, 1981; Belay, 1997). Globalization of national economies, evolution of new media channels, and expansion of social networks allow more

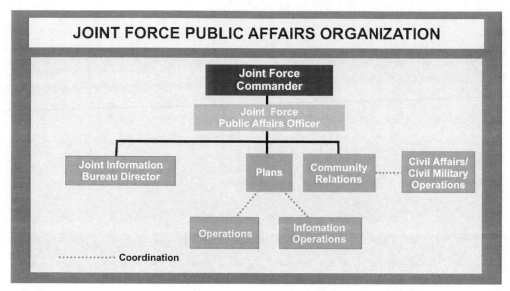

FIG. 39.1   U.S. Joint Force Public Affairs Organization (U.S. Joint Staff, 2005, p. III-3).

actors to participate in international relations. These trends have also given rise to new forms of diplomacy: *public diplomacy, cultural diplomacy, and media diplomacy* (Signitzer and Wamser, 2006).

Public diplomacy consists of direct communication among governments and foreign publics; cultural diplomacy relies on favorable attitudes toward a nation's culture to facilitate diplomatic relations; and media diplomacy utilizes news media channels to conduct open diplomacy (Adelman, 1981; Belay, 1997; Hiebert, 2004; Melissen, 2005; Signitzer and Wamser, 1996). In contrast to diplomacy, which is characterized by discrete, formal, and official communication, public diplomacy and its cultural and media counterparts are open, informal, and mobile (Steinbock, 2003). Public and media diplomacy extend international communication beyond the realm of professional diplomats and other government officials to anyone with access to the Internet or global news media.

To facilitate cultural diplomacy, many countries operate networks of cultural centers around the globe: Chinese Confucius Institutes, French Cultural Centers, German Goethe Institutes, etc. To assure presence abroad, nations also communicate directly or indirectly through broadcast channels and Web-based programs that cross international borders. The British Broadcasting Corporation's World Service seems to be the gold standard, but there are many other examples. The European Commission of the European Union stands behind the EuroNews; the Emir of Qatar enables Al Jazeera's Arabic news network, at least financially; and the Cable News Network could not have succeeded had U.S. administrations not seen the value of the "CNN effect" in promoting foreign policy goals.

Figure 39.2, depicts public diplomacy as seen in actual practice by the UK's Britain Abroad office. Public diplomacy activities are represented by short-term, urgent, but manifest activities (e.g., crisis management, news management) to long-term but latent activities (e.g., student exchange programs).

Recent studies have also addressed post-Cold War international communication concepts like *preventive diplomacy* and *coercive diplomacy*. The former concept uses diplomacy to prevent disputes or escalation of existing conflict (Rubin, 2002). Coercive diplomacy

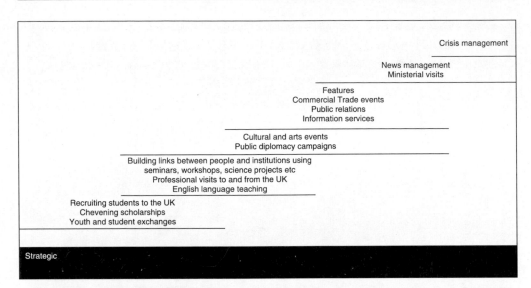

Crisis management

News management
Ministerial visits

Features
Commercial Trade events
Public relations
Information services

Cultural and arts events
Public diplomacy campaigns

Building links between people and institutions using
seminars, workshops, science projects etc
Professional visits to and from the UK
English language teaching

Recruiting students to the UK
Chevening scholarships
Youth and student exchanges

Strategic

FIG. 39.2   Public Diplomacy Spectrum (Reproduced with Permission of the Author, Jonathan Griffin,
Formerly Director of Britain Abroad Task Force)

uses direct measures like threatening an adversary with political, military, or economic
force to prevent conflict or achieve diplomatic goals (Jentleson, 2000; de Wijk, 2003).

Convergence of Public Relations and Public Diplomacy

Signitzer and Coombs (1992) were among the first scholars to explore conceptual relationships between public relations and public diplomacy. Drawing a distinction between
the two fields, they observed, "While public relations theory may be well suited to explain
and to predict the communication behaviors of 'ordinary' organizations . . . diplomacy
theories, for now, are better suited to the understanding of relationships between a nation-
state and its foreign publics" (p. 138).

Questioning the notion that public relations and public diplomacy are separate
functions, Signitzer and Coombs (1992) concluded after an extensive review of research
conducted by U.S. and European scholars that "a relationship between the two areas
does exist" (p. 145). Furthermore, "Public relations and public diplomacy are in a natural
process of convergence" (p. 146). Signitzer and Wamser (2006) explored further this
convergence process and identified similarities between the two functions. They observed
that public relations and public diplomacy are both strategic communication processes that
manage communication, relationships, and consequences among organizations and their
publics; and that both perform research, advocacy, dialog, and counseling. Citing economic and political trends, the authors also concluded that large organizations and multinational alliances are beginning to act like nations, which is causing public relations and
public diplomacy to become "more and more intertwined in our times" (p. 444).

However, audiences differ for public relations and public diplomacy. Notionally, public
relations managers focus on communication among corporate leaders and organizational
publics, while public diplomacy managers focus on communication among national leaders
and foreign publics (Signitzer and Wamser, 2006). For example, the U.S. Department of
State assigns its public affairs managers responsibility to "inform the American people and
to feed their concerns and comments back to the policymakers" (U.S. Department of State,

2008a, p. 2). Its public diplomacy managers communicate with "people throughout the world . . . isolate and marginalize violent extremists . . . [and] foster a sense of common interests and common values between Americans and people of different countries, cultures and faiths throughout the world" (U.S. Department of State, 2008b, p. 2).

In other studies, Peterson (2002) suggested that diplomacy now relies on "a sustained, coordinated capability to understand, inform, and influence people and private organizations, as well as governments" (p. 15); and Melissen (2005) noted that the "modus operandi of the new public diplomacy is not entirely different from the public relations approach" (p. 21). He added that Wilson's (1996) "conclusion on the creation of strategic cooperative communities also applies to public diplomacy" (p. 21). Kunczik (2003), citing the growing importance of strategic publics and international news media organizations in public diplomacy, wrote, "Public relations for states is closely connected to the mediation of foreign policy" (p. 408). Furthermore, Alastair Campbell assigned Britain Abroad responsibility for "rebranding" Britain around the world under the Blair government, which replicated business concepts of branding and re-branding in the international relations of a country (United Kingdom).

Yun (2006) examined conceptual convergence of post-Cold War public relations and diplomacy and found that principles of the excellence theory in public relations also applied to excellence in public diplomacy. Zöllner (2006) also pointed out a convergence of public relations and German public diplomacy after the September 11, 2001 terrorist attacks on the United States. Collins (2003) examined ways that public relations and public diplomacy have converged with other communication functions like psychological operations in NATO's international, political-military alliance. Several other scholars examined how convergence of public relations and public diplomacy influences mediation of messages and perceptions about national policies and values, responses to natural disasters, and conflicts like terrorism (Dutta-Bergman, 2005, 2006; J. Wang, 2007; Zhang, 2006, 2007).

Finally, global games like the 2008 Olympics in China have become a focus of research on public relations, public diplomacy, and soft and hard power. Black and van der Westhuizen (2004) contended that hosting such events is motivated by a desire to promote national identity, fulfill political goals, and expand global markets. Others have linked China's backing of the Olympics and other global events games with the country's increased use of soft and hard power—through public relations and cultural and media diplomacy—to promote national identity and consumer products. According to Y. Wang (2008), "China plans to use both the Olympic Games in 2008 and the Shanghai World Expo in 2010 as opportunities to carry out public diplomacy and promote the China Brand" (Chinese Public Diplomacy Practice, p. 7). This program of research provides opportunities to examine how global games become much more than sporting events. They also are a medium for cultural diplomacy. Just as scholars continue to study the "ping-pong diplomacy" between China and the United States in the 1970s (Wasserstrom, 2000/2001), contemporary scholars will examine the incongruous nature of the 2008 Olympic games as a medium for diplomacy. On one hand, China attempted to use the games to warm its relations with other nations; on the other hand, activists used the same games to discredit China's political policies.

Soft Power and Hard Power

During the 1980s, scholar and diplomat Joseph Nye authored the concept of *soft power* in the field of international relations (Ikenberry, 2004). According to Nye (2004a), "Power is the ability to influence the behavior of others to get the outcomes one wants" (p. 2). Elaborating on this concept, Nye (2003) explained:

> Soft power is the ability to get what you want by attracting and persuading others to adopt your goals. It differs from hard power, the ability to use the carrots and sticks of economic and military might to make others follow your will. (p. 2)

Nye (2004a) traced the foundation of soft power to a nation's "culture (in places where it is attractive to others), its political values (when it lives up to them at home and abroad), and its foreign policies (when they are seen as legitimate and having moral authority)" (p. 11). He also observed that a nation's loss of respect and credibility in the international arena could lead to erosion of this foundation, which weakens the efficacy of soft power and makes use of hard power more likely. Increased use of hard power, often perceived as less ethical than soft power, could lead to further loss of national credibility and increased instability (Nye, 2002, 2003, 2004b, 2004c).

Literature about soft and hard power also suggests that the two concepts are linked and must operate in concert with one another. Van Ham (2005) argued that soft power provides hard power with a "cloak of legitimacy (morally or under international law)" (p. 52), which can help overcome resistance and reduce costs. Conversely, "soft power requires the necessary resources and commitment to put words into actions" (p. 52).

Nye's conceptualization of soft power fits nicely into the Sriramesh–Verčič conceptual framework for analyzing public relations in different countries (see this Handbook, Chapter 1). The concepts of political values, moral authority, culture, and communication resources that underpin soft power correspond with variables related to a country's infrastructure (political system, economic system, level of development, and level of activism), culture, and media environment. The latter framework could be operationalized and made directly relevant for analysis of soft power capacity in a discrete country.

Review of the relevant literature suggests that organizational power (e.g., Mintzberg, 1983), public relations, and public diplomacy share conceptual similarities, at least in terms of their reliance on ethical communication, credibility, and variables like social culture, political systems, and media systems. Nye (2004b) defined soft power in such a way as to make it directly relevant to business communication, therefore aligning international relations with organizational behavior.

Strategic Communication and Information Operations

Strategic Communication

For decades, Western nations have considered strategic communication as a vital element of national power—operating alongside political, economic, and military power. Van Dyke (2001) reported, "The U.S. national security policy even describes information as an element of national power and advocates its use as a means to shape public perception and promote U.S. democratic ideals around the world" (p. 13). This perspective suggests a *perception management* approach to strategic communication adopted by organizations around the world (Collins, 2003; Elsbach, 2006) and by other nations like the United Kingdom (Beelman, 2001). Such "shaping" activities are designed to influence members of foreign publics to adopt attitudes or opinions that are favorable toward the policies or products of an organization or nation. Furthermore, alliances like NATO have incorporated integrated approaches to communication that synchronize these elements of power (Combelles-Siegel, 1998).

The September 11, 2001 terrorist attacks against targets on U.S. soil prompted further study of strategic communication as a practical concept. In a U.S. defense science board task force report, Vitto (2004) underscored the importance of communication as a component of national strategy but warned, "[Strategic communication] is in crisis, and it must be transformed with a strength of purpose that matches our commitment to diplomacy, defense, intelligence, law enforcement, and homeland security" (p. 2). Calling for a more coherent approach to strategic communication, Vitto added, "Public diplomacy, public affairs, psychological operations (PSYOP) and open military information operations must be coordinated and energized" (p. 3).

Subsequently, the U.S. government defined strategic communication as a *focused* or integrated communication management process designed to influence key constituencies. This process consists of four phases (see Figure 39.3), which are comparable to the behaviors in strategic public relations management (Cutlip et al., 2005; Guth and Marsh, 2005; J. Grunig and Repper, 1992). According to the U.S. military's Joint Staff (2007):

> Strategic communication is the focused United States government processes and efforts to understand and engage key audiences to create, strengthen, or preserve conditions favorable to advance national interests and objectives through the use of coordinated information, themes, plans, programs, and actions synchronized with other instruments of national power. (p. xii)

A paucity of scholarly research in this area, especially within the public relations body of knowledge, makes it difficult to locate in theory this international concept of strategic communication. Military scholars are, however, addressing strategic communication from the perspectives of public diplomacy and battlefield management. According to Eder (2007):

> The principal benefit of strategic communication derives essentially from the principle of war called mass. Strategic communication means massing information among all agents of public information at a critical time and place to accomplish a specific objective . . . . Dribbling out mixed, unsynchronized information instead of massing the release of unequivocal messages backed by a substantial body of facts is especially destructive during times of crisis. (p. 62)

Descriptions of strategic communication as a coordinated and synchronized process (Eder, 2007; Vitto, 2004) suggest a scholarly conceptualization of communication described by the excellence theory in public relations (Dozier, 1995; J. Grunig, 1992; L. Grunig,

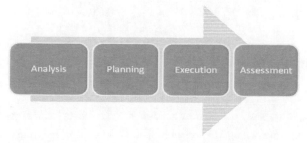

FIG. 39.3   Strategic Communication Process (Adapted from Thorp, 2007).

J. Grunig, and Dozier, 2002). Contemporary definition of strategic communication in the light of public relations theories has been offered by Hallahan, Holtzhausen, van Ruler, Verčič, and Sriramesh (2007, p. 17): "Strategic communication is about informational, persuasive, discursive, as well as relational communication when used in a context of the achievement of an organization's mission." (Cf. also van Ruler and Verčič 2005.)

Information Operations

Information operations (IO) has been defined as integration of "electronic warfare, computer network operations, psychological operations, military deception, and operations security, in concert with specified supporting and related capabilities, to influence, disrupt, corrupt or usurp adversarial human and automated decision making while protecting our own" (U.S. Joint Staff, 2006, p. GL-9). Public affairs (e.g., public information or public relations) and public diplomacy are considered to be among IO's related capabilities (Metz, 2006; U.S. Joint Staff, 2006).

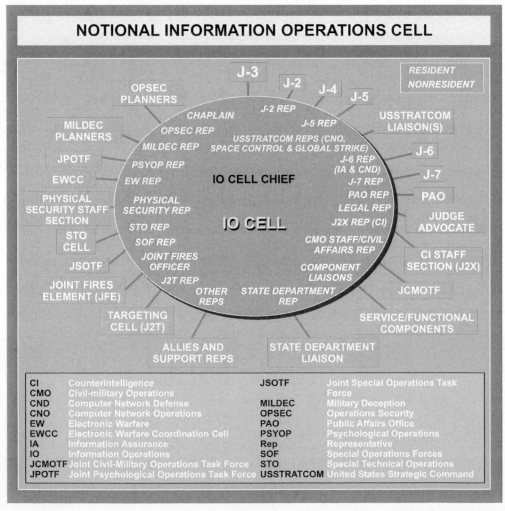

FIG. 39.4   Configuration of a Notional Information Operations Cell, Adapted From U.S. Joint Publication 3–13 [Information Operations] (U.S. Joint Staff, 2006, p. IV-5).

Combelles-Siegel (1998) observed how NATO supported peace operations in Bosnia-Herzegovina with an integrated information campaign that "coordinated and synchronized use of different information activities" (p. 2) like public relations, public diplomacy, and psychological operations. Figure 39.4, above, depicts the configuration of a notional (e.g., typical) information operations cell. The public relations element, labeled as "PAO," is depicted approximately half-way down the right edge of the oval. The public diplomacy representative, or "State Department Liaison," appears near the bottom-right edge of the oval. The psychological operations element, listed as "PsyOp" or "JPO TF," appears opposite public affairs on the left edge of the oval.

The concept of information operations is sometimes associated with *perception management*. Collins (2003) defined perception management as "actions used to influence the attitudes and objective reasoning of foreign audiences and consists of Public Diplomacy, Psychological Operations (PSYOPS), Public Information, Deception and Covert Action" (p. 13).

Contemporary literature has addressed ethical concerns that arise from integration of public relations and public diplomacy with information activities like psychological or deception operations that could be used to confuse, deceive, or even coerce audiences. Van Dyke (2005) studied NATO's public relations management in Bosnia-Herzegovina and proposed an ethical communication model that could be used to guide integrated information activities—even those that engage in coercion. Some nations and international, political-military alliances have enacted policies that keep the public relations (or public information and public affairs) and information operations functions separate but coordinated (Myers, 2004; F. Veltri, personal communication, January 2, 2008). These policies are designed to preserve the "institutional credibility [required] to maintain public trust and confidence" (Myers, 2004, ¶ 1).

DISCUSSION

Analysis of historical antecedents to public relations and public diplomacy indicates, as Signitzer and Coombs (1992) and Signitzer and Wamser (2006) suggested, that these two concepts are in convergence—in practice if not in theory. This discussion will trace these antecedents through the post-Cold War period, demonstrate how war and peace have influenced convergence of public relations and public diplomacy, and identify risks and opportunities associated with this convergence.

Communication in War and in Peace

Revolutions

According to J. Grunig and Hunt (1984), the 18th century American Revolution in the United States was "one of the most important products of public relations-like activities in history" (p. 17). Cutlip et al. (2000) added that "today's patterns of public relations practice were shaped by innovations in mobilizing public opinion" (p. 103) that formed part of Revolutionary War propaganda campaigns. According to Isaacson (2003), Benjamin Franklin performed dual roles as a diplomat (ambassador to France) and journalist-public relations practitioner (writer, printer, and newspaper publisher) in support of the revolution. Thus, Franklin and the American Revolution serve as early examples of how persuasive power can be generated by integrating public relations and diplomacy.

The Industrial Revolution and Information Revolution also promoted convergence between public relations and public diplomacy. The Industrial Revolution increased the need for communication experts and contributed to the growth of professionalism in public relations (Cutlip et al., 2000; J. Grunig and Hunt, 1984). Among these experts was public relations pioneer Edward L. Bernays, who sought to achieve public relations goals through the spread of cultural ideas about art, science, and social programs that would appeal to the mutual interests of organizations and their publics (Brummett, 2000).

Subsequently, the Information Revolution changed the way members of society interacted with each other through the Internet and global social networks. Pratkanis and Aronson (1992) reported, "Western societies experienced a change in the nature of social relationships—from small, cohesive communities emphasizing personal relationships to a web of impersonal, secondary relationships" (pp. 23–24). So, the Industrial and Information Revolutions demonstrated how concepts of public relations and public diplomacy (e.g., cultural diplomacy) were becoming further intertwined.

World Wars I and II

Integration of propaganda and persuasive approaches to public relations continued to gain prominence during and after World Wars I and II. Governments organized groups of journalists and created offices like the U.S. Committee on Public Information in World War I to mobilize domestic and allied support (Cutlip et al., 2000; J. Grunig and Hunt, 1984). Kunczik (2003) explained how combatant nations like Germany, Britain, and the United States used publicity and propaganda to attack the credibility of enemies, cultivate international images, and validate their war efforts. This period also led to further integration of public relations and public diplomacy: "After World War I the character of diplomacy slowly changed. The mediation of foreign policy intensified and today nearly every act in the (open) conduct of foreign policy takes public relations (the effect on the respective image), [sic] into account" (Kunczik, p. 405).

World War II-era public relations and public diplomacy efforts were influenced by public criticism of government control and censorship of information during World War I. This criticism brought into question the integration of propaganda, public relations, and public diplomacy typified by the Creel committee. Crossen (2003) reported: "Controlling information was a touchy subject in the early 1940s. The very word censorship reeked of totalitarianism" (¶ 3). Hence, governments moved to establish offices like the U.S. War Information and the Advertising Council and encouraged journalists to follow a voluntary code of war-time reporting practices (Crossen, 2003). These types of policies represented early government efforts to pursue media diplomacy, to distinguish between propaganda and public relations, and to be seen as responding to rather than manipulating domestic public opinion (Parry-Giles, 2005).

Cold War

After World War II, the threat of nuclear war created an urgent need for careful public communication and diplomacy among nuclear-armed nations. As the Cold War intensified, government leaders increased efforts to integrate public relations and diplomacy while distancing these activities from clandestine propaganda efforts. The demand to manage such conflict encouraged leaders to create specialized information agencies and adopt *strategic communication management* policies that promoted dialog through coordinated communication activities like public relations, public diplomacy, negotiation, persuasion, and coercion.

Cold War-era public relations scholars and political scientists also began to study and apply communication along a continuum of conflict and cooperation—or war and peace. Communication scholars began to study public relations as a strategic management function that could be applied to conflict resolution (Ehling, 1984, 1985, 1992). Development of the excellence theory in public relations also explained how public relations should be kept separate from but integrated with other communication functions (Dozier, 1995; J. Grunig, 1992; L. Grunig et al., 2002). Integration enables coordination but should not subjugate public relations. Information operations should be understood as bringing public relations and psychological or deception operations under the same command—not commanding one or the other. This may be thought of as analogous to the public relations–marketing relationship in a corporate environment. Each function can support the other through integration, but for a corporation to gain the best outcome it must keep separate its public relations and marketing efforts—just as public relations and psychological operations functions must be coordinated and distinct.

Meanwhile, political scientists developed concepts like *preventive* and *coercive diplomacy* that could be used to deter nuclear war (Jentleson, 2000; de Wijk, 2003); and Nye (2002, 2003, 2004a, 2004b) introduced the concept of *soft power* as a cooperative rather than coercive approach to diplomacy.

War on Terror

Public relations and public diplomacy converged further and entered into a controversial reunion with propaganda as information became a weapon in the war against terrorism. According to a U.S. defense science board strategic communication task force report (Vitto, 2004):

> The events of September 11, 2001 were a catalyst in creating a new way to think about national security. The Global War on Terrorism replaced the Cold War as a national security meta narrative. Governments, media, and publics use the terrorism frame for cognitive, evaluative, and communication purposes. (p. 17)

As the Cold War waned, bi-polar conflict between two world super powers ebbed into smaller but more numerous, multi-polar conflicts among many nations and non-state actors. Ironically, the end of the Cold War lulled many political-military leaders into a temporary sense of security, which led former Cold War adversaries to begin a demobilization of many defense and diplomatic capabilities.

The move to demobilize reduced the value of large military forces, diplomatic programs, and soft power (Blinken, 2003; Krauthammer, 2000; Nye, 2002, 2003, 2004b, 2004c). Nye (2004) argued, however, that "soft power was becoming more important, not less" (Nye, 2004, ¶ 8) as new communication technologies like the Internet enabled activist groups and individuals to convert information into power and challenge much larger organizations and states (Armistead, 2004; van Dyke, 2005; J. Grunig and L. Grunig, 1997). Peterson (2002) indicated that individuals now possess "more soft power to influence global affairs directly, indirectly, and through their governments" (p. 15).

Strategies of conflict also became more asymmetrical as non-state actors, radical groups, and terrorist networks began to challenge nations with great military and economic might. As Nemeth (2000) explained, "Without a tactical or strategic edge, adversaries [since Vietnam] have sought means other than equal military strength in order to deny an opponent strength or support" (p. 14). Terrorist groups began to perfect the use of information power to spread fear and intimidation among large populations while nations and alliances used the same power to counteract and even pre-empt terrorist tactics.

The information revolution and war on terror moved public relations practitioners and diplomats to the front lines of conflict. The nature of the post-Cold War era's limited political-military engagements and operations other than war (OOTW)—including *peace* operations—increased the value of public relations, public diplomacy, and other non-lethal soft power elements (Clark, 2000). For example, Phillpot (1996) described a typical NATO military staff meeting that he witnessed in Bosnia-Herzegovina during NATO's first full year of peace implementation operations there:

> Immediately behind [the military commander] Nash, are two rows of staff officers. In war-time, the first row would be operational staff providing instant updates on fire support, air support, armor movements, intelligence, and logistics . . . . Sitting behind Nash instead is a staff more familiar to a big-city mayor: a political advisor, an expert on civilian relations, representatives of two joint commissions, a public affairs specialist, and a staff lawyer. (p. 60)

As planning for the war against terrorism matured, government public affairs specialists and diplomats began working closely with military psychological operations (PsyOps) specialists, who are sometimes perceived as the contemporary equivalent of World War I and World War II era propagandists. Reversing 20th century efforts to separate propaganda from public relations and diplomacy, Western nations and alliances began to integrate these and other communication functions within programs like *information operations*, *perception management*, and *strategic communication*. Some attributed this trend to efforts by nations to control information (Sharkey, 1991); others saw it as a necessary means to consolidate information efforts and coordinate messages (Vitto, 2004).

Integrated Information Activities and Strategic Communication

As in the wake of World War I, government attempts to control messages and media channels in late-Cold War and post-Cold War conflicts resulted in public backlash. Adopting the British model of battlefield information control in the Falklands conflict (1982), the United States attempted to control media access to combat operations in Grenada (1983), Panama (1989), and the Persian Gulf (1990–1991). The United Nations also adopted the British approach to managing news media during its operations in the former Yugoslavia (1991–1995), which drew accusations that military spokespersons "routinely lied to reporters and did so with vigor and the conviction that the importance of an accurate and independent press was subordinate to military strategy and success" (Beelman, 2001, p. 17). News media organizations, frustrated with restrictions imposed by political and military authorities, mounted increasingly stiff opposition to information control.

Mindful of strained relations with news media, the NATO alliance revised its approach to public information, psychological operations, and diplomacy in military operations. These plans were still under revision in late 1995 when NATO launched its peace operations in Bosnia-Herzegovina. NATO quickly approved an integrated information campaign designed to impart timely and accurate information to strategic audiences based on free and open reporting of its operations in the former Yugoslavia.

The NATO model became a predecessor to contemporary information operations and strategic communication programs that integrate and coordinate information activities. The United States published one of the world's first information operations manuals in 1996 (see Beelman, 2001; U.S. Department of the Army, 2003). In 1999, the concept of information operations began to encompass non-military government agencies when U.S. President Bill Clinton established an *international public information* (IPI) program to manage and synchronize messages originating from all U.S. government agencies (Adair and Blanton, 2006). Following the September 11, 2001 terrorist attacks, the United States began development of a broader communication strategy that would evolve into strategic communication (e.g., U.S. Department of State, 2007) and provide a "different and more comprehensive approach to public information efforts" (Bush, 2002, p. 31).

Beyond U.S. borders, other national governments and multinational alliances developed and applied integrated information programs as a primary source of power. These programs were often perceived as types of soft power, since public communication activities can negate the need for harder forms of economic or military power in early stages of conflict and in post-conflict assistance efforts (U.S. Institute of Peace, 1999).

Public Relations and Public Diplomacy: An International Convergence Model

Integrated communication programs like the political-military approach to strategic communication have created a new model of convergence in international relations and organizational behavior. This model explains how public relations and public diplomacy, once considered separate concepts, are now converging within areas described by political-military, strategic communication at an international level.

First, globalization and new forms of media channels have enabled many large organizations to wield types of economic and political influence once reserved for individual nations (Signitzer and Wamser, 2006). Therefore, international relations and organizational activities on a global scale often overlap. Second, scholars and practitioners have demonstrated similarities between public relations and public diplomacy that suggest convergence in practice and in theory. Third, strategic communication's coordinated approach to communication management synchronizes various forms of international and domestic information activities with other elements of national power.

Hence, strategic communication has become the point of convergence for organizational behavior and international relations—and their subordinate functions of public relations and public diplomacy, respectively. Figure 39.5a (below) depicts the general area of convergence among international relations, organizational behavior, public diplomacy, and public relations. Figure 39.5b (below) depicts the specific point within this area where public diplomacy and public relations converge during the coordination of communication plans, processes, themes, messages, and other elements of communication behavior.

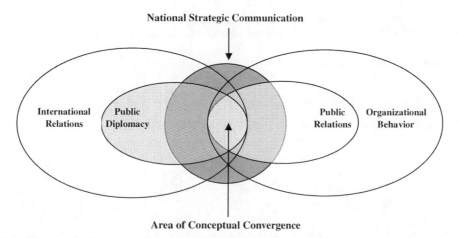

FIG. 39.5a   Van Dyke and Verčič's Model of Public Relations–Public Diplomacy Convergence (Area of Conceptual Convergence).

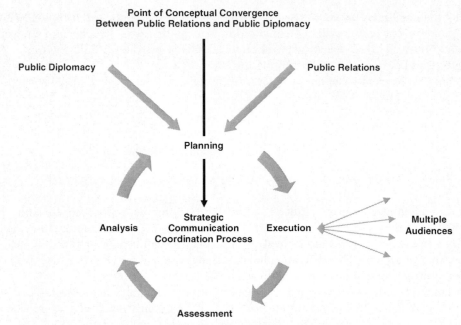

FIG. 39.5b   Van Dyke and Verčič's Model of Public Relations–Public Diplomacy Convergence (Point of Convergence).

Implications

Historical trends provide ample evidence of convergence, at least in practice, between public relations and public diplomacy. Some, like Vitto (2004), have observed this phenomenon:

> Distinctions between public affairs and public diplomacy continue to shape doctrine, resource allocations, and organization charts. But public diplomacy and public affairs practitioners employ similar tools and methods; their audiences are global and local. This conceptual distinction is losing validity in the world of global media, global audiences, and porous borders. (p. 12)

Given this evidence, scholars and practitioners must consider carefully the implications of this trend.

Enhances Value of Public Relations

Strategic communication recognizes public relations' value (van Dyke, 1997, 2005; Jurkowsky and van Dyke, 2000; Kirby, 2000) and gives public relations managers a seat at the decision-making table (Philpott, 1996). Kirby (2000), in a U.S. Naval War College study, acknowledged, "Though controversial, this integration will continue, making PA [public affairs] more than just a bit player" (pp. 3–4). He also concluded that public relations "has become an added capability to IO efforts, aiding in the coordination of themes and messages" (p. 3). This characterization elevates public relations to a "*full-participation* approach" (L. Grunig et al., 2002, p. 383), which assigns public relations responsibility to coordinate messages as part of a strategic decision-making process.

Assigns Public Relations Responsibility for Managing Ethical Communication and Legitimacy of Action(s)

L. Grunig et al. (2002) compared public relations with the conscience of an organization, since it serves as "the management function primarily responsible for introducing moral values and social responsibility into organizational decisions" (p. 554). Involvement in integrated communication programs provides public relations managers with opportunities to introduce a reflexive framework in decisions about applying activities like psychological and deception operations (van Ruler and Verčič, 2005). For instance, NATO public relations managers in Bosnia-Herzegovina counseled allied military commanders on "the ethical nature of [military] actions and how the outcomes of those actions could be perceived by strategic publics" (van Dyke, 2005, p. 306). Lessons learned from NATO's experience in Bosnia-Herzegovina led van Dyke to propose an ethical framework for integrated programs that include a range of communication activities, from dialog to coercion.

Promotes Public Relations as an Integrated but Separate Function

Programs like information operations and strategic communication provide a theoretical and practical "form of structure for integrating communication activities" (L. Grunig et al., 2002, p. 277) that also separates public relations from other functions. Figure 39.4 illustrates how communication functions are integrated in a notional information operation cell. Figure 39.1 depicts how public relations and information operations functions are kept separate and coordinated. NATO has applied a similar structure to its integrated information efforts and maintained a direct line of responsibility between public relations managers and senior leaders:

> PA and Info Ops are separate, but related functions . . . both require planning, message development and media analysis, though the efforts differ with respect to audience, scope and intent . . . . While coordination is essential, the lines of authority will remain separate, the PA reporting relationship being direct to the commander. This is to maintain credibility of PA and to avoid creating a media or public perception that PA activities are coordinated by, or are directed by Info Ops. (F. Veltri, personal communication, January 2, 2008, p. 7)

Potential Loss of Credibility and Public Trust

Post-Cold War employment of public relations and public diplomacy alongside psychological and deception operations has created a controversy reminiscent of the backlash over World War I and World War II propaganda efforts: "Much the same thing occurred in World War II, when [U.S.] congressional leaders scorned the 'unwholesome' domestic propaganda operations of the Office of War Information (OWI)" (Cone, 2007, ¶ 15). Rothrock (1997) warned that such efforts could "conflict with or exceed the imperatives of the national will and the crucial *bond of trust* between people and their government" (p. 223).

The current controversy extends to government offices and programs designed to coordinate public information, diplomacy, and propaganda activities. In 2002, the U.S. government closed its new Office of Strategic Influence, which some watchdogs alleged was providing "news items, possibly even false ones, to foreign media organizations as part of a new effort to influence public sentiment and policy makers in both friendly and unfriendly countries" (Schmitt, 2002, p. 1). Even after this office's closing, U.S. government agencies were still accused of manipulating information, managing perceptions, and influencing foreign news media (Borger, 2002; Gerth, 2005; Schmitt, 2003; Shanker and Schmitt, 2002, 2004). The allegations seem validated, at least in part, by a final approved draft of a U.S.

Army field manual for operations (U.S. Department of the Army, in press) that includes public relations among the *information engagement* activities that are "necessary to influence foreign audiences" (Glossary-7).

Blurring of Conceptual and Disciplinary Boundaries

L'Etang (2004) warned that integration of public relations and diplomacy can obfuscate the relationship between the two concepts. This can create confusion that is not necessarily in the best interests of a nation or the public relations profession. Documenting the convergence of public relations and diplomacy in British history, L'Etang wrote:

> As public relations developed as a discrete occupation, so did its role in national policies. This attracted attention from the media, which became aware that increasing unseen, paid-for interventions by public relations practitioners were taking place within the political process. It also became apparent that some public relations practitioners were becoming involved more directly in international diplomacy, and not always in the British interest. These developments were seen as controversial by the media and, to some extent, within the public relations field itself. (p. 146)

Risk of Communication Errors that Could Escalate Conflict

Practical applications of communication activities that are not guided by theory and ethics (e.g., Bowen, 2000, 2004; Seib and Fitzpatrick, 1995) can be uninformed or, worse yet, catastrophic in terms of escalating conflict and associated costs (Luttwak, 1999). For instance, models of strategic communication that attempt "to create, strengthen, or preserve conditions favorable to advance national interests and objectives" (U.S. Joint Staff, 2007, p. xii) reflect an asymmetrical approach to communication (J. Grunig and Hunt, 1984). Kruckeberg and Vujnovic (2005) warned that overreliance on such persuasive approaches to communication can have dire consequences in a post-Cold War-era, decentralized, global society. These approaches are not as effective in terms of building relationships as symmetrical, or dialogic, approaches to communication that also take into account the interests and objectives of strategic publics (Dozier, 1995; J. Grunig, 1992; L. Grunig et al., 2002).

Hence, mismanagement of information power could erode the value of public relations and diplomacy, undermine public trust in government and private institutions, increase the likelihood that nations will resort to hard power, and prolong or amplify the adverse consequences of conflict. Such outcomes fail to heed the counsel of strategists like Sun-tzu, a Chinese general who wrote more than 2,500 years ago: "To win one hundred victories in one hundred battles is not the acme of skill. To subdue the enemy without fighting is the supreme excellence" (Sun-tzu, 1998/6th century B.C., pp. 64–65).

CONCLUSION

The convergence of public relations and public diplomacy through international strategic communication programs over the last two decades has progressed more rapidly in practice than in theory. Public relations and public diplomacy have a long history of academic study, even though each concept has evolved along different disciplinary tracks. Furthermore, convergence of public relations and public diplomacy has been relegated to limited academic study as a normative concept. Thus, the positive concept of this convergence is being constructed on a shaky theoretical foundation, far from the attention of most public relations scholars. The paucity of scholarly public relations research in this area needs to be addressed, before errors in practical applications become a credibility crisis for public relations and public diplomacy. Future research efforts need to take into account the opportunities and risks associated with convergence and integration.

Conceptual convergence bears witness to the progress of communication management in international relations, on both sides of the public relations and public diplomacy spectrum. In many ways, the centrality of this communication process in contemporary military and political operations parallels the similar entry of communication into the center of many business activities. Practitioners and students of public relations must observe, study, and exploit opportunities offered by these developments through research and case studies. Hence, we propose to overcome the fear of getting hands dirty with reality and start digging.

REFERENCES

Adair, K., and Blanton, T. (2006). *The national security archive: Rumsfeld's roadmap to propaganda*. Retrieved February 8, 2008, from http://www.gwu.edu/~nsarchiv/NSAEBB/NSAEBB177/index.htm.

Adelman, K. L. (1981). Speaking of America: Public diplomacy in our time. *Foreign Affairs, 59*(4), 913–936.

Armistead, L. (2004). *Information operations: Warfare and the hard reality of soft power*. Washington, DC: Brassey's.

Beelman, M. (2001). The dangers of disinformation in the war on terrorism. *Nieman Reports, 55*(4), 16–18.

Belay, G. (1997). Ethics in international interaction: Perspectives on diplomacy and negotiation. In F. Casmir (Ed.), *Ethics in intercultural and international communication* (pp. 227–265). Mahwah, NJ: Erlbaum.

Black, D., and van der Westhuizen, J. (2004). The allure of global games for 'semi-peripheral' polities and spaces: a research agenda. *Third World Quarterly, 25*(7), 1195–1214.

Blinken, A. (2003). Winning the war of ideas. In A. T. J. Lennon (Ed.), *The battle for hearts and minds: Using soft power to undermine terrorist networks* (pp. 282–298). Cambridge, MA: MIT Press.

Borger, J. (2002, March 7). Information is now a casualty of war. *The Guardian Weekly*. Retrieved July 25, 2007, from http://www.guardian.co.uk/GWeekly/Story/0,,662814,00.html.

Bowen, S. A. (2000). A theory of ethical issues management: Contributions of Kantian deontology to public relations' ethics and decision making. Unpublished doctoral dissertation, University of Maryland, College Park.

Bowen, S. A. (2004). Expansion of ethics as the tenth generic principle of public relations excellence: A Kantian theory and model for managing ethical issues. *Journal of Public Relations Research, 16*(1), 65–92.

Brummett, B. (Ed.). (2000). *Reading rhetorical theory*. New York: Harcourt College Publishers.

Bush, G. W. (2002). *The national security strategy of the United States*. Washington, DC: The White House.

Clark, W. (2000, May 22). Visions of the 21st century: How will we fight? *Time, 155*(21), 1.

Collins, S. (2003, Summer). Mind games. *NATO Review*, 13–16.

Combelles-Siegel, P. (1998). *Target Bosnia: Integrating information activities in peace operations*. Washington, DC: National Defense University.

Cone, S. (2007). The Pentagon's propaganda windmills: How "Arkansas' Quijote" tilted against militarism and challenged the marketplace of ideas in America. *Journalism History, 33*(1), 24–41.

Crossen, C. (2003, March 19). In every war but one, the government had media under control. *The Wall Street Journal*, B1.

Cutlip, S., Center, A., and Broom, G. (2005). *Effective public relations* (9th ed.). Upper Saddle River, NJ: Prentice Hall.

Dozier, D. M. (with Grunig, L. A., and Grunig, J. E.). (1995). *Manager's guide to excellence in public relations and communication management*. Mahwah, NJ: Erlbaum.

Dutta-Bergman, M. (2005). Operation Iraqi Freedom: Mediated sphere as a public relations tool. *Atlantic Journal of Communication, 13*(4), 220–241.

Dutta-Bergman, M. (2006). U.S. public diplomacy in the Middle East: A critical cultural approach. *The Journal of Communication Inquiry, 30*(2), 102.

van Dyke, M. A. (1997, May). NATO military public information: IFOR lessons learned. Presentation to Ministry of Defense, Bucharest, Romania.

van Dyke, M. A. (2001, July). From coercion to collaboration: Toward a new communication continuum. Paper presented at the 8th International Public Relations Research Symposium, Bled, Slovenia.

van Dyke, M. A. (2005). Toward a theory of just communication: A case study of NATO, multinational public relations, and ethical management of international conflict. Unpublished dissertation, University of Maryland, College Park.

Eder, M. (2007). Toward strategic communication. *Military Review, 4*(87), 61–70.

Ehling, W. P. (1984). Application of decision theory in the construction of a theory of relationship management, I. *Public Relations Research and Education, 1*(2), 25–38.

Ehling, W. P. (1985). Application of decision theory in the construction of a theory of relationship management, II. *Public Relations Research and Education, 2*(1), 4–22.

Ehling, W. P. (1992). Estimating the value of public relations and communication to an organization. In J. E. Grunig (Ed.), *Excellence in public relations and communication management* (pp. 617–638). Hillsdale, NJ: Erlbaum.

Elsbach, K. (2006). *Organizational perception management*. Mahwah, NJ: Erlbaum.

Gerth, J. (2005, December 11). Military's information war is vast and often secretive. *The New York Times*, p. A1.

Grunig, J. E. (with Dozier, D. M., Ehling, W. P., Grunig, L. A., Repper, F. C., and White, J.). (Ed.). (1992). *Excellence in public relations and communication management*. Hillsdale, NJ: Erlbaum.

Grunig, J. E., and Grunig, L. A. (1997, July). Review of a program of research on activism: Incidence in four countries, activist publics, strategies of activist groups, and organizational responses to activism. Paper presented to the Fourth International Public Relations Research Symposium, Managing Environmental Issues, Lake Bled, Slovenia.

Grunig, J. E., and Hunt, T. (1984). *Managing public relations*. New York: Holt, Rinehart and Winston.

Grunig, J. E., and Repper, F. C. (1992). Strategic management, publics, and issues. In J. E. Grunig (Ed.), *Excellence in public relations and communication management* (pp. 117–157). Hillsdale, NJ: Erlbaum.

Grunig, L. A., Grunig, J. E., and Dozier, D. M. (Eds.). (2002). *Excellent public relations and effective organizations: A study of communication management in three countries*. Mahwah, NJ: Erlbaum.

Grupp, R. W. (2008) Gaining respect through corporate diplomacy [IPRA frontline online]. Retrieved February 18, 2008, from http://www.ipra.org/frontlinedetail.asp?articleid=747

Guth, D. W., and Marsh, C. (2005). *Adventures in public relations: Case studies and critical thinking*. Boston: Pearson.

Hallahan, K., Holzhausen, D., van Ruler, B., Verčič, D., and Sriramesh, K. (2007). Defining strategic communication. *International Journal of Strategic Communication 1*(1), 3–35.

van Ham, P. (2005). Power, public diplomacy, and Pax Americana. In Melissen, J. (Ed.), *The new public diplomacy: Soft power in international relations* (pp. 47–66). Hampshire, England: Macmillan.

Hiebert, R. (2005). Commentary: New technology, public relations, and democracy. *Public Relations Review, 31*(1), 1–9.

Ikenberry, G. J. (2004). Review of the book *Soft power: The means to success in world politics. Foreign Affairs, 83*(3), 136.

Isaacson, W. (2003). *Benjamin Franklin: An American life*. New York: Simon and Schuster.

Jentleson, B. W. (2000). *Coercive prevention: Normative, political, and policy dilemmas* (Peaceworks, No. 35). Washington, DC: U.S. Institute of Peace.

Jurkowsky, T., and van Dyke, M. (2000). *Vision 21: A study of U.S. Navy public affairs in the 21st century*. Washington, DC: Department of the Navy.

Kirby, J. (2000). Helping shape today's battlefield: Public affairs as an operational function. Unpublished manuscript, U.S. Naval War College, Newport, RI, USA.

Krauthammer, C. (1990, March 26). Don't cash the peace dividend. *Time, 135*(13), 88.

Kruckeberg, D., and Vujnovic, M. (2005). Public relations, not propaganda, for US public diplomacy in a post-9/11 world: Challenges and opportunities. *Journal of Communication Management, 9*(4), 296–204.

Kunczik, M. (2003). Transnational public relations by foreign governments. In S. Krishnamurthy and D. Verčič

(Eds.), *The global public relations handbook: Theory, research, and practice* (pp. 399–424). Mahwah, NJ: Erlbaum.

L'Etang, J. (2004). *Public relations in Britain: A history of professional practice in the twentieth century.* Mahwah, NJ: Erlbaum.

Luttwak, E. (1999). Give war a chance. *Foreign Affairs, 78*(4), 36–44.

Melissen, J. (Ed.). (2005). *The new public diplomacy: Soft power in international relations.* Hampshire, England: Macmillan.

Metz, T. (2006, May-June). Massing effects in the information domain: A case study in aggressive military operations [Electronic version]. *Military Review,* 2–12.

Meyers, R. (2004, September 27). *Policy on public affairs relationship to information operations* [Memo CM-2077–04]. Washington, DC: Joint Staff.

Mintzberg, H. (1983). *Power in and around organizations.* Englewood Cliffs, NJ: Prentice-Hall.

Nemeth, C. (2000, November). The winds of change: The role of public information in the era of information operations. *Journal of Peace, Conflict and Military Studies, 1*(2), Article 4. Retrieved July 27, 2007, from http://www.uz.ac.zw/units/cds/journals/volume1/number2/article4.html.

Nye, J. (2002). *The paradox of American power: Why the world's superpower can't go it alone.* New York: Oxford University Press.

Nye, J. (2003, January 10). Soft power: Propaganda isn't the way. *International Herald Tribune,* p. 6.

Nye, J. (2004a). *Soft power: The means to success in world politics.* New York: PublicAffairs.

Nye, J. (2004b). Soft power and leadership. *Leadership,* Spring issue. Retrieved October 15, 2007, from http://hbswk.hbs.edu/archive/4290.html.

Nye, J. (2004c). The decline of America's soft power [Electronic version]. *Foreign Affairs, 83*(3), 16–20.

Parry-Giles, S. (2005). From total war to total diplomacy: The Advertising Council and the construction of the Cold War consensus [Book review]. *The Journal of American History, 91*(4), 1528–1529.

Peterson, P. (2002). Public diplomacy and the war on terrorism. *Foreign Affairs, 81*(5), 74–94.

Philpott, T. (1996, September). Enforcing peace in Bosnia. *The Retired Officer Magazine,* 60–66.

Pratkanis, A., and Aronson, E. (1992). *Age of propaganda: Everyday use and abuse of persuasion* [Electronic version]. New York: Henry Holt.

Robinson, L. (2006, May 26). The propaganda war: The Pentagon's brand-new plan for winning the battle of ideas against terrorists. *U.S. News and World Report, 140*(20), 9–31.

Rothrock, J. (1997). Information warfare: Time for some constructive criticism? In J. Arquilla and D. Ronfelt (Eds.), *In Athena's camp: Preparing for conflict in the information age* (pp. 217–230). Santa Monica, CA: RAND.

Rubin, B. (2002). *Blood on the doorstep: The politics of preventive action.* Washington, DC: Brookings Institution Press.

van Ruler, B., and Verčič, D. (2002, July). The Bled manifesto on public relations. Paper presented at the 9th International Public Relations Research Symposium, Bled, Slovenia.

van Ruler, B., and Verčič, D. (2005). Reflective communication management: Future ways for public relations research. In P. J. Kalbfleisch (ed), *Communication Yearbook 29* (pp. 239–273).

van Ruler, B., Verčič, D., Bütschi, G., and Flodin, B. (2004). A first look for parameters of public relations in Europe. *Journal of Public Relations Research, 16*(1), 35–63.

Schmitt, E. (2002, February 26). Bush seals fate of office of influence in Pentagon. *The New York Times,* p. A1.

Schmitt, E. (2003, December 5). Pentagon and bogus news: All is denied. *The New York Times,* p. A6.

Seib, P., and Fitzpatrick, K. (1995). *Public relations ethics.* Fort Worth, TX: Harcourt Brace.

Seitel, F. S. (2007). *The practice of public relations* (10th ed.). Upper Saddle River, NJ: Pearson.

Shanker, T., and Schmitt, E. (2002, December 16). Pentagon may push propaganda in allied nations. *The New York Times,* p. A1.

Shanker, T., and Schmitt, E. (2004, December 13). Pentagon weighs use of deception in broad arena. *The New York Times,* p. A1.

Sharkey, J. (1991). *Under fire: U.S. military restrictions on the media from Grenada to the Persian Gulf.* Washington, DC: Center for Public Integrity.

Signitzer, B. H., and Coombs, T. (1992). Public relations and public diplomacy: Conceptual convergences. *Public Relations Review, 18*(2), 137–147.

Signitzer, B. H., and Wamser, C. (2006). Public diplomacy: A specific governmental public relations function. In C. Botan and V. Hazelton (Eds.), *Public Relations Theory II* (pp. 435–464). New York: Routledge.

Sriramesh, K., and Verčič, D. (2001). International public relations: A framework for future research. *Journal of Communication Management, 6*(2), 103–117.

Sriramesh, K., and Verčič, D. (Eds.). (2003a). *The global public relations handbook: Theory, research, and practice.* Mahwah, NJ: Erlbaum.

Sriramesh, K., and Verčič, D. (2003b). A theoretical framework for global public relations research and practice. In K. Sriramesh and D. Verčič (Eds.), *The global public relations handbook: Theory, research, and practice* (pp. 1–19). Mahwah, NJ: Erlbaum.

Steinbock, D. (2003). Toward a mobile information society. *Georgetown Journal of International Affairs, 4*(2), 120–126.

Sun-tzu. (1998). *The art of war* (Y. Shibing and J. J. L. Duyvendak, Trans.). Hertfordshire, England: Wordsworth Editions. (Original work published 6th century B.C.).

Thorp, F. (2007). Strategic communication in the [U.S.] Department of Defense. *Sightings, 13*(4), 3–6.

U.S. Department of the Army (2003). *Information operations: Doctrine, tactics, techniques, procedures* [Field manual 3–13/100–6]. Retrieved July 23, 2007, from https://atiam.train.army.mil/soldierPortal/atia/adlsc/view/public/7422–1/fm/3–13/toc.htm.

U.S. Department of the Army (in press). *Operations* [Final approved draft]. Washington, DC: Author.

U.S. Department of State (2007, June). *U.S. national strategy for public diplomacy and strategic communication.* Retrieved February 8, 2008, from www.state.gov/documents/organization / 87427.pdf.

U.S. Department of State. (2008a). *Bureau of Public Affairs.* Retrieved February 12, 2008, from http://www.state.gov/r/pa/.

U.S. Department of State. (2008b). *Under Secretary For Diplomacy and Public Affairs.* Retrieved February 12, 2008, from http://www.state.gov/r/.

U.S. Institute of Peace. (1999, June). Managing information chaos. *Peace Watch 5*(4), 5–8.

U.S. Joint Staff. (1998, October). *Joint doctrine for information operations* [Joint publication 3–13]. Washington, DC: Department of Defense.

U.S. Joint Staff. (2005, May). *Public affairs* [Joint publication 3–61]. Washington, DC: Department of Defense.

U.S. Joint Staff. (2006, February). *Information operations* [Joint publication 3–13]. Washington, DC: Department of Defense.

U.S. Joint Staff. (2007, December). *Joint operation planning* [Joint publication 5–0]. Washington, DC: Department of Defense.

Vitto, V. (2004). *Report of the U.S. Defense Science Board Task Force on strategic communication.* Washington, DC: Department of Defense.

Wang, J. (2007). Telling the American story to the world: The purpose of U.S. public diplomacy in historical perspective. *Public Relations Review, 33*(1), 21–30.

Wang, Y. (2008, March). Public diplomacy and the rise of Chinese soft power. *The Annals of the Academy of Political Social Science, 616*, Annals 257.

Wasserstrom, J. (2000/2001, Winter). Beyond ping-pong diplomacy. *World Policy Journal, 17*(4), 61–66.

de Wijk, R. (2003). The limits of military power. In A. T. J. Lennon (Ed.), *The battle for hearts and minds: Using soft power to undermine terrorist networks* (pp. 3–28). Cambridge, MA: MIT Press.

Wilson, L. (1996). Strategic cooperative communities: A synthesis of strategic, issue management, and relationship-building approaches in public relations. In H. M. Culbertson and N. Chen (Eds.), *International public relations: A comparative analysis* (pp. 67–80). Mahwah, NJ: Erlbaum.

Yun, S. (2006). Toward public relations theory-based study of public diplomacy: Testing the applicability of the excellence theory. *Journal of Public Relations Research, 18*(4), 287–312.

Zhang, J. (2006). Public diplomacy as symbolic interactions: A case study of Asian tsunami relief campaigns. *Public Relations Review, 32*(1), 26–32.

Zhang, J. (2007). Beyond anti-terrorism: Metaphors as message strategy of post-September-11 U.S. public diplomacy. *Public Relations Review, 33*(1), 31–39.

Zöllner, O. (2006). A quest for dialogue in international broadcasting: Germany's public diplomacy targeting Arab audiences. *Global Media and Communication, 2*(2), 160–182.

40

Managing Sustainable Development in Sub-Saharan Africa: A Communication Ethic for the Global Corporation

Cornelius B. Pratt

> *While industry represents perhaps the single biggest threat to society and the natural world, it can also represent one of our greatest allies in our mission to safeguard it and provide for its sustainable development.*
>
> —World Wide Fund for Nature, in Marsden (2000), p. 9

Sub-Saharan Africa faces a litany of developmental challenges, not least its deteriorating environment and ecosystem, its faltering agricultural productivity, its heavy-handed state intervention, its inadequate foreign investment, its improper political governance, its limited public health programs, its narrow business partnerships, and its social strife. Long after the implementation of structural adjustment policies required by the International Monetary Fund (IMF) for its strategic support of teetering African economies and the adoption of investment practices enunciated by both the World Bank and the European Union, those challenges are still far from abating. A statement issued at the conclusion of the U.N. World Summit on Sustainable Development (WSSD), held in Johannesburg, South Africa, August 26-September 4, 2002, underscored the enduring nature of those challenges: "Africa's efforts to achieve sustainable development have been hindered by conflicts, insufficient investment, limited market access opportunities and supply side constraints, unsustainable debt burdens, historically declining ODA [official development assistance] levels, and the impact of HIV/AIDS."

It is against that backdrop that this chapter focuses on the question, How can organizational communication, particularly that undertaken by the global corporation, be used to respond effectively to the challenges of sustainable development in sub-Saharan Africa? It is that question—at the global level—that prompted the Warwick Business School to hold a

Corporate Citizenship Research Conference in July 1998. It explored corporate citizenship and developed an agenda for improving it. Marsden (2000) writes: "Private sector business, particularly . . . [the] large international companies, is increasingly being seen, both by those working inside it as well as outside, as part of the solution to the world's biggest environmental and social problems, rather than just being a part of the problem" (pp. 9-10). More important, however, is the evolving ethic that guides global corporate behaviors: that community involvement, environmental and sustainability initiatives, and stakeholder engagement are gaining momentum (Muirhead, Bennet, Berenbeim, Kao, & Vidal, 2002).

Corporate involvement in communities per se is not new. However, what is refreshing is corporate commitment to (1) a "focus on building bridges between corporations and community" (Vidaver-Cohen & Altman, 2000, p. 145); (2) a recognition of the "mutuality of interests and practices between society and business" (Waddock & Smith, 2000, p. 47); (3) the promotion of "civic engagement . . . to restore neighborhood houses, volunteer in tutoring and mentoring programs, provide impoverished families with . . . vital civic activities" (O'Connor, 2000, p. 142); and (4) the "idea that all those involved in the corporation are potentially members of one community; while they clearly have significantly divergent interests, needs, and values, they also have some significant shared goals and bonds" (Etzioni, 1998, p. 679).

Thus this chapter links three (theoretical) constructs—stakeholder theory, corporate social performance (CSP), and sustainable development—and argues that global organizations apply them *ethically* in their attempt to respond more effectively to the challenges of the societies or nations in which they operate. It argues that business organizations—as harbingers of development in the Third World—apply normative core values of stakeholder theory and those inherent in their social performance to evaluating and responding to community challenges and to collaborating with other organizations and community groups in their contributions to national development. WSSD acknowledged the importance of ethics for sustainable development and emphasized the need to consider ethics in the implementation of "Agenda 21" of the "Rio Earth Summit."

A caveat at this point is necessary: This chapter is neither an add-on to the growing list of strategies for Third World development nor a challenge to the strategies of development agents; rather, it makes the case that stakeholder theory and CSP, as constructs of a communication ethic, frame current programs and extant organizational responses to community challenges.

Understandably, a key principle of effective governance—political, corporate, or organizational—is establishing strong, ethical relationships with one's constituents or publics. The public relations literature is replete with studies that have investigated that principle (e.g., Grunig, 2001; Grunig & Repper, 1992; Ledingham, 2001; Ledingham & Bruning, 1998). Organization-public relationships are all the more critical whenever the principal agent is large or influential globally. For business and major political and community organizations, the emphasis on building firm, dynamic relationships with various publics has morphed into an evolving stakeholder theory, which recognizes the inherent disparate values among an organization's publics. That theory is becoming more relevant today largely because of the social landscape, densely dotted with protest movements, on which major organizations and institutions operate.

THE STAKEHOLDER THEORY

By definition, stakeholder theory has been grounded in functionalist organizational theory (e.g., Freeman, 1984; Freeman & Gilbert, 1988; Freeman & Reed, 1983) and in ethical theory (Argandoña, 1998; Carroll, 1989; Cohen, 1995; Donaldson, 1989; Evan & Freeman,

1988; Phillips, 1997). The former, whose seminal proponent is Freeman (1984), is "about groups and individuals who can affect the organization, and is about managerial behavior taken in response to those groups and individuals" (p. 84). That view defines a stakeholder as "any group or individual who can affect or is affected by the achievement of an organization's purpose . . . [S]ome corporations must count 'terrorist groups' as stakeholders" (p. 53). In general, such groups include shareholders, employees, suppliers, customers, communities in which a firm operates, government agencies, creditors, and competitors. "One of the goals of stakeholder theory," writes Phillips (1997), "is to maintain the benefits of the free market while minimizing the potential ethical problems created by capitalism" (p. 63).

The ethical perspective holds that normative criteria be used by an organization to identify its stakeholders, to allocate rights, and to consider their values in assigning duties (Argandoña, 1998; Donaldson, 1989; Quinn & Jones, 1995); that is, the duty of each stakeholder is to play its part fairly in achieving the organization's common good. An organization should treat its stakeholders as "ends" (Evan & Freeman, 1983).

The stakeholder theory is not without its limitations (e.g., Donaldson & Preston, 1995; Jones & Wicks, 1999). Major issues have been disclosing organizational actions to stakeholders, getting stakeholders' consent, and acting fairly in assigning rights, duties and rewards to stakeholders. Further, Windsor (1998) argued that, because stakeholder theory is at an early stage of development, the identification of stakeholders is very much unresolved. Similarly, Mitchell, Agle and Wood (1997) seek answers to the question, Who or what really counts in a firm's stakeholder environment by using a typology based on one or more of three relationship attributes: power, legitimacy, urgency.

It is argued here that it is the less-than-explicit application of the normative stakeholder theory (Donaldson & Preston, 1995) by the global corporation and its partners that irks anti-globalization activists and spurs protests against business and economic institutions, as routinely occur during annual meetings of the IMF and the World Bank, and as most recently occurred at the WSSD. It is on similar protests that the next section focuses.

PROTESTS AGAINST BUSINESS AND ECONOMIC INSTITUTIONS

Historically, protests are a social movement with which business and government have to contend. They are a tool for exercising citizen rights and for making demands on the power structure. The completion of the first phase of the extensive Lesotho Highlands Water Project early in 1998 attracted the coalescence of several rural and urban environmental groups from both Lesotho and South Africa, to whose governments protests were directed. At issue was the need for further environmental impact analysis, particularly in areas where it was thought that continuing the construction of a dam on the Orange River would cause flooding, damage farmlands and pastures, threaten wildlife and forests, and destabilize rural communities. Even so, the World Bank in June 1998 approved a $45 million loan for constructing the second phase of the dam, further heightening tensions and increasing the call from civic and environmental groups for "environmental justice."

Organizations, particularly those with global operations, confront similar challenges from protest groups. Since 1998, for example, when violent protests rocked the World Trade Organization ministerial conference in Geneva, several protests have been organized against other major global economic institutions—the Group of Eight (Britain, Canada, France, Germany, Italy, Japan, Russia, the United States); the World Bank; the IMF; the World Economic Forum; the European Union—as proxies for attributing blame for Third World poverty and underdevelopment to the perceived failures of the global corporation in protecting and fostering stakeholder interest. Such protests have implications for the perceived failure of global institutions to create broader opportunities for stakeholder input into the governance and policies of global institutions. The criteria for evaluating the social performance of multinational agencies are being expanded to include the human-rights arena. In essence, responsive (global) corporations should *also* be evaluated on their human-rights record, not just on the standard measures of corporate performance. For communication practitioners, that development expands and redefines their boundary-spanning role to relationships with activist groups.

The grievances of activist groups do not have an enduring common theme, but comprise a mixed bag of global issues: labor rights, trade barriers and relations, animal rights, environmental damage (Went, 2000). For the most part, those issues do not frame the traditional discourse on CSP, even though they are the embers over which the fate of the global corporation depends. Yet, they have become the most prominent features of today's economic and political landscape (Held, McGrew, Goldblatt, & Perraton, 1999). For example, November 30 through December 3, 1999, was a watershed in protests against the World Trade Organization, a 135-nation trade group. Protesters got extensive publicity for what they construed as the macabre acts of global corporations—and of their willingness to do business as usual. The sentiments of those protesters rubbed off on the World Economic Forum (January 31-February 4, 2002) in New York City.

WSSD recognized the intersection between development and the environment, as did the Rio de Janeiro Earth summit 10 years earlier. Both summits were fertile grounds for protests. For one thing, the mere mention of "sustainability" attracts the ire of environmentalists worldwide. For the developing nations, that raises gruesome memories of environmental decadence on the rain forests, excessive logging in the Amazon, and the incursions of corporations in pristine homelands. For another, the conferences sought novel partnerships among governments (whose legitimacy is questionable), non-government organizations with competing and sometimes conflicting interests, and foundations and businesses whose investment prospects are narrowly focused on the short term. In the perception of environmental groups a narrow focus translates into a disregard of the concerns and rights of community stakeholders.

CORPORATE SOCIAL PERFORMANCE

Delegates at WSSD reached an agreement on six key issues: water and sanitation, climate change, energy, human and environmental health, sustainable development, and global poverty. The latter is grounded in six issues: that access to markets holds the key to development in many countries; that all export subsidies be phased out; that nations commit to a 10-year framework of programs on sustainable consumption and production; that corporate accountability and responsibility be enhanced; that nations improve their responses to natural disasters; and that a global fund be established to eradicate extreme poverty.

Those agreements suggest a leadership role for business, not least corporate establishments whose headquarters are in the developed nations. For one thing, the economic straits of much of the developing world, particularly sub-Saharan Africa, suggest the presence of economic and political infrastructures that compromise development agendas. For another, it is the ethics-driven global corporation that can serve as a harbinger of, and a vanguard for, development in a complementary mode, assisting national governments and development centers, business roundtables, community groups and other nongovernmental organizations—all in their quest to reverse plummeting economies and stem the incidence of poverty.

WSSD, as it were, set a new tone for global assistance in Third World development, particularly in Africa, where the HIV/AIDS pandemic is robbing the continent of its skilled labor and where political crises and rule by whim are making the region less attractive to global investors. Even so, since the 1990s the region has adopted market-driven economies, most notably by privatizing state-owned infrastructures, and adopting structural adjustment programs by which its economies were liberalized and streamlined.

An earlier summit, the United Nations Conference on Environment and Development held in 1992 in Rio de Janeiro, offered, among other things, a blueprint for sustainable development, the elimination of unsustainable patterns of production and consumption, and the enhancement of the development, adaptation, diffusion, and transfer of technologies.

This chapter argues that corporate governance or CSP is a strategic response to Africa's development problems, particularly those discussed in WSSD. Corporate communicators whose interest should be consistent with those of their key constituents should assist their organizations in framing that response.

CSP, a multidimensional construct (Carroll, 1991; Sharfman, 1996; Wolfe & Aupperle, 1991), has been disaggregated into five most frequently used dimensions: community relations, treatment of women and minorities, product quality, employee relations, and treatment of the environment (Graves & Waddock, 1994; Turban & Greening, 1997; Waddock & Graves, 1997). The last of these dimensions—treatment of the environment—provides a framework for this chapter.

Wood (1991a) defines CSP as the degree to which social responsibility motivates actions taken in behalf of a firm; the degree to which the firm uses socially responsive processes, the existence and nature of policies and programs designed to manage the firm's societal relationships; and the observable outcomes (i.e., social impacts) of the firm's actions, programs, and policies. Thus, that definition integrates three principles: corporate social and ecological responsibility; social responsiveness and issues management, outcomes of corporate social impacts, social programs, and social policies (Bansal & Roth, 2000; Stanwick & Stanwick, 1998; Wartick & Cochran, 1985; Wood, 1991a, 1991b). Corporate social responsibility refers to an organization's legitimacy within a society and its public responsibility; that is, corporations have obligations to groups other than their stockholders and beyond responsibilities required by law or employee unions. "The fundamental idea of 'corporate social responsibility,'" writes Frederick (1986), "is that business corporations have the obligation to work for social betterment" (p. 4). Social responsiveness includes corporate environmental assessment, stakeholder management, and issues management. The third principle investigates the impacts of the corporation on social policies and social programs, Thus, CSP reflects a firm's commitment to its social environment and its ability to adapt to institute changes in that environment that benefit stakeholders.

Studies (e.g., McWilliams & Siegel, 2000) show that CSP can have benefits for organizations; other effects have also been observed. Effects of CSP on financial performance, for example, have been associated with significant excess negative returns to shares of companies that announced divestments of business units in South Africa (e.g., Wright & Ferris, 1997); the effects have been neutral (e.g., Aupperle, Carroll, & Hatfield, 1985; Teoh, Welch, & Wazzan, 1999); and positive (Belkaoui, 1976; Frooman, 1997; McNatt & Light, 1998; Meyerson, 1999; Pava & Krausz, 1996; Posnikoff, 1997; Preston, 1978; Waddock & Graves, 1997; Wood & Jones, 1995). Positive relationships have also been observed between CSP and employee morale and productivity (Solomon & Hanson, 1985), and between CSP and organizational attractiveness to new employees, that is, the development of employment-related images of organizations (Luce, Barber, & Hillman, 2001; Riordan, Gatewood, & Bill, 1997; Strand, Levine, & Montgomery, 1981; Turban &

Greening, 1997). Also, a strong relationship has been observed between profitability and CSP, that is, profitability of a firm allows and encourages managers to implement programs that increase the level of corporate social responsibility (Stanwick & Stanwick, 1998; Waddock & Graves, 1997).

THE ENVIRONMENT-DEVELOPMENT LINK

In the annals of the environment-development literature, two concepts are understandably conjoined. One is the protection of the environment; the other, its sustainability and concomitant development. Those two concepts help explain the evolving corporate interest in ecological responsibility and the consumer interest in corporate "greening." The reasons for the upsurge in that interest have been varied. They include legislation, stakeholder pressures, economic opportunities, ethical concerns, critical events, and corporate values (Bansal & Roth, 2000; Dillon & Fischer, 1992; Lawrence & Morell, 1995; Winn, 1995).

Greening, as a global issue, is at the forefront of the agendas of major environmental and community groups—such as Greenpeace, Earth First! and the Sierra Club, with worldwide presence; and the Network for Environment and Sustainable Development in Africa (NESDA), the Landless People's Movement, Anti-Privatization Forum, Earthlife Africa, Lawyers Environmental Action Team, and Advocates Coalition for Development and Environment, all in Africa. So conjoined are sustainability and conservation that it is a fruitless exercise to attempt to delineate one from the other. However, whenever early ecological discourse referred to conservation, it did so bereft of—if not separated from—the evolving companion discourse on sustainability. But McKee (2001) underscores lucidly the inherent synergy between them:

> When an ecosystem becomes unsustainable and collapses, we imperil nature's services and jeopardize our own resources. . . . One possible solution is conservation. People around the world are making noble efforts to set aside lands in which nature can continue its work. Others have identified particular areas of rich biological diversity, some of which have been targeted for conservation. (p. B20)

Africa's responses to environmental issues took root during the June 1972 United Nations Conference on Human Environment held in Stockholm, where social activists from developing countries raised questions on the effects of affluent countries' operations on the environment. Since then African countries have ratified more than a dozen Multilateral Environmental Agreements, indicating their commitment to sustainable development. And since the1992 Earth Summit in Rio de Janeiro, where "Agenda 21: The United Nations Program of Action from Rio" was adopted, African countries have made progress toward implementing actions called for in Sweden and Brazil. They have established political and economic groups such as the Lake Chad Basin Commission, the African Timber Organization, the East Africa Wetlands Program, and the Lake Victoria Global Environment Facility Project.

In the nongovernmental realm, NESDA, an African initiative, is helping countries such as Botswana, The Gambia, Côte d'Ivoire, Cameroon, Ghana, and Ethiopia achieve environmentally sustainable development by assisting them in developing strategies for environmental management and in establishing relations between sub-regional initiatives (e.g., the Eastern Africa Biodiversity Support Program, the Nile Basin Initiative, and the Integrated Coastal Zone Management) and the rest of the continent.

In the political-corporate sector, the New Partnership for African Development (NEPAD) collaborates with the developed countries in fostering international trade and foreign investment. In mid-April 2002, for example, a summit, "Partnership with the Private Sector for Financing Africa's Growth through NEPAD," acknowledged business as a key player in addressing Africa's environmental challenges through international trade and foreign investment.

During WSSD, delegates expected the United States to play a leading role in averting environmental scourge and global warming, particularly because of the country's reluctance to approve the Kyoto Protocol on climate change. Nonetheless, the United States has a commendable history of environmental enhancement—and, some argue, a dismal record on the environment. The leadership role of the United States in ecological responsibility is grounded in the 19th century, an epoch during which the federal government regulated forestlands, with Congress in 1831 prohibiting the removal of timber from public lands. In 1862 it passed the Morrill Act, by which it set aside lands that could be used by states for educational purposes. That act also established the Department of Agriculture to provide oversight for agricultural land use. George P. Marsh's *Man and Nature* (1864) provided a fillip to the conservation movement and contributed to reforms during the United States Reconstruction (1865-1877) by arguing that public land management was for usufruct alone, not for consumption; therefore, humans should stop destroying the earth's (natural) resources. Consequently, in 1930, for example, the U.S. government established a Timber Conservation Board, which called for greater cooperation between government and industry in promoting conservation—a collaboration that was a bellwether for much of the free world.

U.S. political interest in environmental protection was demonstrated in the creation of the Bureau of Land Management in 1946, in the enactment of the Forest Pest Control Act of 1947, and in the founding of the Civilian Conservation Corps in 1933, all of which coalesced in bringing to a head conservation and sustainability.

Therefore, it is perhaps not an exaggeration to conclude that the late Rachel Carson's controversial book, *Silent Spring* (1962), a response to "the senseless, brutish things" that were being done to the environment, set the stage and upped the ante for today's global dialogue on sustainable development. Carson's work sought to establish causal links between the use of DDT and other pesticides *and* damage to the environment, to humans, and to animals.

Five years after *Silent Spring* was published, the United Nations Educational, Scientific and Cultural Organization sponsored an Intergovernmental Conference for Rational Use and Conservation of Biosphere, which held seminal discussions on a then-emerging concept: sustainable development.

Shortly thereafter, several forces, including the sometimes disparate activities of environmental and other national groups, coalesced to provide the impetus for global attention to the health and management of our nation's forests and rangelands. Even so, a few milestones can be identified as making far-reaching inroads into pushing forest and rangeland health into the forefront of national governments' agendas.

For example, in 1969 alone, three U.S. organizations, the Natural Resources Defense Council, Friends of the Earth, and the United States Environmental Protection Agency, were created to focus U.S. attention on the environment. On January 1, 1970, the National Environmental Policy Act of 1969 was signed; it established the Council on Environmental Quality in the president's office. Also in 1970, a global event, "Earth Day," saw more than 20 million people in the United States alone demonstrate peacefully in behalf of the environment.

Additional developments quickly provided further fillip to the cause of sustainable development. In 1993, Canada convened in Montréal a seminar of experts on sustainable development of boreal and temperate forests. Its mandate: To respond to a June 1992 United Nations conference on the environment during which a call was issued on global attention to the importance of sustainable forest management as a strategic response to meeting our current need for forest products and services without jeopardizing those of future generations. Consequently, the nations that participated in the seminar developed national criteria for and national indicators of sustainable forest management; they are more succinctly referred to as the Montréal Process. A sequela of that initiative in developing those measures was the founding in Geneva in 1994 of the Working Group on Criteria and Indicators for the Conservation and Sustainable Management of Temperate and Boreal Forests.

On February 3, 1995, the 10 original members—Australia, Canada, Chile, China, Japan, the Republic of Korea, Mexico, New Zealand, Russia, the United States—affirmed the Montréal Process by issuing the Santiago Declaration, which comprises seven criteria for and 67 indicators of sustainable forest management. (Uruguay and Argentina endorsed the declaration in July and October 1995, respectively.)

The seven criteria (and the number of their indicators):

1. Conserving biological diversity (9 indicators)

2. Maintaining productive capacity of forest ecosystems (5 indicators)

3. Maintaining forest ecosystem health and vitality (3 indicators)

4. Conserving and maintaining soil and water resources (8 indicators)

5. Maintaining forest contributions to global carbon cycles (3 indicators)

6. Maintaining and enhancing long-term multiple socioeconomic benefits (19 indicators)

7. Establishing legal, institutional and economic framework for forest conservation and sustainable management (20 indicators)

The key here is that global interest in the health of the environment is not lost on corporations and on other multinational agencies whose activities have been criticized as being unhealthful for the ecosystem. Ecosystem regulations aside, it behooves the multinational organization to adhere voluntarily to practices that, at the minimum, are demonstrably reflective of their governments' commitment to sustainable development within their borders.

Since that historic event of 1995, 11 U.S. federal government agencies have entered into a Memorandum of Understanding (initially signed October 16, 2000), which seeks to resolve federal agency responsibilities related to continually collecting, monitoring, analyzing, reporting, and distributing data on the Montréal Process.

A number of reports and technical documents have been issued by the group; and a number of roundtables have been organized for (a) sharing information and perspectives (community of interests) on the sustainable management of our forests (a community of place); and (b) providing dialogues that will move the United States toward sustainable forest management. Such roundtables will, for example, facilitate communication with stakeholders interested in tracking the roundtables and in fostering participation by key constituents. For example, the Sustainable Minerals Roundtable is identifying the status of minerals in sustainable development and is formulating agreed-upon, nationwide indicators for sustaining minerals. Similar efforts are being undertaken for sustainable rangeland management.

The agendas of those groups—as well as those of several others—suggest areas rife with corporate communication opportunities and challenges. To what extent, for example, do key publics know about, let alone support, sustainable development? How much can a nation—and domestic environmental and interest groups and companies—benefit from both a pervasive public and a systemwide understanding of sustainable development? Both those questions suggest opportunities—as well as challenges.

THE TRIONYM OF SUSTAINABLE DEVELOPMENT

Although there are disparate definitions of sustainability, there is some general agreement on what it means. By definition, sustainable development, as noted above, has been associated with concepts such as environmental sustainability; conservation; corporate, social or national responsibility; general do-gooderism; and ecological sustainability. Even though there is disagreement over the meaning of sustainable development, there is comparatively little disagreement about the implications of sustainable development for national development. One coexists with the other, making any difference between them nuanced.

Perhaps a much-earlier description of sustainability was implied in a 1905 letter written by United States Secretary of Agriculture James Wilson and addressed to Gifford Pinchot, the first chief of the new United States Forest Service, to which authority over 86 million acres of federal forest lands had just been transferred from the Forest Reserves. The letter stressed that "all land is to be devoted to its most productive use for the permanent good of the whole people, and not for the temporary benefit of individuals or companies" (Pinchot, 1974, p. 261). It also stated in part:

> The permanence of the resources of the reserves is therefore indispensable to continued prosperity, and the policy of this department for their protection and use will invariably be guided by this fact, always bearing in mind that the conservative use of these resources in no way conflicts with their permanent value.

The World Commission on Environment and Development (commonly known as the Brundtland Commission) proffered a mantra of sorts on sustainable development: to meet communities' current needs without compromising the ability of future generations to meet theirs. Similarly, the National Research Council Board on Sustainable Development (1999) described it as meshing, in the long run, society's developmental goals with its environmental limits and noting that effective efforts at sustainability require society's collective, uncertain and adaptive behaviors vis-à-vis its goals and modus operandi. Both descriptions indicate the trionym of sustainable development, most commonly referred to as the three E's—economic opportunity, environmental protection, social equity (e.g., Fedkiw, 2001):

- Economic opportunity sustains a healthy economy that will create meaningful jobs, reduce poverty, and provide high quality of life in an increasingly competitive global environment.
- Environmental protection ensures the availability of a healthy ecosystem.
- Social equity ensures that all people have access to justice and have the opportunity to achieve economic, environmental and social well-being.

That trionym is inarguably consistent with the concerns of Africans for healthy economies and environments that meet the dire needs of the present generation, as well as those of the future, while pari passu enhancing the quality of the environment. It also has major ethical implications for the regnant actions of corporations in their midst. Such implications are even more important when cast in a historical context: At the turn of the 20th century, corporations tended to disregard the public interest willy-nilly. And even as recently as one-half century ago, corporations had so much power over the marketplace and so little responsibility to society (Bowen, 1953; Eberstadt, 1977; Elbing & Elbing, 1967; Levitt, 1958).

A GLOBAL ETHIC

The Montréal Process, world summits on the environment, and protest movements point to a ferment in the investigation of corporate behavior vis-à-vis sustainable development. Stakeholder theory and CSP, together, provide the framework for communicating with multiple audiences. Stakeholder theory has attracted its own debates on its ethical foundation and the issue of who stakeholders really are. On the one hand, Ulmer and Sellnow (2000) argue that it lacks a normative foundation. On the other, Donaldson and Preston (1995) argue that the theory is both functionalist and normative and suggest that one way to construct that foundation is to connect the theory with more fundamental philosophical concepts.

A second criticism is that stakeholders are not always clearly defined. Mitchell, Agle, and Wood (1997) state that to identify stakeholders and ascertain their salience require a consideration of their influence, legitimacy of relationship with corporation, and urgency of their claim on a company. Therefore, the implications of stakeholder theory and of CSP for fostering an ethic for the global corporation's contribution to sustainable development are subsumed under five non-discrete elements, as a communication ethic: communitarianism, community engagement, mutuality of interests, the common good, commerce and citizenship.

Communitarianism

For the African, the very notion of the self is counterproductive to her or his penchant for communitarianism, which, in turn, explains the African penchant for tribal institutions and her or his strong loyalty to the tribe in preference to the nation. Moemeka (1997, 1998) distinguishes among individualistic, collectivist, and communalistic cultures and concludes that in African societies the latter are supreme: "I am because we are." An African takes action or expresses an opinion based on its implied consistency with norms and thought patterns in a group (Nwankwo & Nzelibe, 1990). Obeng-Quaidoo (1985) referred to that phenomenon as the non-individuality of the African.

Communitarianism—what Moemeka (1997) refers to as the supremacy of the community—gives the community pride of place as supreme authority over the individual, who, whenever necessary, defers to community interest. "The value of such a communalistic principle," writes Moemeka, "lies in the unity that it sustains, the selfless service that it generates, and the valor (honor) that it inspires" (p. 174). Similarly, Traber (1997) argues that communitarian rationale "does not *simply* mean that the community is supreme and that individuals have to subordinate themselves to it. It does, however, mean that there is a moral commitment to community, aiming at both civic order and civic transformation" (emphasis added, p. 339). Preconditions for being-in-community, as Traber (1997) puts it, are truth-telling, social justice, solidarity, and human dignity.

For a corporation to adopt communitarianism requires that it unify with its stakeholders who are also community residents; that it seek out areas where its citizenship can be most creatively accomplished; and that it set itself as a model of exemplary corporate behavior by telling the truth, engaging in a struggle for equitable social order and embracing the ethical norm of human dignity. Global corporations that disregard the cultural attributes of

African thought and behavioral patterns or whose management styles run afoul of cultural practices perpetuate hostile work environments and earn the ire of local residents, as was the case with the Shell Petroleum Development Company in Nigeria.

Its parent, the Royal Dutch Shell Company Group, had been a target of environmentalists, particularly Greenpeace and the Movement for the Survival of the Ogoni People in southeastern Nigeria, because its actions were largely antithetical to communitarianism. In 1958 Shell began oil exploration in Nigeria's Niger delta, where the company's pipelines, about 18 inches above ground, crisscrossed the Niger delta. Flames from intense heat at points where gas burns made farming difficult and environmental damage palpable. Oil accounts for 90 percent of Nigeria's export earnings. Yet, compensation to the Ogoni people was low; their homeland had been mired in abject poverty; unemployment was high; and environmental damage on, and raids against, Ogoni communities were pronounced. Shell had colluded with Nigeria's late dictator, Sani Abacha, to amass weapons and ammunitions for the Nigerian police, to despoil the Ogoni people's homeland, and to leave them with nothing more than a pittance in royalties. Citizen protests, arrests, assassination, and intimidation were common. Shell Oil was insular, arrogant, inward-looking, defensive, and uncommunicative (Mirvis, 2000).

In 1995, Shell Company and its supporters in Nigeria's then-military government announced that there would be an environmental survey of the Niger delta. The panel was stacked with people sympathetic to both the Nigerian government and the company. The findings of that survey were fraught with irregularities. There were more protests and a call for an end to decades of environmental pollution and the payment of a fair share of oil revenues to the Ogoni people. Shell conceded, promising to respond more effectively to community demands, building schools, hospitals, community centers, and roads. It was reported that there was an overhaul of its culture into which was integrated citizenship strategies (Mirvis, 2000; Vidaver-Cohen & Altman, 2000). Such changes earned it worldwide admiration, the status of Britain's "most admired company," and the rank of top five in Europe (Vidaver-Cohen & Altman, 2000). However, the company's critics still contend that it was all too little, too late, and that real transformation in Shell's environmental and social performance in the Niger delta is yet to come (Mirvis, 2000).

Other oil companies in the delta were also targets. In July 2002, delta women took more than 700 Chevron Texaco workers hostage for the same reasons that Shell Oil had been under community attack. The women threatened to disrobe before their hostages as a cultural shaming experience for them. Chevron Texaco offered to employ 30 villagers, to build schools, community centers and a water-purification system, and to improve public health facilities in villages.

Community Engagement

Organizations use moral reasoning to arrive at organizational decisions, have cultures that embrace rationality and respect, and are dependent on multiple parties to create and recreate their own cultures and communities. As Christians, Ferré, and Fackler (1993) state, "Organizations are cultures in the sense that their members engage in producing a shared organizational reality" (p. 131). Working with communities entails much more than getting involved in community projects; it requires setting up a system for community input well before major projects are under way; it requires searching for channels by which community views are represented in organizational decision-making; it requires that corporations, as moral agencies, enunciate and share their cultures with their stakeholders; it requires that business and community interests be aligned for their mutual benefit; and it requires the sharing of organizational symbolism with all stakeholders and being influenced by that of the latter. It is a mutual process, one that might suggest that corporations "get more of what they want when they give up some of what they want" (Grunig & White, 1992, p. 39).

Engaging the grassroots is illustrated in Kenya's Green Belt Movement, whose operations fan across the entire continent. Began in 1977 when logging and deforestation were factors in the deterioration of the country's ecosystem, it employs some 100,000 people, mostly women, who have planted more than 20 million trees, which, in turn, supply their planters with fruits, leaves, and branches that are sold occasionally to local manufacturers and retailers. The movement also collaborates with global companies to promote organic farming and sustainable practices. The local women, the business sector and the environment benefit from efforts grounded in the local environment.

Key questions have been raised regarding community engagement. For example, What stakeholders should participate in corporate governance, and what are the ways and means of their representation? (Etzioni, 1998). For community representation, Etzioni suggests that communities be granted a voice in approximate proportion to the size and duration of their respective investments in corporations. And Mitchell, Agle, and Wood (1997) point to stakeholder influence, legitimacy and urgency of claim as criteria for determining stakeholder salience.

Mutuality of Interests

From the preceding section, it is clear that the various audiences who comprise an organization's stakeholders do not have equal rank—and do not communicate with the organization with equal intensity. Even if they do, do they have consistent interests? Do investors have the same community-development interests as short-term employees? Do creditors and community residents have mutual interests? And does the corporation use what Post (2000) describes as the "glocal" approach, in which it works with a local partner or builds a visible local presence through activities in the community, thereby recognizing the importance of integrating global business strategies and local interests?

As noted earlier, in June 1998, the World Bank provided a loan for further construction of a dam on the Orange River, a move that irked environmentalists who wanted impact studies on possible environmental damage before project implementation. Residents on the path of the dam saw the project as potentially hazardous to the ecosystem and as a telltale of economic hardships. Such chasm in expectations and possible outcomes is sometimes apparent between employee interest and the direction of organizational investments.

In 1998, T. Coleman Andrews III, a U.S. citizen, was hired as chairman and president of South African Airways (SAA), the national airline that was competing for passengers with a regional airline, Sun Air, and hemorrhaging financially. He flooded South Africa with cheap fares, running black-owned Sun Air into bankruptcy, but was unable to make SAA profitable. In slightly more than three years on the job, Coleman used an assertive, can-do, streamlined management style in his attempt to get the airline into the black. His management style was not driven by the African value of reaching a consensus, of demonstrating deference to authority or seniority, or of listening intently to employee complaints and acting on them. His greatest stumbling block: employees who did not see their own professional interests and cultural values as consistent with those of upper management. Tensions grew and employees embarrassed Coleman with a long list of grievances, forcing him to resign in March 2002.

As noted at the outset, African communities have development challenges, which may seem far-fetched to, say, a creditor of a multinational corporation. But there are areas in which the interests of all stakeholders intersect: All, in some measure, are investors and have a stake in the well-being of a corporation. An African community invests in a company by offering land or space, building roads and making available its labor. An investor does the same thing by giving up initial capital for future profit. Creditors make short- or long-term investments by providing services or products for future cash settlements.

Thus, to the extent that stakeholder theory accepts the legitimacy of *all* stakeholders as investors of sorts in a corporation, it is important that investors be treated as means, not as ends. Investments are a means toward corporate profitability. Therefore, investors should be treated equitable as principals whose interests are consistent with those of the corporation. One element in the trionym of sustainable development is social equity, which means that all stakeholders should have a shot at communication opportunities for social well-being and self-improvement.

Common Good

This has been defined as "everything that is good to more than one person, that perfects more than one person, that is common to all" (Argandoña, 1998, p. 1095). It is the fulfill-ment of a company's purpose as a company, that is, the creation of conditions that enable its stakeholders achieve their personal goals. The good *for* the individual translates into the good *of* the community. The 1905 letter sent by United States Secretary of Agriculture James Wilson on the transfer of authority over national forestlands to the United States Forest Service noted that "all land is to be devoted to its most productive use for the permanent good of the whole people, and not for the temporary benefit of individuals or companies" (Pinchot, 1974, p. 261). The common good, as a communication ethic, transcends the values and interests of any single group.

It can be argued that stakeholder theory is inherently divisive because it categorizes publics in accordance with their influence and legitimacy and the urgency of their corporate claims. It can be viewed as antithetical to the tenets of sustainable development, principles that have been the armor of protest publics. If those were so, then, it stands to reason that organizational communication of the common good be done in a fair, judicious, equitable manner that does not pit one group against another. Inter-group dynamics can determine what group is ahead of other groups in terms of returns on investment—creating group conflicts.

Commerce and Citizenship

Admittedly, public- and private-sector agencies have different goals: the former operates supposedly in the public interest, the latter in that of their investors, that is, to yield returns on their investment. Perhaps that is where the difference ends. In reality, both sectors have more similarities than differences: to serve as good citizens of the societies in which they operate.

An organization's level of social performance is a key measure of its citizenship. But what is good corporate citizenship? Davenport's (2000) Delphi study identified three key indicators of corporate citizenship: (1) the use of rigorous ethical standards in business dealings; (2) company commitment to all stakeholders—community, consumers, employ-ees, investors, suppliers; and (3) company commitment to the environment, that is, through programs such as recycling, waste and emission abatement, and impact assessment through environmental audits. Participants also identified 20 principles of corporate citizenship—such as invests in communities in which a business operates, respects the rights of consumers, invites and engages in genuine dialogue with stakeholders, engages in responsible human-resource management, and engages in fair trading practices with suppliers.

It is critical, then, that global organizations communicate with their stakeholders about their commitment to (1) ethical principles in business conduct, (2) all stakeholders, and (3) to the environment. That communication can be enabled by corporate participation in events or the use of innovative ideas that project activities grounded in ethics and in stakeholder and environmental commitment.

I present here two architectural illustrations of environmental sensitivity. First, in 2001, the United States Department of Agriculture Forest Products Laboratory, in collaboration with the Southern Forest Products Association, the Engineered Wood Association, and the Advanced Housing Research Center, completed a four-bedroom, 2,200-square-foot research demonstration house that showcases moisture-resistant construction techniques, proper building practices for moisture control, the use of recycled materials in home-building, resource sustainability, and energy efficiency. The building sits on a property that adjoins the campus of the University of Wisconsin, Madison. It demonstrates how the use of advanced technologies and alternative methods for home-building can improve energy efficiency, affordability, durability, environmental performance, disaster resistance, and the overall safety of housing.

Second, the use of similar technologies is being planned for urban renewal in South Africa, where Earthlife Africa in 1993 conceived the Greenhouse People's Environmental Center Project. Indigenous technologies and materials will be used to build the house at Joubert Park, in Johannesburg. The house, like that in Wisconsin, will be an epitome of green values and practices. Research on sustainable technologies and materials that will be used in the building is being done at the University of Witwatersrand.

CONCLUDING REMARKS

This chapter is based on the notion that two theoretical constructs—stakeholder theory and corporate social performance—be used as key elements in developing a communication ethic for managing sustainable development in sub-Saharan Africa. Both constructs have ethical underpinnings. In communicating the "good news" about corporate involvement in sustainable development, it is important that communication strategies used acknowledge the shift from information distribution (which, at heart, is publicity or outputs) to organizational positioning and relationship management, the ideals of symmetrical organizational communication.

That shift can symbolize the overarching importance of impressions or images that are often sought, cultivated and influenced by organizational actions. It can also be an indicator of a corporation's deliberate attempt to regulate and control information—and its presentation—so that it is consistent with the mutual interest and common good of all stakeholders. That shift, then, seems well suited to a two-pronged analysis. The first is at the corporate or organizational level, the second at the interpersonal (or individual) level.

ORGANIZATIONAL LEVEL

Communication at the corporate level requires the interplay of three dimensions: (1) visibility, that is, how prominent a corporation is in a community; (2) valence, that is, the tone in which, or the extent to which, a corporation is perceived (or portrayed) in a generally positive or negative light; and (3) public salience, that is, whether it is perceived (or portrayed) as relating directly to the common good of stakeholders.

INTERPERSONAL LEVEL

The corresponding dimensions at the *interpersonal* level, that is, the employee-villager or employee-supplier dyad, are as follows: (1) familiarity, that is, the extent to which a community resident is aware of the commitment of a corporation to the environmental; (2) favorableness, that is, a villager's evaluation of corporate activities; and (3) personal salience, that is, the extent to which corporate activities identify with the well-being or common good of community residents.

All six dimensions—at both organizational and interpersonal levels—bear on a corporation's three goals:

- To generate, through information-sharing, awareness of ethical corporate activities among all of its stakeholders.

- To better position the corporation as a major player in improving ecosystem health, —that is, brand-positioning of its "green" activities.

- To build and strengthen relationships between the corporation and all stakeholders.

RECOMMENDATIONS

The preceding analysis leads to two recommendations. The first is that the application of stakeholder theory and CSP be grounded in a communication ethic that emphasizes ethical relationship-building as necessary for communicating the "good news" of tangible corporate contributions to sustainable development in Africa. It is also advisable that attempts be made to extend that communication to the ideal two-way symmetrical process in which organizations use communication to manage conflict and improve understanding among stakeholders and to promote organization-stakeholder change.

The second is that corporations in sub-Saharan Africa engage in a culture-balancing act by co-opting indigenous cultures into their practices in ways that will foster the common good of all stakeholders, in ways that are consistent with the principles of sustainable development, and in ways that will ensure "the permanent good of the whole people, and not for the temporary benefit" (Pinchot, 1974, p. 216) of those corporations. Such corporate actions will assuage the activist groups, engender better relationships between the global corporation and its stakeholders, demonstrate sensitivity to the environmental impacts of corporate actions, enable a number of global organizations to rise well above their occasional disreputable status, and, above all, foster and sustain a region's much-needed development.

REFERENCES

Argandoña, A. (1998). The stakeholder theory and the common good. *Journal of Business Ethics, 17*, 1093–1102.

Aupperle, K. E., Carroll, A. B., & Hatfield, J. D. (1985). An empirical investigation of the relationship between corporate social responsibility and profitability. *Academy of Management Journal, 28*, 446–463.

Bansal, P., & Roth K. (2000). Why companies go green: A model of ecological responsiveness. *Academy of Management Journal, 43*, 717–736.

Belkaoui, A. (1976). The impact of the disclosure of the environmental effects of organizational behavior on the market. *Financial Management, 5*, 26–31.

Bowen, H. R. (1953). *Social responsibilities of the businessman*. New York: Harper & Brothers.

Carroll, A. B. (1979). A three-dimensional conceptual model of corporate social performance. *Academy of Management Review, 4*, 497–505.

Carroll, A. B. (1989). *Business and society.* Cincinnati, OH: Southwestern.

Carroll, A. B. (1991). Corporate social performance measurement: A commentary on methods for evaluating an elusive construct. In J. E. Post (Ed.), *Research in corporate social performance and policy: A research annual, Vol. 12* (pp. 385–401). Greenwich, CT: JAI Press.

Carson, R. (1962). *Silent spring.* New York: Houghton Mifflin.

Christians, C. G., Ferré, J. P., & Fackler, P. M. (1993). *Good news: Social ethics and the press.* New York: Oxford University Press.

Cohen, S. (1995). Stakeholders and consent. *Business & Professional Ethics, 14*, 3–16.

Davenport, K. (2000). Corporate citizenship: A stakeholder approach for defining corporate social performance and identifying measures for assessing it. *Business and Society, 39*, 210–219.

Dillon, P. W., & Fischer, K. (1992). *Environmental management in corporations.* Medford, MA: Tufts University Center for Environmental Management.

Donaldson, T. (1989). *The ethics of international business.* New York: Oxford University Press.

Donaldson, T., & Preston, L. (1995). The stakeholder theory of the modern corporation: Concepts, evidence, implications. *Academy of Management Review, 20*, 65–91.

Eberstadt, N. (1977). What history tells us about corporate responsibilities. In A. B. Carroll (Ed.), *Managing corporate social responsibility* (pp. 17–22). Boston: Little Brown.

Elbing, A. O., Jr., & Elbing, C. J. (1967). *The value issue of business.* New York: McGraw-Hill.

Etzioni, A. (1998). A communitarian note on stakeholder theory. *Business Ethics Quarterly, 8*, 679–691.

Evan, W. M., & Freeman, R. E. (1988). A stakeholder theory of the modern corporation: Kantian capitalism. In T. L. Beauchamp & N. E. Bowie (Eds.), *Ethical theory and business* (pp. 97–106). Englewood Cliffs, NJ: Prentice-Hall.

Fedkiw, J. (2001, March-April). *Sustainability and the pathway hypothesis.* Paper presented at the American Society for Environmental History/Forest History Society Joint Annual Meeting, Durham, NC.

Frederick, W. C. (1986). *Theories of corporate social performance: Much done, more to do.* Working paper, Joseph M. Katz Graduate School of Business, University of Pittsburgh.

Freeman, R. E. (1984). *Strategic management: A stakeholder approach.* Boston: Pitman.

Freeman, R. E., & Gilbert, D. R. (1988). *Corporate strategy and the search for ethics.* Englewood Cliffs: Prentice-Hall.

Freeman, R. E., & Reed, D. L. (1983). Stockholders and stakeholders: A new perspective on corporate governance. *California Management Review, 25*, 88–106.

Frooman, J. (1997). Socially irresponsible and illegal behavior and shareholder wealth: A meta-analysis of event studies. *Business & Society, 36*, 221–249.

Graves, S. B., & Waddock, S. A. (1994). Institutional owners and corporate social performance. *Academy of Management Journal, 37*, 1035–1046.

Grunig, J. E. (2001). Two-way symmetrical public relations: Past, present and future. In R. L. Heath (Ed.), *Handbook of public relations* (pp. 11–30). Thousand Oaks, CA: Sage.

Grunig, J. E., & Repper, F. C. (1992). Strategic management, public, and issues. In J. E. Grunig (Ed.), *Excellence in public relations and communication management* (pp. 117–157). Hillsdale, NJ: Lawrence Erlbaum and Associates.

Grunig, J. E., & White, J. (1992). The effect of worldviews on public relations theory and practice. In J. E. Grunig (Ed.), *Excellence in public relations and communication management* (pp. 31–64). Hillsdale, NJ: Lawrence Erlbaum and Associates.

Held, D., McGrew, A., Goldblatt, D., & Perraton, J. (1999). *Global transformations: Economics, politics and culture.* Cambridge: Polity Press.

Jones, T. M., & Wicks, A. C. (1999). Convergent stakeholder theory. *Academy of Management Review, 24*, 206–221.

Lawrence, A. T., & Morell, D. (1995). Leading-edge environmental management: Motivation, opportunity, resources, and processes. In D. Collins & M. Starik (Eds.), *Research in corporate social performance and policy, supplement 1* (pp. 99–126). Greenwich, CT: JAI Press.

Levitt, T. (1958). The dangers of social responsibility. *Harvard Business Review, 36*, 41–50.

Ledingham, J. A., & Bruning, S. D. (1998). Relationship management in public relations: Dimensions of an organization-public relationship. *Public Relations Review, 24*, 55–66.

Ledingham, J. A. (2001). Government-community relationships: Extending the relational theory to public relations. *Public Relations Review, 27*, 285–295.

Luce, R. A., Barber, A. E., & Hillman, A. J. (2001). Good deeds and misdeeds: A mediated model of the effect of corporate social performance on organizational attractiveness. *Business & Society, 40*, 397–415.

Marsden, C. (2000). The new corporate citizenship of big business: Part of the solution to sustainability? *Business and Society Review, 105*, 9–25.

Marsh, G. P. (1864). *Man and nature; or, physical geography as modified by human action.* New York: Charles Scribner.

McKee, J. F. (2001, January 26). Saving the environment, one (fewer) child at a time. *The Chronicle Review,* p. B20.

McNatt, R., & Light, L. (1998, February 16). Good works—and great profits. *Business Week, 8.*

McWilliams, A., & Siegel, D. (2000). Corporate social responsibility and financial performance: Correlations or misspecification?" *Strategic Management Journal, 21*, 603–609.

Meyerson, A. R. (1999, January 31). Techies discover the joys of giving. *The New York Times*, pp. 1, 11.

Mirvis, P. H. (2000). Transformation at Shell: Commerce and citizenship. *Business and Society Review, 105*, 63–84.

Mitchell, R. K., Agle, B. R., & Wood, D. J. (1997). Toward a theory of stakeholder identification and salience: Defining the principle of who and what really counts. *Academy of Management Review, 22*, 853–886.

Moemeka, A. A. (1997). Communalistic societies: Community and self-respect as African values. In C. Christians & M. Traber (Eds.), *Communication ethics and universal values* (pp. 170–193). Thousand Oaks, CA: Sage.

Moemeka, A. A. (1998). Communalism as a fundamental dimension of culture. *Journal of Communication, 48*, 118–141.

Muirhead, S. A., Bennett, C. J., Berenbeim, R. E., Kao, A., & Vidal, D. J. (2002, July). *Corporate citizenship in the new century: Accountability, transparency, and global stakeholder engagement.* New York: The Conference Board.

National Research Council Board on Sustainable Development. (1999). *Our common journey: A transition toward sustainability.* Washington, DC: National Academy Press.

Nwankwo, R. L. N., & Nzelibe, C. G. (1990). Communication and conflict management in African development. *Journal of Black Studies, 20*, 253–266.

Obeng-Quaidoo, I. (1985). Culture and communication research methodologies in Africa: A proposal for change. *Gazette: International Journal for Mass Communication Studies, 36*, 109–120.

O'Connor, J. (2000, November). Corporate citizenship. *Industrial Distribution, 89*, 142.

Pava, M. L., & Krausz, J. (1996). The association between corporate social responsibility and financial performance: The paradox of social cost. *Journal of Business Ethics, 15*, 321–357.

Phillips, R.A. (1997). Stakeholder theory and a principle of fairness. *Business Ethics Quarterly, 7*, 51–66.

Pinchot, G. (1974). *Breaking new ground.* Washington, DC: Island Press.

Posnikoff, J. F. (1997). Disinvestment from South Africa: They did well by doing good. *Contemporary Economic Policy, 15*, 76–86.

Post, J. E. (2000). Moving from geographic to virtual communities: Global corporate citizenship in a dot-com world. *Business and Society Review, 105*, 27–46.

Preston, L. (1978). Analyzing corporate social performance: Methods and results. *Journal of Contemporary Business, 7*, 135–150.

Quinn, D., & Jones, T. M. (1995). An agent morality view of business policy. *Academy of Management Review, 20*, 22–42.

Riordan, C. M., Gatewood, R. D., & Bill, J. B. (1997). Corporate image: Employee reactions and implications for managing corporate social performance. *Journal of Business Ethics, 16*, 401–412.

Sharfman, M. (1996). The construct validity of the Kinder, Lydenberg, and Domini social performance ratings data. *Journal of Business Ethics, 15*, 287–296.

Solomon, R. C., & Hanson, K. R. (1985). *It's good business*. Atheneum: New York.

Stanwick, P. A., & Stanwick, S. D. (1998). The relationship between corporate social performance, and organizational size, financial performance, and environmental performance: An empirical examination. *Journal of Business Ethics, 17*, 195–204.

Strand, R., Levine, R., & Montgomery, D. (1981). Organizational entry preferences based upon social and personnel policies: An information integration perspective. *Organizational Behavior and Human Performance, 27*, 50–68.

Teoh, S. H., Welch, I., & Wazzan C. P. (1999). The effect of socially activist investment policies on the financial markets: Evidence from the South African boycott. *Journal of Business, 72*, 35–89.

Traber, M. (1997). Conclusion: An ethics of communication worthy of human beings. In C. Christians & M. Traber (Eds.), *Communication ethics and universal values*. (pp. 327–343.). Thousand Oaks, CA: Sage.

Turban, D. B., & Greening, D. W. (1997). Corporate social performance and organizational attractiveness to prospective employees. *Academy of Management Journal, 40*, 658–672.

Ulmer, R. R., & Sellnow, T. L. (2000). Consistent questions of ambiguity in organizational crisis communication: Jack in the Box as a case study. *Journal of Business Ethics, 25*, 143–155.

Vidaver-Cohen, D., & Altman, B. W. (2000). Corporate citizenship in the new millennium: Foundation for an architecture of excellence. *Business and Society Review, 105*, 145–168.

Waddock, S. A., & Graves, S. B. (1997). The corporate social performance-financial performance link. *Strategic Management Journal, 18*, 303–319.

Waddock, S., & Smith, N. (2000). Relationships: The real challenge of corporate global citizenship. *Business and Society Review, 105*, 47–62.

Wartick, S. L., & Cochran, P. L. (1985). The evolution of the corporate social performance model. *Academy of Management Review 10*, 758–769.

Went, R. (2000). *Globalization: Neoliberal challenge, radical responses*. London: Pluto.

Windsor, D. (1998, June). *The definition of stakeholder status*. Paper presented at the annual conference of the International Association for Business and Society, Kona-Kailua, HI.

Winn, M. (1995). Corporate leadership and policies for the natural environment. In D. Collins & M. Starik (Eds.), *Research in corporate social performance and policy, supplement 1* (pp. 127–161). Greenwich, CT: JAI Press.

Wolfe, R., & Aupperle, K. (1991). Introduction to corporate social performance: Methods for evaluating an elusive construct. In J. E. Post (Ed.), *Research in corporate social performance and policy: A research annual, Vol. 12* (pp. 265–268). Greenwich, CT: JAI Press.

Wood, D. J. (1991a). Corporate social performance revisited. *Academy of Management Review, 16*, 691–718.

Wood, D. J. (1991b). Social issues in management: Theory and research in corporate social performance. *Journal of Management 17*, 383–406.

Wood, D. J., & Jones, R. E. (1995). Stakeholder mismatching: A theoretical problem in empirical research on corporate social performance. *International Journal of Organizational Analysis, 3*, 229–267.

Wright, P., & Ferris, S. P. (1997). Agency conflict and corporate strategy: The effect of divestment on corporate value. *Strategic Management Journal, 18*, 77–83.

41

HOW TO MANAGE YOUR GLOBAL REPUTATION: THE PUBLIC RELATIONS AGENCY

MICHAEL MORLEY

The public relations consultancy business (or counseling, as it is known in the USA) is one of the fastest growing businesses. There is every indication that this growth will continue.

The world's ten biggest PR firms in 1990 recorded fee income of $910 million, according to O'Dwyer's *Directory of PR Firms*. Ten years later the top ten fee income had risen to $2.508 billion, as reported by the Council of PR Firms and published in *PR Week*. Since then it has been hard to make reliable comparisons because the majority of the top twenty PR firms stopped providing audited fee income results because they had become subsidiaries of publicly held corporations. Nevertheless, there is every reason to expect this upward trajectory to have continued, after a pause in 2000–2002.

There were two hammer blows to the industry just after the beginning of the new millennium. First was the 'dot-com' bust, which bankrupted many tech PR firms as well as their clients. Then came the destruction of the twin towers in New York on September 11, 2001, which sapped confidence. These two events caused a decline in fees and it took two or three years for agencies to get back to 2000 levels and start growing again. They have done this and growth is once again robust. "The astonishing growth of the PR business over the last decade has not been confined to the US and UK," says Stephen Farish, managing director of *PR Week*. "Similar growth rates have been achieved in major markets like France and Germany, and also in developing markets like Asia and Latin America, albeit from a lower base." "The fact that *PR Week* now has editions in the UK, USA, Germany and Asia is another sign of how the PR industry has become a global phenomenon in recent years. We see that growth continuing and consolidating in the years ahead."

A massive consolidation of the largest PR agencies took place as the twentieth century came to a close, and continued at the beginning of the twenty-first. Larger agencies continued to acquire smaller ones as the principal agency networks sought to flesh out their service to clients geographically and by specialty practice. To this phenomenon, new to the world of public relations (but not to advertising, which had experienced it for many years), was added a series of acquisitions that has created the formation of three global super-groups, each comprising several agency networks or brands. PR agencies owned by Omnicom, Interpublic and WPP each earn about $1 billion in annual fees. These new groupings have made bedfellows of previously fierce competitors such as Hill & Knowlton and Burson-Marsteller, now both owned by WPP, the British-based communications conglomerate.

For the most part, the well-known agency network brands that have gone to form these groups have continued much as before, each with a clear identity. The benefits of common ownership are to be found more in the back office, strategy management and investment in growth than in the more obvious client facing work. But they are increasingly working together in subtle ways to overcome client conflict problems and to create client service teams drawn from different agency brands. An example of this is the virtual team that won a sizable global assignment when IBM decided to have a major realignment and reduction in the number of PR agencies it used. Ketchum led a team composed of members of sister agencies in Omnicom, Fleishman Hillard and Brodeur to achieve a success it might have been unable to manage alone.

It will be interesting to see if this trend may lead to a more formal reorganization of the PR units within Omnicom and WPP in the way that happened within Interpublic under the leadership of PR czar, Larry Weber. Weber is an entrepreneur who by 1997 had built fees in his tech specialist firm up to $61 million, entering the world's top ten for the first time, according to O'Dwyer. He sold out to Interpublic, a laggard in public relations compared with rivals Omnicom and WPP, and quickly moved to acquire Shandwick, which had global reach but had lost its way. Following a series of subsequent acquisitions, the most important being BSMG, he reorganized the brands with a series of internal mergers leading to the first PR agency brand, Weber Shandwick, with annual fees of over $500 million on the day it started trading.

Why this sudden surge of interest in public relations on the part of advertising agencies? Even in the buoyant economy of the 1990s, it was clear that traditional advertising was not growing as fast as other communications and marketing techniques. Direct marketing, public relations and interactive marketing were not only more relevant to meeting the needs of clients but offered greater opportunity for both growth and profit. PR was no longer simply commando support for the heavy guns of advertising, it was now an important offering and business in its own right. Soon, it became apparent to the major communications conglomerates—as happened at Interpublic—that they would be at a severe competitive disadvantage without a high-quality PR component to their business. They would get poor ratings not only from clients but from investors and the financial community as well.

To understand today's universe of agencies it is useful to track its evolution.

HISTORY

The description "consultancy" or "agency," depending on the country concerned, was applied to the firms, individuals, partnerships and companies that established themselves in practice in the early years following the Second World War. At that stage the larger part of the services offered to clients consisted of practical implementation of public relations tactics and there was less emphasis on the analysis of problems and the supply of advice alone, than is the case nowadays. Because several of the early post-war practitioners had a background in journalism—although by no means all of them—the element of consulting and advice grew out of their special knowledge of the working of the media, the correct way to present a story for publication and a feeling for the way in which the public might react to publicity in the media.

A few individuals stand out as major formative figures in the establishment of the public relations consulting and agency profession on an international basis. The father of modern-day public relations in considered by many people to have been Edward Bernays who died in 1995 at the age of 103. He opened for business as a PR Counselor in New York in 1919 and his book, *Crystallizing Public Opinion* was published in 1923. Marion Harper, the creator of Interpublic, based on the international network of McCann Erickson advertising agencies, was an important figure. McCann at one time had what I believe was the largest international PR operation, which operated under the name Infoplan. Its principal offices were in the USA, UK, Germany and France. (A sister company, Marplan, was a force in the world of international market research.) Tim Traverse-Healy built Infoplan into the powerhouse of its time, an early pioneer in multinational programs for its clients, mostly in the field of fast moving consumer goods. Now Professor Traverse-Healy, and teaching at universities in England, Scotland and Ireland, he formed his own consulting company after leaving Infoplan.

The earliest international pioneer among then independent agencies was John Hill of Hill & Knowlton. Hill came from Cleveland, a comparatively small city but one which has been the birthplace of other remarkable world class professional service firms—Ernst & Young, the accountants and management consultants, and the Jones Day law firm, as well as another sizable PR agency.

Hill was a reporter on the *Cleveland Plain Dealer* before crossing the line into PR and establishing the partnership with Knowlton. Hill's client, the Iron and Steel Institute, persuaded him to relocate to New York during the big steel industry strike in 1934. The story is told that, at the time, Hill was eager neither to move nor to undertake the assignment. So when the Institute pressed him hard, he named an outrageously high fee which he was certain they would refuse.

They accepted. Hill relocated. The new New York-based firm, which was to become the industry leader for many years, was born. And John Hill established a pricing policy which ensured he and his associates were paid top dollar. But Knowlton remained in Cleveland and played no significant further role in the growth and success of the firm.

Hill & Knowlton entered Europe in the early 1960s but made a major impact internationally when they acquired Eric White and Associates in 1970, thus gaining a ready-made and strongly established network in the Asia-Pacific region. Eric White, the founder, was an Australian who in a few years established one of the world's most potent networks, including a strong operation in London.

Hill & Knowlton was quickly followed as a firm with international ambitions by Burson-Marsteller and Daniel J. Edelman, Inc., each of which established operations in London in the 1960s.

Harold Burson (the PR half of the partnership; Marsteller was an advertising man) was born in Memphis, Tennessee, and established his firm in New York. Dan Edelman was a New Yorker who established his firm in Chicago. Both had studied journalism and served during World War II in the US Army's psychological (PSYOP) warfare section, perhaps the perfect grounding for the profession both were to enter after the war.

Burson's early strength was its work for industrial companies which were attracted by the combination of media relations, trade press advertising and printed brochures the firm supplied. Edelman, on the other hand, was the acknowledged leader in public relations for consumer products and gained fame in the USA as the creator of the media tour—a PR technique in which a company spokesperson visited key markets, performed store openings, did radio and newspaper interviews and, most important of all, participated in a talk show on local television.

Now both companies offer their clients a complete range of specialist PR services from offices in most key centers around the world.

Another giant of international PR who had his career shaped during the war was France's Jacques Coup de Frejac, who died in 2007. While he always gave recognition to the leadership of the USA in most PR techniques, he opened the minds of many people in France, elsewhere in Europe and beyond, to the importance of communications. Perhaps more important, he played a major role in encouraging clients in the USA and UK to understand the French market and the European movement. De Frejac was the name given to Jacques Coup when he joined the French Resistance. He was only 18 years old when he served as aide de camp to General de Gaulle in the early years of World War II.

In the 1980s Hill & Knowlton, Burson-Marsteller and Edelman were joined by a new and differently constructed competitor—Shandwick. The newcomer was different in two obvious ways. First, it was founded in Britain, by Peter Gummer. Second, it was a publicly held company, its shares listed on the London Stock Exchange. The big three American multinationals were privately held (until Burson-Marsteller was bought by Young & Rubicam and Hill & Knowlton by J. Walter Thompson). Subsequently, both firms became linked under the ownership of WPP, following the merger frenzy of 1999/2000.

Peter Gummer (now Lord Chadlington and head of Huntsworth PLC, trying to replicate the Shandwick success formula) used a strong UK base of operations built from a number of autonomous units practising financial and investor relations, public affairs and consumer PR, and the availability of finance from Shandwick's status as a public company, to launch a major buying spree of 35 agencies in the USA, Europe and the Far East. A combination of Shandwick "paper" and cash enabled Gummer to achieve an international presence in a fraction of the time it had taken others to assemble their networks.

Shandwick owed its strength in the Asia-Pacific region to the vision and industry of another of the titans of international public relations—Taiji Kohara. The Japanese PR doyen was to his region what John Hill, Dan Edelman and Harold Burson were to the USA, Tim Traverse-Healy and Jacques Coup de Frejac to Europe and Eric White to Australia.

Having started his own company in Tokyo in 1968, Kohara went on to establish International Public Relations (IPR), an immensely strong network of offices in 43 countries stretching from Japan to Australia, which Shandwick acquired in 1988 for a price estimated to be $45 million.

The majority of PR budgets in the early years were within the control of the marketing departments of business organizations. Given that they were generally allotted as a tiny percentage of the advertising budgets, it was natural that these public relations or publicity programs were entrusted to the advertising agency. It was, after all, staffed with skilled communicators who were seen as being able to do the job required. Moreover, because they controlled the larger advertising budget, it was often assumed, if not said aloud, that they exercised considerable leverage over the media, and this would ensure the desired level of editorial publicity.

The advertising agencies took on staff as the demand for public relations services increased and established special departments. In due course, these grew into separate subsidiary companies engaged exclusively in public relations. The proper fees and costs could now be established for the services which had grown too great to be given free to large advertisers. Because they were in close contact with client organizations, and they had resources of finance and ancillary services of design, production and printing, the public relations divisions, or subsidiary companies of the large advertising agencies, established themselves as the largest "agencies" in the USA and Western Europe.

While these developments were taking place, a number of independent public relations agencies were launched and were gaining in reputation. Some specialized in a specific branch, others were generalist. They had a great strength building challenge, outside their skills as publicists: They had to survive on what they could earn by providing public relations advice and services. They had to become viable businesses, charging realistic fees covering all their costs and leaving profits for investment. Unless they managed this, they would cease to exist.

Many not only managed to exist—they flourished, and took over the leadership from the advertising agency offshoots. But the advertising agencies were not to be outdone, and ultimately once again achieved a dominant ownership position in the field of public relations. In the early 1980s, three large international PR agencies were acquired by advertising agencies anxious to re-establish themselves in public relations. Further acquisitions of major PR firms took place in the second half of the 1990s. Now, eight of the world's largest PR companies are owned by advertising agencies; another, Incepta PLC, is a publicly traded company on the London Stock Exchange; and Edelman is independent and privately owned by the Edelman family and senior executives of the company.

The description "public relations agency" today is suitable, but still less than accurate, for the majority of firms. While there are a number of people practising as consultants only (they do not engage in the practical implementation of the advice and strategies they recommend), the majority of public relations companies are both consultants and agents. This is the reason why, together with the original ad agency public relations divisions, the public relations agency is usually referred to as "the agency."

For the majority of agencies, there are two clearly defined roles:

1. The provision of expert and objective advice to clients based on a knowledge of the mechanisms that will affect the opinion of key publics, allied to a good knowledge of those clients' organizations, their industries and markets. In this, consultants will draw on their own, and their firm's, experience gained from previous assignments of a similar nature.
2. To act as the public relations agent of the client, assuming responsibility for executing agreed-upon programs on the client's behalf. This might involve, for example, the establishment of an information office for the client, the provision of public relations personnel, the production of various printed and videotaped materials, the execution of events, and the conduct of media relations and publicity efforts.

Often one agency will fulfill both roles, with the senior staff (partners or directors) providing the consulting or counseling service and then involving other executive staff in the agency function. It is not unusual, however, for a client organization to retain the services of more than one agency to meet its needs for advice on the one hand—often specialist in nature—and executional services on the other.

TYPES OF AGENCY

A large proportion of modern agencies could describe themselves as "full service," in that they have staffs with a blend of experience that enables them to offer both consulting and agency services across the different "specialties" within public relations—for example, traditional media relations, online media relation, technical communications, government relations, employee communications, international communications and marketing support. Even if the full range of highly qualified specialist advice is not available within the agency, the "full service" firm will, in most instances, be able to bring the necessary qualified person into its team as a part-time adviser.

The 1970s saw the rapid development of a number of strictly specialist agencies. The description "specialist" can be applied in a number of ways.

There are agencies which specialize in particular branches of industry such as firms which operate exclusively in the field of health and medicine or those which confine themselves to clients involved in travel, tourism and related activities, and yet more which concentrate on fashion, beauty, household products and food.

More generally, however, specialization means that the firm restricts itself to one of the sub-specializations or "practices" of public relations, such a financial communications, government relations, and employee and community relations.

PUBLIC RELATIONS AGENCY STRUCTURES

Although some of the largest PR agencies are now owned by ad agencies or communications conglomerates, most continue to operate as autonomous units. The majority of public relations agencies are privately owned, limited companies. It is perhaps surprising that, with aspirations to professional status, this form of corporate structure for public relations firms should be the norm, rather than the partnership structure to be found in the accounting and legal professions. Whether public, ad agency-owned, or private, most public relations companies have some method of profit-sharing to enable at least the senior staff to participate in the success of the enterprise.

Because the origins of many public relations companies are linked with advertising agencies, it is common, but erroneous, to compare structures and costs between these two branches of communications. Public relations agencies are closer, in many ways, to management consultants, accounting and law firms. They charge fees related to the time spent on client work. Although most agencies charge an additional commission on production costs, this mainly reflects the administrative costs of overseeing production and is not the principal source of income.

There are two main kinds of operational structures within public relations agencies as related to client service. The following examples relate to typical full-service rather than specialist agencies.

The first, and less usual nowadays, is the functional structure. This has an obvious relation to the usual advertising agency structure. Primary consultants and program supervisors are usually called account directors or supervisors. Their job is to advise clients, develop the strategy, budget and method of operation for the programs, and then mobilize the resources of the agency and its subcontractors.

In a functionally structured agency, the staff are specialists in one or another aspect of public relations and invariably work on all the agency's clients, under the supervision of the account director. Take for example a program with extensive demands for a wide range of actions, including an intensive press relations campaign, a strong effort with local radio stations, a briefing for elected officials and an audio-visual presentation for general use. The account director will brief the head of the agency's press office, the specialist whose sole task is working with radio and TV, the public affairs specialist and an executive from the audio-visual and film section.

In my view, while the merits of the functional system are clear, the disadvantages only become obvious in practice. Too many people are involved, those responsible for the actual execution do not have close enough contact with the client and, in general, the time of the account director and the functional executives is spread across too wide a range of projects for sufficient commitment and attention to be given to each. Another problem is that the person aspiring to a broad career in public relations can easily get trapped in a single functional department.

The more usual structure now is that of the account group, in which the account director and one or more executives are responsible for a group of clients whose interests are in some way related.

Many agencies form their account groups by public relations or industry specialty (rather than functional specialty). They will have, for example, account groups for clients whose needs are in investor relations, and others for government relations, technical and industrial public relations, consumer marketing public relations, health care and so on. The heads of these groups might have started as specialists but they will have been trained and have developed over time as competent all-round consultants and executives. Alternatively, they may have started as all-rounders but then developed a specialist skill. In such an agency, the top management will have discussed the client's needs fully with him.

If the work is largely, say, public affairs, the client will be served by the government relations group. The head of this group will offer consulting services and will also undertake or supervise directly much of the day-to-day work of the program. If the client is large and the program involves intensive activity in, say, government relations, investor relations and marketing public relations, the work will be divided into three programs undertaken by three different groups, with a management coordinator appointed to oversee the total quality of service to the client. Such account groups are, in effect, mini-agencies, and in many cases are managed as profit centers. They provide an opportunity to learn teamwork and offer training for senior management positions.

PUBLIC RELATIONS CONSULTANCY COSTS

Agencies are in business to make a profit for shareholders and a good living for their staff, as well as to offer service to clients. In general, they seek to make an overall profit from income of between 10 and 20 percent before tax from the fees they charge clients. Dividends to shareholders and profit-sharing to staff are paid from this profit. The balance goes to finance the growth of the agency and provide it with the necessary reserves to ensure stability. Thus an agency with an income of $10,000,000 per annum might expect to make a pre-tax profit of $1,500,000. A part of that—say, $500,000—might be allocated for profit-sharing or an annual bonus. A prudent board might also have invested say $250,000 in new equipment as the likely profit became known. Of the remaining balance of $750,000, close to 40 percent ($300,000) will go toward taxes, leaving $450,000 to cover dividends and cash to be retained in the business. This will be needed to finance cash flow and growth.

To achieve that profit, however, requires good management and adherence to a pricing policy.

Staff salaries are the largest single cost of an agency. Surveys of members of the Public Relations Consultants Association (PRCA) have shown that in nearly all agencies staff salaries are around 50 percent of income. So our "sample" $10,000,000 agency will have an annual salary bill of $5,000,000. The second largest single cost (usually about 10 percent) is rent. Then come all the other costs, such as telephone, travel, entertaining, hiring and training, which should not amount to more than another 25 percent if 15 percent profit is to be made. When an agency discusses its costs openly with clients, it seldom has difficulties in getting fees appropriate to the assignment. Following are the main fee systems in operation.

Fixed Fee

This is negotiated annually with the client, based on historical knowledge of the volume of work and time involved, or is estimated based on agency experience with similar programs. The fee is usually paid monthly.

Retainer Fee and Hourly or *per diem* Charges

In this system, clients pay a very modest retainer fee, which means they can draw on the agency's services when needed, but the retainer does not automatically "buy" any service and it is payable even if no work is done. When service is needed, an agreed hourly rate is charged to the client. This might be broken down by the hours put in by specific individuals, for example one rate for a senior consultant, another for a junior staff member, and shown as such to the client on the invoice. It is also quite usual for a uniform "team" time rate to be established, which reflects the average of the combined time of senior consultants, executives and support staff. In certain countries, hourly rates are established and recommended by national public relations institutes.

Minimum Fee and Hourly Charges

This approach is often confused with the retainer system because of similarities, but there are significant differences. The minimum fee is invariably more substantial than the retainer. It reflects the fact that the agency has calculated that it is likely to spend a given amount of time each month working for the client and has assigned the staff to do so. The hourly charge comes into operation when the basic time has been used up. Thus, when clients pay a minimum fee of $10,000 per month for, say, 50 hours work at $200 per hour, and the actual time expended in the month is 60 hours, the bill for that month will be $12,000. In a month when only 40 hours work is done, the minimum fee of $10,000 is still payable. Sometimes there is a quarterly "equalization" system built in, to reflect the ups and downs that are inevitable.

It is normal for agencies to charge subcontract, production and out-of-pocket costs, in addition to the professional fee.

WORKING WITH THE CLIENT

In most respects, the working day and practical duties of public relations agency executives are similar to those of their equivalents in the public relations departments of their clients. The likelihood is that the agency people will find themselves working in close cooperation with a public relations professional or at least an experienced communicator within the client organization.

Until the mid-1960s, it was normal for clients embarking on public relations programs to make a decision either to retain an external agency or to employ a public relations executive internally. Now it is relatively common for the larger, forward-looking organizations to have established internal public relations departments and for these to retain the services of agencies in addition. In the case of well-staffed client PR departments, the prime need is for expert, objective external PR consultants. In other cases where the internal staff is small but there is going to be extra work over a defined period, it makes sense to retain specific agency services.

QUALITIES OF GOOD PR CONSULTANTS

Over and above the qualities needed by *all* public relations practitioners, the following are those required of agency executives:

- Observe the successes and failures of techniques employed for other clients and bring this knowledge and experience to bear for the benefit of clients you are currently serving.
- Achieve mastery and knowledge of the subcontracting services available to the agency that will benefit clients.
- Use the resources and expertise of other professionals within the agency when faced with a complex problem.
- Sharpen your creative edge by maintaining regular contact with other professionals in the firm.
- Maintain strong powers of analysis, presentation and creativity, because an agency has to sell its services in competition with other agencies. In short, consultants have to win the right to practise public relations.
- Understand budgeting and business management, vital elements for a career in a PR organization.
- Keep abreast of media developments, new communications techniques and the current mood of public opinion on a variety of issues, if your advice is to be valued as smart, objective and reliable.
- Manage your own time expertly, allocating it appropriately among client contact, program execution, monitoring results, reporting to the client and maintaining direct contact with the media and other publics.

Though difficult, the right time blend must be achieved, because the client pays for a combination of expertise and time.

42

PUBLIC INFORMATION IN THE UNESCO: TOWARD A STRATEGIC ROLE

VINCENT DEFOURNY

The United Nations Educational, Scientific and Cultural Organization (UNESCO) was created in 1946 in response to the emerging needs of the end of World War II and to address the urgent necessity to build peace around the world, develop mutual understanding among people and cultures, and structure international co-operation in specific areas such as education, science, and culture. Although communication is not mentioned at the same level as other disciplines, it has been important to the organization since its inception, as indicated in its constitution:

> ... To realize this purpose the Organization (UNESCO) will: (a) Collaborate in the work of advancing the mutual knowledge and understanding of peoples, through all means of mass communication and to that end recommend such international agreements as may be necessary to promote the free flow of ideas by word and image ... (UNESCO Constitution, article 1) (UNESCO, 2000)

At its inception, the founders hesitated between making UNESCO a purely intellectual organization or an intergovernmental body. They finally adopted a compromise, combining the best of both structures. As a result, the organization has organic links with member state governments, academics, and intellectuals through national commissions, and with what is now called the civil society, with representatives of a large spectrum of international nongovernmental organizations. These constituencies, as well as the Secretariat comprised

---

The views or opinions expressed in this chapter are the author's and do not necessarily represent those of UNESCO.

of approximately 2000 international civil servants based mainly in Paris led by a director-general, have shaped UNESCO's unique profile over more than five decades.

The purpose of this chapter is to propose some milestones and historical references that will be useful, it is hoped, in understanding how UNESCO envisages its international public relations and how these contribute to shaping the actual organization and, thus, to identify emerging organizational patterns. One of the major ideas addressed in this section is that long-lasting difficulties to define and embrace the nature of UNESCO's organizational communication have led to hesitating conceptions and practices of public information and public relations with consequences on UNESCO's image and international influence.

REACHING THE WORLDWIDE MASSES

Founded with the idea that international specialists in education, science, and culture would enlighten national and international policies with their recognized knowledge and moral authority, UNESCO grew with great emphasis being placed on mass communication and other means of communication as major amplifiers for its programs. The first General Conference in 1946, stated the following objectives for the Mass Communication section: "to publicize the program of UNESCO as much as possible and to initiate a program of mass education, in the broadest sense" (UNESCO General Conference, 1st session, Paris, 1946).

As a consequence, the daily publication *UNESCO Monitor* was established. In addition, a weekly 15-minute radio program on education, science and culture—"UNESCO World Review"—was produced in 18 languages for dissemination by stations in 47 countries that agreed to broadcast these programs. In parallel, a survey of technical needs in the press, radio, and film was carried out in 12 countries. National and linguistic adaptations of common universal messages were at the heart of UNESCO's concerns from the beginning. Rapidly, member states realized that such activities were very demanding and two years later the report of the debates of the General Conference stated: "The Committee was emphatic in its assertion that adequate public information services are essential to the success of UNESCO. More than any of the other Specialized Agencies, UNESCO is dependent upon public understanding. The Committee noted with surprise the small staff available for public information services. . . ." (UNESCO, 1948).

The dissemination of the Universal Declaration of Human Rights, very recently adopted by the United Nations, was a major concern. It is also worth noting that the same governing body commissioned two in-depth studies on the origin of Fascism and National Socialism. But the publication of these studies soon became problematic since some countries dismissed the idea of producing them under UNESCO's imprint. The researchers' academic skills were probably not an issue. Rather, the ideological dimensions of these subjects were such that it became almost impossible to obtain universal coverage. In the end, only the analysis of National Socialism, entitled *The Third Reich*, was published by an intellectual partner nongovernmental organization (NGO) with UNESCO's assistance. Its circulation was very limited (Lacoste, 1994, p. 36).

Although political problems such as the former were arising, the prevalent organizational communication culture at that time can be easily compared with the "professional model" of Mintzberg's theory (1979). This model, similar to that usually found in the academic world, is characterized by the separation of intellectual thinking from support services. There is "knowledge" on one side, and on the other the channels by which to transmit it to those who are "ignorant." The communication process is linear and one-way and definitely not far from the "press agentry" model proposed by J. Grunig (1992).

Nevertheless, already at that time one observes that the focus on communication was subject to discussion and debate. According to L'Etang, (1999) John Grierson, the first UNESCO Director of Mass Communications and Public Information, left the Organization after only one year, criticizing the perception that public information entailed acting as "an advocate with a brief for the defense; showing up only the good points, suppressing the weak and, in fact, giving a prejudiced and false picture of the work in hand." For the same reason, he deplored UNESCO's practice of employing former journalists in the division, which he thought inevitably led to a biased approach and an overemphasis on the print media. With a visionary perspective on modern public relations, he wrote: "we need at UNESCO an almost new type of information man with powers of academic and organizational reference as well as skill in one or other of the various forms of public presentation. Such men are obviously rare" (Grierson Archive, G5: 4: 5, p. 4). There is no clear idea of what Grierson had in mind. He was probably seeing the public information officer more as a manager of communication projects than just a good copywriter. We can deduce that the organization has not been capable of drawing the lessons of this departure nor of understanding his rough definition of this new professional profile for UNESCO public information.

SEARCHING FOR THE RIGHT SKILLS

Writing has been the most important skill sought when recruiting public information officers as a result of which numerous former journalists have been recruited over the past 50 years. As a consequence, these former journalists have often had difficulties in defining their roles and positions inside the organization. They tend to believe that writing stories about UNESCO's action in line with organizational strategies is incompatible with their journalistic independence. They perceive it as unprofessional journalism.

This reflects a typical worldwide demarcation between communication specialists and journalists. Public information and public relations are perceived as perverted "journalistic" activities. The situation might find some explanation in some epistemological references. It is the author's view that this conception is directly inherited from a Cartesian understanding of reality in which there subsists the myth of a complete and objective representation of the world. Educated in such a paradigm, journalists consciously or unconsciously pretend to be in that external position from which it seems to be possible to objectively report about real facts. They feel they are in position they can reveal the unbiased truth. Despite its international statute and the multiple origins of its personnel, UNESCO is still strongly influenced by that French classical school of thinking. One reason could be because it is located in Paris. Many of Descartes's and other positivists' ideas are behind a number of UNESCO decisions. However, modern philosophy has demonstrated how reality can be seen as a social construct and how actors are embroiled in the reality they intend to depict. Therefore, a strategic understanding of the role of communication in organizational development is required to give a chance to a less negative approach to public relations activities. It is part of the shared views underlying this volume and one of the key arguments developed later in this chapter. Perhaps Grierson had the intuition that a good UNESCO communication professional would better articulate intellectual, political, and strategic capacities with technical writing skills than with journalistic ones.

In 1948, the *UNESCO Courier* partially replaced the *UNESCO Monitor* before becoming an illustrated magazine in 1954. It had its hours of glory when it was published in 35 different languages, with an overall distribution of more than 1.5 million copies, renowned authors, and largely referreed articles. Its evolution is interesting because it reflects, over the decades, the search for a journalistic identity inside UNESCO's Public Information services. For many years, the magazine was not an institutional publication, but an opinion journal tackling topics covered by UNESCO's mandate but with little reference to activities carried out or official points of view. Journalists were proud of their independence. In 2001, the decision to discontinue the *UNESCO Courier* created such emotion among member state representatives that the director general had to find a compromise in the form of a biannual publication with a new format but with the old title. In fact, the organization was supporting, at high cost, an independent internal magazine. Although its title does not make it clear, this magazine was not the organization's bulletin. This function had to be covered by other magazines such as *UNESCO Monitor* (1948–1955), *UNESCO Chronicle* (1955–1980), *UNESCO Newsletter* (1979–1987), and *UNESCO Sources* (1989–2001). Lines of authority for these periodicals were always subject to discussions and debates, as well as the journalists' administrative status. Now, they are integrated in an editorial team and their role as public information officers appears to be difficult to accommodate with their former professional identity.

In line with what was happening to similar organizations around the world, the development of UNESCO in the fifties and sixties led to the reinforcement of a bureaucratic model with numerous rules and procedures. With a sophisticated administrative manual and code of conduct, UNESCO officials anticipated every situation. There was no room for uncertainty and this led, for example, to the formal adoption of the UNESCO emblem in 1954, although it had already been used the previous year. The UNESCO logo looking like a Greek temple was communicating the greatness and ambition of the organization.

Similarly, in 1958, member states inaugurated a brand new headquarters in Paris. This modernist building, conceived by famous architects, appears as another symbol of the organization's golden age. At this point, UNESCO was well settled and ready to welcome the recently decolonized states. This strength permitted it to become engaged in a type of "pharaoh's work," such as the relocation of the Abu-Simbel Temple in Egypt to preserve it from the rising backwaters of the Aswan dam. The success of this enterprise was the result of an impressive international public campaign led by UNESCO. In March 1960 UNESCO launched an international appeal that invited the world to give financial and technical assistance for the safeguarding of the Nubian monuments. Awareness was raised about the need and urgency to safeguard the antique heritage in the Egyptian cradle of civilization. UNESCO's *public information* model was at its best during this campaign. Similar to the experiences of the government of the United States some decades earlier in mobilizing its population for World War I through public information campaigns, UNESCO managed to have real impact on a critical situation by using communication deftly. As J. Grunig and L. Grunig (1992) stated, the public information model, although related with truth, accuracy and honesty, is still an asymmetrical model because practitioners selectively disseminate information and do not truly engage in dialogue with the public. Although this model is obviously efficient in certain situations such as this, it cannot solve all types of crises. In other periods, UNESCO has had to face situations of great political and ideological complexity in which it was no longer possible to adopt a high and uncontested profile. To be efficient, public information requires this type of asymmetrical relationship between the organization and its audiences.

After this era of successes and achievements, the Cold War context of the sixties and seventies contributed to the freezing of UNESCO's actions. Organizational and political factors simultaneously contributed to the development of stereotyped attitudes and actions in the organization. System theory demonstrated that redundancy and lack of uncertainty inevitably lead to more stable states of a system. That is the reason why bureaucracies slowly evolve to reach the point where the system becomes paralyzed. Considered with some historical distance, a number of UNESCO's positions and activities during that period corresponded to an axiology where no unforeseen events could intervene. For example, it is well known that UNESCO meetings and conferences were among the few where scientists and intellectuals from the Eastern and Western blocs could meet and exchange ideas. There were some other symbolic communication activities that corresponded to this situation such as the direct television link-up between American and Soviet secondary-school children organized under the auspices of UNESCO in the early sixties.

Similarly, the *UNESCO Courier* was one of the rare periodicals authorized to cross the Iron Curtain. For both sides, it provided articles and images from unknown parts of the planet. It was a little window on the outside world. For Nelson Mandela, during his incarceration in South Africa, the *UNESCO Courier* was the sole reading material and contact with the outside world. These bridges across borders were highly appreciated by the individuals who benefited, while for the dominating powers it was a less dangerous way of staying "politically correct," at least in the short run. The public information staff at UNESCO had definitely acquired an art of writing texts that did not disturb the powerful. To prevent any problem, administrative rules very precisely defined who had and who did not have the right to speak to the media.

DIVERGENT OPINIONS

During the Cold War period, UNESCO's conference rooms progressively became an arena for the conflict between Western democratic and Eastern socialistic blocs. In the early 1980a, UNESCO was involved in the debate over the *New World Information and Communication Order* (NWICO). The question, mainly raised by Third World countries, referred to the then-domination of reporting on world issues by media from a few developed countries. Third World countries strongly felt that their views were clearly underrepresented or misinterpreted and they considered the situation unacceptable. The debate pitted two worldviews: one based on free entrepreneurship and marketplace of ideas and the other on state-controlled and planned activities aimed at development. UNESCO's role in this debate is best summed up in its *World Communication Report* (1997):

> The discussions which took place on the subject within UNESCO were extremely stormy. Tension reached a climax in the mid-1980s when the United States (1984) and the United Kingdom (1985) withdrew from the Organization. For their part, a number of international organizations representing professional media circles put all their weight into the balance in order to isolate UNESCO and to make the international community understand that the New World Information and Communication Order constituted an intolerable assault upon press freedom and the free flow of information. (UNESCO, 1997, p. 214)

The crisis about NWICO weakened the position of UNESCO because its credibility had been strongly attacked and its universality questioned. The public information efforts to remedy this situation have not yielded expected results. Instead, they have often been perceived as propaganda for theses advocated by Socialist or Third World countries. Major European newspapers attacked and criticized the director general of UNESCO, at that time, Amadou Mahtar M'Bow of Senegal. The withdrawal of important member states over this debate resulted in massive budget reduction and the resulting morale crisis almost paralyzed UNESCO. Consultative working groups were established to study ways of improving staff management, programming, budgeting, and public information. Such attempts to reform a bureaucratic system hit by a crisis repeatedly occurred in succeeding years, but outcomes and effective results appear to have been very limited. Possibly, the reason may have been that the underlying purpose of these efforts was to restore or readjust the broken system. Staff members who wanted to take initiatives and continue pursuing the original ideals had to invent, as Mintzberg (1979) put it, an *adhocracy*—a system which no longer works with rules and procedures but with personal relationships and inventiveness to bypass the blocking points.

The burial of the NWICO, which was followed by *perestroika* and the falling of the Berlin Wall, as well as the election of a new director-general, Federico Mayor Zaragoza of Spain, in 1987, created the conditions for the renewal of UNESCO. For example, after the NWICO failure, a new strategy for communication was conceived and presented to the General Conference in 1989. The purpose of the new program in the area of "communication in the service of humanity" was to "render more operational the concern of the Organization to ensure a free flow of information . . . and its wider and better balanced dissemination, without any obstacle to the freedom of expression and to strengthen communication capacities in the developing countries, so that they may participate more actively in the communication process." Press freedom continued to be the keystone of the program, entailing not only freedom of expression, but also "independence, pluralism and diversity of the [public, private and other] media." The first 600-page World *Communication Report* (UNESCO, 1997), published that year, served as the underpinning for this new policy. It reviewed recent developments in all aspects of communication throughout the world.

Applying to itself the principles of freedom of expression, diversity, and pluralism, the *UNESCO Courier* underwent a radical change. In 1989, it became an independent magazine with 56–58 pages in full four-color printing and with an editorial policy intended to systematically take an intercultural approach to world issues. It also contained interviews with leading public figures, thinkers, and creative artists. Because the editorial team was not dealing with UNESCO activities but with global issues, there was a proposal to create a new monthly called *UNESCO Sources*, to reflect day-to-day work and improve visibility among partners and the media.

REFOCUSING

Because many friends of UNESCO, including many heads of states such as Vaclav Havel and Nelson Mandela, were rediscovering the preamble of the organization's constitution and mission statement, Director-General Mayor chose to reform the Secretariat not by reorganizing its structures but by rallying energies around a new flagship—the Culture of Peace.[1] As such, this specialized UN agency on education, science, culture, and

---

[1]UNESCO's constitution states: ". . . since wars begin in the minds of men, it is in the minds of men that the defences of peace must be constructed . . ."

communication celebrated its 50th anniversary by paying tribute to the founding fathers who had given UNESCO its clear mandate: to build peace in the minds of people.

Although the United Kingdom rejoined UNESCO in 1997, and UNESCO's image improved, slowly recovering some of its lost prestige, the economic and pragmatic orientations of the 1990s did not favor the success of Mayor's reform.[2] Considered as a missionary or a preacher by some influential member states that first wanted to improve organizational efficiency, the director-general had a difficult time bringing the majority of stakeholders along with him. Too many press releases and speeches condemning peace violators in the most general terms or defending the most difficult causes with abstract words hindered UNESCO's credibility. Within the Secretariat, the existence of a parallel structure assembled under the principle of loyalty to the director-general, as well as the coexistence, in civil servants' minds, of different organizational models—reminiscent of the original *professional model*, formal rules inherited from the *bureaucratic model*, daily practices of *adhocracy*, and the internal break created by the *missionary model*—indicated the need for deep structural reform.

This reform began at the end of 1999 when the new director-general of UNESCO, Koïchiro Matsuura of Japan, was appointed. Public information was one of the pending issues that called for major changes. In their request to address this question, the governing bodies stressed that UNESCO's visibility depended as much on its ability to establish partnership and cooperation ties with social and professional circles sharing common objectives with it as on its media-oriented information policy. It was believed that UNESCO would be appreciated by public opinion, and by the various sectors of the public concerned by whether it was competent, and by its political partners in member states if they could see the usefulness and relevance of its actions.

Such a comprehensive approach to UNESCO's outside communication was not limited only to the Office of Public Information and other dissemination units but also presupposed secretariat-wide mobilization. The need was not merely to improve the organization's capacity to inform but also to get it to transform its capacities to interact with all sectors of the public. This included imparting information, listening to others, and being able to take part in discussions where and when the issues actually arise.

STRENGTHS AND WEAKNESSES

With a view to building a solid communication strategy, a process of external and internal consultations was held and the new plan approved by the executive board in June 2001. A group of prominent experts in communication met twice and addressed a set of recommendations largely integrated in the strategy.[3] This process led to a wide reorganization

---

[2]United States President George Bush announced to the 57th UN General Assembly in September 2002, that the United States would reenter UNESCO.

[3]The president of the group was Nils Gunnar Nilsson (journalist, Sweden) and its membership consisted of José Joaquín Brunner (communication specialist, Chile), Jean-Marie Brunot (former chairman of a press group, France), Tim Cullen (consultant, United Kingdom), Andrej Gratchev (former spokesperson of the head of state, Russian Federation), Manfred Harnischfeger (corporate communication director, Bertelsman Group, Germany), Hisanori Isomura (former director of NHK, Japan), Katherine Smith (specialist in new technologies, United States), Allister Sparks (journalist, South Africa), Ekwow Spio-Garbrah (former Minister of communication, Ghana), Carmen E. Tipling (Head of the national public information agency, Jamaica), Gebran Tuéni (Director of the independent press group An Nahar, Lebanon), Dejan Verčič (researcher and consultant, Slovenia) and Pere Vicens (chairman of the International Publisher Association, Spain).

of the concerned services as well as to the recruitment of a new director for the Bureau of Public Information. The process is still being implemented and therefore it is impossible to determine its efficacy. The following paragraphs will try to depict more precisely the balance of the situation prevailing before the strategy, as well as the main orientations, which are supposed to tackle the unsatisfactory issues.[4]

When addressing the communication problems of an organization such as UNESCO, two major pitfalls must be avoided. The first is restricting the parameters of communication to only the tools and media of information dissemination. The second is employing the term "communication" indiscriminately so that everything by nature becomes communication. While the first pitfall is indisputably reductive, the second can give rise to great confusion. However, the communication and information strategy must cover the whole gamut of actions ranging from the most sophisticated undertakings requiring the involvement of professionals to the everyday practice of all members of staff in their dealings with the outside public. It is through all these channels that UNESCO displays itself to public opinion, and it is on the basis of the totality of signals it emits that the image of the organization is implanted in the minds of those with whom it interacts.

Before assessing the overall results of UNESCO's visibility, it is necessary to briefly review its publics, the major supports utilized, and the objectives pursued. Afterward, results of enquiries and research about UNESCO's exposure and perception will be presented. Although the organization does not use such a typology, one might find it interesting to group the target public with which the organization maintains relations into three major categories forming concentric circles. The first group comprises all persons—and through them, various institutions—that have a formal link with UNESCO. These would include member states through their permanent delegations, governments, the ministries concerned, and their national commissions; intergovernmental organizations; and NGOs. This first group is in a way the internal audience and UNESCO's immediate partners. It represents several tens of thousands of persons.

The second category covers all persons who are more or less part of UNESCO's target constituencies. These are specialized communities of educators, scientists, artists, journalists, or members of society involved in, or even only potentially concerned by, UNESCO's action. These communities all over the world represent several tens of millions of persons and a great many institutions. The final category is somewhat residual. It encompasses all those not belonging to the first two categories. Because under its mandate UNESCO reaches out to all men and women in whose minds the defenses of peace must be constructed through education, science, culture, and communication, the world population should be seen as the organization's constituency, in the broadest sense.

The traditional tools of communication are essentially books, print, and electronic media. But the digital revolution, which has for some years been radically transforming the communication and information scene worldwide, is offering glimpses of new, unsuspected, and promising ways in which the organization can deploy its action and interact with the world. It is no easy matter to give an outline of UNESCO's communication and information activities. They form a very wide-ranging whole that is variable according to one's standpoint. For example, it may be viewed from the standpoint of the media, those at the receiving end, or the objectives or the Organization's internal structures.

---

[4]Parts of the following paragraphs are borrowed from the Official document presented in May 2001 by the director-general to the 161st session of the Executive Board (document 161 EX/43). The author had the privilege of assisting Georges Malempré, assistant director-general, who was entrusted with the mission of preparing the communication strategy presented in that document.

An analytical approach to the question might be to observe the "outlets" and to measure communication outflows. The table below provides some approximate data for the last two years.

UNESCO Publishing	251 new titles (including 14 CD-ROMs) published 2000 titles in the catalog 6 specialized journals	Average print run per language edition: 3000 copies
Monthly Periodicals	The *UNESCO Courier*: 11 issues per year, published in 27 languages + four co-publications in Braille *UNESCO Sources*: 11 issues per year in 5 languages	Combined circulation of the *Courier*: 160,000 copies Combined circulation of *Sources*: 52,000 copies + 400,000 copies of a Chinese-language monthly supplement
Internet	100,000 Web pages online	93,000 visitors per month in January 1999 1,000,000 visitors per month in December 2001
Press	20 press operations 556 press releases in 1998 and 1999	Media coverage: unquantified
Audiovisual	Coproduction of documentary films Production of 15 institutional subjects	Media coverage: unquantified 400 times on CNN
Cultural events	148 exhibitions 108 concerts, shows, or special events	178 member states involved in organizing cultural events at headquarters

In addition to these traditional means of communication, many documents, brochures, folders, and posters are produced by the secretariat at and away from headquarters, many speeches are made by the organization's representatives at many gatherings, and there are various information exchange facilities.

A third way of presenting UNESCO's communication might consist of highlighting the main objectives of all these efforts. A distinction could thus be drawn between activities designed to impart knowledge, raise awareness, mobilize people, or change certain forms of behavior. There is a gradation in the effects sought, which suggests that means should be made consistent with aims. While common sense, which makes it possible to see approximately where one stands in relation to these objectives, governs many communication choices, it must be agreed that very little or no systematic thought is given to the effects sought. Nonetheless, one could expect this to improve in future since over the last three years, UNESCO has been progressively adopting results-based management.

One variant to the *objectives approach* could be to present the functions assumed by communication and information action. They might include, for example, maintaining (or restoring) trust among the main stakeholders, preparing the organization's transparency, increasing UNESCO's credibility, establishing contact among actors at different levels, and exchanging information. But here too, it must be recognized that systematization is more intuitive than rigorous and it would certainly be appropriate to engage in substantial *a posteriori* rationalization to construct a logic of communication action.

ANALYZING THE IMAGE

In spite of all the efforts and supports used to communicate, for several years, the governing bodies have continued to draw the director-general's attention to the fact that UNESCO suffers from a lack of visibility. Recognition of this fact prompted the recent communication strategy elaboration process. If this served to raise awareness, it must be recognized that the organization's visibility is meaningful only if it helps to deal cogently with the issues UNESCO faces by virtue of its mandate. In fact, nothing is to be gained from promoting UNESCO's name if the substance of its action is neither relevant nor credible. The degree of visibility is one consequence of the performance of its mission, but should never be in itself a yardstick of the effectiveness of its action. If there is a "virtuous" circle that leads through efficacy via credibility to visibility, there can also be an infernal spiral that loops around ineffectiveness and poor reputation, or "bad press," and becomes exacerbated with increased visibility.

Despite a biased methodology including limited sampling, an inquiry into how UNESCO is perceived was conducted at the beginning of 2001, at the request of the Swedish National Commission. The study gathered data from opinion-leaders in four countries (Canada, India, Sweden, and the United Kingdom) and officials within the United Nations system. The findings of this study clearly revealed that there was a broad measure of support for the original principles and mandate assigned to UNESCO, but that there were also many signs of frustration and disappointment vis-à-vis an institution that has embarked upon too many different fields, that does not possess resources to match its ambitions, and that tends to be stultified by a degree of bureaucracy. Comparison with other agencies of the United Nations system was distinctly to its disadvantage. In contrast to other organizations of the system, UNESCO could not illustrate its mission by a simple and instantly understandable image. From its multitarious missions there emerged an image that is complex, abstract, and frequently hazy. Moreover, because its mandate is basically intellectual and not so much operational, UNESCO frequently creates the impression of being a remote bureaucracy.

The mission assigned to UNESCO since its creation has nevertheless enjoyed an undeniable aura for a whole range of different sectors of the public. The same appeared true of several of the topics, which it has determined to be its priorities for some years. Some of these topics are: world heritage, education for all, ethics of science and technology, environmental protection, prevention of natural disasters, and conflict prevention. The major thrusts of its new medium-term strategy are those that deal with the most burning issues facing the world today. Many of the programs are favorably perceived in the professional circles concerned. Nevertheless, UNESCO, like other intergovernmental organizations, was feeling the effects of the general disengagement occurring within the public sector, and the organization is in danger of seeing its impact dwindle in a mood of general indifference if it does not succeed in making its action, and its achievements, sufficiently clear and comprehensible.

Another study in the beginning of 2001, was a retrospective analysis of UNESCO's visibility in about 30 international newspapers over a period of two years (from January 1, 1999 to December 31, 2000). The objective was to discover the media outreach, how the image of UNESCO had been projected in the major international press organs, which have a recognized credibility, and, by extension, how world opinion leaders perceive UNESCO based on the information they gathered from the press. More than 2000 articles were analyzed, providing an interesting picture of media portrayal of UNESCO: the organization's

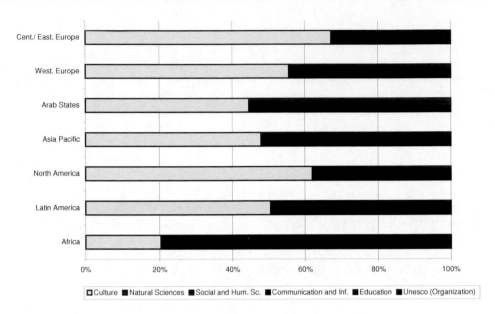

FIG. 42.1.   UNESCO press coverage study 1999—2000. Topics by regions.
(*Note*: **From UNESCO.**)

name is largely associated with world heritage; education is referred to in less than 10% of the articles; there are very few (3%) articles that refer negatively to UNESCO; important UNESCO events such as the Dakar Forum on education, the World Conference on Science, the inscription of new sites on the World Heritage list, and the election of the director-general have had a significant impact in the international press. Besides its innovative methodology, this study showed that the press, according to the geographic region, was not necessarily reactive to the same topics. For example, African newspapers were proportionally more interested by social sciences and communication issues than those from other regions of the world. Figure 42.1 excerpted from the study, illustrates these variations.

Surprisingly, in an organization where cultural diversity was proclaimed as a common wealth, there is no systematic tool to capture and analyze the differences of the reception contexts, or to tailor messages to suit local cultures. In most cases, the same messages are produced in different languages (usually English, French, Spanish, Arabic, and Russian) for different publics around the globe. Experienced journalists from different regions, hired on a permanent basis by UNESCO, revise the translations and sometimes introduce in the texts a few adaptations in order to interest journalists from their region. A relatively small number of national commissions and field offices devote time, skills, and resources to professionally communicate with their local publics. Those who do something can hardly count on guidelines, materials or ideas from headquarters.

SEARCHING FOR CHANGE

If the blurred and splintered image projected by the organization has previously been accentuated by a lack of coordination of its activities as a whole, the services responsible have also suffered for a number of years from a continuous depletion of their means of action. Guided primarily by strategies aimed at making savings and optimizing resources, the organization has been led to undertake structural adjustments of the services concerned, which have not been followed by any clear redefinition of their tasks. By regarding the communication media as a set of program support resources, the tendency has become established, as in most organizations, to reduce communication to the status of a tool and to focus attention too exclusively upon the production and dissemination of information. However, awareness is growing that communication is far more closely bound up with the logic of action. What is the impact produced by such communication media? How do they contribute to achieving the expected results?

Accordingly, if one starts to think about the program in terms of communication and begins to formulate communication in terms of results in relation to set objectives, both communication and public information become strategic components, intrinsically linked to the definition of programs in which the identification, knowledge, and understanding of the target populations always and necessarily precede discussions on the formulation of messages and the choice of means. This change is the linchpin of the communication strategy that the director-general began to implement at the beginning of 2002.

The strategy adopted comprises of 12 major headings that include both strategic principles and practical mechanisms. They are briefly presented hereafter.[5]

- *Anchoring communication activities in the program.* This implies discovering the communication dimension in the substantial activities and managing it in such a way that it directly serves the results that are expected.

- *Distinguishing substantive communication from institutional communication so that they are better coordinated.* The amalgam of the two components of the organization communication has led to confusion and non assumed or badly assumed responsibilities.

- *Establishing a structure to manage communication in a strategic perspective.* Communication and public relations are not just instruments—they require professionals able to adjust them to the overall organizational strategy.

- *Making communication a two-way process through responsiveness to target audiences.* Listening is part of the communication process and gaining the attention to the public is the starting point of a successful communication process.

- *Developing a communication culture inside the secretariat.* Good internal and external communication first requires communicating attitudes and shared values regarding the virtue of openness and dialogue.

- *Spreading the load by involving partners in communication activities.* It is quite obvious that the UNESCO Secretariat cannot support alone the promotion of the organization's objectives. Many partners from the public and private sectors could be involved to disseminate the key messages.

- *Establishing an effective system of editorial and graphic identity (one that is understandable, consistent, and eloquent).* The "temple-like" logo does not communicate what the organization intends to be and its use has been so anarchic that a renewed design is badly needed to graphically deliver key and central messages.

- *Refocusing relations with the press.* Credibility in international public opinion will be gained by good press relations: activities, efforts, and products adapted to media constraints and logic in which UNESCO's views on issues relevantly contribute to public debate.

---

[5]The full document is available online at http://unesdoc.unesco.org/images/0012/001225/122549e.pdf Retrieved January 5, 2003.

- *Publishing a high-quality periodical.* This item originated a number of passionate discussions among the governing bodies because the *UNESCO Courier* was implicitly to be discontinued. Finally, it was decided that a new *UNESCO Courier* would be published twice a year and widely circulated, free of charge, among the far–ranging UNESCO community through the channel of the national commissions.

- *Refocusing publishing activities (printed, audiovisual, and multimedia productions) to reach target groups more effectively.* Since its creation, UNESCO has published almost 10,000 titles, in all its fields of competence, in 70 languages, to be distributed all over the world. Publications should be better articulated with projects and programs so that the principal criteria for UNESCO publishing should no so much be the intent to sell the maximum number of books but to reach the right publics. When targeting large audiences, partnerships with international publishers should be sought.

- *Coordinating Websites and expanding Web communication in the future.* With its growing potential, the Internet is not just a new worldwide medium, but it is also another way to reach and interact with publics. To take full advantage of the Internet is a challenge that starts with the transformation of the present Website, which is an unbalanced patchwork quilt, into a dynamic whole with a greater coherence.

- *Organizing cultural activities, at and away from headquarters, that reflect the creative diversity of UNESCO.* Cultural events use the universal language of art and aesthetics. They say something about the organization as well as contributing to a better understanding of foreign cultures.

UNDERSTANDING UNESCO'S COMMUNICATION ROLE

The historical references evoked different aspects of UNESCO's approach to communication. Simply put, there are three major facets. First, because of the organization's nature, all types of communication practices are central in most of UNESCO's actions. UNESCO does not build roads or hospitals. It is a worldwide forum that brings people together and creates the conditions under which ideas and experiences can be exchanged. The responsibility to facilitate communication crosscuts all entities (headquarters, field offices, central services, and others). Second, UNESCO has a mandate to develop communication in the world. It defends the free flow of ideas and press freedom as well as promoting access for all to information. Communication is one of the major action areas, parallel to education, culture, and science. The Communication and Information Sector is in charge of this dimension with international standard-settings, professional, and academic developments. Third, UNESCO's communication is a permanent process of (re)explaining its institutional dimension, its *raison d'être*. It is the "corporate" communication arm of the organization. Most of the time, this component is internally called "public information" to avoid confusion with the other facets of communication. It principally falls under the responsibility of the Bureau of Public Information, which is supposed to be expert in dealing with the public.

It is relatively easy to make these conceptual distinctions. Most of the examples briefly presented above demonstrate how these three facets are interwoven and overlap. Many of the reforms to improve the effectiveness of UNESCO's communication have had the intention of separating and distinguishing these facets. Public information activities were repeatedly reduced to manage some of the communication instruments used by the organization (books, audiovisual media, press releases, etc.) and intended for the external public. The public information focus has often been "instrumentalized." Over the last 50 years, the promising developments and potentialities in the information and communication area

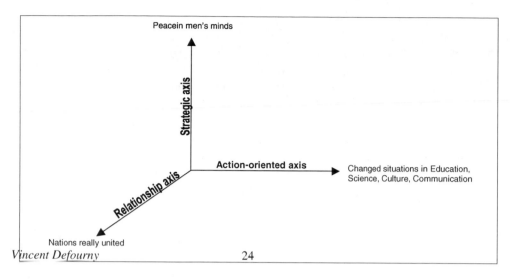

FIG. 42.2. UNESCO and its three driving forces.

(film, radio, television, Internet, and so on) have misled a number of senior managers and member state representatives. Probably influenced by advertising and marketing success stories, they thought that the use of a particular tool or the technology would almost automatically serve UNESCO's interests. The problem lay not so much in reaching the public at large, but in developing a context favorable to the achievements of the organization's objectives. In other words, the organization had to develop the strategic use of communication. The present author believes that a complex goal such as developing UNESCO's communication strategy requires recognizing and better understanding its complexity. The new communication strategy adopted in 2001 intends to follow these lines and principles, and is to be directly plugged into the medium-term strategy covering the period 2002–2007.

The following representation based on system theory, of what UNESCO as an organization is and what its communication role is, is relevant to visualizing some of the key ideas of this chapter.

First, it is necessary to draw three axes, corresponding to three organizational driving-forces (Figure 42.2): (1) the strategic axis with the guiding principle of UNESCO's mandate (peace in the minds of men); (2) the action-oriented axis leading to the fulfillment of all the expected results of its program (education for all throughout life, sound press freedom, preserved and respected world heritage, etc.); and (3) the relationship axis looking toward the achievement of international solidarity (the real United Nations).

The end points of these dimensions belong to utopia, but they definitely organize and structure the mobilization of resources and ideas. Of course, today's UNESCO is still far from reaching these targets, but it is not difficult to observe that, since its foundation, the organization has made significant strides toward reaching them.

Second, interactions between these three subsystems are interesting to consider. (1) People's aspirations find their way in the projection of the relationship axis toward the strategic axis. National and regional consultations preceding the elaboration of the medium-term strategy and the definition of strategic objectives are good examples of this process through which stakeholders collectively place their aspirations in a common document. (2) It is also well known that concrete action and activities find their inspirations in great ambitions: the strategic axis must feed the action-oriented one. For example, in Bosnia and Herzegovina, the reconstruction of the old bridge at Mostar was much more than a heritage preservation activity. It was a way of building peace and dialogue in a war-torn region.

(3) Lastly, concerted actions are much more effective than any other. The action-oriented axis finds its real deployment through the relationship dimension. This third movement can be called "conspiracy/conspiration." So these three key movements (aspiration, inspiration, and "conspiracy/conspiration") linking the three fundamental dimensions (strategy, action, and relationship) represent the organizational "respiration," the repeated and permanent movement that keeps the organization alive (Figure 42.3).

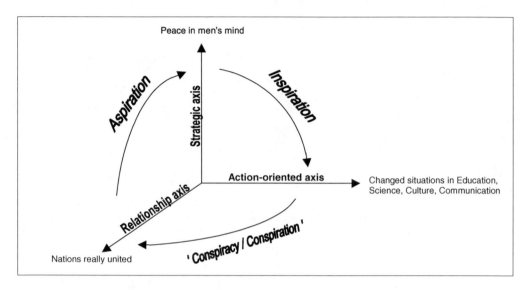

FIG. 42.3.   The organization "respiration."

It is the purpose of communication to stimulate this respiration in such a way that a given situation for the organization—say, the circle joining points A, B, and C placed on the three axes—will be enlarged and improved by a spiral movement produced by the dynamic of strategic communication (Figure 42.4).

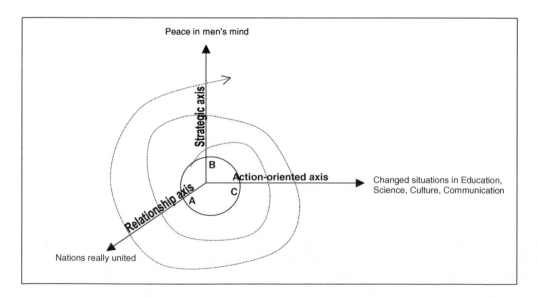

FIG. 42.4.   The role of strategic communication.

In practical terms, this means communicating from the heart of the organization and in line with organizational strategy, objectives and results-orientation by establishing bi-directional communication with constituencies. This should contribute to channeling public aspirations, providing meaning and understanding to large and small-scale projects, as well as consolidating communities. The implementation of the communication strategy during the coming years will be critical and results will have to be carefully analyzed to detect its real strengths and weaknesses.

REFERENCES

Grierson J. Archive, University of Stirling, G5.

Grunig, J. E. (Ed.) (1992). *Excellence in public relations and communications management.* Hillsdale, NJ: Lawrence Erlbaum Associates.

Grunig, J. E., & Grunig, L. A. (1992). Models of public relations and communication. In Grunig, J. E. (Ed.), *Excellence in public relations and communication management* (pp. 285–325). Hillsdale, NJ: Lawrence Erlbaum Associates.

Lacoste, M. C. (1994). *The story of a grand design—UNESCO 1946–1993.* Geneva: UNESCO.

L'Etang, J. (1999). John Grierson and the public relations industry in Britain. In *Screening the Past (electronic journal),* Melbourne: La Trobe University. Retrieved January 15, 2003, from http://www.latrobe.edu.au/screeningthepast/firstrelease/fr0799/jlfr7d.htm

Mintzberg, H. (1979). *The structuring of organizations: A synthesis of the research.* Englewood Cliffs, NJ: Prentice-Hall.

UNESCO (1997). *World communication report.* Geneva: UNESCO.

UNESCO (2000). Basic Texts, Paris.

UNESCO (1948). Records of the general conference of UNESCO, third session, Beirut, Resolutions.

43

THE UNITED NATIONS DEPARTMENT OF PUBLIC INFORMATION: INTRACTABLE DILEMMAS AND FUNDAMENTAL CONTRADICTIONS

SETH A. CENTER

> One trouble with the UN is that it cannot successfully engage in public relations or advertising, like a Government or commercial business does, because it has many different points of view, and it's extremely difficult to get these all into a coherent, saleable position which could be put out there . . . It's an almost impossible task to promote the UN, to make people understand why it is needed. But someone has to do it.
>
> Sir Brian Urquhart (Former UN Under-Secretary-General)[1]

The United Nations has been vexed by questions of public relations since its inception. For both practical and philosophical reasons, the international organization has a vested interest in protecting its global image and communicating its purposes and ideals throughout the world. At the same time, overt propagandizing on behalf of the organization or the political causes espoused within it risks compromising the United Nations' unique position in world politics. While the UN General Assembly is infamous as a forum for member states' propaganda, the United Nations bureaucracy maintains, at least in principle, an ethos of impartiality in global affairs, a culture of deference to its member states, and an adherence to the principle of state sovereignty. This situation has produced intractable dilemmas in the formulation and execution of UN information policy.

Virtually every United Nations' department, fund, programme, and agency has a public information capability, but the burden of reconciling the organization's information policy

---

[1] "Peace Keeping: We Need Serious Rethinking," Interview with Brian Urquhart. *The UN Chronicle* XXXV, No. 3 (1998) [http://www.un.org/Pubs/chronicle/1998/issue3/398p36p.htm].

falls to the Department of Public Information (DPI). The DPI is often referred to as the United Nations' "voice," "megaphone," and "torchbearer" in "telling the UN story." The department is guided by a mission statement to "help to fulfill the substantive purposes of the United Nations by strategically communicating the activities and concerns of the Organization to achieve the greatest public impact" (Activities of the DPI, Corrigendum, 2007). The DPI's purposes and communication strategy have not been nearly as self-evident as these short-hand descriptors and the concise mission statement would suggest. Indeed, despite widespread acknowledgement throughout the UN family that the DPI performs a necessary function, the department has confronted something of an identity crisis throughout its existence.

As a general proposition, the need for effective public diplomacy to ensure the United Nations' success is a rare point of consensus at the organization. Lacking the conventional military and economic power of a state, the United Nations must rely on persuasion and publicity to promote its ideals and multifaceted social, economic, cultural, and political agenda. As the Under-Secretary-General for Public Information remarked in 1988, "[The United Nations] has no authority except the power to convince; to convince the peoples of the world of the value of nourishing a vision of a more harmonious world; to convince through discreet and public diplomacy; and to convince through professional information services and communications campaigns with the goal of reaching out to the peoples of the world" (Committee on Information, 1988, p. 25). Because the organization depends on public funding and global support, it must continuously justify its relevance by communicating to the world that it is a necessary, even irreplaceable institution.

Consensus and clarity quickly dissipate, however, as soon as the subject of public information engages questions of methods, content, and objectives. Throughout the organization's history, UN officials have consistently expressed ambivalence about deploying the methods of public relations professionals. Foremost, they have denied that the United Nations information policy is akin to that of a state propaganda agency and they have consistently disavowed political activism as a part of the DPI mission. As Secretary-General U Thant (1961–1971) stated, the UN neither could nor would "conduct an intensive information campaign such as sovereign Governments sometimes employ." Because of the diversity of views of the member states, he averred, "The United Nations, in its public information activities, can only attempt to give an objective and factual record of what is happening . . . ." (Thant, 1970). Information dissemination rather than promotion was the DPI *modus vivendi*, Thant maintained, because the United Nations served all nations. It had "no 'face' to lose and no victory of its own to win" (UN Monthly Chronicle, 1964).

The dilemma created by the ethos of impartiality is exacerbated by the UN organization's deference to member states and its adherence to the principle of state sovereignty. Early in the DPI's existence observers noticed the fundamental contradiction between the desire to reach the peoples of the world and the department's ultimate subservience to the countries comprising the General Assembly (Gordenker, 1960). Corey (1953) argued that the DPI would not "bring pressure on recalcitrant nations or initiate steps which would strengthen the United Nations at the expense of national sovereignty." As a consequence its editorial independence and freedom to operate were "strictly bounded" by member states. The DPI could only hope to play the "honest broker" to avoid criticism and uphold the impartiality of the Secretariat (pp. 231, 242). Swift (1960) concluded that the DPI was a "servant" to its member state "masters," thus the DPI could not possibly "indulge in the sensational trappings and stereotypes of the more popular broadcasters and writers" (p. 90).

The UN professional staff's determination to maintain the organization's impartiality and its cautious dealings with member states led to substantial and enduring criticism of the DPI's communication strategy by those supportive of a more vigorous public relations strategy. The United Nations' information structure and policies, critics allege, have been plagued by passivity, fragmentation, and an institutional approach to information dissemination. Alleyne (2003) concludes that the "gun-shy" DPI never implemented a "meaningful" public diplomacy program. The "unity and decisiveness" necessary were "beyond" the United Nations (pp. 46–56). The DPI served more as a government printing office, library, and reference source for member states, the press, and the interested public than as an energetic, media savvy, public relations machine pursuing a strategic agenda to advance UN ideals and bolster the United Nations' image.

DPI STRUCTURE AND ORGANIZATION

In the past twenty years the DPI has undergone at least seven reorganization efforts to improve its effectiveness and efficiency in response to internal and external criticism. The most recent reform, beginning in 2002, was designed to ensure the successful transition away from passive information dissemination to a "more strategic approach" to communications that focused on establishing clear goals, identifying target audiences, and providing better guidance for other UN agencies and re-disseminators. The reform spirit also spurred a "culture of evaluation" to ensure that information programs were rationally designed, distributed, and funded. Reformers envisioned establishing a unified communications strategy projected into the world by a common UN voice and an information structure organized within clearly delineated bureaucratic roles and lines of communication.

In its newly defined role, the DPI acts as the "service provider," while the 50 departments, offices, and the 26 field missions are identified as "clients." The relationship is designed such that the "clients" generate the content—the "raw materials," setting the priorities and messages—and the DPI repackages the content for target audiences and promotes it around the world (Tharoor, 2006). To ensure coordination and a unified message, the 2002 reforms established the United Nations Communications Group (UNCG) under the chairmanship of the head of the DPI. In addition to the DPI, its membership includes representatives from the Secretary-General's office and the information heads of the other UN agencies, funds, and programmes. The UNCG holds weekly meetings at headquarters and an annual conference. The group is also replicated at the regional and national levels to provide the same policy coordination for local activities (Activities of the UNCG, 2004).

In 2006–2007, the DPI operated with a budget of $177 million, representing 4.7 percent of the total UN budget. Its staff of 761 officials works in New York, Vienna, Geneva, and UN information centres and offices around the world. The department is divided into three subprogrammes. The Strategic Communications Division is devoted to broadening understanding of and support for the work of the United Nations on priority thematic issues with a focus on improving media coverage of the organization, meeting the "client" needs, and building local support. The News and Media Division provides basic news and information about the organization's activities, meetings, and assemblies to media outlets through press conferences, partnerships with radio and television stations, and UN websites. The Outreach Division focuses on building partnerships with civil society— NGOs, the academic community, educational institutions, and depository libraries— through conferences, exhibits, teaching material, webcasts, and other outlets.

A few brief statistics provide a sense of the scale of DPI operations. It has 44,217 subscribers to its news centre email service; 412,042 annual visitors to UN headquarters for tours; it is responsible for 84 publications and its flagship journal *UN Chronicle* has a circulation of 716,997; and it produces radio and television programs that reach, in partnership with state and private media, an estimated 600 million listeners and viewers each week (Assessing the Effectiveness, 2006). The DPI currently maintains websites in the six official UN languages (Arabic, Chinese, English, French, Russian, and Spanish) and 29 non-official languages. The DPI relies heavily on its "collaborators"—information centres, other UN organizations ("clients"), and the network of 1,500 DPI-accredited civil society organizations. These "collaborators" act as "re-disseminators and multipliers" and help the DPI reach a wider audience through the media and direct grassroots outreach than its own limited communications capabilities would permit (Tharoor, Statement to the COI, 2006). Its 63 information centres and offices give a local "accent" to UN ideas and translate products into local languages, organize community events, and build ties to local media and opinion-makers.

Even as the DPI has attempted to put its own house in order, most observers acknowledge that the UN family—especially the General Assembly—has been equally responsible for the shortcomings in UN information policy. Faced in recent years with some 120 General Assembly mandates and 60 formal activities, as well as ad hoc requests, the quest for a mission and target audience, let alone a comprehensive communications strategy, has proven elusive and unrealistic, especially given the United Nations' perpetual fiscal problems. One outside observer charged that member states hamstrung the DPI with "ridiculous chores and reports to write" rather than putting the emphasis "where it counts"—on effective communications strategies and a full embrace of the media age (World Press Freedom Day, 2007). The Secretariat's own frustration has also been evident. Reports from the DPI frequently allude to the fact that the department is stretched to the limit by expanding mandates and missions and concomitantly stagnant budgets and unchanged staffing levels. "The principal reason" for the DPI's over-extension and fragmentation, the Secretary-General explained in 2002, was the endless mandates that ranged from far too general to unattainable to so specific that they were tantamount to micromanagement (Reorientation of United Nations activities, 2002).

While questions of structure and organization are important, the dilemmas of UN information policy are rooted in culture, philosophy and politics as much as they are in bureaucratic structure and technical questions. As we shall see, the public information programme is trapped between overlapping, but not necessarily complementary, demands to advance the principle of freedom of information, act as the "mouth piece" for the social, cultural, political, and ideological causes of the world body, and help to shape the overarching image of the United Nations.

ORIGINAL INTENT: THE CREATION OF THE DPI

For practical reasons, public relations were central to the creation of the United Nations in 1945. The United States government secretly undertook a massive media campaign in preparation for the San Francisco Conference to ensure the United Nations would avoid the same fate that befell the League of Nations in U.S. public opinion. But the belief in the power of public opinion to determine the success or failure of the new United Nations was not just an American phenomenon. It was widely shared by its international supporters.

The founders vested enormous hope in the power to communicate directly with the people of the world. Many saw the League of Nations' failure in the interwar years, in part, as a result of having "lost touch with the world of publicity." Its successor organization needed an information service capable of reaching the "farmer in Nebraska, the shopkeeper in Lyons, the tractor-driver in a Soviet rural community" with "attractive and easily understandable" information programmes (Royal Institute, 1944, pp. 11–18, 36–38, 62–64). Without a world organization, future peace would not be secure. And without sufficient global prestige the new organization could never hope to succeed. As Benjamin Cohen, the first Under-Secretary for Public Information, said in 1946, "If it [UN] is to succeed—and the alternative is the liquidation of all that the civilized world professes to believe in—it will be because the peoples of the world *want* it to succeed" (p. 155).

Fundamentally, the question of public relations and the power of communications more broadly were interwoven in the very fabric of the new United Nations philosophy because of another lesson from the recent past. Nazi Germany stood as a stark reminder of the malignant power of public relations when deployed in the cause of a malicious ideology. The antidote to future "war-mongering" propaganda was to ensure the principle of freedom of information. The UN's ability to educate the world public with all of the "facts" would prevent a future Nazi Germany from exploiting fear and ignorance to foment war. As Trygve Lie (1953), the first Secretary-General, explained, by giving international issues a full hearing and then disseminating to the world all points of view, the United Nations would "contribute in the long-run to understanding and accommodation among the nations of the world" (p. 514).

Precisely because some countries had state-controlled media and all countries had their own biases, UN advocates decided that the organization needed its own means of disseminating independent information to realize the twin goals of freedom of information and sustaining support for the institution. The United Nations could not rely on the goodwill of others. It had to balance nationalistic slants of state-controlled media and profit-driven sensationalism and jingoism of private media outlets with its own "unbiased" accounts of the international organization's deliberations, actions, and ideals. As conceived, its information programme would give it the teeth that the League of Nations had lacked.

In 1946, the United Nations established the Department of Public Information to help realize its ambitions. UN Resolution 13(I) outlined the new department's mandate. While the resolution recognized that "the United Nations cannot achieve the purposes for which it has been created unless the peoples of the world are fully informed of its aims and activities," actual guidelines for information policy were incredibly vague. The DPI should not engage in "'propaganda'" but rather "promote to the greatest possible extent an informed understanding of the world and purposes" of the United Nations. It should "primarily rely upon the cooperation" of established governmental and nongovernmental agencies and media, but it also "should on its own initiative engage in positive informational activities" to supplement these relationships if they proved to be "insufficient to realize the purpose" of the organization's information needs. Such ambiguity left much to be sorted out as the DPI evolved.

Initially, DPI officials earnestly and consistently declared that they did not operate a "propaganda" agency. Cohen (1946) said that the office's mission was to "collect, collate, and give out factual information" about the UN (p. 146). Tamayo (1967) insisted that the DPI played a cautious role—it was a "rich source of information" but still very much "subsidiary" to states, and its main task was to provide "basic reference tools" on the UN's activities (pp. 186, 192). The earnest protestations belied a more complex picture of the DPI's engagement in active public relations campaigns both for itself and for politically charged causes. To say that DPI officials preferred to avoid an activist posture is not to say that the DPI output was purely informative, impartial or politically neutral.

The United Nations quickly found out how difficult it was to balance the principle of freedom of information and the necessity of promotion in shaping the organization's information policy. The enormous hopes placed in the power of freedom of information to secure world peace dimmed quickly as the Cold War divided the world body. Disillusionment and distrust supplanted hope and many complained that the organization's supporters had "oversold" the United Nations. Secretary-General Lie concluded that the nascent organization would have to go on the public relations offensive. It was caught in a "vicious circle of suspicion, ignorance, and fear" that needed to be met with an aggressive "positive" information campaign to counter anti-UN propaganda and correct distortions about the organization (Annual Report, 1948, Chapter V). A true test of a fully informed world public opinion could not fail to bring peace, but neither could world peace be ensured without securing global public support for the organization and rehabilitating the United Nations' image—and that demanded more than disseminating information; it meant advocating for the organization.

As would prove the case in future events, member states played a key role in determining how the DPI balanced competing impulses. While most states supported the concept of public diplomacy in the abstract, when it came to an aggressive public relations campaign, the DPI met with widespread reticence. Protective of their sovereignty and suspicious of any hint of "propaganda" in a milieu still tainted by the memory of Joseph Goebbels, some states earnestly feared the DPI becoming a vast propaganda programme. Other states argued that the idealistic United Nations should not stoop to the methods of Madison Avenue. Substance was more important, Australia's delegate argued in pointing out that more money was spent by the DPI than by the UN's Food and Agriculture Organization. Belgium's representative demanded 80 percent reductions for the DPI, comparing its work to "the huckster song in 'soap operas'" (Fifth Committee, 1950, SR. 247). The Netherlands complained that the DPI seemed too prone to using "commercial methods" and was guilty of "sugar-coating the pill" in its treatment of controversial subjects. The DPI should only disseminate information couched in "sober terms." Was the global public "so stupid," the Dutch delegate wondered, that the UN needed to engage in "feverish activity" to secure its support? (Fifth Committee, 1950, SR. 245)

The DPI did "sugar-coat" the pill and in the process it compromised its determination to disseminate objective information and educate the world with "all the facts." However, it had little choice. Too much "objective" information was sure to alienate one of the two superpowers and lead to charges of partiality. Thus, even as the DPI insisted that "no attempt is made to omit or gloss over awkward incidents or disagreements," that aspiration was untenable in practice (Cohen, 1946, p. 146). During the early Cold War, DPI publications obscured the degree to which the Soviet–American conflict paralyzed the organization, and the DPI largely resisted the demands of the United States to denounce communist aggression, and vice-versa. In seeking to adhere to the ethos of impartiality, the DPI elided controversial issues like assigning responsibility for the Korean War or even clearly explaining the basic facts about international conflict. Indeed, the DPI consistently strove to avoid singling out individual states for approbation in its treatment of global issues because of the implicit challenge to state sovereignty and the exigency of impartiality.

This early controversy illuminated the basic dilemmas of UN information policy embedded in the founding mandate and the competing demands of the organization: the tension between an active public relations campaign to promote the United Nations and a passive system of information dissemination consonant with the principle of freedom of information, and the tension between the DPI and member-states. But the debate over the utilization of public relations to promote the institution proved far less divisive than the relationship between the DPI and the political activism of member states.

THE EMERGENCE OF POLITICAL ACTIVISM

Historically, the key factor in determining the degree and nature of the DPI's activism has been the balance of power in the General Assembly, where political activism is a hallmark. More than a mere "debating society," the General Assembly establishes through resolutions the mandates and instructions for UN information policy. It also maintains oversight over the DPI by requiring the Secretariat to submit reports and DPI officials to attend hearings on questions relating to information. The DPI's culture of deference toward member-states has ensured that to the extent that the General Assembly has been politicized over the years so too has the content of DPI outputs. This pattern is particularly evident in the DPI's treatment of colonialism and the broader neo-colonial debates between the developed and developing world. As one of the most politically-charged and ubiquitous issues confronting the United Nations, the evolution of the North–South debate illuminates the dynamic between the ethos of impartiality, the culture of deference, and political activism in UN information policy.

Prior to 1960, the West, led by the United States, dominated the United Nations. Western governments supported a philosophy of evolutionary change from colonialism to independence that they enshrined in the UN Charter. Administering powers had a "sacred trust" to help prepare dependent peoples for full independence (UN Charter, Chapter XI). Western states envisioned the collection and dissemination of information by the United Nations as aiding the slow transition towards independence. By issuing statistical and technical (but never political) reports on the economic, social, and educational conditions in territories, the United Nations could create a "healthy competition between the colonial powers for the achievement of better conditions" for the dependent peoples (*A Sacred Trust*, 1959, pp. 36–37). The DPI's own output reinforced the political conservatism. It published brochures and pamphlets that celebrated the benefits of trusteeship and conveyed the supposed enthusiasm of dependent peoples as they came to appreciate the economic and educational benefits of the evolutionary transition toward independence. In colonies beyond the control of the United Nations' trust system, the DPI propagated the message that the path to autonomy would be "long and difficult," and the UN's "responsibilities" very "limited" (*Sacred Trust*, pp. 5, 31–37). A conservatively disposed United Nations produced a conservatively disposed communications strategy in content and objectives.

However, in 1960, the rise of newly independent states shifted the balance of power in the General Assembly. These states, from Africa and Asia and supported enthusiastically by the Eastern bloc, demanded immediate independence for all colonial peoples and supplanted the "sacred trust" with the Declaration on the Granting of Independence to Colonial Countries and Peoples. Anti-colonial rhetoric quickly moved to the centre of UN public information policy. The General Assembly approved a cascade of annual resolutions "requesting" the Secretary-General to engage in evermore expansive information campaigns to promote the Declaration and on behalf of the broader decolonization agenda. The Secretariat was directed to "take concrete measures utilizing all of the media at his disposal" to provide ". . . the widespread and continuous publicizing of the work of the United Nations in the field of decolonization of the situation in the colonial Territories *and* of the continuing struggle for liberation being waged by the colonial peoples" (UN

Resolution 2326 XXII). "Arousing public opinion and promoting practical action" became central UN activities (UN Resolution 2621 XXV).

Moreover, member states began to attack the DPI for its impartiality and passivity. UN information programmes could not be "neutral or uncommitted" when it came to the issue of decolonization. The DPI demonstrated an "obvious pro-Western bias" because it refused to single out specific states believed complicit in colonial practices—especially in their political ties with the racist colonial regimes in southern Africa. By not singling out the position taken by UN delegations on specific issues in its publications—literally the "name-calling" debate—the DPI was "whitewashing" the "pro-colonial" stance of the Western world (Special Committee, 1968).

In addition, member states demanded more attention to the art of public relations. India's delegate, for example, suggested that the DPI's output lacked the "dynamism and bite" and the "sell" aspect necessary to gain public attention (Special Committee, 1972, pp. 13–16, 23–26). Developing countries pushed the DPI to move beyond the reportorial to analyze the causes of decolonization, promote liberation movements' critiques of colonialism, and distribute films showing the crimes and brutalities of colonial systems.

Under this pressure to become a full participant in the decolonization movement, the DPI sought to straddle the mandates of the General Assembly and its philosophical opposition to overt political activism. The Secretary-General (1972) conceded that the DPI should adopt a more dynamic and energetic role in promoting the decolonization agenda. However, the DPI was also limited by its own mandate. It could neither gather nor disseminate material on its own initiative. The DPI's effort at maintaining philosophical consistency had little practical effect on what emerged as radically different output. Indeed the DPI's original mandate provided a loophole that was in fact a massive opening for the exploitation of the DPI for the more "active" public diplomacy activities sought by the decolonization movement irrespective of the department's own caution.

The DPI could not make its own arguments without violating its mandate, but it could rely on statements of those in opposition to colonialism. The DPI could publish and disseminate anything that appeared in the public record of a UN committee, conference, or investigation. Thus the DPI would have no technical difficulty in utilizing this "officially sanctioned raw material" in its media outputs, whatever its political content. In effect, this impartial attitude made the department an active supporter of the cause.

By the early 1970s, the DPI had moved even beyond that. It had direct contacts with liberation movements "to ascertain their requirements and to open up new areas of cooperation," and it made them its "principal source" of the information about colonial conditions (Dissemination of Information on Decolonization, 1972). It published booklets and pamphlets, produced radio programmes and films, and hosted conferences that celebrated the successes of liberation movements—even armed struggles against member states. The UN denounced racism and *apartheid* and neo-colonialism with titles such as *A People in Bondage* and *A Trust Betrayed*. The UN's flagship journal *Objective: Justice*, created at the behest of the General Assembly, published the UN's activities and disseminated the opinions of private organizations as well.

As the expression of broader Third World political ideology began to emerge in DPI material, so did an acceptance of the "name-calling" doctrine that it preferred to avoid. For instance, the 1969 *Foreign Economic Interests and Decolonization* republished in "slightly edited" form described the "rapacious exploitation" by the "foreign monopolies" and their suppression of national liberation movements. The booklet singled out the United States and United Kingdom and argued that the Western powers impeded the freedom of black Africans. The DPI's technical effort at "balance" could be found on the last page of the booklet's 32 pages: a half-page summary of the Western rebuttal, which was followed by a rebuttal of the rebuttal (Foreign Economic Interests, 1969).

As the content of UN public diplomacy increasingly reflected Third World perspectives, the target audience shifted North and West. Representatives of the developing world argued that there was no sense "converting the converted" since they already agreed with the decolonization agenda advanced in the General Assembly. The "correct audience" and the "crucial target" for UN public diplomacy ought to be the public in Western Europe and North America. The uneven distribution of information had left the developing world with a "heightened sense of grievances of colonial peoples" but the West remained "conveniently oblivious of the seriousness of the crisis" (Special Committee 873rd Meeting, p. 7) If Western ignorance and indifference about the plight of the Third World could be overcome and public opinion mobilized, then the Western governments that both cooperated with and possessed sufficient power to stop the practices of colonialism would have to take notice.

Concurrently, the Third World feared that the United Nations had become the target of a propaganda attack by South Africa and the Western media that were inherently hostile to the non-aligned world and the organization. The DPI was needed to counteract this propaganda by giving the "correct view" of Third World positions and the "real" role the United Nations played in the world. Indeed, the Third World concluded that the DPI had a "particularly" important responsibility to target its information campaigns in the West (Special Political Committee, 1986, SR. 26). DPI officials generally agreed that the United Nations' story needed to be more effectively told in the West. However, the problem was not resolvable through its own efforts—the DPI already had information centres in the United States and Western Europe. The real problem was that the Western media was not publishing DPI materials with the same enthusiasm as the Third World. It was an "incontestable fact," a DPI official said, that "nothing can persuade a newspaper to print news that it does not want to print" (Committee on Decolonization, 1972, PV.877). The Third World would have to confront the structural inequalities in the international system if it hoped to advance its political causes in the West through the United Nations.

The central threat to Third World sovereignty was the very nature of the existing neo-colonial international economic and information order, which kept the developing world in a state of "semi-colonial" dependence. The Third World formulated two complementary ideological visions to reach full independence: The New International Economic Order (NIEO) and the New World Information and Communication Order (NWICO). Both orders became cornerstones of a new politically active UN public diplomacy programme. As with the case of political decolonization, the Third World brought its grievance and its vision to the General Assembly not merely for debate but for expression. Once the NIEO became institutionalized within the UN mission, the Third World moved to ensure that it received the full support of the UN's information services by passing a series of resolutions calling on the DPI to specifically maximize information programmes in support of the new world order (A/RES/33/115 B and C).

The Third World also specifically challenged the Western concept of freedom of information. The existing communications order permitted the West to overtly propagandize the developing world without fear of retaliation. Everyone was a hostage to the Western media and the West's ideological and political stances. The "free flow of information" celebrated by the West was a canard. It really meant the "freedom of action for imperialist information monopolies in developing countries" to enslave the Third World in a state of "information colonization" and render it a "passive recipient of biased, inadequate and distorted information." Under the guise of the principle of freedom of information the developed world was denying the Third World the "right to inform and be informed object-ively and accurately" (Special Political Committee, 1983).

Until the developing world achieved the technical capacity for information self-reliance, the Third World demanded that the United Nations help fill the void. The DPI would act as an antidote to Western media domination by helping the Third World disseminate "objective" information about developments in the non-aligned world both within develop-ing countries and to the world at large in order to promote the developing world's views of international affairs. The UN needed to create a new information order which, according to the Mongolian delegate, reiterating the now ubiquitous ideological posture, would be used to "eradicate the remaining vestiges of colonialism, eliminate racial discrimination and apartheid and contribute to the social-economic development" of the developing world (Special Political Committee, 1986). The "decolonization of information" and countering the "tendentious reporting and mass media campaigns" directed against Third World movements were two sides of the same coin and both "intrinsically linked" to the estab-lishment of a new international order of which the UN was now the principal promoter and the DPI a key tool (Special Political Committee, 1983).

THE COMMITTEE ON INFORMATION AND THE IMPARTIALITY DILEMMA

To build the NWICO and redefine freedom of information, the Third World sought explicit oversight and control over UN information policy. The General Assembly affirmed by resolution that it would play the primary role in "elaborating, coordinating and har-monizing United Nations policies and activities in the field of information towards the establishment of a new, more just and more effective world information and communi-cation order" (A/Res/34/182). In 1978, the General Assembly created the Committee on Information (COI) to coordinate and evaluate UN information programmes and promote the NWICO. As the Chairman of the COI (1980) explained, the committee's purpose was to ensure UN information policy was "genuinely and specifically appropriate to the needs of developing countries." He also linked the work of his committee with the efforts of the Non-Aligned Movement and the Group of 77, arguing that the United Nations informa-tion policy needed to reflect what was being done elsewhere in the Third World. The overtly political emphasis of the UN's new information agenda, the chairman of the COI (1979) admitted, put the organization's public diplomacy in a "new light." However, given the Western media's "blackout" of Third World problems, the UN had no choice but to inter-cede on its behalf to help promote the realization of a new, more just world order. The NIEO required the NWICO and both required the support of the UN. Logically, the chairman of the COI suggested these ideological visions deserved such support now that the "great majority of [UN] members" were in agreement on the need to "build a more open and more fraternal world." With the Third World in full control of the UN's public diplomacy oversight apparatus, the politicization of the DPI was unavoidable. The emboldened Third World now sought to use the DPI to publicize political causes with temerity.

By the 1980s, Western states were increasingly frustrated with the ideological and political information campaign mandated by the General Assembly, espoused in the Com-mittee on Information, and transmitted via the DPI to the world. While that agenda did represent the will of the majority of member states, it nonetheless was hurting the image of the United Nations in some of the organization's largest financial contributors. The United States complained that the DPI's new mission was a "serious distortion" of its founding principles. As a result of the Third World's determination to focus information policy on a political agenda, the "efficiency and objectivity" of the DPI had "eroded," and it was becoming "steadily less credible" (Special Political Committee, 1984, SR. 26). Worse, Western states argued that the very UN department established to help win world public opinion was in fact exacerbating the lack of public support for the organization. The politicization of the information agenda was hurting the UN's overall image. "The selective treatment of selected topics," Australia's delegate warned, "could only breed cynicism and indifference and an unhealthy perception" of the United Nations (Special Political Committee, 1983, SR.27, SR. 28).

Western delegates suggested that the DPI needed to redefine its priorities. If the DPI could focus on the organization's efforts to help refugees, provide disaster relief, and promote peace-keeping rather than polemics, it could widen its support, especially in the West. Neither the United Nations nor the DPI should get bogged down in "theoretical debates" about international order as the General Assembly had mandated. The solution to the UN's tarnished reputation was more "balance" in DPI output. Rather than focusing on "publicity" for the General Assembly's causes, the DPI should instead prioritize a basic goal of disseminating information about the organization's "concrete achievements" (Special Political Committee, 1984, SR. 26). Essentially, they argued the DPI should depoliticize itself by disconnecting ideological conflict from practical concerns.

The Third World was not swayed. The depoliticization of information was itself a political act that could only serve the neo-colonial agenda. Information was by nature politicized and the United Nations mandate was to keep the world informed of the concerns of the global community. Egypt's delegate articulated the key point: the DPI's activities "reflected the will of the majority of countries composing the United Nations." Therefore, "any attempt to depoliticize information could only be characterized as selective" (Special Political Committee, 1986, SR. 26). The will of the majority and the UN were synonymous and should be reflected in UN public diplomacy.

The DPI continued to try to walk a tightrope between the assertive Third World and the charges levelled by Western states, but its position was transparently constrained. While the DPI strove for impartiality, the instructions of the General Assembly and the COI specifically directed the DPI to engage in more positive information activities to mobilize world public opinion. The DPI had little room to alter the information priorities established. The Secretariat was indeed deferential in its relations to member states, but that deference had increasingly led to more aggressive public diplomacy campaigns. As the head of the DPI explained, the Department would continue to adhere to the "promotional mandates" of the General Assembly and the Committee on Information, while also "striving to preserve its impartial approach." He hoped there was "no contradiction" in these goals (Special Political Committee, 1984, SR. 30).

THE DPI TODAY: ACTIVISM WITHOUT POLITICIZATION

Both the aspirations of the United Nations' founders to win and hold the hearts of mankind and the intractable problems of designing a public relations campaign for a fragmented and politically divided organization with serious budgetary limitations persist to this day. However, the DPI has found a formula that produced an uneasy détente in the historical conflict over the means and ends of UN information policy. The DPI and wider UN information efforts embrace activism in the conduct of information policy, but abjure politicization in the content.

Beginning in the 1990s, UN officials began to accept the central place of public relations methods in the United Nations' own mission. Today, the need for strategic communications is widely accepted and frankly discussed without the same fears of propaganda or distaste for public relations that once restricted the DPI to discussing "basic reference materials." Recognizing the integral work of public information, UN officials put public diplomacy "at the heart" of the organization's substantive work and have worked to create a "culture of communications" that permeates the entire family of departments and offices reaching from the Secretary-General across all senior UN officials (Tharoor, 2006). This enthusiastic embrace of public relations began under the leadership of Secretary-General Kofi Annan (1997–2007). The Ghana-born diplomat's own embrace went so far that he was labelled the "American Secretary-General" because of his "supremely American faith in publicity campaigns" and his propensity to "view all the criticism of the United Nations as a matter of public relations" (Rieff in Alleyne, 2005, p. 177). The emphasis on public relations represents a shift from the reticence and uneasiness with which UN officials, especially within the DPI, historically approached its mission. However, it has not ushered in any revolution. Bureaucratic restructuring designed to enhance efficiency and effectiveness has not fully resolved the intractable problems of constructing a public relations strategy on behalf of the United Nations.

Every Secretary-General and every General Assembly session has lamented the United Nations' tarnished reputation. The United Nations is perceived as an "irrelevant debating society" exploited by states for their own parochial propaganda interests; a "talking-shop" where nothing substantive gets done; a distant, faceless, inefficient, and even corrupt bureaucracy. It suffers from the disillusionment and cynicism born of the failure of collective security during the Cold War, the unending Arab–Israeli conflict, the humanitarian tragedies in Bosnia, Rwanda, and Somalia, and the 2003 Iraq War. Each event created the impression that the organization has never quite matched its ideals and aspirations with effective actions. These familiar image problems have a common denominator: they principally stem from political and security questions.

The prospects for the DPI overcoming political disillusionment through more effective public relations strategies are not good. The department in fact undertakes an active campaign to rebut what are perceived to be unfair criticisms of the organization and its work. DPI products like *Image and Reality* address many common criticisms, but the range of issues is so diverse and originates across such a wide spectrum that a concerted information campaign is nearly impossible. The DPI must simultaneously rebut charges that the United Nations is a tool of the powerful and the opposite charge that developing countries dominate the General Assembly and hence the UN agenda; it must assuage concern that the United Nations threatens state sovereignty while simultaneously confronting the charge that it is not doing enough to defend universal human rights within its member states. The obvious problem is that these criticisms are as much created by philosophical differences about the purposes of the United Nations as they are by misunderstandings to be overcome by more effective public relations campaigns.

Nevertheless, DPI officials are optimistic about the prospects for the United Nations' image. Indeed public faith in the idea of the United Nations remains strong. Polls suggest that most people see the global issues which the United Nations tackles as important and worthy. The paradox, however, is that people often do not realize that the United Nations is in fact actively engaged in these issues. Thus the DPI sees an untapped reservoir of goodwill for the United Nations that can be unleashed if the DPI can effectively convey to the world the United Nations' moral power and substantive successes in these "soft" areas. As Shashi Tharoor (2006), Under-Secretary-General for Communications and Public Information, said, a key challenge for the DPI was to "close this gap and once again make the UN not only a symbol of our collective hope, but also a powerful instrument for translating that hope into everyday reality." In other words, the communications challenge that the DPI faces today is not wholly that of countering criticism or counteracting biases. It is more a problem of overcoming ignorance about the relationship between the United Nations and global causes.

The DPI has developed a communications strategy that embraces the concept of political unbundling: the DPI's thematic priorities have moved away from irresolvable and divisive political issues and toward an emphasis on issues like climate change, poverty, crime, and gender equality that enjoy widespread support in the industrialized and developing worlds alike. Not only does political unbundling obviate the need for the DPI to stake out positions on politically explosive issues, but it also represents an opportunity to offset the United Nations' very real failures in the field of peace and security by reminding the world of its "softer" but substantive roles and triumphs on consensus issues.

Within the General Assembly and the Committee on Information, developing states continue to demand special treatment from the UN information system, greater effort by the organization to help establish a new information and communication order to overcome the "digital divide," and more active measures by the DPI to "assist developing countries to counter misleading propaganda, distorted facts and falsified news created against them by the Western media" (2007 COI Report, 6–7). However, the General Assembly mandates on information campaigns have become far less involved in North–South political activism than in the past. Today the UN Millennium Declaration and General Assembly resolutions provide the framework for an information programme prioritizing the eradication of poverty, conflict prevention, sustainable development, human rights, dialogue among civilizations, the HIV/AIDS epidemic, combating terrorism in all its forms and manifestations, the needs of the African continent, and coverage of United Nations' peacekeeping efforts (Millennium Declaration, Resolution 60/109 A and B, Resolution 60/1, 2005 World Summit Outcome).

The preference for political unbundling has not been without detractors. Foremost, the strategy reinforces the DPI's historic caution in pursuing aggressive communications campaigns that might impinge on state sovereignty or leave the Secretariat vulnerable to charges of partiality. Supporters of a vigorous role for the United Nations in peacekeeping and humanitarian intervention have been disappointed with the organization's reticence to engage in and fund "information interventions" as a vital component of UN peacekeeping missions (Price & Thompson, 2002, pp. 22–25). While the DPI mounts campaigns to sustain support for peacekeeping missions in the international community and in the states that provide the peacekeepers, the United Nations has not deployed communications tools as aggressively as some would hope and coordination between the DPI and the Department of Peace Keeping Operations has not been optimal. That said, the United Nations does operate radio stations as part of many of its peacekeeping missions and awareness of the importance of information strategies has risen within the United Nations (The Role of the DPI in Peacekeeping, 2002).

COLLABORATORS: THE MEDIA AND CIVIL SOCIETY

Returning to the broader practical problem of contemporary information policy, the DPI still faces the challenge of translating support for the UN idea into appreciation for the substantive work of the organization as an actual instrument for advancing and supporting programmes to address very real global problems. The DPI has targeted the media and civil society as key collaborators and disseminators in raising awareness of these activities. The United Nations' relationship with the media has always been marked by both frustration and hope. On the one hand, the DPI relies heavily on the media to report and publicize UN activities and causes and to disseminate media programmes produced and sponsored by the DPI. On the other hand, the DPI mandate includes filling the void left by the lack of coverage, lack of capability, and the perceived biases and distortions of UN actions created by that very same media.

While the rhetoric of the NWICO still influences attitudes at the United Nations about a Western media bias as a root cause of the organization's image problems, the DPI has reframed the issue away from the more polemical charges. Through omission as much as overt biases, the media presents a distorted picture of the United Nations and its activities. The media—especially the "Western" media—focuses too heavily on the "sensationalized" bad news about the United Nations while ignoring the organization's achievements and positive impact on global affairs. While the United Nations and the media have a "shared interest" in conveying UN activities to the world, the media often gives disproportionate attention to "hard" political news at the expense of "soft" news stories at the United Nations. Thus the DPI's job is to "make it easier for [the media] to see that important issues do not fade from the headlines" with promotional activities like its annual list of "Ten Stories the World Should Hear More About" (Ten Stories, 2006).

Even as the DPI courts a media partnership, some members of the media continue to criticize the UN for its inaccessible style and lack of newsworthiness. The organization, Reuters' UN correspondent complained, is "terribly dull to cover." Instead of conveying messages with plain language, the United Nations uses obtuse concepts, acronyms, and when it discusses international conflict it still avoids "naming the enemy" (World Press Freedom Day, 2007). The UN communication style aside, the underlying reason for what UN supporters see as disappointing media coverage of its commemorative events, press briefings, and conferences is that events come in a seemingly endless stream. Not only is the number of causes and issues overwhelming to cover, but the nature of the events exacerbates the public relations challenge. The organization is the master of what Daniel Boorstin (1961) once called "pseudo-events"—events bearing no clear relationship to any underlying reality, created for the purpose of being reported, and designed to become self-fulfilling prophecies. Thus while the causes being celebrated in any given UN event or publication may enjoy widespread support, the media coverage has not always followed because the UN event itself is manufactured for the purpose of drawing attention. As the same Reuters correspondent (2007) explained, "Just because you say it doesn't mean it's news." The DPI challenge, in essence, is to make the United Nations' activities into "news" worthy of sustained worldwide attention.

One UN strategy to overcome the perceived dullness of the United Nations and garner more media attention and hence greater public awareness has been to aggressively enlist celebrity spokespersons. While the UN has utilized famous spokespersons throughout its history, since 1997 the organization has relied on über-celebrities designated as "The Messengers of Peace." Ranging from Muhammad Ali to Luciano Pavarotti, these celebrities have championed everything from endangered animals, to the Millennium development goals, to the Darfur conflict.[2] The decision to put celebrity culture to the use of the United Nations was simple, as Annan explained at a conference attended by celebrity advocates:

---

[2] As of 2007, the Messengers of Peace were Princess Haya Bint Al Hussein, Daniel Barenboim, Paulo Coelho, Midori Goto, Michael Douglas, Jane Goodall, Yo-Yo Ma, and Elie Wiesel.

Whenever you put your name to a message, you raise awareness far and wide, among policymakers and among millions of people who elect them. In an age when the media tends to focus on issues that they may think of as more immediately accessible to the public, our chances of breaking through the barrier of indifference are vastly improved when we have people like you in our corner and for our cause" (Alleyne, 2005, p. 179).

Often, the UN's partnerships with media and celebrities overlap. For instance Secretary-General Ban Ki-moon (2007) was all too happy to offer a message of thanks at an MTV awards show to "My man Jay-Z," the American rapper, for leading the MTV–UN campaign "Water for Life" to help increase global access to clean drinking water.

Non-Governmental Organizations (NGOs) also play a vital role in the United Nations' efforts to promote the UN and its ideals at the national and local level. UN officials view NGOs as an essential ally both in helping to implement substantive programmes and in mobilizing public opinion. Tharoor has argued that the relationship with civil society groups "arguably holds the key to the continued effectiveness of the UN in today's world" (UN News Centre, 2003). In one sense, NGOs work as non-paid employees for the DPI. The DPI accredits (and can disassociate) NGOs as official United Nations partners. In addition to advancing causes of mutual concern, the DPI-accredited NGOs are expected to devote a portion of their information programmes to promoting the principles and activities of the United Nations itself. Moreover, the NGOs' commitment is cemented with quadrennial reports they submit to the DPI that keep the department abreast of their efforts on the United Nations' behalf.

The DPI/NGO relationship is not wholly intended to rein in the NGOs, however. Whereas UN officials are circumscribed by their ostensibly neutral positions, the NGOs can convey ideas on contentious issues without the apolitical restrictions. Their relative freedom makes them a useful asset. As Kofi Annan (2006) said in celebrating the UN–NGO partnership, "You have the capacity to push the envelope and say things that we cannot say . . . and I often love you for it" (Remarks at DPI–NGO Conference). In order to assist its partners, the DPI provides weekly briefings to NGOs and hosts an annual DPI/NGO conference. It also provides communication workshops to train NGOs in effective communications strategies for reaching the public and working with the media.

CONCLUSION: THE DPI CHALLENGE

At the heart of the DPI's strategic challenge are problems that would be intractable for any public relations strategy in any organization. Embedding a "culture of communications" within the organization and a "culture of evaluation" in the DPI does address the long-standing criticisms of the DPI's fragmentation and passivity and will likely improve the efficiency and effectiveness of United Nations public relations methods. However, the intractable ideological problems will undoubtedly endure. The department is criticized for being both too politically active and not active enough; too attuned to public relations at the expense of information dissemination, and not attuned enough; too deferential to member states' political agendas, and not deferential enough. Activism risks violating the inviolability of state sovereignty and the ethos of impartiality, refusing to engage pressing political agendas risks the charge that the DPI is morally obtuse and indifferent to the will of its members. Adhering to a passive programme of information dissemination only yields criticism from communications specialists for not confronting the organization's image problems effectively, but too much strategic communication and the DPI opens its flank to charges of "propagandizing" and belying its objectivity.

These dilemmas get to the fundamental question of the purposes of the United Nations' information apparatus. Should public relations be used to convert the world to a particular vision? Should public relations be used purely instrumentally to best improve the image of the United Nations to target audiences? Or should the DPI merely engage the principle of freedom of information to ensure that the world has access to all of the proceedings and viewpoints expressed at the United Nations by member states and thus hope for global consensus to grow organically? Historically, the DPI has attempted to do all three tasks simultaneously. Even if the DPI possessed the resources to design and implement communications strategies to fulfil the mandates of the General Assembly, tell the story of the activities of the UN family, and buttress the overarching image of the United Nations (which it frankly admits it does not), the tasks are rarely complementary. Indeed, as in the case of the decolonization debate and the North–South divide, the missions worked at cross purposes. While the boundary between the three tasks is often blurry, it is very real and vexing. An active public relations campaign on behalf of the organization cannot be impartial. But no less can advancing the cause of freedom of information be partial. Likewise, if the DPI advances the mandates formulated by the General Assembly it will be impartially fulfilling its statutory mission; however, it will hardly be disseminating impartial information if those mandates themselves represent contentious political-ideological worldviews.

It is a maxim of bureaucratic politics that where you stand depends on where you sit; unfortunately, albeit predictably, the search for the DPI's chair within the UN family has proven elusive. The substantive challenge for the United Nations' communications strategy is as it has always been and will continue to be. The DPI may have a clearer position in the United Nations organization after the recent reforms, but philosophically it does not sit. It still straddles the line between its role as impartial disseminator of information, advocate for the mandates of the world body, and chief custodian of the United Nations' image as a whole. This uneasy position will likely ensure that the historic frustrations of supporters, detractors, and UN officials with the DPI and the wider United Nations information programme will endure as well. Such is the burden of managing public relations for the institution that embodies the aspirations of the entire world.

REFERENCES

Alleyne, M. (2003). *Global lies?: Propaganda, the UN, and world order.* New York: Palgrave.

Alleyne, M. (2005). The United Nations celebrity diplomacy. *SAIS Review* XXV(1), 175–185.

Annan, K. (2006). The Secretary-General's remarks at the 59th Annual DPI-NGO conference, 8 September 2006. Retrieved from the Web 10/20/2007, http://www.un.org/apps/sg/sgstats.asp?nid=2192.

Ban Ki-moon (2007). Secretary-General's video remarks on MTV Networks Award to Jay-Z for United Nations/MTV campaign on Water and Sanitation, 11/14/2007. Retrieved from the Web 11/24/2007, www.un.org/apps/sg/sgstats.asp?nid=2864.

Boorstin, D. (1961). *The image: a guide to pseudo-events in America.* New York: Atheneum.

Corey, R. H. Jr. (1953). Forging a public information policy for the United Nations. *International Organization* 7(2), 229–242.

Gordenker, L. (1960). Policy-making and Secretariat influence in the General Assembly: The case of public information. *The American Political Science Review* 54(2), 359–373.

Price, M. and Thompson, M. (2002). *Forging peace: Intervention, human rights and the management of media space.* Edinburgh: Edinburgh University Press.

Royal Institute of International Affairs (1944). *The International Secretariat of the future: Lessons from experience by a group of former officials of the League of Nations.* London: Oxford University Press.

Swift, R. (1960). The United Nations and its public. *International Organization* 14(1), 60–91.

Tamayo, M. (1968). The United Nations: A rich source of information. In J. Lee (Ed.), *The diplomatic persuaders: New role of the mass media in international relations* (pp. 181–196). New York: John Wiley & Sons.

Tharoor, S. (2006). Statement made at the opening of the twenty-eighth session of the committee on information, 24 April 2006, retrieved from the Web October 25, 2007, http://www.un.org/ga/coi/statements06/tharoor06eng.htm.

UN News Centre (2003). Civil Society Key to Help Prevent Development Goals, 5/27/2003. Retrieved from the Web 10/25/2007, http://www.un.org/apps/news/story.asp?NewsID=7217&Cr=information&Cr1=technology#.

United Nations (1948). Annual Report of the Secretary General on the Work of the Organization. UNGA Official Records: 3rd Sess., Supp. No.1 (A/565).

United Nations (1950). 245th Meeting of the Fifth Committee, 10/12/1950. UN Doc. A/C.5/SR.245.

United Nations (1950). 247th Meeting of the Fifth Committee, 10/13/1950. UN Doc. A/C.5/SR.247.

United Nations (1959). *A Sacred Trust: The United Nations work for non-self-governing lands*, Fourth revised edition. UN Sales No. 59.I.17.

United Nations (1964). *UN Monthly Chronicle* I(2).

United Nations (1968). Verbatim Records of the 593th Meeting of the Special Committee of 24 on Decolonization, 3/29/1968. UN Doc. A/AC.109/PV.593.

United Nations (1968). Verbatim Records of the 598rd Meeting of the Special Committee of 24 on Decolonization, 4/19/1968. UN Doc. A/AC.109/PV.598.

United Nations (1969). *Foreign Economic Interests and Decolonization*. UN Doc. OPI/370–69–15406—13,000.

United Nations (1971). *The United Nations and some problems of public understanding*. UN Doc. OPI/429–01419—January 1971—10M.

United Nations (1972). Report of the Secretary General, Review and Reappraisal of the United Nations Information Policies and Activities, January 17, 1972. UN Doc. A/C.5/1452.

United Nations (1972). Dissemination of Information on Decolonization. Report of the Office of Public Information on the Implementation of General Assembly Resolution 2879 (XXVI), 5/16/1972. UN Doc. A/AC.109/L.791.

United Nations (1972). Verbatim Records of the 873rd Meeting of the Special Committee of 24 on Decolonization, 6/6/1972. UN Doc. A/AC.109/PV.873.

United Nations (1972). Verbatim Records of the 877th Meeting of the Special Committee of 24 on Decolonization, 8/3/1972. UN Doc. A/AC.109/PV.877.

United Nations (1972). Verbatim Records of the 879th Meeting of the Special Committee of 24 on Decolonization, 8/8/1972. UN Doc. A/AC.109/PV.879.

United Nations. Statement by the Chairman of the Committee on Information, April 19, 1979. UN Doc. A/AC.198/2/Corr. 1.

United Nations (1980). Statement of the Chairman of the Committee on Information, May 9, 1980. UN Doc. A/AC.198/14.

United Nations (1983). Special Political Committee, 17th Meeting, 38th Sess.,11/1/1983. UN Doc. A/SPC/38/SR.11.

United Nations (1984). Special Political Committee, 27th Meeting, 39th Sess. UN. Doc. A/SPC/39/SR.27.

United Nations (1984). Special Political Committee, 28th Meeting, 39th Sess. UN. Doc. A/SPC/39/SR.28.

United Nations (1984). Special Political Committee, 30th Meeting, 39th Sess. UN. Doc. A/SPC/39/SR.30.

United Nations (1986). Special Political Committee, 20th Meeting, 41st Sess., 11/13/1986. UN Doc. A/SPC/41/SR.20.

United Nations (1986). Special Political Committee, 26th Meeting, 41th Sess. UN. Doc. A/SPC/41/SR.26.

United Nations (1988). Report of the Committee on Information. UN Doc. A/43/21.

United Nations (2002). Report of the Secretary General on Reorientation of United Nations activities in the field of public information and communications. UN Doc. A/AC.198/2002/2.

United Nations (2002). Report of the Secretary-General, Substantive questions: role of the Department of Public Information in United Nations peacekeeping. UN Doc. A/AC.198/2002/5.

United Nations (2004). Report of the Secretary-General, Activities of the United Nations Communications Group. UN Doc. A/AC.198/2005/5.

United Nations (2006). Report of the Secretary-General assessing the effectiveness of United Nations public information products and activities: the results of a three-year evaluation project. UN Doc. A/AC.198/2006/4.

United Nations (2006). List of "10 stories the world should hear more about." Accessed from the Web November 15, 2007, http://www.un.org/events/tenstories/

United Nations (2007). Report of the Secretary-General, Activities of the Department of Public Information. UN Doc. A/AC.198/2007/4/ and Corr.1.

United Nations (2007). World Press Freedom Day Commemoration, May 3, 2007. UN Doc. OBV/620 PI/1773.

Epilogue

44

THE MISSING LINK: MULTICULTURALISM AND PUBLIC RELATIONS EDUCATION

KRISHNAMURTHY SRIRAMESH

Among other things, the preceding chapters have highlighted the fact that environmental factors have a significant impact on public relations practice around the world. Given the extent of globalization that has occurred especially in the past 10 years, a *majority* of public relations practice in the twenty-first century has, and will continue to, become multinational and multicultural in nature. Therefore, it is not only the "international public relations professional" who needs to be aware of the differences in cultures, political philosophies, and economic systems, but this knowledge needs to be a part of the repertoire of every public relations professional. In other words, every public relations professional needs to become a multicultural communicator in an ever globalizing world. Therefore, it is pertinent to ask: Is the current public relations education system adequately equipped to train students to become effective multicultural public relations professionals?

This chapter attempts to respond to this question drawing on experiences and literature from Asia, complementing the information from Asia that has already been presented in this volume. There are several reasons for critiquing public relations education from an Asian perspective. First, existing public relations literature lacks a reasonable representation of Asian experiences despite the size of the continent in area and population and its sociocultural diversity. For decades, multinational corporations as well as nongovernmental agencies such as United Nations Development Program (UNDP), United Nations Food and Agriculture Organization (FAO), United Nations International

This chapter was revised from Sriramesh, K. (2002). "The dire need for multiculturalism in public relation education: An Asian perspective," *Journal of Communication Management, 7*(1), pp. 54–70.

Childrens Emergency Fund (UNICEF), and the World Health Organization (WHO) have conducted public communication campaigns in this diverse continent to achieve a variety of objectives. However, the vast pool of information from these experiences (with varying degrees of success) has not been incorporated into the public relations body of knowledge or curricula. Second, Asia is emerging as the fastest growing market, attracting the investment of scores of multinational companies. The professionals of these companies can benefit from such knowledge in designing effective strategies for communicating with diverse Asian publics. Third, an Asian country such as Singapore, has used, and continues to use, public communication campaigns successfully to build a modern state in about a generation. Similarly, China has used communication campaigns to build a novel brand of liberalized capitalism without concomitant political liberalization, and established itself as an economic and military power with increasing global outreach. These, and similar, Asian experiences have not been adequately chronicled or integrated into building a multicultural body of knowledge that would contribute to holistic multicultural public relations education and practice. Finally, the author's familiarity with public relations practice and curricula in some Asian countries also contributes to a cogent critique. It is important to note that although Asia is being used as an example in this chapter primarily because of the familiarity of the continent to the author, the themes of the chapter and the issues it raises are undoubtedly relevant to other regions of the world such as Africa, Latin America, the Caribbean, and Eastern Europe, as well. The diversities of these countries have yet to be fully incorporated into existing public relations theorizing and curricula.

With this goal in mind, this chapter begins by highlighting the current American bias in public relations literature as well as curricular content around the world. The chapter cites experiences and examples from Asia to advocate the primary theme: existing public relations literature and educational practices would greatly benefit by incorporating experiences from Asia as well as other regions such as Africa, Latin America, Eastern Europe and the Caribbean that have so far received very little recognition. Finally, the chapter offers some proposals that would help incorporate multiculturalism and holism into public relations education.

CURRENT STATUS OF PUBLIC RELATIONS EDUCATION

Public relations education, as with any branch of education, needs to stand on two principal pillars: a comprehensive body of knowledge and a pool of qualified educators who can impart, and contribute to the building of, this body of knowledge. When we extend this logic to *multicultural* public relations education, it is evident that we need a body of knowledge of *multicultural* public relations and a pool of qualified educators who can impart this *multicultural* knowledge, and contribute to building it as well. There is a dire need for public relations education to identify the characteristics that make for an effective multicultural practitioner, and help impart these to students who, as professionals, will need to operate in multicultural environment.

However, keen observers of public relations education can definitively conclude that there are many chasms in these critical areas of public relations education. Although many books make references (over a few pages) to the need for multicultural public relations perspectives, currently, there are only four books specifically devoted to international public relations (Banks, 1995; Culbertson & Chen, 1996; Moss & DeSanto, 2001; Nally, 1990). Of these, only one (Culbertson & Chen, 1996) has included representative chapters of public relations in a few Asian and African countries. Moss and DeSanto's anthology of international case studies has cases from Europe, the United States, one case from South

Africa, and none from Asia, the Caribbean, Eastern Europe, or Latin America. Although many refereed journals have begun to publish articles on public relations in different parts of the world, there is a scarcity of published literature on international public relations in general and very limited information from Asia, Africa, Eastern Europe, and Latin America, in particular.

This dearth in published empirical studies from several regions of the world is indicative of the current public relations education as a whole, which is dominated by information based on experiences from the United States. European scholars who are currently spearheading the European Body of Knowledge (EBOK) project have contended that public relations education even in European countries is "largely United States centered" (Verčič, 2000; Verčič, van Ruler, Flodin, & Buetschi, 2001). They have remarked that all over Europe, American books have been used to study the concept and practice of public relations. In Asia too, public relations programs exclusively use books written by authors from the United States. These textbooks are presumably aimed at students in the United States, and are based on public relations experiences of professionals in the United States. In a few instances, these books are translated verbatim into other languages without any attempt to align the contents with the environmental contexts of the native country, thus reducing the value of this information to local students.

THE BODY OF KNOWLEDGE OF PUBLIC RELATIONS IN ASIA

Despite the obvious dearth of information on public relations in Asia, public relations has been, and is being, practiced in Asian countries for a long time. Public relations is said to have been practiced in biblical times in the Holy Land (Eshkol, 1992). Kaul (1988) has referred to the rock and pillar edicts set up by Emperor Asoka around 320 B.C. to illustrate the use of public relations in ancient India: "The inscriptions were meant to inform the people about the policies of his [Asoka's] government, to persuade them to carry out certain tasks and to create goodwill amongst them for the establishment. . . ." According to Kaul, Asoka also used these edicts to propagate Budhdhism, a religion to which he had converted later in life. Alanazi (1996) has chronicled numerous examples of public relations practices in the Arabian peninsula since pre-biblical times, noting that "in what today would pass as a 'press release,' a circular handwritten on a crude type of paper told Babylonian farmers, around the year 2000 B.C., how to increase their crop yields." This rich Asian public relations heritage has not been chronicled adequately, or exploited beneficially, by educators in helping students broaden their horizons and become effective multicultural communication professionals.

The body of knowledge of public relations in Asia is young and growing. Most of the empirical studies that have analyzed public relations in Asia have evolved in the last ten years, with contributions predominantly by graduate students from the Asian continent studying in American universities. These, and other, studies have contributed to our understanding of public relations in countries such as Taiwan (Huang, 1990, 2000), India (Bardhan, 2001; Sriramesh, 1992, 1996), South Korea (Jo & Kim, in press; Kim, 1996; Rhee, 1999, 2002), Japan (Cooper-Chen, 1996; Sriramesh & Takasaki, 1999), Saudi Arabia (Alanazi, 1996; Al-Badr, in press; Al-Enad, 1990), Thailand (Ekachai and Komolsevin, 1996), Singapore (Chay, this volume; Tan, 2001), Malaysia (Kaur, 1997); and China (Chen, 1996; Hung, 2002). After obtaining their doctoral degrees, many of these authors have continued their research programs and have continued to build the body of knowledge of Asian public relations using concepts and theories developed in the United States. To this end, one must acknowledge the immense contributions of many American universities in expanding the body of knowledge beyond United States experiences. Many American universities, especially the highly ranked public relations programs, have provided Asian scholars financial help (through fellowships and assistantships), a robust education based on a strong theoretical base, and research and communication skills to enable them to scientifically analyze and report on public relations phenomena in Asian countries. Without the strength of this foundation, one would not have been in a position to contemplate taking public relations education to the next level of making it more multicultural.

Despite these welcome advances, only a few Asian countries are represented in the above list. Whereas these studies are a good foundation on which to build a comprehensive body of knowledge taking into account the complex socioeconomic milieu that is Asia, much more work needs to be done. As already described in earlier chapters of this volume, there is a significant lack of empirical knowledge of public relations practice in Asia (and other regions of the world as already mentioned earlier), including the impact of environmental variables on the profession. This has adversely affected not only students in Asian universities who lack local examples and experiences to which they can relate more readily, but also students in the United States and Europe who can, and need to, expand their horizons in a world that has become much more multicultural and interdependent—which is the central theme of this chapter and book.

What is currently needed are studies that describe the relationship between the complex sociocultural environments of Asia (and the other regions of the world) and public relations practice, with appropriate case studies. These studies should help specify the appropriate communication strategies and techniques for operating in the complex Asian environment. As stated in Chapter 1, currently very few studies exist that have attempted to link public relations practices with environmental variables either in Asia or other regions of the world.

Once established, a comprehensive body of knowledge of Asian public relations would enhance multicultural public relations education in various ways. First, it would help us understand what public relations *is*—the perceived role for the profession in the Asian context and whether it is perceived to serve the same purpose as currently described in the public relations literature. Recent studies (van Ruler, Verčič, Flodin, and Buetschi, 2001; Verčič, van Ruler, Flodin, and Buetschi, 2001) have highlighted the inherent problems of extending United States-based definitions of public relations to Europe. It is not difficult to imagine the problems of exporting these definitions to the even more distant, and diverse, cultures of Asia, Africa, and Latin America. Second, students and practitioners would be able to use this body of knowledge to discern the political, economic, social, and cultural complexities of Asian countries and use appropriate strategies to better relate to their publics in these countries when there is a need to communicate. The need for contextual sensitivity grows with the increasing numbers of foreign organizations entering the emerging markets of Asia and other regions of the world. Third, the importance of interpersonal communication typified by the personal influence model (Huang, 2000; Sriramesh, 1992; Sriramesh, 1996), a key component for success in Asia (and other continents as well), will be made obvious by such a body of empirical knowledge. If public relations involves the management of relationships with key publics through strategic communication (Heath, 2000; Ledingham and Brunig, 2000), interpersonal communication would be an important key in unlocking complex Asian cultures to the outsider and would help increase the efficacy of public relations professionals. Finally, a body of knowledge with relevant Asian case studies would highlight the successes and failures of various communication and public relations strategies and techniques within the complex Asian social and cultural milieu, thereby helping strategic managers to design more efficacious communication programs and campaigns.

CURRENT STATUS OF MULTICULTURAL PUBLIC RELATIONS EDUCATION

Having established the importance of making the public relations body of knowledge multicultural, and emphasized that the existing body of knowledge is predominantly United States-centered, it is pertinent to address the current status of public relations education. There is little doubt that the United States is currently recognized as the leader in providing the most comprehensive public relations education. This reputation has been well earned because many institutions of higher learning in the United States have increased their support for public relations programs, owing among other things, to increased demand at both the graduate and undergraduate levels. Scholars affiliated with public relations programs in the United States have made significant contributions to the development of the body of knowledge of public relations and professional practice. This is the primary reason for Asian students (especially graduate students) to make many sacrifices to study in the United States. As already stated, United States universities, especially those with highly ranked public relations programs, deserve to be lauded for providing the theoretical and methodological foundations for many of these international scholars, thus preparing them to help contribute to building a more multicultural body of knowledge.

Many public relations scholars in the United States have made significant contributions over the past 25 years to building the body of knowledge in this domain. As a result, public relations has achieved recognition as an independent branch of study in many United States universities. Scholars in the United States have also contributed to establishing theoretical concepts specific to public relations such as the models of public relations (J. E. Grunig & L. Grunig, 1992; J. E. Grunig & Hunt, 1984), the roles of public relations practitioners (Broom and Dozier, 1986, Dozier, 1992), the power of the public relations department (L. Grunig, 1992a), the nexus between activism and public relations (L. Grunig, 1992b; Hollahan, 2001), and audience segmentation (J. E. Grunig & Repper, 1992). Several studies have also analyzed the presence of some of these concepts in different cultures (J. E. Grunig, L. Grunig, & Dozier, 1996; J. E. Grunig, L. Grunig, Sriramesh, Huang, & Lyra, 1995; Moss, Warnaby, & Newman, 2000) thereby giving these concepts an international dimension. Despite these significant contributions, it is time for the field to move to the next level and make the body of knowledge of public relations truly multicultural in keeping with the already stated demands of the twenty-first century.

The increasing number of United States students who wish to specialize in public relations, and the almost total reliance in Asia on United States textbooks as well as public relations curricula, compels one to ask whether the United States, as the pioneer and current leader of public relations education, has strong credentials in delivering *multicultural* public relations education as well. Unless the United States education system grows to the next level—by emphasizing multiculturalism in its graduate and undergraduate curricula and delivering such education—it is bound to lose its current international stature as the leader in public relations education. More importantly, it will fail to provide state-of-the-art education to the thousands of eager undergraduate and graduate students in American universities who wish to specialize in public relations. As far back as 1990, a United States public relations professional criticized the ethnocentrism of United States public relations practice (Farinelli, 1990). In 1994, a study noted that of the 119 institutions then offering public relations programs in the United States, only one offered a course on international public relations at the undergraduate level (Sommerness, 1994). There is no empirical evidence on the specific number of universities that currently offer a course in international public relations in the United States but the number does not appear to be very high. Even if a course on international public relations were offered by a significant number of universities in the United States, it will not be sufficient because it is important to go beyond having only *one* course on international public relations. There is a dire need to integrate multiculturalism into other public relations courses as well. Currently, there is very little multiculturalism in United States public relations education as admitted by the Commission of Public Relations Education (CPRE) in its report released in October 1999.

With 48 leading public relations educators and professionals as members, the CPRE was commissioned by the Public Relations Society of America (PRSA) to evaluate the status of education in the United States and make recommendations for improvement. The commission's primary goal was to "determine the knowledge and skills needed by practitioners in a technological, *multicultural and global society* [emphasis added], and then to recommend learning outcomes . . ." (CPRE, 1999). The commission rightly recognized the need to prepare students to operate in a globalized environment. Although the goal of the commission explicitly recognized the need for multiculturalism in public relations education, which is laudable, its recommendations fell far short of proposing adequate representation to *multicultural public relations* education. For example, of the 12 "necessary knowledge" factors that the commission contended public relations graduates ought to possess, "multicultural and global issues" was listed 10th. Further, in the list of 20 "necessary skills" that the commission determined public relations graduates must have obtained at the end of their education, only three directly contribute to multicultural public relations education. They were listed far lower in the list—"sensitive interpersonal communication [13], fluency in a foreign language [14], and applying cross-cultural and cross-gender sensitivity [20]."

If one were to make the reasonable assumption that the placement of an item on the these lists correlates with the relative importance accorded that item, multicultural public relations does not appear to have been accorded a high priority in the commission's recommendations despite the stated goal of preparing students to operate in a "multicultural and global society." In fact, "applying cross-cultural . . . sensitivity," appeared at the end of the list, almost as an afterthought! The lack of importance to multiculturalism in the committee's deliberations is further affirmed when one studies the list of six specific courses the commission recommended for "the ideal undergraduate major in public relations." There is no mention in this list of a course on multicultural public relations or anything remotely connected to international (global) public relations. Similarly, the commission's recommended list of courses for graduate curricula does not have any international or multicultural public relations courses nor does it contain any courses that contribute to expanding the cultural horizons of students. The commission, it is clear, missed an opportunity to increase the significance for multiculturalism in the public relations curricula of United States universities (thereby taking the lead for the rest of the world as well).

An unscientific, but keen, observation of the universities in the United States confirms this lack of importance accorded to international or multicultural issues in most public relations programs. The current president of the Association for Education in Journalism and Mass Communication and the director of a journalism school where public relations programs are typically housed in the United States, observed that the September 11 terrorism story should compel universities (especially journalism and communication schools) to include greater international content in their curricula. He argued that United States television networks' sparse coverage of foreign news prior to the tragic incidents of September 11, "bordered on malpractice" (Campbell, 2002). This criticism can be extended to public relations curricula also because only a few universities currently offer a course on international or global public relations. Fewer still include international issues in other public relations classes. In the rare instances where a course on international public relations is offered, it is taught only as an "elective," attracting only a small number of students who are interested in international issues for their own reasons. There is a need to rethink the course contents of all public relations courses in an effort to include multicultural issues into other public relations courses such as public relations writing, public relations campaigns, and public relations strategies.

To some extent, the lack of emphasis to multiculturalism is influenced by a lack of resources. There are simply not enough educators who have the interest, or the knowledge/experience base required, to teach courses in global public relations. Twelve years ago two leading public relations educators contended that public relations education in the United States was "terrible"(Wright and Turk, 1990). They commented that "there are some places [universities] where the public relations faculty have never published refereed scholarship, and there are institutions who have hired incompetents to teach public relations" (p. 12). The influx of educators from other communication domains into the ranks of public relations educators continues in the United States. Many are readily absorbed by public relations programs in response to the increase in demand for public relations educators. Many of these "switchovers" have neither the practical experience nor the theoretical background that competent public relations educators ought to possess. Some of them have not even taken a course in public relations. In such an environment, multicultural public relations certainly takes a back seat to the more pressing issues of "servicing" the large number of public relations students by offering basic skills courses.

The need for multiculturalism in public relations education is indisputable because public relations, like communication, is a cultural construct:

> However, we foresee an era in which public relations will undergo fundamental changes and become enriched as a profession ... to succeed in their effort to communicate to [with] their publics in a global marketplace, public relations practitioners will have to sensitize themselves to the cultural heterogeneity of their audiences. ... The result will be the growth of a culturally richer profession. (Sriramesh and White, 1992)

Unfortunately, 11 years have elapsed since that statement was made and the public relations education system's progress toward this goal has been painstakingly slow in the United States and around the world. One may ask why this special focus on the United States? Apart from the fact that the United States is considered the *de facto* leader of public relations education, many Asian countries still harbor a "West is best" mentality on many issues including public relations education. They often follow the United States in matters such as curriculum development, course materials, and so forth. To prepare students as multicultural professionals, a comprehensive public relations education should deliver knowledge on the linkage between public relations and the key environmental variables that influence the practice internationally (as already discussed in this volume). The political, economic, legal, media, and cultural factors of a society play a role in the nature of public relations practice, as discussed in Chapter 1. Communication aspects, especially interpersonal communication, need to be addressed as well when one analyzes multiculturalism and public relations. In the next sections, this chapter will review some of these environmental factors giving Asian examples as a prelude to making propositions that would help enhance the multiculturalism of public relations education.

DEFINITION AND NOMENCLATURE ISSUES IN PUBLIC RELATIONS

Having reviewed the predominant American influence on public relations education around the world, it is pertinent to ask whether there are similarities between the United States and the culturally closer European (at least Western European) conceptualizations of the public relations profession and education as a prelude to linking it to Asia, a more distant culture. The ongoing EBOK study did just this, asking "whether public relations is just an Anglo-American concept or whether there is (also) a European authenticity of public relations" (van Ruler, Verčič, Flodin, and Bütschi, 2001). To answer this research question, the authors conducted a Delphi study of 37 public relations academics and professionals from 25 European countries, which led them to conclude that "public relations is not a very widely used name for the field in Europe, not in practice but especially not in science [academe]" (p. 4). The authors also observed that in many European languages, there is no equivalent for the term "public relations." Some of the preceding chapters in this book also have made references to this.

A similar conceptual extension needs to be made regarding the definition and social role of public relations in Asian settings, which are even more distant from United States culture. But how is the definition of public relations in Asia different? Although the term "public relations" itself is widely used in Asian countries, it is often indicative of "spin doctoring" or mere self-serving publicity by the source of the message. Further, it is important to recognize that unlike in some Western European and United States contexts, the *parameters* of public relations practice in Asia are often limited to maintaining good relations between the client/organization and one specific public: the government. Establishing an Asian definition of public relations invariably leads one to recognize the influence of the political system over the public relations profession.

POLITICAL PHILOSOPHY AND PUBLIC RELATIONS IN ASIA

Some Asian examples help illustrate the political system–public relations linkage. We know from chapter 6 in this volume that public relations has often been characterized as *Gong-Bo* (public relations by government) in South Korea, denoting the almost total control the government wields over much of the society's activities including organizational public relations. This situation has required that public relations professionals liaise almost exclusively with the government, thus making the government the only public—contrary to the multiple "relevant publics" approach that United States textbooks recommend. After the liberalization of the economy and democratization brought on by the 1988 Seoul Olympics, the South Korean public relations field has acquired a different name—*Hong-Bo*, which means "disseminating information in a wide coverage" or "make organizations or persons known to the public broadly" (Jo, 2001). Park's study of the coverage of public relations in three major South Korean newspapers led him to conclude that the term *Hong-Bo* is used more frequently than the term "public relations" to refer to the profession, denoting that public relations and publicity are often seen as synonyms in South Korea (Park, 2001). Park also found that regardless of the term used, the public relations profession was viewed negatively by journalists.

Hong-Bo has its roots in, and is indicative of, an authoritarian government and its arm, the *Chaebol* system (Sriramesh, Kim, & Takasaki, 1999). First instituted in the 1960s in South Korea, the *Chaebol* system has its roots in the Japanese *chaibatz* system (see also the chapter 4 in this volume), which disappeared in Japan after World War II when General Douglas McArthur spearheaded the democratization of Japan. The *Chaebol* system consists of a small group of business conglomerates that have dominated the South Korean economy for decades. The underlying philosophy of this system was laudable—to bring the corporate system and the government together to work in unison to build a strong nation. However, in practice, it turned out to be a system that promoted cronyism. After the 1961 revolution led by Park Chung-Hee (who ruled South Korea from 1961 to 1979) the *Chaebol* system rapidly expanded its outreach with Park's express consent. Both sides benefited from this arrangement because the *Chaebol* had a near monopolistic control over different sectors of the economy while the economic development it brought helped Park stay longer in power. The hugely unpopular *Chaebol*s needed *Hong-Bo* to evade, or counter, negative media coverage.

The government was, and to a large extent continues to be, the significant player in India also. Until the economic liberalization of 1991, most of the critical sectors of the economy were controlled by the government through public sector enterprises. The few private sector monopolies that also operated in tandem with public sectors were controlled by rich family-owned firms. These families had close ties to their benefactors in the government, developed through a system of interpersonal friendships and *quid pro quo* personal influence. Eleven years after liberalization, all sectors of the economy have not yet been opened to competition and many industries still trudge on as inefficient public sector enterprises. Indian public relations continues to be oriented toward maintaining a strong relationship with one key public: the government. Public relations, then, becomes a synonym for government relations (Sriramesh, 1996).

The political system in Singapore also has a great influence on the role of public relations in the society. Although Singapore is a democratic republic, many observers take a contrary view of Singapore's version of democracy. In chapter 5 in this volume, Chay has cited Yuen (1999) and Ho (2000) to substantiate this point. Tan (1994) observed that whatever influence corporations have on public policies is derived primarily from their use of the *personal influence* model. A relatively recent example from Singapore also highlights the direct influence that the political system of the country has on media culture. The acting minister for information exhorted the media to play their "social role" as partners in nation building despite the "pressures" of globalization: "Our local media have played an important role in building modern Singapore. By communicating the government's message across to the people, it has [sic] helped to rally support for policies that have brought us progress and prosperity" (*Straits Times*, March 8, 2002).

It is clear from these examples that the definition and scope of public relations is greatly influenced by the political system in these Asian countries. There can be no doubt that establishing robust government relations is crucial to the strategic management of public relations in Asia, unlike the popular United States concept of public relations where the government is but one relevant public with whom the organization has "enabling linkages" (J. E. Grunig and Hunt, 1984) but the organization must also establish strong linkages with many other critical publics in order to maintain an equilibrium with its environment.

Public relations concepts developed in the United States and transported to Western Europe are based on the fact that they will be practiced in an environment that harbors a particular type of democracy—the free marketplace of ideas. Issues management literature (Heath & Causino, 1990; Jones & Chase, 1979) is replete with references to a healthy public debate occurring before governmental policies are enacted. In fact, the *issue lifecycle* that Crable and Vibbert (1985) proposed assumes that multiple players such as political opinion leaders, the media, activist groups, and citizens' groups play an active role in an open public policy making process that ends with public policies being enacted in the "critical stage" of the life cycle. However, the assumptions that form the underpinnings of issues management are often really alien to the political systems of many Asian countries as well as the personal experiences of much of the Asian populace. This brief review of the concept of political system and its impact on public relations is the context for one self-reflective question: Do public relations programs currently provide students information on the world's political systems and the relationship between these systems and public relations?

ACTIVISM

Chapter 1 has conceptually linked activism with political systems. Activism is another area that United States-based public relations concepts have considered as being important to strategic public relations management (L. Grunig, 1992b, Dozier and Lauzen, 2000; Hollahan, 2001). This assertion is indisputable when one considers the pressure that activist groups can impose on organizations from within (e.g., employee unions) and from the outside (e.g., consumer advocacy or environmental groups). In pluralistic democracies, activists wield a lot of power especially when they have the strength of public opinion behind them. When viewed from an Asian perspective, however, activism does not appear to play a major role in determining public relations strategies. Many Asian societies do not value pluralism or tolerate open disagreement with established authority, as a result of which activism is either nonexistent, muted, or orchestrated by established authority for self-serving purposes. In the rare instance that one sees popular activism, it is often crushed mercilessly as happened in Tianan men Square in June 1989. However, there are some instances where activists have had successes against giant multinational corporations in a few Asian countries.

Immediately after economic liberalization in India, for example, many American companies such as KFC, Pizza Hut, and McDonald's rushed into the market. These companies were severely resisted, often through violent means, by nationalistic activists whose slogan was "we want computer chips and not potato chips." More recently, South Korea witnessed massive activist pressure from power industry workers opposed to privatization of the industry. President Kim Dae-Jung, in his final year in office (2002), initiated a massive privatization plan of the utilities industry and other inefficient public sector firms much to the chagrin of organized labor. The reality remains, however, that activism is not very apparent in most Asian societies beyond organized labor movements or isolated instances of pressure directed at multinationals, which are easier targets for populist nationalistic movements. Perhaps this is because of a higher level of tolerance in many Asian cultures. It also may be because of the cultural idiosyncracy of deference to authority. More often, it is an outcome of fear of retribution by established political authority. Empirical evidence is needed to identify the nature of activism in Asia and its impact on public relations.

MEDIA SYSTEMS

Chapter 1 has discussed the significance of the media for public relations professionals as well as the confrontational relationship between the two. The Western notion of the media as "watchdogs" of society is not evident in most Asian countries, even those that claim to be democracies. Illiteracy and poverty, two factors discussed in Chapter 1, play a very big role in the subjugation of media by politicians who govern. Illiteracy makes only the urban educated minority the audiences for print media in Asia. Poverty and a lack of infrastructure (such as lack of rural electrification) limits the outreach of the electronic media, which can substitute or complement the print media. As a result of poor audience, many of the media of Asian countries are rarely self-sustaining and depend heavily on government subsidies. Governments use these and other covert means for keeping the media in line.

In March 2002, the World Association of Newspapers and the World Editors Forum, which represents more than 18,000 publications in 100 countries, complained to Thai Prime Minister Mr. Thaksin Shinawata that the proposed expulsion of two correspondents of the *Far Eastern Economic Review (FEER)* ordered by his government constituted "a breach of the right to freedom of expression." The expulsion was the result of the *FEER*'s reporting of the tensions between the Thai monarchy and Mr. Shinawata's administration, based largely on the public comments of King Bhumibol Adulyadej. After an international furore, the government backed down. In this instance, the *FEER* had the will and financial soundness to oppose the strongarm tactics of the government. However, an indigenous media organization, especially one that is financially weak, would not contemplate such media activism.

We need studies that analyze the media in Asia and provide case studies that illustrate the dynamics of the relationship between organizations, political systems, and media operations, as part of an overall body of knowledge of public relations in Asia. Such knowledge should prove useful to students, scholars, and professionals around the world.

CULTURE AND PUBLIC RELATIONS

Communication and culture have a reciprocal relationship. Because communication is the primary activity of public relations professionals, it behooves us to explore the impact of culture on public relations activities (Sriramesh & White, 1992). Being the largest continent in size and population, Asia is also home to a broad spectrum of very diverse cultures and religions. The public relations body of literature has only started focusing on culture as a relevant variable in the past 10 years. Even after a decade, there are very few studies that link cultural variables with public relations variables. The few existing studies have predominantly attempted to link Hofstede's (1980, 2001) dimensions of culture with public relations practice (Huang, 2000; Rhee, 1999; Sriramesh, 1992). Through his seminal study, Hofstede (1980) provided a thorough foundation on which to build culture-related theories of organizational behavior. But Hofstede himself admitted that he had not been able to discern *all* the dimensions of culture accepting that there are many other dimensions of culture that are often unique to individual countries. These certainly have an impact on public relations practice. The field would benefit from having empirical evidence about the nexus between the specific cultural idiosyncracies of individual countries and public relations practice before we can move toward globalizing some of the cultural principles.

The importance of such delineation is very apparent when one analyzes the diverse cultures in Asia, home to established religions such as Hinduism, Islam, Budhdhism, and Jainism. Even within the same national boundary, Asian countries have several distinctively different cultures. Countries such as Malaysia and Singapore are multiracial in nature and have consistently tried to conduct communication campaigns to foster interracial harmony. A review of the cultural dimensions of Asia helps one understand its complexity, which not only highlights the challenges of conducting multicultural public relations in this region, but also stresses the need to address this complexity in the public relations body of knowledge.

Public relations in China and Taiwan as well as in other countries that have a significant Chinese population (such as Singapore and Malaysia), is influenced by *guanxi*. Just as culture is hard to define (Hofstede, 2001; Kroeber and Kluckhohn, 1952), the term *guanxi* defies easy and ready definition because its practice varies from context to context:

No unchanging, single form of *guanxi* exists. [There are] urban *guanxi*, rural *guanxi*, business *guanxi*, all-female *guanxi*, owner/tenant *guanxi*, class *guanxi*, marriage *guanxi*, comrade *guanxi*, husband/wife *guanxi*, mother-in-law/daughter-in-law *guanxi*, classmate *guanxi*, and more. Each of these relationships carries its own connotations and its own social/historical specificity. (Kipnis, 1997)

Despite its complex manifestation, however, *guanxi* is ultimately about building interpersonal relationships with key publics—typified by the *personal influence* model. This is evident when one examines the origin of the term:

Guanxi is composed of two ideographs, "guan," and "xi." "Guan" functions both as an action-verb ("to close," "to lock up," or "to shut down"), and a noun that describes a physical site (a "gateway," "pass," or "checkpoint"), or a state of affairs ("a barrier"). Traditionally (in China), gateways ("guankou") were found at strategic points along the Great Wall which had historically served as a territory marker for country, culture and creed—for example, it drew a line between insiders (the Han Chinese) and outsiders (the "barbarians" who resided beyond the Great Wall). The high walls built around the ancient Chinese cities had a similar demarcation function: people who lived within the walls were granted the status of insiders, while those who lived outside were not. (Aw, Tan, & Tan, 2002)

Just as *guanxi* is idiosyncratic of Chinese culture, Japanese culture also has its own cultural idiosyncrasies that affect public relations practice in that country (Sriramesh & Takasaki, 1999). As mentioned by Inoue in chapter 4 in this volume, the concept of *wa* (harmony with fellow humans) is valued greatly by the Japanese, who are reticent to disagree publicly so as not to deharmonize society. Pegels, who attempted to link Japanese culture with management philosophy, described the profound influence of this concept on Japanese society: "the quest for *wa* is a national cultural philosophy. . . . Attaining *wa* does not allow for individualism—*wa* demands considerable conformity, and the Japanese are trained to conform from early childhood" (Pegels, 1984). Sriramesh, Kim, & Takashi (1999) linked this cultural trait and the high-context communication that Hall and Hall (1990) had identified to the operation of press clubs in Japan.

The above description of the diversity of Asia based on certain environmental variables helps offer the following propositions that should improve public relations education by making it more multicultural. The resulting holistic and multicultural education system should surely produce more effective public relations professionals who will also be more valued by their organizations.

1. *Building a multicultural body of knowledge.* First and foremost, it is important to establish a *holistic and multicultural* body of knowledge of public relations that truly reflects the political, social, economic, and cultural differences that make regions such as Asia different and challenging environments for public relations practice. Among other factors, this body of knowledge should contain information on three key areas. First, it should chronicle the history and development of the public relations profession in different regions of the world. It is hoped that such descriptions would help improve our understanding of a *global* definition and scope of public relations. Next, this body of knowledge should present empirical data about the strategies and techniques public relations professionals operating in different regions of the world employ, especially in response to the diverse environments they face. Finally, this body of knowledge must include case studies explicating the successes and failures of different strategies and techniques around the world. Identifying successes and failures in strategy should contribute to the holistic

development of the public relations industry. These case studies should also analyze the pitfalls of replicating United States (principally) and Western European (to a lesser extent) public relations strategies and techniques in other regions of the world such as Asia. Many multinational corporations have made the mistake of simply replicating their home-country communication strategies in a socially and culturally diverse host country, often with dire consequences.

A comprehensive body of knowledge with this wealth of information would truly help educators around the world in their efforts to train professionals for multicultural public relations practice in the emerging markets of Asia and other regions of the world. As noted earlier in this chapter, public relations theories and constructs developed in the United States have laid the foundation on which to build the body of knowledge of *multicultural* public relations. Now is the time to build on this foundation and establish new, or variations of these, theories and constructs by integrating regional differences and experiences. Such efforts would help reduce, and eventually eliminate, the existing ethnocentricity in public relations theories and education, thereby leading to a holistic and multicultural profession.

For the immediate future at least, much of the theory building of multicultural public relations will continue to originate from international graduate students studying principally in the United States and a few Western countries, as well as from recent graduates some of whom have returned to their home countries. Hopefully, in the future, there will be a sufficient number of strong public relations programs in educational institutions located in other regions of the world such as Asia, Africa, and Latin America where such studies can take place indigenously. Further, one hopes that an increasing number of non-natives will conduct public relations research projects in Asia, Africa, or Latin America, thereby lending an outsider's perspective to such research and further integrating the profession

2. *Building a multicultural curriculum.* As discussed earlier in this chapter, in addition to the current body of knowledge, public relations curricula around the world need to diversify. The overreliance on curricula based on the United States experience deprives the ever-growing number of public relations majors studying in the United States and around the world from expanding their horizons as future *multicultural* professionals. There is a dire need to remedy this situation by introducing greater international content to public relations curricula at both the undergraduate and graduate levels in all countries. Courses with a multicultural focus, such as courses on international public relations, should not be offered merely as electives for students, or superfluous teaching assignments for faculty, as is often the case currently. Instead, these courses ought to be integrated into public relations curricula as an essential knowledge asset that all students should be required to acquire.

Especially at the undergraduate level, public relations students in the United States and other countries ought to receive a broad liberal arts education that includes courses on the different political, economic, media, and legal systems as well as different religious traditions that one encounters around the world. Many students in the United States have very little exposure to international issues as highlighted by Brownlee (1988) who remarked that the typical American college student "does not seem to know the difference between Nigeria and Nicaragua, doesn't know that Mexico is to the south of the United States and Canada to the north. ..." Even after 14 years, this situation persists, as evident in the CPRE's report cited earlier in this chapter.

The ethnocentricity of the United States education system, the current leader in the field of public relations education, has a direct influence on public relations students in many other regions of the world including Asia. Most Asian universities look up to the

United States education system as the model in setting their own curricula and frequently invite American professors as visiting fellows (aided often by benefactors such as the Fulbright Foundation) to help set up their public relations programs. Whereas this practice has many benefits, unless public relations education in the United States becomes more holistic and multicultural, the ethnocentricity in the curriculum just gets extended to other continents as well, inhibiting the holistic growth of public relations education around the world. Further, because Asian universities use United States books almost exclusively, the utility of their content to Asian students is limited to the basic principles of public relations and checklists, with little by way of contextual explication tempered by many environmental factors.

Despite the benefits, one has to recognize that there are practical problems in attempting to make public relations curricula more international and multicultural. The practical, but myopic, world view that public relations education ought to meet the demands of students (as "consumers") that they be taught "basic skills" to get an entry-level job, is the principal obstacle. Whereas there can be little argument that "skills" courses ought to be the necessary foundation of a good public relations education, university decision makers ought to recognize that it is equally essential to include multicultural issues in public relations curricula for the holistic development of students. Further, international experience is not valued adequately by administrators, faculty, or students in most universities, a situation that is changing in a few universities in the United States. There are few financial or other incentives to encourage faculty to include multiculturalism in their course content. Faculty members who wish to teach international public relations courses rarely receive enthusiastic support and resources from their supervisors. Many of these supervisors are more interested in, or are pressured to think about, staffing "required" (mandatory) and "service" (core) courses first and then focus on multicultural courses if resources permit. This is particularly debilitating when there is already a low number of faculty who are interested in, or wish to take on, the challenges of conceptualizing a new course such as international public relations.

Another curricular idea that is worth exploring is to have collaboration among two or more faculty of different countries who can jointly teach classes or specific modules of classes either through online computers or by using new technologies such as videoconferencing. The advancement of technology makes this possible as the least expensive and least disruptive option in encouraging dialogue among students and faculty of different countries or even continents. Of course the technology required for such a link has not diffused adequately for this idea to be feasibly applied in most regions of Africa and Asia. But some urban centers of Asia such as Singapore are certainly well equipped technologically for such joint classroom teaching opportunities. Until videoconferencing is within the reach of many more universities, Web-based instruction can be used collaboratively between institutions from different countries or continents. A course designed to be delivered in this manner is also exciting enough to attract larger numbers of students to sign up for international public relations classes whether these are offered as "electives" or core courses.

When establishing public relations curricula, universities in other regions of the world should try to avoid merely replicating the curricula of public relations programs in the United States based on a "West is best" worldview, which remains a widespread practice. These regional programs would do well to judiciously adopt the elements from United States curricula that are useful to their local environment, of which there are many, but also use the body of *multicultural* public relations to build course content specific to their regions and include information from other regions of the world as well. These programs also need to complement imported concepts by including information on the unique local practices and regional public relations issues and cases as well. The next two propositions, although important, may be harder to implement because of the concomitant constraints.

3. *International Experience.* A different society or culture should become a classroom for an increasing number of public relations students in all countries, if their education is to become truly multicultural. Study abroad (and student exchange) programs and international internships are very helpful in providing students this "field" experience and first-hand knowledge of multiculturalism. However, currently, few students in the United States or Asia take advantage of these programs for a variety of reasons. For most, staying for a period of one or two semesters in an exotic culture has psychological barriers. For others, personal factors such as family and friends pose an impediment. Language has always been a matter of concern to students, drastically reducing the choice of countries where one can study.

Financially, it is relatively easier for students from the United States and Western Europe to study abroad than it is for Asian students, because of the disparity in the cost of living as well as differential currency exchange rates. Even students from Singapore, a relatively affluent country (whose per capita income in 2001 was US $20,892), often decline study abroad opportunities citing financial constraints. Cultural or religious barriers often constrain students from foreign travel as in the case of Western Asia and the Middle East. Many bureaucratic impediments also inhibit the few interested students from availing of study abroad opportunities. In Asian countries, which tend to be more bureaucratic, transferring credits of similar courses has often proved problematic as is the issue of swapping credit hours of courses with similar content but different "contact" hours (the number of hours students spend in the classroom per week). As a result of these constraints, fewer students avail the opportunity of experiencing a foreign culture.

4. *Faculty exchange programs.* Many more faculty members should opt to participate in faculty exchange programs to gain, or enhance, their international experience by teaching abroad for one or two semesters. Currently, United States faculty who undertake international teaching and research opportunities do so almost exclusively during their sabbaticals. As a rule, in the United States, only faculty with tenure, and typically those who have been in residence in the same university for at least six years, are eligible for a sabbatical. This situation restricts junior (untenured) faculty and tenured faculty who change employers from engaging in international teaching or research experiences. These factors have greatly reduced the number of public relations faculty who avail themselves of international teaching and research opportunities. Faculty from Asia rarely seek, or receive, opportunities to teach outside of their regions.

CONCLUSION AND THE FUTURE

As an epilogue to this volume, this chapter has argued that there is a dire need for making public relations education and practice multicultural because we operate in a shrinking world that has fewer trade barriers and faster and cheaper communication technology. It has advocated establishing a comprehensive *holistic and multicultural* body of knowledge of public relations. As a first step in expanding the body of knowledge of public relations and making it more multicultural, there is a dire need for anthologies describing public relations experiences in Asia, Africa, Latin America, and the Caribbean. Such anthologies also need to address the issue of how societal factors such as political, cultural, and economic levels of countries influence public relations practice.

After a sufficiently comprehensive knowledge base has been established, cross-national studies of public relations using the same research protocol can be planned and executed to assess similarities and differences in public relations practice, further enhancing the

body of knowledge. Such projects will also be appropriate opportunities for scholar educators of different countries to collaborate. The body of knowledge that results from these
projects will be useful to public relations educators around the world in building comprehensive public relations curricula that are more multicultural and holistic. Ultimately,
these developments in the body of knowledge and curricula should benefit future students,
researchers, and professionals. This volume, it is hoped, has provided the first forays into a
multicultural body of knowledge of public relations. The proposals made in this chapter, it
is hoped, will pave the way for the public relations profession around the world to become
truly *strategic* as a result of becoming more multicultural.

REFERENCES

Alanazi, A. (1996). Public relations in the Middle-East: The case study of Saudi Arabia. In H. M. Culbertson
    & N. Chen (Eds.), *International public relations: A comparative analysis.* (pp. 239–256). Mahwah, NJ:
    Lawrence Erlbaum Associates.

Al-Badr, H. (in press). Public relations in Saudi Arabia. In K. Sriramesh (Ed.), *Public relations in Asia.*
    Singapore: Prentice Hall.

Al-Enad, A. (1990). Public relations roles in developing countries. *Public Relations Quarterly, 35*(1),
    24–26.

Aw, A., Tan, S. K., & Tan, R. (2002, July 15–19). *Guanxi* and Public Relations: An Exploratory Qualitative
    Study of the Public Relations-Guanxi Phenomenon in Singapore Firms. Paper presented to the Public
    Relations Division of the International Communication Association, Seoul, South Korea.

Banks, S. P. (1995). *Multicultural public relations: A social-interpretive approach.* Thousand Oaks, CA: Sage.

Bardhan, N., & Sriramesh, K. (in press). Public Relations in India. In K. Sriramesh (Ed.), *Public relations in
    Asia.* Singapore: Prentice Hall.

Bardhan, N. (2001). Radicalizing public relations metanarratives: India as a case study. Paper presented
    to the Public Relations Division at the annual conference of the National Communication Association,
    Atlanta, GA.

Broom, G. M., & Dozier, D. M. (1986). Advancement for public relations role models. *Public Relations Review,
    7*(1), 37–56.

Brownlee, B. J. (1988). Main Street America asks students to give international perspective. *Journalism
    Educator, 43*, pp. 17–20.

Campbell, D. (2002). Serious business. *American Journalism Review, 24*, 44–47.

Chen, N. (1996). Public relations in China: The introduction and development of an occupational field. In
    H. M. Culbertson & N. Chen (Eds.), *International public relations: A comparative analysis.* Mahwah, NJ:
    Lawrence Erlbaum Associates.

Cooper-Chen, A. (1996). Public relations in Japan: Beginning again for the first time. In H. M. Culbertson and
    N. Chen (Eds.) *International public relations: A comperative analysis.* Mahwah, NJ: Lawrence Erlbaum
    Associates.

CPRE (1999). Public Relations Education for the 21st century: A port of entry. New York: Public Relations
    Society of America.

Crable, R. E., & Vibbert, S. L. (1985). Managing issues and influencing public policy. *Public Relations Review,
    11*, 3–16.

Culbertson, H. M., & Chen, N. (1996). *International Public Relations: A Comparative Analysis.* Mahwah, NJ:
    Lawrence Erlbaum Associates.

Dozier, D. M., & Lauzen, M. M. (2000). Liberating the intellectual domain from the practice: Public relations,
    activism, and the role of the scholar. *Journalism of Public Relations Research, 12*(1), 3–22.

Dozier, D. M. (1992). The Organizational Roles of Communications and Public Relations Practitioners. In J. E.
    Grunig (Ed.), *Excellence in public relations and communication management* (pp. 327–355). Hillsdale, NJ:
    Lawrence Erlbaum Associates.

Ekachai, D., & Komolsevin, R. (1996). Public relations in Thailand: Its functions and practitioners' roles. In
    H. M. Culbertson, & N. Chen (Eds.), *International public relations: A comparative analysis.* Mahwah, NJ:
    Lawrence Erlbaum Associates.

Eshkol, D. (1992). PR in Israel: An up-to-date overview. *International Public Relations Review, 15*, 5–8.

Farinelli, J. L. (1990). Needed: A new United States perspective on global public relations. *Public Relations Journal, 46* (November), 42, 18–19.

Grunig, J. E., & Grunig, L. A. (1992). Models of public relations and communication. In J. E. Grunig (Ed.), *Excellence in public relations and communication management* (pp. 285–325). Hillsdale, NJ: Lawrence Erlbaum Associates.

Grunig, J. E., & Hunt, T. (1984). *Managing public relations.* New York: Holt, Rinehart, & Winston.

Grunig, J. E., & Repper, F. C. (1992). Strategic management, publics, and issues. In J. E. Grunig (Ed.), *Excellence in public relations and communication management* (pp. 117–157). Hillsdale, NJ: Lawrence Erlbaum Associates.

Grunig, J. E., Grunig, L. A., & Dozier, D. (1996). Das situative model exzellenter public relations: Schlussfolgerungen aus einer internationalen studie' (The contingency model of excellent public relations: Conclusions from an international study). In G. Bentele, H. Steinmann, & A. Zerfass (Eds.), *Dialogorientierte unternehmenskommunikation* (Dialogue-oriented approaches to communication) (pp. 199–228). Berlin: Vistas.

Grunig, J. E., Grunig, L. A., Sriramesh, K., Huang, Y. H., & Lyra, A. (1995). Models of public relations in an international setting. *Journal of Public Relations Research, 7*, 163–186.

Grunig, L. A. (1992a). Power in the Public Relations Department. In J. E. Grunig (Ed.), *Excellence in public relations and communication management* (pp. 483–501). Hillsdale, NJ: Lawrence Erlbaum Associates.

Grunig, L. A. (1992b). Activism: How it limits the effectiveness of organizations and how excellent public relations departments respond. In J. E. Grunig (Ed.), *Excellence in public relations and communication management* (pp. 503–530). Hillsdale, NJ: Lawrence Erlbaum Associates.

Grunig, L., Grunig, J. E. & Verčič, D. (1998). Are the IABC's excellence priniciples generic? Comparing Slovenia and the United States, the United Kingdom, and Canada. *Journal of Communication Management, 2*, 335–356.

Hall, E. T., & Hall, M. R. (1990). *Understanding cultural differences.* Yarmouth, ME: Intercultural Press.

Heath, R. L. (Ed.) (2000). *Handbook of public relations*, Thousand Oaks, CA: Sage.

Heath, R. L., & Causino, K. R. (1990). Issues management; End of first decade progress report. *Public Relations Review, 16*, 6–17.

Hofstede, G. (1980). *Culture's consequences.* Beverly Hills, CA: Sage.

Hofstede, G. (2001). *Cultrue's consequences: Comparing values, behaviors, institutions, and organizations across nations*, 2nd ed.). Thousand Oaks, CA: Sage.

Hollahan, K. (2001). The dynamics of issues activation and response: An issues processes model. *Journal of Public Relations Research, 13*, 27–59.

Ho K. L. (2000). *The politics of policy-making in Singapore.* Singapore: Oxford University Press Pte. Ltd.

Huang, Y. (2000). The personal influence Model and *Gao Guanxi* in Taiwan Chinese public relations. *Public Relations Review, 26*, 216–239.

Huang, Y. H. (1990). *Risk communication, models of public relations and anti-nuclear activities: A case study of a nuclear power plant in Taiwan.* Unpublished Master's thesis, University of Maryland, College Park, MD.

Hung, C. J. (2002). *The interplay of relationship types, relationship maintenance, and relationship outcomes: A dialectical approach on how multinational and Taiwanese companies practice public relations in China.* Unpublished doctoral dissertation, University of Maryland, College Park.

Idid, S. A. (1998). *Beauty, brain and brawn in public relations.* Bangi, Selangor: Universiti Kebangsaan Malaysia.

Jo, S. (2001 May). Models of public relations in South Korea: The difference Between *HongBo* and public relations. Paper presented to the Public Relations Division at the annual conference of the International Communication Association, Washington, DC.

Jo, S., & Kim, J. (in press). Public Relations in South Korea. In K. Sriramesh (Ed.), *Public Relations in Asia: An anthology.* Singapore: Prentice Hall.

Jones, B. L., & Chase, W. H. (1979). Managing Public Policy Issues. *Public Relations Review, 2*, 3–23.

Kaul, J. M. (1988). *Public relations in India.* Calcutta: Noya Prokash.

Kaur, K. (1997). *The impact of privatization on public relations and the role of public relations management in the privatization process: A qualitative analysis of the Malaysian case.* Unpublished doctoral dissertation, University of Maryland at College Park.

Kim, Y. (1996). Positive and normative models of public relations and their relationship to job satisfaction among Korean public relations practitioners. Unpublished master's thesis, University of Florida, Gainesville.

Kipnis, A. (1997). *Producing Guanxi: Sentiment, self, and subculture in a North China Village.* Durham, NC: Duke University Press.

Kroeber, A. L., & Kluckhohn, C. (1952). Culture: A critical review of concepts and definitions. *Papers of the Peabody Museum of American Archeology and Ethnology, 47,* Cambridge, MA: Harvard University.

Ledingham, J. A., & Brunig, S. D. (Eds.) (2000). *Public relations as relationships management.* Mahwah, NJ: Lawrence Erlbaum Associates.

Moss, D., & DeSanto, B. (Eds.) (2001). *Public relations cases: International perspectives,* London: Routledge.

Moss, D., Warnaby, G., & Newman, A. J. (2000). Public relations practitioner role enactment at the senior management level within U. K. companies. *Journal of Public Relations Research, 12,* 277–307.

Nally, M. (1990). *International public relations in practice.* Kogan Page, London.

Park, J. (2001, August). Hong Bo and PR in the Korean Newspapers. Paper presented to the Public Relations Division of the Association for Education in Journalism and Mass Communication (AEJMC), Washington, DC.

Pegels, C. (1984). *Japan vs. the West: Implications for management.* Boston, MA: Kluwer-Nijhoff.

Rhee, Y. (1999). *Confucian culture and excellent public relations: A study of generic principles and specific applications in South Korean public relations practice.* Unpublished Master's thesis, University of Maryland at College Park.

Rhee, Y. (2002, July 16). Culture and dimensions of communication in public relations: An exploratory study of South Korean practitioners. Paper presented to the Public Relations Division, International Communication Association, Seoul.

Ruler, B. van, Verčič, D., Glodin, B., & Bütschi, G. (2001). Public relations in Europe: A kaleidoscopic picture. *Journal of Communication Management, 6,* 166–175.

Sommerness, M. (1994). Back to the future: International education in public relations. *Public Relations Review, 20,* 89–95.

Sriramesh, K. (1992). Societal culture and public relations: Ethnographic evidence from India. *Public Relations Review, 18,* 201–212.

Sriramesh, K. (1992). *The impact of societal culture on public relations: An ethnographic study of south indian organizations.* Unpublished doctoral dissertation, University of Maryland at College Park.

Sriramesh, K. (1996). Power distance and public relations: An ethnographic study of Southern Indian organizations. In H. M. Culbertson & N. Chen (Eds.), *International public relations: A comparative analysis* (pp. 171–190). Mahwah, NJ: Lawrence Erlbaum Associates.

Sriramesh, K., & Takasaki, M. (1999). The impact of culture on Japanese public relations. *Journal of Communication Management, 3,* 337–351.

Sriramesh, K., & White, J. (1992). Societal culture and public relations. In J. E. Grunig (Ed.), *Excellence in public relations and communication management* (pp. 597–614). Hillsdale, NJ: Lawrence Erlbaum Associates.

Sriramesh, K., & Verčič, D. (2001). International public relations: A framework for future research. *Journal of Communication Management, 6,* 103–117.

Sriramesh, K., Kim, Y., & Takasaki, M. (1999). Public relations in three Asian cultures: An analysis. *Journal of Public Relations Research, 11,* 271–292.

Takasaki, M. (1994). *Public relations in Japan.* Unpublished term paper, Purdue University, West Lafayette, IN.

Tan, S. P. (1994). Roles of organized business in public policy making in Singapore: changes and continuities. Academy exercise, department of political science, NUS.

Tan, R. (2001). *The State of public relations in Singapore.* Singapore: Singapore Polytechnic.

Verčič. D. (2000). The European body of knowledge. *Journal of Communication Management, 4,* 341–354.

Verčič, D., van Ruler, B., Bütschi, G., & Flodin, B. (2001). On the definition of public relations: A European view. *Public Relations Review, 27,* 373–387.

Wright, D., & Turk, J. V. (1990). *Public relations education: The unpleasant realities.* New York: Institute of Public Relations Research and Education.

Yuen C. K. (27 Sept 1999). *Leninism, Asian Culture and Singapore.* Available on: http://www.sintercom.org OR www.comp.nus.edu.sg/~yuenck/new.

INDEX

Please note that page references to Figures or Tables will be in *italic* print. PR, where appearing in subheadings, stands for 'public relations'

Sweden, 477–478
theocratic, 9
United Arab Emirates, 206
United Kingdom, 398–399
United States, 628–629
Adams, James Truslow, 773
Adams, Samuel, 628, 773
adhocracy, 875, 876
Adler, N. J., 631
Administrative Courts System, Egypt, 369
advertising, nonstandard, 509
advertising agencies, 864–865
Advertising Law, Russia, 609
advertising value equivalents (AVE), 581
Africa and African public relations, 265–287
  see also sub-Saharan Africa
Africa and public relations: activism, 8
  Africa Communication Index *see* ACI (Africa
      Communication Index)
  agencies, 279–280
  communications infrastructure, 275
  education and training, 275–276
  environmental dimensions, 268–270
  future for PR, 285–287
  GDP discrepancies in states, 266–267
  HIV/AIDS pandemic, 299–300, 301, 306, 847
  managing PR and corporate communications,
      285
  media, 274–276
  19th All Africa Public Relations Conference,
      Johannesburg, 286
  partition of Africa into "spheres of influence",
      308
  political and economic dimensions, 270–274
  professional associations, 278–279
  professional standards and ethics, 278–280
  specialists, 279
  tertiary education, 276–277
  see also Egypt and public relations
      Kenya and public relations
      Nigeria and public relations
      South Africa and public relations
Africa Information Services (AIS), 310
African Independent Television (AIT), 300
African National Congress (ANC), 330, 336, 339
Aftalion, Albert, 783
Agee, W. K., 814, 817
agencies, public relations, 861–869
  Africa, 279
  Chile, 759
  consultancy costs, 867–868
  history, 862–865
  Mexico, *682*
  qualities of good PR consultant, 869
  Slovenia, 51
  structures, 866–867
  types, 865–866
  working with client, 868–869
Agency for Governmental Strategies (ASG),
      Romania, 556
Agency of Quality Assurance (ARACIS), Romania,
      555, 560
Agenda 21, Rio Earth Summit (1982), 809, 844, 848
agenda-setting, 66–67, 170
Aguayo, Carlos Aracena, 754

AIDS/HIV: and Africa, 299–300, 301, 306, 847
  disinformation campaign by KGB, 781–782
AIESEC (Association of Students in Economic
      Studies), 563
AIRP (Associazione Italiana Relazioni Pubbliche),
      Italy, 486
AIS (Africa Information Services), 310
AISM (Italian association of market research
      companies), 488
AIT (African Independent Television), 300
Al Ittihad (editorial), 209
ALACAURP (Latin American Society of Public
      Relations Programs), 721
Al-Ahram (Egyptian newspaper), 373
ALAIC (Latin American Society of Researchers),
      721
Alanazi, A., 363
ALARP, 721
Alexander the Great, 771
Alfonso, B. D., 754
Algeria, media, 274
Al-Hiyat al-Jadida, 234
Al-Jazeera television, Palestine, 235
All Russian Census Campaign (2001), 607
Allende, Salvador, 707
amae, Japanese concept, 12, 51
AMAI (Mexican Association of Marketing
      Research and Public Opinion Agencies),
      679
AMCI (Mexican Association of Internal
      Communication), 679
AMCO (Mexican Association of Communicators),
      677, 698
American Red Cross, 814
Amnesty International, 776
Anania, David, 551
ANC (African National Congress), 330, 336, 339
Andrade, Cândido Teobaldo de Souza, 728
Angola, political and economic dimensions, 272
Annax International Communication Agency, 579
Antimonopoly Committee, Russia, 609
Anti-Right Movements, 180
Anti-Slavery Society, British and Foreign, 808
ANZAC (Australian and New Zealand Army
      Corps), 102
Apex Communication Ltd, Kenyan case study, 326
Apostle Paul, 771
APR (Accredited in Public Relations), 659
Arab Public Relations Society, 367
ARACIS (Agency of Quality Assurance), Romania,
      555, 560
Aramony, William, 814, 817
Araos, C., 757
ARC (Auckland Regional Council), 119, 120
Argentina and public relations: education, 716
  history of Argentina, 705–706
  history of PR, 710
  military, role, 707, 708
  poverty, 709
Aron, L., 607
Aronoff, C., 642–643
Aronson, E., 611, 832
ARRP (Romanian Association of Public
      Relations Professionals), 553, 554, 558,
      560, 563